THE OXFORD HANDBOOK OF
ROMAN PHILOSOPHY

THE OXFORD HANDBOOK OF

ROMAN PHILOSOPHY

Edited by
MYRTO GARANI, DAVID KONSTAN,
and
GRETCHEN REYDAMS-SCHILS

OXFORD
UNIVERSITY PRESS

Oxford University Press is a department of the University of Oxford. It furthers
the University's objective of excellence in research, scholarship, and education
by publishing worldwide. Oxford is a registered trade mark of Oxford University
Press in the UK and certain other countries.

Published in the United States of America by Oxford University Press
198 Madison Avenue, New York, NY 10016, United States of America.

© Oxford University Press 2023

All rights reserved. No part of this publication may be reproduced, stored in
a retrieval system, or transmitted, in any form or by any means, without the
prior permission in writing of Oxford University Press, or as expressly permitted
by law, by license, or under terms agreed with the appropriate reproduction
rights organization. Inquiries concerning reproduction outside the scope of the
above should be sent to the Rights Department, Oxford University Press, at the
address above.

You must not circulate this work in any other form
and you must impose this same condition on any acquirer.

Library of Congress Cataloging-in-Publication Data
Names: Konstan, David, editor. | Garani, Myrto, 1975– editor. |
Reydams-Schils, Gretchen, editor.
Title: The Oxford handbook of Roman philosophy / David Konstan,
Myrto Garani, and Gretchen Reydams-Schils.
Description: New York : Oxford University Press, [2023] |
Series: Oxford handbooks series |
Includes bibliographical references and index. |
Identifiers: LCCN 2022038810 (print) | LCCN 2022038811 (ebook) |
ISBN 9780199328383 (hardback) | ISBN 9780197639832 | ISBN 9780197639825 (epub)
Subjects: LCSH: Philosophy, Ancient.
Classification: LCC B111 .O94 2023 (print) | LCC B111 (ebook) |
DDC 180—dc23/eng/20221020
LC record available at https://lccn.loc.gov/2022038810
LC ebook record available at https://lccn.loc.gov/2022038811

DOI: 10.1093/oxfordhb/9780199328383.001.0001

Printed by Sheridan Books, Inc., United States of America

Contents

Preface   ix
   Myrto Garani, David Konstan, and Gretchen Reydams-Schils
List of Contributors   xiii

PART I. THE ROMAN PHILOSOPHER: AFFILIATION, IDENTITY, SELF, AND OTHER

1. Italic Pythagoreanism in the Hellenistic Age   3
   PHILLIP SIDNEY HORKY

2. Epicurean Orthodoxy and Innovation: From Lucretius to Diogenes of Oenoanda   27
   PAMELA GORDON

3. Ethical Argument and Epicurean Subtext in Horace, *Odes* 1.1 and 2.16   42
   GREGSON DAVIS

4. Seneca and Stoic Moral Psychology   60
   GRETCHEN REYDAMS-SCHILS

5. Marcus Aurelius and the Tradition of Spiritual Exercises   74
   JOHN SELLARS

6. Apuleius and Roman Demonology   87
   JEFFREY ULRICH

7. Philosophers and Roman Friendship   108
   DAVID KONSTAN

8. Debate or Guidance? Cicero on Philosophy   119
   MALCOLM SCHOFIELD

PART II. WRITING AND ARGUING ROMAN PHILOSOPHY

9. The Epicureanism of Lucretius 143
   TIM O'KEEFE

10. Cicero and the Evolution of Philosophical Dialogue 159
    MATTHEW FOX

11. The Stoic Lesson: Cornutus and Epictetus 173
    MICHAEL ERLER

12. Persius's Paradoxes 190
    AARON KACHUCK

13. Plutarch 211
    GEORGE KARAMANOLIS

14. *Parrhēsia*: Dio, Diatribe, and Philosophical Oratory 225
    DANA FIELDS

15. Consolation 240
    JAMES KER

16. The Shape of the Tradition to Come: Academic Arguments in Cicero 256
    ORAZIO CAPPELLO

17. Persius on Stoic Poetics 275
    CLAUDIA WIENER

PART III. INSIDE AND OUTSIDE OF ROMAN PHILOSOPHY

18. Translation 293
    CHRISTINA HOENIG

19. Roman Philosophy in Its Political and Historiographical Context 324
    ERMANNO MALASPINA AND ELISA DELLA CALCE

20. Rhetoric 347
    ERIK GUNDERSON

21. Self and World *in extremis* in Roman Stoicism 361
    JAMES I. PORTER

22. Medicine — DAVID LEITH — 379

23. Sex — KURT LAMPE — 397

24. Time — DUNCAN F. KENNEDY — 412

25. Death — JAMES WARREN — 429

26. Environment — DANIEL BERTONI — 442

PART IV. AFTER ROMAN PHILOSOPHY: TRANSMISSION AND IMPACT

27. Roman Presocratics: Bio-Doxography in the Late Republic — MYRTO GARANI — 461

28. Reading Aristotle at Rome — MYRTO HATZIMICHALI — 491

29. Christian Ethics: The Reception of Cicero in Ambrose's *De officiis* — IVOR J. DAVIDSON — 506

30. Augustine's Reception of Platonism — ANNE-ISABELLE BOUTON-TOUBOULIC — 528

31. Roman Quasity: A Matrix of Byzantine Thought and History — ANTHONY KALDELLIS — 548

32. Latin Neoplatonism: The Medieval Period — AGNIESZKA KIJEWSKA — 568

33. Transmitting Roman Philosophy: The Renaissance — QUINN GRIFFIN — 583

34. "The Art of Self-Deception": Libertine Materialism and Roman Philosophy — NATANIA MEEKER — 599

Index — 615

Preface

ROMAN philosophy? The question is, perhaps, inevitable, even today. Is Roman philosophy anything other than Greek philosophy in a toga? Or still worse, does Greek philosophy cease to be philosophy precisely insofar as it is Roman? We seek to recover from Roman writings whatever information they may provide about Greek philosophical schools, and the dross, as it were, is what is Roman—practical applications, at best, or at worst, misunderstandings and distortions. We raise this question here only to dismiss it. Several decades of scholarship by now have demonstrated that Roman thinkers have developed in new and stimulating directions the systems of thought they inherited from the Greeks, and that, taken together, they offer a range of perspectives that are of philosophical interest in their own right. Do they constitute a single perspective, a kind of Roman school? Certainly not. But then, neither is this so for Greek philosophy. And if Roman texts are in some respects derivative of Greek, this can equally be said of most of modern philosophy. Wherever the word "philosophy" is used, it betrays its debt to Greece.

Nevertheless, problems relating to the definition of Roman philosophy remain. Does it apply only to works written in Latin? This would seem unduly restrictive, since many Romans wrote in Greek—one thinks at once of Marcus Aurelius, for example—and many whose native language may have been Greek were living in Rome, or under Roman rule, and were in close contact with leading Roman intellectuals: Epictetus is a good instance, and Plutarch another. An inclusive approach, such as this book offers, is surely appropriate. A different question arises in regard to Christian thought: is this to be regarded as philosophical—or as Roman? Here the answer would seem to be self-evidently yes, and this volume contains chapters on Ambrose, Augustine, Latin Neoplatonism, and even Byzantine political thought. And yet, we ourselves are perhaps guilty of some equivocation, insofar as these chapters are gathered in a separate part bearing the heading "After Roman Philosophy: Transmission and Impact." And if any eyebrows are raised at the inclusion of Byzantium, let it be recalled that the Byzantine Empire identified itself as Roman.

Even this does not exhaust the questions that our manual might raise, and did raise for its editors. Ought poets who were influenced by philosophical currents, but can hardly be called philosophers, to be represented? There is no difficulty when it comes to Lucretius, of course, and perhaps Persius, as a self-proclaimed Stoic, is unproblematic, but what about Horace? Well, he did call himself a pig from the sty of Epicurus. If such a broad criterion for inclusion seems peculiar to Roman philosophy, and perhaps is even a sign of its eclecticism and want of rigor—after all, the gamut of Cicero's works is no narrower than that of Horace's verses—it is worth recalling that Greek philosophy was no less latitudinarian. The decision, in many surveys of Greek philosophy, to exclude figures such as Isocrates, or Cleanthes, or for that matter Lucian, is a reflection of modern habits of thought more than ancient. So Augustan poetry has a place in this book, and Apuleius receives his due.

Great individuals, especially if there emerged schools bearing their names, like Plato, Aristotle, and Epicurus, readily capture attention, but the focus on specific systems may obscure ways in which they respond to questions that are characteristic of their time. After all, less than a century separates the writings of Plato and Aristotle from those of Epicurus and the early Stoics, and despite many changes in the world around them, they continued to live in an identifiable polis culture with many shared values and presuppositions. Rome was a different place, and from the time when we first have access to their literature to the later Roman Empire there occurred profound, if also subtle, transformations in the perception of such basic categories as time, space, and the conception of the self or subject. The imposition of a universal calendar and the standardization of measures, as well as developments in law, in notions of sovereignty, and in language, had an impact even on the most abstract theories of nature and visions of the human good. Thus, one section of the present volume is devoted to such themes.

When it comes to philosophy, even today, style matters, and in a highly rhetorical culture such as Rome's it mattered all the more. One pointed difference between thinkers writing in Latin and those composing in Greek, even when they were Romanized (if that is the right word), is that the former were deeply conscious of questions of translation. Genre mattered too. Quintilian boasts that satire was a wholly Roman invention, and yet it was a principal vehicle of philosophy, as witnessed by Horace and Persius, and the fragments of the earlier poet Lucilius. Philosophy is communicated in dialogues (Plato was the forerunner, of course), in oratory, and in consolations. What is more, the topics that philosophers treated also varied. Not just translation, but questions about the essence of poetry, or of freedom of speech under monarchies, assumed new forms in Roman reflection and widened the scope of philosophical inquiry.

As the reader will notice at once, there is variety not only in the topics selected for discussion but also in the length and tone of the individual chapters. This was not entirely by design. As drafts were submitted, which for reasons beyond the editors' or the contributors' control took place over several years, it became clear that a single size did not fit all subjects, nor was it either possible or desirable to impose a single format or approach to all the essays. For essays the chapters are, not articles in an encyclopedia, which may aspire to greater uniformity. Roman philosophy is, in one sense, still under construction, and very likely always will be (in a large sense, this is no doubt true of philosophy itself). The reader will find that tendencies, themes, and individuals are treated in several distinct chapters (cross-references are provided), not always from the same perspective. Handbooks today, or "companions" as they are often labeled, are not so much summaries of all that is known as invitations to explore further issues that are not yet wholly resolved. It is in this spirit that the reader is encouraged to approach the several papers collected in this volume.

Introductions often conclude with an overview of the contents of the book, but in a volume such as this, such a guide seemed unnecessary, and perhaps even misleading. The chapter titles and associated abstracts give an adequate indication of the topic. For the rest, the pleasure, we hope, will lie in the fresh encounter with the orientations and methods that inform the several chapters, and precisely for the manner in which they sometimes disagree or even clash.

We conclude by expressing our gratitude to the press, and to our editor Stefan Vranka, for their support for this project, to Rebecca Sausville for her diligent copyediting of the entire manuscript, and to the contributors to the volume for their efforts and their patience.

Myrto Garani
David Konstan
Gretchen Reydams-Schils

List of Contributors

Daniel Bertoni received his PhD from Harvard University with a dissertation on Greek and Roman botany and taught for two years in the Department of Classics at the University of Miami. Subsequently, he received a JD from the University of California, Berkeley, and now serves as a Trial Attorney at the US Department of Justice.

Anne-Isabelle Bouton-Touboulic is Professor of Latin, University of Lille (France). She is the author of *L'ordre caché: La notion d'ordre chez saint Augustine* (2004) and has edited or coedited several volumes, including *Scepticisme et religion* (with Carlos Lévy) (2016) and *L'amour de la justice, de la Septante à Thomas d'Aquin* (2017).

Orazio Cappello is an Honorary Research Associate in University College London's Psychoanalysis Unit. He is the author of several articles on Cicero, Republican and Imperial intellectual history, as well as a monograph on Cicero and skepticism.

Ivor J. Davidson is Honorary Research Professor in Divinity, University of Aberdeen, UK. He previously held chairs in Systematic and Historical Theology at the University of Otago, New Zealand, and the University of St Andrews, UK; at the latter he was also Dean of the Faculty of Divinity, Head of School, and Principal of St. Mary's College. A Classicist by initial training and enduring affections, his publications include the standard modern critical study of the Latin text of Ambrose's *De officiis* (2 vols., 2002).

Gregson Davis is Andrew W. Mellon Distinguished Professor Emeritus in the Humanities at Duke University. He has held joint appointments in Classics and Comparative Literature at Stanford, Cornell, and New York University. His major publications in the field of Latin poetry of the Late Republic include the books: *Polyhymnia: The Rhetoric of Horatian Lyric Discourse* (1991) and *Parthenope: The Interplay of Ideas in Vergilian Bucolic* (2012).

Elisa Della Calce is a postdoctoral research fellow at the University of Turin. Her main research interests are in Latin historiography (Livy in particular), the study of value concepts (*Wertbegriffe*) in Roman thought, and digital humanities. She is currently working on the reception of classical authors in Jesuit texts from the sixteenth and seventeenth century.

Michael Erler was Professor ordinarius of Classical Philology at the University of Wuerzburg, He is presently senior professor and chair of the board of directors of the Siebold Collegium, Institute for Advanced Studies, University of Wuerzburg. He is author of several books and articles on Plato, Platonism, Epicurus and the Epicurean tradition, drama, Hellenistic literature, and literature of imperial times. He is interested in the relationship between literature and philosophy. He was president of the International Plato Society (2001–2004), Gesellschaft für antike Philosophie (2007–2010), and Mommsen Gesellschaft, (2013–2015).

Dana Fields is an independent scholar whose work focuses on the Greek-speaking world of the Roman empire. Her recent book *Frankness, Greek Culture, and the Roman Empire* (2021) addresses the significance of *parrhēsia* and related ideas in later Greek culture.

Matthew Fox is Professor of Classics at the University of Glasgow. He has been exploring the interplay between philosophical and literary in Cicero for over thirty years.

Myrto Garani is Associate Professor of Latin Literature at the National and Kapodistrian University of Athens, Greece. She is the author of *Empedocles Redivivus: Poetry and Analogy in Lucretius* (2007), coeditor with David Konstan of *The Philosophizing Muse: The Influence of Greek Philosophy on Roman Poetry* (2014), and coeditor with A. N. Michalopoulos and S. Papaioannou of *Intertextuality in Seneca's Philosophical Writings* (2020). She is currently working on a monograph on Seneca's *Naturales quaestiones* Book 3 (for the Pierides series) and a commentary on Lucretius's *De rerum natura* 6 (for the Fondazione Lorenzo Valla series).

Pamela Gordon is Professor of Classics at the University of Kansas. She is the author of "Kitsch, Death, and the Epicurean," in Sergio Yona and Gregson Davis, eds., *Epicurus in Republican Rome: Philosophical Perspectives in the Ciceronian Age* (2022), and *The Invention and Gendering of Epicurus* (2012).

Quinn Griffin received her PhD in 2016 from The Ohio State University with a dissertation on classical *exempla* and learned women in the Renaissance. From 2016 to 2021 she served as an Assistant Professor of Classics at Grand Valley State University in Allendale, Michigan, where she continued her research on Renaissance and early modern women with an article on the reception of classical authors in Laura Cereta's "Oration on the Funeral of a Donkey." She explored the reception of funeral orations and adoxography in the Renaissance in a chapter titled, "The Owl and the Pussycat: Following the Trail of a Neo-Latin Mock Funeral Oration." She is currently an e-learning developer in Columbus, Ohio, and continues to engage with her research in the context of fiction writing.

Erik Gunderson is a Professor of Classics at the University of Toronto. His research is loosely centered around the Greco-Roman discourses of the self. He is the author of six scholarly monographs and edited *The Cambridge Companion to Ancient Rhetoric*. His most recent book is *The Art of Complicity in Martial and Statius: The Epigrams, Siluae, and Domitianic Rome*.

Myrto Hatzimichali is Associate Professor in Classics (Ancient Philosophy) at the University of Cambridge and a fellow of Homerton College. She is the author of *Potamo* *of Alexandria and the Emergence of Eclecticism in Late Hellenistic Philosophy* (2011), and has recently contributed to volumes on Plato's Academy, late Hellenistic Greek literature, the *Cambridge Companion to Aristotle's Biology*, and the *Corpus dei Papiri Filosofici*.

Christina Hoenig is an Associate professor in Classics at the University of Pittsburgh. Her main areas of research are the Greek and Roman Platonic traditions. A central theme of interest is the translation of Greek philosophical vocabulary into Latin. Her monograph *Plato's Timaeus and the Latin Tradition* was published in 2018.

Phillip Sidney Horky is Professor of Ancient Philosophy in the Department of Classics & Ancient History, Durham University . In addition to his *Plato and Pythagoreanism* (2013) and edited volume *Cosmos in the Ancient World* (2019), he is currently finishing a source book on Hellenistic and Post-Hellenistic Pythagoreanism. His next project is a book entitled *The Philosophy of Democracy in Antiquity*, for which he received a British Academy Mid-Career Fellowship (2022–2023). For the period 2023–2028, he will be working with Professor Edith Hall (Durham) on a major research project, funded by UK Research and Innovation (UKRI), on Aristotle's writing styles and their reception in antiquity.

Aaron Kachuck is Professor of Latin Authors and Latin Literature at Université Catholique de Louvain (Louvain-la-Neuve). A specialist in Latin literature, and a comparatist by formation, he works at the intersection of literature and religion at Rome. He is the author of *The Solitary Sphere in the Age of Virgil* (2021), and is currently working on a commentary on the *Satires* of Persius (under contract), and on articles, monographs, and collective projects related to cosmography in antiquity and in the classical tradition, to the role of ritual in the poetic imaginary of Latin literature, and to Cynicism in antiquity and its later reception.

Anthony Kaldellis is Professor of Classics at The Ohio State University. He has published widely on many aspects of Byzantine history, literature, and culture, and his recent work focuses on its Roman aspects, especially in *The Byzantine Republic* (2015) and *Romanland: Ethnicity and Empire in Byzantium* (2019).

George Karamanolis is Associate Professor in Philosophy in the Department of Philosophy at the University of Vienna working primarily on ancient philosophy while maintaining research interests in Byzantine and Renaissance philosophy. His publications include the monographs *Plato and Aristotle in Agreement? Platonists on Aristotle from Antiochus to Porphyry* (2006; rev. paperback 2013), *The Philosophy of Early Christianity* (2013; rev. 2nd ed. 2021); and the edited volumes *Studies on Porphyry* (2007, with Anne Sheppard); *The Aporetic Tradition in Ancient Philosophy* (2017, with Vasilis Politis), and *Pseudo-Aristotle On the Cosmos: A Commentary* (2020, with Pavel Gregorić).

Duncan F. Kennedy is Emeritus Professor of Latin Literature and the Theory of Criticism at the University of Bristol. Among his writings are *Rethinking Reality:*

Lucretius and the Textualization of Nature (2002) and *Antiquity and the Meanings of Time: A Philosophy of Literature and Interpretation* (2013).

James Ker is Professor of Classical Studies at the University of Pennsylvania. His main area of teaching and research is the cultural dimensions of Roman literature, and his books include *The Deaths of Seneca* (2009).

Agnieszka Kijewska is Professor of the History of Ancient and Medieval Philosophy at the Faculty of Philosophy at the John Paul II Lublin Catholic University (Poland). She is interested in the medieval Neoplatonic tradition, mainly, St. Augustine, Boethius, Eriugena, the School of Chartres, and Nicholas of Cusa.

David Konstan is Professor of Classics at New York University. He is the author of *Friendship in the Classical World* (1997), *The Emotions of the Ancient Greeks: Studies in Aristotle and Classical Literature* (2006), and most recently *The Origin of Sin: Greece and Rome, Early Judaism and Christianity* (2022). He is a past president of the American Philological Association (now the Society for Classical Studies), and a fellow of the American Academy of Arts and Sciences and an honorary fellow of the Australian Academy of the Humanities.

Kurt Lampe is a Senior Lecturer in Classics and Ancient History at the University of Bristol. He is also a psychotherapist in training at the Bath Centre for Psychotherapy and Counselling. His most recent books are the paired volumes, *French and Italian Stoicisms: From Sartre to Agamben* (ed. Kurt Lampe and Janae Sholtz) and *German Stoicisms: from Hegel to Sloterdijk* (ed. Kurt Lampe and Andrew Benjamin).

David Leith is Senior Lecturer in Classics at the University of Exeter. He has published variously on the Hellenistic and Roman medical sects, especially Herophilus, Erasistratus, Asclepiades, and the Methodists, and has edited medical fragments for the Oxyrhynchus Papyri series. He is currently preparing a collection, with essays and commentary, of the testimonia on Asclepiades of Bithynia.

Ermanno Malaspina is *Academicus ordinarius* at the *Pontificia Academia Latinitatis* and President of the advisory Board of the *Société Internationale des Amis de Cicéron* (www.tulliana.eu). His main interests are Cicero, Seneca, and landscape theories in Rome. He is the editor of Seneca's *De clementia* (2016) and of Cicero's *Lucullus* (forthcoming).

Natania Meeker is Associate Professor of French and Italian at the University of Southern California. She is the author of *Voluptuous Philosophy: Literary Materialism in the French Enlightenment* (2006) and coauthor of *Radical Botany: Plants and Speculative Fiction* (2020). She is currently completing a monograph, tentatively titled *Illusion without Error*, on feminine materialisms in eighteenth-century France.

Tim O'Keefe is Professor of Philosophy at Georgia State University. His publications on Epicureanism include two books (*Epicurus on Freedom*, 2005, and *Epicureanism*, 2009) and articles on topics such as the Epicureans on the mind–body relation, freedom of action, the ontological status of sensible qualities, friendship, justice, and death. He has also published on the Pyrrhonian skeptics, the Stoics, the Cyrenaics, Anaxarchus, and the spurious Platonic dialogue the *Axiochus*.

James I. Porter is the Irving Stone Professor in Literature and Distinguished Professor of Rhetoric and Ancient Greek and Roman Studies at the University of California, Berkeley. He is the author, most recently, of *Homer: The Very Idea* (2021). He is currently completing a study of the self as a problem in antiquity from Heraclitus to the Roman Stoics.

Gretchen Reydams-Schils is Professor in the Program of Liberal Studies at the University of Notre Dame, and holds concurrent appointments in Classics, Philosophy, and Theology. She is the author of *The Roman Stoics; Self, Responsibility, and Affection* (2005) and, most recently, *Calcidius on Plato's Timaeus: Greek Philosophy, Latin Reception, and Christian Contexts* (2020). She directs the Notre Dame Workshop on Ancient Philosophy.

Malcolm Schofield is Emeritus Professor of Ancient Philosophy, University of Cambridge, and Fellow of St John's College, where he has taught for fifty years. He has published widely on Presocratic philosophy, Plato, Aristotle, Stoicism, and Cicero's philosophical writings. His most recent book is *Cicero: Political Philosophy* (2021).

John Sellars is Reader in Philosophy at Royal Holloway, University of London. His recent books include *Hellenistic Philosophy* (2018) and *Marcus Aurelius* (2021).

James Warren is Professor of Ancient Philosophy at the University of Cambridge and a Fellow of Corpus Christi College. His publications include *Facing Death: Epicurus and His Critics* (2004), *The Pleasures of Reason in Plato, Aristotle, and the Hellenistic Hedonists* (2014), and *Regret: A Study in Ancient Moral Psychology* (2021).

Claudia Wiener is Professor of Classical and Neo-Latin Studies at the Ludwig-Maximilians-University of Munich. Her research interests include the influence of Stoic philosophy on Roman literature, textual transmission and medieval and renaissance scholarly commentaries on Latin Classics (esp. Persius), and neo-Latin literature in Germany. She has published inter alia *Stoische Doktrin in römischer Belletristik: Das Problem von Entscheidungsfreiheit und Determinismus in Senecas Tragödien und Lucans Pharsalia*.

Jeffrey Ulrich is an Assistant Professor of Classics who specializes in the ancient novel and the reception of Platonism in Imperial Roman culture. He has written extensively on Platonic elements in Apuleius's novel and broader oeuvre, and is finishing a monograph on philosophical choice and aesthetic experience in the *Metamorphoses*. He is also interested in Roman poetry and satire, and has written on Vergil, Horace, and Petronius.

PART I

THE ROMAN PHILOSOPHER

Affiliation, Identity, Self, and Other

CHAPTER 1

ITALIC PYTHAGOREANISM IN THE HELLENISTIC AGE

PHILLIP SIDNEY HORKY

INTRODUCTION

For the soul is celestial, as it was drawn down from its home on highest and, as it were, buried in the earth (*demersus in terram*), a place opposite to the nature that is divine and eternal. I believe that the immortal gods have sown souls in human bodies so that there might be people to watch over the earth, and who, by contemplating the order of the heavens, might imitate it through moderation and constancy of living. Nor have I been driven to believe this by the force of reason and dialectical argumentation alone, but also by the excellence and authority of the greatest philosophers. I have learned that Pythagoras and the Pythagoreans—practically our own countrymen (*incolas paene nostros*)—who were once referred to as "Italic" philosophers (*qui essent Italici philosophi quondam nominati*), never doubted that the soul we have was culled from the universal divine Mind.

(Cato the Elder, speaking in Cic. *Sen.* 77–78)

GRASPING what is "Roman" about the philosophy in Rome that preceded his own was a project that Cicero undertook with a certain amount of energy and care. Cicero sought to pursue this project by reference to non-Roman philosophy, especially Greek philosophy. The ways in which Greek philosophy, chiefly the philosophical ideas of Plato, the Peripatetics, the Stoics, the Epicureans, and the (skeptical) Academy, came to influence Roman philosophy have been thoroughly treated in scholarly literature. However, despite Cato the Elder's assertion that the philosophy of the "Pythagoreans," those "who were once (*quondam*) referred to as Italics" and were "practically" (*paene*) countrymen of the Romans, provided him with the proper understanding of death, modern studies on the importance of "Italic" philosophy, especially figured as "Pythagorean," to Roman philosophy are not easy to find.[1] More common are unsubstantiated claims that subvert such a project: as Jonathan Powell asserts, "the Neo-Pythagoreanism of the Roman Republic is an interesting byway, but probably without major influence on the philosophy of the time."[2] Yet Powell's assertion does little to explain the evidence from Cicero's own corpus of the perceived importance of Pythagoreanism for the development of ancient intellectual cultures, both for early Greek philosophers such as Plato, and, as we will see below, for certain paradigmatic Roman heroes of the early-middle Republic.[3] One reason why a proper assessment of the importance of Pythagoreanism for Roman philosophy has not been written is that scholars haven't quite mapped out the parameters of the Hellenistic Pythagoreanism thought to be associated with the Italian peninsula. This chapter aims to address two problems that arise out of this observation: (1) it seeks to delineate what "Italic" philosophy might have been for the Romans, especially given what "Italic" or "Italian" would have meant to a Roman such as Cicero, in the first century BCE; and (2) it seeks to elaborate further on the relationship between "Italic" philosophy, as constructed in the first century BCE, and Hellenistic Pythagoreanism. The project of defining, or at least sketching the broad parameters of, Hellenistic Pythagoreanism remains beyond the scope of this piece, but we can nevertheless make use of textual evidence of and reliable testimony about Pythagoreanism in the Hellenistic age, in our project of attempting to giving shape to "Italic" philosophy.[4]

It has not often been noticed that Cicero actually differentiates the Pythagoreans, whom his authoritative interlocutor Cato refers to as "practically our own countrymen," from the "Italic" philosophers, a name no longer used to describe the Pythagoreans—as if the old nomenclature had lost its value. At the end of this chapter, the deep importance of this temporal qualification will become clear. A straightforward reading of this passage would of course note that Cicero has been reading the work of Aristotle, or something like it,[5] as Aristotle rather routinely conflates Pythagoreans with "Italian" philosophers in his treatises.[6] But what "Italy" was in Cicero's time was not what it had been in Aristotle's, nor yet what it eventually would become under Augustus, who confirmed Italian identity by dividing all of "Italy," understood to include the entire peninsula from Regium to Transpadane Gaul, into eleven regions.[7] As Emma Dench and, more recently, Grant Nelsestuen, have argued, a variety of positions about what constituted "Italy" in the first century BCE can be detected, not without ideological implications.[8] "Italy" was, throughout the Hellenistic and early Roman Republican ages, more of a construct than a place of firm identity, made up of various ethnic groups distributed throughout a loosely shifting geographical space.[9] And, indeed, from the earliest prose writings in Latin, in Cato's *Origines*, a robust discourse on this subject was available to Romans.[10] Contemporaries of Cicero, such as Varro and Dionysius of Halicarnassus, could plausibly construct wholly diverse geographical orientations of "Italy."[11] Thus, various representations from the past or present could have informed Cicero's sense of what it meant to speak of Pythagorean philosophy as having once been considered "Italic," even though it was no longer allegedly so in his (i.e., Cicero's) own day.

Cicero, however, understood "Italic" philosophy to be neither Roman nor Greek, but something in-between—something that could be associated with the values of Cato the Elder (whether qua Roman or qua Tusculan is unclear), and yet not unrelated to the Ionian philosophy evidenced by Pythagoras's relocation from Samos to Croton. Cicero himself may have had particular personal reasons to revive the notion of "Italic" philosophy, which he probably found in Aristotle's works, but equally probably did not find in other works of philosophical history available to him. For "Italic" philosophy as such is notable for its absence just as much as its presence: no evidence of any philosophy, including Pythagorean philosophy, being expressly called "Italic" as such, is to be found from Aristotle to Cicero's time, although interest in this notion explodes after the first century BCE, and the division of philosophy into Ionian and Italian is reinvigorated by figures like Clement of Alexandria and (ps-)Hippolytus of Rome.[12] That Cicero associated "Italic" and "Italian" with those peoples who were neither strictly Greek nor Roman, however, can be inferred from a passage of his *De Haruspicum Responso*, where, by reference to discussion of the Social Wars (which he calls the "*Italici Belli*"), Cicero differentiates Italic peoples from Greeks and Romans, while nevertheless linking them to the Latins.[13] And he may have had good reason to do so: as a *novus homo*, like Cato the Elder before him (and others, as we will see), Cicero laid claim to being a dual-citizen—having both a Roman *patria*, to which he was to claim allegiance, and his native *patria* of Arpinum, which was the land of his ancestors and seat of native cults.[14] His commitment to Rome was best explained by having one fatherland that was given by birth, and the other by law.

But there still remains the issue of Cicero's initial association, and subsequent dissociation (*quondam*), of Pythagoreanism with "Italic" philosophy. In the *Tusculan Disputations*, Cicero argues that Pythagoras came from Asia Minor to Italy, bringing the notion of the immortality of the soul, which he learned from his teacher Pherecydes of Syros, to the Italian peninsula.[15] Many were thought to have come to Pythagoras to become his students, including Romans. Cicero later (*Tusc.* 4.3) ropes in some surprising figures: other people would say that the great Roman king Numa Pompilius was disciple of Pythagoras, but Cicero knows better—the chronology is all wrong.[16] Even so, the great Cato the Elder, in his *Origines*, evidenced Pythagorean tendencies, and the paradigmatic republican statesman Appius Claudius Caecus was no less than a bona fide Pythagorean himself. Thus, according to Cicero, did Pythagoreanism come to inform early philosophy of the Romans of the late fourth and third centuries BCE. But what about "Italic" philosophy? We see this taken up in Cicero's presentation of the development of Roman philosophy: for, in Cato the Elder's account of his youth in *Sen.* 39–41, he claims to have heard a debate, passed down through oral traditions in Tarentum, which involved not only the famous Pythagorean statesman Archytas of Tarentum and Plato but also a remarkable figure known as Herennius Pontius, a *Samnite* philosopher who was a contemporary of Archytas and Plato. How can we account for this Samnite philosopher's presence in Cicero's text? We are encouraged to consider not only the philosophy that flourished in the emigration of Pythagoreanism from Ionia to Italy but also something that Cicero would have recognized as uniquely "Italic"—a philosophy that is considered to have employed the language and concepts of Greek philosophy, but that retained its own native genius.[17] And, as we will see, much of what survives of "Italic" philosophy, in the writings associated with the Lucanians Aesara/Aresas, Occelus, and Eccelus, and in the fragments of Ennius of Rudiae, is often linked with Hellenistic Pythagoreanism, representing less a subcategory of the Pythagoreanism known to Cicero and others than a novel aspect that Hellenistic Pythagoreanism took on sometime before the end of the second century BCE.

LUCANIAN PHILOSOPHY (1): ARESAS/AESARA

Lucania was an area in southern Italy that maps roughly onto modern Basilicata, forming a house-shaped space that ranged roughly from Thurii in the southeast, to Metapontum in the northeast, to Venusia in the north, Paestum in the northwest, to Laos in the southwest. This area had been substantially overcome around 420 BCE by non-Greeks who spoke a language called Oscan. A Sabellic language spoken in southern and central Italy by Lucanians and Samnites alike, Oscan is mostly known from inscriptions that predate the Social War (91–88 BCE).[18] Oscan and Greek are understood to have coexisted for a long time in Lucania. A number of Lucanian philosophers are attested, and some texts purporting to have been written by these figures survive. Their imprint was left on Aristoxenus of Tarentum, who, writing in the late fourth century BCE, included a number of non-Greek philosophers who hailed from Italy in his list of Pythagorean philosophers.[19] He refers to two brothers named Occelus and Occilus of Lucania, as well as their sisters Occelo and Eccelo. Texts survive under the name of Occelus and a certain Eccelus (see below), which might have originally been an unnecessary correction of Eccelo, although nothing survives for Occilus or Occelo. Additionally, Aristoxenus refers to two other Lucanian philosophers by name: a Cerambus, otherwise totally unknown, and a certain Aresandrus, whose name might have been corrupted to become "Aresas," a figure who is better known, and to whom a substantial fragment of a work titled *On the Nature of the Human* has been attributed by modern scholars.[20] The historical Aresas of Lucania was considered the last "diadochy" or leader of the school that traced itself back to Pythagoras, who then imparted his learning to Diodorus of Aspendus, a heretic who was thought to have publicized the Pythagorean *acusmata/symbola* widely in Greece.[21] Plutarch (*De Gen.* 13) believed that Aresas was one of the last Pythagoreans to stay in western Greece, remaining in Sicily after the Cylonian conspiracy tore the Pythagorean communities apart, and visiting with Gorgias of Leontini. If this information is to be trusted, it would place the historical Aresas in the early part of the second half of the fifth century BCE.

The surviving fragment of pseudo-Aresas/Aesara, from a work called *On the Nature of the Human*, features an inquiry into human nature that focuses on human psychology, by reference to law and justice (ps-Aresas/Aesara of Lucania, *On the Nature of the Human* fr. 1, pp. 48.22–49.8 Thesleff):[22]

> The nature (*physis*) of the human being seems to me to be a standard (*kanôn*) for law and justice, and for the household and the city. For if someone were to follow the tracks in himself, he would make a discovery in his search: the law (*nomos*) is in him, and justice (*dika*) is the orderly arrangement (*diakosmasis*) of the soul. Indeed, being threefold, it has been organized for three functions: <the intellect> effects judgment (*gnôma*) and intelligence (*phronasis*); <the spirit> [effects] prowess and power; and desire [effects] love and kindliness. And all these [parts] of it [sc. the soul] are arranged relative to one another in such a way that what is best leads, what is worst is ruled, and what is in the middle occupies the middle place, i.e., it rules and is ruled.
>
> Φύσις ἀνθρώπω κανών μοι δοκεῖ νόμω τε καὶ δίκας ἦμεν καὶ οἴκω τε καὶ πόλιος. ἴχνια γὰρ ἐν αὐτῷ στιβαζόμενος εὔροιτό κά τις καὶ μαστευόμενος· νόμος γὰρ ἐν αὐτῷ καὶ δίκα ἀ τᾶς ψυχᾶς ἐστι διακόσμασις. τριχθαδία γὰρ ὑπάρχοισα ἐπὶ τριχθαδίοις ἔργοις συνέστακε· γνώμαν καὶ φρόνασιν ἐργαζόμενος <ὁ νόος> καὶ ἀλκὰν καὶ δύναμιν <ἁ θύμωσις> καὶ ἔρωτα καὶ φιλοφροσύναν ἁ ἐπιθυμία. καὶ οὕτω συντέτακται ταῦτα ποτ' ἄλλαλα πάντα, ὥστε αὐτᾶς τὸ μὲν κράτιστον ἀγέεσθαι, τὸ δὲ χεῖρον ἄρχεσθαι, τὸ δὲ μέσον μέσαν ἐπέχεν τάξιν, καὶ ἄρχεν καὶ ἄρχεσθαι.

Ps-Aresas/Aesara expands on the Platonic theory of the tripartition of the soul, using the same terms Plato employed in the *Republic*, but adding concepts and vocabulary from the Peripatetic tradition—adapting ideas that are found equally in Aristotle's *Politics* and, perhaps closer to this text, the *On Law and Justice* attributed to the Pythagorean Archytas of Tarentum, which may be among the earliest of the Pythagorean pseudepigrapha.[23] Moreover, ps-Aresas/Aesara associates the gift of law and justice to humans by God, echoing similar ideas in the so-called Great Speech of Protagoras, and the defense of law and justice in the work known as Anonymus Iamblichi, sometimes thought to be a student of Protagoras.[24] In this way, ps-Aresas/Aesara appears to combine doctrines about the importance of law and justice, familiar from the Sophistic and Socratic traditions, with a hybrid Platonic-Pythagorean presentation of the soul.

Things get more interesting philosophically a bit further down in the fragment, after ps-Aresas/Aesara has described how the various parts of the soul must relate to one another when the disposition of the soul is properly harmonized (ps-Aresas/Aesara of Lucania, *On the Nature of the Human* fr. 1, p. 50.6–22 Thesleff):

> What is more, a certain concord and agreement accompanies this sort of arrangement. For this sort [of arrangement] could justly be said to be the "good law (*eunomia*) of the soul"—regardless of whichever should additionally confer the strength of virtue (the better part ruling or the worse part being ruled). And friendship, love, and kindliness, cognate and kindred, will sprout from these parts. For the intellect that closely inspects persuades, desire loves, and the spirit is filled with might: [once] seething with enmity, it becomes friendly to desire. Indeed, the

intellect harmonized what is pleasant with what is painful, blended the tense and impetuous with the light and dissolute part of the soul, and each part was distributed with respect to its kindred and cognate forethought (*promatheia*) for each thing: intellect closely inspecting and tracking things; spirit conferring impulse and might upon what is inspected; and desire, being akin to affection, adapts to the intellect, exalting pleasure as its own and surrendering circumspection to the circumspect part of the soul. By virtue of these things, the way of life (*bios*) seems to me to be best for humans when what is sweet is blended with what is good (*spoudaios*), i.e., pleasure with virtue. The intellect is able to adjust these things to itself, becoming lovely for its education and virtue.

καὶ μὰν ὁμόνοιά τις καὶ ὁμοφροσύνα ὀπαδεῖ τᾷ τοιαύτᾳ διατάξει. τὸ δὲ τοιοῦτον δικαίως κα λέγοιτο εὐνομία ἤμεν τᾶς ψυχᾶς, ἅτις ἐκ τῶ ἄρχεν μὲν τὸ κάρρον, ἄρχεσθαι δὲ τὸ χέρειον κράτος ἐπιφέροιτο τᾶς ἀρετᾶς. καὶ φιλία δὲ καὶ ἔρως καὶ φιλοφροσύνα σύμφυλος καὶ συγγενὴς ἐκ τούτων ἐξεβλάστασε τῶν μερέων. συμπείθει μὲν γὰρ ὁ νόος ὁραυγούμενος, ἔραται δὲ ἁ ἐπιθυμία, ἁ δὲ θύμωσις ἐμπιπλαμένα μένεος, ἔχθρᾳ ζέουσα φίλα γίγνεται τᾷ ἐπιθυμίᾳ. ἁρμόσας γὰρ ὁ νόος τὸ ἁδὺ τῷ λυπηρῷ συγκατακρεόμενος καὶ τὸ σύντονον καὶ σφοδρὸν τῷ κούφῳ μέρει τᾶς ψυχᾶς καὶ διαχυτικῷ· ἕκαστόν τε ἑκάστῳ πράγματος τὰν σύμφολον καὶ συγγένεα προμάθειαν διαμεμέρισται, ὁ μὲν νόος ὁραυγούμενος καὶ στιβαζόμενος τὰ πράγματα, ἁ δὲ θύμωσις ὁρμὰν καὶ ἀλκὰν ποτιφερομένα τοῖς ὁραυγασθεῖσιν· ἁ δὲ ἐπιθυμία φιλοστοργίᾳ συγγενὴς ἔασσα ἐφαρμόζει τῷ νόῳ ἴδιον περιποιουμένα τὸ ἁδὺ καὶ τὸ σύννοον ἀποδιδοῦσα τῷ συννόῳ μέρει τᾶς ψυχᾶς. ὧνπερ ἕκατι δοκέει μοι καὶ ὁ βίος ὁ κατ' ἀνθρώπως ἄριστος ἤμεν, ὅκκα τὸ ἁδὺ τῷ σπουδαίῳ συγκατακραθῇ καὶ ἁδονὰ τᾷ ἀρετᾷ. ποθαρμόξασθαι δ' αὐτὰ ὁ νόος δύναται, παιδεύσιος καὶ ἀρετᾶς ἐπήρατος γένομενος.

Ps-Aresas/Aesara continues the mapping of politics onto psychology, referring to the disposition of the harmony of the parts of the soul as its *eunomia*, a word whose value to philosophical traditions seems to emerge from Sparta in the eighth century BCE, to obtain confirmation as early as Solon, and to flourish among the Socratics, especially Xenophon and Plato, and figures arguably associated with Socratics, such as Anonymus Iamblichi.[25] In ps-Aresas/Aesara's text, however, something unique is advanced: the state of the soul being properly harmonized is called "well-lawed," which is explained as the disposition in which the better element rules, and the worse is ruled. Some version of this thought is found in Plato's *Republic* (462e), where Socrates and Glaucon conclude that a city-state which is well-lawed (*eunomos*) will, like the soul of an individual person, share in its affections. Similarly, the virtue of temperance, which is applied across the entire city-state of Callipolis and throughout the entire individual soul, is understood to be "a concord between naturally worse and naturally better as to which of them should rule" (*Resp.* 432b). There is a catch, however, as Socrates later (*Resp.* 605b–c) clarifies: in a well-lawed city, those poets who might stimulate and arouse the worse part of the city-state to attack its "rational" part should not be allowed to remain, for the reason that the rational part of the city-state, as well as the rational part of the soul, would be under threat.

Thus ps-Aresas/Aesara, the Lucanian Pythagorean, espouses a tripartite structure of the soul, without any reference to bipartition that would eventually come to be understood as the "truer" version of the Platonic soul in Plutarch (*De virtute morali* 3.441d–442a), in the late first century CE, and that can be found in some parts of the corpus of Pythagorean pseudepigrapha.[26] The notion that Pythagoras initiated the claim that the soul is tripartite is advanced by Posidonius, writing sometime around 100 BCE, citing some writings of Pythagoras's pupils that cannot be identified with confidence.[27] A distinct version of tripartition is also attested in a similar format by one of the best sources for Hellenistic Pythagoreanism, Alexander Polyhistor, in his *Successions of the Philosophers*, where he claims to have obtained the information from a work known as the *Pythagorean Notebooks* (*Pythagorika Hypomnêmata*), which also seem to date from the late second-/mid-first-century BCE (Diog. Laert. 8.25, 8.30). The fragment of ps-Aresas/Aesara represents what is perhaps the most complete surviving evidence for the psychological theory of the Hellenistic Pythagoreans. Indeed, ps-Aresas/Aesara shows us a very original psychological theory, for he claims that three goods, friendship, love, and kindness, sprout *from all three parts* of the soul. How does this happen?

According to ps-Aresas/Aesara, the three parts of the soul, when they have been harmonized into *eunomia*, work quite effectively together. Each performs its own duties, preserving the "justice" so defined as "minding one's own business" in Plato's *Republic* (433b–d). The intellect performs preliminary inspections, and manages to persuade the other parts of the soul to act on its preliminary inspections; desire, persuaded to act, seeks to protect its own interests by pursuing courage, which, properly persuaded by the intellect, acts to defend the whole, and to attack the (external) enemy. How does the intellect accomplish this? Interestingly, ps-Aresas/Aesara claims that it mixes together pleasure and pain and, by doing so, effects the adjustment of the courageous part of the soul (called "tense and impetuous"), where pain belongs, to the desirous part (called "light and dissolute"), where pleasure is located. The consequence of this adjustment, which finally leads to total psychic harmonization, is that the courageous and desirous parts of the soul obtain their own peculiar types of reason, exemplified by their capacities for diverse types of "forethought" (*promatheia*). The intellect inspects and tracks objects it pursues; courage impels the soul toward things being further inspected and endures what is to come; and desire discovers its own important role in this process, which is to acquire pleasure and refer intellectual pleasures, which belong not to itself, upward to the intellect. Ps-Aresas/Aesara claims that humans are at their best when they combine the objects of contemplation and enjoyment together in this psychic system. This is no discourse of the intellect enslaving or controlling the lower parts of the soul—the intellect's primary role in "ruling" the lower parts is to get the ball rolling in the process of inquiry, rather than to supervise at all times each part of the soul's activity, or to chastise the other parts of the soul for being disobedient. There is no familiar moderation of emotions, nor yet their extirpation, as one would find elsewhere in Hellenistic philosophy: the Pythagoreans of this period advocated a psychology of blending and harmonization of the parts, to achieve maximal performance across the whole system.[28]

Lucanian Philosophy (ii):
Occelus and Eccelus

The familiar combination of politics and ethics, which we have seen appealed to in the philosophical theory ascribed to Aresas/Aesara of Lucania above, recurs in the writings of two figures thought to be brothers: Occelus and Eccelus of Lucania. The latter figure is poorly attested, and, except for a single fragment of a work entitled *On Justice*, we know nothing about him except that he was a Pythagorean.[29] This fragment from the Pythagorean pseudepigrapha expresses a complete and wholly original thought, focused on the nature of justice in relation to the other canonical virtues (ps-Eccelus of Lucania, *On Justice* fr. 1, pp. 77.16–78.16 Thesleff):

> It seems to me best to address the justice (*dikaiosyna*) among men as the mother and nurse of the other virtues. For no [man] is able to be temperate (*sôphrôn*), courageous (*andreios*), or intelligent (*phronimos*) without it. Indeed, harmony is peace, with measured cadence, for the entire soul. The power of this [sc. justice] would become clearest to us if we were to examine the other states. For they offer a partial benefit, and [only] for one thing. But it [sc. justice] [offers benefit] for whole systems (*systêmata*), and widely. So, then, in the cosmos, forethought and harmony, justice (*dika*) and the intellect of one of the gods, assume the role of authority over things in their entirety, when one of the gods distributes the lots this way; in the city, it is justly called peace and good order (*eunomia*); in the household, it is unanimity (*homophrosyna*) of the husband and wife towards one another, and goodwill (*eunoia*) of slaves towards the master, as well as care of masters for their servants; in the body and the soul, it is life (*zôa*), first and most beloved to all, and health and soundness, and wisdom (*sophia*) among humans, which arises out of knowledge (*epistama*) and justice (*dikaiosyna*). And if it [sc. justice] educates the whole and the parts and preserves them by making them unanimous and mutually agreeable to one another, how could it not be called the mother and nurse of all and with every vote?

> Δοκεῖ μοι τῶν ἀνδρῶν τὰν δικαιοσύναν ματέρα τε καὶ τιθήναν τᾶν ἀλλᾶν ἀρετᾶν προσειπέν· ἄτερ γὰρ ταύτας οὔτε σώφρονα οὔτε ἀνδρεῖον οὔτε φρόνιμον οἷόν τε ἤμεν. ἁρμονία γάρ ἐστι καὶ εἰράνα τᾶς ὅλας ψυχᾶς μετ' εὐρυθμίας. δηλοφανέστερον δέ κα γένοιτο τὸ ταύτας κράτος ἐτάζουσιν ἀμὶν τὰς ἄλλας ἕξιας. μερικὰν γὰρ ἔχοντι αὗται τὰν ὠφέλειαν, καὶ ποθ' ἕνα· ἁ δὲ ποθ' ὅλα τὰ συστάματα, καὶ ἐν πλάθει. ἐν κόσμῳ μὲν ὦν αὐτὰ τὰν ὅλων ἀρχὰν διαστραταγοῦσα πρόνοιά τε καὶ ἁρμονία καὶ δίκα καὶ νῶς τινὸς θεῶν οὕτω ψαφιξαμένω· ἐν πόλει δὲ εἰράνα τε καὶ εὐνομία δικαίως κέκληται· ἐν οἴκῳ δ' ἔστιν ἀνδρὸς μὲν καὶ γυναικὸς ποτ' ἀλλάλως ὁμοφροσύνα, οἰκετᾶν δὲ ποτὶ δεσπότας εὔνοια, δεσποτᾶν δὲ ποτὶ θεράποντας καδεμονία· ἐν σώματι δὲ καὶ ψυχᾷ πράτα μὲν ἁ πᾶσιν ἀγαπατοτάτα ζωά, ἅ τε ὑγίεια καὶ ἀρτιότας, σοφία τ' ἐκ τᾶς ἐπιστάμας τε καὶ δικαιοσύνας γενομένα ἁ παρ' ἀνθρώποις. εἰ δ' αὐτὰ τὸ ὅλον καὶ τὰ μέρεα οὕτω παιδαγωγεῖ τε καὶ σῴζει ὁμόφρονα καὶ ποτάγορα ἀλλάλοις ἀπεργαζομένα, πῶς οὔ <κα> μάτηρ καὶ τιθήνα πασᾶν τε καὶ πάντων παμψαφεῖ λέγοιτο;

Ps-Eccelus's text argues, somewhat provocatively, that justice is the chief virtue, on the grounds that the other cardinal virtues—temperance, courage, and wisdom—cannot exist apart from it. Ps-Eccelus obliquely qualifies this claim by noting that harmony, of which he must assume justice to be the cause, is the soul's condition when it is at peace and in rhythm with the cosmos. He further elaborates by arguing that justice works at all levels of the macrocosm/microcosm, which he refers to as "systems" (*systêmata*): its benefits are universal, guaranteeing proper rule within the cosmos, and they work in the city-state to promote *eunomia* (the similarity here to the fragment of ps-Aresas/ Aesara of Lucania above might not be incidental); in the household to support marriage, as well as master–slave relations; and in the soul and body, to encourage health, which sustains life. Importantly, ps-Eccelus argues, justice encourages both wholes and parts to be "unanimous and mutually agreeable to one another." Justice here evinces a pre-Socratic—one might say Anaximandrian—tenor, occupying the place of what, in other Pythagorean pseudepigrapha, would be "god" or the "monad"—it is indeed interesting that "Eccelus" holds that justice is the forethought, intellect, righteousness, and harmony "of a certain god," whom he doesn't quite identify.[30] Justice thus construed appears to be an instrument of this anonymous god, which reflects his rationality.[31]

If "Eccelus" is understood to be the brother of Occelus of Lucania, then the former's obscurity contrasts with the high relief of his brother's popularity within the imagination of philosophers in the late Roman Republic and early Roman Empire. Occelus is cited, for example, by Philo of Alexandria (fl. first half of the first century CE) for being (according to some) one of the Pythagoreans who first advanced a theory that the universe is both ungenerated and indestructible; and Philo himself claims to have read the work *On the Nature of the Universe*, which he credits with having not only stated this doctrine, but having proven it through demonstrations (δι' ἀποδείξεων), as we will discuss below.[32] But Occelus's popularity is probably best exemplified by a series of letters, purported to be between Archytas and Plato, concerning the works of Occelus. The series of letters is demonstrably a forgery in which "Archytas," at the behest of "Plato," reports the discovery of the works of Occelus of Lucania (Diog. Laert. 8.80, p. 46.1–7 Thesleff):

> We attended to the matter of the notebooks (*hypomnêmata*) and went up to Lucania, where we happened upon the progeny of Occelus. Moreover, we ourselves have obtained the works *On Law*, *On Kingship*, *On Piety*, and *On the Generation of the Universe*, which we have sent to you. We haven't been able to discover the rest at this time, but if they should be found, you will have them.

Interestingly, in this remarkable historical fiction, the early fourth-century BCE philosopher Archytas of Tarentum is said to have gone from Tarentum to Lucania to find the "notebooks" (*hypomnêmata*) which the students of Occelus, who were understood to be still active in Lucania, were still preserving. Ps-Archytas's tantalizing reference to the "notebooks" recalls the works that Alexander Polyhistor apparently excerpted, the "Pythagorean Notebooks" (*Pythagorika Hypomnêmata*), which date to before the first century BCE; and, indeed, the consensus is that the work of Occelus of Lucania known to Philo of Alexandria as *On the Nature of the Universe* is to be dated from the mid-second century BCE to the mid-first century BCE.[33] It seems probable, then, that the pseudepigrapha circulating under the name "Occelus of Lucania," and known to the author of the epistles between "Archytas" and "Plato," are to be dated to the same period, and that correspondence between "Archytas" and "Plato" functioned as cover letters, in an attempt to authenticate the work of Occelus as both (1) anticipating some aspects of Aristotle's physics (it quotes and adapts parts of Aristotle's *On Generation and Corruption*) and (2) influencing Plato's own writings (especially, one might think, the *Timaeus*). Indeed, when "Plato" responds to "Archytas" in the *12th Epistle*, he praises the works of "Occelus" as being by "a man worthy of his ancient forebears," those Trojans who, under compulsion by their king Laomedon, immigrated to Italy in the generation before the Trojan War.[34]

The first work of "Occelus of Lucania" on the list given by "Archytas" is *On Law*, which survives in one fragment quoted by Stobaeus in order to show that, for "Occelus," "a cause (*aition*) is that through which something comes to be (*di' ho ginetai ti*)", an argument developed by Plato, elaborated and qualified by Aristotle, and assigned significant importance by the Stoics (ps-Occelus of Lucania, *On Law* fr. 1, pp. 124.18–125.7 Thesleff):[35]

> For life (*zôa*) holds the bodies (*skanea*) of animals together, and its cause is soul; harmony holds the cosmos together, and its cause is God; concord (*homonoia*) keeps the household and city together, and its cause is law (*nomos*). So what is the cause and nature, whereby the cosmos is fully harmonized and never falls into disorder, and the city and household are [not] ephemeral? Well, then, those things which are generated and mortal by nature, the matter from which they are composed, have the same cause of [their] dissolution; for they are composed out of what is mutable and perpetually passive. Indeed, the destruction of generated things entails preservation of the matter that generated them. And what is eternally in motion governs, whereas what is eternally passive is governed; in capacity, the former is prior, and the latter posterior; the former is divine, possesses reason, and is intelligent (*emphron*), whereas the latter is generated, irrational, and mutable.

> Συνέχει γὰρ τὰ μὲν σκάνεα τῶν ζῴων ζωά, ταύτας δ' αἴτιον ψυχά· τὸν δὲ κόσμον ἁρμονία, ταύτας δ' αἴτιος ὁ θεός· τοὺς δ' οἴκως καὶ τὰς πόλιας ὁμόνοια, ταύτας δ' αἴτιος νόμος. τίς ὦν αἰτία καὶ φύσις τὸν μὲν κόσμον ἁρμόχθαι διὰ παντὸς καὶ μηδέποτ' ἐξ ἀκοσμίαν ἐκβαίνειν, τὰς δὲ πόλιας καὶ τὼς οἴκως ὀλιγοχρονίως ἦμεν; ὅσα μὲν ὦν γεννατὰ καὶ θνατὰ τὰν φύσιν, ἐξ ἧς συνέστακεν ὕλας, τὰν αὐτὰν αἰτίαν ἔχει τᾶς διαλύσιος· συνέστη γὰρ ἐκ μεταβαλλοίσας καὶ ἀειπαθέος. ἡ γὰρ τῶν γεννωμένων ἀπογέννασις σωτηρία τᾶς γεννάτορος ὕλας. τὸ δὲ ἀεικίνατον κυβερνεῖ, τὸ δ' ἀειπαθὲς κυβερνεῖται· καὶ τὸ μὲν πρῶτον τᾷ δυνάμει, τὸ δὲ ὕστερον· καὶ τὸ θεῖον καὶ λόγον ἔχον καὶ ἔμφρον, τὸ δὲ γεννατὸν καὶ ἄλογον καὶ μεταβάλλον.

Here we see some interesting examples of anti-Aristotelian claims being advanced by way of Aristotelian terminology. Soul is understood to be the cause of "life" in animals, a claim that ultimately derives from a thought found in Aristotle's *On the Soul* (1.1), where Aristotle claims that soul is "as it were, a principle of animals"; but note that ps-Occelus also argues that "life" has a middle part to play, as what "holds together" the bodies of animals teleologically. So, for ps-Occelus, "soul" seems to be the efficient cause of life, and life appears to play the role of formal cause of living beings. Similarly, in a markedly anti-Aristotelian moment, ps-Occelus claims that god is the cause of harmony, and harmony functions as the formal cause that gives arrangement to the cosmos; finally, law takes on the role as cause of concord, which then renders the household and the city-state properly arranged.

One possible reason why the triad of objects compared with the cosmos, body—household—city-state, is to be found here is that it is found elsewhere in the Pythagorean pseudepigrapha, in a text that comes down to us as ascribed to Archytas and entitled *On Law and Justice*: this text shows similarities to the writings of Aristoxenus and employs demonstrably Aristotelian language in order to develop a "Pythagorean" account of a democratic mixed constitution.[36] Law there is key as a guarantor of the success of that order, as in the *On Law* of ps-Occelus and in *On the Nature of the Human* of ps-Aresas/Aesara discussed above, as it functions to regulate what parts of the city-state, and the soul, ought to "rule," and what parts ought to "be ruled."[37] Thus, we see that in the Hellenistic Pythagorean traditions, close relationships are drawn between the Tarentine philosopher-politician and the philosophical traditions associated with Lucanians—both intertextually, and in the fictional epistolary correspondence between "Archytas" and "Plato."

Ps-Occelus raises another question, however, that aims to differentiate the cosmos from household and city-state (and, presumably, body): in a Platonic vein, ps-Occelus claims that the cosmos is "universally harmonized and never falls into disorder,"[38] unlike the household and city-state, which are described as "short-lived." Does this cast a negative light on law, which is supposed to be the cause of the concord that sustains both household and city-state? Not according to ps-Occelus: he claims that it is the *material cause*, the nature from which both household and city-state are constituted, that is responsible for their being subject to generation and corruption, unlike the cosmos. For ps-Occelus, however, it is precisely the corruption of generated things, such as households and city-states, *that preserves matter as such*—nature continues to function as nature so long as the objects it generates are corrupted. Ps-Occelus displays an obvious adherence to the two-principle theory that is to be found in some Pythagorean pseudepigrapha, and which may ultimately derive from the works of the Pythagoreanizing Platonist Xenocrates.[39] The rational, intelligent, divine cause is mind, and the irrational, mutable, and generated cause is the receptacle. The closest comparison I can find to this description is the *On Principles* of ps-Archytas (fr. 1, p. 19.5–13 Thesleff):

> It is necessary that there be two principles of beings: one governs the column of things that are ordered and definite, and the other governs the column of disordered and indefinite things. And the former is expressible and rational, and keeps together the things that are, and it gives definition and order to all things that are not (for, in

its continuous application to generated things, it reduces them rationally and with measured cadence, and it gives a share of the universal substance (*ousia*) and form (*eidos*)). The other is irrational, inexpressible, and causes damage to what has been ordered, and utterly destroys those things that arrive at generation and existence (for, in its continuous application to objects, it assimilates them to itself).

Ἀνάγκα δύο ἀρχὰς εἶμεν τῶν ὄντων, μίαν μὲν τὰν συστοιχίαν ἔχουσαν τῶν τεταγμένων καὶ ὁριστῶν, ἑτέραν δὲ τὰν συστοιχίαν ἔχουσαν τῶν ἀτάκτων καὶ ἀορίστων. καὶ τὰν μὲν ῥητὰν καὶ λόγον ἔχουσαν καὶ τὰ ἐόντα ὁμοίως συνέχεν καὶ τὰ μὴ ἐόντα ὁρίζειν καὶ συντάσσειν (πλατιάζουσαν γὰρ ἀεὶ τοῖς γινομένοις εὐλόγως καὶ εὐρύθμως ἀνάγειν ταῦτα καὶ τὸ καθόλω οὐσίας τε καὶ εἴδεος μεταδιδόμεν)· τὰν δ' ἄλογον καὶ ἄρρητον καὶ τὰ συντεταγμένα λυμαίνεσθαι καὶ τὰ ἐς γένεσίν τε καὶ ὠσίαν παραγινόμενα διαλύειν (πλατιάζουσαν γὰρ ἀεὶ τοῖς πράγμασιν ἐξομοιοῦν αὐτᾷ ταῦτα).

Even despite the obvious similarities here, there are important differences: ps-Occelus argues, quite originally in my opinion, that the passive cause sustains its own existence *as matter* which is subject to ordering by the motive cause by subjecting generated objects to alteration and destruction. Contrast this position with that of ps-Archytas, which, developing the traditions that stem back to Aristotle's account of the Pythagorean Table of Contraries,[40] associates matter with the "unlimited" first and foremost, and says nothing about the unlimited sustaining its own existence through deformation of composite objects—although it does argue that matter assimilates generated objects to itself continuously.[41]

The other surviving text attributed to Occelus of Lucania, the treatise known as *On the Nature* (or *Generation*) *of the Universe*, is more extensive than *On Law*, and it shares many themes with it. There, ps-Occelus argues extensively that the universe is both ungenerated and incorruptible, taking various dialectical positions against his argument and demonstrating that they always end in contradictions. Note that while *On Law* does admit that god is the cause of harmony in the cosmos, it does not imply that the cosmos itself has been generated by god or any other efficient cause, and hence it is entirely plausible that the two texts are building off of one another's arguments. In *On the Nature of the Universe*, ps-Occelus argues that we can draw inferences from things we perceive in order to draw conclusions about the universe's immortality and incorruptibility, focusing on the persistence of its identity (7–10, p. 126.30–127.24 Thesleff):

(7) At any rate, the totality and the universe afford no such indication of anything [like this] to us: for we neither see it being generated, nor yet changing to the better or the greater, nor ever becoming worse or lesser, but it always subsists in itself, in the same way, itself both equal and similar to itself. (8) The signs and indications of this are clear: the orders [of things] are symmetries, figures, positions, intervals, powers, fast and slow motions relative to one another, the circuits of numbers and temporal periods—all things of this sort admit of change and diminution in accordance with

their generative nature's transition: for things that are greater and better tend towards the prime [of life] owing to their power, but those that are smaller and worse tend towards decay owing to their weakness.

(9) The totality and the universe are what I refer to as "the whole cosmos"; for it is through (*dia-*) this term [sc. *kosmos*] that this [meaning] conforms with its denomination: adorned with everything (*hapantôn diakosmêtheis*). After all, the system of the nature of the totality is self-sufficient and perfect, since nothing exists outside the universe. For, if something exists, it is in the universe, and the universe exists with it, and it comprehends all things within itself—some as parts, and others as outgrowths.

(10) The things that are contained in the cosmos feature harmonization (*sunharmogê*) with it, whereas the cosmos [harmonizes] with nothing else, but [only] itself with itself. For all other things have been constructed in such a way that they do not have a complete nature, but they require additional harmonization with their environment, e.g., animals with air; sight with light—and the other senses with their proper objects of sensation; plants with nutrients; the sun, moon, planets, and fixed stars [with the cosmos] according to their allotment of the general arrangement (*koinê diakosmêsis*). But the cosmos itself [harmonizes] with nothing [else], but [only] itself with itself.

(7) τὸ δέ γε ὅλον καὶ τὸ πᾶν οὐδὲν ἡμῖν ἐξ αὐτοῦ παρέχεται τεκμήριον τοιοῦτον· οὔτε γὰρ γενόμενον αὐτὸ εἴδομεν οὔτε μὴν ἐπὶ τὸ βέλτιον καὶ τὸ μεῖζον μεταβάλλον οὔτε χεῖρόν ποτε ἢ μεῖον γινόμενον, ἀλλ' ἀεὶ κατὰ ταὐτὸ καὶ ὡσαύτως διατελεῖ καὶ ἴσον καὶ ὅμοιον αὐτὸ ἑαυτῷ. (8) τὰ σημεῖα δὲ καὶ τεκμήρια τούτου ἐναργῆ· αἱ τάξεις αἱ συμμετρίαι σχηματισμοὶ θέσεις διστάσεις δυνάμεις, ταχυτῆτες πρὸς ἄλληλα καὶ βραδυτῆτες, ἀριθμῶν καὶ χρόνων περίοδοι· πάντα γὰρ τὰ τοιαῦτα μεταβολὴν καὶ μείωσιν ἐπίδεχεται κατὰ τὴν τῆς γενητῆς φύσεως διέξοδον. τῇ μὲν γὰρ ἀκμῇ διὰ τὴν δύναμιν τὰ μείζονα καὶ τὰ βελτίονα παρέπεται, τῇ δὲ φθίσει διὰ τὴν ἀσθένειαν τὰ μείονα καὶ τὰ χείρονα.

(9) Τὸ δέ γε ὅλον καὶ τὸ πᾶν ὀνόμαζω τὸν σύμπαντα κόσμον· δι' αὐτὸ γὰρ τοῦτο καὶ τῆς προσηγορίας ἔτυχε ταύτης, ἐκ τῶν ἀπάντων διακοσμηθείς. σύστημα γάρ ἐστι τῆς τῶν ὅλων φύσεως αὐτοτελὲς καὶ τέλειον. ἐκτὸς γὰρ τοῦ παντὸς οὐδέν· εἰ γάρ τι ἔστιν, ἐν τῷ παντί ἐστι, καὶ σὺν τούτῳ τὸ πᾶν, καὶ σὺν τουτῷ τὰ πάντα ἔχει[ν], τὰ μὲν ὡς μέρη τὰ δὲ ὡς ἐπιγεννήματα.

(10) Τὰ μὲν οὖν ἐμπεριεχόμενα τῷ κόσμῳ πρὸς τὸν κόσμον ἔχει τὴν συναρμογήν, ὁ δὲ κόσμος πρὸς οὐδὲν ἕτερον ἀλλ' αὐτὸς πρὸς αὑτόν. τὰ μὲν γὰρ ἄλλα πάντα τὴν φύσιν οὐκ αὐτοτελῆ ἔχοντα συνέστηκεν, ἀλλ' ἐπιδεῖται τῆς πρὸς τὰ ἐχόμενα συναρμογῆς, ζῷα μὲν πρὸς ἀναπνοήν, ὄψις δὲ πρὸς τὸ φῶς, αἱ δὲ ἄλλαι αἰσθήσεις πρὸς τὸ οἰκεῖον αἰσθητόν, τὰ δὲ φυτὰ πρὸς τὸ φύεσθαι, ἥλιος δὲ καὶ σελήνη καὶ οἱ πλάνητες καὶ οἱ ἀπλανεῖς κατὰ τὸ μέρος μὲν τῆς κοινῆς διακοσήσεως· αὐτὸς δὲ πρὸς οὐδὲν ἕτερον ἀλλ' αὐτὸς πρὸς αὑτόν.

Ps-Occelus's commitment to an ungenerated and incorruptible universe is confirmed by the fact that even the mathematical structures of the universe, especially the motions of the heavenly bodies, admit of irregularities, with some bodies rising higher and obtaining more precision, and other bodies achieving less impressive circuits: this, according to ps-Occelus, is a consequence of their need to adjust to the part of the cosmos to which they naturally belong. Such adjustments to, or harmonizations with, what is "external" are similar in kind to those of other parts of the natural world: everything in nature needs to adjust to the objects by which they can successfully perform their functions: animals to breathing, senses to the perceptibles that are particular to them, and plants to their local habitats. How can such an "adjustment" work, at least in the case of those parts of the universe that are subject to generation and corruption? In another section of the same treatise, ps-Occelus claims that it is by ascetic training of the "material" elements of the compound (the "man" and "wife" in the family, and the "families" in the city-state) that happiness is to be achieved (*On the Nature of the Universe* 51, pp. 136.30–137.5 Thesleff):

> (51) And in the arts (*technai*), too, the first principles (*prôtai archai*) cooperate greatly towards the good or bad completion of the whole work; for example, in the case of a building, the laying of the foundations; in the case of ship-building, the keel; in the case of harmony and lyric song, the articulation of voice and pitch; so too, then, in the case of a constitution, [whether it] have good or bad laws, the establishment and harmonization of households has the greatest effect.

> (51) καὶ ἐν ταῖς τέχναις δὲ αἱ πρῶται ἀρχαὶ μεγάλα συνεργοῦσι πρὸς τὸ καλῶς ἢ τὸ κακῶς τὸ ὅλον ἔργον συντελεσθῆναι· οἷον ἐπὶ μὲν οἰκοδομίας θεμελίου καταβολή, ἐπὶ δὲ ναυπηγίας τρόπις, ἐπὶ δὲ συναρμογῆς καὶ μελοποιίας τάσις φωνῆς καὶ λῆψις· οὕτως οὖν καὶ ἐπὶ πολιτείας εὐνομουμένης τε καὶ κακονομουμένης οἴκων κατάστασις καὶ συναρμογὴ μέγιστα συμβάλλεται.

Ps-Occelus appears to be responding to the arguments found in Aristotle's *Parts of Animals* 1.1, concerning the problem of priority and causation in the formation of generated bodies: whereas Aristotle speaks of the "art" (*technê*) as the cause[42] that acts on the matter that receives it, giving it its proper shape and function throughout the process of its making, ps-Occelus, by contrast, considers the material parts (the "first principles" from which the composite is developed) to be the most influential to the success of the composite.[43] According to ps-Occelus earlier on in his treatise, these material parts of the familial and civic compositions advance toward perfection through "the law," with the added support of "temperance and piety."[44] Close attention to the parts themselves, and especially to harmonizing them both internally, and relative to one another, contributes to the success and happiness of the family, as well as (by extension) of the city-state. Only the universe itself, by dint of its being properly "adorned" as perfect and complete, is not subject to such requirements. Indeed, ps-Occelus argues that we can infer from the attributes of the universe, i.e., from its circular figure and motion, temporal infinity, and insusceptibility to change substantially, that it alone is without beginning or end.

Oscan/Messapian Philosophy

It is a remarkable theory of natural physics that attaches to the final subject of our analysis, the poet Ennius. Originally from Rudiae, a Messapian city-state to the south of Tarentum (near present-day Lecce), Ennius famously obtained his Roman citizenship with the help of Q. Fulvius Nobilior, possibly in 184 BCE, and knew Latin and Greek, in addition to his native Italic language of "Oscan" or "Messapic." In this way, Ennius had two fatherlands, like Cato the Elder (who was born in Tusculum) and Cicero (who was from Arpinum). Indeed, Aulus Gellius notes that the poet himself celebrated his "three hearts" (*tria corda*), which Gellius thought referred to his ability to speak Greek, Oscan, and Latin.[45] Other evidence collected by Emily Gowers suggests that Ennius did indeed focus on the multilingualism of native Italic peoples, such as the Bruttii, and that later Roman poets also embraced this tradition.[46] It was also part of the popular Roman imagination to associate Ennius with Pythagoreanism, to such an extent that Horace (*Epistles* 2.1.50–52) claimed that Homer's soul (*anima*) came into Ennius's body (*corpus*) "according to the doctrine of Pythagoras" (*secundum Pythagorae dogma*), a commonplace thereafter adapted by Persius in his *Satires* (6.9–11). Thus, the association of Ennius with Pythagoras obtained by the end of the first century BCE, at the very latest, but it is not clear that it would have held before then (especially since Cicero, who makes Cato the Elder a quasi-Pythagorean, does not associate Ennius with Pythagoreanism).[47]

Regardless of the historical validity of this association with Pythagoreanism, it is clear that Ennius wrote philosophical poems, including a work called *Epicharmus*, which was considered in antiquity to represent, perhaps to the Romans, the natural philosophy of the Greeks. A probable guess is that it was based on portions of the *Pseudepicharmea*, which were being produced as early as the end of the fourth century BCE and are mentioned by Aristoxenus of Tarentum.[48] It is difficult to know with precision what Ennius's *Epicharmus* looked like, but a reasonable conjecture is that, at the beginning of the poem, the poet Ennius is guided by the sage Epicharmus in his pursuit of knowledge of the natural world.[49] The Epicharmus of the Hellenistic age was a suitable candidate to guide the Oscan poet through the workings of nature: he was probably considered a "Pythagorean" by the beginning of the third century BCE, and the fragments that come down associated with Epicharmus, both those which are considered authentic and those which are not, show an interest in natural philosophy.[50] In his work *Epicharmus*, mostly preserved by Varro, Ennius imagines, while asleep, that he "seemed to be dead" (*videbar somniare med ego esse mortuum*), in marked contrast to the beginning of the *Annales* where, in another dream, Ennius imagines that Homer comes to his side (*visus Homerus adesse poeta*).[51] Varro ascribes to the *Epicharmus* four elements of the universe (*principia mundi*), which Ennius calls "water, earth, soul, and sun" (*aqua terra anima sol*), a unique combination not found anywhere else in antiquity, although Vitruvius preserves something similar by reference to "Pythagoras, Empedocles, Epicharmus, and other natural scientists and philosophers" (*De arch.* 8 *praef.* 1).[52] No other fragments concerning water per se survive, although, in another fragment of this work, we hear that nature "mixes heat with cold, dryness with moisture" (*frigori miscet calorem atque humori aritudinem*) in the process of generation (possibly of a human being)—that is, a mixture of the aspects of the sky-soul (*calor*) with that of earth-body (*frigor*), as well as those of the sun (*aritudo*) and the water (*humor*).[53] Thus, the order "*aqua terra anima sol*" would imply that the inner pair of principles in the list, *terra* and *anima*, are conjoined in the mixture, as are the outer pair, *aqua* and *sol*. Ennius has more to say about earth: also apparently called Ceres (which would correspond with the Greek goddess Demeter), the earth "produces all the people from the lands and, once again, takes them back" (*terris gentis omnis peperit et resumit denuo*), just as it appears to do with fruit (*quod gerit fruges, Ceres*).[54] It is also understood to be "body," just as fire is "mind" (*terra corpus est, at mentis ignis est*).[55] The "mind-body" dichotomy is, perhaps surprisingly, not common in ancient literature (with, for example, philosophers after Plato and Aristotle preferring the "rational-irrational" modality). Ennius further suggests that mind obtained its fire from the sun (*istic est de sole sumptus ignis*), and that sun is "wholly mind" (*isque totus mentis est*), implying that it is the sun that produces human intelligence, a notion that is not far from a sentiment found in ps-Archytas's *On Law and Justice*.[56] Hence Ennius finds multiple ways to demonstrate the interrelationships between his four elements in the introduction to his natural philosophy, appealing to the mixing of their attributes in order to demonstrate elemental change in action.

Following the precedent set especially by Empedocles, Ennius shifts to a discussion of the names of the gods that are associated with the elements of the universe. According to Varro, who quotes the following long section, sky-soul is to be identified with Jupiter, and earth with Juno (Enn. Unidentified Works fr. 9 Manuwald and Goldberg = Varro, *Ling*. 5.65):

> That is this Jupiter, of whom I speak, whom the Greeks call
> "*aer*" [air], who is wind and clouds, and afterwards rain,
> and cold out of rain, then becomes wind, *aer* once again.
> Therefore, these things that I mention to you are Jupiter;
> They give aid to mortals and cities, and beasts—all of them.

Here we see the cycle that Jupiter, as "*aer*," undertakes over time: he is first changed into winds and clouds, then becomes rain, followed by cold, which gives rise to wind, which is once again *aer*. Plutarch interestingly preserves some Pseudo-Epicharmean lines that attest to the same sort of process, by reference specifically to spirit (πνεῦμα in Greek, a possible translation of Latin *anima*) and earth (γᾶ in Greek, a likely translation of *terra* in Latin), leading one to speculate that Plutarch's source might have derived these lines from Ennius's account, or perhaps Ennius was reading the same Pseudepicharmean text as Plutarch (Epicharmus fr. 213 Kassel-Austin = Plut. *Consolatio ad Apollonium* 15, 110B):

> It is combined and it is separated, and returns whence it came—
> earth to earth, and spirit on high; what is difficult about this? Not even one (thing).
>
> συνεκρίθη καὶ διεκρίθη καὶ ἀπῆνθεν ὅθεν ἦνθε,
> γᾶ μὲν εἰς γᾶν, πνεῦμ' ἄνω· τί τῶνδε χαλεπόν; οὐδέν

Such changes of attributes, whereby *aer* (or soul-spirit) changes into various natural forces, can be associated with the mid- or late-fifth-century BCE natural philosopher Diogenes of Apollonia, who understood *aer* to be the intelligence that is "manifold" (πολύτροπος), since it can become warmer or colder, drier or moister, more stationary or quicker in motion, among other attributes.[57] Diogenes also apparently praised Homer for associating Zeus with *aer*, as Philodemus attests (*On Piety* 6b).[58] Indeed, this association of Zeus with *aer* among some Presocratic natural philosophers was confirmed with the publication of the Derveni Papyrus, first anonymously in 1982, and in the "official" edition of Kouremenos, Parássoglou, and Tsantsanoglou in 2006.[59] The Derveni Papyrus, which dates to the mid-fourth century BCE with the text originally written in the late fifth century BCE, presents an allegorizing exegesis of the poem of Orpheus, focusing on the generation of the natural universe, in a mode similar to other Presocratics, especially Diogenes of Apollonia.[60] There, we hear, in a description quite close to that of Ennius's Jupiter, that "all things were called Zeus" (Col. XIX). This presents a problem for the Derveni Author, since the main element of the universe, *aer*, along with "Moira" (Fate), seem to have preexisted Zeus (Cols. XVII–XVIII). The Derveni author offers a solution: the mind of Zeus was originally called "Moira" *before* the name "Zeus" was attached to it (Col. XVIII); after the name "Zeus" was attached to this immortal and ungenerated intellective force, the constituents of the universe, called the "beings" (ἐόντα), were dashed together according to the will of Zeus's intellect (i.e., "Fate"), effecting the construction of the universe in *aer*, the cosmic space which is identical to Zeus himself (Cols. XIV–XVI). Indeed, it is the sun that Zeus employs instrumentally in order to effect the striking of the "beings" together, as fire is understood to be the force that keeps things separated (Col. XVI). The cosmology of the Derveni Papyrus is, to be sure, not precisely that of Ennius's *Epicharmus*; but both assume that all things are called by the name of sky-god (Zeus or Jupiter), the spirit that infuses the entire universe; show similar inclinations toward etymologization of divine names and assignment of divine names to various aspects of nature; and concern themselves with how the various elements of the cosmic systems interrelated, especially the sky-soul/Zeus, and the earth/Juno.

Conclusions

> Many are the aspects of our customs that have been derived from them [the Pythagoreans], which I pass over, lest we seem to have learned those things from elsewhere which we ourselves believe to have discovered. But to return to the purpose of our speech: how many great poets, how many great orators, have sprung up among us in such a short time!
>
> —Cic. *Tusc.* 4.4–5

Cicero's final historical account of Pythagoreanism in the *Tusculan Disputations* leaves us without a final word for its significance to the development of Roman philosophy. But it does leave us with a final word on what happened in Italy. For Cicero (*Tusc.* 4.6–7) laments the fact that after Pythagoreanism's heyday, in the time of Appius Claudius Caecus and Cato the Elder, Stoic and Peripatetic philosophy were not taken up in the Latin language.[61] In the absence of these philosophical schools, Epicureanism, especially under the influence of C. Amafinius, took hold not just in Rome, but throughout all of Italy as well. Indeed, when Cicero goes on to claim that anonymous writings indebted to Amafinius's watered-down version of Epicureanism "seized all of Italy" (*Italiam totam occupaverunt*), it becomes clear why, at the end of the second century BCE, Pythagorean philosophy could no longer be called "Italic": it had been superseded by a popular form of Epicureanism. Readers will here recall Lucretius's citation of Ennius's fame, which he obtained by propagating the notion of the transmigration of the soul, at the beginning of his *De rerum natura*. There (1.116–119), Lucretius lumps Ennius with those who cannot explain, nor obtain certainty about,

> whether it miraculously (*divinitus*) steals its way into other creatures,
> As our Ennius sang, he who first brought down
> From lovely Helicon a crown of perennial leafage,
> To ring out his fame among throughout all the Italic peoples.

From there, Lucretius sets out to correct Ennius, and to show his reader why his Epicurean atomism is better at explaining the nature of the soul than Ennius's theory of transmigration, which is at odds with his eschatology.[62] On the account given by Cicero, then, Pythagoreanism had ceased to be "Italic" simply because *Italy was no longer Pythagorean*. If this is to be believed, we should be inclined not to assume with too much haste that Hellenistic Pythagoreanism was "invented" by Posidonius of Apamea or Eudorus of Alexandria, as is sometimes thought, but rather that their testimonies reflected an older tradition of Pythagoreanism, with roots in the earlier Hellenistic age, that had lost its significance around the beginning of the first century BCE in the Italian peninsula. What better for this tradition to do in order to survive than, in programmatic Pythagorean form (at least according to Cicero), migrate from one patch of earth to another?

Cicero's *Tusculan Disputations* also shows us that the construction of an account of the history of Roman philosophy requires us to take stock of the Pythagoreanism that came before it. In order to do so, however, one is required to grasp what relationships obtained between Pythagoreanism of the sort advocated by influential Greek philosophers such as Plato, Aristotle, and Archytas of Tarentum, and preserved in various accounts by Pythagoreanism's historiographers and pseudepigraphers who forged texts in their names, and the Italic peoples who were thought to have given rise to Pythagoreanism. Whatever the historical "truth" of the actual lives of the Lucanians Aresas/Aesara, Occelus, and Eccelus, the Hellenistic traditions which situated their philosophical ideas within contemporary Platonic, Peripatetic, and Stoic views helped to create the image of a native-grown philosophical school, which was purported to have influenced the development of Platonic and Aristotelian philosophy generations before these great philosophers undertook philosophical inquiry in Athens. The pseudepigrapha that were manufactured in the names of these Italic figures featured developments primarily of Platonic and Peripatetic ideas about psychology, ethics, physics, with a directed focus toward the sorts of theories about cosmic justice that were generated especially by the Presocratics. Finally, the imprint of Empedocles of Agrigentum and Diogenes of Apollonia was left on *noster Ennius*, the primogenitor of Latin poetry, philosophy and history, and paradigm of the dual-citizen that blazed a trail for the *novi homines* Cato the Elder and Cicero—although Ennius betrays no direct knowledge of the tradition of the Hellenistic Pythagorean pseudepigrapha (with the exception of the *gnomai* associated with the Syracusan Epicharmus—but this represents a special case).[63] In diverse ways, Cicero and Lucretius express a sort of nostalgic fondness for—and substantive disagreement with—the lost native Pythagoreanism that had been celebrated by their grandparents' generation. But, as Lucretius famously sets down as his *principium*, "nothing ever springs miraculously out of nothing" (*nullam rem e nihilo gigni divinitus umquam*).[64] Pythagoreanism was, for Cicero and Lucretius, a philosophy which had had its day; and as a new sun rose over the rolling stretches of Italian *terra*, a new seed had taken root.[65]

Notes

1. Exceptions include Volk (2016); Sassi (2011); Horky (2011); Dench (1995); and Mele (1981).
2. Powell (1995) 12n29.
3. E.g., Cic. *Tusc.* 1.38, where one of Cicero's interlocutors claims, "[Pythagoras] came to Italy when Tarquinius Superbus was king, and held what was called Magna Grecia both through the reputation of his teaching, and through his authority. And for many generations to come the name of the Pythagoreans thrived to such an extent that no others were thought to be learned." In the following section, the interlocutor goes on to explain how Plato came to Italy to learn the Pythagorean doctrines from the Pythagoreans. Hence, Cicero's interlocutor embraces a tradition arising out of the seventh Platonic *Epistle*.
4. Recent attempts to illuminate parts of Hellenistic Pythagoreanism include Horky and De Cesaris (2018) (epistemology), Hatzimichali (2018) (metaphysics), Ulacco (2017) (metaphysics and epistemology), and Horky (2015) (metaphysics). For an excellent, synoptic account, see Centrone (2014).
5. Possibly Aristotle's student, Aristoxenus of Tarentum, had something to offer here. On Aristoxenus's importance to this tradition, see Sassi (2011) 26–27, Horky (2011) 137–140, and below.
6. Arist. *Metaph.* 1.5–6, 987a10–31, and 1.6, 988a26; *Mete.* 1.6, 342b30; *Cael.* 2.13, 293a20. See Horky (2011) 124 and Sassi (2011) 23–26.
7. On which, see Nicolet (1991) 171–183.
8. Generally, see Nelsestuen (2015) Chapter 3.

9. Dench (2005) 131 notes the difficulty with which Romans, after the enfranchisement of the Italic peoples to Roman citizenship around 90 BCE, sought to "remap" the Italian peninsula.
10. For a sensible treatment of the fragments concerning Italy and Italic peoples in Books 2 and 3 of Cato's *Origines*, see Cornell (2013) 205–213. He concludes: "That [Cato] saw Italy as in some sense a cultural unit, despite its ethnic and linguistic diversity, is possible, especially in view of Servius's comment (T11e) that he praised the *disciplina* and *vita* of Italy." Cicero's Cato also praises the *vita* exemplified by Platonist-Pythagorean philosophy at *Sen.* 77 as "only worth being counted as such (*sola numeranda*)."
11. As noted by Nelsestuen (2015) 88–92. Dionysius of Halicarnassus (1.37.2) maps out "Italy" geographically as occupying center of the Italian peninsula: there is Campania in the center-west, Messapia to the southeast, Daunia in the center-east, Sabine country in the center, Etruria to the northwest, Alba Longa in the center-west, and Falernia to the center-west, but a bit further to the south of Alba Longa. Varro *Rust.* 1.2.1ff., by contrast, understands "Italy" to refer to areas in the central part of the peninsula (Campania and Apulia, and regions around Falernum and Venafrum) and those to the north, including those regions to the northeast (the Ager Gallicus) and the northwest (the Ager Faventinus) of Rome. As Nelsestuen aptly notes, Varro's configuration is Romanocentric, based on the roads that extended from the capital city (the Via Appia, Via Latina, Via Flaminia and Via Aemilia).
12. Cf. Sassi (2011) 22–23 and 25.
13. E.g., Cic. *Har. resp.* 9, where Cicero refers to the *Italici ipsi ac Latini*.
14. See Cic. *Leg.* 2.5.
15. Cic. *Tusc.* 1.38.
16. One wonders about whether or not Cicero obtained his sense of what counted as "Pythagorean" from his friend P. Nigidius Figulus, whom Cicero credits (*Timaeus* 1 = Test. 9 Swoboda) with reviving the Pythagorean *disciplina*, which "thrived in Italy and Sicily in another age" (*aliquot saecula in Italia Siciliaque viguisset*).
17. See Horky (2011) for a thorough analysis of Herennius Pontius the Samnite and his presentation in Cicero, Cassius Dio, and Appian.
18. On the Oscan language in Lucanian inscriptions, see Isayev (2007) 28–30 and MacDonald (2015).
19. In his catalog of Pythagoreans at the end of Iamblichus's *On the Pythagorean Life* (267). On the catalog, see Zhmud (2012) 109–119. Still, it is unclear whether the entire contents of the catalog should be associated with Aristoxenus, or whether Iamblichus (or his source) has manipulated an original list.
20. The manuscripts clearly ascribe the work to a female writer, Aesara (see Thesleff [1965] 48 with n21). Hence, I will refer to the author of the fragment *On the Nature of the Human* as "pseudo-Aresas/Aesara."
21. Iambl. *VP* 266, which appears to derive ultimately from the writings of Timaeus of Tauromenium (see Horky (2013) 127–128 with n5).
22. Since the texts from the Pythagorean pseudepigrapha are not often well known or easy to access, I include the Greek from Thesleff's edition.
23. See Horky and Johnson (2020).
24. See Pl. *Prt.* 327b and Iambl. *Protrepticus* 20, pp. 100.15–101.6 Pistelli. On Anonymus Iamblichi, see Horky (2020).
25. Cf. Horky (2020) 268–272. I make the case for associating Anonymus Iamblichi chiefly with the Socratics in Horky 2021.

26. Bipartite soul: Aëtius 4.7.5, Timaeus Locrus, *On the Nature of the Universe and the Soul* 46 (p. 218.5–11 Thesleff), Cic. *Tusc.* 4.5.10; tripartite soul: Aëtius 4.4.1, ps.-Theages, *On Virtue* fr. 1 (pp. 190.1–191.21 Thesleff), ps-Metopus, *On Virtue* fr. 1 (pp. 119.12–26 Thesleff).
27. Posidonius T 151. On Posidonius and Hellenistic Pythagoreanism, see Ju (2013).
28. Also see ps-Theages, *On Virtue* fr. 2 (pp. 192.5–193.16 Thesleff). For the cosmic version of the same theory, see ps.-Damippus, *On Prudence and Prosperity* fr. 1 (pp. 68.19–69.19 Thesleff).
29. "Eccelus" is Praechter's emendation, where the Mss. have versions of "From Polus" (ἐκ πώλου). But Eccelus is clearly attested as a Pythagorean by Iamblichus (*VP* 267).
30. Contrast, for example, Alexander Polyhistor, who claims that "the just" is oath-bound, and that "virtue" is "harmony, health, the good entire, and god" (Diog. Laert. 8.33).
31. Compare the Stoic Cornutus (9.2), who, by reference to the many attributes of Zeus, says, "the number of such names for him being infinite, since he extends to every capacity and state and is the cause and overseer of all things. Thus he was said to be the Father of Justice as well, because it was he who brought community to the affairs of men and ordered them not to do each other wrong" (tr. Boys-Stones).
32. This would make Occelus a "mathematical" Pythagorean, in contrast to those who merely "stated" (ἀπεφαίνετο) the doctrine, i.e., the "acousmatics." Occelus is also known by Censorinus's source (probably Varro) to be a Pythagorean along with Archytas of Tarentum (Censorinus 4.3). For a list of testimonia, see Thesleff (1965) 125 with n14.
33. For a useful overview, see Sandbach (1985) 63–64. It is likely that the author of the correspondence between "Archytas" and "Plato" knew this work as *On the Generation of the Universe*.
34. Diog. Laert. 8.81.
35. Differentiation of the "fact" (*hoti*) from the "why" (*dioti*) is fundamental to the classification of the two types of Pythagoreans, according to Aristotle. See Horky (2013) Chapter 1. The Stoics associated demonstration with Zeus (e.g., Diog. Laert. 7.147 = *SVF* 2.1021). For this etymologization and its roots in Plato's *Cratylus*, see Horky (2013) 168–169.
36. See ps-Archytas, *On Law and Justice* F 4d Horky and Johnson (p. 35.10–16 Thesleff), where the progression is body-household-army-city. On the connections to Aristoxenus, see Horky and Johnson (2020) 458–460 and 477–481.
37. Ps-Archytas, *On Law and Justice* F 1 Horky and Johnson (p. 33.9–15 Thesleff).
38. The mixture of the cosmic portions of the Same, Different, and Being in the world-soul are given harmonic order by the demiurge in Plato's *Timaeus* (36a–b). Even so, in the *Timaeus*, the world-soul is eternal but generated (cf. *Tim.* 37c–e).
39. See Dillon (2003) 99–109. Also see Diog. Laert. 3.69, where Plato's universal principles are said to be "god" and "matter," the former of which is described as "intellect and cause," and the latter as "shapeless and unlimited" (following *Tim.* 50d–51a, although "matter" is not mentioned by Plato). Diogenes returns to this claim later on, when he speaks of god-the paradigm and matter (Diog. Laert. 3.76, although there may be textual corruption—see Dorandi *ad loc.*) as the preouranian causes, and he introduces a third postouranian cause, the Forms (3.76–77), for the composition of natural objects.
40. Arist. *Metaph.* 1.5, 986a22–b2. Compare with Eudorus of Alexandria fr. 5 Mazzarelli = Simplicius, *Commentary on Aristotle's Physics* I p. 181.19–30 Diels: "I declare, then, that the followers of Pythagoras admit that the One is the principle of all things, but according to another mode, they introduce two highest elements. They refer to these two elements with many predicates; for, among these, the former is called ordered, definite, knowable, male,

odd, to the right, and light, whereas the latter is called not-ordered, indefinite, unknowable, female, to the left, even, and dark."
41. Aëtius (1.3.8) associates the Pythagorean material cause with the visible cosmos.
42. It isn't entirely clear whether Aristotle is referring to the formal or the final cause here, but, given similarities with *Gen. an.* 2.1, 734b34–735a4, we may infer that he is actually speaking about the formal cause.
43. Arist. *Part. an.* 1.1, 640a27–b5.
44. Ps-Occelus, *On the Nature of the Universe* 43, p. 135.9–11 Thesleff.
45. See Gowers (2007) 28–29.
46. Ibid., citing *Ann.* 477: "*bruttace bilingui.*"
47. See above, although Lucretius does (see below). For a good discussion of the problems here, see Vesperini (2012) 27–61.
48. F 45 Wehrli. See Horky (2013) 131–132, with nn24–25. On the *gnomai* of Epicharmus, which were collected in the late fourth century BCE, see Battezatto (2008).
49. The most recent edition of the fragments is that of Manuwald and Goldberg (2018). Also useful are Kassel-Austin (2001), Courtney (1993), Vahlen (1928), and Diels-Kranz (DK) (^{6}1952).
50. See the association of Epicharmus with *polymathia* in P. Hibeh 1 (early third century BCE).
51. Ennius, *Epicharmus* fr. 1 Manuwald and Goldberg (+ *Annals* fr. 3) = Cic. *Acad. Pr.* 2.51.
52. Ennius, *Epicharmus* fr. 4 Manuwald and Goldberg = Varro, *Rust.* 1.4.1. In Vitruvius's text, however, the terms in order are *aer* (instead of *sol*), *ignis, aqua, terra*. Cf. Vahlen (1928) ccxix. Ennius follows Empedocles in positing four elements, although the latter has them as (in this order) Zeus, Hera, Aidoneus, and Nestis, which are, according to Hippolytus (DK 31 A 33; a different account is offered by Aëtius 1.3.20) the respective names of the elements fire, earth, air, and water. Diogenes of Apollonia as "earth, water, aer, and fire," in that order (DK 64 B 2).
53. Ennius, *Epicharmus* fr. 2 Manuwald and Goldberg (+ *Annals* fr. 7) = Varro, *Ling.* 5.59–60. Varro interprets the passage slightly differently, understanding earth-body to be both wet and cold, and sky-soul as hot. Courtney associates *frigus* with *aer* (by reference to F 39 Courtney), but in the latter scenario *aer-anima* appears to be adopting the attributes of the other elements.
54. Enn. Unidentified Works Manuwald and Goldberg fr. 9 = Varro, *Ling.* 5.64–65. For a useful explanation of the etymologies, see Courtney (1993) 35–36.
55. Enn. *Epicharmus* fr. 5 Manuwald and Goldberg = Priscian, *GL* II, p. 341.18–22. Priscian, the source for this fragment, claims that Ennius is poetically supplementing "*ignis mentis*" for "*mens.*"
56. Ps-Archytas, *On Law and Justice* F 4e Horky and Johnson = p. 35.24–27 Thesleff. On this fragment, see Horky and Johnson (2020) 481–483.
57. DK 64 B 5.
58. DK 64 A 8; also see B 8.
59. The most recent edition is Kotwick and Janko (2017).
60. For the date of the text and the papyrus, see Kouremenos, Parássoglou, and Tsantsanoglou (2006) 8–10. One wonders whether the *Epicharmus* of Ennius also featured Orphic precedents: the etymologization of Proserpina (*Epicharmus* fr. 3 = Varro, *Ling.* 5.68) as the moon, which creeps forward subterraneously (from "*serpens*"), recalls the Orphic theogony, in which Zeus and Selene give birth to Dionysus (cf. Cic. *Nat. D.* 3.58 = OF 497i Bernabé).

61. The advent of Stoic and Peripatetic philosophy in Cicero's account are associated with the famous embassy of Carneades, Critolaus, and Diogenes to Rome in 155 BCE.
62. Lucr. 1.120–126. On Lucretius's response to Ennius's cosmos, see Nethercut (2020) 45–75 (although he does not discuss the *Epicharmus*).
63. On Epicharmus and Pythagoreanism, see Horky (2013) 131–148. A comprehensive, balanced account of Empedocles and Pythagoreanism remains to be written. In the absence of direct knowledge of the Pythagorean pseudepigrapha, one wonders whether most of those texts were written after Ennius's death, but before Cicero's life (e.g., in the last half of the second century BCE).
64. Lucr. 1.150.
65. This chapter was originally written sometime in 2015 and subsequently revised several times over the years. Such revisions cannot be assumed to have removed all errors of knowledge or judgement from it. It has benefited especially from substantive suggestions for improvement by Myrto Garani, whom I kindly thank. I also want to thank Joe Farrell and Grant Nelsestuem, who read an early version of the paper and offered encouragement and support.

References

Battezatto, L. (2008). "Pythagorean Comedies from Epicharmus to Alexis." *Aevum Antiquum* 8: 139–164.
Bryan, J., R. Wardy, and J. Warren, eds. (2018). *Authors and Authority in Ancient Philosophy*. (Cambridge).
Centrone, B. (2014). "The Pseudo-Pythagorean Writings," in Huffman, 315–140.
Cornell, T. J. (2013). *The Fragments of the Roman Historians*, vol. 3. (Oxford).
Courtney, E. (1993). *The Fragmentary Latin Poets: Edited with Commentary*. (Oxford).
Dench, E. (1995). *From Barbarians to New Men: Greek, Roman, and Modern Perceptions of Peoples from the Central Apennines*. (Oxford).
Dench, E. (2005). *Romulus' Asylum: Roman Identities from the Age of Alexander to the Age of Hadrian*. (Oxford).
Diels, H., and Kranz, W. [= DK] (^{6}1952). *Die Fragmente der Vorsokratiker*. (Berlin).
Dillon, J. (2003). *The Heirs of Plato: A Study of the Old Academy (347–274 B.C.)*. (Oxford).
Gowers, E., and W. Fitzgerald, eds. (2007). *Ennius Perennis: The Annals and Beyond, Cambridge Classical Journal Supplementary Volume*. (Cambridge).
Gowers, E. (2007). "The Cor of Ennius," in Gowers and Fitzgerald, 17–37. (Cambridge).
Hatzimichali, M. (2018). "Pseudo-Archytas and the *Categories*," in Bryan, Wardy, and Warren, 162–83.
Horky, P. S., and G. De Cesaris (2018). "Hellenistic Pythagorean Epistemology." *Lexicon Philosophicum 2018 (Special Issue: Hellenistic Theories of Knowledge)*: 221–262.
Horky, P. S. (2011). "Herennius Pontius: The Construction of a Samnite Philosopher." *Classical Antiquity* 30(1): 119–147.
Horky, P. S. (2013). *Plato and Pythagoreanism*. (Oxford).
Horky, P. S. (2015). "Pseudo-Archytas' Protreptics? *On Wisdom* in Its Contexts," in Nails and Tarrant, 21–39.
Horky, P. S. (2020). "Anonymus Iamblichi, *On Excellence (Peri Aretēs)*: A Lost Defense of Democracy," in Wolfsdorf, 262–292.

Horky, P. S. (2021). "Law and Justice among the Socratics: Contexts for Plato's *Republic*." *Polis* 38(3): 399–419.
Horky, P. S., and M. R. Johnson (2020). "*On Law and Justice* Attributed to Archytas of Tarentum," in Wolfsdorf, 455–492.
Huffman, C., ed. (2014). *A History of Pythagoreanism*. (Cambridge).
Isayev, E. (2007). *Inside Ancient Lucania: Dialogues in History and Archaeology*. (London).
Ju, A. E. (2013). "Posidonius as Historian of Philosophy," in Schofield, 95–117.
Kassel, R., and C. Austin, eds. (2001). *Poetae Comici Graeci 1: Comoedia Dorica, Mimi, Phlyaces*. (Berlin).
Kotwick, M., and R. Janko, eds. (2017). *Der Papyrus von Derveni: Griechisch-deutsch*. (Berlin).
Kouremenos, T., G. M. Parássoglou, and K. Tsantsanoglou (2006). *The Derveni Papyrus*. (Florence).
MacDonald, K. (2015). *Oscan in Southern Italy and Sicily*. (Cambridge).
Manuwald, G., and S. Goldberg, eds. (2018). *Fragmentary Republican Latin, Volume 1: Ennius, Testimonia, Epic Fragments*. (Cambridge, Mass.).
Mele, A. (1981). "Il Pitagorismo e le Popolazioni Anelleniche d'Italia." *AION* 3: 61–96.
Nails, D., and H. Tarrant, eds. (2015). *Second Sailing: Alternative Perspectives on Plato*. (Helsinki).
Nelsestuen, G. (2015). *Varro the Agronomist: Political Philosophy, Satire, and Agriculture in the Late Republic*. (Columbus, Ohio).
Nethercut, J. S. (2020). *Ennius Noster: Lucretius and the Annales*. (Oxford).
Nicolet, C. (1991). *Space, Geography, and Politics in the Early Roman Empire*. (Ann Arbor, Mich.).
Powell, J. G. F. (1995). *Cicero the Philosopher*. (Oxford).
Primavesi, O., and K. Luchner, eds. (2011). *The Presocratics from the Latin Middle Ages to Hermann Diels*. (Stuttgart).
Sandbach, F. (1985). *Aristotle and the Stoics*. (Cambridge).
Sassi, M. M. (2011). "Ionian Philosophy and Italic Philosophy: from Diogenes Laertius to Diels," in Primavesi and Luchner, 19–44.
Schofield, M., ed. (2013). *Aristotle, Plato, and Pythagoreanism in the First Century BC*. (Cambridge).
Ulacco, A. (2017). *Pseudopythagorica Dorica: I trattati di argomento metafisico, logico ed epistemologico attribuiti ad Archita e a Brontino*. (Berlin).
Vahlen, J. (1928). *Ennianae poesis reliquiae*. (Leipzig).
Volk, K. (2016). "Roman Pythagoras," in Williams and Volk, 33–49.
Thesleff, H. (1965). *The Pythagorean Texts of the Hellenistic Period*. (Turku).
Vesperini, P. (2012). *La Philosophia et ses Practiques d'Ennius à Cicéron*. (Rome).
Williams, G. D., and K. Volk, eds. (2015) *Roman Reflections: Studies in Latin Philosophy*. (Oxford).
Wolfsdorf, D. C., ed. (2020) *Early Greek Ethics*. (Oxford).
Zhmud, L. (2012). *Pythagoras and the Early Pythagoreans*, transl. K. Windle and R. Ireland. (Oxford).

CHAPTER 2

EPICUREAN ORTHODOXY AND INNOVATION

From Lucretius to Diogenes of Oenoanda

PAMELA GORDON

RECENT years have brought a sea change in Epicurean studies, and not only because new texts have emerged from Herculaneum and Oenoanda. The field has also been invigorated by an increased attention to the originality of later Epicurean figures, and by a growing recognition that much modern scholarship on Epicureanism reflects a robust anti-Epicurean tradition, particularly as articulated by Cicero, Plutarch, and Seneca. Happily, modern agreement with the ancient detractors who found Epicurean thought stagnant, dogmatic, and unimaginative is no longer the norm.[1] This chapter on Roman receptions of Greek Epicureanism offers a brief survey, with attention to the question of whether there were developments in Epicureanism after the lifetime of Epicurus. But it also considers the possibility that Epicureanism offered an alternative to the values of the dominant culture and what might be called—in shorthand—Roman modes of masculinity.

The post-Hellenistic Epicurean texts that have survived in full or in significant fragments are by Lucretius, his contemporary Philodemus (first century BCE), and Diogenes of Oenoanda (second century CE). Scholars have often mined these texts for information about Epicureanism as it existed centuries earlier in Greece. Innovation is admittedly difficult to document: we have extensive, well preserved Roman sources, but relatively few intact, readily deciphered texts by Epicurus (341–270 BCE). But although strict orthodoxy is often assumed, scholarship has begun to describe more creative Epicurean traditions.[2] Most Epicureans may have been conservative, but ancient stereotypes that mock the Epicureans for being incapable of independent thought have too often swayed scholarly opinion. A more Epicurean-friendly approach opens alternative possibilities.

Greek and Roman Epicureanism taught that pleasure is the *telos* (the end, or fulfillment of life). Outsiders in antiquity were suspicious of pleasure-seekers, but friendly observers knew that Epicurus had contextualized the question: "whenever we say that pleasure is the *telos*, we mean not the pleasures of degenerates and pleasures that consist of physical enjoyment . . . but the absence of pain in the body and distress in the spirit" (*Ep. Men.* 131). Epicureanism stressed scientific knowledge, healthy pleasures, and the avoidance of pleasures that soon cause distress. But public opinion was often negative. Significantly, the most unfriendly Roman sources present Epicureanism as the antithesis of manliness, a crucial issue to which I return after surveying innovation in Lucretius, Philodemus, and Diogenes of Oenoanda.

LUCRETIUS

Lucretius (died c. 50 BCE) was a Roman poet who composed our primary source of information on Epicurean physics, a six-book hexameter poem in Latin called *De rerum natura*, or *On the Nature of Things*.[3] Engaging a broad literary heritage that included Ennius, Empedocles, Homer, Hesiod, and Lucilius, Lucretius's work is a radical departure from the prose of Epicurus, who—if we are to believe Cicero and other hostile witnesses—devalued poetry as well as traditional education.[4] Scholarship on Lucretius has long been divided by debates over orthodoxy versus heterodoxy. The conception of Lucretius writing as if in a vacuum was pervasive until recently, but some late twentieth-century scholarship maintains that Lucretius offers tacit critiques of Stoic philosophy or of later skepticism, that he responds to newer developments in science, or that he is aware of later Epicureanism.[5] But David Sedley invigorated the argument for orthodoxy by adducing recently discovered fragments of Epicurus's *On Nature*.[6] For Sedley, Lucretius is a "fundamentalist" who unfolds Epicurean science essentially as it appears in *On Nature*, unmediated and in isolation from contemporary philosophical discourse.

Even Sedley's "fundamentalist" view allows for originality in Lucretius's proems, diatribes, finales, and poetic expression. The poem opens with allusions to current civil strife, and offers Epicureanism as the answer to the cultural disasters of the late Roman Republic. The threat of violence hanging over the poem is intelligible whether we follow the traditional date of 55 BCE or posit that Lucretius is writing in 49/48.[7] Lucretius's caustic treatment of erotic passion has strong Roman overtones (Lucr. 4.1121–1192), he deplores Roman augury (e.g., 6.83–89), and he engages contemporary poetics and rhetoric.[8] But recognition of Lucretius's Roman outlook can be stated more strongly. For Kirk Summers, the *De rerum natura* "attacks the totality of the Roman religious experience" and "derides current religious practice," in ways that cannot be harmonized with the religious ideas of Epicurus.[9] Elizabeth Asmis has affirmed: "Lucretius seeks to shift humans from their position in the Roman social and political order to a place in the natural order of things."[10] In her view, the surface structure of the *De rerum natura* follows Epicurus's exposition of physics, but its deeper structure uses a particularly Roman conception of a natural treaty "to reshape Epicurean physics into an ethical text."[11] Recognizing a yet more fundamental departure, Don Fowler describes how Lucretius's rich language suggests "multiple approaches to the world," whereas Epicurus, as a reductionist, offered "one true story."[12] Fowler senses a tension between Epicurus and Lucretius that renders the poem "as deeply un-Epicurean as it is deeply Epicurean."[13] Several recent essays have suggested that traditional *Quellenforschung* is inadequate. For Alison Sharrock, recent work recognizes in the work of Lucretius a poetic logic, "which does not mean simply 'illogic' but a process of argumentation and legitimatization that proceeds in paradoxical ways."[14] Laying out ways to view Lucretius "as a philosopher in his own right," Tim O'Keefe proposes that Lucretius's use of rhetorical and literary modes is as philosophically significant as Cicero's use of dialogue to present the arguments of various schools. O'Keefe nonetheless finds that Lucretius's sensitivity to the needs of his audience makes the poem "a more effective embodiment of Epicureanism than anything written by Epicurus."[15] But Andrew Morrison, cautioning us not to lose sight of the strangeness of Lucretius's use of poetry, draws attention to the ways the poem resists univocal interpretation and accommodates a plurality of readers.[16] David Konstan suggests that Lucretius added a new dimension to Epicurean ethical theory by describing how one's awareness of one's own misdeeds in the past may result in remorseful mental affliction in the present, "something very like the modern idea of conscience."[17] If Konstan is right, Lucretius makes two subtle references to what might be called a guilty conscience. First, in one of his examples of the soul's vulnerability (among the proofs of the mortality of the soul), Lucretius describes how the recollection of past wrongdoing "bites repeatedly" or "gnaws" (*remordent*) on the soul (3.827). Similarly, in his diatribe against erotic passion, Lucretius uses the same verb to describe the lover's contrition about his wasted life (4.1135).

Philodemus

Epicureanism flourished across the Mediterranean, including in Syria, the birthplace of the Epicurean scholar and poet Philodemus. Philodemus studied in Athens under Zeno of Sidon, and apparently lived near the Bay of Naples during the 60s through 40s BCE. Philodemus's philosophical works (in Greek prose) are known only from the substantially carbonized book rolls found in the so-called Villa of the Papyri at Herculaneum, a city destroyed by Vesuvius over a century after the death of Philodemus. Many scholars connect Philodemus himself with this largely Epicurean library, identifying the villa owner as the Roman statesman L. Calpurnius Piso Caesoninus, an enemy of Cicero, and Philodemus's student and patron.[18]

Like Lucretius, Philodemus promoted early Epicureanism. But unlike Lucretius, who extolled Epicurus as the sole font of Epicurean wisdom (e.g., Lucr. 1.66; 5.7–12), Philodemus recognized four first-generation founders, whom he valorized emphatically as οἱ ἄνδρες ("the men," with the connotation of "The Great Men"): Epicurus, Hermarchus, Metrodorus, and Polyaenus. Philodemus researched the early texts of the Garden, as is evident from his *Works on the Records of Epicurus and Some Others* (*PHerc.*

1418 and 310). Though adamant that the texts of "the men" were essential, Philodemus composed original treatises, preserved Zeno's innovative work, and responded to later critiques of Epicureanism. Thus Philodemus's departures from orthodoxy can sometimes be identified more securely than is possible in the case of Lucretius.

But Philodemus felt that some Epicureans strayed too far. Apparently paraphrasing Zeno's lament over deteriorating Epicurean values, Philodemus writes that "some of those who call themselves Epicureans say and write many things that they have gathered, but also much that is their own, yet not in agreement with the writings" (*PHerc.* 1005, fr. 107.9–16, Angeli; tr. Asmis (1990)). He adds that "the most atrocious thing" regarding most Epicureans is their "unpardonable laziness" (i.e., lack of research) "in the [original] books" (*PHerc.* 1005, col. XIV 14.13–18, Angeli). Elsewhere he calls some Epicureans who disagreed with Epicurus "almost parricides" (*Rhetorica* I, col. VII.18–28 Longo Auricchio).

Philodemus's fragmentary work *On Methods of Inference* demonstrates developments in Epicurean science. Philodemus reformulates Epicurean scientific method, presenting it as wholly inductive, always beginning from concrete observations. But it was most likely Zeno and his associates—not Epicurus—who first reduced all scientific inference to induction.[19] Epicurus apparently adopted two methods: deduction about what is unobserved on the basis of observations; and inductive inferences based on similarities among observed things. Both are based on a distinction between the observed and what cannot be observed. The later Epicureans accepted this distinction. However, "very differently from Epicurus, they built a transition from the one kind to the other by allowing sufficiently tested empirical judgements to become, in the end, judgements about what is unobserved."[20] The argument in *De signis* responds to critiques of Epicurus's epistemology, thus demonstrating how Epicureans modified Epicurus's original position as they responded to negative appraisals. Thus there may be some truth to Seneca's remark: "Among those people, whatever Hermarchus said, whatever Metrodorus said, is ascribed to one man; everything anyone in that brotherhood says is spoken under his authority and control alone" (*Ep.* 33.4).

Diogenes of Oenoanda

Undeterred by the Epicurean recommendation to renounce ambition and "live unknown" (λάθε βιώσας), Diogenes of Oenoanda broadcast the wisdom of Epicurus in stone, displaying hundreds of lines of Greek prose across a surface that was perhaps eighty meters long and four meters tall.[21] Diogenes is known only from this monumental urban inscription discovered in 1884 in Oenoanda, a city in Lycia (now in Turkey). The resemblance of the carved lettering to another, securely dated inscription suggests that Diogenes' inscription belongs roughly to the reign of Hadrian.[22]

Diogenes' extraordinary epigraphical invitation to Epicureanism includes a broad array of texts, among them letters addressed to Diogenes' friends that attest to

Epicurean circles in Athens, Chalcis, Thebes, and the nearby islands. Arranged mostly in narrow columns as if on a papyrus roll, several texts were composed exclusively for the inscription. As Diogenes explains: "I wished to use this stoa to advertise publicly the [medicines] that bring salvation" (fr. 3). Stone was a considered choice: "Epigraphy is clearly the medium in which civic values were projected at this time, and so Diogenes uses this very medium on a gargantuan scale to launch his counter-attack."[23]

Scholarship sometimes uses Diogenes' text to fill our gaps in Epicurean doctrine, or, conversely, focuses on reconstructions of the inscription that rely on texts of Epicurus. But despite Epicurean conservatism, Diogenes is sui generis. In one eccentric contribution, he seems to imagine the possibility of an Epicurean future when humankind will take up the life of the gods. People would study philosophy and farm together (without slaves, according to Martin Ferguson Smith's supplement to a lacuna in fr. 56, col. 2). In that world, "everything will be full of justice and mutual love, and there will come to be no need of fortifications or laws" (fr. 56, tr. Smith 1993). Although the attempt to achieve the happiness of the gods was an Epicurean ideal, no other Epicurean text suggests the possibility of a future Golden Age. Jürgen Hammerstaedt (forthcoming) has recently proposed, however, that the text refers merely to a theoretical hypothesis that Diogenes rules out because not all human beings are capable of philosophy.

Other aspects of content and form place Diogenes firmly in an imperial context. His inscription has been compared to the Column of Trajan (erected 106–113 CE): "In both cases, the reader is impressed, almost bludgeoned with a 'rhetoric of stone' that conveys a magnificent weight and monumentality."[24] Related to its monumentality is its location in the urban center alongside Oenoanda's "Esplanade."[25] According to Clement of Alexandria, Epicurus asserted that Greeks alone are capable of philosophy (*Stromata* 1.15), but Diogenes "shouts" his Epicurean message "to all Greeks and non-Greeks" (fr. 32). Reflecting the cosmopolitanism of the high empire, Diogenes hopes to reach "those who are called foreigners, though they are not really so." He continues: "The whole compass of this world gives all people a single country, the entire earth, and a single home, the world" (fr. 30). Also reflecting the urban life of the Greek East, Diogenes styles himself as a benefactor. But his disparagement of theaters and baths—the more conventional public benefactions—may have been "truly subversive."[26]

A key example of the elasticity of Epicurean texts is Diogenes' version of the *Principal Doctrines*, a collection of sayings attributed to Epicurus that Diogenes displayed prominently in a continuous line running across the inscription. Part of the Oenoanda version matches the now canonical text of the *Principal Doctrines* preserved by Diogenes Laertius (possibly a century later). Yet eight of the Oenoanda sayings are unique. Nonetheless, the sayings all appear in the same prominent band, as though they formed a single, authoritative collection. Thus, Diogenes Laertius and Diogenes of Oenoanda present us with two versions of the *Principal Doctrines* that had equal claims to authenticity. Imitating Epicurus—but not competing with him—Diogenes adds his own collection of maxims elsewhere, in multiline columns.

Perhaps the strongest indication of Diogenes' cultural location is his critique of oracular prophecy (fr. 23 and NF 143). Epicurus rejected all types of divination (Diog.

Laert. 10.135), but oracles in particular may not have attracted his attention, as the Greek oracles were relatively reticent during Epicurus's era. But the oracles of the Greek East rose sharply in popularity in the first centuries of the Empire.[27] Like Lucretius, who takes Epicurus's teachings as the foundation for his censure of Roman augury (e.g., Lucr. 6.83–89), Diogenes makes traditional Epicurean theology relevant to his own audience by attacking oracular practices. Diogenes may also be reacting to the "epigraphical genre" of inscribed oracular utterances, contemporary examples of which are found in Oenoanda.[28]

Diogenes' commentary on the traditional iconography of divinities is also without parallel. Unlike the vengeful gods of traditional Greek culture, divinities as conceived by Epicurus are contented, benign beings (*Principal Doctrines* 1). Thus, instead of arming them with a bow (traditional for Apollo, Artemis, and Herakles) or depicting them guarded by wild beasts (traditional for Cybele), Diogenes asserts: "we ought to make statues of the gods genial and smiling, so that we may smile back at them rather than be afraid of them" (fr. 19). Diskin Clay suggests that Diogenes' assertion may be a response to Christian and Jewish rejection of "graven images."[29]

Also of particular interest is the *Letter to Mother* (frr. 125–126). Responding to his mother, a student of philosophy writes that her nightmares are meaningless: her son is becoming "as joyful as the gods" (an Epicurean ideal). His reassurances accord with the Epicurean explanation that dreams are not divine messages, but are merely streams of fine simulacra that flow from the actual object or person, entering the dreamer's mind along with any distortions that conditions induce. As Diogenes writes elsewhere, dreamers may misinterpret their experience, "for the means of testing the opinion are asleep at the time" (fr. 9).

Is the *Letter to Mother* by Epicurus a letter from Diogenes to his own mother, or is it a fiction?[30] It has been attributed to Epicurus, but signs of late composition include the way it combats anti-Epicurean clichés, paraphrases Epicurus's *Principal Doctrines*, and resembles pseudepigraphical philosophers' letters.[31] Even its interest in dreams may indicate a second-century context, as many among Diogenes' non-Epicurean contemporaries regarded dreams as "a preferred medium of divine communication."[32] Epicureans were allegedly profligate, but this philosophy student pleads, virtuously: "But in heaven's name, do not be so generous with the contributions which you are constantly sending us, for I do not want you to go without anything so that I may have more than enough" (fr. 126). More than the presentation of an Epicurean theory of dreams, the *Letter to Mother* offers a portrait of a loyal Epicurean that challenges negative stereotypes. While hostile observers attributed the inclusion of women in the Garden to Epicurean licentiousness, this letter treats a woman as capable of wisdom.[33] This harmonizes well with New Fragment 186 (discovered in 2010), which refers to Epicurean studies undertaken by some unnamed women. In this fragment, attributed by Smith to a letter by Diogenes, the writer appears to promise assistance to "them" (feminine), and adds: "For indeed they happen already to have done some tasting of the doctrines of Epicurus." Both the pronoun and the (feminine) participle "tasting" identify these newcomers as women, but the badly damaged second column of this fragment reveals little else. Diogenes also refers in fr. 122 to his convalescence under a woman's care in Rhodes, and it is tempting to identify her as a member of his circle of Epicurean friends.

New Fragment 157, discovered in 2008, is relevant to any discussion of Epicurean attitudes toward sexuality. Here Diogenes says that "those who are sick with the passion of love" are unaware "that they derive pleasure to the highest degree from looking even without copulation, while the sexual act itself, whether one's partner has a superior or inferior figure, is the same" (tr. Hammerstaedt and Smith (2014)). For Smith, Diogenes' position on sex is "generally orthodox," but Hammerstaedt finds Diogenes' "positive attitude to the pleasure obtained from looking at an attractive person" at odds with Lucretius's exposé of the unhealthy connection between vision and desire in his attack on erotic love (Lucr. 4.1037–1287).[34] For Lucretius, images of the beloved are deceptive and unsatisfying, but Diogenes presents the beholding of beauty as an untainted pleasure.

Diogenes laments the superstition (ψευδοδοξία) of his contemporaries "who suffer from a common disease, as in a plague . . . and their number is increasing (for in mutual emulation they catch the disease from one another, like sheep)" (fr. 3). He does not specify particular superstitions, but identifies two ethnic groups as "the most fearful of divine power" (δεισιδαιμονέστατοι). Improvising on the Epicurean view that fear of the gods brings no societal good, Diogenes writes: "A clear indication of the complete inability of the gods to prevent wrong-doings is provided by the nations of the Jews and Egyptians, who, while being the most superstitious of all peoples, are the vilest of all peoples" (NF 126). This hostility toward Judaism has been explained variously.[35] Similar sentiments appear in many post-Hellenistic authors, who call the Jewish creed a superstition, and in Rome both Egyptians and Jews were sometimes regarded as practitioners of unwelcome alien cults.[36]

Did Diogenes, in promoting his Epicurean learning so extravagantly, violate an Epicurean teaching to "live unknown"? Geert Roskam has argued that Diogenes' establishment of a public monument does not represent a departure from Epicurean quietism.[37] My own sense is that Diogenes included the following statement to avoid the impression of a contradiction: "In this way, [citizens,] even though I am not engaging in public affairs, I say these things through the inscription just as if I were taking action" (fr. 3).

Epicureanism and Roman Manliness

Among Greek Epicureans, the word for pleasure is ἡδονή. A straightforward Latin equivalent might be *voluptas*, a word Roman Epicureans took as the logical opposite of *dolor* (pain). But *voluptas*—as the examples below demonstrate—often connotes more strongly the pleasures of the body, and thus complicates the contextualization offered by Epicurus (at *Ep. Men.* 131, quoted above). Cicero had a sophisticated understanding of the hazards of translation, so he sometimes used several words to translate one Greek word, or simply transliterated the original Greek when necessary (*Fin.* 3.15). But when fulminating against Epicureanism, Cicero proclaims that ἡδονή provides a special case: "No other word can be found that signifies a Greek word in Latin more exactly than *voluptas* does" (*Fin.* 2.13). With rhetorical incredulity, he protests: "Do I not understand what ἡδονή is in Greek, and what *voluptas* is in Latin? Which language do I not know?" (*Fin.* 2.12).

By insisting that *voluptas* is an Epicurean term, Cicero—like Seneca a century later—emphasizes the Epicureans' alleged sensuality. Harsh condemnation was the point, as is clear from Cicero's summation of *voluptas*: "the name is odious, notorious, suspect" (*invidiosum nomen est, infame, suspectum*; *Fin.* 2.12). The next step was to propose a new polar opposite to *voluptas*. In a peculiar shorthand, the inverse of Epicureanism becomes *virtus*, a masculine quality that Cicero describes as "peculiar to the Roman genus and race" (*Phil.* 4.13). Wordplay was everything: the repetition of *v*, *u*, and the liquids *r* and *l*; the echoing of *tut* with *tat*, or *tus* with *tas*. *Virtus* is a powerful word in Latin, and the English derivative "virtue" does not fully capture its gendered quality, as Cicero and Seneca make clear. Thus, Cicero asserts (with etymological precision) that *virtus* comes from the word "man" (*ex viro virtus*; *Tusc.* 2.43). "Manliness" is a better translation of *virtus*, in light of Roman claims that courage and ethically appropriate behavior—along with particular types of comportment and appearance as described below—are manly traits.

Whenever the paronomasia produced by *virtus* and *voluptas* is unmistakable in Roman texts, Epicureanism is virtually always the subject.[38] To cite a few examples: in *On Moral Ends*, Cicero reconfigures the disagreement over Epicureanism between himself and Torquatus as a competition not between the two men, but between *virtus* and *voluptas* (*Fin* 2. 44). Cicero also asserts: "You Epicureans, by running your lives according to *voluptas*, are unable to cultivate or retain *virtus*" (*Fin.* 2.71). Contrasting himself with Epicurus, Cicero writes: "To my thinking the highest good is in the mind; to his thinking in the body; to mine in *virtus* to his in *voluptas*" (*Tusc.*3. 50). A century after Cicero, Seneca offers an extended elaboration that highlights the gender of Epicureanism (*De vita beata* 7.3):

> *Virtus* is something exalted, something elevated and regal, unconquered, unfaltering; *Voluptas* is lowly, servile, feeble, and decaying, whose hovel and staging-ground are the brothels and the taverns. *Virtus* you will find in the temple, in the forum, in the senate house, defending the city walls, dusty and sun-burnt, hands callused. *Voluptas* you will find most often seeking out darkness, lurking around the baths and sweating rooms and places that fear the magistrates; soft, languid, reeking of wine and perfume, pallid or else painted and made up like a corpse.

Exploiting gendered distinctions between public and private, vigor and weakness, bravery and cowardice, ruddiness and pallor, Seneca excludes the Epicureans from the realm of the elite Roman male. Thus—through the partisan translation of a single Greek word, a bit of word play, and remarkable oratorical skill—Cicero and Seneca portray Epicureanism as the antithesis of traditional Roman values.

How did Epicureans respond when their compatriots claimed that *virtus* and *voluptas* are irreconcilable? We have the unequivocal response of one particular Epicurean, who wrote to Cicero in January of 45 BCE. The letter is from Gaius Cassius Longinus, soon to be involved in the assassination of Julius Caesar, an issue to which I shall return. Earlier that month, Cicero had described Cassius's turn toward Epicureanism as his "divorce" from *virtus* in favor of inglorious *voluptas* (*Fam.* 15.17.3). In a trenchant rejoinder that quotes Epicurus, Cassius code-switches in a particularly pointed way. Declining to translate ἡδονή, he splices Latin with Greek when he mentions "pleasure," and reclaims *virtus*, justice, and the good for Epicureanism: "but it is both true and demonstrable that ἡδονή and tranquility are to be obtained through *virtus*, justice, and the good" (ἡδονὴν vero et ἀταραξίαν *virtute, iustitia,* τῷ καλῷ *parari et verum et probabile est; Fam.* 15.19.2). Cassius again avoids the word *voluptas* and asserts that an Epicurean has *virtus* when he contradicts Cicero by writing that Pansa, his fellow Epicurean and Roman statesman, "follows ἡδονήν, but retains *virtus*" (*Fam.* 15.19.3).

Did other Epicureans reject the codes of "manliness" as conceived by Cicero and Seneca? Before addressing this question, I ask: Why did Cicero and Seneca associate Epicureanism with the feminine? And why was the cliché vigorously promoted by other writers during the Roman Empire such as Plutarch and Epictetus?[39] It was not a matter of simple name-calling. Rather, Epicureanism confronted Rome with a constellation of attributes that were incompatible with traditional conceptions of the duties and prerogatives of elite Roman males. Most prominently, the Epicurean goal of spiritual tranquility (ἀταραξία in Greek; sometimes rendered as *quies* in Latin) promoted the wisdom of withdrawal from public life as opposed to engagement with the *cursus honorum* through which Roman men competed for military and political honors. Epicurean doubts about the wisdom of marriage and the begetting of children were also discordant with the respect accorded to the ideal *paterfamilias*. In Hellenistic Athens, the Garden inspired jokes and polemics, but apparently not in such gendered terms. Another of Cicero's riffs on the radical divide between Roman manliness and Epicurean *voluptas* is instructive: "My entire oration is on the side of *virtus*, not indolence; on the side of dignity, not *voluptas*; on the side of those who believe they were born for their country, for their compatriots, for esteem, for glory; not for sleep, for feasts, and for gratification" (*Sest.* 66.138). The Stoic philosopher Epictetus chose the metaphor of castration: "Epicurus chopped off everything that has to do with being a man, everything to do with being the master of a household, with being a citizen, with being a friend." (Arr. *Epict. diss.* 2.20.2).

Lucretius certainly questions the *cursus honorum* when he condemns political ambition, a theme he addresses passionately. For him, avarice and "blind lust for political office" are lifetime wounds (*honorum caeca cupido . . . vulnera vitae*; Lucr. 3.59–63, tr. Bailey), the true Sisyphus is a grasping politician who has created his own hell on earth (3.995–997), and fame and political power cause pain and bring no security to men "as they struggle to rise to the highest honor" (*ad summum succedere honorem certantes*;

5.1123–1124).⁴⁰ Yet Lucretius does not flinch at the word *voluptas* when he associates "pleasure" with Rome (1.1). There he boldly unites *voluptas* with Roman patriotism by addressing Venus as "Mother of the sons of Aeneas and the pleasure of gods and men" (*Aeneadum genetrix, hominum divumque voluptas*). Stressing Rome's need during the current period of violent upheaval, Lucretius asks for Venus's aid in stilling war and bringing peace (1.29–43). Moreover, although Lucretius evinces a patriarchal outlook elsewhere, his invocation to Venus and his recognition of the power of Mother Earth and *Natura* champion a "feminine principle."⁴¹

Most Epicureans may have recommended withdrawal, but quietism was not the only way an Epicurean might respond to social and political turbulence. Writing during the last years of Mussolini's regime, Momigliano described Cassius's "double conversion to Epicureanism and *libertas*" as the impetus behind his role in the conspiracy to rid Rome of Julius Caesar.⁴² In Momigliano's view, Cassius, as liberator, enacted a "heroic Epicureanism" that reversed orthodox Epicurean strictures against engaging in political activity (157). Cassius's co-conspirator Brutus had secretly tested another, more traditional Epicurean friend before excluding him from the plot. Cicero reports (*Rep.* 1.10) that the Epicurean creed allowed involvement in politics in the case of extreme crises, but another Epicurean, a man named Statilius, was passed over when he spoke approvingly of the wisdom of withdrawing from the fray instead of getting involved in danger and turmoil "for the sake of bad and foolish people" (Plut. *Vit. Brut.* 12.2).

Another statesman who may have integrated his commitment to serious Epicurean values with his politics and comportment is the man Cicero portrays as a hideous voluptuary "from the sty, not the school" of Epicureanism. This is L. Calpurnius Piso Caesoninus, consul of 58 BCE, and one of Cicero's energetic denouncers after the illegal execution of the Catiline conspirators. Cicero offers a memorable caricature in *Against Piso* (55 BCE), a "masterpiece of misrepresentation,"⁴³ but he had begun his attack earlier in the *Post reditum in senatu* and the *Pro Sestio*. Piso, according to Cicero, was under the sway of *Graeculi* ("little Greeks") and had joined "those who argue that no hour should be devoid of *voluptas*" (*Post red.* 14). He was listening to the philosophy of these Greeks "in the brothels, in debauchery, over food and drink" (*Pis.* 42). But Piso's physical appearance apparently fit a stereotype of Roman manliness. This presented a challenge that Cicero faced by alleging that Piso's was a counterfeit hypermasculinity providing a cover for an effeminate interior: "How foul, how fierce, how formidable he is in appearance as he marches along. You would have guessed he was one of our bearded forefathers, a model of the power of old, the image of antiquity, a pillar of the state" (*Sest.* 19).

According to Cicero's report, Piso—upon his return to Rome from Macedonia—voiced objections to the celebration of a military triumph, perhaps the quintessential display of manly success (*Pis.* 56). Cicero implies that the senate would deny a triumph to so detested a governor, but reveals that Piso articulated philosophical reasons for not wanting a triumph. In response to Piso's unrecorded remarks, Cicero sneers: "You have heard, Conscript Fathers, the voice of a philosopher" (*Pis.* 56). The philosophical position is not as fallacious as Cicero implies, and Piso may well have agreed with Lucretius in valuing Epicurean tranquility over displays of power (Lucr. 2.37–46). In fact, there are traces of Epicurean ethics—such as a belief in clemency, commitment to friends, and avoidance of strife—throughout Piso's portrait as offered by Cicero, the historian Cassius Dio, and Plutarch.[44] Piso's revulsion at the execution of the Catilinarian conspirators may also indicate an Epicurean outlook, despite the fact that Cicero treats Piso's remark that he has "always been inclined toward mercy" as specious (*Red. sen.* 17). Perhaps Piso's apparently Epicurean approach was shaped in part by Philodemus, who dedicated to Piso his essay *On the Good King According to Homer*. According to Philodemus, Homer presented the Phaeacian king Alcinous as an ideal ruler: just, wise, and desirous of peace. Mildness is an attribute that Diogenes Laertius saw in Epicurus, whom he praised for his ἡμερότης (gentleness; Diog. Laert. 10.10.). Some people may have considered the gentleness of Epicurus to belong not to historical reality, but to a habit of idealization, as suggested by *Sententia Vaticana* 36: "The life of Epicurus, when compared to the lives of others, might—because of its gentleness and self-sufficiency—be thought to be a fiction."

Writing to his Epicurean friend Atticus months after the death of Caesar, Cicero indicates that Atticus had sent him some apparently Lucretian advice: "You cite Epicurus and dare to tell me to stay out of politics?" (*Att.* 14.20.5). Atticus's abstention from the political and military paths chosen by Cassius and Piso harmonizes with Epicureanism as presented by Lucretius, though some scholars contrast Atticus with "extremists" like Lucretius.[45] But Atticus was no ideologue, as is clear even from his friendship with Cicero. Some Epicureans may have intoned "Do everything as though Epicurus were watching," as Seneca claims (*Ep.* 25.5). But new cultural and political contexts gave Epicureanism new meanings, and not all practitioners responded in unison. The diversity of historical Epicureans that emerges from the pages of Cicero, like the diversity of Epicurean texts from the Roman Republic and Empire, belies the stereotype of the unimaginative Epicurean, and suggests further that, in adapting Epicureanism to the Roman context, Epicureans under the Empire reformulated traditional doctrines in new ways.

Notes

1. For reference, see especially: Campbell (2020), Essler (2019), and Verde (2019).
2. See Fish and Sanders (2011) and O'Rourke (2020), for example.
3. Hutchinson (2001) argues that Lucretius was writing in or after 49 BCE. For a response, see Volk (2010).
4. For poetry and education, see Asmis (1995) and Morrison (2020). Geller-Goad (2020) and Nethercut (2020) offer major reassessments of the roles of Lucilius and Ennius, respectively. Taylor (2020) explores Lucretius's linguistic innovation.
5. E.g., Kleve (1978); Asmis (1982); Clay (1983); Algra et al. (1997).
6. Sedley (1998).
7. For reference, see McConnell (2012).
8. See Gale (2020).
9. Summers (1995) 34. This issue is complicated by Rider (2019), who traces Lucretius's abhorrence of animal sacrifice to Empedocles.
10. Asmis (2008) 141.

11. Ibid., 142.
12. Fowler (2002) 442.
13. Ibid., 443.
14. Sharrock (2013) 14 is referring to essays by Holmes and Kennedy in Lehoux, Morrison, and Sharrock, eds. (2013).
15. O'Keefe (2020) 194.
16. Morrison (2020).
17. Konstan (2019).
18. Against this consensus, see Porter (2007).
19. Asmis (1990) 2380–2381.
20. Asmis (1999) 294.
21. The inscription was dismantled in antiquity, and the over 300 known fragments represent a fraction of the original. Here I cite the texts and translations of Smith (1993) and (2003) and Hammerstaedt and Smith (2008) and (2014). Hammerstaedt and Smith (2014) list all editions, now to be supplemented with the latest significant fragments published in Hammerstaedt and Smith (2018).
22. Smith (1993) 40–43.
23. Warren (2000) 148.
24. Snyder (2000) 62; cf. Warren (2000).
25. Smith (1993) 54–56.
26. Bendlin (2011) 184.
27. See discussion in Bendlin (2011).
28. Warren (2000) 148.
29. Clay (2000) 89–91.
30. See Smith (1993) 555–558.
31. Gordon (1996) 66–93 and Fletcher (2012).
32. Bendlin (2011) 181.
33. Gordon (2012) 72–108.
34. Hammerstaedt and Smith (2014) 88–93.
35. See Smith (1998) 140–142.
36. See Gruen (2002) 43 for superstition and Jewish creed; see 30–33 and 52–53 for the alienness of Egyptians and Jews at Rome.
37. Roskam (2007) 143.
38. Gordon (2012) 109–138.
39. As described in Gordon (2012).
40. For a recent interpretation see Fish (2011).
41. Fowler (1996).
42. Momigliano (1941) 153.
43. Nisbet (1961) xvi.
44. Cf. Griffin (2001) 88–91.
45. Lindsay (1998) 335.

References

Algra, K. A., J. Barnes, J. Mansfeld, and M. Schofield, eds. (1999). *The Cambridge History of Hellenistic Philosophy*. (Cambridge).

Algra, K. A., M. H. Koenen, and P. H. Schrijvers, eds. (1997). *Lucretius and His Intellectual Background*. (Amsterdam/New York).
Angeli, A, ed. (1988). *Filodemo. Agli amici di scuola (PHerc. 1005). La Scuola di Epicuro, 7.* (Naples).
Asmis, E. (1982). "Lucretius' Venus and Stoic Zeus." *Hermes* 110: 458–470.
Asmis, E. (1990). "Philodemus' Epicureanism." *ANRW* II 36(4): 2396–2406.
Asmis, E. (1995). "Epicurean Poetics," in Obbink, 15–34.
Asmis, E. (1999). "Epicurean Epistemology," in Algra, Barnes, Mansfeld, and Schofield, 260–294.
Asmis, E. (2008). "Lucretius' New World Order: Making a Pact with Nature." *CQ* 58: 141–157.
Auvray-Assayas, C., and D. Delattre (2001). *Cicéron et Philodème: La polémique en philosophie.* (Paris).
Bailey, C. B. (1947). *Lucretius:* De rerum natura. 3 vols. (Oxford).
Bendlin, A. (2011). "On the Uses and Disadvantages of Divination: Oracles and Their Literary Representations in the Time of the Second Sophistic," in North and Price, 175–250.
Campbell, G. L. (2020). "Lucretius." *Oxford Bibliographies Online: Classics*, February 26. http://dx.doi.org/10.1093/OBO/9780195389661-0034 (accessed November 14, 2021).
Clay, D. (1983). *Lucretius and Epicurus.* (Ithaca, N.Y.).
Clay, D. (2000). "Diogenes and His Gods," in M. Erler and R. Bees (eds.), *Epikureismus in der späten Republik und in der Kaiserzeit* (Stuttgart), 76–92.
Coates, V. C. G., and J. L. Seydl, eds. (2007). *Antiquity Recovered: The Legacy of Pompeii and Herculaneum.* (Los Angeles).
Essler, H. (2019). "Philodemus of Gadara." *Oxford Bibliographies Online: Classics*, February 27. http://dx.doi.org/10.1093/obo/9780195389661-0246 (accessed November 14, 2021).
Fish, J. (2011). "Not All Politicians Are Sisyphus: What Roman Epicureans Were Taught about Politics," in Fish and Sanders, 72–104.
Fish, J., and K. Sanders, eds. (2011). *Epicurus and the Epicurean Tradition.* (Cambridge).
Fletcher, R. (2012). "Epicurus's Mistresses: Pleasure, Authority, and Gender in the Reception of the *Kuriai Doxai* in the Second Sophistic," in Holmes and Shearin, 52–88.
Fowler, D. (1996). "The Feminine Principal: Gender in the *De rerum natura*," in Giannantoni and Gigante, 813–822.
Fowler, D. (2002). *Lucretius on Atomic Motion: A Commentary on* De rerum natura *Book Two lines 1–332.* (Oxford).
Fowler, D. (2007). "Lucretius and Politics," in Gale, 397–431.
Gale, M. (2007). *Oxford Readings in Classical Studies: Lucretius.* (Oxford).
Gale, M. (2020). "Lucretius," in Mitsis, 430–455.
Gellar-Goad, T. H. M. (2020). *Laughing Atoms, Laughing Matter: Lucretius'* De rerum natura *and Satire.* (Ann Arbor).
Giannantoni, G., and M. Gigante, eds. (1996). *Epicureismo greco e romano.* (Naples).
Gordon, P. (1996). *Epicurus in Lycia: The Second-Century World of Diogenes of Oenoanda.* (Ann Arbor, Mich.).
Gordon, P. (2012). *The Invention and Gendering of Epicurus.* (Ann Arbor, Mich.).
Griffin, M. (2001) "Piso, Cicero, and Their Audience," in Auvray-Assayas and Delattre, 85–100.
Gruen, E. (2002) *Diaspora: Jews amidst Greeks and Romans.* (Cambridge, Mass.)
Hammerstaedt, J. (forthcoming). "Epicurus and His Doctrine in the Inscription of Diogenes of Oinoanda," in Heßler, Erler, and Petrucci.

Hammerstaedt, J., and M. F. Smith (2008). "Diogenes of Oinoanda: The Discoveries of 2008 (NF 142–167)." *Epigraphica Anatolica* 41: 1–37.
Hammerstaedt, J., and M. F. Smith (2014). *The Epicurean Inscription of Diogenes of Oinoanda: Ten Years of New Discoveries and Research.* (Bonn).
Hammerstaedt, J., and M. F. Smith (2018). "Diogenes of Oinoanda: New Discoveries of 2017 (NF 214–219), with New Surprises and a Reedition of fr. 70–72." *EA* 51: 43–79.
Heßler, J., M. Erler, and F. Petrucci, eds. (forthcoming) *Authority and Use of Authoritative Texts in the Epicurean Tradition.* (Cambridge).
Holmes, B., and W. H. Shearin, eds. (2012). *Dynamic Reading: Studies in the Reception of Epicureanism.* (Oxford).
Hutchinson, G. O. (2001). "The Date of *De Rerum Natura*." *CQ* 51: 150–162.
Kleve, K. (1978). "The Philosophical Polemics in Lucretius," in O. Gigon (ed.), *Lucrèce: Huit exposés suivis de discussions* (Geneva), 39–75.
Konstan, D. (2019). "Lucretius and the Conscience of an Epicurean." *Politeia* 1: 67–79.
Lehoux, D., A. D. Morrison, and A. Sharrock, eds. (2013). *Lucretius: Poetry, Philosophy, Science.* (Oxford).
Lindsay, H. (1998). "The Biography of Atticus: Cornelius Nepos on the Philosophical and Ethical Background of Pomponius Attic." *Latomus* 57: 324–336.
Longo Auricchio, F. (1978). "La scuola di Epicuro." *Cronache ercolanesi* 8: 21–37.
McConnell, S. (2012). "Lucretius and Civil Strife." *Phoenix* 66: 97–121.
Mitsis, P., ed. (2020). *Oxford Handbook of Epicurus and Epicureanism.* (New York).
Momigliano, A. (1941). "Epicureans in Revolt." *JRS* 31: 149–157.
Morrison, A. D. (2020). "Arguing over Text(s): Master-Texts vs. Intertexts in the Criticism of Lucretius," in O'Rourke 2020, 157–176.
Nethercut, J. S. (2020). *Ennius Noster Lucretius and the Annales.* (Oxford).
Nisbet, R. G. M., ed. (1961). *In L. Calpurnium Pisonem Oratio.* (Oxford).
North, J. A., and S. R. F. Price, eds. (2011). *The Religious History of the Roman Empire: Pagans, Jews, and Christians.* (Oxford).
Obbink, D., ed. (1995). *Philodemus and Poetry: Poetic Theory and Practice in Lucretius, Philodemus, and Horace.* (Oxford).
O'Keefe, T. (2020). "Lucretius and the Philosophical Use of Literary Persuasion," in O'Rourke, 177–194.
O'Rourke, D., ed. (2020). *Approaches to Lucretius: Traditions and Innovations in Reading the* De rerum natura. (Cambridge).
Porter, J. (2007). "Hearing Voices: The Herculaneum Papyri and Classical Scholarship," in Coates and Seydl, 95–113.
Rider, Z. (2019). "The Failure of Sacrifice in the *De rerum natura*." *TAPA* 149: 1–26.
Roskam, G. (2007). *"Live Unnoticed" (λάθε βιώσας): On the Vicissitudes of an Epicurean Doctrine.* (Leiden).
Sedley, D. (1998). *Lucretius and the Transformation of Greek Wisdom.* (Cambridge).
Sedley, D. (2011). "Epicurus' Theological Innatism," in Fish and Sanders, 29–52.
Sharrock, A. (2013). "Introduction," in Lehoux, Morrison, and Sharrock, 1–24.
Smith, M. F. (1993). *Diogenes of Oinoanda: The Epicurean Inscription.* (Naples).
Smith, M. F. (1998). "Excavations at Oinoanda 1997: The New Epicurean Texts." *Anat. St.* 48: 125–170.
Smith, M. F. (2003). *Supplement to Diogenes of Oinoanda: The Epicurean Inscription.* (Naples).

Snyder, H. G. (2000). *Teachers and Texts in the Ancient World: Philosophers, Jews and Christians.* (New York).
Summers, K. (1995). "Lucretius and the Epicurean tradition of piety." *CPh* 90: 32–57.
Taylor (2020). *Lucretius and the Language of Nature.* (Oxford).
Verde, F. (2019). "Epicureanism." *Oxford Bibliographies Online: Classics*, March 27. http://dx.doi.org/10.1093/obo/9780195389661-0202 (accessed November 15, 2021).
Volk, K. (2010). "Lucretius' Prayer for Peace and the Date of *De rerum natura*." *CQ* 60: 127–131.
Warren, J. (2000). "Diogenes Epikourios: Keep Taking the Tablets." *JHS* 120: 144–148.

CHAPTER 3

ETHICAL ARGUMENT AND EPICUREAN SUBTEXT IN HORACE, *ODES* 1.1 AND 2.16

GREGSON DAVIS

HORATIAN lyric discourse is eudaimonist in its main thematic focus. This ethical dimension is by no means unique to the *Odes*, for in all the other genres represented in the poet's corpus there is an undercurrent of philosophical engagement that may be characterized as an ongoing "conversation" with Epicurean systems of thought.[1] Irrigating this flow of conversation are allusions to certain extant writings of Epicurus and to those of major Republican thinkers who channel and elaborate on his precepts, chief among them the influential emigré Greek teacher Philodemus of Gadara and the Latin philosopher-poet Lucretius. Cicero's critical accounts of Epicurean thought in his philosophical works, especially his *On Ends*, supplement this network of allusions. This chapter will analyze two principal odes that best illustrate Horace's lyric "conversations," namely, 1.1 and 2.16.[2]

Before I document core aspects of the Epicurean subtext of these odes, a brief disavowal is in order. I will eschew any attempt to answer the frequently posed question, "Was Horace an Epicurean?" on the grounds that an unambiguously positive answer would disregard the poet's own robust disavowal of adherence to any philosophical school: *nullius addictus iurare in verba magistri* ("[I have not] sworn an oath of allegiance to any master").[3] My rather different interrogation will be aimed at illustrating the scope and depth of the Horatian lyric dialogue with the founder of the Garden.

ἡδονή/*VOLUPTAS*: *ODES* 1.1

After two opening lines in praise of his intimate friend and patron, Maecenas, Horace resorts to the conventional rhetorical scaffolding of the priamel, in which he constructs an elaborate "foil," consisting of the lifestyle choices of "others," before capping it with the different (and, by implication, superior) choice espoused by the speaker.[4] There is a salient, recurrent leitmotif throughout the poem that focuses on the motivation undergirding the choices of representative lifestyles and embodied in both foil and cap, viz. the pleasure they bring to their respective practitioners. The leitmotif is initiated in the very first item of the foil, where the pleasure experienced by the victor in the Olympic games is marked by the verb *iuvat* (3–6):[5] "Some men **find pleasure** in churning up dust-clouds at Olympia with their chariots, and in grazing the turning-post with red-hot wheels; the palm of victory elevates them to divine status as masters of the earth" (*sunt quos curriculo pulverem Olympicum / collegisse* **iuvat** *metaque fervidis / evitata rotis palmaque nobilis / terrarum dominos evehit ad deos*).

The motif signal, *iuvat*, is carried through the next two items via the grammatical device of a double ellipsis, whereby the verb is to be supplied in the two successive clauses introduced by *hunc* and *illum* (7–10): "[**It pleases**] one person if the mob of fickle Romans vies to exalt him to the three highest offices of state; [it **pleases**] another if he has amassed within his private grain silo all that is swept from Libya's threshing-floors" (*hunc, si mobilium turba Quiritium / certat tergeminis tollere honoribus; / illum, si proprio condidit horreo / quicquid de Libycis verritur areis*).

The next exhibit continues the leitmotif with the occurrence of the verb *gaudeo*, positioned at the head of the line and functioning in this context as a synonym for *iuvare* (11–14): "The farmer who **enjoys** tilling with the hoe his ancestral clods you'd never move with all the wealth of Pergamum's dynasts to cleave through the Myrtoan sea—a fearful sailor in a Cypriot bark" (***Gaudentem*** *patrios findere sarculo / agros Attalicis condicionibus / numquam demoveas, ut trabe Cypria / Myrtoum pavidus nauta secet mare*).

As if to underscore a central point in the poem's argument, the key word *iuvare* is reiterated in verse 23, which parades the lifestyle of the dedicated soldier (23–25): "Many **find pleasure** in soldiers' barracks, the cacophony of clarions and bugles blaring together, and wars that mothers hate" (*Multos castra* **iuvant** *et lituo tubae / permixtus sonitus bellaque matribus / detestata*). In light of this conspicuous replication, the reader is led to assume that the pleasure motif is also implicit in the account of the other items that make up the foil: the incorrigible merchant seaman (16–18), the solitary winebibber (19–22) and the passionate hunter (25–28).

As is well known, the Epicureans held as their paramount ethical tenet that the pursuit of pleasure (ἡδονή), along with the complementary avoidance of pain, is the fundamental goal of human behavior. Cicero and Lucretius both translate this fundamental Epicurean principle by the Latin term *voluptas*, the latter famously in the first line of the hymn to Venus that launches his *On the Nature of Things* (*De rerum natura*, or *DRN*): *Aeneadum genetrix, hominum divumque* **voluptas** ("Mother of Aeneas and his race, delight of men and gods").[6] The concept of the fundamental role of pleasure is hypostasized in the very name of one of the two Muses that Horace selects to decorate the closing lines of the poem, Euterpe (cognate with τέρπειν: "to take pleasure in"). The naming of Euterpe, coupled with Polyhymnia, emphasizes the programmatic significance of the inaugural ode, which promulgates the practice of enlightened hedonism that is at the core of Horace's eudaimonist orientation.

Is the mere presence of the "particular pleasure" leitmotif enough to characterize the speaker's comparative evaluation of lifestyles as "eudaimonist"? On a superficial reading, the articulation of particular pleasures in the priamel may appear to be more compatible with the Cyrenaic than with the Epicurean theory of pleasure, since the prevailing view among scholars of Hellenistic philosophy is that the former school is fundamentally "anti-Eudaimonist." Tim O'Keefe summarizes this view: "One of the most striking features of Cyrenaic ethics is their assertion that "particular pleasure" and not happiness, is the highest good. [. . .] Happiness, the sum of all these particular pleasures, is choice-worthy only because of particular pleasures."[7] A closer examination of certain of the foil items, however, makes it clear that the creator of *Odes* 1.1 regards the choice of a particular pleasure as reflective of a wider ethical outlook that typifies the chooser's attitude to virtue and the good life.[8]

The observation that the speaker's presentation of others' choices is far from neutral is essential to understanding the underlying critique of those choices. The pejorative rhetorical slant that Horace imparts to his typological description is subtly conveyed by means of irony and hyperbole. The aspiring Olympic victor, for instance, is represented as "churning up dust-clouds" in the chariot-race—hardly a pleasant prospect on the face of it; the dedicated soldier, who engages in "wars that mothers hate," has to endure routinely in camp the cacophony of war trumpets. A closer scrutiny of the diction employed in the taxonomy of lifestyles discloses a negative undercurrent that follows a demonstrably Epicurean course.

To begin with the second item in the foil: The ambitious politician is portrayed as utterly dependent on the votes of "the mob (*turba*) of fickle Romans (*mobilium . . . Quiritium*)." Among the adherents of the philosophy of the Garden, the seeker of high echelon political offices is a standard target of detraction. Horace's sardonic verses chime with the motif as employed in more than one instance by Lucretius. Especially relevant is the famous passage of *DRN* that maligns the seeker after the Roman *fasces* by figuring him as the mythical Sisyphus (3.995–1002):

> Sisyphus in vita quoque nobis ante oculos est,
> qui **petere a populo fasces saevasque secures**
> imbibit et semper victus tristisque recedit.
> **nam petere imperium, quod inanest** nec datur umquam,
> atque in eo semper durum sufferre laborem,
> hoc est adverso nixantem trudere monte
> saxum, quod tamen e summo iam vertice rusum
> volvitur et plani raptim petit aequora campi.

> Sisyphus also appears in this life before our eyes, athirst **to solicit from the people the lictor's rods and cruel axes,** and always retiring defeated and full of gloom: **For to solicit power, an empty thing,** which is never granted, and always to endure hard toil in pursuit of it, this is to push laboriously up a hill the rock that still rolls down again from every top, and in a rush recovers the levels of the open plain.

The Sisyphus figure in the Lucretian account shares with Horace's representation the idea of the intrinsic *insecurity* of the position of the person who attains the *fasces*, as captured in the epithet *mobilium* ("fickle") applied with trenchant sarcasm to the pristine designation of the Roman mob as *Quiritium*.

The complex example of the farmer merits a deeper examination in this regard. It is altogether plausible, in my view, to understand the poet as taking a jaundiced view of the joyful toil of the small landowner who cannot be dislodged—even "with all the wealth of Pergamum's dynasts"—from tilling hard clods on his ancestral plot with a primitive mattock (11–14). Despite the tell-tale hyperbole, most commentators are inclined to see the depiction of the small landowner's stance in an unequivocally favorable light. It is worth noting against the grain, however, that this particular *modus vivendi* is expressly downgraded by none other than the Epicurean philosopher, Philodemus, in his treatise *On Property Management*. In his comparative assessment of sources of income in so far as they contribute to the sage's happiness, he puts forward the view that:

> Cultivating the land oneself in a manner involving work with one's own hands is also wretched, while cultivating it "using other workers as if one is a landowner" is appropriate for the good man. For it brings the least possible involvement with men from whom many disagreeable things follow, and a pleasant life, a leisurely retreat with one's friends, and a most dignified income to [those who are moderate].[9]

This recommendation on the part of Philodemus is based on the assumption that one's choice of vocation or avocation is important to the successful achievement of the *summum bonum*.

In the case of the solitary winebibber, it is crucial to Horace's argument for the reader to recognize the ethical deficiencies exposed in the chosen lifestyle, even though it is seductively drawn and set in a *locus amoenus* (19–22):

> Est qui nec veteris pocula Massici
> nec partem solido demere de die
> spernit, nunc viridi membra sub arbuto
> stratus, nunc ad aquae lene caput sacrae.

> Then there's the fellow who does not refrain from poaching from
> the solid daylight hours, imbibing cups of well-aged Massic wine,
> now lying, limbs laid back, beneath the green arbutus bush,
> now prostrate near the source of a numinous, gently flowing spring.

Quite apart from the fact that the logic of the priamel foil, as Horace deploys it, implies an underlying devaluation of the alternative lifestyles, it is clear that the sympotic ideal that he advocates throughout the *Odes* is consistent in stressing the enjoyment of wine in the company of friends (*amici/sodales*).[10] The unflattering example of the person who inappropriately chooses to imbibe Massic wine all by himself in the middle of the day—a habit that is glaringly inappropriate (ἄκαιρος), despite the refined taste of the drinker—brands him as an immoderate pleasure-seeker of the kind espoused by the "everyday hedonism" of the Cyrenaic variety. This image of the solitary drinker obliquely supports a holistic critique of the type on eudaimonist grounds.[11]

The most overtly ethical judgment that Horace delivers on the subject of the existential consequences of a chosen lifestyle occurs in the example of the merchant-seaman (*mercator*) in verses 16–18: "The merchant seaman **when in dread** of winds that scuffle with Icarian waves praises **the tranquility** of his hometown and countryside; but in short order he sets out to repair his battered barks, **unschooled to endure a frugal mode of life**" (*Luctantem Icariis fluctibus Africum / mercator* **metuens otium** *et oppida / laudat rura sui; mox reficit rates / quassas,* **indocilis pauperiem pati**).

The merchant's occupational hazard lies in encountering a dangerous storm at sea that exposes his emotional vulnerability to the recurrent fear of death (implied in the participle *metuens*, 16). Anxiety about one's death was regarded as anathema to a happy life in the Epicurean ethical canon, which perceived it as a primary obstacle to ἀταραξία (freedom from mental perturbation). Although the *mercator* intermittently proclaims his nostalgia for the "tranquility" (*otium*)[12] of his rural home at those moments when he is caught in a violent storm, he is so obsessed with the pursuit of profit that he hastens to refit his storm-battered ships and sets out to sea "in short order" (*mox*) even after near-disaster. Horace identifies the ethical shortcomings of the *mercator* with the terse characterization: **indocilis pauperiem pati** ("**unschooled** to endure a frugal mode of life"). The speaker's editorial comment is framed in Epicurean doctrinal terms that strongly advocated a modest lifestyle (Latin *pauperies*).[13] In the *locus classicus* of this advocacy (Epicurus *Ep. Men.* 131), plain living is specifically and robustly put forward as an antidote to the misfortunes dealt to mortals by τύχη): "Therefore, becoming accustomed to simple, not extravagant ways of life, makes one completely healthy . . **and makes man fearless in the face of chance**"[14] (τὸ συνεθίζειν οὖν ἐν ταῖς ἁπλαῖς καὶ οὐ πολυτελέσι διαίταις καὶ ὑγιείας ἐστὶ συμπληρωτικὸν . . . καὶ πρὸς τὴν τύχην ἀφόβους παρασκευάζει). The fearful *mercator/nauta* who quakes during the misfortune of a life-threatening storm is chastised, in Horace's text, for his flagrant "inability to learn" (*indocilis*) the value of plain living—the very same ethical linkage made in Epicurus's admonition.

The lifestyle that constitutes the cap of the priamel boldly proclaims the superiority of the choice of speaker by elevating the poet to virtually divine status (29–36):

> Me doctarum hederae praemia frontium
> dis miscent superis, me gelidum nemus
> Nympharumque leves cum Satyris chori
> secernunt populo, si neque tibias
> Euterpe cohibet nec Polyhymnia
> Lesboum refugit tendere barbiton.
> Quod si me lyricis vatibus inseres,
> sublimi feriam sidera vertice.

> [My pleasure lies] in the ivy garlands awarded to those well-versed
> poets who enjoy the company of the gods supreme; the cool grove
> is mine, and the light dances of Nymphs and Satyrs,
> setting me apart from the mob, so long as Euterpe does not
> withhold her oboe, nor Polyhymnia her Lesbian lute.
> But if you place me in the lyrists' canon,
> I shall strike the stars with head held high.

To enjoy the company of gods (*dis miscent superis*), as manifested in privileged membership in a Dionysian entourage of nymphs and satyrs, is to live "as a god among men" in the memorable words of Epicurus.[15] From the exalted conception of the poet as *vates*, we are expected to deduce that the educated and acclaimed lyric practitioner (cf. ***doctarum hederae praemia frontium***) transcends the mere acquisition of technical skill to achieve the status of a prophet, sage, and teacher. The *poeta doctus* thereby stands in deliberately sharp contrast to the ***indocilis mercator*** of the foil discussed above.

The scope of the poet's apotheosis conspicuously trumps that attained on earth by the Olympic victor who introduces the priamel (***terrarum dominos*** *evehit ad deos*, "[the palm of victory] uplifts them to divine status **as masters of the earth**"), for the lyrist is imagined as soaring upward away from the earth toward the empyrean in the poem's closing line: *sublimi feriam sidera vertice*," ("I shall strike the stars with head held high").[16] The higher plane of existence into which the poet flies is conceptually far beyond the Olympus of conventional myth; rather, it is meant to evoke the region of ethereal *intermundia* that is the privileged *sedes* of the gods as imagined by Epicurus and his disciple, Lucretius. This celestial existence in the outer regions of space is as far removed as possible from those earthbound pinnacles of success admired by the *vulgus*. The interstellar cosmic location of Horace's ultimate destination is, at bottom, a concrete metonym for an ontological state that conjures up the secluded existence led by the Epicurean divinities as sketched in a passage by Lucretius (2.646–48): "For the very nature of divinity must necessarily enjoy immortal life in the deepest peace, **far removed and separated from our affairs**" (*omnis enim per se divom natura necesset / inmortali aevo summa cum pace fruatur / **semota ab nostris rebus seiunctaque longe***).

The extended priamel that structures the argument of the inaugural ode is framed, at beginning and end, by "ring-compositional" apostrophes that laud Horace's patron and intimate friend, Maecenas. The phraseology of the second line of the opening address (*O et **praesidium** et dulce decus meum*) deserves close inspection, for it is partially couched in the jargon of Epicurean friendship,[17] the significance of which has, to my knowledge, hitherto gone unnoticed in the exegetical literature relating specifically to the *Odes*. Although several commentators have noted that *praesidium* and *decus* are paired in a passage in Lucretius,[18] a nuanced affiliation of *praesidium* with the technical vocabulary of friendship as preached by the Garden may be deduced from the speech allocated to the Epicurean spokesman, Torquatus, in Cicero's philosophical dialogue *De finibus*. In the context of a disquisition that culminates in the central importance of friendship within the Epicurean system of values, Torquatus is moved to cite the founder "almost verbatim" (*his paene verbis*) on the subject (1.68):

> Quaeque de virtutibus dicta sunt, quemadmodum eae semper voluptatibus inhaererent, eadem de amicitia dicenda sunt. Praeclare enim Epicurus his paene verbis: "Eadem," inquit, "scientia confirmavit animum, ne quod aut sempiternum aut diuturnum timeret malum, quae perspexit in hoc ipso vitae spatio **amicitiae praesidium esse firmissimum**."

> All that has been said about the intrinsic connexion between virtues and pleasures must also be said about friendship. For Epicurus notably stated (here I cite his words almost *verbatim*): "The same understanding has strengthened our courage to surmount all fear of eternal or long-lasting misfortune [sc. after death] by the perception that **friendship is our strongest safeguard** in this present span of life."

The lexeme, *praesidium* ("safeguard"), is not to be construed as a mere metaphorical cliché, since Cicero's persona is quoting an extant dictum of Epicurus in which it is evident that the Latin term *praesidium* translates the original Greek ἀσφάλεια (Epicurus RS 28): Ἡ αὐτὴ γνώμη θαρρεῖν τε ἐποίησεν ὑπὲρ τοῦ μηθὲν αἰώνιον εἶναι δεινὸν μηδὲ πολυχρόνιον, καὶ τὴν ἐν αὐτοῖς τοῖς ὡρισμένοις ἀσφάλειαν φιλίαις μάλιστα κατεῖδε συντελουμένην ("The same understanding produces confidence about there being nothing terrible which is eternal or [even] long-lasting and has also perceived **that security amid even these limited misfortunes is most easily achieved through friendship**").[19]

The other term that complements *praesidium* in the opening apostrophe to the poet's friend and patron, Maecenas, is *dulce decus meum*. The epithet *dulce*, in conjunction with the possessive *meum*, characterizes the special "pleasure" (*dulcedo*) that attends intimate friendship; at the same time, it foregrounds the central leitmotif of pleasure that structures the ensuing priamel. The conjoining of two aspects of friendship, namely, *voluptas/dulcedo* and *praesidium*, resonates with deep Epicurean convictions regarding the convergence of the *utile* and the *dulce*—a convergence that is enthusiastically defended by Torquatus (and challenged by Cicero in his rejoinder) in the coda to his exposition of the high value placed on friendship in the dialogue. It is fitting that the nature of Horace's friendship with Maecenas should stand out as a perfect embodiment of the Epicurean model so eloquently articulated by Cicero's Epicurean spokesperson.[20]

ἀταραξία/*OTIUM*: ODES 2.16

Whereas the program ode of the collection centers, as we have shown, on the Epicurean *telos* of ἡδονή/*voluptas*, *Odes* 2.16 (*Otium divos*) elaborates on the equally fundamental doctrine of ἀταραξία. That the lexeme, *otium*, in the thematic context of the latter ode, is best understood as the technical equivalent of ἀταραξία, may be substantiated in the evolving argument of the ode, which relies on a plurality of direct allusions to passages in Lucretius and Epicurus's *Letter to Menoeceus*, as well as to a number of aphorisms attributed to Epicurus (*Principal Sayings* and *Vatican Sayings*). These references and intertexts suffusing the ode have been copiously documented in the insightful interpretations of H. P. Syndikus.[21] His insight is amply endorsed in the commentary of Nisbet and Hubbard, who aptly apply the sobriquet, "Horace's Ode on Tranquility" to *Odes* 2.16 (Nisbet and Hubbard (1978) 252–256).

Horace foregrounds the concept in an incisive manner through anaphoric repetition in the opening two stanzas of the poem (1–8):

> **Otium** divos rogat in patenti
> prensus Aegaeo, simul atra nubes
> condidit lunam neque certa fulgent
>   sidera nautis;
> **otium** bello furiosa Thrace,
>   **otium** Medi pharetra decori,
> Grosphe, non gemmis neque purpura ve-
>   nale neque auro.

> For **tranquility of mind** the sailor prays to heaven the moment
> he is caught in a bad storm on the open Aegean, when a dark cloud
> has buried the moon, and the stars fail to shine
> brightly for mariners.
> For **tranquility of mind**, when the battle rages, the Thracians pray;
> for **tranquility of mind** the Medes resplendent with their quivers,
> Lance, my friend—**a tranquility** that cannot be **purchased**
> with gems, nor with purple robes, nor yet with gold.

Of the many connotations of the lexeme, *otium*, in Latin literature, the pertinent signification operative in *Otium divos* is to be sought not in an *external* condition, but rather in an *internal* state of mental security. This precise connotation (*otium* = ἀταραξία) becomes transparent in the third stanza (9–12):"Neither great wealth nor the lictor who escorts a consul can clear **doleful perturbances of mind, anxieties** that flit around grandiose empaneled ceilings" (*Non enim gazae neque consularis / summovet lictor **miseros tumultus / mentis et curas** laqueata circum / tecta volantis*).

The term *miseros tumultus mentis* ("doleful mental perturbations") aptly renders the ταραχαί that Epicurean teachings characterize as fatal to the achievement of ἀταραξία.[22] As Julia Annas has astutely pointed out, the term ἀταραξία is "negatively defined" as "the state of not having ταραχαί or troubles."[23] That such an undisturbed state of mind cannot be artificially obtained by the accumulation of excessive wealth (here made graphic in Horace's evocation of "grandiose empaneled ceilings") is a sentiment succinctly expressed in the last of the *Vatican Sayings* ascribed to the Epicurean founder: "The disturbance [ταραχή] of the soul will not be dissolved nor will considerable joy be produced by the presence of the greatest wealth, nor by honor and admiration among the many."²⁴ The metonym of the richly ornate (*laqueata*) ceilings of the affluent is a patent allusion to the diction employed by Lucretius in the famous proem of *DRN* 2, in which the *iucunda voluptas* of the Epicurean sage is contrasted with its absence inter alia from the luxurious villas of the opulent (20–27).²⁵

Horace's coupling of *tumultus mentis* (= ταραχαί) with *curas* ("anxieties") sets up a close affinity, if not a virtual equivalence, between *tumultus* and *curas*—an equivalence that is grammatically registered insofar as the genitive *mentis* may be construed as modifying both nouns. The idea of persistent anxieties (*curae*) in the psyche of the unenlightened plays a conspicuous role in the imagery of the sixth strophe, where they reappear in personified form—this time as a collective singular—vividly portrayed as shadowing both the sea-captain and the cavalry commander (21–24): "**Aberrant Care** mounts galleons bound with bronze, nor does it leave alone whole squads of cavalry, Care speedier than deer, speedier than the East Wind driving the clouds" (*Scandit aeratas* **vitiosa** *navis* / **Cura** *nec turmas equitum relinquit,* / *ocior cervis et agente nimbos* / *ocior Euro*). The epithet *vitiosa* links the notion of relentless internal anxiety in a non-trivial way with a moral deficiency (*vitium*).

The deliberate cross-reference that Horace makes to the *mercator/nauta* in the priamel of *Odes* 1.1.15–18 (discussed above) furnishes additional corroboration of the claim that the intended signification of *otium* in *Otium divos* is Epicurean ἀταραξία: "The merchant seaman when in dread of winds that scuffle with Icarian waves praises **the tranquility** of his hometown and countryside, but in short order he sets out to repair his battered barks, **unschooled to endure a frugal mode of life**" (*Luctantem Icariis fluctibus Africum* / *mercator metuens* **otium** *et oppida* / *laudat rura sui; mox reficit rates* / *quassas,* **indocilis pauperiem pati**). By the same token, the shared connotation of *otium* in the two odes under comparison implies that *voluptas* (the leitmotif of the programmatic poem) is closely affiliated with the state of ἀταραξία, in so far as it is the very absence of disturbances (such as fear) that enables the achievement of unalloyed pleasure.²⁶

The summarizing gnome that initiates the fourth strophe also enunciates the teaching that credits a modest lifestyle as conducive to *otium* (13–16): "**The good life is enjoyed with modest means** by the person whose inherited saltcellar glitters **on his frugal table**; he is not deprived of smooth sleep by fear or demeaning greed" (***Vivitur parvo bene,*** *cui paternum* / *splendet in* **mensa tenui** *salinum* / *nec levis somnos timor aut cupido* / *sordidus aufert*). The phrase *mensa tenuis* is a concrete figuration of the idea of *paupertas*—the very lifestyle that is treated as intolerable by the *mercator* of *Odes* 1.1. The virtue of "plain fare" (ἁπλῆ δαίς = *mensa tenuis*) is probably an allusion to a passage in the *Letter to Menoeceus*, as we have seen above, and its reprise in 2.16 is carefully prepared in the preceding two strophes, in which the antipodal lifestyle of luxurious living based on extreme wealth is devalued in no uncertain terms.

The coherence of Horace's argument in these opening stanzas is most evident when the foundational Epicurean tenet of the limit of pleasure is taken into consideration. This tenet is a cornerstone of the so-called *tetrapharmakon* or "four-part cure" that has been preserved in *RS* I-IV as well as in a Philodemus fragment.²⁷ In the trenchant formulation of *RS* 3: "The removal of all feeling of pain is the limit of the magnitude of pleasures." The consequence of this natural limit, in the Epicurean scheme, is that pleasure, such as that derived from a meal, cannot be increased indefinitely once a certain level of fulfillment is reached. The key principle is also articulated with greater nuance in the *Letter to Menoeceus* (130):

> And we believe that self-sufficiency is a great good, not in order that we might make do with few things under all circumstances, but so that if we do not have a lot we can make do with few, being genuinely convinced that those who least need extravagance enjoy it most; and that everything natural is easy to obtain and whatever is groundless is hard to obtain; and that simple flavors provide a pleasure equal to that of an extravagant lifestyle when all pain from want is removed.

Overly sumptuous meals are the province of the rich and powerful of the type targeted in the ethical prescriptions of the second strophe, in which the poet playfully emphasizes the idea of futile extravagance by the metrical ruse of letting the divided syllables of the word *ve-nale* ("able to be purchased") run over into the following verse (6–8): *otium Medi pharetra decori, / Grosphe, non gemmis neque purpura ve- / nale neque auro* ("**a tranquility of mind** that **cannot be purchased** with gems, nor with purple robes, nor yet with gold"). The underlying critique of immoderate accumulation of wealth and sumptuous banquets is clearly indebted, as several scholars have noted,[28] to the thought as well as diction, of a Lucretian proem (2.20–28):

> **ergo corpoream ad naturam pauca videmus**
> **esse opus omnino**: quae demant cumque dolorem,
> delicias quoque uti multas substernere possint
> gratius interdum, neque natura ipsa requirit,
> si non aurea sunt iuvenum simulacra per aedes
> lampadas igniferas manibus retinentia dextris,
> lumina nocturnis epulis ut suppeditentur,
> **nec domus argento fulget auroque renidet**
> **nec citharae reboant laqueata aurataque templa**
>
> **Therefore we see that few things altogether are necessary for the bodily nature**, only such in each case as take pain away, and can also spread for our use many delights; nor does nature herself ever crave anything more pleasurable, if there be no golden images of youths about the house, upholding fiery torches in their right hands that light may be provided for nightly revelings, **if the hall does not shine with silver and glitter with gold, if no crossbeams paneled and gilded echo the lyre.**

In the context of a dinner invitation extended to his extremely wealthy patron, Maecenas, Horace foregrounds the potential attainment of tranquility that is the gift of the modest board (*Odes* 3.29.13–16): "Oftentimes changes [sc. of lifestyle] give pleasure to the wealthy, **and plain meals in the lowly homes of men of modest means**, served without purple hangings, **loosen anxious brows**" (*Plerumque gratae divitibus vices /*

*mundaeque parvo sub lare pauperum / cenae sine aulaeis et ostro / **sollicitam explicuere frontem***). In this strategically placed penultimate ode of the *tribiblos*, which contains an epitome of the poet's eudaimonist thought, the friendly *paraenesis* to the rich patron resonates with both the Lucretian and Epicurean passages we have cited above.

In Horace's reworking of the Lucretian intertext in *Odes* 2.16, the *curae* that haunt the rich and impede their ἀταραξία are framed in a land/sea universalizing "complementary" that maps on to the equally conventional *domus/militiae* (home/abroad) dichotomy.[29] The *curae* are initially represented in the third strophe as winged bat-like creatures flitting around the paneled ceiling of a luxurious mansion (11–12); they are reimagined in the sixth strophe as a singular phantom personification (*Cura*) that climbs aboard battleships and shadows cavalry squadrons (21–24).

Although this double incarnation pictures "cares" as external agents, the argument of the poem conceives them as projections of interior, intrapsychic states. The imagistic externalization is rhetorically comparable to the Lucretian interpretation of mythical sinners like Tityus and Tantalus, who suffer grievous punishment for their high crimes in the underworld. At the climax of Book 3 of *DRN*, the persona of *Natura* expounds a psychological insight not unworthy of a Sigmund Freud in regard to punishments beyond the grave, as in this excerpt regarding the fate of Tantalus (978–983):[30]

> Atque ea ni mirum quae cumque Acherunte profundo
> prodita sunt esse, in vita sunt omnia nobis.
> nec miser inpendens magnum timet aëre saxum
> Tantalus, ut famast, cassa formidine torpens;
> sed magis in vita divom metus urget inanis
> mortalis casumque timent quem cuique ferat fors.

> And assuredly whatsoever things are fabled to exist in deep Acheron, these all exist for us in this life. There is no wretched Tantalus, as the story goes, fearing the great rock that hangs over him in the air and frozen with vain terror; rather it is in this life that the fear of gods oppresses mortals without cause, and the fall they fear is any that chance may bring.

The argumentative aim of *Otium divos* is to debunk the common misconception that peace of mind and happiness can be secured through the acquisition of material goods instead of by philosophical enlightenment.

The touchstone for the attainment of inner tranquility is metonymically depicted in the ode (15–16) as the enjoyment of a "smooth sleep" (*somnus levis*), undisturbed by unsettling "fear or mean desire" (*timor aut cupido sordidus*). The *topos* may be paralleled from a passage in Vergil's *Georgics*, a poem that is also engaged in intermittent "conversations" with Epicurean ethics (2.468–471):

> **O fortunatos nimium, sua si bona norint,**
> **agricolas!** quibus ipsa procul discordibus armis
> fundit humo facilem uictum iustissima tellus.

> si non ingentem foribus domus alta superbis
> mane salutantum totis uomit aedibus undam,
> nec uarios inhiant pulchra testudine postis
> inlusasque auro uestis Ephyreiaque aera,
> alba neque Assyrio fucatur lana ueneno,
> nec casia liquidi corrumpitur usus oliui;
> **at secura quies et nescia fallere uita,**
> **diues opum uariarum, at latis otia fundis,**
> **speluncae uiuique lacus, at frigida tempe**
> mugitusque boum mollesque sub arbore somni
> non absunt;

> **O farmers, happy beyond measure, could they but know their blessings!** For them, far from the clash of arms, most righteous Earth, unbidden, pours forth from her soil an easy sustenance. If no stately mansion with proud portals disgorges from its halls at dawn a flood of those who have come to greet its lord, if they never gaze at doors inlaid with lovely tortoiseshell or at draperies tricked with gold or at bronzes of Ephyra, if their wool's whiteness is not stained with Assyrian dyes or the service of their clear oil is not spoiled with cassia: **yet they have sleep free from anxiety, a life that is innocent of guile and rich with untold treasures. The peace of broad domains, caverns, and natural lakes, and cool vales, the lowing of oxen, and soft slumbers beneath the trees** – all are theirs.

Vergil's praise of the ideal farmer's lifestyle which incorporates *secura quies* (a life free from anxiety), pastoral *otium*, and *molles somni* (soft slumbers) follows on the famous (and philosophically related) excursus on the blessings of Epicurean enlightenment (2.490–499):[31]

> **Felix, qui potuit rerum cognoscere causas,**
> atque metus omnis et inexorabile fatum
> subiecit pedibus strepitumque Acherontis avari.
> **fortunatus et ille, deos qui novit agrestis,**
> **Panaque Silvanumque senem Nymphasque sorores.**
> illum non populi fasces, non purpura regum
> flexit et infidos agitans discordia fratres,
> aut coniurato descendens Dacus ab Histro,
> non res Romanae perituraque regna; neque ille
> aut doluit miserans inopem aut invidit habenti.

> **Blessed is he who has succeeded in learning the laws of nature's working**, has cast beneath his feet all fear and fate's implacable decree, and the howl of insatiable Death. **Happy also is he who knows the rural gods, Pan and aged Silvanus and the sisterhood of the Nymphs.** Him no honors the people give can move, no purple worn by despots, no strife which leads brother to betray brother; untroubled is he by Dacian incursion swooping down from a Danube leagued in war, untroubled by Rome's policies spelling doom to kingdoms; if he has not felt pity for the poor, he has never envied the rich.[32]

To judge by their similarity in thought, no less than in diction, it is altogether plausible that the *Georgics'* *loci* share the same Lucretian intertext—and presumably the Epicurean philosophical sources—as the strophe of *Odes* 2.16 under consideration.

The observation that the entire ode may be read as a coherent precis of ethical values is buttressed by the rhetorical questions that frame the fifth stanza (17–20): "Given our brief life span, why do we take aim at so many targets? Why do we exchange our own country for those warmed by a different sun? **What expatriate is ever able to escape himself?**" (*Quid brevi fortes iaculamur aevo / multa? Quid terras alio calentis /sole mutamus?* **Patriae quis exul / se quoque fugit?**).[33] The self that proves inescapable is the *moral self*; for the would-be escapee carries his debilitating baggage of *vitia* along with him wherever he goes. The imagery of unsuccessfully attempting to flee one's moral self (*se fugere*) is all of a piece with the diction that the poet habitually uses to describe opposing ethical goals in his *Satires* and *Epistles*, where the metaphor of "fleeing vice and pursuing the good" is a standard formulation. Chief among the embedded *vitia* of the restless *exul* is his obsessive anxiety, as implied in the phrase, *vitiosa cura,* that the poet uses to characterize the ineluctable fate of the naval commander already quoted (21–22).

Corroboration of the notion that *the moral self* is at stake in the expression *se fugere* is provided by the rather similar diction of Vergil in the *Georgics* passage cited above that details the defects of unenlightened others, including politicians seeking popular acclaim (2.509–512): *exsilioque domos et dulcia limina mutant / atque alio patriam quaerunt sub sole iacentem* ("and they **exchange** their homes and sweet thresholds **for exile** and seek a country lying beneath an alien sun"). The Vergilian and Horatian moral allegories of futile self-escape are both indebted to the Lucretian intertext at the close of *DRN* 3, where the unenlightened, unschooled other is roundly berated (3.1068–1070): **hoc se quisque modo fugit, at quem scilicet, ut fit, / effugere haud potis est,** ingratis haeret et odit, / propterea morbi quia causam non tenet aeger ("**Thus each man tries to flee from himself, but to that self, from which of course he cannot escape,** he clings against his will, and hates it, because he is a sick man that does not know the cause of his complaint").

The two gnomes that occupy the seventh strophe of the ode chime with the Epicurean tenet that the happy life entails focus on the present rather than on the unknowable and irrelevant future (25–28): *laetus in praesens animus quod ultra est / oderit curare et amara lento / temperet risu; nihil est ab omni / parte beatum* ("**The mind that is focused on present joys eschews anxiety about what lies ahead** and tempers bitter events with a resilient smile. Nothing is uniformly happy"). In his treatise *On Tranquility of Mind*, Plutarch attributes a parallel aphorism to Epicurus:[34] ὁ τῆς αὔριον ἥκιστα δεόμενος," ὥς φησιν Ἐπίκουρος, "ἥδιστα πρόσεισι πρὸς τὴν αὔριον ("'The person who has least need of tomorrow,' as Epicurus says, 'approaches tomorrow with the most pleasure'").

At this fulcral point in the ode Horace embroiders a smooth suture between the Epicurean subtext we have been delineating and the thematic tapestry of his carpe diem philosophy. The injunction to eschew knowledge of the future and harvest the present hour is parsimoniously formulated in *Odes* 1.11 in the iconic words: *carpe diem,* **quam** *minimum credula postero* ("Harvest the present day, **trusting as little as possible in tomorrow**"). The archaic Greek models of Horatian lyric—chiefly Alcaeus and Sappho—are manifestly the main fountainhead of the complex of motifs that constitute Carpe Diem poetry "*avant la lettre*." However, a crucial dimension of Horace's appropriation of the motif pattern is the seamless integration he accomplishes in the *Odes* between Epicurean ethical norms and the lyric values of his Greek predecessors.[35] This harmonious integration of worldviews stemming from lyric poetry, on the one hand, and the Garden, on the other, is further elaborated in the two heroic *exempla* that are meant to substantiate the insight of the second gnome that closes the stanza: *nihil est ab omni / parte beatum* ("nothing [in human life] is uniformly happy") (29–32): *abstulit clarum cita mors Achillem, / longa Tithonum minuit senectus, / et mihi forsan, tibi quod negarit, / porriget hora* ("An early death overtook illustrious Achilles; an eternal old age wasted away Tithonus; and time perchance will offer me what it has denied you").

How do these legendary heroes' lives exemplify the underlying message of the gnome? To confront a misfortune with a "resilient smile" (*lento risu*) is the schooled response of the Epicurean sage who is mentally fortified against τύχη. To understand the futility of hoping for a long or even endless life (Achilles; Tithonus[36]) is to have absorbed the *carpe diem* admonition that receives incisive expression in *Odes* 4.7.7–8: *immortalia ne speres monet annus et almum / quae rapit hora diem* ("to eschew hope for immortality is the lesson of the seasonal cycle and time that snatches away the nurturing day"). The practitioner of a *carpe diem* philosophy, in Horace's inflection of the lyric tradition, maintains a tranquil equilibrium (ἀταραξία) by relinquishing vain hope for a future of uninterrupted bliss. In short, it is the quality of one's life, not its length per se, that confers happiness on mortals.

The ode's closure manifests a distinctly Epicurean tenor. The speaker implies that his "modest lifestyle" (*parva rura*) and his lyric craft are accompanied, if not enabled, by his "avoidance of the miscreant mob" (*malignum spernere vulgus*) (37–40): *mihi **parva rura** et / spiritum Graiae tenuem Camenae / Parca non mendax dedit et **malignum / spernere vulgus*** ("Upon me unerring 'Parsimonious,'[37] has bestowed **a small country estate**, exquisite inspiration from a native Greek Muse, and the insight to **eschew the miscreant mob**"). Although he ascribes his accomplishments to destiny (*Parca*), his commitment to *paupertas* and the poetic vocation are enlightened choices he has autonoDmously made. Among these, his eschewing of the "crowd" (*vulgus*) is best understood in the context of a philosophical posture that is well characterized by Cicero in his reference to followers of the Garden who denigrate "the unenlightened minds of the crowd" (*volgi animos non sapientium*).[38]

The final verse of the ode encapsulates a precept that is well summed up in a dictum ascribed to Epicurus, in which the avoidance of wealth—a motif prominent in the earlier strophes of the ode—is connected with the gesture of separating oneself from the mob: ἐλεύθερος βίος οὐ δύναται κτήσασθαι χρήματα πολλὰ διὰ τὸ τὸ πρᾶγμα <μὴ> ῥᾴδιον εἶναι χωρὶς θητείας ὄχλων ἢ δυναστῶν, ἀλλὰ συνεχεῖ δαψιλείᾳ πάντα κέκτηται· ("A free life cannot acquire wealth, because the task is not easy **without slavery to mobs** or those in power; rather it already possesses everything in constant abundance").[39]

To conclude: The arguments of the two odes we have analyzed in this chapter are strikingly similar in their philosophical outlook. Both the programmatic inaugural poem and the "Ode to Tranquility" are built on a foundation of Epicurean ethical precepts. The ensemble of motifs and *topoi* framing these precepts contain systematic allusions to Epicurean, Lucretian, and Vergilian *loci* which, taken together, present a coherent view of the preconditions for human "flourishing" (εὐδαιμονία).

Notes

1. Horace's dialogue with leading Hellenistic schools includes engagements with Stoics, Cyrenaics, and Academics, especially in the *Satires*, which he refers to as "Conversations" (*Sermones*). On the crucial role played by Epicurean thought in the latter, particularly as refracted in the philosophical corpus of Philodemus, see Armstrong (2014); Yona (2018). There is now textual evidence from the Herculaneum papyri linking Horace and his circle of fellow poets (including his "soulmate" Vergil) with the Epicurean teacher, Philodemus. See, e.g., Janko (2000) 6.
2. This chapter elaborates on the ethical subtext of the Odes along the lines grossly sketched in Davis (2020) 465–467. On the premise, fully endorsed here, that "philosophizing" is endemic to Latin poetry, see the essays collected in Garani and Konstan (2014).
3. Hor. *Epist.* 1.1.14.
4. Elroy Bundy introduced the useful terms "foil" and "cap" to describe key elements of the Pindaric priamel (Bundy (1986) 5–10).
5. The Latin text of Horace's *Odes* is cited in the Teubner edition of Klingner (1982). English translations are my own.
6. Excerpts of the Latin text of *DRN* and the accompanying English translations are quoted from the Loeb edition of Rouse as revised by Martin Ferguson Smith (Rouse (1982)). The Ciceronian use of the technical term *voluptas* is exemplified in the defense of the Epicurean school attributed to the interlocutor Torquatus in *Fin.* 1–2 (passim).
7. O'Keefe (2002) 395. His view is challenged by Lampe (2015) 92–100.
8. In the Horatian inflexion of the concept of *hēdonē*, the choice of a poetic vocation presented in the cap of the priamel is thoroughly consistent with the pursuit of *ataraxia*. Although "orthodox" Epicurean thought is reputed to have downgraded the utility of poetry to the achievement of enlightenment, Philodemus exemplifies the compatibility of the pursuit of the arts and the school's doctrine by virtue of his own practice as a composer of elegant epigrams (see the edition of Sider (1992), while his treatise *On Poems* provides the theoretical justification for this compatibility (cf. Summers (1995); Janko (2000)). Further corroboration is to be found in an extant passage in Diogenes of Oinoanda, on which see Taylor (2014).
9. Philodemus's treatise is cited in the translation of Tsouna (2013) xxxix.
10. It is worth emphasizing in this context that the literal meaning of *sym-posion* (Latin *convivium*) is "drinking **together**." In the motif universe of the *Odes*, the symposium functions as an emblem of the happy life (on which see further Davis (2007). An intimation of the drinker's lack of restraint (compounding his isolation) is implied in *nec spernit*. This critical reading of the position of the solitary drinker revises that put forward by the author in an earlier study Davis (1991) 4.

11. An Epicurean counterimage to that of the solitary tippler occurs in the proem to Lucr. 2.29–3, where a group of friends joyfully take part in a communal drinking-party set in a *locus amoenus* on a riverbank: "*cum tamen inter se prostrati in gramine molli / propter aquae rivum sub ramis arboris altae / non magnis opibus iucunde corpora curant.*"
12. *Otium* in this programmatic context is to be understood in a deeper sense than as the mere opposite of *negotium*, as will become clear in our discussion below of *Odes* 2.16.
13. That the Augustan social program also advocated plain living in no way detracts from the primarily philosophical tenor in the critique of the *mercator* in this poem, which, in the use of the epithet, *indocilis*, stresses his lack of ethical insight and knowledge.
14. Translations of Epicurus's extant writings are from Inwood and Gerson (1994) with slight modifications. An Epicurean subtext that advocates modest living as an ethical buttress against misfortune is also made by Vergil at the conclusion of *Ecl.* 1, on which see Davis (2004) 63–74.
15. Epicurus *Ep. Men.* 134. The Epicurean ideal of virtual godhead is thoroughly discussed in Konstan (2008).
16. The humorous tone adopted in Horace's prediction of his own immortality in this ode has seemed to some readers to verge on caricature, but it is worth remembering that his tongue-in-cheek description here is entirely consonant with the description of his becoming immortal in the form of a bird in *Odes* 2.20.
17. I owe this observation, along with the textual references to excerpts from Cicero and Epicurus that corroborate it, to Erickson Bridges, currently a doctoral student in Classics at Duke University. This connection is discussed within the context of Horace's *Satires* in Yona (2018) 164–165, where the passages cited above are examined.
18. See, e.g., the commentaries of Nisbet and Hubbard (1978) and Mayer (2012) ad loc.
19. The English translation of *RS* 28 by Inwood and Gerson has been slightly modified. The "complementary" *praesidium/dulce* is also attested, though in a different context, at Lucr. 2.643.
20. On the exalted role of friendship in the Epicurean universe of values, see also *RS* 27.
21. Syndikus (1972) 439–454.
22. On the Epicureans' custom of reaching out to the unenlightened who suffer mental disturbances, see *P.Herc.* 1232, fr. 8 col.1; Philodemus: *On Piety* (Obbink (1996) 126, col. 31, 879–889); Clay (1998) 80–83.
23. Annas (1995) 238.
24. Epicurus *Sent. Vat.* 81. Tr. Inwood and Gerson (1994).
25. See the commentaries of Kiessling-Heinze and Nisbet-Hubbard ad loc.
26. In the Epicurean ethical system, which distinguished between "katastematic" (static) and "kinetic" pleasures, *ataraxia* is conducive to the attainment of the former. On the nuances of this taxonomy, see Woolf (2009); Taylor (2014).
27. *P.Herc.* 1005, col. 4.10–14.
28. E.g., Syndikus (1972) 441, who cites additional echoes of passages in *DRN*.
29. "Complementary" is the term I have adopted for the common framing device for which Elroy Bundy coined the phrase, "universalizing doublet." The purpose of these dichotomies is to extend the ethical critique to include *all* unenlightened others.
30. Cf. Lucretius's treatment of the Sisyphus figure as allegory of the overambitious politician in the same passage as discussed above. On this psychologically sophisticated mode of interpretation of mythical figures on the part of Lucretius, see also the discussion in Konstan (2008) 61–65.

31. For an unconventional analysis of these much-discussed passages that interprets the enlightened philosopher (*felix qui potuit rerum cognoscere causas*) and the potentially enlightened farmer (*fortunatus et ille*) as pursuing parallel, rather than opposing, routes to happiness, see Davis (2012) 6–7 and 76–77.
32. Translations of *Georgics* excerpts are from the edition of Fairclough as revised by Goold (Fairclough (1999)).
33. As my translation registers, *fugit* is best construed in this aphoristic context as a "gnomic perfect."
34. Plut. *De tranq. anim.* 474c. The persona of Natura in her apostrophe at Lucretius 3.957–958 utters a similar sentiment.
35. On the philosophical grounding of Horatian *carpe diem* poetry, see Davis (1991) 145–188.
36. The example of Tithonus is ostensibly paradoxical, but fully consistent with Horace's underlying message: An old age that lasts forever deprives the recipient of the pleasure that is the true goal of life in the Epicurean system.
37. My rendition registers the clever wordplay on the name of the Fate, *Parca*, signifying "Parsimonious."
38. Cic. *Fin*.1.19.43.
39. On the advantages of withdrawal from the crowd, see further Epicurus *RS* XIV.

References

Annas, J. (1995). *The Morality of Happiness*. (Oxford).
Armstrong, D, J. Fish, P. Johnston, and M. Skinner, eds. (2004). ***Vergil, Philodemus, and the Augustans*** (Austin, Tex.).
Armstrong, D. (2014). "Horace's Epicurean Voice in the Satires," in Garani and Konstan, 91–127.
Bundy, E. (1986). *Studia Pindarica*. (Berkeley/Los Angeles).
Clay, D. (1998). *Paradosis and Survival: Three Chapters in the History of Epicurean Philosophy*. (Ann Arbor, Mich.).
Davis, G. (1991). *Polyhymnia: The Rhetoric of Horatian Lyric Discourse*. (Berkeley/Los Angeles/Oxford).
Davis, G. (2004). "Consolation in the Bucolic Mode: The Epicurean Cadence of Vergil's First *Eclogue*," in Armstrong, Fish, Johnston, and Skinner, 63–74.
Davis, G. (2007). "Wine and the Symposium," in Harrison, 207–220.
Davis, G. (2012). *Parthenope: The Interplay of Ideas in Vergilian Bucolic*. (Leiden/Boston).
Davis, G. (2020). "Epicureanism in Horace and Vergil," in Mitsis, 455–475.
Fairclough, H. R. (1999). *Eclogues, Georgics, Aeneid 1–6*. G. P. Goold, rev. (Cambridge, Mass.).
Garani, M., and D. Konstan, eds. (2014). *The Philosophizing Muse: The Influence of Greek Philosophy on Roman Poetry*. (Newcastle upon Tyne).
Harrison, S., ed. (2007). *The Cambridge Companion to Horace*. (Cambridge).
Inwood, B., and L. P. Gerson, eds. (1994). *The Epicurus Reader: Selected Writings and Testimonia*. (Indianapolis/Cambridge, Mass.).
Janko, R. (2000). *Philodemus: On Poems*. (Oxford/New York).
Kiessling, A., and R. Heinze (1961). *Q. Horatius Flaccus*. (Berlin).
Klingner, F. (^{6}1982). *Horatius Flaccus*. (Leipzig).
Konstan, D. (2008). *A Life Worthy of the Gods: The Materialist Philosophy of Epicurus*. (Las Vegas/Zurich/Athens).

Lampe, K. (2015). *The Birth of Hedonism: The Cyrenaic Philosophers and Pleasure as a Way of Life.* (Princeton).
Mayer, R., ed. (2012). *Horace: Odes I.* (Cambridge).
Mitsis, P., ed. (2021). *The Oxford Handbook of Epicureanism.* (Oxford).
Nisbet, R. G. M., and M. Hubbard (1978). *A Commentary on Horace's Odes, Book II.* (Oxford).
Obbink, D. (1996). *Philodemus, "On Piety," part 1: Critical Text with Commentary.* (Oxford).
Obbink, D. (1995). *Philodemus and Poetry: Poetic Theory and Practice in Lucretius, Philodemus and Horace.* (Oxford).
O'Keefe, T. (2002). "The Cyrenaics on Pleasure, Happiness, and Future-Concern." *Phronesis* 47(4): 395–416.
Rouse, W. H. D., and M. F. Smith (^{2}1982). *Lucretius:* **De rerum natura.** (Cambridge, Mass.).
Sider, D. (1992). *The Epigrams of Philodemus.* (Oxford).
Sider, D. (1997). "Epicurean Poetics: Response and Dialogue," in Obbink (1995) 35–41.
Summers, A. (1995). *Philodemus' "Peri Poematon" and Horace's "Ars Poetica": Adapting Alexandrian Aesthetics to Epicurean and Roman Traditions.* Dissertation: University of Illinois at Urbana-Champaign.
Syndikus, H. P. (1972). *Die Lyrik des Horaz: Eine Interpretation der Oden*, vol. 1.(Darmstadt).
Taylor, B. (2014). "Diogenes of Oinoanda on the Meaning of 'Pleasure' (*NF* 192)." *ZPE* **191**: 84–89.
Tsouna, V., ed. (2013). *Philodemus: On Property Management.* (Atlanta, Ga.).
Warren, J., ed. (2009). *The Cambridge Companion to Epicureanism.* (Cambridge).
Woolf, R. (2009). "Pleasure and Desire," in Warren, 158–178.
Yona, S. (2018). *Epicurean Ethics in Horace; The Psychology of Satire.* (Oxford).

CHAPTER 4

SENECA AND STOIC MORAL PSYCHOLOGY

GRETCHEN REYDAMS-SCHILS

ONE is immediately struck by the apparent absence in Seneca's extant works of many of the technical aspects of Early Stoic psychology. Seneca does not dwell, for instance, on the intricacies of how impression, assent, and impulse are supposed to function together under the general guidance of reason in adult human beings. He does not provide finely tuned overviews of the different types of impressions, nor does he, for the most part, analyze in great detail the psychological mechanisms that are responsible for the passions.

Yet as recent scholarship has increasingly emphasized, one should not conclude on the basis of this feature of Seneca's writings that his work can be reduced to mere popular moralizing, even if it is intended for a broader audience, or that he had only a superficial knowledge of Stoic doctrine.[1] Rather, it makes sense in Seneca's case to focus on *moral* psychology because his analysis of the workings of the human soul serves his deliberate emphasis on an ethics in action. The technical aspects of Stoic psychology on which he does choose to dwell, as we will see, should be interpreted in the light of this emphasis as well. Thus, in order to find one's way to the full philosophical implications of Seneca's work, one cannot simply rely on the safety rail of a system of Stoic technical notions, as developed especially by Chrysippus.

The first part of this chapter addresses the question of the influence of Platonic psychology on Seneca. Seneca has often been interpreted as "eclectic," and so in order to assess the extent of his commitment to Stoic views, we need a sense of how he handles material from other schools of thought, and especially Platonism. In the second part, we will take a closer look at one of his more technical expositions, his analysis of the pre-emotions and anger. Such accounts, however, need to be balanced with other features of his writings. The range of expressions that Seneca uses in his *On Tranquility of Mind* to capture the different ways in which a human being can relate to him- or herself provides a good window onto his overall approach. Finally, no picture of Seneca's moral psychology would be complete without addressing how a human being relates to others and to the order of the *cosmos*.

Seneca and Platonic Psychology

Whereas older scholarship has tended to emphasize the influence of Platonic psychology on Seneca's views (often seen as mediated by Posidonius[2]), more recent work has focused instead on analyzing how Seneca co-opts Platonic material into an overall Stoic framework. This latter strategy allows for much more consistency in Seneca's psychology than the traditional interpretation that sees his work as eclectic, or more or less loosely cobbled together out of elements from different origins. (The dynamic of co-optation was one of the main vehicles through which the protracted rivalry between the schools expressed itself.) The focal question for our purpose here is to what extent Seneca injects features of Platonic dualism into his view of the human soul. The first crucial distinction one needs to make in this respect, as Brad Inwood has rightly pointed out, is between different kinds of dualism, notably between, on the one hand, a dualism of soul and body, and, on the other, a dualism of rational and nonrational factors within the soul itself.[3]

When it comes to the distinction or even opposition between soul and body (a point of view which Seneca shares with Epictetus and Marcus Aurelius[4]), Seneca freely borrows language that is highly reminiscent of Plato's *Phaedo*. In his consolation addressed to Marcia, for instance, he tells her with characteristic vividness of detail that her son in dying has been freed from the chains and darkness which the body imposes on the soul. In life these chains crushed, suffocated, and tainted the soul, and kept it from the truth and its fitting higher abode. After death, Seneca says, the young man's soul no longer needs to struggle against the weight of the body that always dragged him down, and his true self has survived; what he left behind was only an image (*effigies*) or a mere outer wrapping, like a set of clothes (*Consolatio ad Marciam* 24.5–25.1; see also *Ep.* 58, 65, 79.12, and 92, see below).[5]

At first glance it does seem odd for a Stoic to rail so intensely against the body, given that according to standard Stoic doctrine corporeality is, after all, a hallmark of existence (LS 27, 162–166), as manifested too in the divine, active principle and in the principle of passive matter, or in the fact that the soul itself is corporeal. But like their Socratic-Platonic counterparts, the Stoics endorse a turning away from the wrong attachments to the body and externals toward the supremacy of reason. In a different context, however, Seneca, contrary to Plato, still considers the soul itself, as well as its ruling principle, the *hêgemonikon*, to be corporeal (*Ep.* 50.6, 106.5). Second, even though Seneca at times catches himself dreaming about Platonic immortality (*Ep.* 102.1–2), he adheres to the Stoic doctrine that at most posits a temporary survival of the soul after death (as in *Consolatio ad Marciam* 26.4–6). Third, in line with original Stoicism, Seneca endorses a unified psychology, not a part-based one (although Seneca at times appears to be making concessions to Platonic psychology, see below). Fourth, the "core" of a human being is fundamentally "integrated," that is, the mind or *hêgemonikon* is integrated into the soul as a whole, the soul into the body, and individual human beings into the nature and ordered universe that surrounds them. On the relation between soul and body, Seneca states, in line with orthodox Stoicism: "one's constitution (*constitutio*) consists of a ruling power in the soul which has a certain relation towards the body" (*Ep.* 121.10). Finally, the later Stoics have a "robust" sense of self with distinctive content (see below), for which there is no counterpart in the Platonic view of human rationality because of the latter's focus on the relation between reason and the Forms.[6]

The second type of dualism, of rational and nonrational components within the soul itself, would be more of a challenge if it were present in Seneca's writings, given the Stoics' strong commitment to psychological monism. This view stipulates, in a nutshell, that the passions and other aberrant human behavior do not require other factors in the soul that can rebel against reason or tie it to their own purposes, but should be explained, rather, as resulting from reason not working properly.

There are passages in which Seneca appears to be using language that points to this second type of dualism. In the first book of his *On Anger*, for instance, Seneca talks about reason "ruling" the passions, holding the "reins" (*De ira* 1.7.2–4 a very faint echo of the charioteer image of Plato's *Phaedrus*). Anger needs to "listen to reason," not to act on its own (*De ira* 1.9.2–4; see also 18.1–2). But if one looks more closely at the context of the Platonic echoes, one notices how Seneca recasts this language in terms of Stoic psychology. First, Seneca resorts to the notion of excessive impulses, that is, impulses that, once set in motion by the *wrong assent* of reason (see below), cannot easily be stopped and seem to take on a life of their own, so to speak (*De ira* 1.7.4). He uses the example of a body hurled from a precipice that cannot halt its downward motion. In a famous analogy Chrysippus himself compares an excessive impulse to a runner overtaken by the impetus of his motion (LS 65J, K; see also 65A).

Second, after having prepared the ground with the genuinely Stoic notion of excessive impulse, Seneca points out that once the mind has misjudged, it has great difficulty recovering from *its own* mistake and regaining its proper functioning. Why? Precisely because "the mind is not set apart (*sepositus*), nor does it view the passions merely from the outside (*extrinsecus*), thus not allowing them to advance farther than they should, but is itself transformed into the passion" and "passion and reason constitute a change of the mind for better or worse" (*De ira* 1.8.2–3). The risk that mind itself could "become" the passion is one of the main reasons why Seneca rejects what he describes as the Aristotelian view that anger is beneficial when it is used in moderation. In this instance, then, it is hard to see how Seneca could have been any more explicit about Stoic monism.

A greater challenge, however, is posed by the opening of *Letter* 92, which has been the subject of considerable scholarly debate (*Ep.* 92.1):

> You and I will agree, I think, that one pursues outward things for the body's sake, that one cares for the body in order to show respect for the mind, and that the mind includes subservient parts, responsible for our motor and nutritional functions, which are given to us on behalf of the directive faculty itself. This directive faculty includes both a non-rational and a rational component. The former is at the service of the latter, which is the one thing that does not look to anything else but rather

refers everything else to itself. As you know, divine rationality is similarly at the head of all things, subordinate to none of them; and this rationality of ours, which derives from that divine rationality, is just the same. (tr. Graver and Long)

There is a clear progression in this passage, and much of it coincides with Stoic orthodoxy: Seneca moves from externals, to the body, to an equivalent of what a Stoic would consider the lower soul parts of the five senses, speech, and reproduction (LS 53) that serve its ruling part (the *hêgemonikon*)—except for the fact that he lists the subservient functions in Peripatetic terms, "motor and nutritional functions," rather than the Stoic counterparts—and finally to the ruling part itself. The progression does not end there, because Seneca goes on to mention that human reason is derived from the divine reason that commands the entire universe, a theme that underscores the importance for humans of the contemplation of the order of nature (*Ep.* 92.6; more on this below) and leads to a grand finale in this *Letter* that is very similar to the ending of the consolation addressed to Marcia, discussed above.

An orthodox Stoic would stumble, however, over the claim that the directive faculty of the soul is divided into a rational and a nonrational component. To complicate matters further, in this letter Seneca goes on to claim that the nonrational component in turn can be subdivided into spirit and appetite (*Ep.* 92.8):

> The mind's non-rational part has itself two parts—the one part spirited, ambitious, and wayward, consisting in emotions, the other base, idle, devoted to pleasures. Setting aside the former, which, though unruly, is at least superior, and certainly bolder and worthier of a man, these people have deemed the latter, which is spineless and abject, to be essential to the happy life. (tr. Graver and Long)

If we have reason, spirit, and appetite in place, we now do appear to have a view of the soul that looks very Platonic.

Yet here too we can detect how cleverly Seneca sets up the terms of the discussion. Going back to a debate that figures prominently also in Cicero's *On Moral Ends*, Seneca here takes issue with a certain (perceived) Academic-Peripatetic alliance (predominantly Peripatetic in this case).[7] This view allegedly holds that for a human being to be happy in the plenary sense, or to reach the supreme good (*summum bonum*), he or she needs more than virtue defined as the sole good and consisting of the perfection of reason. It is in this polemical context, in which he counters the views of "these people," that Seneca borrows the particular division of the nonrational part into spirit and appetite: he adopts the terms of his opponents merely to turn these against themselves. The polemical nature of Seneca's move is underscored by the fact that it would be distinctly odd for a Platonist to set the nobler part, spirit, aside for the lower one, desire.

To this argument against a genuine concession to Platonic psychology one could reply, in turn, that in the immediate context of the passage, Seneca cites Posidonius (*Ep.* 92.10), who is often taken as a Platonizing Stoic. According to Galen at least, primarily in his *De placitis Hippocratis et Platonis*, Posidonius diverged from the main line of Stoic thinking on psychology by reintroducing the Platonic notions of spirit and appetite. But one should take Galen's account with a grain of salt: it serves his purpose of establishing Plato's superiority both to heighten as much as possible any divergences between Chrysippus and Posidonius and to claim Posidonius as an ally for his position.[8] Moreover, Seneca's quotation of Posidonius in his letter does not bear out the interpretation that Posidonius is meant to represent a Platonizing position. Seneca merely uses Posidonius to highlight the superiority of virtue (in the soul) over the body (as a step in the argument that the *summum bonum* consists of virtue alone): "Attached to it [virtue] is unserviceable and unstable flesh, a mere repository for food, as Posidonius calls it" (*Ep.* 92.10). In other words, here Seneca emphasizes unity in the Stoic camp, not internal divisions, nor does he himself endorse a divergent view. (If any Stoic could be said to differ from the main line of thinking in this letter, it would be Antipater, who is said to attribute some slight importance to externals, *Ep.* 92.5.)

If we do not have to read the division into rational and nonrational components in the directive faculty of the soul exclusively in terms of Platonic psychology, then the Stoic notion, which we have already seen in Seneca's *On Anger*, of impulses (dis)obeying reason could fit the bill.[9] The polemic in this particular letter does not hinge on different psychological models, but on different views of the good. Thus, at the opening of this letter Seneca, I would suggest, is availing himself of a doxographical pattern that can also be seen at work in Philo and Calcidius (as well as Cicero, Arius Didymus, and, to a lesser extent, Augustine), with a framework that is meant to capture as many features as possible of different psychological models. Notice for instance that the lower functions of the soul that serve the mind are also "responsible for our motor and nutritional functions" (*Ep.* 92.1), language that has distinct Peripatetic overtones.

So, under the nonrational component of the soul, one could list, as Calcidius does (see for instance chs. 182, 220, 223), Stoic impression and impulse (functions that animals have too), together with the senses, speech, and reproduction; Platonic spirit and appetite; or functions listed by the Peripatetics, having to do, for instance, with growth and nutrition. One could protest that such a grouping rests on an equivocation in the use of the label "irrational," but the equivocation is deliberate, in order to blur distinctions. (Other common ways of accomplishing the same goal hinge on the choice of vocabulary, in both Greek and Latin, for notions such as desire, pleasure, or impulse.) An equivocation is clearly at work in Seneca's use of *inrationale* too, which he applies not only to a component of the directive faculty of the soul, but also to externals (*Ep.* 92.4). Often when ancient philosophers are not engaging in a polemic, they try to establish as much common ground as possible between their own views and those of other schools of thought, in order to preserve a sense of the unity of truth, provided, of course, that their view comes out on top, as is the case too, I would argue, with the Stoic view of the good in Seneca's letter.

The Pre-Emotions and Anger

If we turn our attention now from the manner in which Seneca relates to the Stoic tradition to matters of content, his work *On Anger* provides a good starting point.[10] Seneca clearly demonstrates his mastery of some of the more technical aspects of Stoic psychology in his discussion of the so-called pre-emotions (*propatheiai*), in Book Two of his *On Anger* (see also *Ep.* 89.14–15). The passage in question, which has been subjected to much scholarly debate, is not very long (*De ira* 2.1–4), but it presents a detailed and sophisticated account, and one of the best we have extant on this subject, of the difference between involuntary psychosomatic reactions, such as turning pale at the presence of a threat, and the passions. Succinctly put, as Cicero had also pointed out already (*Tusc.* 3.52ff.), a passion requires an evaluative proposition and the assent of the mind to that proposition. Seneca's analysis, I would argue, makes most sense if we assume that by "judgment" (*iudicium*) in this context Seneca also means the evaluative assessment implied in the propositional content of the relevant (hormetic) impressions, before assent occurs.[11]

Seneca renders the Stoic notion of "impression" (*phantasia*) as *species* and "impulse" (*hormê*) as *impetus*—but with the crucial nuance that for Seneca *impetus*, in this context, appears to stand for "excessive impulse" (see above). Thus the term can in itself already carry a negative connotation (as in 2.3.5, for instance). Seneca renders passions as *adfectus*, and the pre-emotions as *principia proludentia adfectibus* ("beginnings that are preludes to the passions"; see also the first motion of 2.4.1: *praeparatio adfectus et quaedam comminatio*).

Seneca uses a wider range of Latin vocabulary to render the required operations of reason: first, an evaluative assessment, which translates the impression into propositional content reflecting the value beliefs of the person articulating the impression, and second, an assent (*sunkatathesis*) to propositions of this kind, which triggers the impulse to set an action in motion. (Latin can also rely on the semantic connections between *sentire, sensus*, and *adsentiri, adsensus*; for the use of *sensus*, see for instance *De ira* 3.10.1, and on the latter, see below.) As we can tell based on Cicero's and Seneca's evidence, the evaluative proposition in question is twofold, both that something is bad or good (for instance, a death, an insult, or a monetary gain) and that a certain response is called for (mourning, revenge, or elation). It is essential for my argument here that an evaluative assessment of this type, while cognitive in the sense of reflecting the propositional content of an impression, does not yet have to entail assent. I take Seneca here to say something along the lines of Epictetus's well-known recommendation that we can train ourselves to tell our impressions to "wait a little" and to hold off on assent while we examine the evaluative assessments implied in this type of impression more closely, only to discover that we tend to get these fundamentally wrong—i.e., we have a tendency to assign the wrong value to the wrong things, often because of received opinion.[12]

In Seneca's account we find *iudicium* for judgment (also *opinio*, or a verb such as *putare*, which indicates that evaluative assessment is included among the meanings of "judgment" he has in mind here) and *adsensus mentis* (*adsentiri, adprobare*) for "assent" (*sunkatathesis*). But he also uses the pair judgment and "will" (*voluntas, voluntarius*; 2.3.5). The latter, I suggest, starts with the second type of evaluative assessment, that a certain response would be appropriate, rather than with assent and impulse (or at most with a preliminary impulse, *Ep*. 113.18). This distinction is the clearest when Seneca states: "suppose that someone has *reckoned* (*putavit*) he was harmed [i.e., thinks that something bad has happened], *wants* to (*voluit*) take revenge [i.e., thinks that a certain response is appropriate], and then immediately calms down when some reason urges against it" (2.3.4, tr. Kaster, and 2.4).

Seneca uses this language of "will" because, as Brad Inwood claims, he wants to emphasize the need for self-control and thus enhance the voluntarist features of this analysis of the passions.[13] Such language also allows Seneca to emphasize the active nature of the passions: they are up to us, that is, they do not just happen to us as a result of accidental occurrences, and therefore can be prevented. But as Inwood also rightly cautions, this language does not imply that Seneca has a strong notion of the "will" as a separate entity in its own right and something over and beyond these other functions of the mind; rather he has what Inwood calls the notion of a "summary will," an "instrumental summary reference to a more complex set of *explanantia*."[14]

In a helpful overview Rainer Zöller points out that there are four main areas in Latin renderings of Stoic psychology in which the notion of *voluntas* asserts itself: (1) as a rendering of the good emotion βούλησις (more on this below); (2) in the complex interaction of impression, assent, and impulse (as is the case in the passages *On Anger* under discussion); (3) as a fundamental orientation and commitment to the good (especially important for one making progress; for instance, in Seneca *Ep*. 37.4, 71.36, 80.4); (4) or as what we may call the intention as opposed to the outcome of an action (for instance, in Seneca *Ben*. 1.15.6).[15]

As we have seen, in this context too, Seneca uses the language of anger "succumbing to reason" (*rationi succumbet*), of reason "persuading" (*ratio persuadet*), or of anger "vanquishing" reason (*rationem evicit*), as if anger and other passions were some kind of independent entities. Yet all the language pertaining to motion (*motus*) and excessive motion—with echoes of Chrysippus's runner image in verbs such as "rushing forth"(*excurrere*[16])—again indicates that Seneca has the doctrine of excessive impulses in mind.

But in this analysis of anger, Seneca gives us an additional perspective on the language of obeying or rebelling against reason. He allows us to imagine three scenarios. A sage (presumably, because Seneca does not explicitly discuss the Stoic sage in this context) would be liable to the pre-emotions, like other human beings (see, for instance, also *Ep*. 71.29), but would not make erroneous evaluative assessments: for instance, she would not consider death an evil nor acknowledge an insult as lessening her worth. A fool, in Stoic terms, would make the wrong evaluative assessments repeatedly, assent to them, and run headlong into the passions. But what about someone willing to change his or her behavior and making progress, the category of people to whom Seneca addresses his writings and in which he places himself? We could imagine such a person going back and forth between different evaluative assessments, and as long as that person's assent has not come down like a hammer, or his repeated wrong choices have not been sealed into a habit, he would still be open to counterarguments (see also the distinction between "receiving the impression of an offense," *speciem iniuriae accepit*, versus approving it, *adprobavit*, De ira 2.3.5). We can construct an imaginary conversation in such a person's head or with a friend who is trying to talk reason into her: "so and so has wronged me and that's bad" with the response "no, he did not wrong you, you're misinterpreting the situation, or if he did, it doesn't matter"; and "[it is appropriate to exact revenge and thus] I want to kill the bastard" with the response "hold on, that makes no sense, and you'll only harm yourself in the process."

In this imaginary dialogue, reason would stand for the *right* kind of evaluative assessment with assent, not just any reasoning process, and we can see the correct assessment winning or being defeated by the wrong one (yielding the third motion of *De ira* 2.4: *qui rationem evicit*; parallel to 2.3.4–5: *illa est ira, quae rationem transilit, quae secum rapit*: "anger is something that leaps clear of reason, that snatches reason up and carries it along," tr. Kaster). If the right assessment wins out, the passion anger is still averted. Moreover, in this scenario it makes sense to call the mistaken assessment "[it is appropriate for me hence] I want to kill the bastard" a "not unruly volition" (*voluntas non contumax*, 2.4) as long as it can be countered by the right one. Or, to quote the relevant passage again: "Suppose that someone has *reckoned* (*putavit*) he was harmed [i.e., thinks that something bad has happened], *wants* to (*voluit*) take revenge [i.e., thinks that a certain response is appropriate], and then immediately calms down when some reason urges against it. I don't call this anger, I call it the movement of the mind still obedient to reason" (*De ira* 2.3.4, parallel to the second motion of 2.4, tr. Kaster). We know that the Stoics in general explained inner conflict as an oscillation, that is, "a turning of the single reason (*logos*) in both directions, which we do not notice owing to the sharpness and speed of the change" (Plut. *De virtute morali* 446F-447A = LS 65G).[17] But whereas in the scenario which Plutarch envisages this oscillation happens unconsciously, Seneca (and Epictetus, see above) present us with the option of consciously and deliberately countering our own mistaken value assessments. And so, it makes sense for Seneca to conclude that "this motion [passion], which *originates with* judgment, is removed by judgment" (2.4, *alter ille motus, qui iudicio nascitur, iudicio tollitur*): as long as assent has not occurred in a given instance the erroneous value assessment can be replaced by the correct one.

The rhetorical force of Seneca's depiction of anger should not be underestimated here. If we are tempted to downplay the harm done by "ordinary" forms of anger, Seneca suggests that any anger is much closer than one may be willing to admit to the excesses displayed by a Phalaris (*De ira* 2.5), which are merely a hardening produced by frequent indulgence in anger. Anger is by nature excessive, and tends to eclipse the very process of giving reasons for one's behavior (2.4: *sed utique*), at which point it is no longer amenable to reason. Therefore it is crucial for the sake of therapy to catch someone or oneself right before the passion of anger manifests itself, or, in other words, to intervene between the initial impression with its accompanying evaluative assessments and assent.

Moral Psychology and Self

In this example from *On Anger*, we see Seneca handling a complex array of technical notions. Yet it would be a mistake to assume that he is at his best, or at his most "philosophical," when he writes in this mode. For a counterexample one can take a closer look at his penetrating portrayal in *On Tranquility of Mind* of the all too human hesitation between a good resolve (*bona mens*) and the temptation of other motives that distract one from that resolve, or, in a different scenario, as Seneca puts it, "the weakness of a mind that leans strongly neither to good nor to evil" (1.4), described as a fluctuation or oscillation (*fluctuatio* 1.17; see also *De vita beata* 8.5–6, *Ep.* 95.57). As in his *On Anger*, Seneca addresses here a form of oscillation of which one can be aware.

The text opens with a self-diagnosis by Seneca's addressee, Serenus. Serenus finds himself in some kind of intermediate state between being not completely freed of his vices yet not entirely in their grip anymore. He illustrates his condition with three examples, of loving frugality, yet still being dazzled by the magnificence he encounters; of wanting to take on responsibility in public life, yet longing for the peace and dignity of leisure; and of leaning toward a simple and direct style in his studies and writing, yet being swept away by grander forms of expression and thought.

This psychological portrait of a man who turns to Seneca for help is in itself already quite compelling. It is not a coincidence that the work starts with Serenus's self-examination (*inquirenti mihi in me* . . .), because the language of "self," rather than more technical Stoic vocabulary, guides the entire exposition.[18] It is quite striking how many variations on this theme Seneca manages to devise. Serenus asks for Seneca's help because he is worried that his condition may actually be more serious than he thinks, for who has the courage "to tell himself the truth" (1.16: *quis sibi verum dicere ausus est*). The therapeutic exchange is set in motion by the diagnosis of Serenus's self-examination and self-doubt.

In order to treat his "patient," Seneca starts by restoring his self-confidence: Serenus has already made considerable progress, and no longer needs to scold and berate himself (2.2: *ut alicubi obstes tibi, alicubi irascaris, alicubi instes gravis*) but should have faith in himself (*ut fidem tibi habeas*; see also *Ep.* 75.13). As his next step Seneca provides a more general diagnosis of the condition of fickleness: a form of dissatisfaction with oneself (*sibi displicere*, 2.7) and a lack of resources in oneself (*parum in se solaciorum habens*), so that one hates being left to one's own devices (*invitus aspicit se sibi relictum*, 2.9). This kind of discontent one cannot run away from, because wherever one goes, one is always accompanied by oneself, a most insistent travel companion (*sequitur se ipse et urget gravissimus comes*, 2.14–15). With this broader diagnosis Seneca has cast a wider net to address both himself and his audience. Serenus's condition affects most, if not all, of us.

As the diagnosis suggests, it is the relation to oneself that needs to be healed, starting with the realization of the invaluable good of a "good conscience" (*bona conscientia*, 3.4–5) if one does participate in public life. Yet, while one has to be careful with the entanglements of a public career, a life that is completely turned toward itself (*vivimusque in nos tantum conversi*, 3.7), without social interactions, is neither satisfying nor appropriate. This insight opens the door to ways of assuming one's social responsibilities even if one is not active in politics (see below). But the key to the right choice in such matters is to assess one's abilities properly (*necesse est se ipsum aestimare* 6.1–2), and to discern whether one's disposition is more suited for an active or for a contemplative life (7.2). Seneca also underscores the value of friendship.

Returning to the topic of how people tend to go astray, Seneca treats wealth and its attendant miseries, and contrasts that condition with self-sufficiency: "How much more happy the man who owes nothing to anyone except himself, whom he can so easily refuse!" (8.8–9, tr. Fantham). We need to seek our "riches in ourselves" (*divitias a nobis*, 9.2) rather than rely on Fortune. A sage can also be described as one who counts not only all his possessions, social position, and body but even "his own self as mere contingencies of chance, and lives as if he has it on loan and is ready to return it without sadness to those who claim it back" (tr. Fantham, 11.1). Over and against busybodies who restlessly run from one activity to the next and are always driven by the actions of others or the turns of Fortune, Seneca urges that the mind "be called back into itself from all externals. Let it have faith in itself, rejoice in itself, respect its own qualities, and as far as possible withdraw from what is alien to it and focus on itself, not feeling losses, interpreting kindly even adversities" (tr. Fantham, 14.2).

Finally, reconnecting with Serenus's opening self-assessment, Seneca sets up the contrast between the honesty of his interlocutor and people who continually put up a front to impress others, and therefore always have to watch themselves in order not to fall out of character (this is an instance of a negative use of *persona*, in the sense of a mask, 17.1). And as he builds up to his conclusion, Seneca enjoins again that one "often ought to withdraw into oneself" (*multum in se recedendum est*, 17.3).

To assume that all these expressions for one's relation to oneself are mere literary flourishes or rhetorical tools underscoring the message is seriously to underestimate their philosophical significance.[19] Like "will," the "self" is not some kind of entity in its own right, set over and above the functions which the Early Stoa already attributed to the ruling principle of the soul or mind. Yet it expresses a very important perspective on how the mind is supposed to function, and is as such much more pervasive than the will in Seneca's writings. One could perfectly render in Stoic technical terms the kind of oscillation and indecisiveness that Seneca addresses, just as one can express how the soul and the mind are supposed to function from an objective, third-person point of view. But in his *On Tranquility of Mind* and many other contexts Seneca prefers to start with the first-person perspective of lived experience: how this condition comes across to an individual like Serenus who struggles with ongoing challenges.

Moreover, this approach locates both the power of and the duty and responsibility for moral progress squarely within the individual him- or herself. Like other Stoics of the

Roman imperial era, including Epictetus,[20] Seneca does not want to create a permanent dependence on an outside authority, whether himself or the founders of Stoicism, nor promote a (semi)permanent attachment to a philosophical school. Stoic teachings are meant to be eminently portable in one's soul. Any therapeutic relationship is only temporary, and the cure is not complete until the conversation with oneself takes over from external authority. An overreliance on external authority would create the same alienation that any hankering after the wrong values would.

Self, Others, and Cosmos

In his *On Tranquility of Mind* and *On Leisure*, as in some of the letters to Lucilius (as in *Ep.* 8, 10, and 14), Seneca appears at times to recommend withdrawal from an active presence in society, as might also be suggested by the language of "withdrawal into oneself." In truth, however, sociability always remains essential to the good life as Seneca envisages it—and on this point he is agreement with the other Stoics of the Roman era.[21] Even a silent person can affect public life merely by setting an example, because "the service of a good citizen is never useless" (*Tranq.* 4.6). By engaging in studies, teaching, or even such activities as framing laws (*Ep.* 14.14), a philosopher always serves the common good: *numquam privatum esse sapientem* (Cic. *Tusc.* 4.51; the same idea expressed in Sen. *Tranq.* 4). In a striking instance of this perspective Seneca projects onto Socrates, who finds himself "in the thick of things" during the regime of the Thirty Tyrants, the modes of engagement with others that he, Seneca, recommends, as in *Ep.* 94 and 95, (*Tranq.* 5.2):

> Yet Socrates was openly out in public life (*in medio erat*) and comforted (*consolabatur*) the mourning fathers and exhorted men (*exhortabatur*) despairing of the state, and reproached (*exprobrabat*) wealthy men fearing the consequences of their riches because they came too late to regret the dangers brought on by their greed; he bore himself as a mighty example for those willing to imitate him, walking as a free man among the thirty masters. (tr. Fantham)

Even in extreme conditions such as exile a Stoic sage never falls exclusively back on himself (Sen. *Ep.* 68.2):

> Besides, we assign to the wise man a state worthy of him, that is, the whole world. Thus he is not outside the state even if he does retire ... the sage is never more active than when things divine and human come into his view. (tr. Graver and Long)

In our relations with others, the Stoic notion of "good emotions" (*eupatheiai*), which are concomitant with the correct functioning of reason, plays a key role, especially "wish" (*boulêsis*), the subkinds of which are all forms of affection for and goodwill toward others.[22] There are three good emotions that correspond to three of the four main passions: "wish" already mentioned as a positive future-oriented state is a counterpart to "desire"; "caution" is a counterpart to the negative future-oriented emotion of "fear"; and "joy" is the positive reaction to a present condition that corresponds to "elation." Only "distress," as a negative response to a present condition, does not have a counterpart because a sage, as a matter of principle, has no use for it.

Seneca for his part leaves room for a form of sorrow and mourning that comes close to providing an *eupathic* counterpart to "distress."[23] His approach to the mourning of the death of a loved one (see *Ep.* 99 and the *Consolatio ad Marciam*) accounts for (1) tears as an involuntary reaction along the lines of the pre-emotions described above; (2) a shift away from grief toward love for and joy in memory of the deceased; but also (3) a dignified form of mourning. Thus, in a creative appropriation of the Stoic tradition, Seneca can bring himself to write about the weeping sage (*Ep.* 99.20–21):

> One can be tranquil and composed even in the midst of tears. The wise have often shed tears without detriment to their moral standing and with such restraint as to maintain both dignity and humanity. I repeat: one can be obedient to nature and still maintain one's decorum. I have seen people who command respect even at the funeral of a family member, when love showed on their faces without any false semblance of grieving, and all that was there was stirred by genuine emotion. There is seemliness even in grief, and that is something the wise person must preserve. Enough is enough, in tears as in everything else. Excessive griefs, like excessive joys, belong to the foolish. (tr. Graver and Long)

As the passage from *Letter* 68 discussed above already indicates, for the Stoics sociability is ultimately anchored in the community of gods and men, at the level of the cosmos. The relation between human rationality and the reason that permeates the entire universe as the divine active principle is most clearly present in the *Prefaces* of Seneca's *Natural Questions*.[24] Ethics is not complete without adding the perspective of the ordered whole that is the universe, and the study of nature properly understood is meant to reinforce the injunctions of ethics. And thus in the *Preface* to the third book of his *Natural Questions* Seneca establishes the inextricable connection between "having seen the universe in your mind" and "having subdued your vices" (10).[25]

Seneca's moral psychology, for all its gestures toward Platonic (and, occasionally, Peripatetic) elements remains fundamentally Stoic. His more technical analyses, such as his treatment of the pre-emotions in his *On Anger*, ultimately serve the purpose of an ethics in action, by promoting a human being's right disposition toward him- or herself, a disposition that, in turn, also governs one's relations with others and reflects the rational order of the *cosmos*.

Notes

1. Recent scholarship includes Wildberger (2006); Hadot (2014).
2. See, for instance, Fillion-Lahille (1984) and Zöller (2003).
3. Inwood (2005) 23–64.

4. For which, see Long (2017).
5. On the importance of the *Phaedo*, see also Boys-Stones (2013), with bibliography.
6. Cf. Reydams-Schils (2010) 200–201.
7. Cf. Graver (2017).
8. Cf. Tieleman (1998).
9. Graver (2017) points to the absence of the potential for conflict between the different components of the soul in Seneca's wording, and interprets the passage as a "deliberate accommodation to Peripatetic thought." This position argues against Inwood (2005) 38–41 and Setaioli (1988) 304–305 and (2014) 246n49.
10. For a recent assessment of this work, see Laurand, Malaspina, and Prost (2021) and Wiener in this volume.
11. For the debate on the number of stages Seneca discerns in the development of anger, see Graver (2007) 125–132 versus Sorabji (2000) 61–63; my position here differs from that of both, as well as from Konstan (2016), in that I assume that *iudicium* can have a sense that precedes assent, as does Gartner (2015). For additional bibliography, see also Kaufman (2014) 119–126.
12. Compare for instance Sen. *De ira* 2.29, 3.10.1–2 with, for instance, Epict. *Encheiridion* 1, 20; Epict. *Diss.* 1.20, 26; 2.8, 18; 3.12.
13. Inwood (2005) 143.
14. Ibid.
15. Zöller (2003) 85–93; on this topic see also Hadot (2014) 292–312; Wildberger (2006) 338–341.
16. See above; or his *efferantur* in 2.4.1, which is an echo of Chrysippus's *ekpheresthai*, Graver (2007) 127, with references to Galen *De Placitis Hippocratis et Platonis* 4.2.16, 4.6.35; see also *De ira* 2.35.
17. Plutarch talks about an oscillation in the passions, includes opinions and judgments, and mentions 1. inclinations and yieldings; 2. assents; and 3. impulses; *pace* Gartner (2015) I accept the oscillation thesis.
18. Bartsch (2006) 244–255, also with a good overview of the secondary literature.
19. Reydams-Schils (2005) 134–141; Graver (2007) 99–101, 196–206; Erler, Porter, and Sellars in this volume.
20. Cf. Reydams-Schils (2011).
21. Cf. Reydams-Schils (2005).
22. See Graver (2007) 51–60; 173–211.
23. For consolation, see Ker in this volume (especially his notes 14 and 15).
24. On which, see Williams (2012).
25. I thank Richard Fletcher, Margaret Graver, James Ker, David Konstan, Anthony A. Long, Aldo Setaioli, Will Shearin, and Jula Wildberger for their comments on drafts of this chapter, and especially for their graciousness in cases in which my interpretation differs from theirs, as indicated in the notes.

References

Bartsch, S. (2006). *The Mirror of the Self: Sexuality, Self-Knowledge, and the Gaze in the Early Roman Empire*. (Chicago).
Boys-Stones, G. (2013). "Seneca Against Plato: *Letters* 58 and 65," in A. G. Long (ed.), *Plato and the Stoics* (Cambridge), 128–146.

Fillion-Lahille, J. (1984). *Le De ira de Sénèque et la philosophie stoïcienne des passions*. (Paris).
Gartner, C. (2015). "The Possibility of Psychic Conflict in Seneca's *De ira*." *British Journal for the History of Philosophy* 23: 213–232.
Graver, M. (2007). *Stoicism and Emotion*. (Chicago).
Graver, M. (2017). "Seneca's Peripatetics: *Epistulae Morales* 92 and Stobaean Doxography 'C,'" in W. Fortenbaugh (ed.), *Arius Didymus on Peripatetic Ethics: Text, Translation and Discussion* (New York), 309–342.
Hadot, I. (2014). *Sénèque, direction spirituelle et pratique de la philosophie*. (Paris).
Inwood, B. (2005). *Reading Seneca: Stoic Philosophy at Rome*. (Oxford).
Kaufman, D. (2014). "Seneca on the Analysis and Therapy of Occurrent Emotions," in J. Wildberger and M. Colish (eds.), *Seneca Philosophus* (Berlin), 111–135.
Konstan, D. (2014). "Senecan Emotions," in S. Bartsch and A. Schiesaro (eds.), *The Cambridge Companion to Seneca* (Cambridge), 174–184.
Konstan, D. (2016). "Reason versus Emotion in Seneca," in D. Cairns and D. Nelis (eds.), *Emotions in the Classical World: Methods, Approaches, and Directions* (Heidelberg), 231–243.
Laurand, V. E. Malaspina, and F. Prost, eds. (2021). *Lectures plurielles du* De ira *de Sénèque: Interprétations, contextes, enjeux*. (Berlin).
Long, A. A., and D. N. Sedley [= LS] (1987). *The Hellenistic Philosophers*. (Cambridge).
Long, A. A. (2017). "Seneca and Epictetus on Body, Mind, and Dualism," in T. Engberg Pederson (ed.), *From Stoicism to Platonism: The Development of Philosophy, 100 BCE –100 CE* (Cambridge), 214–230.
Reydams-Schils, G. (2005). *The Roman Stoics: Self, Responsibility, and Affection*. (Chicago).
Reydams-Schils, G. (2010). "Seneca's Platonism: The Soul and Its Divine Origin," in A. Nightingale and D. Sedley (eds.), *Ancient Models of Mind: Studies in Human and Divine Rationality* (Cambridge), 196–215.
Reydams-Schils, G. (2011). "Authority and Agency in Stoicism." *GRBS* 51: 296–322.
Setaioli, A. (1988). *Seneca e i Greci: Citazione e traduzione nelle opere filosofiche*. (Bologna).
Setaioli, A. (2014). "Ethics I: Philosophy as Therapy, Self-Transformation and *Lebensform*," in G. Damschen and A. Heil (eds.), *Brill's Companion to Seneca, Philosopher and Dramatist* (Leiden), 239–256.
Sorabji, R. (2000). *Emotion and Peace of Mind: From Stoic Agitation to Christian Temptation*. (Oxford).
Tieleman, T. (1998). *Galen and Chrysippus on the Soul: Argument and Refutation in the* De Placitis, *Books II–III*. (Leiden).
Wildberger, J. (2006). *Seneca und die Stoa: Der Platz des Menschen in der Welt*. Untersuchungen zur Antiken Literatur und Geschichte 84.1–2. (Berlin).
Williams, G. D. (2012). *The Cosmic Viewpoint: A Study of Seneca's* Natural Questions. (Oxford).
Zöller, R. (2003). *Die Vorstellung vom Willen in der Morallehre Senecas*. (Munich).

CHAPTER 5

MARCUS AURELIUS AND THE TRADITION OF SPIRITUAL EXERCISES

JOHN SELLARS

THE *MEDITATIONS* OF MARCUS AURELIUS

THE book that we now know in English as the *Meditations* of the Roman emperor Marcus Aurelius was given that title by Meric Casaubon when he published his translation in 1634.[1] Over the centuries it has been given a variety of titles in modern European languages, including *Thoughts*, *Commentaries*, *Pensées*, *Reflexions*, and *Ricordi*.[2] None of these really captures the sense of the Greek title that is preserved in the manuscript tradition, *Ta eis heauton*, which might best be translated as *To Himself*.[3] Although it is unlikely that this title was devised by Marcus himself,[4] it is nevertheless apt and offers a way in to thinking about what Marcus was doing when he was writing these notes.

With the exception of Book 1, which may have been composed separately,[5] the *Meditations* presents itself as a series of occasional reflections on a wide range of personal and philosophical topics in no particular order and with no obvious structure. There is no reason to think that the text was intended as anything other than a series of notebook reflections on topics preoccupying the author. What we have, then, is a series of private notes in which Marcus is in dialogue with himself.[6]

With a private text like this it can be difficult to know for sure what the author was trying to do. Helpfully Marcus gives us his own account of what he was doing (M. Aur. *Med.* 4.3).[7] Some people look for retreats from the pressures of everyday life by withdrawing to the countryside, but as a philosopher Marcus can simply retreat into himself (*eis heauton anachôrein*). He writes, "Continually, therefore, grant yourself this retreat and repair yourself (*ananeou seauton*)." This is not a permanent retreat but simply a brief period of rest and reflection before returning to the business of everyday life. What is the purpose of this retreat? It is to reflect on "brief and fundamental truths" (*brachea kai stoicheiôdê*) already within the mind in order to "wash away all distress" (*to pasan lupên apoklusai*) and to attain "perfect ease" (*eumareia*), which he identifies with "good behavior" (*eukosmia*). He then gives us a couple of examples of what he has in mind, such as reminding himself that he is by nature a social animal in order to keep in check any anger he might feel toward people who behave poorly. He goes on to suggest that there are two fundamental ideas that must be kept "ready to hand" (*procheiros*): (1) that mental disturbances are the product not of things but of our judgments (*hupolêpsis*), and (2) nothing is stable and everything passes, subject to universal flux (*metabolais*). He then summarizes (4.3.4) these two principles as concisely as possible, presumably in order to aid memorization: *ho kosmos alloiôsis, ho bios hupolêpsis*, which we might translate expansively as "the cosmos is in continual change; the concerns of human life are the product of opinion."[8] When Marcus was writing the *Meditations* he was engaged in a practice of reminding himself of these and other central philosophical principles, in order (as he tells us) to overcome distress (*lupê*) and to cultivate a state of complete ease (*eumareia*).[9]

In his monograph on Marcus Aurelius titled *The Inner Citadel*, Pierre Hadot characterized this sort of therapeutic self-dialogue as a spiritual exercise.[10] Hadot borrowed the phrase "spiritual exercise" from Ignatius of Loyola but both the phrase and the sorts of practices it refers to have ancient precedent.[11] In the next section I shall examine the tradition of spiritual exercises in ancient thought before Marcus, beginning with an ancient discussion of the idea. Then in the section after I shall return to the *Meditations* and consider some of Marcus's own spiritual exercises in more detail.

Spiritual Exercises before Marcus

Marcus is explicit about his debt to his Stoic predecessor Epictetus, whose *Discourses* (recorded for us by Arrian) he tells us he read (M. Aur. Med. 1.7). Epictetus was himself influenced by another Stoic, Musonius Rufus, whose lectures he attended at Rome. Notes from those lectures were recorded by Musonius's student Lucius, and the notes from one of those lectures have come down to us under the title *On Exercise* (*Peri askêseôs*).[12]

Musonius's interest in exercise (*askêsis*) stems from his conviction that philosophy is not merely a theoretical discourse but, fundamentally, an activity aimed at transforming one's life. The study of virtue, he suggests, ought to be conceived as something akin to the study of medicine or music, namely something we study in order to gain a practical skill.[13] Like a student of medicine or music, "a man who wishes to become good not only must be thoroughly familiar with the precepts which are conducive to virtue but must also be earnest and zealous in applying these principles."[14] This is where exercise comes in: first one studies the principles or precepts (*mathêmata*); then one undertakes a period of training or exercise (*askêsis*).[15] Musonius goes on to claim that this period of exercise is more important for the student of philosophy than it is for the student of any other art or craft, insofar as philosophy is the most difficult discipline to master.[16] By philosophy he means the task of becoming a good, virtuous person.

What form should this exercise take? Musonius notes that because human beings are comprised of both body and soul it will be necessary to undertake exercises appropriate to both. It is at this point that Musonius introduces the idea of what he calls *askêsis tês psuchês*, which we might translate as "exercise of the soul," "mental training," or, indeed, "spiritual exercise." We might expect this to be contrasted with a fairly straightforward notion of physical exercise, but instead Musonius proposes a composite form of training: "there are two kinds of training, one which is appropriate for the soul alone, and the other which is common to both soul and body."[17] This second type of training works on both the body and the soul at once and includes things like avoiding physical pleasures, testing oneself in extremes of cold and heat, training to cope with thirst and hunger, and practicing endurance in the face of suffering. These sorts of practices benefit the body and soul at once. But what of purely spiritual exercises? These work on the soul alone and, although Musonius thinks both types of exercise are essential for anyone who aspires to become a good human being, these spiritual exercises are, he suggests, fundamental to philosophy. Musonius gives us an extended definition of what these spiritual exercises involve:

> Training which is peculiar to the soul consists first of all in seeing that the proofs pertaining to apparent goods as not being real goods are always ready at hand and likewise those pertaining to apparent evils as not being real evils, and in learning to recognize the things which are truly good and in becoming accustomed to distinguish them from those that are not truly good. In the next place it consists of practice in not avoiding any of the things which only seem evil, and in not pursuing any of the things which only seem good; in shunning by every means those which are truly evil and in pursuing by every means those which are truly good.[18]

The central task of spiritual exercises, then, is to keep philosophical principles (in this case, Stoic principles regarding what is and is not good) "ready to hand" (*procheiros*).[19] In so doing one will be better placed to become accustomed (*ethizesthai*) to acting in accordance with those principles. It will also involve the practice (*meletê*) of actions that embody those principles. In short, spiritual exercises offer the training necessary to transform oneself according to a set of philosophical ideas so that one consistently lives according to those ideas.

Musonius does not mention any sources for his account, although we might note that the distinction between mental and physical/mental exercises had been made well before by Diogenes of Sinope, who was eulogized at length by Musonius's pupil Epictetus.[20] We shall come back to this Cynic ancestry later. It is striking, though, that Musonius makes no mention of his near contemporary in Rome, Seneca. Yet Seneca also engaged in spiritual exercises and he tells us that this was a practice he learned from someone called Sextius (*De ira* 3.36.1–3):

> All our senses must be toughened: they have a natural endurance, once the mind has ceased to corrupt them; and the mind must be called to account every day. This was

Sextius's practice: when the day was spent and he had retired to his night's rest, he asked his mind, "Which of your ills did you heal today? Which vice did you resist? In what aspect are you better?" Your anger will cease and become more controllable if it knows that every day it must come before a judge. [...] I exercise this jurisdiction daily and plead my case before myself. When the light has been removed and my wife has fallen silent, aware of this habit that's now mine, I examine my entire day and go back over what I've done and said, hiding nothing from myself, passing nothing by. (tr. Kaster and Nussbaum)

This is an example of keeping one's guiding precepts "ready to hand" and it also prefigures the practice of self-dialogue that Marcus engaged in when writing the *Meditations*. The Sextius mentioned by Seneca is Quintus Sextius, founder of a philosophical school in Rome where two of Seneca's own teachers, Fabianus and Sotion, had studied.[21] The practice of daily self-examination that Seneca recounts and attributes to Sextius appears to have been Pythagorean in origin, and it is described in the Pythagorean *Golden Verses* (*Carmen aureum*):

> Do not welcome sleep upon your soft eyes
> before you have reviewed each of the day's deeds three times:
> "Where have I transgressed? What have I accomplished? What duty have
>   I neglected?"
> Beginning from the first one go through them in detail, and then,
> If you have brought about worthless things, reprimand yourself, but if you
>   have achieved good things, be glad.[22]

As well as recommending this practice of evening self-examination, the *Golden Verses* also describe a series of mental and physical/mental exercises of the sort outlined by Musonius, exhorting the reader to become accustomed (*ethizesthai*) to acting in accordance with a series of moral precepts.[23]

A number of scholars have suggested that the *Golden Verses* is a relatively late text, perhaps dating from the Imperial Period.[24] However, as Johan Thom has pointed out, there is evidence to suggest that the text is earlier than that and that it was known to early Stoics such as Cleanthes and Chrysippus, both of whom draw on it.[25] If the early Stoics did know this relatively short text then no doubt they would have been familiar with its recommendation of this spiritual exercise.

As well as appealing to these Pythagorean practices, Seneca also comments with approval on Cynic exercises. According to Seneca (*Ben.* 7.1.3–4)., Demetrius the Cynic held that it was far better to have just a few philosophical doctrines (*praecepta sapientiae*) ready to use than many of no practical purpose and so, like a wrestler, one ought to be carefully trained (*diligenter exercuit*) in just a handful of essential skills. The beginning philosopher, says Demetrius (Sen. *Ben.* 7.2.1), must make those few, essential doctrines "a part of himself, and by practicing them daily (*cotidiana meditatione*) get to the point that healthy thoughts come of their own accord" (tr. Griffin and Inwood).[26]

Seneca was of course by no means alone among Stoics in turning to Cynic predecessors for inspiration. The influence of Cynicism on the early Stoa went well beyond Zeno's supposedly youthful *Republic*,[27] and as we have already noted Diogenes of Sinope is reported to have drawn a distinction between mental and physical/mental exercises prefiguring the account in Musonius Rufus. Diogenes Laertius (6.70) writes of Diogenes of Sinope that:

> He used to affirm that training was of two kinds, mental and bodily: the latter being that whereby, with constant exercise, perceptions are formed such as secure freedom of movement for virtuous deeds; and the one half of this training is incomplete without the other, good health and strength being just as much included among the essential things, whether for body or soul. And he would adduce indisputable evidence to show how easily from gymnastic training we arrive at virtue. For in the manual crafts and other arts it can be seen that the craftsmen develop extraordinary manual skill through practice. Again, take the case of flute-players and of athletes: what surpassing skill they acquire by their own incessant toil; and, if they had transferred their efforts to the training of the mind, how certainly their labors would not have been unprofitable or ineffective. (tr. Hicks)[28]

The resonances with the account of exercises in Musonius Rufus are clear. Both draw a distinction between mental and physical exercises, insisting that they are equally essential, but both also acknowledge the mental benefits that come with various forms of physical training.

We can see connections, then, between later Roman Stoic accounts of spiritual exercises by Musonius and Seneca on the one hand, and earlier Pythagorean and Cynic traditions of mental training on the other. Although it is difficult to be sure, given the fragmentary nature of the evidence, the presence of both Pythagorean and Cynic influences on the early Stoics makes it not unreasonable to suppose that they too may have been concerned with spiritual exercises as an important part of philosophical education.[29] We do know that some early Stoics wrote books devoted to the topic of *askêsis*, notably Herillus and Dionysius.[30] If this is right, then the concern with spiritual exercises that we find in Roman Stoics such as Seneca, Musonius Rufus, and Marcus Aurelius was not a late innovation but rather a theme running through Stoicism from the outset.

Spiritual Exercises in the *Meditations*

While we find descriptions of spiritual exercises in a number of ancient texts, the *Meditations* of Marcus Aurelius stands out as a text that is itself an extended spiritual exercise. What we find is Marcus engaging in the sort of self-dialogue proposed in the *Golden Verses* and taken up by Sextius and Seneca. Rather than merely mentally rehearsing the difficulties of everyday life, Marcus's mode of self-dialogue involves writing his thought processes down. It may well be that others produced these sorts of written exercises as well, but the *Meditations* is unique as the only example of such writing to come down to us. In this sense the *Meditations* taken as a whole is an example of a series of written spiritual exercises.[31] There are various features of the text that support this, such as the repetition of phrases like "always remember,"[32] and it also helps to explain the lack of structure and the repetition of topics. Indeed, the repetitive character of the text, once judged a stylistic weakness, can now be seen as an essential feature of this unique work.[33]

As well as being able to consider the *Meditations* as a whole as a form of spiritual exercise, it is also possible to pick out a number of specific exercises in the text. Putting aside Book 1, the *Meditations* opens proper with the first chapter of Book 2, which begins: "Say to yourself in the early morning: I shall meet today inquisitive, ungrateful, violent, treacherous, envious, uncharitable men."[34] This mental rehearsal of potentially unpleasant events to come is an example of *praemeditatio futurorum malorum*, a common theme in Hellenistic philosophy and discussed at length by Cicero, who reports that Chrysippus had made use of this technique.[35] Cicero notes that Chrysippus held the view that "what is unforeseen strikes us with greater force" than what we have already rehearsed in our minds.[36] Although, as Cicero makes plain, the technique was not original to the Stoics, it was an established Stoic practice long before Marcus took it up in the *Meditations*.[37]

In Marcus's version here, he responds to his opening rehearsal of the difficulties he might expect to encounter in the coming day by reminding himself of a number of key Stoic doctrines that ought to inform his response. He opens with the thought that the behavior of the unpleasant people he might encounter is ultimately the product of their ignorance (*agnoia*), and so not deliberate on their part. Marcus himself, however, is not ignorant of how he ought to behave so he has no justification to respond in kind. On the contrary, he knows that he and these others share the same nature and that all share in a divine nature, and so, no matter how they behave, he ought to treat them as kinsmen (*sungenês*). Using an analogy with parts of a single organism, Marcus suggests that to work against other people is to act contrary to Nature (*para phusin*), and he concludes by saying that to respond to the negative emotions of others with negative emotions of one's own would also be against Nature.

As we can see, Marcus is implicitly drawing on a range of Stoic ideas in a way that highlights the interconnectedness of the Stoic system. He appeals to (1) central ideas in Stoic physics, to give him the resources (2) to avoid jumping to rash judgments that might generate negative emotions, which will in turn mean that he can (3) act toward those whom he meets in the ethically appropriate way. In particular he presupposes a number of Stoic claims: that only virtue is good, that emotions are the product of errors in judgment, and that all humans are part of a single, rational community. By prerehearsing encounters with the worst sorts of people he might meet and reminding himself of both the appropriate way to behave in response and the philosophical principles that underpin that response, Marcus is training himself not to rush into making negative judgments about unpleasant people that would, in turn, generate negative emotions, lead to inappropriate behavior, and, ultimately, compromise the integrity of his character and the rationality of his soul. This early morning reflection on the day ahead complements the evening review of the day described by Seneca and both offer very practical examples of philosophical training in action.

Another specific exercise we find in the *Meditations* is often called "the view from above."[38] There are a number of examples throughout the text,[39] of which here is just one representative example:

> Watch and see the courses of the stars as if you ran with them, and continually dwell in mind upon the changes of the elements into one another; for these imaginations wash away the foulness of life on the ground. Moreover, when discoursing about mankind, look upon earthly things below as if from some place above them—herds, armies, farms, weddings, divorces, births, deaths, noise of law courts, lonely places, divers foreign nations, festivals, mournings, market places, a mixture of everything and an order composed of contraries.[40]

This passage and others like it appear to be doing a number of things at once. First there is a meditation on universal flux and the impermanence of all things, designed to offer consolation for loss of various kinds and ultimately consolation for death. Second there is an attempt to see Nature as a whole and to grasp it as a single interconnected system. Third there is an effort to put into a much wider context everyday human cares and concerns in order to minimize their significance.[41] This goes hand in hand with offering a series of dispassionate, physical descriptions of things that are often taken to be very important in everyday human life, again in order to downplay their significance. Thus, for example, countries, over which wars are fought, are merely lumps of mud around a pond.[42] This single mental exercise of viewing things from above does, then, a number of things at once, implicitly appealing to a range of claims from Stoic physics along the way. The frequency with which Marcus repeats or alludes to this vision from above in the *Meditations* highlights the significance he attached to it. In one passage he includes it among three things that he must keep "ready to hand" (*procheiros*), confirming its central place in his repertoire of spiritual exercises.[43]

Marcus's reflections on "the view from above" also form an example of the way in which many of his spiritual exercises ultimately depend on doctrines in physics and, although his aim is entirely practical, it is potentially misleading to characterize his exercises as merely "practical ethics," if that is taken to mean the practical application of ethical principles. In the *Meditations* it is the practical application of epistemological and physical doctrines that recurs again and again.[44] In one particularly striking passage Marcus reflects on the contrast between seeing objects from a purely physical perspective and seeing them overlaid with cultural significance (M. Aur. *Med.* 6.13):

> Surely it is an excellent plan, when you are seated before delicacies and choice foods, to impress upon your imagination that this is the dead body of a fish, that the dead body of a bird or a pig; and again, that the Falernian wine is grape juice and that robe

of purple a lamb's fleece dipped in a shell-fish's blood [...]. Surely these are excellent imaginations (*phantasiai*), going to the heart of actual facts (*pragmata*) and penetrating them so as to see the kind of things they really are.

Elsewhere Marcus offers a description of this technique of describing objects from a physical perspective, a technique clearly aimed at undermining excessive attributions of value to such things (M. Aur. *Med*. 3.11):

> Always make a figure or outline of the imagined object as it occurs, in order to see distinctly what it is in its essence (*kat' ousian*), naked, as a whole and parts; and say to yourself its individual name and the names of the things of which it was compounded and into which it will be broken up. For nothing is so able to create greatness of mind as the power methodically and truthfully to test each thing that meets one in life, and always to look upon it so as to attend at the same time to the use which this particular thing contributes to a Universe of a certain definite kind, what value it has in reference to the Whole, and what to man.

This technique of physical description has the virtue not only of ensuring that objects are valued correctly but also of enabling one to grasp objects as they are in themselves, which is an important end in itself. Many of the spiritual exercises we find in the *Meditations*, including "the view from above," employ this kind of physical perspective on the world, both for its own sake and for its therapeutic benefits.[45]

Concluding Remarks

By way of conclusion there are two points that might be emphasized. First, for Marcus and the other Stoics discussed here—let alone all ancient philosophers—there is no suggestion that philosophy was merely a series of spiritual exercises. Musonius Rufus is quite explicit that this sort of mental training comes *after* the study of philosophical theories, on which it is grounded. Philosophy remains an activity devoted to rational inquiry into what exists and what has value. Musonius's point is that the study of, say, virtue ought to be not merely for the sake of being able to supply a definition of virtue but ultimately for the sake of becoming a virtuous person.[46] In this he is at one with Socrates. Spiritual exercises to do not challenge or replace the sort of rational inquiry usually identified with philosophy, they supplement it. In the *Meditations* Marcus refers to philosophy as an art,[47] to which his spiritual exercises contribute along the lines that Musonius suggests. First one studies philosophical theory and only after that does one undertake the exercises necessary to digest that information and so transform one's behavior.[48] As Marcus himself puts it, it is a task of dyeing one's soul a new color,[49] something that requires the repetition of key ideas, and something that Marcus himself does throughout his own notes to himself. This is analogous to the practical training that a student of an art or craft must undergo after they have studied its basic principles. Thus spiritual exercises are the practical training that forms just one part of philosophy conceived as an art of living.[50]

As a book of such exercises, it is important also to remember that, second, Marcus's *Meditations* is an idiosyncratic and partial book. It comprises a series of spiritual exercises about topics that were of particular importance to Marcus at the time he was writing. It does not pretend to offer a complete or comprehensive account of all the possible spiritual exercises a Stoic philosopher might deploy, much less the theoretical principles on which those exercises are grounded. Insofar as these exercises are designed to put philosophy to work in order to overcome some of Marcus's personal problems, it inevitably focuses on a range of negative issues in his own life. These ought not to be taken as a complete account of either Marcus's outlook on life or his conception of Stoicism. Indeed, it would be a mistake for detractors or admirers to think that the *Meditations* straightforwardly presents us with Marcus's own version of Stoic philosophy. The philosophical precepts, doctrines, and arguments on which Marcus's spiritual exercises depend remain on the whole unstated.[51] Of course it is possible to try to reconstruct Marcus's philosophical views from passing remarks, implicit assumptions, and the wider background of Stoic philosophy to which he seems clearly committed,[52] but the task of the *Meditations* is not to present us with Marcus's unique brand of Stoicism; instead it is to help the author transform himself in the light of the philosophy that, in this text, goes without saying.[53]

Notes

1. See Casaubon (1634), who went on to publish an edition of the Greek text in 1643. In what follows I have in general relied on the text and quote from the translation in Farquharson (1944), occasionally modified. There is a more recent edition in Dalfen (1987) and the first volume of a new edition in Hadot and Luna (1998). Material in this chapter has also been incorporated, in a slightly different form, in Sellars (2021).
2. For titles of translations up to 1908, see Wickham Legg (1910).
3. The title is recorded in the *editio princeps*, which was based on the now lost Palatine manuscript (on which see Ceporina (2012) 55–56). Many have assumed that the title was taken over from the manuscript, although Ceporina (2012) 47 suggests that it may have been added by Xylander. It is literally rendered by a few translators; see, e.g., Rendall (1898). When translated into Latin it is usually, though not universally, translated literally as *ad se ipsum*. It is worth noting that Casaubon's full title in English was *Meditations Concerning Himselfe*.
4. The title is first mentioned by Arethas of Caesarea (c. 850–935), *Scholia in Lucianum* 207, 6–7 Rabe, quoted in Farquharson (1944) 158. An earlier mention of the text by Themistius, *Orationes* 6.81c (dated 364; see Farquharson (1944) xv) does not use the title but instead calls the work *Precepts* or *Admonitions* (*parangelmata*). In the *Meditations* Marcus refers to his own writings as *hupomnêmatia* (little notes), at 3.14.
5. On the distinctive character of Book 1, see Rutherford (1989) 48–125; Hadot and Luna (1998) xli–clxxxiii; Gill (2013) lxxv–lxxxiv.

6. On the *Meditations* and self-dialogue, see van Ackeren (2011) 1.206–287. For a wider discussion of the concept of self in Roman Stoicism, see Reydams-Schils (2005).
7. All passages in the remainder of this paragraph come from here. For commentary, see Farquharson (1944) 309–311; Gill (2013) 120–122. Brunt (1974) 3 says of this passage, "Here surely is the key to the *Meditations*."
8. As an aside from our central concern here, it is worth noting that these two fundamental principles that Marcus thinks he ought to keep ready to hand are not ethical principles relating to conduct. Instead one is logical (conceived broadly), the other physical. Marcus *is* interested in logic and physics—not logical and physical theory, but rather living in accord with a series of logical and physical claims central to Stoicism. In 4.3 as a whole he shows us how reflecting on doctrines in Stoic epistemology and physics might contribute to the cultivation of a mind at complete ease and in good order.
9. Distress (*lupê*) is one of the four principal types of emotion (*pathê*) the Stoics sought to avoid. It is, on their account, a belief (or the product of a belief) in a present evil. See, e.g., Diog. Laert. 7.110–111, Cic. *Tusc.* 3.24–25 [= *SVF* 3.385], 4.14 [= *SVF* 3.393] (where it is rendered into Latin as *aegritudo*), with discussion in Sorabji (2000) 29–32.
10. See Hadot (1992). Hadot first used the phrase "spiritual exercise" in relation to Marcus Aurelius in Hadot (1972).
11. See Hadot (1977), citing Rabbow (1954), with discussion in Sellars (2009) 110–118. Note also Pavie (2012) 19–24.
12. Stobaeus 3.29.78 (3,648–651 WH) and excerpted in Hense (1905) 22–27. The title may well have been added by Stobaeus. It is translated in Lutz (1947) 53–57, from which the translations here are taken. For discussion of this passage, see van Geytenbeek (1963) 40–50.
13. See Muson. fr. 6 (Hense (1905) 22.7–9). Further Musonius references are to fragment, page, and line numbers in Hense (1905).
14. Muson. 6.23.1–3.
15. Muson. 6.23.14–16. On this two-stage conception of philosophical education in Stoicism, see Sellars (2009).
16. See Muson. 6.23.17–24.1. He explains why this is the case: "men who enter the other professions have not had their souls corrupted beforehand [. . .] but the ones who start out to study philosophy have been born and reared in an environment filled with corruption and evil, and therefore turn to virtue in such a state that they need a longer and more thorough training."
17. Muson. 6.25.4–6.
18. Muson. 6.25.14–26.5.
19. The topic of keeping principles *procheiros* recurs throughout the works of Musonius's pupil Epictetus (see, e.g., the titles of *Epict. Diss.* 1.27 and 1.30) and is echoed in the title of Epictetus's *Encheiridion* compiled by Arrian (a connection noted by Simplicius, *in Ench. praef.* 18–20 Hadot).
20. See Diogenes Laertius 6.70, with Goulet-Cazé (1986) 195–222. Diogenes draws a distinction between mental and physical exercises but goes on to suggest, like Musonius, that physical exercises also benefit the soul. For Epictetus on Cynicism, see *Diss.* 3.22, which is examined in Billerbeck (1978).
21. On the school of Sextius, see Lana (1992); on Seneca's teachers, see Sellars (2014) 99–102.
22. *Carmen aureum* 40–44 (translation from Thom (1995) 97). As Thom notes ((1995) 37), these lines are quoted or alluded to by a wide range of ancient philosophical authors,

including Cicero (citing Cato the Elder as his source), Seneca, Plutarch, Epictetus, Galen, Porphyry, and Diogenes Laertius.

23. See, e.g., *Carmen aureum*. 9, 14, 35.
24. Thom (1995) suggests that Nauck's proposal of the fourth century CE is the *opinio communionis*.
25. See Thom (2001), elaborating on points first made in Thom (1995). For Chrysippus compare Gell. *NA* 7.2.12 [= *SVF* 2.1000] with *Carmen aureum* 54, and for Cleanthes compare *Hymn to Zeus* 23–25 [= *SVF* 1.537] with *Carmen aureum*. 55–56.
26. Note also Sen. *Ep*. 16.1.
27. See Goulet-Cazé (2003) for discussion of Cynic themes in the early Stoa. Later Stoics, embarrassed by the seemingly Cynic doctrines of Zeno's *Republic*, tried to present it as a work of Zeno's youth, written under the influence of his teacher Crates but later disowned. But, as Goulet-Cazé shows, Cynic ideas permeated the early Stoa more widely than that.
28. This passage is discussed in detail in Goulet-Cazé (1986) 195–222.
29. See in particular the previously unpublished essay "Chrysippus on Practical Morality" in Brunt (2013) 10–27. Brunt suggests that Chrysippus may have shared more in common with Epictetus than is usually supposed, and that "by systematically omitting homiletic material von Arnim induces a false conception of old Stoic morality" (11).
30. See Diog. Laert. 7.166–167.
31. For further elaboration of these claims, see Sellars (2012).
32. Brunt (1974) 3 (also reprinted in Brunt (2013) 365) notes that phrases such as "always remember" (*memnêso aei*) are repeated some forty times; see the Index Verborum in Schenkl (1913) s.v. *memnêsthai, memnêso* to which Brunt refers, and now Rigo (2010) 129 who lists 46 instances s.v. *mimnêskô*.
33. See further Giavatto (2012) 339–342.
34. M. Aur. *Med*. 2.1. Other examples of morning exercises are described at M. Aur. *Med*. 5.1 and 10.13.
35. For the phrase *praemeditatio futurorum malorum*, see Cic. *Tusc*. 3.29. For the mention of Chrysippus, see *Tusc*. 3.52 [= *SVF* 3.417]. For further discussion, see Newman (1989) 1477–1478. On its prehistory, see Hadot (1969) 60–62, referring to Pythagorean practices described in Iamblichus *Vit. Pyth*. 196 (DK 58D6).
36. Cic. *Tusc*. 3.52 [= *SVF* 3.417].
37. There are a number of previous Stoic instances, such as Sen. *Ep*. 78.29, 91.3–4, *De vita beata* 26.1. See further Newman (1989), who contrasts Stoic *meditatio* with earlier versions.
38. See, e.g., Hadot (1995) 238–250, discussing Marcus Aurelius alongside a wide range of other thinkers, and also Rutherford (1989) 155–161, focusing on parallels with earlier ancient literature. For this phrase in Marcus, see M. Ant. *Med*. 9.30.
39. As well as 7.47–48 quoted below, see, e.g., M. Aur. *Med*. 3.10, 5.24, 6.36, 9.30, 9.32, 10.15, 11.1, 12.24.
40. M. Aur. *Med*. 7.47–48. In modern editions this passage is divided into two chapters, but this dates back only to Gataker (1652). In the earlier edition by Casaubon (1643) they are printed as a single chapter, "7.27." There are no chapter divisions in the Greek text printed in Xylander (1559), although his Latin translation is divided into unnumbered paragraphs, where he prints 7.47–49 as a single paragraph. The earliest edition containing chapter divisions I have seen is the reprint of Xylander's text and translation published in Lyon in 1626 (full details in Wickham Legg (1910) 35–36).

41. In a number of passages (e.g., M. Aur. *Med.* 3.10, 5.24, 6.36, 9.30, 9.32), human life is put into a wider temporal as well as spatial context.
42. See, e.g., M. Aur. *Med.* 6.36.
43. See M. Aur. *Med.* 12.24.
44. See, e.g., 4.3.4 and 2.1, discussed above.
45. For further discussion of this kind of physical description, see esp. Hadot (1972), but note also Hadot (1992) 122–123, Gill (2013) xl–xliv.
46. The same point is made throughout Epictetus; see, e.g., Arr. *Epict. diss.* 2.19, 3.21.
47. See, e.g., M. Aur. *Med.* 4.2, 5.1, 6.16, 6.35, 7.68, and 11.5, with Sellars (2012) 453–454.
48. The comparison with digestion can be found in Seneca (*Ep.* 2.2-4, 84.5–8) and Epictetus (Arr. *Epict. diss.* 2.9.18, 3.21.1–4, *Ench.* 46) and is discussed in Sellars (2009) 121–122.
49. See M. Aur. *Med.* 5.16.
50. For an extended discussion of the (primarily Stoic) conception of philosophy as an "art of living," see Sellars (2009).
51. A similar view is expressed in Brunt (2013) 447.
52. For some doubts about Marcus's commitment to Stoicism, see Rist (1982); for rejoinders, see Gill (2007) and Sellars (2021).
53. For a similar assessment, see Roskam (2012) 94.

References

Billerbeck, M. (1978). *Epiktet, Vom Kynismus* (Leiden).
Bonazzi, M., and C. Helmig, eds. (2007). *Platonic Stoicism—Stoic Platonism: The Dialogue between Platonism and Stoicism in Antiquity.* (Leuven).
Brunt, P. A. (1974). "Marcus Aurelius in His *Meditations.*" *Journal of Roman Studies* 64: 1–20.
Brunt, P. A. (2013). *Studies in Stoicism.* (Oxford).
Casaubon, M. (1634). *Marcus Aurelius Antoninus The Roman Emperor, His Meditations Concerning Himselfe.* (London).
Casaubon, M. (1643). *Marci Antonini Imperatoris De Seipso et Ad Seipsum Libri XII.* (London).
Ceporina, M. (2012). "The *Meditations*," in van Ackeren, 45–61.
Dalfen, J. (²1987). *Marci Aurelii Antonini ad se ipsum libri XII.* (Leipzig).
Damschen, G., and A. Heil, eds. (2014). *Brill's Companion to Seneca: Philosopher and Dramatist.* (Leiden).
Farquharson, A. S. L. (1944). *The Meditations of the Emperor Marcus Antoninus.* 2 vols. (Oxford).
Gataker, T. (1652). *Marci Antonini Imperatoris de rebus suis, sive de eis qae ad se pertinere censebat, Librii XII.* (Cambridge).
Giavatto, A. (2012). "The Style of the *Meditations*," in van Ackeren, 333–345.
Gill, C. (2007). "Marcus Aurelius' *Meditations*: How Stoic and How Platonic?," in Bonazzi and Helmig, 189–207.
Gill, C. (2013). *Marcus Aurelius: Meditations Books 1–6.* (Oxford).
Goulet-Cazé, M.-O. (1986). *L'Ascèse cynique: Un commentaire de Diogène Laërce VI 70–71.* (Paris).
Goulet-Cazé, M.-O. (2003). *Les Kynica du stoïcisme.* (Wiesbaden).
Griffin, M., and B. Inwood (2011). *Seneca: On Benefits* (Chicago).
Grimal, P., ed. (1992). *La langue latine, langue de la philosophie.* (Rome).
Haase, W. (1989). *Aufstieg und Niedergang der römischen Welt II 36.3* (Berlin).

Hadot, I. (1969). *Seneca und die griechisch-römische Tradition der Seelenleitung.* (Berlin).
Hadot, P. (^{3}1972). "La physique comme exercice spirituel ou pessimisme et optimisme chez Marc Aurèle." *Revue de Théologie et de Philosophie* 3rd ser., 22: 225–239; repr. in Hadot (1993).
Hadot, P. (1977). "Exercices spirituels." *Annuaire de la Ve Section de l'École pratique des hautes etudes* 84: 25–70; repr. in Hadot (1993).
Hadot, P. (1992). *La Citadelle intérieure: Introduction aux Pensées de Marc Aurèle.* (Paris).
Hadot, P. (1993). *Exercices spirituels et philosophie antique.* (Paris).
Hadot, P. (1995). *Philosophy as a Way of Life.* (Oxford).
Hadot, P., and C. Luna (1998). *Marc Aurèle: Écrits pour lui-même, Tome I.* (Paris).
Hense, O. (1905). *C. Musonii Rufi Reliquiae.* (Leipzig).
Kaster, R. A., and M. C. Nussbaum (2010). *Seneca: Anger, Mercy, Revenge.* (Chicago).
Lana, I. (1992). "La scuola dei Sestii," in Grimal, 109–124.
Lutz, C. E. (1947). "Musonius Rufus, 'The Roman Socrates.'" *Yale Classical Studies* 10: 3–147.
Meyer, B. F., and E. P. Sanders, eds. (1982). *Jewish and Christian Self-Definition, Volume Three: Self-Definition in the Graeco-Roman World.* (London).
Newman, R. J. (1989). "*Cotidie meditare*: Theory and Practice of the *meditatio* in Imperial Stoicism," in Haase, 1473–1517.
Pavie, X. (2012). *Exercices spirituels: Leçons de la philosophie antique.* (Paris).
Rabbow, P. (1954). *Seelenführung: Methodik der Exerzitien in der Antike.* (Munich).
Rendall, G. H. (1898). *Marcus Aurelius Antoninus to Himself.* (London).
Reydams-Schils, G. (2005). *The Roman Stoics: Self, Responsibility, and Affection.* (Chicago).
Rigo, G. (2010). *Marcus Aurelius Antoninus: Index verborum in opus quod inscribitur Ta eis heauton.* (Hildesheim).
Rist, J. M. (1982). "Are You a Stoic? The Case of Marcus Aurelius," in Meyer and Sanders, 23–45.
Roskam, G. (2012). "Siren's Song or Goose's Cackle? Marcus Aurelius' *Meditations* and Ariston of Chios," in van Ackeren and Opsomer, 87–109.
Rutherford, R. B. (1989). *The Meditations of Marcus Aurelius: A Study.* (Oxford).
Schenkl, H. (1913). *Marci Antonini Imperatoris in Semet Ipsum Libri XII.* (Leipzig).
Sellars, J. (^{2}2009). *The Art of Living: The Stoics on the Nature and Function of Philosophy.* (London).
Sellars, J. (2012). "The *Meditations* and the Ancient Art of Living," in van Ackeren 453–464.
Sellars, J. (2014). "Seneca's Philosophical Predecessors and Contemporaries," in Damschen and Heil, 97–112.
Sellars, J. (2021). *Marcus Aurelius.* (Abingdon).
Sorabji, R. (2000). *Emotion and Peace of Mind: From Stoic Agitation to Christian Temptation.* (Oxford).
Thom, J. C. (1995). *The Pythagorean Golden Verses.* (Leiden).
Thom, J. C. (2001). "Cleanthes, Chrysippus and the Pythagorean *Golden Verses*." *Acta Classica* 44: 197–219.
van Ackeren, M. (2011). *Die philosophie Marc Aurels.* 2 vols. (Berlin).
van Ackeren, M., ed. (2012). *A Companion to Marcus Aurelius.* (Chichester).
van Ackeren, M., and J. Opsomer, eds. (2012). *Selbstbetrachtungen und Selbstdarstellungen: Der Philosoph und Kaiser Marc Aurel im interdisziplinären Licht.* (Wiesbaden).
van Geytenbeek, A. C. (1963). *Musonius Rufus and Greek Diatribe.* (Assen).
Wickham Legg, J. (1910). "A Bibliography of the *Thoughts* of Marcus Aurelius Antoninus." *Transactions of the Bibliographical Society* 10: 15–81.
Xylander, G. (1559). *M. Antonini Imperatoris Romani, et Philosophi De seipso seu vita sua Libri XII.* (Zurich).

CHAPTER 6

APULEIUS AND ROMAN DEMONOLOGY

JEFFREY ULRICH

APULEIUS occupies a unique and fringe place in the history of Roman philosophy. On the one hand, he is a cultural and linguistic outsider: born and reared in a backwoods town in North Africa (Madauros) and educated in Carthage (with a stint in Athens),[1] he writes as a nonnative speaker of an "African"-inflected Latin,[2] and frequently translates Greek works into Latin for a Carthaginian audience. But on the other hand—and more significantly, for the purposes of this handbook—he is our only fully extant representative of a Roman demonology developed and written in Latin before the fourth century CE, when the late Middle Platonist Calcidius translated Plato's *Timaeus* into Latin.[3] Moreover, while Apuleius has never found himself situated in the pantheon of great philosophers—indeed, historians of philosophy often complain of his inconsistencies, his lack of systemization, and his superficial, "popularizing" form of philosophy[4]—nonetheless, his *de deo Socratis* (hereafter, *Soc.*)—a treatise that has Greek counterparts in Plutarch's *de genio Socratis* and Maximus of Tyre's *Or.* 8 and 9[5]—provides the most comprehensive treatment, in either Greek or Latin, of Middle Platonic demonology in the second century. Therefore, although from the standpoint of the history of philosophy our Madauran *Platonicus philosophus* makes no significant contributions or innovations of his own in Middle Platonic demonology,[6] he remains vital for the reception of Platonism in Late Antiquity and Early Christianity, especially when we consider how influential the *Soc.* was on that other great North African rhetor, Augustine of Hippo.[7] It is thus fitting in a volume on Roman philosophy to focus exclusively on Apuleius's Roman demonology, and specifically, on the ways in which he translates Platonic ideas about human interactions with the divine through various kinds of intermediaries.

However, while I explore in this chapter Apuleius's particular method of translating Platonic demonology across his corpus, I may note it is also *à propos* that this chapter invites reflections on affiliation, identity, self, and other. For as everyone familiar with the so-called rhetorical works in Apuleius's corpus knows, the other unique fact about the Madauran Platonist is that he is the only writer of Latin to be included without qualification in the Imperial resurgence of *Greek* culture labeled (for better or worse) the Second Sophistic.[8] As the subtitle to Stephen Harrison's full-corpus study testifies to, Apuleius is sui generis because he is a "Latin sophist." Any philosophical pretensions he displays have traditionally been viewed as precisely that: epideictic display. Thus, Apuleius *affiliates* himself with Plato—according to the school of criticism pioneered by Gerald Sandy (1997) and Stephen Harrison (2000)—as a method of "self-fashioning": he adopts the moniker *Platonicus philosophus* to advertise "his brand" within this sophistic revival.[9] Anachronistic consumer and corporatist metaphors notwithstanding, this paradigm for reading the Apuleian corpus, which had its *floruit* in the late nineties and early aughts, has found few dissenters among literary scholars and has only recently been nudged (ever so slightly) in the direction of taking Apuleius's philosophical pretensions more seriously.[10]

Therefore, rather than performing another exercise in *Quellenforschung*, in which I piece together the sources which influenced Apuleius's unique syncretic doctrine of demonology,[11] I hope in this chapter to offer a response (albeit a partial one due to limitations of space) to the "self-fashioning" mode of criticism by demonstrating how carefully and meticulously this peripheral North African figure translated Plato into a specialized Latin discourse for his own native Carthaginian audience. By doing so, I suggest that Apuleius acts precisely as a *daemon* for his readers and listeners, manifesting or reincarnating Socrates, as it were, in his exegesis of Plato. Indeed, as I will argue, he plays an intermediary role in the very same way that Plato does vis-à-vis Socrates: just as Plato places a representation of Socrates and his absurd, "naked speeches" (*Symp.* 215c7) before our eyes and compels us to decide how we will engage with them—whether as laughable spectacle or divine intermediary—so also, Apuleius, in his role as Madauran Platonist and *Socrates Africanus*,[12] represents a version of philosophizing discourse for his own local audience—a discourse that is rhetorically rich and often ludic or ridiculous, but with the potential nonetheless for mediating the divine. In this respect, I pick up and expand on Richard Fletcher's analysis of Apuleius's "methodological Platonism."[13] However, whereas Fletcher elucidates how Apuleius understood himself to be working in a Platonic tradition—i.e., by labeling Apuleius's approach to Plato, as his subtitle suggests, "the impersonation of philosophy" (with all the theatrical baggage that the notion of "impersonation" entails)[14]—I intend to look carefully at Apuleius's precise and varied translations of some of the most famous demonological discussions in the Platonic corpus. How Apuleius adapts his language to the occasion—e.g., by quoting Latin epic refracted through the Roman philosophical tradition or by repurposing archaic Latin terms from Roman comedy—is invaluable for understanding his role as *interpres*, situated at a temporal and geographical crossroads in Imperial Latin and playing the role of intermediary of Platonic ideals for his own community.[15]

Interrogating the Source of the Divine: Plato's *Phaedrus* in *Soc.*

The best place to begin any analysis of Apuleius's Romanization of Plato's demonology is to look at his popularizing lecture *Soc.* delivered in Carthage at some point in the mid-second century CE.[16] However, rather than opening where most interpreters do—i.e., with an analysis of Apuleius's translation of the most famous passage on demonology from the *Symposium*[17]—I would like first to consider an unrecognized allusion to Plato's *Phaedrus*, which Apuleius weaves into the middle of his translation of the *Symposium*'s discussion of *daemones*.[18] For in the midst of offering a near-verbatim reworking of Diotima's refutation of Socrates, Apuleius digresses into a long tangent on oath-making. In a paradigmatic Romanization of Greek philosophy, Apuleius reinterprets Platonic demonology for his audience in terms of famous oaths made in Latin poetry (*Soc.* 5)—two from Vergil's *Aeneid* (i.e., Ascanius swearing by his own head and Mezentius swearing by his sword as a god)[19] and one from an otherwise unknown Ennian tragedy where a character swears by Jupiter.[20] Finally, Apuleius returns to his formal translation of the *Symposium* with the following segue (*Soc.* 5): *Quid igitur censes? Iurabo per Iovem lapidem Romano vetustissimo ritu? Atque si Platonis vera sententia est, numquam se deum cum homine communicare, facilius me audierit lapis quam Iuppiter.* ("What then do you think? Shall I swear by the Jupiter stone according to the most ancient Roman ritual? And if the opinion of Plato is true—namely that God himself never communicates with humans, then a stone could more easily hear me than Jupiter.")[21]

Key to this passage is the fact that Apuleius *seems* to be superimposing an ancient ritual practice familiar to a Latin-speaking audience—the "most ancient Roman ritual" of swearing by the Jupiter stone—onto the most well-known Platonic demonological treatment of antiquity. Translation is a cultural as well as a linguistic or semantic act. Thus, Apuleius strives to translate Plato not only word-for-word, but also in terms of religious practices and poetic references that are meaningful for his readers/listeners.[22]

However, in my view, Apuleius is simultaneously fusing onto Diotima's discussion of the *Symposium* another famous moment from the dialogues—namely, the close of the *Phaedrus*, where Socrates develops his paradoxical *Schriftkritik*.[23] Indeed, in a criticism of all forms of secondary representation, Socrates fashions a μῦθος about the invention of writing, and Phaedrus jests in a playful rebuttal that Socrates contrives "Egyptian tales" (*Phaedr.* 275b3–4: Αἰγυπτίους... λόγους) for pleasure. To this, Socrates responds (275b5–c1):

> But those [priests] in the shrine of Zeus Dodona, my friend, claimed that the first prophetic utterances came from an oak. Indeed, to the people in that time, insofar as they were not "wise" like you young folk today, it sufficed to listen to an oak or a stone because of their simplicity, if only it spoke the truth; but to you, perhaps it matters who the speaker is and where he is from.

οἱ δέ γ᾽, ὦ φίλε, ἐν τῷ τοῦ Διὸς τοῦ Δωδωναίου ἱερῷ δρυὸς λόγους ἔφησαν μαντικοὺς πρώτους γενέσθαι. τοῖς μὲν οὖν τότε, ἅτε οὐκ οὖσι σοφοῖς ὥσπερ ὑμεῖς οἱ νέοι, ἀπέχρη δρυὸς καὶ πέτρας ἀκούειν ὑπ᾽ εὐηθείας, εἰ μόνον ἀληθῆ λέγοιεν· σοὶ δ᾽ ἴσως διαφέρει τίς ὁ λέγων καὶ ποδαπός.

We will return to this passage again at the end of this chapter, as I argue that it informs the *daemonic* interpretation of the *Metamorphoses*.[24] Indeed, in a text that foregrounds the question of "who is speaking" (*Met.* 1.1: *quis ille?*; cf. τίς ὁ λέγων) and makes the geographical origins (cf. ποδαπός) of the narrative voice a suspiciously moving target for its readers, the "true words" (11.23: *quae vera sunt*) which Lucius speaks about the divine in the Isis-book are nonetheless ventriloquized through the mouthpiece of a "philosophizing ass" (10.33: *philosophantem nobis asinum*).

However, for now, it is worth spending a few moments meditating on Apuleius's particular method of mediating Platonic demonology here. In keeping with B. L. Hijmans's assessment of Apuleius as a translator/adaptor,[25] the performer of *Soc.* emphasizes human actors rather than abstract, metaphysical concepts. That is to say, whereas the priests of Jupiter in Plato's tale seek only to hear the voice of the divine and are willing to passively "listen to a stone" (πέτρας ἀκούειν) in order to discern the truth, Apuleius is concerned with the god's capacity to hear *his* voice and thus, he swears by a stone as an intermediary that will "hear [him] more easily than Jupiter" (*facilius me audierit lapis quam Iuppiter*). Indeed, reversing the direction of traffic between human and divine, Apuleius focuses on "our prayers and petitions" (*Soc.* 6: *hinc precum . . . hinc petitiones*) in order to reinterpret the Platonic *locus classicus* in a theological framework comprehensible to a Latin-speaking and broadly Roman audience.

However, just as Socrates rebuts Phaedrus's clever sophistry by alluding to archaic religious praxis, Apuleius too seeks to illuminate these mediators between the heavens and earth in terms of the "most ancient Roman ritual" (*Romano vetustissimo ritu*). For that reason, he quotes three important moments of oath-taking in Latin poetry, which (in the case of Vergil) juxtapose Trojan and Etruscan religious practices, and which hearken back to the earliest Roman (and proto-Roman) ideas about the gods.[26] Moreover, while the absurdity of Socrates's example relies on the "gullibility" (εὐήθεια)[27] of ancient priests—the same gullibility for which Lucius-*qua*-priest of Osiris is often criticized in the satirical school of interpretation of the *Met.*[28]—Apuleius sets up the ridiculous proposition of a *lapis* hearing his prayers more readily than Jupiter in order to "arrogate"—to borrow an oft-used term from Fletcher[29]—the role of "high priest" for his audience.[30]

In other words, whereas Plato himself is represented as a divinity of sorts in both *de Platone* (hereafter, *Pl.*) and *Soc.*—one born from divine parentage (*Pl.* 1.1) and "endowed with a heavenly eloquence, equal in his discourse with the gods" (*Soc.* 3.5: *caelesti facundia praeditus, aequiperabilia diis immortalibus disserens*)—Apuleius self-consciously plays the role of mediating that divine discourse for the masses. In this case, by alluding to the Jupiter stone and its ability to hear prayers in a context that evokes Plato's own priests of Zeus who would "listen to a stone" provided it spoke the truth, Apuleius sets the stage for his very next sentence in which he, as the "voice" (*Soc.*

6: *mea voce*) through which "Plato responds" (*responderit . . . Plato*) to hypothetical interlocutors, will function as *interpres* of Platonic truth. Although any form of representation is inadequate, according to Socrates's *Schriftkritik*, because it cannot defend itself from the attacks of putative interlocutors without "the help of its father" (*Phdr.* 275e4: τοῦ πατρὸς . . . βοηθοῦ), the Madauran Platonist offers the next best thing to *his* philosophical father—namely, speaking "on behalf of [Plato's] opinion" (*Soc.* 6: *pro sententia sua*).

In this context, we may compare how Apuleius polishes off his opening encomium to Plato's rhetorical transcendence in *Soc.*: he claims to "sing a retreat" (3.7: *receptui canam*) due to his "middling status" (*mediocritas*), and in turn, to "call his speech down from heaven to earth" (*tandem . . . orationem de caelo in terram devocabo*). In short, Apuleius himself exists in the "middle" between his philosophical master and his audience— where *mediocritas* highlights his didactic position in the *medietas loci* (cf. *Soc.* 9). His popularizing role, so often disparaged in criticism as a sign of unseriousness (cf. Swain's "playboy . . . hack" philosopher in n4 above), is in fact a method of using *oratio* to make the divine manifest "on earth." And it is worth noting here that *devocare* is a term used in Apuleius's philosophical and poetic predecessors of figures that hover in the space between humans and the divine.[31] In poetic discourse on magic, for instance, witches "call down" (*devocare*) spells from heaven.[32] But alternatively, in Cicero's archaeology of the origins of philosophy in the *Tusculan Disputations*, *devocare* is deployed to describe Socrates's unique mediating function in the evolution of the discipline: "Socrates . . . was the first to call down philosophy from heaven (*primus philosophiam devocavit e caelo*) and place it in the cities and even lead it into homes, forcing [people] to seek out answers about life and customs, and about good and evil" (*Tusc.* 5.10). Therefore, in *his* role of translating the divine Plato—of "calling *oratio* down from heaven to earth"—Apuleius hovers between magician and philosopher; and thus, he manifests in his performance in Carthage the same *persona* that Socrates himself had, not only in his reception in the Latin tradition (evidenced by Cicero's claim above), but also in the dialogues themselves.[33]

Translating *Daemones* into Latin/Roman

Apuleius's terminological discussion, in which he attempts to translate the Greek concept of a *daemon* for a Latin-speaking audience, is spread across two different philosophical treatises: *Pl.* introduces the issue but focuses primarily on the relationship between cosmology and demonology (i.e., the specific location of *daemones* in the cosmos); *Soc.*, on the other hand, elaborates in detail different names and origins in Latin for the Greek category of *daemones*, and in so doing, develops what Christopher Jones labels an "overly schematic" taxonomy for the Roman analogues to the Greek concept.[34] It is worth spending some time in this section breaking down the complex schema in order to appreciate more fully the protreptic impulse of *Soc.* and Apuleius's intermediary role in its performance.

I begin first, however, with Apuleius's cursory treatment of *daemones* in *Pl.* because there he appropriates an obscure, archaic Latin term from comedy to name this particular species of divinity: *medioximi*.[35] This term represents, on the one hand, a catch-all in Apuleius's framework for the multiple subcategories of *daemones* on which he will elaborate later in *Pl.* (and even more so in *Soc.*). But simultaneously, it emphasizes the cosmological and metaphysical position of these animate beings "in the middle." After elucidating the locations of the "highest god" and the second race of "heaven-dwellers" (*caelicolae*), such as the stars who live below the disembodied supreme deity, Apuleius explains (*Pl.* 1.11): "Those [divinities] hold the third place that the ancient Romans (*Romani veteres*) call 'middling' (*medioximos*) because they are less than the highest gods both in their reasoning (*ratione*) and in place and power (*loco et potestate*), but absolutely greater than the nature of humans." Just as we saw above in *Soc.*, where Apuleius reworks a Platonic intertext by reference to the "most ancient Roman ritual," so also here, he reaches back to an archaic term we find in Plautine comedy to translate a Platonic concept. Significantly, in Plautus's *Casket Comedy* or *Cistellaria* an *adulescens* swears an oath by "the gods and goddesses—the ones above, those below, and those in the middle" (*Cist.* 512: *di deaeque, superi atque inferi et medioxumi*). In other words, for Apuleius's broadest, all-encompassing category of *daemones*, he deploys terminology borrowed from the genre of comedy that, even to an erudite and elite reader, hearkens back to ancient Roman praxis of oath-swearing, and that simultaneously emphasizes through its etymology the "middling" nature of these divinities.[36]

Apuleius's discussion of *daemones* in *Pl.* does not end there. He further subcategorizes demons into *Genii* and *Lares*, which he explains are "ministers of the gods and guardians and interpreters for humans" (*Pl.* 1.12: *ministros deorum . . . custodesque hominum et interpretes*). And it is important to keep this cursory treatment from *Pl.* in mind, as the role of minister, guardian, and interpreter is slowly taken over by Apuleius in his exegetical role in *Soc.* (not to mention by Lucius in his priestly role in the *Met.*). But we should turn at this point to Apuleius's more schematized taxonomy in his attempt to translate the concept of *daemones* in *Soc.*, which is, by his own admission, an act of "interpretation" fraught with the potential for category confusion.[37]

Just as we saw above in the first section, Apuleius opens his Romanizing taxonomy of the Platonic *daemon* in *Soc.* likewise by quoting Latin poetry—once again, from book 9 of Vergil's *Aeneid*. Indeed, in explicating how every human soul has the capacity to become a good *daemon*, Apuleius quotes a passage from Vergil's *Doloneia* in which Nisus, the older lover in an idealized Platonic *erastēs*/*erōmenos* relationship,[38] questions the origins of and distinction between "passion" and "desire" (*Aen.* 9.185 [*Soc.* 15]): "do the gods put this passion (*hunc ardorem*) in our minds, Euryalus, or does one's own harsh desire (*dira cupido*) become a god to each person?" Significantly, Apuleius refers to this Vergilian distinction between negative and positive desires—itself an interpretation and dramatization of Diotima's *daemon* in the *Symposium*, *Erōs*—in order to distinguish bad *daemones* from good ones. And in its original context in the *Aeneid*, Nisus's question is already embedded in a long history of post-Homeric allegorical interpretation, which in this case is further shot through with Lucretian language about the power of *dira cupido*.[39] In other words, when Apuleius attempts to translate the Greek concept of *eudaimonia* into Latin by reference to its etymological root in the *daemon*,[40] it is significant that he does so once again by alluding to an archaic Roman tradition of appropriating Greek poetic and philosophical ideas, refracting Plato, as it were, through Lucretius and Vergil (*Soc.* 15): "some believe that the blessed are called *eudaemones* ... because their good daemon (*daemon bonus*)—that is to say, their soul (*animus*)—has been perfected with virtue (*virtute perfectus est*). In our language, as I **interpret** with a translation that is perhaps not good (*ut ego <u>interpretor</u>, haud sciam an bono*), but nonetheless something I'll hazard, you could call this [*daemon*] a *genius*."

Genii, which is one subcategory of *medioximi* in *Pl.*, is further subdivided in *Soc.* into the archaic Roman category of *Lemures*, which constitute souls that have "repudiated their bodies after finishing service in life" (*Soc.* 15: *emeritis stipendiis vitae corpori suo abiurans*). These, in turn, can be labeled *Lares* or *Larvae*, depending on their role and function in domestic life. However, generally indeterminate *daemones* are named *Manes Dei*, and importantly, these *Manes* are a global, transcultural phenomenon, from Amphiarus in Boeotia to Mopsus in Africa, from Osiris in Egypt to Asclepius everywhere (*Soc.* 15).

Once again, Apuleius's innovation here is not in developing a new approach to demonology or even in articulating it in a philosophically consistent or systematic way. Indeed, he acknowledges as much with the claim that his translation/interpretation is "perhaps no good" (*haud sciam an bono*). Rather, Apuleius's goal here is to render Platonic demonology into a discourse familiar to his audience by overlaying archaic Roman religious practice onto a Platonic superstructure; and moreover, he garners authority for doing so by grounding his discussion at the outset in Vergil's dramatization of idealized Platonic *Erôs*. Apuleius thus aims to offer a syncretic, transcultural, and popularizing portrait of how individuals, through the pursuit of philosophy, can be transformed themselves into *daemones*.

Most importantly, the human souls that "repudiate their bodies," and thereby become a species of *daemones*, set the stage both for Apuleius's own transformation, in which he takes up the mantel of *interpres* for Plato, and for the ultimate *daemonic* representative and central figure of his popularizing lecture: Socrates.[41] Indeed, *Soc.* adopts an elevated, didactic tone immediately after Apuleius has explicated his overly schematized taxonomy. At that point, he turns to his audience and exhorts them as follows (*Soc.* 16):

> Therefore, all of you who listen to this divine opinion of Plato, with me as his exegete (*me interprete*), form your souls (*animos ... formate*) in whatever you do and think in such a way that you know that a man keeps no secret from these guardians (*prae istis custodibus*), neither within his soul nor outside, but rather, that this [*daemon*] curiously partakes of all things: he sees all, he understands all, and

dwells within the very deepest recesses (*in ipsis penitissimis mentibus*) of [people's] minds, like a conscience.

The goal of *Soc.*, in short, is "(trans)formation" (*formate*) of the soul, which, if stripped of its external accidental features (e.g., "birth," "lineage," "wealth," etc.), can itself become a *daemon*. Therefore, after acting as Plato's priestly *interpres*, Apuleius turns to a series of *exempla*, which culminates in the figure of Socrates—a "man completely perfected and judged wise in the estimation of Apollo" (*Soc.* 17: *vir apprime perfectus et Apollinis quoque testimonio sapiens*). Socrates cultivated his *custos* to the point of calling it a *Lar familiaris* and eventually even became "equal [himself] to a most magnificent divinity" through the "dignity of his wisdom" (*Soc.* 20: *amplissimo numini sapientiae dignitas coaequarat*).

Thus, Apuleius displays the perfection of Socrates through cultivation of his *daemon* as a paradigm or protreptic model for his audience (*Soc.* 20–21):

> For nothing is more similar to god (*deo similius*) and more favorable than a man entirely good in soul (*vir animo perfecte bonus*), who surpasses other men more than he himself stands apart from the immortal gods. Why then are we not also raised up by the model and recollection (*exemplo et commemoratione*) of Socrates, and why don't we entrust ourselves to a favorable zeal for an equal philosophy, desiring to become similar to divinities (*similis numinum [c]aventes permittimus*)?[42]

In the end, the didactic impulse of *Soc.* is a familiar *topos* from Platonic discourse, and indeed, a popular(izing) motif in the Second Sophistic: ὁμοίωσις θεῷ (cf. *deo similius*).[43] Socrates achieved this "similarity to God," Apuleius explains, by intentionally cultivating his *daemon*—giving "care in accordance with zeal" (*Soc.* 21: *cura pro studio*), just as an athlete takes pains to look after the *membra* he uses to compete. Through such intentional habituation, Socrates eventually became an intermediary himself. So also, we readers of this text, Apuleius suggests, should pursue "the good life" (22: *bene vivere*) by disregarding all "externals" (*aliena*)—i.e., "nobility" (23: *generositas*), "lineage" (*prosapia*), "forebears" (*natales*), "wealth" (*divitiae*), and any other accidental features of life—and in turn, by cultivating an "oath of allegiance to philosophy" (22: *philosophiae sacramentum*).

This analysis represents, once again, a complex fusion and brilliant Romanization of the Platonic project. For on the one hand, *aliena* is a key term in the New Comic discourse of πολυπραγμοσύνη/*curiositas*—a discourse inherited, we may note, from the Aristophanic sycophant in *Acharnians* and *Plutus*; the term thus recurs often in moralizing contexts in Plautus and Terence.[44] However, the rejection of *aliena* (or in Greek, ἀλλότρια)[45] also represents a foundational principle of the Platonic project, both in Socrates's own defense of himself (*Apol.* 19b), where he denies a charge of meddlesomeness, and in his pursuit of self-knowledge and attempt to define justice in other dialogues. Socrates's interpretation of the Delphic oracle's famous dictum in the *Phaedrus*, for instance, is phrased in terms of not "inspecting those things outside of oneself" (*Phdr.* 230a1: τὰ ἀλλότρια σκοπεῖν). Moreover, in the *Republic*, one of the primary definitions of justice is "to be busy with one's own affairs, and not to play the busybody" (*Resp.* 433a8–b1: τὸ τὰ αὑτοῦ πράττειν καὶ μὴ πολυπραγμονεῖν); in a well-balanced soul, this means "not busying one's self with other people's business" (*Resp.* 443d2: μὴ ... τἀλλότρια πράττειν).⁴⁶ However, Socrates's defense for his own πολυπραγμοσύνη in the *Apology*, as Matthew Leigh has shown,⁴⁷ is derived from Old Comedy's obsession with busybodies and sycophants—from Dicaeopolis's individual market which excludes πολυπράγμονες from participation in *Acharnians*, to the play with sycophants and justice in *Plutus*. Thus, in filtering Plato through the genre of Roman comedy, Apuleius reproduces—or we may say, *represents*—a procedure that Plato himself deployed vis-à-vis comedy. Indeed, in his closing *exemplum* of the *daemonic* Socrates in *Soc.*, Apuleius replicates Plato's incorporation of Aristophanic comedy into his rejection of *aliena* by rephrasing the introspective pursuit of the Platonic project in the language of Roman comedy, and moreover, by appealing to exemplarity (a fundamentally Roman concept with origins also in New Comedy).⁴⁸ In so doing, he again plays *interpres* for his Carthaginian audience, translating Platonism into a discourse familiar to them, exhorting them to pursue ὁμοίωσις θεῷ through exemplarity, and finally, embodying or manifesting Socrates in his performance of a thoroughly Roman demonology.

QUAEDAM DIVINAE MEDIAE POTESTATES: THE *DAEMONIC* READING OF THE *METAMORPHOSES*

In the previous two sections, I set out to demonstrate that Apuleius's innovation in demonology lies not so much in any doctrinal developments or systematic philosophical articulation, but rather in his unique reframing of a Platonic tradition in a thoroughly Romanized (and especially Roman comic) discourse. Living himself on the periphery of the Roman empire and writing in a hybridized, "African"-inflected style of Latin, Apuleius embodies the role of *daemon* in his status as local philosopher and translator of a foreign philosophical tradition. In this sense, much like Cicero's Socrates, the Madauran Platonist "calls philosophy down from heaven" (*Soc.* 3: *orationem de caelo ... devocabo*; cf. *Tusc.* 5.10: *philosophiam devocavit e caelo*). Given more space, one could trace this intermediary role across the rest of Apuleius's corpus, showing, for instance, how he disregards "externals" (*aliena*) in the *Apology*,⁴⁹ such as beauty and wealth, and ultimately reveals his own religious cultivation of a *daemon* in the form of his "little statuette of Mercury."⁵⁰

However, with the limited space that remains, I may only gesture toward a *daemonic* reading of Apuleius's burlesque novel, the *Met.*, where a self-styled philosophical narrator⁵¹ is transformed into an ass and endures many trials and travails until he finally reaches Cenchreae and undergoes an unanticipated conversion to the Egyptian goddess Isis. A holistic reading of the *Met.* would, for instance, account for the many intermediary *daemones*, often in the form of surrogate goddesses, that offer Lucius at least partial access to the divine. The statuary ensemble in Byrrhena's atrium is a case in point: according to Lucius-*auctor*, the central figure in the display, a Parian marble statue of Diana, holds "the middle of the whole place in balance" (*Met.* 2.4: *libratam totius loci medietatem*). Significantly, our asinine narrator uses the same phrasing here that Apuleius himself uses in *Soc.* to exemplify how a *daemon* might inhabit a "balanced middle" (*Soc.* 10: *librata medietas*) in the realm between heaven and earth. Lucius characteristically misses the warning or prophetic value of this mediating *daemon*,[52] but the opportunity for him to encounter the goddess is nevertheless available and accessible to him through the statuary ensemble.[53] It is no coincidence, moreover, that in every subsequent encounter with a surrogate goddess in the *Met.*, the representation of the divine is placed emphatically in the "middle" of Lucius's field of vision, thereby dramatizing in narrative form *Soc.*'s demonological doctrine (cf. *Soc.* 6: *quaedam divinae mediae potestates*).[54] However, most important to the *daemonic* reading of the *Met.* is the fact that, in Lucius's first initiation to Isis, we readers—much like the audience of viewers *inside* of the novel—encounter the recently retransformed ass-man set up as a *simulacrum* together with a representation of Isis "in the very middle of the sacred temple" (11.24: *in ipso aedis sacrae meditullio*).[55] Lucius becomes, in short, a *daemon* together with Isis— both of them standing on a pedestal and representing *simulacra deorum*.

Now, I do not naïvely suggest without qualification that Lucius encounters these divinities sincerely and has a legitimate (or unproblematic) religious experience or conversion.[56] However, I would venture to propose that Apuleius, by representing Lucius as a *daemon* at the close of the novel, is once again playing the role of Platonic *interpres* for his local community—in this case, by inviting us to meditate on a self-styled (albeit buffoonish) Socrates and thereby forcing us to choose how we will respond to the implicit demands of the novel. Indeed, I have argued elsewhere that the stripping of Lucius's ass hide in book 11, taken together with this closing scene in his initiation to Isis, reenacts the portrait of Socrates at the close of the *Symposium*, where the philosopher is stripped of his asinine exterior and reveals "statues of gods" (215b3: ἀγάλματα. . . .θεῶν) buried within.[57] Here, at the close of Apuleius's masterwork, we likewise encounter an *actual* ass stripped of his hide in order to reveal *simulacra deorum* standing "in the middle" of *our* field of vision.

In my view, then, the portrait of the converted and retransformed ass-man declaiming in Rome as a priest of his *daemones*, Isis and Osiris, functions as yet another intermediary for Apuleius's readers. Whether or not we interpret Lucius's conversion as a sincere expression of religious transformation, the mediating *pastophoros*—"guarding the holiest divinity" (*Met.* 11.25: *numen . . . sanctissimum . . . custodiens*) like a *daemonic custos* deep within "the secret places of his heart" (*intra pectoris mei secreta*) and thus dramatizing the principle of *Soc.* that *daemones* "live in the very deepest recesses of people's minds" (*Soc.* 16: *in ipsis penitissimis mentibus . . . deversetur*)—translates, once again, the figure of Socrates into a context familiar and accessible to a Madauran readership.

Therefore, I would like to close this chapter with a reading of Lucius as a *daemonic* figure, and to do so, I turn to the much-debated final line of the *Met*. In a well-known problem of anticlosure,[58] Lucius moves to Rome, where he has a third initiation to the cult of Osiris. He shaves his head once again and travels about the capital of the empire in a seemingly delusory joy (11.30): *Rursus denique quaqua raso capillo collegii vetustissimi et sub illis Sullae temporibus conditi munia, non obumbrato uel obtecto calvitio, sed quoquoversus obvio, gaudens* **obibam** ("Finally, with my head once again shaven completely and with my baldness neither covered up nor hidden, but exposed wherever I went, I was joyfully **fulfilling** the duties of that ancient priesthood, which was established in the time of Sulla").

While there is much to say about this notoriously problematic ending—Lucius's baldness, for instance, seems at odds with his earlier obsession with hair (cf. *Met.* 2.9) and leaves him hovering ambivalently between a serious portrait of Socrates and a buffoonish mime actor[59]—I only have the space here to focus on the final verb of the text, *obibam*, the tense and meaning of which have provided a cornerstone to the deconstructionist and satirical readings of book 11.

On the one hand, the imperfect tense of *obibam*—which seems an *à propos* anticlosure for a novel that opens in medias res (1.1: *at ego*)[60]—has provided fodder to those who see Lucius's multiple initiations as a satirical statement about his gullibility and susceptibility to greedy priests.[61] The process of Lucius's transformation remains incomplete, and thus continues beyond the bounds of the text.[62] But more importantly for interpreters who take a more skeptical view of Lucius's redemption in book 11, a semantic possibility for the verb *obire*—"to die"—*seems* to be at play, thereby associating conversion with death. This reading has found favor especially with scholars who want to see something of a literary *sphragis*, where *obibam* (*Met.* 15.879) functions as an inverted allusion to the closing verb of Ovid's *Metamorphoses—vivam* ("I will live").[63]

However, as the Groningen commentators note, this semantic valence of *obire* can at best be secondary here, since it is "grammatically impossible."[64] Indeed, in the context of this sentence, *obibam* takes *munia* as its direct object, thus complicating the primary idiom associating *obire* with "death,"[65] which the satirical interpretation of Lucius's conversion requires. Instead, it must mean something like "to fulfill one's duties," as I have translated above.[66] Therefore, rather than reaching back to Ovid's *Metamorphoses* for an inverted intertext that makes little contextual sense (except as a literary *sphragis*), we may cite as a meaningful *comparandum* a passage within Apuleius's own corpus: namely, the conclusion of *Soc*.'s translation of the *Symposium*, in which Apuleius explicates how *daemones* are tasked with various "duties, works, and cares" (*Soc.* 7.1: *munus atque opera atque cura*)[67] to carry out the will of "heavenly divinities." Indeed, after explicating how different *daemones* have various (Roman?) *provinciae*—some being tasked with sending dreams, while others manipulate entrails or bird omens, etc.—Apuleius explains (*Soc.* 7.3): *Quae omnia, ut dixi, mediae quaepiam potestates inter homines ac deos obeunt* ("All of these are duties which, as I have said, certain intermediary powers between men and gods **fulfill**").

Although it has gone curiously overlooked, the primary antecedent of *quae* here is the phrase *munus atque opera atque cura*, which is expanded on with specific examples thereafter. In other words, the very idiom with which Apuleius ambiguously concludes *Met.* in an anticlosural gesture—"to fulfill one's duties" for a divinity (*munia . . . obire*)—functions as the closural device for Apuleius's translation and exposition of the *Symposium*'s demonological doctrine. Taking other instances of this idiom in Apuleius into account,[68] in sum, Lucius exists at the end of *Met.* precisely "between men and gods" in his role as a member of the *pastophori* and a priest in the *collegium* of Isis. Bald like Socrates and uncovering his head in a Platonic gesture of revelation,[69] he embodies both a buffoonishly laughable philosopher and a *simulacrum dei*—the very same spectacle that Plato puts on display in the figure of Socrates vis-à-vis the audience of the *Symposium* at Agathon's banquet. In that dialogue, which most clearly articulates Plato's demonological doctrine, Socrates becomes the mouthpiece for Diotima's discussion of *Erôs* as a *daemon* and is, in turn, eventually transformed in Alcibiades' speech into a *daemonic* embodiment of *Erôs*, traveling around shoeless and mediating ἀγάλματα θεῶν for Plato's readers.[70] So also, Lucius closes out the *Met.* performing the very same function for Apuleius's Carthaginian audience—"fulfilling his duties" as a seriocomic spectacle. If we so choose, we can look on and laugh, along with the *populus* inside of the text who "wander around [the spectacle] for a glance" (11.24: *in aspectum populus errabat*); or alternatively, we can strive to see the divine representations hiding underneath.

Conclusion

In the end, this inevitably brings me back to Socrates's praise of the priests of Dodona in the *Phaedrus*, to which, as we saw above in section 1, Apuleius obliquely alludes in *Soc.*'s translation of Diotima's demonology. For we may recall, it is only the "wise" (σοφοί) who concern themselves with "who is speaking" (τίς ὁ λέγων) and "where s/he is from" (ποδαπός); those ancient priests of Jupiter, however, through "simplicity/gullibility" (εὐήθεια), do not concern themselves with such "externals"—details figured as ἀλλότρια in the Platonic corpus (or *aliena* in Apuleius's). For decades now, Apuleius scholars have been trying desperately to establish precisely "who is speaking" (1.1: *quis ille?*)[71] the *fabulae* of *Met.* and where s/he is from. The text begins with a character claiming an elite and erudite background, with "ancient lineage" (1.1: *vetus prosapia*) in the great cultures of Athens, Sparta, and Corinth, with educational credentials and philosophical affiliations to boot (1.2), and with noteworthy external beauty recognizable to everyone.[72] Lucius-*actor*, however, is stripped of all these external features—the same "externals" labeled *aliena* in *Soc.*: the priest of Isis notes in his interpretation of books 1–10 that Lucius's "birth" (*natales*), "nobility" (*dignitas*), and "education" (*doctrina*) did not benefit him on his journey (11.15). And in fact, even within the text, Lucius's cultural affiliation—his *vetus prosapia*, which includes Plutarch, a philosopher who also wrote about demonology (*Met.* 1.2)—shifts imperceptibly from the most famous ancient cities of Greece to a rather insignificant town in North Africa. Indeed, in a notorious problem of inconsistency, Lucius-*actor* in book 11 is unexpectedly labeled "a very poor man from Madauros" (11.27: *Madaurensem, sed admodum pauperem*),[73] thus exposing the chasm between the narrator of 1.1 and the character meandering around Corinth and Rome at the end of book 11.

Rather than obsessively focusing on "who is speaking" and "where s/he is from," as the "wise" scholars of the deconstructionist tradition do, the *daemonic* reading of Lucius's transformation compels us to search for what is true in the text, even if it is spoken by a "rock" or an "oak"—or, according to Lucius's own phrasing, by a "philosophizing ass" (10.33). Moreover, on a cultural level, by shifting this "Greek-ish tale" (1.1: *fabulam Graecanicam*) into a Roman discourse and one accessible to a Latin-speaking North African audience—indeed, even paradoxically transposed onto a Madauran narrator at the end of the story—Apuleius is once again functioning as philosophical *daemon* for his Carthaginian readers. By stripping the ass-man of his external hide and revealing (even if ironically) the *simulacra deorum* underneath, Apuleius is putting on display an alternative paradigm of ὁμοίωσις θεῷ, inviting us in a different way to undergo our own transformation. Perhaps the meaningful question, then, is not "who is speaking?" but rather, "who is reading?"

Notes

1. On Apuleius's life and background, see Harrison (2000) 1–10 (with bibliography). On Apuleius's liminal identity, see *Apol.* 24, where he famously claims to be "half Numidian" and "half Gaetulian" (*seminumidam . . . semigaetulum*). Apuleius not only had a likely educational pilgrimage to Athens but also spent significant time in Rome (see *Fl.* 17). If Filippo Coarelli's thesis is correct (Coarelli (1989); cf. Beck (2000) and Graverini (2012) 68–69 for assessment), he may have owned a villa in Ostia.
2. On Apuleius's "African-ness" in general, see Lee, Finkelpearl, and Graverini (2014); on *Africitas*, in particular, see the contribution of Silvia Mattiacci in that volume (Mattiacci (2014)).
3. The most comprehensive treatment of the reception of demonology in Middle Platonism to date is Timotin (2012). See also Dillon (2004) and Donini (2004) for two targeted studies of reception. Moreschini (1989) and (2015) 117–145 are also invaluable. On Apuleius's influence on Calcidius (and the Latin tradition), see Karfíková (2004); cf. also Reydams-Schils (2020).
4. On Apuleius and "popular" philosophy, see now Moreschini (2015) 29–57 (with bibliography). Swain's tongue-in-cheek assessment of Apuleius remains *en vogue*: "[Apuleius] was a showman and a playboy, clever but shallow. . . . Intellectual vanity made him write a hack account of *Socrates and His Deity*. Finally, his talents found a legitimate outlet in a comic novel about a man's life as an ass (the *Metamorphoses*)" (Swain (2001) 269). Cf. Dillon (1977) xiii for a withering assessment of Middle Platonism as a whole. However, for a useful recent reassessment of Apuleius's philosophical credentials, see Roskam (2017).

5. On the comparison of which, see Moreschini (1989), Trapp (2007), and Benson (2016).
6. Consider Dillon's lukewarm regard for Apuleius: "we must always bear in mind . . . that Apuleius, despite his protestations, is not a philosopher" (Dillon (1977) 311). Cf. also Trapp (2007).
7. See August. *De civ. D.* 8 and 9 for Augustine's lengthy polemic against Apuleius (on which, see Karfíková (2004)).
8. For the first proponents of this view, see Sandy (1997) and Harrison (2000). Indeed, Sandy labels Apuleius an *Orator/Philosophus Sophisticus Latinus*. But these labels have started to mutate and verge on the ridiculous, such as Núñez's "Apuleius: Orator Metasophisticus" (Núñez (2009)). For a nuanced and thorough corrective, see Moreschini (2015) 29-57.
9. Harrison does, indeed, use the language of marketing in his discussion of "self-fashioning" (e.g., (2000) 7, where he labels the *Apologia* "an impressive advertisement of Apuleius's talents as a public speaker"). Even in more recent discussions, Apuleius scholars still speak, e.g., of Apuleius's "idiosyncratic *brand* of Platonism" (Fletcher (2014) 7; my italics).
10. See, e.g., Fletcher (2014), Moreschini (2015), and Benson (2016) and (2019). On Apuleius's Platonism in general and in *Soc.* in particular, see Hijmans (1987) and Habermehl (1996), who offer more sympathetic readings. Cf. also Roskam (2017).
11. The *Quellenforschung* approach to Apuleius's demonology has already been thoroughly covered and there is no need to rehash the doctrinal origins here. See, e.g., Dillon (1977) 317-320, Gersh (1986) 228-236, Donini (2004) (together with Dillon (2004)), Timotin (2012) 112-120 and 259-286, and Moreschini (2015) 117-145. Beaujeu (1973) 3-18 also remains indispensable. On comparison of Apuleius's and Maximus of Tyre's demonological treatments, see Trapp (2007) and Benson (2016). On Apuleius's and Plutarch's demonology, see Moreschini (1989).
12. On which, see Riess (2008).
13. Fletcher (2014) *passim* for the phrase.
14. See, e.g., Fletcher (2014) 16-20, in which he explores the "theatrical concept" of impersonation, "whereby the ideas of acting and remaining yourself, of performing and living, remain in constant tension" (p. 16). Moreover, for Fletcher, the concept of an "impersonator" also functions "as shorthand for imposter," which explains why skeptical criticism on Apuleius's philosophical credentials abounds. For my own critique of Fletcher's evasive elision of Plato himself in his study of "Apuleius's Platonism," see Ulrich (2016) 318.
15. As may be clear from my introduction, I am more sympathetic in my interpretation of *Soc.* to readers such as Habermehl (1996) and Hoenig (2018). That Apuleius plays the role of *daemon* for his readers aligns, to a certain extent, with the overall approaches of Fletcher (2014) and Benson (2019).
16. On the original performance context and Latin-speaking audience for the lecture, see Harrison (2000) 136-140, who proposes that it was likely delivered in Carthage in the 160s (in the same period as the *Florida*).
17. See *Soc.* 6 and *Symp.* 202e. See, e.g., Dillon (2004) 123-124 on the special significance of this passage from the *Symp.* for the demonological tradition.
18. On Apuleius's method of fusing passages from dialogues together, see the careful analysis of Hoenig (2018) 121-124. From a doctrinal stance, this method of fusion was already recognized by Gersh (1986) 229-230.
19. See *Aen.* 9.300: *per caput hoc iuro, per quod pater ante solebat*; and *Aen.* 10.773-774: *Dextra mihi deus et telum, quod missile libro—nunc adsint!*
20. See fr. 184, Jocelyn (1967) 147: *o Fides alma apta pinnis et ius iurandum Iovis*.

21. All translations in this chapter are my own. Latin text of Apuleius's *philosophica* comes from Magnaldi (2019); that of the *Met.* from Zimmerman (2012).
22. Indeed, as Harrison (2000) 138–139 notes, most of Apuleius's quotations to garner authority in *Soc.* come from distinguished Latin writers, and the one quotation from Homer is "ostentatiously" delivered via Apuleius's *Latin* translation.
23. It is no stretch of the imagination to believe Apuleius alludes to this episode from the *Phaedrus* in the midst of his exposition of the *Symposium*. This moment from the *Phaedrus* is generally agreed to have influenced Apuleius's representation of the *Met.* as written on an "Egyptian papyrus" (*Met.* 1.1: *papyrum Aegyptiam*): see, e.g., Trapp (2001), Kirichenko (2008), and Ulrich (2017).
24. Cf. Benson (2019) 28–61, who offers the attractive suggestion that the elusive narrative voice of the *Met.* is meant to be *daemonic* in its invisible, yet intermediary function for the reader.
25. Hijmans (1987) 399–406.
26. For instance, in Cicero's testimonium, whence we find the Ennius fragment (*Off.* 3.104), he connects it to the ancient "faith" (*fides*) that "[Roman] ancestors" (*maiores nostri*) placed in the Capitoline Jupiter.
27. Admittedly, I am translating εὐήθεια tendentiously here. However, even within the Platonic corpus, the distinction between "simplicity" (as here) and "gullibility" is a matter of perspective. Thus, Thrasymachus in *Resp.* 1 snidely refers to justice as "a very 'noble' simplicity" (348c10: πάνυ γενναίαν εὐήθειαν).
28. See, e.g., van Mal-Maeder (1997) and Harrison (2000) 238–252 on Lucius's gullibility (on which, more below).
29. For this phrasing, see Fletcher (2014) 17 (*et passim*).
30. See now Hoenig (2018) 108–112 on Apuleius's role as "high priest" for the divine Plato.
31. On which, see *TLL* 5.1.868.55–60.
32. Thus, the narrative voice of Tib. 1.2 waxes poetic about the capacity of the *saga* to "call bones forth" (1.2.48: *devocat ossa*) from a funeral pyre, and that of Hor. *Epod.* 17 begs Canidia to use the books of her songs "to pluck out the stars and call them down from the sky" (*Epod.* 17.5: *refixa caelo devocare sidera*).
33. It is worth recalling that Socrates is labeled a magician or "sorcerer" (γόης) in *Meno* (80b) and is said by Alcibiades in the *Symposium* to have an enchanting and overpowering effect on his listeners (215c–d). See Belfiore (1980) for discussion.
34. See Jones (2017) 378n29. Fuller discussion can be found in Dillon (1977) 319–320, who traces the origins of Apuleius's schema.
35. For a comprehensive discussion of Apuleius's use of this term, see Fowler (2016) 171–172 (with n126). The only other extant attestation of this word prior to Apuleius appears in a vexed fragment from Varro's *Menippean Satires* (*apud* Non. 141), where the narrator speaks of the Delphic oracle's proclamations.
36. It is interesting to speculate that *medioximi* may have been Plautus's translation of the Greek original *daemones*, as the *Cist.* is one of the few Plautine plays for which we have a definitive and single Menandrean original. In short, Apuleius may be appropriating Plautus's Latin translation for his broadest category of demons.
37. I should note here that, while *interpres/interpretari* are words regularly used for "translator" and for "translation" from one language to another (*TLL* 7.1.2262.31–2263.3), the primary meaning of these terms concerns exegesis and interpretation (*TLL* 7.1.2258.25–51, where *interpretari* is labeled *i. q. explicare, intellegere, accipere*); in my view, Apuleius

self-consciously plays in both of his demonological treatments with the slippage between these two meanings. Hence, the term *interpretes* which he uses for *daemones* (*Pl.* 1.12; *Soc.* 6) functions as his translation of the Platonic ἑρμηνεῖς (*Symp.* 202e)—a concept that clearly has as much to do with exegesis as it does with translation.

38. On the origins of Nisus's and Euryalus's love in Plato's *Symp.*, see Makowski (1989).
39. See Hardie (1994) 109 *ad loc. Aen.* 9.184–185 for discussion of post-Homeric allegorical readings and of Lucretian echoes.
40. As Dillon (1977) 319 notes, Apuleius inherited this notion from Xenocrates's etymological derivation of εὐδαίμων (fr. 81 Heinze) and shares this "commonplace" association with Albinus.
41. Harrison (2000) 139 interestingly points out that Apuleius has reversed the order of his exposition from that of Maximus of Tyre in *Or.* 8, who begins his lecture with Socrates's relationship with his δαιμονίον as a case study from which to extrapolate. Apuleius, perhaps for didactic purposes, concludes with the *exemplum* of Socrates as an exhortation to the study of philosophy, which Fletcher (2014) 168–171 views as a rhetorically protreptic maneuver.
42. There is a textual issue in this second sentence, but I follow the text of Magnaldi's recent edition (2019). For fuller analysis of the textual and interpretive issues at stake in this line, see my review of the new OCT in Ulrich (2021). The conjecture by Beaujeu (1973) 41 *ad loc.* of *similitudini numinum* for the closing phrase is attractive, however, insofar as it strengthens the connection to the Middle Platonic appropriation of ὁμοίωσις θεῷ (on which, see below).
43. The *locus classicus* in Platonic discourse is *Tht.* 176b–c. On its reception in Middle Platonic discourse, see Donini (2004) 144. See also Fowler (2017) 224–225 (with footnotes) for all the references to the *Theatetus* passage in the Second Sophistic.
44. See Leigh (2013) *passim*, but esp. 60–65 on the Roman comic realization of the *curiosus*. See also Labhardt (1960) 206–207 (cited by Leigh (2013) 62n43).
45. See *TLL* 1.1567.21, which glosses *alienum* with the Greek ἀλλότριον.
46. The *Republic*'s discourse of πολυπραγμοσύνη and its influence on Middle Platonism (and Apuleius's *Met.* in particular) has been well treated by DeFilippo (1990).
47. Leigh (2013) 30–34.
48. See, e.g., Cicero's assessment of the value of comedy, a *locus classicus* on comic production of *exempla* (*QRosc.* 47): "for I think that [comic plots] were fashioned by the poets in such a way that we see our habits (*nostros mores*) represented in the *personae* of others (*in alienis personis*) and we see, as it were, the expression of an image of our daily life." On the value of Terence's characters as moral *exempla* in later antiquity, see Müller (2013) 374–377.
49. Cf. *Apol.* 16, where Apuleius mocks his accuser for "tracking down the faults of others" (*aliena indagare*), again deploying the Platonic discourse of ἀλλότρια.
50. See *Apol.* 64, where he links his *sigillum dei* to the "upper realm" of Plato's *Phaedrus*. In my current book project, I give a fuller treatment of the demonological elements of the *Apology*.
51. Cf., e.g., *Met.* 1.2, where Lucius-*auctor* claims Plutarch and Sextus as his forebears.
52. In case we readers miss the prophetic value of the atrium scene, Byrrhena famously spells it out in 2.5 with her exegesis for Lucius: "everything you see is yours" (2.5: *tua sunt... cuncta quae vides*). Winkler (1985) 168 calls this phrase "a lovely ambiguity, read as hospitable by the first-reader, as ominous by the second-reader." See also James (1987) 128, who notes that "Actaeon's fate, brought about by an illicit curiosity, prefigures Lucius's unfortunate

transformation." Cf. Heath (1992) 102–121 for a thorough discussion of Lucius's impending Actaeonic fate.

53. That we are to read Lucius's gazing in this way is reinforced by an Apuleian coinage—*rimabundus*—used of Lucius's gawking at the statue of Diana. The only other extant occurrence of this term in Latin is found in *Soc.*, when Apuleius describes how we ought to contemplate the gods (*Soc.* 2): *intellectu eos rimabundi. . . .<contemplamur>*. Many have also seen in the statue of Diana a foreshadowing of Lucius's relationship with Isis, either sincerely (see, e.g., Laird (1997)) or satirically (e.g., Slater (1998)).

54. Indeed, all the goddesses who appear to Lucius thereafter—Epona (3.27), Venus (10.32), and Isis (11.24)—are viewed "in the middle of his field of vision." A fuller treatment will again be found in my current book project.

55. We may add to this list of "middling" divinities, which Lucius encounters, the divine palace (*regia*) of Cupid at the opening of *Met.* 5, which is said to be situated in the "midmost middle of the grove" (5.1: *medio luci meditullio*) and to have been built "not by human hands, but by divine arts" (*non humanis manibus sed divinis artibus*).

56. The sincerity of Lucius's conversion is an issue far beyond the scope of this chapter. For a survey of recent approaches to the Isis book, see Keulen et al. (2015) 2–8. See also Benson (2019) 184–238, who offers an interesting attempt to reframe the debate, and also contains most of the relevant bibliography.

57. See Ulrich (2017) 220–228.

58. On which, see Finkelpearl (2004).

59. Lucius's baldness has long caused interpreters consternation. Winkler (1985) 224–227 read it as an ambivalent marker, which signals either a sincere initiate of Isis or a buffoonish mime. Cf. Egelhaaf-Gaiser (2012) and Ulrich (2017) 726–727, who see a Socratic resonance in Lucius's closing baldness.

60. On the Platonic gesture of the in medias res opening, see de Jonge (2001) and Ulrich (2017) 728–729. On the relationship between the Prologue's *at ego* and the concluding chapter, see Laird (2001). On the way in which the closing chapters of book 11 compel a "cyclical reading" in a manner akin to Plato's *Resp.*, see Ulrich (2020) 692–693.

61. See esp. van Mal-Maeder (1997), Harrison (2000) 238–252, Murgatroyd (2004), Libby (2011), and MacDougall (2016), all of whom emphasize that Lucius appears in the closing chapters of book 11 to be a dupe suffering at the hands of manipulative religious authorities.

62. In fact, in Winkler's narratological reading of the *Met.*, the imperfect functions as a knowing "taunt" to the reader about the chasm between the recently converted Lucius and the narrating Lucius (see Winkler (1985) 224, citing Callebat (1968) 500 on "*le sourire complice du narrateur*"). See Penwill (1990) 24n70 for skepticism about the limits of Winkler's narratological approach in this reading. Cf. also Finkelpearl (2004) for a more balanced interpretation of the multiple epilogues.

63. See, e.g., Penwill (1990) 24n70. Tilg (2014) 144–145 pushes the interpretation that this is a *sphragis*.

64. See Keulen et al. (2015) 516 *ad loc.* 11.30 for the admission that one cannot read *obire* here with the semantic valence of "death." See also Finkelpearl (2004).

65. The idiom is derived from the phrase *obire mortem* (on which, see *TLL* 9.2.46.16–48) and develops an intransitive usage in later Latin (*TLL* 9.2.48.45–50), but *neither* usage makes sense in our context in the Isis book.

66. Cf. *TLL* 9.2.47.19–41. Cf. Winkler (1985) 224, who feels the need to translate *obibam* twice (i.e., "I was performing the duties. . . .I was. . . .going about") in order to obviate his overreading.
67. I depart from Magnaldi (2019) 17 here, as she brackets [*atque opera*] with little explanation.
68. This idiom would also be fresh in the reader's mind, as Lucius deploys it a few chapters earlier (11.22): *obibam culturae sacrorum ministerium*. Fulfilling *ministerium*, we may recall, is a primary function of *daemones* in *Soc*.
69. In my book, I treat Lucius's baldness as a specific revelatory Platonic gesture—alluding, as it does, to the moment in the *Phaedrus* when Socrates uncovers his head before delivering a Palinode—and I argue that this line demands a cyclical, or "Palinodic," reading from us.
70. For a particularly useful analysis of how Socrates comes to embody the role of Erôs in *Symposium*, see Sheffield (2006) 187–188.
71. The *quis ille?* of the Prologue has also been a thorny issue for scholars. See Keulen (2007) 11–13 for a thorough treatment of the *status quaestionis*. For my part, I am attracted to Fletcher's solution that this "reads as a rephrasing of basic issues of impersonation at the heart of philosophical writing and identity" (Fletcher (2014) 266–267), and I believe it can be further read as a Platonic gesture of symposiastic dialectic (see Ulrich (2017) 729–730).
72. See *Met*. 2.2, where Byrrhena describes Lucius's beautiful external appearance. See also Keulen (2006), who analyzes how Lucius's beauty perfectly accords with the requirements of physiognomic treatises in the Second Sophistic.
73. See Keulen et al. (2015) 465–467 for a comprehensive state of the scholarship. However, I know of no one who has suggested a reader-response approach, in which the sudden shift in identity incorporates the local Madauran reader. I expand on this proposal more fully in my book.

References

Agoustakis, A., and A. Traill, eds. (2013). *A Companion to Terence*. (Malden, Mass.).
Baltes, M., and M. -L. Lakmann, eds. (2004). *Über den Gott des Sokrates*. (Darmstadt).
Beaujeu, J. (1973). *Apulée: Opuscules Philosophiques (du dieu de Socrate, Platon et sa Doctrine, du Monde)*. (Paris).
Beck, R. (2000). "Apuleius the Novelist, Apuleius the Ostian Householder, and the Mithraeum of the Seven Spheres: Further Explorations of a Hypothesis of Filippo Coarelli," in Wilson and Desjardins, 551–557.
Belfiore, E. (1980). "'Elenchus, Epode,' and Magic: Socrates as Silenus." *Phoenix* 34(2): 128–137.
Benson, G. (2016). "Seeing Demons: Autopsy in Maximus of Tyre's *Oration* 9 and Its Absence in Apuleius' *On the God of Socrates*." *Ramus* 45(1): 102–131.
Benson, G. (2019). *Apuleius' Invisible Ass: Encounters with the Unseen in the* Metamorphoses. (Cambridge).
Callebat, L. (1968). *Sermo Cotidianus dans les Métamorphoses d'Apulée*. (Caen).
Coarelli, F. (1989). "Apuleio a Ostia?." *DArch* 7: 27–42.
DeFilippo, J. (1990). "*Curiositas* and the Platonism of Apuleius' *Golden Ass*." *AJPh* 111(4): 471–492.
de Jong, I. (2001). "The Prologue as a Pseudo-Dialogue and the Identity of its (Main) Speaker," in Kahane and Laird, 201–212.
Dillon, J. M. (1977). *The Middle Platonists: 80 B.C. to A.D. 220*. (Ithaca, N.Y.).

Dillon, J. M. (2004). "Dämonologie im frühen Platonismus," in Baltes and Lakmann, 123–141.
Donini, P. (2004). "Sokrates und sein Dämon im Platonismus des 1. und 2. Jahrhunderts n. Chr.," in Baltes and Lakmann, 142–161.
Egelhaaf-Gaiser, U. (2012). "The Gleaming Pate of the Pastophorus: Masquerade or Embodied Lifestyle?," in Keulen and Egelhaaf-Gaiser, 42–72.
Finkelpearl, E. (2004). "The Ends of the Metamorphoses (Apuleius *Met*. 11.26.4–11.30)," in Zimmerman and van der Paardt, 319–342.
Fletcher, R. (2014). *Apuleius' Platonism: The Impersonation of Philosophy*. (Cambridge).
Fowler, R. C., ed. (2016). *Imperial Plato: Albinus, Maximus, Apuleius: Text and Translation, with an Introduction and Commentary*. (Las Vegas).
Fowler, R. C. (2017). "Variations of Receptions of Plato during the Second Sophistic," in Tarrant et al., 223–249.
Gersh, S. (1986). *Middle Platonism and Neoplatonism: the Latin Tradition. Vol. I*. (South Bend, Ind.).
Graverini, L. (2012). *Literature and Identity in the Golden Ass of Apuleius.* (= (2007) *Le Metamorfosi di Apuleio. Letteratura e Identità*. (Pisa)), tr. B. T. Lee. (Columbus, Ohio).
Habermehl, P. (1996). "*Quaedam divinae mediae potestates*: Demonology in Apuleius' *De deo Socratis*," in Hofmann and Zimmerman, 117–142.
Hardie, P. (1994). *Vergil:* Aeneid *Book IX*. (Cambridge).
Harrison, S. J. (2000). *Apuleius: A Latin Sophist*. (Oxford).
Heath, J. (1992). *Actaeon: The Unmannerly Intruder: The Myth and Its Meaning in Classical Literature*. (New York).
Hijmans, B. L. (1987). "Apuleius: *Philosophus Platonicus*." *ANRW* II 31(1): 395–475.
Hoenig, C. (2018). *Plato's* Timaeus *and the Latin Tradition*. (Cambridge).
Hofmann, H., and M. Zimmerman, eds. (1997). *Groningen Colloquia on the Novel* 8. (Groningen).
James, P. (1987). *Unity in Diversity: A Study of Apuleius'* Metamorphoses *with Particular Reference to the Narrator's Art of Transformation and the Metamorphosis Motif in the Tale of Cupid and Psyche*. (Hildesheim).
Jocelyn, H. D. (1967). *The Tragedies of Ennius: The Fragments Edited with an Introduction and Commentary*. (Cambridge).
Jones, C. P. (2017). *Apuleius:* Apologia. Florida. De deo Socratis. (Cambridge, Mass.).
Kahane, A., and A. Laird, eds. (2001). *A Companion to the Prologue of Apuleius'* Metamorphoses. (Oxford).
Karfíková, L. (2004). "Augustins Polemik gegen Apuleius," in Baltes and Lakmann, 162–189.
Keulen, W. (2006). "*Ad amussim congruentia*: Measuring the Intellectual in Apuleius," in Keulen, Nauta, and Panayotakis, 168–202.
Keulen, W., ed. (2007). *Apuleius Madaurensis: Metamorphoses. Book I: Text, Introduction and Commentary*. (Groningen).
Keulen, W., R. Nauta, and S. Panayotakis, eds. (2006). *Lectiones Scrupulosae: Essays on the Text and Interpretation of Apuleius'* Metamorphoses *in Honour of Maaike Zimmerman*. (Groningen).
Keulen, W., and U. Egelhaaf-Gaiser, eds. (2012). *Aspects of Apuleius' Golden Ass. Volume III. The Isis Book*. (Leiden).
Keulen, W., et al., eds. (2015). *Apuleius Madaurensis. Metamorphoses. Book XI*. (Groningen).
Kirichenko, A. (2008). "*Asinus Philosophans*: Platonic Philosophy and the Prologue to Apuleius' *Golden Ass*." *Mnemosyne* 61: 89–107.

Labhardt, A. (1960). "*Curiositas*: Notes sur l'histoire d'un mot et d'une notion." *MH* 17: 206–224.
Laird, A. (1997). "Description and Divinity in Apuleius' *Metamorphoses*," in Hofmann and Zimmerman, 59–86.
Laird, A. (2001). "Paradox and Transcendence: The Prologue as the End," in Kahane and Laird, 267–281.
Lee, B. T., E. Finkelpearl, and L. Graverini, eds. (2014). *Apuleius and Africa*. (New York).
Leigh, M. (2013). *From Polypragmōn to Curiosus: Ancient Concepts of Curious and Meddlesome Behaviour*. (Oxford).
Libby, B. (2011). "Moons, Smoke, and Mirrors in Apuleius' Portrayal of Isis." *AJPh* 132(2): 301–322.
MacDougall, B. (2016). "The Book of Isis and the Myth of Er." *AJPh* 137(2): 251–285.
Magnaldi, G. (2019). *Apulei: Opera Philosophica*. (Oxford).
Makowski, J. F. (1989). "Nisus and Euryalus: A Platonic Relationship." *CJ* 85(1): 1–15.
Mattiacci, S. (2014). "Apuleius and *Africitas*," in Lee, Finkelpearl, and Graverini, 87–111.
Moreschini, C. (1989). "Divinazione e demonologia in Plutarcho e Apuleio." *Augustinianum* 89: 269–280.
Moreschini, C. (2015). *Apuleius and the Metamorphoses of Platonism*. (Turnhout).
Müller, R. (2013). "Terence in Latin Literature from the Second Century BCE to the Second Century CE," in Agoustakis and Traill, 363–379.
Murgatroyd, P. (2004). "The Ending of Apuleius' *Metamorphoses*." *CQ* 54(1): 319–321.
Núñez, L. (2009). "Apuleius: *Orator Metasophisticus*: Miroirs d'un orateur," in van Mal-Maeder, Burnier, and Núñez, 285–316.
Penwill, J. (1990). "*Ambages Reciprocae*: Reviewing Apuleius' Metamorphoses." *Ramus* 19: 1–25.
Riess, W. (2008). "Apuleius *Socrates Africanus*? Apuleius' Defensive Play," in Riess, 51–73.
Riess, W., ed. (2008). *Paideia at Play: Learning and Wit in Apuleius*. (Groningen).
Reydams-Schils, G. (2020). *Calcidius on Plato's Timaeus: Greek Philosophy, Latin Reception, and Christian Contexts*. (Cambridge).
Roskam, G. (2017). "Cupid's Swan from the Academy (*De Plat.* 1.1, 183): Apuleius' Reception of Plato," in Tarrant et al., 156–170.
Sandy, G. (1997). *The Greek World of Apuleius: Apuleius and the Second Sophistic*. (Brill).
Sharples, R., and R. Sorabji, eds. (2007). *Greek and Roman Philosophy: 100 BC–200 AD. Vol. 2*. (London).
Sheffield, F. (2006). *Plato's Symposium: The Ethics of Desire*. (Oxford).
Slater, N. (1998). "Passion and Petrifaction: The Gaze in Apuleius." *CPh* 93(1): 18–48.
Swain, S. (2001). "Apuleius Sophista." *CQ* 51: 269–270.
Tarrant, H. et al., eds. (2017). *Brill's Companion to the Reception of Plato in Antiquity*. (Leiden).
Tilg, S. (2014). *Apuleius' Metamorphoses: A Study in Roman Fiction*. (Oxford).
Timotin, A. (2012). *La démonologie platonicienne: Histoire de la notion de daimōn de Platon aux derniers Néoplatoniciens*. (Leiden).
Trapp, M. B. (2001). "On Tickling the Ears: Apuleius' Prologue and the Anxieties of Philosophers," in Kahane and Laird, 39–46.
Trapp, M. B. (2007). "Apuleius of Madauros and Maximus of Tyre," in Sharples and Sorabji, 467–482.
Ulrich, J. P. (2016). "Review of R. Fletcher's *Apuleius' Platonism: The Impersonation of Philosophy*." *Gnomon* 88(4): 313–320.
Ulrich, J. P. (2017). "Choose Your Own Adventure: an *Eikōn* of Socrates in the Prologue of Apuleius' *Metamorphoses*." *AJPh* 138(4): 707–738.

Ulrich, J. P. (2020). "Hermeneutic Recollections: Apuleius' Use of Platonic Myth in the *Metamorphoses*." *CPh* 115(4): 677–704.

Ulrich, J. P. (2021). "A New Text of Apuleius' *Philosophica.*" *Classical Review* 71(1): 117–119.

van Mal-Maeder, D. (1997). "*Lector, Intende: Laetaberis*—The Enigma of the Last Book of Apuleius' *Metamorphoses*," in Hofmann and Zimmerman, 87–118.

van Mal-Maeder, D., A. Burnier, and M. Loreto Núñez, eds. (2009). *Jeux de Voix: Enonciation, Intertextualité et Intentionalité dans la Littérature Antique*. (Bern).

Wilson, S. G., and M. Desjardins, eds. (2000). *Text and Artifact in the Religions of Mediterranean Antiquity: Essays in Honour of Peter Richardson*. (Waterloo).

Winkler, J. J. (1985). *Auctor and Actor: A Narratological Reading of Apuleius'* Golden Ass. (Berkeley).

Zimmerman, M., and R. van der Paardt, eds. (2004). *Metamorphic Reflections: Essays Presented to Ben Hijmans at His 75th Birthday*. (Leuven).

Zimmerman, M. (2012). *Apulei*: Metamorphoseon *Libri XI*. (Oxford).

CHAPTER 7

PHILOSOPHERS AND ROMAN FRIENDSHIP

DAVID KONSTAN

FAR the most important philosophical treatment of friendship by a Roman thinker is Cicero's *De amicitia*, and this will be the focus of the present chapter.[1] Cicero composed it in 44 BCE, when he had withdrawn from politics after Julius Caesar's defeat of Pompey and his assumption of total power in Rome. This was not long after Cicero's beloved daughter, Tullia, died in childbirth, and shortly before Cicero returned to the forum with the series of brilliant orations in which he denounced Marc Antony, and which cost him his life. The work is dedicated to Cicero's lifelong friend, Titus Pomponius Atticus, a wealthy devotee of Epicureanism who took no active role in politics but stood by Cicero during his ups and downs, and hosted him in his home after Tullia's death, where Cicero consoled himself by immersing himself in the books in Atticus's library and writing several philosophical masterpieces.[2] Cicero's essay thus engages critically with the Greek philosophical tradition, but it also responds to the political crisis of his own time and takes account as well of his personal experience of friendship. Even his grief for his daughter has a subtle influence on the text, for, as we shall see, it betrays a complex connection between friendship and parental affection.

Cicero's essay takes the form of a dialogue, set in the previous century.[3] The main speaker is Gaius Laelius (the treatise bears the alternative title *Laelius*), a Roman aristocrat who studied with the Stoic philosopher Panaetius and who rose to the office of consul. His interlocutors are his two sons-in-law, Gaius Fannius Strabo, who also achieved the consulship and was himself a student of Stoicism, and Quintus Mucius Scaevola, who like the other two was elected consul and was especially famous for his expertise in law. As Cicero tells it, Scaevola recounted the conversation to him when Cicero was a youth (he had been placed by his father under Scaevola's tutelage); Cicero in turn has reproduced it, with some changes and compression, as a tribute to Atticus. By exploiting the dialogue form, moreover, Cicero could distance himself to some extent from the opinions espoused by Laelius, who has too often, perhaps, been taken to represent Cicero's own views in an unmediated way. There is a distinct Stoicizing tone to

Laelius's discourse, whereas Cicero's own commitment was rather to skeptical Platonism (though he was sympathetic to certain aspects of Stoicism).[4] Furthermore, Laelius's dismissal of Epicureanism seems rather curt in a work celebrating the friendship between Cicero and the Epicurean Atticus. The conversational quality of the dialogue and the ostensibly impromptu nature of Laelius's discourse contribute to the work's essayistic style, with its shifts of topic and apparently lax structure, and this too places a burden on the interpreter; for even more than in most philosophical dialogues, the dramatic setting is relevant to understanding Cicero's position.

It is remarkable that a study of friendship should take as its point of departure an episode in which this bond was ruptured. What moved Scaevola to relate Laelius's lecture was, Cicero explains, a quarrel between two friends, one a consul, the other a tribune of the people, who had loved each other dearly but in the end conceived a mortal hatred for one another (the rupture took place around the civil wars involving Marius and Sulla). Atticus himself, indeed, was on close terms with one of the two men involved, as Cicero reminds him. A relationship that should have been above politics thus seems to have fallen victim to partisan strife. Laelius's conversation with his sons-in-law also took place in the immediate aftermath of loss, since its dramatic date is a few days after the death of Scipio Africanus, the great general and twice consul whose friendship with Laelius was proverbial—and whose own death, it was suspected, might have been brought about by his enemies.[5] In life, however, no divergence of views ever drove them apart, and when Laelius comes round to proposing a definition of friendship he affirms: "For friendship is nothing other than agreement on all things divine and human, together with goodwill and affection" (20). Although this idea was something of a commonplace (Sallust put in the mouth of Catiline the statement, "to like and dislike the same things—that, finally, is what a firm friendship is," *Catiline's War* 20.4),[6] nevertheless, when expressed so categorically, it would seem to set the bar very high and to run counter to the intuition that friendship should be able to accommodate differences of opinion. Cicero himself would not have shared Atticus's Epicurean views on the gods or the nature of human virtue.[7] Cicero seems to be imagining an ideal friendship in a bygone epoch, or else ascribing to Laelius an overly strict conception of what such a relationship should be like.

The grounds for Laelius's view lie in Stoicism, with its radical insistence that only those who are perfectly wise and virtuous can be friends (wisdom and virtue imply one another). Stoic sages cannot disagree on significant matters: both will have perfect understanding, and so will be in accord on the nature of things, whether divine or human. But such figures are rare, according to the Stoics, if any have ever existed at all. Laelius, as Cicero represents him, steps back from such philosophical rigor and centers the discussion on the kind of virtue that is within human reach, and was embodied in distinguished aristocrats in Rome's past; as he puts it, "we should look to the ordinary circumstances of life, not those that are imagined or wished for" (17). This concession has a bearing on Laelius's own reaction to the death of his friend Scipio. For according to a strict Stoic conception, such a loss should be borne with perfect equanimity, given that the only good for human beings is virtue, and the deprivation of virtue is the only harm. But Laelius acknowledges that he indeed misses Scipio, whatever "the wise"—that is, hardline Stoics—may think (10).[8] However, he does not let the pain of this loss interfere with his duties: he had missed a meeting of the augurs because he was ill, and not, as some had imagined, out of grief. He thus rejects the sobriquet "wise," which had conventionally been applied to him, and ascribes it rather to Cato, for he endured the loss of a son who was in the prime of life (9). Cicero would appear to be hinting that the death of a child is the greatest test of human wisdom, beyond even the loss of one's best friend. I suspect that he has unconsciously let intrude a recollection of his own inconsolable grief at the death of Tullia;[9] otherwise, he may be intimating the analogy, to be developed later, between kinship and friendship.

Laelius, at all events, consoles himself with the thought that nothing bad has befallen Scipio; thus any pain he feels is for himself, not for his friend—and to suffer on one's own account is shallow egotism. He adds two further considerations that moderate his sorrow. First, Scipio has led a brilliantly successful life, achieving such glory that nothing more could have been added to it, had he lived longer. Second, Laelius is convinced that the souls of good men outlive the body, and so Scipio has not truly perished. There may be a polemical edge to these arguments, since Laelius will later reject the view that he ascribes to certain unnamed Greek philosophers (perhaps the Cyrenaics, though they maintained that friendships should be formed solely on the basis of self-interest), according to which one's own affairs are trouble enough and it is senseless to concern oneself with those of others as well (45). The Epicureans, for their part, denied that the soul could survive the death of the body, and would have looked down at the idea that honors and offices contributed anything significant to human happiness. Broadly speaking, Laelius is staking out an anti-Epicurean position, or at least one hostile to those schools, including both Epicureans and Cyrenaics, that placed a premium on pleasure. But his arguments for equanimity upon the death of friends work only for a special class of people: those who have enjoyed the privileges of exalted rank and have hopes for an afterlife based on their noble achievements.[10] Friendship might still be worth cultivating for lesser folk, but it will bring them pains that may undercut its value. Laelius has thus introduced a kind of modified Stoic elitism, based on a practical conception of civic virtue rather than the unattainable philosophical ideal. Good people, defined now as the respectable class of leading citizens (a common sense of *boni* in Cicero's writings), may be assumed to share traditional values and religious beliefs, and hence can enjoy happy friendships that outlast even the death of one of the parties.

The emphasis on virtue, so conceived, as the basis of friendship will subtend the entire essay, which concludes with Laelius's resounding exhortation to his sons-in-law: "I urge you so to value virtue, without which friendship cannot exist, that, apart from virtue, you deem nothing more worthy than friendship" (104). Laelius praises friendship to the skies as the most valuable gift of the gods to mankind, barring wisdom, and one that bears with it numerous advantages, even to the point of overcoming death because friends abide in memory. The crowning benefit of friendship is that without it, no house, no city could survive (23); Laelius even invokes Empedocles' doctrine that the entire universe is united by friendship (or love). But this extension of friendship to encompass any form of natural or social attraction (the Greeks sometimes attributed this power to *erôs*, e.g., Eryximachus's speech in Plato's *Symposium*) is something of a rhetorical flourish, and is not wholly consistent with Laelius's argument, which looks to intimate personal relationships. What is more, Cicero, unlike Aristotle, does not otherwise equate friendship with social harmony or solidarity.[11] Still, the claim foreshadows, as we shall see, the crucial problem that friendship poses for governing the Roman state.

Having indicated his high estimation of friendship, Laelius continues, at the urging of Fannius and Scaevola, to investigate the subject in greater depth, and turns first to the question of origins and causes. There are two contending accounts: one locates the source of friendship in utility, and the other derives it from a natural inclination to affection. As Laelius puts it, on one view friendship is desired on account of weakness and poverty, which can be minimized by the exchange of necessities, whereas an older and finer theory holds that love (*amor*), which is etymologically related to friendship (*amicitia*), is the primary cause of goodwill (26), and that advantage follows from such affection, rather than the other way around. In a general way, these two positions represent the Epicurean and Stoic views of the origins of friendship, but with substantial differences. Laelius takes the utilitarian account to mean that we form friendships simply by calculating their usefulness (27), which would indeed leave them vulnerable to rupture when circumstances changed. Epicurus's own view was rather that mutual need originally gave rise to valuing friendships in human society, but that they are now perceived as virtues (*aretai*, or as desirable, *hairetai*, according to Usener's emendation) in their own right (*Sent. Vat.* 23), and he held that one might even sacrifice one's life on behalf of a friend (Diog. Laert. 10.120–121). The Stoics, for their part, located the basis of affection for others in what they called "appropriation" or "affiliation" (*oikeiôsis*), which is an instinctive sense of what is one's own, beginning with one's body (and hence the impulse to self-preservation) and extending outward to include first offspring, then kin, and finally all of humanity.[12]

Laelius develops the idea in a different way. He takes the mutual affection between parents and their young in animals as a sign that love for others is natural (a characteristic noted by many, including Aristotle), and affirms that this tendency is still more apparent in human beings. We see this in the first instance from the affection (*caritas*) that obtains between children and parents, which, he says, "cannot be destroyed except by some abominable crime" (again, the filial relationship is treated as prior to friendship). A further indication of love's nature is the fact that a feeling of love arises when we encounter someone of similar character and temperament, "since we seem to perceive in that person, so to speak, the light of uprightness and virtue; for nothing is more lovable than virtue" (27–28). Aristotle had discriminated lovable things into three categories: the useful, the pleasing, and the good, and he proceeded to eliminate the useful, since what is useful is loved as a means to what is either pleasing or good (*Eth. Nic.* 8.1155b27). He further maintained that the highest kind of friendship was based on affection for goodness in another, which is to say, for that person's virtue. But this kind of love or friendship is quite different from the instinctive affection for one's offspring, as Laelius implicitly acknowledges by remarking that parental love among humans may be extinguished if the child proves vicious, albeit only in extreme cases. Love of virtue is strictly a human phenomenon. The centrality of virtue is good Stoic doctrine, but it is not continuous with kin-based affection: it is not natural in this broad sense of the term.

Indeed, Laelius is aware that bonds of friendship or love can lead people astray, inducing them to favor loyalty over the good; if love is natural, it is not always motivated by what Laelius considers to be virtuous actions. Thus, he turns next to limits on the claims of friendship. Laelius begins by observing that friendships are subject to many strains, since friends may cease to share the same views about the state, or they may find themselves in competition for a woman, or money, or, among the best, for honor and office (34), dangers that the Stoic Epictetus emphasized as well (Arr. *Epict. diss.* 2.22). But the real problem with friendship derives from its strength, rather than its fragility, since the refusal to assist a friend even in a wrong cause may be seen as a betrayal of the bond. Laelius recounts the story, which had become proverbial (cf. Val. Max. 4.7.1), of the loyalty of the Stoic Gaius Blossius to Tiberius Gracchus, whom Laelius, like Cicero himself, regarded as a dangerous revolutionary and anything but virtuous as a statesman. Blossius begged Laelius, as advisor to the consuls, to pardon Tiberius on the grounds that he so admired Tiberius that he thought it incumbent on himself to do whatever Tiberius wished. "Even if he had wished you to put a torch to the Capitol?," Laelius asked; to which Blossius replied: "He would never have wished that, but if he had, I'd have obeyed" (37).

Aristotle, in the two books devoted to friendship in the *Nicomachean Ethics*, did not treat the tension between loyalty to friends and doing what is just in any detail. However, his successor Theophrastus did so in the first book of his treatise *On Friendship* (*Peri philias*), according to Aulus Gellius (*NA* 1.3.9), who tells us that the question, "whether one ought to assist a friend contrary to what is just and to what extent and in what ways," was a popular topic in the philosophical schools. Gellius notes that Cicero discussed the issue summarily, simply indicating that one may, in matters of life and death, support a friend's unjust ambitions, provided that this does not entail serious disgrace (Gell. *NA* 1.3.13; cf. *Amic.* 61), whereas Theophrastus allowed that moderate dishonor might be counterbalanced by an important service to a friend (1.3.21–26). The problem clearly looks back to the quarrel between the former friends, one a tribune, the other a consul, that provided the occasion for Scaevola's rehearsal of Laelius's disquisition when Cicero was resident in his household. Laelius thus affirms: "Let this law be ordained in friendship, that we neither request disgraceful things nor perform them if requested" (40; cf. 44). But Laelius is not thinking primarily of private wrongs, but rather of offenses against the state; as he immediately notes, "it is a disgraceful and utterly unacceptable excuse in other transgressions, but especially if one professes to have acted against the state for the sake of a friend," and he adds that these are perilous times for the Republic. Needless to say, Laelius's concerns are analogous to Cicero's own. It is impossible to say whether Theophrastus placed a similar emphasis on crimes against the state, but it is likely that this is Cicero's own contribution to the theme of friendship.

Laelius now picks up the defense of friendship against those who would sacrifice it for the sake of freedom from perturbation (*securitas* [47], Cicero's rendition of the Epicurean *ataraxia*); giving up friendship because it may entail anxiety for a friend is like abandoning virtue, Laelius affirms, because it sometimes causes bother (48). In fact, he says, there is nothing more pleasurable than friendship (49; cf. 51). What is more, like naturally attracts like, and thus goodwill among good men (*boni*) is practically inevitable. Such goodness (*bonitas*) pertains even to the masses, since virtue is not haughty or inhumane (50). It is rather tyrants who are deprived of friends (52–54; compare Xenophon's dialogue, *Hiero*), and yet a life without friends is the most miserable of all. This interlude, recapping topics raised earlier in the dialogue, reaffirms the value of friendship both to the individual and the community, even as it finesses issues such as the rareness of virtue and hence the possibility of genuine friendships among the larger mass of mankind.

Laelius then turns again to the limits (*fines et termini*, 56) of friendship, a topic particularly urgent to him and, we may assume, to Cicero. He first rejects three common views: that we should feel toward friends as we do toward ourselves; that our goodwill toward friends should be in proportion to theirs toward us; and that our friends should value us as we do ourselves. As to the first, we often deprive ourselves for our friends' sake, and do things for friends that we would refrain from doing for ourselves; the second makes of friendship an economic transaction; and the third is worst of all, since friends should be encouraging just when we are down about ourselves. Nor should we adopt a provisional attitude toward friends, in accord with the proverbial advice that we should love as though we might someday hate and hate as though we might in the future love (59–60). Laelius is here, I think, and Cicero with him, exploring fresh territory in the matter of friendship. A friend is not simply another self, in the formula that Aristotle made familiar and that Laelius himself endorses in a different context, where he is arguing that just as we love ourselves without regard to profit, so ought we to love a friend, who is an *alter idem* (80). In fact, it is the lack of identity between friends that makes friendship special, the fact that others can see value in us when we least perceive it in ourselves, and will do for us things that we would be ashamed to do on our own behalf. Laelius speaks here as a man who has had experience of depression, his own and that of others, and appreciates that friends can buoy us up just when we would fail ourselves; I think we can hear the personal voice of Cicero coming through the text at this point.

It is here, moreover, that Laelius returns to the question of acceding to a friend's wishes (cited by Gellius), affirming that even though there should ideally be a complete consensus of views among men of good character, yet when this consensus fails and our friends wish a favor that is less than wholly just, we should oblige them and deviate from the narrow path, provided that the utmost disgrace not result from it (61). One must have regard for one's reputation, and not consider the goodwill of one's fellow citizens to be a trivial weapon. There is no way of knowing whether Laelius had in mind some compromise of perfect virtue in his own relations with friends, for their sake or for his, but there can be little doubt that Cicero would have been conscious of having made such allowances over the course of his career.

In real life, then, love does override regard for virtue, and though we may recognize extreme situations in which we ought to break with friends, Cicero refrains, as Aulus Gellius complained, from offering any but the vaguest guidelines on how or where to draw the line (Gellius says that Theophrastus did better in this regard). To avoid such conflicts, Laelius recommends great care in the initial selection of one's friends; let them be unwavering and dependable. Yet there is a dearth of such people, and what is more, one cannot put them to the test except when they are already friends; thus, as Laelius puts it, "friendship outruns judgment" (62). We must, accordingly, try to rein in the impulse to affection and goodwill, for almost everyone will place, if not money, then at all events honor and advancement ahead of friendship; that is why it is all but impossible to find true friends in the governing class (*qui in honoribus reque publica versantur*, 64), for such men are so rare as to seem divine. We are back, then, at the paradox that has animated the dialogue from the beginning: practical experience confirms the Stoic doctrine that friendship can exist only among the virtuous, which is to say, the wise, and such paragons are vanishingly scarce; yet friendship is both natural and the greatest boon in life.

Laelius now introduces two complementary rules for friendship: the first is complete candor, and the second is complete trust and absence of suspicion. Frankness and the danger of hypocrisy will form the final part of Laelius's discourse, but before entering upon this topic, he pauses to consider two subsidiary matters, both discussed in some detail by Aristotle and very likely by Theophrastus as well, and perhaps too by Panaetius, whom some scholars take to be the source for much of Cicero's analysis. The first concerns old friends versus new (cf. Sen. *Ep.* 9.6–7). Laelius dispatches this one rather summarily, affirming that old friendships age like good wines, though neither are new ones to be spurned: not very helpful advice, it must be said, though Laelius, in his meandering way (governed to some extent by the principle of ring composition), will take the question up again a little later. Laelius next treats friendships among people of unequal social status, and he affirms categorically that "the higher one must be on a par with the lower" (69). Just as superior friends must put themselves on the same level as their inferiors, so too the lesser parties to a friendship must not resent the achievements and abilities of their betters. Yet it is the duty of the more favored not just to lower themselves but also to raise up the lesser, who are likely to feel slighted just because they think they deserve better (72)—an insight that is perhaps to be attributed to Laelius, or Cicero, although Aristotle had noted that people take umbrage the more readily to the extent that they have doubts about themselves (*Rh.* 2.2, 1379a36–b2). Still, as Laelius wisely observes, there are limits to what can be done to elevate one's friends: not everyone can be made a consul. Despite Laelius's inclusive sense of friendship, however, it is noteworthy that he refers to Terence, the gifted young playwright and ex-slave who was on intimate terms with both Scipio and Laelius (cf. Suet. *Vita Terenti* 1), as *familiaris* rather than *amicus* (89). The nuances of *familiaris* are difficult to capture, since they range from "member of the household" to "intimate acquaintance," but it may be significant that Laelius refrains from identifying a man of such modest social status straightforwardly as a "friend."[13]

Laelius now warns that childhood affections cannot be the basis for adult friendships, for if the mere antiquity of a relationship were what counted, we should be best of friends with our nurses and tutors. Not that they should be wholly dismissed from our consideration, but they are to be appreciated in a different way, for there will be an inevitable disparity of character and interests (cf. Arist. *Eth. Nic.* 9.3, 1165b13–22). Laelius goes on to urge that we not let a sentimental attachment hinder the advancement of our friends: here too, one must be careful about what asks of friends or suffers to be asked by them (76). But friendships must sometimes be terminated—this is the real world, after all—and Laelius recommends that one dissolve them gradually and avoid, to the extent possible, the kind of rupture that leads to open hostility, save where the offense is utterly intolerable. Still, political differences, though they may disrupt a friendship, need not result in enmity, and one must take care not to reach the point of open abuse—though if it happens, one ought to endure even this out of respect for the former friendship. Here again we may detect the voice of the Roman statesman, who knows that quarrels among powerful friends can damage the republic itself, even if they sometimes prove inevitable. It is worth recalling that Cicero felt obliged to defend himself against the charge of breach of friendship when he launched the attacks against Marc Antony that would cost him his life (*Phil.* 2.1–9).

The upshot, according to Laelius, is that it is best to take one's time and be sure those you will love are worthy of your friendship, especially since such people constitute a rare species (78–79). Most, however, have no idea what real friendship is like, and their unconditional self-love does not extend to include others; they want friends who are good, but neglect to be good themselves. Laelius recapitulates the qualities of a proper friend, and insists that true friends will not only love but also revere one another for their good qualities (82). In fact, the very purpose of friendship is to enhance virtue, since on its own, that is, in a solitary individual, virtue cannot reach the highest level (83). Virtue, in turn, is the condition for friendship (84): although Laelius does not spell it out, this reciprocal implication is another of the chicken and egg dilemmas associated with friendship, like the injunction, which Laelius proceeds to quote, to love after you have judged, not the reverse (the source is Theophrastus; cf. Sen. *Ep.* 3). For, as Laelius has already mentioned, one can only put a person to the test after a friendship has been formed.

Even if people are heedless about what friendship requires of them, everyone believes, according to Laelius, that friendship, or at least the existence of another with whom to share one's thoughts, is essential to a happy life. Nature instructs us on the need for friends, but people are somehow deaf to its voice. One reason why is the candor that friendship requires, since criticism of our faults is difficult to endure and indeed may inspire hatred, and Laelius now offers advice on how to be frank without causing offense and warns of the danger of hypocritical flattery. It is a canny transition, for there really is no good answer as to why people neglect friendship if its benefits are so manifest. Since the need to distinguish true friends from pretenders who insinuate themselves into one's graces by flattery was a standard topic in Hellenistic and later treatises (e.g., by Plutarch and Themistius; cf. also Philodemus's tract, *On Frank Speech*), Laelius annexes this issue at the point where it may seem to provide an explanation why (this is almost certainly an innovation of Cicero's). Laelius affirms that anyone but a fool can perceive when someone is fawning openly (99), and sincerity wins out over demagogy even in public discourse, but flatterers are a sophisticated bunch and can win you into their confidence by simulating disagreement. Again, there is no good answer to this problem (it was highlighted by Plutarch and other writers who contrasted the frankness of *parrhēsia* of the true friend with self-interested flattery), and Laelius simply checks himself for having wandered off into ordinary friendships.[14] He concludes by returning to the friendships of the wise (in the humanly possible sense of wisdom) and pronounces a passionate eulogy of virtue, for it is the sight of virtue that ignites love (the language here is borrowed from the sphere of erotic passion, which responds to the sight of beauty, and it has a Platonic ring). Since the memory of Scipio's virtue has not died, the love that Laelius bore him also lives on.

Laelius's lecture, as Cicero transcribes it, is an attempt to adapt Stoic conceptions of virtue and the friendship of the wise to the political realities of Rome's ruling class. The move was facilitated by the partisan use of "the good people" to signify the conservative faction in government, but this risked reducing the idea of friendship to a bond uniting a particular clique, whether that of Laelius and Scipio in their conflict with the Gracchi and their supporters or Cicero's own party as opposed to that of Caesar and Marc Antony. Yet clearly there were friendships on the other side too: the problem with love, then, is that it outpaces judgment and generates loyalty, which is the very essence of friendship, to the wrong people and causes (as Laelius and Cicero perceive them). This risk requires that limits be placed on the duties of a friend; yet constancy is a value in itself and may sanction some deviation from the true path, although how far is hard to determine (not to mention the question of who is to judge). Exhortations to choose one's friends carefully, like advice to break off friendships gently and in such a way as not to generate rancor, are all well and good, but virtuous people, Laelius insists, are an extremely rare breed, and so no amount of circumspection is likely to safeguard one against unworthy friendships. Yet friends are indispensable for happiness, and nature itself has planted in human beings, as in other animals, the impulse to love others. Laelius's twists and turns call into question the possibility of harnessing friendship to virtue in the affairs of everyday life.

This is not to say that Cicero's essay is philosophically deficient or without interest: defining the nature of friendship is intractable enough, and many have stumbled in the attempt, even without tying it in with politics. Although Cicero eschewed writing a systematic treatise, perhaps in the knowledge that friendship did not lend itself to such an exposition, he advances the discussion by noting the primacy of love over utility and courageously confronting the consequences of this view, which include the justification for wrongdoing on the grounds of fidelity to friends. He is, to be sure, quick to denounce such an excuse, but he knows that the boundaries are fuzzy. *De amicitia* is powerful and enduring because of the way it struggles with these questions, limning an ideal friendship between Laelius and Scipio that seems itself to be a thing of the past. What of the intimate bond, finally, between the Stoicizing Platonist Cicero, statesman and defender of tradition, and the Epicurean Atticus, who abstained from politics and was a friend to all? Perhaps they would, if pressed, have approved the words of Montaigne on his friendship with La Boétie: "Because it was he, because it was I."

Notes

1. For a reliable translation with commentary, see Powell (1990); a more extensive commentary, in German, is Neuhausen (1981). For the Greek background to ideas on friendship, see Konstan (1997); van Berkel (2019). On friendship in Cicero's correspondence, see Citroni Marchetti (2000). For Roman friendship generally, see Williams (2012). On Cicero's own contribution to the concept of friendship in *De amicitia*, see Pangle (2003); Nicgorski (2008); Prost (2008); Lockwood (2019).
2. There were some ups and downs in their relationship; see Evangelou (2019).
3. On Cicero's use of the dialogue form, see the chapter by Fox in this volume.
4. See the chapter by Schofield in this volume.
5. See Plut. *Vit. Rom.* 27.4–5; App. *B. Civ.* 1.20. Cicero alludes to the rumor cryptically at *Amic.* 12: *quo de genere mortis difficile dictu est, quid homines suspicentur, videtis.*
6. Cf. Aris. *Eth. Nic.* 9.1166a, Cic. *Inv. Rhet.* 2.166.
7. Evangelou (2018) argues that Cicero's target in this essay was not Epicureanism as such but rather a narrowly utilitarian conception of friendship.
8. But see Sen. *Ep.* 63.1, who notes that it is appropriate to be stung (the verb is *vellico*) by the loss of a friend, provided one does not give way to inordinate grief; this is in line with the Stoic view of so-called pre-emotions, instinctive reactions, like shivering with cold or turning pale at danger, that even the sage may experience. See Reydams-Schils in this volume.
9. For further discussion of this point, see Konstan (2017).
10. The Stoics maintained that the soul could outlive the body, and longer for the virtuous; cf. Sen. *Consolation to Marcia* 26.
11. Whereas *homonoia* or concord in Aristotle is regarded as a kind of *philia*, *amicitia* was not usually treated as operating across class lines and so uniting the entire body politic. For this, Cicero invoked the notion of *concordia ordinum*, or harmony among the several social strata (senators, knights, and the common people). See Konstan (2010).
12. Cf. Hierocles *Elements of Ethics* cols. IX–XI; Cic. *Fin.* 3.62; Cicero recapitulates this idea at 81, below, but only to show how most human beings fail to make the transition to a wider affection.
13. Rank may not be the only impediment to full friendship or *amicitia*. At the end of his discourse, Laelius declares that he cherished (*dileximus*, 101) Cato and other elders for their goodwill, but this affection stands out more among coevals; now that he is old, he enjoys the affection (*caritas*) and intimacy (*familiaritas*) of younger men, like his sons-in-law. Once again, Laelius seems to avoid using the term *amicus*, which would indeed seem out of place in reference to kin, including kin by marriage, or to a relationship between men of very different ages.
14. Cf. Plutarch, *How to Distinguish a Flatterer from a Friend*; Themistius *On Friendship*. Maximus of Tyre, *By What Means One May Separate a Flatterer from a Friend* (*Or.* 14), etc. For further discussion, see Fitzgerald (1996).

References

Citroni Marchetti, S. (2000). *Amicizia e potere nelle lettere di Cicerone e nelle elegie ovidiane dall'esilio.* Studi e Testi 18. (Florence).

Evangelou, G. (2018). "Reconciling Cicero's Anti-Epicureanism in *De Amicitia* with his Friendship with Atticus." *Latomus* 77: 991–1012.

Evangelou, G. (2019). "The Use of Emotion as Persuasion in Cicero's Letters to Atticus," in Papaioannou, Serafim, and Demetriou, 153–167.
Fitzgerald, J. T., ed. (1996). *Friendship, Flattery, and Frankness of Speech: Studies on Friendship in the New Testament World.* (Leiden).
Konstan, D. (1997). *Friendship in the Classical World.* (Cambridge).
Konstan, D. (2010). "Are Fellow Citizens Friends? Aristotle versus Cicero on *Philia, Amicitia,* and Social Solidarity," in Rosen and Sluiter, 233–248.
Konstan, D. (2017). "Cicero's Two Loves." *Ciceroniana On Line* 1: 291–305. https://doi.org/10.13135/2532-5353/2502 (accessed November 16, 2021).
Lockwood, T. (2019). "Defining Friendship in Cicero's *De Amicitia*." *Ancient Philosophy* 39: 1–18.
Neuhausen, K. A., ed. (1981). *M. Tullius Cicero: Laelius.* (Heidelberg).
Nicgorski, W. (2008). "Cicero's Distinctive Voice on Friendship," in von Heyking and Avramenko, 84–111.
Pangle, L. S. (2003). *Aristotle and the Philosophy of Friendship.* (Cambridge).
Papaioannou, S., A. Serafim, and K. Demetriou, eds. (2019). *The Art of Persuasion across Genres and Topics.* (Leiden).
Powell, J. G. F., ed. and tr. (1990). *Cicero: Laelius on Friendship and the Dream of Scipio.* (Warminster).
Prost, F. (2008). "La philosophie cicéronienne de l'amitié dans le *Laelius*." *Revue de Métaphysique et de Morale* 57: 111–124.
Rosen, R., and I. Sluiter, eds. (2010). *Valuing Others: Papers from the Penn-Leiden Colloquium V.* (Leiden).
van Berkel, T. (2019). *The Economics of Friendship: Conceptions of Reciprocity in Classical Greece.* Mnemosyne Supplements, vol. 429. (Leiden).
von Heyking, J., and R. Avramenko, eds. (2008). *Friendship and Politics: Essays in Political Thought.* (South Bend, Ind.).
Williams, C. A. (2012). *Reading Roman Friendship.* (Cambridge).

CHAPTER 8

DEBATE OR GUIDANCE? CICERO ON PHILOSOPHY

MALCOLM SCHOFIELD

Introduction

In his essay "Making the World Safe for Utilitarianism,"[1] the political philosopher Jonathan Wolff highlights a contrast between the credit rating of utilitarianism—or of what he calls maximizing consequentialism—in philosophical ethics, and its standing where decision-making in matters of public policy is concerned. "Utilitarianism," he comments, "has been out of favour in philosophy for some time." Certainly there are a number of alternative approaches to ethics which attract greater interest and more support in contemporary philosophy, all typically occasioning subtle and vigorous debate in the journals and on the conference scene. On the other hand: "While philosophers have turned away from maximizing consequentialism, public policy decision making it has embraced it. Many areas of public policy are dominated by cost-benefit analysis, which at least in its purest form is a particularly crude form of consequentialism: consequentialism of money." Philosophers, Wolff suggests, should find this worrying; "some," he goes on, "have duly reported themselves worried."[2] However what he himself concludes (and there are similar remarks in others of his writings) is that "while there are plenty of more appealing approaches to personal morality, we do not seem to have many candidate alternatives for public policy decision making."[3]

I am going to be discussing a similar phenomenon in the philosophical writings of Cicero, in the first instance precisely in discussion of the political sphere and of a much discussed passage of *De legibus*.[4] More generally, we find in him a tension between a conception of philosophy and of philosophical ethics as in its very nature a debate, and the idea that the point of doing philosophy is to find and advocate a sound basis for living our lives. To amplify a little, on the one hand, as Cicero sees it, some views in ethics have more going for them, some less, but to the mind of the Academic skeptic that he is, none has established itself as beyond serious intellectual challenge. To do ethics properly means understanding the main ethical systems that have been or could be proposed, and getting involved in the intricate and apparently unending debate over their merits and demerits.[5] But on the other hand, if philosophy is to deliver on its main function—to supply foundations both for our common existence and for our lives as individuals—it looks as though we must settle for embracing some particular ethical position, despite our recognition that doing so must be problematic.

The general point can conveniently be illustrated from the *Tusculan Disputations* (45 BCE), a sequence of dialogues to which I shall return in due course.[6] Here Cicero speaks of philosophy itself in contrasting modes. On the one hand, in the preface to Book 2 he says that while in the *Academic Books* (written earlier in the same year) he has set out the case for Academic skepticism with all due precision, nothing would be more welcome than some counterargument. The characteristic activities that gave Greek philosophy its vitality were the disputes and disagreements of thinkers who really understood the subject (*Tusc.* 2.4). On the other hand, the preface to Book 5 assures us that philosophy is the guide for life, the explorer of virtue, the expeller of vice: human life is dependent on it (*Tusc.* 5.5). The five books of the work taken together "have made apparent the things most necessary for living happily" (*Div.* 2.2). Or as Book 3 of *De finibus* (another of the dialogues of 45 BCE) had put it, philosophy is the *art* of living a life (*Fin.* 3.4; cf. *Tusc.* 1.1, *Off.* 2.6).

The tension between the two ideas is obvious. If philosophy is to guide us, it must tell us something definite and convey at least the appearance of definitiveness: that death is something that should not trouble us, or that virtue is uniquely sufficient in itself to give us happiness. But if philosophy is to work out answers to the questions people ask about these and similar topics, it needs to debate them vigorously and to welcome challenges to any conclusions it may reach—without the debate it will lose its vigor and thereby its capacity to guide us. But the definiteness and definitiveness philosophy needs if it is to provide people with firm ethical guidance will be hard to come by if debate brings—as it characteristically does—disagreement, still more irreconcilable disagreement.

It is not just that this tension in Cicero's discussions of philosophy and philosophical ethics is apparent to us his readers. He was himself acutely aware of the difficulty, articulates it in different ways at different points in his writings, and develops different strategies—explicitly or implicitly theorized as such—for coping with it in different contexts. One place where Cicero's sense of the problem emerges with special clarity is in the *Lucullus* (again 45 BCE), in the course of a long critique of the discussions of dogmatic philosophers that constitutes the final main section of the skeptical reply to the Stoicizing epistemology which had been developed in the first main part of the dialogue. A particularly good example is the treatment, developed in a characteristic stretch of distinctively Ciceronian philosophical rhetoric, of divergences between Stoic and Peripatetic ethics (*Luc.* 133–34):

> The Stoics hold that all moral errors are equal, but with this Antiochus[7] most forcefully disagrees. Then please may *I* be allowed to consider which of the two views I should follow? "Cut it short," he says. "Do for once decide on something or other." Even given

that the arguments on either side appear to me acute and of equal weight? ... Here's an even bigger disagreement. Zeno thinks the happy life is found in virtue alone. What does Antiochus say? "Yes," he says, "the happy life, but not the happi*est*." ... I am torn. Sometimes one view seems more persuasive to me, sometimes the other. Yet unless one or other of them is right, I think that virtue lies utterly prostrate.

And so it goes on for several pages more, even if at one point Cicero owns to finding it not easy to tear himself away from Antiochus's Peripatetic conception of the ends of life—"I haven't to date found anything more persuasive" (*Luc.* 139).

Perhaps the most succinct and explicit statement of the problem he faces given his own philosophical outlook comes in the preface to Book 2 of *De officiis* (44 BCE), the last of Cicero's philosophical writings (*Off.* 2.7):

> An objection is brought against me—by educated men, indeed—who ask whether I think my behavior is altogether consistent. For although I say that nothing can be known for certain, nonetheless I am in the habit of holding forth on various subjects, and on this occasion I am engaged in formulating advice (*praecepta*) about our obligations.

I have now mentioned three of the four texts—*De legibus*, *Tusculan Disputations*, and *De officiis*—that will be my case studies in this chapter (the fourth will be *De republica*). I shall tackle first a remarkable passage from Book 1 of *De legibus*, where in fundamentals of public policy silencing of debate is advocated. Next I turn more briefly to Book 3 of *De republica*, in which by contrast Cicero stages a confrontation between two views on justice, here as in Book 1 of *De legibus* taken to be the value that political philosophy needs to make central. The final text to examine in any detail will be the most complex of them all, calling accordingly for the fullest treatment: the remarkable attempt he makes in the *Tusculan Disputations* to harmonize conflicting philosophical positions in the service of ethical guidance for the individual. Then we shall consider briefly Cicero's approach to individual guidance in a different literary genre, as exemplified by *De officiis*, in which debate is alluded to but not conducted. Some brief concluding remarks will round off the chapter.

Silencing Debate

One of the most intriguing moments in all Cicero's philosophical writing comes in Book 1 of *De legibus*, a dialogue probably unfinished and unpublished, and usually dated to around 51 BCE.[8] It occurs at the point where, following the first main sequence of argument in the dialogue (*Leg.* 1.16–34), Cicero says that he is now going to make some remarks on his principal thesis: that justice is rooted in nature. The other discussants—his brother Quintus and his close friend Atticus—consider this completely unnecessary.

The arguments they have just been given by Cicero have already convinced them of the truth of the thesis; and Atticus briefly recapitulates them in explaining why (*Leg* 1.35). Cicero replies that though they are right to think the conclusion follows from those arguments, he is going nonetheless to follow the scholastic method favored by some philosophers (doubtless he means the Stoics: cf., e.g., *Tusc.* 5.18–19), and dedicate a separate treatment to the topic.

Atticus exclaims (*Leg.* 1.36): "I take it your own freedom as to how to discuss things has gone missing—or else you are the sort of person not to follow your own judgment in a debate, but to submit to the authority of somebody else." In other words, Atticus is accusing Cicero of abandoning—temporarily or permanently—the freedom the Academic skeptic claims to consider any philosophical question on its merits and as he judges best, in contrast to adherents of the other schools. Other philosophers are standardly represented in the dialogues as required to tackle them only by the methods sanctioned in their schools, and only on the doctrinal basis accepted by them. "We alone are free." Cicero will say in Book 5 of the *Tusculan Disputations*, whereas others are subject to "laws imposed on the way they debate" (*Tusc.* 5.33). The echo of Academic skeptic talk in Atticus's intervention here, and its confirmation that Cicero is already an Academic skeptic at the time of writing, were not often picked up by scholarship until Woldemar Görler pointed out what he rightly called this "massive indication" in a brilliant article of 1995.[9] Once noticed, it is indeed decisive for interpretation.

Cicero does not altogether deny Atticus's charge, although he makes it clear that he is not abandoning Academic independence of judgment as a general policy (*non semper*). Why, then, does he bow to authority (to the extent that he does) on this occasion? Because he is embarked on a specific project in applied political theory, which has the *practical* aim of "putting commonwealths on a firm footing, bringing stability to cities, maintaining every kind of people in a sound condition" (*Leg.* 1.37). That requires in the first instance positing basic principles that are aptly supplied and assiduously investigated (*bene provisa et diligenter explorata*). Such a stipulation in fact impeccably parallels Academic methodology, although Cicero does not emphasize the point. The testing of impressions that Academics insist on when the stakes are high requires "meticulous consideration" (*accurata consideratio*) and "most assiduous exploration" (*diligentissime circumspexerit*: *Luc.* 36). The importance of the political project he articulates is presumably what dictates the need for just such a careful and dedicated treatment of its ethical foundations.

So how does one do that? Here Cicero's policy will be to identify principles that commend themselves (*probentur*) to those who think that what is morally admirable is either the only good or an incomparably great good—i.e., the Stoics or the Platonists and Aristotelians (*Leg.* 1.37–8)—whose differences on that issue are subsequently to be treated as verbal, not substantive, in line with the view of the nonskeptical Academic Antiochus (*Leg.* 1.54–55). Yet here, too, is another echo of Academic skeptic methodology. Such Academics do not claim certain knowledge. What can command their assent is whatever line of thought seems most *persuasive* or *deserving of approval* (*probabile*) or seems *nearest* the truth. But there is in the present case a crucial variation—constituting the degree of surrender of his own judgment that Cicero is admitting. As we have seen, identifying a theory of justice that will support construction of a good constitutional system requires acknowledgment that we are to be concerned with the public sphere, and with practice as well as theory. Once this thought is registered, it will not suffice for Cicero and his interlocutors to agree (or disagree) among *themselves* about what seems most probable or nearest the truth: that would be too fragile a basis for the enterprise. The theory to be proposed should have the approval of a broad swathe of thinkers who all accept that what is good or in itself desirable is the morally admirable alone, or incomparably more so than anything else.

In other words, the right thing is to make sure one has *their probatio*, not—as standardly in Academic scepticism—simply to make one's own mind up. That said, however, as Jed Atkins has pointed out, we should recall that it was precisely the mutual corroboration of witnesses required in the determination of important legal cases to which Carneades appealed in explaining the Academic method: a method described as the rigorous testing of impressions that we engage "in matters that contribute to happiness," to ensure so far as we can that they are "undiverted and throughly explored" (Sex. Emp. *Math.* 7.184). Moreover, as Atkins also observes, Cicero does *choose* to take this approach, and thus "in a manner of speaking" exercises his free judgment.[10] Indeed, in a rather similar context in the preface to *De officiis*, he insists (*Off.* 1.6) that in relying on the same philosophical tradition as is called in aid here, he does so "using my own judgment and discretion" (*iudicio arbitrioque nostro*).

There is a further and more unsettling dimension to the stance Cicero is adopting. He next tells us (*Leg.* 1.39) not merely that it means rejecting—unsurprisingly—the views of the Epicureans, whose hedonistic conception of the good and pursuit of pleasure leaves them (he insinuates) without any understanding of what involvement in the public sphere entails, and who had better stay away from it. More startlingly, those views must be rejected in this context *even if true*:—even if they *say* (*dicunt*, indicative mood) what is true, and not (as we might have expected) if they *were to be saying* what is true (though editors have proposed emending to get the subjunctive *dicant*). The passage echoes one in *De oratore* (55 BCE) where a similar treatment is accorded to Epicureanism in the context of enquiry "not into what is the truest philosophy, but the one most closely tied to the orator." We should warn Epicureans to keep quiet about their doctrine—"as if it were a holy secret"—that there is no role in public affairs for the wise person, "even if it is (*est*: once again some editors substitute the subjunctive, *sit*) absolutely true (*verissimum*)" (*De or.* 3.64). This might be regarded as Cicero's version of Plato's Noble Lie, or more particularly of the variant in Plato's own *Laws*, where after a stretch of dialogue developing the case for thinking that the just life is pleasanter than the unjust, the Athenian Visitor proposes that even if that weren't the case, any lawgiver who was even the slightest use—assuming he was prepared for a good purpose to lie to the young—could devise no more profitable or persuasive *falsehood* (Pl. *Leg.* 2.663D–E).

The final price to be paid by Cicero the Academic in launching into the serious political project which he is undertaking—and the final stage in the surrender of his own judgment—is that he will have also to ask the skeptical Academy of Arcesilaus and

Carneades to "stay silent": they throw all these matters into total confusion (*Leg.* 1.39). In other words, what would be totally unhelpful would be for the statement of principle underpinning the political project he is undertaking to be met by a classic Academic *counterargument*, e.g., to the effect that wisdom dictates pursuit of self-interest, not what is alleged to be "natural" other-regarding justice, the position that will however be affirmed by Cicero himself for his own part in De *officiis*.[11] Not wanted, in short, would be any repeat of Carneades' reputed delivery on successive days at Rome in 155 BCE of speeches first for and then against justice, an episode already familiar to the reader of *De legibus* from Book 3 of *De republica* (54–2 BCE), which is replicated there in the debate between Philus and Laelius that Cicero makes the centerpiece of that whole dialogue, and to which we shall be returning shortly. All the same, says Cicero, "I would like to conciliate it [sc. the new Academy]. I don't dare push it aside" (*Leg.* 1.39). For of course, Academic skeptics aren't *committed* like Epicureans to *doctrines* incompatible with those which the *De legibus* project is to take as its basis. It is open to them to approve whatever in the end seems to them most probable or persuasive or nearest the truth (cf., e.g., *Div.* 2.150, *Off.* 3.20).

In this manner Cicero concludes a remarkable passage of philosophical writing. To summarize, he here temporarily abandons full-blooded Academic skepticism to undertake a practical project in applied political theory: establishing a philosophical foundation—the doctrine of the natural basis of justice—for "putting commonwealths on a firm footing, bringing stability to cities, maintaining every kind of people in a sound condition." Such an enterprise requires observance of a number of constraints:

- *Pragmatism*: the foundational principle need not be true, but must be fit for purpose.
- *Authority*: the appropriate principle must be accepted on the authority of philosophers who have shown it to be carefully considered.
- *No debate*: dissent or query regarding the principle is to be "silenced"—these form no part of the relevant methodology.

There is an evident similarity with Jonathan Wolff's attitude toward utilitarianism and cost-benefit analysis in the article of his to which I have been referring.

However, Wolff stresses that he is defending utilitarianism and cost-benefit analysis in public policy decision-making as decision procedures rather than as moral theories, and as decision procedures "only under certain highly constrained conditions."[12] Elsewhere in discussing risk management he talks of laying the groundwork "so that the moral questions appear in clear focus," not of offering answers to those questions, or of articulating "the normative framework" for the enterprise.[13] Cicero might have found those statements somewhat pusillanimous. If utilitarianism is what public policy decision-making is principally to rely on, other conflicting stances in philosophical ethics are to that extent being put aside. So even if utilitarianism is called in aid only because it enables the adoption of a decision procedure which can be claimed to be objective, plausibly enough for the purpose of achieving a result that will gain a measure of public acceptance, it is hard to see how it is not effectively being treated as its "normative framework."

At the same time, Cicero has his own ways of indicating the theoretical limitations of the approach to political theory he is advocating in this *De legibus* passage. The account of its content just given above shows him not only flagging up his marginalization of Epicurean and Academic skeptic stances, but conceding the possibility that there may in truth be greater validity in what they claim or argue than in the position he is embracing. As Raphael Woolf puts it: "One might say that to announce loudly that one is closing down debate is itself to initiate a debate." Woolf goes on to add a further apt comment:

> Cicero, I suggest, is using the notion of uniformity of outlook to illustrate a crucial feature of the theory he is advocating. The idea of natural law is precisely the idea that there is a universal set of normative principles applicable in all contexts. If this idea is correct, then there is indeed no room for divergence of opinion about what justice is.[14]

It is also significant that Cicero makes the Epicurean Atticus his principal interlocutor in Book 1 of *De legibus*.[15] *De legibus*, after all, is a dialogue, indeed one of Cicero's liveliest dialogues, not a treatise propounding its proposals dogmatically. Nor does Cicero simply ignore Atticus's own philosophical commitments. When he invites him to sign up to a basically Platonic and Stoic thesis on the rule of nature by god or nature, Atticus makes it clear that he does so for the sake of the argument to be developed on its basis, and explicitly brackets his own Epicureanism (*Leg.* 1.21–22). As I point out elsewhere,[16] when he offers a summary of that argument, he does so in terms which abstract from its specifically Stoic commitments (*Leg.* 1.35). And when in the sequel to the passage we have been considering, Cicero mounts against cultural relativist versions of legal positivism a defense of the view (couched in essentially Stoic terminology) that "there is only one justice, which constitutes the bond among humans, and which has been constituted by the one law, which is right reason in commands and prohibitions" (*Leg.* 1.42–48), he has already clearly been attacking the Epicurean view of justice in some detail (*Leg.* 1.40–41, where the manuscript text resumes after a lacuna). Atticus is not made to offer any direct comment on Cicero's extended assault on other views such as these when eventually it is brought to a close (*Leg.* 1.52). Perhaps trying to rekindle a sense of genuine dialogue at this point, Cicero announces that the next topic will be the dispute between the Old Academy and the Stoics on the good. Urbanity and a different perspective are not however restored until Atticus's next intervention: a sardonic anecdote about disagreement in philosophy, which was told him—he says—by Phaedrus: tellingly enough, an Epicurean, like himself (*Leg.* 1.53).

One might suggest at this point something that could appear to pose a more troublesome objection both to Cicero's procedure and to the conclusions he draws from its employment. If his objective is the achievement in practice of a consensus on foundations for a stable and sound political settlement, it might be argued, does he not need to persuade citizens at large of his proposals? Finding a cluster of good philosophical schools with whom they would meet with approval is one thing. Getting them actually implemented is quite another. For a reply to this purported difficulty that we could offer to Cicero, it will suffice to distinguish between the basis on which his political recipe is recommended (its principles would be approved by a consensus of the soundest philosophers in the Platonic and Aristotelian tradition) and the audience to whom it is being recommended. That audience consists of the nonphilosophers Atticus and Quintus within the frame of the dialogue, but as the projected readership of its text he is addressing the Roman political elite. Conceivably Cicero hoped that if sufficient numbers of his peers took its proposals to heart, whether immediately or at some future date, a consensus on their implementation might—in some form or to some extent—emerge among those best placed and equipped to bring about political reformation.

Full-Throttled Debate

Cicero sometimes writes as though political theory—discussion of the best form of *res publica* or of what laws and customs are beneficial—belongs within the intellectual province of the experienced statesman, whereas treatment of what is good or bad, of obligation, and of how we should live (*bene vivendi ratio*) is for the philosopher to work at and then carry through into practice (*De or.* 1.209–13, *Div.* 2.9–12). He credits Carneades with this division of labor (*Div.* 2.9), which belonged within a broader survey of professions that is executed in Socratic style. Such a survey was designed for use in skeptical critique of overweening pretensions entertained by some one among them. One thing clear about the contrast is that it is not to be construed as a sharp division between theory and practice. The assumption is rather that experience needs to inform political theory, and that philosophical findings can and should shape our lives.[17] Another thing obvious enough (cf. *De or.* 1.214–18) is that there is no reason in principle why someone might not become equipped with capacities for both political theory and for philosophy, and achieve accomplishment in each. Then again, doing good political theory might require good philosophical reflection: as Cicero clearly indicates in his treatment of justice in Book 1 of *De legibus*, and especially in his explicit references to philosophical schools and traditions at *Leg.* 1.37–9 (discussed above in "Silencing Debate").

But does the philosophy called in aid of political theory necessarily have to exclude debate (as in that *De legibus* context)? The evidence of *De republica*, to which *De legibus* is presented as the companion dialogue, suggests that Cicero thought otherwise. In a letter dated to October or November 54 BCE to his brother Quintus, he described the topic of *De republica* as "the best system for a citizen body (*civitas*) and the best citizen (*civis*)" (*QFr.* 3.5.1). The participants in the conversations it purports to describe were Scipio, Laelius, and other leading political figures from two or three generations earlier, gathered in 129 BCE at what is represented as a critical moment for the Roman Republic, a few days before Scipio's sudden death (*Rep.* 1.14–18, *Lael.* 14). It was constructed on a grander scale than any of Cicero's other writings, in six books, apparently conceived as three pairs. Books 1 and 2 dealt with "the best system," Books 5 and 6 with "the best citizen," while the central books (as in Plato's *Republic*) addressed more foundational topics: Book 3 justice as the foundation of political order, Book 4 the institutions, customs, and practices needed to bring virtuous citizens up properly.

Book 3 survives only in fragmentary form. However it had been known for centuries—from a report by Augustine in the *City of God*—that at the end of Book 2 Cicero had left hanging for the next phase of the discussion a key question about justice. Is it impossible to conduct the *res publica* without injustice? Or does its conduct on the contrary require justice of the highest order? According to Augustine Book 3 went on to pursue that question by staging a major debate (*magna conflictio*) in which Philus, one of the discussants, argued the case for the unavoidability of injustice, to be answered by Laelius putting the opposite case (August. *De civ. D.* 2.21). A few extracts along with other information about the content of the two speeches were available elsewhere in Augustine, and in other later authors, most importantly Lactantius. Lactantius focused on Philus's arguments, but also (*Div. inst.* 5.14.3–5) records the important information[18] that Cicero was here modeling his treatment on what he represented as the Academic skeptic Carneades' delivery of opposed speeches on justice (though first the positive, then the negative case) while on a diplomatic mission sent by the Athenians to Rome in 155 BCE. Then in 1819 substantial portions mostly of Philus's speech became known through the discovery of a palimpsest containing sections of *De republica*, including most notably much of the first two books. At that point it became clearer than ever that Cicero wanted his readers to side with Laelius rather than Philus, who made it plain from the outset that he dissociated himself from the immorality of the view he was about to advance *argumenti causa* (*Rep.* 3.8). Evidently, however, he thought that the debate needed to be heard.

Reconstruction of how either Philus or (still more) Laelius organized his argument is difficult and has any way to be conjectural; scholarly agreement has accordingly proved hard to achieve. For our purposes, all that we need to note is that the material Cicero included in those arguments contained a good deal of philosophical argumentation on ethical fundamentals. To quote a recent summary of one reading of Philus's case, offered by James Zetzel:[19]

> moving from the grandest idea of law and justice being identical, through the more cautious Aristotelian idea of justice as another's good—already rejected by Thrasymachus in *Republic* 1—to the vulgar consequentialism of the Epicureans, ending with the picture of a world in which only a fool would pay any attention to moral standards, and in which . . . a monarch is no better than a brigand.

By contrast: "Laelius starts from this utter negation of morality and reverses it: by the time he is finished, we can again believe in justice, this time as a transcendent moral standard independent of any human failings."

So presentation of philosophical debate can be important in Ciceronian political theorizing as in every area of his philosophical enquiries. How then to account for its presence at the very heart of *De republica*, but its exclusion from *De legibus*? The obvious and simple answer is that the two dialogues constitute examples of two different genres. While neither excludes philosophy (as understood in the terms referred to at the beginning of this section), *De republica* is a work primarily of political theory as theory, whereas *De legibus* works out a practical legislative project. Here Cicero replicates in his own fashion a salient difference between Plato's *Republic* and *Laws*, very much the models for *De republica* and *De legibus*.

The philosophical debate between Thrasymachus and Socrates in Book 1, together with the challenge reformulating Thrasymachus's stance thrown down to Socrates by Glaucon and Adeimantus at the beginning of Book 2, is what fuels the entire trajectory of the *Republic*, whose main purpose is in fact not to develop a political theory but to illuminate the nature of justice and the good. The *Laws*, by contrast, is shaped by the legislative project to which it gradually works its way round. The conversation represented in the dialogue is dominated by an anonymous Athenian Visitor, who more resembles a Solon than a Socrates, even if his identity as an Athenian thinker is crucially shaped by Socratic ethics. It contains plenty of theoretical reflection, but virtually no philosophical debate. There is occasional and not insignificant disagreement on topics such as tolerance by society of drinking and again of homosexual practices, and in Book 4 we get a reminiscence of Socrates's debate with Thrasymachus in Book 1 of the *Republic*. It is true that argument against other philosophical views from time to time is of crucial importance in enabling the Athenian to set out fundamental ideas governing the whole framework of the project. His critique of a militarist conception of the proper goal for a *polis* at the beginning of Book 1 is what is made to trigger his account of the values that will inform his own view of its proper goal. The attack on atheism in Book 10 provides argument for the religious structure that shapes the life of the good city that he delineates and its constitutional, institutional, and legislative provisions. Nowhere, however, is there two-sided philosophical debate.

A picture begins to form. In the sphere of politics, debate is called for when discussion is at any rate primarily conducted at the level of theory. But when political theory is to be applied in a practical project of legislation, debate will be unwelcome, as liable only to muddy the waters or blunt the message.[20] In his own political life, admittedly, Cicero did indeed from time to time find the waters thoroughly murky, as above all in the agonizing—evidenced in his letters to Atticus of the time—which he articulated often in philosophical terms in the early months of 49 BCE, as civil war between Caesar and Pompey loomed ever closer, and he debated what course he himself should follow.[21] But that mental condition he would no doubt have attributed to human weakness (cf., e.g., *Tusc.* 5.3–4).

Academic Therapy

That is the picture is Cicero seems to leave us with in the dialogues of 55–51 BCE. But when he returned to writing philosophy in 46–44 BCE, we come upon one composition clearly conceived as practical in intent where there is debate in profusion, even though the overall objective is persuasion and guidance. The five dialogues that make up *Tusculan Disputations* (45 BCE) constitute a work that, together with *De officiis*, comes as close as Cicero gets to a personal manifesto in his philosophical writings (despite a disclaimer at *Tusc.* 5.11). Their practical intent is apparent from the account of their scope and purpose that Cicero was to give in the retrospective catalog of his philosophical writings presented in the preface to Book 2 of *De divinatione* (composed in the spring of the following year) (*Div.* 2.2):

> My five subsequent books of *Tusculan Disputations* explained the key prerequisites of a happy life. The first is about making light of death, the second is on putting up with pain, the third deals with the alleviation of distress, and the fourth with other mental disturbances. The fifth covers the subject which sheds more light than any other on the whole of philosophy. It teaches that virtue is sufficient on its own for a happy life.

The philosophy of the *Tusculans* is not merely practical. It is represented as a sort of medicine, an art or science of healing the mind (*Tusc.* 2.43, 3.6: *animi medicina*; cf. e.g. 4.58–61, 83–4). This distinctive conceptualisation of how ethics has practical effect was common ground between Hellenistic philosophers, as amply discussed in recent scholarship. Epicurus ended his ethical *Letter to Menoeceus* by promising his addressee that if he practiced all the *Letter*'s teaching night and day, he would never be deeply disturbed, but live a godlike existence among humans (*Ep. Men.* 135). Elsewhere, explicitly invoking the medical analogy, he pronounced as empty the discourse of a philosopher that provides no effective treatment for any human passion (Porph. *Ad Marcellam* 31 [= LS 25C]). The fourth of the books of Chrysippus's *On Emotions*, which seems also to have enjoyed a separate life as *Therapeutics*, followed the theory of the first three books (which it seems to have recapitulated) with therapeutic advice (Galen *De loc. aff.* 3.1 [= SVF 3.457], *PHP* 5.6.45 [= SVF 3.458]). Cicero's own teacher, the Academic Philo of Larissa, mapped the different modes of philosophical discourse by deploying an elaborate comparison with the corresponding jobs a doctor has to perform (Stob. *Ecl.* 2.39.20–41.25).[22]

Both Epicurus and Chrysippus had worked out a body of ethical and psychological doctrine from which therapeutic consequences readily flowed, and could then be formulated in appropriate advice. The Academic skeptic holds no such doctrines. Debate and questioning are his métier. Cicero might have decided, as earlier in *De legibus* and subsequently (as we shall see) in *De officiis*, to bypass the debate, and instead to report his own conclusion on which school had the more persuasive view on the topics pursued in each of the *Tusculans*' five books. He might then have gone on to articulate therapeutic advice on that basis. In fact he undertakes something methodologically bolder and intellectually more challenging, in the Socratic spirit he invokes at the outset (*Tusc.* 1.8; cf. 5.11). He allows plenty of divergent views to have their voices, rehearses debates between them, and engages in such debate with them himself.

In short, philosophical debate is what drives a good deal of the *Tusculans*' theoretical argumentation (with Book 2 constituting something of an exception), albeit that practical guidance remains the overall objective. This attempt to combine the two modes of debate and guidance, along with other distinctive features of the *Tusculans*, goes to make these dialogues one of the most innovative and experimental works in the Ciceronian corpus.[23] It is as though, at any rate within the sphere of personal ethics, he had come to think that a more flexible and imaginative approach to the requirements of guidance could be attempted than he had taken for politics in *De legibus*.

For practical purposes the controversy Cicero thus places center stage does require some form of resolution. One option would presumably have consisted in plumping for one or other of the views discussed as the more persuasive (and showing it to be so). It is often wrongly supposed that the *Tusculans* do take this path, and can best be described as Stoic (true with some qualifications only of Books 3 and 4). Alternatively—and this turns out to be a closer general approximation to the truth—he might engineer a degree of harmony between discordant philosophical voices, replicating in a different mode the policy that he had adopted in Book 1 of *De legibus* for laying foundations for applied political theory.[24] He would then need to devise a determinate and suitably persuasive therapeutic recipe accordingly.

The *Tusculans* constitute an extensive, complex, and highly nuanced text, and any halfway adequate attempt at a summary of the variety of the ways in which Cicero tackles such challenges would require a full essay all to itself.[25] A first observation, however, is that with the first of the dialogues he certainly represents himself as having delivered the therapy he talks of. Thus at the beginning of Book 2, this is how Cicero's quite lively adolescent interlocutor of the first two books (cf. *Tusc.* 2.15, 28) responds to Book 1's treatment of the fear of death (*Tusc.* 2.10; cf. 1.119): "From this kind of anxiety, believe me, I have been so freed that I consider nothing to be less in need of concern." And at the conclusion of the argument of Book 2 against the view that pain, to be characterized in Book 5 as "virtue's fiercest antagonist" (*Tusc.* 5.76), is the worst thing that can happen to us, he is made to say that over the two days occupied by the two dialogues, he hopes he has been freed from the two things he most feared (*Tusc.* 2.67).

How has the respondent in Books 1 and 2 been brought to such a point of unconcern? Cicero at the outset emphasizes that philosophy in its fully finished form (*perfecta philosophia*) must be able to deploy "abundant and embellished" speech (*copiose . . . ornateque dicere*), and presents the lectures of the *Tusculans* as illustrative of philosophy so conceived: the declamations of his old age, as he puts it (*senilis . . . declamatio*: *Tusc.* 1.7). There has certainly been plenty of rhetoric in Book 1, initially rhetoric in the service of a philosophical argument, mostly designed to present the case for the immortality of the soul and its ultimate freedom from the limitations of the body, as articulated above all by Plato. Then, in the last thirty or so increasingly anecdotal paragraphs, its deployment is intensified and serves chiefly to stiffen our resolve.

The same is even more emphatically true of Book 2. Here the philosopher most prominent in Cicero's discussion is Epicurus, credited with the view (subjected to mocking refutation: *Tusc.* 2.44–45) that pain is "the only bad thing and the worst of all bad things" (*Tusc.* 2.17). Otherwise, apart from giving short shrift to the Stoic view that pain is not something bad at all (*Tusc.* 2.29–30, 42), he says remarkably little about philosophy and philosophers (except for the moral heroism of a minority among them: *Tusc.* 2.52, 61). The direction of his thinking is pithily expressed as follows (*Tusc.* 2.28, just before he attacks the Stoics' *ratiunculae*, "mini-ratiocinations"; cf. *Tusc.* 2.42): "The right question is not so much whether pain is bad, but how the soul is to be strengthened for the endurance of pain." The focus throughout Book 2 is accordingly virtue and its development, as what we need if we are to make a proper evaluation of pain and cope with it in practice.

Cicero does expound a philosophical basis for the recipe he provides. Having dealt with Epicureanism and Stoicism, he sketches an account of self-mastery that draws on Platonic and Aristotelian thought (without mentioning any names) as what is needed for the purpose. The soul has two parts, and it is for reason to prompt or direct or restrain the part that lacks reason into conformity with its grasp of what is honorable (*Tusc.* 2.47–53). But convincing someone to take to heart self-mastery so understood calls not for cool and precise philosophical argumentation (that is not how he dispenses with either Epicurean or Stoic positions) but for a sustained and varied flow of rhetoric. The rhetoric depends heavily on appeal especially to historical examples of courage and endurance, seldom represented as the fruit of philosophy. Nor indeed would it have been in the least plausible to construe them in that light. Their message in a nutshell is: "pull yourself together."

Cicero had in Book 1 achieved a sort of consensus about "making light of death," among philosophers who otherwise hold sharply opposed views on the fate of the soul. Either Plato is right that it is immortal, or if it perishes with the body, as Epicurus and others held, death is no evil.[26] But in Book 2 the only philosophers he really engages with are convicted of propounding nothing but false doctrines and palpably inadequate arguments, which make the right attitude to pain harder to achieve.

Books 3 and 4, however, supply a much more challenging philosophical diet. These two books—though not devoid of characteristic Ciceronian tropes—are almost wholly preoccupied with Greek philosophical debates about distress (in Book 3) and other mental disturbances (in Book 4), the pros and cons of the various positions taken, and the extent of agreement or otherwise between the different schools, both on the phenomena themselves and on appropriate therapies.[27] One way in which Cicero marks the shift in register is by a different handling of the function of interlocutor. He had written the concluding words of Book 2 (*Tusc.* 2.67) as though the next dialogue will be conducted with the same interlocutor as in the first two books. But at the end of the preface to Book 3 he represents himself simply as calling on "one of those present" for a topic to discuss (*Tusc.* 3.7; similarly in Book 4: *Tusc.* 4.8). Cicero restricts the roles these volunteers play simply to stating the views that he will go on to refute at length, and allowing them none of the interventions in the subsequent discussion or the concluding responses made by the interlocutor of Books 1 and 2, nor indeed anything resembling the particularly active engagement of the discussant in the final Book 5. The extended passages of stirring rhetoric that fill the final sections of the other three books are also notable by their absence in Books 3 and 4. Cicero treats his audience (or better, his readership) more like fellow therapists needing a practitioner's handbook than as patients potentially in need of therapy themselves.

A. E. Douglas found so little that was distinctively Ciceronian in these books that he suggested that their subject matter must have been regarded by the author as "less important than the conquest of the fear of death and the endurance of physical pain," death and pain certainly being treated as the subjects of our greatest fears (*Tusc.* 4.64).[28] Such an inference, however, would conflict with Cicero's own words at the end of Book 1, where of the discussions he projects for the following books he singles out as especially important those that are to deal with "the alleviation of distress, fears, lusts: the most abundant fruit produced by all of philosophy" (*Tusc.* 1.119). And as Stephen White points out, of all the mental disturbances to which humans are subject, Cicero defends the decision to make distress the single topic of Book 3 as "the worst thing a person can feel," and "the very well-spring of misery" (*Tusc.* 4.82–3).[29] In the last sentence of the entire work he refers to its writing as providing alleviation from "the bitter sorrows and the host of troubles that beset me on every side" (*Tusc.* 5.121).

Moreover, it was not many months since in grief over the death of his daughter Tullia he had composed a *Consolation*, to which he refers here (*Tusc.* 3.76, 4.63; cf. 1.65, 76); and consolation for grief (*dolor, maeror*) is what figures most prominently in the therapeutic section of Book 3 (*Tusc.* 3.71–9), as often earlier too. Cicero was himself, of course, no securely imperturbable sage (as he observes in commenting on the composition of the *Consolation*: *Tusc.* 4.63; cf. 3.76, 5.3–4). So when he observes that the enquiry of Book 4 (the same would be true of Book 3: cf. *Tusc.* 3.80) is proposed not so much with the wise (i.e., perfectly rational) person in mind, but for the benefit of the inquirer (*Tusc.* 4.58–59), we might not unreasonably read his remark as effectively relating to himself as much as to the interlocutor.

The main body of Book 3, however, is full of technical philosophy. Cicero puts painstaking care into explaining and weighing the merits and demerits of a wide range of views—Stoic, Peripatetic, Epicurean, but also those of the Cyrenaics and Carneades (and among the Stoics the positions of Cleanthes and Chrysippus get separate attention). Scholars often treat Books 3 and 4 as basically Stoic. So they are, in their basic contentions that the cause of all emotional disturbances is a belief, and that belief is always voluntary (*Tusc.* 3.24, 82–83, 4.65, 83). But if the voluntariness of belief is certainly something on which the Stoics differed from the Peripatetics, the treatment of emotion as or involving belief turns out not to be anything on which the leading schools disagree. It is simply that the Stoics offer much the most throrough, precise, and convincing account of the kinds of belief that emotions consist in. So the discussion in each of the two books begins with presentation of Stoic syllogisms (*Tusc.* 3.13–21) or classifications and distinctions (*Tusc.* 4.11–33, where however the extensive detail of the analogy Stoics draw with physical sickness receives criticism: *Tusc.* 4.23, 27). In both books Cicero reverts in due course to his preferred expansive, "freer" mode of argument in more Peripatetic style (*Tusc.* 3.22, 4.9, 4.33), even though specific Peripatetic doctrine on these topics is rejected as inferior to what the Stoics taught (*Tusc.* 3.22, 74, 4.38–46). Moreover, as usual he flags his own general stance as Academic, not "tied to the tenets of a single school," but looking for "the most persuasive answer on each topic" (*Tusc.* 4.7, 47).

Cicero takes distinctly differing approaches to appropriate therapies for emotional disturbances in Book 3 and in Book 4. Book 3's review of the teachings of Epicurus, the Cyrenaics, and Carneades is much preoccupied with the stances they take on therapy, and on pointing out what he sees as their inadequacies, without suggesting that they are entirely without merit. At the end of the book (*Tusc.* 3.75–79) he structures the job of those who are offering consolation as an ordered hierarchy of options: removing distress altogether, getting it to subside or diminish, keeping it within limits, diverting it elsewhere. He sums up the techniques favored by the major schools of philosophy, itemizes the chief considerations worth advancing in consolation, and comments that "different methods work for different people" (he had used them all in his own *Consolation*; cf. also *Tusc.* 4.59). He does endorse Chrysippus's view that the core of the problem is that someone who is grieving, or in some other distressed state of mind, believes their reaction to what has happened to them to be appropriate. So convincing them that it isn't, and that they can stop thinking it is, should be the real key. But at the same time he recognizes that this is a counsel of perfection: its application to the occasion of distress is "difficult" (*Tusc.* 3.79; cf. 82–83).

In Book 4 discussion of therapy is largely confined to its final section, dedicated to that topic, which includes subsections on a number of individual emotions, notably erotic love (the Stoics' position on the topic is interestingly treated as implausibly idealistic: *Tusc.* 4.72). Little, though, is otherwise said here about the views associated with particular schools. Cicero is much more intent than in Book 3 on distilling a single basic method, on which all schools ought to be able to agree, and on presenting this as the voice of reason (echoing his eloquent account, earlier in the book, of virtue as right reason: *Tusc.* 4.34). Such a method should concentrate on teaching that "emotional disturbances are wrong in and of themselves and have nothing natural or necessary about them" (*Tusc.* 4.60; cf. 61–62). We need "to show that they are a matter of belief and are voluntary, and that we experience them because we think it appropriate to do so: it is this error which philosophy promises to eradicate," as "the root of all evils" (*Tusc.* 4.83).

The main tendency of Book 3, then, is to suggest rather pragmatically that, whatever limitations may be found in their theorizing, most philosophical schools have something therapeutically useful to offer, especially since "different methods work for different people." Book 4, on the other hand, as Raphael Woolf points out, more ambitiously extracts from philosophical debate the possibility of a consensus on one single most important task for philosophy: the eradication of error (*Tusc.* 4.61).[30] Its evident idealism foreshadows the theme of the final book: that virtue is sufficient for happiness.

Book 5 is composed on a larger scale. In length it exceeds any of the three preceding books, and bids to rival Book 1. The retrospect in *De divinatione* singles out its subject matter as shedding "more light than any other on the whole of philosophy" (*Div.* 2.2). Book 5's preface soon launches into an extraordinary prose hymn to philosophy as "guide to living a life," couched in rhetoric of an extravagance unparalleled in Cicero's other surviving theoretical writing (*Tusc.* 5.5). His unidentified interlocutor is written as livelier, sharper, and harder to convince than any other in the sequence. He maintains his role through to the book's watershed (*Tusc.* 5.83), when Cicero exploits an opportunity to develop an extended final exhibition of philosophical rhetoric, surpassing in ambition any other stretch of argument in the entire sequence of the *Tusculans*. But philosophical discussion has begun with subtle debate on the pros and cons of the Stoic and Peripatetic conceptions of happiness and the good. In short, Book 5 more than any other of the five dialogues is a tour de force, designed to display the varied argumentative repertoire Cicero could command in writing philosophy for Romans as he thought it should be written.

Its basic structure consists in a simple bipartition. After indicating as usual his own Academic stance in the preface (*Tusc.* 5.11), the first main section sees Cicero arguing the Stoic case that, provided what is morally admirable is the only good, virtue is all we need to guarantee a life of happiness (*Tusc.* 5.15–82). In the second section, he undertakes the job of showing how not only the Peripatetics, who recognise also goods of the body and of fortune, but virtually all philosophical schools whose views on what is good and bad still merit attention, and above all Epicurus, can argue for the sufficiency of virtue or reason and wisdom for happiness, despite their acknowledgment of things good and bad other than virtue (*Tusc.* 5.82–118).[31] Much of the keenest debate in Book 5, however, is prompted by the questions the interlocutor puts at various junctures during Cicero's development of the Stoic position (*Tusc.* 5.13, 17–18, 21, 32, 73, 82). These constitute a device for creating two levels of Ciceronian discourse. At the main level we increasingly get Ciceronian philosophical eloquence, with recourse to episodes from Roman and then Greek history (the story of the sword of Damocles, followed by that of Cicero's own discovery of the crumbling tomb of Archimedes, is compellingly told: *Tusc.* 5.57–66). The subsidiary level consists of responses to those questions framed by the interlocutor, which are very much focused on divergences between different philosophical schools on key points, and more particularly on how far their positions are internally self-consistent.

Cicero expressly endorses the Stoic theory, which he commends both for its courage and—"unless you can produce something better"—its truth (*Tusc.* 5.82). At this point one might suppose that the dialogue has established what it set out to establish—and could therefore be drawn fairly swiftly to a conclusion. Had it done so, however, the force of the promise that *philosophy* is the guide to happiness would have been severely weakened. It would leave Book 5 and indeed the whole work ending up with a narrower view of philosophy than it looked as though Cicero wanted when he hymned its history and achievements in the preface (*Tusc.* 5.5–11). And there would of course be many likely to find deeply unattractive the suggestion that it is in truth only on Stoic premises that happiness for the virtuous is assured. Here is where Cicero makes the interlocutor launch one last sally on his consistency theme. Is there not a way, the discussant asks in effect, in which the Peripatetic position can without losing self-consistency be made to equate with the Stoic (*Tusc.* 5.82)?

In response Cicero devotes only a paragraph or two to reconsideration of the views of the Peripatetics. Within a few paragraphs he is launched into a powerfully eloquent exposition, sustained with all the devices of rhetoric at his disposal, of how and why even Epicurus thinks that the wise person will remain happy whatever happens to him, and however many of the five senses he comes to lose (*Tusc.* 5.89–118). Even Epicurus is to be brought under the umbrella of true philosophy, and of what it can teach us about the way to achieve happiness, though of course for a hedonist such as him virtue holds no interest in and of itself at all. That the Stoic case is in effect counterbalanced in the end by a sympathetic account of Epicureanism represents an extraordinary outcome for Book 5 and the sequence of dialogues as a group.

Philosophical readers of Book 5 are apt to find Cicero's exposition of views alternative to the Stoic position—that nothing else counts for happiness but virtue—puzzling and unsatisfactory. He makes no attempt to mount a defense of the Peripatetic stance that could compare in detail and rigor with the basic case he develops for the Stoic theory (*Tusc.* 5.21–31, 40–54). Much of the dissatisfaction may be due, however, to misunderstanding of the way Cicero wants his endorsement of the Stoic view (as quoted above p. 26: *Tusc.* 5.82) to be taken. He was emphatic early on that he sees the Stoic position as essentially no different from Plato's in the *Gorgias* and *Menexenus* (*Tusc.* 5.34–36). Moreover, having initially invoked Plato's *auctoritas* (much greater, he insinuates, than the Stoic Zeno's), he concludes with the promise that "my whole speech will flow from what might be described as the sacred and revered spring that is Plato's." A little later he will be ascribing the same view to Aristotle and all the leading figures in the Old Academy (*Tusc.* 5.39). So, as he represents it, the position he endorses as Stoic is not unique to Stoicism. It is the shared property of all the major schools (including here the Stoics) in the broadly Platonic tradition.

Where he thinks the Peripatetics and Old Academy (at any rate as represented by Antiochus) have gone astray is in holding that, unless someone possesses goods of the body and of fortune as well as virtue, happiness in its fullness (being not just *beatus* but *beatissimus*) is not possible (*Tusc.* 5.22–23, 40, 51, 75–76). At the beginning of the second main section of Book 5, the interlocutor challenges him to show how they might consistently take that stance (*Tusc.* 5.82). Understandably Cicero has no interest in doing that. Instead he takes the line that, provided they maintain that the virtuous person will despise pain however extreme (and any other ills of the body or of fortune), they may perfectly reasonably claim that happiness will not be affected (*Tusc.* 5.85). In effect they would be embracing the view that he earlier associates with Carneades' Peripatetic contemporary Critolaus (*Tusc.* 5.51). Although Cicero does not say as much, their position will then be just the same as the Stoics', with purely verbal differences between them all that remains: Carneades' verdict, as we are explicitly reminded at the end of Book 5 (*Tusc.* 5.119–20).[32]

So it is true that Cicero does not mount much of a defense of the Peripatetic position on happiness in the second main section of Book 5. But citing and then expatiating on the view shared by them and (more usefully for therapeutic rhetoric) Epicurus, that the virtuous or wise person is indifferent to ills of body and fortune, might reasonably have seemed to him more to the point. It is, to say the least, piquant that Epicurus and Carneades, whom *De legibus* did not allow to speak at all, are left the final say at the end of the *Tusculans*.

One implication might be that philosophy gets obsessed with minor distinctions and with the interlocutor's problem of consistency—of logic. From one point of view consistency, and debates turning on it, matters hugely. And Cicero duly rehearses the debates with appropriate vigor and ingenuity. But in the end Book 5 suggests that they are in danger of diverting us from philosophy's primary task: the guidance we look to philosophy to supply. For that, philosophical rhetoric (harnessed to Academic judiciousness) will need to be called into service: *perfecta philosophia*. It can build on the consensus that most powerful philosophers, despite their differences, do manage to achieve on all the questions debated in the *Tusculans*, from realizing that death holds no terrors to registering the sufficiency of virtue for the good life.

Coda

It is not only when developing the basis for a practicable legislative project for the *res publica* that Cicero thinks it best to eschew debate. Philosophical debate is for the most part and of set purpose excluded in *De officiis*, the last of his philosophical writings on ethics, or indeed on any topic: a book of advice (*praeceptio*, *Off.* 1.6) on our principal moral obligations, not a dialogue but expounded in the literary form of an extended letter to his son Marcus.[33] Guidance, untrammeled by any promise to engage with the disagreements between the philosophical schools over its subject matter (cf. *Off.* 1.6), is uncomplicatedly what it is. We might ask: is there then anything that marks it out as a work of *Academic* philosophy—for which debate is the best way to get at the truth or the best approximation to it—in any sense at all?

To this question the answer is an unequivocal "Yes." Here the preface to the whole work is a key text. For while it does not launch any debate between the schools about the questions Cicero will be engaging with, he sets the scene by *recalling* his own staging of such debates elsewhere (he means principally *De finibus* and *Tusculan Disputations*). It is not that those questions of practical ethics in business deals and in politics do not sometimes pull an agent pondering them or a philosopher thinking about them in different directions. Indeed Book 3 of *De officiis* is devoted to consideration of such issues, particularly the apparent conflict between the honourable and the advantageous course. But it is indicative that the one really philosophical debate he reports in its course is between two members of the same Stoic school—Diogenes and Antipater—who, as he is anxious to stress, do not disagree on the need, dictated by their common philosophy, to do nothing dishonourable, but only on what would actually be a dishonourable thing to do (*Off.* 3.49–53). He dismisses the views of Epicureans and similar schools out of hand, although in the last pages of the work he will judge it prudent to line up some arguments against them, presumably just in case Marcus might feel tempted to waver from the instruction with which he has now been supplied (*Off.* 1.5, 3.116–19). Then he proposes that the business of giving advice is best regarded as the territory of the Stoics, Academics (here he means the Old Academy of Speusippus, Xenocrates, and Polemo: *Leg.* 1.38), and the Peripatetics, ruling out Ariston, Pyrrho, and Erillus, whose views simply leave no scope for that kind of philosophizing (cf. *Fin.* 2.43, 5.73). In the event he will in what follows be presenting a Stoic treatment of the issues—as it quickly transpires, largely in Panaetius's version. But he will do so not slavishly as a translator, but "as I am used to doing, drawing on those sources according to my own judgment and decision (*iudicio arbitrioque nostro*), to the extent and in the manner that will seem best" (*Off.* 1.6; cf. 1.7–10).

These last remarks indicate to the reader that this *is* to be a work by Cicero the Academic skeptic. He refers to his usual practice, in terms that recapitulate elements of the classic statements of Academic methodology in the dialogues (*Nat. d.* 1.11–12, *Div.* 2.150). That he should find a Stoic presentation of the subject most appealing will not surprise readers of his ethical dialogues, nor that he likes Panaetius's version best, while allowing that either a Peripatetic or a Stoic basis for the business in hand would suffice (*Off.* 3.33). Book 4 of *De finibus* had concluded with praise of Panaetius as a Stoic who in style and doctrine alike was close to the Old Academy and the Peripatetics (*Fin.* 4.79). The way Cicero puts the point, however, makes it clear that he himself is by no means to be perceived *as* a Stoic now, a message reinforced in the prefatory sections of Books 2 and 3.

That is in effect the kind of reply he makes explicitly at the beginning of Book 2 to the objection that back in our introductory section we saw him registering. Contrary to the objection, he says, Academic skeptics are not left with no views, or no practical options for living. Academics say that some things are persuasive (*probabilia*), some not, even if certainty is unavailable. And there's no reason why he shouldn't go for what seems persuasive to him, while avoiding the arrogance of flatly asserting or denying things. At this point he refers for a fuller discussion to his *Academic books* (*Off.* 2.7–8). For now what is more important is that the kind of philosophical guidance attempted in *De officiis* can best proceed having given just a few mentions of debate, now recollected in tranquillity: very differently than the *Tusculans*.

The *Tusculans*, however, share with *De officiis*, and with *De legibus*, too, the conviction that in the practical sphere it is important to achieve as much consensus as possible if philosophy as such is to speak with authority. Our examination of these writings suggests that Cicero would have wholeheartedly agreed with Jonathan Wolff: "Philosophers find it hard to compromise.... Without pure philosophical reflection, and the dogged pursuit of what may seem to others crazy ideas, intellectual discussion would be flat and static." But he would also have agreed with Wolff's assessment of philosophy's best strategy for moving the development of policy forward in matters of applied moral and political theory: "to draw more people into a consensus view, so that policy can be more widely endorsed, even if different people's reasons for the policy differ." Kantians and utilitarians can "agree that it is wrong to murder innocents when no good could come of it" (although presumably a Kantian would not put the point in that consequentialist style).[34]

Cicero's social and intellectual world was very different from our own. His ideal of *perfecta philosophia*, in particular, strikes few contemporary resonances, even if the importance of good and well-written philosophy by public intellectuals and others that can speak to readers beyond the academy has often been recognized. Yet his pioneering attempts to tackle a fundamental problem about the reconciliation of debate and guidance in the practical application of ethical and political philosophy, particularly in the *Tusculan Disputations*, should earn him philosophical respect.[35]

Notes

An earlier version of this article was published as Schofield (2021a); use of it is made courtesy of the Institute of Classical Studies, University of London, with thanks.

1. Wolff (2006a).
2. Wolff (2006a) 2–3.
3. Wolff (2006a) 19.
4. The same general issue is interestingly pursued, particularly with reference to politics and to this same passage of Book 1 of *De legibus*, in Nicgorski (2016) 15–58.
5. For the Academics' encyclopedic method, see, for example, Algra (1997).
6. See the section titled "Academic Therapy," pp. 128–136.
7. Antiochus was a member of the Academy active in the late second and early first centuries BCE, with whom Cicero studied in Athens in 79 BCE (*Brut.* 315), and someone he forever after greatly admired. Antiochus had come to believe that its skepticism was a betrayal of the Academy's true philosophical tradition, as represented by Plato's early successors, who for him constituted the "Old Academy." His own teaching was effectively a synthesis of the views of the Old Academy and the Peripatetics (the school founded by Aristotle), and in epistemology the Stoics, whose position on the good, however, he rejected. See further Allen (2018); more comprehensively, Sedley (2012).
8. On the dating, see Dyck (2004) 5–12.
9. Görler (1995) 103 [= Görler (2004) 257–258].
10. Atkins (2013) 183–185.
11. On justice as natural, or more broadly, on a natural sociable impulse to foster community which justice (together with liberality) perfects, see *Off.* 1.11–15, 20–22, 3.21–28, with Schofield (2021b) 159–166; as wisdom's principal focus, see *Off.* 1.153–155, with Reydams-Schils (2015) 95–99.
12. Wolff (2006a) 3.
13. Wolff (2006b) 410, 427.
14. Woolf (2015) 117.
15. So Woolf (2015) 116–117.
16. Schofield (2021a) 114–117.
17. We might compare the opening pages of *De officiis*, where its topic of obligation is said to involve two kinds of question: one relating to the criteria for what things are good (*finis bonorum*: see Allen (2014) for the explanation of this expression, frequently employed by Cicero), the other to rules of guidance (*praecepta*) (*Off.* 1.7).
18. Recently argued in Powell (2013) to be fanciful misinformation, if taken at all literally.
19. Zetzel (2017) 318. I discuss Laelius's reply in Schofield (2017).
20. On philosophical debate on matters of practice in politics, see "Coda," below, pp. 136–138.
21. See Schofield (2021c) 197–206.

22. The recent literature includes notably Nussbaum (1994) and Sorabji (2000). For Chrysippus's *On Emotions*, see Tieleman (2003); for Philo, see Brittain (2001) 255–295.
23. See the important monograph of Gildenhard (2007) for treatment of the distinctiveness of the *Tusculans*.
24. See the discussion above in "Silencing Debate," pp. 121–126.
25. My observations in this section are much indebted to the ample and reflective discussion of the work in Woolf (2015), and they are largely congruent with the subtle treatment of *Tusculans* in Görler (1996) [= Görler (2004) 212–239]. In making the final revision of the fourth section ("Academic Therapy"), I hope I have profited from the discussions of the *Tusculans* conducted at the Symposium Hellenisticum held in Cambridge in July 2019.
26. See the chapter by James Warren in this volume.
27. See the translation and commentary by Graver (2002).
28. Douglas (1990) 77.
29. White (1995) 226.
30. Woolf (2015) 240–241. As he points out, however, Stoics and Peripatetics would not agree on what counts as "error" or irrational emotional disturbance.
31. At *Tusc.* 5.28 Cicero makes the programmatic statement, "It is clear who are the persons I am calling good. We call people who are equipped and adorned with all the virtues we call sometimes wise, sometimes good." From *Tusc.* 5.68 on talk of the wise person predominates.
32. I discuss Carneades' "neutralizing" argument in Schofield (2012).
33. See Gibson and Morrison (2007) 9–13.
34. Wolff (2011) 4–5.
35. This chapter is a revised and expanded version of a Keeling Lecture delivered in 2011: my thanks to Fiona Leigh for the honor of the invitation. Some of its material has also been presented to audiences in Oxford, Cambridge, Glasgow, Princeton, Athens, and Toronto. I am grateful for comments made on all these occasions. The essay mostly retains its original lecture style, and is lightly annotated accordingly. It has been slightly expanded at a few points for the present volume.

References

Algra, K. (1997). "Chrysippus, Carneades, Cicero: The Ethical *divisiones* in Cicero's Lucullus," in B. Inwood and J. Mansfeld (eds.), *Assent and Argument in Cicero's Academic Books* (Leiden), 107–139.

Allen, J. (2014). "Why There Are Ends of Both Goods and Evils in Ancient Ethical Theory," in M. Lee (ed.), *Strategies of Argument: Essays in Ancient Ethics, Epistemology and Logic* (Oxford), 231–254.

Allen, J. (2018). "*Aporia* and the New Academy," in G. Karamanolis and V. Politis (eds.), *The Aporetic Tradition in Ancient Philosophy* (Cambridge), 172–191.

Atkins, J. W. (2013). *Cicero on Politics and the Limits of Reason*. (Cambridge).

Brittain, C. (2001). *Philo of Larissa*. (Oxford).

Douglas, A. E. (1990). *Cicero*: Tusculan Disputations II & V. (Liverpool).

Dyck, A. R. (2004). *A Commentary on Cicero* De legibus. (Ann Arbor).

Gibson, R. F., and A. D. Morrison (2007). "Introduction: What Is a Letter?," in R. Morello and A. D. Morrison (eds.), *Ancient Letters: Classical and Late Antique Epistolography* (Cambridge), 1–16.

Gildenhard, I. (2007). *Paideia Romana: Cicero's* Tusculan Disputations. (Cambridge).
Görler, W. (1995). "Silencing the Troublemaker: *De Legibus* I.39 and the continuity of Cicero's skepticism," in Powell, 85–113.
Görler, W. (1996). "Zum literarischen Charakter und zur Struktur der *Tusculanae disputationes*," in C. Mueller-Goldingen and K. Sier (eds.), *Lenaika: Festschrift für C. W. Müller* (Stuttgart/Leipzig), 189–215.
Görler, W. (2004). *Kleine Schriften zur hellenistisch-römischen Philosophie*. (Leiden).
Graver, M. (2002). *Cicero on the Emotions*: Tusculan Disputations *3 and 4*. (Chicago).
Graver, M. (2007). *Stoicism and Emotion*. (Chicago).
Nicgorski, W. (2016). *Cicero's Skepticism and His Recovery of Political Philosophy*. (New York).
Nussbaum, M. (1994). *The Therapy of Desire*. (Princeton).
Powell, J. G. F., ed. (1995). *Cicero the Philosopher*. (Oxford).
Powell, J. G. F. (2013). "The Embassy of Three Philosophers to Rome in 155 BC," in C. Kremmydas and K. Tempest (eds.), *Hellenistic Oratory: Continuity and Change* (Oxford), 219–247.
Reydams-Schils, G. (2015). "Teaching Pericles: Cicero on the Study of Nature," in G. D. Williams and K. Volk (eds.), *Roman Reflections: Studies in Latin Philosophy* (Oxford), 91–107.
Schofield, M. (2012). "The Neutralizing Argument: Carneades, Antiochus, Cicero," in Sedley, 237–249.
Schofield, M. (2017). "Cicero on Imperialism and the Soul," in R. Seaford, J. Wilkins, and M. Wright (eds), *Selfhood and the Soul: Essays on Ancient Thought and Literature in Honour of Christopher Gill* (Oxford), 107–124.
Schofield, M. (2021a). "Debate or Guidance? Cicero on Philosophy," in F. Leigh (ed.), *Themes in Plato, Aristotle, and Hellenistic Philosophy: Keeling Lectures 2011–18*. BICS Supplement 141. (London), 131–148.
Schofield, M. (2021b). "Atticus in *De legibus* and *Brutus*," in G. M. Müller (ed.), *Figurengestaltung und Gesprächsinteraktion im antiken Dialog* (Stuttgart), 109–126.
Schofield, M. (2021c). *Cicero: Political Philosophy*. (Oxford).
Sedley, D., ed. (2012). *The Philosophy of Antiochus*. (Cambridge).
Sorabji, R. (2000). *Emotion and Peace of Mind: From Stoic Agitation to Christian Temptation*. (Oxford).
Tieleman, T. (2003). *Chrysippus' On Affections: Reconstruction and Interpretation*. (Leiden).
White, S. (1995). "Cicero and the Therapists," in Powell, 219–246.
Wolff, J. (2006a). "Making the World Safe for Utilitarianism," in A. O'Hear (ed.), *Political Philosophy* (Cambridge), 1–22.
Wolff, J. (2006b). "Risk, Fear, Blame, Shame, and the Regulation of Public Safety." *Economics and Philosophy* 22: 409–427.
Wolff, J. (2011). *Ethics and Public Policy: A Philosophical Inquiry*. (London).
Woolf, R. (2015). *Cicero: The Philosophy of a Roman Sceptic*. (London).
Zetzel, J. (2017). "The Attack on Justice: Cicero, Lactantius, and Carneades." *Rh. Mus.* 160: 299–319.

PART II
WRITING AND ARGUING ROMAN PHILOSOPHY

CHAPTER 9

THE EPICUREANISM OF LUCRETIUS

TIM O'KEEFE

What is distinctive about Lucretius's version of Epicureanism? The answer might appear to be "nothing," for two reasons. First, Epicureanism in general is doctrinally conservative, with followers of Epicurus claiming to follow his authority. Second, Lucretius in particular claims to be merely transmitting the arguments of his beloved master Epicurus in a pleasing manner. He is eager to extol his poetic accomplishments in presenting these arguments, but specifically claims that the arguments themselves are not his own.

I will argue that these considerations do not prevent *De rerum natura* (*DRN*) from presenting a distinct version of Epicureanism. Its arguments in physics are almost certainly drawn from Epicurus himself, either directly or as mediated by later Epicurean sources. But in the examples Lucretius uses to illustrate these arguments, as well as in his descriptions of things like the fear of death and the formation of society, Lucretius delivers unexpected insights into human psychology, ones that are not clearly present in the other sources we have on Epicureanism. Furthermore, the way in which Lucretius presents his arguments can rightly be considered original philosophically and not just poetically.

Obstacles to Considering Lucretius a Distinctive Philosopher

While Lucretius is one of our main sources on Epicureanism, he has not been much studied as a philosopher in his own right. This neglect is understandable. Later Epicureans regarded Epicurus not merely as a person with some important insights, but as the savior of humanity, and they wished to say nothing that would contradict him.[1]

Medical advances after Epicurus's time established that, if the mind has a bodily seat, it is in the head and not the chest, as Epicurus had said. Rather than simply admitting that Epicurus had been mistaken on this specific issue, later Epicureans struggled with how to reconcile these advances with their respect for Epicurus's authority.[2] And Lucretius proclaims of Epicurus, "you are our father and the discoverer of truth: you supply us with fatherly precepts; and from your pages, illustrious master, like the bees which in flowerful vales sip each bloom, we sip on each golden saying—golden and ever most worthy of eternal life" (Lucr. 3.9–13).[3]

However, from the mere fact that later Epicureans claim to be faithful to Epicurus, it does not follow that they have nothing distinctive to say. Later Epicureans had to contend with philosophers Epicurus did not. For instance, Philodemus (c. 110–c. 30 BCE) grappled with the Stoics on the basis for inductive generalizations in his treatise *On Signs*, and Colotes (*fl.* c. 310–260 BCE) argued that the Academic skeptics destroyed the basis for action. Also, it's not as if everything Epicurus said was entirely clear or that he had definitively settled every question. Epicureans vigorously disagreed about how to properly understand Epicurus's doctrines and how to apply them to specific cases. For instance, at *Fin.* 1.65–70, Cicero relates that various groups of Epicureans advanced three different accounts of the origins of friendship and the way in which a friend could be said to love his friend as much as himself, and rival factions of Epicureans argued over whether the wise person would ever experience anger, and if so, what kinds of anger.[4]

But Lucretius appears to be in a weaker position than Epicureans like Philodemus when it comes to philosophical originality. Philodemus may pledge fealty to Epicurus, but he is self-consciously trying to interpret Epicurus correctly against rivals and extend Epicurus's thought into new areas, whereas Lucretius says at 3.1–30 that he is not trying to compete with Epicurus in discovering anything new but is merely transmitting the golden truths that have been revealed to him by Epicurus his "father," and at 5.55–56 he says he has been treading in Epicurus's footsteps and following his doctrines. If we take Lucretius at his word, he is not trying to devise any arguments of his own, and it may seem that in order to discover which "version" of Epicureanism is contained in his poem, we should engage in *Quellenforschung*, i.e., we should try to discern what sources Lucretius drew on to compose *DRN*.

The search for Lucretius's sources, however, has been inconclusive and is likely to remain so. The primary obstacle is that almost all of the sources Lucretius may have had at hand—such as Epicurus's *On Nature*, or the treatises of later Epicureans—are lost to us. In the absence of such sources to check *DRN* against, looking at the content of *DRN* itself does not show whether Lucretius drew exclusively on Epicurus himself or also on later sources. It was once thought that Lucretius's polemics against divine providence and teleology in biology were aimed against the Stoics, and hence drew from a source after Epicurus. But the Stoics themselves drew on earlier philosophers such as Plato, especially his creation myth in the *Timaeus*. And when criticizing other philosophical positions, Lucretius generally advances generic "catch-all" arguments—ones that can target both Platonist and Stoic providentialist theologies, teleological biologies of various stripes, and all those who cast doubt on the senses as sources of knowledge.[5] Given this procedure, we would equally expect to find the sorts of arguments we do find in *DRN*, whether Lucretius is drawing on Epicurus himself or a later source.[6]

In any case, even if we concede that the specific arguments in *DRN* are unlikely to be original, it does not follow that philosophically Lucretius is acting merely as the mouthpiece for whatever text he happens to be versifying. Unless you are transmitting somebody's words verbatim, any attempt to explain another person's philosophy will inevitably also be an interpretation of that philosophy. When I present Aristotle's physics or ethics to my students, I am not trying to do anything at all original; instead, I want to explain Aristotle's own views on the four causes or other topics in a way that is accurate, understandable, engaging, and memorable. But in my choices regarding which parts of Aristotle's text to emphasize and which to pass over, how I try to present a systematic account that addresses apparent gaps, ambiguities, and contradictions in the argumentation, the examples I construct to illustrate his views, and in a myriad of other ways, my students will receive a version of Aristotle that is different from the version of Aristotle in other ancient philosophy classes. Furthermore, the examples a person gives may implicitly contain psychological, ethical, or political content of their own, apart from the philosophical points they are meant to clarify. For instance, if I spell out a detailed scenario of a person becoming angry when somebody makes fun of their daughter's speech impediment in order to illustrate Aristotle's ideas about the causes of anger and when it is appropriate to feel it, the example may contain ideas about how people do and should treat those with disabilities, unrelated to Aristotle's ethics.

And so, neither the general doctrinal conservatism of later Epicureans, nor the fact that Lucretius specifically claims not to be offering original arguments, bars Lucretius from presenting his own distinctive version of Epicureanism in *DRN*.

Lucretius on Human Psychology

In order not to give a misleading impression when making a case for a distinctively "Lucretian Epicureanism," it's important to note first that, by and large, what we get in *DRN* is no different from what all of our other sources on Epicureanism give us. According to the Epicureans, the highest good is pleasure, and everything else we do—including philosophizing—is done for the sake of obtaining pleasure and avoiding pain. But a truly pleasant life is not filled with the titillations of luxurious food, fine wine, and orgies. Instead, it is founded on peace of mind (*Ep. Men.* 131–132). In order to obtain peace of mind, we must eliminate the fears that plague humanity, and a correct understanding of the world is required to eliminate these fears. As Lucretius puts it, in a leitmotif of *DRN*, we must study the underlying principles of nature in order to dispel the terrifying darkness that covers our minds (Lucr. 1.146–148, 2.59–61, 3.91–93, 6.39–41).

So, Lucretius tries to demonstrate that the world consists fundamentally of bodies traveling through empty space (a.k.a. void), with the bodies we see composed of indivisible bits of matter (a.k.a. atoms). Everything that occurs is the result of atoms moving in the void. After establishing the basic tenets of atomism, Lucretius spends most of *DRN* showing how this worldview can account for the operations of the mind, the formation of the cosmos, the origin of species, and celestial and terrestrial phenomena like eclipses, thunderbolts, and earthquakes. Two crucial consequences follow from the Epicurean view of the world. The first is that death is annihilation, because the mind is a bodily organ that dies along with the rest of the body. And if death is annihilation, it is not bad for anybody: not for the living, because they have not died, and not for the dead, because they do not exist, and a person must exist in order for something to be bad for them (*Ep. Men.* 125; Lucr. 3.861–869). The second is that the gods have nothing to do with the creation of the world or with the events that occur within it. Explanations of phenomena like thunderbolts in terms of the motions of atoms are supposed to displace ones that appeal to the will of Zeus or other deities, and the random way thunderbolts hit both the guilty and innocent, uninhabited deserts, and even the shrines to the gods show that they are not the result of any divine purposes (Lucr. 6.219–422). And so, we have no reason to fear death or the gods.

Because we have lost most of Epicurus's own writings, as well as those of later Epicureans, Lucretius is our main source for many important parts of Epicurean physics. These include the infamous occasional sideways "swerve" of atoms, which is supposed to be necessary for the formation of the cosmos and the ability of animals to act freely (Lucr. 2.216–93), and the initial creation of life from the earth and the subsequent process of natural selection that resulted in the existence of the species we see today (Lucr. 5.783–924). *DRN* also contains specific arguments not available elsewhere, such as ones against the notion that the soul is immortal and undergoes a cycle of reincarnation from life to life (Lucr. 3.670–783).

However, if we're interested in trying to discern which parts of *DRN* give a distinctively *Lucretian* version of Epicureanism, the examples above are unlikely to be original to Lucretius. After all, as noted above, Lucretius specifically claims that the arguments in *DRN* are Epicurus's. While it is possible that Lucretius's own explanations of Epicurus's arguments introduce interesting new wrinkles to his source material, where we do have the corresponding arguments in Epicurus's summaries of his physics and accounts of meteorological phenomena (the *Letter to Herodotus* and the *Letter to Pythocles*), Lucretius seems to follow Epicurus, although Lucretius's treatment is typically more detailed than the one in Epicurus's letters.[7]

It is not in his physics that Lucretius is most likely to be presenting something distinctive, but in his psychology. Lucretius's manner of presenting the Epicurean positions on the fear of death, the formation of society, and many other topics seems to presuppose a more complicated view of human psychology than we might expect from other texts reporting Epicurus's views. Let me briefly sketch out the picture of Epicurean psychology present in other texts, before turning to the ways Lucretius seems to be distinctive. (By "psychology," I mean topics such as human motivation, beliefs, emotions, etc., not ones such as the material makeup of the mind or the atomic basis for processes like perception.)

The Epicureans are psychological hedonists: they think that all of our actions are explained by our desire for pleasure, our aversion to pain, and our beliefs about how best to obtain pleasure and avoid pain (Epicurus, *Ep. Men.* 128; Cic. *Fin.* 1.23, 1.30, 1.46). From birth, humans and all other animals instinctively pursue pleasure and shun pain, driven by their natural desires for the necessities of life, like food, drink, and shelter from the elements (Cic. *Fin.* 1.30; Diog. Laert. 10.137). However, as humans mature, they acquire beliefs about the way the world works, and this shapes their behavior and their desires. This development can be useful, as adults are able to engage in cost-benefit analysis and accept pain in the short term for the sake of more pleasure in the long term, e.g., having dental work done to avoid worse problems down the road (*Ep. Men.* 129–130). But it also opens up the possibility of corruption. People engage in wrongdoing and acquire harmful desires because they have incorrect beliefs about what will bring them pleasure. (Epicurus, *RS* 7, 10, *Sent. Vat.* 16; Cic. *Fin.* 1.32–33, 1.55). For instance, some people raised in a materialistic society might believe that having great wealth brings security and allows them to fulfill their desires. This false belief makes them greedy, and they are willing to act unjustly to obtain wealth. But having that sort of character and living that kind of life will bring them nothing but misery.

Fortunately, our reason gives us control over our beliefs. We can learn to distinguish which of our desires are for things we really need, and which desires cause us harm, and thereby reject the harmful desires (Epicurus, *RS* 18–22, 29–30). Using our reason, we can overcome hate, envy, contempt, and other emotions that might lead us to wrongdoing (Diog. Laert. 10.117). So Epicurean ethical philosophy is a kind of cognitive-behavioral therapy, in which you seek to uncover and eradicate the false beliefs and dysfunctional behaviors that prevent you from obtaining what you really want.

Furthermore, while our possession of reason means that there are distinctively human emotions and desires, the Epicureans stress the continuity between humans and other animals. The Epicureans distinguish between bodily and mental pleasures and pains. Bodily pleasures and pains are confined to the present, in the sense that they arise only from the present state of the body, such as the sweet sensation of a back massage or the ache of hunger. Mental pleasures and pains, by contrast, are not confined to the present, but can arise from the recollection or anticipation of pleasures and pains. The anticipation of a beating can cause anxiety now, and the Epicureans think you should train yourself to recall sweet memories and anticipate future pleasures, so that you can always have pleasure available to you (Cic. *Fin.* 1.57). However, while the mental pleasures and pains are much more important for determining whether your life is happy (Diog. Laert. 10.137; Cic. *Fin.* 1.55–56), mental pleasures and pains *arise* from bodily pleasures and pains (Cic. *Fin.* 1.25, 1.55). For example, the mental pain of anxiety can be based on the anticipation of the bodily pain of a beating, and the fear of death is predicated on the false belief that you will suffer pain when dead. And even in a case where somebody is anxious because they are afraid of losing some coveted political office, the desire for political power is itself based on the belief that gaining power is an effective means of gaining security against other people (Epicurus, RS 6–7), and so the anxiety *indirectly* depends on the anticipation of bodily pain. (The rival hedonists the Cyrenaics disagree with this thesis, giving the counterexample that we can take joy simply in the well-being of our fatherland, just as we do in our own well-being: Diog. Laert. 2.89).

Lucretius does not disagree that the desire for pleasure is what ultimately motivates humans, that our reason gives us control over our beliefs and desires (Lucr. 3.288–322), and that we need to uncover and eradicate the false beliefs that prevent us from attaining happiness. However, he introduces elements to human psychology that one might not anticipate from the above thumbnail sketch of Epicurean psychology. Furthermore, he seems to be one of those later Epicureans—whom the Epicurean spokesman Torquatus says in Cicero's *De finibus* 1.55 exist but speak with no authority—who do not believe that all mental pleasures and pains arise from bodily ones.

Here is a brief summary of some of what Lucretius says regarding human psychology.

Subconscious beliefs. Lucretius thinks that we do not know ourselves well, and that we are often driven by subconscious beliefs and desires. The man who recoils in horror at the thought of his corpse being torn apart by a pack of wild dogs may believe that he believes that death is annihilation, but his horror shows that unconsciously he still has some unacknowledged belief that a part of him survives his death (Lucr. 3.870–893). And we are often unaware of the irrational causes of our beliefs and desires. Infatuated lovers, through a process of selective perception or motivated reasoning, turn their beloved's flaws into assets—Lucretius gives a scathing catalog, with "the fiery-tempered gossip" becoming a "sparkler," while "another, fighting a losing battle with bronchitis, is 'a delicate creature'" (Lucr. 4.1160–1169).[8] Lucretius also gives the example of a bored, restless, and dissatisfied man, dashing back and forth from his mansion to his country home, who does not know the cause of his psychic illness, which is rooted in his fear of death (Lucr. 3.1053–75).[9]

Awe before nature. Many people view nature with a combination of wonder, awe, and fear. Unless we have a proper account of the nature of things, these feelings can be dangerous, leading us in our ignorance to attribute the workings of the world to the gods (Lucr. 5.1183–1240). For most of his audience, these feelings are now bound up with false religion or with viewing nature anthropomorphically. While Lucretius argues that the earth and celestial bodies are not sentient or divine (Lucr. 5.110–145), he shares his audience's feelings of wonder before nature and thinks they are perfectly appropriate. At 2.1030–1037, Lucretius says that nothing more marvelous than the spectacle of the sun, moon, and stars can be imagined, but familiarity has deadened us to its wonders, and at 3.28–30 he says that having the workings of the world revealed to him by Epicurus fills him with a "divine pleasure" (*divina voluptas*) and a "shuddering" or "trembling awe" (*horror*).[10]

Parental love, compassion, and guilt. Infamously, Epicurus denies that humans love their offspring by nature. Instead, just like the virtues and friendship, parental love arises from a calculation of self-interest, e.g., thinking that cherishing your children will bring you security in your old age.[11] But Lucretius describes how, among animals, offspring and mothers naturally and instinctively recognize and bond with one another. If a calf has been slaughtered in a stupid religious ritual, its bereaved mother will wander the fields searching for its offspring (Lucr. 2.349–370). And since the Epicureans think that nonhuman animals do not engage in deliberation about what is in their self-interest, the mother's love, grief, and search for its calf are not motivated by such a calculation.[12]

Lucretius does not explicitly contradict Epicurus by stating that humans naturally have affection for their offspring, just as some other animals do. The first humans were solitary and self-sufficient individuals, striving to benefit themselves alone and with no concern for the benefits of cooperation (Lucr. 5.958–961). No mention is made of how children were cared for. A crucial change later comes over the human race, however. Men and women begin to live with one another, use fire, and raise their children together. The use of fire makes their bodies less tough and resistant to the elements, and "the children with their charming ways easily broke down the stern disposition of their parents" (Lucr. 5.1011–1018). Once the men were softened in these ways, they began to form mutual pacts neither to harm nor to be harmed, and "claimed protection for their children and womenfolk, indicating by means of inarticulate cries and gestures that everyone ought to have compassion on the weak." Without these pacts, the human race would have gone extinct (Lucr. 5.1019–1027). Here, Lucretius is largely following Epicurus's description of justice as an agreement not to harm one another, entered into because of its usefulness to the parties to the agreement (*RS* 31). But Lucretius adds an important element to this account: the men who were parties to this agreement, whose spirits had been softened by the charms of children, were also motivated by compassion for those under their care.[13]

David Konstan argues that Lucretius, in passing, also puts forward a distinctive conception of guilt and conscience.[14] At 3.824–829, Lucretius describes how the consciousness of past misdeeds afflicts a person with remorse, and in the middle of a description of how romantic love ruins a person (Lucr. 4.1141–1191), Lucretius remarks that "perhaps his conscience experiences a twinge of remorse at the thought of a life spent in sloth and squandered in debauchery" (Lucr. 4.1135–1136). Epicurus believes that acting unjustly is not bad per se; instead, what makes it bad is punishment and the fear of punishment (*RS* 34). He adds that, even if you "get away" with your injustice, you can never be certain that you will not one day get caught, and so you still will suffer the pain of fear (*RS* 35). This fear of detection and punishment, however, is quite different from the pain of *guilt*, a distress caused by the conviction that you have done something wrong.

Attitudes like awe before nature, parental love, grief, and guilt are not themselves desires, although they can shape our desires. And so, Lucretius's inclusion of these attitudes is not inconsistent with Epicurus's psychological hedonism, i.e., his insistence that all human action is ultimately motivated by the desire for pleasure. But these attitudes can widen the scope of objects we take pleasure or pain in, and they can shape our beliefs about what will bring us pleasure or pain. Furthermore, it is initially difficult to square things like feeling a divine pleasure at beholding the wonders of nature with the thesis that all mental pleasures arise from bodily ones. Likewise, it is not inconsistent with psychological hedonism to think that our beliefs are often hidden from ourselves and have subterranean, irrational sources. But if many of our beliefs are like that, it complicates the therapeutic process of uncovering and eliminating the false beliefs that lead to misery.

While Lucretius does seem to have some noteworthy and distinctive psychological insights, we should not overstate what is there. *DRN* contains some theses about human psychology, but it puts forward nothing like a full-blown theory. And unlike his assertions that atoms occasionally swerve to the side or that the gods are not responsible for what happens in our world, Lucretius does not give spelled out arguments for these ideas. Instead, they are contained in descriptions of people, animals, and his own attitudes, which makes it more difficult to pin down precisely what they are.

The Philosophical Use of Literary Persuasion

In the previous section, I outlined the ways in which the *content* of *DRN* might be distinctive. In this section, I turn to considering the *manner* in which Lucretius presents his arguments in his poetry and how it may be philosophically distinctive. Before making my case regarding Lucretius, let me briefly sketch out an instructive parallel case, that of Cicero. Cicero was long treated mainly as a source of information on other philosophers because he claimed that his philosophical dialogues contained little original argumentation (*Att.* 12.52.3).[15] But Cicero is increasingly treated as a significant philosopher in his own right.

Sometimes this is done by claiming that Cicero has staked out noteworthy philosophical positions and arguments of his own, or at least that the manner in which he articulates the philosophical positions of others is distinctive. For instance, his *On Laws* presents a theory about the relationship of law to ethics that is indebted to the Stoics but is still Cicero's own, and Pamela Gordon has argued that Cicero's Stoic-inspired criticisms of the Epicureans for subordinating virtue to pleasure is modulated by a Roman conception of *virtus* as not merely generic virtue but as "manliness," and hence Cicero views Epicureanism as not merely vicious, but also effeminate.[16]

Another thing that makes Cicero philosophically distinctive, however, is the literary form he uses to present his ideas, dialogues in which the spokesmen for various philosophical schools put forward their arguments. Although they consist mainly of long stretches of exposition, the participants do question and criticize one another. The dialogue form reflects Cicero's own conviction, as an Academic skeptic, that you should engage in inquiry by undogmatically considering all of the pertinent arguments on a topic. Cicero also often puts himself within his dialogues as a character, where he expresses his opinions about the positions articulated—not in order to convince his reader to agree with him by appealing to his authority, but to illustrate the skeptical thesis that he is free to give his provisional assent to whatever seems to him to be the most reasonable position after engaging in inquiry. If we ignore his manner of presenting his arguments, we miss something important about Cicero as a philosopher.[17]

Similarly, the way Lucretius uses poetry to present Epicurean arguments is philosophically significant. Lucretius himself at 4.10–25 explains his choice of poetry to express his arguments: like a doctor who persuades a child to drink some nasty-tasting medicine by smearing the lip of the cup with honey, Lucretius coats the healing message of Epicurus in poetry, since many people find attending to philosophical arguments unpleasant. Working through explanations of the atomic basis for hunger can be difficult, but the aesthetic pleasure of poetry helps keep you going. On this model, the persuasive work is done by the arguments, with the poetry playing only an ancillary role of helping you attend to the arguments.

However, this view of what Lucretius accomplishes with his poetry risks selling him short. *DRN* is filled with literary and rhetorical methods of persuasion. Without giving a complete catalog, let me note a few examples, and then describe their significance:

> *Using vivid imagery to evoke emotions.* De rerum natura tries to get its readers to repudiate traditional Greco-Roman religion. The opening of the poem contains a full-throated condemnation of the evils such religion has caused (Lucr. 1.80–101). But Lucretius does not merely list these evils and explain how religion causes them; instead, he gives a heartrending description of the sacrifice of Iphigenia by her father, Agamemnon, in order to appease the anger of Artemis. This description evokes pity for Iphigenia and indignation at Agamemnon, so that the reader shares Lucretius's outrage.[18] Another example occurs in Lucretius's description of sex. The Epicureans hold that sexual intercourse never helped anybody, and that you are lucky if you are not harmed by it (Diog. Laert. 10.118). Lucretius condemns in particularly strong terms romantic infatuation. In his denunciation, Lucretius presents a disturbing description of frenzied lovers having sex, in which they intermingle their saliva and crush lips with teeth, making their consummation repellent and disgusting (Lucr. 4.1037–1191).
>
> *Raising and redeploying powerful cultural tropes.* In one of his eulogies of Epicurus, Lucretius surprisingly describes the theoretical intellectual activities of Epicurus, who investigated the causes of natural phenomena, in terms of the deeds of epic heroes (Lucr. 1.62–79): when we were grovelling in the dust under the weight of traditional religion, Epicurus dared to raise his eyes to challenge it. He boldly burst through the gates of nature and roamed throughout the cosmos in order to cast down traditional religion at our feet and liberate us from it.[19] Elsewhere Lucretius maintains that what Epicurus has done for us is far greater than any of the deeds of Heracles (Lucr. 5.22–54). In these passages, Lucretius evokes the awe and admiration we feel toward epic heroes and redirects them toward a quite different object. Another surprising comparison is Lucretius's extended description of the earth as a mother goddess, awesome and worthy of respect—a metaphor he defends using,

even though he admits that it is dangerous and literally false, as the earth is neither divine nor sentient. (Lucr. 2.594–660) Here, Lucretius evokes the feelings of awe people have toward the earth conceived of as a mother-goddess and redirects them toward the earth as understood by the Epicureans—as a nonsentient, nonpurposive conglomeration of matter.[20]

Ridicule. One of Lucretius's targets, when trying to establish that death is annihilation, is the theory that the soul survives the death of the body and lives again when it unites with a new body, in a cycle of reincarnation. Lucretius presents a wide array of arguments against the theory, but he also mocks it. He says that it is ridiculous to imagine innumerable immortal souls gathering around a pair of rutting animals, jostling one another in order to be the first one in when new life is conceived; he suggests that maybe the souls avoid this conflict by agreeing to a "first come, first served" policy (Lucr. 3.776–783). Here, Lucretius tries to discredit the theory of transmigration by making it look silly.[21]

Lucretius's use of nonrational methods of persuasion such as appealing to emotions and ridicule may appear nonphilosophical, or even antiphilosophical, if philosophy is in part defined by a commitment to rational persuasion. After all, the appeal to pity is fallacious, and concluding that the doctrine of transmigration is false because a mocking depiction of it makes it seem silly is invalid.

Martha Nussbaum accuses the Epicureans generally of committing this sort of intellectual sin, a willingness to use effective but irrational methods of persuasion, which is based on their therapeutic conception of argumentation, combined with their hedonistic conception of the human good.[22] Epicurus holds that philosophy produces mental health (*Sent. Vat.* 54), and the Epicureans compare philosophy to medicine: just as medicine derives its value entirely from its effectiveness in driving out bodily disease, philosophical arguments derive their value entirely from their effectiveness in driving out psychic diseases (Porph. *Ad Marcellam* 31). And because happiness consists primarily in freedom from mental turmoil, the Epicureans have no reason to respect the rationality of their interlocutors, if using irrational means of persuasion effectively promotes their peace of mind. Nussbaum claims that, if we look at the actual practices recommended and followed by the Epicureans, we will see that they are willing to violate the norms of rational discourse for the sake of therapeutic effectiveness.[23]

But a willingness to use rationally dubious methods of persuasion does not fit with other important commitments of the Epicureans, including Lucretius. As noted above, Lucretius believes we must study the underlying principles of nature in order to dispel the terrifying darkness that covers our minds, and Epicurus thinks that only the wise person is unshakably persuaded of anything (Plut. *Adv. Col.* 1117F). So if I believe that transmigration is false only because a mocking description of the cycle of rebirth made it seem silly, such a belief cannot serve as a secure foundation for peace of mind. Instead, I must understand the reasons why the *animus* is material, and hence mortal, including the reasons for rejecting transmigration. Lucretius does not merely mock transmigration; he also gives arguments against it.

Fortunately, I think that Epicurean ethical views generally, and Lucretius's views on human psychology in particular as outlined in the previous section, show how Lucretius can use literary and rhetorical methods of persuasion while insisting that we need a reasoned understanding of the workings of the world in order to secure happiness.

The Epicureans believe that, as members of a sick society, we have absorbed false beliefs and misguided attitudes that make us suffer. We think that money and social status are the keys to happiness, and we envy the unscrupulous businessman who gets ahead. We revere jealous and capricious gods who do not merit reverence. As noted above, Lucretius adds that we do not know ourselves well, that we are often driven by subconscious beliefs and desires.

These false beliefs and misguided attitudes block us from accepting Epicurus's healing message. Lucretius uses literary and rhetorical methods of persuasion to counter such beliefs and attitudes and thus open up his reader to his arguments. And so these methods do not displace argumentation; instead, they work together with it. Let me briefly discuss how this would work in the examples above.

Typical Romans, even if they do not believe in the literal truth of all of the traditional stories about the gods, probably have a reflexive and deep-grained reverence for the gods as traditionally depicted.[24] They know about stories such as Agamemnon sacrificing Iphigenia but aren't bothered by them. To break through this harmful cultural conditioning, Lucretius vividly portrays what this story really involves, in order to bring home its horror. The emotional reactions of pity and indignation that Lucretius's poetry produces are apt and do not produce an irrational belief in the evils religion causes. Instead, they help counter an irrational complacency that the reader previously had, a deadening of their sensibilities.

Similar considerations explain Lucretius's mockery of transmigration. Many people view transmigration with a misplaced sense of respect and reverence—it seems sublime and befitting the dignity of the soul to move from life to life. Mocking the doctrine deflates this misguided sense of awe, lessening a person's emotional attachment to the doctrine and making them more open to the arguments against it.

In the case of romantic love, maudlin popular celebrations lead people to view it with a sentimental attachment, and they may even think of the consummation of their love in quasi-divine terms, as in Aristophanes' myth of erotic reunification in the *Symposium*. Lucretius's harsh depiction of infatuated lovers as frenzied, dissatisfied animals acts as a corrective to such attitudes.

Greek and Roman culture also contains a broad strain of anti-intellectualism, celebrating virile men of action, while pitying the impractical philosopher with his head in the clouds. Callicles' denunciation of philosophy as unfit for a grown man (Pl. *Grg.* 484c–486d) and the story of Thales falling into a well as he was gazing at the stars (Diog. Laert. 2.4–5, Pl. *Tht.* 174a) exemplify the attitude. For Lucretius, this gets things deeply wrong, because the actions of the epic heroes were usually destructive, whereas Epicurus's intellectual work has a tremendous positive impact. Accordingly, in his poetry Lucretius evokes the trope of the epic hero and redirects the admiration it elicits to a more appropriate object.

Finally, Lucretius's depiction of the earth as mother-goddess is one of a number of passages in which he deploys figures of traditional religion or otherwise personifies nature, including the opening invocation of Venus (Lucr. 1.1–43) and Nature's chastisement of those who fear death (Lucr. 3.931–77). Lucretius is doing multiple things by deploying these images, and he doesn't have a single set of purposes across all these passages. But one purpose he probably has is to help convince his reader that atomism need not lead to the disenchantment of nature.

As noted in the previous section, many people view nature with wonder and awe, feelings that Lucretius shares. By evoking the feelings of awe associated with traditional tropes like the earth being our mother, and transferring them to the dancing of atoms in the void, Lucretius reduces one source of resistance to Epicureanism: the sense that the Epicurean view of the world is cold and shorn of wonder.[25] To evoke these feelings while explaining the Epicurean worldview is much more effective than just giving an argument that you can, without impropriety, both believe that the heavenly bodies are insentient and behold them with awe.

The way in which Lucretius presents his Epicurean arguments is informed by his understanding of human psychology and of the point of philosophical argumentation. As noted above, Epicurus stresses that the point of philosophical arguments is to help heal people from the psychic diseases of false beliefs, empty desires, and destructive emotions. Philodemus, in his *On Frank Speech*, discusses in detail how an Epicurean pedagogue will take into account a person's particular psychological profile when interacting with them.[26] In his *On Anger* he says that sometimes imagery is more effective therapeutically than argumentation: a person prone to harmful bouts of anger may not appreciate how badly off they are if their philosophical "doctor" merely reasons with them about the effects of anger, whereas if the doctor brings the badness of anger before their eyes via a vivid depiction of its effects, he will make them eager to be treated.[27]

But Epicurus's *On Nature* and the works we have of Philodemus are standard philosophical treatises. Philodemus describes how a pedagogue may use imagery as a tool of persuasion, but he doesn't employ this tool in what we have of his writing. Epicurus shows some sensitivity for communicating effectively to a wide audience: the *Principal Doctrines* are handy for memorizing important points of dogma, and Epicurus notes that he composed the *Letter to Herodotus* as a summary of the main points of Epicurean physics for those unable to work through the long treatises (*Ep. Hdt.* 35–36). Yet the *Letter to Herodotus* is an unadorned presentation of doctrines and arguments, and is at points obscure for beginners. In his use of literary and rhetorical methods of persuasion alongside his argumentation, Lucretius alone among the Epicureans shows a sensitivity to the need to present his arguments in a way that also takes into account the biases, stereotypes, and other psychological factors that hinder his audience from accepting the healing gospel of Epicurus. In this respect, *DRN* is a more effective embodiment of Epicureanism than anything written by Epicurus.[28]

NOTES

1. For more on Epicurean reverence of their master and how it led to an unwillingness to contradict him, see Sedley (1989).
2. Sedley (1998) 68–72 explains this controversy in more detail. Lucretius himself seems unaware of the problem, confidently asserting that the mind is in the chest and that it would be equally ridiculous to suppose that the mind is in the head as in the feet (Lucr. 3.788–793), which Sedley gives as one reason to think that Lucretius draws exclusively from Epicurus himself in composing *DRN*. I have my doubts on how conclusive this argument is; see O'Keefe (2020) 182–183.
3. Translations of Lucretius are from Smith (2001).
4. For Philodemus and his arguments with other Epicureans on anger, see chapter 9 of Tsouna (2007) 195–238. The papers in Fish and Sanders (2011) show that later Epicureanism was not philosophically stagnant.
5. An instructive contrasting case is Velleius's Epicurean critique of the theologies of a wide range of philosophers in Cicero's *De natura deorum* 1.10–15. Velleius goes through these philosophers by name and gives criticisms of their doctrines keyed to particular things that they say, e.g., in *Nat. D.* 1.12, where he criticizes Empedocles for saying that the four elements are divine even though they come into being, perish, and lack all sensation.
6. Campbell (1999) is responsible for dubbing Lucretius's arguments "catch-all." Furley (1966) presents a convincing rebuttal of earlier arguments that Lucretius is targeting the Stoics in particular. Sedley (1998) is the most influential argument that Lucretius is an Epicurean "fundamentalist," drawing exclusively on Epicurus for his arguments. See Asmis (1982), Clay (1983), and Schrijvers (1999) for arguments that Lucretius also draws on later Epicureans. For more on my own doubts regarding the viability and fruitfulness of the search for Lucretius's sources, see O'Keefe (2020) 177–184.
7. However, see Hankinson (2013) for one possible exception, in the doctrine of "multiple explanations." The Epicureans believe that many cosmological and meteorological phenomena are consistent with multiple physical explanations, and in such cases, we should be content with disjunctively listing all of the possible explanations ("Eclipses are caused by X or Y or . . .") rather than settling on just one (Epicurus, *Ep. Hdt.* 79–80; *Ep. Pyth.* 85–88, 92–115; Lucr. 5.592–770). Hankinson argues that, while Lucretius largely follows Epicurus in his presentation of this doctrine, they differ in a crucial way: for Epicurus, the multiple explanations may be only physically possible, whereas Lucretius commits himself to thinking that each of these possible explanations are, at some point in time and space, actual.
8. The infamous and scathing indictment of romantic love that closes book 4 of *DRN* (1037–1287) is full of details on the irrationality of those blinded by their infatuation, including the thesis that a lover really wishes to possess and consume his beloved, but sex fails to fulfill this desire (Lucr. 4.1058–1120). For more on Lucretius's denunciation of romantic love, see Brown (1987), chapter 5 of Nussbaum (1994) 140–191, and Gordon (2002). For the Epicurean attitude on sex in general, see Arenson (2016). See Brown (1987) 128–132 and 280–294 for possible Greek sources, including Plato, of Lucretius's litany of lovers' deluded epithets for their beloved.
9. For more on the topic of Lucretius on unconscious motivation, see Jope (1983).
10. On Lucretius on the sublime in these and similar passages, see further Most (2012) and Porter (2007).

11. Cic. *Att.* 7.2.4; Arr. *Epict. Diss.* 1.23; Plut. *De amore prolis* 495A–C, *Adv. Col.* 1123A; Lactant. *Div. Inst.* 3.17.5. For much more on Epicurus and Lucretius on parental love, see McConnell (2018); my account here is indebted to his.
12. See Konstan (2013) for more on the Epicureans on grief.
13. In addition to McConnell (2018), a good starting place for more on these issues (along with many references to other literature) is Holmes (2013). Campbell (2003) offers a detailed commentary on these sections of *DRN*.
14. Konstan (2019).
15. See Striker (1995) for a summary of the reasons for not thinking highly of Cicero as a philosopher and pushback against them, and Schmidt (1978–1979) for an account of how Cicero fell into philosophical disrepute after previous esteem.
16. A good recent paper on Cicero's *On Laws* is Asmis (2008). Cicero's most sustained critique of Epicurean ethics is *Fin.* 2, especially *Fin.* 2.45–77. See Gordon (2012) 109–138 on Cicero's gendered polemics against the Epicureans. An excellent example of presenting Cicero's philosophy as a whole on its own terms, without attempting to titrate out what is original, is Woolf (2015).
17. See Annas and Woolf (2001) x–xvii for a brief explanation of Cicero's use of the dialogue form along these lines, and Schofield (2008) for an in-depth consideration.
18. Morrison (2013) shows how Lucretius evokes emotions here and in other passages describing death, and how the evoked emotions are supposed to help persuade his readers to accept the Epicurean message.
19. For detailed consideration of this metaphor, see Buchheit (2007).
20. For a much more in-depth treatment of Lucretius's usage of these mythological tropes that partially overlaps with the approach taken in this chapter, see Gale (1994), esp. 129–155. See Taylor (2016) for a detailed examination of how Lucretius uses allusions to comedy and tragedy in the theater, including the sacrifice of Iphigenia, in his mission to relieve his readers of false and damaging beliefs.
21. See Gellar-Goad (2012) for much more on Lucretius's use of ridicule and satire.
22. Nussbaum (1986).
23. These practices include threats of shunning, informing on wrongdoers, and encouragement of uncritical adulation of authority figures. Nussbaum's main source for such practices is Philodemus's treatise *On Frank Criticism*, although she draws on Epicurus and Lucretius. Tsouna (2007) 91–118 offers a useful overview of Philodemus's treatise and argues against some of Nussbaum's characterizations of Philodemus's therapeutic practices.
24. See Gale (1994) 85–98 for more on the complicated topic of the religious positions of Romans at the time. She concludes that belief in the literal truth of "superstitious" myths regarding the gods may have been widespread among the lower classes but was relatively rare among the elite. However, even the elites generally regarded historical myths (e.g., about the founders of Rome) as accurate and treated the traditional stories regarding the gods with respect as an important part of civic *religio*.
25. For more on this topic, see O'Keefe (2003) 57–60.
26. For instance, he will have to decide whether to use mild or stringent reproofs and how much praise to mix in alongside criticism, and these decisions will be based on both his experience of how a person's age, social standing, and gender effect the way they react to criticism, and on his knowledge of the individual. For more detail, see Tsouna (2007) 91–125.
27. Phld. *De ira* IV 4–19. For more on this technique, see Tsouna (2007) 204–209, and more generally on the treatise *On Anger*, pp. 195–238.

28. I would like to thank David Konstan and Gretchen Redams-Schils for their feedback on this chapter, and David for his unfailingly cheerful encouragement. Much of this chapter, especially in the final section, is adapted from O'Keefe (2020).

REFERENCES

Annas, J., ed., and R. Woolf, tr. (2001). *Cicero: On Moral Ends*. (Cambridge).
Arenson, K. (2016). "Epicureans on Marriage as Sexual Therapy." *Polis: The Journal for Ancient Greek Political Thought* 33(2): 291–311.
Asmis, E. (1982). "Lucretius' Venus and Stoic Zeus." *Hermes* 110(4): 458–470.
Asmis, E. (2008). "Cicero on Natural Law and the Laws of the State." *Cl. Ant.* 27(1): 1–33.
Brown, R. (1987). *Lucretius on Love and Sex*. (Leiden).
Buchheit, V. (2007). "Epicurus' Triumph of the Mind (Lucr. 1.62–79)," in Gale, 104–131. Originally published in 1971, "Epikurs Triumph des Geistes (Lucr. I, 62–79)." *Hermes* 99: 303 323.
Campbell, G. (1999). Review of *Lucretius and the Transformation of Greek Wisdom*, by D. Sedley. *Bryn Mawr Classical Review*, October 29. http://bmcr.brynmawr.edu/1999/1999-10-29.html (accessed November 9, 2021).
Campbell, G. (2003). *Lucretius on Creation and Evolution: A Commentary on* De rerum natura, *Book Five, Lines 772–1104*. (Oxford).
Clay, D. (1983). *Lucretius and Epicurus*. (Ithaca, N.Y.).
Fish, J., and K. Sanders, eds. (2011). *Epicurus and the Epicurean Tradition*. (Cambridge).
Fredrick, D., ed. (2002). *The Roman Gaze. Vision, Power and the Body*. (Baltimore).
Furley, D. (1966). "Lucretius and the Stoics." *BICS* 13: 13–33, reprinted in his *Cosmic Problems* (1989): 183–205 (Cambridge).
Gale, M. (1994). *Myth and Poetry in Lucretius*. (Cambridge).
Gale, M., ed. (2007). *Oxford Readings in Classical Studies: Lucretius*. (Oxford).
Gellar-Goad, T. (2012). *Lucretius'* De rerum natura *and Satire*. Dissertation: University of North Carolina at Chapel Hill.
Gillespie, S., and P. Hardie, eds. (2007). *The Cambridge Companion to Lucretius* (Cambridge).
Goldhill, S., ed. (2008). *The End of Dialogue in Antiquity*. (Cambridge).
Gordon, P. (2002). "Some Unseen Monster: Rereading Lucretius on Sex," in Fredrick, 86–109.
Gordon, P. (2012). *The Invention and Gendering of Epicurus*. (Ann Arbor, Mich.).
Griffin, M., and J. Barnes, eds. (1989). *Philosophia Togata*. (Oxford).
Hankinson, R. (2013). "Lucretius, Epicurus, and the Logic of Multiple Explanations," in Lehoux, Morrison, and Sharrock, 69–98.
Holmes, B. (2013). "The Poetic Logic of Negative Exceptionalism in Lucretius, Book Five," in Lehoux, Morrison and Sharrock, 153–191.
Holmes, B., and W. Shearin. (2012). *Dynamic Reading: Studies in the Reception of Epicureanism*. (Oxford).
Jope, J. (1983). "Lucretius' Psychoanalytic Insight: His Notion of Unconscious Motivation." *Phoenix* 37(3): 224–238.
Konstan, D. (2013). "Lucretius and the Epicurean Attitude toward Grief," in Lehoux, Morrison, and Sharrock, 193–209.
Konstan, D. (2019). "Lucretius and the Conscience of an Epicurean." *Politeia* 1(2): 67–79.
Lehoux, D., A. Morrison, and A. Sharrock, eds. (2013) *Lucretius: Poetry, Philosophy, Science*. (Oxford).

McConnell, S. (2018). "Lucretius on the Nature of Parental Love." *Antichthon* 52: 72–89.

Morrison, A. (2013). "Nil igitur mors est ad nos? Iphianassa, the Athenian Plague, and Epicurean Views of Death," in Lehoux, Morrison, and Sharrock, 211–232.

Most, G. (2012). "The Sublime, Today?" in Holmes and Shearin, 239–266.

Nussbaum, M. (1986). "Therapeutic Arguments: Epicurus and Aristotle," in Schofield and Striker, 31–74.

Nussbaum, M. (1994). *The Therapy of Desire: Theory and Practice in Hellenistic Ethics*. (Princeton).

O'Keefe, T. (2003). "Lucretius on the Cycle of Life and the Fear of Death." *Apeiron* 36(1): 43–65.

O'Keefe, T. (2020). "Lucretius and the Philosophical Use of Literary Persuasion," in O'Rourke, 177–194.

O'Rourke, D., ed. (2020). *Approaches to Lucretius: Traditions and Innovations in Reading* De rerum natura. (Cambridge).

Porter, J. (2007). "Lucretius and the Sublime," in Gillespie and Hardie, 167–184.

Schmidt, P. (1978–1979). "Cicero's Place in Roman Philosophy: A Study of His Prefaces." *CJ* 74(2): 115–127.

Schofield, M. (2008). "Ciceronian Dialogue," in Goldhill, 63–84.

Schofield, M., and G. Striker, eds. (1986). *The Norms of Nature*. (Cambridge).

Schrijvers, P. (1999). *Lucrèce et les sciences de la vie*. (Leiden).

Sedley, D. (1989). "Philosophical Allegiance in the Greco-Roman world," in Griffin and Barnes, 97–119.

Sedley, D. (1998). *Lucretius and the Transformation of Greek Wisdom*. (Cambridge).

Smith, M. F., tr. (2001). *Lucretius: On the Nature of Things*. (Indianapolis).

Striker, G. (1995). "Cicero and Greek Philosophy." *HSCPh* 97: 53–61.

Taylor, B. (2016). "Rationalism and the Theatre in Lucretius." *CQ* 66(1): 140–154.

Tsouna, V. (2007). *The Ethics of Philodemus*. (Oxford).

Woolf, R. (2015). *Cicero: The Philosophy of a Roman Sceptic*. (Abingdon).

CHAPTER 10

CICERO AND THE EVOLUTION OF PHILOSOPHICAL DIALOGUE

MATTHEW FOX

PHILOSOPHICAL dialogue has a long history—stretching from Plato in the fourth century BCE to Hume in the eighteenth century, and beyond. The genre displays a remarkable degree of continuity, and each new writer of dialogue negotiates their own relationship with the tradition. It is the aim of this chapter to discuss the place of Cicero within that history. As Cicero was unambiguously the pioneer of philosophical dialogue written in Latin, and, with only Lucretius as his rival, the initiator of philosophy in Latin altogether, it is his ambitions in relation to the context in which he was working that determine the orientation of my discussion. So this treatment takes a different perspective from one centered on the evolution of Greek dialogue. There is much to say within that tradition about responses to Plato, and about their role in the evolution of Greek philosophical schools, but taking the long view of Latin dialogue, little of that tradition is relevant.[1] Likewise, while Cicero is of vital importance to all post-Classical dialogue in Latin simply by virtue of the popularity of a few of his dialogues as central school texts in the early modern era, the Greek dialogue tradition effectively died out in the second century CE. Although it is not impossible that Cicero's approach to dialogue influenced some Greek writers, that is in itself a short-lived legacy, and one that is hard to find concrete evidence for, given that his dialogues are barely mentioned by any extant Greek writers.[2]

Our knowledge of the dialogue tradition, especially at the point in time when Cicero encountered it, is hampered by the loss of many texts. To understand both which dialogues Cicero could read and what effect his works had in turn on their readers, we lack important material that did not survive past antiquity. The most significant loss is of the dialogues of Aristotle, none of which survived. Ancient readers regarded them as more important and representative of Aristotle's ideas than the treatises we are able to read today. The situation is similar for the period following Cicero. Few dialogues written in Latin are preserved from antiquity, so evidence for Cicero's influence is hard to evaluate.[3] These factors mean that we have to deal with Cicero on his own terms. The nature of his contribution to the tradition can, however, be interpreted on the basis of the evidence provided by his own writings. Because these are mostly well-preserved, that is not really a disadvantage, but it does require us to abandon a particular habit of scholarship which seeks the explanation for all literary practice in lost antecedents, and requires corroborative evidence to support claims of originality. So I leave aside the aspiration to look at Cicero's interventions in terms of his close predecessors and successors, to focus instead on the character of Cicero's encounter with the tradition of dialogue, and I examine its most significant aspects. Cicero's major contributions to the form of dialogue can be summarized as follows: he is the first to use the different speakers in dialogues to act as representatives of different philosophical schools;[4] he adds a particular kind of preface, situating philosophical conversation within a specific historical and political setting; by these means he emphasizes the practical and contingent aspects of philosophy, sometimes at the expense of the abstract; he uses historical references both to highlight the need for philosophy and also to keep readers aware of the artificiality of his textual practice, and the conventional quality of the form itself. A more detailed examination of these topics makes up the remainder of this chapter.

Method and Authority, and the Origin of the Dialogue

The emergence of the literary form that we recognize as "philosophical dialogue" is closely linked to the figure of Socrates—and to Plato's extensive production in that form. I begin by exploring Socrates, Plato, and other Socratic writers, and how they shaped the genre. As I have suggested, there is a significant difference between the view of dialogue we derive from reading Plato and Xenophon, and how that tradition looked to Cicero. We can ourselves make a partial judgment about what distinguished the different Socratic authors from each other based on the contrast between Plato and the dialogues of Xenophon, the only intact material from a fertile first generation. Xenophon, in his *Memorabilia* and *Estate Manager*, makes the Socratic conversation more anecdotal than Plato. He is more attentive to the personal foibles of Socrates's friends and interlocutors, and is interested in the application of Socrates's wisdom and argumentative method to everyday problems of Athenian life. Likewise, Xenophon contains little of the tenacious seeking after philosophical first principles that is so important a part of Plato.[5]

Plato's record of Socrates can rightly be regarded as the starting point for philosophy as a recognizable educational discipline. At the time Plato was writing, dialogue was the most natural form in which to use the written word to act as an educational medium. For all the Socratic writers, the impulse to write dialogue had two main causes: the commemoration of Socrates, and the related idea that a textual reconstruction of a conversation was a better way of encouraging readers to participate in the relatively new project of philosophy. Dialogues were demonstrations of philosophy in action, written in a form that would provide a model philosophical conversation. That conversation could take a variety of forms, and recent readings of Plato have made clear how varied even his practice was in the authority granted to different speakers, and, correspondingly, the amount of work left over for the reader in the search for philosophical lessons.[6] Plato was Cicero's most important model, but in his letters he mentions both the dialogues of Aristotle and those of Heraclides of Pontus as influences, and the names of Xenophon and Aeschines also appear.[7] The kind of education that dialogue aimed to provide, however, and the relationship between philosophical mission and textual form became an object of contention. In essence those disputes are still with us, most prominently over the way in which Plato should be used to try to uncover the thinking and teachings of the historical Socrates.

The debate in the period closest to Socrates himself, and around the works of Plato and his successors (the philosophical tradition known as "The Academy"), concerns not the method itself, but a more general question about the authority of the figures who speak within the dialogues, and the manner in which dialogue transmitted authority. The authority of Socrates was the initial focus for the different ways of using dialogue, but the debate continued for many of Plato's successors in the Academy. Likewise, in the other Hellenistic philosophical schools, there was an explicit choice between monologic writings (such as the treatises of Aristotle or Epicurus), and the dialogue tradition, which was in general more interested in open-ended philosophical conversation than in purveying a clear doctrine or philosophical system.[8]

Fortunately a passage from Cicero tells us what his conception of the Academic tradition was at the point where he was set on importing it for a Roman readership. In the preface to his *On the Nature of the Gods*, Cicero gives a brief history of the fate of Plato's philosophical school. It is a history that centers on a particular approach to Plato, and on the question of how to read philosophical dialogues (*Nat. d.* 1.10–12).[9] Cicero distinguishes between two different possibilities, one of which is more faithful to the Academic tradition, with its commitment to leaving open the fundamental questions of philosophy and presenting multiple answers to difficult questions. That approach regards it as the function of the literary dialogue to provide a model of philosophical conversation which encourages readers to imitate that conversation. It accepts—an important aspect of the method of the Academy—that in philosophical enquiry certainty is often impossible. Dialogue is a form that helpfully presents readers with debate, without necessarily resolving that debate into clear lessons or philosophical doctrines.[10] The alternative tradition, which Cicero criticizes as a symptom of the "slowness of humanity" is to look upon dialogue as a literary convention, and to see in all philosophical writing the disguised doctrines of the teacher. This tradition views dialogue as providing a coded guide to the teachings of the master. It accepts that those teachings require perseverance, so the point of the dialogue form is to add the opacity necessary to turn reading into a quest for the truth.

This text is an important piece of evidence. It reveals a key theme in the history of dialogue: the tension between philosophical authority and the recording of that authority in texts. The Academic tradition was in Cicero's eyes at a crucial juncture. As he makes clear, the skeptical way of treating dialogue as a process that encouraged readers' own philosophical development through suspension of judgment had already fallen out of fashion. It was to be replaced, in the generations that followed, with the movement that we know today as Platonism, which in effect read Plato's writings as a repository of almost mystical truths. Cicero had little interest in philosophical activity of that kind, but in his own writings he was to experiment with different ways of conveying philosophical authority. Some of his dialogues, indeed, are barely dialogues at all—*Tusculan Disputations*, for example. In others (*De senectute* or *De amicitia*), the interlocutors only seem to exist in order to provide a platform for the central speaker—who performs the same kind of monologue that we get from Cicero's own character in the Tusculans. The variety that his works display is itself a response to the literary tradition that he was familiar with—but not a direct response in terms of imitation of particular predecessors. As far as we can tell, Cicero's use of different types of dialogue to explore different versions of textual authority does not have a parallel in any Greek forerunner. This eclecticism in method, even within the dialogue form, is an important part of his contribution to the evolution of dialogue, and it reveals as much about his own concerns with authority, and with the intersection between rhetoric and philosophy, as it does about a critical engagement with the Greek texts that inspired him.[11] At the start of *Tusculan Disputations* Cicero explicitly weighs up the relative merits of a philosophical conversation and philosophical monologue, and argues that experience in rhetorical improvisation is useful for providing the skills required to give lectures on philosophical themes (*Tusc.* 1.6–8). This is a very different approach from the one which he adopts in, for example, *De finibus* or *De natura deorum*, where the dialogue form is used to contrast the different approaches to particular issues of the main philosophical traditions. Certainly, the use of dialogue in these works, where individuals act as spokesmen for different philosophical schools (Epicurean, Stoic, Academic), must be seen as one of the major contributions of Cicero to the form. It was a product of Cicero's ambition to summarize the different Greek schools for a Roman readership. Such works aimed to provide a short-cut for those unacquainted with the different traditions, and the decision to construct dialogues that divide speeches up between individuals on the basis of their doctrinal affiliations is an important moment in the history of ancient philosophy. Although too little evidence survives to say with much assurance how far Cicero was the main innovator here, it is certain that his work looks forward to the tradition of philosophical doxography that becomes our main source for the views of so many Greek thinkers.[12]

It was Cicero's own fondness for the skeptical Academy, combined with his sense that Greek philosophy requires mediation to reach a Roman readership, that produced this innovation. Indeed, these specific conditions have a huge bearing on the significance of Cicero's work in general. So I will now turn to Cicero's philosophical ambitions, since in understanding how Cicero thought philosophy could be best brought to Rome, we can also get a clearer idea about how Cicero's educational mission related to his ideas about his own authority, and about the way in which Roman traditions could intersect with Greek.

Romanizing Philosophy

Romanization is a process that Cicero discusses in a number of the prefaces to his dialogues, always at the start of the works and often of the individual books within them. Here he writes in his own voice, before the introduction of other speakers, and discusses the ambitions of his philosophical project. These prefaces constitute another clear addition to the tradition of philosophical dialogue, though again that development is caused not so much by philosophical as by personal considerations. Malcolm Schofield invites us to read this prefatory material as part of a project to insert what he labels "Ciceronian Presence" into philosophy.[13] To cast himself as a teacher and philosopher is a central part of Cicero's ambitions, and Schofield's reading shares the emphasis of some recent work that sees Cicero's concern for his posthumous reputation as a compensation for his start in life on the political margins, as a *novus homo*.[14] That assessment is especially true of the aspiration to produce a complete philosophical curriculum in the years of Caesar's dictatorship—from the end of 46 BCE—beginning with the lost *Hortensius* and ending with Cicero's death. This project is undoubtedly shaped both by Cicero's sense of his own identity and by the political situation. Nevertheless, in terms of the development of the dialogue, this strong personal dimension, residing in Cicero's use of prefatory introductions to his dialogues, does constitute an important intervention, and is one that had a lasting effect.

In essence, the prefaces problematize the task of making philosophy Roman, and show that regardless of Cicero's intentions, he was fully aware of the possibility for failure and the dangers of a hostile reception. The opening of *De finibus* (1.1) expresses those concerns clearly:

> I was not unaware, Brutus, that, when I committed into Latin what philosophers had handled with the highest genius and the finest erudition in the Greek language, it would turn out that my work would come up against a range of objections. Some people entirely disapprove of philosophy, and not because they are ill-educated. Others do not object to it so much as long as it is done in a more relaxed way, but do not think that so much enthusiasm and effort should be spent on it. There will even be some—themselves well read in Greek literature—who despise Latin literature, and say that they would rather make the effort to read in Greek. Finally I think there will be some who will demand different books from me, and that, elegant though it may be, will say that this type of writing does not belong to my character and station. I think I must briefly say something to refute them.

The passage reiterates ideas expressed in other texts, most closely the opening of *De natura deorum*.[15] In that work we find the same concern for the difficulty of rendering Greek ideas into Latin, with Cicero concluding that improvements in Latin vocabulary have now made it a language as effective at conveying philosophical ideas as Greek, and linking his contribution to that process with his other contributions to the improvement of the state of the res publica. In *De finibus* the emphasis is essentially the same: Cicero launches into a defense of Latin literature based on the translation of Greek models, points out the absurd fashion of those Romans who habitually denigrate Latin literature, and draws an equivalence between his contribution to the res publica in politics, and his role as an educator of his people.[16] A little further on in the same preface (*Fin.* 1.10), we find the culmination of this argument in a particularly succinct form:

> Indeed, since in forensic activities, labours, and dangers, I do not see myself having abandoned the stronghold in which I was placed by the Roman people, I should also surely, as much as I can, strive for citizens to be more learned by my application, enthusiasm, and hard work. And I won't argue with people who prefer to read in Greek, as long as they do read those things, and don't pretend; rather I will serve those who either wish to make use of both literatures, or, if they have their own, don't feel greatly the lack of the other [i.e., Greek].

Here we find the idea of Cicero's philosophical efforts as a compensation for his political marginalization working in tandem with his activities as a translator, translator in the broad sense of bringing Greek ideas into Latin. If he cannot make the citizens of Rome safer, he can at least make them *doctiores*, better educated, by giving them access to Greek philosophy in a way that had not been possible before. In the process, he draws attention to a debate that we do not see otherwise in this form: a debate about the relative value of Greek and Roman literature. There is also a presentation of the major risk that Cicero must overcome: the production of a version of philosophical writing that makes Roman readers reach for a Greek original. The translation to which Cicero aspires does not look like one. That is the context in which we should understand Cicero's careful work with his cast of characters drawn from different periods in Rome's past, as, indeed, with his use of his own contemporaries as speakers in the dialogues. Although he accepts that Roman philosophy will be derivative, it must be carefully naturalized if it is to do its job.

It is tempting to treat these preoccupations with the comparative status of Greek and Latin *litterae* as commonplaces, especially given what we know about the slapdash manner in which Cicero composed his prefaces, and the casual manner in which he repeats material among them.[17] But they do put the dialogues that follow on a different footing, and in fact set up a way of thinking about the processes both of writing philosophy, and of reading philosophical dialogues, which constitutes a dramatic intervention in the genre. As I have already said, the dialogue tradition available to Cicero had a rich and various history, and there were a number of different options available to him in composing dialogues. It is also clear that Greek theoretical and technical writing took a varied approach to the function of the preface.[18] But as far as we can tell, none of these predecessors seem to have used their preface as a direct commentary on the act of doing philosophy and on the context in which that philosophy was being written or read. All of Cicero's dialogues have some kind of preface—and this prefatory material is rather different from that familiar from Plato's dialogues, in which the characters and setting of the conversation are established. Cicero also follows Plato's lead, but as in the passages already discussed, the setting of the stage in the Platonic manner is usually preceded by a commentary on the writing of philosophy itself. Cicero makes an opportunity to speak directly to the reader about the nature of the work in question, and giving them the opportunity to think more widely about the nature of his philosophical project, even before the specific topic and the chosen speakers are introduced.

The transportation of an entire discipline between languages and cultures does go some way to explain what appears to be a new feature within the genre. But it remains difficult to be certain exactly how far this originality extends. We can gain a little more insight by examining one aspect of Cicero's use of Greek antecedents. The evidence concerning the prefaces to Aristotle's lost dialogues, which Cicero apparently had in mind as a model, is contradictory. In a letter to Atticus describing the evolution of *De republica* (*Att.* 4.16), Cicero says that he is making use of *prooimia* (prefaces) in the manner of Aristotle in his *exoteric* dialogues. Although the opening of the *De republica* is lost, the lengthy philosophical polemic that does survive is rather different from the more muted rhetoric of the later prefaces. That perhaps reflects the fact that this was both Cicero's most extensive philosophical endeavor and also his earliest, and it was also no doubt influenced by the popularity of Epicureanism in Rome, which Cicero evidently feels the need to attack. The preface to *De republica* is a kind of exhortation to philosophy, arguing for philosophy as a form of education directly related to political life.[19] But what kind of precedent did Aristotle provide? A rather later source for Aristotle's dialogues, St. Basil, casts doubt on the entire process. Basil points out to his correspondent that Aristotle's dialogues entirely lacked the dramatic scene- and character-setting of Plato, and had nothing in the way of *prooimia*.[20] So if Cicero himself tells us they were his model, either Basil's reading is based on a misunderstanding, or we are looking for Aristotelean influence in the wrong place. That contradiction remains intractable, but the details of Basil's comment raise a different, but important issue: that of literary self-confidence. Basil thinks that both Aristotle and Theophrastus recognized that they fell rather short in terms of the Platonic graces (*endeia ton chariton Platonicon*), and that was why, in their dialogues, they just plunged straight into the *pragmata* (the real subject matter).[21] Cicero evidently did not share their sense of falling short, and his confidence manifests itself in his engagement with a range of generic predecessors. His letters, as well as his pointed use of the same characters across different dialogues, give us plenty of material to observe his concern with the artifice of the dialogues himself. If he shared Basil's critical sensibility, we can take it as a sign of his literary prowess that he could rise to the challenge set by Plato.[22]

To bring the argument back to Cicero: though we cannot know what the thematic content of Aristotle's prologues was, nor what it was that Cicero was imitating, Cicero's prefaces express a concern with the status of philosophy that actually changes the nature of philosophy itself. They do so by drawing attention to the genre, and pointing out the historical and cultural circumstances in which philosophical conversation becomes possible. They even leave room, as in the opening of *De finibus*, for the repudiation of philosophy as a worthwhile activity. Furthermore, beginning in *De republica*, they consistently plead for a close connection between political activity and philosophical insight. This extension of the philosophical project beyond philosophy, and into the cultural reception and public role of philosophy, stems from the project of translation, as importing a foreign way of thinking about ideas. That move in itself may not seem like a particularly philosophical intervention. But if we put it the other way round, and consider the prefaces not so much as a way into the philosophical projects, but rather as an obstruction that stands in the way of the reader's initial engagement with a set of philosophical questions, Cicero's intervention becomes more striking. The prefaces act to detain readers, before they become involved in the philosophical discussion itself. Before being introduced to the material of the dialogue (what Basil calls *pragmata*), the student of philosophy needs to confront the problem of doing philosophy at Rome, and the foreignness of that tradition. That approach may indeed have been something that Cicero took from Aristotle—his *Protreptikos* is thought to be the model for Cicero's *Hortensius*, a work dedicated to persuading the skeptical Roman reader of the relevance of philosophy.[23] However, Aristotle will not have had to contend with Cicero's patriotic critics, nor, given the intellectual traditions of Athens, is he likely to have needed to refute the argument that philosophy was entirely irrelevant. Cicero's prefaces, therefore, do force the reader to confront the need to do philosophy, and think about the relationship between life and philosophy. And although they are rich in polemic against a restricted view of the capacity of Roman literature and of the role of philosophy, the fact remains that, as well as just quashing that view, the prefaces set up the reader to test the efficacy of Cicero's translation, and weigh his success. That is, I would argue, why their reception since the Enlightenment has been so varied—they do not sit comfortably with readers who see philosophy itself as an activity that floats in an ideal world of nonhistorical dialectic.

Historicism and Meta-Romanization

To understand Cicero's practice better, we need to consider the role of historicism: the process through which he anchors philosophy in the historical texture of Roman culture and history. The practice cannot be separated from what, for convenience, I label "Meta-Romanization"—the commentary that the works also provide on the problematic nature of the process of cultural transfer. Cicero's dialogues do not just translate; as the comments in the prefaces discussed above show, they also provide a critical perspective for the process of Romanization, not just in the prefaces but also within the dialogues themselves. Cicero deals with the idea of philosophy as an alien, non-Roman discourse in two ways: by using significant historical figures (Cato, Scipio, Laelius, et al.) as characters, and by littering the philosophical conversation with Roman historical *exempla*, implementing techniques Cicero had honed in his speeches. However, he also draws his readers' attention to this process, by referring directly to the idea of using historical *exempla*. This passage from the second book *De finibus* is fairly typical. The context is Cicero (speaking as a character in his own dialogue) rebutting the arguments of his first interlocutor, Torquatus. Torquatus had spent much of book 1 extolling the Epicurean system—a system that Cicero represents as a barely disguised form of morally reckless hedonism (*Fin.* 2.62):

> I'll restrain myself from using examples. The Greeks have a few: Leonidas, Epaminondas, three or four others. If I were to count up ours, I could get Pleasure to hand herself over to Virtue as a prisoner, but I would run out of daylight. Aulus Varius, who was regarded as a rather harsh judge, used to say to his colleague on the bench, when new witnesses were called in addition to those who had already spoken, "Either we have had enough evidence, or I don't know what enough is." Just so, I have already given enough evidence. Well then; was it pleasure that caused you, in a manner most worthy of your ancestors, when still a youth to snatch the consulship from Publius Sulla?

Torquatus, it would seem, has been chosen as a character for one purpose: he was an Epicurean, whose famous ancestors and noble family can be used repeatedly to demonstrate the idea that the great Romans of the past provide no support whatever for Epicurean philosophy. On that basis alone, one could make a good argument for the self-consciousness of Cicero's procedure, and for the deliberate artificiality of his use of historical *exempla*. A few lines before this passage, Cicero posed to his interlocutor a rhetorical question: would your great ancestor have approved of your speech in favor of pleasure, or mine in favor of disinterested self-sacrifice to his country (2.60)? Torquatus himself had made use of his ancestors to support the claims of pleasure as a motivating force for good in the previous book (1.23, 1.34–36). What we find in this passage is a discussion of the whole question of the application of historical *exempla* to provide evidence for a philosophical position. The words, "I'll restrain myself from using *exempla*" (*contineo me ab exemplis*) have a certain irony to them, in that, if he is moving away from employing examples, he is, nonetheless, about to discuss their use. In the process, he makes an even greater claim for the exemplary quality of Roman history. He also brings in the jurist, Aulus Varius, as an *exemplum*, one who emphasizes a different, more homespun idea of wisdom, coming from the Roman legal tradition. This approach was often a resource for the idea of an intellectual tradition at Rome that had a value that was complementary to Greek philosophy. First, however he makes a comparison between the histories of Greece and Rome: the latter is abundant in examples that refute the Epicurean position.

It is no coincidence that book 1 of *De finibus* not only contains most of that work's contemplation of the problems of translation of philosophy from Greek to Latin, but is also dedicated to the presentation of Epicureanism as a system. The refutation in book 2 is not just directed toward Epicureanism but is also a convenient way of demonstrating how perfectly suited Roman history, and Roman cultural norms are, to the discussion of philosophical ideas, thus reinforcing not just the general relevance of philosophy to Rome as an educational resource but also its concrete application to specific historical contingencies. The fact that here Cicero is able to move from historical heroes to his contemporary, Torquatus, using both as *exempla* for the superiority of virtue over pleasure, shows that philosophy can work in the present as well as prompting a reconfiguration of history to act as a form of philosophical inspiration. That move entails the same polemic that Cicero had taken up in the preface. Cicero is giving a persuasive demonstration of the susceptibility of Roman values to philosophy. The popularity of Epicurus at Rome, as exemplified by the energetic and endearing, but evidently misguided, Torquatus, is an easy target, as Cicero then goes on to say in the opening remarks to book 3. But the debate about Epicureanism is also a well-chosen opportunity to realize the aspirations of the preface, to provide a kind of philosophy that does not make you feel the want of a Greek original.

This passage demonstrates well Cicero's multilayered handling of the adaptation of Greek philosophy for Roman readers, one that takes account of the particular cultural conditions of the period. I now explore another passage that provides more detail to the process of meta-Romanization (*Fin.* 2.66–67):

> When Lucretia was raped by the king's son, she proclaimed the wrong done to her before her fellow citizens, then took her own life. The indignation that her fate aroused in the Roman people led to the nation's liberation under the leadership and guidance of Brutus. Her husband and her father became the Republic's first consuls in her memory. Sixty years after our freedom had been won, Lucius Verginius, a poor and humble man, killed with his own hand his virgin daughter, rather than allow Appius Claudius, who at the time held the highest office of state, to have his lustful way with her. Either you must denigrate their actions, Torquatus, or you must give up your advocacy of pleasure. What kind of advocacy is it, what sort of case does pleasure have, if no witness or supporter can be found among those of greatest renown? On my side the historical record brings forth people who spent their whole life striving for glory and were deaf to the call of pleasure. In your argument, history is silent. I have never heard Lycurgus mentioned in Epicurus's school, or Solon, Miltiades, Themistocles or Epaminondas, all of whom receive due acknowledgment from other philosophers. Now that we Romans have begun to philosophize as well, our friend Atticus can supply us with a vast quantity of heroic names from his treasuries. (tr. Woolf)

It is most interesting to notice how much of what Livy later does with Lucretia is already visible in embryonic form in this passage. Nor should we overlook the resonance with Brutus, the assassin of Julius Caesar, who is the dedicatee of the work. But the crucial part is the deliberation here on the way in which history can act to justify a philosophical position.[24] It would be interesting to explore further why Cicero uses these two specific examples to make this point. Perhaps Verginia just follows Lucretia through an association of ideas of women as sacrificial victims.[25] Lucretia's role as the inaugurator of the Republic is easier to explain: she sets the standard for the life of the res publica that is her immediate legacy. I would also draw attention to the recurrence of the Roman legal metaphor: Torquatus's "advocacy of pleasure," *patrocinium voluptatis*, is a phrase almost unthinkable in Greek, one that reinforces the idea that philosophical debate is thoroughly naturalized within Roman institutions. However, the high point of the argument occurs when, reverting to that list of notable Greek examples of historical self-sacrifice, he says, "In your argument, history is silent" (*in vestris disputationibus historia muta est*). This claim is a dramatic statement of his own aspirations to ground philosophical conversation in history. Epicureans do not even bother to make use of the few examples that might be available to them. The next step in the argument is another moment of high artificiality, one that effectively fractures the fictional framework of the dialogue by referring to Atticus's *Liber Annalis*. Perhaps (as Woolf argues) the reference is a sideswipe at Atticus's own Epicureanism.[26] At all events, it is a clear reference to what was effectively Cicero's main source book for the details of the lives of many of the historical figures he was to write about. The passage continues by way of more wordplay, this time on Themistocles, as Cicero launches into an attack on the Epicurean version of the historical *exemplum*. The case concerns one Themista, an early adherent to the Epicurean cause; a female nonentity, in other words, in sharp contrast to Lucretia and Verginia, as well, of course, to Themistocles himself.

We have a choice, I think, about how to interpret such a passage. We can immerse ourselves fully in the fictional world of the dialogue, and just weigh up the arguments as presented in the texts on the basis of the evidence brought in to support them. Or we can stand back and evaluate the construction that Cicero has placed before us, remain aware of the strong role of *exempla* in the rhetorical tradition, and think about how that tradition might inflect philosophical argument. It seems to me that the reasons in favor of the later position are much stronger. We should consider the process of translating Greek philosophy to Rome which so dominates the preface, and observe how the text also integrates that process in a conversation about philosophy. Such an approach becomes easier if we look back particularly to *De republica*, a text in which the contrast between the intellectual life of the Greeks and the practical life of the Romans is given a much more dominant role, and also a text where the fictionality of the speakers, along with the creation of the myth of the Scipionic circle, is likewise given much greater prominence. Without going into detail, in the later dialogues like *De finibus*, where the dressing of the scene is less careful, and the distancing of the characters in terms of chronology is less extreme, there is a corresponding ease of access to the ironic fracturing of the fiction of the dialogue.

I have mentioned the Academic procedure of stating incompatible positions and leaving their resolution to the reader. I have also brought up the matter of how the history of rhetoric at Rome is to be squared with the arrival at Rome of philosophy. These are big questions, but ones on which Cicero has a fairly consistent position. In writing philosophy for Romans, he is drawing on the stylistic and argumentative skills refined in the course of a long legal and political career. The Academic interest in "the probable" as the way out of skepticism fits well with that training, as it does with the distance that Cicero creates, largely through the framing device of the prefaces, between the actual conditions of Roman society and the work of philosophy.[27] In the passages discussed, we can see Cicero reflecting on his earlier textual labors, and on the way they have shaped the discourse about political and cultural values in Rome. In this late dialogue, as elsewhere, we can detect his own commentary on that history, and see the way in which philosophy can be made to work at Rome, as well as the difficulties inherent in that process.

Conclusion

Cicero gives the dialogue form a new potential. His innovations, however, are not abstract in origin, nor do they stem from the desire to set philosophical method on a different basis. They are the result of a fortuitous combination of circumstances. The most significant of those circumstances must be his own affection for the skeptical academic tradition. That propensity lends itself well to contextualizing the philosophical project, which is central to the transfer of the discipline of philosophy to Rome, and to the manner in which different philosophical positions are presented and interrogated. Cicero's approach produces a form of dialogue that takes the reader away from a self-contained treatment of philosophical abstractions, but for that reason, it also makes philosophy more, rather than less, accessible. By insisting on the contingent quality of philosophical conversation, Cicero wrote in a manner that is less appealing to the professional philosophers of today's academy. His poor reputation among figures such as Kant and Hegel has ensured that professional philosophers mostly consider him important merely as a repository for the doctrines of the Hellenistic schools. However, it is easy to see why, on the basis of his techniques, he was for centuries so important a figure in European education. By including in his dialogues the philosophical history of previous generations, and by connecting abstract argument both to the concrete realities of his own day and to popular moralizing historiography, of a kind so familiar in the exemplary tradition, he could appeal to a wide range of readers, and demonstrate the relevance of philosophy to everyday life. It is true that his most significant legacy was his *On Duties*—the exception to his output in that it takes the form of a letter, rather than a dialogue. But his dialogues too have had an influential history, and it is they that constitute his most sophisticated and complex literary achievement.

Notes

1. Brittain (2001) contains an account of Cicero's interaction with the Academic tradition. Fuller, but less accessible, is Lévy (1992).
2. The essays in Goldhill (2008) give an account of the evolution and demise of dialogue in antiquity. The specialist collection Föllinger and Müller (2013) covers more diverse subjects, and illuminates many aspects of both Greek and Latin traditions.
3. The main exception is Tacitus's *Dialogue on the Orators*. The work is complex, and its reception of Cicero hard to describe; but see Levene (2004) and van den Berg (2014).
4. To some extent, the different philosophers who act as Socrates's interlocutors in Plato and Xenophon are a model. But Cicero's approach reflects the establishment of rival institutions

and traditions for philosophical education that took place later. Mediating the differences between rival schools was evidently important both to Cicero and his Roman audience.
5. For a useful summary of Xenophon's approach to philosophy and philosophers, see Dorion (2016). Waterfield (2004) analyzes the contrasting Socrateses in Plato and Xenophon.
6. See Blondell (2002); Long (2008).
7. This is not Aeschines the orator, but Aeschines of Sphettus, sometimes called Socraticus (Giannantoni VI.A). According to some ancient testimony, he was the writer whose works most closely captured the manner of speaking and character of Socrates. For references, see Hirzel (1895) vol.1, 129, and for the full testimonia, Giannantoni (1990) 593–629.
8. Jazdzewska (2014) is a useful account of the terminology employed within Greek dialogue to describe itself. Her account makes clear that the philosophical method of dialectic, explored by Plato in the *Phaedrus*, should be kept separate from the more varied question-and-answer structure characteristic of dialogues. On the methodological implications of Plato's use of the dialogue form, see also Kahn (1996).
9. I discuss this passage more fully in Fox (2007) 45–49.
10. See Capello in this volume.
11. For rhetoric, see Gunderson in this volume. For more detail on Cicero's skeptical use of dialogue as a response to Greek traditions, see Wynne (2019) 28–46.
12. See Mansfeld (2022).
13. Schofield (2008) 74–81.
14. Notably, Dugan (2005) and van der Blom (2010).
15. *Nat. d.* 1.4–5; see also *Luc.* 5–9; *Tusc.* 2.4–5.
16. See Hoenig in this volume, for the question of translation.
17. Schofield (2008) 77. For a more detailed discussion, see Wynne (2019) 5–18.
18. See Janson (1964) 19–24. Wynne (2019) 29 stresses that the dialogue was not popular in Greek literature at the time Cicero was writing.
19. On the preface, see Blößner (2001).
20. Basil's comment comes in the context of discussion of the dialogues sent him by his correspondent, Diodorus, who in 378 became bishop of Tarsus. He views Plato's works as the most effective in the genre, and makes some interesting recommendations on the value of different approaches to the dramatic use of speakers, and on the question of digression. Rigolio (2019) 96–97 summarizes the letter as evidence for the dialogues of Diodorus.
21. St. Basil, ep. 135 (Migne) cited by Hirzel (1895) vol. 1, 295n2.
22. Hirzel (1895) vol. 1, 488–490 stresses the literary advance that Cicero makes, casting him as the forerunner of more novelistic developments made by Dio Chrysostom and Plutarch.
23. See Turkowska (1965). For Aristotle, *Protreptikos*, see Hutchinson and Johnson (2017). Surviving testimonia, minimal though they are, do confirm that the Aristotle conceived of the objection to doing philosophy as itself a philosophical, rather than a historical, political, or social issue. See Hutchinson and Johnson (2017) 4–6.
24. Readers will find more examples of this process discussed in Fox (2007). *De finibus*, however, is not discussed there.
25. Cf. Livy 3.44.1 for the historian's interpretation of the connection between the two women.
26. Woolf (2001) 49n51.
27. For more detail on how Cicero's own academic training fitted with rhetorical theory, see Reinhardt (2000).

References

Blondell, R. (2002). *The Play of Character in Plato's Dialogues*. (Cambridge).
Blößner, N. (2001). *Cicero gegen die Philosophie*. (Göttingen).
Brittain, C. (2001). *Philo of Larissa: Last of the Academic Sceptics*. (Oxford).
Dorion, L.-A. (2016). "Xenophon and Greek Philosophy," in Flower, 37–56.
Dugan, J. (2005). *Making a New Man: Ciceronian Self-Fashioning in the Rhetorical Works*. (Oxford).
Flower, M., ed. (2016). *The Cambridge Companion to Xenophon*. (Cambridge).
Föllinger, S. and G. M. Müller, eds. *Der Dialog in der Antike*. (Berlin).
Fox, M. (2007). *Cicero's Philosophy of History*. (Oxford).
Giannantoni, G. (1990). *Socratis et Socraticorum Reliquiae*. Vol. 2. (Naples).
Goldhill, S., ed. (2008). *The End of Dialogue in Antiquity*. (Cambridge).
Hirzel, R. (1895). *Der Dialog: Ein Literarhistorischer Versuch*. (Leipzig).
Hutchinson, D. S., and M. R. Johnson, eds. (2017). *Aristotle: Protreptikos or Exhortation to Philosophy*. http://www.protrepticus.info (Accessed October 3, 2022).
Janson, T. (1964). *Latin Prose Prefaces*. (Stockholm).
Jazdzewska, K. (2014). "From *Dialogos* to Dialogue: The Use of the Term from Plato to the Second Century CE." *GRBS* 54: 17–36.
Kahn, C. H. (1996). *Plato and the Socratic Dialogue: The Philosophical Use of a Literary Form*. (Cambridge).
Levene, D. S. (2004). "Tacitus' *Dialogus* as Literary History." *TAPA* 134: 157–200.
Lévy, C. (1992). *Cicero Academicus: Recherches sur les* Académiques *et sur la Philosophie Cicéronienne*. (Paris).
Long, A. G. (2008). "Plato's dialogues and a common rationale for dialogue form," in Goldhill, 45–59.
Mansfeld, J. (2020). "Doxography of Ancient Philosophy." *Stanford Encyclopedia of Philosophy*, Fall 2022 edition, https://plato.stanford.edu/archives/fall2022/entries/doxography-ancient/ (accessed October 3, 2022).
Reinhardt, T. (2000). "Rhetoric in the Fourth Academy." *CQ* 50: 531–547.
Rigolio, A. (2019). *Christians in Conversation: A Guide to Late Antique Dialogues in Greek and Syriac*. (Oxford).
Schofield, M. (2008). "Ciceronian dialogue," in Goldhill, 63–84.
Tuplin, F., ed. (2004). *Xenophon and His World*. (Munich).
Turkowska, D. (1965). *L'Hortensius de Cicéron et le* Protreptique *d'Aristote*. (Warsaw).
van den Berg, C. S. (2014). *The World of Tacitus'* Dialogus de Oratoribus. (Cambridge).
van der Blom, H. (2010). *Cicero's Role Models: The Political Strategy of a Newcomer*. (Oxford).
Waterfield, F. (2004). "Xenophon's Socratic Mission," in Tuplin, 79–113.
Woolf, R., tr. (2001). *Cicero: On Moral Ends*. (Cambridge).
Wynne, J. P. F. (2019). *Cicero on the Philosophy of Religion*. (Cambridge).

CHAPTER 11

THE STOIC LESSON

Cornutus and Epictetus

MICHAEL ERLER

Introduction

In the Stoic tradition Cornutus and Epictetus deserve special attention. Both were famous Stoics at their time, with great influence and important pupils. Cornutus was the teacher of the satirical poet Persius.[1] Although a former slave, Epictetus was a tutor of the historian Arrian and many others. Both Cornutus and Epictetus were involved in the political life of the time,[2] and are important because of their relationship to imperial ideology in Rome and the contribution they make possible toward a better understanding of the Stoic teachings used by Latin poets such as Lucan.[3] Most importantly, both presented their teachings in literary formats that are early examples of educational treatises and, though they are to be understood in the context of Roman Stoic philosophical education, were also of great influence in antiquity and beyond. The so called *Epidrome* of Cornutus and the *Manual* or *Encheiridion* of Epictetus, which was composed by Arrian but was based on Epictetus's teachings, both belong in the tradition of systematic handbooks.[4] They are comparable to introductory literature in the Platonic tradition such as, for instance, Sallustius's *De dis* in philosophy or Cicero's *Topica* or his *Partitiones oratoriae*, in the field of rhetoric.[5] The handbooks of Cornutus and of Arrian aim at introducing readers to Stoic philosophy or special aspects of this school. In addition to these handbooks, we have four out of the eight books of the *Dissertations* of Epictetus, written down again by Arrian. They present the content of Epictetus's Stoic teachings, but they also reflect Epictetus's teaching method. Thus, the dissertations provide a glimpse of Epictetus's classroom.

The texts of Cornutus and Epictetus therefore are of both philosophical and of literary interest. The two are related, because philosophy was regarded by the Stoics—as by most Hellenistic philosophers—as a specialized science (*technē*, *ars*) of right living. What counts for them is not only knowledge of the philosophical doctrine but also the ability to let the school dogma become the maxims of practical action in life in every possible situation. Stoic texts often not only convey Stoic doctrines but also support the reader's or listener's efforts to translate these doctrines into practice. Writing but also reading of texts becomes a philosophical exercise in itself, for which Epictetus even claims Socrates as a paradigm (Arr. *Epict. diss.* 2.2.32–3 (hereafter *Diss.*)). Accordingly, some types of texts, such as the letter, the compendium, and the dissertation or treatise, with their own specific structures of composition, are chosen because they serve best the goal of this kind of transfer of knowledge and because they assist the reader with making correct decisions by applying general principles in given situations, i.e., combining philosophy with life practice. This is the purpose of the texts of Cornutus and Epictetus, as the latter often indicates in his *Manual* and in the *Dissertations*, and Cornutus at the end of the *Epidrome*, where he suggests that more material could be offered to the reader as exercises.

Cornutus's Lessons

Introduction

Lucius Annaeus Cornutus flourished in the reign of Nero.[6] He probably was the freedman Nero is said to have asked for literary advice, but this did not prevent him from banishing Cornutus in 66 or 68 CE. Thereafter nothing is heard of him. Cornutus might not play a major role within the Stoic tradition, but he deserves attention. He, of course, came to be known as an expert in allegory because of his *Epidrome* of true theology, the *Theologiae Graecae compendium* (the Greek title is uncertain), which is a handbook on Stoic allegoresis in Greek, the only work of Cornutus that has survived intact.[7] Although Cornutus's authorship is not undisputed, it seems most probable that the treatise was written by him.[8] From works that are known to us only by quotations or by title we also learn that Cornutus dealt with philosophical topics such as Aristotle's categories,[9] and was critically engaged in a philosophical dispute about some problems in physics. He therefore bears witness that Stoic circles of that era were not focusing on issues of practical ethics only, as is often claimed. They also were interested in philosophical theory. Additionally, Cornutus was a literary critic, who published in Greek and Latin and influenced literary circles in Rome as a teacher of Persius and Lucan. He wrote various rhetorical works in both Greek and Latin, such as *De figuris sententiarum* or *Ars rhetorica*. Finally, he is of interest as a philosophical writer because his *Epidrome* can be regarded as the first *exemplum* of the genre of philosophical handbook.

The *Epidrome* is intended for students and is a didactic composition. It offers insights into the etymological and symbolic interpretations of the Stoics, and helps us to understand better some of the Latin poets of the time, in that it illustrates how they made use of Stoic doctrine.[10] According to his own words, Cornutus does not offer new insights.

He rather claims to follow the Stoic tradition of applying allegorical commentaries to poetry in order to reveal the true nature of the gods. In doing so, Cornutus see himself as summarizing what his predecessors have already said. The *Epidrome* collects moral or naturalistic interpretations of gods or episodes in Greek myths. This summary is especially welcome, because less has been preserved of allegorical interpretation in the Stoic tradition than we might wish.[11]

The text is basically a compilation from works of earlier philosophers. Cornutus drew on material not only from literature, but also from visual arts or from cult practice. He borrowed from different fields, including geography, meteorology, mathematics, and medicine. In doing so, Cornutus seems to have followed the advice that Balbus gives in Cicero's *De natura deorum*, that Stoics should acquire information on the gods from all sources available.[12]

Cornutus might also have had Plato's teachings in mind. It has been argued that there are allusions to and connections with Plato's *Timaeus*.[13] Plato's teachings in other fields as well seem to have been a focus of Cornutus's criticism. His theory of forms, for example, was discussed by Cornutus, who interpreted them as concepts and not as substances.[14]

The interpretations that Cornutus offers show that for Stoics like him the world of phenomena can be understood either literally or by looking below the surface, because the phenomena are associated with divinities and therefore can be regarded as riddles. The goddess Rhea, for instance, was connected with flowing (from *rhei*, "it flows"). The traditional connection of the olive, and hence olive oil, with Athena derives from the fact that it does not mix with other things.[15] In most cases though— for instance when analyzing Oceanus—it is difficult to recognize the etymology of the name, and alternative explanations are offered.[16] Poems are regarded as a *thesaurus* in which mythmakers enshrined what Cornutus seems to have regarded as ancient or mythic truth.

Literary Form and Philosophical Teaching

One of the explicit aims of Cornutus's tract is to help his young readers understand better the religious tradition by explaining names or expressions that might seem difficult to them.[17] No special knowledge of Stoic philosophy is expected of the reader. Here the *Epidrome* differs from other examples of philosophic introductions such as, for instance, the treatise *De dis* of Sallustius, which seems rather to presuppose a reader who already has been taught the basic doctrines of Platonism[18] but is not expected to become a specialist in philosophy. Arrian's *Encheiridion* is addressed to a wider audience, although it is not a popular book. The didactic intention of the *Epidrome* accounts for its structure.[19] The treatise is arranged by chapters that deal with individual divinities. The first chapters (1–8) discuss the gods Uranus, Zeus, Hera, Poseidon, Hades, Rhea, Cronus, and Oceanus, as well as cosmological gods; in chapters 9–16 Zeus and divine figures like the Erinyes, Litai, Moirai, Muses, and Hermes are analyzed. Chapter 17 contains an excursus on method and a discussion of poets, for example Hesiod. Chapters 18–21 discuss more gods. including Prometheus, Hephaestus, Athena, Ares, and Enyo. Chapters 22–29 are about Poseidon and gods who are related to the affections: Poseidon, Nereus, Aphrodite, Eros, Atlas, Pan, Demeter, Hestia, and Horai. The last chapters 30–35 discuss Dionysus, Heracles, Apollo, Artemis, and finally Hades. An interesting conclusion (chap. 35) explains why some material is dealt with here even if it has been treated by others more extensively. The aim of the treatise is to offer a young man (*pais*) useful information, which he should have at hand.[20]

Some features of the text are familiar from other didactic texts or poems. For instance, a person in the text is addressed, although here the addressee is not named, while in other didactic texts, for example Lucretius's *De rerum natura*, this person is identified by name, i.e., Memmius.[21] Cornutus obviously desires brevity,[22] and offers cross-references[23] or helps the reader by marking transitions to other topics. All this might elicit the reader's interest because it gives an impression of coherence to the argument.[24]

The text also offers moral statements, for example, about reason coming about with age, or about the importance of education and scholarship. Advice is given not to drink too much. Hard work is praised, punishment is justified, education and scholarship are regarded as important, although it means a partial withdrawal from everyday life.[25] The didactic intention of the text might be responsible for the fact that Stoic logic and ethics are absent from the treatise, whereas physics is present, because theology is the main topic of the treatise, which for the Stoics belonged with physics. The reason for this focus on physics, or rather a special aspect of physics, was that the Stoics were convinced that knowledge of physics does contribute to happiness. According to a Stoic like Cornutus, it is essential to live according to nature in order to become happy, a position shared by other Hellenistic schools, for instance, the Epicureans. Both Lucretius, in his poem *De rerum natura*, and Diogenes of Oenoanda, in his monumental inscription, offer teachings on physics as a start for those who wish to achieve *eudaimonia*.[26] Although Cornutus does not expect his reader to be well acquainted with Stoic doctrines, he obviously presupposes knowledge of Greek authors like Homer or Hesiod and their myths, inasmuch as he paraphrases parts of their poems and comments on them.

On the other hand, one gets the impression that Cornutus is not very interested in really analyzing the etymologies. Rarely does Cornutus reduce a word to its basic constituents, as one might expect,[27] but he is often content to offer alternative explanations and only occasionally does he indicate what his preference is, or which of the etymologies he regards as the right one.[28] This approach has puzzled interpreters; some have ignored the variants, while others have felt that some alternatives are unsuitable and have bracketed them as interpolations. But this is based on a misunderstanding of Cornutus's method.[29] Although Cornutus's approach does differ from what can be observed in earlier Stoics, his method of *accumulatio* in regard to etymological explanations is similar to what one finds in Lucretius, in the writings of Sextus Empiricus, or in the *Meditations* of Marcus Aurelius. When discussing natural phenomena or, for instance the mortality of the soul, these authors too offer chains of alternative arguments or explanations, without giving any hint as to which they prefer. This method of adding argument upon argument stems from rhetorical contexts and found its way in philosophical discourse as early as Plato.[30] Interesting from a methodological point of view too is the fact that Cornutus, at the end of the *Epidrome*, expresses the hope that the addressee will interpret other myths about the gods along the lines of the models that he has displayed.[31]

It is clear that in his treatise Cornutus wished to provide the reader both with a method and with illustrations of how the method should be applied. The examples that are discussed are meant as blueprints for the interpretation of mythical stories and names, which the reader may apply on other occasions. This combination of method and illustrative applications is reminiscent of Lucretius's approach in *De rerum natura* and of Epictetus's in his *Diatribai*, as well as in the *Meditations* of Marcus Aurelius.[32]

Epictetus's Lessons

Epictetus the Stoic

Epictetus's lectures on philosophy and his *Manual* combine dogmatic material with remarks on method. They also illustrate how this material might be applied in everyday challenging situations. Like Cornutus's *Epidrome*, Epictetus's lectures and his handbook or *Manual*, are of importance for both the tradition of Stoic philosophy and the history of philosophical literature.

Epictetus, a freedman[33] who lived c. 50–125 CE, was in many ways an orthodox Stoic. He ran a school in Rome, but was exiled by Domitian together with other philosophers (93/4 CE), and opened a new school in Nicopolis in Epirus. His teachings were focused on central topics of Stoic ethics and doctrines, such as the question of freedom, of will or *prohairesis*, and of judgment.[34] He probably would not have claimed to have made original contributions to the Stoic tradition, but he did modify certain doctrines to some extent. For instance, he seems to have been less exigent in terms of rationality, because he accepted that no human being is without error.[35] He also preaches tolerance toward all people.[36] The main focus of his teaching is practical ethics. Even if he discusses physics, psychology, or logic, he does so with respect to what these imply for a good life. Teaching philosophy for him means equipping his students with an art of living that enables them to achieve autonomy and deal with difficult circumstances in life.[37]

Epictetus was a great admirer of Socrates, and he considered it beneficial always to test oneself and others and to remember everything Socrates did and said, since Socrates's life and death and his way of doing philosophy were crucial to Epictetus.[38] But it has to be kept in mind that Epictetus's Socrates was different from the one Plato presented in his early dialogues. Epictetus's Socrates is not an aporetic or ironic philosopher, but an *exemplum* of the good life, achieved by controlling emotions and keeping oneself free of wrong judgments. Epictetus's Socratic philosophy includes encouragement to philosophize and offers help toward ridding oneself of false beliefs.

Epictetus is convinced that everyone can live a happy life, if he or she is able to recognize what is up to us and what is not, to assess the value of any given thing, and to adopt an appropriate motivation toward things.[39] The basis of this approach seems to be the rule (*kanon*) that only judgment is in our power and that everything else is not and precisely for this reason is morally indifferent. To be able to follow this rule means to be educated in such a way as to achieve real freedom. Those who are not educated philosophically are in danger of being disturbed by phenomena, although there is no justifiable ground for such responses. Epictetus wants his students to learn how to deal with death or other challenges life offers. In order to bring about this outcome, Epictetus asks young students first to prepare themselves for philosophy by learning to control their desires and emotions "and to live according to nature." Next, he wants them to study rhetoric, logic, and literature.[40]

Epictetus's *Dissertations*: Arrian's Texts

Epictetus follows his teacher Musonius, and most of all, Socrates, his master, in that he—as far as we know—wrote nothing for publication,[41] although in one school lecture Epictetus affirms, that Socrates did write hypomnemata or "notes" of a sort himself (see Arr. *Epict. diss.* 2.2.32–3), in part as an exercise in (self-)refutation.

However, we do have the *Discourses*, which were edited by Lucius Flavius Arrianus, who wrote in Attic Greek and joined Epictetus in Nicopolis, perhaps during the years 105–113 CE. Arrian affirms that these are accurate records of Epictetus's lessons. Four books are preserved out of an original eight. Arrian himself states that he did not "compose the discourses (*logoi*) of Epictetus in the way one might 'compose' such works, nor have I published them myself; for I do not claim to have composed them at all. Rather, I tried to write down whatever I heard him say, in his own words as far as possible, to keep notes (*hypomnêmata*) of his thought and frankness for my own future use" (letter to Lucius Gellius).[42] We also have the *Handbook* or *Manual* (*Encheiridion*), which Arrian compiled out of these "dissertations." It is disputed how far the *Dissertations* and the *Manual* can be regarded as authentic testimonies of Epictetus's teachings. It has been argued that Arrian's claim in the letter to Gellius has to be seen as a literary strategy to persuade the reader of the authenticity of the report, which might nevertheless be fictitious. A close analysis has also suggested that the editor might have added things or arranged the material in a certain order.[43]

Epictetus's *Dissertations*: Title, Structure, Function

Title

The discourses most commonly are called *Diatribai*—informal talks. They are often named *dissertationes* in Latin or *dialexeis* in Greek. We also hear of Epictetus's lectures (*scholai*) or records (*apomnemoneumta*).[44] This variety suggests that they did not have an official title. This point is important because it alerts us to the need to interpret Epictetus's discourses in view of what we know about the literary genre of diatribe. There are without any doubt affinities with Cynic diatribes in style, topic, and other stylistic and methodological aspects. But one should not overlook differences. For instance, Epictetus's dissertations offer a more philosophical or analytical approach. Their repertoire of topics includes theoretical and methodological questions, psychology, and social problems, and is broader than in the diatribes of the Cynics. Socrates plays an important role, as does Musonius.[45] As to the audience of Epictetus's lectures, Epictetus was a famous teacher at his time, as Simplicius tells us.[46] He attracted a large number of pupils, many of them well-to-do youths from Rome and elsewhere, who often had a distinguished career ahead of them.[47] It would therefore not be right to expect Epictetus to promote a kind of popular philosophy, although Epictetus was later contrasted with Plato as someone admired by ordinary people, who believe they profit from reading his works. Epictetus seems to distance himself from the philosophical teaching at his time, and from the manner in which philosophers invited students to their lectures.[48]

Structure

Reading the *Dissertations* one is aware of their loose and somewhat associative structure. This structure has suggested to some interpreters that Epictetus was not interested in a systematic approach to philosophical problems at all, but that he rather aimed at solving practical problems, very much as Socrates did in the earlier Platonic dialogues. It has to be kept in mind, however, that Epictetus's dissertations themselves show that he read and interpreted classical Stoic texts together with students in his classes—a kind of teaching that is not illustrated by the dissertations. There is one scene, for instance, in which a pupil is interpreting a text on Stoic logic while being supervised by an older pupil. We also learn that Epictetus thought in the morning about what text or author he would read or interpret in the afternoon, together with his students.[49] It follows that the dissertations reflect only partially what and how Epictetus taught his students, because they only represent one of Epictetus's teaching methods. Their unsystematic character does not prove that Epictetus was unsystematic as a philosopher.

Function

Epictetus's diatribes formed part of his program to stimulate his students to free themselves from mental weaknesses and to practice what would help them to live a happy life. He was convinced that to defeat bad habits one must acquire the contrary habit; one can only gain tranquility of mind (*ataraxia*) by distinguishing what is one's own, or in one's power, from what is not.[50] Epictetus's *Dissertations* not only illustrate the application of this kind of exercise in everyday life, they also exhibit Stoic doctrines and the methods by which they are applied. Because of their exemplary character, the discourses can be regarded as an appeal to the reader to practice what is illustrated in the text. These calls to engagement reflect oral philosophical conventions and are models intended for further application. They should be understood not just as conveying the *topoi* of the diatribe form but as an invitation to apply doctrine to life in order to handle difficult situations. Further inducements to meditation are the maxim, the *exemplum*, and even prayer, which is part of an exercise for life.[51] The *Dissertations* thus turn out to be a reservoir of incentives originating in oral instruction. They give readers the chance to test themselves and others out loud, at home or in the classroom.[52]

This is just what Epictetus thought books were for. He did not like reading books just for entertainment or for instruction. He held that books should support living a good life, in the same way that Epicureans or Marcus Aurelius wanted their books to be read. According to Epictetus, texts serve to apply general rules to special situations. This is why we should read Homer or tragedy, and this is why it is useful to write texts.[53] Interestingly, as mentioned already, Epictetus refers to Socrates to justify this kind of philosophical writing and reading of books. Epictetus argues, surprisingly, that Socrates wrote so much because he was always busy examining his own opinions, but at times he did not have partners at hand for test-conversations.[54] Only for this reason would a philosopher write books. Socrates, the master of the oral search for truth, becomes a self-therapist and regards books as substitutes for speaking partners.

Epictetus's *Manual*

Besides the *Dissertations*, we possess a small book entitled *Manual* (*Encheiridion*).[55] It is a brief summary of the central philosophical topics of the dissertations, although lacking the literary qualities of the discourses. According to the late Platonist Simplicius, who wrote a commentary on the *Manual*, the title *encheiridion* signals the purpose of the book: "The aim of the book—if it meets with people who are persuaded by it, and do not merely read it but are actually affected by the speeches and bring them into effect—is to make our soul free (. . .). It is titled 'The Handbook,' because it ought always to be to hand or ready for those who want to live well."[56] The *Manual* contains the fundamental teachings of Epictetus and extracts taken from his dissertations, which often are modified.⁵⁷ The pamphlet is well structured. As in the *Dissertations* one can observe a kind of *Ringkomposition*: in the first and last chapter of the *Manual* the focus is on the claim that one must distinguish between what is up to us and what is not, and in the last chapter many quotations are introduced to support this claim.⁵⁸

As Max Pohlenz saw, the other chapters of the *Manual* seem to present the reader with the three areas of study (*topoi*) that form the basis of Epictetus's practical ethics and help the student to reach happiness. They concern human inclination, choice, and intellectual assent, and are practical disciplines that help the student to apply the Stoic principles in daily life. Epictetus describes this procedure in a little scene in one of his dissertations (1.4.10–11):⁵⁹

> "Are you not willing to show him the work of virtue, that he may learn where to look for his progress?" Look for it there, wretch, where your work lies. And where is your work? In desire and aversion, that you may not miss what you desire and encounter what you would avoid; in choice and in refusal that you may commit no fault therein; in giving and withholding assent of judgment, that you may not be deceived. (tr. Oldfather)

These three forms of exercises or *topoi* indeed structure the *Manual*. Chapter 1 of the *Manual* is an introduction; chapters 2–29 deal with the first *topos*; chapters 30–51 deal with the second *topos*; chapter 52 with the third *topos*; and chapter 53 refers back to chapter 1. In the *Manual* we therefore see a systematic structure, which suggests, in addition, that the work might have been addressed to a reader who was already familiar with Stoic teachings. It is meant to function as a mnemonic device. Although there are question- and answer-passages in the *Manual*,⁶⁰ the dialogical structure of these passages is less clear here than in the diatribes. The style is rather that of a treatise. There are no anecdotes or dialogues with fictional heroes. In the last chapter, Socrates is given the final word⁶¹ and the reader is asked to emulate the paradigm of Socrates: "Socrates fulfilled himself by attending to nothing except reason in everything he encountered. And you, although you are not yet a Socrates, should live as someone who at least wants to be a Socrates."⁶² Again, the *Manual* gives the reader good advice for putting Epictetus's teachings into practice, as when he says: "Don't ask that events should happen as you wish; but wish them to happen as they do and you will get on well."⁶³

With good reason the *Manual* has been called a *vade mecum* for people who wish to live a happy life.⁶⁴ It might be of use for those who wish to make progress in Stoic philosophy, but it is also helpful for beginners even in Neoplatonic circles. In Athens, Simplicius regarded the manual as a textbook for beginners in philosophy, to function as a *praeparatio philosophica* in that it helps to achieve a disposition that will enable the student to embark on a philosophical education. The *Encheiridon* was part of the philosophical curriculum in late antiquity, and is mirrored in the structure of Boethius's *Consolatio philosophiae*.⁶⁵ The handbook exerted great influence in later antiquity and beyond.⁶⁶

Philosophy as Exercise: Elements of Exercise

"Is it possible to be free from fault altogether? No, that cannot be achieved, but it is possible ever to be intent upon avoiding faults."[67] From this claim it follows that exercise was of greatest importance for Epictetus in the context of practical ethics, as it had been for his teacher Musonius. For both define philosophy not as mere theoretical investigation in order to expand our knowledge but as a practice that can provide virtue through training (*askesis*).[68] Epictetus's concept of exercise is different from that of Musonius in that he stresses the role of shame or respect (*aidos*) as the aim of practice (*askesis*) far more than Musonius does. Epictetus argues that in order to become wise and virtuous one must perform exercises that concern the soul. This approach is regarded as necessary, because the Socratic conviction that correct knowledge ipso facto leads to action had come to be seen as problematic (askesis receives far greater emphasis in Xenophon's representation of Socratic instruction). Epictetus's teachings aim at instilling an attitude by which to convert knowledge into a *habitus* of the agent, which will enable him or her to deal with challenging situations. The insights that Epictetus offers are not to be consumed passively by students or readers but rather must be used as means for pursuing happiness in life.[69] His lessons are useful in that they not only illustrate spoken philosophical exercises but also show how they must be practiced effectively in order that the pupil or reader may become "dyed with"—to use a metaphor which is also familiar from Seneca and Marcus Aurelius—the wisdom or idea that is needed for living a good life.[70] This approach is what Epictetus wishes to teach his students in the classroom.

The methodological basis for Epictetus's teachings is the so-called *kanon*,[71] a standard question that one should always have ready: "What belongs to me?"; "What does not belong to me?"; "What is given to me?" Epictetus expects one to practice conversation with oneself first in oral and written form, and then to proceed to practical application. All this should enable the student to distinguish between what is up to us, that is, within our power, and what not. The aim of these exercises is tranquility of mind, not to be disturbed by challenges. In order to reach this goal Epictetus demands that exercises be at hand day and night.[72] There are three main fields of exercise, dealing first, with passions, second, with positive or negative impulses, and, third, with unexamined impressions. These three fields correspond to the three activities of the soul. These exercises are practiced as tests of sense impressions, so as to rid oneself of wrong evaluations of the phenomena and avoid bad feelings that may result from them. Epictetus often presents *paradoxa* as a form of practice,[73] because what at first sight seems paradoxical to the inexperienced can be explained on a rational basis and so loses its paradoxical character and thereby eliminates the disturbing element. Epictetus teaches his students: "Bear in mind that it is not the man who reviles or strikes you that insults you, but it is your judgement that these men are insulting you. Therefore, when someone irritates you, be assured that it is your own opinion which has irritated you. And so make it your first endeavour not to be carried away by the external impression" (*Ench.* 20).[74] This kind of exercise is documented in the *Discourses* as well, with a view to stimulating the reader to practice the exercises themselves.[75]

Epictetus's diatribes illustrate how to apply Stoic teachings in everyday life. In doing so, they describe different aspects of self-help in discourse, intended to make Epictetus's philosophy useful in difficult or challenging situations.[76] Fictive dialogues between Epictetus and another person, but also soliloquies or conversations with oneself in written form, give a blueprint for how the reader himself should behave. In this connection, there are many reminiscences of Platonic dialogues, which, besides being literary motifs or allusions, again function as exercises that can be imitated by the reader. Epictetus's way of conducting conversations indeed is similar to Socrates's mode in Plato's dialogues. However, Epictetus's partners in his dissertations seem to be less independent than Socrates's interlocutors are—at least in some dialogues; they rather behave like figures in the later dialogues of Plato, simply foils for the lecturer. Epictetus also imitates Socrates in presenting monologues, as does Marcus Aurelius.[77]

Epictetus contrasts the Socratic kind of dialogue with the bad method of a Stoic who is not able to guide his partner to the truth:[78]

> What a man ought to learn before he will know how to conduct an argument has been precisely defined by the philosophers of our school; but as to the proper use of what we have learned we are still utterly inexperienced (. . .). How did Socrates act? He used to force the man who was arguing with him to be his witness, and never needed any other witness. . . . For he used to make so clear the consequences which followed from the concepts, that absolutely everyone realized the contradiction involved and gave up the battle.

Additionally, Epictetus makes use of prayer as meditative device, as well as *sententiae*, *exempla*, and monologues. For instance, the reader is asked to bring to mind on any occasion the verses of Cleanthes about Zeus. Moreover, Epictetus formulates prayers that turn into meditations and thereby become part of the philosophical exercise.[79] *Exempla* are taken from myth, but most importantly from the life of Socrates, for example, in order to suggest to the reader how to behave when confronted with a judge or in front of the powerful, or to underline one of Epictetus's theses. Sometimes Epictetus adds contemporary anecdotes, like the one about Thrasea.[80] The *Dissertations* therefore are a thesaurus of situations that are to be kept in mind and will help the reader when dealing with difficult situations. Exhortations like, "Say this whenever something occurs to you," demonstrate the close connection between the oral style of the text and the response expected of the reader.[81]

Socratic Elements and Epictetus's Method

Socrates was Epictetus's hero also with respect to philosophical method.[82] Epictetus did not wish to lecture in order to impress or entertain an audience like a rhetorician using epideictic rhetoric, as other philosophers did.[83] But he did seek to influence his students by the use of rhetorical devices or certain styles as instruments. As he himself says in a dissertation titled, "To those who make a display of lecturing and discussing," Epictetus prefers what he calls an elenchtic, a protreptic, and a doctrinal style. The first two signal Epictetus's commitment to the Socratic heritage.[84] The *elenchos* is understood by Socrates as a means to examine his interlocutors' opinions and personality, and to prepare them for discovering truth. Socrates achieves this by showing them that they are confused, though they think they know something, for instance, what bravery is. Socrates undermines his interlocutors' confidence by putting their opinions to the test. Epictetus follows Socrates and indeed sharpens his point by affirming flatly that every error involves a contradiction.[85] Epictetus illustrates this approach by referring to Euripides' *Medea*.[86] Again and again, Epictetus gets his partner to assent to propositions that contradict the opinion asserted at the beginning of the conversation. In doing so, Epictetus does not wish to attain only negative results, but to open the way for a better understanding of the problems under scrutiny, and to indicate how to make the right choices in life. Epictetus's Socratic method therefore is related to practical considerations. As he says: "I invite you to come and hear that you are in a bad way; that you are attending to everything except what you should be concerned about; that you are ignorant of what is good and bad; and that you are thoroughly unhappy and wretched."[87]

Summary

The different views in the philosophical schools on how to convey knowledge led to a variety of literary forms for presenting philosophical doctrine and methods, which not only illustrated the therapeutic intention of Stoic philosophy but also supported its practice. According to Stoics like Epictetus, it is useless to read books just to gain theoretical knowledge. Reading is supposed to prepare for life and to help evaluate the impressions that assail people. It also should help to make correct decisions by giving readers the opportunity to test themselves and others. The social significance of philosophy in the first century CE can be seen not least in the fact that it is not limited to schools and specialists. Rather, as a mediator of life orientation and personality formation, philosophy and philosophical texts had a broad impact beyond the school, in life and often in literature as well. The *Epidrome* of Cornutus and Epictetus's *Manual* and dissertations played a key role in this process, and are important for the history of philosophical literature and its uses.[88]

Notes

1. Berdozzo (2009) 6–13; cf. Pers. 5.19–29 and 5.45–51; cf. Most (1989) 2043–2059.
2. Griffin (1989); Most (1989) 2034–2043.
3. Morford (1989).

4. Fuhrmann (1960).
5. Nock (1931) 1003; Most (1989) 2029.
6. Hays (1983).
7. Lang (1881); Ramelli (2003). A new edition is in preparation for Teubner by Most.
8. Berdozzo (2009) 17–22.
9. Porph. *In Aristotelis categorias* = *Comm. in Arist. Graeca* IV.1 p. 59, 10–11.
10. Cf. esp. Boys-Stones (2001) 56–58.
11. Steinmetz (1986) and modifying his position, Most (1989) 2023–2024.
12. Cornutus, *Theol. Graec.* 35, p. 76, 6–8 Lang; cf. Most (1989) 2015.
13. Boys-Stones (2009).
14. Cf. Syrianus, *In Aristotelis Metaphysica* = *Comm. in Arist. Graeca* VI.1 p. 106, 5–10.
15. Cf. for Rhea Cornutus, *Theol. Graec.* 6, p. 5, 9 Lang; Athena 20, 39.1–3 Lang (hereafter "L").
16. For Oceanus, see *Theol. Graec.* 8. For some helpful observations, see Buffière (1965) 60.
17. Most (1989) 2030; Berdozzo (2009) 22.
18. Sallustius 1.1.
19. Boys-Stones (2007) 86–88.
20. Berdozzo (2009) 22ff.
21. Mitsis (1993).
22. E.g., *Theol. Graec.* 35, p. 76, 6–8.
23. *Theol. Graec.* 7, 7.22–28 L; 14, 17.15–16 L; 15, 18.14 L; 22, 41.19 L.
24. *Theol. Graec.* 22, 41.18–19 L; 28, 52.4–5 L.
25. *Theol. Graec.* 30, 60.4–9 L; 14, 15.10–13 L.
26. Diogenes of Oinoanda, Fr. 2 II 11–III 4 Smith; cf. Erler (1993).
27. Cornutus, *Theol. Graec.* 8, 8.13 L, for the method applied, see Most (1989) 2027–2029.
28. *Theol. Graec.* 3, 4.5 L; 28, 56.20–22 L and 57.3–4; Hays (1983) 16ff.
29. Lang (1881) felt that this method might be unfitting and bracketed some passages; a misunderstanding of Cornutus's method is suspected rightly by Most (1989) 2028 ann. 107; see next note.
30. Erler (2013).
31. Cf. Cornutus, *Theol. Graec.* 35, 75.18–76.2 L and Boys-Stones (2007).
32. Erler (2012).
33. Gell. *NA* 1.2.1–13; 2.18.10.
34. Long (2002) 27ff.
35. *Diss.* 4.12.19.
36. *Diss.* 1.18.3–4.
37. Cf. Erler (2012) 355–359.
38. For Socrates and Epictetus see Hershbell (1989) 2153–2155; Long (2002) 67–96.
39. *Diss.* 3.2.1–15.
40. *Diss.* 2.1.
41. Cf. Fuentes Gonzáles (2000) 122–123.
42. The translation is borrowed from Long (2002) 39.
43. Cf. Wirth (1967) 149–189, 197–216; discussion by Long (2002) 40.
44. For the passages, see Schenkl (^{2}1916) ii–xv, xxxiii–xxxv; discussed in Long (2002) 42.
45. *Diss.* 3.23.29; Erler (2007).
46. Simpl. *Commentaria in Epicteti Encheiridion* 275, 42–45 Hadot.
47. Cf. *Diss.* 1.25.26; 2.14.1; regular hearers cf. 3.5.12–13; occasional visitors cf. 1.10.2; Hijmans (1959) 2ff.

48. *Diss.* 3.23.27–29.
49. *Diss.* 1.26.13; 1.10.8.
50. Cf. *Diss.* 1.27.4.
51. *Diss.* 1.6.37; 2.16.41ff.; 3.24.9–12.
52. *Diss.* 1.1.1–25; cf. 2.1.29ff..; 4.4, *passim*.
53. *Diss.* 4.4.16; Homer or tragedy cf. 4.10.31ff.; cf. Erler (2012).
54. *Diss.* 2.1.32, on which, see Wehner (2000) 84n17.
55. Cf. Boter (2007).
56. Simpl. *Commentaria in Epicteti Encheiridion* 193, 18–25 Hadot; transl. by Brennan and Brittain (2002) 37.
57. Boter (2007) xi ff.
58. Wehner (2000) 251.
59. Cf. Arr. *Diss.* 3.2.1; Pohlenz (^{5}1980) 162.
60. Arr. *Epicteti Encheiridion* 24.1 (hereafter *Ench.*).
61. Cf. *Ench.* 53.4; see Pl. *Cri.* 43d; *Ap.* 30c–d.
62. Translation borrowed from Long (2002) 69.
63. *Ench.* 8; translation borrowed from Long (2002) 8.
64. Barnes (1997) 65.
65. Simpl. *Commentaria in Epicteti Encheiridion* 195, 61–81 Hadot, and cf. Erler (1999).
66. Boter (1999); Spanneut (1962).
67. *Diss.* 4.12.19; translated by Oldfather (1925/8) 429.
68. Gourinat (2012) 433; for Musonius Rufus cf. p. 22, 7–23, 3 Hense.
69. Erler (1998).
70. Cf. Sen. *Ep.* 71.31; M. Aur. *Med.* 5.16.
71. *Diss.* 4.4.29.
72. *Diss.* 3.24.103.
73. *Diss.* 3.2.1; for *paradoxa* see *Diss.* 1.25.32ff., exercise cf. Hijmans (1959); Newman (1989) esp. 1496–1506 (Epictetus).
74. *Ench.* 20; translation by Oldfather (1925/1928) 499.
75. *Diss.* 4.4.14.
76. Cf. Erler (2012) 353.
77. *Diss.* 2.5.4; cf. Wehner (2000) 79–105.
78. *Diss.* 2.12.1–7; translation by Oldfather (1925/8) 291; for soliloquies or fictive dialogues with a man in power, see Wehner (2000) 104ff., 134ff.
79. On the meditative function of philosophical prayer see Erler (2001).
80. *Diss.* 2.2.15; anecdotes cf. *Diss.* 1.1.27ff.; and Döring (1974); Wehner (2000) 226.
81. *Ench.* 9 and Erler (2012) 351–354.
82. Long (2002) 79.
83. *Diss.* 3.23.27–29.
84. *Diss.* 3.23.33.
85. *Diss.* 2.26.1.
86. *Diss.* 1.28.6–8.
87. *Diss.* 3.23.27–29; translation borrowed from Long (2002) 52.
88. I thank Marion Schneider, David Konstan, and Gretchen Reydams-Schils, for improving the English and for their suggestions.

References

Allen, J. (2005). "The Stoics on the Origin of Language and the Foundations of Etymology," in Frede and Inwood, 14–35.
Asper, M. (1998). "Zu Struktur und Funktion eisagogischer Texte," in Kullmann and Althoff, 309–340.
Barnes, J. (1997). *Logic and the Imperial Stoa.* (Leiden).
Berdozzo, F. (2009). "Einführung," in Nesselrath, 3–28.
Boter, G. J. (1992). "Epictetus, *Encheiridion* 27." *Mnemosyne* 45: 473–81.
Boter, G. J. (1999). *The Encheiridion of Epictetus and Its Three Christian Adaptations. Transmission and Critical Editions.* (Leiden).
Boter, G. J., ed. (2007). *Epictetus,* Encheiridion. (Berlin).
Boys-Stones, G. R. (2001). *Post-Hellenistic Philosophy: A Study of Its Development from the Stoics to Origen.* (Oxford).
Boys-Stones, G. R. (2003). *Metaphor, Allegory, and the Classical Tradition: Ancient Thought and Modern Revisions.* (Oxford).
Boys-Stones, G. R. (2007). *"Fallere Sollers*: The Ethical Pedagogy of the Stoic Cornutus," in Sorabji and Sharples, 77–88.
Boys-Stones, G. R. (2009). "Cornutus in His Philosophical Context: The Antiplatonism of the *Epidrome*"/"Cornutus und sein philosophisches Umfeld: Der Antiplatonismus der *Epidrome*," in Nesselrath, 141–161.
Boys-Stones, G. R. (2018). *L. Annaeus Cornutus, Greek Theology: Fragments, and Testimonia.* (Atlanta).
Brennan, T., and C. Brittain (2002). *Simplicius. On Epictetus' "Handbook 1–26."* (Ithaca, N.Y.).
Brunt, P. A. (1977). "From Epictetus to Arrian." *Athenaeum* 55: 19–48.
Buffière, F. (1965). *Les Mythes d'Homère et la pensée grecque.* (Paris).
Busch, P., and J. K. Zangenberg, eds. (2010). *Lucius Annaeus Cornutus: Einführung in die griechische Götterlehre.* (Darmstadt).
Carlini, A. (1995). "Osservazioni sull' Epilogo del *Manuale* di Epitteto." *Stud. Ital.* 13(2): 214–225.
Cattin, E. (1997). *Arrien, Manuel d'Epictète.* (Paris).
Donini, P. (1994). "Testi e commenti, manuali e insegnamento: La forma sistematica e i metodi della filosofia in età posthellenistica." *ANRW* II, 36(7): 5027–5100.
Döring, K. (1974). " Sokrates bei Epiktet," in Döring and Kullmann, 195–226.
Döring, K. (1979). *Exemplum Socratis: Studien zur Sokratesnachwirkung in der kynisch-stoischen Philosophie der frühen Kaiserzeit und im frühen Christentum.* (Wiesbaden).
Döring, K., and W. Kullmann, eds. (1974). *Studia Platonica: Festschrift für H. Gundert.* (Amsterdam).
Duhot, J.-J. (2003). *Épictète et la sagesse stoicienne.* (Paris).
Erler, M. (1993). "*Philologia medicans:* Wie die Epikureer die Texte ihres Meisters lasen," in Kuhlmann and Althoff, 281–303.
Erler, M. (1998). "Einübung und Anverwandlung: Reflexe mündlicher Meditationstechnik in philosophischer Literatur der Kaiserzeit," in Kullmann, Althoff, and Asper, 361–381.
Erler, M. (1999). "Hellenistische Philosophie als '*praeparatio platonica*' in der Spätantike (am Beispiel von Boethius' *Consolatio philosophiae*)," in T. Fuhrer and M. Erker, eds., *Zur Rezeption der hellenistischen Philosophie in der Spätantike* (Stuttgart), 105–122.

Erler, M. (2001). "Selbstfindung im Gebet. Integration eines Elementes epikureischer Theologie in den Platonismus der Spätantike," in T. Szlezak, ed., *Platonisches Philosophieren* (Hildesheim/Zurich/New York), 155–171.

Erler, M. (2007). "Death Is a Bugbear: Socratic 'Epode' and Epictetus' Philosophy of the Self," in Scaltsas and Mason, 99–111.

Erler, M. (2012). "Aspects of Orality in (the Text of) the Meditations," in van Ackeren, 346–361.

Erler, M. (2013). "Chain of Proof in Lucretius, Sextus, and Plato: Rhetorical Tradition and Philosophy," in Marchand and Verde, 25–43.

Erler, M. (2018). "Glück aus Tugend durch Übung ohne Philosophie? Platons Übungsbegriff zwischen Sophistik und hellenistischer Philosophie," in A.-B. Renger & A. Stellmacher (eds.), *Übungswissen in Religion und Philosophie. Produktion, Weitergabe, Wandel* (Berlin), 21–33.

Everson, S., ed. (1994). *Language*. (Cambridge).

Frede, D., and B. Inwood, eds. (2005). *Language and Learning: Philosophy of Language in the Hellenistic Age*. (Cambridge).

Fuentes González, P. P. (2000). "Épictète." *Dictionaire des philosophes antiques* 3, 106–151.

Fuhrmann, M. (1960). *Das systematische Lehrbuch—Ein Beitrag zur Geschichte der Wissenschaften in der Antike*. (Göttingen).

Gill, C. (2005). "Stoic Writers of the Imperial Era," in Rowe and Schofield, 597–615.

Gourinat, J.-B. (1998). *Premières leçons sur le Manuel d'Épictète*. (Paris).

Gourinat, J.-B. (2012). "Ethics," in van Ackeren, 420–436.

Graeven, I. (1891). *Cornuti artis rhetoricae epitome* (Berlin).

Griffin, M., and J. Barnes, eds. (1989). *Philosophia Togata I: Essays on Philosophy and Roman Society*. (Oxford).

Griffin, M. (1989). "Philosophy, Politics, and Politicians at Rome," in Griffin and Barnes, 1–37.

Hadot, P. (1978). "Un clé des *Pensées* de Marc-Aurèle: Les trois topoi philosophiques selon Épictète." *Études Philosophiques* 33: 65–83.

Hadot, P. (1981). *Exercices spirituels et la philosophie antique*. (Paris).

Hadot, P. (1992). *Lá citadelle intérieure: Introduction aux Pensées de Marc Aurèle*. (Paris). (M. Chase, tr. (1998): *The Inner Citadel: The Meditations of Marcus Aurelius*. (Cambridge, Mass.)).

Hadot, I. (1996). *Simplicius: Commentaire sur le Manuel d'Épictète*. (Leiden).

Hays, R. S., ed. (1983). *Lucius Annaeus Cornutus' Epidrome. Introduction to the Traditions of Greek Theology*. Dissertation: University of Texas at Austin.

Hense, O. (1905). *C. Musonii Rufi Reliquiae*. (Leipzig).

Hershbell, J. P. (1989). "The Stoicism of Epictetus: Twentieth Century Perspectives." *ANRW* II, 36(3): 2148–2163.

Hijmans, B. L. (1959). *Askesis: Notes on Epictetus' Educational System*. (Assen).

Jagu, A. (1946). *Épictète et Platon: Essai sur les relations du stoicisme et du platonisme à propos de la morale des Entretiens*. (Paris).

Jagu, A. (1989). "La morale d'Épictète et le christianisme." *ANRW* II, 36(3): 2164–2199.

Kraft, P. (1975). *Die handschriftliche Überlieferung von Cornutus' Theologia Graeca*. (Heidelberg).

Kullmann, W., and J. Althoff, eds. (1993). *Vermittlung und Tradierung von Wissen in der griechischen Kultur*. (Tübingen).

Kullmann, W., M. A. Althoff, and M. Asper, eds. (1998). *Gattungen wissenschaftlicher Literatur in der Antike*. (Tübingen).

Lang, K., ed. (1881). *Cornuti Theologiae Graecae Compendium*. (Leipzig).

Long, A. A. (2000). "Epictetus as Socratic Mentor." *PCPS* 46: 79–98.
Long, A. A. (2002). *Epictetus: A Stoic and Socratic Guide to Life*. (Oxford).
Lutz, C. (1947). "Musonius Rufus: 'The Roman Socrates.'" *YClS* 10: 32–147.
Marchand, S., and F. Verde, eds. (2013). *Épicurisme et scepticisme*. Rome.
Mitsis, P. (1993). "Committing Philosophy on the Reader: Didactic Coercion and Reader Autonomy in *De rerum natura*." *MD* 31 ("*Mega nepios*: Il destinatario nell'epos didascalico"): 111–128.
Morford, M. (1989). "Nero's Patronage and Participation in Literature and the Arts." *ANRW* II, 32(3): 2003–2031.
Most, G. W. (1989). "Cornutus and Stoic Allegoresis. A Preliminary Report." *ANRW* II, 36(3): 2014–2065.
Nesselrath, H.-G., ed. (2009). *Cornutus: Die griechischen Götter*. (Tübingen).
Newman, R. J. (1989). "*Cotidie meditare*: Theory and Practice of the *meditatio* in Imperial Stoicism." *ANRW* II, 36(3): 1473–1517.
Nock, A. D. (1931). "Kornutos." *RE* Suppl. 5: 995–1005.
Oldfather, W. A. (1925/1928). *Epictetus: The discourses as reported by Arrian, the Manual, and fragments, with an English translation by W. A. Oldfather*, 2 vols. (Cambridge, Mass.).
Pohlenz, M. (⁵1980). *Die Stoa: Geschichte einer geistigen Bewegung*. (Göttingen).
Rabbow, P. (1954). *Seelenführung: Methodik der Exerzitien in der Antike*. (Munich).
Ramelli, I., and G. Luchetta, eds. (2004). *Allegoria*. Vol. 1: *L'età classica*. (Milan).
Ramelli, I. (2003). *L. Anneo Cornuto, Compendio di teologia greca: Saggio introduttivo e integrative, traduzione e apparati di Ilaria Ramelli*. (Milan).
Ramelli, I. (2007). *Allegoristi dell'età classica: Opere e frammenti*. (Milan).
Reydams-Schils, G. (2005). *The Roman Stoics: Self, Responsibility, and Affection*. (Chicago).
Reydams-Schils, G. (2011). "Authority and Agency in Stoicism." *GRBS* 51: 296–322.
Reydams-Schils, G. (2018). "Cornutus, Epiktet," in C. Riedweg, C. Horn, and D. Wyrwa (eds.), *Philosophie der Kaiserzeit und der Spätantike: Grundriss der Geschichte der Philosophie* (Basel), 140–143 and 163–170.
Scaltsas, T., and A. S. Mason, eds. (2007). *The Philosophy of Epictetus*. (Oxford).
Smith, M. F. (1993). *Diogenes of Oinoanda: The Epicurean Inscription*. (Naples).
Schenkl, H. (²1916). *Epicteti dissertationes ab Arriano digestae*. (Leipzig).
Sorabji, R., and R. W. Sharples, eds. (2007). *Greek and Roman Philosophy 100 BC–200 AD = BICS* Supplement 94. (London).
Souilhé, J. (1948). *Epictète: Entretiens*, vol. 1. (Paris).
Spanneut, M., (1962). "Epiktet." *RAC* 5: 599–681.
Steinmetz, P. (1986). "Allegorische Deutung und allegorische Dichtung in der Alten Stoa." *Rh. Mus.* 129: 18–30.
Tate, J. (1929). "Cornutus and the Poets." *CQ* 23: 41–45.
van Ackeren, M., ed. (2012). *A Companion to Marcus Aurelius*. (Malden, Mass.).
Wehner, B. (2000). *Die Funktion der Dialogstruktur in Epiktets Diatriben*. (Stuttgart).
Wirth, T. (1967). "Arrians Erinnerungen an Epiktet." *MH* 24: 149–189.

CHAPTER 12

PERSIUS'S PARADOXES

AARON KACHUCK

Introduction

> In taking over the term paradox, we have lost its connection with *doxa*, and so we tend to think of philosophical paradoxes as either mere puzzles or perversity. But a paradox is literally a thought that is incongruous with commonplace beliefs... Plato's *Republic* is a gigantic paradox in the Greek sense that I have explained. The ethical and political writings of Aristotle are not.[1]

AULUS Persius Flaccus (b. December 4, 34 CE, d. November 24, 62 CE), student (with the poet Lucan) of the Stoic philosopher Lucius Annaeus Cornutus, owner (per the *Life of Persius* 38–39 Clausen (hereafter *Vita Pers.*)) of Chrysippus's complete works (in 705 rolls), and friend of noted leader of the "Stoic opposition" under Nero, Thrasea Paetus (*Vita Pers.* 29), was, despite such connections, not a philosopher.[2] Certainly, if one stumbled upon Persius's *Satires* in an anthology of Stoic poetry, just after reading, say, the *Hymn to Zeus* of Cleanthes of Assos (c. 330–230 BCE) or Manilius's *Astronomica* (early Principate), one would be in for a shock: Cleanthes' pious epithets and clear tripartite structure (Invocation, Argument, Prayer) might be said to embody a well-ordered Stoic universe, while Manilius's didactic austerity—"Do not look here for sweet songs—my subject, content to be taught, refuses to be adorned" (Manil. 3.38–39 *nec dulcia carmina quaeras: / ornari res ipsa negat contenta doceri*)—seem, too, close to the Stoic party line on verse's educative functions.[3] Persius's *Satires*, by contrast, seem a mess of obscurity, metaphor, and contradiction.[4] So Kenneth Reckford has called Persius "an anti-aesthetic artist";[5] Shadi Bartsch has seen his *Satires* as "determinedly sensory in a way that is only *negative*, every drop of saliva, every foul-smelling belch... an onslaught of images that remind us of what not to be;"[6] Kirk Freudenburg, replicating a charge that Persius allows "one of the hairy race of centurions" (3.77 *aliquis de gente hircosa centurionum*) to make of himself, namely that philosophers do nothing but "labor over the dreams of some sick old man" (3.83 *aegroti ueteris meditantes somnia*)—sees Persius's *Satires* as landing us "in that *aegri somnia* of Horace, *Ars Poetica* 7, a Daliesque world of psychedelic images, disjointed, cluttered, and frequently pornographic."[7] Not exactly what one would expect of "The Philosopher Satirist,"[8] as conciliatory critics have called Persius; indeed, "the work of such a sobriquet might be to point up, rather than to defuse, paradox."[9]

This chapter shows in what ways, to paraphrase J. L. Austin, Persius's *Satires* teach poets and people how to do things with philosophy, and with philosophers.[10] These are tasks for which Roman satirists were, perhaps, uniquely suited: as Isaac Casaubon put it in the *Prolegomena* to his 1605 commentary, "Both satire and ethical philosophy treat of *mores*," but Persius's *Satires*, Casaubon goes on to say, go above and beyond *officium*'s call: Persius is "more philosophical" (φιλοσοφικότερος) than Horace (and, by extension, Horace's satiric predecessor, Lucilius) but he is also a more stable support for the Stoic porch than Chrysippus, or even Zeno, the school's founder, himself! Certainly, Persius is, of all the satirists, the most devoted to a single school of philosophy, let alone the Stoics. For although one finds evidence of Stoic vocabulary and thought in the surviving Roman satiric corpora, it is only Persius who counts himself a member of the *Stoa*: so Horace, one of whose satires takes aim at the perfection of the Stoic sage (*Serm.* 2.3.7), swears himself a servant of no master (*Epist.* 1.1.14 *nullius addictus iurare in uerba magistri*), and Juvenal, whose tenth *Satire* semi-Stoically attacks nonvirtuous desires and whose thirteenth alludes to Stoic emotional therapies, swears, all the same, with ingenious insincerity, that he is one "who reads neither Cynics nor Stoic dogmas—distinguishable from Cynics by their dress—nor regards happy Epicurus amid the plants of his narrow garden" (*Serm.* 13.121–123 *et qui nec Cynicos nec Stoica dogmata legit / a Cynicis tunica distantia, non Epicurum / suspicit exigui laetum plantaribus horti*). Where Horace is sworn to no master, and Juvenal is illiterate (he claims!) in all the masters' works, Persius actually opens his fourth *Satire*, an invitation to Stoic self-therapy, in his master's bearded master's voice, that of Socrates himself (4.1; cf. 5.37).[11] In addition, the *Satires* make mention *nominatim* of Cornutus (5.23, 37), Cleanthes (5.64), Chrysippus (6.80), and of the Painted Porch (3.54). This last reference, to the Stoa Poikile in Athens, comes in the midst of a speech Persius depicts Cornutus giving to the poet, in which that philosopher adds some local color to our picture of Persius and his fellow Stoic students, down to their hairstyle (3.54 *detonsa*, "shaven-haired") and their diet (*siliquis et . . . polenta*, "lentils and groats").

Yet although Persius is, in his way, a Stoic satirist, little in his works reflects the podium-to-pew sermonizing one might expect of the Stoic sage. Contrast, for example, the thirteen-line panegyric to *Virtus* penned by Persius's satiric predecessor, Gaius Lucilius (fr. 1326–1339 M *apud* Lactantius, *Div. inst.* 6.5.2) with Persius's one and only use of any form of the Stoic (and Roman) keyword *uirtus*,[12] in a compact four-word self-enclosed and epigrammatic line whose context, fittingly, most closely recalls Cleanthes' *Hymn*: *uirtutem uideant intabescantque relicta*, "Let them [tyrants] behold virtue, its loss repine" (Pers. 3.38). Four words, tightly interlocked by syntax and sound, present a surprising fusion of figurative sight and physicalized consumption: observing this difference, one is reminded of how Cicero described Stoic argumentation as proceeding by way of "tiny little interrogatory pin-pricks,"[13] a style he found "subtle (*subtile*) or, rather, thorny (*spinosus*),"[14] a characterization that no doubt helped inspire John Dryden's description of Persius, famously, as "crabbed"[15]: certainly, compared to Lucilius, Persius, with his combination of pith, syntactical misdirection, and bodily corruption, is one who "knows a hawk from handsaw," but won't let you in on the secret unless you grasp it for yourself.

Casaubon had his own reasons for painting Persius as Stoic hero, but he was not wholly off the mark, particularly when it comes to paradoxes: although Stoic paradoxes make periodic appearances in the satires of Horace,[16] and perhaps Varro before him, in the works of Persius they are what hold the poet's scattered satiric persona, and poetic corpus, together, from puzzling start to quizzical conclusion. They are central to his poem's "paradoxical capability," designed, like A. A. Long's Hellenistic philosophers, "to challenge and intrigue and undermine complacency."[17] Shadi Bartsch's recent nuancing of conciliatory readings is no doubt correct: because the Stoics only worried about poetry's allurements when it was seducing people toward wickedness, Persius's *Satires* need not "line up with the traditional Stoic views on how to read poetry safely . . . precisely because he is not writing unsafe poetry in the first place," unlike, say, the works of Homer, Euripides, or Vergil, whose works, she adds, require the steady, guiding hand of Stoic allegory if they are to serve philosophical ends.[18] But this does not exhaust the intense oddity of Persius's works, nor their obsessive interest in paradox, contradiction, and irresolvable puzzles of language and thought.

As a whole, this chapter aims to take up Persius's challenge to establish and provoke connections between Latin literature and Greek and Roman philosophy. It opens with a summary account of the positive philosophical content of Persius's paradoxes by way of a coordinated reading of Cicero's *Paradoxa Stoicorum*. It then proceeds to demonstrate how paradoxes inflect the total structure of Persius's *Satires*, and, in particular, their beginning and end. As a whole, this chapter's explorations move from the philosophical at the beginning toward the more allusive literary-philosophical at the end. In all of what follows, "paradox" will entail four distinct, but related senses. First, both ancient and contemporary philosophy divides paradoxes, as challenges of thought, into (1) sequences of otherwise reasonable propositions that *seem* to yield untrue conclusions, but, on further (often semantically clarifying) consideration, do in fact make sense (i.e., the Simpson's paradox of modern statistics, or the so-called Stoic/Socratic paradoxes/wonders of the ancients), and (2) sequences of thought that yield apparently untrue conclusions whose problematic character cannot be (so easily) resolved (i.e., the famous "sophisms"/"intractable arguments," such as the Liar, Nobody, Veiled, Harvester, and Horn problems often attributed to the Stoics, but in fact much older).[19] Alongside these technical meanings, there is also (3) the rhetorical concept of *sustentatio*, or "suspension," leading to a surprising answer (or question, as in the so-called paradox epigram),[20] and, finally, as A. A. Long has reminded us, the sense of hostile wonder one associates with the counterintuitive thought of a Plato or a Parmenides, and that is captured well by received English usage, at least since Dr. Johnson's 1755 dictionary:

> Pa'radox. n.s. [paradoxe, Fr. παράδοξος.] A tenet contrary to received opinion; an assertion contrary to appearance; a position in appearance absurd.

Persius's Poems by Way of Cicero's Paradoxes

Like Lucretius, Persius can be described usefully, as Roland Mayer (2005) 155 has put it, "as a poet whose philosophical conviction defines his persona"—his persona, and his oeuvre: although Persius did not follow Lucretius in exhaustively systematizing his school's thought in verse, his six *Satires* can be roughly mapped (if not with too literal a spirit) onto the six paradoxes covered by Cicero's *Paradoxa Stoicorum* (hereafter *Parad.*).[21] Cicero wrote this playful treatise (*Parad.* 3: *ludens conieci*) in early 46 BCE, divided into six sections for those six paradoxes of the Stoics that were, to his eyes, the most Socratic, hence, by far, the most true (*Parad.* 4: *longeque uerissima*), an assumed filiation that Persius, too, shares: the very bosom of his Stoic teacher Cornutus is Socratic (5.37 *Socratico, Cornute, sinu*).[22] In his court case *Pro Murena* (63 BCE), Cicero had mocked these same paradoxes; as he later confesses, he was speaking, then, to the ignorant in order to defame Cato the Younger's character; in other words, he was "playing to the crowd,"[23] made easier by the fact that, in the words of Kenneth Reckford, "No Roman, certainly no Roman satirist, could fully accept the Stoic paradoxes."[24] Freed of such juridical constraints, Cicero aimed, in the *Paradoxa Stoicorum*, to give a fuller treatment to these paradoxes—or, as he called them elsewhere, "wonders" (*Luc.* 136 *mirabilia*; *Fin.* 4.73 *admiribilia*)—to see if they might be introduced "into the light, that is, into the forum (*in forum*) . . . or whether learning has one style of discourse and ordinary life another" (*Parad.* 4). As we shall see, Persius aims to bring Stoic paradoxes into good Roman garb, as Cornutus notes (hopefully): "You aim at the words of the toga, skilled at the sharp metaphor" (5.14 *uerba togae sequeris iunctura callidus acri*). Paradoxically, though, Persius accomplishes both Cicero's goal and its opposite: he brings these paradoxes into the forum (*uerba togae*), but does through an *oratio* that is neither *erudita* nor *popularis*, but, properly speaking, and despite his protestations to the contrary, poetic.

Persius's six *Satires*, by way of Cicero's counterintuitive paradoxes, can be (philosophically) summarized (in order) as follows:

1. "Virtue is the only good": most human obsessions are pointless, and so, naturally, is the kind of poetry they like, and want everyone else to like, too, with many a "bravo and beautiful" (1.49 *"euge" tuum et "belle"*) wantonly shouted, even, or especially, when not worthy—"for shake out this whole 'beautiful!' and what couldn't be found within?" Nobody will read these poems, since everyone in Rome has ass's ears, and, instead of reading the truth (1.55 *uerum*) by way of Persius's honesty, they will much prefer "edict in the morning, *Calliroe* [i.e., romances] by night" (1.134 *mane edictum, post prandia Calliroen*). This preference for pleasure over virtue, however, will leave them short of the "paternal testicles" (1.103 *testiculi . . . paterni*) that allowed the great men of Roman history to accomplish what they did (*Parad.* 10–13).

2. "Virtue is sufficient for happiness": most people, my dear friend Macrinus, pray for fine things like "a sound mind, fame, good credit" (2.8 *mens bona, fama, fides*) out loud, but murmur wicked venal prayers to themselves, but this is a kind of sickness associated with the erroneous idea that the gods themselves like gold, rich fat, expensive aromas. The truth is, however, that no matter how rich or powerful, "no wicked, foolish, idle man can be happy" (*Parad.* 19), and what one should pray for are things no decadent Messala can offer on a wealthy plate: "ordered justice and right in my soul, the recesses of my mind sacred, and a breast braised in noble honor—let me offer these in the temples, and I'll sacrifice with spelt" (2.73–75).

3. "All vices are equal, all right actions equal": Wake up late, and hungover, then making up excuses for not writing, even if you come (like Persius) from millennium-old Etruscan stock, turns out to be . . . fatal. "It's a small matter" (*Parad.* 20 *parua . . . res est*), you say, "It's nothing" (3.94 *nihil est*), and then . . . "savory morsels drop out of his relaxed lips, whence trumpet, torches, the dearly departed at last laid out on a bed and smeared with greasy creams" (3.102–104). You think you're in the clear, just because you've got *most* things right? When a dancer misses his cue, or an actor his beat, they're cast from the stage (*Parad.* 26): and you, who think yourself virtuous, would you stay so if you "caught a glimpse of gold, or the pretty girl next door smiled sweetly?" (3.109–110). Surely, you'd shiver, boil, "say things, do things, that insane Orestes himself would swear were signs of insanity!" (3.117–118).

4. "All fools are madmen," or, "The sage alone is a citizen, the fool an exile":[25] "So you want to run the state?" (4.1), asks Socrates of a Romanized Alcibiades (cf. 4.8); your love of the insane crowd, your desire to stick out your tail for them (4.15), your lack of philosophical learning (4.10–13), recommends "unadulterated draughts of hellebore" (4.16), classic cure for the insane. Remember: "What is a city? Every gathering of beasts and savages? . . . Surely not!" (*Parad.* 27). What you need to do is descend into your self (4.23), and realize that the true sage is at home wherever he may be (*Parad.* 31–32): "Spit out what is not *you*. Let each workman bear his own tools. Live with yourself (*tecum habit*): you will realize how poorly you are equipped" (4.51–52).

5. "Only the sage is free": Poets need "a hundred mouths and a hundred tongues" (5.1–2) to offer "lumps of solid song" (5.5), but Persius needs no such assistance to speak to Cornutus, and "show how large a part of me is yours" (5.23–24). Cornutus, "you took up my tender years in your Socratic bosom" (5.35–36), and taught me that, although "Thousand are the faces of men, diverse their lives' color" (5.52), philosophy, especially "the seed of Cleanthes" (5.64) helps one understand that "Freedom is what is needed" (5.73 *libertate opus est*). "What is liberty (*quid est enim libertas*)? The power to live as you will (*potestas uiuendi ut velis*)" (*Parad.* 34), but "If I can live as I wish (*licet ut uolo uiuere*), then am I not freer than Brutus?" (5.84–85). Only if it is a sage's freedom: for otherwise "you are torn apart by a double hook . . . [and] with alternating enslavement, you must by turns submit to your masters, by turns desert them" (5.154–156), when all know that to escape the slavery of a

tyrant only to run into the slavery of tyrannical desires is the mark of one who "wants to change his master, and not be free" (*Parad.* 41).[26]

6. "Only the wise man is rich": Winter may have already brought you, Caesius Bassus, to your Sabine hearth, but why don't you come to Luna—which Ennius recommended after a Pythagorean transmigratory dream—and join me in a happily moderate holiday? My heir wants me to make more money, and stop spending it, but who's to know how much is enough? Although Crassus claimed that "no one is wealthy save one who can fund a legion," but why not six legions (*Parad.* 45), just as a father is rich with one daughter, richer still with two, or, like Danaus, 50 (*Parad.* 44)? By which logic, Crassus, the proverbially wealthy, is not, himself, wealthy. Double, triple, quadruple your wealth: "Tell me where I might stop; and then, Chrysippus, a finisher of your heap will have been found!" (6.80).

Kenneth Reckford was right that "the Stoic paradox provides a traditional frame for Persius's essential revelation, of the insubstantiality of most human endeavor"; even more, it was the frame and structure for each and every one of his poems. Persius's *Satires*, in this sense, through quickly juxtaposed portraits, vignettes, and images of daily life, shows us how the Stoic paradoxes, although seemingly nonsensical, are, in fact, the best way to lead one's life. Indeed, ideally, Stoic dialectic as practiced by a philosopher should, as Mario Mignucci has written, "not only distinguish sophistical from good arguments but also be able to solve them by showing what is wrong with them in such a way that any embarrassment is dispelled."[27]

Persius, however, was not a philosopher, nor was he, in any strict sense, a dialectician, and, correspondingly, his poems tend, as often as possible, to heighten contradiction and maximize embarrassment. In this sense, the role of paradox in Persius's *Satires* is well characterized by Cicero's description of Stoic fallacies (specifically the "Sorites" and the "Liar") as "those traps that the Stoics have laid against themselves" (*Luc.* 147 *plagas ipse contra se Stoici texuerunt*). In what follows, we will focus on how two unsolvable "paradoxes of quantity"—the classic *sophismata* of "No Man" and "Sorites"—that fall on either side of Persius's satiric book allow Persius to lay traps for himself, his poems, and their readers. When it comes to reading Persius's paradoxes, one does well to recall Mignucci's warning: "It is not without sacrifices that we resolve paradoxes."[28]

THE NOBODY PARADOX

Persius recognized Lucilius and Horace as his two satiric forbears (1.114–118), and recognized, too, that they wrote for different, and differently sized, audiences. Where Horace aimed, as the last poem of his first book of *Satires* shows, for the few, but the best (Hor. *Serm.* 1.10.81–90), Lucilius, the founder of Roman satire as we know it, aimed for the generous middle: "I do not write for the most learned, nor for those too unlearned.

I do not want Manilius Persius to read this . . . I do want Iunius Congus!"[29] In a fragment cited by Pliny, the line is even more telegraphic: "I don't want Persius to read me—I do want Decimus Laelius!"[30] As Cicero later explained, this Persius was "our most learned man."[31] From the perspective of generic history, then, if the first surprise twist of Persius's *Satires* is that someone named Persius is trying to write (Lucilian) *Satires* at all, and if the second surprise is that his first line of satiric poetry is, as the *Commentum Cornuti* may suggest (*ad* 1.2), a direct citation of Lucilius's poetry,[32] then the third, and most important, surprise is that Persius, unlike Horace and Lucilius, aimed at an audience of . . . zero, as his syntactically surprising opening lines express in a paradoxical, and sophismatic, form (1.1–3):

> Oh cares of men—oh how much emptiness is in everything!
> Who'll read this?—You're saying this to me? Nobody, by Hercules.—Nobody?—
> Either two people or nobody—Shameful and miserable—Why?
>
> *O curas hominum! o quantum est in rebus inane!*
> *"quis leget haec?" min tu istud ais? nemo hercule. "nemo?"*
> *uel duo uel nemo. "turpe et miserabile." quaere?*

There are as many ways of not only punctuating but also assigning these words to speakers as there are editors and scholars, an *embarras de richesses* usefully outlined in tabular form by Walter Kißel.[33] This confusing press of voices, somehow embodying the poems' philosophical program, gives a message similar to that which Seneca had attributed to a source of debated provenance, but which source, given the lexical parallels, one could imagine being Persius himself: "Enough for me are few, enough is one, enough is none" (*satis sunt . . . mihi pauci, satis est unus, satis est nullus*).[34] Certainly, as compared to this "facile epigrammatic jingle,"[35] Persius's programmatic opening lines outline a sharper paradox for the reader *qua* reader:

1. No one will read this
2. Someone (i.e., the reader) is reading this
3. Therefore, Someone is No One (or not reading this)

Even as it falls short of the syllogistic rigor of Stoic paradoxes and unsolvables, Persius's puzzle reaches back to the nominal confusions depicted in Homer's *Odyssey* (9.360–412)—Odysseus is Οὖτις (Mr. Nobody) to Polyphemus, Οὔ τις (no body) to the other cyclopes—and to the opening line of Horace's *Satires*, which, in asking how it is that "nobody (*nemo*) lives content with life," anticipates Horace's transformation of himself into the unknown nobody that concludes *Satire* 6.[36] Indeed, Andrea Cucchiarelli has seen Persius's strained combination of Stoic philosophy with Horatian imitation as being at the heart of Persius's paradoxical "speaking from silence."[37] As one would expect, then, Persius pushes Horace's looser suggestion into a tighter form of paradox resembling the No Man (Greek: Οὖτις) problem described by Diogenes Laertius (7.61), and best represented as follows (*ap.* Simp. *In Aristotelis Categorias commentaria* 105.7–20, with lacuna):

1. If someone (τίς) is in Athens, someone is not (οὐκ ἔστιν) in Megara
2. Someone (τίς) is in Athens
3. Therefore, No One (Οὔ τις) is (= "Someone" is Not) in Megara.

Philosophical interest in the No Man puzzle is driven by the fact that, as Mignucci has put it, although the argument is sound, "the false conclusion simply shows that a general term cannot be taken as referring to a particular."[38] This, however, does not solve Persius's problem, as the interlocutor notes, thus yielding a change to the paradox's parameters:

1. No one, or two people, will read this
2. Someone is reading this
3. Therefore, a second someone must be reading this, too.

This is not a sophism, though it still does hint at a mystery: who is this second reader? Later in the poem, Persius will suggest that the interlocutor is nobody but an extension of himself, or, as Persius calls him, "Whoever you are, oh you whom sometime I made speak opposite me" (1.44 *quisquis es, o modo quem ex aduerso dicere feci*). The logic is essentially that of a different form of the No Man paradox found in Aulus Gellius (*NA* 18.2.9): "Whatever I am, you are not; I am a man; therefore you are not."

But for now, perhaps the two are meant to be *me*, the reader, and the interlocutor, a nobody as insubstantial as myself (whom Persius has, as well, made speak opposite him?). When Persius goes on to explain to the disbelieving interlocutor why the approbation of the crowd means so little to him, he begins to delimit the range of our guessing-game (1.8–12):

> For at Rome who doesn't . . . ah, if it's allowed to say it . . . but it *is allowed*,
> at least while I'm looking at the grey-head and this, our sad way of life,
> and whatever we do now with our marbles given up,
> while we smack of stern uncles . . . then, then—forgive me, all of you
>   (I don't want to,
> what should I do?) but I'm in wanton humor . . . I guffaw!

> *nam Romae quis non—a, si fas dicere—sed fas*
> *tum cum ad canitiem et nostrum istud uiuere triste*
> *aspexi ac nucibus facimus quaecumque relictis,*
> *cum sapimus patruos. tunc tunc—ignoscite (nolo,*
> *quid faciam?) sed sum petulanti splene—cachinno.*

So if Persius is to be read, he will not be read at Rome, which might create a sophistical dilemma for a hypothetical Roman reader:

1. No one at Rome will read this
2. I am at Rome and reading this
3. Therefore, I am no one.

At least according to the ancient *Life of Persius*, this kind of thought might have been widespread, as Persius's works were an immediate, if bewildering, hit: "As to the published book—immediately, people began to marvel at it (*mirari*), and snatch it up wherever they could (*diripere*)" (*Vita Pers.* 48–49 Clausen).

Meanwhile, Persius's initial aposiopesis—the rhetorical device of breaking off midspeech that Cicero supposedly Latinized as *reticentia* (Quint. *Inst.* 9.2.54), here the hesitancy, then laughter, that breaks off the announcement about that which is ubiquitous at Rome—leads to a paradox of a different kind, what the rhetoricians called *sustentatio*, "suspension," whereby one is kept at attention, waiting to see what surprise is in store for the completion of this sentiment. And complete the sentiment Persius's first *Satire* does, at least in a manner of speaking (1.119–123):

> May I not mumble? in private? in a ditch? nowhere?
> Here, still, I'll start digging. I saw it, I saw it myself, oh my booklet:
> Who doesn't have the ears of an ass? This, my secret, I . . .
> this my laugh, such a nothing . . . I sell it to you for no
> Iliad.

> *me muttire nefas? nec clam? nec cum scrobe? nusquam?*
> *hic tamen infodiam. uidi, uidi ipse, libelle:*
> *auriculas asini quis non habet? hoc ego opertum,*
> *hoc ridere meum, tam nil, nulla tibi uendo*
> *Iliade.*

Persius's experiment—writing "such a nothing" (*tam nil*) for "nobody" (*nemo*) that he would exchange for "no *Iliad*" (*nulla . . . Iliade*)—twists the gently ironized self-deprecation of the *Ars Poetica*, when Horace claims, "I teach obligation and duty, while writing nothing myself" (*Ars P.* 306 *nil scribens ipse*). For Persius, though, nothingness was more properly the object of his Stoic attention, as we can see in the mouth of one of Persius's many misologists, "someone from the hairy tribe of centurions" (3.77 *aliquis de gente hircosa centurionum*), who wonders why, since what he knows is enough for him (3.78 *quod sapio, satis est mihi*), he should imitate one who "gnaws murmurs and rabid silences [?] with himself, and weigh his words on a puckered lip, meditating the dreams of a fevered man, that nothing comes from nothing [*gigni / de nihilo nihilum*, 3.83–84], that nothing may return into nothing" (*in nihilum nil posse reuerti*, 3.84). One cannot, of course, be held liable for teaching nothing to nobody, and one suspects that Persius, who claims in his choliambic prologue that "I bring our song to the orgies of the sacred bards" (Pers. *Choliambi* 7, *ad sacra uatum carmen adfero nostrum*), was aware of how dangerous teaching secret knowledge could be, as one of Chrysippus's youthful paradoxes makes clear (Diog. Laert. 7.186): "Now this philosopher [Chrysippus] used to delight in proposing questions of this sort. The person who reveals the mysteries to the uninitiated commits a sin; the hierophant reveals them to the uninitiated; therefore the hierophant commits sin?"

The puzzle: how is the uninitiated supposed to gain knowledge required for initiation, unless someone teach him? From its first lines, Persian pedagogy models the "descent into the self" that is so central to Seneca's frequent prosaic dilations: *tecum habita*, "live with yourself," writes Persius (4.52), and, says Stoic wisdom, you will find the answers within, and find, as well, the capacity to read the poems of this, the *semipaganus* who has brought them to you.[39] Hence, as well, another reason for Persius's opening gambit: he is a satirist who writes, potentially, for nobody; or perhaps we should paraphrase with the help of another all but contemporary wisdom tradition, for there is nobody "unless he is a sage who already understands on his own."[40]

Why Persius should have wanted to share this "nothing" with "nobody," or rather, with "two people or nobody," can be best understood against the backdrop of three rather strange corners of Stoic learning Persius may have explored by way of Cornutus and, by extension, Chrysippus. First, etymologically, as R. A. Harvey noted, "either two or none" is "an evidently unique phrase... partly modeled on the Greek ἤ τις ἤ οὐδείς ['either someone or nobody']," but for someone trained on Cornutus's anagrammatical and etymological method—his only surviving work, *Epidrome*, a "Summary of Traditions of Greek Theology," derives, for example, "Zeus" from ζῆν (l. 2 "to live") and "Asia" from ἄϊστος (l. 13 "unseen"), Atlas from ἀταλαίπωρος, (l. 26 "without tiring")—it would be only natural to transform οὐδείς [nobody] cross-linguistically into "*duo-eis*," which is to say, two.[41] Second, conceptually, it was only one step from Chrysippus's insistence (*apud* Gell. *NA* 11.12.1 [= *SVF* 2.152]) that "every word is by nature ambiguous"[42] to the argument, which Plutarch has Chrysippus borrowing from Epicharmus, that "each of us is a pair of twins, two-natured and doubled... and that the one is always in flux and motion ... that we are born double, always in flux with one part of ourselves, while remaining the same people from birth to death with one another";[43] i.e., if there is somebody, then there are two bodies, which comes as close as anything to explaining the insistent, confusing dialogism of Persius, which so frustrates (and ensorcels) editors.[44]

Finally, one possibility emerges from one of the few single-argument formulations of the Sorites paradox, the problem of the heap:[45] "It is not the case that two are few and three are not also; it is not the case that these are few and four are not also (and so on up to ten thousand). But two are few: therefore ten thousand are also" (Diog. Laert. 7.82, with μυρίων/μύρια for δέκα/δέκα).[46] In the shadow of the inflationary Sorites, Persius's audience can jump from 0 to 10,000 in under one *metron*; but the Sorites has a deflationary mode as well, often called the Bald Man paradox, or, as Horace put it, the problem of the horse's tail and "the logic of the crashing heap" (*Ep.* 2.1.47, *ratione ruentis acerui*). Take one hair from a horse, then another, then another—at what point is it no longer a tail? Take one grain of sand from a heap of sand, then another, then another—at what point is it no longer a heap? Take one reader away from a poem's audience, then another, then another—when is there no longer an audience? In the end, as Persius knew, and as Cicero makes explicit, Stoic paradoxes start happily enough (Cic. *Luc.* 92 *festiue*) with the elements of discourse, but the turn to solving ambiguities and theorizing always ends up in the same place (Cic. *Luc.* 92): "By small accretions, the discussion comes to the Sorites—a slippery and dangerous place" (*lubricum sane et periculosum locum*). Dangerous for philosophers, as Chrysippus knew, dangerous, too, for satirists, which is why Chrysippus and his heap, shadow presences of the *Satires*' opening, bring Persius's book as a whole to its sudden close, as Persius and his heir dispute just how much money how many times multiplied would be enough.[47]

CHRYSIPPUS AND THE *FINITOR*

> Sell your soul for money, trade, and, expert, shake out
> A whole side of the world, lest anyone be more prominent
> At slapping fat Cappadocians on the rigid slave-stage.
> "Double the worth—I did—now triple, now, for me, quadruple,
> Now tenfold it returns to my wallet. Let me know where I should stop—
> Discovered, Chrysippus, is a completer [*finitor*] of your heap."

> *uende animam lucro, mercare atque excute sollers*
> *omne latus mundi, ne sit praestantior alter*
> *Cappadocas rigida pinguis plausisse catasta,*
> *rem duplica. "feci; iam triplex, iam mihi quarto,*
> *iam decies redit in rugam. depunge ubi sistam,*
> *inuentus, Chrysippe, tui finitor acerui."*

Thus comes to a close Persius's book of *Satires* (6.75–80), at least as edited (supposedly) by Cornutus.[48] By closing with Chrysippus's heap, Persius lays down a *punctum* (<*depunge*) that aims to end not only his own *Satires*, but those, as well, of Horace, whose first *Satire* had, like the two *Satires* that follow, ended, writes Emily Gowers, "with a sideswipe at the Stoics' prolixity or moral dogmatism":[49] "It's already enough: Lest you think I mean to pile on the bookshelves of bleary-eyed Crispinus, I won't add another word more" (Hor. *Serm.* 1.120–121)—this he writes just before adding another nine poems to this book! Indeed, Horace's first *Satire* is crammed with heap-related words (32 *congesta cibaria*, 34–35 *aceruo / quem struit*, 42 *immensum . . . pondus*, 44 *constructus aceruus*). As Freudenburg has noted, the reference to "bleary-eyed Crispinus" may conceal a cryptogram of Chrysippus's name (*Crispini* + *lippi*), but even more than this, the *Sorites* paradox is, in a way, programmatic for Horace's definition of *Satura*, etymologically, the "'heaped high' and/or 'stuffed full' (*satur*)" genre, and a possible lexical connection between Latin *satura* and Greek σωρός may be visible between the *Saturae* of Ennius and the epigram-collection by Posidippus which seems to have been known as "The

Pile."[50] For Persius to end on the heap is therefore a way of finishing off what (and where) Horace started, and a way, as well, of telling Horace that, if he had planned on opposing prolixity (as his mockery of Lucilius suggests), he should have quit while he was ahead.[51]

Horace, Chrysippus, and Persius shared one thing at least: contempt for the multitude. When reproached for not attending the lectures of Ariston, who was quite popular at the time, Chrysippus is said to have replied: "If I had attached myself to the multitude, I would not have been a philosopher" (Diog. Laert. 7.182 εἰ τοῖς πολλοῖς προσεῖχον, οὐκ ἂν ἐφιλοσόφησα). But in respect of quantity, Persius is Chrysippus's precise opposite: where Persius, says the *Life*, "wrote both rarely and slowly" (*Vit. Pers.* 41 Clausen *raro et tarde*), Chrysippus, writes Diogenes Laertius (7.179), was "the most industrious of men, beyond all others [πονικώτατός τε παρ' ὁντινοῦν], as is clear from his writings, which number more than 705." If the report of Chrysippus's old maidservant is correct, then Persius's entire *Satires* amount to just over the 500 lines Chrysippus would write in a single day! More than that: Chrysippus repeatedly addressed the same problem from various angles in multiple works, quoting numerous sources at great length. This approach could go to rather absurd lengths: Chrysippus had, in one of his works, "quoted almost the entirety of Euripides' *Medea*," such that, when asked what he was carrying around, Chrysippus is said to have replied, "Chrysippus's *Medea*"—a Pierre Menard *avant le lettre*, perhaps, but also representing a model of verbal imitation wholly the consistently clipped and clipping use of sources evinced by Persius, as studies from the *Persiana Horatii Imitatio* appendix of Casaubon (1605) to Daniel Hooley (1997) make wonderfully clear.

But in addition to highlighting Persius's relative condensation—a quality that was central to Persius's reception in antiquity[52]—Chrysippus's heap is also the only way to end a book of *Satires* that, according to its opening gambit, never meant to be read in the first place. As Cicero notes (*Luc.* 93), Chrysippus thought there was only one way to avoid being put, or putting oneself, into a Sorites trap: "to grow quiet, or, as they say in Greek, ἡσυχάζειν."[53] This, however, won't protect the respondent, as Cicero goes on to say, from Carneades' attack: "You could be snoring for all I care (*per me uel stertas licet*), but you won't stay asleep (*non modo quiescas*) . . . for someone will follow who will wake you from your sleep" and continue the interrogation upwards or downwards to absurdity. Like Carneades, Persius enjoys breaking in on those who snore (3.3, 3.58, 5.132), but he associated snoring with the origins of Roman poetry: so, just as Ennius's dreams had teed off the *Satires* in the choliambs—"I never touched my lips to the Fountain of the Nag, nor of having slept on twin-peaked Parnassus do I have any recollection, that thus, suddenly, I'd emerge as a poet!" (Pers. *Choliambi* 1–3)—so in the sixth *Satire*, Persius invites Bassus to join him on the Ligurian coast at Luna, "moon-land," where "Quintus Maeonides snored himself off the Pythagorean peacock (6.10–11)" i.e., as the scholiast explains the soul of Homer (*Maeonides*) achieved its fifth (=*Quintus*) transmigration: (1) peacock, (2) Euphorbus, (3) Homer, (4) Pythagoras, and (5) Ennius. Persius does not remember having dreamt as Ennius (dreamt),[54] but might this allusion to Homer's five transmigrations, found in Persius's sixth and final poem, suggest that Homer's soul has found at least one more possible *angulus* of repose, albeit in a repose as troubled as the "dreams of a fevered man" (*aegri somnia*) which Horace's *Ars Poetica* sought to avoid (7)?

Sleep and Sorites are related because, as Antiochus argues in the attack on the paradox Cicero puts in Lucullus's mouth (*Luc.* 49), effacing the difference between a heap and a non-heap would do the same to wolves and dogs, and, worse, between projected mental images and reality, between dreams and waking life. There is good reason to think that this anxiety is alive already in the distinction Persius's prologue slyly makes between what he has not done (drunk from the Nag Fountain of inspiration) and what he "cannot recall" (2–3 *nec... memini*) having done (dreamt on Parnassus). For, while the end of *Satire* 6 attempts to short-circuit the additive (future-oriented) paradox of the heap by following Chrysippus's advice and going quiet, the *Prologue*, by insisting on the poet's own amnesia, aims to foreclose the possibility of an infinite regression, of the kind favored by Anaximander's paradox-ridden quest for the beginnings of beginnings. Bounded by paradox on all sides, Persius's poetry is caught, in Cicero's apt phrase, in traps of its own devising.[55]

CORNUTUS, OR, HOW TO GIVE A MAN HORNS

Persius seems to lay the credit (or blame) for these traps at the doorstep of the Stoics, or, more precisely, his Stoic teacher, Cornutus. The Chrysippan end of the sixth *Satire* is suggestive: Persius's closing image is that of an unfillable *rugam*, as Conington and Nettleship (1893) translates, "the fold of the garment," comparing Pliny *HN* 35.8.34, where *sinus* is used of a purse. But this *ruga*, which is in fact a *sinus*, turns us back to Persius's own account of his philosophical conversion (5.36–37), which occurs when "You, Cornutus, bear (*suscipis*) my tender years in your Socratic bosom (*sinu*)."[56] In fact, though, Cornutus taught Persius the special Stoic lesson that Susanne Bobzien has called "How to Give Someone Horns." Cornutus would be the natural person to give such a lesson: the Latin word for Ὁ κερατίνης, "The Horned Paradox," is... *Cornutus* (cf. Varro, *Ling.* 7.25). The *Cornutus* was one of those problems in which Chrysippus took an active interest, and, like the Liar, Nobody, Veiled, Harvester, and Sorites, the Horn Paradox was, not only a fallacy and sophism (Diog. Laert. 7.43–44), but also one of the "intractable arguments" (Diog. Laert. 7.82 ἄποροι λόγοι), which, as Bobzien writes, are not simply "mildly puzzling, yet readily resolvable," but, rather, the kind of problems in which there remains "disagreement about what the resolution consists in."[57] Seneca provides its basic form (*Ep.* 49.8): *quod non perdidisti habes; cornua autem non perdidisti; cornua ergo habes*:[58] "What you have not lost, you have. But you have not lost horns. Therefore, you have horns."

This trap works because the mechanism of dialectic allows only yes/no, and does not permit what Chrysippus and other would call "split answers": i.e., I did not lose my horns, but I never had horns to begin with. What this means is that there is no escape from the syllogism's attack, making it a "horned" dilemma in a more figurative sense:

everyway you turn, you are, as the ancient association with "horns" would have it, "cuckolded."[59]

In the fifth *Satire*, Cornutus gives Persius his horns. The poem opens with the epic "'Many-Mouths' Cliché,"[60] but in such a way as to lead all fair readers to expect to see this cliché as the butt of Persius's satiric vitriol. Unfortunately for Persius, his audience turns out to be Cornutus, who reveals himself, through his misplaced rebuke, to be one of those characters in the *Satires* all too eager to deliver their (often hypocritical, often Stoic) diatribes (5.5–18):[61]

> Where's all this heading? How many lumps of solid song
> Are you hefting, so many that they'd need a hundred-throater to struggle
>   with them?
> Let such as would speak grandiosely gather clouds on Helicon,
> If there's anyone for whom any pot of Procnes or Thyestes
> Will still boil, to be eaten at the frequent boring feasts of Glyco.
> But you don't expel winds from the breathy bellows, while ore
> Is smelted in the forge—nor, hoarse from pent-up murmuring,
> Do you in any way caw to yourself loud and vain
> Nor aim to burst your chubby cheeks with a pop.
> You follow the words of the toga, skilled at sharp conjunction,
> Polished with a moderate mouth, skilled at scraping pallid morals
> And at pinning down fault with natural wit.
> Bring from here what you say, and leave behind the Mycenaean tables,
> Head and feet, and a plebeian meal come to know.

> *quorsum haec? aut quantas robusti carminis offas*
> *ingeris, ut par sit centeno gutture niti?*
> *grande locuturi nebulas Helicone legunto,*
> *si quibus aut Procnes aut si quibus olla Thyestae*
> *feruebit saepe insulso cenanda Glyconi.*
> *tu neque anhelanti, coquitur dum massa camino,*
> *folle premis uentos nec clauso murmure raucus*
> *nescio quid tecum graue cornicaris inepte*
> *nec scloppo tumidas intendis rumpere buccas.*
> *uerba togae sequeris iunctura callidus acri,*
> *ore teres modico, pallentis radere mores*
> *doctus et ingenuo culpam defigere ludo.*
> *hinc trahe quae dicis mensasque relinque Mycenis*
> *cum capite et pedibus plebeiaque prandia noris.*

Inter os atque offam multa interuenire potest, went the old Latin proverb (Gell. *NA* 13.18.1): "There's many a slip 'twixt bite [5.5 *offas*] and lip [5.15 *oris*, 5.18 <u>*noris*</u>]!" Cornutus's speech combines great insight into Persius's poetics—*iunctura callidus acri* in particular has often been taken as Persius's most pointed act of self-definition—with complete ignorance of the Persius that we have seen: this is a poet who, since *Satire* 1, is the kind who murmurs hoarsely to himself, bursting his cheeks all the while! While Cornutus praises

Persius for following "the words of the *toga*," i.e., good Roman vocabulary, he also, in order to explain the kind of poetry he believes Persius does *not* write, coins the neologism *cornicaris* ("to caw like a crow").[62] "Crow poets and magpie poetesses" were the negative (cupidinous, ventriloquous) exemplars, recall, of Persius's choliambic poem (*Choliambi* 13–14), but there is yet more to this: for this word *cornicaris* also foreshadows this interjector's still-hidden identity (*cornicari* and *Cornutus*).

The presuppositions out of which Persius must (but, dialectically, cannot) slip, constitute Cornutus's concrete objection. What Cornutus asks Persius—"Where's this heading? And how many gobs of solid song are you bringing, so as to try and equal a hundred-throater?" (5.5–6)—functions as a trap because quantity (*quantas*) presupposes existence, which is to say, Cornutus asks, not *whether* Persius is bringing "gobs of robust song" (i.e., epic mumbo-jumbo), but *how much* he is already bringing. Similarly, "leave behind the Mycenean tables" presupposes that Persius had set his hands to their cannibalistic feast, when, in fact, Persius has something very different in mind, as all questions of quantity, it turns out, return to a constrained unity of Persius and Cornutus (5.21–24)—evoking a cannibalism different from that imagined by Cornutus—and that force that encourages their unity, the *Camena* (5.21) . . . the Latin spirit of poetry. It is not so much that Persius splits the question, as Chrysippus sometimes advised, as that he absorbs its terms and changes it into something novel.

Bifurcation of the fields of Latin literature and Hellenistic philosophy has played its part in obscuring how the philosophies (and received life-legends) of Hellenistic philosophers like Chrysippus can play a major role in the interpretation of Persius's *Satires*.[63] The end of Persius's *Satires* furnishes one final example of Persius's philosophical dovetailing, for concluding his sixth and final poem with Chrysippus (and perhaps with Cornutus's help!) is a reminder, long missed, of how this book of poetry, and Persius himself, might be seen as, if not dead-on-arrival, then at the very least as already heading to doom. According to an account attributed to Hermippus of Smyrna, Chrysippus died after guzzling too much wine (Diog. Laert. 7.184, cf. *Anth. Pal.* 7.706), but an alternative popular account had him "die laughing (γέλωτι)": "seeing his ass eating figs, he told his old serving-woman, 'Give the ass unmixed wine to drink now,' and, laughing to excess (ὑπερκαγχάζω), he died."[64] The word for Chrysippus's death-laughter—ὑπερκαγχάζω> καχάζω ("laugh aloud," likely onomatopoeic for χὰ χά "ha! ha!")—is cousin to Latin *cacchino*, precisely the word that put an end to the hectic hesitations of Persius in the first *Satire*, as the poet attempted to silence his own admission that "Everyone at Rome has . . . ass's ears" (1.121): "Then, then—forgive me, all of you (I don't want to—what should I do?) but I'm in wanton humor (*petulanti splene*, 1.12)—I guffaw (*cachinno*, 1.12)!" (1.11–12) Whether one takes this syntax as "broken"[65] or, albeit asyndetic and complex, as essentially continuous,[66] it is a phrase whose ugliness itself "has expressive value as a mirror of the self-consciously staccato progression toward the harshness of *cachinno*."[67]

The fatal shadow that hangs over Persius's cachinnation means that this "staccato progression" has even darker implications: certainly, the legendary death of Chrysippus sheds a morbid light on Persius's hung-over Etruscan doppelgänger in the third *Satire*, who is told the story (3.88–106) of the man who died from alcohol poisoning (like Chrysippus) and over-bathing (the cardinal luxury-sin of Persius's grammar instructor, Palaemon).[68] But the thought that Persius might have died an asinine, Chrysippean death in the opening lines of his first *Satire* should make us think, as well, of the skeletal philosophers continuing their debates, eternally, in the afterlife of the Boscoreale silver cups.[69] Who could ever bring an end to such a heap of conflicting ideas? As Chrysippus's own advice went, and as the structure of Persius's poems demonstrates, when it comes to paradox—"to which it is difficult to put an end, because it grows little by little, and never ceases to insinuate" (Sen. *Ben.* 5.19.9, *cui difficile est modum imponere, quia paulatim surrepit et non desinit serpere*)—the only way for a satirist to stop is just to . . . stop. Even then, paradox, like the practice of the moral life itself, "even now, even now, must be rushed forward, on a sharp wheel, molded without end (Pers. 3.23–24, *nunc nunc properandus et acri / fingendus sine fine rota*)": *sine fine*, indeed.[70]

Notes

> I am grateful to Leon Grek, David Kaufman, Dunstan Lowe, and to the editors of this volume for reading and commenting on various drafts of this chapter: all errors are my own.

1. Long (2006) 14.
2. Kißel (1990) is the essential companion for all studies of Persius; for philosophical comparanda, Casaubon (1605) remains the richest source, Harvey (1981) the best commentary in English. For close literary and cultural readings of Persius's *Satires*, see Hooley (1997), Reckford (2009), and Bartsch (2015, with bibl.). On Persius and (esp. Stoic) philosophy, see Ramelli (2008), and, for a rich documentation of philosophical and other debates between 1964 and 1983, Saccone (1985); for a compelling alternative approach to Persius and (certain) Stoic paradoxes, see Cucchiarelli (2005). For Persius and Stoic poetics, see Wiener in this volume. On Roman satire and philosophy, see Mayer (2005), and on Roman satire more generally, see Freudenburg (2001) and the essays in Freudenburg (2005) and Braund and Osgood (2012a). For the *longue-durée* of Stoicism in European literature from antiquity to the middle ages, see Colish (1985), esp. vol. I, pp. 194–203 on Persius. Persius's *Satires* are cited from Clausen (1992); translations are by the author. On Cornutus, see Nock (1931), Most (1989), Ramelli (2003), and Erler in this volume.
3. On Cleanthes's hymn, see Colish (1985); on hymnic structure, see Furley and Bremer (2001) 51. On Manilius and Stoicism, see Volk (2009) 226–234 and Ramelli (2014).
4. On obscurity and Stoic notions of *parrhēsia* ("freedom of speech") in Persius, see Pia Comella (2014).
5. Reckford (2009) 340.
6. Bartsch (2015) 179.
7. Freudenberg (2001) 127. On disjunction in Horace's own poetic persona, see Kachuck (2021b).
8. See Ramage (1974); cf. Jenkinson (1980) 4.
9. Henderson (1991) 124.
10. Austin (1962).
11. On Lucilius and skepticism, see Goh (2018).

12. On Roman manliness and *uirtus*, see McDonnell (2006); Raschke (1990) is circumspect regarding the Stoic affiliations of Lucilius's *uirtus*.
13. Cic. *Paradoxa Stoicorum* 2: *minutis interrogatiunculis quasi punctis*.
14. Cic. *Fin.* 3.3.
15. On Dryden and Roman satire, see Braund and Osgood (2012b).
16. See, e.g., Hor. *Serm.* 2.3.82 (Damasippus quoting Stertinus on "most men are mad"; for hellebore cure, cf. *Ars P.* 300); 2.7.83–88 ("only the wise man is free"); *Epist* 2.1.45–9 (descending Sorites). We look forward to Kirk Freudenburg's discussions of these paradoxes in his commentary.
17. Long (2006) 15.
18. Bartsch (2015) 173.
19. Diog. Laert. 7.82 ἄποροι λόγοι; cf. 7.43–44, on which, see Bobzien (2012).
20. On the paradox epigram, see Feeney (2009). For *sustentatio*, see Quint. *Inst.* 9.2.22–23.
21. Mayer (2005) 155. On Cicero's *Paradoxa Stoicorum*, see Ronnick (1991) and Mehl (2002); on links between Cicero's paradoxes and Varro's Menippean Satires (with a possible common source in Hecaton Rhodius's Περὶ παραδόξων), see Sigsbee (1976). On the Stoic paradoxes more generally, see *SVF* 3.524–530, 545–684; Barnes (1997) 76–77; Mignucci (1999). For a reading of the storm-scene in Lucr. 2.1–19 as refracted through Pers. 6.27–37 to Juv. 12.17–61, cf. Gellar-Goad (2018). On Cicero's *paradoxa*, see now the edition, with commentary and translation, by Galli (2019).
22. On how Cornutus's *Socraticus sinus* represents a "correction" of Socrates's implied inappropriate relationship with Alcibiades in *Satire* IV—and serves, as a result, as a central *locus* for Persius's relationship with Stoic and Socratic philosophy—see Bartsch (2015) 96–122, condensed in Bartsch (2014).
23. Cic. *Pro. Mur.* 74.
24. Rockford (1962) 492. On satirists' mockery of Stoic paradoxes, see Sigsbee (1968).
25. *Parad.* 27 opens with the first paradox, but, after a lacuna, seems to have switched its focus to the second: Persius's fourth *Satire* takes up both, and, in doing so, perhaps alludes to Alcibiades' eventual fate as an exile. On Alcibiades's "insanity," see Bartsch (2015) 103.
26. Reckford (1962) 493n3 notes that the fifth *Satire* is particularly rich in Stoic terminology in lines 73–131 (treating the paradox), including: *colligis, licet, stultis, officia, ratio, uitiabit, natura, recto, sequenda, euitanda, sapiens, peccas, stultitia, recti*.
27. Mignucci (1999) 157.
28. Ibid., 176.
29. *Apud* Plin. *HN praef.* 7. On the more solitary side of Horace's poetic *persona*, see Kachuck (2021a) 151–198.
30. Lucil. fr. 635 (W) *apud* Cic. *Orat.* 2.25 *Persium non curo legere... Laelium Decumum uolo*.
31. Cic. *de Orat.* 6.25 *omnium fere nostrum hominum doctissimus*.
32. On the *Commentum Cornuti*, a ninth-century CE compilation of ancient scholia, see Zetzel (2005); whether this notice refers to 1.1 or 1.2, or even to Lucilius or Lucretius, remains controversial, on which, see Kißel *ad* 1.1, and, more recently, the intriguing revisionist theory of Sosin (1999).
33. Kißel (1990) 107.
34. Sen. *Ep.* 7.11. On the paradox of solitary literary postures, see Kachuck (2021a) 1–44.
35. Hooley (1997) 37.
36. Cf. Gowers (2012) 214.

37. Cucchiarelli (2005). The most compendious list of Persius's debts to Horace remains the appendix ("Persiana Horatii imitatio") to Casaubon's commentary.
38. Mignucci (1999) 161.
39. See Reydams-Schils in this volume for Senecan psychology.
40. cf. Mishnah Hagigah 2.1; translation author's own.
41. Harvey (1981) *ad* 1.3; cf. Bartsch (2015) 114.
42. For the philosophical and semantic implications, see Atherton (1993) 298.
43. Plut. *Comm. not.* 1083a–1084a.
44. Cf. 5.47–51 (Persius and Cornutus's shared star-signs); on the difficulties of punctuating Persius, see Feeney (2011).
45. On the *sorites* paradox in Persius, see Feeney (2011) 89–91.
46. Cf. Mignucci (1999) 172.
47. Cf. Beikircher (1969) 125; Morford (1984) 69; and Henderson (1991) 146n106: "Cornutus' (presumably abrasive?) editing made 'Persius' even more purely 'Persius' than Persius had managed/imagined."
48. Cf. *Vit. Pers.* 41–43 Clausen *hunc ipsum librum inperfectum reliquit. uersus aliqui dempti sunt ultimo libro, ut quasi finitus esset.*
49. Gowers (2012) *ad* Hor. *Serm.* 1.120.
50. Freudenberg (2001) 41 and 27–29.
51. Juvenal's adaptation of these lines for the conclusion of his fourteenth *Satire* (noted by Casaubon *ad* 6.80) indicates its useful ending-power.
52. Cf. Quint. *Inst.* 10.1.94; Martial 4.29; cf. Henderson (1991) 145n77.
53. On comparable Stoic responses to so-called Changing Arguments, see Barnes (1997) 99–125.
54. On Persius's Ennian/Hesiodic dream, see Miller (2010).
55. On dreaming and self-entrapment, see Kachuck (2020).
56. On Cornutus, see Erler (in this volume).
57. Bobzien (2012) 166.
58. For a slightly different form of the "Horned Paradox," cf. Gell. *NA* 18.2.9.
59. See Bobzien (2012) 182–183.
60. Cf. Gowers (2005).
61. Cf. 4.33–36, 4.42–45, 5.85–86; on the self-defeating quality of such diatribes, see Bartsch (2014).
62. Scholia *ad* 5.12.
63. Shearin (2012) on Atticus's Epicurean death (*apud* Cornelius Nepos) represents an exemplary corrective to this split, and a model for the way forward.
64. The New Comic poet Philemon is said to have died under circumstances similar to those that killed Chrysippus (cf. Val. Max. 9.12, ext. 6; Luc. *Macr.* 25), with both stories, as the Editors of this volume have kindly pointed out, playing on the aural association in Greek of the words for donkey (ὄνος) and wine (οἶνος). On the role of the figs in these donkey-stories, see Beard (2014) 179–181.
65. Bramble (1974) 70.
66. Kißel (1990) *ad loc.*
67. Bramble (1974) 71.
68. On Palaemon, see Kaster (1995) *Suetonius* 23, and, for further reflections on historiographic context and impact, Barwick (1967) and Baratin (2000).
69. On the skeletons on the Boscoreale silver cups, cf. Dunbabin (1986), esp. 224–230.
70. On punctuation and death, see Armstrong (2004) 52.

References

Armstrong, D. (2004). "Horace's *Epistles* 1 and Philodemus," in Armstrong, Fish, Johnston, and Skinner, 267–298.
Armstrong, D., J. Fish, P. Johnston, and M. Skinner, eds. (2004). *Vergil, Philodemus, and the Augustans* (Austin, Tex.).
Atherton, C. (1993). *The Stoics on Ambiguity*. (Cambridge).
Austin, J. L. (1962). *How to Do Things with Words*. (Cambridge, Mass.).
Baratin, M. (2000). "À l'origine de la tradition artigraphique latine, entre mythe et réalité," in S. Auroux, E. F. K. Koerner, H.-J. Niederehe, and K. Versteegh (eds.) *History of the Language Sciences / Geschichte der Sprachwissenschaften / Histoire des sciences du langage* (Berlin), 459–466.
Barnes, J. (1997). *Logic and the Imperial Stoa*. (Leiden).
Bartsch, S. (2014). "Persius' Fourth Satire: Socrates and the Failure of Pedagogy," in Garani and Konstan, 245–268.
Bartsch, S. (2015). *Persius: A Study in Food, Philosophy, and the Figural*. (Chicago).
Barwick, K. (1967). *Remmius Palaemon und die römische Ars grammatica*. (New York).
Beard, M. (2014). *Laughter in Ancient Rome*. (Berkeley).
Beikircher, H (1969). *Kommentar zur 6. Satire des A. Persius Flaccus*. (Vienna).
Bobzien, S (2012). "How to Give Someone Horns: Paradoxes of Presupposition in Antiquity." *Logical Analysis and History of Philosophy* 15: 159–184.
Bramble, J. C. (1974). *Persius and the Programmatic Satire: A Study in Form and Imagery*. (Cambridge).
Braund, S. M., and J. Osgood, eds. (2012a) *A Companion to Persius and Juvenal*. (Chichester).
Braund, S. M., & J. Osgood (2012b). "Imperial Satire Theorized: Dryden's Discourse of Satire," in Braund & Osgood, 409–435.
Casaubon, I. (1605). *Auli Persii Flacci satyrarum liber*. (Paris).
Clausen, W., ed. (1992). *A. Persi Flacci et D. Iuni Iuvenalis saturae*. (Oxford).
Colish, M. L. (1985). *The Stoic Tradition from Antiquity to the Early Middle Ages*. (Leiden).
Conington, J., and Nettleship, H. (^{3}1893). *The Satires of A. Persius Flaccus*. (Oxford).
Cucchiarelli, A. (2005). "Speaking from Silence: The Stoic Paradoxes of Persius," in K. Freudenburg, *The Cambridge Companion to Roman Satire*. (Cambridge), 62–80.
Dunbabin, K. M. D. (1986). "'Sic erimus cuncti . . . The Skeleton in Graeco-Roman Art." *JdI* 101: 185–255.
Feeney, D. (2009). "Catullus and the Roman Paradox Epigram." *MD* 61: 29–39.
Feeney, D. (2011). "*Hic finis fandi*: On the Absence of Punctuation for the Endings (and Beginnings) of Speeches in Latin Poetic Texts." *MD* 66: 45–92.
Freudenburg, K. (2001). *Satires of Rome: Threatening Poses from Lucilius to Juvenal*. (Cambridge).
Freudenburg, K., ed. (2005). *The Cambridge Companion to Roman Satire*. (Cambridge).
Furley, W. D., and J.M. Bremer (2001). *Greek Hymns: Selected Cult Songs from the Archaic to the Hellenistic Period*. (Tübingen).
Galli, D. (2019). *Cicero's Paradoxa stoicorum: Text and Philological Commentary*. (Rome).
Garani, M., and D. Konstan, eds. (2014). *The Philosophizing Muse: The Influence of Greek Philosophy on Roman Poetry*. (Newcastle upon Tyne).
Gellar-Goad, T. H. M. (2018). "Trouble at Sea in Juvenal 12, Persius 6 and the Proem to Lucretius, *De rerum natura* 2." *Cambridge Classical Journal* 64: 49–69.

Goh, I. (2018). "Scepticism at the Birth of Satire: Carneades in Lucilius' *Concilium Deorum*." *CQ* 68 (1): 128–142.
Gowers, E. (2005). "Virgil's Sibyl and the 'Many Mouths' Cliché (*Aen*. 6.625–7)." *CQ* 55(1): 170–182.
Gowers, E. (2012). *Satires. Book 1*. (Cambridge).
Harvey, R. A. (1981). *A Commentary on Persius. Mnemos*. Suppl. 64. (Leiden).
Henderson, J. (1991). "Persius' Didactic Satire: The Pupil as Teacher." *Ramus* 20: 123–148.
Hooley, D. M. (1997). *The Knotted Thong: Structures of Mimesis in Persius*. (Ann Arbor, Mich.).
Jenkinson, J. R. (1980). *Persius: The Satires*. (Warminster).
Kachuck, A. J. (2020). "Ovid's Dream, or, Byblis and the Circle of Metamorphoses", in A. Sharrock, D. Möller, M. Malm (eds.) *Metamorphic Readings: Transformation, Language, and Gender in the Interpretation of Ovid's Metamorphoses*. (Oxford).
Kachuck, A.J. (2021a). *The Solitary Sphere in the Age of Virgil*. (Oxford).
Kachuck, A.J. (2021b). "Exit Pursued by Horace: A Classical Archaeology of Shakespeare's Bear." *Classical Receptions Journal* 13(1): 86–106.
Kaster, R. A. (1995). *C. Suetonius Tranquillus: De grammaticis et rhetoribus*. (Oxford).
Kißel, W. (1990). *Satiren*. (Heidelberg).
Long, A. A. (2006). *From Epicurus to Epictetus: Studies in Hellenistic and Roman Philosophy*. (Oxford).
Mayer, R. G. (2005). "Sleeping with the Enemy: Satire and Philosophy," in Freudenburg, 146–159.
McDonnell, M. A. (2006). *Roman Manliness: Virtus and the Roman Republic*. (Cambridge).
Mehl, D. (2002). "The Stoic Paradoxes According to Cicero," in C. Damon, J. F. Miller, and K.S. Myers (eds.), *Vertis in usum: Studies in honor of Edward Courtney* (Munich), 39–62.
Mignucci, M. (1999). "Logic: The Stoics: Paradoxes," in K. Algra, J. Barnes, J. Mansfeld, and M. Schofield (eds.) *The Cambridge history of Hellenistic Philosophy* (Cambridge), 157–176.
Miller, P. A. (2010). "Persius, Irony and Truth." *AJPhil*. 131(2): 233–258.
Morford, M. (1984). *Persius*. (New York).
Most, G. (1989). "Cornutus and Stoic Allegoresis." *ANRW* II, 36(3): 2014–2065.
Nock, A. D. (1931). "Kornutos." *RE Suppl*. 5: 995–1005.
Pia Comella, J. (2014). "Parrhésie et obscurité poétique dans les Satires de Perse: L'arrière-plan stoïcien." *Rev. Ét. Lat*. 92: 197–220.
Ramage, E. S. (1974). "Persius, the Philosopher-Satirist," in E. S. Ramage, D. L. Sigsbee, S.C. Fredericks (eds.), *Roman Satirists and Their Satire: The Fine Art of Criticism in Ancient Rome* (Park Ridge, N.J.), 114–135.
Ramelli, I. (2003). *Compendio di teologia greca: Bompiani Il pensiero occidentale*. (Milan).
Ramelli, I. (2008). *Stoici romani minori*. (Milan).
Ramelli, I. (2014). "Manilius and Stoicism," in Garani and Konstan, 161–186.
Raschke, W. J. (1990). "The Virtue of Lucilius." *Latomus* 49: 352–369.
Reckford, K. J. (1962). "Studies in Persius." *Hermes* 90: 476–504.
Reckford, K. J. (2009). *Recognizing Persius*. (Princeton).
Ronnick, M. V. (1991). *Cicero's "Paradoxa stoicorum": A Commentary, an Interpretation and a Study of Its Influence*. (Frankfurt am Main).
Saccone, M. (1985). "La poesia di Persio alla luce degli studi più recenti (1964–1983)." *ANRW* II, 32(3): 1781–1812.
Shearin, W. H. (2012). "Haunting Nepos: Atticus and the Performance of Roman Epicurean Death," in B. Holmes and W. H. Shearin (eds.), *Dynamic Reading: Studies in the Reception of Epicureanism* (Oxford), 30–51.

Sigsbee, D. L. (1968). *The Ridicule of the Stoic Paradoxes in Ancient Satirical Literature.* (Ann Arbor, Mich.).
Sigsbee, D. L. (1976). "The Paradoxa Stoicorum in Varro's Menippeans." *C.Phil.* 71: 244–248.
Sosin, J. D. (1999). "Lucretius, Seneca and Persius 1.1–2." *TAPA* 129: 281–299.
Thom, J. C. (2006). *Cleanthes' Hymn to Zeus: Text, Translation, and Commentary.* (Tübingen).
Volk, K. (2009). *Manilius and His Intellectual Background.* (Oxford).
Zetzel, J. E. G. (2005). *Marginal Scholarship and Textual Deviance: The Commentum Cornuti and the Early Scholia on Persius.* (London).

CHAPTER 13

PLUTARCH

GEORGE KARAMANOLIS

Plutarch's Platonism

Plutarch of Chaeronea (c. 45–120 CE) is an important Platonist philosopher, but also a significant historian and essayist, well known for his *Parallel Lives*, the paired biographies of Greek and Roman statesmen and military leaders. In this chapter I focus on certain distinctive features of Plutarch's Platonist philosophy, which, I suggest, make him an important figure of the period of Roman philosophy.[1]

Plutarch's Platonism is marked by the following distinctive features: first, Plutarch sets out to do justice to Plato's work as a whole and to create a coherent philosophical system out of it by relying mainly on the *Timaeus*. This is an important shift of focus in the history of Platonism from the appreciation of Plato's ethics and epistemology by Antiochus of Ascalon to a more holistic approach to Plato's philosophy on the basis of his cosmology and metaphysics. In this respect Plutarch is a forerunner of Numenius and Plotinus. Presumably under the influence of Neopythagorean philosophy, which was flourishing in his age, Plutarch champions a literal interpretation of the *Timaeus*, according to which the world has come about from two principles, the demiurge and the indefinite dyad; while the demiurge accounts for order and intelligibility of the world, the indefinite dyad accounts for disorder and multiplicity, as disordered matter, which the demiurge needs to overrule and put in order by creating the world. Plutarch is thus a representative of principle dualism (see section "Metaphysics").

Second, Plutarch extends this principle dualism also to psychology and ethics; he maintains that the human soul consists of a rational and nonrational part and, furthermore, that it always retains a nonrational aspect, as it is derivative from the world soul. The world soul initially was nonrational, and despite its being made rational by the demiurge, retains traces of its original nonrational character (see section "Psychology and Ethics"). Third, as a champion of a holistic approach to Plato's philosophy, Plutarch has an appreciation of the aporetic element in Plato, which the earlier generation of Platonists, including Antiochus and Eudorus, rejected or neglected. Plutarch avoids the dilemma posed by the skeptical academy and Antiochus that one needs to decide between Plato's skepticism and Plato's doctrines. Plutarch does not see the two as standing in opposition, and he makes an effort to do justice to Plato's aporetic element while also valuing the doctrines he finds in Plato's texts. Accordingly, Plutarch maintains the unity of Plato's Academy, including the early doctrinal stage and the skeptical academy, which Antiochus considered an aberration from Plato's philosophy.[2]

In accordance with Plutarch's conception of Plato's philosophy as one that accommodates both a doctrinal character and an aporetic spirit, Plutarch writes, on the one hand, exegetical works on certain accounts by Plato, such as *On the Generation of Soul in the Timaeus* and the *Platonic Questions*, where he sets out to outline and expound Plato's doctrines, as well as dialogues, which, like Plato's, are either dramatic (e.g., *De cohibenda ira*), narrated (e.g., *De sera numinis vindicta*), or mixed (*De genio Socratis*), and they aim to maintain and imitate Plato's aporetic spirit. Often speakers in these dialogues give long speeches in favor of a certain position,[3] but it remains unclear whether Plutarch sympathizes with any specific view, despite the fact that sometimes he appears as character in some dialogues (e.g., *On the E at Delphi*). Moreover, Plutarch, following Plato again, often uses myths, metaphors, and analogies, and it is not always clear how exactly the reader should construe them. Interesting examples are the work *On Isis and Osiris*, which tells the myth of the two Egyptian gods, but also revisits the account of creation in the *Timaeus*, and the *On the Face Which Appears in the Orb of the Moon*, which centers on the role of the moon in the world and its role in the life of souls. Plutarch's dialogues and mythological works present a challenge to the reader and must be read with caution, as it is not always clear to what extent they host Plutarch's own views.

Fourth, Plutarch is also a skilled polemicist. He aims not only to interpret but also to defend Plato, mainly against criticisms on the part of the Epicureans and the Stoics. Several of his works contains polemics directed especially against the Stoics and the Epicureans.[4] These works are marked by recognizable polemical strategies and often do not give the opposed view a fair hearing.[5] In this respect Plutarch is similar to earlier Platonists like Antiochus and Cicero. Finally, Plutarch also exhibits an interest in the history of philosophy, as Porphyry will do later, and he writes a number of works on aspects and figures of the history of philosophy, all lost today, such as *On What Heraclitus Maintained*, *On Empedocles*, *On the Cyrenaics*, *On the Difference between Pyrrhonians and Academics*, and *On the Unity of the Academy since Plato*.[6]

METAPHYSICS

As a Platonist, Plutarch typically distinguishes between the intelligible and the sensible realms and he also holds that the former is ontologically and causally superior to the latter; that is, the intelligible realm is the source of being, order and intelligibility, which it transmits to the sensible realm. As already mentioned, Plutarch acknowledges two principles, God and the indefinite Dyad. These two principles are antithetical and constantly opposing each other, but they also collaborate in the creation of the world (*De Is. et Os.* 369C-D, *De def. or.* 428E-429A). Plutarch's principle dualism was not new. The same two principles, God and the Dyad, were apparently assumed by the Pythagoreans[7] and were attributed to Plato[8] by Pythagorean Platonists such as Eudorus and Moderatus.[9] Plutarch identifies the two principles with the Limited and the Unlimited of the *Philebus* (he calls the Indefinite Dyad "limitlessness," *apeiria*; *De def. or.* 428F). On this view, God is real being, unchangeable, simple (*De E apud Delphos* 392E-393B), and good (*De def. or.* 423D), the cause of order, intelligibility, stability, and identity in the universe, which is why God is the object of striving for all nature (*De fac.* 944E). The Indefinite Dyad, on the other hand, is the principle of nonbeing, multiplicity, disorder, irrationality, and evil (*De def. or.* 428F). Plutarch describes it as being identical with matter and as inherently disordered (*De Is. et Os.* 369D-F), yet ordered by God (*De def. or.* 428F-429D) or by its *logoi* (*De Is. et Os.* 373A-C). Apparently Plutarch holds that God informs and molds matter, which suggests a one way causality between the two principles that points to the superiority of the forming principle, God. The implication, however, is that God's power is constrained by matter and in this sense God is not absolutely free.[10]

The two first principles do not act alone, but rather relate to the universe through intermediaries: God relates to the world through the rational world soul, while the Dyad does so through the nonrational world soul. Plutarch maintains that before the world has come into being as a result of the intervention of God, it was animated by a nonrational world soul, which was responsible for the disorder (*De an. procr.* 1014B-E).[11] One might object here that, while Plato does speak of a rational world soul in the *Timaeus*, he never speaks of a nonrational world soul. Plutarch makes an interpretative move here; he postulates a nonrational soul which he identifies with the "disorderly and maleficent soul" of *Laws* X (896e-897d; *De an. procr.* 1014B-E, *De Is. et Os.* 370F) and with the "inbred character" of the *Politicus* (272d, 273b). Nowhere in these passages, however, does Plato speak of a nonrational precosmic soul.[12]

Plutarch's interpretative move regarding the world soul is part of an overall interpretation of the world's coming into being as described in the *Timaeus* which we could term literal, to the extent that it assumes a generation of the world, that is, the coming into being of order from disorder. Plutarch outlines and justifies his interpretation mainly in his work *On the Generation of Soul in the Timaeus* (*De animae procreatione in Timaeo*, hereafter *De an. procr.*), a commentary on *Timaeus* 35a1-36b5.[13] Plutarch opposes the interpretation of most Platonists of his time who refused to understand creation in terms of an actual generation (*De an. procr.* 1013E); he argues instead that the cosmogony of the *Timaeus* must be understood in the sense that the world had a temporal beginning.[14] One reason in favor of his interpretation is that it explains Plato's claim that the soul is "senior" to the body (*Ti.* 34c), and that it initiates all change and motion (*De an. procr.* 1013D-F; cf. Pl. *Phdr.* 245c, *Leg.* 896a-c). Another reason in support of Plutarch's interpretation is that the demiurge in the *Timaeus* (35a) does not create the substance of the soul but fashions the world soul by blending indivisible with divisible being, which

Plutarch identifies with the divine intellect and the nonrational world soul respectively (*De an. procr.* 1014D–E). Third, if no motion is possible without a principle of motion (Arist. *De an.* 402a6–7) and this principle is identified by Plato with the soul, then the disordered motion of matter before the cosmogony needs also to be accounted for by a soul, which must, then, be a precosmic one (*De an. procr.* 1015E). Finally, Plutarch's interpretation provides an answer to the paradox that the soul in Plato is said to be both uncreated (Pl. *Phdr.* 245c–246a) as well as created (Pl. *Ti.* 34b–35a; *De an. procr.* 1016A) and also a mixed entity composed of indivisible being (the intellect) and divisible being (i.e., the nonrational precosmic soul; Pl. *Ti.* 35a; *De an. procr.* 1014D–E, 1024A).

Plutarch maintains that the world soul becomes rational and replaces the nonrational world soul to the extent that is informed by God's reason, that is, it is shaped by a "portion" (*moira*) or "efflux" (*aporrhoê*) of God (*De Is. et Os.* 382B).[15] As such, Plutarch claims, the world soul is part of God (*De sera* 559D; *Quaest. Plat.* 1001C) and becomes assimilated to God (*homoiôsis*; *De sera* 550D). We still may wonder how exactly we should understand the process of making the world soul rational. Plutarch appears to maintain that the world soul becomes rational by being shaped when receiving the intelligible Forms from God (*De an. procr.* 1024C). Once it has received the Forms and has become rational, the world soul then transmits these further to matter (*De Is. et Os.* 373A; *De Pyth. or.* 404C). The world soul becomes then an instrument of God. The transmission of Forms from the world soul may well imply a cosmogony in stages, which in Plutarch's view is suggested in the *Timaeus*. First, the rational world soul comes into being and facilitates the realization of Forms in matter.[16] Then Forms inform matter so that primary bodies, such as water and fire, come about (*Ti.* 53bd, 69bc; *De an. procr.* 1025A–B; *Quaest. Plat.* 1001D–E); finally, the imposition of further Forms on matter brings about different kinds of objects, which make up the cosmos (*De Is. et Os.* 372E–F, 373E–F). Based on this explanation the world's order is due to God's wisdom and goodness. Therefore, an appeal to natural causes alone is insufficient, Plutarch argues, since such an explanation ignores the agent (God) and the end for which something happens in the world (*De def. or.* 435E).[17]

Plutarch provides a mythological analogy of the cosmogony and, more precisely, of the way the intelligible principles shape the world in his *De Iside et Osiride*.[18] Osiris is a divine intellect that brings everything into being by having sown in matter, that is, in Isis, the reasons (*logoi*) of himself (*De Is. et Os.* 372E–F), eventually producing Horus, i.e., the world (*kosmos, De Is. et Os.* 374A; *De an. procr.* 1026C). Osiris is identified with the good itself (372E), to which Isis always inclines, offering herself to be impregnated "with effluxes and likenesses in which she rejoices" (373A). Apparently Osiris stands for the creator God of the *Timaeus* and the Form of the Good of the *Republic* (cf. *De an. procr.* 1017A–B)—which explains why Osiris constitutes the object of desire by nature and Isis (*De Is. et Os.* 372E–F; cf. *De fac.* 944E), while Isis obviously stands for the receptacle or matter (*De Is. et Os.* 372E–373C; *De an. procr.* 1026C; Pl. *Ti.* 49a, 51a). The Forms existing in the soul of Osiris (*De Is. et Os.* 373A) are imposed on Isis, that is, matter, which suggests that Plutarch maintained that the Forms exist in God, presumably as his thoughts, (cf. Pl. *Ti.* 39e), a view upheld by several other Platonists in late antiquity.[19]

This interpretation is corroborated by the fact that Plutarch sometimes speaks of God and the Forms as a unity (*paradeigma*; *De sera* 550D).[20]

However rational the world soul becomes through the intervention of the supreme God and the imposition of the Forms, Plutarch still maintains that its initial nonrational character is not entirely eradicated (*De an. procr.* 1027A). He argues that this nonrational character accounts for occurrences of wickedness in the world, such as accidents and natural catastrophes. Otherwise we should assume that God is responsible for such phenomena, which hardly fits God's goodness (*De an. procr.* 1015A–B), or they must happen without cause, which inevitably diminishes God's ruling power (*De an. procr.* 1015C). It is important to note here that Plutarch does not associate wickedness with matter, as later Platonists do (e.g., Numenius, Plotinus), but rather with the nonrational world soul.[21]

Plutarch was especially interested in the nature of the divine, as we would expect from someone who served in various positions in Delphi, including that of the priest of Apollo (*Should Old Men Take Part in Affairs of State?* 792F), and wrote several works about Delphi and the local sacred rituals (*On the E at Delphi, On Oracles at Delphi, On the Obsolescence of Oracles*). Plutarch was actually very interested in religion, and the evidence of his work suggests that he was sympathetic to different religious traditions existing at his time, such as the Egyptian, the Iranian, and Mithraism.[22] He actually appears to maintain that religious mysteries reveal aspects of the divine, that all of them converge toward the same view about the divine, and that for this reason they can function as an introduction to philosophy.[23] Plutarch distinguishes between God or the divine (*theos, to theion*) and gods in plural. He claims that the highest God must be distinguished from the deities of the Greek pantheon, and suggests that the highest God can take different names. Thus, he sometimes names Apollo as the supreme God (*De E apud Delphos* 394A) and at other times Zeus (*De fac.* 927B). Plutarch considers the supreme God as a unity of utter simplicity, which includes all divine beings (*De Is. et Os.* 377F) and is identified with the Good and with Being (*De E apud Delphos* 393B–D).[24] Apparently Plutarch identifies the supreme God with the Form of the Good of the *Republic* and the demiurge of the *Timaeus*, which, as mentioned earlier, is the source of order and intelligibility. And like the Form of the Good in the *Republic*, the supreme God is "beyond everything" (*epekeina tou pantos*; *De E apud Delphos* 393B).

Following the *Timaeus* (42e) Plutarch also acknowledges the existence of lesser gods, who, as in the *Timaeus*, mediate between the supreme God and the sensible world, and he acknowledges other divine entities as well, namely the demons.[25] The latter play a role in extending God's providence to human beings.[26] Plutarch provides us with evidence according to which the role of demons consists in communicating God's will to humans, since demons are bestowed with prophetic powers and inspiration (*Amat.* 758E, *De gen.* 580C, *De fac.* 944C–D), in taking care of humans when they are needy (*Amat.* 758A–B), in taking care of the sanctuaries and the sacred rites (*De def. or.* 417A–B), but also in punishing humans and avenging human bad acts (*De def. or.* 417A–B). The latter is the work of the bad demons. Plutarch distinguishes between good and bad demons, claiming that demons exhibit different degrees of virtue and vice, as is the case with men too (*De def. or.* 417B; *De Is. et Os.* 360E).

Plutarch is concerned with the issue of divine punishment and with the issue of theodicy more generally, which was becoming central in his age. In his work *On the Delays of the Divine Vengeance* (*De sera numinis vindicta*) Plutarch addresses the question whether the delays of divine punishment speak against the existence of divine providence (550C). Plutarch answers this question in the negative on the grounds that God acts always following reason and not on impulse, and his punishment is never vengeful (551A, 557E), which makes God a model for us humans. Plutarch also argues that human wickedness is not always to be punished, as some of us think or want, because wickedness itself already ruins those who engage in such acts, and this is a sufficient punishment (556D–E). Finally, Plutarch suggests that the divine punishment can take place in the afterlife of the soul, as is suggested in *Republic* 10. Thus, Plutarch claims that "it is one and the same argument . . . that establishes both the providence of god and the survival of the human soul" (560F).

Theory of Knowledge

Plutarch's theory of knowledge was shaped, on the one hand, by his distinction, which I described in the previous section, between the intelligible and the sensible realms and, on the other hand, by his commitment to accommodate the Socratic aporetic spirit and adopt, at least partly, the skepticism of the New Academy.

In accordance with the traditional Platonic division between two ontologically separate realms, the intelligible and the sensible, Plutarch distinguishes between intelligible and sensible knowledge (*Quaest. Plat.* 1002B–C). Plutarch indeed speaks of two distinct faculties of human knowledge, the sensory and the intellectual, each of which grasps the corresponding part of reality (*Quaest. Plat.* 1002D–E). The intellect knows intelligible entities and predates the embodied soul (*De an. procr.* 1026E; *Quaest. Plat.* 1001C, 1002F); it is familiar with notions or concepts (*ennoiai*), apparently identifiable with the Forms (*Quaest. Plat.* 1001E); that is, the embodied soul recollects what it knows from its inherent previous familiarity with the intelligible realm, as Plato argued in in the *Meno* (*Quaest. Plat.* 1001D, 1002E).[27] The sensory faculty, on the other hand, comes about when the soul enters the body (*De morale virtuti* 442B–F), and grasps the objects of the physical world as they appear to our senses.

In accordance with his Platonism, Plutarch considers the knowledge of intelligibles superior to the knowledge of sensibles, because it amounts to knowledge of being, not of the world of change and corruption. (*De Is. et Os.* 382D–383A). The former kind of knowledge can make us understand even the divine realm (*Quaest. Plat.* 1002E, 1004D). Plutarch argues that this is the kind of knowledge that Socrates possessed, who was able to understand his *daimôn* because he had purified his soul (*De gen.* 588E). Sensory knowledge instead cannot rise above the level of belief (*pistis*) and conjecture (*eikasia*;

Quaest. Plat. 1001C). This view, however, does not amount to a complete dismissal of sensory knowledge, as Colotes objected to Plato (*Adv. Col.* 1114D–F), let alone a dismissal of the being of the sensible entities (*Adv. Col.* 1115C–1116A). Plutarch claims instead that the senses are of limited use because they can at best inform us only about the sensible world, which is a world of generation, of appearances, not of being (*De E apud Delphos* 392E).

Knowledge of intelligibles, however, is possible only when "our souls are free to migrate to the realm of the indivisible and the unseen" (*De Is. et Os.* 382F). This is the main task of philosophy for Plutarch, who is in this respect guided by the conception of philosophy in the *Phaedo*. Yet Plutarch specifies that philosophy must be inspired by the Socratic practice of inquiry, and this practice amounts to the continuous search for truth, which presupposes that, following the example of Socrates, one admits ignorance (*Adv. Col.* 1117D; *De adulatore et amico* 72A). If Plutarch defends knowledge of intelligibles that can give us access to divine truths, one wonders how he can also defend academic skepticism. Plutarch indeed defends suspension of judgment (*epochê*).[28] He argues that this is a method of testing and evaluating knowledge obtained through the senses (*Adv. Col.* 1124B). This method is necessary, he claims, not only because the senses often deceive us but also because the world is a place that cannot be known perfectly (*De primo frigido* 952A; *De E apud Delphos* 392E). Plutarch argues that suspension of judgment saves us from making mistakes (*Adv. Col.* 1124B) and indeed advances knowledge because it removes opinion (*doxa*) as well as vanity (*kenophrosynê*), both of which prevent us from finding the truth (*Quaest. Plat.* 1000C). This is why, Plutarch argues, Socrates uses this method; he uses it as a "purgative medicine" (*kathartikon pharmakon*; *Quaest. Plat.* 999E–F), trying to remove false opinions and deception from the souls of his interlocutors (*Quaest. Plat.* 1000B, 1000D).[29] Plutarch claims that skepticism of this kind does not affect our actions. He argues against the Stoics that assent to the truth of sense impressions is not required for action (*Adv. Col.* 1122C–D) and that suspension of judgment does not prevent us from acting but only eliminates opinions (*Adv. Col.* 1122B).[30] Plutarch steers, then, away both from the Stoic position that requires assent to sense impression before acting and from the Epicurean position that sense-experiences are always true. He maintains instead that suspension of judgment promotes the search for knowledge, which is what Plutarch himself practices in his own scientific writings such as *De primo frigido*. Plutarch concludes this work by pointing out to Favorinus, a skeptic, that his theory about the principle of cold should not be regarded as certain and he recommends after all suspension of judgement (*Adv. Col.* 955C).[31]

Soul, Body, and Intellect

As a genuine Platonist Plutarch is very concerned with the status and the operation of the soul. Like most ancient philosophers, he regards soul as the principle of motion and life.[32] The world soul, for instance, is responsible for disorderly motion before the world's coming into being and for orderly motion when the world comes about. With regard to individual souls Plutarch appears to distinguish soul from intellect, and he speaks of three aspects of the human constitution, body, soul and intellect. In *De fac.* 943A he argues as follows:

> Most people rightly think that a human is composite, but wrongly think that the composition is only of two things. They think that the intellect is a sort of part of the soul, a mistake which is as bad as the view that the soul is part of the body. Intellect is superior to soul—as much as soul is superior to body: better and more divine. (tr. Boys-Stones)

Plutarch actually turns against the Stoics here, who analyze the nature of man as consisting of two components, body and soul, accusing them of disregarding the intellect (*De fac.* 943AB). Elsewhere, though, Plutarch seems to suggest that the intellect is the part of the soul that does not "sink into the body" (*De gen.* 591E).[33] This passage, however, is ambiguous and can be interpreted in the sense that the soul always presupposes an intellect, which is a Platonic view.[34] However that may be, Plutarch clearly maintains that both the world soul and human souls become rational by coming into contact with the intellect (*Quaest. Plat.* 1001C, 1003A). Plutarch argues in particular that all ensouled beings, including animals, exhibit the presence of the divine intellect (*De Is. et Os.* 382A–B). The degree though in which a soul partakes of intellect varies (*De gen.* 588D, 591D–E), depending on how much the body is purified from emotions and vice (591D).[35] However, an element of nonrationality always remains in souls (*De an. procr.* 1027A).

Plutarch adopts the view we find in Aristotle that the soul engages with the body by developing faculties such as the nutritive and the perceptive (*De morale virtuti* 442B, 450E, 451A; *Quaest. Plat.* 107E–1009B),[36] while thinking and understanding are carried out by the intellect (*De gen.* 589A) or the intellectual faculty (*noêtê kai noêra dynamis*; *Quaest. Plat.* 1002E), which is the only one able to perceive the intelligibles. Following Plato, Plutarch identifies the intellect with our true self (*De fac.* 944F–945A; cf. Pl. *Ti.* 90a–d). He actually appears to distinguish between man as a biological entity and as a thinking entity, and he distinguishes accordingly two kinds of death: first, when intellect leaves soul and body, second when soul leaves body (*De fac.* 943A–B). The separation of intellect from soul and body happens "by love for the image of the sun . . . for which all nature strives" (*De fac.* 944E).[37] The ascent to the sun as the goal of intellect symbolizes the human being's assimilation to the divine (see below, section on Ethics). Plutarch illustrates this point with a myth presented in *On Delays in Divine Punishment*: a certain Aridaeus died but has come back to life to narrate his experience after death, like Er in the *Republic*. Plutarch explains his death as the fall of the intelligent part of his soul (*to phronoun*; *De sera* 563E–F, 566A), through which humans partake of the divine (564C), with the soul remaining behind (*allê psychê*) as an anchor in the body (564C; cf. 560C–D). The latter is the nonrational part of the soul, bound to the body (*sômatoeidês*; 566A) and inclining the entire soul toward earthly concerns (566D; cf. *Phaedo* 82d-e, 83b-e).

Ethics and Politics

Plutarch exhibits a strong interest in ethics, which is characteristic of his age. His predecessors Antiochus and Cicero as well as his contemporaries the Stoics Seneca (c. 4–65) and Epictetus (c. 50–135) show a similar tendency. It is not accidental that Plutarch takes Stoic ethics seriously into account, and it is in dialogue with these views and also with Epicurean ethics, as I will presently explain, that he shapes his own positions in ethics.

Plutarch's strong concern with ethics and politics can be seen not only in his philosophical works but also in his *Lives*, his forty-four biographies of historical figures from the Greek and the Roman world, arranged in pairs. As he explains in the beginning of his *Life of Alexander*, he aims not to write history but to present a given person's life, especially his virtue (*aretê*) and vice (*kakia*), traits which are not always evident in important deeds but often reveal themselves in events of everyday life. In order to carry out this task, Plutarch explains, one needs to go into the details of the traits of someone's soul, in the same way that the painter needs to pay special attention in depicting someone's face and eyes (*Alexander* 1). Central to Plutarch's *Lives* is the idea that humans have a given nature (*physis*) from which they develop a character (*êthos*) through education, role models, or good and bad habits.[38]

As one can surmise, here Plutarch betrays the influence of Aristotle's ethics, which he takes to be a systematic form of Plato's ethics.[39] The crucial feature that Aristotle shares with Plato, in Plutarch's view, is the belief in a soul that is divided between a rational and a nonrational part. This is precisely the main difference between Platonic and Stoic ethics according to Plutarch; for in his view Plato and Aristotle have a different view of human agency than the Stoics. The nonrational part of the soul accounts for uncontrolled actions, while in his view the Stoic conception of human agency as deriving from reason alone fails to account for such actions. Plutarch's definition of virtue relies heavily on Aristotle's *Nicomachean Ethics*, which, as I said, he takes to express Plato's ethical views in systematic form. Plutarch defines virtue as a state (*hexis*) in which reason succeeds in steering emotion in the right direction, while vice arises when reason fails to do so (*De morale virtuti* 443B–D, 444B–C). Plutarch argues then that virtue lies in the mean between two opposite extreme emotions (*De morale virtuti* 443D–444D; *Quaest. Plat.* 1009A; Arist. *Eth. Nic.* 1107a6–8). Courage, for instance, lies in the mean between fear and fearlessness (*De morale virtuti* 451E–452A); that is, courage results from the subordination of fear to a goal set by reason, such as fighting for one's country or family. In this sense moderate emotion plays a role in the constitution of virtue. Plutarch actually suggests that virtue is the state in which emotion is present as matter and reason as form (*De morale virtuti* 440D), a view inspired by Aristotle (*Eth. Nic.* 1104b13–30). Plutarch follows Aristotle also in two other regards, in maintaining that the temperate person is less virtuous than the person who has practical wisdom, the *phronimos* (*De morale virtuti* 445C–D; Arist. *Eth. Nic.* 1151b25–1152a9), and in the belief that there are things beneficial to us other than virtue, such as health, beauty, family. Plutarch considers such goods as completing happiness (*symplêrotika*; *Comm. not.* 1060B–E). In this connection Plutarch relies again on Aristotle in order to criticize the Stoics for contradicting themselves when they argue that the highest end is life according to nature yet admit only virtue as being good, thereby rejecting things such as health for which we strive because they are also natural to us.[40]

Since for Plutarch virtue is a state in which reason informs and guides emotion, it follows that we need training in order to learn how to apply reason to emotion and order it properly. In his work *On Progress in Virtue* Plutarch argues against the Stoic view that virtue does not admit of degrees of perfection (Arr. *Epict. diss.* 1.4; Sen. *Ep.* 75.8); he maintains, instead, that we learn virtue in stages from our parents and teachers, from the virtuous actions of the people around us (*Comm. not.* 1069A), through the law of the cities (*De morale virtuti* 452D; cf. Arist. *Eth. Nic.* 1180a21–1181b12), and also through philosophy, poetry, and history (*De prof. virt.* 79B–80B). Plutarch sets out to provide the education required for acquiring virtue through a number of works such as *On the Control of Anger*, *On Curiosity*, *How to Tell a Flatterer from a Friend*, *Precepts of Marriage*, and *To an Uneducated Ruler*.[41] Plutarch actually undertakes to provide or at least to outline the kind of education that both Plato in the *Republic* but also Aristotle (e.g., *Eth. Nic.* 1080a10–18) deemed essential for the upbringing of a good citizen.

Plutarch, however, could not possibly neglect an alternative conception of *eudaimonia*, which we find highlighted in Plato and in Aristotle, namely a life of contemplation or thinking.[42] This is a life similar to God's mode of being (*homoiôsis*; *De sera* 550D–E), which amounts to the intellectual side of humans being dominant (*Non posse suaviter vivi secundum Epicurum* 1092E). In this regard we are supposed to follow cosmic nature, which strives to imitate the creator God and become like him (*De fac.* 944E).[43] To achieve this goal, one should be guided by intellect alone and attain theoretical virtue (*Non posse suaviter vivi secundum Epicurum* 1092E). Like Aristotle, Plutarch associates the highest kind of happiness with a special kind of virtue, theoretical virtue. By distinguishing two distinct levels of happiness and two levels of virtue, practical and theoretical, Plutarch anticipates Plotinus's distinction of two kinds of life, a political and a theoretical one, and also the hierarchy of virtues that we find in Plotinus and in later Neoplatonists, which pertain to these kinds of life. For Plutarch, however, the theoretical life, the life of inquiry and reflection, is not necessarily detached from society. Quite the opposite is the case. The philosopher in particular, given the picture presented in the *Republic*, is required to assist his fellow citizens and be involved in public affairs. Plutarch actually criticizes the Stoics in this regard for refusing to engage in politics.[44]

Conclusion

As emerges from the above exposition, Plutarch marks an important shift in Platonism to the extent that he makes metaphysics the center of his philosophy, but also to the extent that he, unlike Antiochus, set out to do justice to Plato's philosophy as a whole, its skeptical and dialectical aspect as well as its doctrines. Furthermore, with his *Lives* and his writings on practical ethics Plutarch tries to reach a wider audience, to make Platonism more accessible, but also to realize to some extent at least Plato's educational ideal outlined in the *Republic* in particular. Plutarch also tried to defend Plato's philosophy against Stoic and Epicurean criticisms of Plato and their own alternative theories, and to show that Plato's philosophy is more plausible and a better guide to life than theirs. Plutarch anticipates several of ideas that we find articulated later in Platonism, such as the convergence of various religious traditions toward the same truth about the divine, articulated in the second century by Numenius, the inferior role of nature compared with that of the intelligible causes, the distinction of two kinds of life and the employment of aporetic methodology in his dialogues, all of which we find in Plotinus's work. Yet Plutarch is at the opposite end of Numenius, Plotinus, and later Neoplatonists, however, in that he is a principle dualist, while Plotinus at least defends a strong monism. Plutarch's dualism represents an important alternative interpretation of Plato's philosophy as a whole. It was presumably in reaction against this interpretation that Plotinus honed his monistic view.

Notes

1. For an overview of Plutarch's philosophy and of his place in Platonism, see Dörrie (1971), Dillon (1977), Opsomer (2007b), and Karamanolis (2014). Most useful is now Boys-Stones (2017) with his succinct notes on various topics in Plutarch's philosophy.
2. See mainly Opsomer (1999), and also Karamanolis (2006) chapters. 1 and 2, and Babut (2007).
3. See Russell (1973) 34–36.
4. Against the Stoics are the works *On the Self-Contradictions of the Stoics* (*De stoicorum repugnantiis*), *On the Common Notions against the Stoics* (*De communibus notitiis*), *On the Cleverness of Animals* (*De sollertia animalium*), *On Moral Virtue* (*De virtute morali*); against the Epicureans *That One Cannot Live Happily Following Epicurus* (*Non posse suaviter vivere secundum Epicurum*), *Against Colotes* (*Adversus Colotem*), *Is "Live Unnoticed" Well Said?* (*An recte dictum sit latenter esse vivendum*).
5. See Warren (2011) 290–293 and Kechagia (2011) 135–294 for two different evaluations of Plutarch's polemics.
6. For a reliable presentation of Plutarch's oeuvre, see Ziegler (1951).
7. Diog. Laert. 8.24–25; Sext. Emp. *Math.* 10.261–284; Nicomachus, *Introduction to Arithmetic* 2.18.4. See, further, Dillon (1977) 342–343, 354.
8. Simplicius, *in Phys.* 453.25–27; cf. Pl. *Prm.* 149D2.
9. Simplicius, *in Phys.* 181.7–30, 231.8–9. See Kahn (2001) 105–110.
10. Plutarch's cosmology and metaphysics is well presented by Ferrari (1995) and (1996a). Specifically on Plutarch's conception of the One and the Dyad, see Opsomer (2007b). See also Boys-Stones (2017) chapters 3, 4, and 5.
11. In Plutarch's words, "what preceded the generation of the world was disorder, disorder not incorporeal or immobile or inanimate, but of corporeality amorphous and incoherent,

and of motivity demented and irrational, and this was the discord of soul that has not reason" (*De an. procr.* 1014B; Cherniss's tr. altered).
12. H. Cherniss, *Plutarch Moralia*, Loeb vol. XIII.1, 140.
13. For an analysis of the structure and content of Plutarch's *On the Generation of the Soul*, see Hershbell (1987).
14. *Quaest. Plat.* 1001B–C; *De an. procr.* 1013C–1024C; cf. Pl. *Ti.* 30a, 52d–53b. Plutarch's literal interpretation is confirmed by Proclus's report *In Tim.* I.381.26–388.12, translated in Boys-Stones (2017) 121.
15. Plutarch anticipates Numenius who also speaks of two world souls; Proclus, *In Tim.* II.153.17–154.4; Numenius fr. 39 Des Places. For a commentary, see Boys-Stones (2017) 224–225.
16. *De an. procr.* 1023 B–C with Boys-Stones (2017) 213.
17. This view anticipates Plotinus's argument for the secondary role of nature in the explanation of the order and all events in the world in *Ennead* 3.8.
18. On the cosmological theory conveyed in this work, see Petrucci (2016).
19. See, e.g., Alcinous, *Didascalikos* 163.11–17 with Dillon (1993) 93–96. On Plutarch's view of the Forms, see Ferrari (1996b).
20. See Helmig (2005) 20–26.
21. See also Boys-Stones (2017), 109–114 with further references.
22. See *De superst.* 166A, 169C; *De Is. et Os.* 363C–D; *Quaestiones conv.* 4.6, 671CD, 669B–672C; *Amat.* 771C. I owe the references to Bonazzi (2021) 268.
23. See, for instance, *De Is. et Os.* 378A and the discussion of Bonazzi (2021) 270–273.
24. On Plutarch's conception of the divine, see Brenk (2005), Ferrari (2005), and Opsomer (2009) 158–160.
25. Plutarch explores here a tradition that goes back to Empedocles, Plato (*Symp.* 202D–203E; *Phd.* 107D, 113D; *Resp.* 427B, 620D; *Ti.* 90AD), and Xenocrates, on whose work he particularly draws. See *De Is. et Os.* 360E; *De def. or.* 416C–D.
26. See Dillon (1977) 216–218.
27. See Opsomer (1999) 193–198.
28. On Plutarch's skepticism, see Donini (1986), Boys-Stones (1997a), Opsomer (1999).
29. See Opsomer (1999) 145–150.
30. Opsomer (1999) 88 has rightly noted that Plutarch's argument is very similar to that of the Pyrrhonian skeptics.
31. On this see further Boys-Stones (1997b).
32. On Plutarch's view on the soul, see Deuse (1983) 12–47; Karamanolis (2014), section Psychology; Boys-Stones (2017) chapters. 9 and 10. See also Bonazzi (2010), who focuses on the fragments of Plutarch's *Peri Psychês*.
33. See Boys-Stones (2017) 267.
34. Cf. Pl. *Phlb.* 30c; *Soph.* 248d–249a, *Ti.* 46d–e. Plutarch claims the following: "Every soul partakes of intellect: there is no soul without reason and intellect" (*De gen.* 591E). He repeats the latter part of this claim in *Plat. Quaest.* 1002F–1003A.
35. See Dillon (1977) 212–213.
36. See Karamanolis (2006) 109–115.
37. On this see, further, Brenk (1994).
38. *Life of Pericles* 38; *Life of Alcibiades* 2; *De sera* 551E–F, 552C–D.
39. On this, see Karamanolis (2006) 115–123.
40. Plutarch's criticism is similar to that of Cicero in *Fin.* 4.20–41 in this regard.

41. On these works and Plutarch's practical ethics, see van Hoof (2010).
42. Cf. Pl. *Phd.* 82c–83b; *Tht.* 176ab; *Ti.* 90bc; Arist. *Eth. Nic.* 1177a12–1178a8.
43. Cf. *De virtute morali* 444D; *De def. or.* 470E.
44. Cf. *De Stoicorum repugnantiis* 1033A–1034C; *Adv. Col.* 1126B–1127E; *Ad principem ineruditum* 780C–F.

References

Babbitt, F. C. (1936). *Plutarch's* Moralia, vol. 5. (Cambridge, Mass.).
Babbitt, F. C. (1938). *Plutarch's* Moralia, vol. 6. (Cambridge, Mass.).
Babut, D. (1969). *Plutarque et le Stoicisme.* (Paris).
Babut, D. (2007). "L'unité de l'Académie selon Plutarque," in M. Bonazzi, C. Lévy, and C. Steel (eds.), *A Platonic Pythagoras: Platonism and Pythagoreanism in the Imperial Age* (Turnhout), 63–98.
Bonazzi, M. (2010). "Plutarque et l'immortalité de l' âme," in A. Giavatto and X. Brouillette (eds.), *Les dialogues platoniciens chez Plutarque: Stratégies et méthodes exégétiques* (Leuven), 81–97.
Bonazzi, M. (2021). "Plutarch and the Mysteries of Philosophy," in N. Belayche, F. Massa, and P. Hoffmann (eds.), *Les mysteres au IIe siècle de notre ère: Un tournant* (Turnhout), 267–278.
Boys-Stones, G. (1997a). "Thyrsus-bearer of the Academy or Enthusiast for Plato?," in J. Mossman (ed.), *Plutarch and His Intellectual World* (London), 41–58.
Boys-Stones, G. (1997b). "Plutarch on the Probable Principle of Cold: Epistemology and the *de primo frigido*", *Classical Quarterly* 47, 227–238
Boys-Stones, G. (2017). *Platonist Philosophy 80 BC to AD 250. An Introduction and Collection of Sources in Translation.* (Cambridge).
Brenk, F. (1994). "The Origin and the Return of the Soul in Plutarch," in M. G. Valdés (ed.), *Studios sobre Plutarco: Ideas religiosas; Actas del III Simposio Internacional sobre Plutarco* (Madrid), 3–24.
Brenk, F. (2005). "Plutarch's Middle-Platonic God," in Hirsch-Luipold, 27–49.
Cherniss, H. (1976). *Plutarch's* Moralia, vol. 13.1. (Cambridge, Mass.).
Cherniss, H. (1976). *Plutarch's* Moralia, vol. 13.2. (Cambridge, Mass.).
Cherniss, H., and W. Helmbold (1957). *Plutarch's* Moralia, vol. 12. (Cambridge, Mass.).
De Lacy, P., and B. Einarson (1959). *Plutarch's* Moralia, vol. 7. (Cambridge, Mass.).
Deuse, W. (1983). *Untersuchungen zur mittelplatonischen und neuplatonischen Seelenlehre.* (Wiesbaden).
Dillon, J. (1977). *The Middle Platonists. A Study of Platonism 80 BC to 220 AD.* (London).
Dillon, J. (1993). *Alcinous: The Handbook of Platonism.* (Oxford).
Dillon, J. (2002). "Plutarch and God: Theodicy and Cosmogony in the Thought of Plutarch," in D. Frede and A. Laks (eds.), *Traditions of Platonism: Studies in Hellenistic Theology, Its Background and Aftermath* (Leiden), 223–237.
Donini, P. L. (1986). "Lo scetticismo academico, Aristotele e l'unita della tradizione platonica second Plutarco," in G. Cambiano (ed.), *Storiografia e dossografia nella filosofia antica* (Turin), 203–226.
Dörrie, H. (1971). "Die Stellung Plutarchs im Platonismus seiner Zeit," in *Philomathes: Studies and Essays in the Humanities in Memory of Ph. Merlan* (The Hague), 36–56.
Einarson, B., and P. de Lacy (1967). *Plutarch's* Moralia, vol. 14. (Cambridge, Mass.).

Ferrari, F. (1995). *Dio, idee e materia: La struttura del cosmo in Plutarco di Cheronea*. (Naples).
Ferrari, F. (1996a). "La generazione precosmica e la struttura della materia in Plutarco." *MH* 53: 44–55.
Ferrari, F. (1996b). "La teoria delle idee in Plutarco." *Elenchos* 17: 121–142.
Ferrari, F. (2005). "Der Gott Plutarchs und der Gott Platons," in Hirsh-Luipold, 13–25.
Helmig, C. (2005). "Die Weltentstehung des *Timaios* und die platonische *Homoiosis Theôi*— Zum kosmologischen Hintergrund von Plutarch *De sera numinis vindicta* 550D–E," in T. Leinkauf and C. Steel (eds.), *Platon Timaios als Grundtext der Kosmologie in Spätantike, Mittelalter und Renaissance* (Leuven), 13–35.
Hershbell, J. (1987). "Plutarch's *De anima procreatione in Timae*: An Analysis of Structure and Content." *ANWR* II, 36(1): 234–247.
Hirsch-Luipold, R., ed. (2005). *Gott und die Götter bei Plutarch*. (Berlin).
Kahn, C. (2001). *Pythagoras and the Pythagoreans: A Brief History*. (Indianapolis).
Karamanolis, G. (2006). *Plato and Aristotle in Agreement? Platonists on Aristotle from Antiochus to Porphyry*. (Oxford).
Karamanolis, G. (2014). "Plutarch." *Stanford Encyclopedia of Philosophy*, November 4. https://plato.stanford.edu/entries/plutarch/ (accessed November 15, 2021).
Kechagia, E. (2011). *Plutarch against Colotes. A Lesson in History of Philosophy*. (Oxford).
Opsomer, J. (1999). In *Search of the Truth: Academic Tendencies in Middle Platonism*. (Leuven).
Opsomer, J. (2007a). "Plutarch on the One and the Dyad," in R. Sorabji and B. Sharples (eds.), *Greek and Roman Philosophy 100 BC–200 AD* (London), 379–395.
Opsomer, J. (2007b). "The Place of Plutarch in the History of Platonism," in P. Cacciatore and F. Ferrari (eds.), *Plutarco e la cultura della sua età* (Naples), 283–309.
Opsomer, J. (2009). "M. Annius Ammonius, A Philosophical Profile," in M. Bonazzi and J. Opsomer (eds.), *The Origins of the Platonic System. Platonisms of the Early Empire and Their Philosophical Contexts* (Leuven), 123–186.
Petrucci, F. (2016). "Plutarch's Theory of Cosmological Powers in the *De Iside et Osiride*." *Apeiron* 49: 329–367.
Russell, D. A. (1973). *Plutarch*. (London).
Sandbach, F. H. (1969). *Plutarch's Fragments*. (Cambridge, Mass.).
van Hoof, L. (2010). *Plutarch's Practical Ethics*. (Oxford).
Warren, J. (2011). "Pleasure, Plutarch's *Non Posse* and Plato's *Republic*." *CQ* 61 (1): 278–293.
Ziegler, K. (1951). "Plutarchos." *RE* 21: 636–962.

CHAPTER 14

PARRHĒSIA

Dio, Diatribe, and Philosophical Oratory

DANA FIELDS

Dio Chrysostom occupies a place close to the beginning of Philostratus's *Lives of the Sophists*, an account of the revival of sophistic rhetoric that the biographer identifies as occurring shortly before his own time in the third century CE. This early appearance is not due to Dio's centrality to the cultural development that Philostratus names the Second Sophistic, but rather his marginality; the biographer classifies Dio among "the philosophers who articulated their theories with fluency" and therefore seemed to be sophists and came to be called sophists, even though they were not actually sophists (*VS* 484). Philostratus's introduction to the section on Dio also conveys the problem of finding an adequate label: "I do not know what one ought to call him, on account of his excellence in all matters" (*VS* 486).

The difficulty of categorizing Dio and his rhetorical output has led scholars, starting with Synesius in the fourth century CE, to posit a conversion to philosophy and an accompanying disavowal of his youthful rhetorical pursuits.[1] However, this view has been debunked in an important article by John Moles, arguing that Dio himself purposely creates the conversion narrative in order to manipulate his self-presentation. In fact, most of what we know about Dio's life is drawn from his writings.[2]

Born around 40 CE into a wealthy and privileged family in Prusa, in the Roman province of Bithynia, Dio came from a background in which young elite men were expected to master reading, then literature and grammar, and finally rhetoric.[3] Within this educational model, philosophy played a peripheral role, though perhaps not as peripheral as once thought. But even if less central than rhetoric, the philosophical study could be incorporated into a conventional rhetorical education, and it played a central part in imperial-era *paideia* (understood as the educated culture drawn from Classical learning).[4] The true mark of the cultured man, the *pepaideumenos*, in the Greek-speaking centers of the Roman empire was rhetorical skill coupled with literary knowledge, and contemporary philosophical training would presuppose both of these, as reflected by Dio's writings.

In spite of the image of imperial Greek elites performing elaborate yet sterile display speeches,[5] Dio's corpus is markedly heterogeneous, encompassing both epideictic and practical orations delivered across the empire. It includes topics as wide-ranging as advice to cities, advice to the emperor,[6] the protection of his own political or economic interests, philosophical discourses with notably Stoic and Cynic inflections, literary criticism, and paradoxical themes. What is more, these subjects do not necessarily form discrete categories: philosophical ideas find their way into political orations, and speeches on philosophical themes tend to engage with questions that are also political, such as the legitimate use of power, the meaning of sovereignty, and the political advantages of self-control.[7]

Philosophical Rhetoric— a Contradiction?

Going as far back as Plato, philosophy and rhetoric have often been viewed as fundamentally antithetical,[8] and the Platonic dialogues are an inevitable reference point for any ancient writer addressing such matters. In particular, rhetoric is typically seen as the antithesis of Socratic dialectic, and, while this generalization is largely true, it does not quite give the full picture. Plato's dialogues occasionally leave open the possibility of a philosophical rhetoric, defined in the *Gorgias* as concern for the audience and a desire to make them better (502e–503a) as well as a willingness to displease them for their own good (521a), themes that play a large part in Dio's writings, as we will see. Furthermore, in the *Phaedrus*, the good orator must know the truth (262b-c, 273d), and Socrates's own speeches within the text (which he claims are better than that of the speechwriter Lysias) are identified as dialectic, thus assimilating good rhetoric and philosophy (265e–266d). However, we cannot be certain whether we should take this ideal rhetoric to be purely theoretical, since Socrates makes clear in both dialogues that such rhetoric could only come into being provided just the right speaker, if indeed it could exist at all.[9] *Gorgias* and *Phaedrus* will be discussed further in the remainder of this chapter, but for now it is enough to note that in Plato no one could be a good rhetorician who was not also a philosopher on the model of Socrates.

The Cynic and Stoic traditions can be traced ultimately back to the Socratic,[10] but there is one crucial difference between Socratic dialectic and Dio's ethical advice: Dio typically addresses himself to a crowd.[11] While early-imperial Platonists could give a more positive value to rhetoric by comparison with Plato himself,[12] it is clear that ambivalence persisted among Dio's near-contemporaries. We might compare the view traditionally attributed to the neo-Pythagorean holy man Apollonius of Tyana, a friend to Dio (at least according to Philostratus's *Life of Apollonius*). In *Epistles of Apollonius* 10,[13] addressed to Dio, the sage writes:

> Some people look for the reason why I have stopped speaking before large audiences. Well, here is the answer for those who care to know such a thing. Every argument is

incapable of helping unless it is singular and addressed to a single person. Therefore one who discourses in any other way presumably does so from love of reputation.[14]

Apollonius's insistence on one-on-one communication recalls both Socratic dialectic and a particular point in Plato's *Phaedrus*, when Socrates claims that the good orator must be able to identify the various kinds of soul and then use the particular speech that will be most convincing to each type of soul (271d–272a), a demand that is impossible to meet when speaking to a crowd. The barbed comment at the end of the letter also echoes the *Gorgias*, in which Socrates denies the existence of any orator who sought the public good rather than his own advancement (503b). Given that Dio is the letter's addressee, Apollonius's claim about the base motivations of public speakers seems an implied critique of his friend.

While *Epistles* 10 does not deny that Dio is a philosopher, Philostratus's *Life of Apollonius* raises questions about the validity of combining philosophy and rhetoric: "Dio however had a philosophy that Apollonius thought too rhetorical (ῥητορικωτέρα) and too directed toward giving pleasure.... Often in his letters to Dio he criticizes this demagoguery" (*VA* 5.40).[15] One such letter is *Epistles* 9, which sets up a stark opposition between pleasure-giving and truth:

> Apollonius to Dio: Soothe with the pipe and the lyre, not with language (λόγῳ), for the former are instruments of pleasure, and the art of playing them is called music, where language finds truth. That is what you must practice, that is what you must speak, if truth is your reason for being a philosopher.

Here it is assumed that truth is something unwelcome to its listeners. Apollonius therefore sets up an equivalency between critical frankness, truth-speaking, and philosophy. By contrast, he depicts rhetoric as devoid of value and aimed only at the self-promotion of the speaker (as suggested by the conditional nature of the final statement in the letter).

One of the problems philosophical oratory faces is the close association between rhetoric and flattery or pandering, as suggested by the mention of pleasure in the passages just discussed. Dio tries to counter this suspicion in *Oration* 77/78, *On Envy*, asserting that the wise man is incorruptible and incapable of flattery, "being austere by nature and a friend of truth, making no secret of his thoughts... nor will he ever be warped through want or dishonor or change his own character, becoming a toady and cheat instead of noble and truthful" (33). The piece takes the form of a discussion between Dio and an interlocutor, purportedly before a large audience, thereby melding Platonic dialogue and rhetorical performance.[16] Similarly, the wise man who is the subject of much of the discourse combines these methods of reaching the public: he is described as trying to lead all men to virtue, "taking them aside privately one by one and also admonishing them in groups" (38). We are led to conclude not only that the same man can carry out Socratic dialectic and perform speeches before large audiences, but that each of these is a valid means of accomplishing the goals of philosophy. The wise man's way of speaking also blends rhetorical pleasure and (beneficial) philosophical pain: he tries to improve his interlocutors or listeners "partly by persuading and exhorting, partly by abusing and reproaching" (38).[17] This pedagogical combination of enticement and correction forms the model for Dio's self-presentation as a benefactor of mankind. It is called spending one's life "caring for human beings" (39). The participle that means "caring" here, κηδόμενος, is the same one used at *Gorgias* 503a to express the notion (a theoretical one, as it turns out) that an orator might have genuine concern for his audience's wellbeing. Whether or not Dio is directly responding to Plato in this passage, it is clear that his text proposes an alternative mode of philosophy, one that can more easily include rhetoric.

The Diatribe

Modern usage has identified a popular-philosophical harangue as a "diatribe," especially when given by a Stoic or Cynic philosopher.[18] But is diatribe a helpful category for discussing the works of Dio Chrysostom? Diatribe has a range of meanings in Dio's corpus including pastime or amusement (4.94, 9.3.1, 20.18, 32.45, 67.4), general way of life (33.48), lecture or lecture hall (12.26), theme (7.103), and discussion (1.9, 7.131, 60.10), but it is not a term Dio typically uses to express anything qualitative about his own rhetoric.[19] It may simply be the case that its ancient points of reference are too broad to be interesting at all. Yet identifying in Dio's works elements of "diatribe" (in its modern sense) helps us to contextualize him within a larger tradition of philosophical oratory, both in contrast to the Socratic dialectical ideal and as a possible instantiation of the good rhetoric hinted at in *Gorgias* and *Phaedrus*. Without a fully articulated concept of abrasive and moralizing public address, the closest equivalent in Dio's terms may be the famous Cynic *parrhēsia* ("frankness"). And, while "diatribe" does not describe any category of his speeches (even the philosophical ones, as they too have political and literary themes), it does fit the moralizing elements of Dio's speeches, and especially his bluntly critical tone in orations like the ones addressed to the Alexandrians and the Tarsians (*Orr.* 32–34).

While thinking in terms of "diatribe" can help us situate Dio against the background of other Cynics and Stoics, it is nevertheless important to note that he takes great care to set himself apart from other public speakers with their own claims to philosophy. He particularly criticizes them in the *Alexandrian Oration* as having failed to fulfill their duty of making the population accustomed to critical speech:

> And perhaps this situation is not of your making, but you will show whether it is or not if you bear with me today; the fault may lie rather at the door of those who wear the name of philosopher. For some among that company do not appear in public at all and prefer not to make the venture, possibly because they despair of being able to improve the masses; others exercise their voices in what we call lecture halls, having secured as hearers men who are in league with them and tractable. And as for the Cynics, as they are called, it is true that the city contains no small number of that

sect, and that, like any other thing, this too has had its crop—persons whose tenets, to be sure, comprise practically nothing spurious or ignoble, yet who must make a living—still these Cynics, posting themselves at street corners, in alleyways, and at temple gates, beg and play on the credulity of lads and sailors and crowds of that sort, stringing together rough jokes and much gossip and that talk that belongs to the marketplace. Accordingly they achieve no good at all, but rather the worst possible harm, for they accustom thoughtless people to deride philosophers in general, just as one might accustom boys to scorn their teachers, and, when they ought to knock the insolence out of their hearers, these Cynics merely increase it.

Those, however, who do come before you as men of culture either declaim speeches intended for display, and stupid ones to boot, or else chant verses of their own composition, as if they had detected in you a weakness for poetry. To be sure, if they themselves are really poets or orators, perhaps there is nothing so shocking in that, but if in the guise of philosophers they do these things with a view to their own profit and reputation, and not to improve you, that indeed is shocking. For it is as if a physician when visiting patients should disregard their treatment and their restoration to health, and should bring them flowers and courtesans and perfume. (32.8–10)

Taken as a whole, this passage is not so much about Dio's disdain for the coarse "street corner" Cynics (as is often the focus in scholarly discussion), but rather an illustration of the various ways in which philosophers can go wrong, both by avoiding public speaking and by speaking to the public in the wrong manner. The Cynics are particularly important, however, as rival claimants to the tradition of frank speech. Cynic philosophers are usually infamous for their bold *parrhēsia*,[20] but Dio here characterizes them by their use of empty and deleterious speech, such as deception, jests, and gossip. By contrast, he presents himself as addressing the Alexandrians (and humanity in general) with harsh yet beneficial frankness (11).

Speech as Medicine

The themes of medicine and the physician already appear in the long quote from *Oration* 32 above, in which philosophers who speak publicly with the aim of pleasing their listeners are compared to doctors who give their patients "flowers and courtesans and perfume" instead of what will make them healthier (10). The metaphor of medicine for philosophy is an important trope in earlier philosophy and among Dio's contemporaries.[21] In some of these other works, philosophical medicine takes the form of frank criticism, as it does in Dio. While many of these authors are writing in Greek, a passage from Seneca's *Epistles* reveals that the connection between frankness and philosophical healing also made its way into contemporary Latin writings: "Our words should aim not to please but to help.... Why do you tickle my ears? Why do you entertain me? There is other business at hand; I am to be cauterized, operated upon, or put on a diet. That is why you were summoned to treat me!" (75.5–7). However, it would be difficult to find another writer in which the metaphor is so prominent, well developed, and all-encompassing as it is in Dio, who uses it to express the role of the wise man in his relations with the ruler, the public, and himself.²²

In the conclusion of *Oration* 77/78, Dio compares a wise man to a doctor who uses the strongest medicine on those he loves because, the rhetor implies, he knows the treatment will ultimately do them the most good even if it hurts (43). Likewise:

> Toward oneself first of all, and also toward one's nearest and dearest, one must behave with fullest frankness (παρρησίας) and independence (ἐλευθερίας), showing no reluctance or yielding in one's words. For far worse than a corrupt and diseased body is a soul which is corrupt, not, I swear, because of salves or potions or some consuming poison, but rather because of ignorance and depravity and insolence, yes, and jealousy and grief and unnumbered desires. This disease and ailment is more grievous than that of Heracles and requires a far greater and more flaming cautery; and to this healing and release one must summon without demur father or son, kinsman or outsider, citizen or alien (45).

This passage sets up a fascinating chain of associations. Frankness is a kind of medicine, the characteristics of which are compared not to the gentle correctives of drugs and diet (a metaphor elaborated further in *Oration* 32) but to the severe solution of cautery. Cautery in turn is compared to Heracles' self-immolation, itself both a desperate remedy for intolerable pain and a means of transition to divinity. Thus frankness, it is implied, works by forcing the sufferer to confront his own ethical failings and thereby begin to transform himself into a superior being.

The medical metaphor of philosophy also appears prominently in orations that feature Diogenes of Sinope. Throughout Dio's works, Diogenes recurs as a figure for idealized Cynic *parrhēsia*, as well as a role model and potential alter-ego for the author. In *Oration* 4, *On Kingship*, for example, the Cynic directs his uncompromising frankness toward Alexander the Great, while elsewhere Diogenes offers his advice to a stranger as a doctor might offer unsolicited medical counsel (*Or.* 10.1). But it is in *Orations* 8 and 9 that he most explicitly takes up the role of frank-speaking physician of the soul.

In *Oration* 8, titled *On Virtue*, Diogenes, while exiled from Sinope, decides to make his home in Corinth, "for he observed that large numbers gathered at Corinth on account of the harbors and the prostitutes, and because the city was situated as it were at the crossroads of Greece." In doing so, he compares himself to a doctor setting up his practice where the patients are located: "Just as the good physician should go and offer his services where the sick are most numerous, so, said he, the man of wisdom should take up his abode where fools are thickest in order to convict them of their folly and reprove them" (5). However, Diogenes soon finds that people are more interested in taking care of their bodies than in curing their souls of vice. When he calls himself a dentist or an eye doctor or any other kind of specialist, people flock to him to take care of their physical problems:

> But when he declared that all who should follow his treatment would be relieved of folly, wickedness, and intemperance, not a man would listen to him or seek to be

cured by him . . . as though it were worse for a man to suffer from an enlarged spleen or a decayed tooth than from a soul that is foolish, ignorant, cowardly, rash, pleasure-loving, illiberal, irascible, unkind, and wicked, in fact utterly corrupt. (7–8)

Similarly, *Oration* 9, the *Isthmian Oration*, revolves around Diogenes' attempt to persuade spectators at the Isthmian games that such a pastime is silly and does not celebrate what is truly valuable. The purpose of Diogenes' frankness in this discourse is to humble those who are puffed up over something insignificant, an action that Dio compares to the art of medicine and characterizes as a service to humanity (9.21). As in *Oration* 8, Diogenes is a healer of sorts, but his self-appointed task as physician of the soul takes a somewhat secondary position; in both these speeches his desire to observe mankind is mentioned before his desire to improve humanity. Dio states that Diogenes goes to the Isthmian Games because "it was his custom at the great assemblies to make a study of the pursuits and ambitions of men" (8.6). Likewise, in the *Isthmian Oration* Dio assumes that the Cynic primarily attends the Isthmian games to observe human idiocy (9.1). Yet Diogenes' role as doctor also emerges in this discourse, in that he is said to reason that people will be easier to heal (εὐιατοτέρους) at such a festival because this is where they reveal themselves most, just as bodily ailments can best be treated when they show forth plainly (9.1–2).

Medicine and Politics

Notably, the medical metaphor is at its most elaborate in some of Dio's civic orations, where Dio seeks to correct his addressees' ethical failings in connection with their political problems.[23] From equating philosophical speech with medicine, it is only a small step to treating ethically oriented public speech as comparably medicinal. In fact, the orator Demosthenes (a frequent model for Dio in his civic orations) provides a precedent: in *On the Crown*, he compares a bad statesman to a bad doctor, implying that the good statesman practices a better form of "medicine" (243).[24] Yet, Dio's role is somewhat different from that of a classical Athenian politician, as he himself notes;[25] the growth of oligarchy and the subjection of Greek cities (even nominally free ones) to Roman rule meant that traveling public speakers were not under the same pressures to ingratiate themselves with the public. There may have been even less pressure for those like Dio who represented themselves as friendly with the emperor. Yet it is clearly important to Dio that he take a confrontational stance, on the model of Demosthenes, and remind his audience that he is different from other speakers who have come before them.

In contrast to the Diogenes orations, Dio speaks *in propria persona* to his contemporary Alexandrians and Tarsians in *Orations* 32–34, warning them of the pitfalls of their lack of self-control in a world where the Roman military can be used to impose discipline on an unruly city.[26] But, like his depictions of Diogenes, the role Dio fills is that of the frank speaker, who seeks to make his fellow men better while taking no heed for his own safety (a self-presentation that unmistakably evokes Socrates).[27]

In *Oration* 32, for example, Dio asks that the Alexandrians accept "frankness whose aim is your own welfare" (5). Likewise, in *Oration* 33, he questions whether the Tarsians can tolerate philosophy, or whether they will mistake it for "abuse and harm" (16). Repeatedly in the civic orations he points out that Classical Athens had institutions in place to safeguard frank criticism, but in the absence of these he offers himself as a substitute for the poet-critic (32.6–7; 33.9–13). Similarly, he criticizes contemporary philosophers for their failure to fill this critical role, but makes clear that he is willing to do so (32.20; 33.14–16, 23).

In the *Alexandrian Oration*, at the same time as he shames other philosophers who have given speeches in the city, he manages to glorify himself as that rare treasure, the true philosopher, without ever explicitly claiming to be one:

> To find a man who speaks his mind with frankness in plain terms and without guile, and neither for the sake of reputation nor for gain makes false pretensions, but out of goodwill and concern for his fellow men stands ready, if need be, to submit to ridicule and to the disorder and the uproar of the mob—to find such a man as that is not easy, but rather the good fortune of a very lucky city, so great is the dearth of noble, independent souls and such the abundance of toadies, mountebanks, and sophists (32.11).

In this passage it becomes clear that taking risks is an important aspect of the role of the frank speaker.[28] No matter how much or how little danger Dio actually faces in addressing criticism to the Alexandrians, he gains an advantage by presenting himself as a risk taker. Another notable feature of this quote is its emphasis on the goodwill of the speaker toward his listeners. Ultimately, this description of the noble rhetor seems aimed at coercing Dio's audience (including those listening in Alexandria, listening in repeat performances elsewhere, and/or reading a circulated text of the speech)[29] into feeling the appropriate level of gratitude for his words, which he even goes so far as to suggest are divinely sanctioned (12).

Dio's self-presentation as an altruistic frank speaker is closely connected with the doctor metaphors that appear throughout *Orations* 32–34.[30] He repeatedly contrasts bad doctors with his own role as physician of the soul. In the *Second Tarsian Oration*, Dio once again stresses the importance and difficulty of finding a good advisor (34.27–30), and compares this advisor to the physician: "For the physician who has investigated minutely the symptoms of his patient, so that nothing can escape him, is the one who is likely to administer the best treatment" (26). On the other hand, the men who are usually seen as appropriate to advise cities are actually just self-promoters and fame seekers: "it is with mouth agape for the clamor of the crowd, and not at all from sound judgment or understanding, that they speak" (31).

Likewise, in the *First Tarsian*, Dio excoriates rhetoricians who speak as a form of "spectacle or parade," comparing them with "so-called doctors" who perform "exhibitions" (ἐπιδείξεσι) instead of the beneficial tasks of a real doctor: prescribing, controlling diet, and surgery (33.6). Dio sets himself apart from these men, declaring that his task in speaking to the Tarsians is not to give pleasure, as is the implied purpose of a medical exhibition, but instead to give them truth (ἀληθείας), and he asks for their forbearance so long as he avoids using too much frankness toward them (7).[31] We can see from the *Second Tarsian* that this style of public speaking fits the ideal statesman, who is compared to a pilot, steering his ship without any concern for the applause of his passengers.[32] Rather:

> The counselor who is a good counselor and fit to be leader of a city should be prepared to withstand absolutely all those things which are considered difficult or vexatious, and especially the vilifications and the anger of the mob . . . and he should be wholly unaffected by such outbursts, and neither if they applaud him, should he on that account be elated, nor, if he feels he is being insulted, should he be depressed. (34.33)

By calling attention to his own frankness, Dio sets himself up as just such a statesman, having constructed the role so as to be in no way contradictory to his self-presentation as a philosopher.

Kind and Unkind Cuts

Dio sometimes expands his medical metaphors using the language of cutting and cautery, images which express the severity of the treatment he prescribes for the city. For example, he tells the Tarsians that "Physicians too . . . have to touch their patients' sore spots and even cut them as treatment, even though it causes pain. Likewise I will not stop talking until I cause you pain, but all the same my medicine is milder than your disease deserves" (33.44). In this passage, a straightforward comparison is drawn between frank speech and the most painful medical treatments.

By contrast, Dio's most elaborate discussion of different types of medicine complicates this schema: "there are two systems for the treatment of vice and its prevention, just as there are for maladies in general: the one may be likened to dieting and drugs, and the other resembles cautery and the knife." According to Dio the harsher remedies of surgery are the domain of "magistrates and laws and jurymen . . . whose business it is to remove growths that are abnormal and incurable" while the gentler medicine belongs to "men who have the power through persuasion (πειθοῦς) and reason (λόγου) to calm and soften the soul." It is implied (and will soon be stated) that these "saviors and guardians of all who can be saved" are philosophers, yet the mention of persuasion suggests that rhetorical skill is a crucial part of their ability to save (32.17–18).

Next, however, Dio adds a twist: while the magistrate or "prince" (ἡγεμόνος) should use his harsh methods gently, the philosopher should use his gentle methods more harshly! The reason for this stance is that punishment applied with too much severity is harmful, but in the hands of a philosopher "severity of speech is by nature salutary" for the prevention and early treatment of vice (18). Unfortunately, Dio laments, the public does not seem to appreciate what is good for it, and such frank speakers' services are repaid in "hatred, abuse, and reviling" (19). In this way, the philosopher's use of rhetoric resembles medicine (albeit a mild form) more than it resembles Lucretius's famous description of poetry as the "honey on the cup" that makes philosophy more palatable (Lucr. 1.936–950).

Taken together, these images recall a theme from Plato's *Gorgias*, in which philosophy is compared to medicine and Socrates himself to a doctor. Near the end of the dialogue, Socrates lays out two ways of ministering to the city: "struggling hard, like a doctor, with the Athenians to make them as good as possible" or "seeking to serve their wants and humor them at every turn" (521a). The path Socrates chooses is that of the doctor: "as the speeches that I make from time to time are not aimed at gratification, but at what is best instead of what is most pleasant... I shall be like a doctor tried by a jury of children on a charge brought by a cook" (521d–e).[33] Socrates expects that the children (standing in for the Athenian citizens) will dislike him because of his practice of "cutting and burning" them, as well as his prescriptions of bitter medicine and other unpleasant remedies (521e–522a).[34]

What is more, even though rhetoric is compared to false medicine in the *Gorgias* (464b–465c), Dio's manipulation of the medical metaphor to include rhetoric is already prefigured in Plato. In the *Phaedrus*, Socrates compares rhetoric to medicine, stating that the latter aims "to impart health and strength to the body by prescribing medicine and diet," while the former tries "by proper discourses and training to give the soul the desired belief and virtue" (270b).

Conclusion: The Politics of Virtue

Dio frequently claims that the ethics of a political actor have significant consequences for his political fortunes.[35] Philosophy is not a discrete sphere of activity for Dio (as it was not for Plato);[36] rather, it informs all aspects of life and imposes on the philosopher a duty to improve those around him. For this reason Dio suggests that the philosopher has an important role to play in the management of the city, by correcting the public and calling attention to their faults (which, not coincidentally, is just what he presents himself as doing in the civic orations).

When we turn to the *Second Tarsian Oration*, we can see how he envisions the civic role of a philosopher in the Roman empire. He chides the cities for getting into petty quarrels among themselves (comparing their lack of power to that of fellow slaves in a dispute over "glory and preeminence") (34.48–51). But, in keeping with contemporary Stoic attitudes, he does not present the philosopher in this world as someone divorced from civic concerns.[37] On the contrary, Dio provides an object lesson in the political wisdom of philosophers, by urging the Tarsians not to let themselves be motivated in their conduct toward other cities by "vanity and self-deception and empty, foolish pride" but rather to use "goodwill" and live up to their "reputation for superiority in virtue and kindliness" (47–48). When Dio calls upon the Tarsians to strive after virtue, he is therefore not suggesting that they withdraw from political life (a view he attributes to "many," who believe philosophers are harming the cities by causing a slackening of practical affairs) (52). Instead, we can see in his metaphor of tuning a stringed instrument an ideal of rebalancing the priorities of the city and incorporating more philosophic values into public life (52–53).

Ethical concerns take many forms in Dio's works, but even when he addresses ethics on a small scale, he emphasizes the larger effects of individual actions. For instance, in *Oration 77/78*, *On Envy*, the philosopher is, in Abraham Malherbe's words, "concerned with the virtue of individuals, yet takes special care to contrast antisocial vices with social virtues."[38] At other times, Dio stresses collective ethics, as in the *Alexandrian Oration*, where he returns to the medical metaphor in order to compare public vice to a plague, while that of an individual is more like an unremarkable illness (32.91–92). He notes, "all varieties of human weakness might be found anywhere at all, and drunkards, perverts, and woman-crazed wretches are present in every city; and yet not even that condition is disturbing or beyond endurance; but when the malady becomes prevalent and a common spectacle, then it becomes noteworthy and serious and a civic issue" (91).

While the *Second Tarsian* has generally been considered the more political of the two orations addressed to that city, the *First Tarsian* also acknowledges the political consequences of a city's ethics. This speech is ostensibly an attack on the widespread, mysterious (and apparently immoral) practice of "snorting" that is giving the city a bad reputation.[39] The text is somewhat unclear, but Dio seems to suggest that the Tarsians' behavior is affecting their relations with other cites (33.51), as is only natural, since "while this nasal affliction is wholly manifest, it is inevitable that everything else also must be a fit accompaniment for a condition such as that" (50). Thus any ethical failing on the part of the body of citizens affects (one might even say infects) their standing in the wider world.

Dio gives his most vivid picture of the impossibility of separating ethics from politics in the *Alexandrian Oration*, when he criticizes the citizens for their bad habit of getting too worked up at public performances and races. He argues that this activity can have dire consequences, giving as an example an embarrassing military defeat that he attributes to their childlike lack of seriousness in everyday life (32.72). He goes on to explain that such disasters are:

> the natural outcome of this disorderliness that rules your lives. For it is not possible that those who get so excited over trifles and things of no importance, those who behave so thoughtlessly and with such lack of self-control in these matters of daily life, should be temperate in other matters and competent to plan wisely regarding things of greater moment. For the frivolity of your conduct and your lack of reason do not permit you to call a halt at things of minor importance, and the folly of your misconduct knows no bounds, but instead goes right on to any length without

discrimination, and touches everything with equal recklessness. So do not think that a man is dealing with trifles when he speaks to you about your disorders in the theatre (73–74).

This passage reveals clearly what is at stake in a city's attention or inattention to its own collective ethics. The Alexandrians' childlike frivolity cannot be isolated to unimportant matters, but inevitably determines who they are and therefore their capacity for action as a city.

These texts also make clear what is at stake for Dio in his presentation of philosophy as a kind of medicine. In his role as a public speaker, he claims the ability to save the Greek cities of the Roman empire from themselves, both by offering political advice and by making the citizens better people. This improvement in turn makes them more capable of maintaining not just self-respect, but respect from other cities and the imperial authorities as well. At times he even goes so far as to hint that the Roman domination of Greek cities like Alexandria can be explained by their decadence. According to the holistic vision of ethics that Dio presents, the philosopher as doctor plays a hugely important civic role. By attacking ethical failings, he heals the soul and thereby heals the city.

Notes

1. Von Arnim (1898) even identifies a third period in which Dio disavowed Cynicism but engaged in both rhetoric and Stoic-tinged philosophy. However, it is now generally accepted that Dio's philosophy can best be characterized as eclectic, with prominent Cynic, Stoic, and Platonic elements (Berry (1983)). See also Brancacci (2000) on Platonic elements as mediated through the Cynics; Trapp (2000) on the influence of Plato; Reydams-Schils (2016) and (2017) on Stoic themes. On eclecticism among Dio's near-contemporaries, see also Dillon and Long (1988).
2. Moles (1978). For biographical studies, see Jones (1978); Bekker-Nielsen (2008) 119–146.
3. See Gunderson in this volume.
4. On rhetorical and philosophical education, see Marrou (1982) esp. 194–216, 284–291; Morgan (1998) esp. 190–239 (questioning the utter dominance of rhetoric at 193–196 and discussing the role of virtue in rhetorical training according to Quintilian at 226–239).
5. On the rhetorical culture known as the Second Sophistic, see Whitmarsh (2005) esp. 13–40.
6. Whether or not he actually delivered these speeches before the emperor; for an in-depth review of the evidence, see Whitmarsh (2001) 325–327.
7. Lauwers (2013) calls attention to the problem of drawing normative distinctions between sophistry and philosophy in the imperial era, proposing instead that we approach the two as distinct but interacting cultural subsystems within a larger system of privileged Greek *paideia* (hence the wildly varying connotations of the term "sophist" in contemporary texts).
8. For a history of the traditional antipathy between philosophy and rhetoric, see Lauwers (2015) 15–124.
9. In fact, the *Gorgias* is often read as demonstrating the impossibility of Socratic persuasion; see, e.g., Scott (1999); Woolf (2000); Klosko (2007); Moss (2007).
10. See Long (1996a); Long (1996b) 1–34.

11. While any real evidence for performance is scanty, Swain (2000) 5 notes the discourses' self-presentation as performances.
12. As demonstrated by Hadot (1984) 76–83, 88–100.
13. On the question of these letters' authenticity, see Penella (1979) 23–29.
14. All translations are adapted from the Loeb editions.
15. Cf. Philostratus's own characterization of Dio in *Lives of the Sophists* (and while several members of this family were literary men, these two works belong to the same author; see "Philostrati" in OCD⁴).
16. It is not clear whether this work was performed, and if so we do not know whether there would have been a real interlocutor on stage or whether Dio performed both parts. We might note, however, that by writing a dialogue for himself, he is playing both Socrates and Plato.
17. See also Dio's comparison of this man to the two Ajaxes spurring on their compatriots with a quote from *Iliad* 12.267: "with gentle words at times, at others harsh" (38). On philosophical pain, cf. Arr. *Epict. diss.* 3.23.30 for Epictetus's opinion: "the lecture-room of the philosopher is a hospital; you ought not to walk out of it in pleasure, but in pain!"
18. See van Geytenbeek (1963) 13; Schenkeveld (1997) 230–247; "Diatribe" in OCD⁴.
19. A possible exception is *Or.* 27, "A Discussion (*diatribē*) Concerning the Symposium," which dedicates much of its brief length to railing against various forms of human folly. However, Moles rightly cautions against attributing too much significance to ancient writers' use of "diatribe" as a title ("Diatribe" in OCD⁴) and it is important to remember that this work bears many similarities to others by Dio that are not titled "diatribe."
20. See, e.g., Luc. *Vit. auct.* 7–11.
21. See Moles (1983) 112n73; Luchner (2004) 126–170; Malherbe (2014) 124–129.
22. Besides the works of Dio discussed in this chapter, see also 13.18, 32; 17.2; 23.10–11; 27.7, 10; 48.13; 49.13. For the more general characterization of doctors in Dio's corpus, see 14.7–9, 13; 50.4. See, further, Billault (2002).
23. On Dio's civic speeches, see, further, Salmeri (2000); Bost-Pouderon (2006); Bost-Pouderon (2009); Grandjean (2009); Kasprzyk and Vendries (2012); Fields (2020) 106–141.
24. See also *Against Aristogeiton I* 95; *Third Olynthiac* 33, where the statesman is envisioned as making a prescription for the *dēmos* to enact on itself.
25. "Whenever you see someone who is unkempt and wears his garments closely wrapped about him and has no companions on his walks, a man who makes himself the first target for examination and reproof, do not expect from such a man any flattery or deception, or that clever and seductive language which is most in use in dealing with the masses and satraps and tyrants" (33.14).
26. See esp. 32.51–52, 69–71.
27. Socrates plays a significant part in the *Third Kingship Oration* (3.29–41) and models classical *parrhēsia* at, e.g., 33.9–13. Plato himself reportedly called Diogenes of Sinope "Socrates gone mad" (Diog. Laert. 6.54).
28. See, further, Foucault (2001) 15–17.
29. On the textual history of Dio's speeches, see Bost-Pouderon (2006) 1:44–45; Bekker-Nielsen (2008) 38–39, noting that "despite their 'documentary' appearance, the orations of Dion are literary works, composed or re-composed with a specific public in mind and intended to convey a very specific image of their author." Cf. Desideri (1991) 3916, arguing against reperformance of the civic speeches by contrast with Dio's speeches on kingship.
30. See also *Or.* 38.7, *To the Nicomedians*.

31. A Demosthenic strategy; see, e.g., *Third Olynthiac* 3, *Second Philippic* 31–32, *On the Chersonese* 32, *Third Philippic* 3.
32. The comparison of the statesman to a pilot is another venerable Platonic metaphor that often appears alongside comparisons to medicine.
33. Calling back to 462b–465e, where Socrates sets up a complicated comparison between the sciences of caring for the body and caring for the soul, and the imitation of these sciences by flattery. According to this model, medicine is counterpart to justice, and both of them have a worthless imitator: the former is mimicked by cookery and the latter by rhetoric. Ultimately, Socrates also equates philosophy to medicine (see, e.g., 475d, 478b) and thereby to justice, a subdivision of politics.
34. See also *Resp.* 425e–426a.
35. Besides the civic orations, this theme is especially common in the speeches on kingship (*Orr.* 1–4), which provide an alternative model of the relationship between politics and ethics, centered on the education of the ruler. Frankness directed toward the crown is also frequently set parallel to frankness toward the crowd; see, e.g., 32.26–28, 60.
36. See, e.g., *Resp.* 473c–d, 519c–520c; see also *Grg.* 521d, where Socrates claims to be one of few real practitioners of politics in contemporary Athens.
37. Reydams-Schils (2016) contextualizes Dio's public speeches against the background of Stoic views on political responsibility.
38. Malherbe (2014) 126.
39. On this puzzling oration, see Kim (2013) with further references.

References

Abbamonte, G., ed. (2009). *Discorsi alla prova*. (Naples).
Arruzza, C., and D. Nikulin, eds. (2016). *Philosophy and Political Power in Antiquity*. (Leiden).
Bekker-Nielsen, T. (2008). *Urban Life and Local Politics in Roman Bithynia: The Small World of Dion Chrysostomos*. (Aarhus).
Berry, E. (1983). "Dio Chrysostom the Moral Philosopher." *G&R* 30: 70–80.
Billault, A. (2002). "La médecine et la maladie dans les discours de Dion Chrysostôme," in Defosse, 453–465.
Bost-Pouderon, C. (2006). *Dion Chrysostome, trois discours aux villes*. (Salerno).
Bost-Pouderon, C. (2009). "Entre prédication morale, parénèse et politique: Les *Discours* 31–34 de Dion Chrysostome (ou: La subversion des genres)," in van Mal-Maeder et al., 225–256.
Brancacci, A. (2000). "Dio, Socrates, and Cynicism," in Swain, 240–260.
Branham R. B., and M.-O. Goulet-Cazé, eds. (1996). *The Cynics: The Cynic Movement in Antiquity and Its Legacy*. (Berkeley).
Defosse, P., ed. (2002). *Hommages à Carl Deroux 2*. (Brussels).
Desideri, P. (1991). "Tipologia e varietà di funzione comunicativa degli scritti dionei." *ANRW* II 33(5): 3903–3959.
Dillon, J. M., and A. A. Long, eds. (1988). *The Question of "Eclecticism": Studies in Later Greek Philosophy*. (Berkeley).
Fields, D. (2020). *Frankness, Greek Culture, and the Roman Empire*. (London/New York).
Foucault, M. (2001). *Fearless Speech*. J. Pearson, ed. (Los Angeles).
Grandjean, T. (2009). "Le blâme des cités chez Apollonios de Tyane et chez Dion de Pruse," in Abbamonte, 139–187.

Hadot, I. (1984). *Arts libéraux et philosophie dans la pensée antique: Contribution à l'histoire de l'éducation et de la culture dans l'Antiquité*. (Paris).
Jones, C. P. (1978). *The Roman World of Dio Chrysostom*. (Cambridge, Mass.).
Kasprzyk, D., and C. Vendries (2012). *Spectacles et désordre à Alexandrie: Dion de Pruse, Discours aux Alexandrins*. (Rennes).
Kim, L. (2013). "Figures of Silence in Dio Chrysostom's *First Tarsian Oration* (Or. 33). Aposiopesis, *Paraleipsis*, and *Huposiôpêsis*." *G&R* 60: 32–49.
Klosko, G. (2007). *The Development of Plato's Political Theory*. 2nd ed. (Oxford).
Lauwers, J. (2013). "Systems of Sophistry and Philosophy: The Case of the Second Sophistic." *HSCPh* 107: 331–363.
Lauwers, J. (2015). *Philosophy, Rhetoric, and Sophistry in the High Roman Empire: Maximus of Tyre and Twelve Other Intellectuals*. (Leiden).
Long, A. A. (1996a) "Diogenes, Crates, and Hellenistic Ethics," in Branham and Goulet-Cazé, 28–46.
Long, A. A. (1996b) *Stoic Studies*. (Cambridge).
Luchner, K. (2004). *Philiatroi: Studien zum Thema der Krankheit in der griechischen Literatur der Kaiserzeit*. (Göttingen).
Malherbe, A. J. (2014). *Light from the Gentiles: Hellenistic Philosophy and Early Christianity*. C. R. Holladay et al., eds. (Leiden).
Marrou, H. I. (1982). *A History of Education in Antiquity*. G. Lamb, tr. (Madison, Wis.).
Moles, J. (1978). "The Career and Conversion of Dio Chrysostom," *JHS* 98: 79–100.
Moles, J. (1983). "'*Honestius Quam Ambitiosius*'? An Exploration of the Cynic's Attitude to Moral Corruption in His Fellow Men," *JHS* 103: 103–123.
Morgan, T. (1998). *Literate Education in the Hellenistic and Roman Worlds*. (Cambridge).
Moss, J. (2007). "The Doctor and the Pastry Chef: Pleasure and Persuasion in Plato's *Gorgias*." *Ancient Philosophy* 27: 229–249.
Penella, R. J. (1979). *The Letters of Apollonius of Tyana*. (Leiden).
Porter, S., ed. (1997). *Handbook of Classical Rhetoric in the Hellenistic Period, 330 B.C.–A.D. 400*. (Leiden).
Reydams-Schils, G. (2016). "Dio of Prusa and the Roman Stoics on How to Speak the Truth to Oneself and to Power," in Arruzza and Nikulin, 134–147.
Reydams-Schils, G. (2017). "The Stoics," in Richter and Johnson, 527–537.
Richter, D. S., and W. A. Johnson, eds. (2017). *The Oxford Handbook of the Second Sophistic*. (New York).
Salmeri, G. (2000). "Dio, Rome, and the Civic Life of Asia Minor," in Swain, 53–92.
Schenkeveld, D. M. (1997). "Philosophical Prose," in Porter, 195–264.
Scott, D. (1999). "Platonic Pessimism and Moral Education." *Oxford Studies in Ancient Philosophy* 17: 15–36.
Swain, S., ed. (2000). *Dio Chrysostom: Politics, Letters, and Philosophy*. (Oxford).
Trapp, M. B. (2000). "Plato in Dio," in Swain, 213–239.
van Geytenbeek, A. C. (1963). *Musonius Rufus and Greek Diatribe*. B. L. Hijmans, tr. (Assen).
van Mal-Maeder, D., A. Burnier, and L. Núñez, eds. (2009). *Jeux de voix*. (Bern).
von Arnim, H. (1898). *Leben und Werke des Dio von Prusa*. (Berlin).
Whitmarsh, T. (2001). *Greek Literature and the Roman Empire: The Politics of Imitation*. (Oxford).
Whitmarsh, T. (2005). *The Second Sophistic*. (Oxford).
Woolf, R. (2000). "Callicles and Socrates: Psychic (Dis)harmony in the *Gorgias*." *Oxford Studies in Ancient Philosophy* 18: 1–40.

CHAPTER 15

CONSOLATION

JAMES KER

"They amused, they taught, they consoled, above all they consoled."[1] Momigliano was thinking of the comforts that the first-century CE philosophers could give to the Roman elite under the worst of the Julio-Claudian and Flavian emperors—the period from which Pliny the Younger sought to differentiate the era of Trajan when he observed that during the latter "no one was in need of consolation" (*nemo consolandus fuit*, Pan. 69.1). Not only were Romans of that era banished, executed, or forced to commit suicide: collectively they lacked the political liberty that had characterized the Republic. But Momigliano's words also draw attention to the more basic fact that philosophers at Rome were visible. His emphasis on consolation as conspicuous among their activities might be argued for the Roman world more generally. The focus of Momigliano's essay is Seneca, but Seneca was not the first or the last Roman writer to craft consolations, and the survival of consolations by both major and minor authors, as well as a theoretical discussion in Cicero's *Tusculan Disputations* 3 and more oblique allusions or parodies in other literature, reveal consolation's dynamic role in Roman culture.

TRADITIONS, METHODS, AGENDAS

Philosophers were not the only ones in the ancient world who consoled. Quintilian's praise of Homer's "consolations" (*Inst.* 10.1.47) is somewhat anachronistic, yet already in Achilles' exchange with Priam in *Iliad* 24 (lines 517–551) we find several of the points that would become central to later definitions of the "speech of consolation" (*paramuthêtikos logos*). A recent study of Athenian tragedy shows adviser-figures adopting multiple consolatory strategies and terminology—even if, in the end, tragedy emerges as "a genre that engages with consolation with the express purpose of testing whether it can work at all."[2] Any of the modern schemas listing consolation's main components (arguments, examples, comforting thoughts = *rationes/praecepta, exempla, solacia*), its specific lines of argument (everyone dies; mourning benefits neither you nor the deceased; time heals, but reason heals faster), or more specific strategies that a consoler might adopt (appealing to the mourner's prior resilience or his or her public responsibilities; portraying death as a liberation from life's woes or as a path to immortality either in fact or in the memory of posterity; pointing the mourner toward a particular person as a substitute or toward literature and learning as a comfort; etc.) can be saturated with examples taken from prephilosophical literature.[3] Earlier Greek tradition supplied many of the examples that were commonplace in later consolation, such as the anecdote in which Anaxagoras responds to his son's death by saying, "I knew I had fathered a mortal child" (e.g., Cic. *Tusc.* 3.30, 3.58), a passage from Euripides in which Theseus recalls the advice of a certain wise man to practice imagining the worst misfortunes in advance so as not to be caught unawares (fr. 964 Nauck, e.g., cited by Cic. *Tusc.* 3.29),[4] or the lines from Aeschylus's *Prometheus Bound* drawing an analogy between medicine for the body and words for healing the soul and emphasizing the need for careful timing (*PV* 377–380; cited by Cic. *Tusc.* 3.76). And throughout antiquity, alongside the history of philosophy, we catch many glimpses of broader consolatory social practices, including the funeral speech (*epitaphios logos/laudatio funebris*), gifts of food for mourners, epitaphs that address survivors, and tombs and monuments together with their various commemorative functions.[5]

For any ancient consoler, then, philosophy would never quite be coextensive with consolation, and we find philosophy's place and role being characterized in a variety of ways. When the rhetorician Menander, in his chapter on the speech of consolation, describes how it can be useful "to philosophize" (*philosophêsai*), he means reminding the addressee "about the human condition in general" (2.9). Scholars also view ancient philosophers as having "elaborated and organized the clichés of consolation" and/or as taking the toughest line.[6] Ancient consolatory writers are often found using philosophy's dry or seemingly inhumane doctrines as a foil: Galen points out that it was his father who taught him the most about enduring misfortune, yet his father "did not spend time (*hômilêse*) with philosophers in his youth" (*On Freedom from Distress* 59). Juvenal, drawing a distinction between the precepts of philosophers given "in sacred books" (*sacris . . . libellis*) and what can be learned "from the school of life" (*vita . . . magistra*, 13.19–22), tempts his friend (who has been swindled) to derive comfort from the prospect that the swindler will get his comeuppance and that "vengeance is sweet" (line 180), even though the Stoic Chrysippus would frown on this (184). Writers drawing on philosophy, even if they do not deny that the wise person could respond without grief, are themselves sometimes critical of others who invoke this ideal, as when Seneca confides to Polybius (*De consolatione ad Polybium* (*Dial.* 11) 18.5):

> I know that there are certain men—their thinking is not so much courageous as reckless—who say that the wise person will not grieve. I don't think they have ever encountered such a situation, otherwise fortune would have shaken their arrogant wisdom out of them and forced them against their will to admit the truth.

Seneca wants Polybius to understand that such ambitious philosophizing is at odds with the more humane ideal that lies between the insanity of excessive grief and the impiety of shedding no tears at all.

Consolation as we know it was emphatically a rhetorical project, and many of its salient themes and forms are systematically defined by rhetoricians.[7] In such accounts, consolation is remarkably adaptable: it is a separable discourse but is frequently embedded within a funeral speech or a speech of praise; it may address a public group, family, or individual; its style may be compressed or expansive; it was routinely adapted to suit the personality of the addressee as well as the circumstances of both the life and death of the departed, etc. Tailoring the discourse to the addressee is emphasized also by the rhetorically minded Cicero, who suggests that "just as in arguing cases we do not always use the same strategy . . . but adapt to the time, the nature of the situation, and the person, so in alleviating distress we must see what method of healing each can take" (*Tusc.* 3.79; cf. 3.76, Sen. *De consolatione ad Marciam* (hereafter *Marc.*) (*Dial.* 6) 6.2). When he writes about the diversifying of consolation to address "exile, destruction of one's country, enslavement, maiming, blindness—anything that might be called a 'calamity,'" he refers to these different discourses as *scholae*, a term that evokes rhetorical exercises (*Tusc.* 3.81).

Indeed, much of the innovation we encounter in ancient consolation is couched in terms of rhetorical challenges: being the consoler when you yourself are the one mourning (as in Cicero's *Consolation to Himself* on the death of his daughter Tullia; cf. *Att.* 12.14.3–4), finding the words to console when you are the one whose loss is being mourned (Seneca's *De consolatione ad Helviam* (hereafter *Helv.*) (*Dial.* 12), 1.3), or coming up with an original or cogent consolation when all the arguments are common knowledge and trite. Pliny the Younger challenges his friend, after another friend has died unexpectedly: "Bring me consolations, but not 'He was old, he was weak' (these I know!), but something new, something great, that I haven't heard or read before. For the ones that I've heard and read come straight to mind, but they are overcome by this great grief" (*Ep.* 1.12.13). This last challenge is beguiling if you are consoling someone who has previously played the role of consoler (Cicero, for example), where some version of "Physician, heal thyself" is applicable. In such cases the recipient sometimes appears unable to console himself because the grief is his own and therefore benefits from another's intervention, or sometimes seems to have immunized himself against any benefit (e.g., Cic. *Fam.* 4.5.1, 4.5.5).

In the rhetoricians' accounts these parameters of variation coexist with certain staple strategies for any consolatory discourse, such as the idea that by praising the deceased and yielding somewhat to the survivor's grief as justified, the speaker can get better traction (ps.-Dion. Hal. 281), and also the structural emphasis on the ending of a speech as the time to move toward consolation proper, in a more elevated style, and emphasizing that the soul of the deceased is immortal (283). If Seneca's typical movement in his longer consolations from precepts to examples to comforting thoughts can be taken as a standard consolatory structure (cf. *Marc.* (*Dial.* 6) 6.2; *Helv.* (*Dial.* 12) 19.1), it likely owes more to general rhetorical conceptions of the best way to craft any *monitio* than it does to philosophy as such.

Philosophical Goals

It is also clear that consolation was not necessarily, or not exclusively, about finding a complete solution to grief. A consoler may strive to have the ending of the consolation itself facilitate the ending of the addressee's grief, or at least to anticipate the remedying of grief by reason rather than by time the healer (Cic. *Fam.* 5.16.6; Sen. *Ep.* 63.12). Yet we encounter consolers conceding that they may not "cure" (*sanare*) but merely "alleviate" grief (*levare*, Cic. *Fam.* 5.16.1); that the consolation may have changed a person's facial expression without changing his mind (Cic. *Att.* 12.14.3); that his own experience provides a major counterexample, as when Seneca confesses to have been overcome with grief at the death of his friend Serenus (*Ep.* 63.14); or simply that a given grief (*dolor*, sometimes personified, e.g., Sen. *Helv.* (*Dial.* 12) 2.1) is a mighty opponent.[8] These brushes with failure prompt us to notice what such consolations succeed at nevertheless. They promote specific narratives of personal and cultural identity for all the parties involved—the mourner, the deceased, and the consoler too. They negotiate the meaning of a death, they reestablish the rhythms of exchange among the living, they articulate social expectations based on collective and individual ethical criteria, they both demonstrate and advance an author's public ambitions, and so on.[9]

Within this overall discourse the two main areas of philosophical attention were, first, the ontological question of the nature of death and the afterlife and, second, the moral-psychological question of the analysis and treatment of grief.[10] Since death is the topic of James Warren's chapter in this volume, I limit myself to observing here that in consolatory texts we see philosophical consolers suspending their doctrinal affiliations in favor of an exhaustive set of disjunctions on all the things that death might be—consolation's oft-noted "eclectic" flavor[11]—as well as optimism that the survival of the soul in immortality and divinity is more likely. An influential model for this may be the pseudo-Platonic *Axiochus*, in which Socrates persuades the dying man to rejoice, since death is either annihilation or a happy survival, but asserts that the latter is in fact the case (specifically, an afterlife on the Plain of Truth; cf. Pl. *Phdr.* 248b). As for grief and how it is best overcome, when Cicero remarks that in his self-addressed *Consolation* he "combined pretty much every approach in a single consolation" (*Tusc.* 3.76), or when Seneca says that he "unrolled all the advices of the most illustrious authors, composed for stopping or alleviating grief" (*Helv.* (*Dial.* 12) 1.2), they are alluding to the array of different psychotherapeutic approaches to consolation that follow from the doctrines of individual schools or factions.

The early philosophical terrain can only be glimpsed through one or two surviving works (such as *Axiochus*) and testimonia (mention of consolations by Theophrastus, Epicurus, and Posidonius, among others).[12] But the most influential and admired among the early philosophical consolations was Crantor of Soli's *On Grief* (*Peri penthous*), a work of uncertain form that consoled one Hippocles on the death of a young son. In *Tusculan Disputations* 3,[13] Cicero, from a Stoic perspective, criticizes Crantor's work for its arguments concerning the naturalness and benefits of a moderate amount of grief (*metriopatheia*), but the work is formative for Cicero's thought; he observes elsewhere, "We have all read *On Grief* by Crantor, the Old Academic. The book is not long, but it is golden, and—as Panaetius instructs [Aelius] Tubero—it is to be learned by heart" (*Acad. pr.* 2.135). In his analysis of grief and its treatment, Crantor occupies a middle spot among the spectrum of analyses sketched out by Cicero (*Tusc.* 3.75–76):

> These are the duties of consolers: to remove distress altogether, or to settle it, or to dislodge it as much as possible, or to suppress it and prevent it from flowing very far, or to channel it to other things. For there are those who think the only duty of the consoler is [to show] that it is not an evil at all (the opinion of Cleanthes); others (as do the Peripatetics), that it is not a great evil; there are others who draw [mourners] away from evils to goods (as does Epicurus); there are those who think it sufficient to show that nothing unexpected has happened <as do the Cyrenaics> ... nothing evil.

Cicero mentions that in his *Consolation* he adopted the strategy (as some others had) of throwing every conceivable argument at grief. In the context of *Tusculan Disputations*, however, he has his speaker express a preference for the approach of Chrysippus, that "the main thing in consolation is to dislodge the opinion of the mourner that has him thinking he is discharging a right and necessary duty" (*Tusc.* 3.76), articulating this preference through criticism not only of the more moderate Crantor but also of the more ambitious Cleanthes, who with his ideal of pure Stoic freedom from emotion (*apatheia*) effectively "consoles the wise person, when the wise person does not need consolation" (3.77). The central and most significant concept in Cicero's discussion is that someone who grieves does so as the result of a belief or judgment, and that this belief includes both (1) that the loss they have experienced is a bad thing and (2) that grief is an appropriate response (3.61–67, 79). In siding with Chrysippus, Cicero settles for the more realistic goal of counteracting (2) rather than aiming for the austere axiology of (1). In the course of his discussion Cicero also criticizes the inefficacy of Epicurean diversion or distraction, which is only temporary (3.33–51; cf. Sen. *Helv.* (*Dial.* 12) 17). Cicero gives airtime to the premeditation of future evils supposedly elaborated by the Cyrenaics (3.28, 32, 34, 52) and also articulates the philosophical arguments that might account for the traditional notion of "time the healer": it is not time on its own that heals, but experience and thinking (3.53–54, 74–75). Cicero's survey provides ample illustration of Baltussen's observation that in the philosophers' commandeering of consolatory discourse we see an effort to "redefine or reconceptualize the event" of grief.[14]

Philosophers, however, used consolation for more than one purpose. The ostensible purpose of a given work was typically to help a given individual to overcome their present state of grief, even if this meant acceding to relatively modest goals. For a Stoic such as Seneca, this often meant not aspiring to the ideal of a Cleanthes (with one possible exception: *Ep.* 99) but rather conforming to a "human" middle ground that sometimes resembles Crantor's ideal of *metriopatheia* (see on *Ep.* 18.5 above),[15] sometimes Chrysippus's attack on misguided persistence in grief.[16] To the extent, though, that a philosophical consolation corresponded to a school's doctrine, it might offer a supplement for someone whose imperfect state of philosophical knowledge was not sufficient on its own to show them the right course of action. Seneca, at least, makes it clear that *consolatio*, along with a few other discursive modes such as exhortation, belongs to the category of precepts (*praecepta*) or forms of advice (*monitiones*) that are necessary for anyone, except the wise man, for knowing what to do in a particular situation (cf. *Ep.* 94.21, 34, 39, 49); the wise man alone can do this purely on the basis of foundational doctrines (*decreta*). As regards the mourning addressee, the consolation could advance a school's broader didactic goals—the mourner as student. And distress over death was the emotional problem par excellence, both an a fortiori showcase for the power of philosophy and a gateway to broader ethical topics.[17]

Beyond the addressee herself, a consolation's appearance in literary form also made this transaction both public and iterable as a method for instructing *others*. Cicero admits that he may not have consoled himself very much but that surely others could benefit (*Div.* 2.3), and Seneca openly acknowledges to the secondary reader that his *Consolation to Marcia* is a kind of case-study in how to argue a more specialized case, that of a woman's grief (*Marc.* (*Dial.* 6) 16.1).[18] It is also clear that philosophers writing on moral psychology, such as Chrysippus and Carneades, used the consolatory scenario, and literary commonplaces involving consolation, as a laboratory for the showcasing of specific finer distinctions.[19] In Seneca's *Moral Letters* 99 we apparently see a specific point of Stoic moral theory (that the wise person may shed tears in remembering the deceased) being worked out through a polemical contrast with a deceptively similar position of the Epicurean Metrodorus (*Ep.* 99.25).[20]

Most of the surviving written consolations from antiquity in both Latin and Greek come from the Roman world, which means that a full account of how ancient consolers went about their task would be a matter of looking at how consolation was adapted to address the specificity of grief and death in a variety of Roman literary, social, and political contexts. The corpus of Roman consolatory works has a permeable boundary, since defining a standard form or scope for consolation has proved an elusive task. Even if we focus on those texts that directly address a person's grief rather than deal with the topic of grief more generally (Scourfield terms the latter "metaconsolatory"),[21] we find works of varying length and genre—though epistolography is clearly the most prominent written mode of consolation by philosophers.[22] In the remainder of this survey I briefly sketch the corpus of pre-Christian Roman consolatory writing and identify some of its main concerns.

Cicero

From Cicero's correspondence we have the multiple letters he wrote to friends enduring either exile or death, such as two sent in 52 BCE to his exiled friends P. Sittius and T. Fadius (*Fam.* 5.17, 18) and one sent to Brutus in the summer of 43 following the suicide of Brutus's wife Porcia (*Ad Brut.* 17).[23] There we see the interweaving of Cicero's consoler role with his role as a purveyor of narratives about managing day-to-day public and private life, both others' and his own. This background proved challenging for Cicero's friends as they sought to offer consolation back to the consoler on the occasion of his own exile in 58–57. Cicero systematically repudiates a consolation from Atticus, remarking, for example, that "time not only does not alleviate this grief but actually increases it" (*Att.* 3.15.2).

This is even more the case after the death of his daughter Tullia in February of 45—when letters from Atticus (cf. *Att.* 12.14.3), Caesar (cf. *Att.* 13.20.1), Lucius Lucceius (*Fam.* 5.14), Servius Sulpicius Rufus (*Fam.* 4.5), and Brutus (cf. *Att.* 12.13.1, 12.14.4, 13.6.3) proved only partially effective, as Cicero explains to the writers themselves in his surviving responses (*Att.* 12.14.3 to Atticus; *Fam.* 5.15 to Lucceius; 4.6 to Sulpicius; *Ad Brut.* 17 to Brutus). He does tell Brutus that he was able to pull himself together somewhat, *not* so much because of the arguments that Brutus had made but because of Brutus's personal authority (*Ad Brut.* 17.1). Cicero's most energetic consoler was, of course, himself, in the *Consolation to Himself*, a work that evidently included a pageant of all the different approaches to consolation, examples from Roman history of parents who overcame the deaths of children, and a conclusion on Tullia's worthiness for apotheosis, paralleling the planned shrine to her that was never built.[24] The significance of the remark preserved elsewhere that in the work he "followed Crantor" has been questioned,[25] especially given his comments in *Tusculan Disputations* 3 on the inclusiveness of his approach. The theoretical discussion there is itself highly instructive not only because of its uniquely detailed presentation of Hellenistic philosophy but also for Cicero's retrospective mentions of the *Consolation* and, more generally, for the glimpses it offers of recent collective traumas in the Roman world, such as the experience of enslaved Greeks at Corinth or the psychology of Pompey's men fleeing the battle of Pharsalus (*Tusc.* 3.53, 66). Overall, Cicero's career as giver, recipient, and theorist of consolation has provided scholars with rich material to study everything from the processual "grief work" performed by his various writings in the letters, the *Consolatio*, and *Tusculan Disputations* to the adversarial social dynamics of the consolations received by Cicero from others and his successive responses.[26]

Seneca the Younger

Seneca's consolatory writings extend from his earliest to his latest works.[27] The first of these, *Consolation to Marcia*, dating from the era of Caligula and treating an elite woman's three-year grief over the death of her adult son Metilius, is comparable in many ways to the *Consolation to Helvia* and *Consolation to Polybius* from the period of Seneca's exile under Claudius (treating, respectively, Helvia's grief over her son Seneca's banishment and Polybius's grief over his brother's death). All three are oration-length prose treatments of grief which begin with an elaborate *captatio benvolentiae* and then proceed (with one or two variations) through a relatively clear structure of argument, example, and solace; all are sensitive to the personalities of their addressees, with copious attention to her or his family situation and public profile; all draw on examples both positive and negative from the political worlds of the Republic and early principate, which are often animated through embedded speeches by authoritative figures that include a dead father, an exiled senator, and a living emperor; and all have clear literary ambitions, both in their style and structure and in their rich intertextual engagement with earlier prose and poetry. Each of the works, however, is highly distinctive in its specific arguments and ambitions. *Consolation to Marcia* includes significant attention to Marcia's father Cremutius Cordus, both as an historian of the Roman Republic and as a martyr in the age of Tiberius. *Consolation to Helvia* and *Consolation to Polybius* are characterized by "displacements" (Elaine Fantham's term[28]), such as displacement of Seneca's own experience of exile onto his mother (since it is he himself, the exile, who ought to have been the addressee of the consolation) and displacement of Polybius's needs, as he mourns his deceased brother, by Seneca's own need of consolation by Claudius in the form of a recall from Corsica.

Seneca returns to consolation twice more, briefly, in *Moral Letters*. Letter 63 encourages Lucilius to recover from the death of a friend Flaccus; it is interesting for being the most extensive consolation we possess that deals with the death of someone not related to the addressee and for Seneca's own self-portrait of his relationship with his deceased friend Serenus; and despite its relative brevity, Manning has shown that the letter alludes to an array of different schools, including the Peripatetics, Epicureans, Stoics (specifically, Chrysippus), and Cyrenaics.[29] Letter 99, mentioned above, presents Lucilius with an embedded letter Seneca had sent to Marullus, a friend with some prior knowledge of philosophy, "in which," writes Seneca, "I have not followed my usual manner and did not think he should be dealt with gently, since he deserved not consolation (*solacio*) but castigation (*obiurgatione*)" (*Ep*. 99.1). Seneca takes issue with Marullus's excessive grief over the death of an infant son, belittling such a loss in contrast with the death of a friend, which he describes as "the greatest of all losses" (*damnorum omnium maximum*, *Ep*. 99.3).[30] Letter 99 has prompted different types of scholarly argument about Senecan consolation, ranging from doctrinal analysis to reflections on his use of satire.[31] Further, Seneca's prose consolations, like all of his philosophical writings, should not be read in isolation from the tragedies: there, consolation appears as a futile counter to the passions of the protagonist or sometimes as a perverse rationalizing device for acts of revenge.[32] The diversity of Seneca's consolatory oeuvre shows that Roman audiences witnessed consolation both at its most powerful, seeking to reintegrate the mourner into a normative social world, and at its most impotent or even nefarious.

LITERARY AND SUBLITERARY CONTEXTS

In Latin poetry we encounter a form of consolation that resists being a direct vehicle of philosophical instruction: the poetic consolation is less clearly victorious over lament.

The main texts include Horace's poem to Vergil on the death of Quintilius Varius (*C.* 1.28); Propertius's consolation on the death of Marcellus (d. 23 BCE) (3.18) and his posthumous apology of a deceased Cornelia taking comfort in her well-lived life (4.11); Ovid on the death of Tibullus, who will now join the immortal cohort of Roman poets (*Amores* 3.9), and his *Letters from the Black Sea* on the ineffectiveness of consolations sent to, or by, an exile (*Pont.* 1.3, 4.11); and Juvenal's dubious words of consolation to his swindled friend (Juv. 13). An especially interesting case is that of the elegiac *Consolation to Livia* (authorship and precise date uncertain), in which a speaker of equestrian rank takes it on himself to sympathize with, gently rebuke, and console the princeps' wife after the death of her son Drusus in 10 BCE.[33] The poem includes descriptions of Drusus's death in Germany, his funeral in Rome, and the grief shown by all ranks of Roman society, but concludes with a systematic series of consolations (lines 343–474), some voiced by the deceased Drusus in an imagined speech from beyond. The anonymous author both engages with earlier Augustan poetry and elaborates a context that we know from several different angles: Livia was known to have been consoled by Areus, a philosopher in the house of Augustus,[34] and Seneca in *Consolation to Marcia* reconstructs Areus's consolation and contrasts Livia with the inconsolable Octavia, grieving mother of Marcellus (*Marc.* (*Dial.* 6) 2.2–6.1).[35] Seneca's discussion was likely an inspiration for the poem. There is also Statius's series of consolations (or laments: their labeling has been understandably unstable throughout the tradition)[36] concerning first the deaths of friends' adopted slave-boys, a wife, and a father (*Silv.* 2.1, 2.6, 3.3, 5.1)[37] and then of his own father and adopted son (5.3, 5.5)—a carefully constructed, cumulative series of variations on a theme.

Returning to prose, we find consolation in numerous Roman writers in both Latin and Greek. Pliny the Younger's comments on consolation—he advises a friend that if he writes to their mutual friend grieving the death of his young daughter, he should "remember not to offer a consolation that berates and is too strong, but one soft and human" (*Ep.* 5.16.10; cf. 8.16.4)—are often quoted by scholars as evidence for a turn away from philosophical austerity.[38] Pliny himself innovates as a consoler, as when he explains how after the sickness and premature death of some of his slaves he consoled himself with two thoughts: that he has facilitated his slaves' manumission and that he has allowed them to make wills (*Ep.* 8.16.1–2). Quintilian adds a consolatory note to the preface of *An Orator's Education* 6: he relates the death of his wife and then the deaths of his two sons at ages 5 and 10, but persists in the present work because, as he says, "we must trust the most educated men, who thought the one and only consolation for adversity was literature" (*Inst.* 6 *praef.* 14).[39] A few consolations in Greek all dealing with the death of a young son or daughter present us with a chance to compare some quite different texts.[40] Plutarch's *Consolation to His Wife*, concerning the death of Plutarch's young daughter while he was away on a journey, offers a case-study in matrimonial intimacy, along with self-consolation, conducted before a public audience.[41] Dio Chrysostom's *Charidemus* combines the novelty of an embedded speech of eschatologically optimistic consolation written by the young Charidemus prior to his death with a final confession by Dio that he cannot console the grieving father and son. The *Consolation to Apollonius* (uncertainly ascribed to Plutarch) has often been held at arm's length by scholars due to its lengthy, catalog-like presentation of consolatory arguments. Yet it is arguably the fullest consolatory text and can throw much light on the tradition, not least because of its apparent status as a draft; in its appeal to a *paideia* centering on both Greek and Roman historical examples it espouses a characteristic program for Greek consolation in a Roman context.

A separate cluster of consolatory works in Greek addressing not death but exile offer a still more detailed case-study in theme and variation, and comparanda for Seneca's exile consolations. These include Musonius Rufus's *That Exile Is Not an Evil* and works *On Exile* (*De exilio/Peri phugês*) by Favorinus, Dio Chrysostom, and Plutarch. Galen's recently discovered *On Freedom from Distress* (*Peri alupêsias*) explains the reasoning by which he convinced himself not to be upset at the loss of all his books and medical supplies in the fire of Rome in 192 CE, which occurred while he was away in Campania. It provides an interesting comparison for the other works just mentioned, since Galen concludes by confessing that he thinks he would lack the courage of a Musonius in the face of actual exile (*On Freedom from Exile* 70–72b). Each of these authors finds a distinctive way to perform his self-consolation as a model for others to learn from, though a recurrent theme is the resort to *paideia*, including knowledge of both Greek and Roman examples, as a centering device for the Greek intellectual banished to a periphery of the Roman imperial world. As Tim Whitmarsh observes, exile was "appropriated by its victims . . . as a rhetorical resource through which individual agents could articulate their own philosophical status" and "it is preferable to see these consolations as public dramatizations of the therapeutic process"[42]—a comment that can be illustrated by Favorinus's successive vanquishing of the charges against exile as a series of opponents in "in the temple of Heracles, in the stadium of virtue" (6.3–4).[43]

A dozen letters in Greek on papyrus surviving from Roman Egypt offer a window on the consolatory habit among the local elite. Their many interesting features include their being written often from or to *several* persons, such as a family group; mentions of food accompanying the letter; a strikingly euphemistic approach to referring to death (usually just "the human thing," *to anthrôpinon*); and a focus on the impotence of the individual person in the face of certain realities: "A person can do nothing in the face of such things" (*ouden dunatai tis pros ta toiauta*).[44]

REDIRECTION

A few of the texts already mentioned, as well as some others, may also be categorized as parody, in the sense that consolation's therapeutic ambitions are undermined or repurposed for alternative literary ends.[45] Both epistolography and parody are at play in Ovid's elegiac letter to his friend Gallio over the death of his wife (*Pont.* 4.11), which twists several standard consolatory themes (reciprocation of a previous consolation; time the healer; the need for good timing; the substitution of the deceased with someone new) all to one end: emphasizing the spatial and temporal remoteness of Ovid's exile. Under the heading of parody we may also include Juvenal's *Satire* 13, where Keane observes that Juvenal's speaker uses consolation in a situation that does not necessarily warrant it and also activates a risk inherent to consolation, namely that it can be used as "a tool for competitive self-representation"; the result is "philosophical satire" in which the speaker takes "a philosophical proposition to unforeseen conclusions."[46] In Petronius's version of the Matron of Ephesus tale, the soldier's use of consolation to seduce the grieving matron reveals the potential for a consoler to benefit in a sleazy way from the mourner's reintegration into society, thereby possibly raising suspicions about the motives of *any* consoler—if not for sex or violence, then for power.[47] Petronius invites other observations about consolation, including that its therapeutic potential is an acquired taste: when the matron, because she has never heard a consolation before, is initially shocked by the soldier's arguments (e.g., that "all have the same exit, and the same abode" after death) and goes on to mutilate herself with renewed vigor, we are forced to recognize the violent and potentially alarming nature of what consolers say. Dio Cassius, in turn, exploits the potential of a specific consolatory situation to add to his own literary project when he portrays one Philiscus, who supposedly consoled Cicero on his exile.[48] The final sentences of Philiscus's lengthy speech are conspicuously prescient in their warning to Cicero that if he returns he may have his head cut off and displayed in the forum (Cass. Dio 38.29), so that the speech ironically foreshadows the broader dramatic arc of Dio's narrative. Dio also has Philiscus gesture toward a path not taken: the exiles whom Cicero should most admire are Xenophon and Thucydides, whose exiles were absorbed with the pursuit of historiography (Cass. Dio 38.27). The consoler, then, is plausibly also a self-reflexive mouthpiece for the historian Dio.

We find further evidence of consolation's flexibility when we consider how it was able to mesh with Romans' changing perspectives on the Roman state itself, whether this was embodied in the ideal of the Roman Republic or of the principate or the emperor himself. The Roman Republic, in its various permutations between flourishing and ruin, can occupy virtually every role in the consolatory scenario: as a reason for a consoler's not having written sooner; as an explanation for why the deceased is better off; as the real cause of someone's greater feelings of grief; as something to live for or something to which the mourner has obligations (if flourishing or in peril) or as failing to provide solace (if in ruins); or as immortalized in the afterlife and therefore a better place for the deceased to be. Then, during the principate, it is the principate's (or the emperor's) turn to occupy an array of different positions: Caesars are included among the examples of those who have suffered misfortune (demonstrating their essential humanity) or of those who overcame grief quickly so as to resume their public responsibilities; the deceased is proven to have lived a good life because of a career smiled upon by the emperor or because of tears the emperor himself shed at the funeral; the afterlife is modeled on the apotheosis of Julius Caesar; or Caesar himself *is* the misfortune that provokes grief (in Ovid's maneuver, *Pont.* 4.11.3). Galen even credits the violent reign of the emperor Commodus as having provided him with continual opportunities to premeditate future evils (*On Freedom from Distress* 54). When Pliny the Younger, however, wants to praise the rule of Trajan, the discourse comes full circle: Corellius Rufus dies while "the republic is flourishing" (*florente re publica*, *Ep.* 1.12.13), which makes his death all the more to be lamented.

Christian Consolation

In this context we can only gesture forward to the continuation of consolation in early Christian thought, such as in Jerome's *Letter* 60, addressed to the bishop Heliodorus, and then in humanistic thought, especially in the age of Petrarch.[49] Although these prolific later consolations retained, or worked within, many of the conventions and formulations of Roman consolation, their new ideological frameworks had radically different implications for the status of consolation. Of Christian consolation Scourfield observes the sea-change undergone for consolatory themes: "Christian belief in a single, benevolent and loving God, and in the resurrection, meant that Christian consolees did not face the same difficulty"; yet the same traditional tensions inherent in consolation could exist for a priest who was also someone's father or uncle.[50] McClure, in turn, notes new cultural roles for consolation in secular humanism, where the humanist's ability to render therapy to the mind through consolation represented a distinct sphere of authority situated somewhere between that of the doctor concerned with the body and that of the priest concerned with the soul, and consolation became an important method for exploring and regulating the emotions.[51]

Conclusion

In his casual mention of how philosophers of the first century "amused," "taught," and "consoled," Momigliano evidently sought to register the interpenetration of philosophical practice with ancient rhetoric's three functions of "entertaining, instructing, moving" (*delectare, docere, movere*). As we have seen, however, consolation all on its own could serve all these three functions at once, and more besides.

Notes

1. Momigliano (1969) 239. Recent scholarly approaches to consolation can be sampled in Baltussen (2013); see there especially the introductory chapter by Scourfield, as well as the earlier overview in Scourfield (1993). The philosophical argumentation of consolation is parsed in Johann (1968) and Kassel (1958), while inflections of philosophical argument in the context of Roman culture and society are studied in Reydams-Schils (2005).
2. Chong-Gossard (2013) 37.
3. See, especially, Lattimore (1942) 216n6, using the example of Euripides' *Alcestis*.

4. An instructive case regarding philosophy's attempts to locate a philosophic legacy in this tradition: Cicero takes Theseus to be an autobiographic portrait by Euripides, who learned such things through his contact with Anaxagoras (*Tusc.* 3.30), while Cicero's own translation of the passage introduces language (e.g., *meditabar*) that resonates with the Cyrenaics' premeditation of future evils. The Theseus fragment is central to Galen's discussion in *On Freedom from Distress*: he returns to it twice (52, 77).
5. On consolation and social practice, see in general Scourfield (2013).
6. Nisbet and Hubbard (1970) 280–281; quotation from 280.
7. See, e.g., Menander 2.9, 413–414 and ps.-Dionysius of Halicarnassus 277–283 in the edition of Russell and Wilson (1981).
8. The frequent failure of consolation is noted also by Baltussen (2013) xxi.
9. On the broader "ethical dimension" of ancient consolation, see Scourfield (2013) 5; on face-to-face contact and reintegration in both lament and consolation, Ferrari (2002); on "mediating narratives" of consolatory persuasion, Ker (2009) 91; on textualization of the consoling process, Wilcox (2006); on assertions of social or national identity, Wilson (1997); and on ambitions of publication, Wilson (2013) 112–116.
10. Cf. Scourfield (1993) 22.
11. See, e.g., Baltussen (2013) 90; Scourfield (1993) 22–23.
12. The tradition is sketched by Fitzgerald (2008) 9–10. For reconstruction of Crantor's arguments and sifting of the evidence between the two main sources (*Tusc.* and the *Consolation to Apollonius* ascribed to Plutarch), see Graver (2002) 187–194.
13. The most useful resource for Cicero's discussion in *Tusculan Disputations* 3 along with the earlier philosophical tradition is Graver (2002).
14. Baltussen (2013) xiv–xv.
15. As Manning (1974) 72–73 points out, Seneca is hostile toward *metriopatheia* in doctrinal terms (cf. *Ep.* 85.3–6), but often concedes to it (at least in consolatory contexts) in his activities as "both teacher and physician of souls" (73).
16. E.g., his critique of ostentatious mourning at *Ep.* 63.2, echoing more general mockery of mourning practices most fully realized by Lucian in *On Mourning*.
17. See, especially, Cic. *Tusc.* 3.81–82; on the gateway effect, Boys-Stones (2013).
18. Cf. Wilcox (2006), 75: "Seneca may have seen an additional rhetorical advantage in writing *to* women, but *for* a male audience."
19. See Graver (2002) 205.
20. The two positions are analyzed closely by Graver (2009).
21. Scourfield (2013) 20.
22. Greater nuance on genre-crossing between epistolography and oratory is given by Scourfield (2013) 12.
23. On Cicero's exile letters, see Claassen (1996) 35–39; Hutchinson (1998) 25–48. On the letter to Brutus, see Wilcox (2005b) 252–253.
24. See Baltussen (2013) 67–92, with outline on 75–76; also Kumaniecki (1969).
25. "*Crantorem sequor*," Plin. *HN praef.* 22; with Scourfield (1993) 20; (2013) 23n10.
26. See, respectively, Baltussen (2013) 83 and Wilcox (2005a), (2005b). On Cicero's consolation letters in general, see Hutchinson (1998) 49–77.
27. For the idea of Seneca's "consolatory career" see Wilson (2013) and Ker (2009) 87–89.
28. Fantham (2007).
29. Manning (1974) 77–79.

30. In a contrasting instance in Cicero (*Amic.* 9.6), Laelius applauds Cato's acceptance of the death of his grown son; see Konstan (2017) and in this volume.
31. See, e.g., Graver (2009), Manning (1974), Wilson (1997).
32. See Wilson (2013) 98–104; also Ker (2009) 96.
33. See the edition of Schoonhoven (1992) and studies by Jenkins (2009) and Schlegelmilch (2005).
34. On Areus, see Sedley (2003) 32.
35. On Seneca's version, see Shelton (1995) and Wilcox (2006).
36. Konstan (2018) 152 rightly notes that Statius gives significant license to lament in those moments where the poem envisages a funeral at the very graveside.
37. A useful opportunity to compare Statius's poems with sepulchral epitaph arises in the case of *Silv.* 2.1, where the same death is observed by Martial 6.28, 29.
38. Grollios (1956) 76; Nisbet and Hubbard (1970) 281.
39. Problems in the cultural and rhetorical projections of Quintilian's recovery are explored by Leigh (2004).
40. Such texts provoke the fascinating and complicated question of whether Roman attitudes to infant death were dismissive compared with "ours"; see esp. Bradley (1999) and Golden (1988).
41. See the text, commentary, and interpretive essays in Pomeroy (1999) and Baltussen (2009).
42. Whitmarsh (2001) 133–180, quotations from 135, 140.
43. For Favorinus, see the translation by Whitmarsh (2001) 302–324 and the edition and commentary of Barigazzi (1966).
44. On all these points, see the edition and commentary on these letters by Chapa (1998).
45. On humorous portrayals of consolation, see also Baltussen (2013) xxi.
46. Keane (2007) 33, 35. David Konstan also suggests to me the parallel of Catullus 5, lamenting the death of Lesbia's sparrow.
47. See Ker (2009) 111–112, with references.
48. See Claassen (1996) 41–42.
49. On Jerome and the Christian tradition in general see Scourfield (1993); also, on Augustine, Lössl (2013); and on the Christian tradition, Favez (1937). On the humanists, see McClure (1991).
50. Scourfield (1993) 23–33; quotation from 23. The latter point was made by Scourfield in a paper on Roman bereavement delivered at Temple University in September 2013.
51. McClure (1991) 1.

References

Baltussen, H. (2009). "Personal Grief and Public Mourning in Plutarch's *Consolation to His Wife.*" *AJPhil.* 130: 67–98.

Baltussen, H., ed. (2013). *Greek and Roman Consolations: Eight Studies of a Tradition and Its Afterlife.* (Swansea).

Barigazzi, A. (1966). *Favorino di Arelate, Opere: Introduzione, testo critico e commento.* (Florence).

Boys-Stones, G. (2013). "The *Consolatio ad Apollonium*: Therapy for the Dead," in Baltussen, 123–138.

Bradley, K. (1999). "Images of Childhood: The Evidence of Plutarch," in Pomeroy, 183–196.
Chapa, J. (1998). *Letters of Condolence in Greek Papyri*. (Florence).
Chong-Gossard, J. H. K. O. (2013). "Mourning and Consolation in Greek Tragedy: The Rejection of Comfort," in Baltussen 37–66.
Claassen, J.-M. (1996). "Dio's Cicero and the Consolatory Tradition." *PLLS* 9: 29–45.
Fantham, E. (2007). "Dialogues of Displacement: Seneca's Consolations to Helvia and Polybius," in J. F. Gaertner, ed., *Writing Exile: The Discourse of Displacement in Greco-Roman Antiquity and Beyond* (Leiden), 173–192.
Favez, C. (1937). *La consolation latine chrétienne*. (Paris).
Ferrari, N. (2002). "Le corps consolée : Étude de la consolation privée dans la Rome antique," in P. Moreau, ed., *Corps romains* (Grenoble), 139–160.
Fitzgerald, J. T., ed. (2008). *Passions and Moral Progress in Greco-Roman Thought* (New York).
Golden, M. (1988). "Did the Ancients Care When Their Children Died?" *G&R* 35: 152–163.
Graver, M. (2002). *Cicero on the Emotions: Tusculan Disputations 3 and 4, Translated and with Commentary*. (Chicago).
Graver, M. (2009). "The Weeping Wise: Stoic and Epicurean Consolations in Seneca's 99th Epistle," in T. Fögen, ed., *Tears in the Graeco-Roman World* (Berlin), 235–252.
Grollios, C. C. (1956). *Seneca's Ad Marciam: Tradition and Originality*. (Athens).
Hutchinson, G. O. (1998). *Cicero's Correspondence: A Literary Study*. (Oxford).
Jenkins, T. E. (2009). "Livia the *Princeps*: Gender and Ideology in the *Consolatio ad Liviam*." *Helios* 36: 1–25.
Johann, H.-T. (1968). *Trauer und Trost: Eine quellen- und strukturanalytische Untersuchung der philosophischen Trostschriften über den Tod*. (Munich).
Kassel, R. (1958). *Untersuchungen zur griechischen und römischen Konsolationsliteratur*. (Munich).
Keane, C. (2007). "Philosophy into Satire: The Program of Juvenal's Fifth Book." *AJPhil*. 128: 127–157.
Ker, J. (2009). *The Deaths of Seneca*. (New York).
Konstan, D. (2017). "Cicero's Two Loves." *Ciceroniana On Line* 1: 291–305. https://doi.org/10.13135/2532-5353/2502 (accessed: November 16, 2021).
Konstan, D. (2018). *In the Orbit of Love: Affection in Ancient Greece and Rome*. (New York).
Kumaniecki, K. (1969). "A propos de la '*Consolatio*' perdue de Cicéron." *Annales de la faculte des lettres et sciences humaines d'Aix* 46: 369–402.
Lattimore, R. (1942). *Themes in Greek and Latin Epitaphs*. (Urbana).
Leigh, M. (2004). "Quintilian on the Emotions (*Institutio Oratoria* 6 Preface and 1–2)." *JRS* 94: 122–140.
Lössl, J. (2013). "Continuity and Transformation of Ancient Consolation in Augustine of Hippo," in Baltussen, 153–176.
Manning, C. E. (1974). "The Consolatory Tradition and Seneca's Attitude to the Emotions." *G&R* 21: 71–81.
McClure, G. W. (1991). *Sorrow and Consolation in Italian Humanism*. (Princeton).
Momigliano, A. (1969). "Seneca between Political and Contemplative Life." *Quarto contributo*, 239–256.
Nisbet, R. G. M., and Hubbard, M. (1970). *A Commentary on Horace: Odes, Book 1*. (Oxford).
Pomeroy, S. B., ed. (1999). *Plutarch's Advice to the Bride and Groom and A Consolation to His Wife: English Translations, Commentary, Interpretive Essays, and Bibliography*. (New York).
Reydams-Schils, G. (2005). *The Roman Stoics: Self, Responsibility, and Affection*. (Chicago).

Russell, D. A., and N. G. Wilson (1981). *Menander Rhetor*. (Oxford).

Schlegelmilch, U. (2005). "Was ist und wovon handelt die *Consolatio ad Liviam*?" *WJA* 29: 151–184.

Schoonhoven, H. (1992). *The Pseudo-Ovidian Ad Liviam de Morte Drusi (Consolatio ad Liviam, Epicedium Drusi): A Critical Text with Introduction and Commentary* (Groningen).

Scourfield, D. H. (1993). *Consoling Heliodorus: A Commentary on Jerome Letter 60* (Oxford).

Scourfield, D. H. (2013). "Towards a Genre of Consolation," in Baltussen, 1–36.

Sedley, D. (2003). "The School, from Zeno to Arius Didymus," in B. Inwood, ed., *The Cambridge Companion to the Stoics* (Cambridge), 7–32.

Shelton, J.-A. (1995). "Persuasion and Paradigm in Seneca's *Consolatio ad Marciam* 1–6." *C&M* 46: 157–188.

Whitmarsh, T. (2001). *Greek Literature and the Roman Empire: The Politics of Imitation.* (Oxford).

Wilcox, A. (2005a). "Sympathetic Rivals: Consolation in Cicero's Letters." *American Journal of Philology* 26: 237–255.

Wilcox, A. (2005b). "Paternal Grief and the Public Eye: Cicero, *Ad Familiares* 4.6." *Phoenix* 59: 267–287.

Wilcox, A. (2006). "Exemplary Grief: Gender and Virtue in Seneca's Consolations to Women." *Helios* 33: 73–100.

Wilson, M. (1997). "Subjugation of Grief in Seneca's *Epistles*," in S. M. Braund and C. Gill (eds.), *The Passions in Roman Thought and Literature* (Cambridge), 48–67.

Wilson, M. (2013). "Seneca the Consoler? A New Reading of His Consolatory Writings," in Baltussen, 92–122.

CHAPTER 16

THE SHAPE OF THE TRADITION TO COME

Academic Arguments in Cicero

ORAZIO CAPPELLO

Introduction

From the youthful *De inventione* to the valedictory *De officiis*, Cicero's reflections on method are ubiquitous in the prefaces to his works and have offered an invaluable resource for scholars studying Cicero's intellectual development in terms of the social, political, and personal upheavals of his time.[1] Looking inward to the literary, scholastic, and institutional challenge of making philosophy Roman, these prefaces also develop Cicero's views of philosophy as a discipline with a dynamic tradition that is fundamentally invested in its history. Balancing the descriptive with the prescriptive orientation of his foundational enterprise, the *philosophica*'s introductions and dramatic frames illustrate how Cicero understands philosophy to operate as a practice and as a well-ordered system of knowledge. In reflecting on the treatment of philosophical method, its epistemological grounding and Academic pedigree, this contribution argues that Rome's self-avowed first philosophical author (the first that matters, anyway) actively configures this form of intellectual engagement, (re)creating philosophy as a field of study and of cultural production.

The emphasis on structure, built out of oppositions between ideas, schools, and agents; the codification of normative guidelines for philosophical debate; the definition of external and internal boundaries both to mark out who or what belongs and to classify and exhaust the range of possible positions within philosophy; the frequent, occasionally nostalgic, return to a pure "source"—the constellation of original, generative moments in which philosophy is established and set apart as a unique form of discourse, with its distinctive conditions, parameters, interests, and rules of engagement. Such are the mechanisms and tropes at work in Cicero's philosophical writing (including select letters), the objectives and strategies of which can be helpfully studied within the sociological framework of Pierre Bourdieu's theory of field, specifically as it applies to the production and reception of cultural objects.[2] Cicero's embattled efforts to make room for philosophy at Rome depend on a calculated engagement with the Academy that anticipates elements of Bourdieu's studies of nineteenth- and twentieth-century French literary, artistic, and academic life. Not least, the way in which Cicero carefully organizes and manages historic and continuing relations (read: conflicts) between theories, movements, and philosophers in such a way as to map this intellectual landscape around his Academy.[3]

The preface to the second book of the *Tusculan Disputations* stands out in Cicero's philosophical and rhetorical works for its ambition to define the scope of his philosophical project and its commitment to anchor that vision in the author's philosophical method: the Academic and Peripatetic practice "of arguing about every philosophical topic from opposing perspectives" (*de omnibus contrarias partes disserendi, Tusc.* 2.9).[4] The five books of disputations, written in 45 BCE and canonized as the culmination of Cicero's ethical inquiries at *De divinatione* 2.2, sustain an elaborate reflection on the place of philosophy at Rome, arguing for the discipline's location in the cultural history of Greece and Rome, its efficacy in tackling the anxieties of life, and Cicero's role as interpreter and conveyor of this intellectual practice.[5]

Between introducing his expository approach in the preface to the first book and his reflections on the value of philosophy as "medicine for the soul" (*medicina animi*) in the third book (*Tusc.* 1.1–8 and *Tusc.* 3.1–7), the second preface draws together strands of Cicero's polemic against detractors of Academic philosophy and of philosophizing in Latin to establish the importance of method—specifically Academic method—to the foundational enterprise of his philosophical works of the 40s BCE.

From the first paragraph of *Tusculans* book 2, the reader is confronted with a critique of philosophical amateurism. Echoing Crassus's advice at *De oratore* 3.85–87, Cicero quotes a tragedy of Ennius in which Achilles' son Neoptolemus imposes strict limits on the need for philosophy in life—limits Cicero is loath to accept. Cicero admits that even a "little bit" (*pauca*) of philosophy can be therapeutic for someone whose life, like Neoptolemus's, may be taken up by military or political pursuits, and he argues for the limited efficacy of this approach with reference to the previous book. Dispelling fear of death and freeing man from that fear is, according to Cicero, already an important milestone on the road to the "happy life" (*vita beata*), the central concern of the work (*Tusc.* 2.2; cf. *Tusc.*5 .1).

However, philosophy is not a discipline that lends itself to a piecemeal approach. Cicero indicates two features of the discipline that necessitate a comprehensive treatment: first, selectivity presupposes a broader knowledge of the material from which one makes a selection (*pauca nisi e multis eligi possunt*); second, treatment of a particular topic draws the thinker to work on the rest of the field "with the same keenness" (*eodem studio, Tusc.* 2.2). Philosophy is therefore presented as an integrated subject, each question stimulating the reader to further inquiry, and the effective pursuit of philosophy is predicated on a comprehensive approach.

The reader is an important figure in the preface. Cicero makes use of two foils to address and shape his potential audience: the *populus*, who attended his oratorical displays in Rome, and the Roman Epicureans, who preceded Cicero in composing and circulating philosophical works in Latin. On the one hand, Cicero's *philosophica* are not meant for the multitude, which he portrays as suspicious of and hostile toward this new discipline. Although his oratorical eloquence aimed to please and win over the populace, his present endeavor is an easy target for popular dislike at Rome, in large part also because it does not court this audience (*Tusc.* 2.3–4). This antagonism, coupled with the issue of philosophy's exclusivity, characterizes philosophy's audience as a new social aristocracy of thought whose elite detractors can rely on popular support.[6]

On the other hand, this exclusive social dimension clashes with the inclusivity that Cicero argues is the hallmark of the Socratic tradition. Because of its self-avowed disregard for stylistic and expository care, the existing philosophical literature in Latin, though not negligible (*sane multi libri*), is addressed only to adherents of the school that produced it. This closed circuit is characteristic of Epicurus and Metrodorus of Lampsacus, the Hellenistic Garden School and their Latin interpreters, whose treatises show no desire to broaden access to philosophy and which, accordingly, Cicero refuses to read. Epicurean exclusiveness stands in stark contrast to the universal appeal of Plato, other Socratics, and those who followed in their footsteps whom "everyone reads" (*legunt omnes*). Producing a pleasurable "reading experience" (*lectio*) that is attentive to rhetorical ornamentation sets up philosophy as an inclusive cultural practice not so much interested in transmitting a prepackaged set of beliefs as in opening dialogue between cultured individuals (*Tusc.* 2.7–8).

The cornerstone of this inclusivity is the Academic and Peripatetic "habit" (*consuetudo*) of arguing both sides of every question. This strategy offers Cicero not just a sound epistemological platform from which to launch his philosophical investigations but also an arena within which to train oratorical skills (*maxima dicendi exercitatio*). The relationship between these two aspects of Ciceronian methodology is further explored through its historical development. Aristotle is named as its "first employer" (*princeps usus est*), and Philo of Larissa, with whom Cicero studied, reportedly advanced the tradition by teaching oratorical and philosophical principles at different times (*Tusc.* 2.9). It is precisely the lineage of this practice, this opening of philosophy to rhetorical style and to a broader audience, that connects Plato to Philo and to the *Tusculans* themselves. The dramatic frame of Cicero's treatise is a continuation of that tradition, offering not only philosophical content in the form of epistemological caution but also practical training in oratory.

The dialogic spirit of the Academy underwrites Cicero's approach to his detractors and to the philosophical tradition as a whole. Even as he seals off philosophy against the resistance of the populace at large and against critics of the Academy, he defines his earlier writings, namely *Hortensius* and the *Academici Libri*, as refutations of those adversarial positions (*Tusc.* 2.4). By defining the spirit of his philosophy against the disapproval of others, Cicero situates his activity as a back-and-forth with critics. Furthermore, opposition is not only welcome but actively sought after as the symbol of a dynamic and distinguished tradition. Just as Greek philosophy in its heyday was characterized by debate, so "philosophy is born in Latin literature" (*philosophia nascatur Latinis quidem litteris*) through Cicero's pursuit of debate and his openness "to refute and be refuted" (*redargui refellique*, *Tusc.* 2.5; cf. *Luc.* 7 and *Nat. d.* 3.94)—coming under attack is often in Cicero's prefaces the first and clearest sign of "participation in the struggle," thereby establishing itself as a "criterion" of the treatise belonging "to the field of position-takings and its author to the field of positions."[7] Academic methodology, understood as a critical mind-set, writes the script for the Hellenic performance of philosophy and sets down the rules for staging *philosophia* at Rome. This both for Cicero's dramatic characters and for the first-person quarrels with contemporaries of the prefaces. By defining the operations of the tradition as self-evidently Academic, Cicero legitimates a(n orthodox) discursive form for the renewal of Greek philosophy in a Roman context.

Emphasis on the cooperative attitude required for the discipline to thrive is another prime characteristic of Ciceronian philosophy. To engage in debate requires a particular disposition, a disposition that is shaped by the caution of Academic skepticism toward dogma. Refutation should not, in fact, be a matter of personal hostility but of favoring the best argument, however provisional that approval may be. Academic debate is, in other words, collaborative, insulated from personal "obstinacy" (*pertinacia*) and "anger" (*iracundia*), and based on the sovereignty of "reason" (*ratio*, *Tusc.* 2.5). Nonetheless, a correct philosophical attitude depends neither on reason alone nor on a solipsistic "display of knowledge" (*ostentatio scientiae*, *Tusc.* 2.11). Like the eloquence commanding popular approval, dismissed by Cicero earlier in the preface, philosophy has an important practical dimension. It is a training ground for orators, as well as a cure, a therapy, for those listeners whose *natura* is well disposed toward it (*Tusc.* 2.11). Referring to his interlocutor in the *Tusculans*, the author points to the success of the treatise's first book, whose "discourse" (*oratio*) on death was absorbed by his pupil, as an example of what philosophy could and should achieve when delivered in the right way to the right audience.

Cicero merges rhetoric and philosophy under the aegis of his Academy not simply to give historical legitimacy to his pursuit but also, perhaps more importantly, to elevate Academic arguments to the status of paradigm for engagement with philosophy as a whole, as a practice that is inclusive, comprehensive, authorized by tradition, transformative, and conversant with Roman social and political institutions.

In Utramque Partem and *Contra Omnia Dissertationes*

The composite historical picture of the Academic *consuetudo* at the heart of the *Tusculans*'s second preface embraces two distinct yet complementary methodologies:

debating both sides of a question (*in utramque partem dissertatio*) and arguing against a given proposition (*contra omnia dissertatio*). The distinction between the two methods is implicitly drawn at *Tusc.* 2.9, where Cicero contrasts Aristotle's strategy of evaluating opposing arguments on a particular question with Philo's rhetorically inflected approach of arguing against a thesis (exemplified by the *Tusculans*). He then goes on to develop his reflections on their differences in the opening sections of *De fato*, written and circulated in 44 BCE.

From *De fato*, Cicero looks back to the two earlier works in this triptych on theological questions, *De natura deorum* and *De divinatione*, as examples of a "continuous discourse exploring both sides of the question" (*in utramque partem perpetua oratio*, *Fat.* 1; cf. *Div.* 2.3 on the series). His final work on the topic, a refutation of Stoic determinism that explores divination and the limits of propositional logic, takes a different form. Because of external constraints—a nonspecified accident or event (*casus*, *Fat.* 2)—Cicero explains that Hirtius, his interlocutor in the dialogue, asks him to adopt the disputational style of the *Tusculans*. Hirtius describes this style as "that Academic custom of arguing against a given proposition" (*hanc Academicorum contra propositum disputandi consuetudinem*, *Fat.* 4). The passage characterizes *contra omnia dissertatio* as quintessentially Academic, while also closely connected to oratory. The philosophical exposition Cicero embarks on is introduced by the reassurance that he has not abandoned "rhetorical training" (*oratorias exercitationes*, *Fat.* 3; cf. *Tusc.* 1.7), and by his remarks on the "alliance" (*societas*) between oratory and philosophy in the Academy.

Despite the ostensibly stark distinction between the methods emerging from the comparative description of works in the ongoing cycle, *De fato*'s preface outlines several parallels and correspondences. *Contra omnia* is defined by its conversational tenor and rhythm, triggered by an interlocutor who sets up a thesis for Cicero to argue against, and by its pedagogical dimension as an arena for oratorical improvement. However, differently from the continuous teacher–student interaction in the *Tusculans*, the extant fragments of *De fato* suggest that the back-and-forth between Hirtius and Cicero is somewhat limited. Hirtius recedes into the background after declaring that he will listen to Cicero "as if reading his writings" (*ut ea lego quae scripsisti*, *Fat.* 4). Over the surviving lines of the introductory paragraph, *in utramque dissertatio* is described as an exercise in speech-making in *oratio perpetua*. Cicero's emphasis in the brief description lays the epistemological groundwork for *in utramque*'s balanced structure and reader/audience orientation: Cicero explains its dialogic form as setting out two antagonistic speeches for the sole purpose of allowing the reader to select, or give his approval to (*probaretur*), the side of the argument "that appears most persuasive" (*maxime probabile videtur*, *Fat.* 1).[8] The performance, in Cicero's terse review, is aimed at supporting the reader's ability to make a philosophically informed choice. The structure and objectives of *contra omnia* and *in utramque* are differently articulated, though they are both sustained by a form of opposition between interlocutors, and both cultivate a strong link to rhetoric.

At two points in his earlier works Cicero had provided a more nuanced historical context for the development of these methodologies. In line with his approach to *in utramque* at *Fat.* 1 and to philosophizing in general at *Tusc.* 2.1, in the fifth book of *De finibus* a work completed in the summer of 45 BCE, Cicero has one of his protagonists, Piso, outline the scope of Aristotle's method. According to Piso, *in utramque* is geared toward investigating every aspect of philosophy by setting out all the arguments for and against a particular topic. The focus is on comprehensiveness and argumentative structure; yet Cicero is also keen to differentiate the Aristotelian origin of *in utramque* from Arcesilaus's method of "always speaking against every proposition" (*contra omnia semper* [. . .] *diceret, Fin.* 5.10). Cicero had anticipated this distinction in *De oratore* of the 50s BCE, affirming the genetic and structural differences between the Aristotelian "practice" (*mos*) of developing thorough and competing perspectives "on any question" (*de omnibus rebus*) and the Hellenistic—Arcesilaus's and Carneades's—Academy's predilection for "arguing against every thesis put to them" (*contra omne quod propositum sit disserere, De or.* 3.80).[9]

Alongside these passages where the two methods are contrasted, other prefaces sketch out and reflect on the characteristics of these approaches. Cicero's *philosophica* show an explicit and recurrent preoccupation with methodology, a marked interest both in explaining how the shape of the arguments offers an effective way of dealing with a particular topic and in defending the legitimacy of the expository mechanisms that accord with Cicero's place in the Academic tradition. Overall, Cicero leans on the parallels between the two: *in utramque* is singled out more often as an argumentative structure analogous to Roman rhetorical and judicial disputes, though both methodologies are celebrated as schooling for oratory; both are branches of a shared Socratic pedigree, their separate evolutionary trajectories securely kept within the Academy; a degree of personal investment on the part of the speaker is expected in both performances. However, *in utramque* generally expresses this as a commitment on the part of the philosopher to set out a position in which he believes. And *contra omnia* stages the conditions for one of the disputants to change his mind. In this context, *in utramque* unequivocally orchestrates a conflict between schools—an institutional opposition that is played down in *contra omnia*.

De fato offers only a brief account of *contra omnia dissertatio*. This possibly because of its fragmentary form, which cuts off Hirtius's formulation of a thesis and its initial development, or because of the reference to the *Tusculans* as its formal archetype, which dispenses with the need for further elaboration of its literary form.[10] Nonetheless, it is precisely the reference to the *Tusculans*, in particular to the first book's preface, that defines Cicero's understanding and use of this Academic practice. Hirtius's mention of "oratorical exercises" (*oratorias exercitationes*) and Cicero's discussion of "rhetorical studies" (*oratoria* [. . .] *studia, Fat.* 3) as part of an Academic philosophical curriculum directly echo the discussion of methodology that introduces the *Tusculans*.

Cicero does not use the expression *contra omnia* at *Tusc.* 1.7–8 to explain how he will proceed—a terminology that elsewhere acquires technical status. Instead, he refers to the form of the five books by the terms *exercitatio* ("rhetorical training"), *senilis declamatio* ("speechifying in retirement"; cf. *Tusc.* 2.26), *schola* ("lecture"), and *disputatio* ("debate"). Not only are these expressions drawn from the field of rhetoric and, in the case of *schola*, from Greek practice (*Tusc.* 3.81), but the method itself is historically situated at the crossroads of philosophy and rhetoric. Cicero models his work on the rhetorical inflection of Aristotle's approach to teaching, which, under the influence of the orator Isocrates, undertook "to join wisdom with eloquence" (*prudentiam cum eloquentia iungere*, *Tusc.* 1.7). Furthermore, this Peripatetic interdisciplinarity is shown to be entirely aligned with the spirit of Socratic philosophy, as Cicero qualifies his method in the *Tusculans* as "this old Socratic way of proceeding" (*haec* [. . .] *vetus Socratica ratio*, *Tusc.* 1.8).

The practice is described three times as inviting someone to put forward a thesis, qualified either as an opinion (*quid sibi videretur*) or as a topic of interest (*de quo quis audire vellet*), which cues Cicero's discourse. Additionally, the *Tusculans*'s first preface anticipates the pedagogical orientation and rhetorical origin of *contra omnia dissertatio* of *De fato*. However, Cicero extends the pedigree of this methodology to the Socratic philosophical *ratio*, as well as to the Aristotelian integration of rhetoric and philosophy that emerged as a reaction to Isocrates's "fame" (*gloria*). This dual historical derivation mirrors the rhetorical and epistemological elements of *contra omnia* that *De fato* will keep separate (reserving for *in utramque* all references to epistemology). Socrates is brought in at the end of the passage to define the mode of "arguing against another's opinion" (*contra alterius opinionem disserendi*) as the cautious route to truth or to "what is closest to it" (*quid veri simillimum esset*, *Tusc.* 1.8). The term *opinio*, echoing the earlier expression *quid sibi videretur*, further refines what is at stake in this type of conversation: the personal involvement of the interlocutor, who stands behind his thesis. Subjective investment is, in the later work, associated with the outcome of *in utramque*, through which the audience is expected to select as probable or persuasive one of the two arguments (*Fat.* 1.).

Finally, the preface to the last book of the *Tusculans* echoes the methodological reflections of the first preface. The passage elaborates the historical lineage of this adversarial style of philosophy and emphasizes the epistemological foundations of the Socratic tradition and its therapeutic objective (*Tusc.* 5.11). Shortly after the so-called Hymn to Philosophy (*Tusc.* 5.5–6), Socrates is canonized as the figure who politicized philosophy as an institution (*Tusc.* 5.10) and delivered a "varied approach to philosophical debate" (*multiplex ratio disputandi*)—which Cicero claims to imitate in his work. Imitation of Socrates is not simply the repetition of a foundational gesture, or of a gesture that, as an echo of Carneades, situates Cicero within the Academic tradition. It is also a philosophical attitude supported by Socratic epistemology (presupposing the existence of truth toward an approximation of which the discussion leads, *simillimum veri*), and, as an innovation on the first preface, a therapeutic strategy oriented toward the interlocutor: concealing one's views in order to cure the other's *error* (*Tusc.* 5.11).

This disputational approach, firmly situated within the Academy (cf. *Tusc.* 3.54), is adopted throughout the *Tusculans*, where a thesis acts as a working title for each of the five parts, or *scholae*, against which Cicero argues (e.g., *Tusc.* 1.8; cf. *Div.* 2.2). Each book develops not through a balanced statement of opposing views, but through a series of interconnected approaches to the thesis: analysis of its terms, often including a division of the topic (e.g., death at *Tusc.* 1.18–25, emotions at 3.7–8 and pain at 3.24–27, anxiety at 4.9–28), the proposal of an antithesis (*Tusc.* 1.16; *Tusc.* 5.12) or rejection of the thesis (*Tusc.* 2.14; *Tusc.* 4.8), and the search for and collation of different philosophical arguments and citation of philosophical and historical authorities to refute or support a particular position. The search in book 1 for Greek and Roman *auctores* supporting the theory of the soul's immortality and of death as a good is emblematic—if not programmatic—of this structured approach (*Tusc.* 1.26–81). Each book of the *Tusculans* adopts and adapts philosophical arguments from the Stoa, the Garden School, the Academy, and the Lyceum for its persuasive ends. Doxographies are ubiquitous, to the point where Cicero declares philosophy to be nothing but "a collection of arguments" (*philosophia ex rationum collatione constet*, *Tusc.* 4.84), the work of compiling everything that is relevant to a particular issue (*Tusc.* 5.18).

Beyond the formal principles underlying the development of each *schola*, Cicero is concerned with the attitude of speaker and interlocutor. Although neither teacher nor student put forward or defend a set of tenets linked to a particular school, they are both personally invested in the arguments presented. Cicero often underlines his involvement in the discussion, pointing in book 1 to the need to convince oneself that the dead are not miserable in order to deal with grief more effectively (*Tusc.* 1.111) or to believe the proposition that the wise man is "happy" (*beatissimus*, *Tusc.* 5.34). Similarly, as noted in the reading of *Tusc.* 2.1–13, he insists that his audience must be well disposed to his arguments and offer no resistance (*animoque mihi opus est non repugnante*, *Tusc.* 2.15), coming to the debate with an attentive mindset (*intento opus est animo*, *Tusc.* 4.10). Both of these conditions the student accepts.[11] And the transformative and educative impact of the *scholae* can be appreciated from the dialogue itself. The auditor not only collaborates and accepts that certain theories have freed him from fear (*Tusc.* 1.10), but his ever-more sophisticated participation in the dialogue indicates his "exceptionally steep learning curve."[12]

The most extensive evaluation of *in utramque partem dissertatio* is found in the preface to *De finibus*'s second book. At the heart of a work that Cicero crowns as an exemplar of *in utramque* (*Div.* 2.2 and *Fin.* 3.3), *Fin.* 2.1–17 raises a number of questions about the author's philosophical method and his understanding of the tradition within which he operates.

As Cicero undertakes his refutation of Epicurean ethics, he rejects approaching the debate as a *schola* and situates that rejection at the heart of the Socratic project. Implicitly equating the birth of philosophy with the birth of critical methodology, Cicero tells the story of Socrates, the father of philosophy (*parens philosophiae*, *Fin.* 2.1), ridiculing the sophist Gorgias of Leontini for his use of the "scholastic" method of inviting the audience "to suggest a topic" (*poscere quaestionem*) and discoursing on it (*Fin.* 2.2). Although Cicero "never approved of this method in the slightest" (*magno opere umquam probavi*) and brands it as "shameless" (*impudens*) and "overconfident" (*audax*), he is forced to moderate his criticism because the custom was "thereafter" (*postea*) adopted by his Academy.

The balance between dismissal and acceptance of this practice, which he describes at *Fin.* 2.2 in terms identical to the *contra omnia dissertatio* discussed above, negotiates two of the speaker's objectives. Resistance to *schola* is a gesture of foundational importance in the Academy, marking its Socratic heritage in contraposition to both the sophistic tradition and to later Hellenistic philosophers (*ceteros* [. . .] *philosophos*). Arcesilaus's revival of the practice situates his Academy as direct successor to Socrates, and, consequently, Cicero's own remonstrance locates him in that tradition (*Fin.* 2.2). However, early on in the exchanges between Cicero and his interlocutor Torquatus on the topic of this book (Epicurean pleasure), Torquatus puts a stop to the question-and-answer format (*finem . . . interrogandi*) by expressing his aversion to what he describes as "tortuous dialectics" (*dialecticas captiones*) and steering Cicero to a compromise: to perform his critique of Epicureanism in a continuous speech (*oratio perpetua*), "expressed rhetorically" but in the "rhetoric of philosophers" (*dicamque* [. . .] *rhetorice; rhetorica philosophorum*, *Fin.* 2.17). The practice of expounding on a given topic must therefore be shown to have a role to play within the Academy.

Cicero focuses his reflections on the Socratic spirit of *in utramque*, the essence of which is the question and answer format of dialogue where the "sincerity" of the interlocutor is paramount.[13] Debating views actually held by the conversation partner is crucial, and Cicero underlines its importance in three successive stills from the history of the Academy: first, in the description of Socrates's method of eliciting *opinio* "through investigation and questioning" (*percontando atque interrogando*); second, in the account of Arcesilaus's practice of taking someone's opinion as a starting-point for debate and of giving the interlocutor the possibility of defending it (*Fin.* 2.2); and, finally, in his own satisfaction with the present debate in which Torquatus is taking up a position in favor of Epicurean ethics, not as a dialectician but as a supporter committed to its defense (*Fin.* 2.3).[14]

Critical to this need for sincerity is the back-and-forth of live conversation, where dialogue moves apace, testing each statement for coherence and accuracy, as well as the readiness of the interlocutor to concede or fight back on any given point. This approach stems the tide of oratory with all its rhetorical flotsam, while guaranteeing the relevance of each part of the argument (*Fin.* 2.3). Indifference and superfluity are the shibboleth of Ciceronian methodology.

Until Torquatus moves the discussion to a more treatise-like exchange of speeches at *Fin.* 2.17, what follows is one of Cicero's most dialectical passages, where he exploits the opportunity to practice his ideal philosophical style by bringing his interlocutor repeatedly face-to-face with contradictions inherent in his belief system (*Fin.* 2.9–17).[15] The significance of the transition lies partly in the epistemological framework of *De finibus*. This is a work that expressly "aims for the truth, rather than the refutation of the opponent" (*verum invenire*, not *aliquem convincere*, *Fin.* 1.13; *Fin.* 2.8) by exploring each philosophical school (contrast *Fin.* 5.80). The objective of the treatise finally overrides the methodological reservations and shapes the dialogue according to the principles of comprehensiveness and systematic exploration.

Furthermore, the logical puzzles (*captiones*, *Fin.* 2.17) into which Torquatus feared dialectic was dragging the conversation serve as foil for the development of Cicero's reflections on the relationship between oratory and dialectic. The Socratic injunction to be precise and to define the terms of the debate finds a Roman parallel in the framing of a legal claim through a *formula* that sets down the issue to be tried and that must be accepted by all parties before the *praetor* as a condition to initiate court proceedings (*Fin.* 2.3).[16] Yet Cicero distances his work from that institutional context when he undertakes to move away from the popular oratory of the courtrooms toward the subtle style of the philosophers. By comparing different oratorical contexts, the question of the permeable boundary between oratory and dialectic is shown to be of interest not just to Aristotle and Zeno, but also to belong *de iure* within a Roman context (*Fin.* 2.17).[17]

Such an assimilation situates Cicero's methodology between Greek dialectic and Roman forensic oratory. A practice, in other words, that is at one and the same time familiar to his reader's everyday experience of legal contests in the *forum*, and wholly alien as a performance staging foreign figures.[18] This method also delivers on the promise, made in the first preface (*Fin.* 1.6), to preserve systems of thought worth exploring and, thereby, to shape the readership into a jury charged with evaluating the tradition of Greek ethics. More generally, the display of balanced and exhaustive studies of philosophical questions, framed by epistemological caution as to the attainability of truth, is continuously—often implicitly—defined as a methodology conversant both with Academic tradition and the Roman courtroom. Time and again, Cicero's critical attitude is founded on appeals to the liberty to judge (*iudicium*, cf. *Luc.* 7–9; *Fin.* 1.6; *Nat. d.* 1.10; *Off.* 1.1) and, as in the preface to the second book of *De finibus* (cf. *Luc.* 146), on analogies to forensic or deliberative contexts.

This method is adopted in many of Cicero's later works, from the *Academica* to *De divinatione*, through *De finibus* and *De natura deorum*: all treatises which he openly identifies as examples of *in utramque partem dissertatio*. And there are clearly homologous traits to all these works. Their ambition is to be exhaustive, offering not just thorough investigations of philosophical issues but insights into their historical development (cf. *Fin.* 5.10; *Luc.* 124), and to be educative, providing readers with a comprehensive overview of the question and thus the tools to make a decision.[19] These works are not concerned with persuading the reader to discard a position or to accept a "directed conclusion."[20] Accordingly, *in utramque* dialogues often end without a clear-cut "winner," as in *De divinatione* or *Lucullus*, or with a surprise shift in views, notably Cicero's admission at the end of *De natura deorum* (3.95) that he found the Stoic view more persuasive than the Academic. Furthermore, speakers oppose each other's arguments, rather than cooperate in shaping a single argumentative direction (cf. *Fin.* 2.119 and 4.80), and no debaters ever change their minds or concede defeat (Cicero is not a speaker in *De natura deorum*). Finally, the Aristotelian (and Socratic) origin of this method, along with its frequent association with the skeptical theories and argumentative techniques of Hellenistic Academicians, locate the strategy within the philosophical, rather than oratorical, domain.[21]

At a general level, this investigative attitude can be seen structuring Cicero's thought and operating throughout his philosophical and rhetorical output. Ranging discrete philosophical—primarily Hellenistic—traditions in antagonizing counterpoints over particular questions is common currency in works such as *De fato*, where even the *contra omnia* approach operates as a debate between Stoics and Academics on determinism; and even in works of the 50s like *De republica* or *De oratore*, divergent perspectives voiced by Roman speakers are situated within a Greek tradition of scholastic disagreement. Against the background of this historical and dialogic inflection, Michelle Zerba has claimed that Cicero's philosophical works "constitute, collectively, a kind of high-level engagement in the activity of *in utramque partem*."[22]

THE EPISTEMOLOGICAL FOUNDATION

The overlapping pedigrees of *in utramque* and *contra omnia dissertationes* are written out and explored by Cicero in his *Academica*, where he reconnects them to a common foundation. Composed in the first half of 45 BCE and surviving in two fragmentary editions, the work is concerned with the Academic practice of philosophy. The two surviving fragments, the second book of the first edition (*Lucullus*) and the first book of the second (*Academici Libri*), debate issues of sense-perception and gnoseology, through an intimate and historically oriented engagement with the school to which Cicero declared his affiliation throughout his life: the skeptical Academy of Arcesilaus and Carneades.

As a defense of his philosophical position (*patrocinium*, cf. *Nat. d.* 1.11–12; *Tusc.* 2.4; *Div.* 2.1; *Off.* 2.8) and as a statement of methodology, the *Academica* is of key importance to Cicero's late cycle of works.[23] In this first and full account of (Academic) method in the cycle, Cicero discusses *in utramque* and *contra omnia* as born of the same skeptical heritage, with roots in Socratic (and pre-Socratic) doubt and in Plato's literary practice (*Ac.* 1.44–6). Arcesilaus's philosophy begins with epistemological uncertainty, a radical and corrosive doubt which questions even Socrates's claim to know nothing, leading him to "argue against everyone's views" (*contra omnium sententias disserens*). This attitude amounts to a general "suspension of assent" to mental and physical objects (*akatalēpsia* or *adsensus retentio*) arising from "the equal weight of opposing arguments" (*paria contrariis in partibus momenta rationum*, *Ac.* 1.45). Plato had already created a literary rendition of this *viva voce* performance in his writings, all of which argue about "many things on both sides" (*in utramque multa*) and affirm nothing (*nihil adfirmabatur* [. . .] *nihil certi dicitur*, *Ac.* 1.46).

The unifying foundation of Cicero's general method in philosophy is an epistemological skepticism whose remote source is Socrates and Plato, but which had been revived by Arcesilaus and Carneades, leaders of the so-called New Academy of the Hellenistic period.[24] Cicero defends this skepticism against the dogmatizing tendencies of Lucullus, in the volume that bears this character's name, and of Varro, in the first Academic Book. Both Cicero's antagonists voice the position of the crypto-Stoic Antiochus of Ascalon (*Luc.* 67 and 132), a first-century BCE Academic who rejected "New" Academic arguments against the validity of sense-perception as a stable and secure foundation for knowledge, and plotted a return to the "Old" Academy, a syncretism of early Academic and Peripatetic thought which was then developed and revised—"corrected" even, in Varro's choice expression—by Zeno, the founder of the Stoa (*Ac.* 1.17–42; the terminology of "Old" and "New" also seems to belong to Antiochus, see *Ac.* 1.13).[25]

Defending the views of his teacher Philo (*Fam.* 9.8.1; *Att.* 13.25.3) and those of Arcesilaus and Carneades (*Luc.* 12), Cicero attacks the shortcomings of Stoic empiricism and challenges this school's cast-iron confidence in the truth invested in acts of perception and philosophical speculation. Cicero advocates for a continued and sustained examination and critique of what we perceive to be or construe as true in order to ensure that all assent, however provisional and tentative, is rationally verified and consistent with the evidence available. The preface to the *Lucullus* sets up the dialogue by identifying key aspects of Ciceronian skepticism: like their detractors, Academics want "to discover truth" (*verum invenire*), but they find themselves inevitably hindered by the weakness of human judgment (*in iudiciis* [. . .] *infirmitas*) and by the inaccessibility of truth itself (*in ipsis rebus obscuritas*). Given these conditions making truth unattainable, they can only follow what comes closest to the truth (*ad id [verum] quam proxime accedat*) or what they find most persuasively like the truth (*probabilia multa habemus*). Cautious approval, furthermore, is the result of a process of inquiry (*studioque conquirimus, studium exquirendi, exquirere*), governed by the principle of *in utramque* (*Luc.* 7–9).

Cicero's speech in the *Lucullus* follows the dual path set down in the preface: first, he provides arguments against sense-perception, the reliability of reason and certainty in philosophical inquiry to sustain Arcesilaus's position that nothing can be known and that one should withhold assent in all things (*Luc.* 66–98). Later, he explores Carneades' theory that a provisional and tentative form of assent is rationally admissible (*probabile, pithanón*), allowing the individual to engage in practical and intellectual activity (*Luc.* 98–115). Woldemar Görler's division between the destructive Arcesilean and constructive Carneadean halves of the *Lucullus* captures the method and spirit of research that governs Ciceronian *philosophica*.[26] His writings either present and critique established views or define and follow the position he accepts as most persuasive. They all, however, respond to the call for continued investigation, which constitutes, according to Carlos Lévy, "the only true teaching of the *Lucullus*."[27] Furthermore, as Clara Auvray-Assayas has argued, this probabilistic attitude emphasizes the subjective involvement of the thinker who has to test propositions and perceptions in order to give or deny his approval.[28]

Method as Literary Strategy: The Birth of Roman Philosophy

While the *Academica* underwrites the key epistemological ingredients of *contra omnia* and of *in utramque*, it also defines other elements of these discursive styles in a bid to situate them in the cultural project of founding a Roman philosophy. The fragmentary work represents "something new and foundational"[29] not just for the originality of its form, or its defense of Ciceronian epistemology, but also because it shapes the philosophical tradition in such a way as to authorize Cicero's *philosophica* and legitimize its institution as a continuation of Greek philosophy. Cicero establishes his Academy as the school that both sets the boundaries for and dictates the rules of the game for philosophy at Rome. The gesture of appropriation is accomplished through the structured surveys of all philosophical branches, the portrayal of sects as offshoots of these branches—most clearly the strategy operates through the imitation of practice. And this Cicero achieves by focusing on argumentative method.

The first key principle is debate. Philosophy is a practice that originates from and develops in conversation between two individuals or schools arguing over specific questions, problems, or topics. Cicero's speech in the *Lucullus* identifies the birth and progress of Hellenistic epistemology as a set of related dialogues. The first involves Arcesilaus and Zeno, as they flesh out the terms of the debate (*Luc.* 76–77), and the second pits Carneades against Chrysippus (*Luc.* 98). Even before Academics and Stoics, as Varro notes, Socrates had turned philosophy to ordinary life with his "dialogues" (*sermones*, *Ac.* 1.15–16; see also *Ac.* 1.45; *Luc.* 15 and 74). These Socratic *sermones*—whether they concealed doctrines, as Varro and Lucullus maintain, or genuinely confessed ignorance—established philosophy as conversation.

Beyond the dramatic register that Cicero adopts to translate the live tradition of Athenian debate, he develops the notion of dialogue at a conceptual level as he interweaves ideas and positions from different schools into the fabric of a single argument or section. So, for example, as he sets out the fundamental points of the Academic argument against sense-perception, Cicero shows Lucullus that it can be parsed as a composite of Stoic and Epicurean axioms. He sets out the propositions as follows: (1) false impressions do exist; (2) false impressions cannot be apprehended; (3) when there is no difference between false and true impressions, it is not possible that some can be apprehended and not others; and, (4) there is no true impression originating from sense-perception that is not matched by another impression, which is indistinguishable from it and yet which cannot be apprehended. All schools, Cicero tells Lucullus (and the author shows his readers), agree on the second and third propositions. Epicurus, however, does not think false impressions exist, unlike Stoics and Academics. This focuses the quarrel between the two on the fourth clause, viz., the distinguishability of true and false impressions. Academics believe they are indistinguishable, hence perception has no stable foundation, while Stoics think otherwise (*Luc.* 83). As a response to Lucullus's earlier summary of the argument (*Luc.* 40–2), Cicero portrays the essentials of the Academic argument in terms of other schools' viewpoints, in a three-way contest involving Academy, Stoa, and Garden School.

The doxography that concludes the *Lucullus* provides another example of this conceptual dialogue, while also introducing the second principle of Ciceronian philosophy: historical research. As Alain Michel observes, in orienting his dialogues toward philosophy's past Cicero subjects the history of philosophy to laws similar to those governing Platonic dialogues, where the contours of each school take shape in contraposition to each other. The survey of disagreements among philosophers on physics, ethics, and logic (*Luc.* 116–146) does not merely display the divisions that mark the field, but actually demonstrates its unity: thinkers differ in conclusions and approaches, but they converge on the same philosophical questions.[30] In a narrowly sociological key, Cicero provides an objective outline of the field of philosophy, mapping all possible coordinates as all the positions agents within it have taken—and even, on occasion, positions that do not or have not had a taker but are, by the necessity of his logic, part and parcel of the overall network of differences and so theoretically available to be adopted.[31]

If Academic debate provides the ideal critical method to structure the history of philosophy as a dialogue between diverse positions on shared issues, debate between Academics in the *Academica* unifies the project of philosophy as a whole. The quarrel at the heart of both fragments concerns allegations of heterodoxy within the same school. Antiochus interprets Arcesilaus's skeptical turn as a deviation from Academic thought, identifying in Stoicism the true heir to Plato's tradition ("Two-Academy" theory, *Luc.* 13–15); Philo sees skepticism as a continuation of the Socratic and Platonic spirit, though he brings in certain "innovations" that moderate Academic doubt ("One-Academy" theory; *Luc.* 72–6; *Ac.* 1.13 and 1.46).[32] Presenting rival views on the history of a single school is primarily a way of identifying the Academy as a space within which a plurality of intellectual trends can coexist. Antiochus and Philo are both moving away from what is constructed as the orthodoxy of Arcesilaus and Carneades, both accuse each other of heresy, and both lay claim to the Academy by interpreting its history.

Furthermore, their disagreement is constructed by Cicero in such a way as to assimilate the broader Hellenistic tradition of epistemological debate. One of the puzzling aspects of the *Academica* is that both editions profess to reproduce the quarrel between Antiochus and Philo (*Ac.* 1.13–14 and *Luc.* 11), and yet they appear to sideline this individual antagonism in favor of a broader opposition between Stoics and Academics. Lucullus clearly indicates that he is not interested in Philo's heresy, but in Arcesilaus and Carneades, just before he launches into his description of the Stoic theory of knowledge (*Luc.* 13 and 19–42). Nor does Cicero ground his response in Philo's innovations, but, as discussed above, in Arcesilean and Carneadean dialectics. Similarly, Varro's Antiochian *correctio* theory culminates in Zeno's Stoicism, and Cicero seems to respond with reference to Arcesilaus and Carneades (*Ac.* 1.33–42 and 1.44–46). The *Academica* does not only account for two hundred years of epistemological argument, it compresses into the Academy the entire tradition of disagreement in two of its branches.[33] The dogmatic inflection of Stoicism and the skeptical bearing of the "New" Academy both coexist in Cicero's Academy through the debate between Philo and Antiochus. And, as Auvray-Assayas points out, Cicero keeps both.[34]

This assimilation also occurs at the biographical level. Cicero's first-century BCE Academics display an intellectual development that, in the variety of positions held and arguments deployed, plots the story of the Academy's history. Historians of philosophy like John Glucker and Charles Brittain, who have used the *Academica* as a source for Academic history, have argued that the work embraces discrete theoretical positions held by its protagonists at different times. In Brittain's study of Philo of Larissa, this scholarch is shown to hold three different views, each associated with a stage of Academic thought: his early adherence to the radical skepticism of Carneades as interpreted by his successor Clitomachus, an intermediate position developed by Metrodorus and himself, and finally the so-called Roman views of his later years.[35] Antiochus himself begins as a skeptic, moving further away from that version of the Academy until he integrates a Stoic perspective on knowledge and perception. Cicero never describes these trajectories directly, but allusions (e.g., *Luc.* 18 or 78) create a sense of historical depth in the work that emphasizes the variety and flexibility of Academic thinking. The Academy is thereby shaped into an ideal vehicle to unify the Greek philosophical project and enable its Roman successors to maneuver freely within it. Cicero himself, throughout his *corpus*, fashions an intellectual biography that links him to Phaedrus the Epicurean, the Stoic Diodotus, and both Antiochus and Philo (*Nat. d.* 1.6).

Finally, Cicero equates philosophical thinking with situating oneself in a tradition of interpretation. As discussed above, two versions of Academic history are correlated with two different epistemological positions. However, other Academics mark out their speculative identity through interpretations of important figures in their school, among whom Socrates and Carneades stand out. One of the key concerns of the *Academica* is, in fact, the development of different forms of skepticism: the *Lucullus* presents an extreme form of doubt, which leads to suspension of assent, alongside a moderate form, which allows for limited assent, or assent to persuasive impressions. As critics have debated since Pierre Couissin's classic 1929 article, the status of Carneades' *probabile* sets a challenge to its interpreters: did the Hellenistic Academician affirm and endorse the existence of this kind of persuasive impression, thus producing a kind of dogma, or did he only offer this theory to counter the Stoic critique that Academics would not otherwise be able to (rationally) engage with and act within the world?

The debate between dogmatic and dialectical interpretations of Carneades is not a modern issue.[36] The *Academica* identifies in Clitomachus a champion of the latter view, while Metrodorus and Philo support the former (*Luc.* 78 and 148). Cicero structures the history of the later Academy according to interpretations of Carneades, implicitly suggesting that Academic philosophizing after Carneades consists in positioning oneself as a dogmatic or skeptical interpreter of this inscrutable teacher (cf. *Fin.* 5.6).

Glucker suggests a very similar reading of Cicero's Academy in terms of Socrates and Plato.[37] For Varro and Lucullus, Socrates's confession of ignorance is ironic, a concealment strategy useful to his dialectic insofar as it is centered on freeing the other from his mistakes.[38] Varro also distinguishes him from Plato because of the latter's elaboration of an integrated and positive system of philosophy (*Luc.* 15; *Ac.* 1.16–17). For Cicero, Socrates sets an important precedent in the history of doubt with his claim that nothing can be known, and this realization, in turn, influences Plato's aporetic approach to the dialogue form (*Luc.* 74; *Ac.* 1.46). The Academic then develops his philosophical views partly by aligning himself with a particular interpretation of the founders of the school. In this way, Cicero introduces a hermeneutic element to a practice he has already characterized as intrinsically dialogic and historical.

Conclusion

This contribution set out to interrogate the role and influence of the Academy in Cicero's thought, beyond the usual attempts to interpret his personal viewpoint or survey the epistemological basis of his arguments. Cicero's prefaces evidence a rich and complex engagement with what it means to adopt Academic arguments to write philosophy, and how this approach relates to the epistemic condition of humanity as well as to philosophy as an institution. The author often defends his late cycle of *philosophica* as a service to Rome and to Latin literature. In this respect, his writings and their concern with method and history actively bring to life the philosophical tradition through his Academy—a protean designation for school, method, and privileged position within a field encompassing other positions, histories, and trajectories. Choreographing the struggle between philosophers and schools is the primary dynamic through which Cicero manages this process, priming a conflict with the existing literature of ignorant Stoics and self-serving Epicureans. He takes a position against them, making them antagonists over the question of openness to dialogue and rhetorical craft. It is through dialogue that Cicero appropriates, structures, and originates philosophy as a regimented field of ongoing cultural production tightly entwined with its history. Cicero frames philosophical practice and integrates the project of philosophy within a series of discrete debates, spelling out for his novice audience what philosophy is, what doing philosophy (successfully) looks like, and the rules of engagement by which philosophical thought moves, influences, progresses.[39]

The task of a skeptic is to comprehend and critique all philosophical positions (*Nat. d.* 1.11). And this imperative at the heart of the philosophical discipline amounts to an inclusive performance of philosophy's ideas and debates; it *also* means bringing Philosophy into being as an organized and unified intellectual practice, with its own proprietary canons, interests, and hierarchies.[40] A reading of the *Academica* as a programmatic statement of Ciceronian methodology illustrates the close relationship between Academic arguments and arguments among Academics: the halls of the Academy, as nostalgic as they might appear in the fifth book of *De finibus*, and as fractious and epistemically limiting as they might seem in the *Lucullus*, provide Cicero with the ideal context in which to pursue his far-reaching cultural project of founding Roman philosophy.

Notes

1. See Habinek (1995); Henderson (2005); Schofield (2008); Baraz (2012).
2. Bourdieu (1993).
3. To argue that Cicero sought to secure his place within Rome's elite and establish himself within the oratorical canon by exploiting a range of literary and political strategies is common currency among students of his rhetorical works, speeches, and letters. Many monographs, chief among which John Dugan's *Making of a New Man* (2005), examine this "self-fashioning" and "self-canonization" in terms of Cicero's manipulation of intellectual history and the selection and cultivation of aesthetic criteria.

4. All translations are the author's own, though indebted to Charles Brittain's thoughtful edition of Cicero's *Academica* (2006).
5. See Graver (2003) on books 3 and 4.
6. Cf. Habinek (1995); Gildenhard (2007).
7. Bourdieu (1993) 34.
8. In translating *probabilis* and other cognates of *probo* used in this technical and philosophical sense, I follow Brittain (2006) in using "persuasive" rather than "probable." This rightly privileges the active voice of *probabilis* and the determining role of the subject in responding to arguments, ideas, percepts (Auvray-Assayas (2006) 37–41; Brittain (2006) xl–xli).
9. On Cicero and the Peripatos, see Fortenbaugh and Steinmetz (1989) and Inwood (2014) chapter 4.
10. Hirtius emphasizes again and again his interest in Cicero's written work. While the author differentiates this treatise from the model of *De natura deorum* and *De inventione* (*Fat.* 1), Hirtius informs his interlocutor that he is acquainted with his "rhetorical treatises" (*rhetorica*) and the *Tusculans*, and promises to listen to his speech as if reading his writings (*Fat.* 4). There is a sense in which the author is positioning the present work within a written *corpus* governed by specific compositional principles.
11. Gorman (2005) 70.
12. Gildenhard (2007) 273.
13. Gorman (2005) 93.
14. Cf. Allen (1997) 223.
15. Inwood (1990) 150; Gorman (2005) 61; cf. *Tusc.* 1.9–17.
16. Cf. Crook (1976) 74–77.
17. Cf. Ruch (1969) on the *Lucullus*.
18. Vesperini (2012) 139–165 captures the mixture of bewitchment, confusion, and concern that registered among Romans during the infamous embassy of three leading Hellenistic philosophers to Rome in 155 BCE. As one of the earliest points of contact between Rome and Greek *philosophia*, Carneades, Diogenes, and Critolaus reportedly performed for their hosts and answered their questions, so at *Luc.* 137, Gell. *NA* 6.14.1–2, and Plut. *Vit. Cat. Mai.* 22.1–5.
19. Perhaps one of the most moving instances of philosophy bleeding into real life is a pair of letters dating from 49 BCE (*Att.* 7.11 and 8.3), in which Cicero explicitly co-opts *in utramque* to structure a personal political dilemma about how to engage with the ongoing civil war. Namely, he reflects on the consequences and implications of leaving Italy and following Pompey into war (Michel (1977)).
20. Beard (1986) 35 with reference to *De divinatione*.
21. Cf. Schofield (2008). Tobias Reinhardt has discussed the translation of *in utramque* from a philosophical to a rhetorical context during the so-called Fourth Academy of Philo ((2003) 14) and has argued that Cicero's *corpus*, in particular letters like *Fam.* 9.4.2, testifies to the rhetoricization of this practice ((2000) 541).
22. Zerba (2012) 166.
23. See Steinmetz (1989); Lévy (1992); Griffin (1997) 5–8; Schofield (2008) 81; Thorsrud (2012) 133; Woolf (2015) 10–33; Cappello (2019).
24. See Inwood and Mansfeld (1997); Reinhardt (2000); Brittain and Palmer (2001); Cappello (2019) 261–312.
25. On Antiochus, see Glucker (1978), Barnes (1989), and Sedley (2012).

26. Görler (1997) 38–39.
27. Lévy (1992) 180. Through a close reading of the *Academica*, Tarrant (1985) 26 characterizes the Fourth Academy as a "group of 'examiners.' "
28. Auvray-Assayas (2006) 40.
29. Gildenhard (2007) 58; cf. Michel (1968) 117.
30. Michel (1968) 114.
31. Bourdieu (1993) 30–34, 64.
32. Cf. Glucker (1978) 80; Brittain (2001) 169–252; Cappello (2019) 132–142.
33. Burnyeat (1997) 279.
34. Auvray-Assayas (2006) 36.
35. Brittain (2001).
36. Couissin (1929); Thorsrud (2012).
37. Glucker (1997).
38. Lucullus accused the "New" Academy of concealing "mysteries" (*mysteria*), *Luc.* 60.
39. Cf. Woolf (2015) 10–14.
40. See Schofield (2002).

References

Allen, J. (1997). "Carneadean Arguments in Cicero's Academic Books," in Inwood and Mansfeld, 217–256.
Auvray-Assayas, C. (2006). *Cicéron*. (Paris).
Baraz, Y. (2012). *A Written Republic: Cicero's Philosophical Politics*. (Princeton).
Barnes, J., and M. Griffin, eds. (1989). *Philosophia Togata I*. (Oxford).
Barnes, J. (1989). "Antiochus of Ascalon," in Barnes and Griffin, 51–96.
Beard, M. (1986). "Cicero and Divination: The Formation of a Latin Discourse." *JRS* 76: 33–46.
Bourdieu, P. (1993). *The Field of Cultural Production: Essays on Art and Literature*. (London).
Boyle, A. J., ed. (1995). *Roman Literature and Ideology: Ramus Essays for J. P. Sullivan*. (Bendigo).
Brittain, C. (2001). *Philo of Larissa: The Last of the Academic Sceptics*. (Oxford).
Brittain, C. (2006). *Cicero: On Academic Scepticism*. (Indianapolis).
Brittain, C., and J. Palmer (2001). "The New Academy's Appeal to the Presocratics." *Phronesis* 46: 38–72.
Burnyeat, M. (1997). "Antipater and Self-Refutation: Elusive Arguments in Cicero's *Academica*," in Inwood and Mansfeld, 277–310.
Cappello, O. (2019). *The School of Doubt: Skepticism, History and Politics in Cicero's* Academica. (Leiden).
Clark, G., and T. Rajak, eds. (2002). *Philosophy and Power in the Graeco-Roman World: Essays in Honour of M. Griffin*. (Oxford).
Couissin, P. (1929). "Le stoicisme de la nouvelle Académie." *Revue d'Histoire de la Philosophie* 3: 241–276.
Crook, J. A. (^{2}1976). *Law and Life of Rome*. (Ithaca, N.Y.).
Dugan, J. (2005). *Making a New Man: Ciceronian Self-Fashioning in the Rhetorical Works*. (Oxford).
Fortenbaugh, W. W., and P. Steinmetz, eds. (1989). *Cicero's Knowledge of the Peripatos*. (London).
Gildenhard, I. (2007). *Paideia Romana: Cicero's Tusculan Disputations*. (Cambridge).
Glucker, J. (1978). *Antiochus and the Late Academy*. (Göttingen).

Glucker, J. (1997). "Socrates in the *Academic Books* and Other Ciceronian Works," in Inwood and Mansfeld, 58–88.
Goldhill, S., ed. (2008). *The End of Dialogue in Antiquity*. (Cambridge).
Görler, W. (1997). "Cicero's Philosophical Stance in the Lucullus," in Inwood and Mansfeld, 36–57.
Gorman, R. (2005). *The Socratic Method in the Dialogues of Cicero*. (Stuttgart).
Graver, M. (2003). *Cicero on the Emotions: Tusculan Disputations 3 and 4*. (Chicago).
Griffin, M. (1997). "The Composition of the Academica: Motives and Versions," in Inwood and Mansfeld, 1–35.
Habinek, T. N. (1995). "Ideology for an Empire in the Prefaces of Cicero's Dialogues," in Boyle, 55–67.
Harmatta, J., ed. (1968). *Studien zur Geschichte und Philosophie des Altertums*. (Amsterdam).
Henderson, J. (2005). "From φιλοσοφία into philosophia: Classicism and Ciceronianism," in Porter, 173–203.
Inwood, B. (1990). "*Rhetorica Disputatio*: The Strategy of *De finibus* 2." *Apeiron* 23(4): 143–164.
Inwood, B. (2014). *Ethics after Aristotle*. (Cambridge, Mass.).
Inwood, B., and J. Mansfeld, eds. (1997). *Assent and Argument: Studies in Cicero's Academic Books*. (Leiden).
Leonhardt, J. (1999). *Ciceros Kritik der Philosophenschulen*. (Munich).
Lévy, C. (1984). "La dialectique de Cicéron dans les livres 2 et 3 du *De Finibus*." *Rev. Ét. Lat.* 62: 111–127.
Lévy, C. (1992). *Cicero Academicus: Recherches sur les* Académiques *et sur la philosophie cicéronienne*. (Rome).
Michel, A. (1968). "Doxographie et histoire de la philosophie chez Cicéron," in Harmatta, 113–120.
Michel, A. (1977). "Cicéron, Pompée et la guerre civile: Rhétorique et philosophie dans la correspondence." *Acta Antiqua Academiae Scientiarum Hungaricae* 25: 393–403.
Nicgorski, W., ed. (2012). *Cicero's Practical Philosophy*. (Notre Dame).
Porter, I. J., ed. (2005). *Classical Pasts: The Classical Tradition of Greece and Rome*. (Princeton).
Reinhardt, T. (2000). "Rhetoric in the Fourth Academy." *Classical Quarterly* 50: 531–547.
Reinhardt, T. (2003). *Cicero's* Topica: *Critical Edition, Translation, Introduction, and Commentary*. (Oxford).
Ruch, M. (1969). "La *disputatio in utramque partem* dans le 'Lucullus' et ses fondements philosophiques." *Rev. Ét. Lat.* 47: 310–335.
Schofield, M. (2002). "Academic Therapy: Philo of Larissa and Cicero's Project in the Tusculans," in Clark and Rajak, 91–109.
Schofield, M. (2008). "Ciceronian Dialogue," in Goldhill, 63–84.
Sedley, D., ed. (2012). *The Philosophy of Antiochus*. (Cambridge).
Steinmetz, P. (1989). "Beobachtungen zu Ciceros philosophischem Standpunkt," in Fortenbaugh and Steinmetz, 1–22.
Tarrant, R. (1985). *Scepticism or Platonism? The Philosophy of the Fourth Academy*. (Cambridge).
Thorsrud, H. (2012). "Radical and Mitigated Skepticism in Cicero's *Academica*," in Nicgorski, 133–151.
Vesperini, P. (2012). *La* Philosophia *et ses pratiques d'Ennius à Cicéron*. (Paris).
Woolf, R. (2015). *Cicero: The Philosophy of a Roman Sceptic*. (London).
Zerba, M. (2012). *Doubt and Scepticism in Antiquity and the Renaissance*. (Cambridge).

CHAPTER 17

PERSIUS ON STOIC POETICS

CLAUDIA WIENER

THE only Stoic poet to make programmatic statements about the literature of his own time is the Roman Persius. His first satire, therefore, merits an extensive discussion in this chapter. For a satirist, literary criticism is an important topic—from Lucilius onward, a confrontational stance in the literary scene characterizes the satirical poet. In addition to adopting generic conventions, Persius may be expected to show a fundamentally philosophical attitude in his relationship to poetry, for he models his satirical *persona* after that of a staunch Stoic and conspicuously presents himself in the fifth satire as being of like mind as the Stoic philosopher Cornutus.

By way of contrast, the two major poets of the Neronian period, Seneca and Lucan, have left us no programmatic statements about their own poetry. In his philosophical oeuvre Seneca never refers to his own tragedies; only seldom does he deal with the effect of poetry and then only in passing.[1] In the field of rhetoric, however, coherent comments by him about style can frequently be found. To what extent such statements can be applied to poetry will be discussed in the following. Lucan's epic about the civil war, in turn, diverges so spectacularly from the expectations a reader has of epic poetry that it can be understood as programmatic. But does this mean that we can expect from Lucan an approach to epic poetry that can be described as Stoic?

This brings us to the second problem: Persius is a self-avowed Stoically motivated satirist. But the shocking victory of evil in Seneca's tragedies, dispensing as they do with poetic justice, raises doubts whether a connection can be established with Seneca the philosopher, whose trust in divine providence and in the possibility that mankind can be educated morally appears unshaken. Joachim Dingel (1974) therefore coined the term "the dark side of Stoics" for the tragedies. Alessandro Schiesaro (1997 and 2003) sees in the tragedies the opportunity for Seneca to free himself from the constraints of Stoic ethics and rationality as a poet who reaches the level of divine madness in the Platonic sense (as described in the *Phaedrus*).

Conversely, connections between *Seneca philosophus* and *Seneca tragicus* have been identified precisely in the way he introduces insights from Stoic psychology into the behavior and utterances of his characters (cf. Bäumer 1982; Wiener 2014; Staley

2010; Stroh 2020 discusses the problem exemplarily for Seneca's *Phaedra*), because questions of guilt and determinism are raised (Fischer 2008, Wiener 2006), and because epistemological approaches from Stoa are applied practically (Staley 2010). There is a similar scholarly discussion with regard to Lucan. The opinion that Lucan lost his confidence in the Stoic notion of an ordered course of the world is presented in differing gradations (cf. Johnson 1987, and Sklenář's nihilistic interpretation 2003). Scholars continue to discuss Berthe Marti's view (1945) that Lucan modeled his protagonists on a gradation from the Stoic sage (Cato), through the student on the path to perfection (Pompey), to the antagonist (Caesar). The question of whether Lucan's Cato really represents the ideal of a Stoic sage or whether in this figure Lucan criticizes excesses that can no longer be considered Stoic is dealt with in particular by Wildberger (2005) and D'Alessandro Behr (2007).

Expectations of Stoic Poetics

Before we discuss Persius's first satire, we must ask ourselves whether a Stoic tradition of poetic theory even exists, and what theoretical reflections can be expected of a Stoic "poetics."

Of the works on poetry of Zeno and his pupils, only titles—if that—survive, to which not even extant fragments can generally be assigned with any certainty (Steinmetz (1994) 522: *Zeno, Lecture on Poetics*). The approach of the Stoa to poetics can be most readily inferred in the case of Diogenes of Babylon (Steinmetz (1994) 628–31), since Diogenes Laertius supplies us with the relevant information (esp. Diog. Laert. 7.56–62; *SVF* iii, 221–235). From his report on Diogenes of Babylon's textbook Περὶ τῆς φωνῆς τέχνη (*On the Voice*) and essays on rhetoric (*SVF* iii, 235–243) and music (*SVF* iii, 221–235), we are able to glean some further information on the subject of poetry.

Phillip De Lacy (1948) used Stoic linguistic theory to reconstruct the topics that one might expect to find in Stoic poetics. Stylistic points (word choice and metrical arrangement) would have been handled under ποίημα, and subject matter under ποίησις. The latter was defined by Posidonius as the mimetic representation of anything relating to gods or humans (Diog. Laert. 7.60), and can therefore be expected to have comprised thoughts on characterization and plot structure. This arrangement seems to have been decisive for Hellenistic poetics as well, which, however, developed an additional, third category (ποιητής) concerned with the relationship between the poet's talent (δύναμις ποιητική/*ingenium*) and training (τέχνη/*ars*). This triad is attested for the poetics of Neoptolemus of Parium (Brink (1963) 38–74), which it has been possible to reconstruct from the criticism of him by Philodemus (Asmis (1992 and 1995); Porter (1995) 102–117). The triad has further been recognized by Charles O. Brink (1963 and 1971) as holding the key to understanding the structure of Horace's *Ars poetica*.[2]

Books on ancient poetics do not, as a rule, contain a chapter devoted to Stoic poetics: Manfred Fuhrmann's (³2003) introduction to ancient poetic theory, which has seen several editions since its first publication in 1971, focuses on Aristotle, Horace, and Longinus; Malcolm Heath (2013) discusses the Stoa only as it relates to methods of allegorical interpretation; and Jeffrey Walker (2000) considers—with good reason, although he perhaps attributes too much to the influence of Aristotle—the strongest connections to be those between Stoic poetics, *grammatikê*, and rhetoric (Walker (2000) 290–310). There is thus room for a methodical examination of Seneca's statements concerning rhetoric, too, to see if they can be applied to a reconstruction of his conception of poetry.

Persius: The Poet's *Telos*

In his first satire, or at least in the passages framing it at either end, Persius operates within the generic tradition of satire.[3] The satirist's "traditional dissociation" from the literary scene (Kißel (1990) 104) serves only as a frame for the rest of the satire, though, and the central content is informed by Stoic moral values. The defining characteristic of the satirist Persius is the close connection between literary criticism and the concepts and teachings of Stoic moral philosophy.

As a Stoic, Persius's crucial demand of a poet is that he regards writing poetry as a moral act. The poet must hold himself accountable to himself, i.e., it must be fully clear to him *why* and *for whom* he is writing—and, as a consequence, *how* he should write. Persius's comments on poetics can therefore be expected to represent a Stoic point of view.

Using illustrations from the Roman literary scene, Persius demonstrates that the current relationship between poet and public is not only unsatisfactory but downright repulsive and absurdly insincere. Persius reveals what happens when a poet makes public approval the only measure of his success: not the poet, but the public then ends up deciding what he writes. The public's cries of "bravo!" (*euge! belle!*) become the goal of the poet. But the poet must also analyze the meaning of these cries: *nam "belle" hoc excute totum: / quid non intus habet?* (1.49–50).[4]

Not only the moral-philosophical demand but also the form and method of argumentation that Persius employs can, when compared with Seneca's *Dialogi*, be regarded as typically Stoic. Seneca's argumentation frequently takes as its starting point some indication that a generally recognized opinion or conviction, including those advocated by authority figures, is untenable and even harmfully misleading. Common beliefs about the happy life (*De vita beata*), the usefulness of anger for asserting authority and power (*De ira*; *De clementia*), and misfortune (*De providentia, De constantia sapientis*) are thus rejected and, ultimately, replaced by Stoic views.

In Persius's first satire, even poetic composition, literary criticism, and aesthetic judgments are essentially acts of ethical deliberation, reflecting a conscious decision about how to act in a given situation.[5] Popular success should not become the *summum bonum* of the poet: *sed recti finemque extremumque esse recuso / "euge" tuum et "belle."*[6]

Language reveals a person's inner disposition. Speaking, like any other action, is subject to moral criteria. This fixation on moral-philosophical objectives has been described by J. Bramble as a peculiarity of Persius's conspicuous use of metaphors: "The types of metaphor deployed were not original creations; literary theory explains their pedigree. But what does appear to be original is the way in which he consistently accommodated these metaphors to moralistic ends" (Bramble (1974) 22–23). Shadi Bartsch (2015) goes even further in her analysis of how and why Persius prefers to rely on metaphors of consumption and digestion, sexuality, and medicine. His graphic imagery is meant to evoke disgust and aversion, and thereby to support the poet's argumentative and therapeutic aim of *dissuasio*. The moral-philosophical value of Persius's metaphors lies, according to Bartsch, in their therapeutic and medical effect; Persius demonstrates that there is no simple path to wisdom and that our judgment falters without the guidance of Stoic moral philosophy. Bartsch's analysis is correct: in Persius's first satire, we are told primarily what the poet should *not* do, not what he should do. One need not go as far as Bartsch does in assuming that Persius was using this graphically repulsive imagery to present satire as a dangerous remedy, one which works like the drug *elleborum* when taken incorrectly or in overdose, and from which the reader must therefore eventually be weaned (Bartsch (2015) 210–211). Rather, the reader is trained by the satirist to practice perceiving things in this way by himself.[7]

What Seneca and Persius also have in common is the connection between rational argumentation and psychotherapeutic methods. The satirist brings the reader to a new evaluation of the situation by allowing him to see how his former behavioral patterns appear from the outside. The necessary distance and new angle effect a change of perspective that allows the observer to recognize how ridiculous his own behavior can be, and makes him receptive to the philosopher's advice. Satire is staged as a conversation intended to persuade the interlocutor, who offers resistance every step of the way and must be won over gradually. Persius employs the dialogue format of a diatribe to a large extent, but he also draws attention to its use. He thus emphasizes the introduction of the stubborn interlocutor as a literary device by explicitly addressing him as such: *quisquis es, o modo quem ex adverso dicere feci* (1.44).[8] Persius acts openly and does not conceal his methods, because he wants not simply to persuade but also to convince his addressee rationally. Persius introduces himself as a fellow poet, and yet he does not openly assume the role of a therapist treating a patient, as Seneca might do. He includes himself in these observations and no longer addresses a "you," but refers to "us" (1.9–11: *nostrum istud vivere triste; facimus quaecumque . . . / cum sapimus patruos; scribimus inclusi*).[9] The change of perspective has a quicker effect on him than on his colleagues, however: he is a satirist and breaks into laughter. The "you" of the poem has not quite reached this point, and is unable to muster enough self-irony to laugh at himself. Persius is thus compelled to drag him mercilessly through every inch of the literary scene in order to demonstrate how his idea of the public differs from reality.

Understandably, the poet would like to receive recognition for the time and energy he has put into his work (1.13–14). Persius acknowledges this need for recognition at the end of the scene: he, too, would like to be praised—on the condition that he has actually managed to accomplish something.[10]

The ordinary poet reverses this condition: he believes he has accomplished something when the audience praises him. He takes his public seriously, as his fine robes and solemn entrance show; the listeners are "huge Titusses" (1. 20)[11]. This is where Persius comes in. With his observer's gaze, he exposes the behavior of the audience—and that of the poet, for Persius makes it abundantly clear that such a poet is prostituting himself: the poet's sultry recitations bring the Romans to orgasm,[12] so that the poet himself, exhausted from the labor of writing, must ask them to stop at the climax of pleasure.[13] What mistake has the poet made? He has not recited poems that he considered good, but rather poems that appeal only to the public's senses.

The insulted poet takes offense: why has he bothered learning anything if he is not allowed to show it? Persius counters with a conspicuous polyptoton: *Scire tuum nihil est nisi te scire hoc sciat alter* (1.27).[14] The orator Calvus had memorably made the same play on words when threatening the judges in one of his speeches against Vatinius (Quint. *Inst.* 6.1.13: *Factum (inquit) esse ambitum scitis omnes et hoc vos scire omnes sciunt*):[15] the fact that they know Vatinius is plainly guilty of the crime of *ambitus* ("electoral corruption") cannot be concealed; they must pronounce judgment accordingly. Persius can be trusted to be deliberately picking up the wordplay of Calvus, which also relates to "judging" on the basis of reliable "knowledge," but Persius turns the situation around. It is not knowledge that forces the public to act. The Stoic interprets *scire* from the perspective of moral philosophy: *scire* denotes a potential capability, and this capability is, like every other *virtus*, pointless unless there is a demand and use for it. The poet can therefore also put this capability, i.e., his knowledge, to use. Of course he can—but he does it for the wrong reason if his objective in having knowledge is to win fame. And the manifestation of that fame is that everyone stops and points at the distinguished poet. Still, the poet can cite authorities for his objective: Demosthenes relished his fame, as the anecdote here alluded to shows (e.g., Cic. *Tusc.* 5.103), and Horace praises his Muse for his renown: *quod monstror digito praetereuntium / Romanae fidicen lyrae* (*carm.* 4.3.22–23).[16] Persius, however, introduces other scenes to show us what this fame looks like in reality. To be a school author means to be written down by a hundred children in dictation practice. To be a famous poet means to be recited by an effeminate performer in a magenta-colored robe: what an honor! Violets sprout for joy from the poet's grave (1.39–40)!

What can we glean from these passages about poetics? As far as we may judge, Persius does not belittle his poet's capabilities. He knows that the poet spends a long time on his poetry, and that he can captivate his audience. It is not a matter of needing to take up arms (like Horace) to make poets spend more time polishing their work.

In fact, the criteria by which "the people" (1.63: *quis populi sermo est?*)[17] judge a poet correspond to Horace's advice on painstaking composition, as we shall see. Some may find a negative undertone in Persius's reference to the "flow of the verses in a soft rhythm" (*carmina molli / nunc demum numero fluere*, 1.63–64; Kißel (1990) 193), but the second part of the remark conforms to the demands of Horace (*Ars P.* 292–294): the poems are so well constructed that one could run a finger over them without feeling the seams: *ut per leve severos / effundat iunctura unguis* (1.64–65).[18] Further artisanal metaphors aptly describe proper verse composition: *scit tendere versum / non secus ac si oculo rubricam dirigat uno* (1.65–66).[19]

What conclusions can we draw? Could it be that the public is not so bad after all, and that its judgment can be trusted? No. The people have learned how to praise art—but Persius invalidates their judgment. He divulges to us that the art that they praise is in fact the shoddy workmanship of a dilettante, and that they only praise him because he treats them to a lavish *cena* for it, or gives some poor devil a cloak in return. And when the dilettante is not looking, they make faces at him (1.55–62).

What Persius criticizes about poetry is thus not a lack of technical ability—the poets are almost too well versed in that. It is the content that is wrong. The poets do not choose their material based on its relevance and message but instead take as their criterion the expectation that what they say will be effective. They master the *topoi* of a moral critique of their age: *sive opus in mores, in luxum, in prandia regum dicere* (1.67–68),[20] but without offering competition to Persius—they want to compose *res grandes*, after all. It becomes clear that Persius is referring to the younger generation of poets, who have received the wrong education. He recommends that these poets not yet venture into the loftiest genres (such as epic)—but this is exactly what happens: *heroas sensus afferre docemus* (1.69).[21] There is no transition between *Graece nugari*, that is, light poetry in the Greek style, and the grandiosity of heroic poetry. Is there anything that these artists cannot do? They have mastered a stylistic level void of *pathos*, and nothing more. They are unable to describe a simple grove (1.70: *ponere lucum*) or to extol country life (1.71: *rus saturum laudare*); they immediately introduce subject matter and figures steeped in history (e.g., Remus and L. Quintus Cincinnatus) to raise their description of the rustic Parilia festival to the level of epic and win a coveted "*euge*" from the audience (1.70–75). Persius's stylistic criticism in connection with the poor training of younger poets culminates in the image of a potpourri of styles (1.80: *sartago loquendi*). The most diverse ingredients—including some from the ancient tragedians[22]—are thrown indiscriminately into a stewpot and stirred, since the *patres lippi*, who guide the young generation with failing eyesight, advise it, and because the enthusiastic reaction of the public (depreciated as *trossuli*) offers validation (1.81–82).

In sum, it is evident that Persius acknowledges a high level of technical ability among the poets, which they have gained by imitating diverse literary models that exploit pathos. They do not concentrate enough on content and substance, however, but only on the sensory effect of poetry. Persius demonstrates that these poets lack an appropriate goal beyond mere show. That the audience is excited sexually and even reaches orgasm is certainly not a goal that a Stoic wants to achieve.

There are no suitable criteria for appraising poetry either from the point of view of the producer or from that of the recipient. Persius switches to the field of forensic rhetoric, because there the absurdity of aesthetic assessment becomes still more evident: not even the jury at a trial reaches a rational verdict on the basis of facts and arguments, but it appraises the aesthetic style of the speech for the defense. Persius demonstrates how absurd this criterion is with the examples of the accused Pedius, who was acquitted because he crafted such artfully well-balanced antitheses (1.85–86), and of the successful beggar whose completely fabricated shipwreck story moved everyone to tears—except Persius (1.88–91). What is surprising about the example of the orator Pedius is that the judges are not even manipulated emotionally in a manner of such skillful orators as Antonius, as Cicero renders him in *De oratore*. Rather the judges themselves declare that they are using an aesthetic criterion, which is completely inappropriate in a judicial verdict. The same applies to the success of the beggar, who is similarly honored as an "artist" because he can arouse emotions with his manifestly fabricated tale. In both cases the appraisal criteria which the "audience" apply are out of place.

The ability to elicit an aesthetic effect is only a matter of technical practice. This point is confirmed by the sample verses from a work quoted by the interlocutor as an example of accomplished poetry: *sed numeris decor est et iunctura addita crudis* (1.92).[23] The absurdity of the criteria once again becomes blatantly obvious when the opening of the *Aeneid* is criticized for its infelicitous wording. The overall direction of the statement is clear, even if it is not clear whether this criticism is to be ascribed to the interlocutor or whether the satirist is using the rhetorical question as to whether "Arma virumque" sounds repulsive as a deliberate provocation.[24] The satirist's irony increases when the interlocutor wants to discredit the *Aeneid* as bad poetry. The critics, too, make themselves ridiculous when—like everyone else—they are guided by criteria based solely on formal structure. This judgment also applies to the Greek-sounding verses, which are described as felicitous. Persius is not concerned with finding fault with the verses as too Greek; the lines are well made. He does not wish to deny that formal composition should be mastered; on the contrary, he confirms over and again that it should be! But it represents a mechanical process, something routine in the production of poetry that is superficial and comes "from moistened lips" (1.105). The poet and his poem lack "balls," as Persius himself says in intentionally strong terms: *haec fierent, si testiculi vena ulla paterni / viveret in nobis?* (1.103–104).[25]

What precisely do the poems lack? Persius mentions the hard work of thinking (1.106: *nec pluteum caedit, nec demorsos sapit unguis*),[26] yet this criticism cannot refer to the fine-tuning, but must be directed at the depth and independence of the poet's thoughts. With this remark, the satirist comes to his second program: satire is not easy on the ear; its thoughts are not pleasant to hear, but offend and hurt.

If we are hoping to identify elements of a Stoic poetics in the first century AD, then it is necessary to pay close attention to the proper relationship between style, form (ποίημα), content, and message (ποίησις). The poet and his audience prefer the sensory effect made by a poem the first time they hear it, without the poetic artwork that contains a real message intended to stimulate the intellect. Purely sensory stimulation, which Persius epitomizes in the image of an orgasm, and a smoothly polished surface—a technical skill now mastered by everyone, so that even dilettantes now generate professionally polished works—characterize the superficiality of contemporary poetry. This superficiality compels Persius to take refuge in a diametrically opposed style: his syntax is clumsy and frequently interrupted by anacolutha or a change of speaker; his imagery is taken to extremes, and his shocking metaphors undermine the reader's sense of well-being—they jump at his face, accost him, and force him to think with every verse he reads.

In his first satire Persius justifies not only the choice of genre but also this choice of style for his satires. In this connection he addresses subjects that are to be expected of poetics: questions about the poet's suitability, education, and training, about stylistic treatment, and about an appropriate choice of topic. But he answers them in a completely different way than might be expected of an *ars poetica*. Surprisingly, he asserts that the preconditions for excellent poetry in his age appear to be fulfilled. The poets' suitability and training leave nothing to be desired; they are masters of their craft. Even the audience is educated and knowledgeable as never before. Nonetheless the result is catastrophic, because it is disappointingly superficial. The satire leads to the conclusion that it is not an *ars poetica* that is needed but a moral reorientation.

In the literary scene of his age Persius sees signs of social morbidity. The duty of writers ought therefore to be to counteract this decline. But this will not be possible as long as authors and audiences are locked in a symbiotic relationship and confirm each other in their mistaken view. Accordingly Persius's first satire is a philosophical discourse, which in its analysis and the results of its diagnosis corresponds to discourses by Stoic authors such as Musonius and Epictetus. (Nichols 2013 has identified the second and third satires as diatribes; the same considerations apply equally to the first satire.)

In two of his discourses Epictetus has the same goal as Persius and discusses the relationship between rhetorical expressiveness and the effect on the audience. In Discourse 2.23 ("Of the Faculty of Expression") Epictetus makes it clear from the start that a good turn of phrase is not to be despised but rather to be seen as a gift of God. Nevertheless, in the lecture he proves that eloquence is not a desired quality in itself, but is to be placed on the same level in the Stoics' hierarchy of values as, for example, our senses, whose usefulness is undeniable and which nobody wishes to do without. But still, the power of judgment (προαίρεσις) is superior, because it enables us to determine what is true and what is false, what is good and what is bad. It is moral judgment that forms the basis of all our decisions to take action. Eloquence may be an art and a virtue, but it is not more valuable than the art of the hair stylist. In contrast it is our moral decision that determines the goal for which we make use of art.

If we look for an analogue to Persius's criticism of the literary scene in Epictetus, we can also adduce the latter's Discourse 3.23 ("To Those Who Read and Discuss for the Purpose of Display"). Epictetus, too, emphasizes that the goal of laborious literary training must not be solely to provoke the audience's applause at a public appearance, by showing off one's rhetorical prowess. This criticism of the orator's dependence on the audience's approval and of such appearances as an end in itself will become a programmatic topic of Stoic philosophers in the Second Sophistic, who distance themselves from the increasing success of celebrated orators such as Dio Chrysostomus (cf. Reydams-Schils 2017).

Seeming versus Being: Style as an Expression of Inner Values

These parallels in the Stoics' criticism of poets and orators enable us to evaluate Seneca's statements about rhetoric and see if we can derive from these an interpretative approach to his poetry. Seneca's *Letters* 114 and 115 stress that there exists an indissoluble connection between an orator's rhetorical style and his moral make-up. Seneca proves this theory in *Letter* 114 with a detailed criticism of Maecenas's rhetorical style, documenting his *oratio corrupta* on three stylistic levels: choice of words, word order, and stylistic devices, in particular his use of metaphors. The letter seems to be in line with topics used in debates about the decline of Roman eloquence during the first century CE (thoroughly discussed by Berti (2018) 17–30). But independently of the general criticism of society, which is common in this discussion of the decline of rhetoric, Seneca stresses— as a Stoic moral philosopher—the personal responsibility of every orator, because linguistic style is an expression of one's own personality. Seneca's *Letter* points out that stylistic faults—as a lack of *iudicium*—may reveal a diseased *animus*.[27]

John Sklenář's attempt to relate *Letters* 114 to Seneca's *Oedipus*—as an example of a "diseased *animus*" in "a diseased civic environment" (Sklenář 2017, 17)—is not convincing. His interpretation of Oedipus may be correct in substance, but this diseased condition does not manifest itself in the stylistic composition of the speeches in Seneca's play. Neither in Oedipus nor in the protagonists of Seneca's other tragedies is to possible to find traces of an *oratio corrupta*, such as Seneca detects in Maecenas's style. Conversely, Sklenář would also have to detect a different rhetorical style for morally positive characters. It is not possible, however, to derive in this way an *ars poetica* of tragedy from Seneca's statements about rhetoric.

In the following *Letter* 115 self-indulgence and style assume a different relation to each other. It is not *luxuria* that keeps the students from hard work and proper training. A polished style is rather the symptom of an inner disposition that tends to devote inordinate attention to trivialities (*pusilla*). What might appear to be the virtue of diligence is, surprisingly, turned into the symptom of a *vitium* by Seneca, who sees it as impeding the thought processes characteristic of a *magnus animus*. The best orator is the one who is able to win the trust of his audience with his self-assurance, satisfaction, and positive charisma. This claim can also be seen as an Aristotelian standard for the orator's *ethos*, but in the moral-philosophical context of Seneca, it is justified in Stoic terms. Seneca uses a chain syllogism (*sorites*) intended to prove that oratorical style is a vice: oratorical style is an expression of an inner disposition; a fascination with superficial qualities is the sign of an acquired (i.e., not innate) *vitium*, *luxuria*; *luxuria* ultimately leads to *avaritia*. *Avaritia*, characterized above all by a permanent state of discontent with what one has accomplished, is what stands in the way of a happy life. True happiness lies in being content with oneself, i.e., in recognizing how much one has accomplished by being free from desires (*magnus animus*). In the context of this discussion Seneca adduces a significant anecdote concerning Euripides. For this purpose he translates the provocative hymn to the power of money that Bellerophontes sings in a lost play by Euripides (*Ep.* 115. 14): Money helps its owner better than any human love relationship, and is therefore more valuable. Seneca states that these lines triggered spontaneous indignation in the Athenian audience, and that Euripides was only able to pacify the audience by pointing to the denouement of the tragedy, when the protagonist's view would be proved wrong. We can understand this anecdote as an indication of the type of audience response the tragic dramatist Seneca wanted: moral indignation as a sign of rejection is desirable when his protagonists express views which clearly contradict moral values.

Based on our readings of Persius and Seneca, we may conclude that a Stoic *ars poetica* concerned with linguistic and stylistic details is not to be found in the Roman imperial period, even—indeed especially—when the Roman Stoa was at its height in the first century CE. The Stoic philosophers deemphasize certain areas of more technical inquiry traditionally associated with the school, and concentrate instead on moral education and healing the *psyche* (cf. Reydams-Schils 2015). It is part of the Stoics' program to leave the factual details to experts in grammar and rhetoric, and even to warn others away from pursuing such details, since this can distract from essential responsibilities (Sen. *Ep.* 88).

In contrast to the rhetoricians, Stoic philosophers of the Roman imperial era do not hold society as a whole responsible for the deterioration of rhetoric. The imperial Stoa compels the individual to meet his obligations: each person is responsible for himself. The cycle of mutual interdependence of society and author, which Persius depicted as so dangerous, can in this way be broken.

If we want to derive a central theme for Stoic poetry in the Neronian period, then, it would be an appeal for a responsible relationship between the poet and his audience. Fulfilling the audience's expectations with regard to entertainment and feelings of wellbeing is precisely what the poet must not do. Rather, he must compel listeners to apply their *iudicium* properly and to reach an independent judgment. In this sense we can find in Seneca's plays and Lucan's epic a marked tendency to disturbing provocation which is intended to set this *iudicium* in motion.

Seneca's audience must ask itself how it is to judge the shocking success of his criminal protagonists. They manifest their superior rhetoric and counter every moral objection posed by an interlocutor within the drama. Seneca orchestrates this contrast strikingly by intensifying the dialogue by means of stichomythia (Seidensticker 1968). The superiority of an Atreus or a Medea over anyone who seeks to reason with them is not a function of their formal rhetorical abilities; they are invincible and irrefutable because they have consciously freed themselves from all moral constraints. Bernd Seidensticker (2002) coined the phrase "the Senecan comparative" for this style, with which Seneca's protagonists express their ambition, both unscrupulous and at the same time fascinating. They want to outdo all previous crimes; they want to commit something hitherto unknown (*maius aliquid, inausum*). Seneca knows that this unscrupulous ambition can be misunderstood as greatness. In *De ira* he specifically refers to the mistaken admiration for the character of Atreus in Accius's tragedy and his famous adage *oderint dum metuant* in order to point up this errror (*Dial.* 3.20). That this ambition is not greatness, but is rather based on a severe mental injury as a result of traumatic experiences, is painfully witnessed in Seneca's tragedies. In their utterances the protagonists of these tragedies reveal to the audience their thoughts and the steps leading to the decisions that lead them to commit such heinous crimes.

Epic narrative provides Lucan with an even wider range of creative means to provoke the reader. Studies of Lucan's writing reveals how complex his approach is. Narratological investigations have dealt with the problematic narrator (Leigh 1997; D'Alessandro Behr 2007; Bartsch 2012) and the deliberate use of shifting focuses (Ludwig 2014). Poetological methods of interpretation are revealing as well (Masters 1992): it is ever clearer that the self-characterization of Lucan's protagonists in their speeches is called into question by means of intratextual and intertextual comments. Caesar may stylize himself as a successor to Aeneas, but the epic poet Lucan refutes his protagonist's self-representation by structurally characterizing the events of the civil war as an anti-*Aeneid* (Narducci 1979 and 2002): Caesar is pursuing Rome's downfall. In addition to the *Aeneid* there are numerous intertextual "additional voices" that a reader can distinguish (Hardie 2013 provides a good summary; for intertextual connections beyond the epic, cf. in particular Ambühl 2015; Karakasis 2018 analyzes Lucan's extensive intertextual references for Caesar at the Rubicon). Moreover, the poem questions not merely the protagonists but all the groups involved, in particular the soldiers, whose decision to participate in the *nefas* of the civil war is demonstrated and commented on by the emotional interjections of the narrator. Readers of Lucan cannot even feel secure in their own moral judgments, because even the system of moral values is suspended by the exceptional situation of the civil war. *Fides* leads to crime when the soldiers choose the wrong side. The epic *aristeia* of Scaeva (Luc. 6.1–332) demonstrates how even this bravest of heroes becomes Caesar's stooge. As the example of Domitius shows, Caesar's *clementia* becomes an act of cruel hubris—Lucan here offers an alternative reading to the assessment of Domitius in Caesar's *Commentarii*. Even the interpretation of natural phenomena becomes problematic when the gods choose not to intervene. Caesar survives an unnaturally violent epic storm at sea (Luc. 5. 476–721). Is he right to interpret this as an indication that he has become invincible? Or are such mythological patterns of interpretation refuted by the prognoses, based on science, of the experienced fisherman Amyclas (Meyer 2021)?

Readers of Lucan's epic are constantly confronted with questions that are difficult, if not impossible, to answer; the characters, their utterances, their decisions, and their actions repeatedly require a new and independent evaluation. As I have argued here, this discomfiting pressure for *iudicium* can be regarded as the most salient feature of Stoic poetics in the Neronian period.

Notes

1. In *De Ira* Seneca discuss the effect of literature on the reader: we are reassured that tragedies are not bad for audiences or readers because they excite dangerous emotions; feelings awakened by reading literature are considered to be merely pseudo-emotions (*Dial.* 4.2.5). Seneca uses the figure of the tyrant Atreus (*Dial.* 3.20.4; *Cl.* 2.2.2) to discuss the problem that

criminals can be regarded as false role models; it must be clearly stated that it is a misunderstanding to see the tyrant's provocative utterances as an expression of a *magnus animus*. The effect on the audience of morally dubious speeches in a tragedy by Euripides is raised by Seneca in *Letter* 114, which is discussed below. In his works Seneca likes to cite from other authors. Positive appraisals can repeatedly be found in the *Letters*: even poets can express philosophical truths (cf. *Ep.* 9.21), felicitous *sententiae* are ideal for conveying *praecepta* because they can immediately lead to insights (*Ep.* 94.27). Trinacty (2015) summarizes the central themes. Gregory A. Staley (2010) has systematically searched Seneca's philosophical writings for statements concerning the relationship of philosophy and the poetics of tragedy and has convincingly shown that the Stoic philosopher believes that tragedies cannot serve as a substitute for conveying philosophical content; we can therefore hardly assume that there is any moral philosophical intention. *Seneca philosophus* assigns a subordinate role to the study of literature in the hierarchy of intellectual activities. Philosophy is accorded the highest rank; literary studies have only a propaedeutic function.

2. Manfred Fuhrmann accepts the reconstruction of Neoptolemus's poetics based on Philodemus, but expresses doubt as to whether the triadic schema carries over to Horace's *Ars poetica* (Fuhrmann (1993) 182–193).
3. This has been decisively shown by Walter Kißel in his exhaustive commentary on Persius with the support of parallels from Horace and Juvenal (Kißel (1990) 102–103): the satirist makes himself unpopular by his criticism, even though no one falls victim to his ridicule who does not deserve it. Because it is absolutely necessary for him to get this criticism and ridicule off his chest, Persius cannot help but write satire. The stock character of the admonishing interlocutor, who advises the poet to act more moderately so as to avoid insulting and scaring off everyone, appears in every satirist since Lucilius. The satirist distances himself from normal poets, does not consider himself a poet, and does not take stylistic pains to be seen as a poet. By and large, he does not care whether or not he has readers at all; public success as a poet is not a criterion for him.
4. "Give *Nice* a thorough shake-out: / What isn't in it?" (Lee (1987) 17).
5. *non, si quid turbida Roma / elevet, accedas examenve improbum in illa / castiges trutina nec te quaesiveris extra* (Pers. 1.5–7) "If muddled Rome makes light / Of anything, one shouldn't agree or check the faulty / Tongue in *that* balance or inquire outside oneself" (Lee (1987) 15).
6. "But I deny that the end and object of what's right / Is your *Bravo* and *Nice*" (Lee (1987) 17).
7. See Erler in this volume.
8. "O you the anonymous whom I've just made to object" (Lee (1987) 17).
9. "This (...) dreary 'life' / Of ours"—"what we do (...) when we (...) turn avuncular"—"Cloistered we write" (Lee (1987) 15). Keane (2012) 83 aptly elaborates that Persius is unique in not only establishing a confidential conversational atmosphere between reader and author, but also in suggesting to the reader that he is witnessing an intimate conversation. She points out that "the language of privacy is part of a larger moral theme as well as poetic one. (...) Intimate satire like Persius' is not just about the pleasures of private conversation; it is also about discomfort and self-interrogation and selfknowledge". Mayer (2005) 149–157 emphasises that the Roman satirists all adopted the strategy of the diatribe as a protreptic tool of philosophy. This does not imply any affiliation to a philosophical school, only "Persius sets out to convert all of his readers to Stoicism".
10. *si forte quid aptius exit, quando haec rara avis est* (Pers. 1.45–46) "should it chance to turn out well / (For that's a rare bird)" (Lee (1987) 17).

11. Titus is a common prename, but the bearers of this name evidently feel proud of the first name carrier, the famous king Titus Tatius; Persius gives an ironic confirmation by adding the heroic epitheton *ingens*. In obscene language, however, *titus* is used for phallus, as the scholia explain (cf. Kißel (1990) 139–140).
12. *cum carmina lumbum / intrant et tremulo scalpuntur ubi intima versu* (Pers. 1.20–21), "As poems enter / Their loins and vibrant verses tickle the inmost parts" (Lee (1987) 15).
13. *articulis quibus et dicas cute perditus "ohe"* (Pers. 1.23), "Which you, a wreck in skin and limb, should now refuse" (Lee (1987) 15).
14. "Is your knowledge / Nothing unless another person knows you know?" (Lee (1987) 15).
15. "Calvus (. . .) says, 'You all know that bribery took place, and everyone knows you know it'" (Russell (2001) 23).
16. "that I am pointed out by passer-by as the minstrel of the Roman lyre" (Rudd (2004) 227).
17. "What says the public?" (Lee (1987) 17).
18. "So the juncture smooth rejects / Critical finger-nails" (Lee (1987) 17).
19. "Our poet can lay out / A line as though he ruled it one-eyed with red chalk" (Lee (1987) 17).
20. "Or if there's need to attack the morals, luxury / And luncheons of our 'kings.'" (Lee (1987) 17).
21. "are taught to express / Heroic thoughts" (Lee (1987) 17). Cowan (2017) tries to detect Seneca's reaction to the satiric idea of tragedy as overblown, excessive, and swollen and the Satiric's assertation "that tragedy is irrelevant to real life." Persius's poetics, however, do not blend in: Persius avoids stereotypes; his examples illustrate that any genre is unimmunized and any overambitious poet is prone to superficial exaggeration.
22. The interpretation of verses 1.76–78 is in part disputed, since it is unclear whether Persius is speaking or another interlocutor is making an accusation (cf. the overview in Kißel (1990) 207–208). I here follow the convincing explanation of Kißel, who reasons that *sartago loquendi* must refer to the result, i.e., that the young poets indiscriminately employ the archaic pathos of the ancient tragedians. The imagery that describes the uncritical mixture of all styles cannot be equated with the "potpourri of topics" that Juvenal declares to be the program of his satires (*Sat.* 1.85–86: *quidquid agunt homines, votum, timor, ira, voluptas, / gaudia, discursus, nostri farrago libelli est.*)
23. "'But grace and juncture have been added to raw numbers'" (Lee (1987) 19).
24. For a discussion of this point, cf. Kißel (1990) 230–232.
25. "Would these things be, if any vein of the paternal / Testicles lived in us?" (Lee (1987) 19).
26. "Never bangs the desk or tastes of bitten nails" (Lee (1987) 19).
27. Margaret Graver (2014) 281–284 discusses Seneca's views on the relationship between the *ingenium* and the *animus* itself.

References

Ambühl, A. (2015). *Krieg und Bürgerkrieg bei Lucan und in der griechischen Literatur: Studien zur Rezeption der attischen Tragödie und der hellenistischen Dichtung im "Bellum civile."* (Berlin/Boston).

Asmis, E. (1992). "Neoptolemus and the Classification of Poetry." *Classical Philology* 87: 206–231.

Asmis, E. (1995). "Epicurean Poetics," in Obbink, 15–34.

Bäumer, Ä. (1982). *Die Bestie Mensch: Senecas Aggressionstheorie, ihre philosophischen Vorstufen und ihre literarischen Auswirkungen.* (Frankfurt a.M./Bern).
Baier, Th., ed. (2012). *Götter und menschliche Willensfreiheit: Von Lucan bis Silius Italicus.* (München).
Bartsch, S. (2012). "Ethical Judgment and Narratorial Apostrophe in Lucan's *Bellum Civile*," in Baier, 87–97.
Bartsch, S. (2015). *Persius: A Study in Food, Philosophy, and the Figural.* (Chicago/London).
Bartsch, S., and A. Schiesaro, eds. (2015). *The Cambridge Companion to Seneca.* (Cambridge/New York).
Berti, E. (2018). *Lo stile e l'uomo: Quattro epistole letterarie di Seneca (Sen. epist. 114; 40; 100; 84) introduzione, traduzione e commento.* (Pisa).
Bloomer, W. M., ed. (2015). *A Companion to Ancient Education.* (Chichester).
Bramble, J. C. (1974). *Persius and the Programmatic Satire: A Study in Form and Imagery.* (Cambridge).
Braund, S. M., and C. Gill, eds. (1997). *The Passions in Roman Thought and Literature.* (Cambridge/New York).
Braund, S. M. and J. Osgood, eds. (2012). *A Companion to Persius and Juvenal.* (Chichester).
Brink, C. O. (1963). *Horace on Poetry: Prolegomena to the Literary Epistles.* (Cambridge).
Brink, C. O. (1971). *Horace on Poetry II: The Ars Poetica.* (Cambridge).
Buckley, E., and M. T. Dinter, eds. (2013). *A Companion to the Neronian Age.* (Chichester).
Cowan, R. (2017). "Bloated Buskins: Seneca and the Satiric Idea of Tragedy," in Trinacty and Sampson, 75–117.
D'Alessandro Behr, F. (2007). *Feeling History: Lucan, Stoicism, and the Poetics of Passion.* (Columbus, Ohio).
D'Alessandro Behr, F. (2014). "Consolation, Rebellion and Philosophy in Lucan's *Bellum Civile* Book 8," in Garani and Konstan, 218–244.
De Lacy, P. (1948). "Stoic Views of Poetry." *American Journal of Philology* 69: 241–271.
Dingel, J. (1974). *Seneca und die Dichtung.* (Heidelberg).
Fischer, S. (2008). *Seneca als Theologe: Studien zum Verhältnis von Philosophie und Tragödiendichtung.* (Berlin/New York).
Flashar, H., ed. (1994). *Grundriss der Geschichte der Philosophie: Die Philosophie der Antike. Band 4: Die Hellenistische Philosophie.* (Basel).
Freudenburg, K., ed. (2005). *The Cambridge Companion to Roman Satire.* (Cambridge).
Fuhrmann, M. (1993). "Komposition oder Schema? Zur Ars poetica des Horaz," in Ludwig, 171–206.
Fuhrmann, M. (^{3}2003). *Die Dichtungstheorie der Antike: Aristoteles—Horaz—"Longin"; Eine Einführung.* (Düsseldorf/Zürich).
Garani, M., and D. Konstan, eds. (2014). *The Philosophizing Muse: The Influence of Greek Philosophy on Roman Poetry.* (Cambridge).
Graver, M. R. (2014). "Honeybee Reading and Self-Scripting: *Epistulae Morales* 84," in Wildberger and Colish, 269–293.
Hardie, Ph. (2013). "Lucan's *Bellum Civile*," in Buckley and Dinter, 225–240.
Harrison, S., Frangoulidis, S., and T. D. Papanghelis, eds. (2018). *Intertextuality and Latin Literature.* (Berlin/Boston).
Heath, M. (2013). *Ancient Philosophical Poetics.* (Cambridge).
Johnson, W. R. (1987). *Momentary Monsters: Lucan and His Heroes.* (Ithaca, N.Y./London).

Karakasis, E. (2018). "Lucan's Intra-/Inter-textual Poetics: Deconstructing Caesar in Lucan," in Harrison, Frangoulidis, and Papanghelis, 353–375.
Keane, S. (2012). "Life in the Text: The Corpus of Persius' Satires," in Braund and Osgood, 79–96.
Klees, C., and C. Kugelmeier, eds. (2020). *Seneca und das Drama der Antike*. (Saarbrücken).
Kißel, W. (1990). *Aules Persius Flaccus: Satiren; Herausgegeben, übersetzt und kommentiert*. (Heidelberg).
Lee, G., and W. Barr (1987). *The Satires of Persius: The Latin Text with a Verse Translation by Guy Lee, Introduction and Commentary by William Barr*. (Liverpool/New Hampshire).
Leigh, M. (1997). *Spectacle and Engagement*. (Oxford).
Ludwig, K. (2014) *Charakterfokalisation bei Lucan: Eine narratologische Analyse*. (Berlin).
Ludwig, W., ed. (1993). *Horace: L'oeuvre et les imitations—un siècle d'interprétation; Neuf exposés suivis de discussions*. (Vandœuvres-Geneva).
Masters, J. (1992). *Poetry and civil war in Lucan's 'Bellum Civile'*. (Cambridge).
Mayer, R. (2005). "Sleeping with the enemy: satire and philosophy," in Freudenburg, 146–159.
Meyer, A.-S. (2021). *Die Naturphänomene in Lucans Bellum civile: Darstellung, Wahrnehmungen und Deutungen*. (Basel).
Narducci, E. (1979). *La provvidenza crudele: Lucano e la distruzione dei miti augustei*. (Pisa).
Narducci, E. (2002). *Lucano: Un'epica contro l'impero*. (Roma/Bari).
Nichols, M. F. (2013). "Persius," in Buckley and Dinter, 258–274.
Obbink, D., ed. (1995). *Philodemus and Poetry*. (New York/Oxford).
Porter, J. (1995). "Content and Form in Philodemus," in Obbink, 206–231.
Reydams-Schils, G. (2015). "Hellenistic and Roman Philosophy," in Bloomer, 123–133.
Reydams-Schils, G. (2017). "The Stoics," in Richter and Johnson, 527–538.
Richter, D. S., and W. A. Johnson, eds. (2017). *The Oxford Handbook to the Second Sophistic*. (New York).
Rudd, N. (2004). *Horace: Odes and Epodes*. (Cambridge, Mass./London).
Russell, D. A. (2001). *Quintilian: The Orator's Education, Book 6-8*. (Cambridge, Mass./London).
Schiesaro, A. (1997). "Passion, Reason and Knowledge in Seneca's Tragedies," in Braund and Gill, 89–111.
Schiesaro, A. (2003). *The Passions in Play:* Thyestes *and the Dynamics of Senecan Drama*. (Cambridge).
Seidensticker, B. (1968). *Die Gesprächsverdichtung in den Tragödien Senecas*. (Heidelberg).
Seidensticker, B. (2002). "Senecas 'Thyestes' oder die Jagd nach dem Außergewöhnlichen," in Seidensticker, 115–138.
Seidensticker, B., ed. (2002). *Senecas* Thyestes: *Deutsch von Durs Grünbein; Mit Materialien zur Übersetzung und zu Leben und Werk Senecas*. (Frankfurt a.M.).
Sklenář, R. J. (2003). *The Taste for Nothingness. A Study of Virtus and Related Themes in Lucan's Bellum Civile*. (Ann Arbor).
Sklenář, R. J. (2017). *Plant of a Strange Vine: "Oratio corrupta" and the Poetics of Senecan Tragedy*. (Berlin and Boston).
Staley, G. A. (2010). *Seneca and the Idea of Tragedy*. (Oxford/New York).
Steinmetz, P. (1994). "Die Stoa," in Flashar, 495–716.
Stroh, W. (2020). "Senecas *Phaedra* als Drama eines Stoikers. Mit einer Einleitung: Zur Geschichte der *interpretatio Stoica* von Senecas Tragödien," in Klees and Kugelmeier, 1–130.
Trinacty, C. V. (2015). "Senecan Tragedy," in Bartsch and Schiesaro, 29–40.

Trinacty, C. V., and C. M. Sampson, eds. (2017). "The Poetics of Senecan Tragedy." Special issue. *Ramus* 46 (1 & 2).

Walde, Chr. (2005). *Lucan im 21. Jahrhundert/Lucan in the 21st Century/Lucano nei primi del XXI secolo.* (München/Leipzig).

Walker, J. (2000). *Rhetoric and Poetics in Antiquity.* (Oxford/New York).

Wiener, C. (2006). *Stoische Doktrin in römischer Belletristik: Das Problem von Entscheidungsfreiheit und Determinismus in Senecas Tragödien und Lucans* Pharsalia. (München/Leipzig).

Wiener, C. (2014). "'Stoic Tragedy': A Contradiction in Terms?," in Garani and Konstan, 187–217.

Wildberger, J. (2005). "Quanta sub nocte iaceret nostra dies (Lucan 9,13f.)—Stoizismen als Mittel der Verfremdung bei Lucan," in Walde, 56–88.

PART III

INSIDE AND OUTSIDE OF ROMAN PHILOSOPHY

CHAPTER 18

TRANSLATION

CHRISTINA HOENIG

Introduction

In the field of classical philosophy, as in other disciplines heavily dependent on translation, the assumption prevails that the translator, as a mediator between primary source and academic audience, intends to find a suitable balance between accuracy[1] and accessibility.[2] In this balancing act, the faithfulness to the primary source more often than not remains the assumed priority of the translator, who is expected to yield the stage to the original author.[3] This scenario is intended to preserve the integrity of the source text, and to allow for an authentic reading experience, as much as this is possible, by striving to communicate the original meaning, register, and coloring in the target language.

Glancing over at the academic discipline of translation studies we note that, for some time, focus has been shifting away from the assumed authority of the source text toward the agency of the translator[4] and other factors that may influence, or serve as yardsticks for, the success of a translation.[5] A translator's specific agenda, whether personal or determined by patronage,[6] may lead to purposeful expansion, abridgment, and other modifications of a source text. At the same time translators naturally come with a predetermined linguistic, social, cultural, and ideological mindset. These factors, and many others, give rise to questions regarding the translator's responsibilities toward source text and target audience,[7] and, while obvious, may be useful for us to bear in mind as we engage with our source material, both as translators and as readers of translations that are already available.

Moreover, it is worth reflecting on the significance of a translator's agency and decision-making in the context of philosophical language and terminology, in particular: already the early scientific thinkers of Ionia, as they began to observe human existence from nontraditional angles and formed their conceptions of physical and metaphysical realms, were faced with the task of expanding and adjusting their familiar lexicon.[8] Their habitual manner of expression underwent semantic shifts and was applied to new contexts, thereby giving a voice to early philosophical inquiry.[9] Gradually, and by no means systematically, early philosophical writers in this manner "translated" novel cognitive contents and helped build a more specialized language.[10] The manipulation and expansion of established language as the linguistic raw material for expressing novel ideas came to be the attendant practice of philosophy from its earliest beginnings. Given that many staples of contemporary philosophical curricula are accessed through translation, it is all the more important to remind ourselves that writers of ancient and contemporary texts rely, to a greater or lesser extent, on recycling, manipulating, and stretching[11] familiar expression to convey their ideas, even before their material is further affected by the process of translation.

* * *

It has become a commonplace observation, in the particular case of Greek-Latin translation, that Roman translators generally prioritized literary creativity, invention, and *variatio* over authenticity and faithfulness. Yet, to appreciate their contributions fully, we need to contextualize Roman translators beyond customary references, for instance, to Horace's warning against the all-too-slavish "faithful interpreter" (*fidus interpres*, Ars P. 133), or to Cicero's maxim of translating not "like an interpreter [he means by this 'literally'], but like an orator" (*De optimo genere oratorum* 14, see below). In addition to adjusting our expectations with regard to the equivalence between Greek source text and Roman translation, it is useful to examine the specific manner in which a source text is integrated into a new environment: what parts of the Greek text are translated? Does the source text appear in a new genre? Are speaking parts assigned to a specific character, fictional or otherwise? Does the translation explicate, disambiguate, create new associations, connotations, semantic relations? I shall bring these and similar questions to bear on several writers of Roman philosophy. Before I do so, let me set the scene with some brief introductory notes on Roman translation.

Already Lucretius (1.832, 3.260) had complained about the infamous *patrii sermonis egestas*, the limited suitability of the Latin language as an adequate medium of creative literary expression. The apparent inadequacy of Latin, as contrasted with the more flexible Greek linguistic system, motivated Roman writers to emulate their Greek counterparts by producing a distinctively Latin literature, which, though modeled after Greek source texts, sought to compete with the latter in style and sophistication. Translation became a form of literary *imitatio*[12] aimed not only at reproducing a text but also at improving on it. Far from being considered the derivative activity of a translator, expected to hide behind the original author, translation was perceived as a creative endeavor worthy of critical acclaim.[13] As a part of this agenda, the Roman translator would become visible, or heard, by interfering with the original text. The intention was not to convey the text into the target language in as pure and intact a form as possible, but to invite the reader actively to compare and evaluate the new text in competition with the original.[14] An important requisite was an educated Roman readership with sufficient expertise in Greek to perceive a text's individual style and structure.

No fixed canon of translation theory materialized prior to the early Middle Ages.[15] Roman translators used various terms to define their work, such as *convertere/vertere*, *exprimere, interpretari, tradere, traducere, transferre, transcribere,* and *transponere*,[16] but the use of this terminology was not clear-cut.[17] Some basic precepts or lines of approach emerged and are commonly mentioned in the context of Roman translation. The sense-oriented translation allowed for the abandonment of the syntactical and lexical structures of the source text, thereby achieving a greater level of idiomatic diction in the target language. The alternative, literal rendering would be closely modeled on the source text at the expense of natural and idiomatic diction in the target language. These two lines of approach[18] are described by ancient translators as *interpretari ad sensum* and *ad verbum* respectively.[19] The *ad sensum* approach was the clear favorite. As mentioned previously, Horace in his *Ars poetica* 133 coined the image of the *fidus interpres*, a slavish translator whose technique should be avoided by the style-conscious writer.[20] Gellius informs us (*NA* 1.16.3) about the difficulties a translator may encounter when searching for an *ad verbum* expression, while Seneca demands (*Tranq.* 9.2.3) that not the form (*forma*) of a particular Greek word should be retained in translation, but its force (*res* or *vis*).[21]

Over time, the changes in the linguistic landscape of the later Roman Empire were to impact on the role and function of translation. The end of the second century CE brought a decline of Greek as the lingua franca of the Roman West that, around two hundred years later, resulted in a reduced proficiency in the language, now restricted to aristocratic circles and scholars in fields such as rhetoric, philosophy, and medicine, whose profession required the knowledge of a technical Greek vocabulary.[22] The decline of Greek proficiency particularly in the Western Empire of Late Antiquity was at the root of a development that would lend new significance to translation as a medium of communication between two diverging cultures. We will witness the changing role of translation for Roman philosophical literature as we look at the authors Cicero, Lucretius, Apuleius, and Calcidius. For each of these authors, we will find, translation is a defining factor in their engagement with Greek philosophy.

Finally, a note on my own terminology: I consider it appropriate, in the context of the four authors under examination below, for whom the pursuit of strict equivalence between source text and translation was not a primary concern, to adopt a rather broad definition of "translation" that accommodates looser interpretations we might alternatively describe as "adaptations." Such translations may be marked by invasive methods such as extensive omissions or expansions, a change of authorial perspective, and even a change of genre.[23]

Cicero

I begin with Cicero, whose witness accounts of translation practice[24] make a frequent appearance in the early chapters of translation histories or similar subject-specific compilations.[25] Often cited in this context is his rejection of a literal style of translation, as noted in his *De optimo genere oratorum* (hereafter *Opt. gen.*). Less frequently examined is the specific context of these comments.[26] Cicero's professed aim in this work is to allow Roman readers to experience his recommended style of oratory, the so-called Attic type, whose refinement and purity elevate it over and against the "Asian" type, which is "defective in its exuberance" (*Opt. gen.* 8: *illos potius [imitemur] qui incorrupta sanitate sunt, quod est proprium Atticorum, quam eos quorum vitiosa abundantia est, qualis Asia multos tulit*). Thus far, according to Cicero, error has reigned as to the specific nature of the Attic style, and it is his desire, with the help of translations from suitable Greek sources, to accustom students' ears to it (*Opt. gen.* 13: *in eo magnus error esset quale esset id dicendi genus . . .*).[27] Cicero rebukes his critics' erroneous assumptions that the primary characteristics of this style were mere simplicity and a lack of rhetorical embellishment. He explains (*Opt. gen.* 14) that, in order to offer students as authentic an experience of Attic oratory as possible:

> I translated (*converti*) the most celebrated orations . . . I did, however, not translate them as an interpreter would do, but in the manner of an orator (*nec converti ut interpres, sed ut orator*), with the same meaning and forms (*sententiis isdem et earum formis*) or, so to say, figures of speech (*figuris*), but with expressions that are in accordance with our own usage. For these expressions, I did not think it necessary to translate word for word (*verbum pro verbo*), but I preserved the character and force (*genus vimque*) of the words.[28]

Cicero's method of translating "in the manner of an orator" is tailored to the specific aim of reproducing the true Attic style in Latin, an undertaking prompted by his desire to promote a new stylistic model. Naturally, a cumbersome "word-for-word" approach would be ill suited to the task.

A similar discussion appears in Cicero's *De oratore* 154–155, where Crassus recalls his youthful practice of translating Greek in the hope of refining his style of Latin oratory.[29] Crassus had previously given up on paraphrasing Latin literature, given that eminent Roman authors such as Ennius and Gracchus had already used the "most suitable," "most elegant," and "best" (*propria, ornatissima, optima*) words and left him little room for improvement. Once again, the recommended method is a relatively loose translation ("I decided to unfold [*explicarem*] the most eminent Greek speeches") that aimed at stylistic brilliance and idiomatic Latin, and allowed the forging of new expressions (*quae nova nostris essent*) where appropriate.

Greek-Latin translation became a crucial tool for Cicero also during his later years as a writer of philosophy, when the skills he had developed during his rhetorical practice proved important for the deposition of Greek cultural hegemony.[30] In the preface to his *De finibus* Cicero professes his ambition not merely to perform the role of an *interpres* but to add to the doctrinal material his own "judgment and arrangement" (*iudicium et ordo scribendi*), thus producing "writings that are at once brilliant in style and not only translations from Greek" (*Fin.* 1.6).[31] Cicero is responding here to critics who questioned the use of his philosophical translations, expressing a preference for reading Greek philosophy in its original language.[32] Likely in response to such criticism, Cicero's various philosophical treatises convey an abundance of Greek doctrinal material, rearranged as urbane and learned discussion among luminaries of Roman politics. With his own "judgment and arrangement" added to the Greek material, Cicero positions himself, in the *De finibus*, at the front of a long line of Greek philosophical writers such as Diogenes, Antipater, Mnesarchus, Panaetius, Posidonius, and Theophrastus, each of whom had made use in their own works of material that had already been discussed by previous Greek authors. Cicero feels justified in producing his own, Latin, variations on doctrinal themes[33] since the validity of this practice had been granted in the case of his Greek predecessors. As we continue in the preface to *De finibus* 1, Cicero lists as a further, decisive justification for writing Roman philosophy his patriotic duty, announcing that even a direct translation from Greek has merit: "Even if I were to produce a direct translation (*si plane sic verterem*) of Plato or Aristotle, of the sort the poets have done with plays, I believe I would render a service to my fellow citizens in bringing about their acquaintance with their divine genius" (*Fin.* 1.7).[34] Adding further justification to the practice of literal translation, Cicero at *Fin.* 1.3 professes himself astonished at the "arrogant distaste for domestic products" (*insolens domesticarum rerum fastidium*), given that the Latin language does not suffer from a poverty of words (*Latinam linguam non modo non inopem*), but, in fact, surpasses Greek in its abundance (*locupletiorem*).

We find a useful display of the power dynamics, cultural and intellectual, between Greece and Rome in Cicero's *Tusculan Disputations*. In this work, his appropriation of a whole host of Greek material by means of Latin translation is intended to express not merely Rome's competitiveness, but its superiority as a cultural nation, with the Latin language subduing, harvesting, and finally transcending the voice of the Greek philosophical authors.[35] In the preface to Book 1 of the *Tusculans* Cicero explains his intention of illuminating the subject of philosophy *Latinis litteris*, not because one could not access the subject via the works of Greek authors, but because his fellow Romans "have shown themselves to possess more wisdom than the Greeks in all matters, both in discovering [novelties] for themselves and in improving upon what they had taken over from them, at least in matters they had deemed worthy of pursuit." With Greece already having been defeated in the field of oratory (*Tusc.* 1.5), Cicero intends to take on the so-far-neglected territory of philosophy (*philosophia iacuit usque ad hanc aetatem*) as a service to his fellow countrymen.[36] As in the earlier context of the *De finibus*, Cicero portrays his engagement with Greek philosophy as a patriotic act, intended to remind his fellow citizens of their exclusively Roman virtuous disposition. The weapon with which he furthers his nation's interests is translation, and it is a weapon wielded with astonishing frequency in Book 1 of the *Tusculans* alone, where Cicero integrates into his discussion—partly conducted in the style of Socrates, as Cicero is eager to advertise—translations of varying faithfulness and length from various Platonic dialogues.

For the remainder of this section, I propose to examine how Cicero in *Tusc.* 1, with the help of Greek-Latin translation, uproots Greek material and integrates it into a new context in such a way as to align it with a Roman outlook.[37] More specifically, Platonic material is translated and transformed in a way that allows Cicero, or rather his unidentified mouthpiece "M.,"[38] to pursue an argumentative line in favor of soul's immortality.

This leads to a powerful conclusion in which the role of Socrates is appropriated by Cato, the paradigm of Roman *mores* and virtues, characteristics that ultimately qualify him as the archetypal philosopher.[39]

I begin with a mere snippet of translation, Cicero's rendering of ps.-Plato's second *Letter* 311c, at *Tusc.* 1.31–32.[40] In the original text the author comments on his own prominent relationship with the tyrant Dionysus I, who had complained about having acquired an unfavorable reputation due to slander, of which he accused Plato's associates and Plato himself. Since their relationship is the subject of much talk, ps.-Plato urges that it must remain untainted to ensure that their combined reputation remain favorable even after their death. His observation that base men show no concern, whereas the most decent men do everything in their power to ensure they will be spoken of well after their death, is proof that "the dead have some kind of perception of the affairs here on earth, for the best souls divine that this is so" (Ep. 2, 311c7–d1: ὃ δὴ καὶ ἐγὼ τεκμήριον ποιοῦμαι ὅτι ἔστιν τις αἴσθησις τοῖς τεθνεῶσιν τῶν ἐνθάδε· αἱ γὰρ βέλτισται ψυχαὶ μαντεύονται ταῦτα οὕτως ἔχειν). Accordingly, certain men who have died "would have taken great care to ensure they would be talked of more favorably than it is the case now" (311d4–5: πάνυ ἂν σπουδάσαι ὥστε βελτίω λέγεσθαι περὶ αὐτῶν ἢ νῦν).

At *Tusc.* 1.27, following M.'s doxographical survey on the nature of the soul, his interlocutor "A." demands that M. prove, firstly, that souls survive death and, secondly, that death is free from evil. Engaging with the first request, Cicero transfers ps.-Plato's sentence "and I will take [this] as a proof that the dead have some kind of perception of the affairs here on earth" (ὃ δὴ καὶ ἐγὼ τεκμήριον ποιοῦμαι ὅτι ἔστιν τις αἴσθησις τοῖς τεθνεῶσιν τῶν ἐνθάδε) into a Roman setting that, moreover, serves as a prop for his current program of presenting arguments in favor of soul's immortality. The translation of ἔστιν τις αἴσθησις τοῖς τεθνεῶσιν appears in the following statement, itself loosely adapted from the Greek:

> Thus we find among those men of the past, whom Ennius calls the "ancients," the established view that *there is sensation in death* (*esse in morte sensum*) and that, once life is spent, man is not so destroyed as to pass away entirely. And this can be discerned, as in numerous other cases, in the context of the pontifical law and from burial rites. Men of the most impressive abilities would not have observed these with such great care, nor would their violation have been forbidden by such irreconcilable offense against religious ordinance, unless there had remained fixed in their minds the view that death is not destruction that suspends and destroys everything.
>
> Itaque unum illud erat insitum priscis illis, quos cascos appellat Ennius, esse in morte sensum neque excessu vitae sic deleri hominem, ut funditus interiret; idque cum multis aliis rebus, tum e pontificio iure et e caerimoniis sepulcrorum intellegi licet, quas maxumis ingeniis praediti nec tanta cura coluissent nec violatas tam inexpiabili religione sanxissent, nisi haereret in eorum mentibus mortem non interitum esse omnia tollentem atque delentem . . .

Without acknowledging his source, Cicero transfers the view that sensation exists in death from the context of the Greek author's concern for his reputation to a concern for proper religious practice. This concern, supposedly prompted by the view that soul remains after death, Cicero anchors in the authority of the Roman fathers of the distant past, who, with Ennius's approval, assume the role of ps.-Plato's "best souls" (αἱ βέλτισται ψυχαί). Cicero appeals as a proof to Rome's religious custom and pontifical law, thereby replacing the apparently mundane wish for a good reputation upon death with the Roman virtue of *religio*.

Further into the discussion at *Tusc.* 1.52–53 Cicero renders into Latin Socrates's interpretation of Apollo's oracular utterance "know yourself," such as it appears at *Alcibiades* 1, 130. In his endeavor to discover "whatever we ourselves are" (τί ποτ' ἐσμὲν αὐτοί, 129b1–2) Socrates understands "him who commands us to know ourselves" to be saying, more specifically, that we ought to "know our soul" (130e8–9), observing that "nothing possesses more sovereign power over ourselves than soul" (130d5–6). Soul must look toward soul in order to know itself, and especially toward the seat of its own virtue, wisdom (133b7–10). A soul that fails to know itself is unable also to obtain a full grasp of anything else, and thus unable to hold civic office or any other position of authority.

In the *Tusculans* this passage features in the context of M.'s appeal to various types of authorities, including Plato, who held soul to be immortal. Censuring critics' inability to grasp soul's nature without the body, in other words: their ignorance of their own soul's nature, he appeals to Apollo's oracle: "Therefore, when Apollo [commands] 'know yourself,' he means: 'know your soul' " (*cum igitur [Apollo] "nosce te," dicit, hoc dicit, "nosce animum tuum"*). This statement, a straightforward translation of Plato's *Alcibiades* 1, is then transferred from the context of soul's wisdom as a prerequisite for political office to the more specific purpose of validating the claim that soul is immortal. Only those who know their soul's nature are aware that it is immortal. The force of this claim is increased by a further stretch of translation, a rendering of *Phaedrus* 245c5–246a2, Socrates's proof of soul's immortality. In its original context, this proof is intended to reveal the true nature of soul, the first step of convincing Phaedrus to associate with a true lover who may guide his soul toward virtue. M. uproots the proof of soul's immortality from its original purpose, instead offering a somewhat awkward transition between this and the preceding translated passage from *Alcibiades* 1. There is yet hope for those who fail to know the nature of their own soul. They may infer, instead, from soul's knowledge of its own existence and movement the fact that it is immortal. Even if soul lacked self-knowledge, M. asks, would it also not know of its own existence or movement (*ne esse quidem se sciet, ne moveri quidem se, Tusc.* 1.53)? According to M. it was this very question that prompted Plato's proof of soul's immortality. He next launches into the *Phaedrus* passage, for which Cicero provides a rather close translation,[41] followed by an elliptical summary (1.55): "Soul perceives that it moves. Along with this perception comes another, the perception that it is moved by its own power, not by another. Nor is it possible that it will ever be deserted by itself. From this follows its eternity" (*sentit igitur animus se moveri; quod cum senti, illud una sentit se vi sua non aliena moveri, nec accidere posse ut ipse umquam a se deseratur*). The line of Cicero's narrative in favor of soul's immortality is constructed on the backbone of a patchwork of Greek passages that are clipped together, at times awkwardly so.

As M. duly points out (*Tusc.* 1.53), the current context is not the only one in which the *Phaedrus* passage is put to use. A virtually identical rendering of it had made a previous appearance at the close of Scipio's dream in Cicero's *De republica*. Scipio Africanus's objective in appearing to the younger Scipio at the end of this work was to instill in the latter an increased sense of duty to protect the fatherland (*curae de salute patriae*, 6.29). Following a sobering demonstration of the triviality, from a universal perspective, of mortal fame (*celebritas sermonis hominum*, 6.20), the *Phaedrus* passage follows Africanus's astonishing statement that humans are gods: "Know, therefore, that you are a god, for indeed it is a god who has life, sensation, memory, foresight; who reigns, regulates, moves the body to which it is attached, just as the supreme god and this world" (6.26). Soul itself is immortal and self-moving, as demonstrated subsequently in the familiar *Phaedrus* passage. While at *Tusc.* 1.53 this passage serves the purpose of corroborating M.'s argument in favor of soul's immortality, in the present context it functions as the prerequisite for Africanus's exhortation to make use of the immortal soul for the best possible purpose (*hanc [naturam animi] tu exerce optimis in rebus*), the care for the good of the fatherland. Even though M. at *Tusc.* 1.53 is crediting Plato with the content of the argument (*illa ratio nata est Platonis*), Cicero immediately creates for the reader an intertextual association with one of his own most notable works, in which Plato features in accordance with Cicero's arrangement (*a me autem posita est [illa ratio] in sexto libro de re publica*, 1.53). The *Phaedrus* thus shares a stage with Cicero's *De re publica* while, for the reader of the *Tusculans*, the reference to the striking corollary of Scipio's dream would lend additional conviction to the view of an immortal soul.[42]

At *Tusc.* 1.71 Cicero intensifies his program of appropriation. Pointing to the example of Socrates in Plato's *Apology*, M. observes that the philosopher's conviction regarding soul's immortality allowed him to accept his impending death. After recalling additional details of Socrates's speech, Cicero draws a sudden boundary: "But these are both matters of the past, as well as Greek" (*sed haec et vetera et Graeca*, 1.74). In what follows, Socrates's courageous stance at the prospect of death is appropriated by Cato, the paradigmatic champion of traditional Roman values and virtues. Cato "departed from life in a manner that made him rejoice in having found a reason to die." While it remains a sacrilege to commit suicide without divine prompting, in the case of Cato, as previously with Socrates, "god himself had given a just reason" (*causam iustam*). It is Cato who is foremost in M.'s mind as he renders the famous pronouncement of *Phaedo* 67d8–9, "This is the very exercise of the philosophers, the release and separation of soul from body" (τὸ μελέτημα αὐτὸ τοῦτό ἐστιν τῶν φιλοσόφων, λύσις καὶ χωρισμὸς ψυχῆς ἀπὸ σώματος),[43] in Cicero's words: "The philosophers' entire life ... is a preparation for death" (*tota enim philosophorum vita, ut ait idem, commentatio mortis est*). Cato will soon reappear at *Tusc.* 1.101, where he reiterates, as parallels for his own attitude toward death, the shining example of many Roman legions who marched toward certain doom in high spirits.

Meanwhile, the critical "judgment and arrangement" (recall *Fin.* 1.6) Cicero employs while translating from the Greek appears to have paid off. At *Tusc.* 1.24, A. had expressed the desire to be convinced of soul's immortality[44] but, despite repeated study of Plato's very own *Phaedo*, his conviction of Plato's view wanes as soon as he puts down the book.[45] Having been exposed to M.'s variation on the theme of soul's immortality, however, he is happy to report at *Tusc.* 1.77 that, having understood M.'s arguments, "nobody will dissuade me from [soul's] immortality." Cicero's own philosophical narrative in favor of soul's immortality which, at this point in the discussion, has appropriated several passages from various dialogues of Plato only to culminate in the portrayal of Cato as the archetypal philosopher, has achieved in A. greater persuasion than Plato's works standing by themselves.[46]

The sheer accumulation of Platonic echoes, all of which have been aligned to harmonize with M.'s argumentative line in favor of soul's immortality, fits well with Cicero's professed aim not only of inserting himself into the philosophical tradition but also, at the same time, of positioning himself at its apex. His choice to produce an unusually large number of, at times, rather close translations of Platonic material in *Tusculans* 1 alone, instead of simply alluding to or summarizing their content, serves the explicit purpose of making Plato himself speak on his own behalf, in a powerful validation of Roman philosophical writing.

LUCRETIUS

Lucretius does not often feature in translation histories.[47] This may be due to the fact that he did not produce any longer, coherent stretches of recognizable translation from Epicurean sources. We do, however, find at *De rerum natura* (hereafter *DRN*) 6.1138–1285 a rendering of Thucydides' *History of the Peloponnesian War* 2.47–53, an account of the plague that devastated Athens in 429 BCE. Lucretius's translation of this passage exhibits varying levels of faithfulness. He omits the Greek author's political frame and ethical analysis concerning the erosion of respect for divine law and the resulting pursuit of short-lived pleasure (Thuc. 2.53.1–4). Instead, his focus is on Thucydides' description of the effects of the disease on its victims. Here, Lucretius follows the order of the original text relatively closely,[48] but embellishes it with detailed, graphic sketches of the victims' bodily and mental deterioration.[49] By means of strategic excisions, elaborations, and shifts of emphasis, he prioritizes the Athenians' horror[50] and ignorance,[51] advertised by him in hindsight as consequences of the fact that Epicurean doctrine was not yet available to the Greeks.[52] Having introduced his readers to the Epicurean teachings that culminate in the poem's dramatic ending, Lucretius offers a novel analysis of familiar events for which they may draw on their newly acquired learning. His contemporary audience was well acquainted with Thucydides both through direct access of the Greek and through numerous Latin imitations,[53] and would likely have been all the more sensitive to the manner in which he shed a new Epicurean light on the familiar Athenian plight.

As for Roman acquaintance with Epicurus's writings, Cicero at *Tusc.* 4.6–7 points to the wide circulation of Epicurus's doctrine via Latin prose translations (which he himself considers to be of low quality). Lucretius chooses a different route. He translates the principal tenets of Epicurus's thought[54] in the form of malleable images or metaphors that instantiate the underlying doctrine in multiple forms and shapes,[55] an artistic process that mirrors the basic atomic mechanism at play in the cosmos, as I propose to examine in the remainder of this section. This same mechanism, the rearrangement of stock material, is underlined by his switch to a different language as well as genre. The stock material that is Epicurus's doctrine is restructured and cast into a linguistic and literary form that better matches a Roman setting.

I begin with a well-known passage, the description of Venus in her embrace of Mars at the outset of Lucretius's poem, to examine how the poet first introduces, with the help of these two figures, the central image of union and disunion, an image that illustrates the elementary physical processes of atomic aggregation and segregation at work in the universe.[56] This same image of union and disunion then functions as a unifying theme throughout the work as it is translated, in various forms, into the poem's content, lexicon, and metrical pattern. Lucretius introduces the image of union and disunion at the outset in a striking invocation of Venus, divine *genetrix* (1.1) of the Roman people who, in due course, is joined by Mars. Initially, however, Venus alone is praised for providing the impulse to sexual union and for ensuring future generations for every living species: "Because of you, every species of living creatures is conceived and, once born, sees the light of the sun" (1.3–4). Moreover, Venus is ultimately responsible for the wide variety of species inhabiting the earth: "Earth still young grew grass and bushes first, then gave birth to generations of living creatures, many tribes, in many modes and manners" (*multa modis multis varia ratione coorta*, 5.790–792; cf. e.g. 1.341–342).[57] The term *voluptas*,[58] of course, placed in a prominent position at the end of the poem's first line, would have been recognized by Lucretius's readers as a familiar epithet for the goddess of sexual pleasure. As is frequently noted, however, the poem's Epicurean framework ties Venus's familiar association with sexual union[59] to the Epicurean concept of ἡδονή.

The figure of Venus takes on an additional, political dimension at the end of the invocation where Venus *omnipotens* appeases Mars (merely *armipotens*, 1.33), in a scene rich in sexual connotations. With their bodies entwined (*hunc . . . recubantem corpore sancto circumfusa super*, 1.38–39) Lucretius urges Venus to "sweet talk" Mars so as to allow for peaceful love and care among the Roman people (1.39–40). Venus, now acting as an advocate for political union, temporarily subdues Mars, who, in turn, evokes disunion, disorder, and hostile clashes between warring factions (*belli fera moenera Mavors armipotens regit*, 1.32–33), a sentiment that likely resonated with Lucretius's audience, as set against the current troublesome climate of the Republic (see 1.41–42).[60] Coupled with the appeal for political union, moreover, is Lucretius's gesture toward the equally important binding relationship of *amicitia*. The social ties of family and friendship are shown to be bound up with the wider political community that is urged to join together in peace. Lucretius stresses that the strong bond he shares with Memmius, his dedicatee, provides tranquil pleasure, a state of mind required to carry out his creative work, and fuels his eagerness: "The sweet pleasure (*voluptas*) of your welcome friendship (*amicitiae*) persuaded me to take on any toil" (1.140–42). The imagery of social ties and unions represented by Venus early in the poem resurfaces again later. Men learned to live as a community and to rise above their primitive, violent nature to ensure the future existence of later generations (5.1019–1020, 1024–1027). Excessive political aspiration, often accompanied by violent means, is a sentiment that runs counter to Epicurean tenets and leads to disunion and destruction. Having suffered the consequences of hostile conduct, men of their own accord submitted themselves to the binding "ordinances and the close mesh of law" (*sub leges artaque iura*, 5.1145–1147, tr. Bailey). Tranquility can prevail only where citizens abide by the "common bonds of peace" (*communia foedera pacis*, 5.1154–1155).[61] Lucretius's early introduction of the central image of union and disunion through the archetypal Roman figures of Venus and Mars reappears throughout the poem, translated into images of the bonds and ties of civilized, lawful conduct which may, temporarily, overcome violence and hostility.

This reading of Venus and Mars's embrace as the first of many varying images that render the recurring theme of union and disunion[62] into a language suited to Roman taste—images that serve to instantiate the basic doctrine of atomic compound formation and separation—appears to ignore Lucretius's own warning, at 2.655–660, against a metaphorical use of divine names for worldly phenomena. But he explains that such a strategy is permissible as long as it does not reinforce religious superstition.[63] Indeed, Lucretius's own objective is diametrically opposed to the propagation of religious creed, and his symbolic appeal to Venus and Mars serves to introduce elementary atomic mechanisms, an awareness of which combats religious superstition. Accordingly, Lucretius proceeds to decode the symbolic embrace between Venus and Mars in the subsequent lines. In a crucial step in his artistic undertaking, the interlinked notions of procreative, social, and political union and disunion are followed by the introduction of atomic aggregation and segregation (1.55–60): "The first beginnings of things, from which nature creates, grows, and nourishes all things, and into which nature, in turn, dissolves them when they are perished. These, as we present their account, we are accustomed to call matter, creative bodies and seeds of things" (*rerum primordia . . . / unde omnis natura creet res auctet alatque / quove eadem rursum natura perempta resolvat, / quae nos materiem et genitalia corpora rebus / reddunda in ratione vocare et semina rerum / appellare suemus*). As is frequently noted,[64] the image of *genetrix* implies "mother" (*mater*), which is etymologically tied to the Epicurean *materies*, the atoms. Even though these atoms, unlike their compounds, share with *mater* Venus her divine attribute of immortality (e.g., 1.221; 1.239; 1.245), an understanding of their eternal nature not only does not require superstitious belief, but dispels it. In what follows, Lucretius's choice of expression for atomic compound formation makes for a striking echo of Venus's role as a force of procreative union. The first bodies come together in a "creative gathering" (*genitali concilio*, 1.182–183; and see *materiai concilium* at 1.516–517), with the term *concilium* aptly adding its political connotations to Lucretius's philosophical message.[65]

The figure of Mars, previously introduced as a force destructive to social and political order, is decoded as instantiating the disunion or breaking up of atomic compounds. Forced apart from their connective structures (*dispulsa suo de coetu*, 1.1017) individual atoms travel throughout the void at random. Prior to the formation of the gigantic compound that has become our universe, individual atoms whirled through the void as a newly formed cloud or mass. Due to their dissimilar shapes they remained in discord as if on a chaotic battlefield made up of temporary groupings, interlaced with gaps and thruways and subject to mutual blows, clashes, and commotions.[66] Atoms that are incompatible with one another due to their differing shapes are described by Lucretius as "hostile," fighting wars against one another, with troop set against troop in an eternal struggle without respite, bustling about in their repeated (unsuccessful) attempts at forming factions (2.116–124, cf. 2.569–574). Moreover, any part of a compound that becomes brittle allows for destruction and a new, disorderly multitude of atoms is set free (1.1111–1113). Death is to be thought of as no more than the disunion or scattering of previously connected atomic compounds.[67] As Venus embraces Mars, the two aspects of atomic doctrine, atomic compound formation and destruction, are inseparable. Venus herself as the symbol of union is aptly invoked, however, at the very outset of the poem, given that the Lucretius himself is here only beginning to reassemble the raw material of Epicurean doctrine in a new form.

The chaos of scattered, disorderly, and hostile atoms in a state of war, and the association of this scenario with death, a stock Epicurean tenet,[68] is illustrated in dramatic fashion by Lucretius's description of a pivotal episode of Roman history, the Punic Wars, in a further instantiation of the poem's central theme of disunion (3.830–846):[69]

1	nil igitur mors est ad nos neque pertinet hilum,	Therefore, death means nothing to us and is of no concern
	quandoquidem natura animi mortalis habetur.	since, indeed, the nature of the mind is held to be mortal.
	et velut anteacto nil tempore sensimus aegri,	And even as we felt no ill in the time that has passed,
5	ad confligendum venientibus undique Poenis,	when Phoenicians came clashing together from all sides,
	omnia cum belli trepido concussa tumultu	when all was shaken by the frenzied roar of war,
	horrida contremuere sub altis aeteris oris,	terrified, trembling beneath the high regions of heaven,
	in dubioque fuere utrorum ad regna cadendum	unknown to whose kingdom
10	omnibus humanis esset terraque marique	all life, land, and sea would fall,
	sic, ubi non erimus, cum corporis atque animae	even so, when we are no more, after the dissolution of body and soul by which we are composed as one,
	discidium fuerit quibus e sumus uniter apti,	be sure that nothing whatever can affect us, [us] who will be no more, or stir our senses.
	scilicet haud nobis quicquam, qui non erimus tum,	
15	accidere omnino poterit sensumque movere,	Not unless land will mingle with sea and sea with the heaven.
	non si terra mari miscebitur et mare caelo.	And even if mind's nature and the power of soul have sensation once it has been torn out of our body,
	et si iam nostro sentit de corpore postquam	
	distractast animi natura animaeque potestas,	it will still be nothing to us, [us] who are composed as one by the joining and union of soul and body.
	nil tamen est ad nos qui comptu coniugioque	
	corporis aque animae consistimus niter apti.	

Soul's mortality at the outset of this passage (l.2) is reiterated toward the end, where Lucretius explains further that we ourselves exist and have sensation only when soul and body are conjoined (ll.16–17). When they are not, "nothing whatever can affect us, [us] who will be no more, or stir our senses" (ll.11–12). We can detect the raw material for these verses in Epicurus's *RS* 2: "Death is nothing to us. For that which is rent asunder lacks sensation. But that which lacks sensation is nothing to us" (ὁ θάνατος οὐδὲν πρὸς ἡμᾶς. τὸ γὰρ διαλυθὲν ἀναισθητεῖ. τὸ δὲ ἀναισθητοῦν οὐδὲν πρὸς ἡμᾶς).

A similar sentiment appears in Epicurus's *Letter to Menoeceus*, 124.6–125.9:

> But grow accustomed to the thought that death is nothing to us, since every good and every bad is [bound up with] perception. But death is the loss of perception.... Death is nothing to us. Since, indeed, whenever we exist, death is absent, but whenever death is present, we do not exist. Therefore, [death] is nothing to the living nor to those who have died, since, indeed, it does not attend the former, while the latter no longer are.

> συνέθιζε δὲ ἐν τῷ νομίζειν μηδὲν πρὸς ἡμᾶς εἶναι τὸν θάνατον· ἐπεὶ πᾶν ἀγαθὸν καὶ κακὸν ἐν αἰσθήσει· στέρησις δέ ἐστιν αἰσθήσεως ὁ θάνατος.... ὁ θάνατος οὐδὲν πρὸς ἡμᾶς. ἐπειδήπερ ὅταν μὲν ἡμεῖς ὦμεν, ὁ θάνατος οὐ πάρεστιν, ὅταν δὲ ὁ θάνατος παρῇ, τόθ' ἡμεῖς οὐκ ἐσμέν. οὔτε οὖν πρὸς τοὺς ζῶντάς ἐστιν οὔτε πρὸς τοὺς τετελευτηκότας, ἐπειδήπερ περὶ οὓς μὲν οὐκ ἔστιν, οἳ δ' οὐκέτι εἰσίν.

Lucretius in the above passage of his poem presents what is termed the symmetry argument,[70] according to which nonexistence prior to one's birth is likened to nonexistence following death.[71] Disunion between the atomic compounds soul and body equals nonexistence and the absence of perception, an Epicurean tenet Lucretius associates with a harrowing military conflict, the historic clash between Rome and Carthage. A further effect of this specific image is the Roman reader's realization that even conflicts as destructive as the ones fought against the Carthaginians do not stir us when our soul and body are not united. What is more, the theme of warfare and disunion, whether military or atomic, is translated into incoherent word order (cf. the hyperbaton *omnia . . . oris* spanning over ll. 3.834–835), while the military dimension is reinforced further by the spondaic metrical pattern, in particular, of l.3.833.

Atomic aggregation and segregation is, moreover, famously translated into the very fabric of Lucretius's literary medium (*nunc ut repetam coeptum* **pertexere** *dictis*, 1.415; see also 6.42 and his use of the noun *textura* to describe atomic compounds at 1.246). Initially, the gesture to Ennius's *aeterna versa* at 1.117–126 (*Ennius ut noster cecinit*) confirms didactic poetry as an authentically Roman literary genre. But the switch to a new literary medium is effective also on another level, in that it allows Lucretius to rearrange letters and words in suitable groupings that are aptly fitted and linked together.[72] At 4.524 he initially explains that voice, like all sounds, is perceived when impacting upon our sense organs. Given its ability to exert such an impact, sound is declared to be of corporeal nature. Spoken (*voces*) and written (*verba*) words are made up of corporeal elements (4.533–534). Building on this same notion, Lucretius is later able to point out that he is the first to translate (*vertere*) Epicurus's teachings and, as it were, to "reassemble" them with the help of the *voces* of the Roman forefathers in a novel linguistic and literary shape and form (*hanc [natura haec rerum ratioque] primus cum primis ipse repertus nunc ego sum in patrias qui possim vertere voces*, 5.335–337).

Overall, Lucretius's choice of translating Epicurus's Greek doctrine into a multitude of Roman images, verses, words, and rhythms, instead of producing a straightforward stretch of translation, in a more narrow sense of the word, of any one identifiable Greek source, reinforces the central tenet of Epicurean doctrine, atomic compound formation and separation, an effect that would be lost to readers choosing to study Epicurus's doctrine in its original Greek or in Latin prose translations. On that note, let me point, finally, to Lucretius's strategic use of Greek terms in the poem. At 4.1153–1191 he provides an entertaining catalog of flattering Greek nicknames[73] used by those "blinded by love" (*cupidine caeci*, 4.1153) to praise their sweethearts' undeserving merits. Alongside these Greek labels Lucretius provides Latin "translations" that decode and reassemble them into sober, accurate language expressive of their true properties. Providing a whole battery of Greek terms, along with their Latin interpretation, Lucretius reinforces the inaccuracy[74] and inauthenticity of the Greek epithets, in contrast to their Latin explanations (Greek terms marked in bold) (4.1160–1170):

1	*nigra* **melichrus** *est, inmunda et fetida* **acosmos,**	A dark girl is like "gold-brown" honey, smutty and foul is "effortless,"
	caesia **Palladium,** *nervosa et lignea* **dorcas,**	sharp gray eyes are like Athena's, bones and sinews a "gazelle,"
5	*parvula, pumilio,* **chariton mia,** *tota merum sal,*	the mite and pithy passes for a Muse, "pure and delightful through and through,"
	magna atque inmanis **cataplexis** *plenaque honoris.*	one towering and big is "formidable," a "preeminent beauty."
	balba loqui non quit, **traulizi,** *muta*	A girl who stammers "lisps" instead; she
10	*pudens est;*	who is mute is merely "shy,"
	at flagrans, odiosa, loquacula **lampadium** *fit.*	yet tedious babbling is "fervid fieriness." The "slight sweetheart" is gaunt with
	ischnon eromenion *tum fit, cum vivere*	her skeletal frame; the "slender" one is
15	*non quit prae macie;* **rhadine** *verost iam mortua tussi.*	coughing close to death.
	at nimia et mammosa Ceres est ipsa at Iachho,	Yet one plump and busty is like Ceres feeding Bacchus,
	simula Silena ac Saturast, labeosa **philema.**	the snub-nosed girl is "dear to Silenus and the Satyres," the blubber-lipped is like a "kiss."

Apuleius

With Apuleius of Madauros, a prolific intellectual of the second century CE, we associate a range of literary genres. The ability to express his espoused philosophical outlook in various literary forms while displaying broad learning was part and parcel of

Apuleius's concept of an accomplished philosopher.[75] Alongside his perhaps most widely read novel, *Metamorphoses*, which leads the reader through a cheerful mix of bawdy folktale adventures and myth to religious salvation, feature the *Florida*, a collection of public speeches, his *Apology*, a defense speech against charges of magical practice, the *De deo Socratis* (*DDS*), a lecture devoted to demonology, the *De Platone et eius dogmate* (*DPD*), a handbook summary of Middle Platonic doctrine, and the *De mundo* (*Mund.*),[76] a loose Latin translation of the pseudo-Aristotelian treatise *Peri kosmou* (*Kosm.*) on the physical world that culminates in a theological discussion on the dissemination of divine power throughout the universe. Apuleius's method of translation bears the syncretistic character of imperial philosophical exegesis, incorporating into the work's Peripatetic framework elements of Middle Platonic theology, a method I propose to discuss in this section. Before I turn to this translation, it will be helpful to look at some key passages from his *DPD* that will facilitate an understanding of the interpretation he offers in the *Mund*.

The metaphysical setup presented in *DPD* shows a providential divine administration of the universe in which a hierarchy of agents are responsible for different domains and tasks in the material realm. At *DPD* 1.11.7,[77] Apuleius introduces as subordinates to a highest, transcendent god the heavenly bodies and other divine powers (*numina*),[78] the "heaven dwellers" (*caelicolae*), who appear to be second in rank. Third in the hierarchy, both in terms of location and power, are the "intermediaries" (*medioximi*), who, at the same time, are the connecting link between the divine and the human sphere.[79] Integrated in Apuleius's divine hierarchy is his doctrine of Providence, ultimately rooted in passages such as Pl. *Ti.* 30b–c,[80] and designed to reconcile the transcendent highest god with a providentially governed physical universe. This providential government is executed in the following manner: "divine thought" (*divina sententia*), the source of which is the "most eminent (*exsuperantissimus*) of all gods," is described at *DPD* 1.12.2 as *providentia* and "the preserver of the well-being of that for the sake of which it has assumed such a task" (*conservatricem prosperitatis eius cuius causa tale suscepit officium*). Within the cosmic environment, it becomes divine law (*divina lex*) and Fate (*fatum*),[81] "through which god's inescapable thoughts and plans (*inevitabiles cogitationes dei atque incepta*) are fulfilled." The highest god's *divina sententia* is executed, in the first place, by the heaven dwellers, who are positioned throughout the cosmos and charged with its safekeeping and its beauty. Apuleius at *DPD* 1.12.3–4 further clarifies the highest divinity's providential impact down to the lowest sphere. "By establishing his laws, he assigns to the other gods the task of managing and safeguarding the day-to-day business of those matters that remain" (*fundatisque legibus reliquarum dispositionem ac tutelam rerum quas cotidie fieri necesse est, diis ceteris tradidit*);[82] further, "having received providence [i.e., fate] from this source, the gods hold on to the secondary providence with such zeal that everything, even the heavenly display for mortals, maintains the immutable condition of the paternal government" (*Unde susceptam providentiam dii secundae providentiae ita naviter retinent ut omnia etiam quae caelitus mortalibus exibentur inmutabilem ordinationis paternae statum teneant*).

With this brief description of Apuleius's doctrine on universal Fate and Providence, we turn to his *Mund*. where, at 38.1–5, we find an interesting modification of his Greek source. In the latter, this passage, which marks the work's end, is preceded by a number of Orphic verses that describe Zeus's omnipresence in the cosmos. In the ensuing statement the Greek text retains Zeus as its point of reference, listing as further alternative titles for the god ἀνάγκη ("Necessity"), εἱμαρμένη ("Destiny"), πεπρωμένη ("Fate"), μοῖρα ("Portion"), νέμεσις ("Law"), ἀδράστεια ("Inevitable"), and αἶσα ("Dispensation"). That these names refer to Zeus himself is indicated at the beginning of the list at *Kosm.* 401b7–8, where the author notes, "I believe that [the name] Necessity, too, is used for nothing other than him" (οἶμαι δὲ καὶ τὴν Ἀνάγκην οὐκ ἄλλο τι λέγεσθαι πλὴν τούτον). In a subsequent reference to the three Fates, Atropos, Lachesis, and Clotho, the Greek author concludes, moreover, that "all of these are nothing else than the god, as even noble Plato states." His statement is rounded off by a brief quotation from Plato's *Laws* 715e7–716a3[83] that is merged with a further passage, *Laws* 730c2–3:

[*Laws* 715e7–716a3:] But the god, as told in the ancient story, holds the beginning, end, and middle of all things that are,[84] and he brings them to fulfillment as he moves on the straight path of nature.... Forever following behind him is Justice, avenger of those who turn from the divine law.... [*Laws* 730c2–3:][85] May he who is to be blessed and fortunate share in her from the very beginning.

ὁ μὲν δὴ θεός, ὥσπερ ὁ παλαιὸς λόγος, ἀρχήν τε καὶ τελευτὴν καὶ μέσα τῶν ὄντων ἁπάντων ἔχων. εὐθείᾳ περαίνει κατὰ φύσιν πορευόμενος.... τῷ δὲ ἀεὶ ξυνέπεται δίκη, τῶν ἀπολειπομένων τοῦ θείου νόμου τιμωρός.... [*Laws* 730c2–3] ἧς ὁ γενήσεσθαι μέλλων μακάριός τε καὶ εὐδαίμων ἐξ ἀρχῆς εὐθὺς μέτοχος εἴη.

In this statement, the closing sentence: "May he who is to be blessed and fortunate share in her from the very beginning" is taken from *Laws* 730c2–3, where "her" (ἧς) originally refers to Truth (ἀλήθεια). The role of Truth in this closing sentence is taken over in *Kosm.* by Justice (δίκη), an adjustment to the context of the preceding quotation, where Justice features as the god's entourage. Apuleius, initially, when resuming the discussion after reproducing the verses that list Zeus's various manifestations in the cosmos, does not simply assume the perspective of the Greek author but inserts himself into the text, signaling that he is now reporting a Greek dogma: "The Greeks wish to call Fate 'εἱμαρμένη'" (*"fatum" autem Graeci* εἱμαρμένην ... *volunt dici*), where the reference to the Greeks replaces the Greek author's οἶμαι, "I believe," in this statement. In what follows, Apuleius reproduces the Greek terms εἱμαρμένη, πεπρωμένη, μοῖρα, and ἀδράστεια, but substitutes ἔννομον ("Law") for the Greek νέμεσις.[86] He fails to mention ἀνάγκη, named at the outset of the list of names in the original text. Crucially, all these names are presented by Apuleius as alternative names not for Zeus, the supreme god, but for "Fate" (*fatum*). He next reproduces the Greek description of the three Fates, Atropos, Clotho, and Lachesis, who are "the Fate of" the past (*fatum praeteriti temporis*) and the future (*[fatum] futuri temporis*) and in charge of the present (*Clotho praesentis temporis habet curam*), respectively. He subsequently omits the Greek statement that identifies Zeus with the three Fates and the various names listed previously (compare the Greek "all of these are nothing else than the god, as even noble Plato states"). Instead, Apuleius quotes Vergil's *Georgics* 4.222: "But a man will not believe in vain that 'god walks through all the lands, the currents of the sea, and the boundless heavens' (*deum namque ire per omnes terrasque tractusque maris caelumque profundum*) when he hears these words of Plato," rounding off his translation by reproducing the Greek text's reference to Plato, patched together from the *Laws*—with one modification. In Apuleius's translation, the role of Zeus's attendant falls to yet another candidate, Necessity (*Necessitas*), who comes to displace both Plato's and ps.-Aristotle's Justice. We recall that Apuleius, in the earlier list of titles he associates with Fate (unlike the Greek, which associates the titles with Zeus), had omitted the reference to Necessity altogether.

Let us attempt to unravel Apuleius's reasoning behind his rendering of this passage. Initially, he sets apart his Roman identity from the Greeks, whose views he is about to unfold. Second, the Roman coloring in his translation is reinforced by the quote from Vergil's *Georgics*, which, in essence, matches the contents of a number of the Orphic verses he reproduces at *Mund.* 37.6, where Zeus is described as permeating the material cosmos, representing the foundation of the earth, the heavens, and the sea. To counterbalance this impression of Zeus's involvement in the physical cosmos, however, Apuleius identifies *Necessity* with Zeus's attendant (thus displacing Justice) rather than with Zeus himself, thereby effectively removing the god from the physical universe. At the same time, by associating Necessity with Fate, which, in his *DPD*, he identifies as the highest god's divine Providence at work in the physical universe, he transfers any engagement with the material realm to it and away from Zeus. From this perspective, the translation Apuleius supplies following the Orphic verses may be considered a "decoding" of these verses in terms that align better with a Middle Platonic theological outlook, according to which transcendence is reserved for Zeus the supreme god while his Providence, in the form of Fate, permeates the cosmos. Apuleius's translation lends the passage a distinctively Roman air, while his emphasis on the workings of Necessity or Fate that "follows" the transcendent god is in line with the exegesis we find at *DPD* 1.12.

CALCIDIUS

I close with a brief glance at Calcidius (Cal.), who was probably writing sometime during the late fourth to early fifth century CE. Calcidius's partial translation and commentary of Plato's *Timaeus* were commissioned by a certain Osius, whom he addresses as his dedicatee and superior. Osius's identity poses no smaller riddle than Calcidius's own, but there are reasons to assume that he may have been a Christian of elevated position.[87] Calcidius suggests that Osius had planned to "borrow" Plato's work from the Greeks to be used by a Roman audience (*eiusque [operis] usum a Graecis Latio statueras mutuandum*, Cal. *Epistula ad Ossium* 5.l.8). Osius's commission likely reflects the heightened demand for Latin translations noticeable from this period. Calcidius, accordingly, perceives it as his task to simplify access to the doctrine of the *Timaeus* for a Latin audience. In the preface to his commentary (*Commentarius in Platonis*

Timaeum (=*Comm. in Tim.*) 1.57.1–3), he explains that the commonplace charge against the dialogue's difficulty is not due to Plato's literary style, but due to the fact that the many different areas of expertise covered in the text (2.58.5–8) are discussed by way of technical lexica, an understanding of which requires expert knowledge (1.57.3–5). Thus, to do justice to Osius's request for a Latin version of the dialogue, Calcidius in an often-quoted passage considers it necessary to produce a commentary in addition (*Epistula ad Ossium* 6.6.9):

> Having approached the first parts of Plato's *Timaeus* . . . I have not only translated [the text] (*transtuli*) but have, moreover, composed a commentary on the same parts, in the belief that a copy (*simulacrum*) of an obscure subject matter (*reconditae rei*) without the unfolding of an interpretation (*sine interpretationis explanatione*) would be rather more obscure than the model (*exemplo*) itself.[88]

His commentary, in which he "unfolds his interpretation" serves to preclude the possibility that Plato's text might become more obscure as a result of the translation process. Of course, in introducing his translation as a mirror image or effigy (*simulacrum*) of the "paradigm" that is Plato's original (*exemplum*), Calcidius shows off his expertise as an interpreter of the *Timaeus* by creating a "kinship" between the subject matter and his own explanatory account thereof, a kinship that is duly required by the dialogue's namesake at *Ti.* 29b.[89]

Calcidius's method of illuminating Plato's doctrine with the help of a translation and a commentary is a complex exegetical process. As well as integrating excerpts from his translation into the commentary, Calcidius in his translation modifies the underlying text by way of additions, omissions, and alterations that serve to explain, simplify, and disambiguate Timaeus's account even before the reader consults the commentary.[90] The translation itself thus takes on an exegetical as well as a pedagogical role.[91] In what follows, I propose to single out his rendering of Plato's *Ti.* 27d6–28a4 as an example for the subtle exegetical dynamic between translation and commentary.

At *Ti.* 27d6 Timaeus begins his creation account with a preliminary distinction between the ontological spheres of being and coming to be. In doing so Timaeus prepares his listeners for the subsequent classification of the created universe as a perishable object of sense perception that has come to be, having been formed by the divine architect after an intelligible model whose ontological status, in turn, is that of eternal, unchanging being:

1	τί τὸ ὂν ἀεί, γένεσιν δὲ οὐκ ἔχον, καὶ τί τὸ γιγνόμενον μὲν ἀεί,[92] ὂν δὲ οὐδέποτε;	What is that which always is, having no coming to be, and what is that which always becomes, but never really is?
5	τὸ μὲν δὴ νοήσει μετὰ λόγου περιληπτόν, ἀεὶ κατὰ ταὐτὰ ὄν, τὸ δ' αὖ δόξῃ μετ' αἰσθήσεως ἀλόγου δοξαστόν, γιγνόμενον καὶ ἀπολλύμενον, ὄντως δὲ οὐδέποτε ὄν.	The one is graspable by intellect with the help of reason, always being selfsame. The other is opinable by opinion with the help of sense perception, comes to be and perishes and never really is.

Calcidius's translation:

1	*Quid sit quod semper est carens generatione quid item quod gignitur nec est semper?*	What is that which always is, lacking generation, [and] what in turn is that which comes to be and is not always?
5	*alterum intellectu perceptibile ductu et investigatione rationis, semper idem,*	One is perceptible through the guidance of intellect and the inquiry of reason, and is always the same;
	porro alterum opinione cum inrationabili sensu opinabile propthereaque incertum,	the other, in turn, is opinable by opinion with irrational sense perception and, for this reason, uncertain.
10	*nascens et occidens neque umquam in existendi condicione constanti et rata perseverans.*	It comes to be and perishes and never perseveres in a steady and settled state of existence.

The appearance of *semper* in Calcidius's rendering *quod gignitur nec est semper*[93] for τὸ γιγνόμενον μὲν ἀεί, ὂν δὲ οὐδέποτε (l.2) might suggest, first, that his Greek source featured the second, controversial ἀεί (see n93), with ὂν δὲ οὐδέποτε captured by *nec est*. This, however, would make for a somewhat odd word order (placing *semper* at the end of the rendering instead of with *quod gignitur*) and choice of expression, given that the expected Latin equivalent would presumably be *quod gignitur nec est umquam*. I suggest, alternatively, that Calcidius's phrasing *nec est semper* betrays a specific exegetical intent. In the Greek, τὸ γιγνόμενον is described further in l.8, as ὄντως δὲ οὐδέποτε ὄν, "never truly being," with the addition of ὄντως, "truly," added to Timaeus's previous ὂν δὲ οὐδέποτε, "never being" (l.2). Calcidius, in turn, further describes *quod gignitur* as something that "never perseveres in a steady and settled state of existence" (*neque umquam in existendi condicione constanti et rata perseverans*, ll.10–12), a rather lengthy paraphrase of Timaeus's simple ὄντως. This additional characterization of *quod gignitur* suggests, perhaps more forcefully than the underlying Greek ὄντως, that that which becomes is not strictly denied any degree of being, but merely does not persevere in being. This interpretation aligns with the characterization of *quod gignitur* as it is introduced in ll.2–3, where Calcidius indicates not that *quod gignitur* "never is"—*nec est umquam*—but that "it is *not always*": *nec est semper*.

Calcidius's subtle modification of the Greek in his translation, I suggest, anticipates Plato's introduction of a third ontological category at *Ti.* 50–51. Calcidius, in his commentary on the passage, observes that the Greek text introduces this third category in addition to the two introduced previously, the intelligible "form" or paradigm (falling into the class of "being," τὸ ὄν), and the mirror images shaped in its likeness, i.e., the entirety of created species (falling into the class of "coming to be," τὸ γιγνόμενον). The third category is likened by Plato to a "receptacle," ὑποδοχή, and "space," χώρα. Calcidius (330.324.12ff.) identifies it with "matter," *silva*, "that in which the generated species arise" (*generata videlicet species ... aliud in quo gignitur*).[94] Like Plato, Calcidius illustrates the relations between the three *genera* with the help of a metaphor. That which generates, the paradigm, assumes the role of a father; that which "receives within itself," the receptacle, is the mother; their offspring are the generated species. He concludes that there are three kinds (*erunt igitur tria haec*): (1) *quod semper est* (see the identical phrasing in l.1 above), "what always is," i.e., the paradigm; (2) *quod semper non est*, i.e., the receptacle, *silva*, "what always is not"; and (3) *quod non semper est*, i.e., the mirror images that make up our perceptible realm (cf. l.1: *nec est semper*, "what is not always"). Calcidius's translation may thus anticipate Plato's later characterization at *Ti.* 50f of that which comes to be as the offspring or the generated species that stands between the truly existing nature that is constant and always the same, and that which never is, *silva*. Since generated objects undergo change but cling to at least a temporary existence, Calcidius construes ὂν δὲ οὐδέποτε, "never being" in l.2 above, as *nec est semper*, "that which is not always," a phrasing that, in his view, may have aligned more accurately with his later characterization in ll.10–12 of *neque umquam in existendi condicione constanti et rata perseverans*. In anticipation of *Ti.* 50–51, and perhaps with a nod to his own lengthy excursus on matter in his commentary, Calcidius introduces already at this early stage in his translation τὸ γιγνόμενον as "half-being" between the receptacle and the eternal paradigm, thereby facilitating for the reader an understanding of Plato's metaphysical program later in the dialogue.

Conclusion

The above examples have revealed that translation plays a central role in the philosophical project of each of our four authors. In Cicero's *Tusculans* translation becomes an instrument of appropriation and a symbol of a new power dynamic between Greek and Roman intellectual culture. Greek passages of varying faithfulness are uprooted from their original environment and pay deference to Cicero's chosen line of argument. For Cicero, a close translation of his Greek source, far from signaling acquiescence in the original author's towering legacy, instead expresses a complete appropriation of the latter thinker, who is transformed into a mouthpiece for Cicero's own agenda. Lucretius does not frequently resort to direct translation from his Greek sources, instead producing multiform images of his Greek material that instantiate the underlying doctrine in vivid Latin diction. At the same time, his very method of translation, the reassembling of Greek prose in the form of Latin poetic imagery, is in itself an instantiation of Epicurean atomic doctrine. The negotiation of intellectual hegemony, which, especially in Cicero's case, relies on the audience's acquaintance with the Greek material under siege, disappears in these later writers. Instead, Apuleius's method of translation allows for modifications that help align Greek philosophical doctrine with his own Middle Platonic outlook, no doubt reflective of a broader effort, visible in authors of the early centuries CE, to streamline and systematize Plato's philosophy. At the same time, however, Apuleius keeps Greek terminology "close by," and purposefully inserts his own voice into the translation, reminding his readers of their need for his expertise as a mediator able to decode Plato's wisdom. Finally, Calcidius illuminates his Greek source text with the help of strategic modifications in his translation that foreshadow his complementary exegesis in the commentary. In doing so, he fulfills his primary aim of presenting Platonic doctrine as a coherent and accessible system to a nonexpert audience.

While the genre of Roman philosophy is greatly indebted to the practice of translation, a useful way to conceive of the relationship between Greek philosophical material and its Roman translations may be to think of it not as the type of relationship that holds between an object and its mirror image, but rather as the kind of rapport between raw material and a creative product fashioned from it, with the product's contours and dimensions determined by its creator's adopted purpose.

Notes

1. Of course, this assumption is not universally warranted, as in the case of some dated translations, many of which are still widely available. An example is the 1863 translation of Horace's *Satires* by Christopher Smart, whose discreet omission of Horace's erotic dream at *Sat.* 1.5.84, continues to confound unassuming students scrambling to consolidate their homework.
2. For the present study I will assume (1) that cognitive contents can be expressed by linguistic means, and (2) that these expressions can be successfully understood by the audience. A lack of shared meaning, or of suitable equivalent expressions in the receptor culture or language, may be remedied by explanatory gloss, new word coinage, calques, contextualization, and similar methods. Here I merely note that my view opposes that of deconstructionist scholars of translation, often inspired by an early Derrida, (e.g., Chau (1984), Arrojo (1993), and Arrojo (1996)), for whom meaning can of necessity be neither understood nor communicated. A more optimistic stance may be corroborated by the recent publication—now available in English translation (!)—of the French *Vocabulaire Européen des Philosophies: Dictionnaire des Intraduisibles* (ed. Cassin 2004).
3. See Venuti's *The Translator's Invisibility* (1995), which analyzes contemporary attitudes toward translators.
4. E.g., Inghilleri (2005); Wolf and Fukari (2007).
5. Strict equivalence between source text and translation as the criterion of success went out of fashion some decades ago following a period during which approaches from linguistics dominated the field. In 1984 Berman argued for the purposeful retention and emphasis of "foreign" elements in translations, following in the footsteps of German Romantic authors such as Humboldt and Schleiermacher. The so-called cultural turn (e.g., Bassnett and Lefevere (1990); Venuti (1995)) of the discipline saw scholars becoming more interested in translation as a process that must be approached by taking into account social, cultural, and ideological considerations.
6. In the broadest sense of the word, see Lefevere (1992). Recent studies have examined the dynamics of power that determine a translation process in the context of cultural appropriation or asymmetrical political relations, e.g., Stoll (2004); Branchadel and West (2005).
7. E.g., Newmark (2009). For the wider ethical implications of translation, see Pym (1997) and Pym (2001).

8. See, for instance, Anaxagoras's complaint in fr. B17: "The Greeks do not consider coming to be and perishing correctly.... They would correctly refer to 'coming to be' as 'mixing,' and to 'perishing' as 'being separated'" (all translations are my own unless indicated otherwise). Cf. Empedocles' fr. B8, 6–7, which notes that "birth" (φύσις) is merely the name given to "mixture" (μίξις) by humans.
9. To name but one obvious example, the term κόσμος is used by Homer at *Od.* 7.492 to describe, apparently, the "construction" or "joining together" of the wooden horse at the gates of Troy. It is applied to the orderly universe initially by Pythagoras, as reported by Aët. *Placita* 2.1.1 and Diog. Laert. 8.48. Diogenes reports further that Theophrastus believed Parmenides to be the first, while Zeno suggests it was Hesiod, but no such usage survives for the poet.
10. A practice that led Derrida to point to the "violent difficulty in the transference of a non-philosopheme into a philosopheme" in his discussion of Plato's use of the term φάρμακον in *La Dissémination* (1981) 71–72, tr. Johnson. See also the excellent discussion by Young (2014), esp. 45–46.
11. Cf. Young (2014) 41–45. One might think, for instance, of Heidegger's "*Dasein*" or his "*Bewandtnis*," expressions that require contextualization even for a native audience.
12. A point emphasized by Reiff (1959) passim.
13. A far cry, of course, from our modern sensitivity toward originality and plagiarism. Stemplinger (1912) remains a useful evaluation of literary *imitatio*, for instance: 177, 210–212.
14. See also McElduff (2013): 7–11; Seele (1995) 13. Bassnett-McGuire (1991) 45 aptly likens the activity of the ancient translator to "an exercise of comparative stylistics."
15. Against Rener (1989) who claims that there existed a coherent theory of translation, starting out in Cicero's time, that remains more or less unchanged until the present day. Bassnett-McGuire (1991) 39–42 offers a sensible critique of Steiner's *After Babel* (1998) in which the latter attempts to draw up a chronologically structured history of translation. See also the conclusions of Seele (1995) 19–22. On the development of medieval translation theory, see Copeland (1991).
16. See Puelma (1980) 138 with n1.
17. With the exception, perhaps, of *interpretari*, which frequently describes a more literal translation style. See Powell (1995) 278.
18. Often compared to what has famously been termed "dynamic" and "formal" equivalence in modern translation studies by Eugene Nida, e.g., (1964) 159.
19. The expression *verbum de verbo* first appears in the preface of Terence's *Adelphoe*. See Marti (1974) 64.
20. *Nec verbo verbum curabis reddere fidus interpres* .... In the preface to his translation of Porphyry's *Isagoge*, Boethius confesses to being a *fidus interpres*, in reference to Horace's unfavorable verdict. See Kytzler (1989) 45.
21. Several centuries later even Saint Jerome, ever torn between the *elegantia* of a sense-orientated translation and the *ad verbum* we approach commended for the translation of Scripture, signs up for the former: "I not only confess but declare openly that my translation of Greek texts and of Holy Scripture, whose word order itself is a divine mystery, is not literal but sense-oriented" (*non verbum e verbo, sed sensum exprimere de sensu*, Jer. *Ep.* 57.5).
22. See, e.g., Zgusta (1980) 139.
23. Nord (1997) 93 adopts a broader definition that appears to include "adaptation." For more detailed discussions regarding the relationship between adaptation and translation, see Bastin (1998) and Bastin (2005).

24. As a young man Cicero had produced a verse translation of Aratus's *Phaenomena* (see *Div.* 2.14 and *Nat. D.* 2.104). He also translated Xenophon's *Oeconomicus* (*Off.* 2.87) and Plato's *Protagoras*. For Cicero's dialogues, with some discussion of translation, see also Fox in this volume.
25. From, e.g., Steiner (1998) (first published 1975) to Rener (1989), to Robinson (2002), to Munday (2009), to name very few.
26. An exception is McElduff (2013) 110–115.
27. See also McElduff (2013) 110–115.
28. Cf. *Brut.* 310.
29. McElduff (2013) 99–100. On the paraphrase as a literary device in antiquity, see Fuchs (1982) 10–16.
30. Cf. Hoenig (2018), in particular 42–44, where I argue that Cicero exploits similarities in technical vocabulary between the disciplines of rhetoric and philosophy and, with the help of careful manipulation of his Platonic source text, adds an interpretative layer intended to recruit Plato for the skeptical cause.
31. Nevertheless, in response to Atticus's warning about the difficulty of translating Greek philosophy into Latin, Cicero in a pretense of humility at *Ep. ad Att.* 12.52.3, describes his philosophical works as mere ἀπόγραφα: *minore labore fiunt; verba tantum adfero, quibus abundo.*
32. *Fin.* 1.1: *ii quidem eruditi Graecis litteris, contemnentes Latinas, qui se dicant in Graecis legendis operam malle consumere.*
33. *Fin.* 1.2: "In the case of the Stoics, what did Chrysippus leave untouched? Yet we read Diogenes."
34. See also *Ac.* 1.9–10.
35. See the excellent discussion by Gildenhard (2007), who notes the "complex dynamic of appropriation" (104) in his examination of the prefaces in the *Tusculan Disputations*. See also ibid.: 108, 132.
36. Cicero considers the Latin philosophical texts that were available before he himself took on the subject inadequate either in content (*Tusc.* 4.6) or in literary sophistication (2.7).
37. I leave aside at present the more technical aspects of Cicero's translation practice, e.g., his solutions for rendering the Greek definite article, pre- and suffix, or participial constructions unavailable in Latin. Such aspects are discussed thoroughly, for instance, by Powell (1995) 292–297.
38. "M." and "A." are not Cicero's abbreviations. For a discussion of the interlocutors' identities, see Pohlenz (1911); Gildenhard (2007) 21–34.
39. Gildenhard (2007), esp. 114–118, shows how Cicero ties Greek wisdom to the stock Roman virtues that had, in Cicero's view, come under threat by Caesar's political activities.
40. On the structure of Cicero's Socratic method at the beginning of Book 1, see Gorman (2005) 64–84. On the argumentative structure of Book 1 as a whole, see Koch (2006).
41. For a closer comparison between *Phdr.* 245c5–246a2 and Cicero's translations of the passage at *Tusc.* 1.53–54 and *Rep.* 6.27–28, see Traglia (1971) 318–324. See also Douglas (1985) *ad loc.*
42. As we return to the *Tusculans*, soon after the appearance of the *Phaedrus* passage, Cicero at 1.57 references the doctrine of recollection in the *Meno* and the *Phaedo*, pointing out that soul has divine characteristics such as memory. Soul remembers certain ἔννοιαι (a Stoic coloring) it must have acquired prior to incarnation. To explain that soul could not possibly have acquired its memory of ἰδέαι (Cicero: *species*) while shackled to a human

body, Cicero adds another Platonic echo to his argument, this time likely alluding to the *Timaeus*: "For [Plato] believes that nothing exists that comes to be and perishes, and that only that truly exists, which is always such as it is" (*nihil enim putat esse, quod oriatur et intereat, id que solum esse, quod semper tale sit quale est*). Cicero supplies a similar rendering in his translation of the *Timaeus* proper, cf. his translation of *Ti.* 27d5: *quid est, quod semper sit neque ullum habeat ortum, et quod gignatur nec umquam sit? quorum alterum intellegentia et ratione conprehenditur, quod unum atque idem semper est.* In the Greek text, this passage, of course, describes the ontological nature οὐσία at large instead of a Platonic ἰδέα as such. The *Timaeus* is referenced again at *Tusc.* 1.63, where Cicero puts it to use by adding a twist to the argument from design. Just as the Greek mathematician Archimedes relied on the ingenuity of his divine soul (*divino ingenio*) when creating his animated model of the cosmos, the Timaean demiurge set into orderly motion the physical universe.

43. Cf. *Phaedo* 80e5–81a2.
44. "Indeed, [the hope that soul survives death] delights me, and I would like for this to be the case most of all; but even if it is not, my next wish would be, nevertheless, to be persuaded [of it]."
45. *Tusc.* 1.24: *feci mehercule, et quidem saepius; sed nescio quo modo dum lego adsentior, cum posui librum et me cum ipse de inmortalitate animorum coepi cogitare, adsensio omnis illa elabitur.* Cf. Stull (2012) 38–39. A.'s dissatisfaction echoes that of Simmias and Cebes in Plato's *Phaedo*, a complaint, according to Stull, that is caused by the fact that the *Phaedo* is "too eloquent," a view opposed to Schrenk (1994) 357, who believes that the Greek dialogue is too "philosophical."
46. Socrates is called on again at *Tusc.* 1.97, where, following a number of arguments intended to portray death as a relief from care and anxiety, Cicero provides a rather loose translation of Plato's *Apology* 40c4–42a5. See, for instance, the much simplified version of Socrates's cumbersome hypothesis: "If one ought to pick out the night in which one slept so as to have no dream, and if one ought to compare all the other nights and days of one's life with this night, and if one were to say, upon consideration, for how many days and nights in one's life one had lived in a better and happier way than in this night, I think that not only any private individual, but even the great king [of Persia] himself would find only few in number when compared with the other nights—if, then, death is of such a nature, I, at any rate, call it an advantage. For if this is so, time in its entirety appears to be no longer than one night" (εἴ τινα ἐκλεξάμενον δέοι ταύτην τὴν νύκτα ἐν ᾗ οὕτω κατέδαρθεν ὥστε μηδὲ ὄναρ ἰδεῖν, καὶ τὰς ἄλλας νύκτας τε καὶ ἡμέρας τὰς τοῦ βίου τοῦ ἑαυτοῦ ἀντιπαραθέντα ταύτῃ τῇ νυκτὶ δέοι σκεψάμενον εἰπεῖν πόσας ἄμεινον καὶ ἥδιον ἡμέρας καὶ νύκτας ταύτης τῆς νυκτὸς βεβίωκεν ἐν τῷ ἑαυτοῦ βίῳ, οἶμαι ἂν μὴ ὅτι ἰδιώτην τινά, ἀλλὰ τὸν μέγαν βασιλέα εὐαριθμήτους ἂν εὑρεῖν αὐτὸν ταύτας πρὸς τὰς ἄλλας ἡμέρας καὶ νύκτας—εἰ οὖν τοιοῦτον ὁ θάνατός ἐστιν, κέρδος ἔγωγε λέγω· καὶ γὰρ οὐδὲν πλείων ὁ πᾶς χρόνος φαίνεται οὕτω δὴ εἶναι ἢ μία νύξ). Compare with this Cicero: "Or how many days can be found that are preferable to this kind of a night, and if all of the impending continuity of future time is similar to this night, who is happier than I?" (*aut quam multi dies reperiri possunt qui tali nocti anteponantur, cui si similis futura est perpetuitas omnis consequentis temporis, qui me beatior?*). The mention of a "great king" in the Greek might not have appealed to Cicero, given his political convictions. While he retains the overall Greek framework of the Underworld and enumerates those he will meet upon death: the judges Minos, Radamanthus, Aecus, and Triptolemus, Orpheus, Musaeus, Homer, and Hesiod, and the Trojan heroes Agamemnon, Odysseus, and Sisyphus, he omits the concept of a

"demigod," ἡμίθεος. Unlike Socrates, who refers to "those demigods who had come to be just in their lives" (ὅσοι τῶν ἡμιθέων δίκαιοι ἐγένοντο ἐν τῷ ἑαυτῶν βίῳ), Cicero supplies "those who have lived justly *and piously*" (*qui iuste e cum fide vixerint*), a rendering that rather befits Cato, in that it recalls *fides*, one of the central Roman virtues (see Gildenhard (2007), e.g., 151). Cicero also omits the mention of Socrates's divine sign (41d5–6) and the reference to his sons (41e2–7).

47. An exception is McElduff (2013).
48. For the following, see the discussion by Foster (2011). At 90 with n7, Foster notes that the passages most faithfully rendered by Lucretius are those describing physiological and psychological symptoms.
49. With Thucydides' matter-of-fact description of symptoms at 2.49.2: "The internal parts, the throat and the tongue, would suddenly be bloody and send off a strange and foul odor" (καὶ τὰ ἐντός, ἥ τε φάρυγξ καὶ ἡ γλῶσσα, εὐθὺς αἱματώδη ἦν καὶ πνεῦμα ἄτοπον καὶ δυσῶδες ἠφίει), compare Lucretius's lingering focus on the tongue at 6.1149–1150: "And the tongue, interpreter of the mind, would drip with gore and had grown lame from its afflictions, heavy of speech and rough to the touch" (*atque animi interpres manabat lingua cruore debilitata malis, motu gravis, aspera tactu*).
50. E.g., Lucr. 6.1158–1159: "Fearful anguish and lamentation mixed with groans were the steady companions of unbearable afflictions" (*intolerabilibusque malis erat anxius angor adsidue comes et gemitu commixta querella*), lines that possibly capture Thuc. 2.49.3 where the symptoms are "accompanied by great distress" (μετὰ ταλαιπωρίας μεγάλης).
51. Unlike Thucydides' physicians, helpless at first since they had never before witnessed the symptoms (2.47.4), Lucretius points to the shamed silence of *medicina* who at 6.1179–1181 "would murmur in silent fear at the many rolling eyes, burning from disease, staring wide, deprived of sleep" (*mussabat tacito medicina timore, quippe patentia cum totiens ardentia morbis lumina versarent oculorum expertia somno*).
52. At 2.49.8, Thucydides notes that many escaped the disease by cutting off their fingers, toes, or eyes, an image famously adapted by Lucretius at 6.1208–1211, where the victims self-mutilate their genitalia, hands, feet, and eyes as a direct consequence of the victim's fear of death (*metuentes limina leti*, 6.1208). See Bright (1971) Sedley (1998) 160–165, esp. 161; Gale (1994) 208–228.
53. See, for instance, Samotta (2012), Canfora (2006), and Cicero's own respectful remarks concerning the Greek author at *Orat.* 31.
54. Clay (1983) 267–276 ("Appendix 1") provides passages from Epicurus's writings that may have inspired several key passages in Lucretius. For an assessment of Lucretius's possible source material, see Farrell (2008).
55. Sedley (1998) 38–42 and 44–45 describes Lucretius's use of "a range of his own live metaphors" and "metaphorical diversification" in the context of Lucretius's terminology for atoms and Epicurean εἴδωλα, and stresses the Empedoclean precedent of this method. See also West (1970) for a study of further images.
56. No doubt strongly evocative of Empedocles's principles of love and strife. Lucretius's debt to Empedocles as a literary role model is discussed by Sedley (1998) 1–34, of which 16–21 are in response to the earlier study of Empedoclean influences in Lucretius by Furley (1970). Epicurus mentions atomic aggregation and segregation, for instance, at *Ep. ad Herod.* 40.9–41.7, parts of which Lucretius reproduces closely at 1.483–486; further *Ep. ad Herod.* 54.4–9, which is picked up at Lucr. 2.737–738, 748–756. See Clay (1983) 270, 374–375.

57. At 1.172–174 divine *voluptas* is the guiding principle of life (*ipsaque . . . dux vitae dia voluptas*) who, through sexual union, ensures the future existence of mankind and prevents its extinction. Clay (1983) 82–94 analyzes the figure of Venus in relation to *natura*. See also Gale (1994) 212ff.
58. Argued by Bignone (1945) 437–444. For further comments on Lucretius's use of the key term *voluptas*, see Clay (1983) 256–257.
59. Sexual union driven by excessive passion is portrayed in a negative light. Whoever strives to avoid such base forms of love is still able to enjoy its delights, without enslaving himself to any negative consequences (4.1073), while a reasonable person will remain able to escape the strong bonds of Venus (2.114). See also those defeated by sexual pleasure and tortured by the mutual chains of sexual pleasure at 4.1201–1205. At 3.4 Lucretius cleverly advocates for the "correct" type of desire, which does not impel to strife but to creative imitation. He is not *desirous* of competing with Epicurus because of his *love, non ita certandi cupidus quam propter amorem*.
60. The passage echoes Empedocles' love and strife, which inspired Lucretius's poem and would have been well known to his audience.
61. Social and political relationships are affected negatively at 3.83–84 by superstitious fears. Terrorized by fear men come to detest established social values and to burst the bonds of friendship (*hunc vexare pudorem, hunc vincula amicitiai rumpere . . . suadet*).
62. Gale (1994) 220 notes that Venus and Mars's eternal love symbolizes the unity of the forces of creation and destruction in Lucretius. These two sides of the coin are captured by the role of *natura*, where "Venus *genetrix* and Mavors/ *mors* together represent *natura creatrix* and *perfica*." See ibid. 219–220 with literature and a survey of additional interpretations of Venus, Mars, and *natura*.
63. Lucr. 2.658–60: *concedamus ut hic terrarum dictitet orbem / esse deum matrem, dum vera re tamen ipse / religione animum turpi contingere parcat*. Cf. Gale (1994) 39.
64. E.g., Sedley (1998) 38 (= Sedley (1999) 230) and see Sedley (1998) 194–196 for the sexual connotations of Lucretius's atomic vocabulary. Elsewhere, the image of a mother is linked to the atomic principles even more directly. If there were no generating bodies (*genitalia corpora*) for each thing, how could there be a certain mother (*mater certa*, 1.167–168, 1.171) of things?
65. Note the distinction between individual atoms and atomic compounds, which can both be termed *corpora*. See also 1.483.
66. Lucr. 5.431–448: *sed nova tempestas quaedam molesque coorta, discordia quorum intervalla vias conexus pondera plagas concursus motus turbabat proelia miscens propter dissimilis formas variasque figuras*.
67. Lucr. 3.926–930: *maior enim turbae disiectus materiai consequitur leto*. In Book 6 the disorderly mass of atoms is captured by Lucretius's striking description of the plague that wreaked havoc on Athens: *inhumana iacerent corpora supra corporibus*.
68. For instance, Lucr. 3.147–162; and the preceding lines of the above-quoted passage, 3.806–829.
69. For a discussion of this passage and the symmetry argument in connection with the pseudo-Platonic Axiochus, see Warren in this volume.
70. Similar arguments are found in ps.-Plato's *Axiochus* 365d and in Cicero's *Tusc.* 1.37.
71. The two states of nonexistence are described as mirror images at Lucr. 3.972–975.
72. See West (1969) 115–128.
73. For the detailed background of these Greek terms, cf. Brown (1987) 280–294.

74. Sedley (1999) 238–246 argues that Lucretius employs Greek terms with the intention of creating a "foreign" atmosphere in his poem.
75. Cf. Hoenig (2018) 67–70 with literature, and Hoenig (2019) for a general overview of his Platonism.
76. The work's authenticity work is now generally accepted, see Regen (1971); Beaujeu (1973) xi–xxviii; Hijmans (1987) 408–415; Moreschini (2015) 203–204.
77. Ed. Magnaldi (2020).
78. See also *DDS* 2.4–5. Already Xenocrates, via Aët. *Placita* 1.7.3, had considered the "fiery stars," identified with the Olympian gods) to be divine, alongside demons in the sublunary realm. See also Ps.-Pl. 572f–574a; Moreschini (2015) 233–237.
79. "He names three kinds of gods. The first is the one and only highest god, who is supramundane, incorporeal, whom we have shown earlier to be the father and builder of this divine world. The other kind is that of the stars and other divine powers whom we call 'heaven dwellers.' The third kind belongs to those whom our Roman ancestors called 'intermediate gods,' inferior to the highest gods in terms of condition, habitat and power, yet certainly superior to humans by nature" (*deorum trinas nuncupat species, quarum est prima unus et solus summus ille, ultramundanus, incorporeus, quem patrem et architectum huius divini orbis superius ostendimus; aliud genus est quale astra habent ceteraque numina, quos caelicolas nominamus; tertium habent, quos medioximos Romani veteres appellant, quod est sui ratione, sed et loco et potestate diis summis sunt minores, natura hominum profecto maiores*).
80. There, the cosmos, according to the likely account, is described as having come to be as an ensouled, rational creature through divine providence (οὕτως οὖν δὴ κατὰ λόγον τὸν εἰκότα δεῖ λέγειν τόνδε τὸν κόσμον ζῷον ἔμψυχον ἔννουν τε τῇ ἀληθείᾳ διὰ τὴν τοῦ θεοῦ γενέσθαι πρόνοιαν). For a broader analysis of Apuleian providence, see Regen (1971) 83–91.
81. Fate as divine law ultimately derives from the *nomoi heimarmenoi* at *Ti.* 41e2. See also Alcinous, *Didaskalikos* 16.2.5; Nemesius, *De natura hominis* 38.109.18; Ps.-Plut. *De fato* 568d6.
82. Compare Ps.-Plut. *De fato* 573d–574a.
83. The same passage, in which the Athenian describes how future inhabitants should be addressed upon their arrival, is quoted also at *Kosm.* 397b, the beginning of the work's theological section. This section is thus framed by the same passage, a nod to Zeus, who holds beginning and end of the cosmos.
84. Listed by Kern in his *Orphicorum Fragmenta* (fr. 21, compare 21a) as an annotation to the *Laws* passage by a scholiast.
85. In this part of the dialogue, the Athenian indicates that, following affairs regulated by law, they will discuss those affairs as are regulated by praise and blame, "as the instruments whereby the citizens are educated individually and rendered more tractable and well-inclined toward the laws which are to be imposed on them." The role of Truth is elevated in this context.
86. Apuleius's replacement ἔννομον retains the etymological connection with the Greek that is established through διανέμησις, "distribution."
87. A large number of manuscripts identify Calcidius's Osius with Osius, bishop of Cordoba, an associate of Emperor Constantine, but this view is not unproblematic. For a recent list of possible Osii, cf. Magee (2016) viii–xi. See also Bakhouche (2011) 9n5.
88. Discussed also by Dutton (2003) 189; Reydams-Schils (2007) 305; Hoenig (2018) 103–104.

89. "Now, in regard to every matter it is most important to begin at the natural beginning. Accordingly, in the case of a likeness and its model, we ought to determine that the accounts (τοὺς λόγους) bear a kinship (συγγενεῖς ὄντας) to the subject matters of which they serve as exegetes." See the discussion of Calcidius's authorial voice in chapter 1 of Reydams-Schils (2020), esp. 12.
90. See Bakhouche (2011) 27–30.
91. See Seele (1995) 86–88.
92. The evidence in support of the second ἀεί is inconclusive. Its inclusion, one might assume initially, would have been favored by those Platonists who endorsed a nonliteral reading and thus an everlasting (ἀεί) process of coming to be. It is, however, omitted by the vast majority of the (nonliteral) Neoplatonist tradition and retained, oddly, by Eusebius (*Praep. evang.* XI.9), perhaps also by Plutarch (cf. *De def. or.* 433E), who endorsed a literal reading of the dialogue. Dillon (1989) 62 believes that the second ἀεί was retained among the nonliteralist second-century tradition more frequently than assumed.
93. A small number of MSS read *nec semper est* (Waszink's Cam_2, Br_3, Cam_3, *Bl*, *p*, and *f*).
94. Although the identification of ὕλη with matter and with Timaeus's receptacle, ultimately going back to Aristotle, is a common notion in the Middle Platonist tradition, we do not know any author to have used the Latin term *silva* for ὕλη prior to Calcidius. Cf. van Winden (1959) 31.

References

Adams, J. N., and R. G. Mayer, eds. (1999). *Aspects of the Language of Latin Poetry*. (Oxford).
Arrojo, R. (1993). *Tradução, Deconstrução e Psicanálise*. (Rio de Janeiro).
Arrojo, R. (1996). "Postmodernism and the Teaching of Translation," in Dollerup and Appel, 97–105.
Bakhouche, B., ed. (2011). *Calcidius: Commentaire au* Timée *de Platon ; Texte établi, traduit et annoté. Tome 1: Introduction générale, introduction à la traduction du* Timée*, traduction du* Timée *et commentaire (c. 1–355); Tome 2: Notes à la traduction et au commentaire, indices, annexes, bibliographie générale*. (Paris).
Baltussen, H. (2011). "Cicero's Translation of Greek Philosophy: Personal Mission or Public Service?," in McElduff, 37–47.
Bassnett-McGuire, S., ed. (1991). *Translation Studies*. (London).
Bassnett, S., and A. Lefevere (1990). *Translation, History and Culture*. (London).
Bastin, G. L. (1998). *¿Traducir o Adaptar?* (Caracas).
Bastin, G. L. (2005). "Les Interventions Délibérées du Traducteur." Paper presented at the XVII Conference of the Canadian Association of Translation Studies. (London, Ontario).
Beaujeu, J. (1973). *Apulée : Opuscules Philosophiques (Du Dieu de Socrate, Platon et sa Doctrine, Du Monde) et Fragments*. (Paris).
Berman, A. (1984). *L'épreuve de l'étranger: Culture et traduction dans l'Allemagne Romantique*. (Paris).
Bermann, S., and C. Porter, eds. (2014). *Companion to Translation Studies*. (West Sussex).
Bignone, E. (1945). *Storia della Letteratura Latina* II. (Florence).
Branchadell, A., and L. M. West, eds. (2005). *Less Translated Languages*. (Amsterdam).
Bright, D. F. (1971). "The Plague and the Structure of the *De Rerum Natura*." *Latomus* 30: 607–632.

Brown. R. D. (1987). *Lucretius on Love and Sex*. (Leiden).
Burnet, J., ed. (1902). *Platonis Opera*, vol. 4. (Oxford).
Canfora, L. (2006). "Thucydides in Rome and Late Antiquity," in Rengakos and Tsakmakis, 721–754.
Cassin, B., ed. (2014). *Dictionary of Untranslatables*. (Princeton).
Chau, S. S. C. (1984). "Hermeneutics and the Translator: The Ontological Dimension of Translating." *Multilingua* 3(2): 71–77.
Clay, D. (1983). *Lucretius and Epicurus*. (Ithaca, N.Y.).
Copeland, R. (1991). *Rhetoric, Hermeneutics, and Translation in the Middle Ages: Academic Traditions and Vernacular Texts*. (Cambridge).
de Falco, V., ed. (1971). *Studi filologici e storici in onore di Vittorio de Falco*. (Naples).
Derrida, J. (1981). *La dissémination*. Trans. B. Johnson. (Chicago).
Dillon, J. (1977). *The Middle Platonists: A Study of Platonism, 80 B.C. to A.D. 220*. (London).
Dillon, J. (1989). "Tampering with the Timaeus. Ideological Emendations in Plato, with Special Reference to the Timaeus." *American Journal of Philology* 110: 50–72.
Dillon, J. (^{2}1993). *The Handbook of Platonism: Alcinous*. (Oxford).
Dollerup, C., and V. Appel, eds. (1996). *Teaching Translation and Interpreting*. (Philadelphia).
Douglas, A. E. (1985). *Cicero: Tusculan Disputations 1*. (Warminster).
Dutton, P. E. (2003). "Medieval Approaches to Calcidius," in Reydams-Schils, 183–205.
Farrell, J. (2008). "Lucretian Architecture: The Structure and Argument of the *De Rerum Natura*," in Gillespie and Hardie, 76–91.
Flashar, H., et al., eds. (1983). *Die Philosophie der Antike. Band 3. Ältere Akademie, Aristoteles, Peripatos*. (Basel).
Fleischmann, E., P. Schmitt, and G. Wotjak, eds. (2004). *Translationskompetenz*. (Tübingen).
Foster, E. (2011). "The Political Aims of Lucretius' Translation of Thucydides," in McElduff, 88–100.
Foster, E., and D. Lateiner, eds. (2011). *Thucydides and Herodotus: Connections, Divergences, and Reception*. (Oxford).
Fuchs, C. (1982). *La paraphrase*. (Paris).
Furley, D. J. (1970). "Variations on Themes from Empedocles in Lucretius' Proem." *BICS* 17: 55–64.
Gale, M. (1994). *Myth and Poetry in Lucretius*. (Cambridge).
Gildenhard, I. (2007). *Paideia Romana: Cicero's Tusculan Disputations*. (Cambridge).
Gillespie, S., and P. Hardie, eds. (2008). *The Cambridge Companion to Lucretius*. (Cambridge).
Gorman, R. (2005). *The Socratic Method in the Dialogues of Cicero*. (Stuttgart).
Hijmans, B. L. (1987). "Apuleius Philosophus Platonicus." *ANRW* II, 36(1): 395–475.
Hoenig, C. (2014). "Calcidius and the Creation of the Universe." *Rhizomata* 2: 80–110.
Hoenig, C. (2018). *Plato's Timaeus in the Latin Tradition*. The Cambridge Classical Series. (Cambridge).
Hoenig, C. (2019). 'Apuleius' Platonism,' *Oxford Bibliographies Online*. DOI:10.1093/OBO/9780195389661-0345.
Inghilleri, M. (2005). "The Sociology of Bourdieu and the Construction of the 'Object' in Translation and Interpreting Studies." *Translator* 11(2): 125–145.
Jones, D. M. (1959). "Cicero as a Translator." *Bulletin of the Institute of Classical Studies of the University of London* 6: 22–34.
Kobusch, T., M. Erler, and I. Männlein-Robert, eds. (2002). *Metaphysik und Religion: Zur Signatur des Spätantiken Denkens*. (Munich).

Koch, B. (2006). *Philosophie als Medizin für die Seele: Untersuchungen zu Ciceros Tusculanae Disputationes.* (Stuttgart).
Kytzler, B. (1989). "*Fides Interpres*: The Theory and Practice of Translation in Classical Antiquity." *Antichthon* 23: 42–50.
Lefevere, A. (1992). *Translation, Rewriting and the Manipulation of Literary Fame.* (London).
McElduff, S., ed. (2011). *Complicating the History of Western Translation: The Ancient Mediterranean in Perspective.* (London).
McEldruff, S. (2013). *Roman Theories of Translation: Surpassing the Source.* (New York).
Magee, J., ed., tr. (2016). *Calcidius: On Plato's* Timaeus. (Cambridge, Mass.).
Magnaldi, I. (2020). *Apulei Opera Philosophica.* (Oxford).
Marouzeau, J. (1947). "Latini Sermonis Egestas." *Eranos* 45: 22–24.
Marti, H. (1974). *Übersetzer der Augustin-Zeit.* (Munich).
Moreschini, C. (1966). *Studi Sul "De Dogmate Platonis" di Apuleio.* (Pisa).
Moreschini, C. (1978). *Apuleio e il Platonismo.* (Florence).
Moreschini, C. (2015). *Apuleius and the Metamorphoses of Platonism.* (Turnhout).
Munday, J., ed. (2009). *The Routledge Companion to Translation Studies.* (London, New York).
Neumann, G., and J. Untermann, eds. (1980). *Die Sprachen im Römischen Reich der Kaiserzeit.* (Cologne).
Newmark, P. (2009). "The Linguistic and Communicative Stages in Translation Theory," in Munday, 20–35.
Nida, E. (1964). *Toward a Science of Translating: With Special Reference to Principles and Procedures Involved in Bible Translating.* (Leiden).
Nord, C. (1997). *Translating as a Purposeful Activity: Functionalist Approaches Explained.* (Manchester).
Pohlenz, M. (1911). "Die Personenbezeichnungen in Ciceros *Tusculanen*." *Hermes* 46: 627–629.
Powell, J. G. F. (1995). "Cicero's Translations from the Greek," in Powell, 273–300.
Powell, J. G. F., ed. (1995). *Cicero the Philosopher.* (Oxford).
Puelma, M. (1980). "Cicero als Platonübersetzer." *Museum Helveticum* 37: 137–178.
Pym, A., ed. (1997). *Pour une éthique du traducteur.* (Arras).
Pym, A. (2001). *The Return to Ethics.* Special issue. *The Translator* 7(2).
Ratkowitsch, C. (1996). "Die *Timaios*-Übersetzung des Chalcidius." *Philologus* 140: 139–162.
Regen, F. (1971). *Apuleius Philosophus Platonicus: Untersuchungen zur Apologie und De Mundo.* (Berlin).
Reiff, A. (1959). *Interpretatio, Imitatio, Aemulatio: Begriff und Vorstellung Literarischer Abhängigkeit bei den Römern.* (Cologne).
Rener, F. M. (1989). *Interpretatio: Language and Translation from Cicero to Tytler.* (Amsterdam).
Rengakos, A., and A. Tsakmakis, eds. (2006). *Brill's Companion to Thucydides.* (Leiden).
Reydams-Schils, G. (1999). *Demiurge and Providence: Stoic and Platonist Readings of Plato's* Timaeus. (Turnhout).
Reydams-Schils, G. (2002). "Calcidius Christianus? God, Body, and Matter," in Kobusch, Erler, and Männlein-Robert, 193–211.
Reydam-Schils, G., ed. (2003). *Plato's* Timaeus *as Cultural Icon.* (Notre Dame).
Reydams-Schils, G. (2007). "Meta-Discourse: Plato's *Timaeus* according to Calcidius." *Phronesis* 52: 301–327.
Reydams-Schils, G. (2020). *Calcidius on Plato's Timaeus. Greek Philosophy, Latin Reception, and Christian Contexts.* (Cambridge).

Rosenbaum, S. E. (1989). "'The Symmetry Argument: Lucretius against the Fear of Death." *Philosophy and Phenomenological Research* 50(2): 353–373.
Samotta, I. (2011). "Herodotus and Thucydides in Roman Republican Historiography," in Foster and, Lateiner, 345–369.
Schrenk, L. (1994). "Cicero on Rhetoric and Philosophy: *Tusculan Disputations* I." *Ancient Philosophy* 14: 355–360.
Sedley, D. (1998). *Lucretius and the Transformation of Greek Wisdom*. (Cambridge).
Sedley, D. (1999). "Lucretius' Use and Avoidance of Greek," in Adams and Mayer, 227–246.
Sedley, D. (2007). *Creationism and Its Critics in Antiquity*. (Berkeley).
Seele, A. (1995). *Römische Übersetzer*. (Darmstadt).
Steiner, G. (^{3}1998). *After Babel: Aspects of Language and Translation*. (Oxford).
Stemplinger, E. (1912). *Das Plagiat in der Griechischen Literatur*. (Leipzig).
Stoll, K-H. (2004). "Englisch als Kommunikationsvernichter," in Fleischmann, Schmitt, and Wotjak, 443–461.
Stull, W. C. (2012). "Reading the *Phaedo* in *Tusculan Disputations* 1." *Classical Philology* 107(1): 38–52.
Traglia, A. (1971). "Note su Cicerone Traduttore di Platone e di Epicuro," in de Falco, 305–340.
Van Winden, J. C. M. (1959). *Calcidius on Matter: His Doctrine and Sources; A Chapter in the History of Platonism*. (Leiden).
Venuti, L. (1995). *The Translator's Invisibility. A History of Translation*. (London).
Venuti, L. (2008). *The Translator's Invisibility: A History of Translation*. (London).
Warren, J. (2001). "Lucretius, Symmetry Arguments, and Fearing Death." *Phronesis* 46(4): 466–491.
Waszink, J. H., and P. J. Jensen, eds. (1962). *Plato: Timaeus a Calcidio Translatus Commentarioque Instructus*. (Leiden).
West, D. (1969). *The Imagery and Poetry of Lucretius*. (Edinburgh).
West, D. (1970). "Virgilian Multiple-Correspondence Similes and Their Antecedents." *Philologus* 114: 262–275.
Wolf, M., and A. Fukari, eds. (2007). *Constructing a Sociology of Translation*. (Amsterdam).
Young, R. (2014). "Philosophy in Translation," in Bermann, and Porter, 41–53.
Zgusta, L. (1980). "Die Rolle des Griechischen im Römischen Reich der Kaiserzeit," in Neumann, and Untermann, 121–145.

CHAPTER 19

ROMAN PHILOSOPHY IN ITS POLITICAL AND HISTORIOGRAPHICAL CONTEXT

ERMANNO MALASPINA AND ELISA DELLA CALCE[1]

INTRODUCTION

AFTER a brief survey of the relationship between Greek and Roman political thought and between practical and theoretical approaches to political philosophy, the three central sections of this chapter are devoted respectively to the philosophical background of the historical genre in Rome; philosophical contributions to understanding the nature of the Roman state and to healing its ills, that is, what is today called "political philosophy"; and ethical approaches, predicated on the moral qualities of the citizen or ruler. The final section is devoted to the radical criticism of any commitment to public affairs, both in Epicurean thought and in one strand of late Stoicism. In all these areas, consideration is given not only to recognized philosophical writers, such as Cicero, Lucretius, and Seneca, but also to historians and, more broadly, to what has recently been dubbed "the philosophy of non-philosophers."[2]

GREECE AND ROME, ONCE AGAIN

It is the fate of a culture born in the shadow of another to accept that each of its own achievements will inevitably be evaluated in comparison to the source-culture, particularly if it is older and, if not superior, at all events richer and broader, as was the Hellenistic world in relation to Rome. In the last three centuries, following Horace's aphoristic pronouncement, *Graecia capta ferum victorem cepit* ("Conquered Greece tamed its wild conqueror," *Epist.* 2.1.156), the scholarly tradition has seen in this relationship dependency, even a slavish dependency, of Roman thought on Greek, more often than modification, innovation, and criticism, not to mention independence, and nowhere more than in the domain of philosophy. That one can conceive of a *Handbook of Roman Philosophy*, and one that includes a chapter on politics and history, testifies to a new orientation.[3] And yet, even the ostensibly new approach that treats Roman philosophy as mere "practice" (which we hope is a passing fashion) in fact ends up reducing it to mere trappings, on the part of a people more concerned with the formal imitation of certain styles of behavior than with acquiring authentically new attitudes and visions. In so doing, it reflects the old stereotype of the Roman peasant, unrefined but savvy, in comparison to intellectually sophisticated but ultimately sterile Greeks.[4]

In the area of political philosophy, right down to the seventeenth century it was entirely normal to regard Rome as a source of inspiration at least as important as Greece.[5] But it remains a minority tendency today for scholars of contemporary politics to recognize the indispensability of Latin historiography and Rome's many contributions to political philosophy,[6] even though there are good reasons for acknowledging Rome's exceptional role in the philosophical legacy of the West.

THEORY AND PRACTICE?

The relationship between philosophy on the one hand, and politics and historiography on the other, had a special salience in Rome, and was not deemed to be the exclusive prerogative of the Greek world. As the well-known verses of Vergil put it, Rome's role is to rule others, imposing peace, sparing the defeated and conquering the arrogant (*Aen.* 6.847–853). Such was Rome's image of itself, at least at the time of Augustus. Correspondingly, the activities in which the Greeks excelled (evidently regarded as inferior) are exemplified by the fine arts (*excudent alii spirantia mollius aera; vivos ducent de marmore vultus*), oratory (*orabunt causas melius*) and astronomy (*caeli meatus describent radio et surgentia sidera dicent*). Even so, and well before Vergil, Cicero had constructed an alternative narrative, designed to demonstrate the systematic superiority of Romans in respect to Greeks, at least potentially, and above all in the sphere of language, which, far from being impoverished, as Lucretius complained (*patrii sermonis egestas*, 1.832, 3.260), was in reality far richer and more versatile.[7] Cicero's declared purpose was to reduce the gap even where it was not really possible to maintain that Greece was inferior: *elaborandum est ut hoc* (i.e., Rome's superiority) *non in nostris solum artibus, sed etiam in illorum ipsorum adsequamur.*[8] Clearly, for Cicero it was not only the fine arts and the sciences that counted among the Greeks' own disciplines (*illorum ipsorum*), as in Vergil, but philosophy too, with the exception precisely of political philosophy, which is, as Cicero put it, among "our arts" (*nostrae artes, Tusc.* 1.1–2).[9] Private life, economy, and politics, in an ascending order that is not accidental, are thus the activities in which Romans excel, together with military arts and the exercise of virtues (*gravitas* [...], *constantia, magnitudo animi, probitas, fides* ..., *virtus*).

One might object that Cicero and Vergil do not claim superiority for Roman political philosophy, but only for politics (or, if at all, for political "culture"),[10] just as they do not affirm superiority in military or moral treatises, but only in the exercise of the art of war and virtue. If this were so, we would find ourselves once again facing the traditional opposition between Greek theory and Roman *negotium* or practice, and Roman political thought would end up once more radically scaled back. The close connection with actual politics that is characteristic of Rome would constitute a defect and a limitation. But this view is to be firmly rejected. If in other areas of philosophy it is legitimate and often obligatory to abstract from real life, a political philosophy that adopted such an approach would be doomed to remain utopian. No one reproaches political scientists today for basing their philosophical contributions on an analysis of the *hic et nunc* of actual political systems. One ought then in fairness to maintain the same attitude toward thinkers in ancient Rome, whose commitment to the immediacy of their *res publica* was not a limitation, but provided added value, in comparison with the more abstract theories of the great philosophers of Athens' golden age.

Even in the Greek context, in fact, many scholars have had to reevaluate the role of practice in relation to theory, which has attracted the lion's share of attention in the history of classical political thought. Practical and historical developments in fact often overwhelmed Greek speculation, which could not offer interpretative tools that were consistent and adapted to changing times. One may think here of Aristotle, straddling the classical *polis* and the new global empire. Thus Greek theory, far from acting decisively on real life, or shaping it in accord with Plato's aspirations, was often in the Hellenistic age little more than an a posteriori justification of facts on the ground.[11] Roman political thought, on the contrary, was from the very beginning marked by the massive presence of the *res publica–imperium*. It is no coincidence, indeed, that even after Augustus Roman authors used both words in the same sense, namely to signify the "Roman State,"[12] although nowadays they represent two distinct and in many ways antithetical forms of government.[13] For all that the *polis* was at the center of Greek political reflection for quite a long time,[14] the *res publica–imperium* was a much more totalizing experience for the Romans, and this for two reasons. On the one hand, there is its multinational nature,[15] not *one* form of government among others, but *the* form of world government, without limits in time or space, in the direction of the Stoic *cosmopolis*. While the Latin idea of a "public thing" (*res publica*) is far from the modern notion of a republic,[16] the notion of *imperium*, which originally indicated the power exercised by a Roman magistrate within the province assigned to him, assumed the further sense of territorial dominion as soon as Rome extended beyond the Italian peninsula.[17] Thus, as has been recently reaffirmed, in the spatial or territorial sense the concept acquired a "universal" significance, along with the expansion of Roman hegemony, ideally coming ever closer to that "global" geopolitical space that Cicero sought to define by way of the expressions *societas hominum* and *societas universi generis humani*, which extended to all rational beings, i.e., even the gods.[18] On the other hand, there is the extraordinary continuity of this institution, which lasted for a millennium. In comparison, the *polis* and the Hellenistic empires were not only multiple and not cosmopolitan, but above all were limited in time and space and inextricably linked to Greek tradition, whereas Rome, with its *res publica* and *imperium*, created, in the words of Rutilius Namatianus (1.63), a single nation out of various countries (*patriam diversis gentibus unam*). This view diminishes the precedent of Alexander's universalizing empire, but, arguably, this was too short-lived to become a significant model. In any case, it did not give rise to any high-quality theoretical analysis. We may add that the image of Alexander was quite controversial in Rome, where, apart from his personal defects, thinkers took delight in contrasting the ephemeral results of his conquests, based on the qualities, admittedly extraordinary, of a single man, with the slow but solid achievement of Rome, the fruit rather of the centuries-long *virtus* of an entire people.[19]

Rather than appeal to idealistic abstractions of the "Greek spirit," in the manner of Werner Jaeger or Max Pohlenz, we would argue that the very fact of the *res publica–imperium* sufficiently accounts for why Roman political thought did not elaborate political systems *ex novo*, on the model—often decidedly utopian—of Greek thinkers, starting at least with Plato. Rather, the tools of theoretical reflection were at all times placed at the service of the Roman state, its history, its constitution and evolution, the analysis of its nature, and its diseases and possible remedies, peaking in the first centuries BCE and CE.[20]

The "Past-Present" Dialectic in the Prefaces of Sallust, Livy, and Tacitus

We may begin by examining the nature of political theory as it is exemplified in the Roman historians. For present purposes, we focus on the histories of Sallust, Livy, and Tacitus, and more narrowly, the prefaces to their respective works. Writing history in the Latin tradition was never a matter of simply recounting what happened, but always reflected a profound and complex ideology, in which the material intersected with the lived experience of the historian, despite the *topos* of objectivity that marks every preface. Historical works were thus invested with a plurality of goals, in addition to the most obvious one of memorializing the past. There was also the didactic function of educating readers, along with exhortation and critique, all with a view to exhibiting the discrepancy between the exemplary values of remote times and the corruption of the present era. To cite an example, Polybius, in the Hellenistic period, embraced an ideal of "pragmatic history,"[21] and argued for a clean break with the dramatic and anecdotal approach of some of his predecessors,[22] in a return to what he conceived of as the Thucydidean model. Livy, however, writing in the age of Augustus, even as he exploited Polybius as a source for his account of the Hannibalic War, did not eschew a certain emotional tone in his narration of the facts or the inclusion, albeit mostly limited to the first pentad, of legendary tales.[23] Indeed, his handling of Polybius is often revealing of Livy's ideology, since, wherever it is possible to compare the two, one may see how Livy transforms his source in a way that reflects Roman values.[24]

One fundamental tendency characterizes Roman historiography, though it assumes different forms in the three historians under consideration here: Roman history is a narrative of change. There is invariably an implicit story of decline, though there may be some hope for improvement in the future.[25] A further feature is the role of great individuals who might change the course of history, although here again, there is much variation.[26] Finally, as noted above, there is the claim to objectivity, and the rejection of mythical elements with a view to constructing a plausible narrative, although this does not exclude often tendentious interpretations of events with a pro-Roman bias.[27] With respect to the first characteristic, the Roman historians generally regarded their histories as exemplifying a sequence of regime types,[28] each manifesting a certain set of values;[29] there is inevitably a pattern of decline, which renders possible in turn—though it is by no means guaranteed—a restoration of the *mos maiorum*. Sometimes, there are antecedents for such a renewal. In Livy, for example, the foundation of the *res publica* in 509 BCE is treated as a sign of the rebirth of *libertas*, which had been suppressed under the tyranny of the Tarquins. The celebrated victory of Rome over the Gauls in 390 BCE, in turn, opens a new chapter in Roman history, in which the victorious general, Marcus Furius Camillus, can be seen as a second Romulus (Livy 5.49.7).[30] In Tacitus, however, the advent of the Principate is indeed treated as a new cycle, both painful and inevitable, but the Republic to which it succeeds is now regarded as utterly dead and gone.[31] The contrast between a good leader, who represents the qualities of Cicero's *rector civitatis*,[32] and the popular masses, chaotic and irrational and hence in need of a guide, has its roots ultimately in Plato,[33] but surfaces clearly in Livy.[34] A similar opposition, also due ultimately to Plato,[35] is the antithesis between the soul, inclined to the exercise of virtue, and the body, which tends rather to favor the baser appetites. The proems to Sallust's two historical monographs open on this note.[36]

Taking these features together, we can sketch out an overview of the philosophical and political aspects of the works of Sallust, Livy, and Tacitus. Since all three view the past from the perspective of the present, one must take into account the contemporary political climate for each, along with their individual experiences and beliefs. One immediate distinction among them is that, while Sallust and Tacitus are historians, both were also senators; Livy, on the other hand, devoted his entire life to the composition of his monumental work. As a result, the many books of his *Ab urbe condita* lack the kinds of autobiographical references found in Sallust's proems and the preface to Tacitus's *Historiae*, where both feel the need to justify their decision to write histories and seek to relate it to the current political context. Livy, on the contrary, simply aims to serve his country by preserving the memory of the achievements of the Roman people.[37] And yet, all three share a pessimistic tone in regard to the present. For Sallust, it is irremediably corrupt. Livy seeks refuge in the past from the crises that characterize his own times. And Tacitus shows how an increasing tendency to flattery, over the course of the Principate, has falsified any pretense at objectivity in the historiographical writings of his time.

We begin, then, with Sallust, the most pessimistic of them all. Having observed, as he perceived it, the progressive decline of morals and the crisis of institutions that the Republic underwent,[38] he leaves not the slightest hope of improvement in the present. For him, it is a matter of psychology or ethics: people could have acted in accord with virtue, given the bipartite nature of the soul, but *libido* gained the upper hand over reason, once and for all.[39] It is thus impossible to engage in politics any longer, save corruptly, and so the only option is *otium* and, for Sallust, the career of historian.[40] Historiography, accordingly, has no constructive role but reflects rather a spirit of critique.[41] The pessimism of Livy's *Praefatio* is more attenuated,[42] even though he too lived through the crisis of the civil war. One can perceive a certain eagerness to get to events of the present time (*festinantes ad haec nova, praef.* 4), even if he entertained doubts about the effectiveness of any remedies (*remedia*) for current problems.[43] The word *remedium* has been much discussed, but most likely it refers to the new order of "one-man rule,"[44] and more particularly, that of Octavian. As Livy was writing, Octavian was still putting in place the institutions that would legitimize his supremacy and promised a new social stability.[45] References to the present in the proems to Tacitus's *Historiae* and *Annales* are again different, reflecting his disenchantment with "the pretense or public image (*princeps*) and the reality (*imperium*),"[46] not without reference to his own experience in politics.[47] Yet Tacitus did not simply express criticism, but was also a spokesman for a more constructive vision, whereby honorable individuals might live and serve even after *libertas* had been stifled under tyranny.[48] Hence his description of the reigns of Nerva and Trajan as *rara temporum felicitas* (*Hist.* 1.1.4).

These several conceptions of the present in relation to the past are bearers of implicit political theories. For Sallust, as we have seen, the explanation of social decline is above all moral, the triumph of greed and ambitions in the human soul.[49] Livy, who saw the emergence of Octavian's rule, which put an end to civil wars, was more inclined to a "great-man" conception of history. For this reason, he was especially drawn to *exempla* or models of good leadership (or the reverse), which one should imitate or avoid,[50] and which could nourish the hope of renewal.[51] For Tacitus, above all in the *Annales*, it was more a matter of institutions.[52] The Republic was the locus of the fundamental value of *libertas*, which was trampled by the tyranny of the early empire.[53] Tacitus gives no space in his prefaces to the role of exemplary figures. Certainly, his views evolved between the early *Historiae*, which located a crucial change after the battle of Actium, and the *Annales*, which recognized the presence of *decora ingenia*,[54] who could hold out against the rising tide of adulation.[55] Be that as it may, for Tacitus the empire was a fact. His vision of history was predicated neither on the Platonizing analogy between political regimes and moral or psychological dispositions, nor on the ambiguous compromise between *principatus* and *libertas*, which would bring peace to a world riven by dissension and civil war.[56] What remained, then, was to provide the reader with keys to surviving in the present. This, indeed, is the core of his philosophy of history. Just as the past manifested cruel tyrants but also *decora ingenia*, so too the present, despite the absence of *libertas*, had its positive periods (exemplified by Nerva and Trajan). The role of the historian is thus to remind the reader that even when the present moment is tranquil, there remains always the danger of tyranny, but that in such instances too one may adapt to present circumstances those values which the *decora ingenia* of the past manifested.

Analysis and Therapy of the Roman Empire

We now pass from reflections on historiography to political thought in the narrower sense, but with the same objective, that is, identifying genuine philosophical contributions even independent of Greek sources. Nevertheless, the existence of contacts and philosophical influences deriving from the Greek world is attested from a very early date,[57] even if it is often difficult to distinguish a genuine and knowledgeable report from later reconstructions, which aimed at giving the impression of a Greek lineage even to phenomena that were wholly Roman. An example is the well-known case of Pythagoras, whose connection with Numa had already been refuted by Cicero in his *De re publica* on chronological grounds, but whose connections with Appius Claudius are affirmed in Cicero's *Tusculanae*.[58]

A turning point is undoubtedly represented by the so-called Scipionic Circle of the late second century. This may have happened because by this time contacts with Greek philosophy had ceased to have merely legendary contours and could be shown to be historically well founded. Or else the reason may be found in the ongoing evolution of the Romano-Italic *res publica* into a universal empire, which required a corresponding theoretical effort to adapt its political structures to the new conditions—without, however, repudiating, at least formally, the ancestral *instituta* and *mos maiorum*. This is a disposition that we see still very much alive in Cicero and in Augustus's constitutional reforms.

It is to the period of the "Circle" that we may trace the adoption of the Stoic notion of *kathékon (officium)* as a justification of political engagement and imperialism on the part of Romans—or, better, of the patrician-plebeian elite of the families that shared republican offices associated with *libertas*. The idea of *officium* resonated down to Vergil's *regere imperio populos* and beyond. The time is long gone when *Quellenforschung* posited the dependency on a lost text of Panaetius (or of Posidonius) every time a Latin writer offered an intellectually complex view, in the absence of known Greek sources. Nevertheless, one cannot deny the role of Panaetius, whether in relation to Aemilianus's views or, above all, to the Middle Stoic canonization of *kathékon/officium*.[59] There are other effects as well of Panaetius's influence on subsequent writers (though they are often difficult to define precisely), along with Polybius's ruminations in his *Histories*, which, however, for all their focus on Rome's empire, can only with a good bit of forcing be seen as a product of "Roman philosophy." Polybius's theory of the "mixed constitution" will, nevertheless, remain a fixed point in the Latin tradition down to Varro and Cicero's *De re publica* and beyond.[60] In addition, this period witnesses the beginning of effective collaboration between intellectuals and political figures, represented by the careers of Panaetius himself and of Polybius. There is also a more open interest on the part of the philhellenic *gentes* in the contemporary practices of the absolute monarchies of the Diadochi or successors of Alexander the Great, which implicitly furnished the first *specula principis* for the most ambitious Roman generals, beginning with Scipio Africanus.[61] The entire power struggle with the traditionalist party of Cato may be read, from the point of view of political philosophy, as a clash over the legitimacy of incorporating within the *mos maiorum* the self-interested postures that were modeled on eastern regimes, and that might readily be suspected of concealing aspirations to *regnum* or tyranny.

It is impossible, indeed, to understand Roman political philosophy without considering the role of the *mos maiorum*, which is all the more frequently invoked in just those situations where a precise definition is most lacking. Familial traditions and political customs mix with religious procedures and legal norms to create a prescriptive ethical scenario, which forms the horizon within which, for the Romans, any theoretical reflection must operate.[62] In contrast to Greece, both law, which we know primarily through its much later written systematization, and religion, understood not as personal communication with the divine but as the totality of prescriptions, formulas, and rituals necessary for the preservation of the *pax deorum* and social harmony, had a place in Rome also in the history of political philosophy.[63]

The second half of the second century BCE also set in motion developments that led rapidly to that paroxysm we now call the "Roman Revolution,"[64] and to recurring accusations of aspirations to *regnum* and to intensified individualism on the part of generals. Although these can be read, as we have observed, in the light of the influence of practices typical of the Hellenistic monarchies, there is another factor, philosophically even more significant, namely an acknowledgment of the social and economic crisis of the small landowners, the sinews of the traditional Roman army. This crisis led, among the most discerning minds, to a recognition of the need for changes in the form of the constitution, by introducing guarantees of equality that ran counter to the actual drift of things. This is what lay behind the politics of the Gracchi, who were intimate associates of the Stoic philosopher Blossius of Cumae, a student of Antipater of Tarsus and the teacher of Tiberius Gracchus.[65]

Nevertheless, it is, obviously, only with Cicero that we possess a corpus of philosophical texts in which it is possible to put Roman political thought to the test. The triad *De republica*, *De legibus*, and *De officiis* have been widely studied in this regard,[66] but the investigation needs to be extended to other sources as well, including oratory. All these genres indicate an awareness that the crisis of the republic requires first and foremost a theoretical development—in the realization of which, it goes without saying, Cicero was deeply invested—that could correct negative features in the polity. In this connection, the recent contribution of Benjamin Straumann is especially valuable, as he maintains that Cicero sought first of all a specifically constitutional solution, rising above eudaimonistic prescriptions focused on achieving individual happiness via the exercise of virtue (whether that of the citizen or of ruler), which derived from Greek speculation and which we will examine in the next section. Thus, Cicero sketches in "a specific view of politics that centers on certain rights and norms achieved and guaranteed by a set of higher-order constitutional rules, rules that are understood to have legal character."[67] In the absence of a "Roman constitution" in the modern sense, that is a unified code, fixed and clearly embodied in written laws and considered superior to positive legislation, which is specific and always in the process of change, Cicero sought to propose a "virtual constitution" as preeminent and of higher authority than the various positive norms. This was, he held, more entrenched[68] in the *mos, ius,* and above all the prepolitical right to private property and the laws of nature, ideas that are Stoic in origin.[69] For on this point Cicero registers one of the greatest departures from his repeatedly advertised philosophical posture as an *Academicus*, that is, an adherent of the Platonic school.[70]

To disparage this complex undertaking for its practical deficiencies, in the context of the proscriptions of 43 and the subsequent drift toward monarchy in Rome, would be deeply unfair. As we noted,[71] centuries of republicanism culminating in the foundation of the United States of America, and centuries of natural law theory would never have existed were it not for Cicero's political philosophy and his desperate attempt to save the republic, not with arms, but with political and constitutional theorizing.

Virtue and Nothing Else

If, as we have said, Greece and Rome were different, in that the former (it is said) was the home of political theory while the latter looked to a critical and concrete analysis of the existing state, there was also a third approach to political philosophy, the eudaimonistic privileging of the moral qualities of citizens and/or rulers. This tendency stands out as a remarkable *fil rouge*, with an increasing focus, from the first century BCE onward, on the *princeps* as the sole factor that can guarantee the well-being of the system, regardless of its constitution.

This approach, well known in the Greek literary tradition from the conception of the "good king" in Homer and critiques of the figure of the tyrant in archaic lyric up to Hellenistic *specula principis*,[72] is accompanied, in Cicero, by considerations (cited above) that look rather to constitutional reforms. This more theoretical approach was limited, as we have said, to political treatises, intended for a narrower and higher-class public. On the contrary, the conception of the good ruler, who achieves both his moral nature and his personal *gloria* in serving the interests of his fellow citizens, provincials, and in the final analysis the State, while not absent from the doctrinal works, is most evident in the speeches, which were aimed at a larger public, philosophically less informed and politically perhaps even hostile to Cicero. For this moralizing attitude was close to the stereotype of the good Roman citizen, that is, one who was respectful of the *mos maiorum*: this approach (which is found already in archaic epigraphical *elogia* and became a byword in Cato's definition of the political orator as *vir bonus dicendi peritus*)[73] was wholly centered around the term *virtus*. Needless to say, this typically Roman word, which originally referred to masculine valor (deriving from the root *vir-tus*), a connotation absent in the corresponding Greek term *areté*,[74] had long since acquired specifically Greek philosophical connotations as well. We can see this at least as early as in the abovementioned *elogia* and in verses 1326–1338 (Marx) of Lucilius, that is, the famous fragment containing the "praise of *virtus*" addressed to Albinus.[75]

The eudaimonistic approach is also often manifested in the contrary example of the bad Roman, from Verres to Catiline, from Clodius to Gabinius, and from Vatinius to Antony. Doubtless in the descriptions of these exemplary figures, whether good or bad, political opportunism and the struggle among *factiones* often had the upper hand over staid political analysis. Nevertheless, it would be a mistake to suppose that Cicero left it at that, or that in his constitutional theory he wished to devalue the ethical aspect as nothing more than a bow to moralizing traditionalism and a propagandistic strategy to ingratiate himself, from time to time, with judges, the Senate, the *equites*, or the plebs. That it was rather a sincere component of his political thought is clear both from the well-known and much-discussed figure of the *princeps* in his *De re publica* and perhaps even more so from the long epistle *Ad Quintum fratrem* 1.1.[76] As for the former, everything relating to the true nature of the *princeps* has by now been said: the fragmentary nature of the treatise makes it impossible to define its constitutional character precisely, whereas the moral elements are clear in a portrait characterized by a firm possession of *virtus* in all its facets, always to the benefit of the state.[77] By contrast, it is easier to follow Cicero's advice to his brother when he was governor of the province of Asia, in the winter of 60–59. This is evidently a *Fürstenspiegel* in which the element of *decorum*—that is, the moral duty to pursue virtue at all costs—in fact coincides with the *utile*, that is, with success and the political consensus, in this case with regard to the provincials. Such an agreement between the *honestum* and the *utile*, which Cicero would have clarified with reference to Panaetius in the third book of his *De officiis*, remains a *Leitmotiv* of Roman political thought right down to Seneca's *De clementia* and beyond, in the optimistic conviction that abstract morality can coincide with political advantage, a belief that it would take Machiavelli finally to tear down.[78]

We may end this section on Cicero by recalling how much he cared about the moral education of younger generations, also at the level of political culture, following in the footsteps of Isocrates and holding that *sapientia* is the offspring of *eloquentia*.[79]

In the imperial period the eudaimonistic objective of happiness through virtue remained central, even if the addressees changed. It was no longer the senatorial elite of the republic, which tended to egalitarianism within its own circle, but, on the one hand, the emperor, and, on the other, at a great remove, the citizens, who had become subjects or at best imperial officials. Beyond the borders of the empire, however, one may find among the barbarians a society in which good morals have a natural robustness, precisely because they are removed from the enticements of *humanitas* (Tac. *Agr.* 21), without the need for a specific pedagogy or legal or constitutional correctives. It was Tacitus who expressed this idea in one of his most incisive *sententiae*: *ibi boni mores valent quam alibi bonae leges* (*Germ*. 19.2).

The perhaps ingenuous solution of Quintilian, who returns to Cato's ideal of the *vir bonus* in order to define the new image of the citizen, an honest collaborator with power,[80] has its analogue in Pliny's portrait of Trajan, which sees the perfect prince as the point at which all virtues converge.[81] Common to both, perhaps in part on account of Quintilian's influence as the teacher of the young Pliny, is the formally secondary role that Greek philosophy has in this moralizing picture, according to which, in a line that runs from Isocrates through Cicero, both see philosophy as the *ancilla rhetoricae* and not the reverse. Nevertheless, these two texts, the *Institutio* and the *Panegyricus*, especially if they are compared with what was to follow in late antiquity, that is, the *Panegyrici Latini*, have a depth that renders them the last serious contributions on a theoretical level, albeit with a progressive watering down in conceptual content with respect to Cicero and Seneca.[82]

To Seneca, indeed, we owe a contribution that is an *unicum* in the Latin world. The *De clementia* deliberately excludes any analysis of a constitutional sort and focuses solely on the ethical aspect of the eudaimonistic education of the ideal prince. Behind this approach stand the Latin tradition of the *clementia* of the virtuous commander and the commonplaces of Hellenistic *Fürstenspiegel* (which invariably embraces the pairing of *utile* and *honestum*), as well as the Stoic ideal of the *sapiens*, immune to pity (*misericordia*) but prepared to benefit the world by going beyond *iustitia* pure and simple in the direction of *clementia*. These three themes constitute the disparate ingredients of a cocktail that represents without a doubt the most "philosophical" contribution to political theory in Rome. And yet, it remained almost entirely without an afterlife, whether because it was bound up with the infamous Nero, the emperor who served as its model, or because, being incomplete (of the projected three books there survive only the first and the first seven chapters of the second), it ended in a theoretical dead end. So much for the daring attempt to endow *clementia* with citizen status in Roman Stoicism.[83]

Radical Criticism of Political Engagement

All the philosophical positions examined up to this point share the common assumption, frequently left implicit because it was considered obvious, that both the sage and the common man not only can but actually must engage in public affairs. From the viewpoint of earlier Greek thinkers, the centrality of politics found a powerful philosophical justification in Plato's *Republic*, as well as being inherent in the historical experience of the *poleis*. The subordination, in Aristotle's scale of *eudaimonía*, of political activity to *sophía* as exercised in contemplation[84] reduced the philosophical status of politics, but without ousting it from the range of activities worthy of a free person in classical Greece.

It required, as we have noted, the new relations of power in the Hellenistic monarchies and the birth of philosophies such as cynicism, Epicureanism, and also, in part, Stoicism to legitimize a radical disengagement from politics and indeed to represent it as the best choice for the sage.

This evolution took place in Greece under the broad heading of *bíoi*, or the choice of lifestyle, in particular between the *vita activa* and the *vita contemplativa*.[85] In the optimistic perspective of Cicero, these two options did not constitute a sharp antithesis.[86] Rather, they were understood in a unitary framework, in which, for the statesman, the active life (*negotium*) is dominant, with the proviso that philosophical reflection is the primary commitment in times given over to *otium*. A person's entire existence is thus devoted to higher activities that look to the well-being of the fatherland, whether they are practical in moments of business (*negotium*) or contemplative during periods of leisure (*otium*). This division obtains in Cicero's idealized image of the Scipionic circle, who philosophize at those times of the year that the calendar assigned to *otium* (as is the case in the conversations carried on in the *De re publica*, which Cicero is keen to point out occurred during the *feriae Latinae*, 1.14), or when advancing age gradually hampers physical but not intellectual activity.[87] For Cicero, this holds true—perhaps, sad to say, even more true—when *otium* is not a choice, but is imposed by a tyrant.[88]

Seneca's position on the *bioi* is quite different. We will get to him, however, after finishing the survey of the philosophical downgrading of political commitment in the period of the republic. Based on what has been said above, it is unsurprising that such a deflation ended up in direct conflict with traditional attitudes in Rome.[89] Of the three schools mentioned above, only one seems to have been active in this regard in the republican era: Epicureanism. Stoicism indeed had a strong presence in Rome, but, as was said above, this took the form of the Panaetian variant associated with the "Scipionic circle," which distanced itself from the Stoa of the founders both in treating as primary the *kathékon* of political commitment and in rejecting, among other things, the anarchic and sometimes downright bizarre aspects of the political views of the early Stoa.[90] The Cynic ideal of life, in turn, had least place in the aristocratic culture of the cultivated classes, and a figure such as Diogenes could never serve as a political model worthy of being adopted in the republican period. In fact, it is Cicero himself who testifies, with some discomfort, to the expansion of Epicureanism in Rome by way of translations, apparently quite defective, by otherwise unknown figures such as Rabirius, Gaius Amafinius, and Catius Insuber.[91] Cicero's hostility toward this philosophical doctrine is total and transcends the scope of this chapter, but, to limit ourselves to political philosophy, it is well known the degree to which Cicero's fears were centered on the increasing popularity in Rome of the precept, *mè politéuesthai*, or "do not engage in politics."[92] Cicero's interpretation of the Epicurean position was long accepted uncritically, in line with a partisan view of Epicurus as a socially revolutionary thinker.[93] Today, however, many "political" contributions on the part of Epicurus concerning the concept of security, justice, laws, and social community have been highlighted,[94] which insulate him at least partially against Cicero's criticisms. Leaving aside Epicurus's own ideas, and looking rather at the influence of Epicureanism in Rome, which interests us here, the risk of political disengagement that terrified Cicero does not find much objective historical support.[95] Apart from the case of Atticus,[96] the elite senatorial figures who fully accepted Epicurus's ethical teachings do not seem to have sided with the precept *mè politéuesthai*. Take the example of Lucius Manlius Torquatus,[97] the son of the consul of the same name in 65, and himself praetor perhaps in 49, who committed suicide in the civil war against Caesar. Cicero assigned him the role of defending Epicureanism in the first book of *De finibus*, and political activity was indeed an ineliminable part of his life. Nor is this a matter of an isolated case, but was rather the rule, from the earliest Roman Epicurean who can be identified, that is, the Titus Albucius who was ridiculed by Lucilius.[98] Even Lucretius, who in other respects is a prime source for Epicureanism, is never a spokesman for *mè politéuesthai*. Limiting himself to a generic antimilitarism, he nevertheless recognized that Memmius could not fail to serve the common welfare (*communi desse saluti*) at a critical moment for the state (*patriai tempore iniquo*).[99]

We may find a good-natured recognition of the Epicurean link between wisdom and *mè politéuesthai*, now devoid of the pejorative connotations in Cicero's writings, where historians of philosophy are unlikely to look for it, that is, in the *Silvae* of the poet Publius Papinius Statius. To Pollius Felix,[100] a cultivated individual who belonged to the municipal nobility of Campania and known only thanks to Statius himself, Statius dedicated *Silvae* 2.2, an ekphrastic poem on the villa with a beautiful view that Pollius owned in Sorrento. Pollius is represented as an excellent poet, given to all the genres, and at the same time a follower of Epicurus (who probably would not have appreciated the coupling; v. 113). In the final encomium, in which Pollius is represented as a philosopher sage above the humble crowd (129), the explicit rejection of political engagement is an integral part of his portrait.[101]

It is not unlikely that, in the era of Domitian, the reference to his Epicureanism was also an implicit way of certifying Pollius's loyalty to the empire and his distance from the prosenatorial opposition, which had coalesced around a Stoicizing posture. And with this we may pass to the final part of the chapter, that is, the role of Stoicism under the empire. Here, we may say at once, it is not always easy to distinguish between those who opposed not politics as such, but the political institution of empire, and yearned for a return to republican forms, from those who, more radically, made the doctrine of *mè politéuesthai* their own, even if they were in the Stoic camp. The two variants merge into one only where opposition to the principate is accompanied by a recognition that there are no alternatives, and so it too yields to a radical political pessimism.

We have no theoretical treatments of political dissent, but rather practical evidence of the opposition to tyranny, often consisting in nothing more than silence and in a refusal to join in the celebration of the emperor's misdeeds. Information about this attitude comes from disparate sources, all of them deriving from the lost *exitus illustrium virorum* or deeds of famous men (Plin. *Ep.* 8.12.4), which nevertheless attest to a Stoic and Cynic ethical substratum.[102]

Finally, with respect to *mè politéuesthai*, we come to Seneca, at once a source and a protagonist. At the heart of the recuperation of Cynic maximalist examples of political disengagement is the *Sextiorum nova et Romani roboris secta* or school of the Sextii,[103] which was founded by Q. Sextius Niger, probably in the time of Julius Caesar, and was continued by his son of the same name and above all by Papirius Fabianus. It came to an end well before the death of Seneca, who is practically the only one who mentions it. It is difficult to say exactly what the thinking behind it was, but it is clear that the Sextii succeeded in rendering acceptable to the senatorial elite the political radicalism of the Cynics, giving it an ethical stamp of Stoic nature. This radicalism, however, at the same time distanced itself from the Stoic ideal of collaboration between intellectuals and political leaders,[104] focusing instead on the moral perfection of the individual.[105] What made its success possible was the inexorable reality of the principate, which to many was unbearable, but also the "Roman" nature of the school. Building on a Stoic-Cynic base, with references also to Platonism and Pythagoreanism, it assigned great importance also to formal decorum and rhetorical activity (true especially of Fabianus, who had been a rhetor before "converting" to philosophy),[106] and so in this regard was in conformity with Roman tradition.

Seneca was an intermittent disciple of the Sextii. It is to him that we owe, in his *De clementia*, as we have seen above, the most complete theorization of the collaboration between the (Stoic) intellectual and the (Stoic) emperor, and so at the opposite extreme from what the Sextii preached. However, in the final years of his life, at the time of the *De otio* and the *Epistulae*, Seneca underwent a profound change. He recuperated the cosmopolitanism of early Stoicism and concentrated on the moral goal of the inner development of the *proficiens*, who no longer looks to ameliorating the government of the *res publica* but rather to reaching the sanctity of the *sapiens*. The scope is now, if not directly the *posterorum negotium* (the title of John Eliot's account of Parliament in 1625), at least the *maior res publica* of the Stoics, that one could better serve *in otio*, in agreement, incidentally, with Epicureanism.[107] This change in attitude is not a sign of inconsistency or opportunism on the part of Seneca, but rather of the overriding importance of *prodesse* or service, which depends on what circumstances allow, a concept that goes back to early Stoicism and which demonstrates, if proof were needed, Seneca's substantial loyalty to his school. The apogee of this trajectory, culminating in a radical refusal of politics and the focus of the *sapiens* solely on his own interiority, may be seen, even more so than in the *De otio*, in the magnificent third chorus of the *Thyestes*:

> A king is a man who fears nothing
> a king is a man who wants nothing.
> This kingdom one gives to oneself.
> Let the ruler who wants take his stance
> on the slippery rooftop of rule:
> I'd like to loll in sweet calm.
> Obscurity grants me safe footing.
> Let me relish my easy repose,
> and, known to none of my peers,
> let my life flow by silently.
> And when my days have all passed
> without any hullabaloo,

> let me die both old and a commoner.
> Death only weighs heavy on him
> whom everyone knows far too well
> but who dies unknown to himself.[108]

It marks the conclusion, symbolic as well as practical, of classical Roman political thought.

Notes

1. The authors are pleased to thank David Konstan for the English translation, and Gretchen Reydams-Schils for her penetrating comments. The authors have discussed the entire article; but the fourth section ("The 'Past-Present' Dialectic") is primarily by Della Calce, the rest by Malaspina.
2. See Aubert, Guérin, and Morlet (2019); Volk and Williams (2022).
3. See also, for instance, Griffin and Barnes (1989), Zecchini (1997), Rowe and Schofield (2000), Balot (2009), Hammer (2014), Atkins (2018), and Atkins and Bénatouïl (2022).
4. A summary of this position can be found in Vesperini (2012), on which, see Malaspina (2016).
5. We refer the reader to the very recent Kapust and Remer (2021); see also Atkins and Bénatouïl (2022) 229 and 268–300.
6. See, for example, Viroli (2010) 10 on the idea of liberty in Cicero.
7. *Fin.* 1.10: *ita sentio et saepe disserui, Latinam linguam non modo non inopem, ut vulgo putarent, sed locupletiorem etiam esse quam Graecam*; 3.5, *nos non modo non vinci a Graecis verborum copia, sed esse in ea etiam superiores.*
8. *Fin.* 3.5.
9. *Meum semper iudicium fuit omnia nostros aut invenisse* per se *sapientius quam Graecos aut accepta ab illis fecisse meliora, quae quidem digna statuissent in quibus elaborarent. Nam mores et instituta vitae resque domesticas ac familiaris nos profecto et melius tuemur et lautius, rem vero publicam nostri maiores certe melioribus temperaverunt et institutis et legibus.* See also *Tusc.* 4.1–6, *Rep.* 2.30, and Pohlenz (1965) 35.
10. See Arena, Prag, and Stiles (2022).
11. See Schuller (1988), Laks and Schofield (1995), and Schofield (1999) 739–740.
12. Just to provide some figures, Cicero uses *imperium* a little more than 600 times and *res publica* almost 3,000 times; Tacitus uses *imperium* almost 300 times and *res publica* almost 200; and for Ammianus Marcellinus the figures are 90 for *imperium* and 60 for *res publica*. See Suerbaum (^{2}1970).
13. We do not mean to suggest that between the Roman republic and principate there were not enormous constitutional differences nor that they were unknown to the Romans. We mean only that, despite these, the government of Rome was felt to be an element of constancy and continuity. This sense of continuity was favored too by the formal maintenance of the names of the republican magistracies until the threshold of the Byzantine era.
14. Reference to Aristotle's systematic collection of the constitutions of Greek cities is in order, but the comparative evaluation of the three ideal forms of government (monarchy, aristocracy, democracy) is already present in Herodotus (3.80–82), who certainly cannot be called a philosopher.

15. Romans were well aware that the apparently benevolent universalism of their dominion could be seen as mere propaganda by the subjugated communities: see Sall. *Hist.* 4.69; Tac. *Agr.* 30.
16. As Moatti (2018) has brilliantly explained.
17. Letta and Segenni (2015) 21–22.
18. Reydams-Schils (2005) 93–99, and Pagnotta (2022) 167–168.
19. On Roman evaluations of the character of Alexander, see Fears (1974), Kühnen (2008), and the papers collected in Moore (2018) 162–232; 254–354. The best-known comparison is Livy, 9.17–18; see also *infra* n61.
20. Crucial is the study of the Roman political vocabulary. For the republic, Hellegouarc'h (1972) remains fundamental; unfortunately, we have nothing similar for the empire.
21. Polyb. 1.2.8 and 9.1–2. For a thorough definition, see Walbank (1957) 8n6 and Musti (2010), 17–31.
22. Polybius's critique is directed especially against historians of the fourth and third centuries, such as Theopompus, Timaeus, and Phylarchus.
23. Livy *Praef.* 6–7.
24. Compare, for example, the account of the battle of Cynoscephalae, in which the Romans confronted Philip V of Macedon (197 BCE). In Livy (33.10.3–5), the brutality of the Roman army is mitigated, whereas in Polybius's version the Romans slaughter most of the enemy (18.26.9–12). On this point, see Eckstein (2015) 414–415.
25. See especially Engels (2009) 859–894, and for Livy's *Histories*, Mineo (2015a) 139–152.
26. On the principate, see Syme (1939) 440–458; 513–524, and on the role of the leader in relation to power, Stadter (2009) 456–470.
27. See, for instance, Livy 45.42.10–11, where Romans confer *beneficia gratuita* on their adversaries (45.42.11); cf. Pianezzola (^{2}2018) 73.
28. On the so-called *anacyclosis*, see Polyb. 6.4.7–9 and Cic. *Rep.* 1.41–45. Cf. Walbank (1957) 643–648 and Engels (2009) 866–872.
29. On cycles in Livy, see Mineo (2015a) 140, who emphasizes that "inside each cycle, the reader will notice two historical sequences of equal duration, one an ascending curve and the other a descending curve, depending on whether *concordia* or *discordia* is prevalent at the time."
30. Thus Mineo (2015a) 146.
31. On Tacitus, cf. Syme (1939) 516: "there was no escape. Despite the nominal sovranty of law, one man ruled . . . the more so because a respectable tradition of philosophic thought held monarchy to be the best form of government. It was also primeval, fated to return again when a state had run through the whole cycle of change."
32. *Rep.* 2.51.
33. Cf. Mineo (2015b) 129.
34. See Vasaly (2015) 96–116 and Mineo (2015b) 125–129, 132–134 for the philosophical subtext, inspired by Plato.
35. On the contrast between soul and body, see Pl. *Phd.* 80a with Mariotti (2007) 124–125.
36. *Cat.* 1 and *Iug.* 1–2. On the special nature of Sallust's prologues, see Balmaceda (2017) 50–51 with bibliography.
37. So Vasaly (2015) 23: "he will instead attempt to articulate a proper form for recording events that have been frequently memorialized in the past." Of course, we are missing the books where Livy treated contemporary history. On the composition of the work and the relevant dates, see Luce (2009) 17–47; also Moles (2009) 69: "Livy surely could have

written in such pessimistic terms even after Actium, just as Horace does, for example in *Odes* 3.6, because 'the present' can be a fairly elastic term when the perspective is the whole of Roman history from the foundation of the city, and because, although Actium was indeed a decisive turning-point, the 20s were in fact a very tense political era."

38. Cf. Balmaceda (2017) 81–82.
39. *Cat.* 2.2–6 and *Iug.* 1.3–2.4.
40. *Cat.* 3–4 and *Iug.* 4.1–4.
41. Cf. *Iug.* 3.1: *verum ex iis magistratus et imperia, postremo omnis cura rerum publicarum minume mihi hac tempestate cupiunda videntur, quoniam neque virtuti honos datur neque illi, quibus per fraudem iis fuit uti, tuti aut eo magis honesti sunt.*
42. Thus Balmaceda (2017) 88.
43. Livy *praef.* 9: *donec ad haec tempora quibus nec vitia nostra nec remedia pati possumus.*
44. Moles (2009) 71.
45. Cf. Marcone (2015) 92–94.
46. Goodyear (1972) 94 on *Ann.* 1.1.1: *et Pompei Crassique potentia cito in Caesarem, Lepidi atque Antonii arma in Augustum cessere, qui cuncta discordiis civilibus fessa nomine principis sub imperium accepit.*
47. *Hist.* 1.1.3.
48. Cf. Syme (1958) 548–549; Rutledge (2009) 431.
49. In *Cat.* 10 and *Iug.* 41.2–3 Sallust locates the beginning of moral degeneration in the aftermath of the destruction of Carthage (146 BCE). Cf. Balmaceda (2017) 88 on the contrast with Livy: "for Livy, instead, vices such as ambition and avarice had crept into the city slowly and late."
50. *Praef.* 10: *hoc illud est praecipue in cognitione rerum salubre ac frugiferum. Omnis te exempli documenta in inlustri posita monumento intueri; inde tibi tuaeque rei publicae quod imitere capias, inde foedum inceptu foedum exitu quod vites.* See Chaplin (2000) and Beltramini (2017) 171–174.
51. Innovation based on tradition is a basic premise of Octavian's *restitutio rei publicae*: see Scheid (2018) 120–127, and cf. Balmaceda (2017) 87–91. In this regard, Livy's notion of *exemplum* is not dissimilar from that of Augustus; see Balmaceda (2017) 90 and Beltramini (2017) 193 (with relevant bibliography in n36).
52. Cf. Chilver (1979) 36–37 on Tacitus's change of his original plan (*Hist.* 1.1.4).
53. On *libertas* in general, cf. Arena (2012), Balmaceda (2020), and Schofield (2021) 27–59. On the interpretation of this concept in the prologues of the *Annales* and the *Historiae*, see respectively Goodyear (1972) 88–92, 95–97 and Chilver (1979) 35. On the connection between Tacitus and Augustus, see especially Lyasse (2008) 979–984.
54. *Ann.* 1.1.2: *temporibusque Augusti dicendis non defuere decora ingenia*; *Hist.* 1.1.1: *postquam bellatum apud Actium atque omnem potentiam ad unum conferri pacis interfuit, magna illa ingenia cessere.* Cf. Syme (1958) 364–365.
55. Cf. Goodyear (1972) 96–97: "towards the end of Augustus' life repression begins, with the burning of the writing of T. Labienus ... and the condemnation and exile of Cassius Severus." On the final years of the Augustan principate, see Syme (1939) 486–488.
56. See Augustus, *Res gestae* 1.1 and Tac. *Agr.* 3.1.
57. See the collection of testimonies in Garbarino (1973), a pioneering and still indispensable work, supplemented by Garbarino (2003).
58. *Rep.* 2.28–29 and *Tusc.* 4.2–4, with Horky in this volume. On the story, see Rawson (1989) 236–238; we have already noted (n9) how the denial, wherever possible, of a dependence on Greek sources in Cicero is part of an ambitious project to enhance Romanism.

59. See Barlow (2018), Wildberger (2018) 186–188 and Mitsis (2021).
60. See Pohlenz (1965) 34–35, Lintott (1997) and Schofield (1999) 744–748.
61. For the *imitatio Alexandri* by Scipio Africanus see Tisé (2002); see also Kühnen (2008) with a broader chronological scope on the same subject.
62. Here too the bibliography is enormous; see, at a minimum, Linke and Stemmler (2000) and Sauer (2018).
63. See Zecchini (1997).
64. See Büchner (1984) 53; Syme (1939).
65. Cic. *Amic.* 37; Plut. *Vit. Ti. Gracch.* 8.4–5: see Moatti (2018) 126.
66. The bibliography is huge; see, at a minimum, Büchner (1984) 49–56, who explicitly distances himself from the devaluation of Cicero's theoretical contribution in earlier *Quellenforschung* (49); also Zarecki (2014); Moatti (2018) 187–248; Fox in this volume.
67. Straumann (2016) 11; see also Schofield (2021) 112–125, and above all 232–235.
68. "The fact that certain rules are more entrenched than other rules and less susceptible to change," Straumann (2016) 36.
69. Straumann (2016) 147–161, 191–237. His analysis treats procedural institutions (the *senatus consultus ultimum*, the *provocatio*, the dictatorship, the declaration of a citizen as *hostis*, *imperia extraordinaria*, popular sovereignty with its limitations), in pursuit of higher and, as it were, "nonnegotiable" principles, on which Cicero makes all the rest of his positive legislation depend. These are regarded as barriers against individualistic tendencies on the one hand and the radical demands of the *populares* on the other.
70. Lévy (1992) 59–74; Malaspina (2012–2013); Schofield (2021); Cappello in this volume.
71. See n5.
72. See Schofield (1999) 740–744.
73. *Ad Marcum filium* fr. 14 Jordan = 18 Cugusi, *Orator est, Marce fili, vir bonus, dicendi peritus*, quoted by Sen. *Controv.* 1.*praef.* 9, and Quint. 12.1.1 (*infra* n80).
74. The equivalent to *virtus* is *andréia* rather than *areté* when the sense is "valor" or "courage," especially in battle.
75. See Classen (1996).
76. See Prost (2017) 144–211 and Schofield (2021) 147–184.
77. See Lepore (1954) and Zarecki (2014).
78. It would take us too far afield to enter here into the debate on Roman amoralism that centers on the *Commentariolum petitionis*, and especially its phrase *Alterum est tamen boni viri, alterum boni petitoris* (45). See Alexander (2018), who argues against a proto-Machiavellian vision in Cicero. But the controversy remains very much alive.
79. *Leg.* 3.29: *Cum omni vitio carere lex iubeat, ne veniet quidem in eum ordinem quisquam vitii particeps. Id autem difficile factu est nisi educatione quadam et disciplina.* On the passage, see especially Pagnotta (2022) 64–66; in general, see Michel (1960); also *Part. or.* 79, *nihil est enim aliud eloquentia nisi copiose loquens sapientia*, with Grilli (2002).
80. Quint. 12.1.1: *Oratorem autem instituimus illum perfectum, qui esse nisi vir bonus non potest, ideoque non dicendi modo eximiam in eo facultatem sed omnis animi virtutes exigimus*; see *supra* n73.
81. See for instance Plin. *Pan.* 33–35, 65, 80.
82. See in general Gangloff (2019).
83. Malaspina (2009) 35–70.
84. See, e.g,. *Eth. Nic.* 6.7.1141a, 10.7.1177b.

85. See Schofield (1999) 762–765, Grilli (2002), Laurand (2005) 135–143, Reydams-Schils (2005) 99–113, and Dross (2021).
86. For the agreement between Cicero and Stoicism on this point see Reydams-Schils (2005) 93–99 and (2021) 204–209.
87. Cic. *Sen.* 21–26.
88. Cic. *Div.* 2.5–6: the fact that Cicero devoted himself to philosophy only when he could no longer be engaged in politics is one of the leitmotifs, explicit or implicit, of the prefaces to all the treatises of the period 45–44.
89. However, the problem was also debated in rhetorical exercises, *sitne sapientis ad rem publicam accedere* (Cic. *Top.* 82; see also *De or.* 3.112; Quint. 3.5.6).
90. See Schofield (1999) 756–760, Laurand (2005) 59–77, and Wildberger (2018) 89–116.
91. See *Ac. post.* 5–6; *Tusc.* 4.5–7, *Fam.* 15.16.1; 19.1–2 (testimonies and fragments in Garbarino (2003) 75–83). Cicero says nothing about Lucretius, who however had complained, at least a decade earlier, that Epicureanism had very little following in Rome: *haec ratio plerumque videtur / tristior esse quibus non est tractata, retroque / volgus abhorret ab hac* (1.943–945). But it is understandable that a disappointed supporter and a worried opponent may have quite different views on the matter; see Garbarino (1973) 2.464–465.
92. See Diog. Laert. 10.119 and Cic. *Att.* 14.20.5 (= fr. 8 Usener), with Grilli (2002) 59 ff.
93. See Farrington (1967).
94. See Konstan in this volume, Schofield (1999) 748–756, and Spinelli (2019), esp. 381: "the exercise of politics becomes something very refined and is perceived as a sort of compromise between the respecting of natural urges and a more or less conscious obedience to the laws conventionally established as social norms;" also 394 ff. on justice as a contract.
95. See Griffin (1989).
96. Cic. *Att.* 1.17.5; see Benferhat (2005) 98–169.
97. *RE* 80; *MRR* 2.587.
98. Frs. 88–94 Marx. See Benferhat (2005) 68–69: "le premier exemple de ces hommes qui s'affirmèrent épicuriens tout en faisant une carrière politique conforme à leur origine familiale." For other historical examples, see Benferhat (2005) 69–72 and 233–284, who for the age of Caesar rightly distinguishes between Epicureans belonging to the class of knights, supposedly active only as "conseillers dans l'ombre" (the best-known example being Maecenas in the following generation), and Epicurean *nobiles*, fully engaged in politics. Caesar's philosophical allegiance is more difficult to define: see Benferhat (2005) 284–311 and Garbarino (2010).
99. Lucr. 1.24–43.
100. PIR^1 419; *RE Pollius* no. 2.
101. *Silv.* 2.2.123–127, *quem non ambigui fasces, non mobile vulgus, / non leges, non castra terent; qui pectore magno / spemque metumque domas voto sublimior omni, / exemptus fatis indignantemque refellens / Fortunam*.
102. See Ronconi (1966). The main figure is Thrasea Paetus (PIR^1 938; *RE Clodius* no. 58), author of a life of Cato Uticensis (which Plutarch used as a source) and friend of the poet Persius. Also important are Arulenus Rusticus, Helvidius Priscus, and Demetrius, *Cynicae institutionis doctor* (Tac. *Ann.* 16.34), but still more three generations of women: Arria Maior, wife of Caecina Paetus, her daughter Arria Minor, wife of Thrasea, and her granddaughter, Fannia, wife of Helvidius, genuine exemplars of *virtus*; see Plin. *Ep.* 3.16 with Malaspina (1996).
103. Sen. *QNat.* 7.32.2; see Lana (1992). Testimonies and fragments in Garbarino (2003) 118–136.

104. See above ("Analysis and Therapy of the Roman Empire") in connection with the middle Stoicism of Panaetius.
105. "Il romano Sestio non ignora la realtà politica quale essa è: la riconosce: ma si proclama, rispetto ad essa, indifferente", (Lana (1992) 356); "Non più la libertà . . . *nello* Stato, ma la libertà *dallo* Stato" (359).
106. Sen. *Controv.* 2 *praef.* 1–4 (= Test. 4 Garbarino (2003)).
107. Sen. *De otio* 4.1–2; *Ep.* 8.2: see Dionigi (1983) 66–77, Laurand (2005) 126–135, Wildberger (2018) 190–192, and Mitsis (2021).
108. Vv. 388–403, tr. Bartsch (2017) 205–206: "in the discussion of the leading Stoics of the early Roman empire—Seneca, Epictetus, Marcus Aurelius—the claims of citizenship of the universe come to dwarf those of the existing societies in which we find ourselves: the cosmic perspective increasingly overshadows the vantage point of ordinary life" (Schofield (1999) 770); for Epictetus and Marcus Aurelius, see Erler and Sellars in this volume. We mention, only to reject it, the theory, supported by a few scholars, that Seneca's tragedies were opposition literature, with an implicit antityrannical message; discussion in Malaspina (2004) 292–296.

References

Alexander, M. C. (2018). *Roman Amoralism Reconsidered: The Political Culture of the Roman Republic and Historians in an Era of Disillusionment.* (Self-published). http://hdl.handle.net/10027/22252 (accessed February 14, 2022).
Arena, V. (2012). Libertas *and the Practice of Politics in the Late Roman Republic.* (Cambridge).
Arena, V., J. Prag, and A. Stiles, eds. (2022). *A Companion to the Political Culture of the Roman Republic.* (Chichester).
Atkins, J. (2018). *Roman Political Thought.* (Cambridge).
Atkins, J. W., and T. Bénatouïl, eds. (2022). *The Cambridge Companion to Cicero's Philosophy.* (Cambridge).
Aubert-Baillot, S., C. Guérin, and S. Morlet, eds. (2019). *La philosophie des non-philosophes dans l'empire romain du Ier au IIIe siècle* (Paris).
Balmaceda, C. (2017). Virtus Romana: *Politics and Morality in the Roman Historians.* (Chapel Hill, N.C.).
Balmaceda, C., ed. (2020). Libertas *and* Res Publica *in the Roman Republic. Ideas of Freedom and Roman Politics.* (Leiden).
Balot, R. K., ed. (2009). *A Companion to Greek and Roman Political Thought.* (Chichester).
Barlow, J. (2018). "Scipio Aemilianus and Greek Ethics." *CQ* 68: 112–127.
Bartsch, S., tr. (2017). *Lucius Annaeus Seneca: The Complete Tragedies.* (Chicago).
Beltramini, L. (2017). "Narrazione ed exemplum in Livio." *Eikasmos* 28: 171–194.
Benferhat, Y. (2005). Ciues Epicurei: *Les épicuriens et l'idée de monarchie à Rome et en Italie de Sylla à Octave.* (Brussels).
Büchner, K. (1984). *M. Tullius Cicero*: De re publica. *Kommentar.* (Heidelberg).
Chaplin, J. D. (2000). *Livy's Exemplary History.* (Oxford).
Chaplin, J. D., and C. S. Kraus, eds. (2009). *Oxford Readings in Classical Studies: Livy.* (Oxford).
Chilver, G. E. F., ed. (1979). *A Historical Commentary on Tacitus' Histories I and II.* (Oxford).
Classen, C. J. (1996). "Grundlagen und Absicht der Kritik des Lucilius," in C. Klodt (ed.), Satura lanx: *Festschrift für W.A. Krenkel* (Hildesheim), 11–28.

Dionigi, I., ed. (1983). *Lucio Anneo Seneca,* De otio *(dial. VIII). Testo e apparato critico con introduzione, versione e commento.* (Brescia).
Dross, J. (2021). *Le philosophe dans la cité: Sénèque et l'*otium *philosophique.* (Turnhout).
Eckstein, A. M. (2015). "Livy, Polybius, and the Greek East (Books 31–45)," in Mineo, 407–422.
Engels, D. (2009). "Déterminisme historique et perceptions de déchéance sous la république tardive et le principat." *Latomus* 68: 859–894.
Farrington, B. (1967). *The Faith of Epicurus.* (New York).
Fears, J. R. (1974). "The Stoic View of the Career and Character of Alexander the Great." *Philologus* 118: 126–127.
Garbarino, G. (1973). *Roma e la filosofia greca dalle origini alla fine del II secolo A.C. I: Introduzione e testi; II: Commento e indici.* (Turin).
Garbarino, G., ed. (2003). *Philosophorum Romanorum Fragmenta usque ad L. Annaei Senecae aetatem.* (Bologna).
Garbarino, G. (2010). "Cesare e la cultura filosofica del suo tempo," in G. Urso (ed.), *Cesare: Precursore o visionario?* (Pisa), 207–221.
Gangloff, A. (2019). *Pouvoir impérial et vertus philosophiques: L'évolution de la figure du bon prince sous le Haut-Empire.* (Leiden).
Goodyear, F. R. D. (1972). *The Annals of Tacitus: Books 1-6, Vol. 1.* (Cambridge).
Griffin, M. T. (1989). "Philosophy, Politics, and Politicians at Rome," in Griffin and Barnes, 1–37.
Griffin, M. T., and J. Barnes, eds. (1989). Philosophia Togata: *Essays on Philosophy and Roman Society.* (Oxford).
Grilli, A. (2002). *Vita contemplativa: Il problema della vita contemplativa nel mondo greco-romano.* (Brescia).
Hammer, D. (2014). *Roman Political Thought: From Cicero to Augustine.* (Cambridge).
Hellegouarc'h, J. (1972). *Le vocabulaire latin des relations et des partis politiques sous la République.* (Paris).
Kapust, D. J., and G. Remer, eds. (2021). *The Ciceronian Tradition in Political Theory.* (Madison, Wis.).
Kühnen, A. (2008). *Die* Imitatio Alexandri *in der römischen Politik (1. Jh. v. Chr.–3. Jh. n. Chr.).* (Münster).
Laks, A., and M. Schofield, eds. (1995). *Justice and Generosity: Studies in Hellenistic Social and Political Philosophy.* (Cambridge).
Lana, I. (1992). "La scuola dei Sestii," in P. Grimal (ed.), *La langue latine langue de la philosophie* (Rome), 109–124.
Laurand, V. (2005). *La politique stoïcienne.* (Paris).
Lepore, E. (1954). *Il* Princeps *ciceroniano e gli ideali politici della tarda repubblica.* (Naples).
Letta, C., and S. Segenni, eds. (2015). *Roma e le sue province: Dalla prima guerra punica a Diocleziano.* (Rome).
Lévy, C. (1992). Cicero Academicus: *Recherches sur les* Académiques *et sur la philosophie cicéronienne.* (Rome).
Linke, B., and M. Stemmler, eds. (2000). Mos maiorum: *Untersuchungen zu den Formen der Identitätsstiftung und Stabilisierung in der römischen Republik.* (Stuttgart).
Lintott, A. (1997). "The Theory of the Mixed Constitution at Rome," in J. Barnes and M. T. Griffin (eds.), Philosophia Togata II: *Plato and Aristotle at Rome* (Oxford), 70–85.
Luce, T. J. (2009). "The Dating of Livy's First Decade," in Chaplin and Kraus, 17–48.
Lyasse, E. (2008). "Auguste et le principat: Quelques remarques." *Latomus* 67: 977–984.

Malaspina, E. (1996). "Arria Maggiore: Una 'donna virile' nelle epistole di Plinio? (*Ep.* III, 16)," in De tuo tibi, *Omaggio degli allievi a I. Lana* (Bologna), 317–338.
Malaspina, E. (2004). "Pensiero politico ed esperienza storica nelle tragedie di Seneca," in M. Billerbeck and E. A. Schmidt (eds.), *Sénèque le Tragique* (Vandœuvres), 267–320.
Malaspina, E., ed. (2009). "*La clemenza*," in L. De Biasi, A. M. Ferrero, E. Malaspina, and D. Vottero, eds. *Lucio Anneo Seneca: Opere V* (Turin).
Malaspina, E. (2012–2013). "Cicerone e la verità." Res Publica Litterarum. Documentos de trabajo del grupo de investigación "Nomos": 1–13.
Malaspina, E. (2016). Review of Vesperini (2012). *Revue de Métaphysique et de Morale—Bulletin de philosophie ancienne* 92: 587–592.
Marcone, A. (2015). *Augusto: Il fondatore dell'impero che cambiò la storia di Roma e del mondo.* (Rome).
Mariotti, I. ed. (2007). *Gaio Sallustio Crispo: Coniuratio Catilinae.* (Bologna).
Michel, A. (1960). *Rhétorique et philosophie chez Cicéron: Essai sur les fondements philosophiques de l'art de persuader.* (Paris).
Mineo, B. ed. (2015). *A Companion to Livy.* (Hoboken, N.J.).
Mineo, B. (2015a). "Livy's Historical Philosophy," in Mineo, 139–152.
Mineo, B. (2015b). "Livy's Political and Moral Values and the Principate," in Mineo, 125–138.
Mitsis, Ph. (2021). "Théorie politique stoïcienne," in *Natura aut voluntas? Recherches sur la pensée politique et éthique hellénistique et romaine et son influence* (Turnhout), 167–200.
Moatti, C. (2018). Res Publica: *Histoire romaine de la chose publique.* (Paris).
Moles, J. L. (2009). "Livy's Preface," in Chaplin and Kraus, 49-87.
Moore, K. R. (2018). *Brill's Companion to the Reception of Alexander the Great.* (Leiden).
Musti, D. (2010). "Introduzione," in M. Mari, D. Musti, and J. Thornton (eds.), *Polibio: Storie, Volume I: Libri I–II* (Milan), 5–94.
Pagnotta, F. (2022). *Cicerone e la* societas hominum: *Contesto e funzioni di un concetto politico* (Milan).
Pianezzola, E. (^{2}2018). *Traduzione e ideologia: Livio interprete di Polibio.* (Bologna).
Pohlenz, M. (1965). *Ciceronis Tusculanarum disputationum libri V.* I. (Amsterdam).
Prost, F. (2017). *Marcus Cicéron. Lettres à son frère Quintus I, 1 et 2.* (Paris).
Rawson, E. (1989). "Roman Rulers and the Philosophic Adviser," in Griffin and Barnes, 233–257.
Reydams-Schils, G. (2005). *The Roman Stoics: Self, Responsibility, and Affection* (Oxford).
Reydams-Schils, G. (2021). "Were the Later Stoics Anti-Utopians?" in P. Destrée, J. Opsomer, and G. Roskam (eds.), *Utopias in Ancient Thought* (Berlin), 199–212.
Ronconi, A. (1966). "Exitus illustrium virorum." RAC VI, 48: 1258–1268.
Rowe, C., and M. Schofield, eds. (2000). *The Cambridge History of Greek and Roman Political Thought.* (Cambridge).
Rutledge, S. H. (2009). "Reading the Prince: Textual Politics in Tacitus and Pliny," in W. J. Dominik, J. Garthwaite, and P. A. Roche (eds.), *Writing Politics in Imperial Rome* (Leiden), 429–446.
Sauer, J. (2018). "Römische Exempla-Ethik und Konsenskultur? Philosophie und *mos maiorum* bei Cicero und Seneca," in G. M. Müller and F. Mariani Zini (eds.) *Philosophie in Rom—römische Philosophie? Kultur-, literatur- und philosophiegeschichtliche Perspektiven* (Berlin), 67–95.
Scheid, J. (2018). "La refondation de Rome par Octavien/Auguste : Fiction et invention à la naissance du régime impérial," in S. Segenni (ed.), *Augusto dopo il bimillenario: Un bilancio* (Milan), 120–127.

Schofield, M. (1999). "Social and Political Thought," in K. Algra, J. Barnes, J. Mansfeld, and M. Schofield (eds.), *The Cambridge History of Hellenistic Philosophy* (Cambridge), 739–770.
Schofield, M. (2021). *Cicero: Political Philosophy*. (Oxford).
Schuller, W., ed. (1988). *Politische Theorie und Praxis im Altertum*. (Darmstadt).
Spinelli, E. (2019). "Justice, Law, and Friendship: Ethical and Political Topics in Epicurus," in C. Riedweg (ed.), *Philosophie für die Polis: Akten des 5. Kongresses der Gesellschaft für antike Philosophie 2016* (Berlin), 379–408.
Stadter, P. A. (2009). "Character in Politics," in R. K. Balot (ed.), *A Companion to Greek and Roman Political Thought* (Oxford), 456–470.
Straumann, B. (2016). *Crisis and Constitutionalism: Roman Political Thought from the Fall of the Republic to the Age of Revolution*. (Oxford).
Suerbaum, W. (^{2}1970). *Vom antiken zum frühmittelalterlichen Staatsbegriff: Über Verwendung und Bedeutung von res publica, regnum, imperium und status von Cicero bis Jordanis*. (Münster).
Syme, R. (1939). *The Roman Revolution*. (Oxford).
Syme, R. (1958). *Tacitus. Vols. I–II*. (Oxford).
Tisé, B. (2002). *Imperialismo romano e imitatio Alexandri: Due studi di storia politica*. (Lecce).
Vasaly, A. (2015). *Livy's Political Philosophy: Power and Personality in Early Rome*. (Cambridge).
Vesperini, P. (2012). *La philosophia et ses pratiques d'Ennius à Cicéron*. (Paris).
Viroli, M. (2010). *La libertà dei servi*. (Rome).
Volk, K., and G. D. Williams, eds. (2022). *Philosophy in Ovid, Ovid as Philosopher*. (Oxford).
Walbank, F. W. (1957). *A Historical Commentary on Polybius: Books I–VI*. (Oxford).
Wildberger, J. (2018). *The Stoics and the State. Theory—Practice—Context*. (Baden-Baden).
Zarecki, J. (2014). *Cicero's Ideal Statesman in Theory and Practice*. (London).
Zecchini, G. (1997). *Il pensiero politico romano: Dall'età arcaica alla tarda antichità*. (Rome).

CHAPTER 20

RHETORIC

ERIK GUNDERSON

From a certain perspective philosophy and rhetoric can make for an uncomfortable pair: apples and oranges, as it were. There is a long tradition that would disaggregate the two. And this tradition arises as an element of philosophy's own constitution as an independent, identifiable discipline.[1] Nevertheless, the two are not disparate pursuits at Rome. A variety of institutional factors conspired to unite the two. Political, economic, cultural, and intellectual capital tended to be tightly aligned in this society. Rhetoric and philosophy are prestige disciplines whose production, dissemination, and reproduction are all conducive to the acquisition and maintenance of privilege.[2] Neither pursuit should be reduced to its sociological dimensions, but worldly considerations consistently inform the self-presentation as well as the concrete choices of our sources.[3]

In fact, few freeborn Roman citizens seem to have been exclusively philosophers, and any list of philosophically active Roman gentlemen is always also going to be a list of men who had interests in rhetoric and perhaps also poetry in addition to other learned topics. Indeed, one could turn this around: any list of men active in any sphere is likely to contain a large number of men who were also philosophically engaged.[4] For example, a catalog of Epicureans in the Republican age would include the consuls Piso and Pansa, praetors Albucius, Cassius, and Memmius, and knights Papirius Paetus and Pomponius Atticus. And yet Epicureanism is often thought of as a philosophy that counsels political withdrawal and prudent obscurity.

Rhetorical theorists had long appreciated that there were a number of elements to rhetoric and rhetorical training that converged with topics handled by philosophers.[5] The ethical component of oratory and moral philosophy are obviously congruent, and they are flagged as such in the programmatic opening of Quintilian's *Institutes of Oratory*.[6] Similarly, basic techniques of argumentation and analysis are common to both oratory and philosophy. And if the rhetoricians often encroach on the territory claimed by the philosophers, the converse charge can be made as well. Philosophical literature itself contains extensive meditations on rhetoric.[7] A pointed conflation of the two domains can be seen in Cicero. Cicero's *On the Orator* begins with a very long account of the philosophical pedigree of its own discussion of oratory. And, conversely,

Cicero's *On Duties* opens with the claim that Cicero's son needs to be in possession of a rhetorical articulation of the philosophical material that he is learning in Athens if these lessons are to achieve their full educative potential. Cicero likewise asserts that the best philosophers could have been orators and the best orators philosophers, had they so chosen. And if we set aside for a moment Cicero's strategic and self-serving presentation of the matter, it is nevertheless true that at Rome the same men in fact are often both rhetoric teachers and philosophers.[8]

People who have been trained within the Roman educational system may well be more strongly associated with philosophy than with oratory, but one is probably less surprised by a philosopher who participates within the rhetorical milieu than one who refuses to do so.[9] Roman education was, in effect, a specifically rhetorical education that ideally yielded skilled lawyers and statesmen. To be educated at all implied being trained in rhetoric. By the time any Roman gentleman might be imagined to "choose" to become a philosopher, he would already be more or less qualified to be a practicing orator.

An educated person at Rome was taught rhetoric from an early age. His youthful rhetorical training would have familiarized a gentleman with a specific manner of approaching a number of philosophical issues. In fact, both orators and philosophers work with related-but-different versions of terms like *thesis*, *schola*, diatribe, and disputation.[10] Any absolute distance between the rhetorical meaning of one of these items and the philosophical is likely a lexicographer's distinction.

Even a hypothetical "choice" of philosophy on the part of a Roman that entails a turn away from oratory is itself only going to be a sort of strategic posture. Nobody demanded of a philosopher that he renounce his oratory. A judicious use of philosophical sensibilities can enhance oratory, and speakers feel free to lace their performances with moments that are readily identifiable by the audience as "philosophical."[11] Even today speakers freely move between styles and sound sometimes more academic and sometimes less. Nevertheless, in specifically aesthetic receptions of rhetorical performances complaints about an overly-philosophical presentation can emerge.[12]

The comprehensive—at least according to their own understanding of comprehensiveness—education of Roman gentlemen made transfers between modes quite easy, and it left these men inclined to interpret and to valorize others' performances in light of multiple criteria that for us might be heterogeneous. Pliny praises a contemporary philosopher Euphrates in terms that are almost completely rhetorical: "His arguments were subtle, weighty, and polished."[13] One could just declare that Pliny is inept, and that he cannot really see the philosophy or that Euphrates is no real philosopher, but that sort of approach presupposes a disjunction between philosophy and rhetoric in the face of a variety of Roman efforts to put and to keep the two in communication.[14]

Readers of Latin epistles will have a hard time catching sight of "pure" philosophy. The highly political letters of Cicero themselves transition between rhetorical and philosophical moments freely. Cicero's highly rhetorical letters often read either as mini-speeches or drafts of "talking points" destined for later public presentation, and in them he fuses deliberative oratory and political philosophy: "What is to be done?" The various ethical questions of the civil war period receive a rhetorical work-up in a number of letters, letters that often read like collections of (philosophical) meditations that can be used to (rhetorically) justify various (political) courses of action. See, for example, the various inset philosophical meditations about the by no means abstract topics of civil war and the prospect of life under a tyrant.[15] The correspondence of Fronto also mixes philosophy and rhetoric. His letters to Marcus Aurelius are full of both theoretical and practical demonstrations of erudition. These include accounts of topics like the theory of rhetorical images (Fronto, *Ep.* 3.7–8). But there is also a very long discussion of the erotics of Platonic pedagogy prompted by Marcus's insistence that he loves his teacher.[16] And, as we will see presently, the *Moral Letters* of Seneca are thoroughly saturated with both philosophy and oratory.

In practice Latin philosophical writings seem to cluster around the very same issues where one can note a convergence with oratorical predilections rather than divergence from them. And this does not seem to be just a matter of the accidents of preservation and transmission. Accordingly, we tend to find works that concern themselves with questions of ethics, duty, and citizenship instead of treatises dedicated to logic, metaphysics, or natural history. These last exist, of course, but they do not seem to be the works that most engaged Roman readers and writers. Moreover, both in the more technical works and even in the most metaphysical passages, one readily notes a tendency for key moments of the argument to have a rhetorical articulation. Heated rhetorical and ethical moments of Seneca's *Natural Questions* arrive as the climax of the preceding technical arguments.[17] And so Roman philosophy is often eloquent and stirring. If Aristotle is often terse to the point of obscurity, a Latin author will instead be expansive. In addition to the raw logic, the reader is routinely provided with something more.

This rhetorical "supplement" can, of course, be decried as somehow unserious and unphilosophical, but Roman authors consistently evince a conviction that a symbiosis between rhetoric and philosophy is appropriate. There is a quiet and consistent resistance to the idea that merely knowing better necessarily results in doing better. An orator is instructed that his core aims are to teach, to move, and to delight. Few presentations of philosophical subjects in Latin merely teach and elect to do so dogmatically. They instead contain as well these other two dimensions and are thereby readily identifiable as rhetorical performances. Rhetoric is impressed into the service of aiding an imperfect audience to find the motivation to strive towards what is philosophically better.[18] Consolations are some of the most obvious instances where one finds self-conscious pairings of rhetoric and philosophy.[19]

Rhetoric often finds itself making the case that one should give an ear to the philosophers in the first place. This too has its sociological dimension: politically and culturally deracinated Greek intellectuals circulating around the halls (and richly appointed dinner tables) of the Roman elite were popularly taken as the model of what a philosopher was like.[20] And few Roman gentlemen will want to assimilate themselves to this sort of figure without insisting on a number of key modifications to the standard cultural template.

Even those Roman philosophical texts that address themselves to recondite questions of philosophy that do not have immediate fungibility within the public discourse of civic life nevertheless bear the stamp of rhetorical thinking. And, indeed, the rhetoricity is not just impressed on the text, but it is also clear that natural history and metaphysics themselves might inform rhetorical thought by providing *comparanda*, *topoi*, or even the grounds for arguments. Furthermore, one detects a desire to integrate the various branches of philosophy. A discussion of optics in a technical passage becomes a discussion of mirrors becomes a discussion of "know thyself": that is, natural philosophy transitions into ethics.[21] Most philosophical schools already insist on as much at a theoretical level, but one is more likely to find contemporary Greek intellectuals writing specialized treatments of individual topics while Roman gentlemen gravitate toward more synthetic and comprehensive works. And even if one might quibble with the literal truth of the preceding statement, it nevertheless reflects the manner in which a number of Roman texts themselves opt to portray the Roman relationship to technical questions.[22]

In light of this general overview, I would like to offer three samples of hybrid moments of philosophy and rhetoric from three different authors, genres, and eras: Cicero's *Tusculan Disputations* 1, Seneca's *Moral Letter* 59, and Apuleius's *Apology*. Each is mobilized specifically as a synthesis of modes, and none of them really coheres if the rhetoric is stripped away in order to get at just the philosophy. As a collection they reveal that articulating the proper relationship between rhetoric and philosophy was the name of the Roman game, not segregating philosophy from rhetoric in the name of keeping the former free of the taint of the latter.

In the *Tusculan Disputations* Cicero makes the case for philosophy. In pleading this case, Cicero builds an opposition that is not really an antithesis: the Greeks and the Romans both know a lot about "living well" (*recta vivendi via*, 1.1), a phrase that is glossed as the virtual equivalent of philosophy itself. The Greeks may well have an elaborate intellectual apparatus that articulates how one might go about living well, but the Romans have a variety of native customs and institutions that are conducive to this very same end. There may be a difference in modality, then, but not of aim or product. This distinction between cultures itself offers an allegory for the distinction between philosophy and rhetoric. And the synergy between the two likewise corresponds to Cicero's own sense of the possibility of fusing the two cultural traditions in the name of a higher synthesis.[23]

Cicero argues that Roman culture at an institutional level is excellent at promoting virtue. What has been wanting is an accomplished "discourse of virtue," which, in Cicero's case at least, is effectively a "rhetoric of virtue."[24] Coarse, ill-written books about philosophy hinder the dissemination of philosophy itself. Cicero's own rhetorically informed "eloquent philosophy" will render a service to philosophy. But this favor is really just the repayment of a debt: Cicero's very eloquence flows from philosophical fonts.[25] And it is more or less impossible to segregate the two disciplines if "perfect philosophy" necessarily entails the ability to speak with eloquent abundance about the weighty matters at hand.[26]

At a practical level as well the *Tusculan Disputations* sees itself as a thoroughly rhetorical work about philosophical topics. It purports to be the transcription of a collection of "declamations" (*declamitabam*, 1.7) held over several days. But these exercises are no sooner given a highly technical and specifically rhetorical designation that we are told that they were conversations done in a Socratic mode (*Socratica ratio*, 1.8).[27]

Given such an introductory framework, it comes as no surprise to see that the refutation of the thesis that "Death is an Evil" is thoroughly redolent of rhetorical tactics. Anyone who consulted a handbook on rhetorical theory would immediately recognize in the piece all of the canonical elements of a well-crafted speech. Cicero has covered invention and disposition. There are prologues and perorations. In fact the peroration ends by with the words, "And here you have my peroration."[28] The digressions come where an orator would put them. The style varies, but its rise and fall is perfectly suited to the flow of a good speech.[29]

From the perspective of pure logic, much could be trimmed. Cicero lays out every possible theory of the soul and then proves that no matter which one is correct, one should not fear death: "If we survive death, then that is good; if we do not survive death, then we cannot experience this as bad." (1.25) But a merely syllogistic approach to the topic is by no means his aim. One is treated as well to appeals to authority (1.27), appeals to common opinion (1.31), culturally charged examples of self-sacrifice that betray a disregard of death and belief in immortality (1.33), and meditations on the theory and practice of artists and artisans (1.33–34).

A logician might well cringe at the way Cicero is quick to associate effeminacy and wrong-headedness (*cogitationibus mollissimis effeminamur*, 1.95) and heaps scorn on contrary positions as trifling (*ineptiae*, 1.95). Nevertheless, from a sociological standpoint, Cicero has delivered just what he promised he would. Philosophical meditations have been fused with all of the other valorized elements of gentlemanly culture. Everything one learns in school, both explicitly and implicitly, can be found here. That is, not only is rhetorical culture abundantly on display but so too culture more generally. We are treated to Plato and Aristotle, Homer and Ennius, war heroes and consulars. The point is that all of this can and should work together: the best version of philosophy is perfectly consonant with superlative eloquence (as well as the best poetry in addition to aristocratic virility).

Cicero sometimes asserts the tight relationship between philosophy and rhetoric, and at other times he presupposes this connection and then sets the two affable yokemates to work. Seneca offers the same pairing, but also he meditates on the ability of rhetoric to work against rather than with philosophy. This is not to say that rhetoric is necessarily a problem for the philosopher, only that finding the right sort of rhetoric is every bit as important as determining the best philosophical school.

Seneca's philosophically minded individual lives amid a bustling world of discourses, many of which pull in contrary directions, and few of which are conducive to moral excellence. The common crowd makes a case for pursuing a variety of vulgar ends, and they can lead us astray.[30] But the simple act of sitting at the feet of a philosopher is not necessarily more salutary: it is possible to attend to philosophy in a merely rhetorical manner and to get swept up in a lovely swirl of words that never eventuates in virtue.[31] And yet giving ear to "pure philosophy" while making a radical break from everything else is not held out as the sure path to enlightenment. Instead Seneca valorizes a fusion of philosophy and rhetoric, but with the important caveat that one constantly test the soundness of the fusion by attending to the ends pursued and achieved. They may be a pair, but they are connected more like patron and client than as equal mates. Nevertheless, the net result is a pervasive collection of moments where the interactions between philosophy and artful language are explored.

Seneca frequently finds himself most comfortable with an intimate version of moral exhortation. The public quality of rhetorical speech—a quality that is kept in constant view by Cicero's philosophical rhetoric, even when articulated in moments of leisure and retreat—has been set aside: rhetorical performance is fully philosophical precisely when private and limited in scope. This valorized philosophical rhetoric allows one to persuade a close friend and/or oneself with a vigorous rhetoric of virtue that is fully consonant with a terse and hardy Stoicism. And it is no coincidence that the *Moral Letters* as a whole are formally convergent with this theoretically privileged version of rhetorical intimacy.[32] In them a friend is being exhorted, but he is also being shown how and why certain versions of exhortation are morally efficacious. For example, at *Moral Letters* 108.12 Lucilius is taught how to use poetry to pave the way for rhetorical attacks on vice that serve philosophical ends precisely where the technical application of a philosopher's syllogistic know-how would fall short.

As in Cicero, Seneca's discussions regularly adduce both poetry and rhetoric when discussing philosophy. Again the component parts of the general education of a Roman gentleman are presented as confluent, even if one aspect in particular is being singled out as most important for living well. Seneca's reflections are seldom about education in general, though: he adduces the triad of poetry, rhetoric, and philosophy as part of his investigations of language, investigations that are always consequential for the status of his own linguistic performances.

In *Moral Letter* 59 Seneca reflects on the relationship between wisdom and joy, but he can only do so after a collection of meditations on style that are rhetorically inflected. For example, what is the right word for joy? This is the letter's opening topic. The moment can easily be glossed as a rhetorical and not just a philosophical game by those so trained. A rhetorician would insist that successful *elocutio* (style more generally) requires *perspicuitas* (clarity) which itself requires *proprietas verborum* (apposite word choice).[33] As the letter opens Seneca teases his addressee by using the "wrong" word, *voluptas* and not *gaudium*, "(sensual) pleasure" and not "(abstract) delight": "I got a lot of pleasure from your letter" (59.1). Seneca immediately follows this with a discussion of the technical sense of terms for joy and their relationship to common idiom. In the course of this discussion Seneca ironically praises Vergil's "(rhetorical) eloquence" (*diserte quidem dicit*), but only to note at once that the poet's use of *gaudium* was by no means satisfactory, at least from the standpoint of the proper philosophical meaning of the word (*sed parum proprie*). Eloquent Vergil has, it seems, nevertheless failed when subjected to this rhetorical-*cum*-philosophical analysis. The poet's spurious eloquence has been set against a more substantive philosophical eloquence. The pleasures of Senecan discourse arrive as his style playfully clarifies the apposite words for the very matters under discussion.

These lessons are both distraction and prologue: when Seneca gets back on track (*sed ut ad propositum revertar*), this letter flags language itself as the source of Seneca's "delight" (*delectaverit*) when reading Lucilius's own letter: Seneca was pleased to see that Lucilius "was in control of his words, and his speech did not carry him off or take him anywhere he had not intended to go" (59.5). This does not mean, though, that Seneca is praising Lucilius for writing narrowly orthodox, precise, and technical Latin. Lucilius has avoided being seduced by a pleasing word into saying something he did not intend to say. His language is terse and well-chosen. And, Seneca adds, Lucilius says not just what he wants to say, but he even hints at more than he literally says. This "something more" seems to be the source of Seneca's "delight" (and "pleasure" and "joy"). The fullness of language is being praised and not its narrow precision. In fact Seneca turns the "something more" of language itself into a means of diagnosing a "something more" about the author of that language: Lucilius's mastery of words is a clear sign (*indicium*) of something still greater: he is self-controlled, and his soul has nothing surfeit or swollen to it (59.6).

Authorial mastery of language and the self-mastery of the virtuous soul converge. Moreover Seneca carves out a space for the good reader who can see in language a philosophically crucial beyond, namely the virtue of the soul who promulgates that language. And so even if Seneca does present a version of the distinction between philosophy and rhetoric as well as the superiority of the former over the latter, he nevertheless reinscribes a symbiosis of the two that highlights their congruence at a key juncture.

Seneca is both praising and doing philosophy-and-rhetoric. Throughout Seneca's writing an orator's canonical tripartite duty to teach, move, and delight has turned into a self-aware dialectical process: teaching doctrine, moving the auditor to become attached to wisdom, and revealing the pleasure in knowledge. The letter's initial conceit that a rhetorical analysis offers a means of pursuing ethical analysis is succeeded by a technical analysis of various other tropes and figures. Seneca comments on Lucilius's metaphors, his images, and his similes. And then Seneca reflects on an image used by the philosopher Sextius about the ways in which the wise man should take inspiration from a well-ordered military column. The flow of the letter never lets us see a portrait of philosophy that is not always also a philosophy working in tandem with a sense of language that has been informed by rhetorical training.

Seneca may well see himself as producing a higher synthesis than anything available in the rhetorical schools where one acquires an education that is all too frequently deployed in the service of mere ostentation (59.15), but he is by no means turning away from the basic idea that rhetoric really matters. In fact here and elsewhere he vigorously reinvests in rhetorical criticism: as are the words, so is the man. Stylistic criticism is moral criticism.[34] Rhetoric is no mere distraction. A self-rhetoric is a vital component of moral progress: Seneca adumbrates the talking points for a quasi-senatorial internal deliberative rhetoric (*ipse te consule*) that Lucilius can deploy to fix his attention on true joys and to pull him away from the specious counsels and claims that circulate in the world.

The letter's last portion contains an encomium of *gaudium* that can be used to lend force to this ethical self-rhetoric. And even as a rhetorically inclined reader with a narrow focus might see in the letter's peroration a collection of mere rhetorical effects, the point of all of this rhetoric is decidedly philosophical: the speaker is not seducing us over to some specious cause but instead enabling us to take possession of ourselves by adopting a very specific relationship to language itself.

I would like to round out my discussion by ending with a claim I made at the beginning: the well-educated gentlemen can easily be made to feel at home amidst philosophical discourses. Of course, one could point to the dog-like cynics and other "scandalous" philosophers whose ideas and, more to the point, practices, diverge from the contents of the relatively capacious zone of acceptable elite behavior.[35] Nevertheless much of philosophy can be argued to be consonant with the general tenor of a gentleman's sociopolitical milieu.[36] But rather than myself making this case, I can just turn to Apuleius's *Apology* for a prolix and explicit advocacy of this very position. In the published version of this speech—a speech that may never have been delivered—Apuleius is defending himself on a charge of sorcery. The relatives of his wealthy wife have claimed that a charming young stranger has cast a spell on the woman in order to make her and her estate his own. Apuleius defends himself before the Roman magistrate judging the case with a host of appeals to their shared culture.[37] It is obvious that he cannot be a magician, and any educated man could perceive as much. Doctrine, erudition, learning, wisdom: such terms abound in the speech, and their use always aligns speaker and judge against the prosecution.[38] The boorish, grasping rustics on the other side of the case cannot appreciate what is patent to Maximus: everything that looks like magic to an outsider is really just an element of a variety of philosophical pursuits that are fully normative for a man of Apuleius's station.

As with most orations, the fact that Apuleius conjures the obvious rightness of his own position does not necessarily mean that all of this is necessarily obvious to everyone (or even right in the eyes of anyone). Nevertheless, the educated reader today has a hard time not sympathizing with his claims: indulging a curiosity about optics should not be confused with dabbling in the black arts (13–16). And Apuleius has constructed a judging audience who will inevitably line up with his defense of erudition. He claims that there is cause for confidence and celebration seeing that with you as a judge (*te iudice*) he will get a chance of acquitting philosophy in the presence of uninformed outsiders as well as offering a justification of his conduct.[39] Apuleius's phrasing contains a rhetorically bold (and not necessarily logical) claim: what is true and proven about the man doubles as a defense of the pursuit.[40] And Apuleius is happy to play around with this conceit: the opening of the speech luxuriates in the defense of philosophy rather than the defendant proper, namely the speaker himself.

We are treated to a lengthy discussion of the manner in which philosophy has long been associated with a whole host of socially valorized qualities and pursuits. Apuleius explores the Greek tradition of the good and the beautiful, the *kaloskagathoi* gentlemen who were leading thinkers and leading citizens. Anything and everything that Apuleius does that has been read negatively by the *imperiti* is glossed as an element of a centuries long international consensus about the valorized pursuits of the hegemonic classes. We are most definitely to compare the poetic productions of our philosopher-orator with those of Solon (9). And any sexiness one might find here is not an occasion for scandal. Instead it only recalls the noble pederastic verses of the a number of Greek sages (9). And surely one would never reproach the sort of thing Vergil himself also wrote (10). Why it seems that his accusers would even lay charges against the emperor Hadrian (11). Rhetoric is here insisting on the consonance of philosophy, poetry, and politics.

As with Cicero's *Tusculans*, it is possible to imagine a much more terse style of argument. But rather than a taut demonstration of the logical fallacy of the position occupied by the other side, Apuleius instead offers a rhetorically copious and expansive portrait of the life of the educated elite, a life that the ignorant masses are incapable of parsing, let alone understanding. The published version of the speech is pleased to linger over every flower in the garland of *paideia* that Apuleius has ostentatiously set upon his own brow. Greek and Latin poets, philosophers, and men of letters are cited constantly and often at length. We know Apuleius is not a predatory Lothario using malevolent means to achieve base ends precisely because he can present himself as occupying so many valorized discourses simultaneously.

Apuleius's claim that he is not a magician is (rhetorically) coherent precisely because he relies upon a preexisting postulate of sociocultural coherence, and this putative coherence of the sociocultural field presupposes the relatively free movement between disciplines on the part of gentlemen who are so inclined to move. Certainly there are specialists out there, and indeed one can even find philosophers who speak ill of verse or who malign oratory. Moreover Apuleius himself can author specialist works of philosophy when he wants to.[41] Nevertheless a narrow sliver of cultural and intellectual space is not being mapped out. Instead Apuleius—just as had Cicero and Seneca—opts to move ostentatiously along a much-traveled path where a variety of persons with harmonious interests can all stride together towards a goal that is relatively well agreed upon, namely some version of aristocratic normativity where the better sort of people do the better sort of thing for the better sort of reasons. There is a socio-rhetorico-philosophical sleight of hand here, of course: what is designated as "better" slides between registers quite freely.

Apuleius's *Apology* likely strikes the reader as far less philosophically consequential than Plato's *Apology*. Nevertheless one can observe a sophisticated Platonic and pedagogical depth beneath the glossy rhetorical surface.[42] On the one hand the text is a virtual rhetorical handbook, but, on the other, rhetorical digressions on topics like mirrors are in fact philosophically propaedeutic. What initially strikes us as rhetorical ornament moves us toward enlightenment. Even so, we never sunder ourselves from the educational apparatus, its habits, and its techniques. In fact the speech's structure can recall a school teacher running through a set of formal lessons (and not a philosopher unfolding an argument).[43] In short, rudimentary school lessons and the most sublime teachings of the philosophers can (and perhaps should) all be connected both by and within rhetorical practice.

However for our present purposes even the most superficial version of Apuleius's portrait of a certain kind of man should be taken seriously precisely because of the "common sense" on which it rests: rhetoric and philosophy fit perfectly well together. When we give ear to the manner in which Roman philosophers speak about what they are doing, we seldom hear the voice of rigorous logician, at least when these authors publicly address large numbers of their fellow gentlemen. The philosopher may well embrace the designation philosopher and he might even orient his activity primarily in terms of that designation, but he is seldom seen repudiating outright the rich resources available to him from other domains. He instead capitalizes on the proximity between fields and the free flow between them.

We can return to and modify the idea that opened this essay. Some might consider "philosophy and rhetoric" to be "apples and oranges." An even more hostile appraisal would designate the pair as "baby and bathwater." Ideally, only one of these should be retained. But it seems clear that a variety of Romans for centuries mixed both philosophy and rhetoric to heady and productive effect. The resulting concoction was something like "gin and tonic." And if one were today were to order a gin and tonic with an idiosyncratic demand to the bartender either to hold the gin or the tonic, this unexpected request would evoke a distinctly puzzled response: "OK, but what sort of person would want such a thing?"

Notes

1. See Wardy (2009).
2. Note that youthful rhetorical exercises could include mock debates on the relative social worth of the orator and the philosopher. See (ps?)-Quintilian, *Minor Declamations* 268.
3. See Hine (2015) on a general hesitation on the part of authors to self-identify as philosophers despite praising the pursuit of wisdom and explicitly engaging in all sorts of philosophical activity. And, as Zetzel (2015) notes, a lot of philosophical activity is happening in the Late Republic without people labeling themselves philosophers or their work as philosophical.
4. See the appendix of Gilbert (2015) and also Castner (1988).
5. For a detailed account of the way in which technical terms from rhetoric and philosophy intersect in Cicero, see the second part of Michel (1960).
6. See Quint. *Inst.* 1.pr.9–14.
7. Plato's *Phaedrus* and Aristotle's *Rhetoric* are the most famous. But the index to Diels and Kranz (1996) reveals that rhetoric and philosophy was a topic for the presocratic philosophers as well. Cleanthes and Chrysippus also wrote on oratory (Cic. *Fin.* 4.7). And Quintilian's discussion of the nature of oratory makes it clear that both Stoics and Peripatetics had long been working through the relationship between philosophy and oratory. See Quint. *Inst.* 3.1.15. The Philodemus papyri likewise contain scientific, ethical, and rhetorical writings.
8. See the biographical notices in Suetonius's *On the Grammarians and Rhetoricians* for Aurelius Opilius (6) and Marcus Pompilius Androncus (8).
9. See Seneca the Elder's extensive accounts of the declamations of Fabianus the Philosopher (*Fabianus philosophus*, *Controv.* 2.pr. 1). The Stoic philosopher Attalus is praised as an exceptionally eloquent orator with an unadorned style (2.12.6).

10. See Bonner (1949) 2–11 on the history of institutional intersections between the *theseis* of philosophers and rhetoricians. See Douglas (1995) 201–205 on *schola* and disputation.
11. See, for example, Sen. *Controv.* 1.7.17 and 7.6.18.
12. See, for example, Sen. *Controv.* 1.3.8.
13. Plin. *Ep.* 1.10: *Disputat subtiliter grauiter ornate, frequenter etiam Platonicam illam sublimitatem et latitudinem effingit. Sermo est copiosus et uarius, dulcis in primis, et qui repugnantes quoque ducat impellat.* See Gibson and Morello (2012) 172–179 on this letter.
14. Epictetus's Euphrates is much more of a "philosopher proper," but even Epictetus notes Euphrates's rhetorical power. See Reydams-Schils (2011) 314. She adduces an excited parenthetical recorded both at Arr. *Epict. diss.* 3.15.8 and *Encheiridion* 29.4 in this regard: "Who was his equal as a speaker?" (καίτοι τίς οὕτως δύναται εἰπεῖν ὡς ἐκεῖνος;)
15. See Cic. *Fam.* 6.22 and *Fam.* 9.16.
16. See Fronto, *Additamentum epistularum* 7-8 (ven den Hout). On the love, see Richlin (2006). On the intersection between the quasi-Platonic erotics and the technical discussion of rhetoric, see Taoka (2013).
17. Conversely, note the striking anaphora of "What is of chief importance in human affairs?" The question is repeated seven times at the climax of the preface to the third book of the *Natural Questions*. I agree with Harry Hine: this is in fact the preface to what was once the first book before the manuscripts became confused. Accordingly this rhetorical flourish marks "the end of the beginning" as Seneca launches into this substantial piece of philosophizing. See Hine (1996) xxii–xxv.
18. See Schrenk (1994): Cicero sees himself adding in the necessary rhetorical components whose want vitiates "pure" philosophical treatments since the conviction they produce is merely abstract, and as such it is fleeting. Philosophy fails to achieve its own ends if it works alone.
19. For example, Seneca's *Consolation to Helvia* is self-aware about its literary novelty and contains a variety of flashy sound bites—*sententiae*, to give them their Latin technical name—that cap paragraphs. But the consolation is also full of ethical reflections and metaphysical passages that insist on the value of a turn to liberal study in general and to philosophy in particular. See also Ker (2009) 90: "The tailoring of [their] advice to suit the addressee makes the consolation an exercise in the rhetoric of occasion."
20. But even this portrait can be misleading. Consider the notoriously and multiply hard-to-classify Favorinus of Arles: born in the Gallic north, he gives speeches in Greek, engages in erudite discussions about the Latin language at Rome, is frequently called a "sophist" today given his writings, but is resolutely labeled "Favorinus the philosopher" by Aulus Gellius. See *NA* 14.1 and 20.1. For an account of the complex world of sophists like Favorinus, see Gleason (1995).
21. See Sen. *QNat.* 1.16–17 and Apul. *Apol.* 13–16. The former passage has a rich bibliography, much of it following in the wake of Leitão (1998).
22. See Cic. *De or.* 1.102–112 for an elaborate staging by gentlemen of the problem gentlemanly discourse versus professorial discourse.
23. See Habinek (1994) on the imperialism implicit in Cicero's appropriation of Greek philosophy. The rich in political and social capital are shown how to get still richer by adding philosophy as well to their cultural stores. See the eighth chapter of Bourdieu (1990) for a more general portrait of the manner in which concrete modes of domination are turned into symbolic modes of mastery.

24. Cic. *Tusc.* 5: *philosophia iacuit usque ad hanc aetatem nec ullum habuit lumen litterarum Latinarum.*
25. Cic. *Tusc.* 1.6: *quare si aliquid oratoriae laudis nostra attulimus industria, multo studiosius philosophiae fontis aperiemus, e quibus etiam illa manabant.*
26. Cic. *Tusc.* 1.7: *hanc enim perfectam philosophiam semper iudicavi, quae de maximis quaestionibus copiose posset ornateque dicere.*
27. See Douglas (1995) for more on the relationship between the philosophical content and the rhetorical form.
28. And the reaction to it is, "Yes, and it did (philosophical/ethical) work by bolstering my resolve" (*Et quidem fecit etiam iste me epilogus firmiorem.* 1.119).
29. See Fohlen (2011) vi–x for a rhetorical analysis of the *Tusculans*.
30. See Williams (2012) 88.
31. See the chapter "Misreading Seneca" in Gunderson (2014). The relationship between rhetoric and philosophy in *Moral Letter* 108 is discussed at length there.
32. See Inwood (2005) 31–38 and Bartsch (2009).
33. The vocabulary is all lifted from Quint. *Inst.* 8.1–2.
34. The notorious site of this thesis is the letter assailing Maecenas's moral-and-literary depravity. See Graver (1998).
35. The Roman elite was disinclined to embrace cynicism in any but a highly qualified manner. A cynic's hostility to social conventions, disregard for reputation, and disinclination to participate in political life meant that the average educated gentleman would, unsurprisingly, be little inclined to drop everything and go live in a barrel. See Griffin, (1996) 196–197. Romans were nevertheless interested in the barbed tongues of the cynics, and so were fascinated by it less as a philosophy than as a rhetoric (Griffin (1996) 200).
36. See the seventh chapter of Habinek (1998) on the manner in which Seneca uses upper-class modes and concepts to (rhetorically) transition his readers from a found, empirical aristocracy to an aristocracy of virtue.
37. See Bradley (1997) 212–213.
38. See Bradley (1997) 216. The ignorance of the *imperiti* is a similarly recurrent theme.
39. Apul. *Apol.* 1: *quo ego uno praecipue confisus gratulor medius fidius, quod mihi copia et facultas te iudice optigit purgandae apud imperitos philosophiae et probandi mei.*
40. And so *Apology* 3 makes explicit this notion latent in *Apology* 1: *sustineo enim non modo meam, uerum etiam philosophiae defensionem.* See Fletcher (2008) on the philosophically consequential pairing of biography-and-philosophy in the *Apology*.
41. For Apuleius as a philosopher, see Fletcher (2014).
42. See Fletcher (2008).
43. See Schneider (2009) 398–401 on digressions and philosophy. See the piece more generally for the speech's relationship to *progymnasmata*.

References

Bartsch, S. (2009). "Senecan Metaphor and Stoic Self-Instruction," in S. Bartsch and D. Wray (eds.), *Seneca and the Self* (Cambridge), 188–217.
Bonner, S. F. (1949). *Roman Declamation in the Late Republic and Early Empire*. (Liverpool).

Bourdieu, P. (1990). *The Logic of Practice.* (Stanford).
Bradley, K. (1997). "Law, magic, and culture in the '*Apologia*' of Apuleius." *Phoenix* 51: 203–223.
Castner, C. J. (1988). *Prosopography of Roman Epicureans from the Second Century B.C. to the Second Century A.D.* Studien zur klassischen Philologie, Bd. 34. (Frankfurt am Main).
Diels, H., and W. Kranz (⁶1996). *Die Fragmente der Vorsokratiker, griechisch und deutsch.* (Berlin).
Douglas, A. E. (1995). "Form and content in the *Tusculan Disputations*," in J. G. F. Powell (ed.), *Cicero the Philosopher: Twelve Papers* (Oxford), 197–218.
Fletcher, R. (2008). "Plato Re-Read Too Late: Citation and Platonism in Apuleius' *Apologia*." *Ramus* 37: 43–74.
Fletcher, R. (2014). *Apuleius' Platonism: The Impersonation of Philosophy.* (Cambridge).
Fohlen, G. (⁷2011). *Cicéron. Tusculanes: Tome I. Livres I et II.* (Paris).
Gibson, R. K., and R. Morello (2012). *Reading the Letters of Pliny the Younger: An Introduction* (Cambridge).
Gilbert, N. (2015). *The influence of Roman Epicureans on Cicero's philosophical works.* Dissertation: University of Toronto.
Gleason, M. W. (1995). *Making Men: Sophists and Self-Presentation in Ancient Rome.* (Princeton).
Graver, M. (1998). "The Manhandling of Maecenas: Senecan Abstractions of Masculinity." *AJPhil.* 119: 607–632.
Griffin, M. (1996). "Cynicism and the Romans: Attraction and Repulsion," in R. B. Branham and M.-O. Goulet-Cazé (eds.), *The Cynics: The Cynic Movement in Antiquity and Its Legacy* (Berkeley), 190–204.
Gunderson, E. (2014). *The Sublime Seneca: Ethics, Literature, Metaphysics.* (Cambridge).
Habinek, T. (1994). "Ideology for an Empire in the Prefaces to Cicero's Dialogues." *Ramus* 23 55–67.
Habinek, T. (1998). *The Politics of Latin Literature: Writing, Identity, and Empire in Ancient Rome.* (Princeton).
Habinek, T. (1996). *L. Annaei Senecae Naturalium quaestionum libros.* (Stuttgart).
Hine, H. (2015). "Philosophy and *philosophi*: from Cicero to Apuleius," in Williams and Volk, 13–29.
Inwood, B. (2005). *Reading Seneca: Stoic Philosophy at Rome.* (Oxford).
Ker, J. (2009). *The Deaths of Seneca.* (Oxford).
Leitão, D. (1998). "Senecan Catoptrics and the Passion of Hostius Quadra (Sen. Nat. 1)." *MD* 41: 127–160.
Michel, A. (1960). *Rhétorique et philosophie chez Cicéron: Essai sur les fondements philosophiques de l'art de persuader.* (Paris).
Reydams-Schils, G. (2011). "Authority and Agency in Stoicism." *GRBS* 51: 296–322.
Richlin, A. (2006). *Marcus Aurelius in Love.* (Chicago).
Schneider, C. (2009). "Discours écoutés, discours prononcés dans l'Afrique romaine: L'*Apologie* d'Apulée ou le trompe-l'œil absolu," in G. Abbamonte, L. Miletti, and L. Spina (eds.), *Discorsi alla prova: Atti del Quinto Colloquio italo-francese* (Naples), 391–413.
Schrenk, L. (1994). "Cicero on Rhetoric and Philosophy: *Tusculan Disputations* I." *Ancient Philosophy* 14: 355–360.
Taoka, Y. (2013). "The Correspondence of Fronto and Marcus Aurelius: Love, Letters, Metaphor." *Cl. Ant.* 32: 406–438.
van den Hout, M. P. J. (1988). *M. Cornelii Frontonis* Epistulae. (Leipzig).

Wardy, R. (2009). "The philosophy of rhetoric and the rhetoric of philosophy," in E. Gunderson (ed.), *The Cambridge Companion to Ancient Rhetoric* (Cambridge), 43–58.
Williams, G. D., and K. Volk, eds. (2015). *Roman Reflections: Studies in Latin Philosophy*. (Oxford).
Williams, G. D. (2012). *The Cosmic Viewpoint: A Study of Seneca's* Natural Questions. (Oxford).
Zetzel, J. (2015). "Philosophy Is in the Streets," in Williams, G. D., and K. Volk, eds. (2015). *Roman Reflections: Studies in Latin Philosophy*. (Oxford), 50–62.

CHAPTER 21

SELF AND WORLD *IN EXTREMIS* IN ROMAN STOICISM

JAMES I. PORTER

> You have to begin by analyzing the third person. One speaks, one sees, one dies. There are still subjects, of course—but they're specks dancing in the dust of the visible and permutations in an anonymous babble. The subject's always something derivative. It comes into being and vanishes in the fabric of what one says, what one sees.
>
> —Gilles Deleuze[1]

THE self in Roman philosophy is a booming area of research in Classics today. Historical curiosity and academic fashion are undeniable factors, but they hardly tell the whole story. Similar kinds of inquiry into the self are likewise flourishing in philosophy, in the history of thought, and in popular culture. But the Roman perspective, and Roman Stoicism in particular, has enjoyed an unusual resurgence. One possible explanation is that the writings of the principal exponents of Stoicism under Rome—Seneca the Younger, Epictetus, and Marcus Aurelius (and, to a lesser degree, Musonius Rufus)—happen to be seductive, easily accessible, and more or less completely preserved, unlike the fragmentary and at times forbiddingly academic remains of Zeno, Chrysippus, and Cleanthes, the school's founders. Focused on practical rather than technical issues and attentive to their own praxis as literary works meant to be heard or overheard by readers, the Roman texts have a moving simplicity and directness to them that makes them feel like living documents even today. You don't need a lot of explanatory footnotes and commentary to hear their authors' admonishing and encouraging voices in your ear. But above all, they preach good news.

Welcome to Stoicism

There is no question that the popularity of the Roman Stoics owes much to the ways in which they are read and not only what they have to offer. The general tendency today is to look to the Stoics for comforting lessons on how to withstand the shocks of existence and for advice on how to live, and not only among those readers who follow the approach to self-care inaugurated by Pierre Hadot and Michel Foucault.[2] Up to a point, the makeup of Stoicism's basic teachings encourages this kind of reading. This makeup includes:

The reassuringly providential, rational, and purposive nature of the Stoic universe. The world, in its complete physical and rational coherence, fundamentally makes sense. It is not chaotic or threatening once we perceive its true nature—that is, the cosmic sympathy and immanent divinity of all that exists, call it God, Zeus, Nature, Fate, Necessity, the All, or the Whole.

The suggestion that the Stoic self, subject, individual, person, or agent is defined by its divine rational core, the soul or *hēgemonikon* ("ruling center"), which is genetically identical to the divine and ruling elements of the universe—intelligent, active (*technikon*, i.e., "craftsmanlike" or "designing"), and fiery pneuma whence the *hēgemonikon* was born and to which it returns upon death. Subjects are thus as intelligible as the world they inhabit.

The invulnerability of this inner core to external influences and misfortunes: it is a virtual fortress (an *akropolis* or *munimentum*).

The belief in moral perfectionism: that is, the view that the Stoic subject can perfect itself through the practice of mental exercises that serve to train the often imperfectly rational faculties (for instance, in their emotional and desiderative aspects) and bring them into alignment with the directives of the universe, which inclines its subjects to a life lived in accordance with nature and reason—in contemporary parlance, through the practice of "self-fashioning."

The relative autonomy enjoyed by the rational individual, which can exercise considerable freedom to act on the impressions it receives from within (through the mind) or from without (through the senses). Such action lies within its powers and is indefeasibly "up to us" as responsible agents. This is the guarantor of inner stability and eudaimonic happiness, however much hardship may come one's way.

So described, the Stoic universe is a hospitable and even cheering place in which to be. I want to propose a revised version of the orthodox, welcoming view of Stoicism.

The Stoic Welcome Revised

In contrast to the reassuring view of Stoicism just outlined, there are aspects of the philosophy that point in an entirely different direction. These alternative features exist not to deter adherents from pursuing the school's tenets but to incite and challenge them to produce better, hardier, and worthier versions of themselves. These include the following considerations:

1. Although the Stoic universe is providential, rational, and purposive in nature, it is not reassuringly so on balance. The world is anything but a calm, tranquil, and orderly place. On the contrary, it is characterized by constant and writhing change, movement, and turmoil, not stability, and by more than occasional irregularity (Sen. *QNat.*, passim; *SVF* 1.188 = LS 44D). It passes through cycles of growth and collapse, starting out from a state of absolute purity—primordial fire (*SVF* 1.497) that is so refined as to approach a condition of αὐγή, sheer gleam or brilliant light (*SVF* 2.611; cf. Sen. *Ep.* 65.19: *aliquid igne lucidius*; the term and concept may be Heraclitean [DK 22B118])—that is neither habitable nor inhabited apart from god. It gradually follows a path of imperfection and impurity, though even this is a simplification. For as Seneca says, "The stages of growth (*incrementa*), if you calculate correctly, are actually losses (*damna*)" (*Dial.* 6.21.7). In other words, the way up is simultaneously the way down. Growth not only entails but actually *is* a state of decay and imperfection, if not corruption, that falls away from this original pure state as it involves increasing amounts of complication and differentiation and consumes increasing amounts of material in the process: "The soul of the cosmos [which is god] ... continues to grow until it uses up [or "consumes," καταναλώσῃ] its matter" (*SVF* 2.604; 30 2.1064); "many disadvantageous things accrued as inseparable from her [sc., mother nature's] actual products" (*SVF* 2.1169–1170 = LS 54Q). "The brighter a fire blazes, the sooner it goes out" (Sen. *Dial.* 6.23.4): this is a law of nature that affects all bodies, including those bodies known as souls, and requires that the world should end in a cosmic meltdown that burns off the corrupted parts (the accumulated matter and its resulting complications) and restores the universe to a condition of pristine and primordial divine fire ("no evil at all remains," *SVF* 2.60631)—a state in which there is no activity (Sen. *Ep.* 9.16 = *SVF* 2.1065), because its actuality just is its pure potentiality. That is the fate, necessity, and nature of the universe to which even god must submit. None of this should be taken to imply that the original state of the world is in any way better than its later evolutions.[3] Quite the contrary: the world is always in its best possible state.[4]

Second, there are extraordinary gaps in our picture of the world, a fact that enhances its uncertainty for us. Far from being a knowable and certain place, the universe is completely unfathomable, unless it be by god—but assuredly not for mortals, and not even in their most godlike portion, their minds: "So far the truth has eluded us humans. According to the proverb, 'Certainty is hidden deep'" (Sen. *QNat.* 4a *ad fin.*). All that is certain is that "the whole of the future is uncertain, and fairly certain to get worse" (*Dial.* 6.23.1). This, too, is dictated by the cyclical movement of nature, which is unalterable. Seneca's worldview can at times appear dire and downright pessimistic: "We can go on accusing the fates, but we cannot alter them: they remain harsh and inexorable." And the same is true of humankind: "everywhere you find abundant, constant grounds for tears" (*Dial.* 11.4.1-2). Marcus can be just as dark and despairing: "In human life, the time of our existence is a point, our substance a flux, our senses dull, the fabric of our entire body subject to corruption, our soul ever restless, our destiny beyond divining, and our fame precarious.... Our life is a war, a brief stay in a foreign land, and our fame thereafter, oblivion" (M. Aur. *Med.* 2.17). The world may be rational in theory, but its workings are anything but rational in appearance (*insanit* and *insanis* are not infrequently used by Seneca to describe nature's phenomena), while the truth of that theory has to be taken on faith, but not through a rational grasp of things—for the truth exceeds our grasp, and recognizing this itself requires a degree of irrationality. The gaps in our knowledge are both a boon and a curse. They excite us to press beyond our limits. But as they do, they continually expose us to those same limits. We were born to search, not find (*Dial.* 8.5.1-8); to wonder, not necessarily to understand (*QNat.* 7.1.4); and to surge on the edge of insobriety (*usque ad ebrietatem ueniendum*) and madness (*dementia*) (*Dial.* 9.17.8-10). What is more, every experience of a height entails a crashing fall: "Now your minds are lifted up on high, now dashed down to the depths" (*nunc in sublime adleuatos nunc in infima adlisos*, *Dial.* 7.28.1). By the same token, sublime exaltation is a sign and a product of our belittled status: "We believe [that adverse circumstances but also natural phenomena] are great because we are small; many things derive their greatness not from their intrinsic nature but from our lowly status" (*QNat.* 3.praef.10).

2. The turbulent inconstancy and fluidity of human affairs (*Dial.* 6.22.1) mirror those of nature (*QNat.*, passim), and so too does our death mirror the conflagration (*ekpurōsis*) that restarts the cycle of the universe and its incessant commotion as it runs through its several phases of rebirth (as pure fire), corruption, and purification in rebirth again (*Dial.* 6.26.6–7). "Nothing is ever stable whose nature consists in motion" (*Dial.* 7.7.4). But nature precisely does consist in motion (Philo, *De aeternitate mundi* 52, 54 = LS 52A), in part simply by being unstably composed of contrasting elements (*ex diuersis compositus est*) and in part because two of these, air and fire, are inherently volatile (*in fuga*) (*QNat.* 7.27.3; 7.23.3; cf. 6.18.5; *Dial.* 1.1.2). Nature, too, is a living creature that is affected, or afflicted, with all the circumstances of any living thing: "just like an animal, it will experience equal discomfort all over (*totum uexationem parem sentient*)" the way it does whenever earthquakes strike (*QNat.* 6.14.2). As with the universe, so with each individual living creature, especially ourselves: we begin life in complete purity and innocence; as we mature, we progressively decline, not only towards death but also morally. Thus, "nature's starting points are unperverted" (ἀδιαστρόφους, *SVF* 3.228); "wickedness soon creeps in" (*cito nequitia subrepit*, Sen. *QNat.* 3.30.8); "perfect virtue escapes and vanishes from our sight, and things that ripen early do not keep till the end of the season" (*Dial.* 6.23.3–4). In both cases, it is the same law of physics that is being obeyed: "whatever reaches its climax is close to its end" (*Dial.* 6.23.3–4; cf. M. Aur. *Med.* 3.2). "Nothing is firm" (*nihil stabile est*, *QNat.* 3.27.6) or

fixed in place forever (*Dial.* 12.7.10). And for the same reason, subjects are only as intelligible as the world they inhabit.

Vulnerability and fragility mark the totality of existence, individual lives and selves included. By "vulnerability" I do not mean being exposed to harm but rather being exposed to what lies outside oneself, a mutual conditioning by one's external environment (call it surroundings, others, or nature), and hence an interdependency that reminds us that no one and no things exist autonomously.[5] At the level of the individual person, the Stoic self exists in the tension between its first- and third-personal or impersonal reality: it is part phenomenological "me" and part elemental *daimōn*, and as such it is permanently but also constitutionally vulnerable to expropriation into the impersonal realm of nature.

Differently put, we are ineluctably wedded to our material constitutions; we are individuated in this precise sense: this defines our particular coherence. But part of being is being somewhere and therefore being exposed to other things at all levels in both body and soul, while individuality is permanently challenged by, and hence vulnerable to, expropriation: a self is always an other and always being othered. Autonomy is an unsustainable ideal. For the same reason, virtuous life is not exempt; it is a trial and a contest. And so too, tied to the vicissitudes of life, the virtuous man (*bonus uir*) "must go up and down (*sursum . . . ac deorsum*), he must be tossed by the waves" (*Dial.* 1.5.9). This is his essential activity; and activity is prone to contingency (*Dial.* 1.5.9) and to much more besides—for "who does not find life a torment?" (*QNat.* 5.18.15). Learning to be mindful of this existential fragility is the first and last step of virtue. "How foolish you are, how forgetful of your fragility!" (*QNat.* 2.59.9), a lesson that applies as much to the sage as to the struggling *proficiens*.

For these same reasons, moral perfection is not the final overcoming of obstacles to virtue but a constant confrontation of such obstacles and a permanent testing of one's self. This requires that subjects train themselves in dangers before they arise: they must seek them out before the dangers seek them out (*Dial.* 1.2.2: *omnia aduersa exercitationes putat*; 9.11.8). Flexibility, "surfing" contingency, avoiding fixed plans, and being responsive to chance and to change are the order of the day (*Dial.* 9.14.1). Virtue comes from a direct experience of these torments—this is what it means "to live in accordance with the experience (κατ' ἐμπειρίαν) of what happens by nature." Thus, virtue is "illuminated by the very things with which it is attacked" (*Dial.* 7.27.2). To know the hardness of a rock you have to have been "dashed on it"; consequently, "I offer myself like a lonely outcrop (*rupes aliqua . . . destituta*) in a shallow sea, which the waves keep lashing" (*Dial.* 7.27.2–3). Conversely, tranquility without the experience of fear, danger, or extremity is naïveté, not virtue. "Good fortune that has known no wound (*inlaesa*) cannot endure a single cut [or "blow"] (*ictum*)" (*Dial.* 1.2.6; cf. *Ep.* 13.2). Not even the sage, who after all is human too, is invulnerable to fear (Arr. *Epict. diss.* fr. 9) or wounding: his mind will bear the scars of extreme encounters (*cicatrix manet*) "even when the wound (*uulnus*) has healed" (so Zeno, quoted in Sen. *Dial.* 3.16.7 = *SVF* 1.215). Nor is virtue a permanent possession: it must continually prove itself from one moment to the next. "Without an adversary, [an individual's] manliness (*uirtus*) wastes away" (*Dial.* 1.2.4).

Being a part of nature (*SVF* 3.4), the individual does not enjoy absolute autonomy of any kind but rather partakes of the whole and cooperates with it. Individual responsibility and agency are of course possible; but these are both delimited by the sphere within which actions that are "up to us" are possible. In the bigger picture, there is much more that is not up to us than is.[6] We may call this an ascetic and modest view of agency, which paves the way for an enhanced sense of responsibility, one that is other-directed and not simply egoistic. Our responsibility is to align our natures with the laws and ways of nature, not to act independently of them.

Once they are put on a cosmic scale, we recognize how our responsibilities are owed to and shared with other parts of the world, both animate and inanimate, human and non-human: they are as large as the world itself. Our agency, by contrast, does not follow the same path of enlargement: it shrinks proportionately to our responsibility. The greater our share of responsibility to nature is, the smaller our individual powers of agency can ever be. Such a stance obliges us to recalibrate our place in the world. And because our place in the world is forever changing, so too is the recalibration of ourselves that is required of us. The picture is a dynamic one that keeps us on our toes. But most of all, it reminds us that mirages of agential autonomy must be continually subjected to critique. We cannot simply add a cosmic perspective onto a preexisting foundation of the self as an accessory to selfhood, as though doing so will leave either half of the equation untouched.[7] Neither the first-personal nor the third-personal viewpoint is epistemologically secure or experientially stable. Both are vulnerable to radical questioning. And such questioning is the source of ancient ethics at its finest.

Let us take stock of what has emerged so far. In the place of a single portrayal of the "mood" of Stoic philosophy, we now have two apparently competing portrayals, one welcoming and the other unwelcoming. Assuming that neither portrayal is inaccurate (and there is good evidence to back either view), how can we explain this divergence? I think the answer has to be that Stoicism is open to both kinds of description. If this is right, then we will have to acknowledge that Stoicism is less monolithic and more complex as a philosophy than it is typically understood to be. This is not the same as saying that Stoicism is a label that gets attached to a loose set of teachings or system of precepts that evolves over time, or that Stoicism contains contradictions that it can never abolish, although both of these things are also true. It is rather to say that Stoicism is best characterized as a way of looking at the world that is inherently equivocal: it is a philosophy with two faces. But the two faces can be explained and even reconciled up to a point in the following way.

Whenever Stoicism takes a hard look at the universe, it comes up with mixed results. The world it finds is far from being a quiet place, and the disturbances that run through nature can be disquieting in the extreme. Nature brings injuries and threats into our life, events that it would be false to ignore but wrong to despair of. Without erasing these realities, Stoicism offers a way forward: it asks us to make a mental adjustment and to adapt ourselves to nature. We adapt by looking for a rationale that can be used to explain these predicaments in life and in nature, and we make mental adjustments accordingly—that is, we adjust our picture of nature. Doing so amounts to nothing more than a perspectival shift. Nature's doings are not thereby erased. They are accepted, more than they are explained or justified, with the following kind of logic: Whatever happens, happens for a reason, whether we understand it or not. True understanding requires a cosmic perspective that is unavailable to us but to which we can, and must, nevertheless appeal. Nature, Fate, God, or Teleology are the names we give to this highest-order explanation, or rather inexplicability. Here, the thinking runs from is to ought, not from ought to is. Nature *is*. Therefore, if we wish to make our peace with the world of nature, we *must* live in accordance with it.

The alternative is to state that whatever is, is but for no particular reason, none at least that we should care about. That is the atomistic solution. Stoicism builds into itself a kind of mental ruse that allows us to accept what is given in the world as something that we should honor and not look on with blank indifference. It permits us to take a particular posture toward reality and it encourages an active engagement with reality as opposed to a withdrawal from the world. Whence the second component of the Stoic worldview, namely the notion that whatever happens represents the best state of affairs possible at any given moment. This is not exactly a normative claim about nature. It is rather a claim about the *acceptability* of events in nature: they are now irreversible facts that one can begin to reckon with. In other words, what happens in nature just is its particular order and harmony.

A view like this has psychological and ethical benefit. It gives us grounds for action, whether mental (adjusting our conceptions of the world) or ethical (locating ourselves in the world). And it creates a sense of urgency about the need for action, a kind of raw motivational requirement of the sort that comes from *oikeiōsis*, the instinct for self-preservation realized by attending to one's natural constitution, even more than any urgency for a particular kind of action.[8] No such urgency can be generated out of the first portrayal of Stoicism above, but it can be generated out of the interplay of both portrayals of the school. Of course, if we succeed in this endeavor, we will have accomplished more than a mental shift. We will have altered our view of ourselves as we stand in relation to nature. And that is of the greatest consequence, for it entails our best possible chances for achieving eudaimonic happiness and the most rational grasp of nature that any mortal creature can hope to attain. In sum, we can say that *Stoicism is not merely a theory of the world because it is primarily a stance that is taken towards the world*, one that requires shifting our perspectives to accommodate ourselves to this world. Cosmological ethics ratifies this mental shift and renders it appropriate, acceptable, and actionable.[9] Thus, Marcus writes, encouragingly, "Love only that which happens to you and is spun as the thread of your destiny; for what could be better suited to you?" (*Med.* 7.57; cf. 10.5, 10.7).

In what follows, I want to trace this redescribed ethical practice in the face of nature's twofold aspects in the writings of Seneca, whose challenges to the kindlier and gentler view of Stoicism tend to be downplayed in contemporary treatments of their thought.

SENECA: THE SELF AS EXPERIMENT

Writing under the early principate (4–65 CE), Seneca the Younger recognized the same set of problems as both Epictetus and Marcus Aurelius later would: "We have wasted enough time" (*Ep.* 19.1), the little of it that we have. "Everything else is beyond our grasp [lit., is alien to us and belongs to others: *omnia . . . aliena sun*t]. . . . Time alone is ours" (*Ep.* 1.3; tr. modified), which is to say, that tiny portion of time that we know and have, our present moment: the rest, time in its totality and eternity, is a "deep abyss" (*profunda . . . altitudo*, *Ep.* 21.5). The time we know and can call ours is "a gift" on loan (*Ep.* 1.3; cf. Arr. *Epict. diss.* 4.1.103–106; M. Aur. *Med.* 2.4, 4.50, 12.7). Here we find uncertainty and urgency being held as one. That is because they effectively are one. And so too we can say that the Senecan self is a precarious self. It occupies only the minutest "point in time (*punctum*), and so much less than a point" (*Ep.* 49.3). All around that point lies a ruinous "abyss," mere collapse and waste: "Whatever time has passed is in the same condition: it is observed in the same way and buried together (*una iacet*): everything falls into the same abyss (*omnia in idem profundum cadunt*)" (*Ep.* 49.3). The self stands wincing on the edge of this abyss, which is both the abyss of the universe in all its unfathomability and, crucially, that of the self, a fact that is one of its darkest secrets, as will be seen momentarily.

No one is exempt, not even the bravest among us, and not even a sage. No matter how brave a person may be, he "will wince at grim experiences and shudder at sudden events (*inhorrescet ad subita*) and be blind with dizziness (*caligabit*) if he looks down on an immense depth when standing on its brink (*uastam altitudinem in crepidine eius constitutus despexerit*, *Ep.* 57.4). A fragment from Epictetus clarifies how inevitable this fear is (Gell. *NA* 19.1.17 = Arr. *Epict. diss.* fr. 9):

> So when some terrifying sound comes from the sky or from a falling building, or news of some danger is suddenly announced, or something else of that kind occurs, even the mind of a wise person (*sapientis quoque animum*) is bound to be disturbed, and to shrink back and grow pale for a moment (*paulisper moueri et contrahi et pallescere*), not from any idea that something bad is going to happen, but because of certain swift and unconsidered movements which forestall the proper functioning of the mind and reason.

This response to danger and existential nullity is not one of cowardice; it is a natural and unavoidable feeling, and it cannot be fully addressed by reason (*naturalis adfectio inexpugnabilis rationi*, Sen. *Ep.* 57.4).[10] The self is fashioned up to a point by conscious direction and with the aid of philosophy (*me . . . transfigurari*, *Ep.* 6.1; *animum format et fabricat*, 16.3; *finges*, 31.11; *formauerunt*, 34.1), but its ultimate shape comes not from austere measures or regimens or even dialogue. Rather, it results from the confrontation with limits—its own—in the face of the abyssal character of nature: its endlessness, its sheer meaninglessness (when viewed from the first-personal perspective), and its extremity. For it is only when experiences are had at the limit of what can be experienced—*in extremis*—that the self's true measure can be taken. "Every pleasure saves its sweetest moment for its end (*in finem*). So one's age is most pleasant when it is beginning to go downhill, but not yet headlong, and I judge that even the moment on the brink of collapse (*in extrema tegula stantem*) has its pleasures, or else in place of pleasures comes the very fact of needing nothing" (*Ep.* 12.5).

To stand on the brink of an abyss is to confront the enigma of nature, its vast territory of the unknown. There is much to say about this prospect, but even more to say about Seneca's willingness to approach it, and the degree of self-negation that he is willing to take on as he does. We can start with a passage from his *De providentia*, which will help to illustrate the extremity of Seneca's stance. Partway into the essay, Seneca issues some Stoic boilerplate that suggests an unshakeable confidence in his own moral invulnerability (*Dial.* 1.5.6):

> I am coerced into nothing. I suffer nothing unwillingly. I do not serve god, but rather I agree with him—all the more so because I know that all things come to pass by a law that is fixed and is decreed for eternity.... And however much the lives of individuals seem to be distinguished by great variety, the total comes to one thing: the things we receive will perish, as will we.

Proud and confident in his philosophical beliefs, Seneca approaches his condition with reckless abandon: "Let nature use its bodies as it wants" (*Dial.* 1.5.8). One might suppose that Seneca's boast that he is prepared to give himself over to nature is less bold than it appears. After all, what he is surrendering is a paltry thing, his body. What he is holding in reserve is "the best part of us," his rational being—his living mind—that contains a spark of the divine (*QNat.* 4a.praef.20). Yet even that must perish, at least in the form that is intuitively familiar to Seneca. The mind, too, may be part of nature, but all that exists will eventually come to an end, whether through fire or inundation (*Dial.* 6.26.6; *QNat.* 3.27.1–30.7101), and not even nature and its ruling principle are exempt from the fate that they themselves dictate not just for us alone but for themselves: "Human and divine are carried along equally on a course that cannot be revoked. Yes, the founder and ruler of everything inscribed the fates himself, but he also follows them: having commanded them once, he obeys them always" (*Dial.* 1.5.8). And so, Seneca reasons, as if consoling himself, to die is to repay a debt to the universe: "Nothing perishes that is ours." And by "nothing" Seneca means "everything," our bodies and our minds. That being the case, he is willing "to offer himself up to fate," not just because he has nothing to lose but because there is a grander prospect to be gained in the interim. For "it is a magnificent consolation to be carried away [or "off"] with the universe" (*grande solacium est cum uniuerso rapi*). Seneca expects to be ravished by nature, even if that event takes place in a future that he will never personally experience. At the limit, in the final hour of the universe's destruction before it is reborn once again, well after he has died, there will be nothing to experience and no one to experience it, save if we wish to personify the universe as Zeus or god, something Epictetus was keener to do (*Diss.* 3.13.4) than Seneca is. To be so disposed towards this grand finale is the very height of virtue.

"See how high virtue ought to ascend!" (*Dial.* 1.5.10). The thought of self-abandonment in the name of virtue's highest attainments conjures up an image from myth, namely that of Phaethon as he is swept up into the heavens. Ovid (*Met.* 2.63–69) provides the proof text (*Dial.* 1.5.10):

> The first part of the road [to virtue] is steep, and even fresh in the morning the horses can scarcely struggle up it. The highest part is in the middle of the sky, and to look on the sea and the lands from there is something I myself am often afraid to do, and *my heart trembles in quivering terror*. The road's furthest part is steep and calls for firm control: even then, Tethys looks up from below, *fearing that*, before she receives me in the waves that lie beneath, *I may be thrown headlong* (*ne ferar in praeceps*). (emphasis added)

Standing back from Ovid, Seneca takes the narrative reins again and proceeds to translate for us and for himself in the first person what races through Phaethon's mind, all such fears notwithstanding: "This road appeals to me: I will ascend. So valuable is it to go through those things, *even if I will fall*" (1.5.11; emphasis added). The Sun (Apollo) threatens Phaethon, to no avail. Phaethon insists that he wants "to stand in the place where the Sun himself trembles (*trepidat*)." And so he does, rising and rising, until he can no more.

The image of Phaethon's ascent—or is it an assault?—on heaven is sublime, both in a literal sense and in literary terms. There is a transgressive thrill to the thought of stepping into another realm where one does not rightfully belong. Were Seneca to follow Ovid through to the fated conclusion for Phaethon, with its wrack and ruin, the lesson would be ghastly. The lesson, after all, is about perfecting virtue, not about immolating oneself in the process. But virtue would not be complete without the risk of self-destruction. "No great intellect is without a mixture of craziness (*dementiae*)," Aristotle wrote. Seneca quotes this approvingly and adds that "nothing sublime and set on high (*sublime quicquam et in arduo positum*) can come to it as long as it is at home with itself (*apud se est*); it ought to desert its customary mode and be borne away and bite the bridle and carry off (*rapiat*) its rider and bear him where he feared to rise" (*Dial.* 9.17.1011). As we shall see, virtue cannot even be attempted, in Seneca's mind, without taking on such profound and literally ecstatic risks. The thought is Longinian (*Subl.* 15.4, on Euripides' Phaethon).[11] And yet, the risks are not identical. All that Longinus's poets and readers risk is a failed encounter with sublimity. What is the exact risk that is being envisaged by Seneca? In what does the prospect of a fall consist for him?

There is no single answer, in part because Seneca's image is a metaphor that operates on several different levels of meaning. On one level, what is risked is a failure to attain virtue. But since virtue is perfect only in the Sage, this is not a mortal risk; it is simply a human failing, one that is programmed into our existence. On another level, at risk is the failure to attempt virtue, which requires. courage, fortitude, and any number of other moral qualities. The risk here is the risk of moral failure. On a third and final level, at risk is something grander still, the risk involved in facing the ultimate limit, be this death or an exposure to being "carried away with the universe" (*cum uniuerso rapi*) that entails a radical alteration in or destitution of one's identity, which are in fact one and the same thing. And here we would have to say that Seneca's bet is entirely hedged. After all, he calls this last prospect, which is fated more than it is chosen, "a consolation." Why?

The answer is that to reach one's mortal limits is, as we saw in the case of Marcus, to dissolve into the constituents from which one has been made. Seneca knows that "the human mind is composed of the same elements (*ex isdem . . . seminibus compositum*) as divine beings" (*Dial.* 12.6.8). To be returned to his divine constituents is to be one with them again: "as all matter goes up in flames" (*omni flagrante materia*), upon death "we [too] shall be returned to our original elements" (*in antiqua elementa uertemur, Dial.* 6.26.6–7). But the path to this return is in one significant sense an illusion. For in returning to nature, Seneca is not actually going anywhere that he already isn't. He is, at the very moment of his writing, already a piece of nature and so too constituted out of its original elements. Whenever he conceives of himself in these terms, that is, whenever he recalls that he is made up of physical elements and in this way inscribes himself back into nature, he is merely redescribing himself. And so too, the path of Phaethon, understood in this way, describes a shift in perspective, not a movement to another place. It pictures another view of who Seneca is, be this as a human being attempting or risking virtue or as a piece (a "pinprick," *punctum*) of the natural universe. It is only through such shifts that Seneca can decenter his habitual view of himself and locate it somewhere else. And it is only by accounting for himself along the lines of each of the three levels of meaning gauged by risk just mentioned, each of which implies the other—only by risking himself—that he can practice a virtuous existence.

We should not underestimate the terrifying quality of this shift in perspectives. What Seneca is undertaking is a kind of psychic restructuring, but also a psychic dissolution. His soul, the seat of his first-personal identity, literally goes up in flames the moment he acknowledges that it consists in fiery pneuma. Once it does, all personal characteristics vanish with it: the self, the "I," the *hēgemonikon*, the *mens* and *animus* (the mental or psychic self), and the *anima* (the soul) are no more. All of these dissipate once they are released from the no longer vital body. It is in retracing the path of the divine in the world of the senses and in the world beyond them, a world that can be reached only by means of reason and imagination, that Seneca finds the fulcrum of his beliefs and the ultimate tranquility of his spirit. But such a radical realignment of his view of himself is not risk-free. It does not mean that Seneca has domesticated the scenario of Phaethon risking life and limb to ascend to a height. Quite the contrary: the imaginary identification with Phaethon, indexed by his ventriloquism ("I will ascend . . . , even if I will fall"), is part of the experimentation with his self that Seneca continually undertakes, whether he is suffering real pains or simply imagining them. It is, in fact, part and parcel of his effort to understand nature and his place in it. Phaethon is merely the emblem of this undertaking. The cosmological equivalent to Phaethon's fate is, of course, the circuit taken by the world as it passes into a final dissolution through universal conflagration. The dissolution of the self neatly parallels this cosmic event of nature as a whole. We might call it a "personal conflagration," albeit one that leaves the person behind as little more than a vapor trail.

Approaching nature as a limit to be transgressed takes Seneca well beyond an insight that he stands to gain into the rational workings of the universe. To study nature is to follow a natural impulse, based on *oikeiōsis* (our inborn orientation to nature), that is sparked by wonder and fear (cf. *QNat.* 6.3.4: *nihil horum sine timore miramur*). It is also to follow an impulse to venture into boundary exploration, an effort that nature encourages, ratifies, and rewards. As we pass through boundaries, our minds expand their reach (*crescit animus*, *QNat.* 3.praef.3). However, given the endlessness of the task and its incommensurability relative to our capacities (praef.4), such study is bound to frustrate our attempts. To know nature is by definition beyond the reach of any living individual or entire generations of individuals: its scope is too vast and, as Seneca repeatedly reminds us, the greater part of nature can in any case never be known to us: observation cannot achieve truth but only guesswork and hunches ("we are only permitted to grope around for it [sc., truth] and to advance into the darkness [*ire in occulta*] by means of conjecture," *QNat.* 7.29.3), and "god did not make everything for human beings" to fathom (7.30.3) Simply to recognize this is itself to make a gain: it reminds us of our human limitations. "What is most important? . . . Remembering your human status (*hominis meminisse*)" (*QNat.* 3.praef.15).

Consequently, the study of nature as a useful moral undertaking is not designed to exalt ourselves beyond our human standing. It exists to teach us humility, whether this means diminishing our stature with respect to the universe; exalting us to a point that can only precipitate a fall back into the abyss of contingency and change that attends the world at any moment, including those that are marked by the highest exhilaration (for the highest moments are also the least stable for Seneca); or plunging us back into elemental nature (e.g., *Dial.* 6.26.1–8; *toti se inserens mundo*, *Ep.* 66.6). And so, in the last analysis, the cosmic view is far from providing an alleviating view of nature, unless we understand by this a reconciliation with and submission to the way things are, achieved by accepting fate, mortality, and our native smallness in the greater scheme of things—in other words, by reckoning with every limit that we can know and experience (or simply infer) about the world. Virtue is not a matter of resisting these conditions but of surrendering to them (*Dial.* 11.4.1). One surrenders not only by accepting the inevitability of circumstances but also by convincing oneself about whatever state of affairs obtains at any given moment, whatever happens to us or to the world, that "this is naturally so" (M. Aur. *Med.* 10.7), and by "learning to wish that everything should come about just as it does" (Arr. *Epict. diss.* 1.12.15). Nature, so viewed, is not a source of comfort or solace. It is not redemptive. It does not relieve us of the reality of harsh limits that we have to experience. Seneca puts this somewhat severely when he states that "there is no greater comfort (*sollacium*) in the face of death than mortality itself" (*QNat.* 6.2.6). The only solace we can have, in other words, is to be found in the way things are.

Setting himself as an example, Seneca achieves this perspective on nature by experimenting at the limits of his experience at the two ends of the available spectrum, by confronting both nature as a whole and the conditions of his own mortality and by confronting each of these with the other. Whenever the two insights come together, as they inevitably do, they produce a sense of radical precariousness and moral urgency that gives his writings their compelling quality, and the same is true of his Roman peers. Seneca's self-experimentation accounts for the totality of his philosophical essays, which either record this practice or are its site. Playing with the boundary conditions of his self requires a concomitant self-rifacimento: "So let us shape our minds as if we have reached the end (*tamquam ad extrema uentum sit*)"—the end of life, the end of meaning and of rational understanding—in other words, the limiting conditions of our existence (*Ep.* 101.7). "Our boundary stone (*terminus*) is fixed where the inexorable necessity of the fates has planted it," and it is only in view of this terminus that we can truly fashion a sense of who we are. Better yet, we can do so only in view of another limit, the limit of not knowing, for "none of us knows how near he is to that boundary." The as-if quality runs through every aspect of this encounter. We are to make as if life has reached its end, in an ongoing process that can only generously be called one of self-fashioning or self-shaping, since this shaping is itself an imaginary one: it too has no fixed boundary. Rather, it belongs to a process that is steadily reshaped with every passing moment, permitting nothing more than a provisional outline that needs to be revised at every moment. The outlines are continually being redrawn whenever we reach them in the course of our life for as long as we live, until we no longer can or do.

"How foolish it is to organize one's life when one is not even master of the morrow!"—so Seneca opens this line of thought (*Ep.* 101.4), which extends the letter's original reflection on the brute fact of our own worthlessness and "vulnerability" (*fragilitatis*) that is impressed on us with "every day and every hour": "we are nothing" (*nihil simus*, *Ep.* 101.1, trans. modified). Self-fashioning is an encounter with the threat of self-disorganization and annihilation. More than this, it is an ongoing experimentation with an intolerable prospect, one that we nevertheless are compelled to face both morally and in order to be brutally honest with ourselves (*aliquando te offende*, *Ep.* 28.10). "Imagine this is your last day of life; or if not"—depending on your comfort level—then "the next to last" (*Ep.* 15.11). For we are, in fact, dying every day (*Ep.* 1.2; 24.20). Identically, Marcus Aurelius: "perform every action as though it were your last" (*Med.* 2.5) or "as if you had died" (7.56), because "dissolution is already under way" and "everything is dying" at every moment (10.18; cf. 3.1; 10.29). Imagine that nature is constituted by limits (and limits are both the most real and the most imaginary of mental objects). Or imagine that nature is unbounded, not physically (I am thinking of the way in which the Stoic universe, though surrounded by infinite, extracosmic void, is typically treated as a self-contained entity)[12] but in every other way that matters. This too is another fiction of the mind, an unverifiable premise, but nothing more, albeit one with ethical implications for how we imagine the universe and find a place for ourselves in it.[13]

Setting limits, however provisional, is the way we progress through life and the way we measure that progress, although there is no real progression being made but only a sequence of events that eventually sweeps us away. The fabled attentiveness of the Stoic mind is in fact trained on these imaginary limits: its job is to make these relative measures and limits appear to itself, even as they vanish with every second: "You have gone ahead of yourself. Set a limit (*finem*) which you could not exceed even if you wanted" (*Ep.* 15.11; cf. *Ep.* 49.4 on attending to limits [*lineas*] as they approach, albeit sensed as imminent losses). The self is tempered by such tests—of its virtue, its patience, its endurance, its capacity for expansion but also for contraction, or rather for shriveling into a tiny speck: in a word, its capacity to test what cannot truly be had in experience. *The self is known only in the starkest relation to its own vulnerabilities* (*Ep.* 18.5–13; 26.3–10), because it, too, is a limit. *Experimentum* covers all of these situations. Hovering uncertainly between "test" and "experience," the word in fact stands for an experience of limits, whether self-imposed or imposed from without.[14] The final irony is that these are tests one cannot pass but can only attempt. In their most radical form, they do not test (locate and identify) one's self but only *the limits of experience itself*, so that we may learn what these are. (Here, the self is more of a limit-function than a positive entity.) Their collective record charts the progress of the aspiring philosophical subject. "How much progress shall I make?" "As much as you attempt" (*Ep.* 76.5)—just like nature itself, which is forever in a state of progress (that is, always in process and in motion), never ending, never fathomable, and endlessly receding before us.

The abyssal prospect of nature has its exact mirror in the Senecan self. There exist two abysses, one without, nature's cosmos, and one within, our very own minds. Like infants who only "crudely and superficially and vaguely understand their natural make-up (*constitutionem*),"

> we too know we have a mind, but we do not know what the mind is, where it is, what is its nature and from what source. Just as we are aware of our own mind, *although we do not know its nature and place*, so all animals are aware of their own composition. For they must necessarily feel the organ by which they feel all other things; they must necessarily have a feeling they obey and by which they are governed. No man among us fails to understand that there is something that stirs his impulses; *but he doesn't know what it is*. And he knows he has an impulse, but he does not know what it is or its origin. So infants too and animals have a perception of their governing part, *but it is not yet sufficiently clear or articulate*. (*Ep.* 121.12; emphasis added)

This is one of the more profoundly gripping moments in Seneca's Letters. It has a complement in his *Natural Questions* (7.25.2):

> Everybody will agree that we have a mind, by whose commands we are driven on and called back. But what the mind is, this controller and master of ours, no one will explain to you, any more than he will explain where it is: one person will say that it is breath, another that it is a kind of harmony, another that it is a divine power, a portion of god, another that it is the finest part of the soul, another that it is an incorporeal power; someone will be found to say it is blood or heat. *So far from being able to acquire a clear grasp of other things, the mind is still trying to understand itself* (*adeo animo non potest liquere de ceteris rebus ut adhuc ipse se quaerat*).

The passage from *Natural Questions* brings out what is implicit in letter 121: the obscurity of the mind is rooted in the physics of nature. The mind has a composition (*constitutio*); it is made up of natural elements in virtue of which it enjoys and navigates through life. But against all expectations, the life of the mind operates for the most part instinctively, on the model of an infant and indeed of all animals. The typical Stoic response to this instinctive set of natural predispositions and movements is to focus on "the commanding element in the mind, guiding it in relation to the body" that provides volition and direction to natural impulses (*Ep.* 121.10). Seneca knows this orthodoxy, to be sure, and he is often its exponent. But what is odd in the present case is that he is presenting the orthodox doctrine as an objection to his own argument. Far from being known, the make-up, locus, and nature of this commanding element are shrouded in obscurity. We are unknown to ourselves. In this respect, we are no better off than infants or animals. For if it is the case that an infant "only understands his composition crudely and superficially and vaguely (*obscure*)," it is no less the case that we do too. Such is our "infancy," in the most literal sense of the word. And no matter how hard we try, the opacity of our self to ourselves "cannot be addressed" (or "be expunged and laid to rest") by reason any more than the fear that a brave man experiences while standing on the edge of precipice, as we saw earlier in letter 57.4.

The reference to nature in both cases is the key to understanding Seneca's complex stance, which reflects an unstable blend of precarity, curiosity, pessimism, and confident optimism all at once. It is this precise combination of factors, with nature's inexorable presence standing behind them all, that renders Seneca's outlook an ethical one and not simply an expression of uncertainty, doubt, or philosophical confusion. Differently put, his outlook on nature, as unstable as it appears to be, grounds his ethics. Consequently, we have to acknowledge that what grounds Seneca's ethics or morals is what ungrounds his perception of himself as an intact subject that is transparent to itself, a trait he shares with his Roman philosophical peers. The self for Seneca is not a firm entity. It is a *problem*. And that makes him a representative ancient, and not only a representative Roman Stoic.

Final Coda

Taking its cue from Roman philosophies of the self, this essay points to the need for a larger but also differently conceived inquiry into the self in antiquity—its nature, its boundaries, its conditions of emergence, and the conditions under which it is experienced. If anything of a more generalizable sort results from this brief outing with the Roman Stoics, it would have to be that the self, instead of being an object that is waiting to be described, is for them the source of endless aporias, antagonisms, discomforts, uncertainties, and riddles. But neither is the self the be-all and end-all of their most pressing concerns. The self, not only for the Roman Stoics but elsewhere, is less the starting point of inquiry than the byproduct and residue of a complex set of experiences in the face of nature and society and across any number of flashpoints, from one's own or others' beliefs, actions, values, and relationships to the difficulty of sizing up one's place in the world. At such moments along a path that can be traced from Heraclitus to Augustine, the self comes to light not only as a devilishly elusive and opaque entity—a problem that admits of no solution—but also as an endless abyss that threatens to endanger the subject who is seeking this knowledge.[15]

But this chapter has not been interested in locating the ancient self. It has been interested in exploring how the pressures of natural and ethical considerations among the Roman Stoics put their conceptions of the self at considerable risk. It is here that the Stoics begin to look strikingly modern, even contemporary, above all when they are compared with representatives of recent and current critical ecological theory. In fact, the reverse is the case. It is no accident that current theory can recall Roman philosophies of the self and nature. The ancients knew things that we are just beginning to learn.[16]

Notes

Excerpted from Porter (2020). Thanks to the editors for including it in their volume and for pointers on how best to excerpt the original essay. Translations are drawn from the following: Sen. *Ep.*: Fantham (2010); Sen. *Dial.*: Fantham et al. (2014); Sen. *QNat.*: Hine (2010); Epictetus: Hard (2014); M. Aur. *Med.*: Hard (2011).

1. Deleuze (1995) 108.
2. This includes Neostoic literature (e.g., Irvine (2009), Pigliucci (2017), Sherman (2005)) and recent scholarship on ancient Stoicism (e.g., LS 1.392; Williams (2012) 171, 257; Long (2019) 99). The literature on the Stoic self or sense of self in its relation to nature is vast. The following titles are particularly seminal and/or have been particularly useful to my thinking to date: Bartsch (2006); Bartsch (2015); Foucault (1986); Frede (1999); Gill (2006); Hadot (1995); Inwood (2009b); Long (2002); Reydams-Schils (2005); Sedley (2012).
3. *Pace* Mansfeld (1979).
4. LS 1.392; Long (1985) 25. Bobzien (1998) 32 and Frede (1999) 75–77 usefully complicate this conceit.
5. Vulnerability of this kind is at the heart of contemporary ethical and ecological reflection but is insufficiently attended to in the study of ancient philosophy. See, however, Frede (1999).
6. Cf. Bobzien (1998) 331–338.
7. So Reydams-Schils (2019), esp. 101–102, in line with most scholarship on the ancient self today, for arguments that the "ideal self" of ancient philosophy is "incoherent." But this leaves intact the subjective self that remains protected even after its expropriation by a cosmic perspective.
8. A crude rendering of *oikeiōsis* might be "adapting" to what naturally is by appropriating it and making it one's own. A metaphorical rendering would be "finding one's place or home" in the world. The irony of *oikeiōsis* is that any adaptation we make is to what already is our own place in nature; we simply need to learn to acknowledge that this is the case. Hence, a final rendering of *oikeiōsis* would be "making do" with the world. See esp. Klein (2016); also, Magrin (2018).

9. I borrow the term "cosmological ethics" from Betegh (2003). On the place of Stoic physics in Stoic ethics, see Striker (1991); Hadot (1995) 238–250; Menn (1995); Inwood (2009a).
10. This is an example of what Stoics called *propatheia*, "pre-emotions," though the wide number of synonyms for the term attests to a broad interest in these feelings that could not easily be contained by Stoic psychological and ethical categories. See Inwood (1985), 176–178; Graver (2007), ch. 4 ("Feelings without Assent").
11. See Porter (2016) 345.
12. See Mansfeld (1979) 179, 149n58; Furley (1999).
13. See the salutary comments by Bobzien (1998) 24–25, 43.
14. This, I propose, is the full meaning of Chrysippus's definition of the end, [τὸ] κατ' ἐμπειρίαν τῶν φύσει συμβαινόντων ζῆν (*SVF* 3.4), marking a significant revision of Zeno's formula, ὁμολογουμένως τῇ φύσει ζῆν (*SVF* 1.552).
15. See Heraclitus (DK 22B45), Aristotle (*De an.* 402a10–11), Plato (*Phd.* 88b2–3; *Phdr.*, passim), Lucretius (*De rerum natura* 3), Galen (*De placitis Hippocratis et Platonis* 3.1.15), Plotinus (see Remes (2007), ch. 6, esp. 250–253), and Augustine (*Conf.* 4.4.9; 10.1.2; 10.8.15; 10.17.26; cf. Serm. 340A8). On Heraclitus, see now Porter (forthcoming).
16. See esp. Morton (2007); Braidotti (2013) ch. 1 ("Life beyond the Self"); Braidotti and Bignall (2019). On the relevance of these approaches to antiquity, see esp. Bianchi, Brill, and Holmes (2019).

References

Bartsch, S. (2006). *The Mirror of the Self: Sexuality, Self-Knowledge, and the Gaze in the Early Roman Empire*. (Chicago).
Bartsch, S. (2015). "Senecan Selves," in S. Bartsch and A. Schiesaro (eds.), *The Cambridge Companion to Seneca* (Cambridge), 187–198.
Betegh, G. (2003). "Cosmological Ethics in the *Timaeus* and Early Stoicism." *Oxford Studies in Ancient Philosophy* 24: 273–302.
Bianchi, E., S. Brill, and B. Holmes, eds. (2019). *Antiquities beyond Humanism*. (Oxford).
Bobzien, S. (1998). *Determinism and Freedom in Stoic Philosophy*. (Oxford).
Braidotti, R. (2013). *The Posthuman*. (Cambridge).
Braidotti, R., and S. Bignall, eds. (2019). *Posthuman Ecologies: Complexity and Process after Deleuze*. (London).
Deleuze, G. (1995). *Negotiations, 1972–1990*. M. Joughin, tr. (New York).
Fantham, E., tr. (2010). *Seneca, Selected Letters*. (Oxford).
Fantham, E., H. M. Hine, J. Ker, and G. D. Williams, tr. (2014). *L. A. Seneca, Hardship and Happiness*. (Chicago).
Foucault, M. (1986). *The Care of the Self: Volume 3 of The History of Sexuality*. Robert Hurley, tr. (New York).
Frede, M. (1999). "On the Stoic Conception of the Good," in K. Ierodiakonou (ed.), *Topics in Stoic Philosophy* (Oxford), 71–94.
Furley, D. J. (1999). "Cosmology," in K. Algra (ed.), *The Cambridge History of Hellenistic Philosophy* (Cambridge), 412–451.
Gill, C. (2006). *The Structured Self in Hellenistic and Roman Thought*. (Oxford).
Graver, M. R. (2007). *Stoicism and Emotion*. (Chicago).

Hadot, P. (1995). *Philosophy as a Way of Life: Spiritual Exercises from Socrates to Foucault*. A. I. Davidson, ed., M. Chase, tr. (Malden, MA).
Hard, R., tr. (2011). Marcus Aurelius, *Meditations, with Selected Correspondence*. (Oxford).
Hard, R. (2014). Epictetus: *Discourses, Fragments, Handbook*. (Oxford).
Hine, H. M., tr. (2010). *Lucius Annaeus Seneca, Natural Questions*. (Chicago).
Inwood, B. (1985). *Ethics and Human Action in Early Stoicism*. (Oxford).
Inwood, B. (2009a). "Why Physics?," in R. Salles (ed.), *God and Cosmos in Stoicism* (Oxford), 201–223.
Inwood, B. (2009b). "Seneca and Self-Assertion," in S. Bartsch and D. Wray (eds.), *Seneca and the Self* (Cambridge), 39–64.
Irvine, W. B. (2009). *A Guide to the Good Life: The Ancient Art of Stoic Joy*. (Oxford).
Klein, J. (2016). "The Stoic Argument from *oikeiōsis*." *Oxford Studies in Ancient Philosophy* 50: 143–200.
Long, A. A. (1985). "The Stoics on World-Conflagration and Everlasting Recurrence," *Southern Journal of Philosophy* 23(Supplement): 13–37.
Long, A. A. (2002). *Epictetus: A Stoic and Socratic Guide to Life*. (Oxford).
Long, A. A. (2019). *How to Be Free: An Ancient Guide to the Stoic Life; Epictetus, Encheiridion and Selections from Discourses*. (Princeton).
Magrin, S. (2018). "Nature and Utopia in Epictetus' Theory of *Oikeiōsis*." *Phronesis* 63: 293–350.
Mansfeld, J. (1979). "Providence and the Destruction of the Universe in Early Stoic Thought," in M. J. Vermaseren (ed.), *Studies in Hellenistic Religions* (Leiden), 129–188.
Menn, S. (1995). "Physics as a Virtue," in J. J. Cleary and G. M. Gurtler (eds.), *Proceedings of the Boston Area Colloquium in Ancient Philosophy*, X (Leiden), 1–34.
Morton, T. (2007). *Ecology without Nature: Rethinking Environmental Aesthetics*. (Cambridge, Mass.).
Pigliucci, M. (2017). *How to Be a Stoic: Ancient Wisdom for Modern Living*. (New York).
Porter, J. I. (2016). *The Sublime in Antiquity*. (Cambridge).
Porter, J. I. (2020). "Living on the Edge: Self and World *in extremis* in Roman Philosophy." *Cl. Ant.* 39.2: 225–383.
Porter, J. I. (forthcoming). "How Ideal Is the Ancient Self?," In G. Kroupa and J. Simoniti (eds.), *The Possibility for Idealism in the 21st Century* (Berlin).
Remes, P. (2007). *Plotinus on Self: The Philosophy of the "We."* (Cambridge).
Reydams-Schils, G. (2005). *The Roman Stoics: Self, Responsibility, and Affection*. (Chicago).
Reydams-Schils, G. (2019). "How to Become Like God and Remain Oneself," in M. R. Niehoff and J. Levinson (eds.), *Self, Self-Fashioning and Individuality in Late Antiquity* (Tübingen), 89–104.
Sedley, D. (2012). "Marcus Aurelius on Physics," In M. van Ackeren (ed.), *A Companion to Marcus Aurelius* (Malden, Mass.), 396–407.
Sherman, N. (2005). *Stoic Warriors: The Ancient Philosophy behind the Military Mind*. (New York).
Striker, G. (1991). Following Nature: A Study in Stoic Ethics. *Oxford Studies in Ancient Philosophy* 9: 1–73.
Williams, G. D. (2012). *The Cosmic Viewpoint: A Study of Seneca's Natural Questions*. (Oxford).

CHAPTER 22

MEDICINE

DAVID LEITH

GREEK theoretical medicine had from its beginnings drawn extensively on contemporary philosophical developments. Many treatises that later found their way into the Hippocratic Corpus show a deep engagement with Presocratic philosophy, a phenomenon that was to continue through the fourth century into the Hellenistic period with such figures as Diocles of Carystus, Praxagoras of Cos, Herophilus of Chalcedon, and Erasistratus of Ceus, all finding inspiration on various levels in current philosophical trends.[1] Nor was the line of influence all in one direction: the interests of Plato and Aristotle, for instance, in the work of medical writers and in the contributions they might make to the study of nature are well known.

Such cross-fertilization was to persist after Greek medicine was transplanted to Rome. From the Late Republic on, interactions between medicine and philosophy were principally mediated by the medical *haireseis*, or "sects" as they are conventionally called. Their origins can be traced to early Alexandria, where Herophilus and his pupil Philinus of Cos (see below on the Empiricist sect) in the early and mid-third century BCE gathered adherents who followed their distinctive approaches to medicine and subsequently formed enduring groups with a self-conscious identity. Erasistratus did likewise at around the same time, though it is not clear that he was based in Alexandria (our sources point to connections with Athens and the Seleucid court at Antioch). These groups were professionally successful and intellectually influential, and continued to transmit, develop, and in some respects modify the theories and methods of their founders.[2] The Roman period was a particularly innovative and diverse one for theoretical medicine. As we shall see, further medical sects proliferated in their new Roman context, and reached new levels of doctrinal dispute as they spread further afield throughout the Empire. They were all philosophically informed, in some cases directly appropriating particular theories, yet the story of the medical sects was distinct from that of the Athenian philosophical schools. Epistemological debates on the nature and origin of medical knowledge came to be at the forefront, but disputes naturally also raged concerning the nature of the human body, how it functioned, the causes of disease, and how these sorts of questions must be approached.

In what follows, I shall look in turn at the most important medical sects and authorities of the Roman period—namely the Asclepiadeans, Pneumatists, Empiricists, Methodists, and Galen. I shall try to give a sense of their individuality, how they reacted to each other, and the ways in which they used and manipulated various philosophical theories and interacted directly with the philosophical schools. I shall focus on the sects which either grew up in Rome or which seem to have developed significantly there; hence I shall not have much to say about either the Herophilean sect, which seems to have died out in the first century CE, or the Erasistrateans, who were still prominent in Rome in the late second century, but who exhibit substantial doctrinal continuity with their Hellenistic predecessors.[3]

It should be emphasized at the outset that our picture is overwhelmingly dominated by the evidence of Galen, whose vast output contains a huge amount of polemic directed against his medical and philosophical precursors, especially those of the Hellenistic and Roman periods. His testimony can be tested to a certain extent against the reports of other writers, such as Celsus, Sextus Empiricus, Caelius Aurelianus, and some pseudo-Galenic authors, but it is essential to understand Galen's peculiar preoccupations, biases, and polemical strategies as far as possible.[4]

Asclepiades of Bithynia

Greek medicine established itself in Rome only slowly and fitfully. A rather unsuccessful venture was reportedly made by one Archagathus in the later third century BCE (Plin. *NH* 29.12–13), but it is clear that Greek doctors were arriving in greater numbers in the following century. By the later second century BCE, however, Rome had its own major authority in theoretical medicine, Asclepiades of Bithynia, and to judge from the positive portrayals in the Latin tradition, this was to become, and may well have been already at the time, a source of considerable pride for the Roman aristocracy with interests in intellectual currents.[5] Having spent at least some time in Athens before coming to Rome, Asclepiades developed a systematic medical theory which drew extensively on Epicurean atomism, especially in connection with his theory of matter and his epistemology.[6] According to his doctrine, the human body, as with everything in the universe, is made up of tiny, imperceptible particles called (*anarmoi*) *onkoi*, or "(seamless) masses." These are in perpetual motion, bouncing around forever in void space, without any providential intelligence at work in the universe to guide them. Just like Epicurean atoms, these particles have size and shape, but are devoid of the secondary, phenomenal qualities of color, smell, taste, and so on; such secondary qualities arise only in complex structures of *onkoi* in combination. Asclepiades also employed Epicurean arguments to establish this (cf. Caelius Aurelianus, *Celeres vel acutae passiones* 1.14.106 with Lucr. 2.788–94). Nevertheless, he introduced certain striking modifications to the Epicurean theory, not least in his contention that the *onkoi* were not at all atomic, but physically breakable.[7] All this will have been set out in detail in his treatise *On Elements*, in which he also openly attacked the Stoics' theory of matter (Gal. *Hipp. Elem.* 9.35 [i 489–90 K = *CMG* V 1,2 p. 136 De Lacy]). Asclepiades' theory formed the basis of his physiology and pathology: health is maintained by the free and balanced motion of the *onkoi* through the void interstices (*poroi*) within the body's structure, while disease is the consequence of a blockage or impaction (*enstasis*) of *onkoi* in a particular part of the body, with different diseases resulting from blockages in different parts.[8]

Asclepiades' epistemology was well enough regarded to attract the attention of Antiochus of Ascalon, more or less his contemporary. As reported by Sextus Empiricus, Antiochus had written the following about him in his *Canonica*: "someone else, in medicine second to none, but who tried his hand also at philosophy, believed that perceptions are apprehensions in reality and in truth, while we apprehend nothing at all with reason" (Sext. Emp. *Math.* 7.201). Sextus duly identifies this authority as Asclepiades, and takes the statement to indicate that he, like Epicurus, upheld the senses as the criterion of truth. Yet Asclepiades also believed that the senses were inadequate by themselves to yield the sort of information required for an art such as medicine; for that, one also needed reason, and he mounted a comprehensive attack on the Empiricist medical sect (on which see below) for their claims to be able to do without it.[9]

Asclepiades' physiology, on the other hand, was principally informed by that of his medical predecessor Erasistratus, and this also had important implications for his psychology.[10] For Asclepiades, the substance of the soul was pneuma, and it was composed of especially small, round and smooth *onkoi*, just like the atoms that constituted the Epicurean soul (Calcidius, *Commentarius in Platonis Timaeum* (= *In Tim.*) 215).[11] But Asclepiades adopted a distinctively Erasistratean theory of how this soul-pneuma is generated by means of respiration. Like Erasistratus, Asclepiades held that the inhaled pneuma travels to the heart via the lungs, where it undergoes a first elaboration; some of the pneuma then passes through the carotid arteries to the brain, and at that point, after a second stage of elaboration, it becomes psychic pneuma and spreads throughout the body, mediating sensation and other psychic functions (Calc. *In Tim.* 214). For Asclepiades, this extremely refined psychic pneuma just is the soul. Notably, Asclepiades is the first doctor since the Classical period for whom we have direct evidence for a developed theory on the nature and substance of the soul. By contrast, Erasistratus (along with other Hellenistic doctors) does not appear to have expressed a view on the nature of the soul itself, although the psychic pneuma in his system was responsible for mediating the key capacities of perception and voluntary motion.[12]

Perhaps Asclepiades' most distinctive and original thesis, for which he became best known in philosophical circles, was his denial that the ruling-part-of-the-soul, or *hēgemonikon*, occupied a particular part of the body. This gave him a prominent and outlying place in doxographical surveys of views on the location of the *hēgemonikon* (e.g., Sext. Emp. *Math.* 7.380; Tert. *De anim.* 15). Asclepiades thus rejected Epicurus's location of the rational part of the soul in the thorax. This is perhaps in part the result of tensions between the Epicurean view and the anatomical findings of the earlier Hellenistic physicians Herophilus and Erasistratus, who were able to trace the origins of sensation and voluntary motion, via the nervous system, to the brain or its meninges.

In support of his thesis, Asclepiades pointed to the abilities of animals such as bees or locusts, and crocodiles or goats, to continue carrying out complex psychic functions even after their heads or their hearts had been removed (Calc. *In Tim.* 216; Tert. *De anim.* 15.2).[13]

The Asclepiadean sect was to have considerable success in Rome in the first centuries BCE and CE, including in their number, for example, Augustus's personal physicians Marcus Artorius and Antonius Musa.[14] Galen gives the impression that the sect was languishing in his day, though he mentions in passing his contact with certain unnamed representatives and notes that it maintained a respectable following (e.g., Gal. *Nat. Fac.* 1.13 [ii 34 K = p. 125 Helmreich] and 1.14 [ii 52 K = p. 139 Helmreich]). In terms of Asclepiades' wider influence, we have already observed that Antiochus took notice of his epistemology. Scholars have also tried to find traces of his reciprocal influence on the Epicurean tradition, in particular through Lucretius and Philodemus, although the evidence cited has proved inconclusive.[15]

Athenaeus of Attaleia

A little later, probably some time in the first half of the first century BCE, Athenaeus of Attaleia developed a medical system based on Stoicism, his followers being referred to as Pneumatists.[16] Athenaeus was certainly engaged in criticism of Asclepiades (Gal. *Hipp. Elem.* 9.20 [i 486 K = CMG V 1,2 p. 132 De Lacy]), and it is tempting to wonder whether his own medical project was in part an attempt to do with Stoicism what Asclepiades had done with Epicureanism.

Athenaeus had been a pupil of the Stoic Posidonius (Gal. *CC* 2.1 [CMG Suppl. Or. II pp. 54, 134 = T51 Edelstein-Kidd]), and he analyzed the human body in terms of Stoic elemental theory. He held that, for medical purposes, the elements of the body may be taken to be the elemental qualities hot, cold, wet, and dry (ps.-Gal. *Def. Med.* 31 [xix 356 K]), though he was unwilling to refer to the composition of the cosmos out of the elemental bodies earth, water, air, and fire, as going beyond what was necessary for the medical art (Gal. *Hipp. Elem.* 6 [i 457–473 K = CMG V 1,2 pp. 102–118 De Lacy]).[17] He also adhered to the Stoic theory of pneuma as a substance characterised by a dynamic tension, that permeates, holds together, and sustains the cosmos and everything it contains, including living things. Athenaeus held that this pneuma, which for the Stoics constitutes the substance of animals' souls, is also fundamentally responsible for all disease, for it permeates and regulates all of the uniform parts of the animal body, affecting them directly (ps.-Gal. *Int.* 9.6 [xiv 699 K]). The elemental qualities, hot, cold, wet, and dry, can alter the quality of this pneuma, and when it departs from its natural state to such an extent that the body's functioning is impaired, disease results (Gal. *CC* 2 [CMG Suppl. Or. II pp. 54–56, 134]). The pneuma can be altered either directly by the external environment, for example being heated by the sun or chilled by a cold bath, or internally through excessively hot, cold, wet, or dry fluids that can come to be within the body, such as drugs, venoms, or a surplus of blood.

It was Athenaeus's general analysis of disease causation that was to become one of his most lasting contributions to medical theory. The pneuma, which according to Stoic doctrine holds together and sustains (*sunechein*) the world and its inhabitants, thus became at the human level the "sustaining" (*sunektikon*) cause of disease (and presumably also of health). The external factors that led to alterations of the "sustaining" pneuma's quality, such as heat from the sun, were termed by Athenaeus "antecedent" (*prokatarktika*) causes, while the internal factors, such as drugs, which affected the pneuma from within the body, were termed "preceding" (*proēgoumena*) causes. This intrinsically Stoic analysis was nevertheless reconfigured by later, non-Pneumatist doctors who had no use for natural pneuma or any other Stoicizing elements.[18] Accordingly, the "sustaining" (*sunektikon*) cause came to describe generally, in pathological contexts, any cause that was directly correlated to and cotemporal with the disease it produced, as opposed to the "antecedent" (*prokatarktika*) causes which came earlier in the causal chain, were external, and did not invariably bring about disease—the "preceding" (*proēgoumena*) causes, although referred to by some doctors such as Galen, apparently reflected a distinction which was not found so useful.

Athenaeus was also to side with the Stoics in other philosophical debates in which doctors had increasingly come to be embroiled. A conspicuous example is his location of the ruling-part-of-the-soul in the heart (Gal. *MM* 13.21 [x 929 K]).[19] Athenaeus can thus be seen following in the footsteps of Stoics such as Chrysippus and Diogenes of Babylon, who did not see the anatomy and physiology of the nervous system as fatal to their cardiocentric psychology (for Stoic arguments which apparently seek to reconcile their doctrine with the discovery of the nervous system, see Gal. *PHP* 2.5.69–70, 2.8.44 [*CMG* V 4,1,2 pp. 140, 164–166 De Lacy]).

There is no extant evidence that Athenaeus himself actually went to Rome, but his teachings were to have a significant impact there, especially through the figures of Agathinus of Sparta and Archigenes of Apamea. These doctors, on the other hand, are often referred to as "eclectics" of one kind or another, for adding to their Pneumatist doctrine elements from other medical traditions.[20]

It may be noted that there is no question of Asclepiades or Athenaeus being thought of as Epicurean or Stoic philosophers. Antiochus's reaction to Asclepiades quoted above is illuminating in this regard: for whatever reason, Antiochus apparently chose not to name him, yet recognized him as someone with interesting things to say, though not as a properly philosophical authority. Both doctors seem to have approached philosophical issues from a self-consciously medical perspective, but believed that medicine had a real contribution to make to such questions as the nature of the soul. On the other hand, Asclepiades seems to have been happy to make changes to some fundamental tenets of Epicureanism, while Athenaeus was apparently concerned to defend at least some core aspects of Stoic orthodoxy.

THE EMPIRICISTS

A rather different model of medicophilosophical participation developed within the Empiricist sect in the Roman period. Instead of merely drawing on contemporary philosophical systems, selecting from and modifying them for their own particular medical needs, Empiricists were actually to become merged, in the case of certain individuals at least, with a particular tradition, that of Pyrrhonian Skepticism. By the second century CE at the latest, we see leading figures who are identified not only as Empiricist doctors, but also as Pyrrhonists, the most famous example being Sextus Empiricus.[21]

The Empiricist sect came into being in the early- to mid-third century BCE, in reaction to the new physiologies of Herophilus and Erasistratus, which had been based on a range of groundbreaking anatomical discoveries. A pupil of Herophilus, Philinus of Cos, seems to have rejected their whole approach to medicine, involving as it did an attempt to understand in detail the way in which the body functioned, as a prerequisite for knowing how to cure it when this functioning went wrong. Philinus and his followers maintained that, in order to recognize an effective treatment, it was necessary to observe *that* it worked, not to develop a speculative account of *why* it worked.[22] The only thing that could be relied on invariably was direct experience (*empeiria*, after which they named themselves *Empeirikoi*). In fact, in their view all accepted treatments had been discovered effectively by accident, and they had become accepted only because they had been observed to work on a number of occasions under the same circumstances. Accordingly, the medical art could eventually be fully realized by building up a collection of remedies which were known to be successful for each and every condition, either from one's own personal experience as a doctor, or from the documented and corroborated experiences of others.[23] The whole project of the "Rationalists" (*Logikoi/Dogmatikoi*), as the Empiricists themselves labeled their rivals collectively, to discover the body's functions and the hidden causes of disease was in their view entirely unnecessary.[24] But they also alleged that the Rationalist project was not even *capable* of producing results, since the various representatives, such as Erasistrateans and Herophileans, were unable to reach any agreement about what the hidden causes of disease might be.

While their charge of an undecidable dispute among the Rationalists obviously coheres well with skeptical strategies, there is no sign of any direct connections with the Skepticism developing in the Athenian Academy at this time, and the Empiricists evidently entertained no doubts about the truth of what they ascertained through experience. The roots of Empiricism may lie rather in debates over the relative merits of art vs. experience (*technē* vs. *empeiria*).[25] At the beginning of his *Metaphysics*, for instance, Aristotle distinguished between doctors who rely only on experience of curing individuals and those who have a theory (*logos*) of how their cures work, adding that it is better to have only experience than only theory as far as practice is concerned (*Metaph.* A 1, 981a 12–24). Early surviving Empiricist critiques similarly appear to focus on the Rationalists' rhetorical skill and obsession with theory, and their supposed helplessness when faced with the actual practicalities of healing: they are like those who think they can learn to sail from books.[26] Empiricism certainly became more and more sophisticated throughout the Hellenistic period, primarily in response to sustained attacks from such theorists as Erasistratus, Asclepiades, and Athenaeus. Criticisms often centred around the extent to which the Empiricists were entitled to claim to manage without the use of reason (*logos*), and to rely only on sense perception and memory. At some point, for example, the Empiricists made a concession that there was a kind of reasoning that they employed, but it was only an everyday kind, enjoyed by everyone and licensing only basic inferences concerning observable states of affairs; to this they gave the name *epilogismos*, and contrasted it sharply with the kind of formal reasoning they attributed to the Rationalists, *analogismos*, which involved inference from what can be observed to what is hidden or obscure.[27]

On the other hand, Aenesidemus's development of Pyrrhonian Skepticism in the early first century BCE seems to have been motivated principally by his discontent with the Dogmatic turn taking place within the contemporary Academy, of which he had been a member.[28] Pyrrhonism did not emerge from medical Empiricism, but developed independently and only subsequently joined forces with it.[29] All of these considerations help to explain the rather loose fit that Empiricism and Pyrrhonism appear to exhibit and the tensions that evidently arose when attempts were made to make them cohere. An obvious problem was the Empiricists' apparently unquestioning faith in the data given to them by experience, in contrast to the Pyrrhonists' highlighting of the conflict between sense perceptions. Similarly the Empiricists were said to claim that hidden matters are by nature inapprehensible (cf., e.g., Celsus, *Med.* pref. 27–28 = fr. 14 Deichgräber), in contrast to the Pyrrhonists' universal suspension of judgment. Moreover, Sextus Empiricus seems to run into difficulties in his discussion of sign-inference (*Pyr.* 2.97–133, *Math.* 8.141–299), where he employs the originally Empiricist distinction between indicative signs, which are used to reveal what is nonevident, and commemorative signs, which are used to reveal what is only temporarily or contingently nonevident, but has been observed together with the sign in the past. As has been long recognized, the arguments recorded by Sextus appear to be as damaging to the Empiricists' own use of signs as to that of their stated targets.[30] Yet the Pyrrhonian Empiricists evidently did not regard such problems, insofar as they were acknowledged, as insurmountable, and it is worth noting that the most prominent Pyrrhonian Empiricists, Menodotus and Sextus Empiricus, are said to have "fortified [Empiricism] with precision" (*akribōs ekratunan*) (ps.-Gal. *Int.* 4.2 [14.683–84 K = fr. 6 Deichgräber]). Even if not all Empiricist doctors in the second century CE became Pyrrhonists, nor vice-versa, there was evidently an influential group that identified a common purpose and believed their respective interests could be served through direct collaboration.[31]

The Methodists

Methodism can helpfully be seen as an attempt to circumvent the apparent epistemological impasse reached by the Empiricists and their Rationalist rivals by the end of the Hellenistic era.[32] We are told that Asclepiades' most successful pupil, Themison of Laodicea, made changes to his master's teaching in old age, which we have no reason to believe took place anywhere but in Rome, in the early- to mid-first century BCE. Under the influence of Asclepiades' analysis of the human body as a complex structure of invisible particles rebounding in void space, Themison retained a general conception of it as a sponge-like substance susceptible to being condensed or rarefied. Yet he seems to have divested the analysis of most of its theoretical content: that is, there is no sign that the invisible particles or void of Asclepiades' theory played any direct role in Themison's or his followers' pathology.[33] Later in Rome, during the reign of Nero, Thessalus of Tralles appears to have rejuvenated the sect to an extent and introduced a number of more or less fundamental modifications to the basic system that Themison set up.[34]

The fundamental tenet of Methodism was that there are three basic "common features" (*koinotētes*) that can be observed in all the variety of diseases that befall humans: one is a state of constriction, in which the body is too constricted or compacted to allow the proper movement of bodily fluids; another is a state of laxity or looseness, in which fluids move too easily within the body and are excessively dissipated; while a third state is a mixture of these two, where one predominates in one part of the body, the other elsewhere. These salient common features are not to be thought of as the causes of conventional diseases such as phrenitis or epilepsy, but as concomitant traits that help to account for the impairment experienced in illness (cf., e.g., Sor. *Gyn.* 3.1.2).

Two characteristics of the common features of disease were crucial for the Methodists. The first is the fact that they happen to be evident. It may require some Methodist training to become fully practiced in identifying them correctly in every case, but nevertheless they are there for all to see.[35] The second is that they immediately and straightforwardly indicate to the doctor how they are to be treated, for excessive constriction is obviously to be counteracted by relaxing, and excessive laxity by constriction. By this process of "indication" (*endeixis*) the treatment is immediately and incontrovertibly suggested to the doctor, without the need for rational reflection or any external theoretical support. Nor is it by repeated experience of its effectiveness that the Methodist knows that he must relax a constricted state and constrict a relaxed one—it is simply self-evident.[36]

The observation of these common features therefore represented a kind of methodology which made the epistemological debates of the Rationalists and Empiricists redundant, at least insofar as therapy is concerned. Using their Method, the Methodists felt able to bypass speculative theories about hidden causes or processes such as the Rationalists relied on. They could also claim to be able to come up with a reliable treatment in any given case of disease, without having to resort to lists of recorded therapies or the contingencies of previous experience as the Empiricists did, and for which they were criticized by the Rationalists. The Method enabled its practitioners to discover appropriate treatments for any disease using a straightforward procedure based on direct observation. In consequence, certain Methodists claimed for their brand of medicine the status of a science (*epistēmē*), as opposed to that of a mere craft (*technē*) (ps.-Gal. *Int.* 5.1 [xiv 684–85 K = fr. 284 Tecusan]).

It has often been assumed that the Methodists, like the Empiricists, used skeptical strategies to cast doubt on the Rationalist approach to medicine, and to question their epistemological claims. However, the evidence does not generally appear to bear this out. It seems rather that the Methodists were actively trying to avoid getting embroiled in the epistemological issues that beleaguered the disputes between the Rationalists and Empiricists. While they claimed not to partake in Rationalist inquiries into nonevident matters, they were also concerned to distance themselves carefully from the Empiricists' attitude, as for example Galen confirms (*SI* 6 [1.82 K = fr. 203 Tecusan]):

> [The Methodists] also say that they do not even agree with the Empiricists in the manner in which they occupy themselves solely with what is apparent: for, they say, the Empiricists will have nothing to do with what is not manifest, claiming that it is *unknowable*, whereas they themselves will have nothing to do with what is not manifest because it is *useless*. (tr. Frede)

Hence it was not because of the inherent untrustworthiness of the Rationalists' theories that they were avoided, but simply because they were unnecessary for therapy: the Method offered a much more straightforward route to the correct treatment.[37] The Methodist doctor, in treating patients, is obliged to *ignore* theories about hidden matters, but he is not obliged to *doubt* them. Moreover, there is plenty of evidence confirming that individual Methodists held all sorts of dogmatic views about hidden matters, which, presumably, they did not see as contributing directly to therapy. Soranus of Ephesus (*fl.* c. CE 100) is a prominent example for whom we happen to have a fair amount of evidence. According to Tertullian, who used Soranus's treatise *On the Soul* in composing his own similarly titled work, Soranus believed that the soul is corporeal and nourished by corporeal matter, that it is therefore mortal, and that it has seven parts (Tert. *De anim.* 6.6, 8.3, 14.2, 38.3). Similarly, for example, he argued that the female seed does not contribute to generation (Sor. *Gyn.* 1.12). Geoffrey Lloyd has also drawn attention to the distinctly unskeptical approach Soranus takes in his *Gynaecia* in general.[38] It is very difficult to see how these sorts of views could be at all compatible with a generally skeptical outlook.

The key text which has been thought to reveal a connection between Methodism and Skepticism is Sextus Empiricus's discussion of the relationship between Pyrrhonian Skepticism and medical Empiricism. Sextus states that if Empiricism involves a dogmatic assertion of the inapprehensibility of what is nonevident, then it is not the same as Skepticism, and it would be more appropriate for the Skeptic to follow the Method (*Pyr.* 1.236). Since there were indeed un-Skeptical forms of Empiricism that did involve negatively dogmatic claims of the sort Sextus mentions here, it is possible to read his words as a preliminary to promoting a more Skeptical form of Empiricism that did not involve such assertions. Yet an explicit promotion of this kind never materializes; instead, Sextus immediately goes on to describe in detail at least some ways in which Methodist approaches could be seen to line up quite well with the Pyrrhonist's outlook (*Pyr.* 1.237–241).[39] However, if Sextus was indeed advocating a link between Pyrrhonism and Methodism here, we have little reason to believe that he further developed it in any way. Diogenes Laertius (who may have been a near-contemporary) certainly regarded both Sextus and his pupil Saturninus as belonging firmly to the Empiricist tradition, and as we have noted the pseudo-Galenic author of the *Introduction* described both him and Menodotus as having fortified Empiricism (Diog. Laert. 9.116; ps.-Gal. *Int.* 4.2 [14.683–84 K]). It remains very difficult to be sure just what Sextus had in mind in his discussion of Methodism. Nevertheless, perhaps the more important point for present purposes is that there is no sign whatsoever in our sources of any *Methodists* showing interest in aligning themselves with Pyrrhonism; nor is it easy to see what benefits there could have been for them in doing so, especially given the difficulties faced by the Empiricists.

Galen

By the second century CE, then, the Epicureans, the Stoics, and the Pyrrhonian Skeptics had made a direct impact on a variety of approaches to healing, in the latter case even extending to a partial coalescence with the Empiricist medical sect. Galen of Pergamum, more than any other doctor we know of, embodies the influence of contemporary Platonism and Aristotelianism.[40] Initially trained for a career in philosophy, Galen had been taught in his youth by representatives of all the major schools, before his father received a dream from Asclepius recommending the study of medicine too (e.g., Gal. *Ord. Lib. Prop.* 4.4 [xix 59 K]). His outlook was certainly shaped by the syncretist tendencies of his day, especially within Middle Platonism.[41] His distinctive strategy, however, was to maintain that wherever Plato and Aristotle had got things right (and he certainly did not think that either was always right), they had in fact been anticipated to a considerable degree by the great medical authority of Hippocrates. In practice, then, Galen had a tendency to read chosen Hippocratic texts in light of his own philosophical commitments, and he was more likely to be sympathetic to aspects of his preferred philosophies if he could find plausible parallels in the Hippocratic Corpus, naturally aided by its considerable diversity.[42] Thus, for example, Galen's elemental theory was basically Aristotelian, but he traced it to the Hippocratic treatise *On the Nature of Man*, merging it with the four-humor theory found there.[43] He developed views on a very wide range of subjects in physics and metaphysics, in which his medical theories were firmly grounded, though he refrained from expressing opinions on such questions as the substance of the soul or the origins of the cosmos, which he believed did not admit of certain answers, but which were also, happily, inapplicable to medicine (e.g., Gal. *Prop. Plac.* 1–3, 7 [pp. 172–73, 178–79 Boudon-Millot and Pietrobelli]).

Galen's commitment to Hippocratic authority was matched by his commitment to the findings of anatomy, and naturally he attempted to establish Hippocrates' expertise in this field as well.[44] A resurgence in systematic animal dissection had taken place around 100 CE, and Galen was to follow this trend, making a number of important discoveries of his own.[45] He was eager to apply these results to philosophical questions as far as possible. He believed, for one, that an important use of anatomy was to demonstrate the intelligence and providential artifice of Nature, to which Galen was very strongly committed (*AA* 2.2 [2.286–87 K]). His teleology, with its consciously acting Demiurge, owed more in broad terms to Plato's *Timaeus* than to Aristotle, but his functional anatomy, as set out in his great hymn to Nature *On the Utility of the Parts*, is in the tradition of the latter's *Parts of Animals*, although Galen strove for even greater comprehensiveness than Aristotle in working out the functions of individual anatomical features.[46] Galen also believed that anatomical knowledge could furnish a proof of the Platonic tripartite analysis of the soul. His treatise *On the Opinions of Hippocrates and Plato* contains an extended demonstration, based in part on Herophilus's discovery of the nervous system and its role in mediating sensation and voluntary motion, that the rational, controlling part of the soul resides in the brain; that the spirited soul resides in the heart; and, based on self-confessedly less probative grounds, that the desiderative soul resides in the liver.[47] As the title leads one to expect, this treatise was devoted to establishing not only that Plato was right, but also that Plato had derived his sound theories ultimately from Hippocrates.

Despite Galen's rather eclectic approach, the medical system he constructed was marked by a remarkable internal consistency. Underpinning the whole was Galen's abiding commitment to logic.[48] He wrote a considerable range of logical works, not least his 15-book *On Demonstration*, which is unfortunately lost, although he had little time for logic as a subject of study in its own right, maintaining a firm conviction of its usefulness strictly as a tool for philosophical or scientific discovery.[49] He looked to geometrical demonstration as a paradigm, which he tells us rescued him in his youth from succumbing to Pyrrhonism (*Lib. Prop.* 14 [19.39–40 K]). He drew directly on Peripatetic and Stoic traditions in logic, and the so-called demonstrative or "apodeictic" method that he championed largely developed out of these, though his thinking on logic was not merely derivative, and he made some important contributions.[50]

For Galen, his use of the demonstrative method meant emancipation from the medical sects, which had encouraged, in his view, a kind of uncritical or slavish adherence to a particular approach or set of doctrines. Thus his (lost) treatise *On the Best Sect* in fact contained a defense of the necessity of employing the demonstrative method in medicine in general (e.g., *Ord. Lib. Prop.* 1 [19.50–52 K]). On the other hand, there seems to be little in broad terms to distinguish his own intention to develop a new medical system from the projects of his Rationalist predecessors such as Athenaeus or Asclepiades (although, in contrast to them, the evidence for followers who might have constituted a comparable "Galenist" sect is unclear). His approach was, as he acknowledged, that of a Rationalist, in that he employed reason, but he also had some sympathy for the Empiricists' dependence only on experience, which he felt could indeed produce an adequate medical art, though not a perfected one. His methodological commitment to the need for theories developed by reason to be tested against relevant empirical data has been hailed as an important precursor to the experimental method.

Galen's interests were not confined to the physical and logical branches of philosophy. Unusually for a physician, he also wrote on ethics, and of course believed that it was necessary for the practice of medicine (*Opt. Med.*). Unfortunately, again, most of the relevant writings are now lost (see esp. *Lib. Prop.* 15 and 19 [19.45–46, 48 K]), but there are some important exceptions in moral psychology, such as *Character Traits*, and in the recently rediscovered *On Avoiding Distress*.[51]

The influence which Galenism had on the Western medical tradition can hardly be overstated, but he was also to have an impact on philosophy. For instance, Galen's views on a number of areas were of interest to his contemporary Alexander of Aphrodisias, and although the surviving evidence largely reports Alexander's criticisms, it is clear that Galen was an authority with whom the philosopher needed to engage.[52] Galen was also to have a considerable impact in general on late antique philosophy, in particular Neoplatonism.[53] For example, another, apparently more positive, response to Galen was that of John Philoponus, who wrote commentaries on Galenic works, notably *On the Utility of the Parts*, and praised his expertise in natural philosophy in the context of his medical system.[54]

Throughout the Roman period, the most influential and apparently most successful approaches to medicine deliberately and self-consciously drew inspiration from contemporary philosophies. In the case of certain Empiricists at least, this extended even to amalgamation with Pyrrhonian Skepticism. Otherwise, however, medical practitioners retained a strong sense of their position and role as quite distinct from the philosophers'. Although they felt they had the expertise to encroach on the philosophers' turf in some areas, such as on the soul's interactions with the body, they were also more than content to leave certain inquiries untouched as irrelevant to the goals of the medical art. On some issues they engaged directly in criticizing philosophers, and were at times taken seriously by their philosophical opponents, yet the general impression is of doctors and philosophers operating in largely separate spheres. Nevertheless, there was a clear sense in the Roman period that medicine needed to be philosophically informed, and although there is a willingness to be selective and innovative, when new approaches to healing were developed it was repeatedly to contemporary philosophy that doctors looked for inspiration.

Notes

1. For general overviews, see the introduction to van der Eijk (2005) and van der Eijk (2008).
2. On the changing nature of the medical sects in the Hellenistic period, see von Staden (1982); for the development of medical sects in the first century BCE, see Flemming (2012); for their general expansion and reach, see Leith (2016).

3. For Herophilus and the Herophileans, see esp. von Staden (1989); for Erasistratus, Garofalo (1988).
4. See, e.g., Smith (1979); Tieleman (1996); von Staden (1997); Allen (2001a); Tecusan (2004) 29–36. All references to Galenic and ps.-Galenic writings follow the abbreviations set out in Hankinson, ed. (2008a) appendix 1.
5. On Asclepiades's life and significance, see esp. Rawson (1982) and Flemming (2012).
6. The issue of Asclepiades's debts to Epicureanism has been the subject of considerable controversy: in an important study, Vallance (1990) argued that Asclepiades's theory of matter is not at all to be regarded as Epicurean; in Leith (2009) and (2012) I aimed to demonstrate that the *onkoi* are directly based on Epicurean atoms, and that Asclepiades held a distinctively Epicurean theory of void.
7. See Leith (2009) 305–318.
8. See Vallance (1990) 108–117.
9. For Asclepiades's critique, see esp. John of Alexandria, *In librum de sectis Galeni* 4rb70–4va64 [pp. 49–50, 52 Pritchet]; Gal. *SI* 5 [i 75 K]; Sext. Emp. *Math.* 8.6–7; and the first four chapters of Gal. *Med. Exp.*
10. While Erasistratus had referred much of the fluid motion in the body to the natural tendency of matter to fill up an area that is being vacated, massed void being an impossibility for him, Asclepiades replaced this with a parallel principle based on his own theory of matter, according to which the *onkoi* will naturally drift into an adjacent area of void space, given that they are already in perpetual motion.
11. See Leith (2009) 300–305.
12. For the lack of evidence for Herophilus's and Erasistratus's direct interest in the soul itself, see Leith (2020a) 45–48.
13. The precise implications of this theory are difficult to tease out from the evidence. Polito (2006) makes a case for a radical reconceptualization on Asclepiades's part of the way in which the mind works, with higher mental functions explained ultimately in terms of bodily processes, and anticipating in certain respects modern materialistic accounts of the mind.
14. For Artorius, see Leith (2020b); for Musa, Michler (1993).
15. Sedley (1998) 69n40 and 72n51, effectively counters arguments for Lucretius's engagement with Asclepiades. A more recent attempt to link Philodemus with Asclepiades's account of pain may be found in Pearcy (2012).
16. The fundamental study remains Wellmann (1895); see now Coughlin and Lewis (2020).
17. It is significant too that Athenaeus's Hellenistic predecessors Herophilus and Erasistratus ruled out the inquiry into the fundamental elements as irrelevant to medicine, belonging properly only to natural philosophy: see Leith (2015) esp. 487n57.
18. On the problems in understanding the precise relationship of this scheme to the Stoic analysis of causation, as well as the details of its later influence, see Hankinson (1987a) and (1999).
19. For various aspects of Athenaeus's psychology, see Coughlin (2018).
20. See, e.g., Flemming (2000) 87–88; Coughlin and Lewis (2020). Aretaeus of Cappadocia is often wrongly regarded as a Pneumatist, and his conception of pneuma as inhaled air is quite distinct from Athenaeus's Stoic pneuma: Flemming (2000) 188–190.
21. Diog. Laert. 9.116 provides a list of successors of Pyrrhonism, including a number of people who are identified, or who can be identified from other sources, as Empiricist doctors, such as Menodotus of Nicomedia, Theodas of Laodicea, and Sextus (although, as

we shall see in the next section, his case is not straightforward). On Menodotus, see Perilli (2004).
22. On medical Empiricism, see Hankinson (1987b); Frede (1987a) and (1988); Guardasole (1997). The fragments are collected and discussed in Deichgräber (1965).
23. A third means of establishing effective treatment was distinguished by later Empiricists, namely the "transition to the similar" (*metabasis tou homoiou*), according to which the doctor, when faced with an unfamiliar condition, could test a therapy by trying out remedies which had been successful against a condition which was observed to be similar in some relevant respect.
24. The Empiricists also attacked the practice of dissection, in particular human vivisection, as cruel, misguided and unnecessary (see esp. Celsus, *Med.* pref. 40–44 = fr. 14 Deichgräber; Cic. *Acad. Post.* 2.122 = fr. 66 Deichgräber).
25. See Schiefsky (2005) 345–359.
26. Esp. Polyb. 12.25D. Galen was later to allege that in fact the Rationalists and Empiricists were largely in agreement in terms of the treatments they actually used, differing principally in the path by which they arrived at them (e.g., Gal. *SI* 7 [1.15 K]), but this is likely to reflect Galen's strategy of pairing off the Rationalists and Empiricists against the Methodists. It is clear from such texts as Caelius Aurelianus's *On Acute Diseases* and *On Chronic Diseases*, for example, that there were fierce disagreements between all sects over therapies.
27. The late Hellenistic Empiricists did make some impression on contemporary debates concerning sign-inference, as Philodemus makes clear in his, admittedly rather dismissive, reference to their views at *Sign.* 60 [*P. Herc.* 1065 col. xxxviii 25–32].
28. See Mansfeld (1995), addressing earlier debate.
29. Although Aenesidemus is reported to have been taught by one Heraclides at Diog. Laert. 9.116, there seems no particular reason to identify this individual with the famous Empiricist Heraclides of Tarentum.
30. For a detailed discussion, see Allen (2001b) 87–146.
31. Polito (2006) speculates on the possible benefits in terms of patronage that Pyrrhonists might have gained by being aligned with medical Empiricism.
32. On Methodism in general, see esp. Edelstein (1967); Frede (1987b); Gourevitch (1991); Pigeaud (1993); van der Eijk (2005b). The fragments are collected in Tecusan (2004).
33. Attempts have been made to map the Methodists' common feature of constriction onto Asclepiades's theory of blockage (*enstasis*) as the cause of disease, and the common feature of laxity onto an alternative explanation Asclepiades reserved for certain conditions: see Vallance (1990) 131–143. However, given that most diseases in Asclepiades's pathology involve both blockage and a swift movement of particles toward the affected area, it seems preferable to interpret his influence on Themison in looser, more conceptual terms.
34. On Themison's and Thessalus's respective contributions to Methodism, see Pigeaud (1993).
35. Thessalus, for example, claimed that he could teach medicine in a matter of six months (e.g., Gal. *MM* 1.1 [10.4–5 K = fr. 155 Tecusan]).
36. The Methodists saw their use of "indication" as one of the main points distinguishing them from the Empiricists: cf., e.g., Gal. *SI* 6 [1.82.2–4 K], "however much they may occupy themselves with what is apparent, they are separated from the Empiricists by their use of indication," tr. Frede.
37. Cf. van der Eijk (2005b) 326: "it is simply not true that the Methodists do not wish to commit themselves to the existence, or the occurrence, of unobservable entities or

processes, and there is no indication that they believe that knowledge about the invisible is *impossible*. It is rather that they prefer not to build their therapy on such speculations or commitments; but this is a matter of *preference*, based on the criterion of relevance, rather than a matter of unqualified rejection based on the belief that such commitments would necessarily be uncertain" (original emphasis).

38. Lloyd (1983) 182–200.
39. Allen (2010) examines the potential attractions for the Pyrrhonist of Empiricism or Methodism.
40. For recent studies of his relationship to Middle Platonism and Aristotelian philosophy, see the contributions by Chiaradonna and van der Eijk respectively in Gill et al. (2009); for his attitude to the Stoics, see Tieleman's essay in the same volume. For studies on Galen's relationship to philosophy in general, see Donini (1992); Barnes and Jouanna (2003); Adamson et al. (2014).
41. On Galen's eclecticism, see Hankinson (1992).
42. Smith (1979); Lloyd (1991).
43. See esp. Gal. *Hipp. Elem.*, with Hankinson (2008b) and Kupreeva (2014).
44. Galen makes a number of remarkable claims about the state of anatomical knowledge in Hippocrates's time (e.g., *AA* 2.1 [2.280–83 K]), and he devoted an (unfortunately lost) treatise to showing the superiority of Hippocratic anatomy, *On Anatomy according to Hippocrates*.
45. E.g., Rocca (2008).
46. For the distinctiveness of Galen's teleology, see Schiefsky (2007).
47. For Galen's demonstration in *PHP* and its context, see Tieleman (1996).
48. Morison (2008).
49. Recent reconstructions of various aspects of Galen's *On Demonstration* may be found in Chiaradonna (2009b); Havrda (2011) and (2015).
50. Hankinson (1994).
51. Analyzed and translated in Singer (2013).
52. See recently, e.g., Harari (2016).
53. E.g., Tieleman (1998); Chiaradonna (2009b); Wilberding (2014).
54. Todd (1977); Strohmaier (2003).

References

Adamson, P., R. Hansberger, and J. Wilberding, eds. (2014). *Philosophical Themes in Galen*. (London).
Algra, K., J. Barnes, J. Mansfeld, and M. Schofield, eds. (1999). *The Cambridge History of Hellenistic Philosophy*. (Cambridge).
Allen, J. (2001a). "Galen as (Mis)informant about the Views of His Predecessors," *Archiv für Geschichte der Philosophie* 83: 81–89.
Allen, J. (2001b). *Inference from Signs: Ancient Debates about the Nature of Evidence*. (Oxford).
Allen, J. (2010). "Pyrrhonism and Medicine," in Bett, 232–248.
Ayers, L., ed. (1995). *The Passionate Intellect*. (New Brunswick, N.J.).
Barnes, J., and J. Jouanna, eds. (2003). *Galien et la philosophie*. (Geneva).
Bett, R., ed. (2010). *The Cambridge Companion to Ancient Scepticism*. (Cambridge).
Boudon-Millot, V., and A. Pietrobelli, eds. (2005). "Galien ressuscité: édition *princeps* du texte grec du *De propriis placitis*," *Revue des études grecs* 118: 168–213.

Chiaradonna, R. (2009a). "Galen and Middle Platonism," in Gill et al., 243–260.
Chiaradonna, R. (2009b). "Le traité de Galien *Sur la démonstration* et sa postérité tardo-antique," in R. Chiaradonna and F. Trabattoni (eds.), *Physics and Philosophy of Nature in Greek Neoplatonism* (Leiden), 43–77.
Coughlin, S. (2018). "Athenaeus of Attalia on the Psychological Causes of Bodily Health," in C. Thumiger and P. Singer (eds.), *Mental Illness in Ancient Medicine: From Celsus to Paul of Aegina* (Leiden), 109–142.
Coughlin, S., and O. Lewis (2020). "Pneuma and the Pneumatist School of Medicine," in S. Coughlin, D. Leith, and O. Lewis (eds.), *The Concept of Pneuma after Aristotle* (Berlin), 203–236.
Curd, P., and D. W. Graham, eds. (2008). *The Oxford Handbook of Presocratic Philosophy*. (Oxford).
Deichgräber, K. (^{2}1965). *Die griechische Empirikerschule. Sammlung der Fragmente und Darstellung der Lehre*. (Berlin-Zurich).
Donini, P. L. (1992). "Galeno e la filosofia." *ANRW* II, 36(5): 3484–3504.
Edelstein, L. (1967). "The Methodists," in Temkin and Temkin, 173–191.
Flemming, R. (2000). *Medicine and the Making of Roman Women*. (Oxford).
Flemming, R. (2012). "Antiochus and Asclepiades: Medical and Philosophical Sectarianism at the End of the Hellenistic Era," in Sedley, 55–79.
Frede, M. (1987). *Essays in Ancient Philosophy*. (Oxford).
Frede, M. (1987a). "The Ancient Empiricists," in Frede, 243–260.
Frede, M. (1987b). "The Method of the So-Called Methodical School of Medicine," in Frede, 261–278.
Frede, M. (1988). "The Empiricist Attitude towards Reason and Theory," in Hankinson, 79–97.
Frede, M., and R. Walzer (1985). *Galen: Three Treatises on the Nature of Science*. (Indianapolis).
Garofalo, I. (1988). *Erasistrati Fragmenta*. (Pisa).
Gill, C., T. Whitmarsh, and J. Wilkins, eds. (2009). *Galen and the World of Knowledge*. (Cambridge).
Gourevitch, D. (1991). "La pratique méthodique," in Mudry and Pigeaud, 51–81.
Guardasole, A. (1997). *Eraclide di Taranto. Frammenti*. (Naples).
Hankinson, R. J., ed. (1988). *Method, Medicine and Metaphysics. Studies in the Philosophy of Ancient Science*. (Edmonton).
Hankinson, R. J. (1987a). "Evidence, Externality and Antecedence: Inquiries into Later Greek Causal Concepts," *Phronesis* 32: 80–100.
Hankinson, R. J. (1987b). "Causes and Empiricism," *Phronesis* 32: 329–348.
Hankinson, R. J. (1992). "Galen's Philosophical Eclecticism," *ANRW* II, 36(5): 3505–3522.
Hankinson, R. J. (1994). "Galen and the Logic of Relations," in Schrenk (1994) 57–75.
Hankinson, R. J. (1999.) "Explanation and Causation," in Algra et al., 479–512.
Hankinson, R. J. (2008a). *The Cambridge Companion to Galen*. (Cambridge).
Hankinson, R. J. (2008b). "Philosophy of Nature," in Hankinson, 210–241.
Harari, O. (2016). "Alexander Against Galen on Motion: A Mere Logical Debate?" *Oxford Studies in Ancient Philosophy* 50: 201–236.
Harris, W. V., ed. (2016). *Popular Medicine in Graeco-Roman Antiquity: Explorations*. (Leiden).
Havrda, M. (2011). "Galenus Christianus? The Doctrine of Demonstration in *Stromata* VIII and the Question of Its Source." *Vigiliae Christianae* 65: 343–375.
Havrda, M. (2015). "The Purpose of Galen's Treatise *On Demonstration*." *Early Science and Medicine* 20: 265–287.

Kullmann, W., and S. Föllinger, eds. (1997). *Aristotelische Biologie: Intentionen, Methoden, Ergebnisse.* (Stuttgart).
Kupreeva, I. (2014). "Galen's Theory of Elements," in Adamson et al., 153–196.
Leith, D. (2009). "The Qualitative Status of the *Onkoi* in Asclepiades' Theory of Matter," *Oxford Studies in Ancient Philosophy* 36: 283–320.
Leith, D. (2012). "Pores and Void in Asclepiades' Physical Theory." *Phronesis* 57: 164–191.
Leith, D. (2015). "Elements and Uniform Parts in Early Alexandrian Medicine." *Phronesis* 60: 462–491.
Leith, D. (2016). "How Popular Were the Medical Sects?," in Harris, 231–250.
Leith, D. (2020a). "Herophilus and Erasistratus on the *Hēgemonikon*," in B. Inwood and J. Warren, (eds.), *Body and Soul in Hellenistic Philosophy* (Cambridge), 30–61.
Leith, D. (2020b). "Notes on Three Asclepiadean Doctors," in L. Totelin and R. Flemming, (eds.), *Medicine and Markets: Essays on Ancient Medicine in Honour of Vivian Nutton* (Cardiff), 127–141.
Lloyd, G. E. R. (1983). *Science, Folklore and Ideology.* (Cambridge).
Lloyd, G. E. R. (1991). "Galen on Hellenistics and Hippocrateans: Contemporary Battles and Past Authorities," in G.E.R. Lloyd (ed.), *Methods and Problems in Greek Science* (Cambridge), 398–416.
Mansfeld, J. (1995). "Aenesidemus and the Academics," in Ayers, 235–248.
Meyer, B. F., and E. P. Sanders, eds. (1982). *Jewish and Christian Self-definition,* III: *Self-definition in the Graeco-Roman World.* (London).
Michler, M (1993). "*Principis medicus*: Antonius Musa." *ANRW* II, 37(1): 757–785.
Morison, B. (2008.) "Logic," in Hankinson, 66–115.
Mudry, P., and J. Pigeaud, eds. (1991.) *Les écoles médicales à Rome.* (Geneva).
Pearcy, L. T. (2012.) "Does Dying Hurt? Philodemus of Gadara, *De Morte* and Asclepiades of Bithynia." *CQ* 62: 211–222.
Perilli, L. (2004). *Menodoto di Nicomedia: Contributo a una storia galeniana della medicina empirica.* (Leipzig).
Pigeaud, J. (1993). "L'introduction du Méthodisme à Rome." *ANRW* II, 37(1): 565–599.
Polito, R. (2006). "Matter, Medicine, and the Mind: Asclepiades vs. Epicurus." *Oxford Studies in Ancient Philosophy* 30: 285–335.
Pritchet, C. C., ed. (1982). *Iohannis Alexandrini Commentaria in librum De sectis Galeni.* (Leiden).
Rawson, E. (1982). "The Life and Death of Asclepiades of Bithynia." *CQ* 32: 358–370.
Rocca, J. (2008). "Anatomy," in Hankinson, 242–262.
Schiefsky, M. J. (2005). *Hippocrates, On Ancient Medicine.* (Leiden).
Schiefsky, M. J. (2007). "Galen's Teleology and Functional Explanation." *Oxford Studies in Ancient Philosophy* 33: 369–400.
Schrenk, L., ed. (1994). *Aristotle and Later Antiquity.* (Washington).
Sedley, D. (1998). *Lucretius and the Transformation of Greek Wisdom.* (Cambridge).
Sedley, D., ed. (2012). *The Philosophy of Antiochus.* (Cambridge).
Singer, P., ed. (2013). *Galen: Psychological Writings.* (Cambridge).
Smith, W. D. (1979). *The Hippocratic Tradition.* (Ithaca, N.Y.).
Strohmaier, G. (2003). "Der Kommentar des Johannes Grammaticus zu Galen, De usu partium (Buch 11), in einer unikalen Gothaer Handschrift," in G. Strohmaier (ed.), *Hellas im Islam* (Wiesbaden), 109–112.
Tecusan, M. (2004). *The Fragments of the Methodists. Volume One: Methodism outside Soranus.* (Leiden).

Temkin, O., and C. L. Temkin, eds. (1967). *Ancient Medicine: Selected Papers of Ludwig Edelstein*. (Baltimore).
Tieleman, T. (1996). *Galen and Chrysippus on the Soul. Argument and Refutation in the* De Placitis *Books II-III*. (Leiden).
Tieleman, T. (1998). "Plotinus on the Seat of the Soul: Reverberations of Galen and Alexander in *Enn.* IV, 3 [27], 23." *Phronesis* 43: 306–325.
Tieleman, T. (2009). "Galen and the Stoics, or: The Art of Not Naming," in Gill et al., 282–299.
Todd, R. B. (1977). "Galenic Medical Ideas in the Greek Aristotelian Commentators." *Symbolae Osloenses* 52: 117–134.
Vallance, J. (1990). *The Lost Theory of Asclepiades of Bithynia*. (Oxford).
van der Eijk, P. J. (2005a). *Medicine and Philosophy in Classical Antiquity*. (Cambridge).
van der Eijk, P. J. (2005b). "The Methodism of Caelius Aurelianus: Some Epistemological Issues," in van der Eijk, 299–327.
van der Eijk, P. J. (2008). "The Role of Medicine in the Formation of Early Greek Thought," in Curd and Graham, 385–412.
van der Eijk, P. J. (2009). "'Aristotle! What a Thing for You to Say!' Galen's Engagement with Aristotle and Aristotelians" in Gill et al., 261–281.
von Staden, H. (1982). "Hairesis and Heresy: the Case of the *haireseis iatrikai*," in Meyer and Sanders, 76–100, 199–206.
von Staden, H. (1989). *Herophilus: The Art of Medicine in Early Alexandria*. (Cambridge).
von Staden, H. (1997). "Teleology and Mechanism: Aristotelian Biology and Early Hellenistic Medicine," in Kullmann and Föllinger, 183–208.
Wellmann, M. (1895). *Die pneumatische Schule bis auf Archigenes*. (Berlin).
Wilberding, J. (2014). "Neoplatonism and Medicine," in S. Slaveva-Griffin and P. Remes, (eds.), *The Routledge Handbook of Neoplatonism* (Abingdon), 356–371.

CHAPTER 23

SEX

KURT LAMPE

> One may derive pleasure in a sex act from expressing certain feelings to one's partner or from awareness of the attitude of one's partner, but sexual desire is essentially desire for physical contact itself: it is a bodily desire for the body of another that dominates our mental life for more or less brief periods.
>
> —Alan H. Goldman (1977)

> The truth is that sexuality is everywhere: the way a bureaucrat fondles his records, a judge administers justice, a businessman causes money to circulate; the way the bourgeoisie fucks the proletariat; and so on.
>
> —Gilles Deleuze and Félix Guattari (1983)

BEFORE beginning to discuss the topic of sex in Roman philosophy, we must first ask what we mean by "sex," "sexual desire," "sexuality," and so on. This might appear to be a lexical issue: for instance, when ex-President Bill Clinton said "I did not have sexual relations with that woman,"[1] conventional American usage of the phrase "have sexual relations" should have determined what he meant, and thus whether his later admission of receiving a blow job made him a liar. If word usage were sufficient to identify the intensional and extensional domains of sex words, then in order to specify this chapter's remit, we would merely need to identify the ancient Greek and Latin words with which we were concerned. (Might a Roman Clinton have said *Ista cum muliere nequaquam coii*? In Greek, *ekeinēi g' oudamōs eplēsiasa*?[2])

But as my epigraphs exemplify, there is striking disagreement today about what sex words mean. At the same time, we are all familiar with how almost *any* word can become a sexual innuendo with the right context and intonation. It is this slipperiness that allowed Clinton to claim (however unconvincingly) that "sexual relations" does not include fellatio. Sex pervades language and behavior in complex and mysterious fashions. Theorists such as Alan H. Goldman, Gilles Deleuze, and Félix Guattari respond to this complexity in contrary ways: Goldman aims to clarify and rationalize the mystery, while Deleuze and Guattari want to exacerbate it in order to reform rationality. Between these extremes numerous theories have flourished, most resting on more or less explicit psychologies, philosophies of language, and even ethics, theologies, or metaphysics.

My own position is that the impulse to adjudicate among these popular usages and theories would be misguided. The topic can better be understood through a hermeneutical approach[3] that thoughtfully traces partial convergences as well as divergences in the way "sex" is invoked in different contexts. If space allowed, it would be rewarding to examine texts by authors from various philosophical affiliations and genres, such as Lucretius, Persius, and Plutarch. In this chapter, given space constraints, I focus on a single short text: Musonius Rufus's *On Sex*. I approach this text from three different theoretical perspectives, which I have adapted from virtue ethics, Michael Foucault's genealogy of "sexuality," and Julia Kristeva's psychoanalytic cultural criticism. It is my hope that this methodological diversity will give us a fuller and more flexible understanding of the meanings of "sex" in Roman philosophy.

Sexual Virtue Ethics

One place we might expect sex to be thematized is in discussions of the nature of happiness and the right attitudes and behavior for achieving it. For example, we might expect philosophers to indicate which partners, situations, or reasons for having sex are consonant with virtue, conducive to happiness, and therefore choiceworthy, and which are not. Let us call this "sexual virtue ethics" or simply "sexual ethics" for short.

In fact sustained discussions of sexual ethics are rare in Roman philosophy,[4] so we are fortunate that Stobaeus has preserved Musonius Rufus's *Peri Aphrodisiōn* (fr. 12 ed. Hense[5]). Gaius Musonius Rufus was a politically significant Roman *eques* and influential Stoic teacher of the first century CE, who probably left no writings behind, but about whom memoirs were written (in Greek) by an otherwise unknown "Lucius."[6] Although Lucius's memoirs do not appear to have fully captured the persuasive and intellectual powers of their subject,[7] he is our only source for this topic. Thus for the purposes of this chapter, by "Musonius" I will always mean the implied author of Lucius's reports. *Aphrodisia* etymologically means "things having to do with Aphrodite." Pragmatically speaking we can translate *Peri Aphrodisiōn* as *On Sex*, provided we keep in mind that the Greek word is associated with different ethical challenges and opportunities than the English one.[8]

I will begin by summarizing Musonius's arguments in this excerpt, then offer some thoughts about the sexual ethics that emerges. Musonius starts with the observation that "Not the smallest part of wantonness belongs to sexual pleasures," because wantons are fickle and shameless in their choice of partners (63.10–16). By contrast (63.17–64.4),

> People who aren't wanton or bad should only consider sexual acts to be just when they're carried out in marriage and for procreation, because they're legitimate. Sexual acts that seek mere pleasure are unjust and illegitimate, even if they're in marriage.

There are two key positions here. First, mere pleasure is not a just or legitimate motivation for having sex. Sex is just and legitimate only when it takes place in marriage and for the sake of procreation. It is unclear at this point whether he means that *both* of these conditions must obtain or that *either one* suffices.[9]

Musonius now surveys several classes of unjust and illegitimate sexual acts: adulterous and homosexual "embraces" (*sumplokai*) are "the most illegitimate" (64.4–7), but even nonadulterous heterosexual "intercourse" (*sunousiai*) is "shameful" if "it isn't done legitimately, because it's done through intemperance" (64.7–9). Here "legitimately" appears simply to mean "in marriage," as the sequel reveals: "If he has temperance," Musonius goes on, "no one would endure having sex [*plēsiazein*] even with a prostitute, even with a free woman outside of marriage, even, by Zeus, with his own slave-girl" (64.10–12). At this point it becomes unambiguously clear that Musonius's notional audience is composed entirely of men, for whom no unmarried woman of any kind is a legitimate sexual partner.

Musonius offers two proofs for this audacious claim. The first is that no man has sex with women from any of these categories openly "if he's able to blush even a little. Rather, people venture to do these things covertly and secretly, unless they're totally depraved." "Trying to hide" is an implicit admission of fault (65.14–66.2), so everyone who engages in these acts is at least unreflectively aware that he is somehow at fault. Second, Musonius argues that these sexual acts are unjust. He imagines someone objecting that whereas the adulterer "wrongs the husband of the corrupted woman," a man who sleeps with an unmarried woman or prostitute wrongs no one. Musonius responds that by implicitly admitting his fault, such a man also admits that he makes himself "worse and less honorable" (65.9). In short, he wrongs himself, and thus commits an injustice.

Musonius does not so much expect these initial arguments to be persuasive as to soften his audience for a more forceful attack: "But set aside injustice: certainly it's entirely necessary for intemperance to attach to the person who's overcome by shameful pleasure and delights in filth, like pigs" (65.11–66.2). Since his notional audience doubt extramarital sex is bad, Musonius presumably expects them to be taken aback by this name-calling. He is raising the stakes. But he has a follow-up argument prepared, which revolves around the scenario he expects his audience to find least objectionable: sex with slaves. If Musonius can show that even this is intemperate, a fortiori he will have shown that all sex outside of marriage is intemperate.

"If someone denies it's shameful or out of place for a master to have sex with his slave," he suggests, ". . . let him deliberate how it would appear if a mistress had sex with a male slave" (66.7–10). Well, that would obviously be "unbearable!" (66.11) It is implicit—but perhaps too sensitive to say—that mistresses should restrain themselves, although they may be tempted. So, men should also restrain themselves, especially since "I doubt anyone will esteem men worse than women, less able to train their desires than women" (66.13–15). After all, men claim to be "better" than women and to "be in charge." Training desires is the essence of temperance, just as neither training nor ruling them betokens lack of self-control (66.10–67.2). Thus masters who have sex outside of marriage, even with their slaves, are behaving more intemperately than mistresses who sleep with *their* slaves—i.e., "like pigs."

Setting aside Musonius's apparent sexism[10] and shocking insensitivity to the slaves' point of view,[11] for our purposes what is most noteworthy in this passage is the stringency of its emphasis on marriage and children.[12] Here one might remark that "conjugalist" and "procreationist" tendencies feature prominently in Western sexual morality, including Roger Scruton's relatively recent *Sexual Desire: A Philosophical Investigation*. However, it is important to insist that this superficial similarity rests on dissimilar conceptions of human well-being and its place in the universe.[13] In order to understand Musonius's specifically Roman and Stoic position, we need to consider how his beliefs about psychology, human virtues, and the relation of virtues to happiness underlie his choice of words and sequences of thought.

Let us start with the implicit connection Musonius makes between sexual ethics and psychology. "Not the smallest part of wantonness [*truphē*] belongs to sexual pleasures," he begins (63.10–16),

> because wantons need all sorts of sweethearts, not only legitimate but also illegitimate ones, not only females but also males, seeking different lovers at different times, not satisfied with what's easily available, but yearning for what's scarce, and pursuing unseemly embraces.

On the one hand, Musonius certainly assumes that "wantonness" is intrinsically and axiomatically bad, so that its association with promiscuity discredits the latter.[14] On the other, this passage also hints at a psychopathology common in Roman ethical writing. When people do not regulate their desires with an understanding of true happiness, they get no satisfaction from fulfilling them, so they are driven restlessly from place to place. Thus Musonius's wanton "seeks different lovers at different times." They entangle themselves in unnecessary troubles. Musonius's wanton is "not satisfied with what's easily available, but yearns for what's scarce." They even violate their own standards of decorum and dignity. Musonius's wanton "needs" "illegitimate" lovers (presumably including other people's wives[15]) and "pursues unseemly embraces." This pattern is so familiar to Musonius's listeners that he only sketches it briefly, and leaves its conclusion implicit: that such people, despite their devotion to pleasure, do not enjoy themselves, and ultimately do not even like themselves.[16]

Thus Musonius associates sexual promiscuity with an illness of the soul, which destroys the feeling of well-being. But he places greater emphasis on wantonness's pernicious effect on ethical character, a topic on which he expatiates in another excerpt (20.113.5–114.2):

> As for me, I'd rather be sick than wanton. Sickness only hurts the body, but wantonness corrupts both body and soul, bringing weakness and incapacity to the body and intemperance and cowardice to the soul. Wantonness even produces injustice, because it also produces greed. A wanton person can't help being luxurious; a luxurious person can't keep expenses down; someone with many wishes must try to acquire many things; and whoever tries to acquire many things has to be greedy and unjust,

because he can't get much by just means. There's also another way the wanton would certainly be unjust: he'd shrink from suffering what's fitting for his polis, or else he wouldn't be acting wantonly; and if it were necessary to undergo harm for his friends or family, he wouldn't endure it.

In this passage we see wantonness represented as incompatible with three of the four cardinal virtues to which Musonius constantly returns: courage, temperance, justice, and prudence (e.g., 4.16.10–12, 6.23.3–14, fr. 8 passim). For Stoics "living virtuously" is a common definition of happiness (e.g., LS 63A1, C1–2, D3), so it follows from the "corrupting" effects of wantonness that it destroys happiness.

One might object that not all instances of sexual promiscuity are motivated by wantonness, and thus are not associated with illness, cowardice, injustice, or intemperance. But Musonius also draws a direct connection between extramarital sex and two cardinal vices. The promiscuous man implicitly acknowledges his fault by concealing his behavior, and "whoever commits a fault, inasmuch as he commits a fault, becomes worse and less valuable" (65.9–10). Making yourself worse and less valuable amounts to "wronging" yourself (65.7), and thus to injustice. Extramarital sex also shows a man to be "less able to train his desires" than his wife (66.14–15), and therefore guilty of "intemperance" (*akolasia*, 64.9) and "lack of self-control" (*akrasia*, 66.19–20). Thus extramarital sex manifests two of the cardinal vices, and is incompatible with the happiness that consists of living according to virtue.

Modern readers may find the notions of mental health and virtue in the foregoing rather underdeveloped, culture-bound, and antiquated, so it is important to add that Musonius has one final argument for his position. This argument does not appear in *On Sex*, but can be inferred from *On Whether Marriage Is an Impediment to Philosophizing*. In the course of this vehement defense of marriage, Musonius argues that (14.71.11–72.2):

> Marriage appears to be natural, if anything is. Otherwise why did the craftsman of humanity first cut our race in two, then make two sets of genitalia, one female and one male, and create in us a powerful mutual desire for congress and sharing? And why did he mix in a powerful yearning of each for the other . . . ? Isn't it obvious that he wanted them to be together and live together and contrive a living together, and to cooperate in making and nourishing children?

The valorization of "companionate" marriage in this passage is representative of a trend in surviving Stoic texts, which begins in the second century BCE with Antipater of Tarsus's *On Marriage* and flourishes in the first- and second-century CE Roman Stoicism of Musonius, Seneca, and Hierocles.[17] For Musonius, as for other Stoics, this is once again a matter of living virtuously and therefore happily. "Living naturally," like "living virtuously," is a Stoic definition of happiness (LS 63A1); and since "nature" is simply one of the aspects of god,[18] "living naturally" can be redescribed as "doing everything on the basis of the concordance of each man's guardian spirit with the will of the administrator of the whole [i.e., god]" (LS 63C4). So when Musonius infers the naturalness of marriage from the divine craftsman's workmanship, he is attempting to think, feel, and act in harmony with god's will, and thus to live virtuously and happily. (His numerous references to "legitimate" [*nomimon*] and "illegitimate" [*paranoma*] behavior point in the same direction, since another aspect of god is cosmic "law" [*nomos*]: Diog. Laert. 7.87.)

Let us unpack this argument more carefully. Musonius takes it as given that every feature of our bodies is the result of divine purpose. Any educated Roman would recognize in the image of humanity "cut in two" by Zeus an allusion to Aristophanes' speech in Plato's *Symposium* (190c1–191a5),[19] but Musonius harnesses this complex, whimsical fable to a straightforward, serious claim: human bodies were designed for "congress" (*homilias*), as their "powerful desire" (*epithumian iskhuran*) corroborates. But this desire cannot be fulfilled by bodily congress alone; it is also a desire for "sharing" (*koinōnias*), which Musonius spells out as "being together," "living together," "contriving a living together," and "cooperating in making and nourishing children." This capacious desire for sharing blends with "yearning [*pothon*] for each other," which Valéry Laurand has thoughtfully glossed as "*désir du désir*": not the need to remedy a lack and thus become a unified "whole," as in Plato's *Symposium*, but rather a self-sustaining desire to participate in the conjugal dyad.[20] In short, Musonius has in mind an entire existential project shared by two people, who remain independent. Sex is designed to contribute to this project, which is threatened by whoever perverts this "powerful desire."[21]

Several scholars have noted that as the preeminent interpersonal relationship, marriage begins to occupy the place earlier Stoics often attributed to the friendship of wise men.[22] It also appropriates the role Zeno (the founder of Stoicism) attributed to homoerotic friendship in his lost *Republic*, which was controversial among Roman Stoics and continues to provoke debate today.[23] Like Zeno's homoerotic friendship, Musonius claims that marriage serves a vital political purpose. In fact, he goes so far as to assert that marriage is the necessary foundation for organized and enduring human life:

> Whoever removes marriage from humankind removes also the household, removes the polis, removes the entire human race. Because it wouldn't survive without procreation, nor would there be any procreation without marriage, at least not any just or legitimate procreation. (14.73.11–15)

Here we must be careful: while Musonius helps himself to the cataclysmic rhetoric of annihilation, we should not take him to believe that human organisms would die out without marriage. He is well aware that sex and procreation would still be possible (13A.68.1–4). Rather, we should focus on his final clause, which asserts that no "just or legitimate procreation" could occur without marriage. This at first glance feeble protestation can actually be taken to imply a significant philosophical claim, that only within the social structures of marriage, household, and the polis can human organisms become human beings.[24] In other words, if familial and political relationships generate the obligations and opportunities through which human beings attempt to live naturally and virtuously, then whoever destroys these relationships makes a meaningfully "human" life impossible. Without these structures there are no genuine goods or evils at which to aim. For this reason Musonius says that "human nature is most like the bee, which can't live alone and dies if isolated" (14.72.13–73.1). In sum, not only is sex designed to contribute to the couple's preeminently natural relationship but also both the couple and the family lay the foundations for natural human life.

I wish to emphasize two points by way of conclusion. First, earlier I left open the question of whether Musonius believes that legitimate sex must occur both within marriage and for the sake of children. As Martha Nussbaum rightly argues, he had better not: his sexual ethics rests on his valorization of the marital couple, whose naturally "powerful desire for congress and sharing" would not disappear if one or both were infertile.[25] Second and more generally, Musonius's austere chastity should be understood against the Stoics' broad virtue-ethicist backdrop, not against any belief in the intrinsic badness of sex: first, he connects promiscuity with a subjectively uncomfortable malady of the soul; second, he argues it is incompatible with the objectively desirable virtues of justice and temperance; third, he argues from the experience of sexual desire and the morphology of human bodies that god designed sex to bring and hold lovers together in a fundamental relationship of caring and commitment. So in order to play our proper role in the providential cosmopolis, we ought to associate sex with marriage.

Sexuality and the Aesthetics of Desire

Despite the fact that Musonius is able to mobilize many theoretical and popular considerations to support his position, it may appear to be of "merely historical" interest. Setting aside its theological background (although reports of the death of god look increasingly exaggerated), let us focus on Musonius's emphasis on "wantonness" (*truphē*), "temperance" (*sōphrosunē*), "intemperance" (*akolasia*), and "lack of self-control" (*akrasia*). With the exception of self-control, these evaluative concepts have little resonance in contemporary Western society. *Truphē* in particular is difficult to accommodate: I have translated it with the archaic word "wantonness," although the standard lexicon gives "softness, delicacy, daintiness."[26] In fact it combines luxuriousness, fickleness, pursuit of pleasure, and indulgence of desires in a pejorative psychological and ethical paradigm, which does not map easily onto contemporary conceptual schemes.

In order to see through the opaque historicity of this paradigm and connect it in a philosophically interesting way with Musonius's sexual ethics, we should turn to Michel Foucault's seminal *History of Sexuality*. Foucault argues that the specifically modern concepts of "sex" and "sexuality" conceal a practical and discursive network of processes of power, methods of generating knowledge, and exercises of identity formation or "subjectivation."[27] For example, in the early clinic of "perversion" doctors constructed "truths" about the anatomical and developmental sources of "sexual impulses" that had been "misdirected" (processes of knowledge); they prescribed "remedies" for these "disorders" (processes of power); and their diagnostic labels and descriptions "revealed" their patients' personality and identity (processes of subjectivation). Foucault plausibly argues that none of the "sex" words we have seen in Musonius had a comparable ability to attract and coordinate such overlapping processes of power, knowledge, and subjectivation; rather, these processes were coordinated by a broader problematic of bodily desires and pleasures.[28]

Foucault argues that Romans tend to treat bodily desire as a vehement and unruly force, which requires mastering through subordination to reason and laborious exercises of self-scrutiny and bodily practice. The goal of this rationalization and asceticism is a form of subjectivation: to make yourself "free" from "enslavement" to desire, knowledgeable about your own ethical progress, and ultimately a "nobler" or "more beautiful" individual.[29] Foucault refers to this as "a stylization of attitudes and an aesthetics of existence."[30]

Whatever the shortcomings of Foucault's sweeping analyses with regard to many areas of Greek and Roman cultures,[31] they cast significant light on several elements of Musonius's *On Sex*. For example, Musonius describes having extramarital sex as "being overcome by ugly pleasure" (*hēttomenōi aiskhras hēdonēs*, 66.1). This recalls the Foucauldian theme of "mastery": either you must "overcome" and "rule" your desires, which is represented as "freedom," or else you will "be overcome and enslaved" by them.[32] In order to appreciate the significance of this metaphorical scheme, we must keep in mind the monumental division in Greek and Roman cultures between free people and slaves. (Consider once more Musonius's assumption that his audience would find sex with slaves "harmless.") Note also that Musonius calls these mutinous pleasures *aiskhrai*, a word that may connote both ethical and bodily "ugliness" (64.9); he says earlier that all illegitimate intercourse brings "ugliness" (*aiskhos*, 64.13). Not only do the Stoics in particular claim that "only what is beautiful [*kalon*] is good" (Diog. Laert. 7.100) and "every good is beautiful [*kalon*], and likewise everything ugly [*aiskhron*] is bad" (Arius Didymus, *Epitome of Stoic Ethics* 6e ed. Pomeroy), but in the light of Foucault's research it is clear that the "aesthetics" of enjoyment was a pervasive concern for Greek and Roman ethics.

This also makes sense of an otherwise odd phrase, where Musonius asks, "Surely no one will esteem men . . . less able than women to educate their own desires [*paidagōgein tas heautōn epithumias*], since they are more powerful mentally [*gnōmēn*]" (66.15–16). One way free male citizens legitimated their power over slaves, females, and noncitizens was by representing the latter as unable to govern their own desires.[33] The reason often given for this incapacity was weakness of the reasoning faculty. The "education of *their own* desires" through their superior "minds" was thus an important facet of desiring and enjoying "like a free man."

If we now return to wantonness and temperance, we should find their role in Musonius's sexual ethics more intelligible. Since wantonness involves indulging desires without attempting to educate them through reason, it is slavish, unmanly, and ugly. Indulgence in sex, like any other bodily pleasure, requires self-monitoring and moderation—in short, temperance.

This whole moral, ascetic, and aesthetic complex appears most clearly with regard to another bodily enjoyment, eating. Eating is the preeminent hotspot for intemperance, Musonius argues (18B.101.3–12), because we eat several times a day, and

> every time food is brought, there is not only one danger of error, but many: we risk eating too much, or too fast, or dirtying ourselves with the sauce, or choosing pleasant rather than healthy food, or taking more than our share, or eating at the wrong time.

"Since this is incredibly ugly [*aiskhistou*]," Musonius says, "the contrary would be incredibly beautiful [*kalliston*], namely eating in an orderly and decorous fashion and displaying temperance here first, although it isn't easy: it requires a lot of care and training [*pollēs epimeleias kai askēseōs*]" (100.8–12; cf. 101.16). Musonius's punctilious anxiety, hyperbolic admiration or repugnance, and "care and training" associated with eating would be nonplussing, if we did not keep in mind the importance of self-mastery and decorum during enjoyment. Sex is less socially visible, which helps to explain why it receives less attention, yet the same principles apply.

Thus Musonius's sexual austerity is motivated not only by his Stoic virtue ethics, but also by an ethically and politically embedded aesthetics of enjoyment (albeit one taken to extremes). This emphasis on self-scrutiny and self-stylization does not exclude genuine care for wives. For Musonius, precisely what makes marriage the only "beautiful" place for enjoying sex is its divinely purposed integration of this enjoyment into a caring, committed, and politically beneficial relationship.[34] In other words, virtue ethics and the aesthetics of desire are complementary motivations for Musonius's positions.

Sexual Desire and Meaning

For many intellectuals in the wake of Freud, "sex" cannot be reduced to material for virtuous deportment or aesthetic elaboration. Rather, sexual desire and pleasure can best be understood as paradigmatic transformations of drive energy, which is fundamental for all human experience. For example, the linguist, psychoanalyst, and cultural theorist Julia Kristeva argues that "the *sexual thing*" underlies all meaningful linguistic expression.[35] As the final entry in this selective hermeneutics of Roman philosophy and sex, I will attempt to apply Kristeva's claim to Musonius's text.[36]

I will begin with a brief overview of Kristeva's views on language.[37] She believes that any meaningful language act is dialogical; the enunciating subject speaks or writes for someone, even if the addressee is merely notional.[38] In fact Kristeva argues that language is the last in a series of strategies developed in order to mediate our relationships with other people. The infant begins with an intense, ambivalent, bodily relationship to her primary caregivers. Her experiences in this relationship structure her drives, so that for Kristeva, drives are already other-directed and quasi-meaningful.[39] Kristeva calls this prelinguistic drive system "the semiotic." Language supervenes when the child invests drive energy in the use of socially imposed signifiers and syntax, which Kristeva calls "the symbolic," so that henceforth she can pursue enjoyable relationships through language and linguistically motivated action. Language thus becomes both an instrument for relating to other people and an Other in its own right.[40] This is one reason why Kristeva says that "the sexual thing" underlies linguistic expression: language sublimates the intense bodily joy and frustration (or *jouissance*) of human relationships. The other reason is that this intense drive energy endures as an element *within* language: semiosis underpins symbolic signification as intonation, rhythm, metaphorical polysemy, and "style" quite generally.[41]

I will address just two elements in Musonius's texts that Kristeva's theories can illuminate. The first is his rhetorically polished exposition. For Kristeva, rhetoric aims to accentuate the harmonization of semiotic and symbolic processes in language acts.[42] In other words, it harnesses prelinguistic drive energy to acts of judgment, persuasion, and so on. (By contrast, modern avant-garde literature often uses semiotic processes to *destabilize* symbolic meaning and the language acts relying on it.[43])

Consider the following sentence, which follows Musonius's condemnation of all extramarital intercourse (64.14–17):

> So no one does anything like this openly, if he's able to blush even a little; rather, people venture to do these things covertly and secretly, unless they're totally depraved.

> ὅθεν οὐδὲ πράττειν φανερῶς οὐδὲν ἀνέχεται τῶν τοιούτων οὐδείς, κἂν ἐπ᾽ ὀλίγον ἐρυθριᾶν οἷός τ᾽ ᾖ, ἐπικρυπτόμενοι δὲ καὶ λάθρᾳ οἵ γε μὴ τελέως ἀπερρωγότες ταῦτα τολμῶσιν.

Kristeva might say that my translation captures the sentence's symbolic signification, but not its semiotic underpinning, since I completely change its rhythm, word order, sounds, and penumbra of sensory associations. For example, the first Greek clause is structured around a triple repetition (*oude ... ouden ... oudeis*), which climaxes with the emphatic "no one": *no one* would do this! The jubilant vehemence of this climax bleeds into the corporeal-chromatic imagery of "blushing" or "reddening" (*eruthriān*) in the second clause. The third clause receives the energy of the first by answering "openly" with "covertly and secretly." It withholds its verb (*tolmōsin*) until the last word, thus crowning its periodic momentum with "superegoic" indignation.[44] More subtly, Musonius makes an unnecessary change in its grammatical subject, from "no one" to "people who aren't totally depraved." The enjoyment packed into this nomination is signaled by the particle *ge*, which is difficult to translate into English except by intonation ("*totally* depraved people!")[45]—an exemplary manifestation of semiotic *jouissance*, the sexual excitement embedded in language.

Second, some of Musonius's individual words suggest semiotic investment. For example, "depraved" is at best an approximate translation of *aperrōgotes*, which might more etymologically be translated as "broken off" or "broken down."[46] This word belongs to a metaphorical pattern in Musonius's invective, which comes across most emphatically in his discussion of male grooming (21.116.15–17):

> Some people . . . cut their hair and smooth their cheeks, obviously people who are **shattered** (*houtoi ge kateagotes*) by wantonness, entirely enervated (*ekneneurismenoi pantapasin*), since they tolerate being seen as girly-men and effeminates (*androgunoi kai gunaikōdeis*).

Notice that the adjective "shattered" is preceded by the same particle *ge* as was the phrase "totally broken down" in the previous example. Moreover, the noun "wantonness" (*truphē*) itself derives from the verb *thruptō*, "break into pieces." From *thruptō* Musonius elsewhere borrows the adjective *thruptikos*, "easily broken, delicate, effeminate" (11.58.4).[47] What is the meaning of calling promiscuous or well-groomed men "broken off," "shattered," and "easily broken?" These words have the same illocutionary force as those with which they are associated, like "girly-men," "effeminates," and "enervated": they aim to stimulate shame. But their locutionary connotation is fuzzier, recalling what Kristeva says about obscenity:

> around the object denoted by the obscene word . . . more than a simple context asserts itself—the drama of a questioning process heterogeneous to the meaning that precedes and exceeds [that meaning].[48]

In other words, precisely what makes certain words "obscene" is their impregnation with energy and enjoyment "that precedes and exceeds" articulate values.[49] Musonius stops short of calling these people "*fucking pussies*," but he "gets off" on the name-calling we have seen in a similar (if milder) fashion.[50]

In conclusion, if Foucault's genealogy permits us to go beyond the virtue ethics of intercourse toward an analysis of the networks of power, exercises of subjectivation, and truth-telling games in which desire and pleasure are imbricated, Kristeva extends our investigation in another direction: she allows us to think about how intense bodily need, frustration, and enjoyment permeate discourse. You don't need a Freudian to tell you that a great deal of sexual desire and enjoyment is in the thoughts and images we entertain, not in the motions of our bodies.[51] Therefore an adequate philosophy of sex really does need to address the way a subject thinks, imagines, daydreams, and speaks, not only how they use their body and with whom. As my brief analysis of Musonius's text hopefully exemplifies, it is this *variety* of interpretive approaches that can best support a complex and thought-provoking consideration of sex and Roman philosophy.

Notes

1. A transcript of this famous statement can be found at http://millercenter.org/president/speeches/speech-3930 (accessed November 23, 2021).
2. For the Roman sexual vocabulary, see Adams (1982). The nearest Greek equivalent of which I am aware is Henderson (1975).

3. By "hermeneutics" I particularly have in mind the methodology of Paul Ricoeur.
4. The other prominent example is Lucr. 4.1030–1287.
5. All translations of Musonius are my own. All references are to fragment, page, and line numbers in Hense's 1905 edition.
6. Testimonia not deriving from Lucius's memoirs are preserved in Arrian's memoirs of Epictetus and possibly in Plutarch, Aelius Aristides, and Aulus Gellius. On Musonius's biography and the transmission of the texts ascribed to him, see Goulet-Cazé (2005) 555–564, 567–571.
7. See Hense (1905) xv–xvi on Lucius's free reportage, and Goulet-Cazé (2005) 568 (quoting Lutz (1947) 12) on the difference between Lucius's portrait and that transmitted by Arrian and Aulus Gellius.
8. LSJ s.v. *aphrodisios, a, on* def. II gives "sexual pleasures." On the relation of this phrase to late antique Christian and modern European notions of sex and sexuality, see Foucault (1990b) esp. 35–52.
9. Nussbaum (2002b) 309.
10. Scholars interested in Musonius's stance on gender equality have debated whether he shares these presumptions of male superiority or merely imputes them to his auditors. See Engel (2000) 388; Nussbaum (2002b) 288, 298–299, 303–304; Reydams-Schils (2005) 157.
11. Nussbaum (2002b) 302–303 and Reydams-Schils (2005) 158–159 both associate Musonius's "incomplete feminism" with Seneca's accommodation of slavery in *Ep.* 47. Harper (2013) has argued with great force that Roman sexuality was inextricable from social power hierarchies, especially slavery (e.g., 26–28, 45–50).
12. Compare fragment 13A.
13. Of course, this is one of the principal arguments of Foucault (1990a), (1990b), and (1998).
14. He never says this explicitly, but see 18B.99.4–5: "No one will deny . . . that gluttony and gourmandizing are incredibly shameful."
15. Compare 7.29.3–6.
16. On this pattern, which receives its most striking Stoic expressions in Seneca, see Lampe (2008).
17. On the handling of marriage by Roman Stoics, see the excellent discussion in Reydams-Schils (2005) 143–176. On similar sentiments in Roman culture more broadly, see Treggiari (1991) 245–253, Harper (2013) 61–70.
18. Nature and god are both described as "a designing fire which methodically proceeds toward creation of the world" (LS 46A1, *SVF* 2.1133–4; cf. LS 43A2, 54B).
19. Likewise, the image of a "craftsman" "mixing" ingredients recalls Plato's *Timaeus* 35a1–b3, 41d3–7, although "mixing" also recalls Antipater of Tarsus's *On Marriage* (*SVF* 3 "Antipater Tarsensis" 63), and Stoics often refer to god as a "craftsman" (e.g., LS 44B2, 44E3–4, 44F).
20. Laurand (2001) 98–99. Compare Hierocles: "Nature fashioned us to be not only gregarious, but also inclined to form couples [*sunduastikous*]" (p. 72 ed. Ramelli).
21. Compare Scruton's claim that premarital chastity is necessary in order to safeguard the potential of marriage to redeem our "thrownness" and facilitate our moral growth ((1986) 320, 341–343).
22. Laurand (2001) 104–108, Reydams-Schils (2005) 79, 149. In fact Musonius claims that "everyone considers the friendship of husband and wife the most venerable of all" (14.74.9–10).
23. On Stoic *erōs*, see Schofield (1991) 22–56, Inwood (1997), Nussbaum (2002a) 76–87, Gaca (2004) 82–90, and Graver (2007) 173–190.

24. Similar ideas are common in Greek political philosophy, prominently including Aristotle's *Politics* 1.2 and numerous Stoic texts, as Hense notes in his apparatus criticus.
25. Nussbaum (2002b) 309; see also Musonius fr. 13A.
26. LSJ s.v. *truphē*.
27. See, especially, Foucault (1998) 77–160.
28. This emerges from Foucault (1990a) and (1990b) as a whole, but see, especially, (1990b) 3–32.
29. Foucault (1990a) esp. 39–68. Foucault covers this territory in greater detail in (2005), where he abandons his unhelpfully restrictive focus on sexuality.
30. Foucault (1990b) 92; cf. (1990a): 71 and 185 (quoted below).
31. Bersani (1985) rightly questions Foucault's valorization of Greco-Roman "stylistics" over post-Christian "codifications" of sin, morality, and health; Davidson (2007) 152–166 critiques some of Foucault's claims about Greek "homosexuality"; and Goldhill (1995) addresses the generic homogeneity of the texts on which Foucault focuses. On Foucault and Stoicism, see most recently Mitcheson (2018).
32. Foucault (1990b) 63–93.
33. Foucault (1990b) 72–77, (2005) 32–36, 43–44, 174, etc.; Winkler (1990) esp. 45–70; Davidson (1997) passim. But see n9: Musonius may not *wholeheartedly* share this attitude.
34. On companionate marriage as an element of Roman "aesthetics of existence," see Foucault (1990b) 72–80, 147–185.
35. Kristeva (2009) 28; cf. (1981) 87, (1989) 40–42.
36. Note that Kristeva repeatedly comments on Stoicism herself, as I have elucidated and critically evaluated in Lampe (2016).
37. Kristeva (1984) remains the most thorough discussion, Oliver (1993) esp. 91–113, the best scholarly introduction (though both are slightly outdated).
38. Kristeva (1989) 41; cf. (1984) 43–51.
39. Kristeva (1995) 30–31. This is the realm of "oceanic" mother–child union and love for the "imaginary father" (concisely summarized at (2009) 7–10) and of "abjection" ((1982a) 10–15).
40. Kristeva (1984) 48.
41. It may also implode meaning, but that will not be relevant to Musonius. On "style" as semiosis, see Kristeva (2009) 36–37.
42. Kristeva (1981) 138.
43. Ibid. 131–147; Kristeva (1984) passim (e.g., 217–234); (1982a) 133–206.
44. The pseudo-object of the Kristevan superego is "the abject," one of the manifestations of the "sexual thing" ((1982a) 2, 15).
45. This usage falls between what Denniston classifies as "emphatic" and "limitative" ((1954) 114–150).
46. LSJ s.v. *aporrhēgnumi*.
47. LSJ s.v. *thruptikos*.
48. Kristeva (1981) 143.
49. It is thus extremely interesting that Zeno argues "*nihil esse obscenum, nihil turpe dictu*" (Cic. *Fam.* 9.22)—an argument that deserves a study of its own.
50. For another angle on non-eupathic *jouissance* in Stoicism generally and Musonius particularly, see Lampe (2013).
51. See the devastating critique of Goldman (1977) by Morgan (2001).

References

Adams, J. N. (1982). *The Latin Sexual Vocabulary*. (London).
Bersani, L. (1985). "Pedagogy and Pederasty." *Raritan* 5: 14–21.
Davidson, J. (1997). *Courtesans and Fishcakes: The Consuming Passions of Classical Athens*. (London).
Davidson, J. (2007). *The Greeks and Greek Love: A Radical Reappraisal of Homosexuality in Ancient Greece*. (London).
Deleuze, G., and F. Guattari (1983). *Anti-Oedipus: Capitalism and Schizophrenia*. R. Hurley, S. Mark, and H. R. Lane, tr. (Minneapolis).
Denniston, J. D. (^{2}1954). *The Greek Particles*. (Oxford).
Engel, D. (2000). "The Gender Egalitarianism of Musonius Rufus." *Ancient Philosophy* 20: 377–391.
Foucault, M. (1990a). *The Care of the Self. Volume 3 of The History of Sexuality*. (London)
Foucault, M. (1990b). *The Use of Pleasure. Volume 2 of The History of Sexuality*. R. Hurley, tr. (New York).
Foucault, M. (1998). *The Will to Knowledge. Volume 1 of The History of Sexuality*. R. Hurley, tr. (London).
Foucault, M. (2005). *The Hermeneutics of the Subject: Lectures at the Collège de France 1981–1982*. F. Gros, ed., G. Burchell, tr. (New York).
Gaca, K. L. (2004). *The Making of Fornication: Eros, Ethics, and Political Reform in Greek Philosophy and Early Christianity*. (Berkeley).
Goldhill, S. (1995). *Foucault's Virginity: Ancient Erotic Fiction and the History of Sexuality*. (Cambridge).
Goldman, A. H. (1977). "Plain Sex." *Philosophy and Public Affairs* 6(3): 267–287.
Goulet-Cazé, M.-O. (2005). "Musonius Rufus," in R. Goulet (ed.), *Dictionnaire des philosophes antiques*, vol. 4 (Paris), 555–572.
Graver, M. R. (2007). *Stoicism and Emotion*. (Chicago).
Harper, K. (2013). *From Shame to Sin: The Christian Transformation of Sexual Morality in Late Antiquity*. (Cambridge, Mass.)
Henderson, J. (1975). *The Maculate Muse: Obscene Language in Attic Comedy*. (New Haven, Conn.).
Hense, O. (1905). *C. Musonii Rufi Reliquiae*. (Leipzig).
Inwood, B. (1997). "Why Do Fools Fall in Love?," in R. Sorabji (ed.), *Aristotle and After* (London), 55–69.
Kristeva, J. (1981). *Desire in Language: A Semiotic Approach to Literature and Art*. L. S. Roudiez, tr. (Oxford).
Kristeva, J. (1982a). *Powers of Horror: An Essay on Abjection*. L. S. Roudiez, tr. (New York).
Kristeva, J. (1982b). "Psychoanalysis and the Polis." M. Waller, tr. *Critical Inquiry* 9(1): 77–92.
Kristeva, J. (1984) *Revolution in Poetic Language*. M. Waller, tr. (New York).
Kristeva, J. (1989). *Black Sun: Depression and Melancholia*. L. S. Roudiez, tr. (New York).
Kristeva, J. (1995) *New Maladies of the Soul*. R. Guberman, tr. (New York).
Kristeva, J. (2009). *This Incredible Need to Believe*. B. B. Brahic, tr. (New York).
Lampe, K. (2008). "Seneca's Nausea: 'Existential' Experiences and Julio-Claudian Literature." *Helios* 35(1): 67–87.

Lampe, K. (2013). "Obeying Your Father: Stoic Theology between Myth and Masochism," in V. Zajko and E. O'Gorman (eds.), *Classical Myth and Psychoanalysis: Ancient and Modern Stories of the Self* (Oxford), 183–198.

Lampe, K. (2016). "Kristeva, Stoicism, and the 'True Life of Interpretations.'" *SubStance* 45(1): 22–43.

Laurand, V. (2001). "Souci de soi et mariage chez Musonius Rufus: Perspectives politiques de la κρᾶσις stoïcienne," in F. Gros and C. Lévy (eds.), *Foucault et la philosophie antique* (Paris), 85–116.

Long, A. A., and D. N. Sedley [= LS] (1987). *The Hellenistic Philosophers.* (Cambridge).

Lutz, C. (1947). *Musonius Rufus, "The Roman Socrates."* (New Haven, Conn.).

Mitcheson, K. (2018). "Foucault, Stoicism, and Self-Mastery," in M. Dennis and S. Werkhoven (eds.), *Ethics and Self-Cultivation: Contemporary and Historical Perspectives* (London), 124–140.

Morgan, S. (2001). "Sex in the Head." *Journal of Applied Philosophy* 20(1): 1–16.

Nussbaum, M. (2002a). "*Erōs* and Ethical Norms: Philosophers Respond to a Cultural Dilemma," in Nussbaum and Sihvola, 55–94.

Nussbaum, M. (2002b). "The Incomplete Feminism of Musonius Rufus, Platonist, Stoic, and Roman," in Nussbaum and Sihvola, 282–326.

Nussbaum, M., and J. Sihvola, eds. (2002). *The Sleep of Reason: Erotic Experience and Sexual Ethics in Ancient Greece and Rome.* (Chicago).

Oliver, K. (1993). *Reading Kristeva: Unraveling the Double-Bind.* (Bloomington, Ind.).

Reydams-Schils, G. (2005). *The Roman Stoics: Self, Responsibility, and Affection.* (Chicago).

Schofield, M. (1991). *The Stoic Idea of the City.* (Chicago).

Scruton, R. (1986). *Sexual Desire: A Philosophical Investigation.* (London).

Treggiari, S. (1991). *Roman Marriage:* Iusti Coniuges *from the Time of Cicero to the Time of Ulpian.* (Oxford).

Winkler, J. (1990). *The Constraints of Desire: The Anthropology of Sex and Gender in Ancient Greece.* (London).

CHAPTER 24

TIME

DUNCAN F. KENNEDY

INTRODUCTION: THINKING ABOUT TIME PHILOSOPHICALLY

Like any ground floor philosophical inquiry, that into the nature of time reaches into other fundamental philosophical preoccupations—for example, the nature of change, the fundamental stuff of the world, the relationship between discourse and what it is about, human consciousness... and human freedom.[1]

THINKING about time through to the present day has been inevitably conditioned by Greek philosophical and historical ideas, and, as Raymond Tallis suggests here, a cluster of concerns tend to recur. Those concerns were memorably explored across a range of Latin texts that were powerfully influential in the postclassical age and resonate still. This chapter will focus on three in particular, *On the Nature of Things* by Lucretius (c. 99–c. 54 BCE), (in passing) the *Aeneid* of Vergil (70–19 BCE), and the *Confessions* of Saint Augustine (354–430 CE).

The fourth century BCE had seen the emergence of two distinctive discourses, styles of thinking that remain in tension with each other, "philosophy" and "history." "Philosophy" became strongly associated with the Platonic style of thinking that sought to make the term its own,[2] and which saw as one of its chief concerns the metaphysical question of "what (really) is"—what would come to be termed ontology.[3] In Plato's hands, this opens out a separation of realms, of reality and appearance, spatially imagined as up there and down here, and it guides us to observe the world from two imagined viewpoints, above and below. The solutions suggested to ontological questions are strongly colored by the argument of Parmenides' Way of Truth: "what is uncreated and imperishable, for it is entire, immovable and without end. It was not in the past, nor shall it be, since it is now, all at once, continuous" (fr. B8.3–6). For Parmenides what (really) *is* does not change, and is marked by its stability. When the ontological question is asked of time in texts that see themselves as philosophical, this style of thinking not unsurprisingly is inclined to downgrade time as an aspect of (and along with) human experience (down here) and not a feature of whatever (really) is (up there).

Aristotle begins his seminal discussion in *Physics* 4.10–14 by raising the question of whether time exists, and warns that, from the considerations he is about to present, "one might suspect that either it doesn't exist at all, or only scarcely and dimly" (217b33–34).[4] We become aware of it through motion and change, but time is "a number of movement in respect of the before and after. Time, then is not movement, but it is a feature of movement that makes number applicable to it" (*Ph.* 4.11, 219b1–3).[5] From the perspective of twenty-three centuries later, this characterization of time can be seen to have a profound influence, in two distinct ways that developed in the ancient world but extended far beyond it.

One outcome of the association of time and number is the emergence of more systematic reckonings of the passage of time than traditional means such as the generations of genealogy, royal reigns, or lists of magistrates ever could. The mapping of the passage of time (past and future) on to a numerical sequence, potentially endless in either direction, will lead eventually to the emergence of a chronology that could transcend local traditions of reckoning the passage of time.[6] This feeds into cosmological speculation, and becomes a key feature of anticreationist arguments; but in dispensing with the scale of the human lifecycle, it serves to diminish the place of human experience in the cosmos as it is and how it came to be. A point of perspective that transcends an everyday sense of time and space and its familiar human scale was memorably constructed by Cicero in the Dream of Scipio with which he concluded his *Republic*, an episode that aspired to the level of metaphysical *poiesis* Cicero had encountered in Plato's *Timaeus* and *Republic*. From the vantage point of the Milky Way, Scipio can look upon stars larger than we ever surmised to exist. The earth seems small, smaller still the extent of Roman dominion (*imperium*) upon it, which embraces as it were a point (*quasi punctum*), such that Scipio is induced to rue his previous estimation of it (*ut me imperii nostri . . . paeniteret*, 6.16.16). We cannot hope for a glory that is long-lasting, let alone everlasting, in a Stoic cosmos subject to periodic floods and conflagrations (6.21.23). The human year measured by the circuit of the sun is as nothing to the "great year" when all the stars return to their positions (6.22.24). The Stoics sought to resolve the conundrum of time by rejecting a simple binary ontological distinction (does it exist or doesn't it?), regarding it (like void or place) as an "incorporeal,"[7] and, like Aristotle, as associated with the measurement of movement (Zeno called it a "dimension of movement"). While not existing in the sense that corporeals do (they "subsist"), such incorporeals are not nothing in that they can form the content of thoughts and statements (*lekta*, likewise incorporeal).[8] In turn, *lekta* can use and develop the resources of language to articulate the human experience of time. If the human experience of time is articulated in language, then that experience becomes open to the kind of dizzying, even existentially disorientating, effects Cicero presents here. A generation later, Vergil's *Aeneid* will develop a narrative of *imperium* that seeks to address the sorts of metaphysical challenges encountered in the Dream of Scipio.

Second, it is noteworthy that Aristotle discusses time in that subset of philosophical writing called "physics," the study of nature, or, as it came to be called in the early modern period, "natural philosophy": he thus sets in motion the association of time and measurement that has assumed crucial importance in physics to this day. Historically, the capacity to measure time with increasing precision and to a high level of agreement among observers had to await the development of reliable clocks. The impulse to quantify, and to reduce time, space, and motion to numbers, became the hallmark of what has become known as the "Scientific Revolution." For Galileo, "the Book of Nature is written in the language of mathematics," and the drive of physics toward generalization finds its purest manifestation in the extreme abstraction of equivalences and equations (Newton's $f = ma$ or Einstein's $e = mc^2$). Philosophically, measuring things is one aspect of the process of dephenomenalizing them, of abstracting them ever further from the processes of human observation.[9] When the physical image of the world strives to be at it most comprehensive, it "loses" time:[10] the ontological status of time has been precarious in physics ever since physics emerged as a distinctive discourse and remains a subject of controversy.[11] Quantitative physics and the mathematization of nature can shade into a metaphysical dogmatism that takes the human observer (the one who does the measuring down here) to the very margins, and even out of, the picture it develops; in some cases, this leads to the assumption of a "God's-eye view" or, in the memorable phrase of Thomas Nagel,[12] "the view from nowhere"—and equally "nowhen."

Much of this lies in the future of the Roman philosophies of time we will be considering in this chapter, but the present conditions what we see as the agenda of those philosophies, and the sense of what might be particularly salient in their texts—an issue to which we will return in the next section. Thus the impulse toward extreme abstraction and the pressure to marginalize the human observer feel tangible already in the physics of Lucretius. In his case, these tendencies are expressed not in the language of mathematics, but rather in the ontological assertion that only matter and void, and not time nor any other aspect of human experience (however pressing), exist per se—though he goes to great lengths, as we shall see in the next section, to counter this by the care he takes to explicate and dramatize how the human experience of time permits the observer to theorize the real nature of things.

The drive to "philosophize" time opens a gap that philosophical thinking struggles to bridge, between what could be characterized as the depersonalized and stable third person "is-being" of the world "outside" time that physics seeks to give us (and the intellectual prestige that continues to be associated with it), and the first-person "am-being" of human experience "within" time, and the constraints associated with it. The alienating effect of a physical image of the world that reduces the human and its experience of being in time toward zero underlies, for example, the contention of Paul Ricoeur (who takes his inspiration from the *Confessions* of Augustine, considered below) that philosophy alone cannot vouchsafe a full understanding of time, and that it is through narrative (including the narratives of philosophy's "other," history) that the human experience of time is explored—and can be enriched.[13] The most powerful Roman metaphysical response before Augustine to the human experience of living in time—its imperfect knowledge, the potential disorientation and alienation we saw in Cicero's Dream of Scipio—is developed in the narrative of Vergil's *Aeneid*. It dramatizes a distinction between the timeless and the time-bound respectively in Jupiter, with his all-encompassing "God's-eye" vision of history as Roman *imperium* without boundaries of space and time (*Aen.* 1.278–279) which he can view, as it were as a whole from "outside," and human figures such as Aeneas or indeed the readers of the poem, with their imperfect knowledge of the significance of events when they can only be viewed from points "within" time and history.[14] The interplay of these two viewpoints was to provide the ideological blueprint for the justification of Roman imperial power and the emerging political system of one-man rule, the principate.

Lucretius on Time, the Physical Cosmos, and Human Knowledge

While Cicero's emphasis is on the capacity of mind-boggling *magnitude* to alter understanding and belief, both the Stoics and the Epicureans embraced the notion of the *infinity* of the cosmos. The unboundedness of time and space is as crucial to Epicurean theory as its trademark atomism,[15] and is put to heuristic use that can be by turns settling and unsettling. Lucretius exploits notions of infinite time and infinite space imaginatively as part of his strategy to combat the two major ills he sees as afflicting his society, fear of gods and their supposed intervention in the world, and fear of death.

The fundamental components that make up our world below the threshold of our senses are characterized only by size, shape, weight, and, crucially, movement; they have always existed and will always exist. A cosmos that has no temporal beginning or end can do without the notion of a creator-figure (such as the Demiurge, modeled on a craftsman, in Plato's *Timaeus*) that informs the kind of theological worldview Epicureanism seeks to counter. Unlimited time can explain the universe as we know it and the emergence of complex entities such as ourselves and the world with which we are familiar without recourse to a creator. So important is this that on three occasions, Lucretius emphasizes that, given infinite time, by going through every possible kind of motion and combination, matter of its own accord cannot but come into the sorts of dispositions as constitute our world and the creatures in it (1.102–1028; 5.187–194; 5.419–431).[16] Human beings by their very existence demonstrate the potential of self-organizing matter to form sentient creatures, and were thus going to occur, willy-nilly. Epicureanism thus strips out the temporal aspect associated with "craftsman" theories of the universe: no moment of creation, no end or *telos* toward which the universe or what it contains is directed. Such an argument can have existentially unsettling ramifications. The fifth-century BCE atomist Democritus is reported in Cicero (*Academica* 2.55) as claiming that in an infinite universe, there are infinitely many worlds. Not only that: some of them are not only similar to each other, but utterly completely and absolutely so alike that there is precisely no difference between them. And more: there are infinitely many of those, and likewise the people in them, such that across that infinite number of worlds, there would be a corresponding infinity of people precisely called Quintus Lutatius Catulus, one of the interlocutors of the *Academica*. The immediate context is the perception of identity and difference, and the views of Democritus are introduced so as to have some jollity at their—and Catulus's—expense. There are not many people (perhaps few more than Cicero) who are not protective of their sensed uniqueness.[17]

Lucretius in rather more sober terms acknowledges in 2.1048–1104 that in an unbounded universe ours cannot be the only world there is (2.1056). However, elsewhere he uses the infinity argument not to suggest (as in Cicero) that there are infinite identical worlds existing *simultaneously* (worlds we could never access anyway), but rather that similarities can emerge *serially* over time in this particular world we inhabit. "When you look back," Lucretius says (3.854–858), "on the whole expanse of time *without measure that has gone by* (*immensi* temporis omne / praeteritum spatium, 3.854–855), and consider how varied the movements of matter are, you could easily come to believe that these same seeds from which we are now constituted have often (*saepe*, 3.857) been positioned in the same arrangement as they are now in." "Often," Lucretius says, when strictly speaking he could say that the seeds, the primordial elements that now make up *you*, have been disposed in exactly the same ways infinitely many times in the past (and will be so disposed infinitely many times in the future). However, the point he goes on to make (3.859–861) is that you don't have any memory of those earlier selves who, while in every respect they were constituted out of exactly the same matter moving in exactly the same ways, are not *you*, since a "break in life" (*vitai pausa*) and sensation has been interposed. Infinity throws up this bewildering array of an infinite series of physically identical selves, but Lucretius chooses to highlight the psychological integrity of each individual self, which arises out of the human consciousness of time passing and the operation of memory. As Wilson Shearin puts it, "being an individual, a 'self,' is not merely being a material thing but *acting continually* in the full retrospective knowledge of one's self as a self."[18]

Nonetheless, emphasis on the integrity of the individual self makes palpable the other fear Epicureanism claims to counter, that of death. Ontologically, little feels more "real" to being a human than one's own time-limited existence, the sense that *I am*, but that a moment will come when *I am* no longer. A few lines before this, Lucretius has argued that, just as we feel no distress at our nonexistence in the past, so we should feel no concern at our nonexistence in the future (3.832–842), and he returns to emphasize this point by asking you to reflect on your individual existence within the infinite passage of time (3.972–976): "Look back at how the past duration of everlasting time before we are born has been nothing to us. This therefore nature presents as a mirror-image of the time to come after we die at last. Is there anything gloomy to see there? Is it not freer from care than any sleep?" The appeal to such a familiar personal experience of unconsciousness seeks to counter the way Epicurean thought about death reduces the *person* to their physical body, "I" to "it." Lucretius's emphasis on physical dissolution downplays (indeed ridicules in the finale to Book 3) the individual self's psychological investment in its world, not least in other people and *their* future.[19] The human experience of being-in-time (which is arguably "are" as well as "am," let alone "is") is not adequately addressed in exclusively physical terms. And, at the first-person level (singular *and* plural, individual *and* collective), the experience of time, before and after, past, present, and future, seems inescapable. Lucretius is committed to putting forward "is-being" as fundamental, and the chief philosophical challenge to this (then and now) is negotiating the question of the place of first-person experience, "am-being," in the depiction of "the nature of things." Early on in the poem, Lucretius subjects his readers to an ontological cold shower: time does not exist per se.

Book 1 addresses head-on the ontological issues that are crucial to the Epicurean world picture. Only matter and void *really* exist. Everything else is either "properties" of these two (*coniuncta*, as weight to stones or heat to fire; they are "joined together," and when one disappears, so does the other, 1.449–454), or what Lucretius calls *eventa*. In contrast to *coniuncta*, he says: "slavery, poverty, riches, freedom, war, concord, all else by whose *coming and going* (*adventu . . . abituque*) nature remains intact we are accustomed to call *eventa* (1.455–458)." The examples he uses are some of the most pressing aspects of first-person experience. *Eventa*, formed from the perfect passive participle of *evenio*, are "things that [have] come and go[ne]," their so-called "outcome" known. This term is the context in which he puts forward his theory of time and provides his rationale for understanding it (1.459–463):

> Time *similarly* does not exist in itself, but from things themselves there follows the sense of what has been brought through to an end in the passage of time, then what is pressing upon us, further what is to follow thereafter; it must be admitted that no-one experiences time in itself apart from the movement of things and their calm cessation.
>
> tempus *item* per se non est, sed rebus ab ipsis
> consequitur sensus, transactum quid sit in aevo,
> tum quae res instet, quid porro deinde sequatur;
> nec per se quemquam tempus sentire fatendumst
> semotum ab rerum motu placidaque quiete.

At the level of the two entities that fundamentally exist per se, matter and void, we are asked to imagine a continuum of happening: matter is simply in constant motion. But at the level of human perception, this does not seem to be the case. Human sensation associates cessation of movement with a conclusion, and construes that concluded movement in/as "the past" that is differentiated from an unconcluded movement experienced in/as "the present"—a distinction between a (concluded) event and a (continuing) process that articulates the human experience of time. Humans perceive movement in terms of beginnings and ends that are simply not there and play no part at the level of matter and void. But humans' experience of what they call "time" is crucial to their understanding of what really is, as he will try to explain.

Lucretius cautions his readers not to accept that the rape of Helen or the Trojan War "are/exist [*esse*] per se" (1.464–467). This is not to say that they did, or did not, happen (these are matters of "fact" historians can argue over); rather, philosophically speaking, they are *eventa* construed in the way he has suggested. Lucretius could have said more here, for human thinking about time is beset with confusion. The statement that "the Trojan War lasted ten years" involves a specific temporal experience very different from that of being in the midst of weary years of waging war of uncertain outcome. However, if the statement is thought to be a "fact," it has a quasi-timeless quality: *eventa* that constitute a sense of the "past" can be *spoken of* at any moment felt to be the "present," and this can give rise to the sense Lucretius cautions against, that they exist per se. The *saying* "that such-and-such is the case" (e.g., *that* matter and void are the only things that exist per se) is fraught philosophically no less than historically, and Lucretius must negotiate these difficulties with time in the exposition of his case.

That "'matter' and 'void' are what they are and do what they do" reflects the human encounter with nature that distinguishes temporally what it observes as *eventa*—and expresses what is timeless (the cosmos has no beginnings and no end; no history either) in what I have described as quasi-timeless facts. How does this come about? Human perception can apprehend sequentiality in events that are experienced as shaped by beginnings and ends. Lucretius significantly associates this sense of sequentiality with "what is to follow thereafter" (*quid porro deinde sequatur*, 1.461): thus *eventa* can act as a guide to what may follow hereafter. Such a sense of temporal sequentiality, before *and then* after, underlies perceived regular *relationships* of events so crucial to Epicurean understanding of the physical world: sequentiality shades into a sense of consequentiality. The similarity and regularity of the perceived relationship of events permits a generalized statement that is not tied to one particular sequence at one particular time and so transcends ongoing experience (*quae res instet*, 1.461) and attains a quasi-timeless, abstract character. Lucretius does not say explicitly that causes and their effects are a function of the human sense of time (and so do not exist per se), but this seems to follow from what he has said here. He was willing to accept, as Epicurus had done, that a phenomenon might be open to multiple explanations between which it might be difficult to adjudicate, when one cannot attain a closer view[20] Speaking of the movement of celestial bodies, he offers a number of possible causes (5.509–525), but which of these causes holds sway in our world is, he says, difficult to posit for certain (5.526–527). He sees his task as setting out the many causes (*pluris . . . causas*, 5.529) that may operate in the infinite number of worlds throughout the cosmos, one of which must operate here also; "but which of them it is not the task of one proceeding step by step (*pedetemptim progredientis*) to lay down" (*praecipere*, 5.533–534). Epicurean explanation, compelling as it is felt to be, remains unfinished business; it retains a sense of what presses upon us now.

Elsewhere he speculates that *if* all *motion* is *always* connected, and new motion arises out of old in *fixed order* (*si semper motus conectitur omnis / et vetere exoritur motu novus ordine certo*, 2.251–252), this would result in a wholly deterministic universe. He then introduces the notion (not attested in the extant texts of Epicurus but ascribed to him independently) of swerve to break this rigid determinism. Lucretius makes a subtle shift from "movement" to "cause" by introducing the peculiarly human temporal language of beginnings, of originary moments, that are no part of nature per se (2.253–256): "if the *first-order beginnings* (*primordia*, a term he regularly uses of the constituent matter that makes up the objects we perceive) do not by swerving bring about *some sort of a first stage* of motion (*motus/principium quoddam*) such as to break the binding agreements of fate (*fati foedera*), lest cause follow cause from infinity (*ex infinito ne causam causa sequatur*), whence comes this free will to living things across the earth . . . ?" Movement is thus not entirely subject to prediction, the saying in advance what will be the case. The human detection of *causes* from perceived movement, whilst amenable to progress through accumulated experience, will never be complete or definitive. Thus "what is to follow after" (1.461) remains provisional, the view forward open to revision in the light of events.

Crucially, Lucretius associates a sense of causation and a sense of agency. Speaking of the link between causation and agency, Tallis observes: "Events . . . are seen as effects of what no longer is and as causes of what is not yet. The idea that Event X brings about or could bring about Event Y inspires the idea that *I* could bring about Event Y."[21] Not everything is possible of course. Human agency is in many ways constrained, and it is important to have a firm understanding of what can, and cannot, happen. In practical terms, the sheer multiplicity of possible "events" presented to us by our temporal experience in terms of causes and effects encourages the exercise of choice directed toward a particular "outcome" in any situation that "presses upon" us: "we move forward" (*progredimur*, 2.258) in one direction as opposed to others that we anticipate. Strikingly, it is human experience that warrants attributing indeterminacy to the way fundamental matter moves, and, as Lucretius goes on to suggest (2.259, *declinamus item motus*, "we similarly swerve our motions"), provides a repertoire of images in which we can envisage this important notion. We should avoid taking this in a literally minded way. The limits of human temporal experience may explain the convoluted rhetoric that Lucretius adopts to express the (to him, erroneous) notion of physical determinism—as a hypothesis (cf. 2.251–252, "if all motion is always connected . . . in fixed order") that is gradually rendered counterfactual by the terms in which he is obliged to express it: "a sort of beginning of motion" (*motus/principium quoddam*, 2.253–254). There are no beginnings in fundamental nature! That's temporally conditioned thinking.

The explanation of the world offered by Epicurean thinking is thus an avowedly human construct which, in its precise details at least, Lucretius suggests, is work in progress—as is his own attempt to expound the theory. Famously he presents himself as working deep into the night searching for the words and poetry by which his readers may see into the very heart of things (1.142–145). There is a scholarly debate over whether Lucretius is to be regarded as a largely derivative source for Epicurean thought or an innovative thinker in his own right.[22] It may be helpful to factor time into this argument—as Lucretius himself does, and this can be helpful for considering the question of what his text *is* and what we are doing when we read it. Lucretius presents himself as the devoted follower of Epicurus, using the image of placing "my own footsteps firmly now in your imprinted marks" (3.3–4), his own work an act of love rather than rivalry (3.5–6). However, in matters of *poiesis*, he elsewhere presents himself, again using the imagery of taking steps, as traversing "the pathless places of the Muses trodden by the foot of no-one" before him (1.926–927 = 4.1–2). The world is young, he surmises in 5.330–331; "certain arts are *now* [i.e., in the process of] being finessed, *now* even are in the process of growth (*quaedam nunc artes expoliuntur/ nunc etiam augescunt*, 5.332–333). Temporally speaking, these are examples of *quae res instet* (cf. 1.461), things that are currently pressing on our attention, but are not completed. The last example he gives is "this nature and system of the world [that] has been found recently, and I myself am now found *the first, the very first*, to be able to turn it into the language of my fatherland (*denique natura haec rerum ratioque repertast/nuper, et hanc primus cum primis ipse repertus/nunc ego sum in patrias qui possim vertere voces*, 5.335–337). As the mode of explanation (*ratio*, 5.335) migrates across time (from the lifetime of Epicurus to that of Lucretius) and space (from Greece to Rome), its exposition becomes subject to translation, an issue that currently presses on Lucretius (cf. 1.142–145), but which can be an opportunity for one "progressing step by step." Neither the *ratio* nor his own text is viewed as an *eventum*, equipped with a beginning *and* a conclusion. His claim to being *first* is curiously emphatic: his text is a fresh beginning within a process in which no conclusion has been reached, or is anticipated. From the midst of things where he situates himself and his text, Epicureanism is being finessed and refined. What sort of reader, then, does the poem address? One who regards it as an *eventum*, a product of the past, its sense circumscribed (running the risk of thinking that sense exists per se)? Or a thing of recurring insistence, its meaning (the term has the form of a present participle) provisional, not foreclosed, and ever subject to fresh interpretation?[23]

Lucretius draws specific attention to the task of translation that presses on him. Matter is everlasting and timeless, never created, and, not being subject to infinite division (the quality that prompts the Greek term *atomos*), can never be destroyed. However, he famously never transliterates the Greek term, although Cicero, for one, shows no such compunction.[24] Among the multiplicity of Latin terms he coins, and often deploys to subtle argumentative effect (*semina*, "seeds," *genitalia corpora rebus*, "the bodies that give birth to things," emphasizing becoming rather than being),[25] a couple stand out that are of particular relevance here. One we have met in 2.253, *primordia*, which I translated "first-order beginnings" to capture its etymology. Lucretius introduces a catalog of terms he will use for matter in its "primordial" state in 1.54–61, which includes *rerum primordia*, "the first-order beginnings of things [of the world that we experience]" (1.55) and *corpora prima*, "first bodies, because from them first all things exist" (*quod ex illis sunt omnia primis*, 1.61), for which there is no exact parallel in Epicurus.[26] Lucretius also eschews the use of the singular of these terms.[27] Matter is everlasting, but its movements *initiate* the coming into being and passing away of the things of the world, the temporal, processual aspect that is available to our senses and is invoked in the poem's title, *de rerum natura*, on the birth of things. In turn, the human concern with birth, beginnings, growth, decay, and passing away provides the *ratio*, the style of thinking, that can take you beyond what you can sense. *Ratio* allows one to transcend the barrier between the seen and the unseen, the time-bound and the timeless. It provides the timeless *principles* of the argument, etymologically the things that occupy first place (*primus* + *capio*): they are the starting point of the argument (as Lucretius uses *principium* in 1.149), and whatever phenomenon you wish to explain, you trace it back to those principles, and no further. For all that Lucretius's vocabulary can feel rebarbative (as he himself admits when he talks about its novelty and the poverty of his native tongue, 1.136–139), his language aspires to transparency, so that, as he puts it, "I may be able to open out clear lights before your mind, by which you may see right into hidden things (*clara tuae possim praepandere lumina menti, / res quibus occultas penitus convisere possis*, 1.144–145). In the classic aspiration of realism (< *res*), language is to dissolve before our eyes as time-bound phenomena, as they appear to us, give way to theory (quasi-timeless, albeit open to revision) of what really is, seen in "the mind's eye."[28]

The language of "firsts" invokes the metaphysical tradition associated with Aristotle's *archai*, though Lucretius distances himself from the theologically inflected metaphysics of Plato and Aristotle. An explanation of the universe may see it as boundless, without beginning or end, with no creator figure, and operating with brute and absolute indifference to the conscious beings it has generated and their notions of time and order, both sequential and consequential; but *qua* explanation it is a construction of the human mind and so requires its boundaries, its starting and endpoints, and, as a human construction, itself has a history. In the face of these challenges, Lucretius's recourse is to narrative. His main strategy is to focus on the figure of Epicurus himself, the one who "came upon these things" (*rerum inventor*, 3.9). Crucial is the first encounter with Epicurus, depicted as the savior of mankind from superstition and fear of the gods (1.62–79).[29] He is represented in military terms as a champion of downtrodden humankind, the *first* to break out from our world, under siege by religious superstition (1.66–67). He traverses the cosmos ("the immeasurable everything," *omne immensum*, 1.74) in mind and spirit, whence "he reports back to us what can arise (*quid possit oriri*), what cannot (*quid nequeat*), in short the reasoning by which each thing has its dominion (*potestas*, its 'capacity for being able to') limited and its boundary stone deep-set" (1.75–77). Epicurus brings back not an explanation of each and every phenomenon in the universe (a task that would take an infinity of time and make Lucretius's poem an endless text) but a mode of explanation (*ratio*, cf. 1.77) of what *potentially* can and cannot happen: no matter where, no matter when, this theory lays claim to explain any phenomenon whatsoever.

Epicurean materialism can be seen as a rebuttal of the Platonic worldview, and as part of his expositional strategy, Lucretius eagerly appropriates and repurposes the tropes of Platonizing metaphysics. For Plato, there is a separation of realms, one in which time-bound objects exist, and one in which timeless things (the Forms, mathematical objects) exist. The former is the experiential world of change, the latter is unchanging and associated with the heavens and the gods. Epicurus's journey across the cosmos and his report back to us shares a narrative structure with Plato's myth of the Cave in the *Republic*, where the philosopher leaves the shadows to climb up to the light and then returns to inform those who remained behind. For Lucretius there is no insuperable barrier between the time-bound and the timeless: the journey of Epicurus is a mythical fantasy that elevates his achievement while making key philosophical points. To achieve what he did, he didn't need to leave the human world at all—except in mind and spirit (*mente animoque*, 1.74). In another eulogy he is represented, in imagery that once more evokes the Cave, as the *first* to be able to lift up so clear a light amid such great shadows, throwing light on the amenities of life (*o tenebris tantis tam clarum extollere lumen/qui primus inlustrans commoda vitae*, 3.1–2). His feat may be represented in heroic terms, but there is nothing "super"-human about it. Everything you need to understand the cosmos and your existence within it you can find down here.

If time is a product of human consciousness, explanations of the universe that appeal to a creator figure could be seen as a projection on to "the divine" of the human experience of time and its quest for meaningful order, of beginnings and ends, of relationships between what has happened, what is happening and what will happen. The qualities that are associated with such creator figures are transferred in Lucretius's account to the creator of the explanatory *theory* of the universe, a theory that holds good irrespective of time or place. Epicurus "was a god (*deus ille fuit*) . . . who first discovered that theory of life (*vitae rationem*) which is now called wisdom" (5.8–10). Epicurus may have been mortal, but his "golden sayings" are "ever most worthy of eternal life" (3.12–13). As a human construction, this theory also has a history, emerging at a particular time and place: Athens "when it gave birth to a man . . . who in days gone by poured forth everything (*omnia*) from his truth-telling lips" (6.5–6). Though he is now dead, on account of his "divine discoveries" (*divina reperta*), his glory, spread far and wide in days gone by, is now exalted to the skies (6.7–8). "Down here" and "up there" are repurposed and revalorized.

Augustine: Time, Theology, and Lived Experience

However powerfully we are affected by the magnitudes presented to us as time is reckoned by number—indeed by an infinity of time ("time without measure" in Lucretius; time "without end" in Vergil's *Aeneid*)—this fails to capture important aspects of time. Plotinus, arguing against Aristotle, suggested (*Ennead* 3.7.45) that to reduce time to number, a quantity of change, is not sufficient to grasp its essence. Famously, the *Aeneid* was the favorite reading in his youth of Augustine, and the metaphysical dichotomy of viewing history from the "inside" and the "outside" (or from "up there" and "down here") engineered in Jupiter's prophecy continued to resonate for him in his thinking about history in *City of God*.[30] Although he rejects Jupiter as a false god, and believes that no historical regime can fulfill the Vergilian prediction of "empire without end," he nonetheless retains a commitment to this as a theological idea: "Terrestrial kingdoms undergo change; but he shall come of whom it is said: 'And of his kingdom there shall be no end'" (*Serm.* 105.7.9). But his own experience of transience was the source of anxiety to him. His study of Platonism (especially Plotinus), which was intellectually crucial to his turn to Christianity, underpins the division he is committed to between himself, caught up in time, and God, who is eternal. "May I know you, who know me. May I 'know as also I am known' (1 Corinthians 13:12)" he says at the opening of Book 10 of the *Confessions*, as he struggles to make sense of a relationship with a being who exists outside time, and to understand himself in a way that, he believes, that being knows him. In the first nine books he has attempted to narrate his own story, but his narration is not addressed to God, who is all-knowing: "Lord, eternity is yours, so you cannot be ignorant of what I tell you. Your vision of occurrences in time is not temporally conditioned" (11.1.1). God doesn't narrate: existing outside time, he has no need to. Narration is a characteristically human response to the desire to know and understand, and Augustine's is explicitly directed to his fellow human beings, who share his experience of existing within time (cf. 2.3.5).

For all his efforts (he has narrated his story "to the best of my ability," 11.1.1), Augustine finds himself confronting two problems.[31] The first is the temporal gap in narratives of the self between the narrating self and the narrated self on whom he looks back. The narrating self, with the benefit of hindsight, sees significance in events that was not apparent to his narrated self at the time (for example in the codex his friend Ponticianus picks up and opens in 8.6.14 and which Augustine subsequently picks up and opens in the garden scene in 8.12.29), but a significance that was, in some sense, already there, did the narrated self but know it.[32] On the one hand is the frustration that, from a human perspective within time, one can never know the meaning of an event in its full intentional and consequential significance, which can extend far beyond the lifetime of the individual concerned—indeed, to the very end of time itself. On the other hand is the faith that God, outside time, knows the full meaning of any such event (or such an individual) *sub specie aeternitatis*, and that the human apprehension of a greater significance is a sign of God's providence (i.e., foresight) and an intimation, however slight, of God's omniscience. God knows the "real" meaning that lies outside temporal experience ("You are always the same, and you always know unchangeably the things which are not always the same," 8.3.6), but human beings must *make* the truth (*veritatem . . . facere*, 10.1.1), construct facts as best they might, by *relating* two temporalities of experience of an event (those of the narrating and narrated selves), and trying to divine what significance may emerge between them. And, by implication, *re*make the truth as time passes, and new significances emerge in the light of subsequent events and the fresh perspectives brought to bear. Augustine describes the human experience of time and change in ontological terms, and the terms he uses for time (present; future) are ontologically inflected, formations from the verb "to be." Change is experienced as absences: what was once intensely felt as a presence, but is no longer there (e.g., his beloved mother, Monica); what was present, but not noticed at the time (the significance of the codex Ponticianus picks up). Facts must depend on something to bring them to presence: memory. The self, the soul, is distended across time, never wholly present to itself, in contrast to the ultimate being, seen as one for whom these are *not* issues, existing in a pure state outside time.

The second problem Augustine confronts is language, which he expresses as a distinction between human words and the Word of God. In thinking about the creation of heaven and earth, he rejects the craftsman model. God spoke and heaven and earth were created, he remarks (11.5.7–6.8): "But how did you speak? Surely not in the way a voice came out of the cloud saying: 'This is my beloved Son' (Matt. 17:5). The voice is past and done with; it began and is ended. The syllables sounded and have passed away, the second after the first, the third after the second, and so on in order until, after all the others, the last one came, and after the last silence followed." Words point to the passing of time by the sequentiality of their ordering. His study of the Neoplatonists emphasized for him how language marks the separation of the human from the divine, and is a symptom of humanity's fallen condition: "In the eternal, nothing is transient, but the whole is present. But no time is wholly present" (11.11.13; cf. Plotinus 3.7.3), not at least for the soul, distended across past and future. Strikingly, sound rather than vision (recall the importance of observation in the physical tradition, and the constant recourse Lucretius has to the language of seeing)[33] becomes the dominant sense in thinking about time. Language is not something to be "seen through," but enacted in prayer, preaching, reading and writing, and particularly in the trope that reaches out to God, second-person apostrophe. Language provides the master metaphor for understanding God's purpose: in the beginning was the Word, as the opening of St John's Gospel has it. God's Word is not like the languages of man; it brought time into being with the creation of everything else (11.13.15).

"What then is time?" Augustine asks. "Provided that no one asks me, I know. If I want to explain it to an inquirer, I do not know" (11.14.17). Augustine offers no answer and only briefly and with little evident enthusiasm mentions philosophical discussions that associate time with movement (11.23.29). How can time be said to exist when the past is gone, the future does not yet exist, and the present vanishes in extent toward zero? If we speak, as we do, of a "long" or a "short" time, how do we measure it? Aristotle had tentatively suggested that time is an experience of the soul (*Ph.* 4.14), and Augustine, much more concerned, as we have seen, with how people make sense of the succession of events they experience, both on a local personal scale, and on a grander, historical one, makes this, rather than the definition of time, the focus of his thinking. Augustine's key suggestion is that it is inexact to speak of three times, past, present, and future; rather, in the soul's capacity for continuous attention in a moving present there is a present of things past (memory), a present of things present (immediate awareness), and a present of things future (expectation). In this threefold present, the soul becomes "distended," stretched in memory and anticipation (11.20.26).

If the temporal sequentiality of language poses problems, it can also help to point toward possible ways of understanding the human experience of time. Augustine uses two textual examples to develop his argument. The first is the recitation of a metrical hymn consisting of alternate short and long syllables to suggest that the measuring of the length of the syllables is a function of memory in the continuous attention of the soul in the present—which is what allows one to measure time generally (11.27.35). The distension of the mind over past and future is then illustrated by the recitation of a psalm that, significantly, one knows by heart. One therefore has an expectation of it as a whole before one begins. "The life of this act of mine," he says, "is stretched two ways, into my memory because of the words I have already said and into my expectation because of those which I am about to say. But my attention is on what is present: by that the future is transferred to become the past." This continues until the psalm is finished, expectation is exhausted, and the entire action passes into memory. Augustine then invites his readers to scale that action both down and up: "What occurs in the psalm as a whole occurs in its particular pieces and its individual syllables. The same is true of a longer action in which perhaps that psalm is a part. It is also valid of the entire life of an individual person, where all actions are parts of a whole, and of the total history of 'the sons of men' (Ps.30: 20) where all human lives are but parts" (11.28.38). That will be the preoccupation of *City of God*.

So, in the stretching of the soul that is memory and expectation, people can have a sense not only of their own lives but of time and history as a whole. But that view is from within the flux of time, and the example of the psalm is but a poor analogy to God's knowledge: "Far be it from you to know all future and past events in this kind of sense. You know them in a much more wonderful and much more mysterious way" (11.31.41). God is eternal, and his knowing is not subject to the variation that existing in time brings. Augustine's textual examples have illustrated the capacity of discursive forms to create different effects in the soul. Narrative is the way human beings might seek to *make* the truth as best they might, but it is in the narrative of the self, at least for Augustine, that the distension of the soul is most painfully experienced and the distance from the eternal most acutely felt. Earlier, Augustine has described the eternal as that in which "nothing is transient, but the whole is present" (11.11.13), and when he strives toward that presence discursively, he seeks to eschew narrative in favor of repeated apostrophe, direct second-person address to the deity in the present tense. Language can impose a sense of separation from the eternal—but also orchestrate an intimation of metaphysical presence.

Notes

1. Tallis (2017) 4.
2. Cf. Nightingale (1995) and (2004). Earlier uses of the term *philosophos*, "the lover of wisdom" are explored in Moore (2020).
3. History no less has its ontological concerns; I explore this in Kennedy (2020b).
4. Translations are my own, except in the case of Augustine's *Confessions*, where I use Chadwick (1991).
5. For discussion of what Aristotle means, cf. Coope (2005) 85–98.
6. Cf. Wilcox (1987) 7–8. Kosmin (2018) explores the crucial role of the Seleucid Empire in this development.
7. For the texts, cf. Long and Sedley (1987) 1.162–164.
8. On *lekta*, see Bronowski (2019).
9. Cf. Tallis (2017) 112–118.

10. Tallis (2017) 5. Some prominent physicists (e.g., Weinberg (1993)) see their discipline as having left philosophy behind; and there are some philosophers (e.g., Ladyman and Ross (2007)), who reduce philosophy to physics (naturalism or scientism).
11. Thus Rovelli (2017), who seeks to reconcile quantum mechanics with the general theory of relativity, believes time at the fundamental level is unreal; by contrast Smolin (2013), a cosmologist profoundly skeptical about string theory and the theory of the multiverse, argues that what he calls "the crisis in physics" arises from the failure to acknowledge the reality of time. Unger and Smolin (2015) would like to see the discipline of physics embrace once more the outlook of natural philosophy.
12. Nagel (1986).
13. Ricoeur (1984–1988).
14. Explored in detail in Kennedy (2013a) 44–83.
15. Cf. Bakker (2018) and O'Rourke (2020).
16. Sedley (2007) 133–166 has a fine discussion.
17. For the philosophical implications of the plurality of worlds cf. Warren (2004); and on the history of theories of multiple worlds/universes, Rubenstein (2014).
18. Shearin (2015) 150; emphasis original.
19. Scheffler (2013) sensitively explores this weakness in the Epicurean approach to personal extinction, employing the thought experiment of the imminent extinction of the whole human race to suggest our investment in its continuation after our death.
20. Cf. Hankinson (2013).
21. Tallis (2017) 578.
22. For further discussion about this debate cf. Gordon in this volume and O'Keefe in this volume.
23. This is the stance of Nail (2018), who, from the perspective of quantum field theory and his own concern with developing an ontology of motion, sees as particularly salient the text's concern with flows and folds, and views as an *eventum*, an episode in the poem's reception, the early modern period's concern with particulate matter.
24. Cf. Sedley (1998) 38.
25. Cf. Sedley (1998) 193–198.
26. Cf. Fowler (2002) 174.
27. We should be cautious about speaking of "the atom" when discussing Lucretius's poem. Cf. Nail (2018), referred to in n22 above.
28. On this passage cf. further Kennedy (2020a) 265–266.
29. For further discussion of this passage cf. Kennedy (2013b), which argues that Epicurus is here presented as a philosophical counterpart to Alexander the Great, but far outstrips his achievements.
30. Cf. further Kennedy (2013a) 69–75.
31. For what follows, cf. the more detailed discussion in Kennedy (2013a) 1–42.
32. For a detailed reading of this episode, cf. Kennedy (2013a) 5–7.
33. Cf Lehoux (2013). To show interest in the natural world, as Augustine says he sometimes finds himself doing, is a sinful distraction he calls *curiositas*, which interrupts his prayers (*Conf.* 10.35.57).

References

Bakker, F. A. (2018). "The End of Epicurean Infinity: Critical Reflections on the Epicurean Infinite Universe" in Bakker, Bellis, and Palmerino, 41–67.

Bakker, F. A., D. Bellis, and C. R. Palmerino, eds. (2018). *Space, Imagination and the Cosmos from Antiquity to the Early Modern Period*. (Cham, Switzerland).
Bronowski, A. (2019). *The Stoics on Lekta: All There Is to Say*. (Oxford).
Chadwick, H., tr. (1991). *Saint Augustine* Confessions. (Oxford).
Coope, U. (2005). *Time for Aristotle: Physics 4.10–14*. (Oxford).
Fowler, D. (2002). *Lucretius on Atomic Motion: A Commentary on* De Rerum Natura *2.1–332*. (Oxford).
Furley, D. (1989). *Cosmic Problems: Essays on Greek and Roman Philosophy of Nature*. (Cambridge).
Hankinson, R. J. (2013). "Lucretius, Epicurus, and the Logic of Multiple Explanations," in Lehoux, Morrison, and Sharrock, 69–97.
Kennedy, D. F. (2013a). *Antiquity and the Meanings of Time: A Philosophy of Ancient and Modern Literature*. (London).
Kennedy, D. F. (2013b). "The Political Epistemology of Infinity," in Lehoux, Morrison, and Sharrock, 51–67.
Kennedy, D. F. (2020a). "Plato and Lucretius on the Theoretical Subject," in O'Rourke, 259–281.
Kennedy, D. F. (2020b). "On Not Being Modern: Exploring Historical Ontology with Bruno Latour," in A. Turner (ed.), *Reconciling Ancient and Modern Philosophies of History* (Berlin), 43–81.
Kosmin, P. J. (2018). *Time and Its Adversaries in the Seleucid Empire*. (Cambridge, Mass.).
Ladyman, J., and D. Ross (2007). *Everything Must Go: Metaphysics Naturalized*. (Oxford).
Lehoux, D. (2013). "Seeing and Unseeing, Seen and Unseen," in Lehoux, Morrison, and Sharrock (2013), 131–151.
Lehoux, D., A. D. Morrison, and A. Sharrock, eds. (2013). *Lucretius: Poetry, Philosophy, Science*. (Oxford).
Long, A. A., and Sedley, D. N. (1987). *The Hellenistic Philosophers*. (Cambridge).
Moore, C. (2020). *Calling Philosophers Names: On the Origins of a Discipline*. (Princeton).
Nagel, T. (1986). *The View from Nowhere*. (New York).
Nail, T. (2018). *Lucretius I: An Ontology of Motion* (Edinburgh).
Nightingale, A. W. (1995). *Genres in Dialogue: Plato and the Construct of Philosophy*. (Cambridge).
Nightingale, A. W. (2004). *Spectacles of Truth in Classical Greek Philosophy:* Theoria *in Its Cultural Context*. (Cambridge).
O'Rourke, D, ed. (2020). *Approaches to Lucretius: Traditions and Innovations in Reading* De rerum natura (Cambridge).
O'Rourke, D. (2020a). "Infinity, False Closure and Enclosure in Lucretius' *De rerum natura*," in O'Rourke, 103–123.
Rubenstein, M.-J. (2014). *Worlds without Ends: The Many Lives of the Multiverse*. (New York).
Ricoeur, Paul (1984–1988). *Time and Narrative*. 3 vols. (Chicago).
Rovelli, C. (2017). *The Order of Time*. (London).
Scheffler, S. (2013). *Death and the Afterlife*. (New York).
Sedley, D. (1998). *Lucretius and the Transformation of Greek Wisdom*. (Cambridge).
Sedley, D. (2007). *Creationism and Its Critics in Antiquity*. (Berkeley).
Shearin, W. (2015). *The Language of Atoms*. (Oxford).
Smolin, L. (2013). *Time Reborn: From the Crisis in Physics to the Future of the Universe*. (London).
Tallis, R. (2017). *Of Time and Lamentation: Reflections on Transience*. (Newcastle upon Tyne).

Unger, R. M., and L. Smolin (2015). *The Singular Universe and the Reality of Time*. (Cambridge).
Warren, J. (2004). "Ancient Atomists on the Plurality of Worlds." *CQ* 54: 354–365.
Weinberg, S. (1993). *Dreams of a Final Theory: The Search for the Fundamental Laws of Nature*. (London).
Wilcox, D. J. (1987). *The Measure of Times Past: Pre-Newtonian Chronologies and the Rhetoric of Relative Time*. (Chicago).

CHAPTER 25

DEATH

JAMES WARREN

> *sestertium reliquit trecenties, nec umquam philosophum audivit.*
> — Petron. *Sat.* 71 (Trimalchio imagines the inscription on his tombstone)

THE theme of death and mortality looms large in all literature and philosophy, and it would be a mammoth task to discuss even just the philosophical material written during the period covered by this volume. In this chapter I shall therefore concentrate on exploring just two themes. First, I look briefly at the important continuities between Roman philosophical approaches to death and their Greek antecedents. Second, I discuss the theme of suicide, deliberate and voluntary self-killing, through a discussion of the presentation of the death of Cato the younger in the works of Cicero and Seneca. Throughout, I focus on texts written in Latin, since there was a large degree of continuity in the tradition of Greek philosophical writing on death in the various schools and I am interested in distinctively Roman contribution to these debates. I focus on two such contributions: the deployment of earlier philosophical ideas in the context of standing Roman notions of duty, *pietas*, and courage; and the interest in philosophically sanctioned suicide, often looking back to the models of Socrates and Cato.

THE GREEK BACKGROUND

The important trends in ancient philosophical thanatology were well established before the Roman period.[1] In the first place there was a simple disagreement over the nature of death. There was a division between those who considered death to be the release of the immortal soul from the body—roughly speaking, those working in the Platonist tradition—and those who considered death to be the annihilation of the soul—roughly speaking, everyone else including the Epicureans and Peripatetics.[2] But this disagreement overlay a general agreement that death itself was in fact not something that should be considered a bad thing. True, those who thought that the immortal soul can bear the unfortunate imprint of a badly lived life held that there were some people who would not look forward to an afterlife of bliss, but even they were of the view that death was not itself something terrible. Indeed, it could be a benefit provided one has looked after one's soul while alive. The annihilationists argued that since the person ceases to be at the end of his life, there is no sense in which he can be harmed after death. In this sense, death is not harmful. Both sides agree, furthermore, that what matters is that every person should try to live their life well and that part of living well is thinking properly about human mortality.

The two sides were united in the claim that death is per se nothing to be feared and could, on occasion and sometimes with special permission, even be something that should be pursued. But they were less interested in emphasizing this broad consensus than they were in criticizing their philosophical rivals. Debates between the two camps took the form of each side asking whether the other side's conception of the nature of death was in fact compatible with their preferred stance on its value. For the annihilationists, their opponents' supposition that the soul might continue to exist in some afterlife was hailed as a source of fear and anxiety since no one can be sure what fate will await their soul after death. The annihilationists' preferred view was that death is the absolute end of our existence and they insisted that for that reason there can be no post mortem harm for us to fear. Here is the Roman poet Lucretius's succinct expression of the central idea, which is his version of an argument found in earlier Greek sources (Lucr. 3.830–831):[3] "Therefore death is nothing to us, nor does it matter to us at all, since the nature of the soul is understood to be mortal."

For the supporters of an immortal soul, on the other hand, the idea that the soul perishes along with the body should be seen as a distressing image of finality and destruction. Their preferred view was that the final separation of the immortal soul from the body was, ideally, the culmination of the philosopher's life-long cultivation of his true self and might even be a way in which each of us can aspire to become godlike. Apuleius, for example, writing in the second century CE, explains his Platonist view as follows (*De dog. Plat.* 2.33.253–255):

> It is not merely during his lifetime that every man should act in a manner worthy of the gods and refrain from things displeasing to their greatness, but also when he departs his body (which we will not do unless god is willing). For even if the capacity for death is in his own hands and although he might know that he will obtain better things once he has left behind earthly affairs, he will not arrange his own death unless a divine law has decreed that he must submit to this necessity. Even if the honors of his earlier life make his death a good one, nevertheless the death itself should be more virtuous and win a favorable reputation. When, sure of the future of his descendants, he allows his soul to leave for immortality, he knows that because he has lived piously his soul will inhabit the regions of the blessed, joining with choruses of gods and demigods.

Each side, therefore, could accuse the other of failing to offer a picture of our mortal condition consistent with the presentation of a positive picture of the consequences of mortality for our overall well-being. An important sign that the debate between these two camps had reached a certain stage of maturity by the end of the Hellenistic period is that we then begin to find works that set out to dramatize the contest between the annihilationists and the postmortem survivalists. Indeed, we have two works from around the first century BCE that pit these two visions against one another and compare the psychological effectiveness of their respective points of view. The first is a pseudo-Platonic dialogue, *Axiochus*, whose authorship and place of composition is unknown. There, Socrates first tries to console as old man, Axiochus, who is gripped with fear at the thought of his death, with some Epicurean-style arguments. When these fail Socrates turns to some more effective thoughts based on the idea that the soul will survive Axiochus's death.[4] The second is Cicero's first *Tusculan Disputation*, written in the summer of 45 BCE. It too is a dialogue in which one character, "M.," attempts to persuade the other, "A.," that death is not a bad thing. Initially, this is done through rapid exchanges that are clearly indebted to Epicurean arguments. But this soon gives way to a longer exposition based on the generally Platonist assumption that the immortal soul will survive death.[5] As in the *Axiochus*, this approach turns out to be more effective in assuaging the fear of death.

This interest in staging a contest between the competing approaches to dealing with the fear of death clearly continued beyond the first century BCE. In *Letter 77* Seneca tells Lucilius a story about Tullius Marcellinus (77.5–9). Marcellinus fell ill and became decrepit rather quickly. As a result, he began to think about death. He called together various friends and asked each of them in turn to offer him some reason not to be so afraid of dying. One by one each friend offered some advice. A timid friend tried to persuade Marcellinus of just what he had persuaded himself; another friend tried to flatter Marcellinus by saying what he thought Marcellinus wanted to hear. But only the Stoic friend offered anything that seems to Seneca to be useful advice. The Stoic explained that living or dying is not any great matter and the mere prolongation of life is simply indifferent. So Marcellinus, now resolved, asked the slaves to help him to die. The Stoic friend had to strengthen the slaves' resolve too and explain they would not be held responsible for their master's death but soon enough Marcellinus was sufficiently confident to begin dividing up gifts of his possessions to all those present. He fasted for a few days and then allowed himself to pass away in a hot bath. In Seneca's Rome, of all the various ways of thinking about death that are available to a cultured Roman it is Stoicism—unsurprisingly—that offers the most helpful philosophical approach to dying. More specifically, Seneca assures Lucilius that Stoicism alone offers the noble Roman an intellectual basis not only for not fearing death but also for hastening it and taking charge of when and how it comes by committing suicide.

It is not always possible to know for certain the extent to which our Latin authors are being innovative in their approach to these topics, simply because we do not possess a full sample of the earlier works which influenced them. But it is a reasonable supposition that there is little genuine innovation in the philosophical arguments presented in the Roman period on the topic of the nature of death. The principal questions to be faced are quite clear and had been clearly identified by the Greeks; the relevant issues had already been subjected to continued sophisticated scrutiny. What the later Roman philosophers had to offer to the philosophical discussion of death, therefore, was not so much a set of innovative ideas as a set of different ways to present and explain long-standing debates and opinions, deploy the tools offered by earlier philosophical traditions, and translate these ideas with new examples and new emphases in a different cultural context.[6]

To illustrate the general landscape, we can compare two texts written at around the same time as one another and which both deal with the Epicurean attitude to death. One—Philodemus's *De morte*—is in Greek. The other—Lucretius's *De rerum natura*—is in Latin. Philodemus moved from Athens to Italy sometime around 88 BCE, and some of his works are dedicated to Roman patrons. And although Philodemus was in all likelihood here as elsewhere using material he had picked up from reading Epicurus himself and from listening to Zeno of Sidon, it is reasonably certain that *On Death* was composed in Italy and the date of its composition is usually placed at some time soon after 45 BCE. Nevertheless, a reader of the surviving columns of the work would be hard-pressed to discern any obvious connection with Italy or Rome. What remains we have of *On Death* come from its fourth book (*PHerc* 1005).[7] There, the examples of great men that Philodemus uses to make his various points are all Greek (Themistocles and Pericles at 29.2–15, Socrates and Callisthenes at 33.37–34.29) and the events which he mentions are taken from classical Greek history (Artemisium, Salamis, and Plataea at 33.10–23). For the vast majority of the text, what we are reading could more or less have been composed three hundred years earlier. There is, however, one brief sign of Philodemus's own times. Toward the end of the surviving rolls and the end of the book, Philodemus discusses the question of being caught unawares by death (37.18ff.) and addresses people who seem not to recognize what in fact would make a life complete. He writes (38.3–14):

> But some are such foreigners in human life, not only among common people but also among those said to be philosophers, that they actually arrange for themselves to spend so many years in Athens eager for knowledge, and so many touring Greece and the accessible parts of the non-Greek world, so many discoursing at home, and the rest with their acquaintances; but suddenly, hidden, there approaches, taking away great hopes, necessity. (tr. Henry)

The reference to people taking time out to study philosophy in Athens and to tour Greece is surely not relevant for an Athenian or Greek audience; here Philodemus is addressing those Romans—even those with a philosophical leaning—who might have thought that they could not consider their life complete unless they had gone to study in the home of philosophy and spent some time touring around Greece.

Only parts of the fourth book of Philodemus's *De morte* survive. Time has been even less kind to L. Varius Rufus's Latin poem *De morte* which was probably written at some time in the 40s BCE.[8] But we do have one outstanding Epicurean discussion of death from this period in the third book of Lucretius's *De rerum natura*. Lucretius, for his part, seems to be more concerned here to adapt the argument and the examples he uses to a Roman audience, decisions presumably consequent on his choice of Latin verse as a medium and his choice of a Roman addressee, Memmius. Like Philodemus, Lucretius is heavily reliant on Epicurus's original writings for the content and perhaps even the structure of his work. But he takes care to make the argument relevant for a Roman audience by choosing examples from Roman culture and politics alongside those from Greece and occasionally making obvious changes to the Greek original in his presentation of the argument. For example, in his account of the Epicurean "symmetry argument," Lucretius gives the Punic Wars as an example of events from before our birth which caused us no distress (3.833) and this cannot, obviously, have been the example he found used by Epicurus himself.[9] For the argument to be persuasive the intended audience of the argument should recognize that some terrible event that took place earlier than their own birth was not at the time of its occurrence something that caused them harm. With the addition of the further—and controversial—premise that the time in the future after that person's death is not relevantly different in terms of the potential to suffer harm, the addressee is invited to conclude that postmortem nonexistence is no more capable of harboring potential harms than was prenatal nonexistence. The chosen example cannot be an event too far in the past, since this would leave open room for the objection that, although the remote prenatal past and the remote postmortem future may be harm-free, there nevertheless remains the possibility of some more proximate and harmful postmortem and prenatal nonexistence. (It is perhaps reasonable to think a parent has more reason to think that not seeing his great-great grandchildren born is harmful than not seeing the birth of some very distant descendant.) Here is Lucretius's version with the relevant example (3.832–842):[10]

> And just as in the time that went before we felt no pain—when Carthaginians came from all sides to wage war, and the world struck by the disturbing upheaval of war shook and quivered under the high vault of heaven, and it was unclear to whose kingdom should fall all men on the land and sea —so when we are no more, when the body and soul from which combination we are formed have come apart, then no doubt there will be nothing to us (who will not be then) which will be able to move our senses in the slightest, not even if earth and sea and sky are mixed together.

In contrast, the version of this argument that appears in the pseudo-Platonic *Axiochus*, set dramatically in Athens at the end of the fifth century BCE, refers to "the time of Draco or Cleisthenes" (at 365d7–e2). Perhaps there was an instance of this argument in Epicurus's own writings but, even if there was, we do not know what example he chose. Perhaps he referred to Draco and Cleisthenes too. Nevertheless, the significant point is that Lucretius's innovation is presentational and not philosophical. Lucretius's choice of example makes no difference to the philosophical content or logic of his argument but demonstrates a clear regard for making his argument directly relevant to a Roman audience.

A similar picture emerges from considering those works aimed not at persuading someone not to feel pain in the expectation of his or her own death but rather at consoling a surviving friend or relative grieving on account of someone else's death. It is not easy to determine the precise generic boundaries of what tend to be called "consolations" (*consolationes*) but we have a number of examples from the Roman period of works that fall into this rough category, written in both Greek (e.g., Plutarch's *Consolatio ad Apollonium*) and Latin (e.g., Seneca's *Consolatio ad Polybium*).[11] Cicero famously composed a consolation to himself on the death of his daughter Tullia in February or March 45 BCE (just before he wrote the *Tusculan Disputations*) which might have been rather novel in being a self-addressed example of the form, but unfortunately it has not survived.[12] But here too we know that there were some important Greek precedents of such works and this makes it once again difficult to determine the nature and extent of any later Roman innovations. Epicurus apparently wrote on the occasion of the death of Hegesianax to the deceased's father Sositheus and brother Pryson and made the case for grief at the death of a loved one.[13] The Academic philosopher Crantor (d. 276/5 BCE) wrote a work *On Grief* (*Peri penthous*) that was apparently rather popular in Rome. Unfortunately, only fragments of it survive as quotations in other works.[14] Crantor was certainly an influence on Cicero in composing both his *consolatio* and also the *Tusculans* (see *Tusc.* 3.12 and cf. *Acad.* 2.135).[15] In that case, already by Cicero's time various positions and arguments concerning the nature of the emotions in general and of painful grief in particular had been outlined and defined quite well by earlier Greek authors. It is likely, therefore, that the *consolatio* against grief was another form of writing that came with a ready store of material for the resourceful Roman writer.

Cato and Roman Suicide

The roots of the close association in many Latin writers between Roman nobility, suicide, and Stoicism are to be found in the first century BCE.[16] Marcus Porcius Cato, "Cato the younger" or "Cato Uticensis," fought alongside Pompey in the civil war against Julius Caesar. After defeat at Pharsalus, Cato escaped to Africa. Another defeat at the hands of Caesar's forces at Tharsus led to Cato deciding to take his own life in Utica in April 46 BCE rather than be captured and perhaps pardoned by Caesar. Cato's suicide quickly became a symbol of resistance against tyranny and also a Roman example of philosophically guided noble voluntary death. Indeed, his suicide neatly combines two themes that characterize much of the later discussion by Roman authors interested in the ethics and metaphysics of death.

First of all, Cato provided Romans with a perfect home-grown *exemplum* which could be used in place of more remote Greek cases of noble self-killing such as the death of Socrates. And yet a note of caution is perhaps appropriate here. The use of noble examples from the Roman past as ethical paradigms was a long-standing practice that does not of itself need to be assigned any particular philosophical basis. Indeed, at *Tusc.* 1.89 Cicero's character "M." comments that Romans in fact have no need of philosophy to see that death is not to be feared; the actions of their own ancestors clearly demonstrate the fact. And, what is more, it is possible that suicide was in general a course of action that was more tolerated in Roman culture than it had been in earlier Greek culture. It would be difficult to substantiate such a claim, but it is important to remember that prior Roman social and cultural attitudes had an important role to play in guiding which of the aspects of Greek philosophy were taken up and emphasized by Latin authors and which were not.[17] Certainly, under the Principate it is not always easy to determine whether there was any specifically philosophical basis for a particular case of suicide.[18]

All the same, Cato did fit neatly into a philosophical milieu as well as a more general Roman tradition of moral exemplarity. In particular, he was presented as a Stoic who killed himself in order to safeguard his virtue in the face of insupportable political circumstances. Presentations of Cato's death tend to look back to interpretations of Socrates's death in Platonist and Stoic sources and emphasize the similarities to Socrates's own defiant and fearless attitude to death.[19] As we have already noted, the Platonic and Stoic traditions differ significantly in the metaphysical account of death that they favor. What the two traditions share, however, is the notion that there are occasions on which a person would be doing the right thing by causing his own death, in particular when this is a means of preserving a freedom from being forced to act unjustly or otherwise viciously.[20] It is not surprising, therefore, that Cato became something of a standard-bearer for a broader notion of *libertas* for those in Rome concerned about the erosion of Republican ideas and the growth of monarchic power. He stands for Roman steadfastness and consistency (*gravitas, constantia*) and a Republican distaste for tyranny.[21]

The assimilation of Cato to Socrates begins very early. In Cicero's *Tusculan Disputations*, written just a year after Cato's death, we are told that Cato "departed from life with the joy that he had received a reason for dying" (*Tusc.* 1.74).[22] M. continues by saying that we are in general forbidden from taking our own lives without express divine permission. This permission was given to Socrates in the past and has now been given to Cato. There was, of course, continued philosophical opposition to the permissibility of suicide except in very special circumstances.[23] And here Cicero is heading off any possible criticism of Cato by insisting that his actions had divine blessing. But Cicero is also explicitly connecting Cato with Socrates and, in particular, with the discussion of suicide and the depiction of Socrates's death in Plato's *Phaedo*.[24] This is useful for Cicero since, being no supporter of Stoicism himself, he can look back directly to the Platonic source material in his positive praise of Cato and emphasize the connection with Plato's Socrates. For example, in Cicero's *Tusculans*, the context surrounding the mention of Cato and Socrates is decidedly Platonic, concentrating on death as the release of the immortal soul from the body. Later writers embellish the connection further by claiming that Cato was reading the *Phaedo* before his death, implying that Cato was looking in that work for the justification and resolve to do what was needed.[25] And while the Stoics were also comfortable taking Socrates's divinely sanctioned death as something of a model (see, e.g., Diog. Laert. 7.28 and 7.176), their view of the nature of death is quite unlike Plato's and unlike what is argued for in the *Phaedo*. Nevertheless, it was as a Stoic exemplar that Cato made his great impact on the Roman philosophical imagination. If Cato became the Roman Socrates, then he did so for the most part in the guise of the Stoic Socrates. After the immediate scars of the civil wars had passed, this Socratic air elevated Cato into the position of an exemplar for Roman writers and readers of principled and rational martyrdom in the face of external political pressures.[26]

Seneca should certainly take some of the credit for cementing Cato's place as a Roman Stoic sage. In the *De constantia sapientis* 2.1–3, for example, Cato is compared favorably with the Stoic heroes Ulysses and Hercules for facing down not mere dangerous beasts but the vices of an entire degenerate state. Later, Cato is explicitly offered as a concrete example of a perfect Stoic agent (7.1).[27] Elsewhere in Seneca, Cato continues to appear paired with Socrates.[28] He also appears regularly in passages designed to show that the wise man is always free in the sense that he has in his own hands the means to escape any intolerable circumstances and to preserve control over his own virtue and well-being. In *Letter* 104, for example, Seneca is discussing how difficult circumstances do not detract from a person's happiness or the goodness of his character. He gives an account of the various difficulties that Socrates endured. Then—*vis alterum exemplum?* (104.29)—he turns to Cato. Despite all the upheavals and setbacks in his life Cato too remained constant and unflappable. He determined just what he would do given the available alternatives: he would die if Caesar prevailed and rejoice if Pompey won. And so, Seneca asks, what could frighten such a person who has resolved for himself what he will do under any possible circumstance? When Cato died, he did so "by his own order" and not by Caesar's (104.32).

In *De providentia* 2.9–12 Seneca allows himself to compose Cato's own final words—apparently something that was a common school exercise[29]—while emphasizing how the gods themselves must have looked in a kindly way on these actions. Seneca also notes that Cato did not die quickly and simply—Plutarch's account of Cato's death is also quite grisly—but nevertheless manages to put a positive spin on the scene. Clearly, he says, the gods were so pleased with the sight they could not allow it to be over too soon and, of course, the delay provided an even greater opportunity for Cato to display his virtuous character.

Seneca's *Letter* 70, perhaps his most famous discussion of suicide, has surprisingly little explicit reference to Cato, despite its theme being the relationship between *libertas* and our ability to depart from life whenever we choose. But Cato is nevertheless an important presence in the letter. Seneca discusses the death of Socrates (70.9) but the place of Socrates's usual Roman partner is here taken by M. Scribonius Libo Drusus (70.10–11).[30] This is all part of the letter's general rhetorical strategy. In fact, Seneca cleverly mentions Cato only to pass on to explain how even far less noble examples can demonstrate the same general philosophical point (70.22). (This is where he gives the famous example of the German beast-fighter who kills himself with a toilet sponge: 70.20–21). The reader is therefore invited both to recall the august Cato and also to recognize that Cato stands for a much more general human freedom that is not in the least restricted to noble senators and great political crises.

Seneca himself, it seems, was in turn held up to comparison with Socrates and with his own celebration of Cato.[31] Perhaps these were in part as a result of Seneca's own self-presentation but such comparisons, once invited, are not always welcome. It is hard to live up to such a high standard and Seneca's detractors were not slow to depict his death in terms that were less than noble and laudatory. It is hard to read accounts of Seneca's difficulties when he eventually did decide to commit suicide in the positive way in which Seneca presents even Cato's protracted death. Indeed, perhaps in tandem with the tradition of writing in praise of these fine and upstanding Roman preservers of *libertas*, there was another train of thought which saw these theatrical and self-aggrandizing deaths as empty bids for fame.[32] Certainly, not all Roman attempts to emulate Socrates and Cato were equally successful either in basic practical terms or as enactments of political or philosophical ideas. Compare, for example, the depictions in Tacitus's *Annals* of the deaths of Thrasea Paetus (16.34–35: this is where the extant text of the work breaks off) and of Seneca himself (15.60–64). Both vignettes invite comparisons with Socrates. While Socrates notoriously asks Crito to take Xanthippe away because she is grieving excessively "as women do" (*Phaedo* 60a), Seneca's wife Paulina and Thrasea's wife Arria both try to kill themselves alongside their husbands. Seneca approves of Paulina's choice but she is restrained on Nero's orders (*Ann.* 15.63–64); Thrasea persuades Arria to stay alive for the sake of their daughter (16.34).[33] Otherwise, Thrasea Paetus manages a good Socratic suicide, with the required preparatory discussion (with the Cynic philosopher Demetrius) "about the nature of the soul and the separation of the mind from the body" (16.34) and giving notice of his own performance as an *exemplum* to others.[34] (Thrasea Paetus also composed a biography of Cato, which is likely to have been one of Plutarch's sources.) Seneca, in contrast, finds it hard to hasten his own death and eventually even calls for "the poison given to someone condemned by an Athenian jury" (15.64). But even this final attempt at a Socratic gesture proves ineffective and, in the end, Seneca expires in the bath.[35]

Notes

1. For a recent survey of Greek and Roman philosophical attitudes to death and immortality, see Long (2019).
2. The Stoics are perhaps a difficult case, since there are some sources according to which they allow that souls may last for some time after the destruction of the living person but will eventually—perhaps at the conflagration—also perish (e.g., Cic. *Tusc.* 1.78). I shall not discuss in any detail Christian approaches to death. They fall into the same general camp as the broad Platonic tradition in holding that death is the separation of an immortal soul from the physical body.
3. See Epicurus, *Kyria Doxa* 2 and *Ep. Men.* 125.
4. On the *Axiochus* see now the introduction, text, translation, and interpretative essays in Männlein-Robert et al. (2012).
5. On *Tusc.* 1, see Gildenhard (2007) and Warren (2013).
6. For example, Reydams-Schils (2005) 119–121, 134–141 emphasizes how Roman Stoics (119) "write against the background of a society that highly values the reciprocal, dutiful, and

affectionate bond of *pietas* between parents and children" (119) and a notion of extended bonds of duty to various others.

7. See the edition and translation by Henry (2009).
8. Only a few fragments survive quoted by Macrobius. For the argument that Varius's poem was a philosophical work influenced by Epicureanism, see, e.g., Hollis (1977) and cf. Hollis (2007) for the fragments with commentary.
9. See also Hoenig in this volume.
10. On the symmetry argument in Lucretius and various other examples of it in Greek and Latin texts, see Warren (2004) 57–108 and, for a brief philosophical assessment of the argument and recent attempts to defend or object to it, see Warren (2014).
11. See Reydams-Schils (2005) 119–123 and 136–141, LaBarge (2012), Scourfield (2013), Konstan (2013), and Ker in this volume.
12. See Baltussen (2013). Cic. *Div.* 2.3 explicitly places the *consolatio* within Cicero's conception of his philosophical oeuvre and also suggests that it was at least in part designed for a wider audience than just himself. For evidence of the content of the work see, e.g., *Div.* 2.22; *Tusc.* 1.66, 1.76, 4.63. Various letters in the Ciceronian correspondence also offer some evidence for the content of the lost work. *Att.* 12.14.3 (= Shackleton Bailey 251), written in March 45 BCE, announces that Cicero has been working on the *consolatio* to himself "*quod profecto ante me nemo.*" In April of 45 BCE, Servius Sulpicius Rufus writes a letter of condolence to Cicero (*Fam.* 4.5 = Shackleton Bailey 248). Cicero replies and confesses that he is unable to bear his grief in quite the wise manner his friend recommends (*Fam.* 4.6 = Shackleton Bailey 249). Both of these artful letters should probably themselves be included as examples of the consolatory genre. In that same month, Caesar too sent Cicero a letter of condolence: *Att.* 13.20.1 (= Shackleton Bailey 328).
13. Plut. *Non posse suaviter vivi secundum Epicurum* 1101A. See also Carneiscus's *Philista* (*PHerc.* 1027) and Warren (2004) 34–41.
14. For example: Plutarch's *Consolatio ad Apollonium*: 102D, 104C, 114C, 115B.
15. Cf. Pliny *NH* praef. 22. For a brief account and collection of the evidence for Crantor's work, see Graver (2002) 187–194. The third book of the *Tusculans* is devoted to the question whether the wise man will be subject to emotions (*pathē* or *pertubationes animi*). The Stoics insisted that the wise man will never be subject to such affections since they are all in fact based on false judgments about what is and is not of value. Crantor apparently advocated the view that excessive grief is inappropriate but a moderate affection (*metriopatheia*) is natural and this view was supported by later Peripatetics (see *Tusc.* 3.12, 70–74). Cf. Gildenhard (2007) 279–281.
16. For a detailed and careful account of suicide in Roman literature and philosophy, see Hill (2004), who also includes a helpful discussion of the very notion of "suicide" and its relevance to these cases.
17. Cf. Griffin (1986) 192–194 and Reydams-Schils (2005) 45–48. See, for example, Seneca *Ep.* 24, which combines various exempla, including Socrates and Cato and, for Cato as a general moral exemplar, see also Valerius Maximus 3.1.2a–3 and 3.2.14.
18. Griffin (1986) 197–198: "Obituaries and death scenes of all kinds abound in the literature of the early Empire, and we know of works that dealt specifically with the deaths of famous men. One plausible explanation of this emphasis lies in the restriction of the traditional opportunities for acquiring glory that was imposed by the autocratic system of government. The Roman nobility found it more difficult to live up to the example of their

ancestors in acquiring military and civic fame, but they could still die noble and memorable deaths."

19. For Stoic interest in Socrates's death, see, e.g., Cicero *Fat.* 30 and cf. Sedley (1993) 314–320.
20. It is important to note that there were important *caveats* expressed by Epicureans and Stoics against committing suicide for the wrong reasons. See for example, Lucr. 3.79–82 and Seneca *Ep.* 24.22–25 with Warren (2004) 205–209. Cf. Sen. *Ep.* 70.14. Piso, the Antiochean spokesman of Cicero's *De finibus* 5, argues against self-killing on the grounds that it shows a lack of love for oneself: *Fin.* 5.28–30 (compare Aquinas, *Summa Theologiae* Part II–II, Q. 64 Art. 5 co.).
21. E.g., Cic. *Off.* 1.112: *Catoni cum incredibilem tribuisset natura gravitatem, eamque ipse perpetua constantia roboravisset, semperque in proposito susceptoque consilio permansisset, moriendum potius queam tyranni vultus aspiciendus fuit.* See also Gildenhard (2007) 123–125. Cicero's account of the Stoic justification for suicide is at *Fin.* 3.60–61.
22. In the opening of his *Paradoxa Stoicorum* (1–4) probably written early in 46 BCE, just before Utica, Cicero praised Cato's ability to make plausible paradoxical Stoic doctrines. See Wassmann (1996) 96–138 (esp. 105–132) and Baraz (2013) 131–136.
23. See Hoenig in this volume.
24. See, for the necessity of divine permission: *Phaedo* 62b–e (this view is retained in Apuleius *On Plato and His Philosophy* 2.23, cited above). For discussion, see Warren (2001). Cicero restates this view also at *De republica* 6.15 and at *De senectute* 73, where it is ascribed to Pythagoras. At *Phaedo* 61d–e it is ascribed to the Pythagorean Philolaus. Cf. Augustine *De civ. D.* 1.20–21 for a Christian version of the same idea.
25. See Seneca *Ep.* 24.6: *Platonis librum legentem . . .* ; Plut. *Vit. Cat. Min.* 68 (where the work is referred to as "Plato's dialogue on the soul") and 70. Cf. Rist (1969) 244–246. Zadorojnyi (2007) emphasizes ways in which the Platonist Plutarch makes Cato rather un-Stoic, perhaps to suggest that Cato was in fact a rather better (i.e., less Stoic) person than the Stoics would have it.
26. See Griffin (1986) 195–198; Rist (1969) 246–248. Cato remained a focus for pro- and antimonarchic pamphlets, beginning with Cicero's own *Cato* and Caesar's reply: *Anti-Cato*. Cf. Wassmann (1996) 139–159 and Hall (2009) 94–100. Caesar's conduct toward Cicero's praise of Cato also became a touchstone for later discussions of how emperors might deal with dissent. See Tac. *Ann.* 4.34.
27. Cf. Cicero *Brut.* 118.
28. E.g., Seneca *Ep.* 13.14: *cicuta magnum Socratem fecit. Catoni gladium adsertorem libertatis extroque: magnam patrem detraxeris gloriae*; cf. 67.7 and 104.27–32. See also Seneca *Consolatio ad Helvetia* 13.4.6: Socrates was not disgraced by being imprisoned; similarly, Cato was not disgraced by failing to be elected praetor and consul. Socrates graced the prison by his presence; Cato graced these offices merely by being willing to serve in them.
29. Roman schoolboys learned and recited the speech of dying Cato: Persius 3.44–47.
30. On Socrates's role in this letter, see also Inwood (2005) 241–242. On M. Scribonius Libo Drusus's trial and suicide, see Tac. *Ann.* 2.27–32.
31. See Griffin (1976) 369–388. See also Reydams-Schils (2005) 171–175 with again, a crucial difference: the presence of Paulina.
32. Martial 1.8 cites Thrasea and Cato as people not to emulate: (1.8.5–6: *nolo virum facili redimit qui sanguine famam, / hunc volo, laudari qui sine morte potest*; cf. 6.32). Compare the more positive judgment of Seneca's final hours in Griffin (1976) 383.

33. See Reydams-Schils (2005) 171–175.
34. Thrasea Paetus is said to be the Cato to Nero's Caesar: *Ann.* 16.22.
35. For a rich discussion of the death of Seneca and its afterlife in later sources, together with an account of the theme of death in Seneca's own writings, see Ker (2009).

References

Baltussen, H. (2013). "Cicero's *Consolatio ad se*: Character, Purpose, and Impact of a Curious Treatise," in Baltussen, 67–91.
Baltussen, H., ed. (2013). *Greek and Roman Consolations: Eight Studies of a Tradition and Its Afterlife.* (Swansea).
Baraz, Y. (2013). *A Written Republic: Cicero's Philosophical Politics.* (Princeton).
Brunschwig, J., and M. Nussbaum, eds. (1993). *Passions and Perceptions: Studies in Hellenistic Philosophy of Mind.* (Cambridge).
Dominik, W. J., J. Garthwaite, and P. A. Roche, eds. (2009). *Writing Politics in Imperial Rome.* (Leiden).
Gildenhard, I. (2007). Paideia Romana: *Cicero's* Tusculan Disputations. *Cambridge Classical Journal* Suppl. vol. 30. (Cambridge).
Graver, M. (2002). *Cicero on the Emotions*: Tusculan Disputations *3 and 4*. (Chicago).
Griffin, M. (1976). *Seneca: A Philosopher in Politics.* (Oxford).
Griffin, M. (1986). "Philosophy, Cato, and Roman Suicide." *G&R* 33: 64–77 and 192–202.
Hall, J. (2009). "Serving the Times: Cicero and Caesar the Dictator," in Dominik, Garthwaite, and Roche, 89–110.
Henry, W. B. (2009). *Philodemus,* On Death. (Atlanta).
Hill, T. D. (2004). Ambitiosa mors: *Suicide and Self-Killing in Roman Thought and Literature.* (London).
Hollis, A. S. (1977). "'L. Varius Rufus, De Morte (Frs. 1–4 Morel)." *CQ* 27: 187–190.
Hollis, A. S. (2007). *Fragments of Roman Poetry c. 60 BC–AD 20.* (Oxford).
Inwood, B. (2005). *Reading Seneca: Stoic Philosophy at Rome.* (Oxford).
Kamtekar, R., ed. (2012). *Virtue and Happiness: Essays in Honour of Julia Annas, Oxford Studies in Ancient Philosophy Supplementary Volume* (Oxford).
Ker, J. (2009). *The Deaths of Seneca.* (Oxford).
Konstan, D. (2013). "Lucretius and the Epicurean Attitude towards Grief," in Lehoux, Morrison, and Sharrock, 193–209.
LaBarge, S. (2012). "How (and Maybe Why) to Grieve Like an Ancient Philosopher," in Kamtekar, 321–342.
Lehoux, D. M., A. D. Morrison, and A. Sharrock, eds. (2013). *Lucretius: Poetry, Philosophy, Science* (Oxford).
Long, A. G. (2019). *Death and Immortality in Ancient Philosophy.* (Cambridge).
Luper, S., ed. (2014). *The Cambridge Companion to Life and Death.* (Cambridge).
Männlein-Robert, I., et al. (2012). *Ps.-Platon Über den Tod.* Sapere XX. (Tübingen).
Reydams-Schils, G. (2005). *The Roman Stoics. Self, Responsibility, and Affection.* (Chicago).
Rist, J. M. (1969). *Stoic Philosophy.* (Cambridge).
Shackleton Bailey, D. R. (1965–1970). *Cicero's* Letters to Atticus. 7 vols. (Cambridge).
Shackleton Bailey, D. R. (1977). *Cicero's* Epistulae ad Familiares. 2 vols. (Cambridge).
Scourfield, J. H. D. (2013). "Towards a Genre of Consolation," in Baltussen, 1–36.

Sedley, D. N. (1993). "Chrysippus and Psychophysical Causality," in Brunschwig and Nussbaum, 313–331.
Stacey Taylor, J., ed. (2013). *The Ethics and Metaphysics of Death*. (Oxford).
Warren, J. (2001). "Socratic Suicide." *JHS* 121: 91–106.
Warren, J. (2004). *Facing Death: Epicurus and His Critics*. (Oxford).
Warren, J. (2013). "The Harm of Death in Cicero's first *Tusculan Disputation*," in Stacey Taylor, 44–70.
Warren, J. (2014). "The Symmetry Problem," in Luper, 165–180.
Wassmann, H. (1996). *Ciceros Widerstand gegen Caesars Tyrannis: Untersuchungen zur politischen Bedeutung der philosophischen Spätschriften*. (Bonn).
Zadorojnyi, A. (2007). "Cato's Suicide in Plutarch." *CQ* 57: 216–230.

CHAPTER 26

ENVIRONMENT

DANIEL BERTONI

Cities are built up over ages, but fall in an hour. Fire comes about in a moment, a forest over a long time. Great protections stand and cause everything to thrive, but swiftly and suddenly they tumble down. Anything that nature bends away from this current state of affairs is sufficient for the destruction of human beings.

Urbes constituit aetas, hora dissolvit; momento fit cinis, diu silva; magna tutela stant ac vigent omnia, cito ac repente dissiliunt. Quicquid ex hoc statu rerum natura flexerit, in exitium mortalium satis est.

—Sen. QNat. 3.27.2–3

THE possibility of an inundation that washes away all civilization causes Seneca to betray a fear at the power of nature to wipe out human civilization.[1] Yet nature itself can be changed through human activity. The examples of cities and the ruin of human edifices stress both anthropogenic alterations of the environment (*urbes* and *tutela*) and the power of natural disasters to destroy both them and the naturally growing forest. This interrelationship between human beings and the natural world creates the fluid idea that we call the environment: the interface between civilization and the powers not yet under human control, the part of nature that ordinary people live in, farm, excavate, and pollute, as well as the attitudes they have toward it. It is a difficult concept to define even today, so to determine the environmental sensibilities of the ancient Romans presents a daunting task.[2]

Unlike other English words derived from French, "environment" does not have a clear Latin etymology.[3] It therefore behooves a study of Roman views of the environment to determine exactly which Roman concepts can be mapped onto our developed notions of the environment.[4] Modern environmental studies, environmental history, and literary ecocriticism are vibrant fields, but the extent to which these concepts can be applied to ancient societies can be problematic.[5] Ecocritic Timothy Clark defines "nature" in three ways, and determines that the meaning of nature as that which is opposed to culture is the one most applicable to environmental criticism. Yet in the twenty-first century, part of the new geological era called the Anthropocene by some scholars, Clark argues that the nature–culture division is crumbling, leading to questions of scale and influence: his excellent example is to inquire whether the effect of automobile exhaust on snowpack levels is a "natural" or a "cultural" phenomenon.[6] Was the division clear or muddied in Roman times? Although the Anthropocene is usually defined as beginning in the mid-20th century,[7] humans have been altering the environment since the beginnings of farming and city culture. Yet Romans simply did not have industrial technology to cause environmental harm on the scale that Clark discusses, though, as discussed below, there is evidence (at a minimum) of local deforestation. For this reason, we must be cautious when applying modern ecocritical theories and methods of environmental history.[8] While these methods of analysis may provide insight when applied to classical texts and other aspects of life in the ancient world, the ancient Mediterranean world differs from ours in scope and scale, necessitating a scholarly approach that begins with a fundamental question: what is the environment and is it the same across time and culture?

Coming to Grips with the Environment

Studies of the ancient Mediterranean environment, in the sense of the physical spaces that surround human beings and how these spaces influenced life, abound. Peregrine Horden and Nicholas Purcell's *The Corrupting Sea* (2000) explores how the disparate yet connected microenvironments of the Mediterranean led to a distinctive Mediterranean history. This kind of environmental history requires a lot from its students: experience in archaeology, history, geology, hydrology, and botany all come in handy. These skills, not often found in a single individual, also belong to both sides of the schism between science and humanities.[9] What can we then say about the historical interactions between ancient Romans and the natural world?

To take up a part of this question: did the ancients have a measurable impact on the environment, in terms that we might now call deforestation, pollution, or other environmental damage? For some scholars the answer is indubitably affirmative: J. Donald Hughes details widespread deforestation and erosion primarily caused by obtaining timber for fuel, and includes anthracological data to show that coal productions shifted from oak to holm oak as the former was depleted.[10] Hughes also reports on increased atmospheric lead in ancient times and writes a muckraker's expose on the environmental abuses of silver mines at Laurium.[11] Opposing these ideas, Horace Rackham, responding to the 1983 first edition of Hughes's book, declares that the Greeks "appear to have lived well within the limitations of their environment," particularly in terms of timber use.[12] Similarly, James McGregor posits a concept of "First Nature," which he traces to the Neolithic Period. This "worldview pictured the universe as a partnership between the human and biological communities that was exemplified and symbolized by their meeting place, the landscape shaped for cultivation." This mindset, the claim goes, animated the majority of the Mediterranean population before the industrial age.[13]

On a smaller scale, individual investigations have yielded interesting results, as have complementary studies of the effects of climate change on the inhabitants of the Mediterranean basin.[14] Yet a serious difficulty remains in finding any agreement among scholars. Rackham denies almost all deforestation. John Ward-Perkins traces the deforestation of central Italy, which he believes led to the erosion that created the hilly landscape of Etruria. Arnold Toynbee discusses the timber industry and the stripping of woods near to Rome. This attitude is picked up and amplified by Hughes, who dwells on the consequences of deforestation for erosion and land degradation.[15] William Harris steers a middle course, tracing some areas of deforestation that led to local shortages of wood for fuel and shipbuilding in Egypt and some urban and isolated areas, but no "general crisis of timber-supply."[16] What the nonspecialist can take away is that although many areas undoubtedly lost some trees to be used as lumber and fuel, differences emerge on a case-by-case basis as to whether the cut areas rapidly grew back or caused people to go farther afield for timber.

For a different lens on environmental issues some studies examine how the Romans or Greeks *thought* with the environment. The philosophical concepts of *physis* and *natura* have attracted much study, though the multivalency of these words complicates research.[17] When writing about certain aspects of what we call the environment, Romans might use the word *natura* (often personified and capitalized), though the semantic ranges of the two terms diverge significantly. *Natura* is a dynamic conception rather than a static one; it does not apply to a "snapshot" of the landscape but to the processes of growth and change that the landscape represents.[18] The Greek word *physis*, with its etymological connection via the Indo-European root *bhū- to the verb *phuô/phuomai*, points to how ancient interest in nature grew from the study of processes to investigations of origins and states of being. *Natura*—which is close to an ideal translation of *physis* and has similar linguistic connections to verbs such as *nascor*—covers the same basic categories of inherent nature/character and external nature/universe.[19] Studies of *physis* and *natura* by ancient philosophers yielded the coherent *kosmoi* of Plato and Aristotle, the Stoics and Epicureans, in which the place of human beings in the universe was determined, based on natural law and metaphysical considerations.[20] McGregor believes that Greek philosophy from Empedocles onward substituted this kind of rationalistic worldview for his First Nature ideal,[21] yet, as he acknowledges, these views of the environment were never culturally dominant. The average Roman—even the average elite when not having a philosophical discussion—maintained his or her own environment based on more immediate concerns than the Prime Mover.

These theoretical constructs, in concert with physical natural surroundings, contribute to the idea of the environment as it develops in the individual's mind. The ways this process occurred among ancient Romans is the subject of the remainder of this chapter.

Creating the Environment

Although the blue skies, plants, and mountain vistas have their own existence and can be explained rationally through physical and metaphysical laws, we create our environment through the actions we take and the ideas we develop toward these features. One's conceptualization of the natural world becomes most evident through the ways in which one interacts with it. For Romans, nature was often close at hand, even in city dwellings. Pliny the Elder notes that the urban poor had a view of *imago hortorum*, likely window boxes of plants rather than painted garden scenes (*HN* 15.59).[22] Yet our knowledge of the attitudes and interactions of these multitudes remains scanty. One of the best integrative attempts at describing how the inhabitants of a single city represented the environment they lived in has been the *Natural History of Pompeii*, edited by Wilhelmina Jashemski and Frederick Meyer. This book comprises archaeological evidence, palynology, visual art, and textual descriptions to give a sense of not only what was around the inhabitants of Pompeii but also how they reacted to and interacted with this "environment."[23] The authors of the various chapters, each expert on a particular facet of natural history from soil and plants to insects and birds, combine to produce a synthesis of what is known from the preserved remains. Wall paintings and texts bear witness to 184 plants, and the pollen of an additional 95 was discovered.[24] Based on this and similar evidence, we can add color and verisimilitude to our image of the city's numerous gardens, vineyards, and orchards. Such a comprehensive treatment is outside the scope of this chapter. For reasons of expediency as much as any other, out of the many people and years of ancient Rome, and out of the many places touched by Roman culture, I will maintain a more narrow approach, following the majority of the evidence and focusing on the intellectual elite (mostly male) in Italy in the late Republic and early Empire. This approach is not meant to dismiss the environments constructed by marginalized groups or those from times and places deemed less Classical, but simply to illustrate the best-characterized environment that we can partially reconstruct.

Attitudes toward the environment shift seemingly with the wind, even within a single author, though some trends emerge. A simple, reductionist approach could label environmental attitudes as merely positive or negative.[25] We will see several instances of negative attitudes—fear and pessimism among them—as well as their positive counterparts, including aesthetic appreciation and praise. Yet beyond this single-minded approach to how people react, the environment itself has an impact on those that inhabit it. The dependence of humans on the world around them is a common theme in ancient literature.[26] Rome's excellent natural surroundings—mountains for fortifications, mild climate, a position in the center of Italy and the Mediterranean generally—were considered by Strabo to be a major cause of its growth in power (6.4.1).[27] Therefore, the best way to live within a given environment was to control it to the extent possible. Vitruvius notes not only how buildings should be adapted to suit their local environment, but also how environment affects humans' body size, complexion, pitch of voice, intellect, and temperament (6.1). These ideas have deep roots in Greek thought, including the "environmental determinism" of the Hippocratic *Airs, Waters, Places*—Scythian men, for instance, are effeminate because of their cold and wet climate (*Aer.* 20–22)—and the Persian emperor Cyrus's declaration that soft lands breed soft men (Hdt. 9.122.3).[28] Understanding the environment, then, could be an exercise in understanding the self. The landscape provides a mirror in which the Roman viewer sees reflected philosophical ideas about the nature of life and the soul. A farmer looking at the vineyard might see grapevines that have roots in place of feet, branches for arms, and shoots that reach out instead of hands.[29]

Therefore, any attention that can be paid to the reciprocal relationship of human and environment can lead to a greater understanding not only of history or literature, but of wider contemporary concerns: what sort of environment should we create for ourselves, and how can a study of the Roman environment inform our decisions?[30] In the remainder of this chapter, I present three case studies of the created environment: love of nature and the *locus amoenus*, the gods of nature, and the aesthetics of the fields. Although the mass of omitted topics dwarfs my selections,[31] the chosen themes reveal multiple constructed environments: literary, religious, and aesthetic.

"Love of Nature"

As the industrialization of the West increasingly hid the trees and fields from city-dwellers, and the near-simultaneous Romantic discovery of the Wild urged a fetishization of nature untouched, bouts of sentimental scholarly investigation have from time to time unearthed love of nature in ancient literature. The work of Alfred Biese (1882–1884) tracks a notional development in ancient *Naturgefühl*, from naivety in the Homeric poems through sympathy and sentimentality in Classical and Hellenistic poetry, with a similar development shown in Latin literature to an apex of high sentimentality in the later empire. The teleology of this approach, made yet more evident in Biese's third volume that culminates in the Romantic poets, bespeaks a view of the Romans as proto-moderns, in whose appreciation of the natural world we can see recognizable tendencies of ours. Other similar works of scholarship illustrate the predilections of their authors as much as any true Romanticism among the ancients.[32]

Nevertheless, the *locus amoenus* as a literary landscape often exudes natural bliss of a sort that could cause the most Romantic of critics to lapse into a stupor. Vergil's flowered meadows and the wooded glens of Ovid's *Metamorphoses* distill the concept of "outside" to its essence and present it as an object of admiration. The trope can trace its literary origins to the departure of Socrates and Phaedrus from Athens at the opening of Plato's dialogue *Phaedrus* (227a–230e) and its philosophical grounding to the garden settings of the Academy, Lyceum, and, clearly, Epicurus's Garden. The literary *locus* represents for Latin writers a kind of "poetic geography" in the terminology of Jacqueline Fabre-Serris:

a place of Epicurean repose as well as a site for solitude or romance, a wild place that can be put in opposition to the city.[33] The *locus amoenus* will also be made to resonate with the author's literary themes. For instance, the stream in Ovid's story of Narcissus is as untouched and pure as the young man himself:

> There was a clear spring, glistening with sparkling waves, which had been left untouched by the shepherds or the goats that grazed on the mountain or any other beast. No bird nor wild creature had stirred it up, nor a branch fallen from a tree. There was grass around, which took nourishment from the nearby water, and the forest would not allow the place to grow warm under any sun.
>
> fons erat inlimis, nitidis argenteus undis,
> quem neque pastores neque pastae monte capellae
> contigerant aliudve pecus, quem nulla volucris
> nec fera turbarat nec lapsus ab arbore ramus;
> gramen erat circa, quod proximus umor alebat,
> silvaque sole locum passura tepescere nullo. (*Met.* 3.407–412)

Like Narcissus's pool itself, the environment functions as a mirror: the uninhabited glen reflects the young man's sexual purity; so do the shading trees, which allow no untoward warming.[34] For Ovid as author, the natural beauty of the setting allows thematic elements to be recast in an external guise: Narcissus's character and the place he visits are fundamentally akin. The idea of the mirroring of humans in their environment, illustrated clearly by the story of Narcissus, recurs in other ways of looking at the outside world. And as we have seen, when grapevines have hands and feet, scientific curiosity into the growing of plants reveals more about the investigator than the subject.

Gods of Nature

Perhaps the largest scale on which humans can view themselves in the environment is displayed by the kind (and number) of gods they see there. For the Romans, as well as other ancient Mediterranean societies, the environment was not merely a source of beauty or a place to grow food. It was also the source of portents and omens, such as the eclipses, showers of stones, and springs spouting blood that, for instance, were reported in Italy in advance of the Battle of Cannae (Livy 22.1). These portents could be explained by ancient authorities in multiple ways: as contrary to nature, as following nature, or as representing the direct intervention of humanized gods in nature.[35] Regardless of the explanation, these manifestations in the natural world reflected the eternal and the divine. The environment, therefore, could be not only the interface between the individual person and the world outside, but also the threshold between the supernatural and the natural, a porous boundary where even landscape features could be seen as passages between worlds: the caves at Cumae, the fires of Etna, and the whirlpool of Charybdis all representing gaps in the wall between human and divine.

Thus, as Seneca says, "there is no nature without god, nor god without nature" (*nec natura sine deo est nec deus sine natura*; *Ben.* 4.8.2).[36] The creative impulse of nature, properly divinized, occurs as the divine figure of Venus Genetrix in at the opening of Lucretius's *De rerum natura* and the personified Pax or Roma in the propaganda of the time of Augustus.[37]

In addition to its creative potential, every part of the natural environment was a place for religious activity and a home to gods. Groves and woodlands were the locations for rites, and various gods represented aspects of the natural world, including Pomona, Silvanus, and Mars.[38] The rural god Silvanus was an ancient and popular figure in private cult. Worshipped outside the city, he presided over both the forests and the fields, receiving the fifth most surviving dedications of any divinity, yet he lacked an established cult.[39] Faunus, an earlier and similarly elusive deity, seems to have lacked even definitive iconography, allowing his worship to be replaced by that of Silvanus.[40] The woodlands therefore teemed with a fluctuating array of spirits. In response to this superabundance of nature gods, Lucretius states that the superstition of the *finitimi* ("locals," undoubtedly in a pejorative sense) caused them to imagine Fauni and Pan lest the land be *deserta ab divis* ("abandoned by gods" 4.591).

A land abandoned by gods would no longer be fruitful. In addition to the gods of the forest, agricultural deities abound in Roman religion. On Dumézil's schematic of the functions of archaic Roman gods, the god Quirinus occupies the third spot, which is lowest and humblest: the charge of preserving grain for the masses. Quirinus's duties were shared among a large grouping of other divinities: Ops and Consus among others.[41] Varro begins his *Res rusticae* with an invocation not of the Muses, but of twelve agricultural divinities termed *dei consentes* (councilor gods): Father Jupiter and Mother Tellus, Sol and Luna, Ceres and Liber, Robigus and Flora, Minerva and Venus, and Lympha and Bonus Eventus (*Rust.* 1.1.4–7). These six groups of two represent (1) the great parents, (2) the guides for planting and harvesting, (3) the providers of the necessary fruits, (4) nurturers of flowers and banishers of rot, (5) protectors of olive plantations and gardens, and (6) suppliers of moisture and good issue.[42]

Appeasing these divinities was the duty of specialized priesthoods, chief among which was the Arval Brotherhood. The *Fratres Arvales*, among whose number was the Roman emperor, wore a wreath of corn and, at least originally, led the worship of gods such as Flora and Pomona.[43] In addition, specialized divinities such as Vervactor, Imporcitor, and Sarritor, who governed the appropriate stages of the farming process, were invoked in the worship of Ceres.[44] It is unknown to what extent the god Vervactor was the subject of a genuine cult or existed as more than a name. It is nevertheless safe to say that in most literary texts of the Augustan period and later, the listing of agricultural gods takes on a performative, sentimental tone as the author conjures an imagined lost rustic innocence.[45]

The Beauty of the Fields

In addition to being a source of omens from the gods—which could be considered irregularities in the "natural" way of things—the environment also housed the regular phenomena of seasons, sunsets, and harvests.[46] The Romans took a multifaceted view of a "properly functioning" environment. The very notion of what it means for the environment to function properly could have political, economic, military, or aesthetic implications. Vergil's *laudes Italiae* are famous not solely for descriptions of the beauty of an unspoiled landscape but also for their tribute to olives, flocks of sheep, mines, and peoples of Italy alongside its lakes and harbors. In contrast to portents from the gods, whose oddities spark wonder at the potentialities and powers of nature, these mundane products extracted and harvested from the environment delight as a consequence of their ubiquity. Ensuring that the land performs its proper task of food production always represented a major concern, and the attention paid to agricultural fertility, in particular, exemplifies this importance. Furthermore, it was all the better if the land could not only produce as it ought but also do so in a visually pleasing way. Whether it concerned fields, groves, or gardens, the Roman attitude toward the agricultural environment was aesthetic as well as practical.

To focus on the practical side first, the question of the fertility of the earth was a fraught one in intellectual circles. The agricultural basis of the economy depended on good crop yields, and rulers were hailed as bringers of agricultural abundance.[47] Yet how to account for declining crop yields was an ever-present question. The transition from smallholdings to *latifundia*, which began in earnest in the late Republic, was seen to have resulted in poorer harvests in Italy.[48] Columella records that Italian wheat crops scarcely yield four times the amount used in planting (*Rust.* 3.3.4), whereas Cicero had reported yields of eight- to tenfold in Sicily (*Verr.* 2.3.112).[49] Nowadays we might attribute these difficulties to overplanting, underfertilizing, lack of proper crop rotation, or simple negligence. In Roman times, however, blame was only rarely apportioned to systemic human abuses of these kinds,[50] Pliny's famous (and dubious) report of the extinction of cultivated *silphium* or *laserpicium* notwithstanding (*HN* 15.38–40).[51]

In more philosophical circles, the creation and destruction of the *kosmos* was of more concern than day-to-day changes in the environment, though arguments about one often informed the other.[52] For the first century CE, Stoic and Epicurean ideas of cosmogony and (if I am permitted) cosmolysis were most influential. The physics of the Stoics, with its repeated universal conflagrations (*ekpyrôseis*), tends to support environmental decay, given that their world must react to all physical changes and hurtles from creation toward ruin.[53] Epicurean doctrine also holds that the continuing disintegration of the atomic structure of the earth explains why no new species of animal were being produced and why it seems harder and harder to make the land bear fruit.[54] These kind of arguments can be thought of as environmental: from observation of the surroundings and recent history, it is inferred that the world is perishable. Because visible changes are happening in the environment, for instance the creation of new islands, the world must have had an origin and will also meet its end.[55]

A decaying earth is a potent image, and one that agriculturalists wished to subvert. A popularized version of the above philosophical ideas imputes agricultural difficulties to the advanced age of the (female) earth and her consequent barrenness. So prevalent was this sort of pessimistic Stoic/Epicurean explanation for failed crops that Columella begins his monumental twelve-book *Res rustica* by refuting it and stating that the negligence of landowners is the cause, rather than any inherent weakness of the earth (*Rust.* 1 *praef.*1–3). By blaming human beings rather than the earth, which he declares is blessed with a "divine and eternal youth" (*divina et aeterna iuventa*), Columella's stance at once takes personal responsibility for human interference with the environment and yet denies any possibility of permanent damage. The earth in this view cannot decay irreparably even if mismanaged by its stewards.[56]

While an argument in favor of the earth's inherent fertility could reassure an anxious farmer, extreme fertility could be thought of as negative. Golden-age *topoi* of this sort were associated with the ends of the earth, and carried connotations of danger.[57] India may produce the largest trees, under which bands of cavalry can take shelter and over which one cannot shoot an arrow, but the horrific tribes of the cave-dwelling Troglodytes, dog-headed Cunocephali, and umbrella-footed Sciapodes come from there as well (Plin. *HN* 7.21–32). Conversely, although Vergil's Italy does not sprout ebony, frankincense, or balsam (*G.* 2.116–19), it also lacks dangerous lions and tigers (*G.* 2.150–51). Pushing this kind of natural peril to the edges of the known world is a distancing technique: India is not part of a Roman's nearby surroundings and could hardly be said to be part of the local environment. Therefore the Roman elite allow themselves the intellectual safety of a well-organized and -maintained environment. Rome and Italy in particular were not wild places, for the most part, and a safe aesthetic of the agricultural ideal could grow happily there. A discussion of the crop yields and the practicalities of the fertility of the land then could yield an appreciation of a practical kind of beauty, not entirely divorced from economics. By valorizing the particular qualities of the local environment, often in comparison to a faraway place, a Roman could judge a place not only by its fertility, but by its unique characteristics as well.

The elite fetish for country living, though undoubtedly somewhat for the purpose of overseeing landholdings and escaping the city's hubbub, resulted from these aesthetic considerations of the country as opposed to city, a topic of much scholarly attention.[58] The beauty of the fields could move even the most staid of authors to rhetorical heights. For instance, the following extract from Book 3 of Columella's *Res rustica* glows with an appreciation of the natural loveliness of the well-run farm. The author is in the midst of discussing how a farmer should separate grapeseed to grow each variety in a separate plot:

> For it is the most challenging of all farming tasks, because it both requires the highest attention in selecting the seeds and for separating them there is most often need for the greatest good luck and common sense. But occasionally, as the divine writer Plato

says, the beauty of the matter induces us to pursue even those ends which we are unable to achieve due to the weakness of our mortal nature.

> Est enim omnium rusticorum operum difficillimum, quia et summam diligentiam legendis desiderat seminibus, et in his discernendis maxima plerumque felicitate et prudentia opus est; sed interdum, quod ait divinus auctor Plato, rei nos pulchritudo trahit vel ea consectandi, quae propter infirmitatem commortalis naturae consequi nequeamus. (*Rust.* 3.20.4)

What Columella hints at is a kind of Platonic ideal of the organized landscape. Reminiscent of the class segregation of the *Republic*,[59] proper organization of grape varietals is not only a useful end for the farmer, but also an aesthetic end: *pulchritudo* is the inducement that leads the farmer on, even if mortal flesh is weak. Columella proceeds to state that that, unlike the Platonic forms, the ideal vineyard can be achieved by a *paterfamilias* of sufficient years when knowledge, ability, and will (*scientia, facultas*, and *voluntas*) act together. In the farmer's value system, beauty ranks perhaps lower than profit or the proper use of manure, yet as Columella's economics lesson lapses into aesthetics, his prose is wrapped up in the appreciation of the surrounding environment.

Conclusions

The range of Roman environments surveyed has been brief. Yet a sense of the semantic boundaries of the "ancient Roman environment" emerges. Profit from extractive industry or farming, a connection to the divine, and an appreciation of natural beauty were all present among the attitudes the Romans applied to the physical world around them. These ideas could be based on philosophical foundations, as when Columella creates his Platonic field, or on literary concerns of form and substance, in the trope of the *locus amoenus*.

To complement Seneca's fear and awe at nature's power, with which this chapter began, consider Pliny the Younger's description of the setting of his Tuscan villa:

> A broad and wide-spreading plain is surrounded by mountains, which have lofty and ancient woods on their highest part. The area is thick with varied game for hunting. From there, woods for timber descend with the mountain itself, and among them are rich and earthy hills where rock is not found easily even if one should search. These equal the flattest plains in productivity. They produce their rich harvest later, but ripen their fruit no less. Below these grapevines spread throughout every mountainside, and weave a unified fabric far and wide. At the boundary and, as it were, bottom hem orchard trees grow.
>
> lata et diffusa planities montibus cingitur, montes summa sui parte procera nemora et antiqua habent. frequens ibi et varia venatio. inde caeduae silvae cum ipso monte descendunt. has inter pingues terrenique colles (neque enim facile usquam saxum etiam si quaeratur occurrit) planissimis campis fertilitate non cedunt, opimamque

messem serius tantum, sed non minus percoquunt. sub his per latus omne vineae porriguntur, unamque faciem longe lateque contexunt; quarum a fine imoque quasi margine arbusta nascuntur. (*Ep.* 5.6.7–9)

Aesthetic appreciation there is to be sure, but tempered with a close regard to the productive qualities of the environment. The lofty and ancient woods (*procera nemora et antiqua*) provide hunting (*venatio*), the forests on the mountainside are for cutting down (*caeduae silvae*), the hills are rich and fertile (*fertilitate non cedunt*), and at the lower elevations, Pliny marvels at the aesthetics of the "fabric" of the grapevines, with its hem (*margine*) of trees. Far from a simple view of the environment, emotion as well as concerns for profit are at work in his account. This Tuscan landscape would be less striking—and far more akin to Seneca's destructive nature—without the human touch. It is not an untamed wilderness, but the environment, the thin and tenuous meeting place between nature and culture, that meets with Pliny's approval.

Notes

1. This trope has its most emphatic philosophical grounding in the tales of floods Pl. *Ti.* 22c–25d.
2. Rackham (1996) details the numerous pitfalls facing the potential historian of ecology. Horden and Purcell (2000) 43–49 define their historical ecology as more history than science. For one attempt to interpret ancient attitudes to ecology, see Vögler (2000), a condensed adaptation of arguments from Vögler (1997). Vögler draws together divine forces of nature, myths of creation and human development, and then traces ecological thinking in numerous ancient writers. Hughes (2014) 43–67 surveys ecological ideas before determining that these notions did not prevent ancients from doing harm to the environment.
3. OED^3, s.v. "environment" and "environ." A possible etymon of Middle French *environ* is contained in the words *viriolae* and *viriae*, which Pliny reports are the Celtic and Celtiberian words for "armband" (*HN* 33.12.40).
4. See Thommen (2012) 3–9 on this difficulty.
5. For instance, two handbooks on ecocriticism offer scant attention to Latin or Greek literature outside the pastoral tradition of Theocritus and Vergil: Westling (2013) and Garrard (2014).
6. Clark (2013), especially 78–81.
7. A major factor in separating the Anthropocene from the Holocene are the altered levels of certain radioisotopes in the atmosphere, resulting from nuclear testing. See Waters et al. (2016).
8. For a survey of six major schools of ecocriticism (Romanticism and deep ecology, phenomenology, Marxism, spatiality theory, cultural ecology, and posthumanism), see Goodbody (2013). A good introduction to environmental history is Hughes (2015).
9. Edited collections such as Harris (2013a), with contributions from both sides of the science/history divide, are helping to bridge this gap.
10. Hughes (2014) 69–87.
11. Hughes (2014) 129–149, especially 136–142 on Laurium.

12. Rackham (1996) 41. In Rackham's view, the major environmental changes occurred before the Classical period in Greece, and references to true deforestation with explicit lack of regrowth are limited to Eratosthenes's comment on the growing scarcity of trees on Cyprus (quoted at Strabo 14.6.5). Delano Smith (1996) provides supporting geoarchaeological evidence from the Tavoliere plain that true "wilderness," in the sense of untouched forest, did not exist even in ancient times. Hughes, the main proponent of the opposing viewpoint, argues that Romans' rapacity for exotic beasts led to the extinction or near eradication of several species (2010).
13. McGregor (2015) 95–96.
14. Hughes (2014) and several of the papers in Harris (2013a).
15. Rackham (1996); Ward-Perkins (1964); Toynbee (1965) 594–598; Hughes (^{2}2014).
16. Harris (2013b) 190.
17. The polysemy leads to edited collections on *natura* that discuss the *locus amoenus* alongside Cicero's *De natura deorum* (see Lévy (1996)).
18. Sallmann (2001) 489–490.
19. Pellicer (1966); Naddaf (2005) 11–35.
20. Macé (2019) 42 emphasizes that "calling the universe a '*kosmos*' was once a metaphorical act." For a general history of scholarly views on early Greek *physikoi* and the development of the concept of *kosmos*, see Horky 2019b.
21. McGregor (2015) 125–142. He paints with a very broad brush, for instance ignoring the biological works of Aristotle and declaring "Plato and Aristotle, given their theories, had no real motive to study the raw materials that sustained life or the labor of beasts and humans that transformed those materials into food." Cf. *Part. an.* 644b23–645a4, Aristotle's protreptic to the study of things that take part in coming to be and destruction.
22. Linderski (2001). Von Stackelberg (2009) stresses the "cultural content" implied in Pliny's use of the term *imago*: "a garden was not just a place, it was an idea of a place" (2).
23. Jashemski and Meyer (2002). The editors take their inspiration from the broad sense of "natural history" found in the writings of Pliny the Elder.
24. Jashemski, Meyer, and Ricciardi (2002) give a catalogue of the 184 plants with their occurrences in visual art, preserved remains, and textual descriptions.
25. Thommen (2012) 76–78 summarizes some of these attitudes: pessimism in Lucretius versus the triumphant optimism of Stat. *Silv.* 2.2 and Cic. *Nat. D.* 2.152).
26. A good general overview of this variety of ecological thinking in Greco-Roman antiquity (and in the ancient Near East as well) is Irby, McCall, and Radini (2016).
27. See also Vitr. 6.1.11; Plin. *HN* 37.201–203.
28. For Herodotus and *Aer.* and their connection to fifth-century BCE scientific thought, see Thomas (2000) and Chiasson (2001).
29. This "upright" grapevine inverts the upside-down plants of the Aristotelean paradigm, in which a plant's roots represent its mouth as it feeds from the earth. See *Part. an.* 683b18, 686b35; *IA* 705b2, 706b5; Lloyd (1983) 41–42, Bos (2010) 831–837. Nevertheless, such a comparative description of the plant's humanoid structure is very much in the Peripatetic vein of Aristotle's and Theophrastus's biological works and follows a remarkable passage in which an agricultural author discusses the soul as charioteer and the uniqueness of purpose of each part of the body, calling the living thing an *animans machina* composed of the soul (*sacra illa spiritus elementa*) secreted within the *terrena primordia* (Columella, *Rust.* 3.10.10).

30. Lobbying for a return to a traditional agriculture and an aesthetic of the worked environment, McGregor (2015) 286–304 scorns the idea of the unspoiled landscape in favor of harmonious working within natural constraints. A similar drive also animates works of landscape history such as Agnoletti (2013), which declares that "landscape heritage and the related traditional knowledge are fundamental resources that need to be safeguarded" as a knowledge base for future decision-making (vii).
31. The Roman garden in particular will receive scant attention. For scholarship on this topic, see Pagán (2007), Von Stackelberg (2009), and Coleman and Derron (2014).
32. For instance Geikie (1912), who is more renowned for his work in geology. Fairclough (1930) 9 seeks to demonstrate the "very profound love of nature . . . quite as genuine and significant as any that has been voiced by the most ardent nature-lovers among our poets of the present day." Hyde (1915) examines the "simplicity and freshness" of the Greeks, which induced only a modicum of appreciation for mountains in their poetry, and the "less imaginative Romans," for whom mountains were objects of dread, not beauty. For a survey of earlier thought on the issue, starting from the opposite scholarly pole (Schiller's 1795 declaration of the lack of sentimentality in the way in which ancients regarded nature), see Fairclough (1930) 3–9.
33. Fabre-Serris (1996) 23–31.
34. Cf. the sacred grove in Euripides's *Hippolytus*, where the meadow (*leimôn*) is as pure (*akêraton*) as the goddess Artemis herself (73–81).
35. "Nature" here means not "that which is opposed to culture," but "the normal internal and visible workings of the universe." See Guillaumont (1996) for analysis and classification of portents along these lines. Varro defined portents as "that which seems to arise contrary to nature": *portenta esse Varro ait quae contra naturam nata videntur* (Isid. *Etym.* 11.3.1), whereas Cicero in *On Divination* tends to the rationalist side: *quorum omnium* [sc. *portentosorum*] . . . *una ratio est. quicquid enim oritur, qualecumque est, causam habeat a natura necesse sit.* (*Div.* 2.60).
36. Sallmann (2001) 486. See also Slaveva-Griffin (2016) for a broad survey across various (mostly Greek) thinkers.
37. For the connections among Venus, Natura, and creation (a perceived etymological connection through the verb *nascor*), see Clay (1983). For the use of such imagery on the Ara Pacis Augustae, see Zanker (1990) 177 and Elsner (1991) 57–59.
38. Horden and Purcell (2000) 403–460, and, for Greek use of sacred land, McInerney (2006). For Mars as an agricultural deity, see Cato the Elder's prayer to Mars to ensure agricultural success (*Agr.* 114).
39. The earliest literary evidence for shrines is found at Plaut. *Aulularia* 674–675 and Cato *Agr.* 83. Ranking ahead of Silvanus in number of dedications are Jupiter, Hercules, Fortuna, and Mercury. See Dorcey (1992) 1–13 for a discussion of the literary and epigraphic evidence.
40. Fantham (2009) 17–22.
41. Consus's underground altar at the circus is mentioned by Tert. *De spect.* 5, and Var. *Ling.* 6.21 discusses the worship of Ops Consiva. See Dumézil (1970) 148–175, 246–272, 370–385. Other divinities fulfilling roles in the "third function" include Tellus, Ceres, and Pales.
42. See Dorcey (1992) 136–137, who discusses these divinities as part of the urban imagination of rural life, rather than the more "folksy" religion of Silvanus, who is not included.
43. Plin. *HN* 18.6, cf. Dumézil (1970) 270–271. For comprehensive evidence and analysis of the Arval Brethren, see Scheid (1990).

44. Turning over land, plowing, and weeding, respectively. This list, spoken by the flamen of Ceres, originated with Fabius Pictor's *Libri iuris pontificii* and can be found at Serv. *G.* 1.21. See Dumézil (1970) 34–38 for an assessment of the "limited conceptual zone" these divinities occupy and their position as a quasi-*familia* of the chief goddess, Ceres in this case.
45. See especially Fantham's study of the rural gods in Vergil: (2009) 34–62.
46. For an interesting take on the idea of law in Roman views of nature, see Lehoux (2012) 47–76, who draws on references to the laws of nature (*leges* or *foedera naturae*) especially in Lucretius and Vergil, as well as "lawlike" references to how nature behaves. McGregor (2015) 147–149 sees Lucretius's attention to natural laws as a "celebration" of First Nature.
47. Hor. *Carm. saec.* 29–32, *Carm.* 4.5.17–20; Verg. *G.* 1.26–28; Plin. *Pan.* 29–32.
48. Smallholdings never disappeared entirely, and the term *latifundium* covers a wide range of estates, growing various crops and managed in disparate ways. See White (1970) 384–412.
49. White (1970) 48–49; Garnsey and Saller (2014) 103–107. It should be noted that Columella gives the figure of fourfold yields while trying to promote the economic benefits of viticulture rather than growing wheat. Few other textual references to yield survive. One other example is that Varro notes that bean seeds can yield between ten- and fifteen-fold, depending on location and soil type, with Etruria falling toward the higher end of the scale (*Rust.* 1.44.1).
50. Hughes (2014) 119–124 suggests the monoculture practices on *latifundia* might have been a cause of declining yields.
51. The plant, which was reported to grow only in Cyrenaica, was supposedly made extinct by practice of grazing sheep on the shoots. On the difficulty of identifying the plant and whether it is in fact extinct, see Parejko (2003) and Amigues (2004).
52. For ideas about cosmogony from Hesiod onward, see Gregory (2016) and for creationism Sedley's Sather lectures (2007), though both focus mostly on Greek sources.
53. For sources on the conflagration, see *SVF* 2.596–32. See Long (2006) 256–282 on the "cosmo-biology" of the Stoic view, which infers the world's perishability from the assumption that the same physics operate in both the sub- and superlunary regions.
54. For instance, Lucretius 2.1150–1174. This idea forms a key part of the myth of the Ages, appearing in Hesiod concerning the race of iron: οὐδέ ποτ' ἦμαρ / παύονται καμάτου (During the day they never rest from labor; *Op.* 176–177).
55. Philo of Alexandria, drawing on a lost work by Theophrastus, refutes some of these environmental arguments. In addition to the idea that the sea is being used up because of the creation of new islands and the presence of seashells far from the shore, there is also the notion that the varied terrain of the earth implies its recent creation (*De aeternitate mundi* 118–149). See Sharples (2008), and, for Epicurean responses to Theophrastian ideas in Luc. 5.235–350, Sedley (1998) 166–185.
56. Columella gives a fuller account of the refuted theory at the beginning of Book 2, where he attributes the incorrect view to Gnaeus Tremelius Scrofa, whose work on agriculture is lost, but who appears as a character in Varro's *Res rusticae*. To repair and replenish a field damaged by overworking, manuring is called for (2.1.6–7). For a survey of other Roman authorities and an assessment of their recommendations, see White (1970) 125–144. The true identities of those agricultural sources who believed the earth was in terminal decline remain unknown, though similar statements are made by Lucretius (2.1157–1174) and both Pliny the Elder (*HN* 17.40) and Younger (*Ep.* 6.21.1). See Gummerus (1910) 15–20.

According to Gummerus, Columella's eclectic philosophy is based mostly on Stoic ideas, the major exception being the passage under discussion.

57. Parker (2008); Romm (1992).
58. See Eigler (2002), Dyson (2003), and the papers in Rich and Wallace-Hadrill (1991) and Rosen and Sluiter (2006).
59. In addition to the familiar system described in the *Republic,* compare descriptions of the idealized caste system of India: Diod. Sic. 2.40–41, Strabo 15.1.39–49, Plin. *HN* 6.66–67, Arr. *Indica.* 11–12, Porph. *Abst.* 4.17.

References

Agnoletti, M., ed. (2013). *Italian Rural Landscapes.* (New York).
Alesse, F. (2008). *Philo of Alexandria and Post-Aristotelian Philosophy.* (Leiden).
Amigues, S. (2004). "Le silphium: Etat de la question." *Journal des savants* 2004: 191–226.
Biese, A. (1882–1884). *Die Entwicklung des Naturgefühls bei den Griechen und Römern.* 2 vols. (Kiel).
Bos, A. P. (2010). "Aristotle on the Differences between Plants, Animals, and Humans and on the Elements as Instruments of the Soul (*De Anima* 2.4.415b18)." *Review of Metaphysics* 63: 821–841.
Chiasson, C. C. (2001). "Scythian Androgyny and Environmental Determinism in Herodotus and the Hippocratic περὶ ἀέρων ὑδάτων τόπων." *Syllecta Classica* 12: 33–73.
Clark, T. (2013). "Nature and Post-Nature," in Westling, 75–89.
Clay, D. (1983). *Lucretius and Epicurus.* (Ithaca, N.Y.).
Coleman, K., and P. Derron, eds. (2014). *Le jardin dans l'Antiquité.* (Geneva).
Delano Smith, C. (1996). "Where Was the 'Wilderness' in Roman Times?," in Shipley and Salmon, 154–179.
Dorcey, P. F. (1992). *The Cult of Silvanus: A Study in Roman Folk Religion.* (Leiden).
Dumézil, G. (1970). *Archaic Roman Religion.* P. Krapp, tr. (Chicago).
Dyson, S. L. (2003). *The Roman Countryside.* (London).
Eigler, U. (2002). "Urbanität und Ländlichkeit als Thema und Problem der augustischen Literatur." *Hermes* 130(3): 288–298.
Elsner, J. (1991). "Cult and Sculpture: Sacrifice in the Ara Pacis Augustae." *JRS* 81: 50–61.
Fabre-Serris, J. (1996). "Nature, mythe et poésie," in Lévy, 23–42.
Fairclough, H. R. (1930). *Love of Nature among the Greeks and Romans.* (New York).
Fantham, E. (2009). *Latin Poets and Italian Gods.* (Toronto).
Garnsey, P., and R. Saller. (2014). *The Roman Empire: Economy, Society, and Culture.* (Berkeley).
Garrard, G. (2014). *The Oxford Handbook of Ecocriticism.* (Oxford).
Geikie, A. (1912). *The Love of Nature among the Romans during the Later Decades of the Republic and the First Century of the Empire.* (London).
Goodbody, A. (2013). "Ecocritical Theory: Romantic Roots and Impulses from Twentieth-Century European Thinkers," in Westling, 61–74.
Gregory, A. D. (2016). "The Creation and Destruction of the World," in Irby, 13–28.
Guillaumont, F. (1996). "La nature et les prodiges dans la religion et la philosophie romaines," in Lévy, 43–64.
Gummerus, H. (1910). *De Columella philosopho.* (Helsingfors).

Harris, W. V., ed. (2013a). *The Ancient Mediterranean Environment between Science and History.* (Leiden).
Harris, W. V. (2013b). "Defining and Detecting Mediterranean Deforestation, 800 BCE to 700 CE," in Harris, 173–194.
Horden, P., and N. Purcell. (2000). *The Corrupting Sea: A Study of Mediterranean History.* (Oxford).
Horky, P. S. (2019a). *Cosmos in the Ancient World.* (Cambridge).
Horky, P. S. (2019b). "When Did *Kosmos* Become the *Kosmos*?," in Horky, 22–41.
Hughes, J. D. (2010). "Europe as Consumer of Exotic Biodiversity: Greek and Roman Times." *Landscape Research* 28(1): 21–31.
Hughes, J. D. (^{2}2014). *Environmental Problems of the Greeks and Romans.* (Baltimore).
Hughes, J. D. (^{2}2015). *What Is Environmental History?* (Cambridge).
Hyde, W. W. (1915). "The Ancient Appreciation of Mountain Scenery." *CJ* 11(2): 70–84.
Irby, G. (2016). *A Companion to Science, Technology, and Medicine in Ancient Greece and Rome.* (Chichester).
Irby, G., R. McCall, and A. Radini. (2016). "'Ecology' in the Ancient Mediterranean," in Irby, 298–312.
Jashemski, W. F., and F. G. Meyer. (2002). *The Natural History of Pompeii.* (Cambridge).
Jashemski, W. F., F. G. Meyer, and M. Ricciardi. (2002). "Plants: Evidence from Wall Paintings, Mosaics, Sculpture, Plant Remains, Graffiti, Inscriptions, and Ancient Authors," in Jashemski and Meyer, 80–180.
Lehoux, D. (2012). *What Did the Romans Know? An Inquiry into Science and Worldmaking.* (Chicago).
Lévy, C. (1996). *Le concept de nature à Rome: La physique. Actes du séminaire de philosophie romaine de l'Université de Paris XII-Val de Marne (1992–1993).* (Paris).
Linderski, J. (2001). "*Imago hortorum*: Pliny the Elder and the Gardens of the Urban Poor." *CP* 96(3): 305–308.
Lloyd, G. E. R. (1983). *Science, Folklore and Ideology: Studies in the Life Sciences in Ancient Greece.* (Cambridge).
Long, A. A. (2006). *From Epicurus to Epictetus: Studies in Hellenistic and Roman Philosophy.* (Oxford).
Macé, A. (2019). "Ordering the Universe in Speech: '*Kosmos*' and '*Diakosmos*' in Parmenides' Poem," in Horky, 42–61.
McGregor, J. H. S. (2015). *Back to the Garden: Nature and the Mediterranean World from Prehistory to the Present.* (New Haven, Conn.).
McInerney, J. (2006). "On the Border: Sacred Land and the Margins of the Community," in Rosen and Sluiter, 33–59.
Naddaf, G. (2005). *The Greek Concept of Nature.* (Albany).
Pagán, V. E. (2007). *Rome and the Literature of Gardens.* (London).
Parejko, K. (2003). "Pliny the Elder's Silphium: First Recorded Species Extinction." *Conservation Biology* 17(3): 925–927.
Parker, G. R. (2008). *The Making of Roman India.* (Cambridge).
Pellicer, A. (1966). *Natura: Etude sémantique et historique du mot latin.* (Paris).
Rackham, O. (1996). "Ecology and Pseudo-Ecology: The Example of Ancient Greece," in Shipley and Salmon, 16–43.
Rich, J., and A. Wallace-Hadrill, eds. (1991). *City and Country in the Ancient World.* (London).
Romm, J. (1992). *The Edges of the Earth in Ancient Thought.* (Princeton).

Rosen, R. M., and I. Sluiter, eds. (2006). *City, Countryside, and the Spatial Organization of Value in Classical Antiquity*. (Leiden).

Sallmann, K. (2001). "Der Mensch und 'seine' Natur." *Gymnasium* 108: 485–514.

Scheid, J. (1990). *Romulus et ses freres: Le collège des Frères Arvales, modèle du culte public, dans la Rome des empereurs*. (Rome).

Sedley, D. N. (1998). *Lucretius and the Transformation of Greek Wisdom*. (Cambridge).

Sedley, D. N. (2007). *Creationism and Its Critics in Antiquity*. (Berkeley).

Sharples, R. W. (2008). "Philo and Post-Aristotelian Peripatetics," in Alesse, 55–73.

Shipley, G., and J. Salmon, eds. (1996). *Human Landscapes in Classical Antiquity: Environment and Culture*. (London).

Slaveva-Griffin, S. (2016). "Nature and the Divine," in Irby, 60–75.

Thomas. R. (2000). *Herodotus in Context*. (Cambridge).

Thommen, L. (2012). *An Environmental History of Ancient Greece and Rome*. P. Hill, tr. (Cambridge).

Toynbee, A. J. (1965). *Hannibal's Legacy: The Hannibalic War's Effects on Roman Life*, vol. 2. (London).

Vögler, G. (1997). *Ökogriechen und grüne Römer*. (Dusseldorf).

Vögler, G. (2000). "Dachte man in der Antike ökologisch? Mensch und Umwelt im Spiegel antiker Literatur." *Forum Classicum* 2000(4): 241–253.

Von Stackelberg, K. T. (2009). *The Roman Garden: Space, Sense, and Society*. (London).

Ward-Perkins, B. (1964). *Landscape and History in Central Italy*. (Oxford).

Waters, C. N., et al. (2016). "The Anthropocene Is Functionally and Stratigraphically Distinct from the Holocene." *Science* 351(6269): aad2622. doi:10.1126/science.aad2622.

Westling, L., ed. (2013). *The Cambridge Companion to Literature and the Environment*. (Cambridge).

White, K. D. (1970). *Roman Farming*. (Ithaca, N.Y.).

Zanker, P. (1990). *The Power of Images in the Age of Augustus*. A. Shapiro, tr. (Ann Arbor, Mich.).

PART IV

AFTER ROMAN PHILOSOPHY
Transmission and Impact

CHAPTER 27

ROMAN PRESOCRATICS
Bio-Doxography in the Late Republic

MYRTO GARANI

Prologue

A young Greek named Dioscurus is said to have sent to Saint Augustine a list of questions, both about Cicero's *De natura deorum* and about some of the latter's rhetorical treatises. In his reply, Augustine rebukes him for having recourse to the Ciceronian doxography instead of the Greek primary sources (*Ep.* 118.10):[1]

> Will you say that you preferred to learn these things from the books of Latin rather than of Greek authors? By such an answer you will, in the first place, put an affront upon Greece; and you know how men of that nation resent this. And in the next place, they being now wounded and angry, how readily will you find what you are too anxious to avoid, that they will count you on the one hand stupid, because you preferred to learn the opinions of the Greek philosophers, or, more properly speaking, some isolated and scattered tenets of their philosophy, in Latin dialogues, rather than to study the complete and connected system of their opinions in the Greek originals, and, on the other hand, illiterate, because, although ignorant of so many things written in your language, you have unsuccessfully laboured to gather some of them together from writings in a foreign tongue. Or will you perhaps reply that you did not despise the Greek writings on these subjects, but that you devoted your attention first to the study of Latin works, and now, proficient in these, are beginning to inquire after Greek learning? (tr. Cunningham)

Although in 410 CE Dioscurus was probably able to take Saint Augustine's advice, since he could get hold of and consult the corresponding Greek originals, many centuries later the situation is rather gloomy: with only a few notable exceptions, the students of Presocratic philosophers are faced with a textual vacuum.[2] The reconstruction of the Presocratic doctrines and the access to their original meaning are intrinsically tied to

Latin philosophical or philosophizing authors. An exhaustive mapping of Presocratic references within Roman writers would be far from realistic, since it would require a larger-scale study, still to be done.³ In the absence of such a work, I focus here on three contemporaneous writers who were active in Italy around the end of the Republic, namely, Philodemus of Gadara, Lucretius, and Cicero.⁴ Within these authors, rather than gleaning scattered and isolated references to certain Presocratic thinkers, I prioritize specific passages in which there is some sort of a list of Presocratic philosophers.⁵

The discussion is organized around the works of each author, but the questions to be addressed are common for all three of them. First, I delve into the specific sources from which these authors drew their information and explore whether they relied for their accounts on their exclusive and direct access to the Presocratic doctrines or whether their reading was instead mediated through certain interpretative prisms. As we will soon realize, the formation of what we call "Roman Presocratics," i.e., the distorted image that Romans of the first century BCE had of their Presocratic predecessors, is heavily dependent both on the doxographical tradition and the Hellenistic biographies of the Presocratics, as these are reflected in Diogenes Laertius's *Lives of Eminent Philosophers*.⁶ Both these channels of filtering and transmitting the Presocratic doctrines to Rome are eloquently encapsulated in Marcello Gigante's coinage "bio-doxography."⁷ With this in mind, in what follows I also discuss the purposes that Presocratic references serve in the three authors under investigation, and thus the role that the Presocratics were summoned to play in their new Roman environment. Why would a Roman be interested in the integration of Presocratic ideas into his own system of thought? Should we consider these texts as reliable sources for the Presocratic theories? Or, conversely, had the biased reception of the Presocratics by these Roman authors any particular influence on the way they were themselves appreciated and comprehended in turn by later writers?

PHILODEMUS OF GADARA: WRITING GREEK IN ITALY

Let us first turn to the fragments of Philodemus's voluminous treatises, which were discovered in the volcanic ashes of the Herculaneum library, and examine whether there are any Presocratic references.

Arrangement of the Philosophers (Σύνταξις τῶν φιλοσόφων)

In the tenth book of his *Lives of Eminent Philosophers*, which expounds Epicurus's life (10.3), Diogenes Laertius refers to the tenth book of Philodemus's Σύνταξις τῶν φιλοσόφων.⁸ According to this reference, Diogenes found the statement that

Epicurus's three brothers discussed philosophy with him in Philodemus's work entitled *Arrangement of the Philosophers*, which was written in at least ten books, the tenth of which was probably the one dealing with Epicurus.[9] It is a great misfortune that from the Herculaneum library we have been able to retrieve only part of Philodemus's work, specifically the part that concerns the history of the Academy and the history of the Stoa, the so-called *Index Academicorum* (*PHerc*. 1021 et 164) and *Index Stoicorum* (*PHerc*. 1018), respectively.[10] Taking into consideration what we can extract from the decipherable papyri, Philodemus's work itself appears to have been highly influenced by the Hellenistic genre of philosophical histories called *Successions* (Διαδοχαί) of philosophers. In the *Successions* the philosophers are organized in long lists of pupils or disciples, with the focus placed on the special ties that group together various philosophers in terms of teacher–disciple relationship rather than on individuals.

Before we consider the information that we may gather from Philodemus's fragmentary *Syntaxis*, let us ask how this work could—or does—pertain to "Roman Presocratics." On the basis that both Philodemus's and Diogenes' works are written in ten books, with considerable similarities in terms of content, there are those who plausibly believe that Philodemus's *Syntaxis* offered Diogenes a model of writing and structure.[11] Given the fact that Diogenes' work contains lengthy treatments of Presocratic biographies, which are also organized according to the system of *Successions* (Ionian and Italian), one is easily led to think about a possible corresponding presence of the Presocratics within Philodemus's work. Had it not been destroyed by fire, Philodemus's *Syntaxis* would be highly enlightening with regard to the present discussion. However, the evidence on the Presocratics in this text is not only extremely scanty, but also controversial. Rather than attempt here a summary of the *status quaestionis*,[12] I limit myself to observing that thanks to the paleographical homogeneity with other testimonies of the *Syntaxis*, texts associated with the Presocratics have been identified in—at least—two papyri (*PHerc*. 327 and 1508), which may point to the existence of two Presocratic *diadochai*, likely containing the history of the Eleatic/Abderitic and the Pythagorean School respectively.[13] These papyri were originally published by Wilhelm Crönert, who even argued that Xenophanes, Parmenides, and Democritus would make what is called a "succession book" (cf. Diog. Laert. 9.18–49).[14] In *PHerc*. 327 Crönert read the names of Democritus (fr. 1.3 and 1.5 Crönert) and Xenophanes (fr. 2.3–4 Crönert). With reference to Democritus, Crönert read φιλόπολις (fr. 5.2 Crönert), "the one who loves his country"; in the same fragment, Democritus is also plausibly said to have been buried by the whole town (fr. 5.5 Crönert παν]δημ[ε]ὶ δ' ἐτάφη). In *PHerc*. 1508, in which Philodemus may have turned his attention to the members (doctors) of the Pythagorean school, Crönert read the words ἰατρόν and φύσιν (fr. III 11_{19} Crönert) and the names of Πολυμνάστος and Εὐρυφῶν (fr. IV 3_{26} and $_{28}$ Crönert), which belong to the Pythagorean environment (cf. references to places, e.g., Akragas fr. III 7_{20} and Mytilene fr. III 10_{14}; to people: Apollodorus fr. III 5_{30}, 30 Crönert). Christian Vassallo has now plausibly argued that *PHerc*. 1788 may have been part of the same work. In this papyrus, which also belongs to the tradition of biodoxographical accounts, Empedocles is characterized as arrogant (col. 6 [*olim* fr. 3]) and Democritus as a plagiarist of his alleged master (col. 8 [*olim* fr. 1]).[15]

Bearing in mind that only limited and tentative conclusions can be extracted about the part of the text that does not survive, we may consider the general character of the *Syntaxis* as this can be reconstructed from the study of the Academic and Stoic parts, and Diogenes Laertius's evidence will be called on when appropriate. On the basis of the principle that we may be allowed to apply our general conclusions about the whole work to its parts, we should be able to form at least an idea about Philodemus's alleged treatment of the Presocratics in this context. A major question regarding the *Syntaxis* pertains to its categorization in terms of genre. As Myrto Hatzimichali remarks, whereas some of the material can be traced back to "the tradition of Hellenistic biography of Peripatetic/ Callimachean pedigree," a tradition which intrinsically abounds in anecdotes, nevertheless Philodemus's work should not be considered "simply a work of biography."[16] As far as Philodemus's use of doxography is concerned, scholars are divided. In the remaining fragments of the text as it stands, doxography is mainly absent. Despite this fact, David Sedley has argued for the possibility that the doxographical material was not integrated with the lives of the philosophers in question, but stood self-contained as in Diogenes Laertius.[17]

Whatever the case may be, as scholars have repeatedly pointed out, it is particularly important for the present discussion that the text lacks the "polemical engagement and vigor" otherwise typical of an Epicurean adherent against the rival schools.[18] Hatzimichali aptly considers the absence of doxography as the main cause "for a sense of objectivity and impartiality prevalent throughout the surviving portions of the *Syntaxis*."[19] As for the purpose of such a work by Philodemus, Hatzimichali considers it to be "a way of packaging Greek philosophy in a concise systematic form, targeted at his Italian audience, that is an educated Roman elite," what Gigante defines as "an institutional manual."[20]

Assuming that Philodemus's *Syntaxis* was subsequently so influential as to have plausibly served as the main model for Diogenes Laertius, let us summarize how this same work may have contributed to the formation of "Roman Presocratics" in the first place.[21] Philodemus appears to have had at his disposal wide-ranging biographical material, on which he draws in order to write a work structured according to the *Succession* literature. Whereas one cannot rule out the possibility that doxography may have formed part of the *Syntaxis*, it is important to bear in mind that, despite his Epicurean identity, Philodemus did not approach his philosophical predecessors—Presocratics included—in a polemical spirit, but rather in a historical one. As the next section will demonstrate, Philodemus's attitude was not consistent throughout his writings.

De Pietate (*PHerc*. 1428, cols. 318–33 Vassallo = frs. 7–19 Schober)

Among Philodemus's treatises of which fragments are extant, *On Piety* is perhaps the only one in which the Presocratic presence is indisputably attested at considerable length.²² By means of this treatise, Philodemus responds to a Stoic critique of Epicurean theology. In the first part Philodemus offers a defense of Epicurean religious ideas and practices; in the second, he refutes the mythical conception of the gods promoted by the Greek poets and mythographers and then—of particular interest to us—sharply criticizes the theology of Greek philosophers from Thales of Miletus (6th cent. BCE) and down to the Stoic Diogenes of Babylon. The segment of the list in which Philodemus introduces the "Roman Presocratics" (*PHerc.* 1428, cols. 318–333 Vassallo = frs. 7–19 Schober) starts with Thales and goes down to Diogenes of Apollonia (2nd cent. BCE).²³

As far as the sources of Philodemus's doxography are concerned, Dirk Obbink argues that this passage may have drawn its information from the Epicurean Zeno's of Sidon (now lost) treatise Περὶ εὐσεβείας, in which Zeno attacks contemporary Stoics. As Obbink remarks, there were more such Epicurean treatises, e.g., the Περὶ θεῶν by Phaedrus, who was the head of the Epicurean school before 70 BCE.²⁴ Whatever the case may be, Philodemus builds his refutation on the epistemological basis that, instead of perceiving the true nature of Epicurean gods, these philosophers favored insensate, inanimate, nonanthropomorphic divinities. Contrary to what we have just discussed in connection with his *Syntaxis*, in the present case Philodemus's point of view is distinctly Epicurean. Although all the philosophers who figure in the list were presumably included among the authorities praised by Philodemus's Stoic opponents in support of their thesis, Philodemus himself refers to them in order to criticize the Stoic practice of appropriating traditional ideas about the gods (συνοικείωσις / *accomodatio*).²⁵ As Obbink remarks: "Philodemus's treatment of the pre-Stoics prefaces his engagement with the Stoics in the next section and like the critique of the poets and historians, it is meant to inform the attack on the Stoics who, he notes, habitually cited these figures in support of (or as having prefigured and therefore as confirming) Stoic views."²⁶ In other words, Philodemus employs the refutation of various Presocratic ideas about the gods as a *preparatory stage* in an *argumentative vehicle* in order to undermine the corresponding Stoic theory with which his discussion culminates and to show that this theory is ridiculous and self-contradictory. I postpone further discussion regarding the actual content of the doxographical list, in order to compare Philodemus's list with Cicero's parallel passage below.

LUCRETIUS: THE EPICUREAN

The most elaborate evidence for the Roman reception of the Presocratic philosophers in the late Republic derives from Lucretius's *De rerum natura* (*DRN*), a poetic text with a distinctive Epicurean standpoint and explicit didactic goal. In the first book of his poem, Lucretius expounds the basic principles of the Epicurean doctrine, establishes the existence of matter and void and identifies the atoms along with their properties; he then launches a harsh attack against three particular Presocratic philosophers, i.e.,

Heraclitus (1.635–704), Empedocles (1.705–829), and Anaxagoras (1.830–920), so as to refute monism, finite pluralism, and infinite pluralism respectively.[27]

Various questions related to the so-called Critique have been extensively discussed: for example, scholars have delved into Lucretius's philosophical sources, in order to account for the doctrinal distortion of certain Presocratic arguments. They have also pondered Lucretius's choice to single out just those three Presocratics and to grant the Critique the central place within book 1; last but not least, special attention has been drawn to the rhetorical and persuasive function of such an attack within the framework of his didactic philosophical plan.[28] Whereas a detailed discussion of the Critique falls beyond the scope of this chapter,[29] I focus here rather on the reasons for Lucretius's misunderstanding of certain Presocratic doctrines as well as his possible familiarity with the original Presocratic texts; I also explore whether and why Lucretius further elaborated the information that he derived either directly from the Presocratics or already filtered through an intermediary source. As I show, the Critique bears the strong imprint of the biographical tradition, which Lucretius developed on the basis of a certain doxographical text. Yet Lucretius also infused this tradition with his independent knowledge of the three Presocratics so as to build his own poetic account.

As far as the sources of the Critique are concerned, it should be first pointed out that a similar Epicurean refutation of the Presocratic theories of matter in the form of a doxographical list is found in the fragmentary epigraphical text of Diogenes of Oenoanda (fr. 6 Smith).[30] In his rather compressed list Diogenes states that he will explain the primary and imperishable elements of things, but first he will refute the tenets of others; in line with this intention, in addition to Lucretius's references to Heraclitus, Empedocles, and Anaxagoras, he includes Thales, Diogenes of Apollonia, Anaximenes, and finally Democritus and the Stoics; despite these significant additions, it seems plausible that the two texts are ultimately dependent on the same source. Diogenes also reproduces biographical information present in Aëtius as well (I 3 Mansfeld/Runia)—concerning the Presocratic philosophers' place of origin (e.g., Ἡράκλειτος ὁ Ἐφέσιος, Ἐνπεδοκλῆς ὁ Ἀκράγου, Ἀναξαγόρας δ' ὁ Κλαζομένιος).[31] Still, the question remains: why should Lucretius single out those three specific Presocratics? James Warren summarizes the potential explanations: "These three are intended to stand as proxies for contemporary opponents [...] An alternative interpretation would simply state that although these three are ancient in Lucretius's day, for Epicurus they would have been much closer and perhaps genuine rivals."[32]

Lucretius claims that, since all three of his Presocratic predecessors deny the existence of void and maintain that their primary substances are perishable, they are all equally mistaken.[33] However, in this refutation, Lucretius misrepresents various aspects of the Presocratic doctrines. For example, Lucretius takes it for granted that Heraclitus's material principle was fire, a claim that does not plausibly reproduce Heraclitus's original sayings, but rather their erroneous interpretation by Aristotle and Theophrastus (cf. Arist. *Metaph.* A.3, 983b8). It is probably for the same reason that Lucretius also attributes to Heraclitus the non-Heraclitean theory of creation through rarefaction and condensation (1.645–664).[34] Likewise, Lucretius wrongly claims that Empedocles's elements are perishable (1.753–781; cf. DK 31 B35.14). He also grants him the transformationist theory, according to which fire turns into air, air into water, and water into earth, and then back again in reverse, in a never-ending cycle (1.782–802).[35] Last but not least, Lucretius wrongly refers to Empedoclean *terra, ignis,* and *umor* as examples of Anaxagoras's fundamental stuff (1.841, 1.853).[36] In sum, Lucretius's reading of the three Presocratics noticeably repeats misunderstandings introduced by the Theophrastean doxographical tradition.[37]

However, the question remains: can we track down with even more precision Lucretius's source? In order to account for Lucretius's divergence from the original Presocratic theories, Sedley argues that the Epicurean poet drew his arguments from Epicurus's Περὶ Φύσεως (ΠΦ), Books 14 and 15.[38] Serious objections have been raised to this claim, especially by Francesco Montarese in his recent treatment of the Critique. In particular, the choice of Heraclitus as the only representative of monism by Lucretius and the primary one by Diogenes of Oenoanda suggests that they both must have used a source later than Epicurus, at a time when the Stoics' admiration for Heraclitus was crystallized.[39] Cicero explicitly considers Heraclitus the precursor of the Stoics regarding fire (*Nat. d.* 3.35.2). At the same time, Lucretius strikingly transliterates the Greek work *homoeomeria* (1.830 and 1.834) with reference to Anaxagoras's theory of elements, according to which a portion of everything exists in everything; this is remarkable, while this word is not found in Anaxagoras's extant fragments, in all plausibility it occurs in Epicurus's ΠΦ XIV and XV, used in a sense different from what we read in Lucretius, that is, in the Aristotelian sense, meaning that smaller parts of a substance preserve the same qualities as the substance itself.[40] That is why there are scholars who plausibly claim that, notwithstanding his devotion to his master, in this particular case Lucretius took into consideration later developments in the Epicurean school and made use of a source later than Epicurus. Since it is impossible to reach any specific conclusion about Lucretius's source, it would be best to assume with Jaap Mansfeld that "both Lucretius and Diogenes of Oenoanda depend on an Epicurean exegetic and scholastic tradition which is in turn dependent on the *Placita*."[41]

Scholars unanimously agree that, whatever Lucretius's source, he himself critically tailored his doxographical material, in terms of both content and style; they also underscore Lucretius's remarkably harsh tone. Let us first focus on the parts of the Critique in which Lucretius rejects Heraclitus's and Empedocles's theories respectively. As Robert D. Brown writes, "The first two philosophers, Heraclitus and Empedocles, are introduced by elaborate passages in which a brief transition stating each man's theory about the basis of matter leads into a section of heavily embroidered personal comment by Lucretius on each thinker's personality and achievement. Though he rejects both theories, Lucretius takes a strongly contrasting attitude to each man, of blame and praise respectively."[42]

Lucretius repeatedly states that Heraclitus's doctrine was mere madness (cf. 1.692: *perdelirum*; 1.698: *cum vanum tum delirum*; 1.704: *dementia*). Montarese comments that "there is no evidence that such a damning and derisive attitude towards Heraclitus was customary in the Epicurean school."[43] Turning the focus from the Epicurean reception back to Heraclitus's own writings, Ernst D. Kollmann states that the use of military metaphors in the Critique (e.g., Lucr. 1.638 *dux proelia primus*; cf. also 1.741) are meant to parody Heraclitus's own use of military language (cf. DK 22 B80 and B53) and thus sketch the latter's aggressiveness and sharp criticism.[44] Heraclitus appears to have used opposites, paradoxes, and the oxymoron figure of style, with the purpose of obscuring his thoughts. That is why Heraclitus's obscure style became proverbial among Lucretius's contemporaries.[45] As Kollmann summarizes it, "Language has an important function in Heraclitus's philosophy. The use of antitheses and word-plays is essentially connected with his philosophic system and stresses the unity of opposites and the contradictions in unity."[46] According to Kollmann, it is for this very purpose of reproducing Heraclitus's style that the passage is so burdened with opposites (e.g., 1.639 *clarus ob obscuram linguam*; 1.639–40 *inanes . . . gravis Graios*). Lucretius, therefore, fights Heraclitus by means of the latter's weapons, in order to reject both his personality and his theory of elements. In other words, it could seem plausible that Lucretius had somehow direct access to Heraclitus's writings; in turning Heraclitus's writing against him, Lucretius was going further than Epicurus himself. His hostility to Heraclitus might, then, have been inspired by later developments in Epicureanism, but his strategy may have been his own.

When it comes to the appraisal of Empedocles, Lucretius radically modifies his stance.[47] The narrative space that is devoted to Empedocles's praise is indicative of the analogous debt that the Epicurean poet is about to acknowledge to his literary forebear, as founder of the genre of philosophical poetry (1.716–733). Lucretius explicitly refers to Empedocles's divine heart and his famous achievements (1.731–733).[48] In doing so, he incorporates Empedocles's religious and oracular imagery (cf. DK 31 B112).[49] Given the fact that the Epicureans were rather hostile to the Acragantine philosopher, Lucretius's stance has been considered highly puzzling.[50] To complicate matters further, Sedley has offered a plausible reconstruction of Empedocles's proem to his *On Nature* using Lucretius's opening hymn to Venus on the basis of the claim that it contains tangible Empedoclean echoes. Sedley draws particular attention to what he calls the "Empedoclean fingerprint" (i.e., the use of two compound adjectives within the same verse, translating or paraphrasing the corresponding Empedoclean verses; cf. e.g., Lucr. 1.3 *quae mare navigerum, quae terras frugiferentis*), which leads one to assume that Lucretius had firsthand knowledge of Empedocles's poem.[51] In a similar vein, Lucretius's tableau of Venus holding Mars in her embrace (1.29–43) has been long considered to replicate the Empedoclean cosmological powers of Love and Strife. Last but not least, regarding the creation of species in *DRN* 5, Lucretius seems to have turned to Empedocles as his model for the antiteleological system.[52]

With all this in mind, let us return to the Empedoclean section of the Critique. After the introductory verses about Empedocles's wrong theory, Lucretius proceeds to an elaborate description of Sicily and of Mount Aetna. Lucretius seems to invoke Empedocles's legendary biographical tradition, according to which Empedocles made a fatal leap into Etna to prove his divinity (cf. Diog. Laert. 8.70). This well-established tradition is also found in later Latin poets, such as Horace (*Ars P.* 464–466).[53]

Bearing in mind what is considered to be the standard Epicurean polemical practice regarding Heraclitus and Empedocles, the reader is faced with Lucretius's strikingly different approach: his condemnation of Heraclitus versus his enthusiasm for Empedocles. Without underestimating other reasons that may have influenced Lucretius's stance—such as Heraclitus's association with the Stoics along with Empedocles's ideal poetical style—this attitude strikingly replicates a standard motif easily spotted within the biographical tradition. As Ava Chitwood remarks:

> The biographers' reaction to Heraclitus and to his work was, in fact, generally unfavorable and manifests itself in an unusually hostile biography; hence Heraclitus's refusal to rule becomes another example of the philosopher's misanthropy. Empedocles, on the other hand, in his work addresses his fellow citizens as "friends" and says that the 'best men' become political leaders. His philosophical statements therefore impressed the biographers in a favorable manner and result in a generally *favorable* biographical tradition; his refusal to rule glorifies the philosopher as a selfless, sympathetic, and democratic fellow citizen.[54]

One is thus tempted to believe that it is because Lucretius toys with this influential biographical tradition that he departs from the standard Epicurean polemic, regarding the reception of both Heraclitus and Empedocles.

How does Anaxagoras fit into this scheme?[55] There is no introductory reference to Anaxagoras's personality, such as those that we read in association with Heraclitus and Empedocles; Lucretius appears to limit himself to doctrinal criticism. The omission of any reference to Anaxagoras's personality should not come as a surprise, since a corresponding gap also exists within the biographical tradition.[56] On the other hand, Lucretius's refutation of Anaxagoras's theory once again is not consonant with the Epicurean tradition. According to Diogenes Laertius (10.12), "Of the ancients Epicurus received most favorably Anaxagoras, although he opposed him on certain points, and Archelaus, the teacher of Socrates."[57] What is particularly striking about the criticism of Anaxagoras is the use of the word *homoeomeria*, one of the only two Greek philosophical words within *DRN* that Lucretius transliterates instead of translating (the other one being the word *harmonia* in 3.117 and 131). Sedley justifies Lucretius's choice on the basis that "Anaxagoras's horrible word is glaringly not at home in the Latin language; and that linguistic incongruity in turn foreshadows the fact, which Lucretius satirically develops in the sequel, that the concept underlying it is equally unwelcome." Sedley concludes that in this way Lucretius creates a "link between the alienness of a word and the alienness of the concept it expresses."[58] Still, we should bear in mind that this word, as we have noted above, is not found—at least not with the same meaning—either in Anaxagoras's extant fragments or in Epicurus's writings.[59]

Regarding Lucretius's treatment of Anaxagoras's doctrine, we may note the unusual amount of repetition (e.g., 1.835–837), which may point to his own reading and reproducing of Anaxagoras's style. To quote Montarese: "However Lucretius may have acquired familiarity with Anaxagoras's language, it seems likely that by introducing the long list of examples, he was reproducing and *caricaturing* Anaxagoras's *long-winded, stiff and monotonous style*, and thus silently *condemning* it. As in the case of Heraclitus and Empedocles, so in the case of Anaxagoras Lucretius made his refutation forceful by fusing his *own knowledge* of the Presocratics named with the philosophical material he found in his source [my emphasis]."[60] Even if this assessment holds true, Lucretius's negative appraisal of Anaxagoras's style would once again clash with other ancient evidence. Diogenes Laertius praises Anaxagoras's style (Diog. Laert. 2.6): "He was a pupil of Anaximenes, and was the first who set mind above matter, for at the beginning of his treatise, which is composed in attractive and dignified language, he says, 'All things were together; then came Mind and set them in order.' "[61] Brown underlines the satirical character of the passage, achieved by means of several techniques, and claims that "Lucretius has redirected the inventive imagination which he earlier applied to personal characterization into an entertaining presentation and critique of Anaxagoras's ideas."[62] Therefore, it seems that Lucretius's presentation of Anaxagoras is based on his own assessment of the latter's doctrine and style.

To sum up our findings regarding the Critique, although Lucretius turns to a post-Epicurus doxographical text as his starting point, he nevertheless sets himself apart from the Epicurean school. While he plausibly adopts a harsher voice than his master—or even his source—against Heraclitus and Anaxagoras, he presents us with a heavily biased account, in which he distorts the Presocratic doctrines and imposes his own judgment about his predecessors' personalities and writing style. In doing so, he embeds in his Critique his own direct knowledge of these three Presocratics, along with related information that he draws from the biographical tradition. At the same time, Lucretius the poet allows himself to touch also on themes associated with poetic succession and literary accomplishments. Last but not least, he applies to all three sections of the Critique the vocabulary, poetic techniques and metaphorical imagery that he also deploys throughout his work, so as to highlight that the structure of things is homogenous at all levels, and to facilitate the transmission of the Epicurean truth. As to the question whether Lucretius's bio-doxographical Critique could in any possible way present contemporary and later readers with a reliable image of these Presocratics and more specifically of their philosophical tenets, our answer definitely must be negative. Still, Lucretius's account, and more generally his poem, proved particularly influential, especially as far as the prioritizing of Empedocles over the other Presocratics by the Romans.

Cicero: Reading the Presocratics from an Academic Perspective

In the period after the defeat of Pompey, Cicero was obliged to withdraw from active political life, and he devoted himself to philosophical writing. During an extremely prolific period that extended from February 45 BCE to November 44 BCE, Cicero made an unsurpassed attempt to render Greek philosophy into the Latin language in the form of dialogues, after his Platonic model.[63] Before taking a closer look at the passages in which Cicero cites the names of specific Presocratics, we may first offer a few preliminary remarks. Given that the main focus of Cicero's works is ethical philosophy, concrete references to Presocratic philosophers within his corpus are understandably scarce. We should also bear in mind that, despite his vast knowledge of Greek, because of the speed and haste with which he composed his philosophical dialogues, he was often obliged to turn to handbooks. As for the prospective recipients of his dialogues, to quote Obbink, "The typology of the books of the Herculaneum library contrasts sharply with the publishing ventures of Cicero and Atticus. Cicero's dialogues depict Roman gentlemen engaged in learned yet urbane and witty conversation about the central topics in Greek philosophy of the generation. Philodemus' treatises, on the other hand, promote Epicurean good life for the benefit of the recalcitrant Piso and his sons."[64]

De natura deorum

In his dialogue *De natura deorum* (August 45–early 44 BCE; dramatic date 77–75 BCE),[65] Cicero offers his own version of the history of theology and expounds the philosophical disagreement between the Epicureans and the Stoics on the existence and nature of the gods. In the first book of this work, Velleius, the Epicurean spokesman, presents his school's corresponding views (*Nat. d.* 1.18–56). Just before developing the Epicurean theology, Velleius makes a preliminary attack on the Platonic and Stoic concept of the deity (*Nat. d.* 1.18–24) and then criticizes the theologies of twenty-seven philosophers, in a list that begins with Thales of Miletus and concludes with the Stoic Diogenes of Babylon. The Presocratic doxography, on which we will focus our discussion, covers five paragraphs (*Nat. d.* 1.25–29), in which Velleius discusses the views of twelve Presocratic philosophers (Thales, Anaximander, Anaximenes, Anaxagoras, Alcmaeon of Croton, Pythagoras, Xenophanes, Parmenides, Empedocles, Protagoras, Democritus, Diogenes of Apollonia).[66] Velleius's Epicurean account is followed by Cotta's Academic rebuttal (*Nat. d.* 1.57–124).

As has been long pointed out, the part of Velleius's account that contains the doxography mirrors the concluding section of Philodemus's *On Piety*, even if the former is placed at the beginning of Cicero's work, in an abbreviated form. In fact, the similarity between Philodemus's and Cicero's accounts is so evident that in his *Doxographi Graeci* Diels printed these texts in parallel columns (*Dox. Graec.* 531–550). Despite the similarity with Philodemus's text, the question of Cicero's sources has tantalized scholars. There are those who consider the Epicurean Phaedrus as Cicero's ultimate source.[67] There are others who opt for Zeno of Sidon, the Epicurean teacher of both Philodemus and Cicero. Given that Obbink's new reading of the Herculaneum papyri to be ascribed to Philodemus's *On Piety* yielded more names of philosophers, an even closer correspondence between the two texts was revealed, which made Cicero's dependence on his Epicurean sources closer.[68] This led some scholars to prefer the more economical solution, according to which Cicero expatiated on Philodemus's account, so as to buttress his Academic standpoint.[69] Last but not least, Vassallo pointed out "doxographical analogies and, above all, differences that rule out both Cicero's dependence on Philodemus and the existence of only one source for both authors." As he rightly concludes, "Such a source, if it ever existed, was necessarily mediated by other sources, by the personal selection that the two authors made, and by their efforts to fit them into the different contexts of the two works."[70]

While a systematic comparison of these twin passages is something that remains to be done, I attempt here rather to touch on general issues related to them, with particular emphasis on their similarities or discrepancies; in doing so, I will hopefully demarcate their different roles within the general framework of Romanizing the Presocratics that I am sketching.[71] In a way similar to Philodemus's *Syntaxis* and Diogenes Laertius's *Lives*, the sequence in which the philosophers are refuted is roughly chronological, while there is a clear distinction between two lineages, the Ionian and the Italian; in other words, despite the chronological impossibilities that one may easily spot (e.g., Anaxagoras cannot have been the pupil of Anaximenes), both lists bear the imprint of the successional literature.[72] Regarding in particular Cicero's method of refutation, scholars have drawn attention to two specific facets of his doxographical list: his *misrepresentation* of specific Presocratic views as well as the *sharpening* of his critical tone compared to that of Philodemus.

As far as the doctrinal content of the lists is concerned, the Epicureans appear to disapprove of the Presocratics because of their lack of perception of or knowledge about the true nature of the gods (e.g., *non vidit* 1.26; *non sensit* 1.27; *non intellegens* 1.33).[73] This critique is exercised from a distinctive Epicurean point of view, i.e., the physical belief in προλήψεις about the gods, who are happy and perfect eternal anthropomorphic beings (1.45). In addition, refutation of the philosophers is organized in groups, with the same arguments being directed against two or three different opponents (e.g., Thales, Parmenides, and Empedocles are attacked for their claim that a god has no feelings).[74] Richard McKirahan has demonstrated in detail Velleius's distortion of both Thales's and Anaxagoras's doctrines. According to Velleius, "Thales held that god was the mind that moulded all things out of water" (1.25). While most ancient testimonia make Thales a hylozoist (cf. Arist. *De an.* A5, 411a7–8), in this statement Velleius wrongly attributes to Thales an Anaxagorean mind that acts as a creative principle independent of water. As McKirahan rightly notes, this mistake can be spotted also in Aëtius (1.7.11); this observation points to the fact that this misunderstanding might have already been present in Cicero's source.[75] When it comes to Anaxagoras (1.26), his notion of mind is said to be sentient and an animate being, infinite in extent; it also brings to completion (*conficere*) the order of the cosmos. Although according to the doxography mind is infinite, it is not described as being infinite in extent (DK 59 B12). The idea of Anaxagoras's Mind as an agent with intentions (*dissignari*) does not correspond to what we read in Anaxagoras's fragments, or to what Cicero could have read in Philodemus's *On Piety* [PHerc. 1428, col. 320 20–32 Vassallo (= fr. 9 Schober). Cf. Gomperz 1866 p. 66 with DK 59 B12] or to what he writes about Anaxagoras in his *Academica priora* (2.118.5–7).[76] As McKirahan states, in this particular case Cicero should be considered the originator of this doctrinal misrepresentation.[77] The idea that Empedocles's roots are liable to destruction (1.29), a thesis incompatible with Empedocles's actual beliefs, but one that we have also spotted in Lucretius's Critique (1.753–781), is probably again due to Cicero's doxographical source.[78] Along the same lines, Cicero's list mistakenly presents us with an—otherwise unattested—mythical version of Parmenides's cosmology, according to which god is something fanciful like a wreath that surrounds the sky with a continuous ring of fires (1.28: *commenticium quiddam coronae simile efficit [στεφάνην appellat]*).[79] In this way, Cicero may seek to impose the view that the Presocratic theories have fallen prey to Epicurean hands. Characteristic is the absence of Heraclitus, who more than once is elsewhere said to have been invoked by the Stoics as the predecessor of their views.[80] As far as Democritus is concerned, we should draw attention to the fact that the Academic Cotta also criticizes his doctrine in a similar way in 1.120, this time, however, presenting him as Epicurus's predecessor (cf. 1.73a).

Philodemus's deviations from the actual Presocratic doctrines, as well as Cicero's further adjustment, put us on the alert regarding the reliability of the Presocratic information we may gather from both lists as well as their ultimate objectives. Regarding Cicero in particular, one must consider his specific reasons for revising—instead of just translating, so to speak—Philodemus's doxographical list. Clara Auvray-Assayas argues that Velleius's treatment of the Presocratics aims at forming a unified image of their concept of the divine, which ultimately looks back to Plato's *Timaeus*. Given that at the time of writing his *De natura deorum*, Cicero was also in the process of translating this Platonic work, Velleius's account may be regarded as Cicero's critical appropriation of this particular Platonic work and his interpretation of it within the history of philosophy.[81]

While I revisit Cicero's motives for these doctrinal modifications below, we may now raise the question of whether his doxographical errors had any impact on the subsequent reception and comprehension of Presocratic ideas. Given that Cicero attributes to some of the philosophers that he mentions views which clash with other ancient evidence that we have at hand, McKirahan concludes that some of the inconsistencies in the passage could have been easily spotted by Cicero's readers: "These sophisticated readers would be both amused by the caricatures and made that much more suspicious and ill-disposed to Velleius's subsequent exposition of Epicurean theology."[82] According to him, this dynamic could account for the low reputation of this passage as doxography. The first critical reaction to Velleius's account is already found within the very same treatise, where the Academic Cotta compares the philosophers that figure in the doxographical list to senators, whose decisions may have authority (*Nat. d.* 1.94): "You yourself just now, when reeling off the list of philosophers like a censor calling the roll of the Senate, said that all those eminent men were fools, idiots and madmen. But if none of these discerned the truth about the divine nature, it is to be feared that the divine nature is entirely non-existent." Cotta makes use of a triple alliteration (*desipere delirare dementis*) to underscore the fact that, while Epicureans ridicule other schools, their own anthropomorphism is equally ridiculous.

Scholars also almost unanimously agree that Cicero's critique is sharper than Philodemus's polemical tone.[83] Whereas disdainful references to his predecessors are not absent from Philodemus's writings (cf. in particular his comment against the Stoics in the extant part of the list: *De pietate, PHerc.* 1428, col. VIII.24–28 Henrichs), and we cannot exclude the possibility that more such remarks lurked in the now-lost part of the treatise, Cicero's derogatory expressions are particularly striking.[84] For example Parmenides' beliefs are characterized as "monsters" (1.28 *monstra*); Xenophanes deserves to be severely criticized (1.28 *reprehendetur . . . vehementius*); Empedocles is reproached for having committed foul mistakes (1.29 *multa alia peccans . . . turpissume labitur*); and Democritus is said to have committed the biggest errors (1.29 *nonne in maximo errore versatur*). Velleius concludes that all the ideas discussed in his overview should be considered the dreams of madmen (1.42): "*Exposui fere non philosophorum iudicia, sed delirantium somnia.*" In McKirahan's words, Cicero's list "is marked by a tone of smugness, intolerance and disrespect. [. . .] In sum, passage B [i.e., this list] appears to be partisan, polemical and *prima facie* preposterous."[85] In a similar vein, Carl Classen writes: "While pretending to make both the Epicurean and the Stoic give *instructive* speeches, Cicero in fact depicts Velleius as if he were an advocate, delivering for the most part a *destructive* form of speech which does not correspond to the *instructive* function that the speech is supposed to have. Indeed, here it is the actual form of Velleius's speech that reveals its true (polemical) function."[86] While both these remarks are valid, we ought not to disregard the fact that before launching on Velleius's account, Cicero in his own voice disapprovingly criticizes the Epicurean argumentative method and ironically compares the Epicurean authority to that of their gods, since it does not leave any space for doubt (1.18). Having introduced Velleius's list with this comment, Cicero prepares the reader for the biased account that he is about to offer. At the same time, what is significantly missing from Velleius's account is any specific biographical information—negative or, more significantly, positive—concerning the Presocratics under discussion, such as we saw in Lucretius's Critique and which are scattered elsewhere in Cicero's works.[87] Given that, according to Cicero, the Epicureans made no effort at all to reconcile the Presocratic ideas with their master's truth, leaving absolutely no space for compromises, there is no reason why Velleius's attack against the Presocratics should get personal. Within the Epicurean universe there is no place for *any* of his Presocratic predecessors—or at least this is what Cicero would have them say; they should all be equally ostracized, even if, for this purpose, their views must first be distorted.[88]

Cicero's adjustment of Philodemus's list is particularly revealing, as far as the former's Academic stance toward the Epicureans and, subsequently, his rhetorical method are concerned. In view of the fact that part of the doctrinal distortion is plausibly due to his own intervention, rather than to the Epicurean arguments themselves, Cicero appears to be fighting his philosophical rivals with the same weapons to which the latter resorted in regard to their Presocratic predecessors. In order to show the Epicureans to be unreliable historians of theology and hence refute them, Cicero must first falsify them (cf. Cic. *Acad. pr.* 2.118).[89]

Academica

Academica (May–July 45, dramatic date of the first dialogue: 63–60) is the other key treatise from which we may glean information about Cicero's manipulation of the Presocratics; in this treatise, he discusses the theory of knowledge and various epistemological problems and presents us with a history of the Academic beliefs about perception and truth. The dialogue was written in two stages. The first draft (*Academica priora*) contained two books (*Catulus*, on the Academic theory of knowledge, and *Lucullus*, on Antiochus's epistemological theories), whereas the second—and revised—version consisted of four books (*Academica posteriora*, June 45 BCE). Only the second book of the first edition (*Lucullus*) together with the first book of the second edition (*Varro*, with Varro standing in as the protagonist and Antiochus's spokesman, who converses with Atticus and Cicero) are extant.[90] While in Cicero's *De natura deorum* it is the approach of the Epicureans that dominates, whose only goal was to *refute* the Presocratics and establish Epicurus's sole truth, in his *Academica* Cicero reveals the diametrically opposite Academic attitude, according to which the Presocratic theories, instead of being rejected, are on the whole *accepted*.

In the first book (of the four-volume second edition) Cicero replies to Varro and explains Arcesilaus's "defection" from the old Academy (*Acad. post.* 1.44–45):

> "It was entirely with Zeno, so we have been told," I replied, "that Arcesilaus set on foot his battle, not from obstinacy or desire for victory, as it seems to me at all events, but because of the *obscurity* of the facts that had led Socrates to a confession of ignorance, as also previously his predecessors Democritus, Anaxagoras, Empedocles, and almost all the old philosophers, who utterly denied all possibility of cognition or perception or knowledge, and maintained that the senses are limited, the mind feeble, the span of life short, and that truth (in Democritus' phrase) is sunk in the abyss, opinion and custom are all-prevailing, no place is left for truth, all things successively are wrapped in darkness."

According to Cicero, since all the Presocratics believe that neither reason nor the senses are able to guarantee apprehension of the nature of things, their views resemble the Academic *akatalepsia* thesis and would apparently support it; hence it is absolutely legitimate for the Academics to make an appeal to them, in order to show that there is a historical continuity in their philosophical thought.[91] In this context, the Presocratics are referred to as a group who share specific epistemological ideas in common, without any differentiation in their particular doctrines.

In the second book (of the two-volume first edition), it is the *Antiochean* Lucullus who attacks Academic skepticism and criticizes the Academics' appeal to the Presocratics, namely Empedocles, Anaxagoras, Democritus, and Parmenides (2.13–15).[92] As he argues, given that the ancients were *dogmatic*, when the adherents of the New Academy cite the names of Presocratics in order to buttress their arguments— e.g., Arcesilas together with Democritus—they pervert philosophical history. In order to stress his point, Lucullus compares the Academics with modern demagogues who introduce themselves as democratic statesmen, so as to justify their actions. It should not go unobserved that in this context Lucullus's counterarguments rely on a profound respect for the Presocratics, a respect that Lucullus shares with his opponents. Still, while he underlines Democritus's modesty, he nevertheless hints at Empedocles's madness (2.14 *furere*). Even worse, when Lucullus discusses the Academics' appeal to Democritus in association with their refutation of the Stoic criterion of truth, he accuses his opponents not just of misconstruing but, even worse, of deriding the natural philosophers (*Acad. prior.* 2.55): "Then you fly for refuge to the natural philosophers, the favourite butts of ridicule in the Academy, from whom even you can no longer keep your hands."[93] Lucullus's attack against the Academic method of appropriating the Presocratic theories tailored to their wishes is reminiscent of Cotta's corresponding denigration of Velleius's Epicurean argument. In both cases the "Roman Presocratics" appear to be the product of a misconstrued and biased history of philosophy.

Cicero responds to that criticism and repeats the Academic claim that all Presocratic philosophers were really skeptical, in fact dogmatically skeptical; that is why the Academics aspire to imitate them by embracing their doctrines (*Acad. prior.* = *Luc.* 2. 72–5):

> Our way of first recalling ancient philosophers was like the sedition-mongers' habit of putting forward the names of persons who are men of distinction but yet of popular leanings. Those people although they have unworthy designs in hand desire to appear like men of worth; and we in our turn declare that the views we hold are ones that you yourselves admit to have been approved by the noblest of philosophers. [. . .] Do you agree that I do not merely cite the names of persons of renown, as Saturninus did, but invariably take some famous and distinguished thinker as my model?

Cicero refers to five—instead of Lucullus's four—Presocratics, namely Empedocles, Anaxagoras, Democritus, Parmenides, and Xenophanes.[94] On the one hand he repeats his opponent's claim regarding his incontestable admiration of their predecessors (2.73: "Why, he [Anaxagoras] was a man of the highest renown for dignity and intellect. Why should I talk about Democritus? Whom can we compare for not only greatness of intellect but also greatness of soul?").[95] On the other, he challenges Lucullus's criticism of Empedocles, by underlining the exceptional value of the latter's poem (2.73: "I think that he sends forth an utterance most suited to the dignity of the subject of which he is speaking"). There is, however, a significant absence from Cicero's neo-Academic doxographical survey (1.44, 2.14, 2.72–74): Heraclitus, which is due to his importance for the Stoics as precursor of their dogmatism; given that in the present context the other Presocratics are presented as precursors of the suspension of judgment and the impossibility of accessing the truth, the Academics could not appeal to him.[96]

Conclusion

To summarize our findings, overall, with Philodemus in his historical *Syntaxis* being perhaps the only exception, philosophical and philosophizing writers who were active during the late Republic did not make a great effort to understand the Presocratics for their own sake. While Aristotle consulted his Presocratic predecessors so as to reach the truth, allowing for the fact that each of them had already grasped a segment of it, the Roman adherents of each Hellenistic philosophical school picked up on the Presocratics randomly and selectively, to the extent that Presocratic ideas help them bolster the primacy of their own views over those of their contemporary rivals. In the process of integrating Presocratic wisdom into Roman thought, two opposite trends can be discerned. On the one hand, the Epicureans (i.e., Philodemus, Lucretius, Cicero's Velleius) refute the Presocratics in order to establish their own unique truth; on the other, the Academics (Cicero) cite them positively, since they are interested in showing that there is a historical continuity in their philosophical thought, i.e., the suspension of judgment, which, in their opinion, can be traced back to the Presocratics. Quite paradoxically, however, in both cases the discussion of the Presocratic doctrines is conditioned by prejudice, misapprehension and deliberate misrepresentation. Provided that their Roman contemporaneous readers had limited independent access to the original Greek texts, it was through such a distorting lens that they first became acquainted with Presocratic ideas. As for the channels through which the Presocratics were first transferred to Rome, apart from the Presocratic texts that were firsthand available at least to Philodemus and Lucretius,[97] we have identified two additional routes: Hellenistic doxographical manuals, which were imbued with either Epicurean or Academic criticism, and the Hellenistic biographies circulating at the time.

Augustine, it seems, was wiser than we might have supposed in discouraging his pupil Dioscurus from relying on Cicero's account in his desire to grasp the Presocratic doctrines. It seems, in fact, that we cannot rely on the Republican authors for Presocratic ideas—or certainly not solely on them. To put it another way, if we had no fragments at all or testimonia from the Presocratic writings, the image we would have pieced together of them would be totally distorted and misleading.

Notes

> I sincerely thank Voula Tsouna for her warm encouragement in a very early stage of writing this paper, Stavros Kouloumentas for bibliographical suggestions, and Jaap Mansfeld for sending to me his otherwise inaccessible recent publication. Once again, David Konstan has been a meticulous reader of my work; his advice and support over the last decade have proven invaluable. Many thanks are also due to Gretchen Reydams-Schils for her perceptive comments. Last but not least, I wholeheartedly express my deep gratitude to Christian Vassallo, who painstakingly read an earlier version of this chapter and offered insightful

suggestions, corrections, and updating of the papyrological refences. Needless to say, whatever mistakes remain are my own. An earlier version of this chapter was presented at La Sapienza University (Rome) in March 2016. I thank Alessandro Schiesaro for the honur of the invitation.

1. Shanzer (2012) 167.
2. Runia (1999) and (2008); Mansfeld (1999); Baltussen (2005). Cf. also Mansfeld and Runia (1997).
3. Cf. the notable exception of the book on Heraclitus by Lévy and Saudelli (2014). For Seneca, see Hall (1977) and Setaioli (1988) 91–110.
4. For Lucretius's relationship with Philodemus see Obbink (2007), now also the Prolegomena in Vassallo (2021); see also Delattre (2003). For Lucretius's relationship with Cicero (*ad Q. fr.* 2.9, 10 or 11 February 54), see Pucci (1966), André (1974).
5. For an overview of Roman philosophy, see Long (2003). Discussion of (Neo)-Pythagoreanism falls beyond the limits of this chapter. See Horky in this volume. See also Flinterman (2014).
6. Mansfeld (2012) and (2017). See also McKirahan (2018) 474–480. As for Diels's view, see Zhmud (2013).
7. Gigante (1986). Cf. also the term "biographical doxographers" to distinguish them from "doxographers proper," a collocation first used by Burnet (^{4}1930) 34–37 in connection with the doxographical section in Hippolytus's *Refutatio*, Book 1.
8. For the *Syntaxis*, see Dorandi (1990). See also Giannatasio Andria (1989); Dorandi (1991) and (1994); Arrighetti (2003). See now Vassallo (2017b), with regard to *PHerc.* 1788.
9. Cf. Clay's different translation of the title as "*The Ordering of the Philosophers*" (2004).
10. Several other Herculaneum papyri should be ascribed to the *Syntaxis*. See below and Dorandi (1991). See now the new translation with introduction of Philodemus's *Index Academicorum* (*PHerc.* 1021 and 164) by Kalligas and Tsouna, along with notes by Hatzimichali (2020).
11. Cf., e.g., Gigante (1995) 21. For objections, see now Fleischer (2019).
12. For a *status quaestionis* see Longo Auricchio (2007) 220–221. See also Erler (1994) 297–300.
13. For the presence of Parmenides in Philodemus, see Capasso (1987) 304, Vassallo (2016), and discussion below. For other references to Democritus in Philodemus, who is expected to show his own admiration to Epicurus's predecessor, as Lucretius also does, see Gigante and Indelli (1980). Cf. Phld. *De piet.*, *PHerc.* 1428, col. 329 Vassallo (= fr. 16 Schober), dealing with the origin of religious ideas in men who observe the meteorological and astronomical phenomena), hereto Henrichs (1975a), Vassallo (2018a), and further discussion in the next section; *De mus.* IV, *PHerc.* 1497, col. 150.29-39 Delattre (Democritus is called φυσιολογώτατος in the discussion regarding the problem of the evolution of the society); *De morte* IV, *PHerc.* 1050, cols. 29.27–30.11 and col. 39.6–25 Henry; Cf. also *De adulat.* (*PHerc.* 1457) col. 10, 1–21 Kondo; *De ira, PHerc.* 182, col. XXIX, 17–29 Indelli. For other critical catalogs in Philodemus, see, e.g., *De morte* Book IV, *PHerc.* 1050, col. 35.11–34 Henry (about the courage that Socrates and Zenon from Elea and the atomist Anaxarchus from Abdera faced their death); *De rhet.* IV, *PHerc.* 224, fr. III Sudhaus, with Capasso (1987) 299–301 and Vassallo (2015) 84–107 (Anaxagoras, Metrodorus of Chios, Parmenides, and Melissus, about the relationship between rhetoric and philosophy or rhetoric and political power). For an exhaustive commentary to all this evidence, I refer to Vassallo (2021).
14. Crönert (1906) 127–133.

15. Vassallo (2017b). As he points out ((2017) 41), this is one of the several pieces of evidence for Empedocles in the Herculaneum papyri and the most ancient quotation of Empedocles's Καθαρμοί (DK 31 B112.4). For Empedocles in the Herculaneum papyri, see Leone (2019). For Empedocles's presence in Philodemus's *On Wealth*, see Armstrong and Ponczoch (2011) and (2013); see also Indelli (2007).
16. Hatzimichali (2020) 258–259 for a highly illuminating discussion. Cf. Arrighetti (2007).
17. Sedley (2003a) 31–32. For an overview of the discussion about the alleged existence of a doxographical passage in the lost part of *Syntaxis* see now Hatzimichali (2020) 264–267. Cf. Arrighetti (2003) 18–19n30.
18. Clay (2004) 55, who cites also Comparetti's remark (1875) 471 that the treatise lacks polemical and partisal zeal as well as any sign of having been written by an Epicurean; cf. also Mekler's comment (1902) xxxi–xxxii about the dispassionate and colorless character of the work. In a similar vein see Asmis (1994) 2376. Gigante (1995) 23 also remarks that the *Syntaxis* was not polemical. If Sedley's assumption (2003a) about the doxographical material held true, any Epicurean polemics could have appeared in separate sections. Capasso (1987) 303 remarks that the Epicureans seem to have adjusted their tone toward other philosophers depending the degree of danger.
19. Hatzimichali (2020) 264.
20. As Hatzimichali (2020) 270 summarizes: "We get a picture of peaceful co-existence and friendly relationships on a personal level across the various schools. [. . .] There is not unanimous agreement among modern scholars as to whether the *Syntaxis* was indeed intended for Roman newcomers to Greek philosophy or internally for Epicurean converts, or indeed as to whether it portrayed the Garden as somehow superior to the other schools." See also Gigante (1995) 20–23. Cf. Arrighetti (2003) 18–19; Clay (2004) 57. For the view about Epicurean superiority see Gaiser (1988) 24.
21. Alternative hypotheses on this point have been recently advanced by Fleischer (2019).
22. For the Presocratic section, see Gomperz (1866) and now Vassallo (2018b).
23. Obbink (2002) 190: Catalog of citations (one after another, most without the benefit even of direct quotation, and few equipped with commentary). Philodemus calls it a συναγωγή (*De piet.* I in Obbink 1996 line 2341–2342). For textual problems and readings of new names of philosophers in the papyrus, see Obbink (2002). See now Vassallo (2017a) and (2018b).
24. Obbink (2002) 206 refers also to Diogenes of Babylon's Περὶ τῆς Ἀθηνᾶς. See Henrichs (1972) 81n37 with further discussion. Cf. also Pease (1955) 39–42. Cf. on the contrary Philippson (1939b) 27–31, who believes that both Philodemus and Cicero copied from Phaedrus's Περὶ θεῶν; see also Diels *Dox. Graec.* 126–127.
25. Henrichs (1975b); Obbink (2002) 191.
26. Obbink (2002) 198.
27. Warren (2007) 27. For the particular nature of Lucretius's work, Warren (2007) 25 writes: "*DRN* is not concerned with carving out for the first time particular philosophical theory by engaging in long and complex arguments with alternative views. Nor is it primarily a polemical work addressed to committed adherents of alternative philosophical schools, pointing out the failings in their own theory or answering criticisms launched by them at Epicureanism. Nor is it a dialectical work, whose purpose is to contrast and evaluate competing philosophers. Rather, it is concerned to explain an already completed philosophical system to someone who is as yet uncommitted philosophically." For other—unnamed—references to Presocratics see Mansfeld (1990) 3148–3149, who argues that the

criticism in Lucr. 3.119–129 is derived from doxography. For another instance of Lucretius's usage of doxography in Book 5 regarding the illuminations of the moon see Runia (1997) 95 who notes that "Lucretius's method is dogmatic and refutatory, not dialectical and doxographical." In Book 6, Lucretius lists the doxographical explanations about the meteorological phenomena, but he does not name any specific Presocratic philosopher.

28. See two books published recently, which are devoted to the Critique: Piazzi (2005) and Montarese (2012). See also Piazzi (2008).
29. For Lucretius's eclecticism, see the collection of articles in Algra, Koenen, and Schrijvers (1997). For Lucretius's intertextual relationship with Empedocles, see Garani (2007) and further discussion below.
30. Mansfeld (1990) 3154–3157. For other references to Empedocles in Diogenes, see Gallavotti (1975–1977); Casanova (1984); Smith (1993) 491–493.
31. Mansfeld (1990) 3156–3157; Montarese (2012) 41–42 plausibly points out that there may have been an additional intermediary text, which was followed by one of them. On the contrary, see Érvard (1999), who claims that both Lucretius and Diogenes depend on the very same text.
32. Warren (2007) 26. For Epicurus's philosophical rivals see Sedley (1976) about Timocrates (cf. Plut. *adv. Colot.* 1108 C–D). Sedley (1998) 73 points to the fact that "none of the named philosophers presented, by any stretch of imagination, a live philosophical challenge to the Epicureans in Lucretius's own day." See also Kleve (1978) who argues that the selection of the Presocratics is conditioned in part by the fact that these figures were associated with the Stoics in Epicurean polemics.
33. Denial of void: Heraclitus: 1.655–664; Empedocles: 1.742–745; Anaxagoras: 1.841; perishable first principles: Heraclitus: 1.665–671; Empedocles: 782–793; Anaxagoras: 847–858.
34. In his recent treatment of the Critique Montarese (2012) offers a detailed account of those misunderstandings. See Montarese (2012) 22–27 especially 24: Cf. Arist. *Ph.* A.6, 189b8–10 and *Metaph.* A.8, 988b34–989a1.
35. Montarese (2012) 46–50.
36. Montarese (2012) 28–30.
37. Rösler (1973) 50–53.
38. Sedley (1998).
39. Montarese (2012) 177–178. Montarese (2012) 185: "Whether or not Lucretius's source explicitly mentioned the connection between the Stoics and Heraclitus, Lucretius had the Stoics' veneration of Heraclitus in mind when composing line 635–44." Cf. the word *stolidi* (Lucr. 1.641) plausibly referring to the Stoics with Snyder (1980) 118.
40. Cf. in particular Epicurus *On Nature* XV fr. 25, in which the word is plausibly used with the Aristotelian sense of the word, i.e., that smaller parts of a substance preserve the same qualities as the substance itself. See Montarese (2012) 36–40, 84–119. Cf. Wigodsky (2007).
41. Mansfeld (1990) 3154–3155.
42. Brown (1983) 146.
43. Montarese (2012) 185. Capasso (1987) 101 points to the fact that there is no mention of Heraclitus in Metrodorus, Hermarchus, Colotes. On the contrary, Piazzi (2005) 25–27 appears to think that Lucretius's irony derives from the Epicurean school or even Epicurus himself. According to Diogenes Laertius (10.8), Epicurus appears to have called Heraclitus κυκητής, the Stirrer, in order to refer to the latter's cosmological idea of universal flux. For Lucretius's embracing of Heraclitus's concept of flux and the corresponding imagery

of flowing, even if modified through the Empedoclean pluralistic materialism see Garani (2007) 198–200.

44. Kollmann (1971) 82 refers to Heraclitus B80 and B53. Kollmann (1971) 85 summarizes: "It may well be that Lucretius, the poet, wanted to present before the listener a picture of Heraclitus drawn by Heraclitean means, by his language and his style. They are all in here, the elements important for Heraclitus and known from his fragments: his aggressiveness, sharp criticism, the main characteristics of his language, its difficulty and its beauty, and its importance in Heraclitus' philosophy." Cf. Brown (1983) 146–147, who points to the mock-epic metaphor of battle, the proverbial obscurity as well as the use of oxymoron. See also Tatum (1984) 185 with special emphasis on the language: "For Lucretius there is a mean between the obscurity of Heraclitus and the jargon he associates with Anaxagoras, between the dark and the drab, and that mean is presented through the person of Empedocles." Cf. Montarese (2012) 182–185. For discussion of Lucretius's doxography see also Farrell (2001) 39–51, who characteristically notes [47] "Heraclitus' fame is situated *inter Graios* (and among the *inanis* rather than the *gravis Graios* at that), while Empedocles's proximity to Lucretius is stressed in philosophical, geographical, ethnographical, and linguistic terms." Cf. on the contrary Bollack (1969) 383–392 maintains that the passage demonstrates an instructive progression of advancing and developing philosophical ideas.
45. Cf. also Cic. *Nat. d.* 1.74 about Heraclitus speaking obscurely on purpose; *Div.* 2.133, *Fin.* 2.15.
46. Kollmann (1971) 81. Cf. West (1969) 26: "the specious tortuosities of Heraclitus' style."
47. On the contrary, on the basis of the repetition of verbs meaning "it seems," Edwards (1989) believes that Lucretius's reference to Empedocles is completely ironical.
48. For the discussion about the ambivalent semantic weight of the phrase "*praeclara reperta*," see Garani (2007), who claims that Lucretius praises Empedocles's analogical method.
49. Clay (1983) 49–52; Castner (1987).
50. Cf. Cic. *Nat. d.* 1.93; Diog. Laert. 10.25; Plut. *adv. Colotem* 1123B. For further references in other Epicureans see Garani (2007) 5.
51. Sedley (2003b). See Campbell (2014) about Lucretius's Empedoclean answer to Cleanthes' *Hymn to Zeus*.
52. Campbell (2003) 101–109.
53. Edwards (1989) 109. This is not the only instance that Lucretius takes into consideration Empedocles's biography for allusions to Empedocles's democratic stance. See Garani (2007) 69–71.
54. Chitwood (2004) 3–4.
55. Brown (1983).
56. See, however, reference in Maximus of Tyre 16.1 for the tradition according to which Anaxagoras, like Democritus, gave away all his possession. Cf. Anaxagoras P30 Laks and Most (< A13 = Plut. *Vit. Per.* 16), Democritus P38 Laks and Most (A15 = Philo, *Vita contemplativa* 14), Cic. *Tusc.* 5.66.
57. For Anaxagoras and Epicurus, see Reesor (1983). For Anaxagoras's σπέρματα in Epicurus, see Sedley (1998) 193–198. Sedley (1976) 135–136 remarkably points out that Epicurus's goal may have been to "assume the mantle of Anaxagoras and Archelaus' at Lampsacus." Cf. also Epicurus's spurious fr. 104 Arrighetti, in which someone, possibly Nausiphanes, is reading the works of Anaxagoras and Empedocles. For Lucretius's echoes of Anaxagoras's biological metaphor of *semina*, see Schrijvers (1999) 185–188; Schiesaro (1990) 83–85, 111–122; Fowler (2000) 141–148. On seeds in Lucretius, see also Sedley (1998) 193–198.

58. Sedley (1998) 48–49. See also Wardy (1988).
59. For consideration of the noun's meaning and history see Wigodsky (2007) 536–538.
60. Montarese (2012) 238–239. Cf. Brown (1983).
61. For Anaxagoras's dialect and style see Ugolini (1985), Sider (2005) 22–32, especially 27n14: On philosophical more than stylistic grounds, Aristotle criticizes Anaxagoras for not writing clearly; e.g., *Metaph.* 989b4–19 (A61L). Cf. also Plotinus 5.1.9.1, who says that Anaxagoras did not write clearly δι' ἀρχαιότητα. Simplicius, on the other hand, often says that Anaxagoras writes clearly (163.15, 164.23, 166.17). See also Mejer (1992) 3591–3592 about Anaxagoras in Diogenes Laertius and Hippolytus of Rome.
62. Brown (1983) 151–152. Brown enumerates the techniques: e.g., the list of *adynata* (1.881ff.), the imaginary interlocutor (897), the biological metaphors (901–903), the personified atoms shaking with tears of laughter (919–920).
63. Powell (1995); Striker (1995); Schofield (2013). Cicero calls his works ἀπόγραφα *(Att.* 12.52.3).
64. Obbink (2002) 190. Of course, there were essays addressed to a more general public; for a distinction into two types regarding Philodemus's treatises see Robertson (2016) 72–88.
65. Pease (1955–1958) I 40–41 for the sources.
66. In Cic. *Nat. d.* 1.93 Cotta once again mentions philosophers rejected by Epicurus and his pupils (Pythagoras, Plato, Empedocles, Theophrastus, Democritus) [1.93 *Istisne fidentes somniis non modo Epicurus et Metrodorus et Herinarchus contra Pythagoram, Platonem Empedoclemque dixerun*t]. Cf. Diog. Laert. 10.6–8. Demetrius of Laconia also opposed Empedocles in his writings (fr. 35, fr. 43 and fr. 46 de Falco). Hermarchus wrote 22 books against Empedocles, entitled Ἐπιστολικὰ περὶ Ἐμπεδοκλέους, (Diog. Laert. 10.24–25). On Hermarchus against Empedocles, see also Gallo (1985); Longo Auricchio (1988) 66–73, 92–99 and 125–150; Obbink (1988); Vander Waerdt (1988) 89–90.
67. See Summers (1997) about the books of Phaedrus requested by Cicero (*Att.* 13.39). Cf. also Pease (1955–1958) 40–41.
68. Obbink (2002) 196–197. For comparison of the structure see Obbink (2002) 192.
69. Obbink (2001) and (2002) 193; Dyck (2003) 8–9.
70. Vassallo (2018b) 100. See also Vassallo (2017a).
71. The most comprehensive discussion is that by McKirahan (1996), on which I mostly build my discussion.
72. Dyck (2003) 83–84 also comments that two fifth-century figures, Anaxagoras and Alcmaeon of Croton, are placed too early, ahead of Pythagoras and Xenophanes, and another, Diogenes of Apollonia, is inserted too late, after Democritus. [. . .] The Eleatics, Zeno and Melissus, as well as Heraclitus, Prodicus and Euhemerus are omitted.
73. Dyck (2003) 87. Note that this critique in Cicero's account may follow or precede—as in the case of Parmenides and Empedocles (1.28–29)—the statement of each philosopher's view.
74. Montarese (2012) 27n89: Anaxagoras and Xenophanes are grouped together for considering the concept of mind divine, and Croton and Parmenides for making the heavenly bodies divine.
75. McKirahan (1996) 877: "Cicero altered his source to make passage B more Epicurean, his notion of being more Epicurean apparently involving being less accurate historically and more polemical." 878: "*De natura deorum* discredits the Epicureans both on matters of doctrine and on matters of philosophical and personal style." Cf. Philippson (1939a) 1153, who claims that Cicero inserted this material in order to earmark the Epicureans.
76. Vassallo (2018b) 112–113: Philodemus, *De pietate* (PHerc. 1428, col. 320 20–32 Vassallo): *(c. 20 lines missing)* "the infinite worlds/giving an order] *(1 line and 1 word missing)*, and [he

(*scil.* Anaxagoras) maintains that] it was because of the Mind imposing order [to the universe] that motion always has been and is and will be. And [he further says that] the Mind rules and governs all things, and [that] it ordered the sum total of all things, mixed together *(continues on)*."

77. Cf. McKirahan (1996) 871–873, who cites further ancient testimonia. Regarding the fact that Cicero attributes infinity to the Mind of Anaxagoras, Mansfeld (2019) 627 points to the fact that "Philodemus does not call Mind infinite but applies the epithet to 'all the infinite (s. infinitely many) mixed things Mind sets in order.'" Mansfeld argues that this should not be considered Cicero's inaccuracy or misinterpretation, but an intentional use of the criterium of formlessness to discredit the divinity of a philosopher belonging to the tradition of Anaximenes.
78. For Cicero's appreciation of Empedocles as poet see Cic. *De or.* 1.217.
79. Capasso (1987) 290–299. For Parmenides in Philodemus's *De pietate* (*PHerc.* 1428, col. 324 Vassallo = fr. 13 Schober) see now Vassallo (2016). Cf. also the later testimonium of Aëtius (Aët. 2.7.1 Mansfeld-Runia = D.G. pp. 33–336 = DK 28 A37 = test. 61 Coxon) quoted and commented in Vassallo (2016) 37–39. See also Coxon (²2009) 364 and the commentary *ad loc.* in Mansfeld and Runia (2020).
80. Cf., e.g., Philod. *De piet.*, *PHerc.* 1428, cols. VII.3–VIII.13 Henrichs. Cf. Henrichs (1974) 20; Obbink (2002) 201–203. See now Vassallo (2016) 36. For Heraclitus in Philodemus's *On Arrogance* see Ranocchia (2019).
81. Auvray-Assayas (1996). About Cicero's translation and reception of Plato's *Timaeus* see Lévy (2003), Sedley (2013), Hoenig (2018) 44–100 and Hoenig in this volume.
82. McKirahan (1996) 878.
83. Cotta pays Velleius a compliment about his style (1.58): "I myself, however, though reluctant to praise you to your face, must nevertheless pronounce that your exposition of an obscure and difficult theme has been most illuminating, and not only exhaustive in its treatment of the subject, but also graced with a charm of style not common in your school." Mansfeld (2019) 619 refers to Cicero's strong language, but also to Philodemus's unkind expressions with reference (at least) to the Stoics (Phld. *De piet. PHerc.* 1428, col. XII.8–12 and col. XIV.17–20 Henrichs).
84. Obbink (2002) 193: "Cicero exaggerates and sharpens the level of sharp Epicurean criticism he found in Philodemus. The distortion of Velleius's account is due to Cicero's own polemical strategy." Philippson (1939a) 1153 notes that the invective is mainly due to Cicero. Cf. also Philodemus's other works with Philippson (1939c) 2480. Philippson (1939b) 28–30 remarks that Philodemus also employed this sort of invective. For objections see Auvray-Assayas (2001).
85. McKirahan (1996) 867–868.
86. Classen (2010) 207.
87. For the relation of Cicero's *Nat. d.* with Lucretius's *DRN* see Pucci (1966) especially 101–117. For Anaxagoras's death see Cic. *De or.* 3.138 (= A15), Cic. *Tusc.* 1.43.104 (= A34a).
88. McKirahan (1996) 867 "Passage B sets out from the certainty that Epicurean theology and the physics and ethics on which it depends are correct and proceeds to look for places where the views of earlier philosophers deviate from this truth."
89. Obbink (2002) 187; cf. also *id.* 204–205 with reference to *Nat. d.* 1.41: "Cicero has deliberately over-polemicised his rendition, making his Epicurean spokesman accuse Chrysippus and Cleanthes of something they never did—namely claim that the old poets and philosophers had themselves been Stoics."

90. We now have the second book of the two-volume first edition (*Academica priora* = *Academica* 2 = *Lucullus*) and the half first book of the four-volume second edition (*Academica posteriora* = *Academica* 1). Translations of Cicero's *Academica* are by Rackham (1933).
91. Brittain and Palmer (2001) 45 remark that in the lost book of the *Academica*'s first edition, Cicero presumably had Catulus explain the general nature of the Academics' appeal to the Presocratics.
92. For Cicero's philosophical stance in the *Lucullus* see Görler (1997).
93. Brittain and Palmer (2001) 66.
94. For Anaxagoras see also Cic. *Acad. pr.* 2.100 with Brittain and Palmer (2001) 52–53: "When we come to the second passage which makes use of his denial that snow is white, his view seems to serve more as an embarrassing parallel to the unreasonable dogmatism of the Stoics than as a skeptical precedent,"
95. For Democritus see also Cic. *Acad. pr.* 2.125 *studiosus nobilitatis fui*, *Div.* 2.133, *De or.* 1.42; 3.56.
96. See also Cic. *Nat. d.* 3.35 (about Heraclitus being the precursor of the Stoics); *Fat.* 39.4 (a doxography of academic inspiration about necessity and liberty, citing Democritus, Heraclitus, Empedocles and Aristotle, as philosophers who represent a sort of universal fatalism) with Lévy and Saudelli (2014) 7–24. For further references to Heraclitus, see Cic. *Tusc.* 5.105; *Att.* 16.11.1 (5 November 44); 2.5.1 (April 59).
97. Vassallo (2021).

References

Algra, K. A., M. H. Koenen, and P. H. Schrijvers, eds. (1997). *Lucretius and His Intellectual Background*. (Amsterdam).

André, J.-M. (1974). "Cicéron et Lucrèce: Loi du silence et allusions polémiques," in Boucher, J.-P. Turcan, R. Morel, J.-P. Gros, P. Lavagne, H. (ed.), *Mélanges de philosophie, de literature et d'histoire ancienne offerts à Pierre Boyancé* (Rome), 21–38.

Andria, R. G. (1989). *I frammenti delle "Successioni dei filosofi."* (Naples).

Armstrong, D., and J. A. Ponczoch. (2011). "(Philodemus) *On Wealth* (*PHerc.* 1570 Cols. VI–XX, Pcc. 4–6a): New Fragments of Empedocles, Menander and Epicurus." *Cronache Ercolanesi* 41: 97–138.

Armstrong, D., and J. A. Ponczoch. (2013). "Empedocles and Philodemus in *PHerc.* 1570, col. VI 9–19." *Cronache Ercolanesi* 43: 113–115.

Arrighetti, G. (2003). "Filodemo biografo dei filosofi e le forme dell' erudizione." *Cronache Ercolanesi* 33: 13–30.

Arrighetti, G. (2007). "Anekdote und Biographie: Μάλιστα τὸ μικρὸν φυλάττειν," in Erler and Schorn, 79–100.

Asmis, E. (1994). "Philodemus' Epicureanism." *ANRW* II, 36(4): 2369–2406.

Auvray-Assayas, C. (1996). "Les constructions doxographiques du *De natura deorum* et la réflexion cicéronienne sur la physique," in C. Lévy (ed.), *Le concept de nature à Rome: La physique* (Paris), 67–83.

Auvray-Assayas, C. (2001). "Relire Cicéron pour comprendre Philodème. Réponse à Dirk Obbink," in Auvray-Assayas and Delattre, 227–234.

Auvray-Assayas, C., and D. Delattre, eds. (2001). *Cicéron et Philodème: La polémique en philosophie*. (Paris).

Baltussen, H. (2005). "The Presocratics in the Doxographical Tradition: Sources, Controversies, and Current Research." *Studia Humaniora Tartuensia* 6(6): 1–26. https://www.ut.ee/klassik/sht/2005/baltussen1.pdf (accessed November 30, 2021).
Bollack, M. (1969). "Un désaccord de forme: Lucrèce et Héraclite." *Actes du VIIIe Congrès Association Guillaume Budé* (Paris): 383–392.
Brittain, C., and J. Palmer (2001). "The New Academy's Appeals to the Presocratics." *Phronesis* 46(1): 38–72.
Brown, R. D. (1983). "Lucretian Ridicule of Anaxagoras." *CQ* 33: 146–160.
Burnet, J. (^{4}1930). *Early Greek Philosophy*. (London).
Campbell, G. L. (2003). *Lucretius on Creation and Evolution: A Commentary on Lucretius, De rerum natura 5.772–1104*. (Oxford).
Campbell, G. L. (2014). "Lucretius, Empedocles, and Cleanthes," in M. Garani and D. Konstan (eds.), *The Philosophizing Muse: The Influence of Greek Philosophy on Roman Poetry* (Newcastle upon Tyne), 26–60.
Capasso, M. (1987). "Epicureismo ed Eleatismo: Secondo contributo alla riconstruzione della critica epicurea alla filosofia presocratica," in M. Capasso, *Comunità senza rivolta: Quattro saggi sull'epicureismo* (Naples): 253–309.
Casanova, A. (1984). "La critica di Diogene di Enoanda alla metempsicosi empedoclea (NF 2 + FR. 34 Ch.)," in Vv. A.a., *Studi in onore di Adelmo Barigazzi I (= Sileno 10)* (Rome), 119–130.
Casertano, G., ed. (2007). *Empedocle: Tra poesia, medicina, filosofia e politica*. (Naples).
Castner, C. J. (1987). "*De Rerum Natura* 5.101–103: Lucretius' Application of Empedoclean Language to Epicurean Doctrine." *Phoenix* 41: 40–49.
Chitwood, A. (2004). *Death by Philosophy: The Biographical Tradition in the Life and Death of the Archaic Philosophers Empedocles, Heraclitus, and Democritus*. (Ann Arbor, Mich.).
Classen, C. J., ed. (1986). *Probleme der Lukrezforschung* (Hildesheim).
Classen, C. J. (2010). "Teaching Philosophy, a Form or Function of Oratory: Velleius' Speech in Cicero's *De natura deorum*," in D. H. Berry and A. Erskine (eds.), *Form and Function in Roman Oratory* (Cambridge), 195–207.
Clay, D. (1983). *Lucretius and Epicurus* (Ithaca, N.Y.).
Clay, D. (2004). "Philodemus on the Plain Speaking of the Other Philosophers," in J. T. Fitzgerald, D. Obbink, and G. S. Holland (eds.), *Philodemus and the New Testament World* (Leiden), 55–71.
Comparetti, D. (1875). "Papiro ercolanese inedito." *Rivista di Filologia e di Istruzione Classica* 3: 449–555.
Coxon, A. H. and R. McKirahan (2009). *The Fragments of Parmenides*. (Las Vegas).
Crönert, W. (1906). *Kolotes und Menedemos*. (Leipzig, repr. Amsterdam 1965).
de Falco, V. (1923). *L'Epicureo Demetrio Lacone*. (Naples, repr. New York 1987).
Delattre, D. (2003). "Présence ou absence d' une copie du *De rerum natura* à Herculanum? Réponse à Mario Capasso," in A. Monet (ed.), *Le jardin romain: Épicurisme et poésie à Rome mélanges* (Villeneuve d' Ascq), 109–116.
Diels, H. (1879). *Doxographi Graeci*. (Berlin).
Dorandi, T. (1990). "Filodemo storico del pensiero antico." *ANRW* II, 36(4): 2407–2423.
Dorandi, T. (1991). *Filodemo, Storia dei filosofi: Platone e l'Academia*. (Naples).
Dorandi, T. (1994). *Storia dei filosofi: La Stoà da Zenone a Panezio (PHerc. 1018)*. (Leiden).
Dyck, A. R. (2003). *Cicero, De natura deorum I*. (Cambridge).

Edwards, M. J. (1989). "Lucretius, Empedocles and Epicurean Polemics." *A&A* 35: 104–115.
Erler, M. (1994). "Die Shule Epikurs," in H. Flashar (ed.), *Die Philosophie der Antike* 4/1 (Basel), 203–380.
Erler, M., and S. Schorn, eds. (2007). *Die griechische Biographie in hellenistischer Zeit: Akten des internationalen Kongresses vom 26.–29. Juli 2006 in Würzburg.* (Berlin).
Érvard, É. (1999). "Diogène d' Oenoanda et Lucrèce," in R. Poignault (ed.), *Présence de Lucrèce: Actes du colloque tenu à Tours 3–5 Décembre 1998* (Tours, Centre de Recherches A. Piganiol), 51–63.
Farrell, J. (2001). *Latin Language and Latin Culture from Ancient to Modern Times.* (Cambridge).
Flashar, H., D. Bremer, and G. Rechenauer, eds. (2013). *Die Philosophie der Antike Band 1: Frühgriechische Philosophie.* (Basel).
Fleischer, K. (2019). "Structuring the 'History of Philosophy': A Comparison between Philodemus and Diogenes Laertius in the Light of New Evidence." *CQ* 69: 684–699.
Flinterman, J.-J. (2014). "Pythagoreans in Rome and Asia Minor around the Turn of the Common Era," in C. A. Huffman (ed.), *A History of Pythagoreanism* (Cambridge), 341–359.
Fowler, D. P. (2000). "Philosophy and Literature in Lucretian Intertextuality," in D. P. Fowler, *Roman Constructions: Readings in Postmodern Latin* (Oxford), 138–155.
Gaiser, K. (1988). *Philodems Academica: Die Berichte über Platon und die Alte Akademie in zwei herkulanensischen Papyri*, Supplementum Platonicum I. (Stuttgart).
Gallavotti, C. (1975–1977). "La critica di Empedocle in Diogene di Enoanda." *Museum Criticum* 10–12: 243–249.
Gallo I. (1985). "Ermarco e la polemica epicurea contro Empedocle," in P. Cosenza (ed.), *Esistenza e destino nel pensiero Greco antico* (Naples), 33–50.
Garani, M. (2007). *Empedocles* Redivivus: *Poetry and Analogy in Lucretius.* (New York).
Giannatassio Andria, R. (1989). *I frammenti delle "Successioni dei filosofi.* (Naples).
Gigante, M. (1986). "Biografia e dossografia in Diogene Laerzio." *Elenchos* 7: 7–102.
Gigante, M. (1995). *Philodemus in Italy: The Books from Herculaneum.* D. Obbink, tr. (Ann Arbor, Mich.).
Gigante, M., and G. Indelli (1980). "Democrito nei papyri ercolanesi di Filodemo," in F. Romano (ed.), *Democrito e l' atomismo antico* (Catania), 451–466.
Gomperz, T. (1866). *Philodem: Über Frömmigkeit.* (Leipzig).
Görler, W. (1997). "Cicero's Philosophical Stance in the *Lucullus*," in Inwood and Mansfeld, 36–57.
Hall, J. J. (1977). "Seneca as a Source for Earlier Thought (Especially Meteorology)." *CQ* 27: 409–436.
Hatzimichali, M. (2020). "The Academy through Epicurean Eyes: Some Lives of Academic Philosophers in Philodemus' *Syntaxis*," in Kalligas, Balla, Baziotopoulou-Valavani, and Karasmanis, 256–275 (Cambridge).
Henrichs, A. (1972). "Towards a New Edition of Philodemus' Treatise *On Piety*." *GRBS* 13: 67–98.
Henrichs, A. (1974). "Die Kritik der stoischen Theologie im *PHerc.* 1428." *Cronache Ercolanesi* 4: 5–32.
Henrichs, A. (1975a). "Two Doxographical Notes: Democritus and Prodicus on Religion." *HSCPh* 79: 93–123.

Henrichs, A. (1975b). "Philodems *De Pietate* als mythographische Quelle." *Cronache Ercolanesi* 5: 5–38.

Hoenig, C. (2018). *Plato's* Timaeus *in the Latin Tradition*. (Cambridge).

Indelli, G. (2007). "Filodemo ed Empedocle," in Casertano, 277–288.

Inwood, B., and J. Mansfeld, eds. (1997). *Assent and Argument: Studies in Cicero's Academic Books* (Leiden).

Kalligas, P., C. Balla, E. Baziotopoulou-Valavani, and V. Karasmanis, eds. (2020). *Plato's Academy: Its Workings and Its History*. (Cambridge).

Kalligas, P., V. Tsouna, and M. Hatzimichali (2020). "Philodemus' History of the Philosophers: Plato and the Academy (PHerc. 1021 and 164) [Translated with Introduction by Paul Kalligas and Voula Tsouna, and Notes by Myrto Hatzimichali]," in Kalligas, Balla, Baziotopoulou-Valavani, and Karasmanis, 276–383.

Kleve, K. (1978). "The Philosophical Polemics in Lucretius: A Study in the History of Epicurean Criticism," in O. Gigon (ed.), *Lucrèce: Huit exposés suivis de discussions* (Geneva), 39–71.

Kollmann, E. D. (1971). "Lucretius' Criticism of the Early Greek Philosophers." *Studii Clasice* 13: 79–93.

Laks, A., and G. W. Most (2016). *Early Greek Philosophy*. 9 vols. (Cambridge, Mass.).

Leone, G. (2019). "Empedocles in the Herculaneum Papyri: An Update," in Vassallo (2019), 299–331.

Lévy, C. (2003). "Cicero and the *Timaeus*," in G. J. Reydams-Schils (ed.), *Plato's* Timaeus *as Cultural Icon* (Notre Dame, Ind.), 95–110.

Lévy, C., and L. Saudelli, eds. (2014). *Présocratiques latins: Héraclite; Traductions, introductions et commentaires* (Paris).

Long, A. A. (2003). "Roman philosophy," in D. Sedley (ed.), *The Cambridge Companion to Roman Philosophy* (Cambridge), 184–210.

Longo Auricchio, F. (1988). *Ermarco: Frammenti*. (Naples).

Longo Auricchio, F. (2007). "Gli *studi sui testi biografici* ercolanesi negli ultimi dieci anni," in Erler and Schorn, 219–255.

Mansfeld, J. (1990). "Doxography and Dialectic: The *Sitz im Leben* of the 'Placita.'" *ANRW* II, 36(4): 3056–3232.

Mansfeld, J. (1999). "Sources," in K. Algra et al. (eds.) *The Cambridge History of Hellenistic Philosophy* (Cambridge), 3–30.

Mansfeld, J. (2012). "Doxography of Ancient Philosophy." *Stanford Encyclopedia of Philosophy*, April 17. https://plato.stanford.edu/archives/win2013/entries/doxography-ancient/ (accessed December 4, 2021).

Mansfeld, J. (2017). "Ancient Philosophy and the Doxographical Tradition," in L. Perilli and D. P. Taormina (eds.), *Ancient Philosophy: Historical Paths and Explorations* (London), 41–64.

Mansfeld, J. (2019). "Lists of Principles and Lists of Gods: Philodemus, Cicero, Aëtius, and Others," in Vassallo, 609–630.

Mansfeld, J., and D. T. Runia (1997). *Aëtiana: The Method and Intellectual Context of a Doxographer*. Volume 1: *The Sources*. (Leiden).

Mansfeld, J., and D. T. Runia (2020). *Aëtiana V: An Edition of the Reconstructed Text of the Placita* 4 vols. (Leiden).

McKirahan, R. (1996). "Epicurean Doxography in Cicero, *De natura deorum* Book I," in G. Giannantoni and M. Gigante (eds.), *Epicureismo greco e romano*, vol. 2 (Naples), 865–878.

McKirahan, R. (2018). "The Downside of Doxography," in J. Mansfeld and D. T. Runia (eds.), *Aëtiana IV: Towards an Edition of the Aëtian* Placita (Leiden), 473–502.
Mejer, J. (1992). "Diogenes Laertius and the Transmission of Greek Philosophy." *ANRW* II, 36(5): 3556–3602.
Mekler, S. (1902). *Academicorum philosophorum index Herculanensis.* (Berlin).
Montarese, F. (2012). *Lucretius and His Sources: A Study of Lucretius,* De rerum natura *I 635–920.* (Berlin).
Obbink, D. (1988). "Hermachus, against Empedocles." *CQ* 38: 428–435.
Obbink, D. (1996). *Philodemus* On Piety: *Critical Text with Commentary, Part 1.* (Oxford).
Obbink, D. (2001). "Le livre I du *De natura deorum* de Cicéron et le *De pietate* de Philodème," in Auvray-Assayas and Delattre, 203–225.
Obbink, D. (2002). "All Gods are True in Epicurus," in D. Frede and A. Laks (eds.), *Traditions of Theology: Studies in Hellenistic Theology, its Background and Aftermath* (Leiden), 183–221.
Obbink, D. (2007). "Lucretius and the Herculaneum Library," in S. Gillespie and P. Hardie (eds.), *The Cambridge Companion to Lucretius* (Cambridge), 33–40.
Pease, A. S. (1955–1958). *M. Tulli Cicero.* De natura deorum *libri III.* 2 vols. (Cambridge, Mass.).
Philippson, R. (1939a). "M. Tullius Cicero (Philosophische Schriften)." *RE* 7A1: 1104–1192.
Philippson, R. (1939b). "Die Quelle der epikureischen Götterlehre in Ciceros ersten Buche *De natura deorum.*" *Symb. Osl.* 19: 15–40.
Philippson, R. (1939c). "Philodem." *RE* 19(2): 2444–2482.
Piazzi, L. (2005). *Lucrezio e i Presocratici: un commento a De rerum natura 1, 635–920.* (Pisa).
Piazzi, L. (2008). "Analisi della polemica condotta da Lucrezio contro i filosofi presocratici (Eraclito, Empedocle e Anassagora) in *De rerum natura* 1, 635–920," in M. Beretta and F. Citti (eds.), *Lucrezio: La natura e la scienza* (Florence), 11–25.
Powell, J. G. F. (1995). "Cicero's Translations from Greek," in J. G. F. Powell, *Cicero the Philosopher* (Oxford), 273–300.
Pucci, G. C. (1966). "Echi lucreziani in Cicerone." *Stud. Ital.* 38: 70–132.
Rackham, H., tr. (1933). *Cicero: On the Nature of the Gods; Academics.* (Cambridge, Mass).
Ranocchia, G. (2019). "Heraclitus' Portrait in Diogenes Laërtius and Philodemus' On Arrogance," in Vassallo, 221–247.
Reesor, M. E. (1983). "Anaxagoras and Epicurus," in J. P. Anton and A. Preus (eds.), *Essays in Ancient Greek Philosophy,* Vol. 2 (Albany), 93–106.
Robertson, P. (2016). *Paul's Letters and Greco-Roman Literature: Theorizing a New Taxonomy.* (Leiden).
Rösler, W. (1973). "Lukrez und die Vorsokratiker: Doxographische Probleme im I. Buch von '*De Rerum natura.*'" *Hermes* 101: 48–64; repr. in Classen, 57–73.
Runia, D. T. (1997). "Lucretius and Doxography," in Algra, Koenen, and Schrijvers, 93–103; repr. in Mansfeld and Runia, 255–270.
Runia, D. T. (1999). "What Is Doxography?" in P. J. van der Eijk (ed.), *Ancient Histories of Medicine: Essays in Medical Doxography and Historiography in Classical Antiquity* (Leiden), 33–55.
Runia, D. T. (2008). "The Sources for Presocratic Philosophy," in P. Curd and D. W. Graham (eds.), *The Oxford Handbook of the Presocratics* (Oxford), 27–54.
Schiesaro, A. (1990). *Simulacrum et Imago* (Pisa).
Schofield, M. (2013). "Writing Philosophy," in C. Steel (ed.), *The Cambridge Companion to Cicero* (Cambridge), 73–87.

Schrijvers, P. H. (1999). *Lucrèce et les Sciences de la Vie.* (Leiden).
Sedley, D. (1976). "Epicurus and his Professional Rivals," in J. Bollack and A. Laks (eds.), *Études sur l'Épicurisme Antique* (Lille), 121–159.
Sedley, D. (1998). *Lucretius and the Transformation of Greek Wisdom.* (Cambridge).
Sedley, D. (2003a). "Philodemus and the Decentralisation of Philosophy." *Cronache Ercolanesi* 33: 31–41.
Sedley, D. (2003b). "Lucretius and the New Empedocles." *LICS* 2(4): 1–12.
Sedley, D. (2013). "Cicero and the Timaeus," in M. Schofield (ed.) *Aristotle, Plato and Pythagoreanism in the First Century BC: New Directions for Philosophy* (Cambridge), 187–205.
Setaioli, A. (1988). *Seneca e i Greci: Citazioni e traduzioni nelle opere filosofiche* (Bologna).
Shanzer, D. (2012). "Augustine and the Latin Classics," in M. Vessey (ed.), *A Companion to Augustine* (Chichester), 161–174.
Sider, D. (2005). *The Fragments of Anaxagoras: Introduction, Text, and Commentary. Second Edition.* (Sankt Augustin).
Smith, M. F. (1993). *Diogenes of Oenoanda, the Epicurean Inscription.* (Naples).
Snyder, J. M. (1980). *Puns and Poetry in Lucretius' De rerum natura.* (Amsterdam).
Striker, G. (1995). "Cicero and Greek philosophy." *HSCPh* 97: 53–61.
Summers, K. (1997). "The Books of Phaedrus Requested by Cicero (*Att.* 13.39)." *CQ* 91: 309–311.
Tatum, W. J. (1984). "The Presocratics in Book One of Lucretius' *De rerum natura*." *TAPA* 114: 177–189.
Ugolini, G. (1985). "Appunti sullo stile di Anassagora." *Elenchos* 6: 315–332.
Vander Waerdt, P. A. (1988). "Hermarchus and the Epicurean Genealogy of Morals." *TAPA* 118: 87–106.
Vassallo, C. (2015). "Testimonianze su Anassagora e altri Presocratici nel libro IV della *Retorica* di Filodemo: *Praesocratica Herculanensia* V." *Lexicon Philosophicum* 3: 81–145.
Vassallo, C. (2016). "Parmenides and the 'First God': Doxographical Strategies in Philodemus' *On Piety*; *Praesocratica Herculanensia* VII." *Hyperboreus* 22: 29–57.
Vassallo, C. (2017a). "La 'sezione presocratica' del *De pietate* di Filodemo: Una nuova ricostruzione: *Praesocratica Herculanensia* X (Parte I)." *Archiv für Papyrusforschung* 63: 171–203.
Vassallo, C. (2017b). "P.Herc. 1788 ([Philodemi], [*Philosophorum historia*?]): Introduction, Edition, and Commentary." *Analecta Papyrologica* 29: 7–56.
Vassallo, C. (2018a). "Atomism and the Worship of Gods: On Democritus' 'Rational' Attitude towards Theology." *Philosophie Antique* 18: 105–125.
Vassallo, C. (2018b). "The 'Pre-Socratic Section' of Philodemus' *On Piety*: A New Reconstruction: *Praesocratica Herculanensia* X (Part II)." *Archiv für Papyrusforschung* 64: 98–147.
Vassallo, C., ed. (2019). *Presocratics and Papyrological Tradition: A Philosophical Reappraisal of the Sources.* Studia Praesocratica 10. (Berlin/Boston).
Vassallo, C. (2021). *The Presocratics at Herculaneum: A Study of Early Greek Philosophy in the Epicurean Tradition; With an Appendix on Diogenes of Oinoanda's Criticism of Presocratic Philosophy.* Studia Praesocratica 11. (Berlin).
Wardy, R. (1988). "Lucretius on What Atoms Are Not." *CPh* 83: 112–128.
Warren, J. (2007). "Lucretius and Greek Philosophy," in S. Gillespie and P. Hardie (eds.), *The Cambridge Companion to Lucretius* (Cambridge), 19–32.
West, D. A. (1969). *The Imagery and Poetry of Lucretius.* (Edinburgh).

Wigodksy, M. (2007). "'*Homoiotetes, Stoicheia*' and '*Homoiomereiai*' in Epicurus." *CQ* 57: 521–542.

Zhmud, L. (2013). "Die Doxographische Tradition," in Flashar, Bremer, and Rechenauer, 150–174.

CHAPTER 28

READING ARISTOTLE AT ROME

MYRTO HATZIMICHALI

ROMAN engagement with Aristotle's works took many forms, and our evidence for it points in different directions that suggest a complex set of relationships, exchanges, and appropriations. On the one hand, we have explicit references to books, that is physical copies of Aristotelian treatises, with information about their discovery, transmission, use and abuse, even lamented loss. On the other hand, many Roman authors display familiarity with a wide range of Aristotelian ideas and/or pay homage to Aristotle as one of the main pillars of Greek wisdom without any reference to particular texts; in such cases we often speak of dependence on the mediation of Hellenistic summaries, handbooks and the like—this is another way of reading Aristotle, to be considered alongside those cases where direct consultation seems more likely. In what follows I will trace our evidence in a roughly chronological sequence, in order to interrogate what "reading Aristotle" amounted to for the Romans, from the first century BCE to the late second century CE. Problems of direct vs. indirect access to texts and ideas arise for practically every Greek philosopher with a Roman afterlife, and they are part and parcel with the processes of transmission, translation, and cultural appropriation that attended the development of Roman philosophy. In the case of Aristotle, however, matters are complicated further by Strabo's celebrated tale about the disappearance of the great philosopher's books in a ditch in Asia Minor for the duration of the Hellenistic period and their subsequent re-emergence in Rome in the first century BCE,[1] which forces scholars to ask additional questions about the availability of Aristotle's school treatises. It seems appropriate, therefore, to begin with Strabo's sensational story, with special emphasis on events at Rome.

Sulla's Library and the "Roman Edition"

Strabo informs us that after the death of Theophrastus all of his and Aristotle's books were bequeathed to Neleus, who took them to his hometown of Scepsis in the Troad, and where his descendants kept them hidden in a ditch until they made up their minds to sell them to the rich bibliophile Apellicon of Teos. He made the books public (ἐξέδωκεν), but not before loading them with rash supplements and emendations. According to Strabo, this state of bad transmission continued in Rome. The grammarian Tyrannio, who came to Rome in the early 60s BCE as a captive of Lucullus during the Mithridatic war,[2] handled the collection as an expert with a genuine interest in the content of Aristotle's work. It is also significant from a Roman point of view that Aristotle's treatises excited the interest of commercial booksellers, who set about their hasty and careless (according to Strabo) reproduction. This would imply that there was a reading public keen to acquire these books, even though what we know from Roman authors of the period does not suggest a wide readership. Strabo's text leaves the relationship between Tyrannio and the booksellers quite unclear, and scholars have suspected a lacuna here.[3] It is not at all unlikely that Tyrannio performed an intermediary role, connecting potential buyers (who would have belonged to an educated elite) to commercial producers.[4]

We have thus seen that the arrival of Sulla's library in Rome was accompanied by a commercial interest in Aristotle. As far as the more scholarly aspects are concerned, we learn from Plutarch (*Vit. Sull.* 26) that Tyrannio "arranged" most of the books—elsewhere the same Greek verb (ἐνσκευάζω) means "dress up," "equip." From Cicero's correspondence with Atticus we know that Tyrannio also had a role in setting in order Cicero's own library (*designatio mirifica*, *Att.* 4.4a). This process included gluing loose pieces of papyrus together with the help of specialist clerks (*glutinatores*) and labeling the books. We may suspect that Tyrannio's work in the service of Sulla's librarian was of a similar nature and resulted in improving the physical state of (some of) the manuscripts that Sulla brought from Athens. This type of activity can hardly amount to a "Roman edition" of Aristotle, which is why the scholar credited with such a feat was Andronicus of Rhodes who, according to Plutarch, gained possession of the copies through Tyrannio and made them public.

The significance of Andronicus's achievements has been treated with a lot of skepticism, especially since Jonathan Barnes's demolition job.[5] I have argued elsewhere that Andronicus's main contribution was not a critical edition of Aristotle's texts, but the detailed catalog (the *pinakes*, "lists" mentioned by Plutarch at *Sull.* 26), which probably saw the treatises organized for the first time in something like the shape and order in which we still find them today.[6] Moreover, some scholars are not prepared to place Andronicus's activity in Rome (there is no evidence for this other than Tyrannio's mediation), because other sources mention him as head of the Peripatos at Athens.[7] On the whole, then, the importance and even the very existence of a "Roman edition" of

Aristotle's works is called into question. What we can take away from the celebrated story in terms of Aristotle's fate in Rome is that an important collection of Aristotelian books came from Athens with Sulla in the early first century BCE, and some years later Tyrannio had a hand in restoring and arranging these books. He probably also provided copies to Andronicus (whether the latter was based in Rome or further away in Athens), and must have been the main port of call for any Romans interested in acquiring their own copies—as we saw above, Tyrannio was well known to intellectuals such as Cicero. The absence of an authoritative critical edition of Aristotelian works at Rome is further suggested by the situation described several centuries later by Galen: the works of Aristotle and Theophrastus found in the main Roman libraries were not only obscure and difficult in themselves, but also lacked proper editorial attention, something Galen was preparing to provide himself (*De indolentia* 14). Unfortunately, his labors, along with the older copies, were destroyed in the fire of 192 CE, which devastated the Palatine library as well as Galen's private warehouses on the Via Sacra. It is not unlikely, as Rashed argues, that the old books Galen worked on, which included the very rare Aristotelian *De plantis* (*De indol.* 17), were direct descendants of the collection brought to Rome by Sulla.[8]

This was our direct information on the fate of physical copies of Aristotle's books at Rome; for the readership of these books and the resulting influence of Aristotelian philosophy we must now turn first of all to Cicero.

Cicero

In defense of his project of writing about Greek philosophy in Latin, Cicero singles out Plato and Aristotle as the "divine minds" (*diuina ingenia*) with whom it would be a patriotic service to acquaint his countrymen (*Fin.* 1.7). He contemplates wholesale translation of their works (as in fact he did in the case of Plato with the *Timaeus* and the *Protagoras*[9]) but concludes here in the *De finibus* that the best approach is to borrow selected passages as appropriate. But the fact that he *could* provide full translations of Aristotelian works suggests that he had such works at his disposal:[10] we need to ask, therefore, what works these were, how Cicero used them, and what different approaches to "reading Aristotle" we can detect in the pages of Cicero's voluminous output.

The *De finibus* provides a further piece of evidence, which links back to the question of the circulation of Aristotelian books: at *Fin.* 3.7–10, in the scene-setting of his debate with Cato the Younger on Stoic ethics (dramatic date: 52 BCE), Cicero states that he was visiting the library at the Tusculan villa belonging to the young Lucullus in order to find some "Aristotelian notebooks" (*commentarios quosdam Aristotelios*, *Fin.* 3.10). The young man no doubt inherited the collection of his father, L. Licinius Lucullus, who owned a celebrated library[11] and was also the one who brought Tyrannio to Rome. It is possible, therefore, that Tyrannio procured for Lucullus, with or without the involvement of commercial booksellers, some copies of the manuscripts in Sulla's collection.[12]

It is significant that Cicero refers here to *commentarii*, works of a more informal type, usually not explicitly intended for publication. Such a description would certainly fit the Aristotelian treatises available to us nowadays, which are often much closer to notes (scholars sometimes speak of lecture notes[13]) than to polished texts destined for general circulation. Aristotle had also produced works of the latter kind in dialogue form, and it must be to those that Cicero's praise for Aristotle's style refers, such as the "golden stream of his speech" at *Luc.* 119. Cicero was clearly aware of the distinction: "on the subject of the chief good fall there are two kinds of books, one popular in style, which they called 'exoteric'; the other more refined, which they left in the form of notebooks." (*Fin.* 5.12) Thus at least in the field of ethics Cicero and his associates were aware of two different kinds of Aristotelian books, and perhaps the latter (the ones in the form of notebooks) were harder to access, hence Cicero has to seek them out in the library of Lucullus.[14]

In the same passage of the *De finibus*, Cicero gives an outline of the Peripatetic system (*Peripateticorum disciplina*, 5.9) that shows familiarity with some distinctive features of the work of Aristotle and his followers, such as Aristotle's and Theophrastus's work on politics, including their collections of constitutions, their scientific impetus based on systematic research and observation, and the "division of labour" between Aristotle's work on animals and Theophrastus's on plants (*Fin.* 5.9–11). Elsewhere Cicero cites Aristotle directly for information on cranes' flight patterns (*Nat. d.* 2.125, not attested in any of Aristotle's extant works); many other zoological facts and *mirabilia* from that section of *Nat. d.* may go back to collections of facts about animals that were known throughout the Hellenistic period under the name of Aristotle with titles such as Ζῳικά (*On animals*) and often overlap with our *Hist. an.*[15] There are good reasons for thinking that these collections were more widely known in Rome: P. H. Schrijvers argued that Lucretius's remarks on the animal world owe much to Aristotelian material, and we can fairly safely speculate that Romans (not only those writing philosophy) treated these zoological collections as valuable reference resources.[16]

Other than collections of scientific facts, Cicero was familiar with a number of Aristotelian works that are now lost to us, especially some of the "exoteric" dialogues. In *De natura deorum* in particular, the dialogue *On Philosophy* features several times.[17] The third book is quoted at *Nat. d.* 1.33, where the Epicurean spokesman Velleius accuses Aristotle of various theological inconsistencies. This polemical Epicurean presentation has a close parallel in Philodemus's *De pietate*[18] and therefore raises the possibility that Cicero is indebted here to Philodemus or a common doxographical source.[19]

In *De natura deorum*, in the exposition of the Stoic spokesman Balbus who enlists Aristotle as an ally against the Epicureans, we also find references to two central Aristotelian cosmological doctrines, namely the eternity of the world and the fifth element.[20] At 2.42 we have an a fortiori argument that, since animals are generated in the other elements (earth, water, and air), there must be sentient beings of the greatest intelligence in the zone of ether, endowed with eternal motion.[21] At 2.95–96 Balbus offers a longer quotation, generally agreed to come from *On Philosophy*, which comes very close to an argument from design and thus sounds quite un-Aristotelian. But the providential overtones must be part of Balbus's Stoic reading of Aristotle, whose own focus may have been rather an account of the origins of religious belief (cf. Sext. Emp. *Math.* 9.20–23). Other possible references in Cicero to lost Aristotelian dialogues include *Div*.1.25 to the *Eudemus*; his use of the *Protrepticus* in the lost *Hortensius*; *Rep.* 3.12 to *On Justice*. Finally, Cicero acknowledges a methodological/presentational debt to Aristotle's dialogues, in his choice of longer speeches presenting fully argued positions "on either side" of a question,[22] and in making himself (the author) one of the interlocutors (*Tusc.* 2.9; *Att.* 13.19.4).

In the field of ethics, Cicero was familiar with the Peripatetic view that posits the semidivine life of contemplation as the best possible life: he says that some of the most "splendid and distinguished" work of the Peripatetics is devoted to this topic (5.11). In the writings extant for us now, this view famously appears in Book 10. 7-9 of the *Nicomachean Ethics*, raising serious problems of consistency with the rest of that work, while Cicero was also aware of an intraschool disagreement between Theophrastus and Dicaearchus, who favored the contemplative and the practical life respectively (*Att.* 2.16.3).[23] Cicero appears to have known of the *Nicomachean Ethics* (or something like it under this title), because the interlocutor Piso claims to be following "Aristotle and his son Nicomachus" (*teneamus Aristotelem et eius filium Nicomachum*, *Fin.* 5.12). Cicero's wording here suggests that the authorship of the work was disputed in his time, and tends to favor the son as the true author, unaware perhaps that Nicomachus died very young in battle and must have been rather the dedicatee of the work.[24]

The picture emerging thus far suggests a general familiarity on Cicero's part with the Peripatetic tradition, in terms of both the types of writings produced and their contents. There are elements that go back to Aristotle himself without, however, justifying any firm conclusion that Cicero had read particular treatises. It is also significant that in the context of the ethical debate of *De finibus* 5 Aristotelian/Peripatetic views are of interest mainly to the extent that they were updated by Antiochus of Ascalon in order to make a contribution to the first-century debate on the sufficiency of virtue for happiness. Despite his admiration for Aristotle, in the fields of theology, politics, and ethics Cicero's interests were largely dictated by his even greater admiration for Plato and by the contemporary debates between Stoics, Epicureans, and the "Old Academic" construct of Antiochus of Ascalon.

One area where Cicero could turn to Aristotle for inspiration and material support on issues that were really close to his heart was rhetoric. An important part of Cicero's project throughout his *philosophica* (in which I include works such as *Orator* and *De oratore*[25]) was the attempt to reconcile philosophy with rhetoric, following in the footsteps of Aristotle and Theophrastus, who "united philosophy with rhetorical teaching" (*Div.* 2.4; cf. *Tusc.* 1.7), and to show that a philosophical grounding is essential if one aspires to excellence in oratory (*De or.* 3.71–72).[26] The practical benefit that an aspiring orator can obtain, according to Cicero, from studying the relevant Aristotelian material consists mainly in dialectical expertise, that is the skill of arguing "on either side" (*in utramque partem*) on particular matters (cf. *Fin.* 5.10; *Tusc.* 2.9). A reference in Alexander of Aphrodisias confirms that there were books under the names of Aristotle and Theophrastus designed precisely for training in this pro and contra argumentation.[27] Cicero advocated that this skill and methodology should be applied to rhetorical speeches in Roman law courts (*De or.* 3.80). A further material contribution by Aristotle lies in the discovery of arguments (*inventio*): in his works he provided *topoi* (*loci*) for finding premises relating to abstract questions, which Cicero again thought should be equally applicable to philosophical and to rhetorical/legal argumentation (*De or.* 2.152, *Orat.* 46).

The question of *topoi* brings us to the issue of Cicero's *Topica*. In the scene-setting of that work (*Top.* 1–2), Cicero refers to "something called the 'Topics' of Aristotle" (*Aristotelis Topica quaedam*) that his friend the jurist Trebatius had discovered in Cicero's own library and wanted to learn more. Cicero's *Topica* purports to be an account (admittedly from memory while aboard ship, *Top.* 5) of this Aristotelian work (cf. also *Fam.* 7.21), but a comparison of contents quickly makes clear that it cannot possibly be an account of "our" *Topics*. What, then, did Cicero read and did he even possess a copy of Aristotle's *Topics*? The most recent and in-depth study of the Ciceronian work shows that we are not compelled to identify the book lying in Cicero's library (which could well have been Aristotle's *Topics*) with the source of his own *Topica*. The latter must have had a stronger rhetorical focus, but as a method for discovering arguments it was probably not entirely alien to Aristotle's *Topics*.[28]

We have seen thus far that Cicero found in Aristotle (including what may have been a later tradition drawing on Aristotle's *Topics* and sections of the *Rhetoric* such as 1.7 and 2.23) material for dialectical training and the construction of arguments. A closer engagement with the contents of the third book of "our" *Rhetoric* may be detected in the passages where he discusses prose rhythm (*De or.* 3.182–186). He does not cite any particular Aristotelian work at that point, but the parallels with *Rhet.* 3.8 are unmistakable. It would make perfect sense for Cicero to seek out and consult Aristotle's rhetorical works, which must have been available in Rome for some time: at *De or.* 2.160 he has his speaker Antonius claim that he has read "the book in which [Aristotle] described all of his predecessors' theories of speaking, as well as those in which he gave some views of his own about this same art." These must be references to the *Collection of Arts* (Τεχνῶν Συναγωγή, now lost, but listed at Diog. Laert. 5.24) and some form of the *Rhetoric* respectively. We need not take the claim at face value as far as Antonius himself is concerned, but it shows that Cicero knew these works.[29]

In conclusion, then, Cicero's reading of Aristotle takes many forms: sometimes "Aristotle" is simply synonymous with the Peripatetic tradition and a popular understanding of his thought that does not necessarily imply direct acquaintance with his treatises. In other cases Cicero deploys material from Aristotelian dialogues that are now lost to us and we cannot assess his use of them. But he is also aware of the separate type of *commentarii* and is keen to access them, perhaps with his curiosity heightened by the fact that not all of them were as readily available. He placed particular value on Aristotle's rhetorical work, in which he included a method of discovery of premises that must have owed something to the *Topics*. We must not neglect the fact that Cicero's reading was active and creative enough to make the Aristotelian material his own, thus we should not be too ready to conclude that he did not read certain works if we find him adapting or diverging from "our" Aristotle.[30]

NERONIAN ARISTOTLE

A very different type of engagement with Aristotle can be detected in the fragmentary remains from the work of the Stoic L. Annaeus Cornutus. Cornutus had a flourishing teaching career in Rome, with the poets Persius and Lucan among his more prominent students, until he was banished by Nero in 65 CE. In terms of his writings, which included works in both Greek and Latin, his best-known (and surviving) work is the *Compendium of Greek Theology*, a pedagogical manual characterized by the use of etymological exegesis.[31] He had broader linguistic interests, evidenced in a series of grammatical/rhetorical treatises, and it is to these interests that we can link his engagement with Aristotle's *Categories*. Aristotle's scheme of the ten categories apparently had a broader presence in the Roman rhetorical tradition, as evidenced by Quint., *Inst.* 3.6.23–24. It is introduced there as a list of "elements on which every question seems to turn" and construed as Aristotle's response to the question of how many rhetorical *staseis* (*status*) there are and what topics they cover. Quintilian's Roman source may have been the Augustan Stoic Plautus, who is credited with the translation of *ousia* as *essentia* (*Inst.* 3.6.23), but this sort of use must go back to a long-standing interpretative tradition that treated the *Categories* as a work on dialectic and rhetorical invention, closely associated with the *Topics*.[32]

From fragmentary references in the later Neoplatonist commentaries Cornutus emerges as a critic of Aristotle's *Categories*, alongside his earlier fellow Stoic Athenodorus (probably first century BCE). According to the commentators, they both took the subject of the Aristotelian work to be "words *qua* words" and criticized it for failing to include all verbal expressions under its division into ten classes (Porph. *In Aristotelis Categorias commentarium* 59.9–13; Simpl. *In Aristotelis Categorias commentarium* (= *In Cat.*) 18.17–19.1). Simplicius also reports criticisms by Cornutus on the grounds that the *Categories* lacks thematic coherence, moving indiscriminately between logic, physics, ethics, and theology (*In Cat.* 19.2–7). All this so far suggests that Cornutus engaged with the work as a whole, interrogating its purpose (*skopos*), structure, and overall choice of contents.

Furthermore, Simplicius preserves some detailed remarks by Cornutus, making it clear that he also commented on problems and controversies surrounding the individual categories. For example, on the category of relatives (*pros ti*) Cornutus seems to be at odds with Athenodorus, interpreting relatives in terms of their signification of reality (πρὸς ὑπόστασιν σχέσις) and not just as bare words-*qua*-words (Simpl. *In Cat.* 187.28–35). This made Paul Moraux speak of an ontological turn by Cornutus, away from the standard Stoic linguistic line.[33] With Cornutus, therefore, we have an example of the text-based reading of Aristotle, commenting and raising problems and objections on programmatic as well as detailed points, which became current with the early commentators in the first century BCE.[34] Apart from a direct engagement with Aristotle's text it also involves engagement with the exegetical tradition, and we saw Cornutus reacting to the strictly linguistic interpretation. It is hard to believe that Cornutus was alone in Neronian Rome in his exegetical interests; there must have been some ongoing debate at least on the *Categories*, perhaps on the part of those thinkers who were interested in theories of language, or of rhetoric and argument, as we saw with the evidence from Quintilian.

While Cornutus stands out as an attentive and engaged reader of Aristotle, by far the most prominent philosopher in Neronian Rome was Seneca the Younger. He was of course a Stoic, but he showed considerable interest and was well versed in the philosophy of the other schools. With respect to Aristotle and the Peripatetics, it is clear that he is familiar with a number of their doctrines and that he knows them from his readings rather than from oral teaching, because he is not known to have had any Peripatetic teacher.[35] But it is not always clear what exactly he is reading, or what use he is making of it.

More specifically, he takes issue, as we would expect any committed Stoic to do, with the Peripatetic view on emotions that advocated their moderation rather than elimination (*Ep.* 85.3–4; 116.1). At *De ira* 1.9.2 he attributes to Aristotle (*inquit Aristoteles*) the view that anger is necessary in order to assist performance in battle, as long as it is not allowed to hold sway. There is no such remark anywhere in what we have of Aristotle, which means that Seneca either read a work that is now lost to us, or was happy to ascribe to the master views that perhaps originated with later Peripatetics—on many occasions he speaks of "the Peripatetics" in general.

In *Ep.* 65 Seneca takes Aristotle to task on the number and nature of the fundamental causes operating in the world. The Aristotelian theory is criticized alongside and on the same grounds as the Platonic one—Plato is said to have "added" two further causes to Aristotle's four (65.5).[36] If these ancient authorities understood by "causes" the necessary conditions that need to obtain in order for something to come about, then they have listed too few. If, on the other hand, they were trying to get at the fundamental (to the Stoics) "active" sense of cause, then they listed too great a "throng of causes" (*turba causarum*, 65.11).[37] At 65.4–6 Seneca lists Aristotle's four causes, familiar from *Physics* 2.3, but with the final cause singled out in a way that has puzzled scholars, and with examples that look very un-Aristotelian.[38] These final causes, alongside the exhaustive application of the full set of four causes to the one example of the statue, which is nowhere done by Aristotle himself, suggest that Seneca is drawing on an interpretative tradition that goes beyond the text of the *Physics*.[39]

The work where Seneca's reading of Aristotle comes more strongly to the fore is his *Natural Questions*, which draws substantially on the *Meteorologica*. Even for this work scholars have doubted whether Seneca made direct use of Aristotle's text,[40] but we should keep in mind that divergences from Aristotle (both in wording and in substance) can very plausibly be attributed to independent thinking and critical intervention on Seneca's part. There is no need to appeal to Posidonius or other unknown intermediary source(s) that provided Seneca with Stoic arguments and adapted versions of Aristotelian views, because he must have been capable, as a critical reader with a specific purpose, of making these adjustments himself.

More specifically, there are two passages where we find almost word-for-word translations from the Aristotelian meteorology: at *QNat.* 2.12.4–6, on thunder and lightning, Aristotle is introduced into a doxographical survey of the causes of these phenomena, on the side of those who think fire is "produced for the occasion" (*ad tempus fieri*, 2.12.3) rather than being present in the clouds throughout. What follows is an accurate report of Aristotle's theory of the double exhalation which occurs *passim* in *Mete* and a fairly close quotation from *Mete.* 2.9.369a25–b9. Similarly, at *QNat.* 1.3.7 on the formation of rainbows, Aristotle is inserted in a survey of earlier explanations in support (*Aristoteles idem iudicat*) of the view that rainbows are formed of droplets of water acting as mirrors that reflect images of the sun. This passage parallels *Mete.* 3.4.373a35–b27 fairly closely, leaving little doubt that Seneca made use of Aristotle's own text.

There are a large number of looser references to Aristotle's meteorology, where Seneca makes no claim to be quoting directly, and may be paraphrasing or quoting from memory (e.g., *QNat.* 6.13.1 on earthquakes; 7.5.4 and 7.28.1 on comets). More importantly, as J. J. Hall has noted, the requirements of the context affect Seneca's presentation of Aristotelian material:[41] it is much more faithful when Aristotle is a favorable witness among many in a doxographical survey, but there are departures and adaptations when a particular argument is at stake, for instance when Seneca, contra Aristotle, seeks to promote the view that comets are superlunary phenomena.[42]

On the whole, then, we have seen that for Seneca, as for most Romans, Aristotle was a great authority of the past, but his views were frequently accessed through the lens of a long-standing and ongoing interpretative tradition. They were treated as part of a general Peripatetic "consensus" (especially in ethics), or were included in debates with Platonism almost as part and parcel of the Platonic heritage (especially in metaphysics). Seneca must have turned directly to Aristotle's meteorology for his scientific *Natural Questions*, but even there he was an active reader, less interested in copying "accurately"[43] than in marshalling Greek knowledge in ways that would promote his own purposes.[44]

Aristotle in Antonine Rome and Beyond

The Imperial period has thus far been marked by Stoic readings of Aristotle in the works of Cornutus and Seneca. Stoicism remained prominent in the centuries after these thinkers, not least with its adoption by the emperor Marcus Aurelius. Marcus himself does not appear to have engaged closely with Aristotle, indeed in his *Meditations* he lamented his general lack of opportunities for reading (3.14). He was, however, in contact with philosophers from different schools, including the Peripatetic Gnaeus Claudius Severus (*Med.* 1.14). His commitment to Greek philosophy was also demonstrated in practice by his funding of chairs for all four main schools in Athens.

In order to form a clearer picture of Aristotle's fate in Antonine Rome we may turn to two authors whose careers partly overlapped with Marcus's reign. The first one, Apuleius of Madaura, was an outspoken Platonist, but he is also credited with two works of Peripatetic inspiration, a Latin treatise on logic titled *Peri hermeneias* and a translation of the pseudo-Aristotelian *De mundo*. The attribution of the former to Apuleius is more doubtful, but even scholars who argue against it are prepared to see it as the work of someone close to and influenced by Apuleius, and thus relevant for our purposes.[45] The *Peri hermeneias* is influenced by developments in logic in the centuries after Aristotle (notably Stoic logic), making it much more than a handbook exposition of Aristotelian logic, but it also displays "considerable direct acquaintance" with Aristotle's own works on the subject, including material from *De interpretatione* and *Prior Analytics*.[46]

There is greater consensus for attributing the *De mundo* to Apuleius, where again the author has intervened with a number of additions and embellishments,[47] making his own mark on one of the ways in which Greek philosophy was received in Rome, namely direct translation. The fact that this is a translation is not acknowledged anywhere in Apuleius's Latin version, nor is there any explicit comment on the authorship of the Greek original. In fact the Preface states that the exposition will follow both Aristotle and Theophrastus, perhaps indicating some doubts about the precise Peripatetic pedigree of the Greek *De mundo*. Finally, Aristotle was for Apuleius, as for many other Romans, a great authority on scientific and biological matters, and he claimed to have read his books on *Dissections*, lost to us but listed at Diog. Laert. 5.25 (*Apol.* 36.3, cf. 41.4; 41.6–7).

Apuleius was in all likelihood acquainted with Aulus Gellius, and they both spent time in Athens, where some of their acquaintance with Aristotle and other Greek authors must have taken place. Gellius in his *Attic Nights* is more forthcoming than most of the authors we have encountered so far on the subject of reading strategies and practices and informs us, for example, that he made his own excerpts (*praecerperemus*) from Aristotle's *Problems* (2.30.11). The *Problems* is in fact the Aristotelian work most frequently cited by Gellius, who does not raise any concerns about its authenticity. He must have known a different or larger collection than the one that survives today, because on two occasions (19.5.9; 19.6.1) he quotes Greek passages that do not appear in our *Problems* (frs. 214 and 243 Rose). The citation at 19.5.9 is preceded by the tale of an unnamed Peripatetic philosopher who warned Gellius and his party about the dangers of drinking melted snow; when he was ignored by the party, he produced the relevant tome by Aristotle himself from the library of the temple of Hercules at Tibur! (19.5.4). Consultation of Aristotelian books *On animals* (cited as *De animalibus*) was deemed necessary by Gellius also at 13.7.6, to resolve a disagreement between Homer and Herodotus on the reproductive habits of lions.

Gellius is also an important witness to a crucial development in the ways in which Aristotle was read (not only in Rome), namely the privileging of the "esoteric," "acroamatic" treatises or *commentarii* over the "exoteric" dialogues that were still appreciated, e.g., by Cicero. At 20.5.7–10 Gellius quotes from and appears to take seriously the alleged correspondence between Aristotle and Alexander the Great, where Aristotle purportedly reassures Alexander over the publication of the esoteric works on the grounds that those who have not actually attended his lectures will fail to understand the special wisdom hidden therein. This belief in some exclusive privileged teaching contained only in the esoteric works must lie behind the neglect and eventual disappearance of Aristotle's published output, and we can see from Gellius that it was already current in the intellectual circles of Antonine Rome.

Conclusions

We may now attempt to bring together some of the main ways in which Aristotle was accessed and read at Rome. There was often little or no distinction of Aristotle's thought from the Hellenistic Peripatos—a practice reflected in handbook-type literature such as the ethical doxographies preserved by Stobaeus, which list, e.g., "the doctrines of Aristotle and the other Peripatetics on ethics" (Stob. *Ecl.* 2.7.13; cf. 2.7.5 for Zeno and the Stoics). But many Roman authors, including Cicero and Seneca as well as the authors of the Second Sophistic, would often turn directly to specific Aristotelian treatises, especially for topics where Aristotle was considered an authoritative specialist (animals,[48] meteorology, prose rhythm, invention of arguments, etc.). We have also seen that Cornutus read at least the *Categories* very closely for the purposes of commentary, tackling specific interpretative problems. A further important feature of Roman readings of Aristotle was the extent to which he was read through existing exegetical lenses, which could sometimes mean assimilation to Platonic doctrines, as we saw in Seneca's case. Above all, however, we must keep in mind the independent and sometimes even partisan reading strategies employed by Roman authors, which should prevent us, in cases where Aristotelian ideas are adapted or reported "inaccurately," from concluding that the author in question has not read Aristotle.

Notes

1. Strabo, 13.1.54. A briefer version of the story, but with the crucial additional reference to Andronicus of Rhodes, is found in Plut., *Vit. Sull.* 26. Both are discussed in what follows.
2. He became Lucullus's captive after the latter's victory at Amisus in 70 BCE and was subsequently freed by Murena (*Luc.* 19.7).
3. See Barnes (1997) 19–20.
4. See Dix (2013) 215, with *Suda* s.v. "Tyrannio" (τ 1184).
5. Barnes (1997).
6. Hatzimichali (2013) esp. 18–27. But see now Rashed (2021).
7. See especially Moraux (1973) 48–58.
8. Rashed (2011) esp. 76–77.
9. See Sedley (2013).

10. "I have not done this [sc. full translation] yet, however I do not think that doing it is out of the question," *Fin.* 1.7.
11. Plut., *Vit. Luc.* 42.1–2; cf. Dix (2000).
12. Alternatively, these "Aristotelian notebooks" may have come from Lucullus's booty from the Pontus: *Pontica praeda* (Isid., *Etym.* 6.5.1.). Cf. Barnes (1997) 49, with n. 202.
13. Barnes (1995) 11–13.
14. References to "exoteric" works go back to Aristotle himself, and are found most frequently in his ethical and political works, cf. *Eth. Eud.* 1217b22, 1218b34; *Eth. Nic.* 1102a26, 1140a3; *Pol.* 1278b31, 1323a22. Strabo (13.1.54) claims that only the exoteric works were available, even within the Peripatetic school, during the Hellenistic period.
15. On the transmission of these works see Keaney (1963); Lennox (1994). The remark about a kind of insect at *Tusc.* 1.94 is paralleled at *Hist. an.* 552b18.
16. Schrijvers (1999). Tutrone (2006) tries to take the matter further and argue for Lucretius's direct use of Aristotle's school treatises. But most of his article is devoted to describing the sociocultural conditions indicating that Lucretius *could* have consulted these works. There is not enough close comparative reading of the relevant passages to persuade that he *actually* read them.
17. Admittedly, many passages are attributed to the *On Philosophy* only on the grounds that they appear in *Nat. d.*, see Furley (1989) 209, 211.
18. See Obbink (2001).
19. See Barnes (1997) 47–48.
20. These are referred to explicitly also at *Luc.* 119, *Acad. pr.* 1.26, *Tusc.* 1.70. In the *Acad. pr.* 1 passage and *Tusc.* 1.22 Cicero claims that Aristotle considered the fifth element the matter of the soul as well as the stars (*quintam quondam naturam censet esse, e qua sit mens, Tusc.* 1.22). See Furley (1989) 210.
21. Shortly after this passage (2.44) Cicero states more problematically that Aristotle thought of motions upward and downward as the only two possible natural motions, and ascribed the circular motion of the stars to their will rather than the natural motion of the fifth element. See Furley (1989) 207–209.
22. This is presented by Cicero equally as an Academic practice, see Long (1995) 54–60.
23. On the theoretical life in *Fin.* 5 see Tsouni (2012), and on the "debate" between Dicaearchus and Theophrastus, see McConnell (2012).
24. "Now the elaborate treatise on ethics is attributed to the father, but I do not see why the son should not have matched the father," *Fin.* 12. He was not alone in this in Antiquity, cf. Diog. Laert. 8.88; Barnes (1997) 57–59.
25. See Long (1995) 39.
26. See also Schofield (2008) 68.
27. "There are books written by Aristotle and Theophrastus containing argumentation on opposing sides through received opinions (*endoxa*)," *In Top.* 27.17–18; cf. Long (1995) 56.
28. Reinhardt (2003) 14–17; 177–180. See also Huby (1989) 61–62 for a similar distinction between Aristotle's *Topics* and Cicero's source, and Barnes (1997) 54–57, who is more agnostic.
29. On Cicero's access to the *Rhetoric* see further Fortenbaugh (1989), arguing that it is all indirect; Barnes (1997) 50–54 arguing for the availability of a three-book *Rhet.* in Cicero's time; see Hatzimichali (2013) 24 for some reservations about this.
30. This point is very well made by May and Wisse (2001) 39.
31. On the compendium see Boys-Stones (2007) and (2018), with references to earlier literature.

32. See Bodéus (2001) xxii with n1 and Griffin (2015) 32–79.
33. Moraux (1973) 594. Simplicius reports an *aporia* of Cornutus's on place expressions (*In Cat.* 329.1–5), which is of a grammatical/lexical nature, casting doubt on his ontological interests. But since we do not have the context in which Cornutus raised the issue, we cannot be certain about his thinking on this occasion.
34. For more on the differences of this type of reading from, e.g., Cicero's see Chiaradonna (2013).
35. Inwood (2005) 17.
36. See Inwood (2007) 140 and 144–145 for Seneca's presentation of the Aristotelian theory as included in and subsumed by the Platonic one, and Sedley (2005) 136.
37. See Sedley (2005) 139 for a comparison of this critique with Cornutus's strategy vis-à-vis the *Categories*.
38. 65.4: "a cause is spoken of in three ways . . . a fourth cause is added to these" (sc. the final cause). At 65.6 we find the artist's earnings, glory or piety as final causes for the creation of a statue. See also Sedley (2005) 136n47.
39. See further Inwood (2007) 143, and 147–148 on the question whether a "more Aristotelian" final cause may be behind the additional ("sixth") cause at 65.8 and 65.14.
40. See especially Setaioli (1988) 387–477.
41. Hall (1977) 410–416, esp. 416.
42. See Williams (2012) 279–280.
43. Hall (1977) esp. 410, 414, 421 makes very good remarks on how preoccupation with accuracy and associated value judgments stem from modern priorities that were of no interest to ancient authors like Seneca.
44. Williams (2012) 303.
45. Harrison (2000) 11. It is treated as a work by Apuleius by Sandy (1997) 222–223 and Londey and Johanson (1987).
46. See Londey and Johanson (1987) 4–5 and 20–27.
47. Harrison (2000) 174–183.
48. For the reception of Aristotle's biology at Rome, see Hatzimichali (2021).

References

Barnes, J. (1995). "Life and work," in J. Barnes (ed.), *The Cambridge Companion to Aristotle* (Cambridge), 1–26.
Barnes, J. (1997). "Roman Aristotle," in M. Griffin and J. Barnes (eds.), *Philosophia Togata II: Plato and Aristotle at Rome* (Oxford), 1–69.
Bodéus, R. (2001). *Aristote [Catégories]*. (Paris).
Boys-Stones, G. (2007). "*Fallere sollers*: The Ethical pedagogy of the Stoic Cornutus," in R. Sorabji and R. W. Sharples (eds.), *Greek and Roman Philosophy, 100 BC–200 AD* (London), 77–88.
Boys-Stones, G. (2018). *L. Annaeus Cornutus, Greek Theology: Fragments and Testimonia* (Atlanta).
Chiaradonna, R. (2013). "Platonist Approaches to Aristotle: From Antiochus of Ascalon to Eudorus of Alexandria (and Beyond)," in Schofield, 28–52.
Dix, T. K. (2000). "The Library of Lucullus." *Athenaeum* 88: 441–464.

Dix, T. K. (2013). "'Beware of Promising Your Library to Anyone': Assembling a Private Library at Rome," in J. König, K. Oikonomopoulou, and G. Woolf (eds.), *Ancient Libraries* (Cambridge), 209–235.

Fortenbaugh, W. W. (1989). "Cicero's Knowledge of the Rhetorical Treatises of Aristotle and Theophrastus," in Fortenbaugh and Steinmetz, 23–60.

Fortenbaugh, W. W., and P. Steinmetz, eds. (1989). *Cicero's Knowledge of the Peripatos*. (New Brunswick, N.J.).

Furley, D. (1989). "Aristotelian Material in Cicero's *De natura deorum*," in Fortenbaugh and Steinmetz, 201–219.

Griffin, M. (2015). *Aristotle's Categories in the Early Roman Empire*. (Oxford).

Hall, J. J. (1977). "Seneca as a Source for Earlier Thought (Especially Meteorology)." *CQ* 27: 409–436.

Harrison, S. J. (2000). *Apuleius: A Latin Sophist*. (Oxford).

Hatzimichali, M. (2013). "The Texts of Plato and Aristotle in the First Century BC," in Schofield, 1–27.

Hatzimichali, M. (2021). "The Early Reception of Aristotle's Biology," in S. M. Connell (ed.), *The Cambridge Companion to Aristotle's Biology* (Cambridge), 228–245.

Huby, P. (1989). "Cicero's Topics and Its Peripatetic Sources," in Fortenbaugh and Steinmetz, 61–76.

Inwood, B. (2005). *Reading Seneca*. (Oxford).

Inwood, B. (2007). *Seneca: Selected Philosophical Letters*. (Oxford).

Keaney, J. J. (1963). "Two Notes on the Tradition of Aristotle's Writings." *AJPhil.* 84: 52–63.

Lennox, J. G. (1994). "The Disappearance of Aristotle's Biology: A Hellenistic Mystery," in T. D. Barnes (ed.), *The Sciences in Greco-Roman Society: Apeiron* 27.4 (Edmonton), 7–24.

Londey, D., and C. Johanson, eds. (1987). *The Logic of Apuleius*. (Leiden).

Long, A. A. (1995). "Cicero's Plato and Aristotle," in J. G. Powell (ed.), *Cicero the Philosopher* (Oxford), 37–61.

May, J. M., and J. Wisse (2001). *Cicero on the Ideal Orator*. (Oxford).

McConnell, S. (2012). "Cicero and Dicaearchus." *Oxford Studies in Ancient Philosophy* 42: 307–349.

Moraux P. (1973). *Der Aristotelismus bei den Griechen von Andronikos bis Alexander von Aphrodisias* I. (Berlin).

Obbink, D. (2001). "Le livre I du *De natura deorum* de Cicéron et le *De pietate* de Philodème," in D. Delattre and C. Auvray-Assayas (eds.), *Cicéron et Philodème: La polémique en philosophie* (Paris), 203–226.

Rashed, M. (2011). "Aristote à Rome au IIe siècle: Galien, *De Indolentia*, 15-18." *Elenchos* 32: 55–77.

Rashed, M. (2021). *Ptolémée "al-Gharīb". Épître à Gallus sur la vie, le testament et les écrits d'Aristote*. (Paris)

Reinhardt, T. (2003). *Cicero's Topica*. (Oxford).

Sandy, G. N. (1997). *The Greek World of Apuleius: Apuleius and the Second Sophistic*. (Leiden).

Schofield, M. (2008). "Ciceronian Dialogue," in S. Goldhill (ed.), *The End of Dialogue in Antiquity* (Cambridge), 63–84.

Schofield, M., ed. (2013). *Aristotle, Plato and Pythagoreanism in the First Century BC*. (Cambridge).

Schrijvers, P. (1999). "L'homme et l'animal," in P. Schrijvers, *Lucrèce et les sciences de la vie* (Leiden), 40–54.

Sedley, D. N. (2005). "Stoic metaphysics at Rome," in R. Salles (ed.), *Metaphysics, Soul and Ethics and Soul in Ancient Thought* (Oxford), 117–142.
Sedley, D. N. (2013). "Cicero and the *Timaeus*," in Schofield, 187–205.
Setaioli, A. (1988). *Seneca e i greci: Citazioni e traduzioni nelle opere filosofiche*. (Bologna).
Tsouni, G. (2012). "Antiochus on Contemplation and the Happy Life," in D. N. Sedley (ed.), *The Philosophy of Antiochus* (Cambridge), 131–150.
Tutrone, F. (2006). "Lucrezio e la biologia di Aristotele." *Bollettino della Fondazione Nazionale "Vito Fazio-Allmayer"* 35(1–2): 65–104.
Williams, G. D. (2012). *The Cosmic Viewpoint: A Study of Seneca's Natural Questions*. (Oxford).

CHAPTER 29

CHRISTIAN ETHICS
The Reception of Cicero in Ambrose's De officiis

IVOR J. DAVIDSON

THE *De officiis* of Ambrose of Milan (c. 339–397) has sometimes been said to be the first systematic treatment of Christian ethics.[1] The image may be misleading. Ambrose's treatise scarcely represents the earliest Christian rendition of the metaphysics of morals. Christian thinkers had written plenty on moral themes long before him; their efforts were generally reflective of what their authors took to be an integrated construal of the nature and ends of human agents. Ambrose did not aspire to present a system of ethics as such, some grand theoretical configuration of being and action or general compendium of virtue and its motives. But no surviving early Christian text contains such a self-conscious adaptation of classical Roman thought on moral behavior, its discernment and exemplification. Ambrose's work considers the principles of virtuous conduct in strategic evocation of a philosophical archetype; in that, it affords an exceptional glimpse of how a framework of ethics could be reassembled in a context of cultural transition.

For the historian, thick narration of beliefs and practices involves a great deal more than the reading of landmark conceptual accounts. Expressions of a moral vision are nevertheless important aspects of an historical picture. What was happening to Roman moral philosophy as it fell into—and from—the hands of a creative Christian intellectual in the late fourth century?[2]

CONTEXT

Ambrose was a Latin bishop like none before him.[3] Son of a senior imperial official, he had by his early thirties become consular governor of the province of Aemilia-Liguria, based in Milan. In December 374 he became the city's bishop, leader of a church marked by doctrinal factions. Spiritually he was fairly unprepared. His Christian background was strong, but he had had little or no training in theology; like others in the period, he had first to be baptized in order to proceed to ordination. In terms of immediate ecclesiastical concerns, his loyalties were, however, clear. He was firmly "pro-Nicene": God the Son was coequal in being with God the Father. Milan's recently deceased bishop, Auxentius, had been of a different position: to his critics an "Arian," more accurately one of the many in his time who held the Son to be "like" the Father but inferior in ontological terms.[4] Auxentius had withstood attempts to dislodge him from his see over the best part of two decades. The Nicene cause in the region was animated but fragile. Ambrose was the man to address that challenge. Politics were certainly at play. "Snatched into the priesthood from a life spent at tribunals and amid the paraphernalia of administrative office" (*Off.* 1.4), he had to learn a fair bit on the job. Early years required careful footwork, but he knew what it took to build up a leader's authority; to the demands he brought experience, wealth, bearing, style.

Schooled in the liberal arts in Rome, he had been educated to a high standard in literature, rhetoric, and law; proficient in Greek, he read philosophy, especially of a Platonist provenance. To develop as exegete he studied Philo, Origen, Athanasius, Basil, Didymus, and others, assimilating Greek interpretative techniques in the moralizing exposition of scriptural exemplars. Political constraints did not disappear, but versions of contemporary pro-Nicene reasoning were rapidly absorbed and robustly declared; in an age of high-stakes polemics, manifesto-cum-refutation remained a prominent (if somewhat restricted) genre.[5] His mind was steeped in biblical idiom; poetic imagery and classical allusion were also on easy display. Ambrose was an orator already. His pulpit manner could not fail to impress, accessible and urbane all at once. Its energy could be quite intense: great contrasts between the sensuality and corruption of the world and the calling of the regenerate, in holy ascent to the one true God. Salvation was infinite privilege; its pursuit was serious business. Ambrose's own seriousness, a visibly ascetic devotion, could not be missed. Preaching, writing, liturgy, and spectacle articulated sacred mysteries; moral and pastoral applications were drawn in broadly directive terms.

Ambrose's originality as a theologian would never be as great as some, but his spiritual dedication and commitment to scholarship were real; he was a versatile intellectual and a master of communicative art. His agendas were pursued at large: in doctrinal instruction, in interventions in church affairs elsewhere, in the politics of synods. Privileged as his own path had been, he had known the importance of networking; his ability, in turn, to converse at Milan's new imperial court brought him an image, and sometimes a role, as a significant powerbroker, a lobbyist of the mighty and counselor of their stratagems. Effective political diplomacy incurred debts, some of which might be called in, such as persuading the teenage Valentinian II to refuse restoration of the Altar of Victory to the senate-house in Rome in 384, contrary to carefully reasoned petition for religious toleration from a formidable senatorial voice, Q. Aurelius Symmachus. Ambrose also had his enemies. In 385–386 anti-Nicene energies in Milan gained fresh impetus and some potent support at court, not least in the empress Justina. Ambrose refused to yield his opponents space for public worship, ultimately risking stand-off with the forces of order in defiance of legal edict. There and elsewhere, it may have suited him to elaborate and homogenize the threat posed by "Arian" antagonists so as to enhance his own position;[6] he was also good at seeming most in control when it was least true.

Ambrose was an adept promoter of his church's social presence: an advocate of ascetic consecration, a developer of martyr cults, a public benefactor, a builder of basilicas that colonized the suburbs, a champion of congregational hymn-singing as instrument of pedagogy and cohesion as well as praise. He wrought for himself an image as a pastor who spoke powerfully to and for a people and claimed their loyalty in turn. Consensus as well as opposition could be rhetorically constructed, but his preparedness to resist as well as his capacity to persuade bespeaks a measure of undeniable popular support; an ability also to outclass his critics. Ambrose could seem devoted and remote all at once. The political as well as religious messaging was timely. Among other moves, the flourishing of Nicene confession could be associated with the security of the empire; in the enduring wake of the Roman military fiasco against the Goths at Adrianople in August 378, "Arian" faith and "barbarian" threat were readily aligned.

By the time he produced his *De officiis*, it was fourteen years or so since he had assumed his episcopal role, and much had been achieved. "The time of the Arian onslaught" (1.72) was now somewhat in the past. The invasion of Maximus had given young Valentinian and his entourage more to deal with than the capital's doctrinal squabbles; they fled to Thessalonica, where past allegiances were withdrawn. Theodosius, swift victor over Maximus's forces, would soon assert his own rights in the West: with that, Nicene momentum would prevail. Things for Ambrose were already somewhere on that turn; greater literary productivity than ever before was under way. A modest beginning to an ambitious treatise remained in strategic order (1.1–22), but a measure of didactic boldness was feasible. Personal apologia and a propensity for gesture were part of the equation: justification of his own record where criticisms had clearly been ventured (2.70–71, 136–143, 150–151); thinly veiled censure of his distinguished non-Christian contemporary, Q. Aurelius Symmachus (that man again), for moral failure as urban prefect of Rome a few years earlier (3.45–52).[7]

In the community of Ambrose's faithful, ordinary social distinctions were supposedly overturned: rich and poor worshipped together; the emperor himself might yet do penance. When Ambrose preached, greed, indulgence, and abuse of the vulnerable were roundly condemned; modesty, charity, and mercy celebrated. If Christian behavior in general mattered, how the church's official representatives in particular behaved—and were seen to behave—was crucial. Fundamental to Ambrose's sense of his task as bishop was an effort to raise the bar on clerical standards, to instill in those who held office something of the character he himself brought to his position: a heady mix of gravitas, confidence, self-discipline, and care. At every level, the church's servants were public figures, an index of the relevance and integrity of Christian claims. In a court city, image was of considerable moment. "Those on the outside" (1.247) were watching. Ambrose, "held in honor by the great and powerful,"[8] was as equipped as anyone to know how an individual "of the first rank" (2.67) should conduct himself, to mediate what a "gentleman" (*vir optimus*) might think—and to equate such judgment with the discernment of the morally superior (1.227). He could offer direction in the business of ecclesiastical assurance, the demonstration that Christian moral claims and their clerical enactment bore appeal alongside their alternatives.

The counsel applied not only in cosmopolitan, status-conscious Milan but across quite a large area of Northern Italy, in territories that variously benefited from their proximity to an imperial capital, or contained the great estates of its present and former grandees, and in towns where local elites might slowly be nudged toward more elevated patterns of existence. Ambrose almost certainly had no formal metropolitan role, but he sought to wield a significant level of influence in the region and had early shown his abilities to galvanize its churchmen in potent support of his causes. Trainees in Milan went on to hold episcopal office in towns like Bologna and Modena; in the bishoprics of Como, Brescia, Trent, and Aquileia those who had not necessarily been under Ambrose's initial tutelage but had been installed with his blessing remained recipients of his guidance. Advice to the faithful bishop of Pavia is mentioned in 2.150–151: it was of obvious importance that it had been followed. Through extensive letter-writing and other contacts Ambrose remained an energetic authority-figure, expecting deference from lesser churchmen as interpreter of the Word and the times; sometimes it was all more controversial than he himself was prone to imply. The instruction in *De officiis* was an extension of the work, a further way of setting out his ideals for genuine or assumed satellites and the communities they served.[9] It bore also, in part at least, upon some of the Christian officials, landowners, and businessmen whose ways of life held potential significance in the evolution of local and regional power-structures.[10] It would be considered, too, by plenty of non-Christian as well as Christian *literati* in Milan, Rome, and far beyond, curious to see what a prominent bishop was up to when he discoursed in evocative style on matters of conduct.

For Ambrose, the sketching of a strong vision for Christian ethics was no dilettante affair: intimately connected to his social and political aspirations as churchman, it was a thoroughly practical matter.

Ambrose and Cicero

He turned to the most obvious exemplar he could: Cicero's *De officiis*. Another exercise with political ends firmly in view, it was a staple text, known to men of Ambrose's class as no other Latin work on ethics would have been.[11] A reader of Cicero since schooldays, Ambrose's writing and preaching in general evinced his influence plentifully,[12] though only in writing his own *De officiis* does he mention him by name. Cicero's language was deeply embedded in his memory; some version of the same awareness could be expected in some of those for whom he wrote. Ambrose could evoke the substance of Cicero's arguments by *praeteritio*, "passing over" stories without specific identification of their source, expecting the echoes to be recognized (3.71, 87; cf. also 2.30; 3.66, 70).

In writing on duties he was tackling a theme with an impressive history: Panaetius and his "son" (or former pupil, Posidonius) had written on the subject in Greek, Cicero in Latin; as Cicero had set out to instruct his young son Marcus (and in turn a wider constituency of young Romans aspiring to public office in his time), so too a bishop could endeavor to offer his spiritual "sons" his fatherly guidance (1.24). There is no evidence that Ambrose knew Panaetius or Posidonius except from Cicero. The structure of Ambrose's argument follows the threefold approach to duties Cicero had taken from Panaetius's περὶ τοῦ καθήκοντος:[13] like Cicero, Ambrose considers, in three books, (1) the honorable (Cicero's *honestum* renders Panaetius's καλόν), (2) the beneficial or useful (Cicero: *utile*; Panaetius: συμφέρον), and (3) the relationship between the two. Panaetius had also written in three books, but had never managed to tackle the third question; Cicero had compressed the material Panaetius had treated in three stages into his books 1 and 2, finding some (limited) help in his third book from Posidonius and, it seems, Hecato of Rhodes. For all its qualities, Panaetius's treatment of the honorable and the beneficial had also seemed to Cicero inadequate; Cicero had felt it necessary to give some consideration to *degrees* of the honorable in book 1 and to *degrees* of the beneficial in book 2: more than one thing might be honorable, more than one thing beneficial. Ambrose adopts Cicero's basic three-book plan, but says relatively little about these supplementary questions.

Like Cicero, Ambrose organizes the heart of his discussion of the honorable in book 1 around the four Platonic virtues to which elsewhere he himself is the first to attach the name "cardinal":[14] prudence, justice, courage, temperance. He is conscious that Cicero made various adjustments in handling these themes: justice belonged within a broader treatment of sociability that also included beneficence; courage was magnanimity in particular; due construal of temperance involved expansion of a Middle Stoic emphasis on "the fitting" or "the seemly" (Cicero: *decorum*; Panaetius: πρέπον). Ambrose endorses the fundamental Stoic assumption that the virtues are a unified package; the expression of each mutually implies the presence of the others, an overall orientation toward the good. His definitions are infused with many aspects of Stoic thinking, particularly in the cases of courage and temperance. Ambrose affirms the importance of rational self-mastery and—in general terms at least—of living in accordance with nature.

His treatment is nevertheless immediately distinctive. Prudence (1.122–129), for Ambrose as for Cicero, is essentially a matter of practical wisdom more than theoretical knowledge. But the most practical knowledge of all is, for Ambrose, the knowledge of God. If spiritual piety, faith in God, is the "first source of duty" (1.126), prudence—not justice, as Cicero had assumed—is necessarily the most important of the virtues. Justice (1.130–174), for Ambrose as for Cicero, is divided into strict justice (*iustitia*) and kindness (*beneficentia*), and, like Cicero, Ambrose ranks kindness higher than a basic principle of not doing harm unless one is harmed, or of rendering to each his or her own (*suum cuique*). But kindness is for him a matter of Christian charity, in which right intentions and the following of a Christlike pattern are crucial. In the case of courage (1.175–209), like Cicero, he sees inner fortitude or "greatness of soul" (1.178) as more worthy than physical or martial daring (though he cannot resist celebration of the bodily as well as spiritual valor of biblical characters and Christian martyrs). But rational triumph over irrational forces of fear, pain, or adversity and a proper contempt for externals are closely tied to biblical images of perseverance in hope of eschatological reward. Temperance (1.210–251) consists of modesty and propriety, and as in Cicero this involves the maintenance of harmony, sobriety, tranquility, and due measure in both the individual parts and the whole of one's deportment. But the inner soundness of which outward seemliness is an index derives, for Ambrose, from right relation to God.[15]

When he turns to the beneficial in book 2, Ambrose upholds Cicero's strong interest in the good of human society, and the assumption that honorable behavior equates to behavior that is practically advantageous. The beneficial is not, however, simply a matter of positive worldly advantage, personal or social, but that which contributes to the attainment of eternal life; it is in that state that human community is supremely realized. The truly virtuous person operates by a combination of faith and works, for these are the way in which the ultimate good of eternal, not just temporal, happiness is attained. The path to this end involves suffering, privation, and self-denial in the here and now, but it is marked also by fulfillment in the midst of—even because of—these realities (2.1–21). Individual expressions of the beneficial may reflect many of Cicero's categories—the value of prudent generosity, hospitality, good counsel, right company, fair and sincere treatment—but central to all of these is the principle of serving Christ, of obtaining eternal life and commending it to others. If the most practical thing of all is to be loved (2.29–39), this is secured, in effect, by faithful testimony to God's love for humankind. Ambrose shares Cicero's close interest in temporal and societal image, the acquisition and maintenance of reputation, but in the end expediency is for him about acting in a way that will reflect divine priorities and draw others to God. What is beneficial is eternal and otherworldly in its final orientation.

In his third book, Ambrose follows Cicero's approach that what is dishonorable cannot be beneficial, and that the honorable end must be sought by honorable means. But whereas for Cicero the honorable is aligned with the advantage of pursuing whatever promotes the interests of human cohesion and equity, for Ambrose it is about rightly relating to and attesting the character of God. By God's design the ultimate interests of the individual are consonant with the interests of the universal human family the individual is called to serve. The law of nature, as Cicero argues, is indeed fundamental, but for Ambrose this law coincides with the advantage to be found in following the pattern of Christ, in whom the human image of God—or of human life in accordance with the creature's intended nature—is supremely found. The good of humanity is furthered by the observance of justice, the protection of the vulnerable, and the preservation of what is right and true, but these ends are synonymous with the working out of redemption for both individual and society. The key note in Ambrose's treatment is the supremacy of the honorable rather than a comparison of the honorable and the beneficial as such. As he presents things, there can ultimately be no difference between the two core categories, inasmuch as both alike can only be understood with reference to the purposes of God and the task of inviting others to appreciate these in this world and the next.

Whose Authority?

Cicero's image of the personal and civic obligations of a gentleman resonated deeply; Ambrose found enduring appeal in many aspects of its exposition of manners. He goes to considerable efforts, however, to emphasize that his intellectual authority as teacher of ethics is neither Cicero nor Cicero's Hellenistic predecessors: it is Christian scripture. The theme of duties, *officia*, is for Ambrose legitimized by the use of the word *officium* in the New Testament (1.25, citing Luke 1:23). Under the influence of his Middle Stoic sources, Cicero (*Off.* 1.8) had professed to be interested primarily in "middle" duties rather than "perfect" ones: the original Stoic image of the honorable was an unrealistic ideal, unattainable by the ordinary person; better to focus on those practical obligations of which a rational account can be rendered, the acts by which most people can attain the goal of the public good. This distinction of "middle" and "perfect" duty is echoed by Ambrose, but his justification for it is the gospel story of Jesus's response to the rich young man who had kept the divine commandments but lacked the obedience essential for the possession of treasure in heaven (1.36–37, citing Matthew 19:20–21). To observe the Decalogue is middle duty; the higher path, perfect duty, is to follow Christ's instruction on self-sacrifice and love for enemies, and to imitate divine perfection in the exercise of mercy (1.38).

Both the honorable (1.221) and the beneficial (2.23–27) are justified with scriptural usages of the language. "Seemliness"—a vital feature of Panaetius's and in turn Cicero's depiction of the honorable as being *seen* to do the appropriate thing consistently with one's personal circumstances and abilities, and thus visibly avoid extremes—is validated by references to "fittingness" (Greek πρέπον; Latin *decorum*) in biblical verses (1.30, 221, 223–224).[16] Cicero's attempt (*Off.* 1.93–95) to explain the difference between the honorable and the seemly is again, for Ambrose, bettered by a differentiation established in the scriptures (1.221, citing Psalm 92:1; Romans 13:13; Psalm. 64:2; 1 Corinthians 14:40, and alluding to other texts).

Ambrose's endeavors to establish the philosophical categories biblically involve obvious contrivance. What matters for immediate purposes, though, is his insistence that his concern is not *mere* philosophy. He presents himself as a humble student-teacher of the Bible (1.3); it was, he claims, while meditating on a Psalm (38 [39]) that the idea of writing on duties came to his mind (1.23). Cicero wrote as a father to his son; the apostles wrote to their spiritual children, offering them a deposit of sound teaching to be guarded carefully: Ambrose evokes both registers (1.2–3, 23–24; 3.139). Again and again he stresses where his true authority lies (1.36, 131, 151; 2.3, 5, 65, 113; cf. 1.106): "if we do not find things in the scriptures, how can we make use of them?" (1.102). Biblical truth and exemplars are intrinsically superior to anything offered by the classical tradition—first, because the Bible is of greater antiquity than philosophy and thus deserves the credit for originality; second, because it is the source of many of the philosophers' best ideas. The chronological priority of biblical wisdom is emphasized (1.31, 43–44, 92, 94, 118; 2.6, 48;

3.2, 80, 92); in close connection with this point Ambrose adduces a standard Jewish and Christian apologetic claim: "pagan" insights were stolen from the scriptures (1.31, 79–80, 92, 126, 132–35, 141, 180; 2.43).[17]

Only two of Ambrose's five references to Cicero by name occur in contexts of specific reference to Cicero's text; only one of these (1.82) is direct. For the most part, Ambrose goes to great lengths to avoid naming him or other classical thinkers as source, preferring to hide their identity behind generic plurals: "the philosophers"; "the pagans"; "the men of the world"; "the orators"; "some"; "they"; "those people" (1.27, 29, 92, 94, 102, 118, 122, 126, 130, 131, 132, 186, 207, 252; 2.43; 3.8, 26, 27, 29, 80, 81, 83, 91, 97, 126). Often the vagueness is in the context of mentioning a Ciceronian illustration without naming the author (3.71, 87; cf. also 3.66, 70; 2.30). Such generalizing did not in antiquity always bespeak hostility, but what is striking in *De officiis* is Ambrose's regular combination of oblique references with sharp adversatives, directly contrasting what is said by Cicero and his kind with what is appropriate for Christian instruction and practice, especially in light of scripture (1.27–28, 29, 82–83, 102, 116, 131; 2.3, 4–5; 3.27, 97). Sometimes a classical idea is repudiated completely in favor of an allegedly superior Christian principle (1.131; 3.27); at other times, while there may not be explicit rejection of a philosophical view, an argument from lesser to greater is deployed: if such-and-such is the standard according to worldly wisdom or convention, that can only be a minimal threshold of virtue; how much higher should the ideal be for those who follow Christ (1.185–86; 2.124; 3.26, 65)?

The quest for a theological platform for duties is most obvious in the manner in which Ambrose chooses to fill out his account of the honorable and the beneficial at almost every turn. Cicero's argument is sprinkled with examples from Greek and Roman history, literature, and mythology; Ambrose's with the heroes, heroines, and villains of the Bible. Roman veneration for ancestors and their moral inspiration is transposed to a new setting: the great spiritual family, the people of God. Ancient Israel and those who first followed Jesus or told the world about him are the forebears of a late-fourth-century bishop and his addressees: "the fathers," "ours." The characters in biblical narratives are actors in a drama into which the moral vocations of Ambrose's readers are incorporated. Who are the good and faithful of Northern Italy? The descendants of patriarchs and prophets; the beneficiaries of the ultimate Teacher; the heirs of the apostles and of the communities to which their message gave rise. The whole business of salvation-history is progressive in character, moving from "shadow" (divine revelation to the patriarchs, Israel, and the prophets) through "image" (the gospel dispensation) to "truth" (eschatological fulfillment). The logic facilitates typological and spiritual exegesis of Old Testament texts; it also provides the basis for an implicit correlation of philosophical notions of moral progress (Middle Stoicism) or ascent (Platonism) with respective phases of divine grace (1.233–239).

Where Ambrose does retain Ciceronian stories, particularly in book 3, he mentions only two of the characters by name, Scipio Africanus (3.2) and Gyges (3.29–36) respectively. The rest are to be spotted by allusion. Repeatedly there is emphasis on the superiority of scriptural material (3.1–7, 29–36, 67, 69–75, 77–85, 86–87, 91–97). The individuals depicted in "our" scriptures are the true mirror of moral instruction (1.116; cf. 3.139); it is by studying their example, not that of classical figures, that Christian readers will profit. Being "filled up on the word of God" (1.164) is the goal; this involves the shunning of "art" in favor of "simplicity" (1.29, 116; cf. 3.139). Just as he did in his sermonic exposition and catechesis at large,[18] Ambrose seeks to saturate his moralizing with biblical idiom, to hold up scriptural *exempla* as supreme guide to practice.

There are almost no *exact* quotations from Cicero, only close reminiscences and endless verbal echoes, not always in any clear or logical sequence. The overall presence of Ciceronian language diminishes as the work progresses. Large sections contain none of the core philosophical vocabulary; many passages do not obviously pick up anything at all in Cicero's argument. The honorable does not appear in 1.1–26, 29–73, 103–122, 126–151, 153–174, 223–257; the beneficial is mentioned only once, in passing, in the second half of book 2 (2.138), and disappears entirely in the climax of book 3, where the honorable is presented as the only standard. Even at that, reference to the honorable often seems artificial, an attempt to tie biblical stories loosely to the Ciceronian theme by the insertion of one or two Ciceronian words in the transitions between sections. Cicero's supplements to the Panaetian structure, the respective comparisons of different kinds of honorable things and different kinds of beneficial ones, are known to Ambrose (1.27), but represented only tenuously. Varieties of the honorable are mentioned toward the end of book 1, but it is simply proposed that one should opt for whichever is the more honorable option in any context (1.258). A ranking of beneficials may be necessary (2.22, 28), but it is scarcely explicit in the unfolding of Ambrose's advice; Ambrose conflates the calculus of *utilia* in book 2 with the distinction between the honorable and the fitting in book 1, rather than lining it up, as Cicero does, with the comparison of *honesta*.

In book 1, Ambrose does not get to the cardinal virtues until 1.115 (Cicero introduces the theme at his *Off.* 1.15). Before that, he spends a great deal of time on the themes of modesty (*verecundia*) and seemliness in conduct and speech (1.65–114), which leads him to anticipate material that naturally falls under the fourth virtue, temperance (1.210–251). Drawing twice on Cicero's discussion of temperance, he has two sections on anger (1.90–97, 231–238), several references to the twin movements of the soul, reason and appetite (1.98, 105–114, 228–230), and two passages on speech (1.99–104, 226). In various places he appears to misunderstand, or fails to represent accurately, Ciceronian divisions or points (e.g., 1.105–106; in the distribution of Ciceronian themes in book 2 after 2.29). Within each book there are extended passages that do not obviously evoke Cicero at all: on the virtues of silence as opposed to speech (1.5–22, 31–35), on divine providence and theodicy (1.40–64), on duties especially germane to clerics (1.246–251), and so on. Ambrose's second book opens with a treatment of happiness or the blessed life (*vita beata*) (2.1–21) that finds little basis in Cicero's second book beyond a passing phrase (Cic., *Off.* 2.6);[19] Ambrose's third book climaxes with a lengthy celebration of friendship (3.125–38) that goes far beyond Cicero's in *Off.* 3.43–46, drawing extensively on the much fuller characterization offered earlier by Cicero in his *De amicitia*.

Much more could be said about Ambrose's style, and about his own sensitivity to the potential deficiencies of his arrangement of subjects. At times he draws upon his sermons on biblical texts, or defends his own conduct in recent affairs. Very often he just wanders off-topic, carried far beyond Ciceronian themes by his enthusiasm for biblical material. At the very least, it is obvious that he does not work with Cicero's text to hand but relies on his memory: the results can include a curious pastiche of minor words and phrases recollected alongside major concepts.

Ambrose's Aims

The Christian *De officiis* is, on any reckoning, an amalgam of old and new. But why is it the particular amalgam that it is? What is Ambrose seeking to achieve? It will not do to write him off as an inept plagiarist, clumsily piecing together a mosaic of sentiments from different places, somehow unaware of the distinctive thought-worlds to which they belonged, naïve to the tensions between his philosophical inheritance and his investments as a Christian.

Many interpretative arguments have been ventured; in the end, the options for Ambrose's intentions have generally boiled down to one version or another of the following possibilities: (1) Ambrose aimed to produce a positive synthesis of Ciceronian Stoicism and biblical material, perhaps as a bridge-building exercise, or as a protreptic to Christian belief; (2) Ambrose aspired to replace Cicero's work by effecting significant change to much of its philosophical substance; if intended in part—beyond the fortifying of its primary addressees—for those yet unpersuaded of Christian claims, the approach was as much spirited as soothing. Either way, it is necessary, of course, to differentiate aims from results. Whether Ambrose's effort might be deemed to represent an intellectual success or a failure is not the point. The question is whether, in this adaptation, he wished to point up continuities between Roman philosophy and Christian faith, or to suggest that the latter effectively rendered the former redundant.

The first view has a certain plausibility. Stretching as far back as the apostle Paul, Christian theology and ethics had plenty of connections with Stoicism. Paul deployed argumentative registers familiar to Stoic diatribe; he ventured accounts of sociality, virtue, and vice that evinced at least formal similarities to Stoic assumptions in numerous respects.[20] Musonius Rufus, Epictetus, Justin Martyr, Tatian, Clement of Alexandria, and other writers were well aware of the possible parallels between Christian and Stoic ideas. Tertullian spoke of Seneca as "often ours";[21] the late fourth century yielded a forged set of letters between Seneca and Paul;[22] Jerome could note the "many" instances of agreement between Stoic and Christian thought.[23] Ambrose is hardly the first Christian writer to recognize surface compatibilities between his Christian investments and Stoic teaching on nature as ethical norm (1.33, 77–78, 84, 123–125, 127, 132, 135, 223; 3.15–28), or the unimportance of wealth (1.118), or human society as a body (2.135; 3.17–19), or the ties of goodwill that bind human relations (1.169), or the triumph of the sage (or spiritual leader) over external problems (1.178–95; 2.10–21). His appeals to conscience, to the power of reason to moderate the passions, or to the importance of inner courage or outward *decorum* appear on the face of things to typify standard Middle Stoic themes.

At times, such as when he is talking about private property (1.132), Ambrose can in fact sound closer to orthodox Stoicism than either Cicero or Panaetius does, seeing the evolution of private possession as in conflict with nature's rationale, a matter of unjust acquisition rather than defensible convention. Certainly he attributes such human greed directly to a primitive moral fall, advocating a charitable deployment of property that emulates an original purpose of universal justice as willed by a personal creator; the golden age Ambrose evokes is of a specific kind. In other respects, though, his language about the origins of private right is arguably more classically Stoic than Cicero's.[24] When Ambrose explains how to attain happiness, again, he does not always mention faith: *virtue* is indispensable; it is the key, "the only good, the supreme good" (2.18). What it gains, of course, is at last "eternal life," which is, in Ambrose's perspective, a good deal more than independence from external, temporal circumstances; still, his preparedness to locate the basis of fulfillment in the pursuit of goodness as such can be quite striking, and divine grace is not always invoked as the necessary source of outstanding capacities (e.g., 2.66).[25]

De officiis upholds a plethora of stereotypes. Clerical good conduct involves the manifestation of gentlemanly "virility," an absence of "effeminacy": such soundness of character will be clearly recognizable in body language (1.71–75), tone of voice (1.84, 104; cf. 1.67), and quality of speech (1.76, 99–103, 226; 2.86, 96). Traditional interests in the physiognomy of public figures were already widely assimilated (and sometimes far more heavily recast) in Christian renditions of social semiotics; they remain an obvious feature among Ambrose's ideals of self-fashioning. Embodied virtue will look, sound, and act a particular way—measured, rationally controlled, grave, refined, yet evidently natural and without contrivance (cf. 1.73, 75, 84, 101, 104). The suitably ordered (1.82, 85) person will not come across as uncouth or rustic (1.72, 84, 104).[26] He will avoid anger (1.5–22, 90–97; cf. also 1.31–35, 68, 233–238),[27] flattery (1.226; 2.96, 112–120; 3.134–135; cf. also 1.88, 209, 226; 2.66), and jokes and improper stories (1.102–103; cf. 1.85, 88, 184). He will keep away from dangerous social situations (1.85–87), seek the company of wise elders (1.212; 2.97–101; cf. 1.65–66), and in general use his leisure-time (*otium*) profitably (3.1–7). His view of possessions and wealth will reflect the Stoic axiom that the wise man has the whole world for his own (1.118; 2.66); he will (albeit in accordance with scripture's authority) not be "effete," "soft," "unmanly," or "feeble" in esteem of pleasure or fear of suffering (2.9), nor in desire for power (1.138). His enjoyment of the benefits of friendship and his ways of handling the challenges of intimacy (3.125–138) will have plenty in common with the Stoic and Peripatetic sentiments endorsed by Cicero; in a generalized commendation of Christian unity, stylized celebrations of loyalty, honesty, and altruism merge in the practical interests of clerical harmony rather than a sustained attempt to revolutionize a philosophical theme.[28]

The virtuous cleric is indeed somewhat akin to the Ciceronian *vir bonus*, with at least some of the same responsibilities and attitudes. Ambrose's concern that character be well spoken of not only within the church but among "those on the outside" (1.247) makes biblical allusion (1 Tim. 3:7); the sentiment on public esteem is also entirely traditional (cf. also 1.227; 2.29–39; and the remainder of book 2, passim). Desirous of being useful to all, a wise public servant, the Christian leader is to be generous and smart, compassionate but discerning, neither vainglorious nor elusive, neither miserly nor a soft touch. Classical euergetism is recast as almsgiving, but the clergyman as patron is bound to conventions of prudence aimed in part at maintaining, not compromising, relations of power (1.143–159; 2.76–78, 109–111). Inherited property is valued (2.17; 3.63), commercial money-lending (2.111; 3.20, 41) or greedy mercantile behavior (1.243) condemned in ways reminiscent of Cicero as well as the Bible. Love of country, horror of treason, and esteem for the honor of political involvement are all evocative of Ciceronian inflections of Stoic themes (1.127, 144, 254; 3.23, 84, 127). For Christians, patience, forgiveness, and nonretaliation are crucially important, and Christians, like Stoics, speak of a universal human brotherhood. For Ambrose as for Cicero, this does not rule out the possibility of a just war, or a legitimately violent response to some forms of provocation (1.176–177); here at least, specifically Christian criteria are not much specified (a biblical exemplification of courage suffices).[29]

General similarities between Stoic and early Christian ideas are, however, often overstated; for all the points of contact, the two traditions also exhibit rather profound differences, above all of course in the theological physics to which they appeal. Though the point is often lost on modern-day enthusiasts for an eclectic blend of Stoic and Christian ideals, in antiquity the traditions developed and interacted as often as not as *rival* accounts of the good life and its claims to truth: influences and apologetic gambits notwithstanding, a measure of the perceived *incompatibility* between them, rather than their actual or potential alliance, needs to be reckoned with.[30] In any event: there is very little reason indeed in the text of De officiis to conclude that Ambrose for his part is interested in effecting a positive fusion of Roman Stoicism and the Bible. He is concerned not to emphasize the achievements of philosophical ethics but to outdo them.

The evidence lies not least in his tone. As far as Ambrose is concerned, scripture depicts a far higher standard of duties than any—Stoic or other—offered by "the world" (*saeculum*). The sustained antitheses, the charges of pagan appropriation of biblical truth, the regular depreciation of classical examples all combine to press the point. The references not only to Cicero but to other classical thinkers—Panaetius (1.24, 31, 180), Zeno (2.4, 6), the Stoics in general (1.132–133; 2.4), Aristotle (1.31, 48, 50, 180; 2.4, 6), the Peripatetics (2.4, 6), Pythagoras (1.31), the Epicureans (1.47, 50; 2.4)—are all presented as contrasts with biblical wisdom. Plato's insight was anticipated by Job (1.43);[31] his famous story of Gyges and the ring is juxtaposed with the Bible's "true examples" (3.32).[32] There is one basic dichotomy between all "those men"—regardless of their schools of thought—and the truth (1.47–50). Philosophy specializes in "tortuous, complex, and confused enquiries," "pointless discussions"; scripture offers a simple prescription (2.8).

There is in all this no quest for any ideological merging of philosophy and faith. For Ambrose, "philosophy" as a path leads, in principle, in a different direction from his gospel. In a now lost work he contrasted its falsehoods with the truth attained through baptism, the sacrament of regeneration.[33] Of course it is necessary to recognize that polemic against philosophy in general does not mean necessary hostility to everything philosophers said; as his allusions in other places to Platonist texts might be taken to imply, Ambrose could well assimilate, echo, or reframe ideas while repudiating the realms in which they were advanced. Philosophical cargo of various sorts could also be subtly imported in debts to exegetical and theological authorities. Ambrose no doubt owes his philosophical inheritance as a whole much more than he recognizes or is prepared to admit. But he does not seek to tease out details of Stoic thought as a matter for analysis in themselves (he shows very little interest in the possible relationship between Cicero and his sources, or in the differences between those sources and Stoicism before them), far less suggest that the tradition at large lines up well alongside the Bible. His contention is that the wisdom revealed in his sacred texts is the original, definitive disclosure of reality, that everything finally worth knowing is there, and that the best thoughts of the philosophers have simply been lifted from that source. His ways of reading these scriptures are indubitably affected by enduring Ciceronian and other assumptions, but that is, we might say, merely what he brings by dint of a complex cultural formation to the interpretative process. If he is largely uninterested in reflecting on the layers of intellectual influences that shaped his construal of scripture, even less is he interested in invoking philosophical concepts in the reading of scripture so as to propose a marriage of the two. Rather than suggesting that Roman Stoicism as such holds enduring value, he wishes to construct its general encounter with his theological commitments.

In as much as scripture's instruction is the only foundation that is deemed properly to matter, Ambrose works hard—if not always neatly—to emphasize the differences in, rather than parallels between, his underlying logic and that of Cicero and his predecessors. The discussion of the virtues in book 1 is prefaced with a treatment of core aspects of the theological framework that will immediately mark it as distinctive. Cicero begins his treatise confidently, talking about his literary ability and his contributions to philosophy. Ambrose sets out modestly, praising humility as a spiritual disposition, conscious of his initial lack of preparation and unworthiness as teacher, emphasizing the need for silence before speech, valorizing a self-mastery patterned not on an overcoming of inner passion or a resistance to provocation but on the fear of the Lord; the disposition is expressed with suitable effect by the godly sufferer, supremely by Christ himself (1.1–22). Duty is owed to God and rewarded by God; the standard of what is honorable and seemly is the measure acceptable to future judgment, the attainment of eternal life rather than present enjoyment (1.28–29).

It is appropriate, thus, that Ambrose establishes the nature of divine providence and the spiritual purposes of temporal suffering as preliminary to his treatment of moral obligations. Providence for him is not an impersonal force, but the action of one who establishes all things and is committed to particular ends for them in accordance with his essential love and justice (1.40–64). The world as brought into being has come to be morally broken, and thus nature cannot function as a straightforward or neutral general standard; it is fallen as well as created, a problem to be dealt with as well as a norm to be invoked. The creator is engaged in an unfathomably generous strategy, the personal deliverance of creatures from their self-imposed bondage, the ultimate transformation of everything: nature will yet be as intended.[34]

The stage on which human behavior is enacted is for Ambrose fundamentally constituted by the economy of the God who creates and saves. Christian agents are embraced within the purposes of God and answerable to God. Their desire is to love, please, and honor the one who has made them, resurrected them from death through saving action, and set about the business of bringing them to their true end in fellowship with him. Suffering and service, action and ambition are conditioned accordingly. Obligation is framed in the context of final divine assessment rather than present-worldly criteria (1.40–64; cf. also 1.146–147). It is as the *baptized*—those who by repentance and faith have died and been raised with Christ (the "author of happiness": 2.20), and are now committed to the tasks of his kingdom—that Ambrose's Christian readers are summoned to act. Their moral teleology lies in pursuit of their destiny as the redeemed.

In that light, emphasis on the visibility of virtue in this world is immediately delimited. The first obligation of the believer is to devote to God "the most precious possession" he or she has: the soul; only then will service to others follow in appropriate form (1.253). Admirable conduct derives not from a quest for display but from gratitude and obedience; the new desire of the inner self, love of God, propels action. Interiority is a crucial element in Ambrose's exposition of moral choice, but the structure of due deliberation is specific. If conscience is a judge (1.6; 2.2; 3.24, 29, 31), it functions as such with reference to its source and constant reference-point. With God in view as witness (1.9, 40, 44, 124; 2.96), the intention of the heart stamps the right kind of mark on human work; genuine devotion, compassion,[35] or charity, not desire for worldly praise and glory, drives action. If the gospel is taken seriously, silence and secrecy rather than display may well be the appropriate setting for generous behavior. If there is no point in seeking reward in this world only to lose your soul in the next, better to live in humility here, glory there (1.147; 2.2–3; 3.29–36).

Ultimately for Ambrose redemption is no less physical than it is spiritual: a final restoration of human life to the state of proper unity of body and soul intended by the creator but marred by sin. The relation of such anthropology and eschatology to the legacies of an autarkic psychology of the passions or a Stoic account of the transcendence of physical suffering or loss may never in *De officiis* be fully resolved, but nor is it actively sought. As far as Ambrose is concerned, a biblically shaped narrative of paradise lost and regained remains of basic significance for the challenges faced by seekers of the good in the world as it actually is, and for their capacities to transcend these on a path that leads finally upward to ultimate, embodied freedom and fulfillment. It is not possible to make much sense at all of Ambrose's reckoning of rationally ordered, virtuous behavior in present human existence in any sustained detachment from these theological assumptions. Whatever may be implied *en passant*, the setting for virtue's true expression is for Ambrose only properly found through faith, in participation in a divine work: the regeneration of human existence, a process now begun, yet to be completed. On salvation's road, a new reality obtains, solemn and assuring all at once: the virtuous person is "always with God" (3.7).[36]

Ambrose's gestures in respect of Ciceronian arguments extend well beyond his strained attempts to validate philosophical nomenclature by appeal to biblical verses. There is frequent ambivalence between the Ciceronian and the scriptural senses of terms such as "faith" (*fides*) (1.140, 142, 145–46), "glory" (*gloria*) (1.175, 177, 179, 187, 194–196, 208; 2.2, 14, 81, 90, 153, 156; 3.36, 48, 56, 89–90), or "justice"/"righteousness" (*iustitia*) (1.39, 110, 117, 142, 186, 259; 2.35). Ambrose slides from one register to another and back again within a few sentences, generally aware of what he is about. Challenging as his habits may make things for translators of his text, his moves cannot be trivialized as mere clumsiness: they speak in their own subtle way of his submission that philosophy's coinage is no longer a sufficient currency. If now, for him, "the cause is more splendid" (1.218), the conviction generates a deliberate expansion of the semantics of moral reasoning.

Ambrose variously subverts as well as affirms the content of classical ideals. Not only does he emphasize such things as prayer, sacraments, study of the scriptures, fasting, self-denial, poverty, humility, and chastity; he also ventures a definition of ultimate duty that looks different to anything in his classical predecessors. Not only is perfect duty something taken seriously by just a few (3.10; cf. 3.12; also 1.16, 125, 184, 217–218): it is, specifically, the path pursued by those called to Christian leadership, the "athletes" or "soldiers" of Christ (1.183–187, 238). If the celebrated magnanimity of the virtuous is bound up with a rational apprehension of ultimate truth, it is, as such, also vitally bound up with final scrutiny and pursuit of eternal reward (1.124, 188, 191; 2.3, 96).[37] To such awareness and endeavor all Christians are drawn, but the philosophical sage in particular is recast as the holy man, a Christian gentleman (3.27) distinct even from the community of ordinary believers, whose achievements represent a mere keeping of the commandments. The latter is a serious standard, no doubt, but the fully devoted are, it seems, summoned to a life of special sanctity and self-giving. At the last, "middle" duty is of only relative significance: for the leader of the church, a "man who occupies a position of honor" (2.67), nothing less than perfection will do (cf. 3.12). Whatever may be said of aspects of his moral teaching elsewhere,[38] in *De officiis* Ambrose is especially keen to encourage forms of character appropriate to an identifiable spiritual élite.

The social realities for the practitioners, as well as the commitment expected of them, can be glimpsed here and there. Ambrose himself was rich enough to endow his church handsomely from his own patrimony while retaining enough for his own needs; while a great many of his clergy were not a tiny part so well-off in their origins, he speaks to some at least who remain able to live on the proceeds of what he calls—coyly—their own "little bit" of land as alternative to a church stipend, urging them to be content with one or the other, *sans* supplement from commercial activities on the side (1.184–185). The self-supporting priest or other minister who is able through prudent deployment of personal resources not to be a burden to the church is commended (1.152).[39]

Opportunities to spend well ranged widely. The building and decorating of churches in appropriate style is, alongside caring for the indigent, a priestly use of money worthy of mention (2.110–111), not least because Ambrose's own practices in his equivalent of the Ciceronian politician's schemes of public works were controversial, extending his church's physical presence in Milan in rapid yet elaborate fashion and probably liquidating assets from his immediate predecessor's days in the cause (2.142).[40] Another is hospitality (2.103–108; cf. 1.39, 167), partly in avoidance of extravagant dinner parties at others' houses (1.86). Personal debts can be written off as an act of good will (1.168). Where the church acts as a banker for the deposits of widows and other vulnerable parties, it should do so scrupulously (1.254), in resistance if need be of secular encroachment—again in accordance with Ambrosian example (2.144–151). Where a bishop sits in adjudication of civil cases, as Ambrose did all the time, no partiality is to be shown to the rich or powerful, and sordid financial disputes are to be declined (2.124–125; 3.59). Inheritance-hunting, beloved target of Roman satire, is disgraceful (3.57–58); it was a problem in the church, the need for its increasingly stringent legal restriction a potential threat to valuable income.

Involvement with the powers that be is assumed to be a matter on which a number of Ambrose's clerical addressees might benefit from his considerable experience; unsurprisingly, the right combination of boldness and prudence is deemed important (1.208; 2.150–151). Ambrose seeks to fashion those who, even as they look down on the world's affairs, wealth, and desires (1.184, 192; 2.66), know how to approach its social, economic, and political practicalities in the right style: realistically (1.187). If Christian leadership is to be successful in its moral testimony, its way of enacting the virtues needs to be unambiguously impressive: not only beyond reproach, but astute besides. Perfect duty is ambitious; it is also quite pragmatic.

Ambrose's conception of a vocation to a special existence is perhaps most striking in the area of sexual ethics. On the one hand, he continues to prize a vision of assertive "manliness" that is highly traditional; on the other, he summons his clerical readers to standards of sexual "integrity" (1.249; 2.27) that go well beyond anything required of the conventional Roman gentleman and in various ways subtly "feminize" traditional ideals of masculinity, calling men to epitomize a modesty and submissiveness more usually supposed to be associated with the social obligations of women.[41] Sexual propriety is no longer a matter of showing mere discretion or restraint of appetite, as it was for the young men to whom Cicero addressed himself; for a Christian élite, it is total abstinence. Ministers "at the altars of Christ" (1.88; cf. 1.247), privileged guardians of the "deep things of God" (1.251), are—like Ambrose himself—to live in celibacy, serving with bodies "untainted," "unsullied and undefiled" (2.27; cf. 1.248–249; also 1.68–69, 76–80). It is clear that a number of Ambrose's clergy were already married at the time of their ordination. For them, strict continence is required (1.249). Those married more than once are barred from ordination altogether (1.248). Ambrose is aware of the arduousness of his standards and their deterrent implications for the young (1.218; cf. 3.10); he presses a self-denial that brooks no compromise. Asceticism's denial of the body, as he envisions it, is meant to be seen as far more ambitious than any merely temporal transcendence of the passions. The commitment of the soldiers of Christ to *this* degree of rigor is energized by divine power and oriented toward heavenly recompense: "those men serve for the present, we for the future" (1.218). The clergy will not only match the Ciceronian ideals for temperance: they will substantially exceed them.

In these and other ways, Ambrose's very specific sort of *imitatio* ventures, in and beyond its immediate guidance for clergy, a bold intellectual case: his work ought now to be read *instead of* Cicero's. Unadorned and modest (or rough) his text may be by comparison, but "those who do not read the works of those people will read ours if they wish" (1.29). Those whose memories retain a reasonable stock of Cicero's advice, or whose libraries afford them reference to it, may reflect on the reworking of the old themes, the strategic reconceptualizing of their range, depth, and ultimate purpose. The invitation is presented not by hiding the distinctiveness of the theological investments, still less by pedantically contriving their supposed alignment with the bequest of philosophical ethics at point after point, but by an authoritative proposal: the philosophers' standards can—precisely on the basis of the particular story Christian theology tells—be outdone. Just so, they are superseded. The modesty at the beginning and the end (3.139) is not to be overread.

Just how much Ambrose's annexation of Cicero assisted with his immediate ends as a churchman we cannot exactly say. He undoubtedly had considerable influence as a leader, and his treatise is in its way a distinctly self-conscious expression of his style; the evidence also seems pretty clear that he scarcely succeeded in elevating the clergy of Northern Italy at large to quite his own standards, or transforming all the ways of Christian businessmen or officials, or luring the cultivated away from their philosophy en masse. As the text suggests, the political and symbolic roles played by the churches' leading ambassadors were increasingly significant in society as a whole, the contours of Christian communities were in process of social change; but none of this occurred in any remotely simple fashion, nor indeed did the lifestyles of the privileged in particular always change so dramatically in consequence of Christian profession or episcopal exhortation.[42] Ambrose might seek to fashion as powerful a case as anyone could in his time and place that it was only by the strength of his church's pulse that the entire life of a realm was sustained; the reality was inevitably a little more complicated.

Still: Ambrose's contention that his gospel outbid Cicero's legacy was—of course—heavily rhetorical: a declaration of a cultural claim by one to whom the terms were clear, the moral fruits unarguable. There is very good reason to suppose that it was through the Christian fashioning of a different kind of intellectual relationship with traditional texts and ideas that Christianity did indeed extend its appeal in upper-class late-Roman society, and that it was in no small measure through the symbolic gestures as well as the personal example of confident Christian spokesmen such as Ambrose that aristocratic "paganism," so far from reviving in the period, continued to decline.[43] To such a process the production of a Christian *De officiis*—albeit one that insists on its *differentness*, not its continuity—appears an obviously emblematic contribution.

For all that, it was in the nature of the exercise that the results were mixed. While Ambrose's treatise would have its influences, serious appreciation of his work would always require the continuing study of its classical predecessor. In any contest for general legacy over the centuries, Cicero has beaten Ambrose hands down. If the long-term cultural repercussions of Ambrose's endeavor seem in hindsight inevitable, their reality merely attests the challenges he and other Christians of late antiquity faced in any such aspiration to assume intellectual capital, reshape it, and move on. Roman moral philosophy may supposedly have been passé; its lingering presence amid all the new theology confirmed things could hardly be quite so neat.

Notes

1. So, e.g., Homes Dudden (1935), vol. 2: 502.
2. References in what follows are to the text in Davidson (2002); on the dating, composition, purposes, and influence of the work, see Davidson (2002), vol. 1:1–112. A Latin text is also available in Testard (2000).
3. For modern biography, see McLynn (1994); Ramsey (1997) 1–54; Savon (1997); Moorhead (1999); also Liebeschuetz (2011) 57–94.
4. On the theological background and labels, see Ayres (2004).
5. On Ambrose and "Arianism," see in particular Williams (1995); also Markschies (1995).
6. The general case is pressed quite hard by Williams (2017), somewhat against the grain of other modern scholarly accounts of a serious struggle with "Arian" rivals.
7. Symmachus himself may very well have been envisaged as a reader.
8. Augustine, *Conf.* 6.3.3.
9. One of his final achievements was the installation of another former Milanese, Honoratus, as bishop of Vercelli in 396. On Ambrose's influences in Northern Italy, see Lizzi (1989), Lizzi (1990), Zelzer (1997), Sotinel (2010), Gannaway and Grant (2021); more broadly on the region, see Humphries (1999). Aspects of episcopal relationships have been considered in Svetkovic and Gemeinhardt (2019).
10. Note the advice about the responsibilities of merchants and those involved in financial activities: 1.242–245; 3.37–52, 57–75.
11. It had been exploited already in the cause of a Christian apologetic by Lactantius in the early fourth century. Nelson (1933), however dated, is still quite a useful overview; on the reception of Cicero's writings more broadly, see MacCormack (2013).
12. For some of the debts, see Madec (1974) 141–166; Zelzer (1987); on Ambrose's use of Cicero in his homilies on the death of his brother Satyrus, see Biermann (1995) 24–44, citing earlier studies.
13. The fullest modern treatment of Cicero's influences and argument remains Dyck (1996); see also Newton (2016). Major aspects of the larger cultural psychology of Roman political ethics, honor, and the emotions can be pursued in Barton (2001) and esp. Kaster (2005).
14. Ambrose, *De excessu fratris* 1.57; *Expositio Evangelii secundum Lucam* 5.49, 62; *De sacramentis* 3.9.
15. The best study of Ambrose's treatment of the virtues remains Becker (1994); Colish (1985) 62–70 offers a useful discussion; see also Zelzer (1996).
16. On the background to the expansive (rather than confused) Ciceronian rendition of temperance and seemliness, see Schofield (2012).
17. On the background, see generally Droge (1989); Pilhofer (1990); Ridings (1995). Ambrose has particular debts to Philo, on which see at large Savon (1977); Lucchesi (1977).
18. On postbaptismal instruction, see Satterlee (2002).
19. Cicero had of course addressed the theme earlier, in his *Paradoxa Stoicorum* 6–19, and extensively in *Fin.* and *Tusc.* 5. Ambrose's summary of philosophical views at 2.4 draws directly on Cicero, *Fin.* 5.73.

20. See, int. al., Sevenster (1961); Engberg-Pedersen (2000); Rasimus, Engberg-Pedersen, and Dunderberg (2010); Thorsteinsson (2010).
21. Tertullian, *De anim.* 20.1; cf. also Lactantius, *De inst.* 1.5, 6.24.
22. Römer (1992).
23. Jerome, *In Isaiam* 4.11.6.
24. See further Swift (1979); Wacht (1982).
25. On such features generally, see Colish (1990).
26. On the conventions of *urbanitas*, see Ramage (1973), esp. 52–76.
27. See further Davidson (2006); for a powerful exposition of the classical background, see esp. Harris (2001).
28. Ambrose's treatment has attracted a significant literature; a useful discussion can be found in White (1992) 111–128; on the background, see Konstan (1997), esp. 149–173.
29. On Ambrose as seminal contributor to Christian theorizing on justice and war, see further Swift (1970).
30. The case is put strongly by Rowe (2016).
31. Evoking Plato, *Resp.* 357a ff., esp. 358c–d, courtesy of Cicero, *Rep.* 3.8.
32. Plato, *Resp.* 359c–360d, via Cicero, *Off.* 3.38.
33. Ambrose, *De sacramento regenerationis sive de philosophia*; fragments are found in Augustine: see Madec (1974) 247–337; on baptism as radical alternative, see further Smith (2011), pt. II. On "philosophy" in Ambrose's corpus as a whole, see esp. Madec (1974); Lenox-Conyngham (1993). Among other things, the evidence pushes firmly against certain ways of reading Ambrose's debts to Platonism, a subject too large to explore substantively here.
34. On the reframing of natural law via salvation-history, see Maes (1967).
35. On elements of the construction of affective compassion or pity and its relations to emotional tranquility in early Christian thought, see generally Wessel (2016).
36. The case for Christian specificity with reference to Ambrose's moral teaching at large is made by Smith (2011).
37. On Latin Christian modulations of magnanimity, see Smith (2020).
38. Colish (2005) exceeds the available evidence regarding the social background of Ambrose's "ordinary" addressees on moral themes in other contexts.
39. An astute account of some key themes on Ambrose and wealth can be found in Brown (2012) 120–134, 135–147.
40. On Ambrose's church-building, see esp. Krautheimer (1983) 69–92; also McLynn (1994) 226–237; Humphries (1999) 196–202.
41. On some aspects of this, see Burrus (2000) 167–178; for one way of reading the ideological possibilities that may have attached to Christian reconstructions in the period, see Kuefler (2001).
42. A few examples of the complex social and religious evolution of Western aristocracy (broadly conceived) are explored in Salzman (2002).
43. For a major redrawing of the scholarly picture, see Cameron (2011).

References

Ayres, L. (2004). *Nicaea and Its Legacy: An Approach to Fourth-Century Trinitarian Theology*. (Oxford).
Barton, C. A. (2001). *Roman Honor: The Fire in the Bones*. (Berkeley).

Becker, M. (1994). *Die Kardinaltugenden bei Cicero und Ambrosius,* De officiis. (Basel).
Bernardo, A. S., and S. Levin, eds. (1990). *The Classics in the Middle Ages.* (Binghamton, N.Y.).
Biermann, M. (1995). *Die Leichenreden des Ambrosius von Mailand. Rhetorik, Predigt, Politik.* (Stuttgart).
Brown, P. (2012). *Through the Eye of a Needle: Wealth, the Fall of Rome, and the Making of Christianity in the West, 350–550 AD.* (Princeton).
Burrus, V. (2000). *"Begotten, Not Made": Conceiving Manhood in Late Antiquity.* (Stanford).
Cameron, A. (2011). *The Last Pagans of Rome.* (Oxford).
Colish, M. L. (1985). *The Stoic Tradition from Antiquity to the Early Middle Ages,* vol. 2: *Stoicism in Christian Latin Thought through the Sixth Century.* (Leiden).
Colish, M. L. (1990). "Cicero, Ambrose, and Stoic Ethics: Transmission or Transformation?" in Bernardo and Levin, 95–112.
Colish, M. L. (2005). *Ambrose's Patriarchs: Ethics for the Common Man.* (Notre Dame, Ind.).
Davidson, I. J. (2002). *Ambrose,* De Officiis: *Edited with an Introduction, Translation, and Commentary.* 2 vols. (Oxford).
Davidson, I. J. (2006). "Seeking Perfection: Ambrose on Passion." *Studia Patristica* 43: 345–351.
Droge, A. J. (1989). *Homer or Moses? Early Christian Interpretations of the History of Culture.* (Tübingen).
Dyck, A. R. (1996). *A Commentary on Cicero,* De officiis. (Ann Arbor, Mich.).
Engberg-Pedersen, T. (2000). *Paul and the Stoics.* (Louisville, Ky.).
Gannaway, E., and R. Grant, eds. (2021). *Ambrose of Milan and Community Formation in Late Antiquity.* (Newcastle).
Harris, W. V. (2001). *Restraining Rage: The Ideology of Anger Control in Classical Antiquity.* (Cambridge, Mass.).
Homes Dudden, F. (1935). *The Life and Times of St. Ambrose.* 2 vols. (Oxford).
Humphries, M. (1999). *Communities of the Blessed: Social Environment and Religious Change in Northern Italy, AD 200–400.* (Oxford).
Kaster, R. A. (2005). *Emotion, Restraint, and Community in Ancient Rome.* (Oxford).
Konstan, D. (1997). *Friendship in the Classical World.* (Cambridge).
Krautheimer, R. (1983). *Three Christian Capitals: Topography and Politics.* (Berkeley).
Kuefler, M. (2001). *The Manly Eunuch: Masculinity, Gender Ambiguity, and Christian Ideology in Late Antiquity.* (Chicago).
Lenox-Conyngham, A. (1993). "Ambrose and Philosophy," in Wickham and Bammel, 112–128.
Liebeschuetz, J. H. W. G. (2011). *Ambrose and John Chrysostom: Clerics between Desert and Empire.* (Oxford).
Lizzi, R. (1989). *Vescovi e strutture ecclesiastiche nella città tardoantica (L'"Italia Annonaria" nel IV-V secolo d. C.* (Como).
Lizzi, R. (1990). "Ambrose's Contemporaries and the Christianization of Northern Italy." *JRS* 80: 156–173.
Lucchesi, E. (1977). *L'usage de Philon dans l'œuvre exégétique de saint Ambroise: Une "Quellenforschung" relative aux commentaires d'Ambroise sur la Genèse.* (Leiden).
MacCormack, S. (2013). "Cicero in Late Antiquity," in Steel, 251–305.
McLynn, N. B. (1994). *Ambrose of Milan: Church and Court in a Christian Capital.* (Berkeley).
Madec, G. (1974). *Saint Ambroise et la philosophie.* (Paris).
Maes, B. (1967). *La loi naturelle selon Ambroise de Milan.* (Rome).

Markschies, C. (1995). *Ambrosius von Mailand und die Trinitätstheologie: Kirchen- und theologiegeschichtliche Studien zu Antiarianismus und Neunizänismus bei Ambrosius und im lateinischen Westen (364–381 n. Chr.)*. (Tübingen).
Moorhead, J. (1999). *Ambrose: Church and Society in the Late Roman World*. (London).
Nelson, N. E. (1933). "Cicero's *De Officiis* in Christian Thought: 300–1300," in *Essays and Studies in English and Comparative Literature*, 59–160. (Ann Arbor, Mich.).
Newton, B. P. (2016). *Marcus Tullius Cicero* On Duties, *Translated with Introduction, Notes, and Indexes*. (Ithaca, N.Y.).
Nicgorski, W., ed. (2012). *Cicero's Practical Philosophy*. (Notre Dame, Ind.).
Pilhofer, P. (1990). *Presbyteron Kreitton: Der Altersbeweis der jüdischen und christlichen Apologeten und seine Vorgeschichte*. (Tübingen).
Ramage, E. S. (1973). Urbanitas: *Ancient Sophistication and Refinement*. (Norman, Okla.).
Ramsey, B. (1997). *Ambrose*. (London).
Rasimus, T., T. Engberg-Pedersen, and I. Dunderberg, eds. (2010). *Stoicism in Early Christianity*. (Grand Rapids, Mich.).
Ridings, D. (1995). *The Attic Moses: The Dependency Theme in Some Early Christian Writers*. (Gothenburg).
Römer, C. (1992). "The Correspondence between Seneca and Paul," in Schneemelcher, 46–52.
Rowe, C. K. (2016). *One True Life: The Stoics and Early Christians as Rival Traditions*. (New Haven, Conn.).
Salzman, M. R. (2002). *The Making of a Christian Aristocracy: Social and Religious Change in the Western Roman Empire*. (Cambridge, Mass.).
Satterlee, C. A. (2002). *Ambrose of Milan's Method of Mystagogical Preaching*. (Collegeville, Minn.).
Savon, H. (1977). *Saint Ambroise devant l'exégèse de Philon le Juif*. (Paris).
Savon, H. (1997). *Ambroise de Milan (340–397)*. (Paris).
Schneemelcher, W., ed. (1992). *New Testament Apocrypha*, vol. 2: *Writings Relating to the Apostles: Apocalypses and Related Subjects*. R. M. Wilson, rev. and tr. (Louisville, Ky.)
Schofield, M. (2012). "The Fourth Virtue," in Nicgorski, 43–57.
Sevenster, J. N. (1961). *Paul and Seneca*. (Leiden).
Smith, J. W. (2011). *Christian Grace and Pagan Virtue: The Theological Foundation of Ambrose's Ethics*. (New York).
Smith, J. W. (2020). *Ambrose, Augustine, and the Pursuit of Greatness* (Cambridge).
Sotinel, C. (2010). "The Bishops of Italy in Late Antique Society: A New Elite?" in C. Sotinel (ed.), *Church and Society in Late Antique Italy and Beyond*, pt. VIII: 1–24. (Farnham).
Steel, C., ed. (2013). *The Cambridge Companion to Cicero*. (Cambridge).
Svetkovic, C. A., and P. Gemeinhardt, eds. (2019). *Episcopal Networks in Late Antiquity: Connection and Communication across Boundaries*. (Berlin/Boston).
Swift, L. J. (1970). "St. Ambrose on Violence and War." *TAPA* 101: 533–543.
Swift, L. J. (1979). "*Iustitia* and *Ius Privatum*: Ambrose on Private Property." *AJPhil*. 100: 176–187.
Testard, M. (2000). *Sancti Ambrosii Mediolanensis* De officiis. Corpus Christianorum, Series Latina, 15. (Turnhout).
Thorsteinsson, R. M. (2010). *Roman Christianity and Roman Stoicism: A Comparative Study of Ancient Morality*. (Oxford).
Wacht, M. (1982). "Privateigentum bei Cicero und Ambrosius." *Jahrbuch für Antike und Christentum* 25: 28–64.

Wessel, S. (2016). *Passion and Compassion in Early Christianity*. (Cambridge).
White, C. (1992). *Christian Friendship in the Fourth Century*. (Cambridge).
Wickham, L. R., and C. P. Bammel, eds. (1993). *Christian Faith and Greek Philosophy in Late Antiquity: Essays in Tribute to George Christopher Stead*. Supplements to *Vigiliae Christianae* 19. (Leiden).
Williams, D. H. (1995). *Ambrose of Milan and the End of the Nicene-Arian Conflicts*. (Oxford).
Williams, M. S. (2017). *The Politics of Heresy in Ambrose of Milan: Community and Consensus in Late-Antique Christianity*. (Cambridge).
Zelzer, K. (1996). "L'etica di sant'Ambrogio e la tradizione stoica della virtù," in *L'etica cristiana nei secolo III e IV: Eredità e confronti; XXIV Incontro di studiosi dell'antichità cristiana, Roma, 4–6 maggio, 1995*, 47–56. (Rome).
Zelzer, K. (1997). "Vescovi e pastori alla luce delle lettere ambrosiane," in *Vescovi e pastori in epoca teodosiana: In occasione del XVI centenario della consacrazione episcopale di s. Agostino, 396–1996; XXV Incontro di studiosi dell'antichità cristiana, Roma, 8–11 maggio, 1996*, vol. 2: 559–568. (Rome).
Zelzer, M. (1987). "Ambrosius von Mailand und das Erbe der klassischen Tradition." *Wiener Studien* 100: 201–226.

CHAPTER 30

AUGUSTINE'S RECEPTION OF PLATONISM

ANNE-ISABELLE BOUTON-TOUBOULIC

In the period of late antiquity during which he lived, the Platonism in that part of the western Roman Empire with which Augustine (354–430) had to deal had undergone many transformations over several centuries. First, there was the Roman philosophy of the Republican period, represented to some degree by Varro but above all by Cicero's New Academy, whose influence was still considerable in late antique Africa. Then, in the Imperial period, there followed so-called Middle Platonism,[1] which counted among its adherents Apuleius, the fellow countryman of Augustine. Platonic philosophy and its variants were dominant from the middle of the second century CE on, and were reoriented with the neo-Platonism introduced by Plotinus,[2] who maintained his school at Rome for twenty-five years (244–269). It was his works that fructified Augustine's thought, along with those of his disciple Porphyry. Although in many cases there survive mere fragments of the latter, he has been called the "master of western thought"[3] for this period. Nevertheless, Christian writers in late antiquity could find inspiration in various forms of Platonism of the imperial period.[4]

All these forms of Platonism known to Augustine had been adapted and transformed, but also opposed and contested by Christian writers themselves,[5] some of whom, such as Ambrose, the bishop of Milan, had a direct influence on him, as when he heard some of Ambrose's *Sermons* in 386. Further complicating the reception of Platonism as it evolved over such a long period was, in Augustine's case, the matter of language, since he never mastered Greek sufficiently—at least in the beginning—to be able to access Platonic texts other than those in Latin. He was thus indebted in his reading on the one hand to works written originally in Latin, especially those of Cicero but also of Varro and Apuleius, or again those of earlier Christian writers, not to mention doxographies,[6] and

'I warmly thank David Konstan for having translated my text into English.

on the other hand to Latin translations of Greek works. Thus, translations also mediated his reception of Platonism. Above all, adherence to the Christian faith constituted the major prism—or rather source of antagonism[7]—in regard to this reception, but in Augustine's case, it so happens that his intellectual commitment to Christianity was made possible by the appropriation of certain neo-Platonic concepts, as he himself records in his *Confessions*. This appropriation doubtless explains the controversy that arose among scholars at the beginning of the twentieth century on whether he converted to Christianity or rather to neo-Platonism.[8]

However, Augustine's appropriation of Platonism was selective and critical, and also governed by apologetic purposes. His research into these Platonic philosophies also widened as it became necessary for him, especially in his role as bishop, to deepen the gift of his faith. But his interest in them remained constant, from his earlier works up to, at least, *The City of God*, completed around 426. Did he not in turn effect a "conversion" of what was then the dominant philosophy of paganism?

After examining the way in which Augustine presents Plato and Platonic philosophy in general terms, we shall see in what respect it, and more particularly neo-Platonism, shaped various aspects of his philosophy and his *intellectus fidei*, whether it is a matter of his *conuersio* to God, his representation of the world, his anthropology, or, finally, his theories of the soul. Within the limits of this article, we shall examine certain motifs that serve to highlight the originality of this reception, the variety of his methods and their goals (all the while raising the question of whether one must distinguish between the philosopher and the apologist), and the synthesis that he effected among the several traditions of Platonism. It is a matter, finally, of determining up to what point the expression "the Platonism of the Fathers"[9] applies to Augustine.

Plato and Platonism

Augustine knew that etymologically the Greek word *philosophia* might be rendered in Latin by the expression *amor sapientiae*, and he took over Plato's "erotic" value of the term.[10] From his earliest surviving work, written in 386, the *Contra academicos* (*C. acad.*), a dialogue that looks to refute the arguments of the skeptical New Academy (expounded by Cicero in his *Academica*), he not only assigned Platonism primacy over the other philosophies but he leaned on it so as to understand rationally the gift of faith. Why did he confer this role on Platonism? The "complete system of philosophy"[11] (*perfecta philosophiae disciplina*) which, in his view, is identical with the Christian message, is none other than Platonism, which is characterized by the opposition between two worlds. On the one hand, there is "the intelligible world where truth itself resides"; and on the other, this sensible world which is "only truthlike and made in its image" (*ad illius imaginem factus*), whence only opinion and not knowledge can be engendered in the souls of those who are unwise" (*C. acad.* 3, 17, 37).[12] It is the primacy granted to the intelligible over the sensible, far removed from the "materialist" philosophies (Stoicism and Epicureanism), that gives Platonism this preferential status. "Let us suppose that Plato were still alive,"[13] he states in his treatise *De uera religione* (391). If so, he might give the speech by which Christ himself succeeded in persuading the mass of people: one must adhere to a spiritual truth, and to that end, purify one's spirit of images of sensible objects so as to adhere to "the immutable form of things and to beauty." This latter hypostasis has replaced the "intelligible world"[14] with which, in his early Dialogues (*De ordine* 1.11.31), he identified the "kingdom" of the gospels, which is not "of this world" (Jn 18:36).

Much later, between 415 and 417, in Book 8 of *The City of God*, as he went over the various philosophical schools (Ionian and Italian), he repeated, *à propos* the Platonists, that "they stand closest to us," since they locate the blessedness of mankind in the pleasure taken in God (8.9). Indeed, according to Romans 1.20, "they knew God," an incorporeal and immutable God (8.10), perhaps via access to the holy Scriptures thanks to Plato's voyages to Egypt (8.11). But if Augustine finally rejected the traditional idea that pagan wisdom was "borrowed" from the Bible, he nevertheless was content to connect Genesis with the *Timaeus* and Exodus 3:14 ("I am who I am") with the Platonic philosophy of being (*De civ. D.* 8.11). The Platonists recognized God as being "the cause by which the universe was constituted, the light by which truth is perceived, and the fount at which happiness is imbibed" (*causa constitutae uniuersitatis, et lux percipiendae ueritatis et fons bibendae felicitatis, De civ. D.* 8.10.2, tr. Babcock). We underscore the fact that Augustine's Plato is a dogmatic, not a skeptical Plato, who allowed his views to be perceived despite the Socratic irony and elenchus.[15]

In fact, Augustine considered Plato, of whom he states that he was superior to all his successors (*De civ. D.* 8.12), as the one who, coming after Pythagoras and Socrates, raised philosophy to perfection, by uniting contemplation and action and effecting the systematization of philosophy in three parts (8.4). God is the object of these three parts of philosophy (moral, physical, and logical), and in them the *platonici* recognized the Trinity.[16] In *Ep.* 118 (dated to 410), Augustine had already interpreted in this way Cicero's depiction of Plato.[17]

Plato is thus, in Augustine's eyes, the highpoint in this history of philosophy. In the *C. acad.*, in which he recounted the history of the Academy, he represented him as such, even as he added that the one who incarnated this philosophy henceforward was Plotinus, a philosopher "so like Plato that they seem to have lived at the same time." Augustine borrows here a phrase that was doubtless employed by Porphyry.[18] In Book 8 of *The City of God*, he will expand this list as follows: Among "the more distinguished philosophers of more recent times, who chose to follow Plato . . . , of these the most notable are the Greek Plotinus, Iamblichus, and Porphyry, but the African Apuleius also stands out as a noteworthy Platonist in both languages" (*De civ. D.* 8, 12).[19]

In his *Revisions* (1.1.1), Augustine will reproach himself for having been too laudatory of these pagan philosophers in his early works. But in 387, his friend Nebridius, recalling the letters that he received from Augustine, affirmed: "They will speak to me of Christ, of Plato, of Plotinus,"[20] thereby demonstrating that these two philosophers were regarded in terms of Christian doctrine. Nevertheless, although we may suppose that Augustine had never read the works of Plato himself (except in Cicero's partial translation of the *Timaeus*), he was steeped in Plotinus, of whom he says in *De beata uita* that he had read "a rather small number of his books and had compared them with those that have revealed to us the divine mysteries," with the result that, he continues, "I was so fired up that I wanted to snap all my moorings."[21] This declaration, like the testimony of *C. acad.* 2.5 which mentions *libri quidam pleni* ("certain books brim full"), looks back, according to most commentators, to *quidam Platonicorum libri* ("some books by the Platonists") mentioned at *Conf.* 7.9.13.

THE RECEPTION OF THE NEOPLATONIC BOOKS (*LIBRI PLATONICORUM*) IN THE *CONFESSIONS*

The Identification of the Neoplatonic Books Read in 386: *a quaestio uexata*

Augustine teaches us in the *Confessions*, in fact, that he did procure some books by neo-Platonists (*quidam Platonicorum libri*), translated into Latin by the orator and philosopher Marius Victorinus,[22] "via a certain man grossly swollen with pride" (*Conf.* 7.9.13), that is, undoubtedly by a pagan hostile to Christianity, perhaps a disciple of Porphyry. He thus discovered neo-Platonism during his time in Milan (384–386), a city where there must have existed, if not a neo-Platonic "circle," at all events some Christian personages who were imbued with this philosophical current. Several times Augustine attests to the "shock"[23] that this reading produced in him, rekindling the passion for wisdom that his reading of Cicero's *Hortensius* had wakened in him when he was 19 years old (*Conf.* 3.4.7–8).

Paradoxically, however, the decisive influence of these books on Augustine does not reduce the mystery concerning their nature,[24] their authors (Plotinus only, Plotinus and Porphyry, or only Porphyry)[25] or their precise contents, a mystery that has not ceased to provide food for learned arguments for over a century. How may we identify these *Libri* and their authors (the *Platonici*)? Augustine does not name these *recentiores Platonici* (more recent followers of Plato) until later in *De civ. D.* 8.4, as we have seen. We must indeed include Plotinus among them, as the early Dialogues explicitly invite us to do (*De beata uita* 1.4), in a passage where we may detect numerous reminders of Plotinus; but we may ask in what form he was read by Augustine in 386, since his disciple Porphyry provided the *Enneads*, which he had arranged and edited, with commentaries and summaries (*Plot.* 26 and 30),[26] and which he had paraphrased, in the form of brief sentences, in his *Aphormai pros ta noêta* (*Sententiae*). Did Augustine have an anthology of Plotinus at hand, or else some treatises commented on by Porphyry, or again

Porphyry's *De regressu animae*, which abounds in extracts from Plotinus and other Platonists?[27]

I have emphasized also the bias that the Latin translation, which has not survived, might have introduced into Augustine's reading of Plotinus' texts,[28] and so it may seem hazardous, in respect to Porphyry, to suppose that Augustine had already read in 386 all those works that he only mentions in that late text, *The City of God*: the *Letter to Anebo* (*De civ. D.* 10.11); *De imaginibus* (*De civ. D.* 7.25); the *De regressu animae*, a treatise named only by Augustine (*De civ. D.* 10.29), and that he certainly knew in 386; and the *Philosophy of Oracles* (*De civ. D.* 19.23).[29] The very name of the Tyrian philosopher is only cited for the first time in the *De consensu euangelistarum*, which dates to 400. Nevertheless, thanks to textual and conceptual parallels, one can draw up a list, in part, of some of the *Enneads* that were undoubtedly read quite early (I.2 [19]; I.3 [20]; I.4 [46]; I.6 [1]; I.8 [51]; III.2–3 [47–48]; IV.3 [17]); V.1 [1]; V.2[11]; V.3 [49]; VI.6 [34]; VI.9 [8],[30] and include already in this period his reading of Porphyry's *Sententiae* and *De regressu animae*.[31] No doubt Augustine continued and deepened his reading of the neo-Platonists.[32] It is also possible that he got from Porphyry some bits of his commentary on Plato, for example that on the *Phaedo*.[33]

Augustine's Reception of the Libri Platonicorum, *According to the* Confessions

In Milan, Christian intellectuals with whom Augustine associated had thus already adapted Platonism to the new Christian religion. For example, Simplicianus congratulated him (*Conf.* 8.2.3) on having read these *Libri Platonicorum* and not those of philosophers who were "full of fallacies and dishonesties that smacked of the principles of this world" (Colossians 2:8). For in the former, on the contrary, one could recognize "the truth of God and his Word" (tr. Boulding). A Platonist could indeed say that the preface to the Gospel of John should be inscribed in golden letters in every church (*De civ. D.* 10.29.2). The *Sermons* of Ambrose, bishop of Milan, delivered in the spring of 386 (*De Isaac, De bono mortis*), are full, as Pierre Courcelle has shown,[34] of "Christianized" reminiscences of Plotinus on the nature of evil, the ascent of the soul to the Good, and on the "good" that death constitutes.

How did Augustine, for his part, conceive of such an appropriation? In Book 7 of the *Confessions*, he presents in the form, *ibi legi/ibi non legi*, both what he took from these *Libri platonicorum* (*ibi legi*), which will become the principal axes of his thought, and, under *non legi*, what belongs properly to Christian doctrine, as opposed to philosophy. He is glad to have read Saint Paul only afterward, and to have found there what was truthfully said by the neo-Platonists, but this time uttered "from your gift of grace" (*Conf.* 7.21.27). What was the content of these insights?

It refers to the teaching that the nature of the divine is incorporeal (*Conf.* 7.20.26), eternal, and immutable. God is defined as being itself (as in Porphyry, while in Plotinus it is the One, beyond being), on which other beings depend by means of participation. The corruption that can affect these latter is a "privation of being," a "deficiency" (*elleipsis* according to Plotinus, *Enn.* I.8 [51].5.6; cf. Ambrose, *De Isaac* 7.60). Thus evil is not a substance (*Conf.* 7.12.18), contrary to what Manichean dualism maintains, which imagines two opposite substances. The entirety of creation, composed of unequal elements but each located according to its function, is good (cf. Plot., *Enn.* III.2 [47].3). This reading brought Augustine, who had had a corporeal conception of God, close to Stoic pantheism (*Conf.* 7.1.2), the idea of a spiritual substance. But in his *Sententiae*, Porphyry established a fundamental opposition between the intelligible, whose parts are internal to one another, and the corporeal, whose parts are external to one another (*Sent.* 33).

Conversion and Ascent to God

Now, the soul is itself a spiritual substance, capable of participating in the intelligence from which it emanates; the soul's superior part coincides with the intellect (Plotinus, *Enn.* IV.8 [6].1.3). Thus, for Plotinus "to discover the divine is neither more nor less than discovering oneself."[35] In Plotinus' treatise *On the Beautiful*, the huge influence of which on Augustine is well known,[36] it is thus a matter of "fleeing toward our most precious part," toward "our father who is below."[37] In his understanding of the return movement toward its origin, Augustine retains this much: To reach God, one must go by way of a *conversio*, a "return" (*epistrophê*) of the soul to its creator, which completes the simple creation and gives the creature its form, and its fullness of being (*Conf.* 13.2.3). Just as in Plotinus, after the process of the *proodos* (that is, the derivation from the first cause), the "return" of the soul and its gaze upon the One subsequently constitute the second hypostasis as Intelligence (*Enn.* V.2 [11].1.9–10).

Now, this return involves a movement toward interiority: "warned by these writings that I must return to myself, I entered under your guidance the innermost places of my being" (*Conf.* 7.10.16). According to Plotinus, it is a matter of seeing beauty in oneself, which he compares to the work of a sculptor: "Go back into yourself and look; and if you do not yet see yourself beautiful, then, just as someone making a statue which has to be beautiful, cuts away here and polishes there . . . , so you too must . . . never stop 'working on your statue' till the divine glory of virtue shines out on you" (Plot., *Enn.* I.6 [1].9.7–11).[38]

The soul must gather itself and withdraw from the senses, and not disperse its desire in what would be an impoverishment, a scattering of its being far from the divine unity. This is a theme that is again indebted to Porphyry's *Sententiae* (37.l.45–50),[39] and which is also found in the prologue to the *De ordine*, a youthful dialogue composed in 386. Augustine there compares the midpoint of a circle to the spiritual center of our life, that is, to God.[40] The influence of Plotinus and Porphyry is palpable in this image of the circular movement of the soul, rotating around a midpoint from which is generated the entire circle, and also in the idea that the soul issues forth from unity, which signifies both multiplicity and a loss of being.[41]

His reading of the neo-Platonists thus revealed to Augustine the immense value of this interiority.[42] In fact, God is simultaneously immanent in the soul and transcendent, "more intimately present to me than my innermost being, and higher than the highest peak of my spirit" (*Conf.* 3.6.11).[43] In gathering into itself, the spirit discovers the divine transcendence that grounds it and draws it to God (*Conf.* 1.1.1: *fecisti nos ad te*)—but with Whom it does not merge: "I saw the immutable light far above my spiritual ken, transcending my mind; not this common light which every carnal eye can see ... but greater" (*Conf.* 7.10.16). But he still finds himself very far from God, "far away from you in a region of unlikeness" (*Conf.* 7.10.16),[44] an expression that goes back to Plato (*Pol.* 273D–E: "bottomless sea of unlikeness"), via Plotinus, *On the Origin of Evils* (*Enn.* I.8 [51]). According to Plotinus, if the soul descends into vice (*kakia*), it "becomes it and enters altogether into the region of unlikeness," falling into the "mud of darkness" (cf. Plato, *Phaedo* 69C), identified with matter (*Enn.* I.8 [51].13.16–19). The soul, then, must rely on the hierarchy of beings to try to rise to its creator. Having thus arrived at "that which is," "in the flash of a tremulous glance" (*in ictu trepidantis aspectus*), it is then driven back by its weakness (*Conf.* 7.17.23). The height of that "ecstasy at Ostia"—an experience that recalls the goal of union with the One in Plotinus—which Augustine shared with his mother Monica (*Conf.* 9.9.24–25) is itself marked by reminiscences of Plotinus,[45] as Suzanne Poque has shown, who examined this four-stage model of ascent (sensible world / intelligible soul / God / descent), as it is developed in these two latter texts from the *Confessions* and in his sermons.[46] The idea of the "illumination" of the soul by the divine principle is itself explicitly attributed to Plotinus in *De civ. D.*[47]

STRUCTURES OF HIERARCHIZED BEING

The Criterion of Mutability

Augustine also inherited in part the hierarchized structure of the world as it was conceived by the neo-Platonists—who were in general "enamored of hierarchical models"—and in particular the version of Porphyry. The definition of being involves the notion of immutability, and mutability characterizes the condition of creation. As heir to the Platonic distinction between being and becoming, Augustine made it the touchstone not only of the dichotomy between the Creator and his creation, but also further subdivided the nature of the mutable according to the categories of time and place, so as to form a hierarchy governing all creatures. Thus, taking his inspiration from Porphyry (*Sententiae* 44), Augustine established the hierarchy God—soul—body, based on the degree of mutability in time alone (the soul), in time and space (the body) or without any mutability at all (God), as in Letter 18, composed in 388.[48]

Such a hierarchical representation, which was already present in the works he composed in Thagaste (388–390), was then complicated with the supplementary distinction in the cause of motion, since the soul and God are both such causes.[49] Besides, nothing in the divine substance is less in the part than in the whole (*De Genesi ad litteram* 8, 15, 38), which looks to *Sentence* 22 of Porphyry, for whom the intellective essence is "homeomeric," "such that in any one of its parts whatsoever, the whole is present" (Porphyry, 441F Smith[50]).

The Intermediate Place of the Soul

Probably inspired once more by Porphyry, for whom "All body is in a place, but none of those things that are in themselves incorporeal, as such, is in a place" (*Aphormai* 1, tr. Dillon), Augustine confers on the soul an intermediate position: it is "something in the middle" (*quiddam medium*), an affirmation one finds in Porphyry[51] and in Plotinus, evoking its "middle rank" (*Enn.* IV.8.7.6: μέση τάξις). These concepts are put in the service of the allegorical method of biblical exegesis. Thus, "the tree of knowledge of good and evil . . . planted in the middle of Paradise" signifies "the halfway centrality of the soul, its integrity in the due order of things."[52] If the soul is ignorant of the dynamic that orients it toward God, and is situated "with its back to God" and "wants to enjoy its own power without reference to God," it commits a sin (it loses its equilibrium) and receives a punishment that marks the end of this orderly integrity, that is, it undergoes an ontological regression (synonyms, for Augustine, of mortality and the weakness of the will).

"Flee the Body Entirely"?

According to his biographer Porphyry, Plotinus "seemed ashamed of being in a body" (Porph., *Plot.* 1). One of the core points in the confrontation between Christian doctrine and Platonism is without a doubt the question of the body, since we know from Augustine that Porphyry proclaimed in *De regressu animae*, "*omne corpus fugiendum est*" (Smith 297F, 21).[53] Augustine himself seems to have been at first receptive to this type of sentiment, as indicated by his *Soliloquies* (*Sol.*), composed in 387, where he affirms: "Sensible things should be utterly fled from." (*Sol.* 1.14.24)[54] In his *Revisions*, at the end of his life, he regretted that view (I.4), ascribed there to "the false philosopher Porphyry," and he corrected it: it is not a matter of fleeing "all sensible things" but only "these things," that is, "corruptible things" (tr. Babcock).

It is true that in his early works, the body could be seen as an obstacle to the contemplation of the truth (cf. *De Genesi contra Manichaeos* 2.20.30). Augustine adopts the same Orphic-Platonic image of the "prison" (*carcer*) to describe the body in relation to the soul (*C. acad.* 1.3.9), which one must escape.[55] But later he distances himself from this view[56] and distinguishes the body of human beings before sin and the fall, on the one hand, and, on the other, the postlapsarian "corruptible" body, which "weighs down the soul," according to his interpretation of Wisdom 9:15,[57] and which is the only one that "one must flee" to achieve blessedness (*De civ. D.* 13.17.2). After death, the soul has as a support for some of its activities "a certain similarity to its body" (*similitudo corporis sui*), an idea that evokes the (pneumatic) vehicle of the soul, an extremely fine "airy, luminous substance," a notion found in Porphyry.[58] The last category, that of glorious or spiritual bodies, pertains to saints after the resurrection.

The theme of the resurrection of the body is itself also one of the key points in the anti-Christian polemic to which Porphyry testifies in *Contra Christianos*, an objection taken up by his supporters and reflected in Augustine's *Epistle* 102 to Deogratias (408),[59] his *Sermons* 240, 241, 242 and 243 of 418,[60] and in Books 13 and 22 of *The City of God*. Augustine notably charges Porphyry with the following contradiction, arising from a comparison that he himself, rather than Porphyry, makes between two of Porphyry's works. Why, he asks, is Porphyry hostile to the idea of resurrection in the *Philosophy of Oracles*, maintaining too that "one must flee the body entirely" in the *De regressu animae*, all the while admitting the existence of the bodies of the blessed immortals located in the celestial realms?[61] How can one accommodate the representation, deriving from Plato's *Timaeus*, of the world as an animated being, altogether happy and eternal, if, in order to be happy, one must entirely flee the body?[62] And how can one reconcile, once again, this hostility to the idea of resurrection with the discourse of the Demiurge in *Timaeus* 41AB, who grants incorruptibility to the lower gods, a passage that Augustine loved to quote, in Cicero's translation?[63]

Furthermore, in this apologetic use of Platonic works, Augustine sets the various *Platonici* against one another, and is grateful to Porphyry for having "corrected" his predecessors, Plato and Plotinus, in denying the metensomatosis that they accepted (*De civ. D.* 10.30; 13.19 = Smith 300bF).[64] He even tries to combine different aspects of their respective views (those of Plato and Porphyry, and even that of Varro), so as to forge a distinctly Christian viewpoint (only an incorruptible body can offer the guarantee of happiness that is promised to souls after death),[65] as if these pagan writers had had a presentiment of this "truth."

Objections Concerning the Divine, Its Nature, and Its Role

Grace

These objections, offered from an apologetic perspective, are expressed especially in *The City of God*, where the principal interlocutor is Porphyry, who had composed the *Philosophy of Oracles* and a *Contra Christianos* in which he gave support to contemporary criticisms of Christianity that Augustine was led to refute.[66] Porphyry had in fact testified to his concern for the health of the soul and for various religious traditions and practices, such as theurgy (which he criticized in his *Letter to Anebo*), that were uniquely able, according to him, to purify the "spiritual" part of the soul (*De regressu animae* = Smith 289b F). This, according to Augustine (*De civ. D.* 10.16), was too obliging a step toward theurgy, since Christ offers purification simultaneously to the intelligence, the spirit, and the body (*De civ. D.* 10.27). In this same book, Augustine brings up what is sometimes called Porphyry's "pessimism"[67]: only a small number of people can join God by virtue of their intelligence, an opinion that Augustine shared in the beginning (*De ordine* 2.5.16). Here, however, he makes an effort to see in these propositions of Porphyry the Christian idea of grace, by way of a specific claim: "You do, however, admit that there is such a thing as grace, for you say that it has been granted (*esse concessum*) only to a few to attain to God by the power of intelligence" (*De civ. D.* 10.29.1 = Smith 297F). Augustine asserts that Porphyry relied on Plato (*Phaedo* 66B) to defend this view, in *De regressu animae*,[68] where he affirms that the soul, because of the body, cannot arrive at the perfection of wisdom, but that it will be able to after death.

The "uia uniuersalis"

Again, Augustine affirms that Porphyry claimed (in *De regressu animae*) that he failed to find the *uia uniuersalis* that he had likewise sought via *cognitio historialis*,[69] and he declared that "no view containing a universal way of the soul's liberation has as yet been received into any specific philosophical school—not from any supremely true philosophy, nor from the morals and practice of the Indians, nor from the initiations of the Chaldeans—and that no such way has as yet come to his knowledge from his historical inquiries" (*De civ. D.* 10.32.1 (tr. Babcock) = fr. 12 Bidez = 302 F Smith = 15 A Madec-Goulet-tr. Goulet, p. 159–161).

Now, that was doubtless not the meaning of the original Greek that lay behind the expression *uia uniuersalis* ("way of salvation").[70] For Augustine, Porphyry simply did not wish to see the universal *uia*, that is, the one accessible to all that Christ offers. This is of a piece with the distinction in *Conf.* 7.20.26 between "those who see the goal but not the way to it and the Way to our beatific homeland, a homeland to be not merely described but lived in." With this double image, which is a leitmotif of his œuvre, in which the *uia* of John 14:6 leads straight to the "homeland" that Plotinus desired, Augustine opposes the pride of the neo-Platonists to the humility of Christ. He is probably referring, in fact, to Plotinus, *Enn.* I. 6 [1].8: "Our country from which we came is there. Our Father is there."[71] And he takes from him the idea that one cannot approach God by means of spatial motion (on foot, by chariots, or ships: *Conf.* 1.8.28, *Conf.* 8.8.19: *non illuc ibatur nauibus aut quadrigis aut pedibus*). One approaches God, Augustine adds, by one's "will," one of his chief concepts.

The Nature of the Divine

Moreover, Augustine could not identify the Trinity, composed of three equal Persons, with the strongly hierarchical structure of Plotinus' three hypostases, The One, intelligence, and the soul.[72] In fact, he observes, Plotinus located the nature of the soul after the second hypostasis, which Porphyry, for his part, calls "paternal intelligence" (*patrikos nous*, translated as *paternus intellectus* or *paterna mens*). Porphyry places between the Father and the Son a "middle," which Augustine, however, refuses to identify with the Holy Spirit (*De civ. D.* 10.23 = Smith 284 F).[73] For him, it is not a matter of affirming "two or three principles" or "two or three gods" (*De civ. D.* 10.24). Nevertheless, Augustine does identify the Son with the divine Intellect, which contains, as Plotinus too held, the eternal *rationes* of mutable beings.[74]

Esse-vivere-intellegere

Plotinus inherited, as we know, the intelligible triad *esse-uiuere-intellegere* from an earlier Platonic tradition, which was based on the *Sophist* 248E, and he defined complete or plenary being of the second hypostasis (the Intellect) as the simultaneous possession of being, life, and intelligence (*Enn.* V.6 [24].6.20–24). Augustine for his part took up this "triad"[75] in order to define, in *De Trinitate* (*Trin.*) 6.10.11, the Form (*Species*), that is to say, the divine Word, but also to imagine God himself, in whom "to be, to live, and to think" are mutually implied and form an indivisible and indissociable unity. This unity stands in stark contrast to what happens in creation, where the three are disposed hierarchically and separately.[76] Nevertheless, around the year 400, there obtruded a different triad in connection with the "psychological analogy" of the Trinity in the *mens* (*memoria, intellegentia, uoluntas*): *esse, nosse, uelle* (*Conf.* 13.11.12), a formula that corresponds to the increasing importance of the concept of the will in Augustine's thought after the *De libero arbitrio*, and which had, instead, a Ciceronian precedent.[77]

Providence

The reception of providence is always critical where Christian dogma is directly in play. Augustine proclaimed his proximity to Plotinus on the matter of a Providence that extends "from the supreme God whose beauty is intelligible ... to the lowly and earthly things" (*De civ. D.* 10.14),[78] and in fact he took from the *Peri pronoias* many images (the color black, the choryphaeus) intended to show that the order of the world as a whole is always preserved. But his conception of a Providence connected to the will of a personal God distanced him, in turn, from Plotinus, who rejected the idea of a universal providence "that belongs to the individual, and which is a calculation before action," in the sense of "a foreseeing and calculation (*logismos*) on God's part about how the All might come into existence and how things might be as good as possible" *(Enn.* III.2 [47].1.11–12 and 18–19).

The Incarnation and the True Mediator

The Incarnation of Christ is part of what Augustine did not find in the *Libri Platonicorum* (*ibi non legi*), and there certainly lies the major stumbling block. He could not help but collide with the *Philosophy Drawn from the Oracles*, where Porphyry saw in Christ nothing more than a man of outstanding wisdom, a wonderworker whose disciples went astray.[79] It is all the more interesting to note that, precisely in order to legitimize the idea of the Incarnation, Augustine made use of a Porphyrean notion, that of a "union without mingling" (ἀσύγχυτος ἕνωσις), which allows each substance in the mix to retain its integrity. Porphyry no doubt developed this idea in his *Zêtêma* "On the Union of the Soul and the Body,"[80] and which Augustine appropriated in order to conceive of the "mixture" of two incorporeal substances, in this case the divine Word and the human soul (*Ep.* 137 to Volusianus). We have here an example of *retorsio*, that is, showing that a claim is self-defeating. But, in a more positive way, Augustine also resorted to this Porphyrean idea to imagine, in Book 9 of *De Trinitate*, an *unio inconfusa*, which is neither *iunctio* (addition) nor *commixtio* (mixture)—connecting the human *mens*, its *notitia* and its *amor* in the trinity of the human soul, created in the image of the divine Trinity.[81]

Another example of this recourse to Platonic motifs is the way that Christ, and not the demons, is, in Augustine's eyes, the true mediator between God and human beings, which allows him to bridge the gap between the eternal and the temporal, since he is eternal like God but was incarnated historically. Now, in *Cons. euang.* 1.35.53, Augustine justified the mediation of Christ, as he would do in *Trin.* 4.18.24, by relying on the same quotation of *Timaeus* 29C: "As eternity is related to that which is created, so is truth to faith," in Cicero's translation.[82] And in Book 9 of *The City of God*, he cited the Latin translation of Plotinus *Enn.* I.6.8 (*Fugiendum est ad carissimam patriam*), and recalled the requirement of *Theaetetus* 176B (*similem Deo fieri*, "become like God"). But according to Augustine, only Christ, who became "like us" by virtue of his humanity, can cure and liberate the soul.[83]

Cognitive Activity and the Immortality of the Soul

Augustine is seen to emulate Plotinus especially in his analysis of sensible perception, which the soul does not, according to him, undergo passively but in which, on the contrary, it manifests its activity.[84]

We know too that Porphyry had a marked influence on Augustine very generally in the area of psychology.[85] In the course of studying his analysis of *uisiones* (corporeal, spiritual, intellectual) from this angle,[86] Stéphane Toulouse concluded that, without borrowing the notion of the "imaginative soul," "Augustine derived from the neo-Platonists the form of knowledge that is specific to the soul at the level at which it exercises its cognitive activity, and this permitted him to hierarchize the various types of visions, all the while maintaining the psychic unity of the individual consciousness thanks to the notions of *uoluntas* and *intentio*."[87] As we can see from *Trin.* 11, whether for sensation or for thought, it is the *intentio* (which recalls the notion of *prosochê* in Porphyry (*Abst.* 1.41.5) or *uoluntas* that ensures consciousness in individual experience.[88]

In his youthful works, Augustine could adopt the Platonic theory of reminiscence (*Meno* 81D and *Phaedo* 72E), which he knew *via* Cicero (*Tusc.* 1.57–58). Thus, in *De quantitate animae* 34, he writes: "what is called learning is nothing else than the act of recollecting and remembering." That is one proof of the immortality of the soul, based on the idea that "truth is internal to the mind."[89] Nevertheless, he later criticized this theory as potentially implying the idea of the pre-existence of souls,[90] and he therefore preferred the theory of illumination.[91] Furthermore, in *De immortate animae* 6—a text that is a sketch for a future Book 3 of the *Soliloquies*—Augustine connects this theory of knowledge as reminiscence to the proof of the immortality of the soul: since it finds in itself a knowledge of eternal things, it can only be immortal.

We have further evidence on this topic of the complexity of the Augustinian synthesis in comparison to his neo-Platonic sources. As Christian Tornau has shown, the proof of the immortality of the soul in the *Soliloquies* (according to the argument *in subjecto esse*) is not of Porphyrean inspiration, but arises from an interpretation—erroneous, as it happens—of the *Categories* of Aristotle[92] *via* the *Isagogē* of Porphyry.[93] However, out of a wish to strengthen his proof, Augustine, in the *De immortalitate animae* 14, appeals to a concept of causality that indeed betrays an allegiance to neo-Platonism (Plotinus), namely the eternal presence of its own cause in the *ratio* of the human soul.

Conclusion

It is necessary to insist on both continuity and difference in Augustine's reception of Platonism. His appropriation of Plato was indirect, via Cicero and neo-Platonism. He saw in Platonism above all the opposition between the intelligible and the sensible, and the affirmation of transcendence. If we look to the neo-Platonism of Plotinus and Porphyry, many aspects of his thought bear its traces and were nourished by it, beginning with his philosophical and spiritual program of conversion. This influence is operative also in his ontology and his assertion of the goodness of creation, as well as in his description of life and the activities of the soul (in the *Confessions* and the *De Trinitate*), and even in his understanding of the divine. To be sure, as his thought evolved he came to favor a critical approach to those aspects of neo-Platonism that were least compatible with Christianity (the hierarchized hypostases, the procession model, the role of matter), and he gave more space to apologetics and indeed to polemics. This latter is especially noticeable in *The City of God*, whose very structure proceeds by way of a critical reading of Porphyry. All in all, we may say that the special achievement of Augustine is that of having "transformed" Platonism by virtue of a new interest in the finite subjectivity of mankind. He thus offered a new description of interiority in respect to transcendence, as it was reconceived at the dawn of Christianity. This was anything but a superficial appropriation that may be dismissed as just some "Church Father Platonism."

Notes

1. Dillon (1977); Moreschini (2015).
2. O'Meara (2015)
3. Courcelle (1943) 440.
4. As Köckert (2009) showed in connection with the influence of Platonic interpretations of the *Timaeus* on the cosmology of the Greek Fathers (Origen, Basile, Gregory of Nyssa). For Neoplatonism into the medieval period, see Kijewska in this volume.
5. Daniélou (1961); de Vogel (1985); von Ivánka (1964).
6. Solignac (1957).
7. See de Vogel (1985).
8. Alfaric (1918) vs. Boyer (1920); Madec (1994); see Bouton-Touboulic (2004b).
9. Madec (1994) 27–43.
10. *De ordine* 1.11.32; cf. Catapano (2018) 719. This information can be found in Cicero; see *Conf.* 3.4.8.
11. Tr. King (1995) 87.
12. Tr. King (1995), modified.
13. *De uera religione* 3.3.
14. Cf. Hadot (2010).
15. *De civ. D.* 8.4: from the *C. Acad.* (386) onward, this is how he interprets Plato, by adhering to the idea of a "closet (esoteric) dogmatism," concealed behind the facade of the skepticism of the New Academy; cf. Lévy (1978); Bouton-Touboulic (2018) 238.
16. Fuhrer (1997) 89.
17. *Ep.* 118.20: *sapientia diuina* is the final goal of this threefold division. Cf. Hadot (2010) 274; Testard (1958) II.97.
18. *C. acad.* 3.19.41. Cf. Courcelle (1943) 165.
19. Tr. Babcock (2012) 256. He does not appear to have known the works of Iamblichus.
20. August., *Ep.* 6.1, tr. Teske (2001) 25.
21. *De beata uita* 1.4. There is the same image of fiery enthusiasm in *C. acad.* 2.2.5.
22. *Conf.* 8.2.3. Marius Victorinus's theological oeuvre is itself influenced by Porphyry. Cf. Hadot (1968).
23. Lane Fox (2005) 25–29.
24. Hadot (1960) 243, Erler (2018) 763. According to Smith (1987) 769–770, the only acceptable conclusion is a *non liquet*. See Cary (2000) 33.

25. Henry (1934) 105–106 defends the view of an essentially Plotinian influence, whereas Theiler (1966 [1933]) argues for Porphyry's influence. But undoubtedly one must factor in both. On these three interpretations, see Beatrice (1989) 248–250.
26. Goulet-Cazé (1982) 306–307 and 322–323: Porphyry added to his edition of the *Enneads* commentaries, summaries, and arguments (*epicheirêmata*).
27. Hadot (1960) 241; with a few exceptions (Solignac (1957); Smith (1974)). The general view, in line with Courcelle (1943), appears to be that Augustine had read the *De regressu animae* in 386. Some scholars (O'Meara (1959)) have posited that this work is the same as *Philosophy of the Oracles*.
28. Clark (2007) 128.
29. O'Meara (1959) maintains that Augustine read only Porphyry's *Philosophy from Oracles*; Beatrice (1989) argues that this book may be identified with some others works by Porphyry (among them *De regressu animae*, *Letter to Anebo* and *Contra Christianos*). This latter is mentioned in *Ep.* 102.8, composed in 408; on its possible presence in the *City of God*, see Clark (2011).
30. Henry (1934); du Roy (1966) 70–71; Solignac (^{2}1992) 110–111; Beatrice (1989) 251; Cary (2000).
31. Courcelle (1943); Madec (1992) vs. Solignac (1957) 461; Smith (1987) 770.
32. See Cary (2000) 34, according to whom Augustine will establish his "distinctive program of inward turn" beginning only with his deeper readings in the following decade; cf. Lane Fox (2005) 26; Catapano (2006) cxxiv.
33. Mommert (1907) xxvi–xxvii. Cf. Hadot (1956) on Ambrose, who allegedly integrated aspects of commentaries on Plato and Plotinus which he would have found in *De regressu animae*.
34. Courcelle (^{2}1968)
35. Laurent (1999) 17.
36. Henry (1934) 105–119.
37. *Enn.* I.6 [1].8.16; 20; summarized by Augustine in *De civ. D.* 9.17:
38. Tr. Amstrong (1966) 259. Cf. Plot. *Enn.*, I.6 [1].7.4–6: in reascending toward the Good, one has to remove this clothing. The image of undressing as a form of purification and return to oneself recurs in Augustine *De ordine* 2.2.6.
39. Ed. Brisson (2005). The soul is thus called sometimes *Penia*, sometimes *Poros*, names derived from Plato's *Symposium*. Cf. also Porph., *Sententiae* 40.3–5.
40. *De ordine* 1.1.3.
41. Solignac (1957)
42. 460. See Madec (1994) 152.
43. Taylor (1989) 176 emphasizes this difference with Plato ("Le principal chemin qui nous mène à Dieu ne passe pas par le domaine de l'objet mais 'à l'intérieur' de nous-mêmes"), and argues that Augustine initiates a "position de réflexivité radicale."
44. The parable of the prodigal son adds another layer to this echo of Plotinus.
45. Mandouze (1954).
46. Poque (1975); *Conf.* 7.17.23; *Conf.* 9.10.24–25; *Serm.* 52.16–17; *Enarrationes in Psalmos* 41.7–8; *In Iohannis euangelium tractatus* 20.11, 12, 13, a text in which a mediating influence of Basil of Cesarea can be detected, (*Homilia* 15 *De fide*), who in turn was influenced by Plotinus.
47. *De civ. D.* 10.2.
48. *Ep.* 18.2, tr. Teske (2001) 51.

49. *De Genesi ad litteram* 8.20.39; see Bouton-Touboulic (2004a) 112; *Serm. contra paganos* (= *Serm.* Dolbeau (^{2}2009) 26.28) preached in 404.
50. Pépin (1999) 98–99.
51. *Sententiae* 5: "The soul is something intermediate (μέσον τι) between the indivisible essence and the divisible essence in the domain of the body." See Theiler (1966) 184–186.
52. *De Genesi contra Manicheos* 2.9.12, tr. Hill (1991) 79.
53. See *De civ. D.* 10.29. We know the title of the work only thanks to Augustine.
54. *Sol.* I.14.24. See also *De quantitate animae* 33.76, composed in 388.
55. Courcelle (1965) 230.
56. Russell (1981) 164.
57. Bochet (2011).
58. 185F Smith, 4–6. This vehicle is the recipient of the soul's punishment after death, since Hell is not a physical place in *De Genesi ad litteram* 12.32.60. Cf. Chase (2005) 239; Toulouse (2009) 240–241; Pépin (1993) 297.
59. Written around 408 in order to respond to questions of a pagan friend that someone sent him, "some of which," he says, "were posed by the philosopher Porphyry" (*Retract.* 2.31). See Bochet (2011).
60. Pépin (1964) 423–461 has shown that the objection against the resurrection that rests on the order of the elements, discussed in *Sermon* 242, originated with Porphyry and probably his *Contra Christianos*.
61. *De civ. D.* 10.29.2. Hadot (1960) 218.
62. Ibid. and *De civ. D.* 13.17.2 (example of the World Soul, with the world itself identified with Jupiter; Augustine paraphrases Plat. *Ti.* 36E). See Bochet (2009) 291.
63. *De civ. D.* 13.16; cf. *De civ. D.* 22.26; *Serm.* 241.8. Cf. Cic., *Timaeus* 11.40. See Testard (1958) II.58–59; Hadot (1960); TeSelle (1974) 136; Sodano (1965) 22; Russell (1981) 164; Bochet (2009) 278.
64. *Conf.* 7.12.18.
65. *De civ. D.* 22.25–28. See Hadot (1960) 218–220.
66. As in *De consensu euangelistarum* I.23; see Madec (1992); or the *quaestiones* at *Ep.* 102 (cf. Bochet (2011)); on "Porphyrius Siculus," see *Retract.* 2.31.
67. Cipriani (1997).
68. See Clark (2007) 134.
69. The meaning is a matter of debate; Studer (1996) sees in the passage an allusion to an interest Porphyry may have had in history; O'Daly (1999) 133n45 reads the passage differently: "study/investigation of (scholarly) evidence."
70. Cf. Clark (2007) 136–137: "it means that Porphyry expected a narrow range of people who could attain liberation of the higher soul, but a wide range of ethnic traditions that provided ways to liberation."
71. *Enn.* I.6 [1].6.19–20: "the soul's becoming something good and beautiful is being made like God" (cf. Plat. *Tht.* 176B), tr. Amstrong (1966), 256 and 251.
72. *De civ. D.* 10.23. O'Meara (2015) 323.
73. See Porph., *De regressu animae* fr. 8. Cf. Fokin (2013) who establishes a connection between this notion, which is distinctive of Porphyry, and the "intelligible triad" (*esse uiuere intellegere*).
74. See *Diu. Quaest.* 83.46, 2 *De Ideis*.
75. See du Roy (1966) on the different formulations of the Trinity involved in creation, which correspond to the threefold ontological dimension of the created realm: *esse, species, ordo*;

Theiler (1966) 32–35 argues for a connection between the latter formula and Porphyry's version (*ousia, eidos, taxis*).
76. *De diversis Quaestionibus octaginta tribus* 83.51.2. See Fokin (2013) 61.
77. That is *memoria, intellegentia, prouidentia*. See Ayres (2010) 134–135; 308–309.
78. *Enn*. III.2.13.18–29. Henry (1934) 122–123. Augustine here quotes *Matthew* 6:28.
79. Madec (1992).
80. *Ep*. 137.11. Cf. Pépin (1964); Fortin (1954).
81. *De Trinitate* 9.4.7. Pépin (1977) 254–260.
82. *De consensu euangelistarum* 1.35.53 (tr. Paffenroth (2014) 167): *Quantum ad id quod ortum est aeternitas ualet, tantum ad fidem ueritas*. Cf. Cic. *Timaeus* 3.8. See Madec (1992) 27–28.
83. *De civ. D*. 9.17. Henry (1934) 107.
84. O'Meara (2015) 315.
85. Theiler (1966); Smith (1974) 771; Chase (2005) 241.
86. Dulaey (1973) had already made the case for Porphyry's influence on the three visions—corporeal, spiritual, noetic—which Augustine distinguishes in *De Genesi ad litteram* 12.
87. Toulouse (2009), 245–246; Alici (2008) 663: "in the more mature psychology of *trin*. Augustine unifies the entire spiritual life, from sense perception to *uoluntas*."
88. Toulouse (2009) 246.
89. Catapano (2013) 116. See also *Ep*. 7.2 (and the note in Bermon 2011: 551–552).
90. *Retract*. 1.1.4.
91. *De Trinitate* 12.15.24. Catapano (2013) 116.
92. He read the *Decem Categoriae* in a Latin translation in his youth (see *Conf*. 4, 16, 28); on the identification of this text and its possible "background" in Porphyry, see Lössl (2012).
93. Tornau (2017).

References

Alfaric, P. (1918). *L'évolution intellectuelle de Saint Augustin*. (Paris).
Alici, L. (2008). *s.v. intentio*. In C. Mayer et al. (eds.), *Augustinus Lexikon* 3 (Basel), 662–665.
Ayres, L. (2010). *Augustine and the Trinity*. (Cambridge).
Babcock, W., tr. (2010). *Saint Augustine*, Revisions. R. Teske, intr. *Works of Saint Augustine (WSA)* I/6. (New York).
Babcock, W., tr., intr. (2012). *Saint Augustine*, City of God (De civitate Dei *I–X*). B. Ramsey, notes. *WSA* I/2. (New York).
Beatrice, P. F. (1989). "*Quosdam Platonicorum libros*: The Platonic Readings of Augustine in Milan." *Vig. Chr*. 43: 248–281.
Bermon, E., and G. O'Daly, eds. (2012). *Le De Trinitate de saint Augustin: Exégèse, logique et noétique*. (Paris).
Blumenthal H. J., and R. A. Markus, eds. (1981). *Neoplatonism and Early Christian Thought: Essays in Honour of A. H. Armstrong*. (London).
Bochet, I. (2009). "Résurrection et réincarnation: La polémique d'Augustin contre les platoniciens et contre Porphyre dans les *Sermons* 240–242," in Partoens, Dupont, and Lamberigts, 267–298.
Bochet, I. (2011). "Les *quaestiones* attribuées à Porphyre dans la *Lettre* 102 d'Augustin," in Morlet, 371–394.
Boulding, M., tr. (1997). *Saint Augustine*, The Confessions. *WSA* I/1. (New York).

Bouton-Touboulic, A.-I. (2004a) *L'ordre caché: La notion d'ordre chez saint Augustin* (Paris).
Bouton-Touboulic, A.-I. (2004b). "L'approche philosophique de l'œuvre d'Augustin au miroir de la *Revue des Études Augustiniennes*." *Revue des études augustiniennes et patristiques* 50(2): 325–347.
Bouton-Touboulic, A.-I. (2018). "'*Os illud Platonis*': Platonisme, scepticisme et néoplatonisme dans le *Contra Academicos* d'Augustin," in Guillaumin and Lévy, 233–256.
Boyer, C. (1920). *Christianisme et Néo-platonisme dans la formation de saint Augustin.* (Paris).
Brisson, L., ed. (2005). *Porphyre*, Sentences. J. Dillon, English tr. (Paris).
Cary, P. (2000). *Augustine's Invention of the Inner Self: The Legacy of a Christian Platonist* (Oxford).
Catapano, G. (2006). *Agostino, Tutti i Dialoghi.* (Milan).
Catapano, G. (2013). "The Epistemological Background of Augustine's Dialogues," in Föllinger and Müller, 107–122.
Catapano, G. (2018). s.v. *Philosophia.* In R. Dodaro, C. Mayer and C. Müller (eds.), *Augustinus Lexikon* 4 (Basel), 719–741.
Chase, M. (2005). "Porphyre et Augustin: Des trois sortes de 'visions' au corps de résurrection." *Revue d'études augustiniennes et patristiques* 51: 233–256.
Cipriani, N. (1997). "Il rifiuto del pessimismo porfiriano nei primi scritti di Agostino." *Augustinianum* 37(1): 113–146.
Clark, G. (2007). "Augustine's Porphyry and the Universal Way of Salvation," in Karamanolis and Sheppard, 127–140.
Clark, G. (2011). "*Acerrimus inimicus*? Porphyry and the *City of God*," in Morlet, 395–406.
Courcelle, P. (1943). *Les Lettres grecques en Occident: De Macrobe à Cassiodore.* (Paris).
Courcelle, P. (1965). "Tradition platonicienne et tradition chrétienne du corps-prison (*Phédon* 62b; *Cratyle* 400c)," *Rev. Ét. Lat.* 43: 406–443.
Courcelle, P. (^{2}1968). *Recherches sur les Confessions de Saint Augustin.* (Paris)
Daniélou, J. (1961). *Message évangélique et culture hellénistique aux IIe et IIIe siècles* (Paris).
de Vogel, C. J. (1985). "Platonism and Christianity: A Mere Antagonism or a Profound Common Ground?" *Vig. Chr.* 39: 1–62.
Dillon, J. (1977). *The Middle Platonists* (London).
Dolbeau, F., ed. (^{2}2009). *Augustin d'Hippone, Vingt-six sermons au peuple d'Afrique* (Paris).
Dulaey, M. (1973). *Le rêve dans la vie et la pensée de saint Augustin.* (Paris).
du Roy, O. (1966). *L'intelligence de la foi en la Trinité selon saint Augustin.* (Paris).
Erler, M. (2018). "*Platonicorum Libri.*" In R. Dodaro, C. Mayer, and C. Müller (eds.), *Augustinus Lexikon* 4 (Basel), 762–764.
Fokin, A. R. (2013). "The Doctrine of the 'Intelligible Triad' in Neoplatonism and Patristics," in M. Vincent (ed.), *Neoplatonism and Patristics*. Studia Patristica 68(6). (Leuven): 45–71.
Föllinger, S., and G. M. Müller, eds. (2013). *Der Dialog in der Antike: Formen und Funktionen einer literarischen Gattung zwischen Philosophie, Wissensvermittlung und dramatischer Inszenierung.* (Berlin).
Fortin, E. L. (1954). "Saint Augustin et la doctrine néoplatonicienne de l'âme." *Augustinus Magister* 3: 371–380.
Fuhrer, T. (1997). "Die Platoniker und die ciuitas Dei. (Buch VIII–X)," in Horn, 87–108.
Goulet-Cazé, M.-O. (1982). "L'édition porphyrienne des *Ennéades*. État de la question," in L. Brisson, M.-O. Goulet-Cazé, R. Goulet, and D. O'Brien (eds.), *Porphyre, La Vie de Plotin I, Travaux préliminaires et index grec complet* (Paris): 280–327.

Goulet-Cazé, M.-O., G. Madec, and D. O'Brien, eds. (1992). *SOFIHS MAIHTORES*. *"Chercheurs de sagesse": Hommage à Jean Pépin*. (Paris).
Guillaumin, J.-B., and C. Lévy, eds. (2018). Plato Latinus: *Aspects de la transmission de Platon en latin dans l'Antiquité*. (Turnhout).
Hadot, P. (1956). "Platon et Plotin dans trois *Sermons* de s. Ambroise." *Rev. Ét. Lat.* 34: 202–220.
Hadot, P. (1960). "Citations de Porphyre chez saint Augustin (À propos d'un ouvrage récent)." *Revue d'études augustiniennes et patristiques* 6: 205–244.
Hadot, P. (1968). *Porphyre et Victorinus*. 2 vols. (Paris).
Hadot, P. (2010). "La présentation du platonisme par Augustin," in P. Hadot, *Études de patristique et d'études des concepts* (Paris), 273–281.
Henry, P. (1934). *Plotin et l'Occident: Firmicus Maternus, Marius Victorinus, Saint Augustin et Macrobe* (Louvain).
Hill, E., tr. (1991). *Saint Augustine*, The Trinity. *WSA* I/5. (New York).
Horn, C., ed. (1997). *Augustinus, De ciuitate dei*. (Berlin).
Karamanolis, G., and A. Sheppard, eds. (2007). *Studies on Porphyry*. (London).
King, P. tr. (1995). Augustine, *Against the Academicians and the Teacher*. (Indianapolis).
Köckert, C. (2009). *Christliche Kosmologie und kaiserzeitliche Philosophie* (Tübingen).
Lane Fox, R. (2005). "Movers and Shakers," in Smith, 19–50.
Laurent, J. (1999). *L'homme et le monde selon Plotin*. (Paris).
Lévy, C. (1978). "Scepticisme et dogmatisme dans l'Académie: 'L'ésotérisme' d'Arcésilas." *Rev. Ét. Lat.* 56: 335–348.
Lössl, J. (2012). "Augustine's use of Aristotle's *Categories* in *De Trinitate* in the Light of History of the Latin Text of the Categories before Boethius," in Bermon and O'Daly, 99–121.
Madec, G., and R. Goulet (2012). "Porphyre de Tyr, *Sur le retour de l'âme*: Un recueil provisoire des témoignages et fragments avec une traduction française et des notes," in I. Bochet (ed.), *Augustin philosophe et prédicateur: Hommage à G. Madec* (Paris), 67–184.
Madec, G. (1992). "Augustin et Porphyre: Ébauche d'un bilan des recherches et des conjectures," in Goulet-Cazé, Madec, and O' Brien, 367–382.
Madec, G. (1994). *Petites études Augustiniennes*. (Paris).
Mandouze, A. (1954). "'L'extase d'Ostie': Possibilités et limites de la méthode des parallèles textuels." *Augustinus Magister* 1: 67–84.
Mommert, B., ed. (1907). *Porphyrios*, Sententiae ad intelligibilia ducentes. (Leipzig).
Moreschini, C. (2015). *Apuleius and the Metamorphoses of Platonism*. (Turnhout).
Morlet, S., ed. (2011). *Le traité de Porphyre contre les chrétiens: Un siècle de recherches, nouvelles questions*. (Paris).
O'Daly, G. (1999). *Augustine's City of God*. (Oxford).
O'Meara, D. J. (2015). "Plotinus," in L. P. Gearson (ed.), *The Cambridge History of Philosophy in Late Antiquity*, vol. 1 (Cambridge), 301–324.
O'Meara, J. J. (1959). *Porphyry's "Philosophy from Oracles" in Augustine*. (Paris).
Paffenroth, K., tr. (2014). *Saint Augustine*, Agreement among the Evangelists. *WSA* I/15. (New York).
Partoens, G., A. Dupont, and M. Lamberigts, eds. (2009). Ministerium sermonis: *Philological, Historical and Theological Studies on Augustine's* Sermones ad populum. (Brepols)
Pépin, J. (1964). *Théologie cosmique et théologie chrétienne (Ambroise Exam. I, 1–4)*. (Paris).
Pépin, J. (1977). Ex Platonicoroum persona. *Études sur les lectures philosophiques de saint Augustin*. (Amsterdam).

Pépin, J. (1993). "Pourquoi l'âme automotrice aurait-elle besoin d'un véhicule? (*Nouveaux schèmes porphyriens chez saint Augustin*, II)," in J. J. Cleary (ed.), *Traditions of Platonism: Essays in Honour of J. Dillon* (Aldershot), 293–305.

Pépin, J. (1999). "La hiérarchie par le degré de mutabilité (Nouveaux schèmes porphyriens chez s. Augustin." *Documenti e studi sulla tradizione filosofica medievale* 19: 89–107.

Poque, S. (1975). "L'expression de l'anabase plotinienne dans la prédication de saint Augustin et ses sources." *Recherches augustiniennes* 10: 187–215.

Russell, R. (1981). "The Role of Neoplatonism in St. Augustine's *De ciuitate dei*," in Blumenthal and Markus, 150–170.

Smith, A. (1974). *Porphyry's Place in the Neoplatonic Tradition*. (The Hague).

Smith, A. (1987). "Porphyrian Studies since 1913," *ANRW* II, 36(2): 717–773.

Smith, A., ed. (1993). *Porphyrii Fragmenta*. (Leipzig).

Smith, A. (2005). *The Philosopher and Society in Late Antiquity: Essays in Honour of Peter Brown*. (Swansea).

Sodano, R. (1965). "L'interpretazione ciceroniana di 'Timeo 41A7–B6' nella citazioni testuali di Sant'Agostrino." *Revue d'études augustiniennes et patristiques* 11, 15–24.

Solignac, A. (1957). "Réminiscences plotiniennes et porphyriennes dans le début du *De ordine* de saint Augustin." *Archives de philosophie* 20: 446–465.

Solignac, A. (^{2}1992). *Œuvres de saint Augustin, Les Confessions*. Bibliothèque Augustinienne 13. (Paris).

Studer, B. (1996). "La *cognitio historialis* di Porfirio nel *De civitate dei*," in E. Cantarelli (ed.), *Il De civitate dei: L'opera, le interpretazioni, l'influsso* (Rome), 51–65.

Taylor, C. (1989). *Sources of the self*. (Cambridge, Mass.) (C. Melançon, tr. (1998): *Les sources du moi: La formation de l'identité moderne*. (Paris)).

TeSelle, E. (1974). "Porphyry and Augustine."*Augustinian Studies* 6: 113–145.

Testard, M. (1958). *Saint Augustin et Cicéron*. 2 vols. (Paris).

Theiler, W. (1966 [1933]) "Porphyrios und Augustin," in W. Theiler, *Forschungen zum Neuplatonismus* (Berlin), 160–248.

Tornau, C. (2017). "*Ratio in subjectio*? The Sources of Augustine's Proof for the Immortality of the Soul in the *Soliloquia* and Its Defense in *De immortalitate animae*." *Phronesis* 62: 319–354.

Toulouse, S. (2009). "Influences néoplatoniciennes sur l'analyse augustinienne des *visiones*." *Archives de Philosophie* 72: 225–247.

von Ivánka, E. (1964). Plato Christianus: *Übernahme und Umgestaltung des Platonismus durch die Vater* (Einsiedeln). (E. Kessler-Slotta, R. Brague, and J.- Y. Lacoste, tr. (1990): Plato Christianus. *La réception critique du platonisme chez les Pères de l'Église*. (Paris)).

CHAPTER 31

ROMAN QUASITY
A Matrix of Byzantine Thought and History

ANTHONY KALDELLIS

SCHOLARS of ancient Rome have discussed, but not yet named, a legal move that operated in many domains of ancient Roman thought and practice, enabling the Romans to treat one thing as if (quasi) it were another. That maneuver is here baptized quasity and studied as a matrix of important aspects of Byzantine (east Roman) history and social practice. Specifically, it enabled the east Romans to treat Constantinople as if it were Rome; to venerate icons of Christ and the saints as if they were the holy figures that they depicted (but knowing that ontologically they were not); to create fictive kinship in legal, monastic, and religious relations; and to assimilate foreigners into Roman society.

Byzantium is the modern name for the eastern half of the ancient Roman empire that survived until the fifteenth century, a full thousand years after the fall of the western Roman empire in the fifth century. It was predominantly Greek-speaking and Christian Orthodox, but regarded itself fundamentally as a Roman polity. Its political thought and institutions were derived from ancient Rome, as were its laws and social orders. The ethnic identity of the majority of its population was Roman and the name that they gave to their state and society was *Romanía*. This aspect of its civilization was long denied in the West in order to enable Western institutions to lay exclusive claim to the Roman legacy. The Byzantines were instead recast as "Greeks," and their thought was studied exclusively within a Greek or Christian matrix. This was a mistake for, their language notwithstanding, the Byzantines did not self-identify as Greek and traced many of their fundamental modes of thought back to Roman traditions. Now that these ideological blinkers are being removed, the Roman aspects of Byzantine civilization are finally being studied.[1]

It is an open question how many east Roman thinkers practiced philosophy as opposed to the scholarly study of ancient philosophy and theology (including paraphilosophical moves made to advance a theological agenda).[2] The domains of their thought that were most overtly Roman in inspiration included their political system (the Roman *res publica*) and their system of law, as Byzantine law was but Roman law in Greek translation (and in continuous evolution, as systems of law always are).[3] It is a matter of definition whether this body of thought merits the title of philosophy. Ulpian, at any rate, regarded jurists and lawyers as "priests of the art of the good and the fair," and, as that art made men good, its devotees "professed a true philosophy, not a pretended one."[4]

This chapter will, for the first time, attempt to excavate one of the Roman foundations of Byzantine thinking that was so deeply embedded that it has not yet been identified. The Byzantines inherited it directly from ancient Roman law and practice and they applied it to many areas of their life, political, social, and religious. Calling it a mode of thinking is perhaps not entirely accurate, for it was in addition "a power that transforms the order of things, that remodels them,"[5] and so it was an activating force behind the history of Byzantium in many respects. But at heart it was a conceptual move that originated in a feature of Roman law that I call "quasity," from Latin *quasi*. This was the ability of Roman law to treat a thing fully "as if it were" a different species, to subsume it under a category to which it did not belong "by nature" and thereby to normalize it within a preexisting order. This legal fiction enabled the imperial court (or other controlling legal authority) to act on the basis of a state of affairs that was not, strictly speaking, true or real, but that served the purposes of policy or convenience, or extended the applicability of a certain rule or power into territory that it could not otherwise claim. "Legal fictions" are a recognized, albeit minor problem in the philosophy of law.[6]

Quasity therefore has two fundamental components: an act of the imagination that enables one to fictively transfer a thing between categories within a taxonomy, followed by a legal and social practice which treats that conceptual transference as an accomplished fact and respects it as fully real. It is aware of, but pragmatically overlooks, its fictive origins. A mere thought experiment or literary metaphor does not count, for the fictive act must also become a social fact.

The ancient Romans deployed quasity to treat noncitizens as if they were citizens for the purposes of adjudicating a dispute; to adopt non-kin and treat them as if they were kin; to create promagistrates, who did not hold a certain office but were treated as if they did; to cope with the complex diversity of cults and social orders among the subjects of their empire; and in other contexts where a faulty interface between reality and legal norms created dark spaces that needed to be bridged by legal fictions. Such fictions were, however, feats of the imagination that constituted much of Roman life and history.[7]

The Romans were not the only ones to deploy quasity. In 1903, when the United States leased the land on which the Panama canal was built (after inciting the people of Panama to rebel and secede from Colombia), the treaty gave the United States all the rights in perpetuity that it would have "if it were the sovereign of the territory," without, of course, giving it actual sovereignty (the zone was returned to Panama in 1999).[8] We will henceforth focus here only on east Roman examples. Quasity is not a well-known aspect of Roman thinking to begin with, which is why a name for it had to be invented here, and it is completely unknown in the field of Byzantine studies. The focus of this chapter will be on certain domains in which the Romans (and by extension the Byzantines) showed "a remarkable commitment to the social consequences of legal facts."[9]

As we will see, quasity shaped para-philosophical or theological debates in Byzantium too, but it is unclear whether it itself can be classified as "philosophy." That is because it is difficult to classify as a mode of thought. It was a conceptual move that occurred within and between the legal taxonomies through which the Romans approached their world and that enabled them to change and govern it. It was, at any rate, a distinctively Roman cognitive move with almost no analogue in the other traditions that the Byzantines inherited. This should partially relieve us of the anxiety that accompanies many discussions of Roman thought and philosophy, namely whether it was authentically Roman or something Greek in Latin disguise. Quasity was Latin and Roman in origin. In this and other ways, Byzantium was a Roman civilization disguised as a Greek one. Many of its fundamental terms, such as *politeia*, appear to be Greek on the surface but turn out to have a Latin meaning (in this case, res publica). This area of research has just begun. As a proof of concept, this chapter will examine the following specific domains of quasity: how the Romans made a New Rome in the east that they treated and built up as if it were Rome itself; how icons came to be venerated as if they were the holy people that they depicted; and how a network of fictive-spiritual relations spread across the face of Byzantine society and treated as if they were relations of biological kinship.

The Making of a New Rome

Byzantine history is inconceivable apart from its capital city, Constantinople or New Rome, built on the site of the city of Byzantion, on the Thracian Bosporos, and inaugurated by Constantine on May 11, 330 CE. Its foundation has been studied from many angles—the events that surrounded it as well as the city's monuments, institutions, and logistics—but one underlying question has not been asked with the clarity it deserves: What conceptual matrix enabled Constantine and his planners to imagine not just a new city named after a ruler (for there had been many of those), or even a city to serve pragmatically as a new capital in the east, but a branch-office of Rome, a copied-and-pasted simulation that mimicked its institutions, name, and identity and was treated, for all intents and purposes, as a New Rome? If not right from the start, Constantinople quickly acquired the legal designation of a "new," "other," or "second" Rome, along with the institutions that went with the name, such as a Senate, a prefect (with jurisdiction out to 100 miles), a Milion that marked the empire's symbolic center-point, and a grain dole for its citizens, in addition to a palace adjacent to a hippodrome ("perfectly alike to the one in Rome"), fourteen regions, and the requisite imperial monuments. Over time New Rome even acquired a mythic history that matched that of Rome, and, in the Byzantine imagination, even seven hills. By the sixth century, it was believed that Constantine had transferred the Palladium (a sacred protective talisman) from Rome to his own foundation.[10]

Constantinople functioned so effectively as Rome that, after 476, Romulus's city looked to Constantine's to confirm its own Romanness.[11] The people of New Rome, who were addressed in imperial law as *cives Romani*, increasingly took on the functions of the Roman *populus* under the imperial monarchy, including the sovereign right to acclaim and thereby create new emperors in the hippodrome, the forum of Constantine, or, later, in Hagia Sophia. Records of these acclamations and the verbal exchanges that took place between the emperor and the *populus* reveal that the Constantinopolitans spoke on behalf of the Roman people, just as had once happened in the assemblies of Rome.[12] They enjoyed Roman-style chariot racing, not Greek athletic games, and celebrated the *kalends*, *Brumalia*, *Vota*, and *Lupercalia*, in their mutated later forms, to be sure.[13]

History appears to admit of no precise parallel to this unique project: no other imperial metropole generated a "new" version of itself in a former province to function there as it itself had once ruled over the entirety of its empire. (The relationship between Nanjing and Beijing acquired a similar aspect under the Ming dynasty, though both were preexisting cities.)[14] Moreover, despite the tremendous effort expended in the creation of New Rome, the idea itself appears to have been effortless and the commitment to it by all Romans both then and thereafter was nearly total (the sole exception being some bishops of Rome who objected to the near-parity bestowed on the two Romes in the ecclesiastical rankings). The making of a New Rome was imagined, probably accurately, by one Church historian as a legal-fictive act by Constantine that was publicly posted in the new city.[15] His subjects then easily made the leap from one sense of "fictive" (an act of the imagination) to the other (a fashioning that creates a new reality). This reality manifested itself as what we call "Byzantine history" because the Romans committed to it and did not question whether New Rome was "really" Rome, as modern historians do, who are not, in this matter, thinking like Romans. When the emperor Justinian declared in 530 that all cities must follow the laws of Rome, he clarified that by Rome "we mean not only the old city but also our royal one," i.e., Constantinople, as Old Rome had ceased to be an imperial capital.[16] According to the emperor Herakleios (early seventh century), Constantinople was "the common fatherland of all." This appropriated (and cast in Greek) what a Roman jurist had declared in Latin in the third century, that "Rome is our common fatherland."[17]

The duplication of Rome echoed, likely responded to, and was perhaps even conceptually homologous to the prior duplication of the imperial office itself. The philosopher Themistios, a leading senator and orator of New Rome in the fourth century, and an Aristotelian scholar, captured this conceptual confluence in Greek philosophical terms. He said that Constantine's city, "through her virtue, became a partner in empire along with the great city [Rome]," exactly in the same way that Theodosius I (379–395), whom the orator was addressing, had become emperor: it was because of his virtues that Theodosius was appointed to that office by Gratian (367–383), even though he was not biologically related to him. Yet through the metaphorical language of "father" and "son," Themistios gestures toward a fictive kinship between the two emperors, though, because Theodosius was older and the addressee of the moment, the orator coyly implies that

Theodosius was the father in this relationship.[18] Just as Gratian and Theodosius were "co-emperors," Rome and Constantinople were "co-ruling" imperial cities.[19]

A Constantinopolitan poet of the sixth century, Paulos the silentiary, configured the relationship between Rome and Constantinople as that between mother and daughter, though, he adds, the latter now shines more brilliantly than the former, a success that is, after all, every parent's delight.[20] But this is a poetic flourish: there is no indication that the relationship was legally or administratively treated as that of a metropolis to its colony. It was rather that of a mirror-image: Rome and Constantinople even shared in the same "fortune," or *Tyche*, as if they were animated by one and the same spirit. New Rome's sacred name, *Anthousa* ("Blooming"), was a translation of that of Rome, *Flora*.

The idea for a New Rome did not, however, burst out of Constantine like Athena from the mind of Zeus. Treating places that were not Rome "as if" they were Rome had a long prehistory and was spurred by the fact that the Romans imagined themselves first and foremost as a legally constituted community, a *populus* or *res publica*, and not as an agglomerate who merely happened to live in a particular place. A Rome, or quasi-Rome, could be reconstituted wherever the Romans gathered for a common purpose.[21] This tendency expanded dramatically during the third century CE, when citizenship was extended to all free inhabitants of the empire. The whole empire was thereby constituted as a vast Roman community, and soon, possibly already in the later third century, acquired the name *Romanía*. Rome became a highly portable idea, a matrix of thought that could be applied to virtually any place that the Romans wished to treat as their "capital." Consider how the emperor Gordian I, who rebelled in North Africa in 238, treated the city of Carthage, once the arch-enemy of Rome, and note the density of the language of simulation, or quasity, in the account by the contemporary Greek historian Herodian (7.6.1–2):

> Gordian knew that Carthage was the largest and most populous city [in North Africa], so that he could act there *as if* he were in Rome. For that city was second only to Rome in terms of its wealth, population, and size, and was competing for second place with Alexandria in Egypt. He was followed by a full imperial retinue, the soldiers who were stationed there, and the tallest young men of the city walked ahead of him *in the guise* of the bodyguard at Rome. The *fasces* were garlanded with laurel wreaths, which is the mark that distinguishes an emperor from a private citizen, and a fire was carried before him in the procession, so that the city of the Carthaginians *bore the visage and shared in the standing* of Rome itself, at least for a short time and *by way of a replica*.

This mental technology of fictive yet effective simulation was in place long before Constantine brought his engineers to the Bosporos, and it survived elsewhere even after 330 CE. In the fifth century, the preacher Salvian in southern Gaul called Carthage "the greatest rival of Rome and a kind of Rome of the African world"—*quasi Romam*.[22] Absent this distinctive way of thinking, what we call "Byzantium" would never have existed.

The Veneration of Icons

One of the most distinctive and well-studied aspects of Byzantine civilization was the veneration of icons, that is of images of holy figures such as Christ, his mother the Virgin Mary, and the saints. In the eighth and ninth centuries, this veneration elicited pushback in the form of iconoclasm, which was an effort by a number of emperors to curtail this practice and possibly to remove images from churches and prominent public places. This effort failed. The iconophiles won and proceeded to rewrite the history of iconoclasm as one of vicious persecution and resistance by the pious champions of the icons. Scholars today are trying to identify and correct all the distortions that this narrative introduced into the historical record.[23] Be that as it may, the Byzantines themselves hailed the final restoration of icons in 843 as the Triumph of Orthodoxy and celebrated it on the first Sunday of Lent (and many Orthodox Churches still do so). Thus, the Orthodox identity of Byzantium was tied to the vindication of icons. Accordingly, icons are the prime focus of the discipline of Byzantine art history, and some would argue that the Byzantines' theorization of the religious icon is among their most powerful and distinctive contributions to world civilization.[24] This section will link that theorization to the mental matrix of Roman quasity.

The chief objection against the religious use of icons that was brought by the first iconoclasts, especially the emperor Konstantinos V (741–775), was that it was a form of idolatry, similar to that of ancient paganism (at least as Christians regarded the latter). In other words, the believer was worshipping a material thing, such as a panel of painted wood, not the Creator himself, who was an immaterial being of an altogether different nature who should be the sole object of Christian worship. This condemnation of icons was enshrined in the iconoclastic Council of Hiereia held in 754 at a palace near Constantinople. According to this Council, icons "drag down men's minds from the exalted worship appropriate to God to an earthy and material worship of things created."[25] Hiereia was overturned in 787 by the iconophile Council of Nicaea II. Its bishops offered up a number of minor arguments in favor of the use of icons in worship (for example, their pedagogical, mnemonic, and emotional value) but their major argument was that "the honor paid to the image ["honor" being the "content" delivered by worship] passes over to the prototype." That is, the worship is not directed *at* the icon itself but rather *through* the icon *to* its prototype, Christ or the Virgin. And this, by and large, remained the Byzantine Orthodox position after the restoration of icons in 843.[26]

For this theory, iconophiles relied on a single patristic source, the *Treatise on the Holy Spirit* written by the fourth-century bishop Basil of Caesarea, whom the Byzantines regarded as a saint, an authoritative theologian of the Trinity, and a model bishop. One passage in particular from his *Treatise* was cited repeatedly at Nicaea II and by other defenders of icons, such as saint John of Damascus (in the mid-eighth century) and Theodoros of Stoudios (in the early ninth). That passage is not concerned with religious images but with defining the relation between Father and Son within the Trinity and explaining how they were distinct persons even though they constituted one entity. Basil did this by pointing to the image of the emperor:

> How, then, are these not two gods? In the same way that the image of the emperor is also called "the emperor": they do not make two emperors. His power is not divided, nor is his glory split in two. The power that governs us is one ... for the honor paid to the image passes over to its prototype.[27]

As an argument for the oneness of the three members of the Trinity, this is weak. But as an argument for the veneration of images it is quite strong and draws on an experience embedded in the political and legal life of the empire, namely the fiction that, under certain circumstances, the image of an emperor could be treated *as if it were* the emperor himself, while everyone knew that ontologically speaking they were distinct entities. (Cf. attitudes toward Santa Claus: children know that the man in the department store is enacting Santa, but they think of him as Santa and ask for gifts with sincerity; nor is this notion shaken when they see several other Santas gathered outside.)[28]

Imperial portraits, which were ubiquitous in the early empire, functioned as the emperor's legal and personal stand-ins. They received acclamations, presided over the formal proceedings of Roman magistrates, were addressed by speakers in the second person, and citizens could request asylum or make petitions by speaking to them as if they were the emperor present in person. Conversely, insults to the imperial portrait—such as taking a coin with the imperial visage into the bathroom—could be construed as acts of treason against the emperor. Rebellions often began by tearing down an emperor's images.[29] A protest in Antioch in 387 against a new tax turned into a tense political crisis when the protesters tore down the emperor's statues. Eastern provincials of the Christian empire had fully absorbed the legal implications of this form of Roman quasity. Severian of Gabala (c. 400), a native Syriac-speaker, told an audience in Constantinople that "if the emperor is absent, an image takes his place . . . and the people venerate it not as if it were a wooden board but as if they were seeing the visage of the emperor, not in person, but in representation."[30]

Roman and Byzantine authors discussing the legal standing of the imperial image were aware of the ontological difference between the lifeless object on the one hand and the emperor himself on the other, but insisted that, under certain conditions, the former had to be treated exactly as if it were the latter. In another text, St. Basil argued that pointing to a panel and saying, "This is the emperor," does not set up another emperor or strip the flesh-and-blood emperor of his title.[31] Thus the Byzantine defense of religious icons can be traced genealogically, through an argument about the members of the Trinity, to a Roman legal fiction that enabled the emperor to be present everywhere while being absent in all places but one. The same logic applied to both cases. Compare these two: a Roman jurist opined that no charge of treason applied if one repaired an imperial statue that had "fallen into disrepair with age" (even if it meant striking its face with a chisel), and a theologian quoted at Nicaea II also noted that an image of Christ can be burned, without disrespect, once it becomes too faded to be usable.[32] As the iconophile theologian Theodoros of Stoudios put it, it is not the "essence" of the wood that is venerated, only that of Christ, through his image.[33] Relying on the Christian Platonist pseudo-Dionysios, the iconophiles insisted that "one entity can be taken for the other, though in essence they are in fact different."[34]

The "genealogy" posited here was not merely an intellectual one, in which theoretical arguments were recycled and put to new use in different contexts. It was a genealogy that carried ideas within the bounds of a specific domain, namely the legal standing of images of authority in Roman society. The modalities governing the treatment of the imperial image were extended to images of Christ, the Virgin, and the saints. The comparison had already been drawn before the outbreak of the iconoclastic controversy in the 720s,[35] and Christians were approaching images of a holy person "as if he were present." Today, a powerful strand of scholarship argues that many pre-iconoclastic texts about images were forged or tampered with during and after the controversy itself, and that they are not reliable evidence for the period before it. This does not ultimately affect the present argument for the continued deployment of Roman modes of thinking, yet two such texts that are unimpeachably authentic contain that distinctively quasic language. One of them is a Latin account of a western traveler who came to Constantinople in the 680s that could not have been tampered with by a post-iconoclastic Byzantine apologist. That visitor documents a developed cult of images, with icons that performed miracles, were venerated, and were spoken to "as if it were saint George present in person."[36]

LEGAL AND SPIRITUAL KINSHIP

Nearly all ancient and medieval societies allowed adoption in one way or another as well as forged bonds of spiritual kinship such as ritual brotherhood, confraternities, or the symbolic redeployment of kinship terms to other kinds of relationships. All these practices embodied quasic thinking, as they entailed a commitment to treat an unrelated person as a related one. Among these societies, the Romans (and by extension the Byzantines) had developed the law and practice of adoption to the greatest degree; they had probably the most extensive and diverse types of spiritual kinship; and they gave the most explicit legal validity to them.

Adoptive quasity became so refined and elastic in Roman thinking that imperial dynasties were based on adoption (the Julio-Claudians) before biology (the Flavians). In the late second century, one dynasty (the Severans) retroactively adopted itself into a prior one (the Antonines), a fiction to which early Byzantine society actively subscribed: when Caracalla bestowed Roman citizenship upon the empire in 212, all those emancipated by this decree (the "Antonine Constitution") henceforth bore the name Aurelius, not Septimius. Thus, when Byzantine history (notionally) begins a century later, well over half its population were Aurelii.[37]

On the more mundane level of private citizens, the Roman law of adoption was both more elaborate than that of other ancient societies and legally more committed to the fictive kin-relations that it established. Thus, for example, it was possible to adopt a grandson "on the fiction (*quasi*)" that he was born of one's son; he would be a *quasi-nepos* born from a *quasi*-son (because one might not even have a biological son).[38] But at the same time, in contrast to the socio-legal systems that formerly prevailed in the Greek provinces of the empire, adoptive relations in the Roman system were treated as fully real, so that marriages between adopted and natural children were deemed incestuous for as long as the adoption was valid, that is before emancipation from paternal authority.[39]

We know the Roman law of adoption best through the *Digest*, which was compiled under Justinian in the late 520s and 530s and subsequently translated into Greek. In some instances, we can observe moves toward greater quasity in the Byzantine modifications to Justinianic law. For example, Justinian had decreed that "adoption mirrors nature" and so a younger man cannot adopt an older one; a eunuch cannot adopt anyone because he is unable to have children of his own; and a woman also cannot adopt because she cannot exercise paternal authority.[40] However, the emperor Leon VI (886–912) struck down this logic for both eunuchs and women, arguing that the law should not imitate nature but seek to correct its defects. Eunuchs more than anyone, he declared, need "child-making via the law." And the requirement to hold paternal authority, Leon points out, even contravenes the criterion of "nature" that Justinian set down. So these groups too may adopt someone "to have the place of a son," the legal term in Byzantine law for an adoptee.[41] Unfortunately, we lack conclusive evidence that eunuchs (who were few in number anyway) took advantage of this law.[42] Be that as it may, the principle behind Leon's modifications was to extend the domain of legal parenthood in a direction of greater inclusivity.

There is at least one case of a younger man adopting an older one: Michael III, who was without children, adopted Basileios I in 866 and then elevated him to the rank of co-emperor. Basileios expedited the transition of power the next year by murdering Michael and starting his own dynasty (the Macedonian one).[43]

The spiritual relationships created by Christianity considerably expanded the scope of fictive kinship in the Roman empire, and they were quickly housed within the regulatory mechanisms of the canon law of the Church (an imperial institution) and Roman law generally, so they were absorbed into the prevailing modes of legal thinking. Specifically, godparenthood—sponsoring a child at its baptism—established a fictive parity between the godparent and the biological (or adoptive) parent as "co-parents" of the child (*synteknoi*). After the sixth century, the Byzantines increasingly committed to the legal consequences of this definition, eventually banning marriages to the seventh degree of relation between the kin of the parent and the kin of the godparent, i.e., exactly as if their relationship were familial (the Church calculated degrees of kinship by using the ancient Roman method of counting the generations, inclusively, up from one person to the first common ancestor and then down to the other person). The premise was that spiritual relationships were just as consequential and valid as biological ones (and metaphysically superior). Moreover, baptism was regarded by the Church Fathers as a kind of adoption and, conversely, the language associated with adoption in Byzantium took on some of the attributes of baptism, including its consummation via a Church service that was mandated by a law of Leon VI.[44] In a letter to the pope, the emperor Konstantinos IV (668–685) referred to his "spiritual adoption" by Christ (presumably his baptism), which had inspired him to crack down on heresy in order to become worthy of this "elevating divine kinship" and the "nobility bestowed by this adoption." But here we have left social practice behind and entered the stratospheric level of imperial rhetoric.[45]

Adoption, both legal and spiritual, enjoyed a resurgence as a strategy of dynastic succession in the eleventh century,[46] and there is even a case of a man being retroactively adopted into the family-name of a deceased person on the "fictional pretense [hôs dêthen] that he was descended from him."[47] As a dynastic strategy, adoption was made largely obsolete by the fecundity of the Komnenoi in the twelfth century, which was unprecedented among Roman ruling families and ushered in a period of intense fixation on biological *genos*.[48] Among the general population, adoption was surely uncommon but baptism was universal, meaning that Byzantine society was crisscrossed by a network of spiritual relations that functioned legally and socially (*thesei*, "by arrangement/placement") as if they were biological ones (*physei*, "by nature"). Moreover, there was a specialized practice and ritual for "brother-making" (*adelphopoieia*), which was used to form alliances or pacts of solidarity, and these were often treated as spiritual relationships on a par with the rest, such as godparenthood.[49] Specialized texts (*On Degrees of Kinship*) emerged to keep track of such relationships, in part because spiritual-legal relations imposed restrictions on potential marriages. In the eyes of canon and state law, fictive kinship blocked potential biological relations. We can see in this a Christian extension of ancient Roman practice, which recognized that changes in legal status potentially disrupted kinship structures, enabling the social to override the natural.[50]

I mention in conclusion the spiritual relationships that were established by joining a monastic community ("brother," "son," and "father" for the men). This was a metaphorical language that did not entail a change in legal status, although monks, because they now belonged to a new community, were not supposed to become godparents (in practice they sometimes did).[51] The monastery replaced the monk's biological family, although this did not entail legal restrictions. Monks even took on new names upon joining. The monastic reformer of the early ninth century, Theodoros, the abbot of the monastery of Stoudios, told his monks in c. 800:

> You have come here after renouncing your parents and brothers and relatives— indeed, the whole world itself—and you were then born as my spiritual children who were reconfigured toward a more holy life. Wherefore, you don't allow yourself to be called by the name of this or that of your corporeal forebears, but only your spiritual fathers and forefathers, thus demonstrating that you broke with your nature (*physis*) and embraced your new, chosen rebirth.[52]

Laymen often had "spiritual fathers," which could be one's godfather or a priest who took confession. The result was a highly complex "social imaginary." It is therefore often unclear in Byzantine sources what kind of relationship is meant when a source refers to someone's "brother" or "father."[53]

Making Romans

The ultimate factitive power of Roman law was to render people subject to its domain, that is to make them Roman citizens and to treat them as such, regardless of who or what they had been before (foreigners, slaves). Before the universal extension of citizenship to all nonslaves in the empire in 212 CE, there were many contexts in which noncitizens could be treated as if they were citizens, such as for the purpose of resolving a legal dispute, for convenience, or as a favor. The emperor Claudius once granted citizenship to a group who had mistakenly thought that they had citizenship and had been living under, and according to, that error for some time. Hadrian not only granted citizenship to some soldiers, he retroactively redefined their careers in the Roman army as if they had been citizens ever since they joined the ranks.[54] The Antonine Constitution of 212 created millions of new Romans, a legal fact to which the administration of the empire adjusted instantly with no known "nativist" Roman backlash. Half a century before that, a Greek orator had praised the emperors for ruling "as if the entire empire were a single city," "as if it were a single household."[55]

Romans were made not just by decree but by treating non-Romans as if they were Romans, which assimilated them to imperial society. The philosopher-Senator Themistios argued for such a treatment of the Goths who had entered the empire in 376, defeated the imperial armies at the battle of Adrianople in 378, and had fought a four-year war against the emperor Theodosius I. Now, in 382, they had signed a peace treaty and Themistios was trying to sell it to the Senate on the emperor's behalf. The Goths could and would be assimilated, he argued, if they were treated accordingly by the authorities. He raised the example of the Galatians of Asia Minor (*Or.* 16.211c–d):

> Look at the Galatians. . . . These men crossed over into Asia under the law of war [in the third century BCE]. . . . Neither Pompey nor Lucullus destroyed them, although this was possible, nor Augustus nor the emperors after him; rather, they forgave their sins and assimilated them into the empire. And now no one would ever refer to the Galatians as barbarian but as thoroughly Roman. For while their ancestral name has endured, their way of life is akin to our own. They pay the same taxes as we do, they enlist in the same ranks as we do, they accept governors on the same terms as the rest, and abide by the same laws (tr. modified from Heather and Moncur).

Themistios was talking not about citizenship but cultural assimilation, a more far-reaching policy, and he hoped that "we will soon see the same happen with the Goths. To be sure, we have recently been clashing with them, but before long they will share in our offerings, meals, military campaigns, and public service."[56] Treat them as if they are Romans and eventually they will become that, he seems to be saying.

The law of Roman citizenship in Byzantium was liberal and based on the Antonine Constitution: "all who are in the Roman world are Roman citizens," with the gloss: "Those who live within the circumference of the Roman world, namely those who are under the authority of the Romans, even if they do not live in Rome, are still Roman citizens on the basis of the decree issued by the emperor Antoninus."[57] This meant that non-Romans henceforth could enter the empire in only two ways: by migration or by the conquest, absorption, or annexation of their territories by the empire. Now, it should be added that in the middle Byzantine period, if not earlier, Romanness had become an ethno-cultural identity and was not merely legal. It was understood by the Romans and their neighbors as a function of language (Greek), religion (Chalcedonian Orthodoxy), law, custom, dress, political culture (*Romanía* or "the polity of the Romans"), and sometimes ancestry. It was criteria such as these and not the fact of citizenship that primarily distinguished ethnic Romans from, say, Slavs, Bulgarians, Armenians, Georgians, Franks, and Arabs. These lines of distinction could even be drawn in stark racial terms. The emperor Konstantinos VII in the tenth century argued that all these nations were like different species of animal, with different habits, laws, and institutions, and therefore they should not intermarry; he made an exception only for Franks and Romans.[58] In this respect he was like Augustus, another race theorist who restricted grants of citizenship so as not to "dilute the purity of Roman blood."[59]

Yet, in the matter of foreign admixture, pragmatism prevailed in New Rome just as it had in Old Rome. When it came to small or mid-sized groups who sought to immigrate to the empire, imperial policy tended to follow the argument made by Themistios. Over the course of two or three generations, this policy transferred the newcomers across "the taxonomic divide" from foreigner to Roman.[60] Countless examples can be cited. A striking instance was an army of 30,000 Iranian refugees, the Khurramites, whose beliefs were a mix of Islam and folk Zoroastrianism, and who had been fighting a losing war against the caliphate. The emperor Theophilos (829–842) allowed these refugees to enter the empire, enrolled them in the Roman army (with salaries and offices), brought their leaders into the court system, and even required provincial Roman women to marry them in order to accommodate them and facilitate their assimilation. The ethnic profile of these people was wholly foreign, and there was a nativist reaction against this policy, which forced Roman women into marriage with "barbarian" men. Theophilos was also accused by some of his subjects of being a "lover of ethnic foreigners." But the policy worked: some two generations later, the Khurramites had gone "extinct" as a distinct group inside the empire. Their descendants were mainstream Romans, just like the descendants of other groups that had been absorbed in similar ways.[61] If you treat people as if they belong, even if culturally and ethnically they do not, eventually they will.

The point has recently been made—correctly—that grants of citizenship are not in themselves legal fictions. Becoming a citizenship literally is to be the recipient of such a grant, which is a factitive act.[62] Yet in a Byzantine context, Romanness entailed far more than just citizenship: it was also an ethnic identity, and belonging (or not) to the group was judged on the basis of the relevant indicia, including language, dress, customs, and comportment. It was well understood that these did not change automatically by legal fiat: ethnic qualities were expected in the long term. Thus, treating foreigners presumptively and in anticipation as ethnic Romans through the bestowal of citizenship counts as a form of quasity. It signaled that we will treat you legally as an insider until you actually become one.

Repeatedly we find emperors willing to treat foreign groups or individuals as if they were Romans in order to "graft their wild strain onto our civilized one," as another imperial orator of the twelfth century put it. Grafting implies that the two are not of a different species. The emperor in question, Manuel I Komnenos (1143–1180), encouraged certain foreign groups

> to make a foreign land [i.e., the empire] their home, deeming as their fatherland any place in which they eventually prospered. . . . These men came to populate cities, and their lives became entwined in the fabric of life. They left behind manifold descendants . . . transplanted into our land from the land out of which they were uprooted, producing a flourishing crop.[63]

According to the taxonomies of Roman life, these foreigners had to be treated as Romans in order to be transplanted.

Another emperor of the twelfth century made that point explicitly. Isaakios II Angelos (1185–1195) allowed the Venetians to establish their own quarter in Constantinople, a city that was not normally open to foreigners. Though his motivation was pragmatic, his legal reasoning is quasic: we don't normally allow foreigners (*gentes*) to settle in our great city, he says, but Venetians we regard not as foreigners but just as if they were native Romans, who fight and suffer on behalf of *Romanía* just as much as do the Romans themselves. This is a logical tangle and historical falsehood that makes sense only when quasity cuts through the Gordian knot of reality: Isaakios was redefining the Venetians for the purposes of a legal-diplomatic act, not giving a historically grounded account of who they were.[64] In a number of legal contexts, the emperors of this period treated Venetians as if they were imperial subjects, even though they were not.[65]

It is often said that the United States is a country created by immigrants and that it should therefore remain open to them now and in the future. A comparable statement for Byzantium would be that New Rome and *Romanía* were created by feats of the imagination that replicated, extended, and naturalized Roman orders (including citizenship) among lands and people where they had previously never existed. Legal fictions and equations, backed by social and political resources and commitments, called the east Roman world into being and sustained it during its thousand-year journey. The first principles of this distinctively Roman approach were encoded in the narrative myths of the foundation of Rome itself.[66]

Conclusions

Let us sketch, in conclusion, the philosophical contours of Byzantine quasity. It was a legal tool of duplication, extension, and identity that created social facts via legal reasoning. It tended to abstract and dematerialize identities, associations, and practices so that even a thing such as the city of Rome could be *here* as well as *there*; so that kin relations could "break away from nature" (as Theodoros of Stoudios put it) and become "reconfigured" (*anamorphosis*) in extended and spiritual ways that were no less real or ethically compelling; and so that foreigners could be grafted onto the nation through a legal and political process that, over time, created ethnic facts that violated the premises of racial thinking. Conversely, it could materialize the abstract, so that Christ, an invisible deity who was only once present on this earth, could be worshipped in the form of physical icons, allowing the material, bodily practice of worship to be infinitely replicated.

Quasity could also be used to ill effect. For example, new heresies (such as the Paulicians in the ninth century) could be falsely but legally equated with old ones (in this case the Manichaeans), enabling their lethal repression.[67] But even in this dark domain of Byzantine civilization, the opposite move could also be made: for the purposes of social peace and prosperity, society and the court could treat old heretics (e.g., Syriac Monophysites) as if they were orthodox, and so we find Romans intermarrying with them and allowing them to testify in the courts of law, even though, as some fundamentalist bishops complained, that was prohibited by imperial law itself.[68] Quasity was a tool of both power and accommodation. The two aspects were combined in the quasi-sacerdotal status that the Church was willing to grant to the emperor, treating him, technically a layman, "as if" he were a priest in certain contexts. Thus dynamic tension shaped a great deal of Byzantine history, and its roots should be sought in Roman thinking too, not just in the Old Testament.[69]

The widespread application of quasic modes of thinking created a society that was both legalistic and imaginative, rule-oriented and flexible. The combination of these qualities was one of the factors that enabled the Roman empire to survive for two thousand years, a duration which, depending on how we define certain key terms, was longer than any other state in human history. Over that time span, it gradually but flexibly changed its geographical locale, capital city, language, religion, culture, and human stock, and adjusted to changing circumstances, all the while preserving its identity and coherence. This might also be called an anti-essentialist project, at least insofar as it flouted the limitations of race, kinship, and place, which ostensibly value "nature" over social agreement. Yet Roman identity and institutional continuity survived. The Romans were more adept at this than many modern societies, which fail to overcome the cognitive limitations of race and place. Historians too are trapped in modern racial thinking when they fail to accept the Byzantines as "real" Romans. We typically think of Byzantium as a conservative and even unimaginative pre-modern society, but its accomplishment in this area was radical and enabled by the cognitive tools of Roman law. These tools exerted perhaps a greater impact on people's lives and their thinking than their more overtly philosophical counterparts.

Notes

1. For an introduction to these issues, see Kaldellis (2019).
2. Gutas and Siniossogou (2017), which will provoke further discussion.
3. Politics: Kaldellis (2015) for the Roman aspect; and Dvornik (1966), for the Greek and Christian aspects; law: Stolte (2017).
4. Ulpian in *Dig.* 1.1.1.1.
5. Thomas (1995) 19–20.
6. Fuller (1967); Del Mar and Twining (2015).
7. Richardson (1995); Ando (2015a), (2015b), (2020); Koortbojian (2020) 41, 93–94, 141. My understanding of the Roman background is fundamentally indebted to Cliff Ando's work, which inspired me to explore its Byzantine extensions. I thank him for that, and for his valuable comments on an earlier version of this chapter. He is not responsible for any remaining fictions in it.
8. Immerwahr (2019) 114. Likewise, the Four Corners Monument was geographically misplaced, but the U.S. Supreme Court decreed that its location satisfied legal criteria and so must be treated as if it were geographically accurate too.
9. Cliff Ando, pers. comm.
10. The fundamental study is Dagron (1974); New Rome from the start: Lenski (2015); "perfect likeness": Ioannes Malalas, *Chronicle* 13.7, ed. Thurn (2000) 245–246; history: Kaldellis (2005).
11. Kruse (2019).
12. Kaldellis (forthcoming). Many acclamations and exchanges are recorded in the *Book of Ceremonies* compiled by Konstantinos VII in the tenth century: ed. and tr. Moffatt and Tall (2012).
13. Graf (2015).
14. I thank Qianyi Fu and Shao-yun Yang for instructing me on the use of the two cities as parallel primary and "back-up" capitals.
15. Socrates, *Hist. eccl.* 1.16.
16. Justinian, *Deo auctore* 10, pref. to the *Dig.* (*debere omnes civitates consuetudinem romae sequi, quae caput est orbis terrarum, non ipsam alias civitates. Romam autem intellegendum est non solum veterem, sed etiam regiam nostram*).
17. Modestinus in *Dig.* 50.1.33; Herakleios in Zepos and Zepos (1931) 33.
18. *Them. Or.* 16.182a–183a; cf. Vanderspoel (2012).
19. *Them. Or.* 23.298b.
20. Paulos Silentiarios, *Ekphrasis of Hagia Sophia* 150–151, 164–167, ed. de Stefani (2011).
21. For an extended treatment, see Kaldellis (2020).
22. Salvian, *On the Governance of God* 7.16.67, ed. Lagarrigue (1975).
23. Brubaker and Haldon (2011).
24. Barber (2002); Mondzain (2004).

25. Only the definition of faith (and not the Acts) survives from the Council of Hiereia, quoted in session six of the iconophile Council of Nicaea II that overturned Hiereia in 787: ed. Lamberz (2008–2016) v. 3, 600–792; tr. Price (2018) v. 2, 425–546, quotation from 456.
26. Minor arguments: Lamberz (2008–2016) v. 3, 826; tr. Price (2018) v. 2, 564–565. "Honor passes over:" Lamberz (2008–2016) v. 2, 398; v. 3, 684, 744; tr. Price (2018) v. 1, 312–313; v. 2, 483, 518; and passim.
27. Basil of Caesarea, *Treatise on the Holy Spirit* 18.45, ed. Pruche (1946) 194; cf. also Athanasios of Alexandria, *Against the Arians* 3.5, ed. Opitz (1940).
28. This analogy was helpfully provided by the volume editors.
29. Ando (2000) 228–253; Kitzinger (1954) 122–123.
30. Severianos of Gabala, *On the Cross*, in John of Damascus, *Orations on the Images* 3.123, ed. Kotter (1975); on John, see Louth (2002). Antioch: van de Paverd (1991).
31. Basil of Caesarea, *Against the Sabellians, Areios, and the Anhomeans* 4, in Migne, *PG* 31: 608, also cited at Nicaea II.
32. Marcianus in *Dig.* 48.4.5; Leontios of Neapolis, *Against the Jews*, quoted at Lamberz (2008–2016) v. 2, 350–352; tr. Price (2018) v. 1, 292.
33. Theodoros of Stoudios, *Letter 57* (*To Plato on the Veneration of Images*), ed. Fatouros (1991); see Tollefsen (2018).
34. Parry (2018) 273.
35. Kitzinger (1954) 124–125.
36. Adamnán of Iona, *De locis sanctis* 3.4–5, ed. and tr. Meehan (1958) 110–119; the other text is an epigram by Agathias (sixth century): *AP* 1.34. Skepticism: Brubaker (1998), relying on the many works of Paul Speck.
37. Adoptive dynasties: Richardson (1995) 128–129; Antonine Constitution: Ando (2016); Imric (2018).
38. *Dig.* 1.7.6, 1.7.43.
39. Huebner (2013) 516; cf. *Dig.* 23.2.17, 23.2.55.
40. *Inst. Iust.* 1.11.4–10, tr. Birks and McLeod (1987) 45; but cf. Gaius's *Institutes* in *Dig.* 1.7.2.1: eunuchs can adopt; in general, see Macrides (1990).
41. Leon VI, *Novel* 26–27, ed. and tr. Troianos (2007) 110–119.
42. Tougher (2008) 66.
43. Konstantinos VII, *Life of Basileios I* 18, ed. and tr. Ševčenko (2011) 70–71.
44. Macrides (1987) 142–143 (adoption), 146-147 (godparenthood); Leon VI, *Novel* 24, ed. Troianos (2007) 104–107.
45. Riedinger (1992) 894.
46. Shepard (1996) 108–113.
47. Skylitzes, *Synopsis*, p. 483, ed. in Thurn (1973).
48. Leidholm (2019).
49. Rapp (2016).
50. Ando (2020) 48–49.
51. Rapp (2016) 101–103, esp. ch. 5 for the rules; for spiritual monastic relations, see Morris (1995) 92–107.
52. Theodoros of Stoudios, *Great Catechesis*, tr. Hatlie (2007) 297; onomastics: Talbot and McGrath (2006).
53. E.g., Masterson (2019) 408.

54. Ando (2019) 185–188.
55. Aristid. *Or.* 26: *To Rome*, passim; for a translation, see Behr (1981) 73–97.
56. Them. *Or.* 16.211d (my tr.).
57. Ulpian in *Dig.* 1.5.17; Greek version: *Basilika* 46.1.14, eds. Scheltema and van der Val (1953–) v. 6, 2119; Greek gloss: Holwerda and Scheltema (1953–) v. 7, 2732–2733.
58. Konstantinos VII, *De administrando imperio* 13.104–200, ed. Moravcsik and tr. Jenkins (1967) 70–77. For Roman ethnic identity in this period, see Kaldellis (2019).
59. Suet. *Aug.* 40.3; cf. Gaius, *Institutes* 4.103-105 for more Augustan legal restrictions.
60. The phrase is from Ando (2015a) 298.
61. The sources for the Khurramite assimilation are presented in Kaldellis (2019) 127–132.
62. Berthelot (2021) 394.
63. Eustathios of Thessalonike, *Funeral Oration for Manuel Komnenos* 18–19, ed. and tr. Bourbouhakis (2017) 16–21. (mod.).
64. Tafel and Thomas (1856) no. 74, p. 208: *Quamquam enim graue celsitudini nostre uidetur, latitudinem infra magnam urbem gentibus exhibere; uerumtamen, quia non ut alienigenas, immo ut aborigines Romanos genus Veneticorum nostra serenitas reputat, tantumque pro Romania dolent, quantum et ipsi Romani*, etc. For the context, see Magdalino (2007).
65. Burgmann (1997) 79.
66. Konstan (1986); Dench (2005).
67. Kolbaba (in progress).
68. Synodal Memorandum, September 1039, in Ficker (1911) 28–42.
69. Dagron (2003).

References

Ando, C., ed. (2016). *Citizenship and Empire in Europe 200–1900: The Antonine Constitution after 1800 Years*. (Stuttgart).
Ando, C. (2000). *Imperial Ideology and Provincial Loyalty in the Roman Empire*. (Berkeley).
Ando, C. (2015a). "Fact, Fiction and Social Reality in Roman Law," in Del Mar and Twining, 295–323.
Ando, C. (2015b). *Roman Social Imaginaries: Language and Thought in Contexts of Empire*. (Toronto).
Ando, C. (2019). "Race and Citizenship in Roman Law and Administration," in F. M. Simón, F. P. Polo, and J. R. Rodríguez (eds.), *Xenofobia y racismo en el mundo antiquo* (Barcelona), 175–188.
Ando, C. (2020). "The Future's Past: Fiction, Biography and Status in Roman Law." *AC* 63: 43–55.
Ayres, L., ed. (1995). *The Passionate Intellect: Essays on the Transformation of Classical Traditions Presented to Professor I. G. Kidd*. (New Brunswick, NJ).
Barber, C. (2002). *Figure and Likeness: On the Limits of Representation in Byzantine Iconoclasm*. (Princeton).
Behr, C. A., tr. (1981). *P. Aelius Aristides: The Complete Works*, vol. 2. (Leiden).
Berthelot, K. (2021). *Jews and Their Roman Rivals: Pagan Rome's Challenge to Israel*. (Princeton).
Birks, P., and G. McLeod, tr. (1987). *Justinian's Institutes*. (Ithaca, N.Y.).
Bourbouhakis, M., ed. and tr. (2017). *Not Composed in a Chance Manner: The Epitaphios for Manuel I Komnenos by Eustathios of Thessalonike*. (Uppsala).

Brélaz, C., and E. Rose, eds. (2021). *Civic Identity and Civic Participation in Late Antiquity and the Early Middle Ages*. (Turnhout).

Brubaker, L. (1998). "Icons before Iconoclasm?." *Settimane di Studio del Centro Italiano di Studi sull'Alto Medioevo* 45: 1215–1254.

Brubaker, L., and J. Haldon (2011). *Byzantium in the Iconoclast Era, c. 680–850: A History*. (Cambridge).

Burgmann, L. (1997). "Chrysobull gleich Privileg? Beobachtungen zur Funktion einer byzantinischen Urkundenform," in Dölemeyer and Mohnhaupt, 69–92.

Dagron, G. (1974). *Naissance d'une capitale: Constantinople et ses institutions de 330 à 451*. (Paris).

Dagron, G. (2003). *Emperor and Priest: The Imperial Office in Byzantium*. J. Birrell, tr. (Cambridge).

Del Mar, M., and W. Twining, eds. (2015). *Legal Fictions in Theory and Practice*. (Boston).

de Stefani, C., ed. (2011). *Paulus Silentiarius: Descriptio Sancta Sophiae*. (Berlin).

Dench, E. (2005). *Romulus' Asylum: Roman Identities from the Age of Alexander to the Age of Hadrian*. (Oxford).

Dölemeyer, B., and H. Mohnhaupt, eds. (1997). *Das Privileg im europäishen Vergleich*, vol. 1. (Frankfurt am Main).

Dvornik, F. (1966). *Early Christian and Byzantine Political Philosophy: Origins and Background*. (Washington, D.C.).

Fatouros, G., ed. (1991). *Theodori Studitae epistulae*. 2 vols. (Berlin).

Ficker, G., ed. (1911). *Erlasse des Patriarchen von Konstantinopel Alexios Studites*. (Kiel).

Fuller, L. (1967). *Legal Fictions*. (Stanford).

Grig, L., and G. Kelly, eds. (2012). *Two Romes: Rome and Constantinople in Late Antiquity*. (Oxford).

Grubbs, J. E., and T. Parkin, eds. (2013). *The Oxford Handbook of Childhood and Education in the Classical World*. (Oxford).

Gutas, D., and N. Siniossogou (2017). "Philosophy and 'Byzantine Philosophy,'" in Kaldellis and Siniossogou, 271–295.

Graf, F. (2015). *Roman Festivals in the Greek East: From the Early Empire to the Middle Byzantine Era*. (Cambridge).

Hatlie, P. (2007). *The Monks and Monasteries of Constantinople, ca. 350–850*. (Cambridge).

Heather, P., and D. Moncur (2001). *Politics, Philosophy, and Empire in the Fourth Century*. (Liverpool).

Holwerda, D., and H. J. Scheltema, eds. (1953–) *Basilicorum libri LX., Series B*. 9 vols. (Groningen).

Huebner, S. R. (2013). "Adoption and Fosterage in the Ancient Eastern Mediterranean," in Grubbs and Parkin, 510–531.

Immerwahr, D. (2019). *How to Hide an Empire: A History of the Greater United States*. (New York).

Imric, A. (2018). *The Antonine Constitution: An Edict for the Caracallan Empire*. (Leiden).

Kaldellis, A. (2005). "The Works and Days of Hesychios the Illoustrios of Miletos." *GRBS* 45: 381–403.

Kaldellis, A. (2015). *The Byzantine Republic: People and Power at New Rome*. (Cambridge, Mass.).

Kaldellis, A. (2019). *Romanland: Ethnicity and Empire in Byzantium*. (Cambridge, Mass.).

Kaldellis, A. (2020). "How Was a 'New Rome' Even Thinkable? Premonitions of Constantinople and the Portability of Rome," in Kim and McLaughlin, 221–247.

Kaldellis, A. (2021). "Civic Identity and Civic Participation in Byzantium," in Brélaz and Rose, 93–110.

Kaldellis, A., and N. Siniossogou, eds. (2017). *The Cambridge Intellectual History of Byzantium*. (Cambridge).

Kaplan, M., ed. (2006). *Monastères, images, pouvoirs et société à Byzance*. (Paris).

Kim, Y. R., and A. E. T. McLaughlin, eds. (2020). *Leadership and Community in Late Antiquity: Essays in Honour of Raymond Van Dam*. (Turnhout).

Kitzinger, E. (1954). "The Cult of Images in the Age before Iconoclasm." *Dumbarton Oaks Papers* 8: 83–150.

Kolbaba, T. (in progress). "Why Read Heresiology? What Anti-Heretical Texts Can Contribute to Historical Understanding."

Konstan, D. (1986). "Ideology and Narrative in Livy, Book I." *Cl. Ant.* 5: 197–215.

Koortbojian, M. (2020). *Crossing the Pomerium: The Boundaries of Political, Religious, and Military Institutions from Caesar to Constantine*. (Princeton).

Kotter, P. B., ed. (1975). *Die Schriften des Johannes von Damaskos*, vol. 3. (Berlin).

Kruse, M. (2019). *The Politics of Roman Memory from the Fall of the Western Empire to the Age of Justinian*. (Philadelphia).

Lagarrigue, G. (1975). *Salvien de Marseille: Oeuvres*, vol. 2. (Paris).

Lamberz, E., ed. (2008–2016). *Concilium Universale Nicaenum Secundum*. Acta Conciliorum Oecumenicorum ser. 2, vol. 3. 3 vols. (Berlin).

Leidholm, N. (2019). *Elite Byzantine Kinship, ca. 950–1204: Blood, Reputation, and the Genos*. (Leeds).

Lenski, N. (2015). "Constantine and the Tyche of Constantinople," in Wienand, 330–352.

Louth, A. (2002). *St John Damascene: Tradition and Originality in Byzantine Theology*. (Oxford).

Macrides, R. (1987). "The Byzantine Godfather." *Byzantine and Modern Greek Studies* 11: 139–162.

Macrides, R. (1990). "Kinship by Arrangement: The Case of Adoption." *Dumbarton Oaks Papers* 44: 109–118.

Magdalino, P. (2007). "Isaac II, Saladin, and Venice," in Shepard, 93–106.

Masterson, M. (2019). "Nikephoros Ouranos, Eunuchism, and Masculinity during the Reign of Emperor Basil II." *Byzantion* 89: 397–419.

Meehan, D. ed. (1958). *Adomnan's* De locis sanctis. (Dublin).

Moffatt, A., and M. Tall (2012). *Constantine Porphyrogennetos: The Book of Ceremonies*. 2 vols. (Canberra).

Mondzain, M.-J. (2004). *Image, Icon, Economy: The Byzantine Origins of the Contemporary Imaginary*. (Stanford, Calif.).

Moravcsik, G., ed., and R. J. H. Jenkins, tr. (1967). *Constantine Porphyrogenitus: De administrando imperio*. (Washington, D.C.).

Morris, R. (1995). *Monks and Laymen in Byzantium, 843–1118*. (Cambridge).

Mullett, M., and D. Smythe, eds. (1996). *Alexios I Komnenos*. (Belfast).

Opitz, H. G., ed. (1940). *Athanasius Werke*, vol. 2.1. (Berlin).

Parry, K. (2018). "Theodore the Stoudite: The Most 'Original' Iconophile?" *Jahrbuch der österreichischen Byzantinistik* 68: 261–275.

Price, R. (2018). *The Acts of the Second Council of Nicaea (787)*. 2 vols. (Liverpool).

Pruche, B., ed. (1946). *Basile de Césarée: Traité du Saint-Espirit.* (Paris).
Rapp, C. (2016). *Brother-Making in Late Antiquity and Byzantium: Monks, Laymen, and Christial Ritual.* (Oxford).
Richardson, J. S. (1995). "The Roman Mind and the Power of Fiction," in Ayres, 117–130.
Riedinger, R. (1992). *Concilium Universale Constantinopolitanum Tertium*, vol. 2. Acta Conciliorum Oecumenicorum ser. 2, vol. 2.2. (Berlin).
Scheltema, H. J., and N. van der Val, eds. (1953–) *Basilicorum Libri LX, Series A.* 8 vols. (Groningen).
Ševčenko, I., ed. and tr. (2011). *Chronographiae quae Theophanis Continuati nomine fertur liber quo Vita Basilii imperatoris amplectitur.* (Berlin).
Shepard, J. (1996). "'Father' or 'Scorpion'? Style and Substance in Alexios' Diplomacy," in Mullett and Smythe, 68–132.
Shepard, J., ed. (2007). *The Expansion of Orthodox Europe: Byzantium, the Balkans and Russia.* (Aldershot).
Stolte, B. (2017). "Legal Thought," in Kaldellis and Siniossogou, 141–166.
Tafel, G. L. F., and G. M. Thomas, eds. (1856). *Urkunden zur älteren Handels- und Staatsgeschichte der Republik Venedig*, vol. 1 (Vienna).
Talbot, A.-M., and S. McGrath (2006). "Monastic Onomastics," in Kaplan, 89–118.
Thomas, Y. (1995). "*Fictio legis*: L'empire de la fiction romaine et ses limites médiévales." *Droits* 21: 17–63.
Thurn, I. (1973). *Ioannis Scylitzae Synopsis historiarum.* (Berlin).
Thurn, I. (2000). *Ioannis Malalae* Chronographia. (Berlin).
Tollefsen, T. T. (2018). *St Theodore the Studite's Defence of the Icons: Theology and Philosophy in Ninth-Century Byzantium.* (Oxford).
Tougher, S. (2008). *The Eunuch in Byzantine History and Society.* (New York).
Troianos, S. N., ed. (2007). Οι Νεαρές του Λεόντος ς του Σοφού. (Athens).
van de Paverd, F. (1991). *St. John Chrysostom, The Homilies on the Statues: An Introduction.* (Rome).
Vanderspoel, J. (2012). "A Tale of Two Cities: Themistius on Rome and Constantinople," in Grig and Kelly, 223–240.
Wienand, J., ed. (2015). *Contested Monarchy: Integrating the Roman Empire in the Fourth Century AD.* (Oxford).
Zepos, P., and J. Zepos (1931). *Jus Graecoromanum*, vol. 1. (Athens).

CHAPTER 32

LATIN NEOPLATONISM
The Medieval Period

AGNIESZKA KIJEWSKA

The continuation of the Neoplatonic tradition in the Middle Ages is a complex problem that has been the object of many studies. Stephen Gersh, in his comprehensive monograph devoted to Middle Platonism and Neoplatonism in the Latin tradition, summed up the results of this research and introduced a number of essential distinctions. One of the most widespread beliefs concerning the nature and development of Platonism in the Latin Middle Ages is that this tradition was mediated by late antique reinterpretations of Platonic thought, and that the availability of Plato's own dialogues in the medieval Latin milieu was slight.[1] The question that immediately arises is whether medieval Platonism is in fact indistinguishable in its doctrinal content from Neoplatonism. This question is part of a larger problem, namely, to what extent Platonism and Neoplatonism can be regarded as two distinct currents of thought, each with an evolution of its own, rather than two sides of a single current.[2] Gersh sums up his own view of this problem as follows: "One can perhaps conclude from even this brief discussion that the proposed definition of Neoplatonism as that philosophy which is concerned with the elaboration of certain underlying tendencies in Plato's own teaching has a number of advantages."[3]

Taking this quasi-definition of Neoplatonism as my point of departure, in what follows I will propose certain distinctions pertaining to medieval Latin Neoplatonism. I hope that these distinctions, despite a certain oversimplification, may prove helpful in providing a synthetic grasp of the variety of Latin Neoplatonism and its roots in ancient thought. This in turn may be helpful in eliminating some prejudices concerning this period and in finding a guiding thread to represent the complex issues involved.[4]

The distinguished medieval scholar, Joseph Koch, in his 1956 study of medieval Platonism, identified two fundamental forms of Platonism as pursued and developed in the Middle Ages, namely the Augustinian and Dionysian tendencies.[5] There seem to be good reasons to add to this division a third, distinct form of Platonism present in the Middle Ages, namely that which has its origin in Boethius.[6] Each of these three forms of Neoplatonism was started in Christian antiquity by a "founding father" of its own, was continued and developed by some medieval followers, and had its roots in the philosophical schools of pagan antiquity.

A body of philosophical writings which Augustine described as *libri platonicorum*, without specifying either the authors or the titles (so it is still open to debate what these items were), played a decisive role in the intellectual evolution of Augustine's thought. We may be certain that among those texts were excerpts from Plotinus's *Enneads* in the Latin rendering of Marius Victorinus. Possibly Augustine's readings may also have included sections of Porphyry's treatise *De regressu animae*.[7] Thus it is plausible to conclude that Augustine's thought was shaped by ideas formed in the Roman school of Neoplatonism founded by Plotinus, with contributions from Porphyry and passed on to the Latin intellectual milieux by Marius Victorinus. In Porphyry's interpretation, the triadic structure of reality as conceived by Plotinus was further subdivided into an enneadic or nine-fold scheme, headed by the first element, the One, which is identical with the Being. On this view, Porphyry's first triad, the intelligible One, comprised three hypostases: Being, Life (or Power), and Intelligence. These three elements, as reinterpreted by Augustine in the light of the Prologue to the Gospel of John, were seen as an apt way of articulating the Christian doctrine of the Trinity. We may draw several conclusions.

1. Augustine's interpretation of the Christian trinitarian conception in philosophical terms, without asserting the primacy of the One over Being, is one of the most distinctive features of Augustinian Neoplatonism.
2. Another such feature is Augustine's transformation of the emanationist model of the evolution of reality from the One (later summarized in the concise formula *mone-proodos-epistrophe*/remaining-procession-reversion) into a creationist and non-emanationist view:[8] the automatism of the necessary process of outflowing was replaced by God's voluntary act of creation.
3. It follows necessarily from this last point that material reality, being the work of God, projected and executed by Himself, is of necessity good in itself. In this perspective, evil as such has no real substance, no independent being, but only a tenuous and dependent existence of privation, a lack of the requisite good.
4. The material world, being a projection of the system of ideas as subsisting in God's own Mind (exemplarism), has an anagogical function: it works as a set of symbols whose true meaning is the reality of God Himself; the corporeal world is like a book that should be read and whose reading will lead mankind back to the source of all reality.
5. The privileged locus of this reading and ascent to God is the interior of the human mind, the *cogito*; since sensible things have a better existence as known by the human mind than in themselves, it can legitimately be said that the human mind is foundational with respect to the material world.
6. Human nature, nevertheless, good as it is in itself, has been corrupted as a result of original sin, and therefore truly intelligent cognition of things can only be

accomplished with the assistance of special divine enlightenment, which alone enables man to assess the cognized things in the light of their eternal, divine archetypes.
7. Augustine's essential assumption concerning human nature was that, since man was created in God's image and likeness, his nature is a reflection of God's triune nature, the human soul being one in itself and yet comprising three distinct powers of memory, intelligence and will.
8. The effective remedy for the crippling effect of original sin upon man, and especially upon human will, is divine grace, which is absolutely necessary for human conversion and reformation.

These essential ideas of Augustine's, as summarized in the eight points above, formed a doctrine that was influential ever since in the Latin Christian tradition, and had a particularly powerful impact on the thought of the Middle Ages. These ideas were taken up and developed by Alcuin, St. Anselm of Canterbury, the school of Saint Victor, and in the thirteenth century by St. Bonaventure and the Augustinian current of that century as represented by John Peckham and Peter Olivi.

Dionysian Neoplatonism penetrated into the intellectual milieux of the Latin West owing to the translation of the *Corpus Dionysiacum* into Latin in the ninth century. The enigmatic author of that body of writings, probably a Syrian monk, who depended heavily on the ideas of Proclus, one of the leading representatives of the Neoplatonic school of Athens, styled himself a disciple of St. Paul, converted by the apostle at the Areopagus in Athens (Acts 17). The first ascertainable reference to him in the Latin West is found in the *Homilies on the Gospels* by St. Gregory the Great.[9] The *Corpus Dionysiacum* itself made its way into the Latin West only in 827, when a copy was sent as a gift for the emperor Louis the Pious by the Byzantine ruler Michael the Stammerer. The first Latin translation of this body of writings was the achievement of Hilduin, the abbot of Saint-Denis, but it proved unsatisfactory, and so John Scotus Eriugena was commissioned to prepare a new Latin version, which he did in 862. In the twelfth century John Sarrazin and in the thirteenth Robert Grosseteste produced new translations of Pseudo-Dionysius's work, but it is Eriugena's version that came to be regarded as the "Latin Dionysiac Vulgate."[10]

Pseudo-Dionysius, following Proclus's ideas, asserted the absolute transcendence, ontological as well as cognitive, of the inaccessible First Principle—the One, which is a reality beyond and above being itself. This transcendent Divine Principle cannot be known for what it is, for nothing can legitimately be predicated of it in the affirmative; we can only know it for what it is not, since only predication in the negative is allowed of it.

1. Such a radically apophatic approach can be regarded as one of the most salient distinctive features of Pseudo-Dionysius's conception. In this theory, God emerges from His mysterious depths in the process of positing beings and in this way reveals Himself and makes Himself nameable and cognitively graspable through the intermediary of the realities He calls into being.

2. Thus, the reality posited in the process of God's self-manifestation is a theophany, a revelation, albeit imperfect, of the hidden, inaccessible Source, which in this way becomes graspable within the framework of a cataphatic theology.
3. The process of divine self-revelation, which is identical with the creation of knowable reality, follows a definite order and its result is a hierarchically arranged world comprising both intelligible and sensible beings, to which correspond the concepts of the celestial and the ecclesiastical hierarchy respectively.
4. The reality posited in this way forms an orderly structure, which is symbolic in its function in that its elements always point to some reality beyond, ultimately to the reality of the transcendent First Principle; finding the meaning of these symbols is the task given to mankind.
5. In this metaphysical vision man is assigned a very special place and function: being located between the sensible and intelligible spheres of reality, human beings are called on to reverse the process of the flow of being out of and away from the First Principle and to return to the Source and unite with it (henōsis).
6. This reverse movement is accomplished through intellectual cognition: it begins with reading the symbols constituting perceptible reality, and an understanding of their meaning provides the light which enables the human intellect to step onto the path of mystical ascent toward the One, which comprises the successive stages of purification, illumination, and perfection.[11]

The ideas of Pseudo-Dionysius had a significant impact on medieval intellectual tradition, and its influence is particularly noticeable in medieval mysticism and aesthetics. After Eriugena completed his translation of the Dionysian corpus and supplemented it with his commentary on *The Celestial Hierarchy*, and until the twelfth century, when Hugh of Saint Victor published his exposition of the same work, *The Celestial Hierarchy* was the most studied treatise among Dionysius's works, providing the Latins with a guide to representing the structure of the spiritual Universe. In the thirteenth century the interest of the Latin scholars shifted to another treatise, namely *The Divine Names*, already commented on in the twelfth century by William of Lucca. This work attracted the attention of such thinkers as Albert the Great and Thomas Aquinas, who wrote expository treatises on it. In the fourteenth and fifteenth centuries yet another of the Dionysian works came to the fore, namely *Mystical Theology*, which became the focus of debates on mystical experience and learned ignorance as a path to mystical unknowing.[12]

Over and above these two currents in the reception of Neoplatonic ideas there existed in the Middle Ages yet another tendency whose proponents studied and developed conceptions and methods put forward in the Neoplatonic context of late antiquity. This third current has been aptly named "Boethian Neoplatonism." Anicius Boethius, an illustrious descendant of an ancient Roman aristocratic family and one of the most erudite men of his generation, probably acquired his learning in the Neoplatonic schools of Alexandria. His work, which proved so influential in medieval schools, consisted in a large part of translations of some logical works of Aristotle and Porphyry and extensive commentaries on these,[13] yet he was also an ingenious thinker in his own right, as his "sacred opuscules" and the famous *Consolation of Philosophy* prove, and he was the chief transmitter of much of the ancient logical, philosophical, and scientific legacy to the schools of the Middle Ages.[14] The essential features of the intellectual tradition passed on by Boethius to medieval scholars are as follows.

1. An emphasis on logical, philosophical, and scientific erudition, including insistence on logical precision and methodological systematicity: some of Boethius's works were composed "in a geometric manner" (*more geometrico*), on the model of Proclus's *Elements of Theology* and Euclid's *Elements*.
2. The interpretation of Aristotle's tripartite division of theoretical philosophy into physics, mathematics, and theology in a Platonic spirit as a description of the ascent of the human intellect toward immediately grasping the pure form of Godhead, starting from forms immersed in matter (physics), via forms abstracted from matter (mathematics) and finally arriving at the realm of purely formal being. Thus, the ultimate goal of theology is the intellectual vision of the pure immaterial being, God, which means that intellectual discourse ends in theology in an act of pure contemplation.
3. An important intermediary role in the ascent of the human mind to the contemplation of God is played by mathematics, which is the proper domain of the faculty of reason (the discursive faculty of the human mind as opposed to intellect, which is the faculty of immediate comprehension), which purifies the eye of the human mind of all sense images and enables it to comprehend purely nonsensual reality; one can say that mathematics plays a propaedeutic role with respect to theology.[15]
4. Such an epistemology, related to Platonic ontology, raises the question of the ontological structure of the human being, and especially of the nature and origin of the human soul. At the outset of his discussion of human cognition, Boethius employs the language of Aristotelian genetic empiricism, as he states that our senses are the only source of cognitive material for our imagination and reason, yet he soon goes on to state that the concept of pure and simple form is only grasped by the eye of intellect, which is an innate faculty of the human mind and is set off by sense stimuli but does not depend on the senses for the comprehension of its object.[16]
5. When considering the origin of the human soul, Boethius seems to assert the soul's priority in time with respect to its body: the soul descends or "falls" into the body from heaven.[17] This view of the human soul he expresses mainly in the *Consolation*, a work that used to be regarded with suspicion on account of its allegedly pagan content, yet the riddle of the origin of the human soul was regarded as notoriously hard to solve and even. Augustine, in his attempts to find an answer to that question, admitted the plausibility of even very odd theories, and his conception of "heaven of heavens" can be said to represent a theoretical acceptance of the preexistence of the human soul.[18]
6. While emphasizing the fundamental importance of the intellectual sphere in man (as shown in his celebrated definition of the person),[19] Boethius did not leave out of account the human will and its place in the structure of human faculties. He

considered acts of the will to be analogous to natural desires in animals; an act of the human will, when supported by a judgment of reason and in the absence of external compulsion, is an act of free choice (*liberum arbitrium*).[20] Man enlarges the extent of his freedom as he comes closer to God's vision of things; however, when he departs from the spiritual perception of reality and falls to the level of corporeal life, he becomes enslaved in natural necessity and comes to be a prisoner of his own freedom.[21] With this idea Boethius bequeathed to scholars of subsequent generations the problem of the relationship between human freedom and divine prescience and Providence.[22]

Boethius's approach, and in particular his methodology and conception of philosophical knowledge, with mathematics providing the link between the study of the visible cosmos and that of the spiritual domain, found its followers above all in the twelfth century. Boethius's attempt to conjoin faith and reason in one overarching cognitive movement, leading ultimately to a contemplative grasp of God as the proper object of the human intelligence, found a congenial reception in such thinkers as Thierry of Chartres, William of Conches, Gilbert of La Porrée, Alain of Lille, and others. In this intellectual environment mathematics was applied to cosmological speculations, but also to theological ones, especially in those currents that David Albertson has described as "mathematical theology," represented by Thierry of Chartres in the twelfth and by Nicholas of Cusa in the fifteenth.[23]

The tripartite scheme delineated above might be modified in a number of ways: new elements might be added to it, and emphases might be shifted. Yet on the whole it provides a useful guide to the rich legacy of medieval Neoplatonism.

In the following section I give an example of an application of the above scheme to one particular problem. A well-known formula summarizing the process of reality as envisioned in Neoplatonism is the triadic expression *mone-proodos-epistrophe* (remaining-procession-reversion). Christian thinkers, in adopting the overall scheme captured by this formula, had to replace its emanationist construal as implicit in pagan conceptions with a creationist one. Another crucial modification introduced by Christians was to shift the most important caesura dividing reality from the borderline separating the corporeal sphere from the spiritual world to that separating the Creator from His work as a whole, which comprised both sensible and intelligible beings. In creating the material world God produced the most perfect work of art as a book, in which a well-prepared reader can read God's Power, Wisdom, and Graciousness. In this spirit Hugh of Saint Victor wrote:

> For this whole sensible world is a kind of book written by the finger of God, that is, created by divine power (*virtus*), and each creature is a kind of figure, not invented by human determination, but established by the divine will to manifest and in some way signify the invisible wisdom of God. However, just as an unlettered person sees an open book and notices the shapes but does not recognize the letters, so stupid and carnal people, who are not aware of the things of God, see on the outside the beauty

in these visible creatures but they do not understand its meaning. On the other hand, a spiritual person can discern all things. When he considers externally the beauty of the work, he understands internally how wondrous is the wisdom of the Creator.[24]

As the designated reader of the book of the world, mankind occupies a special position within this created world[25]. The Book of Genesis has him created on the last, sixth day of creation, as if to imply that man is the sum and crown of creation. In terms of Neoplatonic anthropology, man comprises in his nature both sensible and intelligible reality: *kosmos aisthetos* and *kosmos noetos*; in point of fact man constitutes the only link between these two universes. As a sum of all of created reality, albeit in miniature, he is aptly described as microcosm (Pl. *Timaeus* 31C). The description of man as microcosm goes back to Plato, whose philosophy was an attempt to demonstrate that all spheres of human life, in particular the moral and social spheres, should be modeled after the structure of the human soul and be in agreement with the structure of the material universe. Being a miniature summary of the whole universe, man has the task of perfecting the process of reality by bringing the universe back to its source[26]. The analogy between man and the universe at large may be seen in terms of the structure of the human body (cosmological aspect) or of the human soul (psychological aspect), or else in terms of the dynamic psychophysical unity of the whole human being (dynamic-organological aspect). The distinction among these different aspects presupposes the theory of psychophysical dualism of man as proposed by Plato; for this reason Aristotle and those who subscribed to his anthropology rejected the explanation of the human being in terms of microcosm.[27] Specification of diverse conceptions of man proposed by the several medieval currents of Neoplatonism as aspects of the microcosmic theory allows us to highlight the theoretical points they have in common as well as differences between the three species of medieval Neoplatonism sketched above.

St. Augustine, in his *Soliloquies*, in an inner dialogue[28] (1.2.7) declares: "I desire to know God and the soul. And nothing more? Nothing whatever." This statement, often construed in terms of exclusive theocentrism and contempt for the profane world of our ordinary experience, contains a concise summary of Augustine's engagement with theories of reality and of knowledge. It presupposes a conception of man as a being located between two distinct realms of the universe and constituting the mediating link between them. This supposition is made explicit in his *On the Magnitude of the Soul*, where he attempts a definition of the human soul, modeled on the one widely accepted in the Platonic tradition (*Alcibiades* 129c–130c): "It seems to me to be a certain kind of substance, sharing in reason, fitted to rule the body."[29]

When treating the human soul, Augustine uses the terms *anima*, *animus*, *mens*, or *spiritus*, while the term *ratio* or "reason" refers to power within the soul. He is very firm on the substantiality of the soul and its essential independence from the body. The human soul is a substance that not only possesses being, in common with all other beings, including inanimate bodies, but also life, in common with animals, and, above all, the faculty of intellectual vision, which is a common feature of spiritual beings. As the soul possesses life in its own right, it can impart life to its associated body, while the human mind's ability to know intelligible, incorporeal essences clearly shows that it is incorporeal itself and, consequently, immortal: being the principle of life, the mind cannot die itself.[30] Not only is the human soul capable of performing acts of intellection and willing on its own, without participation of the conjoined body, but it is immediately aware of itself in performing these acts. Thus, while the existence of every object of our experience can in principle be doubted, the existence of the soul as the thinking subject is beyond reasonable doubt; Augustine points to this fact in a number of contexts, establishing in this way the model for the Cartesian *cogito* argument.[31] He was much occupied by problems concerning the human soul: its origin, its ontological nature, its faculties and functions, the interplay of the acts it can perform simultaneously, and the connection and distinction of its faculties within the simple nature of its substance, which for him formed the clearest model available to us of the Trinity of Divine Persons within the unity and simplicity of the Divine Substance:

> We are inquiring, of course, about the power of the soul, and the soul has the power to perform all these acts simultaneously, although it may think that it is really doing only that act which implies some effort, or, at least, some fear. For it performs that act with greater attention than the rest. To teach these grades to anyone, let the acts of the soul, from the lowest to the highest, be called, first, Animation, the second, Sensation; the third, Art; the fourth, Virtue; the fifth, Tranquility; the sixth, Approach, the seventh, Contemplation. They can be named also in this way: "of the body," "through the body," "about the body," "toward itself," "in itself," "toward God," "in God."[32]

The journey of the soul toward God begins at the level of sense experience: the soul perceives the material reality and, awakened by this experience, returns into itself, whence it can begin its ascent toward spiritual knowledge of God. Augustine calls the soul in so far as it performs its lower, biological functions, such as the vegetative function of animation and of sensation, the "outer man," recalling the Pauline distinction between "inner" and "outer" man.[33] However, even these lowest biological functions, when performed by the human soul, are executed in a distinctively human way, and they contribute to the functioning of the power which Augustine calls "lower reason" (*ratio inferior*), whose proper task is acquisition of "science," that is knowledge about the world of sense experience.[34] When the human mind turns its attention to eternal essences, which are ideas subsisting in God and can be known by human beings thanks to divine enlightenment, it employs the power which is called "higher reason" (*ratio superior*), and which belongs to the "inner man." Other terms used by Augustine to refer to the spiritual faculty are "mind" (*mens*), intellect, and "eye of the mind" (an expression perhaps coined by Plato, *Resp.* 533c–d), always turned toward what is eternal and immutable, that is to divine ideas. The knowledge this "higher reason" achieves is wisdom (*sapientia*) properly so called, and in its light the achievements of the "inferior reason" are judged and assessed:

> But it is the province of the superior reason to judge of these corporeal things according to incorporeal and eternal reasons, which, if they were not above the human mind, would certainly not be unchangeable (. . .) But we judge of corporeal things

according to the standard of dimensions and figures, which, as the mind knows, remain unchangeable.³⁵

Corporeal realities, when known by the human mind, acquire a "better," more unified mode of being than that they had outside the mind. Thus the movement from the external to the internal is a progress from the "inferior" to the "superior," a movement of approach toward God. The path of human ascent leads from sensible reality via the human spirit toward the reality that surpasses human spirituality. Now it is clear why the cognition of one's own soul was so crucial for Augustine: it is the soul that relates the acquired knowledge of the sensible world to the eternal patterns existing in God and thus to God Himself. Whatever is of any importance for progress toward mankind's ultimate goal can be reduced to these two objects of human knowledge: God and the soul.

Hugh of Saint Victor, undoubtedly much under Augustine's influence, envisioned the itinerary of human progress toward God in an analogous way. This representative of the twelfth century revival of speculation and letters discovered images and similitudes of transcendent realities even in the material world; for instance, he found a reflection of the Trinity of Divine Persons in the structure of the human body.³⁶ He laid particular stress on the human mind, "created wisdom" being an image of the "uncreated wisdom," the Wisdom of God:

> Therefore, the first and principal representative of uncreated wisdom is created wisdom, that is, the rational creature, which because in one aspect it is visible and in another invisible, becomes a door and path of contemplation. It is a door insofar as it is visible, it is a path insofar as it is invisible (...), It is a door because in some fashion it shows invisible things visibly. It is a path because it leads those going from the visible through the invisible to see the One who is Creator equally of the visible and the invisible. One can recognize this in oneself. No one is wise at all who does not see that he exists. Nevertheless, if one begins to pay attention to what one truly is, one will understand that he is none of all the things that are or can be in him. For truly that in us that is capable of reason, although that is, so to speak, infused into and mixed with the flesh, can distinguish itself by its own reason from the substance of the flesh and understand that the latter is foreign to it. Why then does anyone have any doubt at all about the existence of invisible things, when he sees that what is truly human, whose existence no one can doubt, is itself invisible? Therefore the door to contemplation opens for one, who, under the guidance of reason, enters to know himself.³⁷

No one can miss the unmistakably Augustinian flavor of the quoted passage, which contains some of the most essential points of the Augustinian representation of the cognitive ascent of the human spirit toward God. Likewise, a century later, St. Bonaventure described the "itinerary of the mind to God" as consisting of a passage from imprints of Divine Wisdom in the material world to the interior of the human mind and from there, progressively, to the contemplation of the divine attributes of Being and Goodness:

> Some created things are vestiges, others images; some are material, others spiritual; some are temporal, others everlasting; some are outside us, others within us. In order

to contemplate the First Principle, who is most spiritual, eternal, and above us, we must pass through his vestiges, which are material, temporal and outside us. This means to be led in the path of God. We must also enter into our soul, which is God's image, everlasting, spiritual and within us. This means to enter in the truth of God. We must go beyond to what is eternal, most spiritual and above us, by gazing upon the First Principle. This means to rejoice in the knowledge of God and in reverent fear of his majesty.[38]

There is a very curious elaboration of the idea of man as microcosm in the work of John Scotus Eriugena, who, as the translator of Pseudo-Dionysius's writings, familiarized himself thoroughly with his thought. Eriugena locates man on the borderline between the sensible and intelligible realms of being as a reality straddling the dividing line between them. In his famous *Homily on the Prologue of St. John's Gospel*, he calls man a "third world," consisting of the elements of the first and second worlds. The former is the spiritual universe, filled with the substances of immaterial and pure spirits, which are close to the divine light itself. Opposed to that realm of light is the second world, the one of matter, comprising all corporeal entities. The third world is the one constituted in man, whose soul is taken from the spiritual and body from the material universe. Comprising in a way both worlds in his constitution, man forms the link between them, a crucible, in which all created elements are melted together to produce one reality. The injunction in the Gospel of Mark (Mark 16:15), "Preach the gospel to all creation," is a commandment to evangelize mankind, since man is in fact all creation.[39] Man's central position in the universe entitles him to the description, "workshop of all creatures," as all creatures have been made fit to constitute his nature.[40]

All the descriptions that Eriugena attributes to man as the centerpiece of all created orders presuppose that man is an agent participant in the process of creation. For it is in the human intellect that God posited all things as possible objects of knowledge. In its essence God's creative act is an act of intelligence, and so Eriugena can name God's creative wisdom a *Virtus Gnostica*, and claim that the human intellect participates in this "gnostic power" as conscious activity constituting the things of the created universe. In Scotus, the conscious mind, the *cogito*, is not only the source of certainty in the thinking subject, as it was in Augustine; it is also a manifestation of the "power" of comprehension, which is the force positing things as correlates of conscious intentional acts.[41] The Book of Genesis indicated this in its story of Adam giving names to all those creations, which he had been called on to supervise and take care of. The act of giving a name to a thing presupposes on the part of man possession of the concept of the thing he names. The concept of a thing as posited by God in the human mind determines the true substance of that thing, whereas the concept of man is only present in God's mind and thus has a part in God's unknowability. One may say, therefore, that the human *cogito* is also a revelation of the hidden God:

> For I understand the substance of the whole man to be nothing else but the concept of him in the Mind of his Artificer, who knew all things in Himself before they were made; and the very knowledge is the true and only substance of the things known,

since it is in that knowledge that they are most perfectly created and eternally and immutably subsist.[42]

The whole nature of man comprises the "outer man," which is the body composed of the four elements and the form which unites them, and the "inner man," comprising in turn the senses: the inner sense and the outer senses, vital movement, reason, and intellect.[43] All the lower ontological elements constituting man are contained in an eminent way in the human intellect, as the ontological principle that governs this philosophy states that all inferior elements exist in a better way in superior elements. Seen in this perspective, human nature is said to contain all ontological layers of created reality in a perfect way and, as such, is called Paradise. Outside that Paradise, that is outside the human intellect, nothing exists. However, original sin, that is, the irrational motion of the soul, was brought about the fall of man and, consequently, the whole of creation. The present predicament of man, that is, being in a "worse" state than the original condition assigned to man by God, imposes upon man the obligation to effect the restoration of himself and of the whole creation to the primeval perfection of Paradise. Thus the history of human progress is the history of the cosmic return of the whole of created reality to its original perfection; man is the moving spirit behind this return. There are, moreover, two forms of cosmic return: there is universal return of the universe of all things to the original condition of perfection and there is special return of the elect. The latter consists in mystical union of the chosen with the transcendent and impenetrable God. Eriugena provides an illustration of the difference between the two kinds of return by reference to the parable of the ten virgins (Matthew 15:1–13): while all the virgins come to the wedding, only the wise ones, who brought oil, are admitted to the banquet. Likewise, while all humans will be renewed in their natural constitution and the natural gifts they are endowed with, only those who provided themselves with the oil of good deeds and clean conscience will be admitted to communion with the Bridegroom, that is to mystical marriage.[44]

The dynamic vision of reality presented in Eriugena's works found few adherents and followers; it was only the movement of German idealism in the first half of the nineteenth century that brought a new appreciation and highly positive evaluation of the ideas of that genius of the Early Middle Ages.[45]

In contrast to the tradition of Neoplatonic metaphysical speculation which inspired Eriugena, Boethius focused on the moral dimensions of the theory of man as microcosm, especially in relation to the psychological version of that theory, which highlighted the likeness of the human soul to the universe. In a famous scene of his *Consolation*, Lady Philosophy appears to the imprisoned Boethius, who is plunged in despair after having been accused of the worst crimes and having lost his high standing in the world. The personified Philosophy undertakes to cure the illness of her pupil, an illness which she diagnoses as lethargy and forgetfulness of himself.[46] The course of therapy she proceeds to apply consists in an extensive argument designed to demonstrate to the despairing Boethius the falsehood of the beliefs concerning the supreme good, the world and man, that he had inadvertently accepted. An authentic human existence consists in coming to know the form of true good, the good that is the source of life, because it introduces unity in whatever it informs. When a human being departs from that good and unity, he loses the kind of life that is properly human and falls to the level of animal existence and possibly even lower:

> And so it comes about that anyone whom you see metamorphosed by vices you can no longer judge to be a human being. One man, a savage thief, pants after and is ravenous for the goods of other people—you can say that he is like a wolf. (...) Another wallows in foul and unclean lust—he is held under by the physical delights of a filthy sow. And so it is that anyone who has ceased to be a human being by deserting righteousness, since he has not the power to cross over into the divine condition, is turned into a beast.[47]

What Boethius presents here is a moral interpretation of the doctrine of reincarnation: when a human being fails to live up to the moral exigencies imposed by his rational nature, he becomes an animal and exemplifies the irrational and beastly aspects of animal nature. Thus, it is crucial for man to come to know his true position in the universe and to accept the true hierarchy of goods, and embrace those goods that are the proper objective of human striving and define the essence and dignity of humanity. It is vital for man to realize that only the possession of the Supreme Good will give him the fullness of power, independence, and self-sufficiency, whose possession amounts to happiness. Paradoxically, even the animal aspect of human nature is only brought to perfect realization when a human being, by overcoming his limitations, comes to be a god by participation:

> Therefore, every truly happy person is God. But, to be sure, God is one by nature; however, nothing prevents there being as many gods as you please by participation.[48]

The selected topics from the Latin tradition of Neoplatonism and discussed here may give the reader some idea about the richness and variety of that tradition. The authors chosen belong to late antiquity and the early Middle Ages, and represent the three currents of the Neoplatonic tradition that developed in this period: Augustinian, Dionysian, and Boethian Neoplatonism. All three revolved around the same major theme, namely, man as microcosm, yet each of them stressed a different aspect of that rich subject. Moreover, they presented their thoughts in a literary form that is both instructive and beautiful, although that is the topic for another study. May these ideas be a help to us, like the wings offered by Dame Philosophy to Boethius, in our own efforts to find the true meaning of our lives:

> See what I have: These are swift-beating wings for you,
> Alert to rise to heaven's heights;
> Swift-thinking mind, once these wings are attached to it,
> Looks down the earth in vast disgust.[49]

Notes

1. See Gersh (1986) 2–3.
2. Gersh (1986) 39.
3. Gersh (1986) 45.
4. See Kijewska (2020) 355–378.
5. See Koch (1969) 317–342.
6. See de Libera (1999) 159–181; Kijewska (2012) 35f.
7. See O'Meara (1997) 172–183; Courcelle (1968) 157. See Bouton-Touboulic in this volume, 1, 5–6.
8. See Gersh (1978) 217–218.
9. Poirel (2013) 273.
10. See Théry (1931) 274.
11. See Sheldon-Williams (1967) 457–472.
12. See Poirel (2013) 387.
13. See Marenbon (2003) 10–14.
14. Boethius's writings combined with Calcidius's *Commentary* on Plato's *Timaeus* became the pillars of Chartrian wisdom in the 12th century: Jeauneau (1975) 19–54; Dutton (2003) 183–205.
15. Giulio d'Onofrio names this doctrine an "eidetic nativism"; See d'Onofrio (2008) 116.
16. Boethius, *Consolatio Philosophiae* (= *Consolatio*) 5.4.
17. Boethius, *Consolatio* 3.9, tr. Stewart and Rand; Gersh (1986) 711–714.
18. August. *Conf.* 12.15 (ed. O'Donnell); Teske (2000) 39–42.
19. Boethius, *Contra Eutychen* 3.
20. Boethius, *Commentarii in librum Aristotelis Peri hermeneias* 3 (ed. Meisner); Marenbon (2003) 123–124.
21. Boethius, *Consolatio* 5.2.
22. Marenbon (2003) 121–124.
23. Albertson (2014) 12–17.
24. Hugh of Saint Victor, *On the Three Days* 4. 3 (tr. Feiss); *De tribus diebus* 814b (ed. Poirel).
25. Kijewska (2021) 49–56.
26. Kurdziałek (2014) 210.
27. Kurdziałek (2014) 210.
28. Augustine regarded Cicero as his master, especially in the field of a literary style. See Fox in this volume.
29. August., *The Magnitude of the Soul* 13.22, tr. McMahon.
30. August., *The Immortality of the Soul* 9.16.
31. See *De trinitate* 10.10.14.
32. August., *The Magnitude of the Soul* 35.79, tr. McMahon.
33. August., *De trinitate* 12.1.1, tr. McKenna. See D. F. Kennedy in this volume.
34. August., *De trinitate* 12.3.3; *The Magnitude of the Soul* 27.53.
35. August., *De trinitate* 12.2.2.
36. See Hugh of Saint Victor, *On the Three Days* 7.2.
37. Hugh of Saint Victor, *On the Three Days* 17.1–17.2, tr. Feiss; *De tribus diebus* 824D–825A.
38. *The Soul's Journey* 1.2, tr. Cousins.
39. Eriugena, *Homilia* 19.294A–B, ed. Jeauneau.
40. Eriugena, *Periphyseon* 3.733B, ed. Jeauneau, tr. O'Meara.

41. See Eruigena, *Periphyseon* 1.490B; Stock (1977) 327–335.
42. Eriugena, *Periphyseon* 4.768B, tr. O'Meara.
43. Eriugena, *Periphyseon* 5.874A.
44. *Periphyseon* 5.1011A–1012B; see Dietrich and Duclow (1986) 41–43.
45. See Beierwaltes (1973) 190–199.
46. Boethius, *Consolatio* 1.2.
47. Boethius, *Consolatio* 4.3, tr. Relihan.
48. *Consolatio* 3.10, tr. Relihan.
49. *Consolatio* 4.1, tr. Relihan.

References

Albertson, D. (2014). *Mathematical Theologies: Nicholas of Cusa and the Legacy of Thierry of Chartres.* (Oxford).
Beierwaltes, W. (1973). "The Revaluation of John Scottus Eriugena in German Idealism," in J. J. O'Meara and L. Bieler (eds.), *The Mind of Eriugena* (Dublin), 190–199.
Courcelle, P. (1968). *Recherches sur le Confessions de Saint Augustin.* (Paris).
Cousins, E. (1978). *Bonaventure: The Soul's Journey into God, The Tree of Life, The Life of St. Francis.* (Mahwah, N.J.).
de Libera, A. (1999). "Genèse et structure des métaphysiques médiévales," In J.-M. Narbonne and L. Langlois (eds.), *Métaphysique. Son histoire, sa critique, ses enjeux* (Paris), 159–181.
Dietrich, P., and D. Duclow (1986). "Paradise and Eschatology: Symbolism and Exegesis in *Periphyseon* V," in G.-H. Allard (ed.), *Jean Scot—Écrivain* (Montreal), 29–49.
d'Onofrio, G. (2008). Vera Philosophia: *Studies in Late Antique, Early Medieval, and Renaissance Christian Thought.* J. Gavin, tr. (Turnhout).
Dutton, P. (2003). "Medieval Approaches to Calcidius," in G. Reydams-Schils (ed.), *Plato's Timaeus as Cultural Icon* (Notre Dame, Ind.), 183–205.
Feiss, H., tr. (2011). "Hugh of St. Victor: 'On the Three Days,'" in B. T. Coolman and D. M. Coulter (eds.), *Trinity and Creation: A Selection of Works of Hugh, Richard and Adam of St. Victor* (New York), 49–102.
Gersh, S. (1978). *From Iamblichus to Eriugena. An Investigation of the Prehistory and Evolution of the Pseudo-Dionysian Tradition.* (Leiden).
Gersh, S. (1986). *Middle Platonism and Neoplatonism. The Latin Tradition*, vol. 1. (Notre Dame, Ind.)
Jeauneau, É. (1975). "L'héritage de la philosophie antique durant le haut moyen âge," in *La cultura antica nell' Occidente latino dal VII all' XI secolo* (Settimane di studio del CISAM, XXII, Spoleto), 19–54.
Jeauneau, É., ed. (1996). *Iohannis Scotti seu Eriugenae*, Periphyseon: Liber primus. (Turnhout).
Jeauneau, É. (1999). *Iohannis Scotti seu Eriugenae*, Periphyseon: Liber tertius. (Turnhout).
Jeauneau, É. (2000) *Iohannis Scotti seu Eriugenae*, Periphyseon: Liber quartus. (Turnhout).
Jeauneau, É. (2003). *Iohannis Scotti seu Eriugenae*, Periphyseon: Liber quintus. (Turnhout).
Jeauneau, É. (2008). *Iohannis Scotti seu Eriugenae,* Homilia super "In principio erat Verbum" et Commentarius in Euangelium Iohannis. (Turnhout).
Kijewska, A. (2021). "John Scottus Eriugena and Hugh of Saint Victor: Readers of the Book of Nature and the Book of Scripture," in D. Poirel, M.J. Janecki, W. Bajor, and M. Buraczewski

(eds.), *"Omnium expetendorum prima est sapiential":* Studies on Victorine Thought and Influence (Turnhout), 33–62.

Kijewska, A. (2012). "Ksiądz Profesor Marian Kurdziałek—promotor neoplatonizmu boecjańskiego" [Rev. Prof. Marian Kurdzialek—Promoter of Boethian Neoplatonism]. *Roczniki Filozoficzne* 60 (3): 31–51.

Kijewska, A. (2020). "Platonizm średniowieczny," in S. Janeczek and A. Starość (eds.), *Dydaktyka filozofii,* vol. 10: *Historia filozofii* (Lublin), 355–378.

Koch, J. (1969). "Augustinischer und Dionysischer Neuplatonismus und das Mittelalter," in W. Beierwaltes (ed.), *Platonismus in der Philosophie des Mittelalters* (Darmstadt), 317–342.

Kurdziałek, M. (2014). "Mediaeval Doctrines on man as image of the world." *Roczniki Filozoficzne* 62 (4): 205–246.

Marenbon, J. (2003). *Boethius.* (Oxford).

Matthews, G. B., ed., and S. McKenna, tr. (2002). *Augustine,* On the Trinity. (Cambridge).

McMahon, J., tr. (1947). "The Magnitude of the Soul," in *The Writings of Saint Augustine, Vol. 2* (Washington, D.C.), 59–149.

Meiser, C., ed. (1880). *Boethius:* Commentarii in librum Aristotelis Peri hermeneias. (Leipzig).

O'Donnell, J. J., ed. (1992). *Augustine:* Confessions. 3 vols. (Oxford).

O'Meara. J. J., tr. (1987). *Eriugena:* Periphyseon (*Division of Natures*). (Montreal).

O'Meara, J. J. (1997). *La jeunesse de Saint Augustin: Introduction aux Confessions de Saint Augustin.* J.-H. Marrou, tr. (Fribourg).

Poirel, D., ed. (2002). *Hugonis de Sancto Victore:* De tribus diebus. (Turnhout).

Poirel, D. (2013). *Des symboles et des anges: Hughes de Saint-Victor et le réveil Dionysien du XIIe siècle.* (Turnhout).

Relihan, J., tr. (2001). *Boethius,* Consolation of Philosophy. (Indianapolis).

Schopp, L., tr. (1947). "The Immortality of the Soul," in *The Writings of Saint Augustine, vol. 2* (Washington, D.C.), 15–47.

Sheldon-Williams, P. I. (1967). "The Pseudo-Dionysius," in A. H. Armstrong (ed.), *The Cambridge History of Later Greek and Early Medieval Philosophy* (Cambridge), 457–472.

Stewart, H. F., and E. K. Rand, tr. (1968). *Boethius: The Theological Tractates; The* Consolation of Philosophy. (Cambridge, Mass.).

Stock, B. (1977). "*Intelligo me esse:* Eriugena's 'Cogito,'" in R. Roques (ed.), *Jean Scot et l'histoire de la philosophie* (Paris), 327–335.

Teske, R. (2000). "The Heaven of Heaven and the Unity of St. Augustine's *Confessions.*" *American Catholic Philosophical Quarterly* 74: 29–45.

Théry, G. (1931). "Scot Erigène traducteur de Denys." *Bulletin du Cange* 6: 185–278.

CHAPTER 33

TRANSMITTING ROMAN PHILOSOPHY
The Renaissance

QUINN GRIFFIN

INTRODUCTION

THE philosophical writings of the Renaissance display several general tendencies that can be traced to their origins in the humanist movement. The civic nature of Italian humanism, a movement that sought the return of a Classical "golden age" through the restoration of ancient texts, prompted a shift toward moral and political philosophy. Scholasticism and Aristotelianism were still the subject of study for many, but other schools, such as Stoicism, Epicureanism, and Skepticism received increased attention, in part due to the rediscovery of lost texts as well as the improved ability of Renaissance scholars to read and produce Latin translations of Greek authors.[1] As Jill Kraye notes, however, editions and translations were not the only way in which humanists engaged with ancient philosophy—their works "entailed other types of *transformation* as well."[2] Kraye identifies, using the categories devised by the *Sonderforschungsbereich* 644 (a collaborative research group out of Humboldt University of Berlin),[3] a number of other interactions between humanists and ancient philosophy, such as appropriation and assimilation. These practices are evident in the works of some of the best-known writers of the era, including Machiavelli, Petrarch ,and Lorenzo Valla. It was not solely the "great men," however, who engaged with the Roman philosophical tradition in this period. The wider availability of philosophical texts and the growing practice of providing training in Latin, and more rarely, Greek, to the daughters of the merchant classes and the elite allowed for the phenomenon of the Renaissance "learned lady" to emerge.

The relationship of these women to the humanist movement has undergone substantial reevaluation throughout the modern era, from Jacob Burkhardt's late nineteenth-century assessment of Vittoria Colonna's poetry, to Albert Rabil's editions of the works of Cassandra Fedele and Laura Cereta, to Diana Robin's translations and commentaries on the same.[4] These works have demonstrated that women humanists had command of several languages and literary genres, both secular and sacred, ancient and vernacular; participated in public intellectual exchanges with both men and women, whether through oratory or in published writings; and finally, perhaps most importantly, argued eloquently for their right to do so.

This chapter will use two philosophical letters written by Laura Cereta of Brescia as a case study for the reception of Roman philosophy in this period. These letters are an excellent example of the difficulties attaching to Renaissance reception studies, particularly regarding Roman philosophy. Readers like Cereta were certainly aware of the separate traditions of Roman and Greek philosophy; yet they received much of their knowledge of Greek authors through Latin texts, whether in translation from the original Greek, as with Ambrogio Traversari's Latin edition of Diogenes Laertius, or descriptions of the schools written by Roman authors, as with Seneca's comments on Epicurus.[5] In addition, Cereta seldom quotes her sources directly, but rather uses paraphrases with similar vocabulary to convey the sense of the intended reference. These factors make for a complex relationship between the author, her sources, and her audience.

Laura Cereta was born in 1469 to a noble family. She received her earliest instruction from her father and a certain tutor identified only by her title, *praeceptrix*. Cereta then spent two years studying in a convent, resuming her studies independently at home afterward. Her letters demonstrate a firm grasp of the Latin language and knowledge of philosophy, mathematics, astrology, and religion. She mentions Cicero fondly and demonstrates familiarity with authors closer to her time such as Boccaccio, Petrarch, and Valla. Her letters, personally selected and edited in 1488, circulated among the humanists of Brescia, Verona, and Pavia during her lifetime.[6] Among others, she corresponded with Angelo Poliziano and Cassandra Fedele of Venice (though Fedele never reciprocated).

Giacomo Filippo Tomasini of Padua published the contents of a now-lost manuscript containing Cereta's letters as well as her *Oration on the Funeral of Donkey* in 1640. The 1640 edition includes a *vita* by Tomasini himself and Cereta's letters, though not the funeral dialogue. Two other manuscripts exist; Rabil argues that all of these copies were made from an unknown archetype. One is currently held in Venice,[7] written in a humanist hand and missing several folios—the index states that the *Oration on the Funeral of Donkey* begins on folio 7, but the first folio is numbered 11. The most complete manuscript resides in the Vatican.[8] This edition includes all the material in Tomasini in addition to the dialogue and seven more letters. Beyond these written works, Cereta's other scholarly activities are more difficult to establish. She may have lectured on philosophical theses at the age of eighteen and taught publicly in Brescia between the ages of twenty and twenty-seven.[9] Rabil suggests that she may have tried her hand at poetry before her efforts were cut short by her death at the age of thirty.[10]

Cereta's works reveal an intriguing stage in the reception of Roman philosophy. Rather than subscribing to any one philosophical school, Cereta envisions a larger context for her works: a *muliebris respublica* (republic of women) which Robin identifies as a "variation on the humanist commonplace *respublica litterarum* (republic of letters), a metaphor for the notion that there is an imaginary city of men who share a commitment to the study of literature."[11] Though Cereta never succeeded in creating a concrete version of this community among her contemporaries, she laid the groundwork for one by arguing that men and women were equally capable of participating in such a venture. If some women remained outside of the academic community, it was not by nature, but by choice, as she describes in one of her letters: "Nature has sufficiently bestowed her gifts upon everyone. She has opened the gates of their own choice to all" (*Donavit satis omnes Natura dotibus suis. Omnibus optionis suae portas aperuit*).[12]

This argument runs counter to much of the rhetoric surrounding the learned women of the Renaissance. Most often, they were represented as exceptions to the rule: women who managed to defy their weaker nature and rise to the level of men. Cereta, in contrast, argues against this exceptionality by referencing in one of her letters an intellectual lineage made up of approximately twenty women from Sappho and Leontium to Cereta's contemporary, Cassandra Fedele of Venice.[13] These women prove for Cereta that *ingenium* is not the sole province of men, but in fact quite common among women. Elsewhere, Cereta envisions herself as an addition to this lineage, writing to her cousin,

> My mind burns for fame, whence the noble hope of being an *exemplum* for eternity is nourished: since the name of the Amazons is extinct, and since those warlike women have returned their bows and their weapons to the temple of Bellona, I have recalled my entire mind from feminine concerns to the love of learning.
>
> ardens animus fama, unde ad perpetuitatis exemplum spes generosa nutritur: sed quantum iam extinctum sit nomen Amazonum, quantumque belligerae undecumque mulieres arcum atque arma templo Bellonae reddiderunt, revocavi penitus totum animum a foemineis curis ad litterarum amorem.[14]

For this reason, many have identified Cereta as a "proto-feminist;" she tends, however, to ascribe only intellectual equality to women, noting occasionally that they are inferior in other ways. Furthermore, her emphasis on choice as the deciding factor in women's academic inclusion overlooks the systemic inequalities that prevented many from doing so. Cereta herself, for instance, had to study at night after her housework was done, unlike the men of her class who could pursue writing and study as their main occupation.

Still, Cereta's understanding of her own intellectual potential, and that of other women, seems to have influenced her approach to classical sources. The community she envisions transcends the boundaries between philosophical schools and is united instead by a proto-feminist philosophy of intellectual equality. As such, Cereta is not wholly devoted to any one school of ancient philosophy, referencing most of the major philosophers and their schools in her works. Furthermore, the ideas of these schools appear fully digested and integrated into her work. Ancient philosophy is not a source of absolute authority for Cereta; the authors and texts are subject to her own interpretation, which is often influenced by the Christian context in which she wrote. The incompatibility of paganism with Christianity was in fact a constant source of tension between the Christian author and her sources throughout the early modern period, and it often necessitated some justification or explanation on her part. The authors of the period resorted to many different strategies, as R. G. Witt has described: some simply ignored the incompatibility, choosing only the passages that suited their needs; others insisted that offensive pagan myths and religious practices were really complicated allegories containing universal truths; still others rejected pagan authors outright, or only drew from them for knowledge they considered to be purely secular.[15] Cereta's method is more straightforward: she acknowledges that the philosophers committed certain errors and then extracts what she finds to be useful and true.

CERETA, SENECA, AND LUCRETIUS

Cereta tends to favor Stoicism and Epicureanism in her writings and often borrows ideas and rhetorical strategies from Seneca and Lucretius. She would have had exposure to both schools of thought in her education and her independent studies. Stoicism had remained popular throughout the Medieval and Renaissance periods, with the fictitious correspondence between Seneca and Paul providing an argument for the compatibility of his philosophy with Christianity. In addition, Petrarch had set a precedent for this compatibility with his 1366 work, *Remedies for Good and Bad Fortune*.[16] Though humanists such as Lorenzo Valla eventually began to question the authenticity of the letters between Seneca and Paul, and at times were critical of Stoic philosophy, there remained a sense that Stoicism was not altogether inconsistent with Christianity, and Seneca was among the most influential authors for the humanists, as Fothergill-Payne notes:

> Seneca's influence on the humanists can hardly be overestimated. The growing neo-Stoic movement chose the Roman philosopher as its preferred teacher on ethics, while his eminently portable and quotable sentences continued to be a rich source of epigrams, mottoes, and other notable sayings.[17]

Cereta thus would have had relatively easy access to Seneca's letters, which circulated even throughout the Medieval period, as well as the dialogues and tragedies.[18]

Little was known of Epicurus or Lucretius until the rediscovery of Diogenes Laertius's *Lives* in the fifteenth century and Poggio Bracciolini's famous recovery of Lucretius's *De rerum natura* in 1417, dramatized by Stephen Greenblatt in *The Swerve*.[19] Humanist scholars struggled at times to reconcile the so-called hedonism of the Epicureans with their own literary interest in the newly recovered text, and Lucretius appears frequently on lists of banned books in this period; however, as Ada Palmer points out,

> Lucretian ideas were considered dangerous in the hands of unsupervised students and the less educated, not in the hands of scholars like Giordano Bruno who were expected to see through the holes and errors in Lucretius's system.[20]

Palmer's 2014 volume *Reading Lucretius in the Renaissance* in fact demonstrates that most readers focused primarily on the poetic, rather than philosophical, aspects of the work, particularly the invocation to Venus, with a few notable exceptions: Lorenzo Valla's 1431 work *On Pleasure* rehabilitates the philosophy by redefining Epicurean pleasure as divine, rather than earthly,[21] while Marsilio Ficino's late-1450s work of the same title points out rightly that Epicurean pleasure could more accurately be described as the absence of pain. That being said, Cereta's entry into this conversation, as a young woman approaching the text largely on her own, would have been inherently controversial given her gender, which would automatically qualify her in many Renaissance minds as one in whose hands Lucretius's ideas might be "dangerous."

The particular combination of Stoicism and Epicureanism found in Cereta's letters is indicative of her reception of both schools through Latin sources: primarily Seneca and Lucretius. The former is especially important. Though critical of Epicurus at times—he calls him a *magister voluptatis* in letter 18.9, and effeminate in letter 33—Seneca was, on the whole, an admirer of the man. He often closes his correspondence with a quotation from him, acting as a "spy in enemy camp" (*Ep.* 2). He even goes so far as to exhort his correspondent, "Do everything as if Epicurus is watching you" (*Ep.* 25.5: *Sic fac . . . omnia, tamquam spectet Epicurus*). In fact, Seneca references Epicurus by name almost fifty times in Volume 1 of the letters alone, and the quotations he attributes to him span a variety of topics. For example, in the letter quoted above (28.9), Seneca writes: "Epicurus, it seems to me, said a noble thing: 'The beginning of good health is the recognition of error'" ('*Initium est salutis notitia peccati.*' *Egregie mihi hoc dixisse videtur Epicurus*), a very general statement that could be applied to any number of philosophies, even Christianity, where *peccatum* would carry overtones of "sin." To cite a few other examples, Seneca quotes Epicurus on the importance of dedication to philosophy (letter 8); on the importance of friendship (letter 9); on the utility of *exempla* (letter 11); on living in accordance with nature (letter 16); and on the troubles associated with wealth (letter 17), among other topics. These *sententiae* are drawn from a variety of sources; Alessandro Schiesaro finds that Seneca is aware of at least five of Epicurus's letters, and probably also drew on an unidentified collection of his sayings arranged by subject.[22]

Seneca explicitly defends his use of Epicurus's words in several of the letters. The general argument is that all wisdom is public property and can be borrowed by anyone regardless of philosophical affiliation. Seneca writes in letter 8, for instance:

> It may happen that you should ask me why I refer to the many fine sayings of Epicurus rather than to those of our own school. Why would you suppose that there is any saying that belongs only to Epicurus, and not to the public?
>
> *Potest fieri, ut me interroges, quare ab Epicuro tam multa bene dicta referam potius quam nostrorum. Quid est tamen, quare tu istas Epicuri voces putes esse, non publicas?*[23]

Seneca applies this theory outside of references to Epicureanism as well, stating further in letter 12.11 that the best ideas belong to everyone (*sciant, quae optima sunt, esse communia*). Cereta's approach to philosophy is remarkably similar. Her acknowledgment of "Epicurus's error" (in her letter to Francesco Fontana, cited below), clears the way for Cereta to reinterpret his doctrine, with the help of Seneca and Lucretius, in a way that does not conflict with Christianity. Seneca also uses his own reinterpretation of Epicurean doctrine to contextualize his use of the philosopher's *sententiae* in a passage that may have inspired Cereta. According to Seneca's letter 85, Epicurus believed that pleasure came from virtue, but did not consider virtue alone sufficient for a happy life. Seneca's own reading of Epicurean doctrine, however, leads to the conclusion that virtue alone should be sufficient for a happy life.[24] Cereta seems to agree with Seneca on this point, emphasizing in another letter (to one Martha Marcella) the importance of virtue in Epicureanism:

> Even the doctrines of Epicurus hope that the wise man is able to be content with himself alone: for virtue is sweeter than any friend, since our happiness proceeds not from a spouse, or gold, or any other delight, but from virtue. What profit can a pleasure that is tangled and knotted with passion hold?
>
> vult enim Epicuri doctrina sapientem posse se ipso esse contentum: nam omni prorsus amico dulcior est virtus, quippe quod ex virtute, non ex marito, vel auro, ullave delectatione felicitas nostra procedit. Quid enim fructus habet implexa passioni innodataque voluptas?[25]

Any understanding of Epicurus or Epicureanism gained from the letters is thus skewed by Seneca's methodology in choosing his quotations. His selection is not random; rather, he chooses general maxims that are suited to the Stoic themes of his own letters and his own voice as an author. Margaret R. Graver describes this as a process of "digestion": "This is to say that a writer should not merely string together quotations from older works but should develop a voice of his own which will be recognizable to readers."[26] This method of reading and writing has much in common with the strategies of the Renaissance reader; Palmer has described the tendency to read Lucretius's *De rerum natura*, for instance, only for what was useful, and to downplay radical elements of the text in favor of useful moral and scientific material.[27]

Epicurus and Epicureanism are thus transmitted to Cereta largely through the voice of a Roman Stoic, whose intertextuality serves a very particular agenda, as described by Jula Wildberger:

> Intertextuality [in the letters] is a social phenomenon of generic transformation. L. Annaeus adapts a kind of writing that for a member of his class constitutes suitable reading but not something dignified enough for him to produce himself. This undertaking is part of an overall agenda of promoting the role of philosophy in the lives of his peers and those Romans aspiring to attain his rank.[28]

The version of Epicureanism that Cereta encounters here has therefore already undergone a transformation as Seneca adapts his work to an elite Roman audience. Furthermore, while Cereta would have been familiar with the general principles of Epicureanism through other sources, such as Valla's *On Pleasure* and Lucretius's *De rerum natura*, her use of Stoic ideas within a text defending Epicurus suggests that the two authors and schools were linked in her mind, most likely by Seneca's letters, and the two authors' shared epistolary genres.[29] In addition, these two letters demonstrate Cereta's engagement with the larger issues surrounding Roman philosophy in the Renaissance. The rediscovery of Lucretius's *De rerum natura* inspired debates on the nature of Epicureanism and its potential for undermining the Christian worldview. Cereta's identification of Epicurus's "error," and her subsequent attempt to correct it by placing pleasure in a Christian and Stoic context, can be counted as part of the humanist reaction to the recirculation of the text.

The two letters by Cereta that I have selected, in order to explore issues in the reception of Stoicism and Epicureanism, were both written in 1487. In the first, Cereta draws on Lucretian themes to combat the forces of fortune and superstition; she then uses Stoic concepts of self-regulation to console herself over the unfortunate death of her husband, who succumbed to illness just one year after their marriage. The second letter is a defense of Epicurus, whom Cereta's sister Deodata must have disparaged in a lost letter or conversation. Drawing again on Lucretian and Senecan elements, Cereta argues here that pleasure is not inherently connected with vice, and furthermore, that the pleasure of the Epicurean lies not in earthly delights, but in quiet contemplation of God.

LUCRETIAN *RELIGIO* AND STOIC CONSOLATION: LETTER TO FRANCESCO FONTANA, APRIL 13, 1487

This letter[30] is an *execratio* against the goddess Fortuna that relies on three arguments: first, that worship of the goddess inspires ridiculous and dangerous practices; second, that what humans call Fortune is actually coincidence, as demonstrated by the ability of misfortune to affect even good people; and finally, that worship of Fortuna as a goddess is just another form of pagan idolatry. Cereta supports these arguments using a Lucretian critique of superstition (*religio*) and a Stoic understanding of a good death. The letter is typical of Cereta's approach to philosophy in several ways. First, in referring to these pagan authors, she is careful to distance herself from their religious beliefs while borrowing their examples and rhetorical strategies. For instance, though she believes that Epicurus and his philosophy were in error regarding the nature of the divine and Fortune, Cereta still finds it useful to appeal to Lucretian vocabulary and rhetoric in her argument, particularly on the theme of *religio*. Next, Cereta is careful to align her philosophy with Christian doctrines. Cereta denounces the pagan concept of Fortuna and replaces her with the concept of *accidens*, emphasizing the presence and concern of a Christian God while acknowledging that chance plays a prominent role in human life. Finally, the letter ends with a self-consolation for the loss of her young husband that relies more on elements of Stoic than Epicurean philosophy, demonstrating her willingness to appeal to motifs of different schools of philosophy as she finds them useful even in a single context, rather than make use of only one school's principles or strategies.

To illustrate her first point regarding the types of behaviors inspired by the worship of Fortuna, Cereta cites the supposed Euboean practice of sacrificing foreigners to the goddess (possibly relying on Pliny the Elder, *HN* 36.17), and the story of Alexander the Great carrying a statue of the goddess on his head to frighten the enemy. Cereta will later identify this kind of behavior more explicitly with *religio*, superstition, making her strategy quite Lucretian. Recall that for Lucretius, *religio* leads to strange, useless, or even dangerous practices, as in *De rerum natura* 1.62–101, where he describes the sacrifice of Iphigenia and blames *religio* for the travesty. She then makes the cult of Fortuna responsible for "the first blasphemies following the Devil," emphasizing the harmfulness, in her view, of the worship of Fortune as a goddess.[31] It is most of all people who have experienced very negative, sudden events, Cereta tells us, who turn to this practice, attributing their misfortune to a vengeful figure who needs to be appeased. Cereta argues that inquiry into the matter shows otherwise:

> It is granted to be known to those who seek out the truth, explore it and mull it over, and weave the causes back together, that this [goddess] is the occurrence of things.
>
> qui veritatem conspicantur, explorant, et retorquent, rursusque texunt causas, quibus cognosci datur hanc ipsam esse rerum eventum.

Cereta's use of the phrase "*rerum eventum*" emphasizes that the occurrences driving some to think of Fortune as a goddess are not a matter of Fate, but chance. Cereta then uses a long list of examples drawn from Cicero, Livy, and Quintilian to illustrate the kinds of events she means: Hannibal the Elder's destruction, Regulus dying in chains, Alcibiades in exile, and the varying fortunes of Cyrus. As she argues, bad and good things can happen to all people, and happenstance is outside our control—and even the Christian God's:

> It ought to be enough for my argument to show that it is not Fortune who troubles us, but rather chance (*accidens*), which, when what is contingent has been set in order, either Nature or God directs. But really what we call Fortune is none other than an image of empty terror.
>
> Satis ad argumentum videri debet, quod non est ea, quae nos vexat, Fortuna, sed accidens, quod super contingenti disposito vel Natura, vel Deus inclinat. Quod

vero dicimus ipsi Fortunam, id ipsum omnino nihil est aliud, quam imaginatio vani terroris,[32]

Cereta's arguments here reveal that there are three possible forces at work in her world: God's will, which is often beyond our comprehension; *accidens*, chance, a random force over which humanity has no control; and Fortuna, the personification of chance as a vengeful goddess. For Cereta, the first and last of these are incompatible, as are the pagan and Christian religions. She in fact places worship of this *imaginatio* at the bottom of a long catalog of other practices that she deems ridiculous, including the worship of animals, firmly placing the goddess in the camp of the pagans.

Cereta's rejection of the goddess Fortuna in favor of the morally neutral *accidens* so far sounds rather Lucretian. Cereta, however, finds that Epicurus goes too far in placing chance at the root of all occurrences. This is one of the few places in her letters where she calls out an ancient author by name (*Epistolae*, 53):

> Nevertheless the enormous fact of Epicurus . . . being refuted can be attributed to his own error, namely denying that God has concern for the world, and affirming that everything happens by chance or accident. All the other philosophers spit on Fortune.
>
> Et quamquam confutati Epicuri . . . in errorem suum illa revolvatur enormitas, qua, Deo Mundi curam esse negantes, omnia fortuitu et contingenti quodam evenire firmarunt; reliqui tamen omnes in Fortunam conspuere philosophi.

Cereta identifies two of the Epicurean ideas that most disturbed Renaissance readers: lack of divine involvement in human life and the attribution of all occurrences to chance. Palmer includes both in her list of "proto-atheist arguments" appearing in Lucretius's *De rerum natura*, arguing that, while Epicureanism is not atheist in the modern sense of the word, it contains ideas that could lead to loss of faith;[33] hence Cereta's careful denial of her belief in these two aspects of the philosophy. Cereta's efforts to distance herself from Epicurus do not, however, prevent her from drawing on Lucretian themes and vocabulary in her attack on fortune, particularly the concept of *religio*, which Cereta uses in the Lucretian sense. Cereta writes: "Fear is excited in times of grief, and superstition in times of fear" (*Epistolae*, 52: *sub dolore, timor excitur, et ex timore Religio*). Similarly, a passage from *De rerum natura* reads (3.52–53): "They bring offerings to the dead and turn their minds to superstition / Much more ardently in troubled times" (*inferias mittunt multoque in rebus acerbis / acrius advertunt animos ad religionem*).

Cereta explains further that this type of *religio* is false, likening it to what she considers idolatry in the religions of ancient Rome, Egypt, Crete, India, and elsewhere. Cereta makes this connection as well when she cites human sacrifice, which she associates with pagan religions, as one of the consequences of the worship of Fortuna.

The close of the letter marks a shift in the subject matter. Cereta ends with a reflection on the death of her own husband, in which she appeals to elements of Stoic philosophy. She considers the instability of human fortune and emphasizes her own ability to calm and console herself through meditation, concluding (*Epistolae*, 54–55):

> Death is a fate common to all; but a happy death belongs alone to a virtuous man. Fortune then neither curses nor blesses the just, and every outcome in death depends on virtue or vice.

> Mors communis est omnibus casus; sed unus innocentis foelix est obitus. Non ergo justos infoelicitat Fortuna vel beat: a vicio atque virtute omnis in morte pendet eventus.

Cereta's thoughts echo Seneca's letters to Lucilius on death and dying. For Seneca, as Russell Noyes has argued, "Dying not only represented a trial of a man's soul but also a final judgment of its strength."[34] We can see these ideas developed in the letters, "where *meditatio mortis* (death rehearsal) becomes a serialized habit,"[35] that develops, as James Ker argues, not only throughout the correspondence, but within the structure of each individual letter. In letter 66 Seneca reflects, for instance, on the different times and methods of death, and ultimately concludes that death is the great equalizer (*Ep.* 66.43):

> Dying is the same for everyone. As to the methods, it may differ; but in the event, it is one and the same. No death is lesser or greater; its measure is the same for all, to have ended life.

> Mors quidem omnium par est. Per quae desiliunt, diversa sunt; in quod desiliunt, unum est. Mors nulla maior aut minor est; habet enim eundem in omnibus modum, finisse vitam.

The only distinguishing factor in the final moment is then revealed in letter 70: "It does not matter whether one dies early or late, but rather whether one dies well or badly. And dying well means escaping the danger of living badly" (*Citius mori aut tardius ad rem non pertinet, bene mori aut male ad rem pertinet. Bene autem mori est effugere male vivendi periculum*).

As Catharine Edwards notes on this point, "Only the wise man, one who is conscious that he has used his time well, can approach death with a steady step."[36] For both Seneca and Cereta, then, a good death depends not on external factors, but only on virtue. Death itself is not a misfortune, since the virtuous person is always prepared for the ups and downs of fate. Fortune, therefore, loses all its power in regard to the wise person. Cereta's *execratio* of Fortuna thus relies on both a Lucretian critique of *religio* and Stoic views of a good death, even as her argument rejects the far-removed atomic gods of the Epicureans in favor of a Christian worldview where human free will and chance are still at play.

A Defense of Epicurus: Letter to Deodata di Leno, December 12, 1487

Cereta's use of Epicurean and Stoic themes continues in a letter to her younger sister, Deodata di Leno, whom she identifies as a nun. In this letter,[37] Cereta considers several philosophical issues central to the study of Epicureanism in the Renaissance: the nature of pleasure; its relationship to Christian virtue; and the path to true happiness, which Cereta identifies with the Christian God. In the course of the discussion she also defends her interest in Epicurus against her correspondent, who, it is implied, expressed criticism in an earlier letter.

Deodata's criticism stems from her understanding of Epicurean pleasure, which Cereta seeks to redefine (*Epistolae*, 169):

> You silently impugn pleasure when you attack my enjoyment of Epicurus, but I would not attribute pleasure so easily to vice. The philosopher finds pleasure not in the delight of the senses, but in the gratification of a contented mind.

> Tacite sub nostro illo gaudio Epicuri voluptatem impugnas. Hanc tamen ipsa tam facile vicio non dederim; quantum Philosophus illam non in delectationum sensibus, sed in animi contenti satietate locaverit.

Much as Valla does in *On Pleasure*, Cereta refocuses *voluptas* around the mind instead of the body. To illustrate her point, Cereta sets out on an imaginary journey. She describes an ascent up a mountain through a pastoral setting evocative of the Epicurean garden. The author and her companions take pleasure in the simple things of nature: grapes on the vine, milk, and the antics of various animals. The group bathes in a pond, sleeps by a stream, and then dines on simple foods, since the wise person is satisfied with a frugal meal.[38]

At this point Cereta begins to discuss philosophy more explicitly. She exhorts Deodata and herself to recognize that the enjoyment, *jucunditas*, of this tranquil walk up the mountain is worth very little. Cereta evokes a passage from Lucretius's *De rerum natura* in order to make her point. She asks,

> What does a refreshing tranquility, looking down on the fields from the mountains, now do for the supreme happiness of the mind? What does the quiet ebullience of a content heart give us, by which we looked over the mountains we've wandered over without any noise, or any injury of fate?

> Quid facit nunc ob beatitudinem animi respirans illa videndi e promontoriis arva tranquillitas? Quid contulit quietior illa nobis consolati cordis effusio, qua pervagatos montes sine strepitu ullave Sortis iniuria lustravimus?[39]

This passage reworks the opening to Book 2 of *De rerum natura* (2.4.8):

> It is pleasing to watch the great battle lines of war
> Drawn out across the field, without any part in the danger;
> But nothing is sweeter than to hold the high plains,
> Serene and well-fortified by the learning of the wise,
> From where one may look down and see others wandering here and there
> Drifting about, seeking the path of life.

> suave etiam belli certamina magna tueri
> per campos instructa tua sine parte pericli;
> sed nihil dulcius est, bene quam munita tenere
> edita doctrina sapientum templa serena,
> despicere unde queas alios passimque videre
> errare atque viam palantis quaerere vitae.

Cereta reinterprets this passage, however, by combining elements of two experiences: that of the wise person looking down from the mountain and of the people searching down below. Cereta, it seems, has been wasting time searching for a place like Lucretius's "serene temple," noting of her journey (*Epistolae*, 173–174),

> Against the precepts of Philosophy I thought that by traveling I was crossing a more secure threshold, and one of peace.... We have wandered here and there enough on account of this changing of places.

> quod contra Philosophiae praecepta crediderim isto discursu quietis securius limen intrare.... Satis ex hac locorum mutatione huc atque illuc erravimus.

Cereta draws on Seneca for this passage, recalling his comments on travel in one of the letters; which itself borrows a phrase from Horace's *Epistles* (1.11.27 *Caelum non animum mutant qui trans mare currunt*):

> You wander, and going on you change from place to place, when that which you seek—to live well— is located everywhere.

> erras et agens ac locum ex loco mutas, cum illud, quod quaeris, bene vivere, omni loco positum sit.[40]

As Martin Stöckinger et al. point out in their introduction to *Horace and Seneca*, "Ep. 28 starts at the point where the Horatian letter ends: Seneca's addressee, Lucilius, has undertaken a *mutatio caeli* and yet experienced no *mutatio animi*."[41] Cereta places herself in the same situation in her letter, and further develops this theme into a Christianized version of Seneca's view that only a contented mind enables the individual to live well. She writes that true pleasure can only be found in a mind content with God's love rather than the enjoyment of fleeting physical pleasures: "This one thing is the greatest pleasure of the contented mind ... by which we are led safely towards God on the path of faith" (*Epistolae*, 177: *Haec una illa est et summa animi contenti fruitio ... qua ad Deum tuto fidei calle perducimur*).

Epicurean pleasure, then, is not found in the absence of pain, but in the presence of God, an argument which allows Cereta to make her case to Deodata that her study of Epicurus (and by extension, Lucretius) is not in conflict with Christian values.[42] Her descriptions of the philosopher add to her case as well, opposing the criticisms leveled in her earlier letter. Here Cereta praises Epicurus as a temperate man of great moderation, explaining how he curbed his appetites and thus broke the cycle of always desiring more, and furthermore, how he believed that misguided attempts at finding comfort would be punished.[43]

Cereta's journey up the mountain, reported in the first half of the letter, thus gives way to a metaphorical road to salvation guided, ironically, by a philosophy often branded as atheist in the Renaissance, but reconfigured around Christian values. At the same time, while she is indebted to Lucretius for much of the imagery in this letter, she also relies, as she often does, on Seneca, adding to the sense that Cereta's approach to philosophy is largely practical, motivated by the desire to "live well" rather than adhere to the tenets any one school. Cereta sums up this blend of Stoic, Epicurean and Christian worldviews best when she writes near the end of her letter: "There exists in life a pleasure unknown to the people at large: a divine one, which, indifferent to human affairs, is bought with the currency of virtue" (*ignota est vulgo viva voluptas, quae humanorum negligens divina virtutis pre[t]io mercatur*).[44]

Cereta neatly recasts *voluptas*, the highest good of Epicurean philosophy according to some Renaissance readings of the text, as pleasure in the presence of the divine (*divina*) and makes virtue (*virtus*), the highest good of Stoic philosophy as Cereta understands it, the currency used to purchase it. The consonance she creates with repetition of the *-v-* sound further emphasizes the compatibility in her view of the three systems of thought; and the fact that some of her exposure to Epicurean thought came about through Seneca likely further encouraged her to blend these philosophies as she saw fit. *Virtus*, *voluptas*, and the divine thus come together in her letters to clarify Cereta's view of humanity's place in the world and the relevance of ancient philosophy for the life of the author.

Notes

1. See Vasoli (1990), 55–74.
2. Kraye (2019) 151.
3. See Kraye (2019) 149n1. On the categories developed by the *Sonderforschungsbereich* 644, see Bergemann et al. (2011) 39–56.
4. Burckhardt (1990) 251; Rabil (1981); Robin (1997).
5. See Kraye (2007) 97.
6. See Robin (2002) 83–108.
7. Biblioteca Nazionale Marciana. Marc. Cod. Lat., XI, 28 [4186] mbr. XV, 154 fols.
8. Vat. Lat. 3176, cart. XVI, 73 fols.
9. Rossi (1620).
10. Rabil (1981) 22.

11. Robin (1997) 74.
12. Cereta, *Epistolae*, 192–193. All translations mine.
13. Cereta and Tomasini (1640) 187.
14. Letter to Bernardino di Leno, 1486. Cereta, *Epistolae*, 73.
15. See Witt (2000) 245–246.
16. For a full discussion of the revival of Stoicism in this period see Kraye (2007) 99–102.
17. Fothergill-Payne (1991) 121.
18. See Reynolds (1965) 37–39.
19. Greenblatt (2011). For a full discussion of the textual tradition, see Hankins and Palmer (2008) 34–36.
20. Palmer (2020).
21. Joy (1992) 576–577.
22. Schiesaro (2015) 239.
23. Sen. *Ep.* 8.8. Thank you to the editors for their translation suggestions here.
24. Sen. *Ep.* 85.13: *Epicurus quoque iudicat eum qui virtutem habeat, beatum esse, sed ipsam virtutem non satis esse ad beatam vitam, quia beatum efficiat voluptas, quae ex virtute est, non ipsa virtus. Inepta distinctio. Idem enim negat umquam virtutem esse sine voluptate; ita si ei iuncta semper est atque inseparabilis, et sola satis est. Habet enim secum voluptatem, sine qua non est, etiam cum sola est.*
25. Cereta, *Epistolae*, 142.
26. Graver (2014) 285.
27. See Palmer (2014b) 233–241.
28. Wildberger (2020) 82.
29. Thank you to the editors for pointing out this last connection regarding genre.
30. Cereta, *Epistolae*, 47. *Ad Regium Oratorem Franciscum Fontanam. Laurae Ceretae Execratio contra Fortunam /Epist. XXIV.* April 13, 1487.
31. *primas citra Daemonem . . . blasphemias*, Cereta, *Epistolae*, 47.
32. Cereta, *Epistolae*, 52. Thank you to the editors for their translation suggestions here.
33. Palmer (2014b) 21–32.
34. Noyes (1973) 233.
35. Ker (2010) 147.
36. Edwards (2014) 324.
37. Cereta, *Epistolae*, 168. *Ad sororem Deodatam Leonensem Monacham Laura Cereta Topographia, Epicurique Defensio./Epist. LXIII.* December 12, 1487. Also found in Vt 75, Ve 65.
38. Robin notes that this half of the work is indebted to one of Petrarch's letters, in which the author climbs a mountain while meditating on the divine, while the second half of the letter owes more to Lorenzo Valla's *On Pleasure*, in which Valla redefines Epicurean *voluptas* to agree with Christian values, focusing not on sensual pleasure, but on the bliss of being close to God. See Robin (1997) 115–116.
39. Cereta, *Epistolae*, 173. Tomasini's edition reads *ab beatitudinem*; I have corrected to *ob* for sense. Thank you to the editors for their translation suggestions here.
40. Sen. *Ep.* 28.5. Thank you to the editors for pointing out the parallels with Horace.
41. Stöckinger, Winter, and Zanker (2017)
42. These arguments were not original to Cereta. Other humanists, including Valla, Francesco Filelfo, and Pico della Mirandola, came to the same conclusion. See in general Allen (1944).
43. Cereta, *Epistolae*, 174.
44. Cereta, *Epistolae*, 177. Thank you to the editors for their translation suggestions here.

References

Allen, D. C. (1944). "The Rehabilitation of Epicurus and His Theory of Pleasure in the Early Renaissance." *Studies in Philology* 41: 1–15.
Baker, P., J. Helmrath, and C. Kallendorf, eds. (2019). *Beyond Reception*. (Berlin).
Bartsch, S., and A. Schiesaro., eds. (2015). *The Cambridge Companion to Seneca*. (Cambridge).
Bergemann, L., M. Dönike, A. Schirrmeister, G. Toepfer, M. Walter, and J. Weitbrecht. (2011). "Transformation: Ein Konzept zur Erforschung kulturellen Wandels," in H. Böhme et al. (eds.), *Transformation: Ein Konzupt zur Erforschung kulturellen Wandels* (Munich), 39–56.
Bridenthal, R., and C. Koonz, eds. (1977). *Becoming Visible: Women in European History* (Boston).
Burckhardt, J. (1990). *The Civilization of the Renaissance in Italy (1860)*. S. G. C. Middlemore, tr. (London).
Celenza, C. S. (2004). *The Lost Italian Renaissance: Humanists, Historians, and Latin's Legacy*. (Baltimore).
Cereta, L., and G. F. Tomasini (1640). *Laurae Ceretae Brixiensis feminae clarissimae epistolae jam primum è MS in lucem productae*. (Padua).
Churchill, L. J., P. R. Brown, and J. E. Jeffrey, eds. (1994). *Italian Women Writers: A Bio-Bibliographical Sourcebook*. (New York).
Cox, V. (2008). *Women's Writing in Italy, 1400–1650*. (Baltimore).
Edwards, C. (2014). "Ethics V: Death and Time," in Heil and Damschen, 323–341.
Fleischmann, W. B. (1971). "Lucretius Carus, Titus." *Catalogus translationum et commentariorum* 2: 349–365.
Fohlen, J. (2002). *Biographies de Sénèque et commentaires des Epistulae ad Lucilium (Ve–XVe s.)*. (Rome and Padua).
Fothergill-Payne, L. (1991). "Seneca's Role in Popularizing Epicurus in the Sixteenth Century," in Osler, 115–133.
Fubini, R. (2003). *Humanism and Secularization: From Petrarch to Valla*. (Durham).
Garani, M., A. N. Michalopoulos, and S. Papaioannou, eds. (2020). *Intertextuality in Seneca's Philosophical Writings*. (London/New York).
Garin, E. (1961). *La cultura filosofica del Rinascimento Italiano ricerche e documenti*. (Florence).
Gillespie, S., and P. R. Hardie, eds. (2007). *The Cambridge Companion to Lucretius*. (Cambridge).
Gordon, P. (2012). *The Invention and Gendering of Epicurus*. (Ann Arbor, Mich.).
Grafton, A., and L. Jardine (1988). *From Humanism to the Humanities*. (Cambridge).
Graver, M. (2014). "Honeybee Reading and Self-Scripting: *Epistulae Morales* 84," in J. Wildberger and M. L. Colish (eds.), *Seneca Philosophus* (Berlin), 269–294.
Greenblatt, S. (2011). *The Swerve: How the World Became Modern*. (New York).
Hadzsits, G. D. (1935). *Lucretius and His Influence*. (New York).
Hankins, J., ed. (2007). *The Cambridge Companion to Renaissance Philosophy*. (Cambridge).
Hankins, J., and A. Palmer (2008). *The Recovery of Ancient Philosophy in the Renaissance: A Brief Guide*. (Florence).
Hardie, P. R., V. Prosperi, and D. Zucca, eds. (2020). *Lucretius: Poet and Philosopher; Background and Fortunes of* De rerum natura. (Berlin)
Haskell, Y. (2007). "Religion and Enlightenment in the Neo-Latin Reception of Lucretius," in Gillespie and Hardy, 185–201.
Heil, A., and G. Damschen, eds. (2014). *Brill's Companion to Seneca*. (Leiden).

Hieatt, A. K., and M. Lorch, trs. (1977). *L. Valla's* On Pleasure/De voluptate. (New York).
Jardine, L. (1985). "'O decus Italiae Virgo,' or The Myth of the Learned Lady in the Renaissance." *The Historical Journal* 28: 799–819.
Joy, L. S. (1992). "Epicureanism in Renaissance Moral and Natural Philosophy." *Journal of the History of Ideas* 53: 573–583.
Kelly-Gadol, J. (1977). "Did Women Have a Renaissance?," in Bridenthal and Koonz, 137–164.
Ker, J. (2009). *The Deaths of Seneca.* (Oxford).
King, M. L. (1980). "Book-Lined Cells: Women and Humanism in the Early Italian Renaissance," in Labalme, 66–90.
Kraye, J. (2002). *Classical Traditions in Renaissance Philosophy.* (Aldershot).
Kraye, J. (2007). "The Revival of Hellenistic Philosophies," in Hankins, 97–112.
Kraye, J. (2019). "Renaissance Humanism and the Transformations of Ancient Philosophy," in Baker, Helmrath, and Kallendorf, 149–162.
Labalme, P. H., ed. (1980). *Beyond Their Sex: Learned Women of the European Past.* (New York).
Lehnerdt, M. (1904). *Lucretius in der Renaissance.* (Königsberg).
Lorch, M. L. (1991). "The Epicurean in Lorenzo Valla's *On Pleasure*," in Osler, 89–114.
Noyes, R. (1973). "Seneca on Death." *Journal of Religion and Health* 12: 223–240.
Osler, M. J., ed. (1991). *Atoms, Pneuma, and Tranquillity: Epicurean and Stoic Themes in European Thought.* (Cambridge).
Palmer, A. (2014a). *Lucretius Carus, Titus: Addenda et corrigenda.* (Washington, D.C.).
Palmer, A. (2014b). *Reading Lucretius in the Renaissance.* (Cambridge).
Palmer, A. (2020). "The Persecution of Renaissance Lucretius Readers Revisited," in Hardie, Prosperi, and Zucca, 167–198.
Prosperi, V. (2007). "Lucretius in the Italian Renaissance," in Gillespie and Hardy, 214–226.
Rabil, A. (1981). *Laura Cereta: Quattrocento Humanist.* (Binghamton, N.Y.).
Rabil, A. (1994). "Laura Cereta (1469–1499)," in Churchill, Brown, and Jeffrey, 67–75.
Reeve, M. D. (1980). "The Italian Tradition of Lucretius." *Italia Medioevale e Umanistica Padova* 23: 27–48.
Reeve, M. D. (2007). "Lucretius in the Middle Ages and Early Renaissance: Transmission and Scholarship," in Gillespie and Hardy, 205–213.
Reynolds, L. D. (1965). *The Medieval Tradition of Seneca's Letters.* (London).
Robin, D., tr. (1997). *Laura Cereta: Collected Letters of a Renaissance Feminist.* (Chicago).
Robin, D. (2002). *Women Writing Latin.* (Abingdon).
Rossi, O. (1620). *Elogi historici di Bresciani illustri: Teatro di Ottavio Rossi.* (Brescia).
Schiesaro, A. (2015). "Seneca and Epicurus: The Allure of the Other," in Bartsch and Schiesaro, 239–254.
Schmitt, C.B., J. Kraye, E. Kessler, and Q. Skinner, eds. (1990). *The Cambridge History of Renaissance Philosophy.* (Cambridge).
Stöckinger, M., K. Winter, and A. T. Zanker, eds. (2017). *Horace and Seneca: Interactions, Intertexts, Interpretations.* (Berlin).
Vasoli, C. (1990). "The Renaissance Concept of Philosophy," in Schmitt, Kraye, Kessler, and Skinner, 55–74.
Weiss, R. (1969). *The Renaissance Discovery of Classical Antiquity.* (Oxford).
Wildberger, J. (2020). "Seneca and the Doxography of Ethics," in Garani, 81–104.
Witt, R. G. (2003). *In the Footsteps of the Ancients: The Origins of Humanism from Lovato to Bruni.* (Leiden).

CHAPTER 34

"THE ART OF SELF-DECEPTION"
Libertine Materialism and Roman Philosophy

NATANIA MEEKER

What makes a materialist a libertine? Is libertinism the practice and materialism the theory? Does the philosophical doctrine emerge from an acknowledgment of desire? Or does becoming a materialist instead entail disciplining the body and its urges, so that desire becomes sublimated in thought?[1] These questions, which have ancient origins, are the object of strenuous debate in early modern Europe. Across these debates, libertine materialism emerges as an ambivalent and sometimes uncomfortable melange of convictions, behaviors, and approaches—perhaps best described as what Alexandra Torero-Ibad calls a "pratique du collage."[2] For all its diversity, however, libertine materialism nonetheless owes a specific debt to Roman philosophy, and in particular to the work of the first-century BCE poet Lucretius, whose poem *De rerum natura* (*DRN*) functions as both a *topos* and a methodological inspiration. The figure of the libertine materialist is on the one hand that of a "bad" or improper materialist, one who appears to follow the shifting inclinations of a desire that always threatens to lead them astray.[3] Read through the lens provided by Lucretius in *DRN*, however, libertine materialism takes on if not an order at least a certain coherence. First, it prioritizes a critique of religion and sentimental love as forces that structure human desires. And, second, it is a resolutely *poetic* materialism, finding in the image—both literary and visual—a crucial tool for the cultivation of pleasures across different kinds of bodies and envisioning what will come to be called "illusion" as an instrument of delightful dispossession.[4]

The pairing of libertines with materialism is an uneasy one. To begin with, the very term "libertinism" (or libertinage) carries with it an implication of disorder, whether in body or in mind. For instance, Pierre Bayle famously explores the distinction between a "libertinage of the senses" and a "libertinage of the mind" in the *Pensées diverses sur la comète* (1682–1683) and later at more length in the *Dictionnaire historique et critique* (1697).[5] Although the two categories—libertine sensualist and free-thinking philosopher—are often conflated, hedonistic behavior does not necessarily derive from an application of materialist principle, Bayle argues. Bayle is particularly interested in ridding the new science and philosophy of his time of the "suspicion of immorality,"[6] but, as he points out, the figure of the virtuous materialist has important classical antecedents in both Stoic and Epicurean philosophy. Diogenes Laertius, in his famous defense of an honorable and restrained Epicurus against those who portrayed him as debauched, stresses the benevolence, good will, and even the piety of Epicureanism's founder.[7] The Stoic program of extirpating and subduing the harmful passions also suggests that it is a mistake to equate materialism generally with the indulgence of either feeling or appetite. While Stoics and Epicureans alike stress the importance of the close connection between ethics and physics, both forms of classical materialism tend toward an end—*apatheia* on the one hand, *ataraxia* on the other—that emphasizes the careful management of the passions, not their indulgence. This ancient tradition of materialism as a mode of self-governance makes its way into early modern Europe in part as a set of techniques for fostering the virtuous self through the cultivation of knowledge (including scientific knowledge). In the early modern framework, Bayle points to many examples of materialists whose lives seem to have been anything but debauched (including Pierre Gassendi, known as the christianizer of Epicurus; Baruch Spinoza; and Lucilio Vanini, the latter executed for atheism in 1619).

In short, for Bayle there is no easy or inevitable passage from materialist thought to libertine action.[8] The yoking of materialism to impious or improper behavior is instead part of a long history of efforts to discredit philosophical schools that have taken a materialist position. As Bayle writes in the article on "Arcesilaus" from the *Dictionnaire*:

> Be that as it may, the true principle of our morals is so far from residing in the speculative judgments that we make about the nature of things, that there is nothing more ordinary than orthodox Christians who live poorly, and libertines of the mind who live well.[9]
>
> Quoi qu'il en soit, le vrai principe de nos mœurs est si peu dans les jugemens spéculatifs que nous formons sur la nature des choses, qu'il n'est rien de plus ordinaire que des Chrétiens orthodoxes qui vivent mal, & que des libertins d'esprit qui vivent bien.

Here Bayle pries apart a libertine ethics from a materialist physics, suggesting that "speculative judgements" may have no moral effects whatsoever. Furthermore, as Bayle's taxonomy suggests, libertinage itself is an extraordinarily vexed category, precisely because the ascription of libertine tendencies to a philosophical approach suggests a kind of divagation or *dévoiement*—an excessive freedom that manifests itself in belief and action.[10]

Bayle's distinction between free thought and licentious behavior solidifies over the course of the eighteenth century. Denis Diderot[11] attempts to delimit the two categories ("materialist" and "libertine," respectively) in the entry on *"matérialistes"* from the *Encyclopédie* (1751–1772). The entry reads:

> Name of a faction. The ancient church called *materialists* those who, cautioned by Philosophy that nothing comes from nothing, had recourse to an eternal matter worked upon by God, instead of believing in the system of creation, which admits of God alone as the sole cause of the existence of all things.... Today we still give the name of *materialists* to those who argue that the soul of man is material, or that matter is eternal, and that it is God; or that God is only a universal soul spread throughout matter, which moves and orders it, either to produce beings, or to give shape to the various configurations that we see in the universe. See Spinozists.
>
> Nom de secte. L'ancienne église appelloit *matérialistes* ceux qui, prévenus par la Philosophie qu'il ne se fait rien de rien, recouroient à une matiere éternelle sur laquelle Dieu avoit travaillé, au-lieu de s'en tenir au systeme de la création, qui n'admet que Dieu seul, comme cause unique de l'existence de toutes choses.... On donne encore aujourd'hui le nom de *matérialistes* à ceux qui soutiennent ou que l'ame de l'homme est matiere, ou que la matiere est éternelle, & qu'elle est Dieu; ou que Dieu n'est qu'une ame universelle répandue dans la matiere, qui la meut & la dispose, soit pour produire les êtres, soit pour former les divers arrangemens que nous voyons dans l'univers. Voyez Spinosistes. (Diderot and d'Alembert (1751–1772) 10:188)

The importance of Spinoza to this definition is obvious even before the cross-reference appears, as are the resonances with Stoicism, which Bayle also notes as characteristic of Spinoza's thought in his article on the philosopher from the *Dictionnaire*.[12] But throughout the entry, Diderot highlights the continuity between ancient and modern materialisms, allowing the reader to imagine a materialist tradition that stretches from the ancient past into the present, one organized around coherent (if not always consistent) principles and arguments.

Perhaps predictably, then, Diderot's emphasis on a series of specific materialist arguments about the nature of matter—and his initial qualification of "materialist" as originally constituting its own "name of a faction"—stands in implicit opposition to his presentation of libertinage as rooted in an attitude of inconstancy.[13] Of libertinage, he writes (9:476):

> It is the habit of yielding to the instinct that leads us toward the pleasures of the senses; it does not respect moral conventions, but it does not pretend to challenge them outright; it is without delicacy, and is only justified in its choices by its inconstancy; it strikes a balance between voluptuous pleasure and debauchery; when it is the effect of age or temperament, it doesn't rule out either talents or good character.... When libertinage inheres in the mind, when one seeks to gratify needs more than pleasures, the soul is necessarily without taste for the beautiful, the great, and the true. The table, as well as love, has its libertinage; Horace, Chaulieu, Anacreon were libertines in every sense; but they injected so much philosophy, so much good taste

and wit into their libertinage, that they could be forgiven for it all too well; they even had imitators whom nature destined for wisdom.

> C'est l'habitude de céder à l'instinct qui nous porte aux plaisirs des sens; il ne respecte pas les mœurs, mais il n'affecte pas de les braver; il est sans délicatesse, & n'est justifié de ses choix que par son inconstance; il tient le milieu entre la volupté & la débauche; quand il est l'effet de l'âge ou du tempérament, il n'exclud ni les talens ni un beau caractère.... Quand le *libertinage* tient à l'esprit, quand on cherche plus des besoins que des plaisirs, l'ame est nécessairement sans goût pour le beau, le grand & l'honnête. La table, ainsi que l'amour, a son libertinage; Horace, Chaulieu, Anacréon étoient libertins de toutes les manieres de l'être; mais ils ont mis tant de philosophie, de bon goût & d'esprit dans leur *libertinage*, qu'ils ne l'ont que trop fait pardonner; ils ont même eu des imitateurs que la nature destinoit à être sages.

Libertinage according to this definition extends to both body (or "instinct") and mind in ways that blur Bayle's distinction between the two types. But in either instance the term suggests a condition that, although not utterly incompatible with philosophy (in the cases of Horace, Chaulieu, and Anacreon, for example), tends to counteract and undermine reflection, judiciousness, and tact. Even as Diderot is at least partially sympathetic to libertine inclinations, he reads libertinage as at its heart non-philosophical ("only justified in its choices by its inconstancy"). For Diderot, the libertine adopts not a series of arguments but an attitude, a mode of being and of feeling that draws him toward pleasure and away from conventional morality.

Moving from the seventeenth into the eighteenth century, from Bayle to Diderot, it seems then as if the definitions of libertinage and materialism do not so much dovetail neatly as increasingly pull apart. Where the first connotes a range of practices, the second suggests a mode of speculation; where the one evokes a world of sensualism and refined pleasures, the other retains a certain austerity in the face of the passionate intensity of desire. More crucially, where materialism supposes the taking of a position—the commitment to a consistency of argument and explanation—libertinage presumes the refusal to attach, the resistance to dogma, a style of nonadherence ("inconstancy," as Diderot puts it) that extends from modes of justification into the delights of love (and, in Diderot's example, those of the table as well). Perhaps an earlier "*revendication de liberté*" characteristic of seventeenth-century libertine thought[14] is gradually morphing into a demand for the freedom *not* to think—a style, in the modern sense of a way of being in the world, rather than a position.

A final tension reveals itself here. Ultimately, where materialism has ancient origins, libertinage tends toward modernity in multiple senses. First, the use of the term "libertine"—while derived from Latin legal terminology—is tied from the sixteenth century onward to forms of dissidence and heterodoxy that will become the free thought of later periods. (Thus, while the Latin *libertinus* is an enslaved person who has been manumitted, the early modern libertine, famously named as such in 1544 by Jean Calvin in an attack on Anabaptist sects, has freed him- or herself in mind, if not always in body, from orthodoxy.) Second, the seventeenth-century libertine's motto—*Intus ut libet, foris ut moris est* (inside, think what you will; outside, follow the custom)—suggests the extent to which libertinage is oriented toward a kind of split subjectivity that, for all its ancient roots, is distinctively modern in nature.[15] Against the putative constancy of the ancient materialist—loyal to his principles and coherent in his logic—libertines increasingly seem to cultivate the ephemeral commitments, uprooted subjectivity, and alienation typical of a modernity that, in the seventeenth and eighteenth centuries, was still in the process of realizing itself. For his critics, the libertine appears not as a person but a persona or an impersonator—conscious of the illusion(s) that constitute him as a social being but unable to fully free himself from them.

How then to account for the influence of Roman philosophy on a textual legacy that has long been marked by its failure to remain faithful, even to itself? I will suggest here that it is by means of a return to Lucretius that the category of libertine materialism recovers a certain consistency, with *DRN* as a crucial ancient source for later materialisms both inconstant and coherent.[16] The Lucretian presentation of Epicureanism in *DRN*, framed by the invocation to Venus on the one hand and the spectacle of the devastation caused by the plague of Athens on the other, allows the reader to connect the critique of superstition to a celebration of pleasure and an attachment to life in the face of human mortality.[17] It also posits what Duncan Kennedy has called the "textualization of nature" as important to the evolution of a community for whom acts of reading and writing become part of the fostering and dissemination of a materialist attitude. Later on, libertine versions of this community will be cultivated in the space opened by literary and poetic modes of representation, which promises its own revelation of the flexibility of the material world and of the diverse bodies that move through it.[18]

While Lucretius is not always cited by name in many of the works that are traditionally identified as libertine, this extraordinarily varied corpus—ranging from the excursions into natural philosophy of the *libertins érudits*[19] to the often more frankly erotic sensualism of mid- to late eighteenth-century libertine texts—reveals a persistent debt to *DRN*, and not just because libertines both fictional and actual tend to be interested, as Lucretius is, in the transmission of pleasurable feeling by means of the written word.[20] In her essay "The Materialist World of Pornography," Margaret C. Jacob argues on behalf of an analogy between the atomic particle animated in Epicureanism and the physical bodies animated in early modern pornography.[21] Christophe Girerd, in *La sagesse libertine*, plays on this comparison with his assertion that *"le libertin ressemble à l'atome"* (the libertine resembles the atom).[22] And Thomas M. Kavanagh describes the French eighteenth century as "a century of Pleasure," thereby invoking both what he calls "the Epicurean goal of maximizing pleasure" and "the Stoic's distance and control."[23] This gradual move toward what Anne Deneys-Tunney and Pierre-François Moreau have referred to as a kind of libertine hedonism can seem to extend to the human body a new set of possibilities—an energetic embrace of the *potentia* that inhabits everyone. But, for all its emphasis on the rejection of religious authority in favor of an investment in bodies and sensations, libertine neo-Lucretianism posits *voluptas* not as the final affirmation of a secular human subject but as this subject's delightful dissolution or dispossession. Pleasure is the Epicurean response to a world in which humans recognize their own contingency, where in the words of Diderot's dreaming philosopher d'Alembert, "All beings circulate through one another; consequently all species . . . all is in perpetual flux. . . . Every animal is more or less human; every mineral is more or less vegetable; every vegetable is more or less animal" ("*Tous les êtres circulent les uns dans les autres; par conséquent toutes les espèces . . . tout est en flux perpétuel. . . . Tout animal est plus ou moins homme; tout minéral est plus ou moins plante; toute plante est plus ou moins animal*").[24]

Although the development of a Lucretian libertinage is in many ways most significant in France, where libertine thought originates and flourishes (often clandestinely),[25] the libertine turn to Lucretius is transnational and transgenerational, knitting together seventeenth- and eighteenth-century philosophies of pleasure, a *libertinage érudit*, and an enlightened libertinism preoccupied with the mechanics of the erotic encounter. Take as an example the two passages from *De rerum natura* that John Wilmot, Earl of Rochester, translates in the second half of the seventeenth century: namely, the opening and concluding lines of the apostrophe to Venus Genetrix with which the poem opens. Rochester's brief translations reveal the scope and paradoxical attachments of a Lucretian Epicureanism that attempts to diminish the anxiety of human existence and instead cultivate the pleasures that are made available to humans in the world limned by the poem. These pleasures accompany the reader in the attack on superstition by way of a description of the detachment of the Epicurean gods—"Rich in themselves, to whom we cannot add: / Not pleas'd by *Good* Deeds; nor provok'd by *Bad*"—as in the invocation of Venus in her most generative form, as "Greate Mother of Eneas and of Love, . . . / Who all beneathe those sprinkl'd dropps of light / . . . do'st bless, sinc 'tis by thee / That all things live, which the bright sunn do'es see."[26] Both passages hint at the role of Lucretius as a philosopher who prioritizes the radical undoing of the integral human subject in favor of a voluptuous flexibility in which literature (and other arts) participate.[27] They also anticipate the twin preoccupation of later libertinisms with institutional critique on the one hand and erotic delight on the other—often in conjunction with one another.

Increasingly, in the eighteenth-century libertine reception of Lucretius, we see the evolution of a materialism that embraces the power of poetic language to transfigure humans as beings constituted in the flux of things (and thereby radically dehumanized at the atomic level). Mediated through Lucretius, libertinage is something other than a celebration of sensual enjoyment as the birthright of human nature. Out of the struggle against the erroneous belief that humans are necessarily more than mortal bodies, not just one life form among others, simulacral "illusion" (what Gilles Deleuze in his essay on the Lucretian simulacrum calls "phantasms") becomes the instrument of the pleasurable dispossession of the libertine self and a mechanism for the formation of a libertine community of letters. Thus, for Julien Offray de La Mettrie in his essay *L'école de la volupté*, "*c'est ainsi que la volupté même, cet art de jouir, n'est que l'art de se tromper*" ("it is thus that sensuousness itself, this art of enjoyment, is nothing but the art of self-deception").[28] Throughout this tradition, inconstancy positively defines the movement of libertinage—from the poetic rendering of the natural world in which feeling is mediated through acts of reading and writing, to an experience of sexual desire as both inspired by and managed in its representations.

Lucretius is well-known for his critique of the errors—and anxieties—engendered by religion (1.100–106): "By Superstition we are driven to deeds of such great evil. / Someday even you may listen to one of these priests' empty threats and, in need or a moment of weakness, / be tempted to listen as they conjure their vain dreams and sow seeds of doubt" (tr. Slavitt). Priestly myths, with their images of the torments that come after death, trouble those who believe in them; the fear of eternal punishment in the afterlife encourages submission to those authorities who claim to explain the ways and desires of the gods. In his attack on superstition, Lucretius describes Epicurus as defying religious authorities with "the lively force of his mind" and "forcing a breach through the flaming walls of the world / to travel the universe in thought and imagination" (1.71–74). This journey beyond the boundaries of the known allows Epicurus to convey to his followers "the prize of knowledge of what can come into being and what cannot, the limits of the powers of things and their clear and orderly boundary lines" (1.75–77). On the one hand, the Epicurean universe is characterized by regularity and orderliness: Lucretius is careful to explain that, while atoms are in constant movement, bodies do not generate themselves haphazardly, but instead follow (reassuringly) predictable patterns in the ways that they come to be. On the other, the series of examples that Lucretius offers of the process of generation posits an equivalence among sets of bodies that might otherwise appear to be unlike, including animal, human, and vegetal bodies: everything is derived from seeds (*semina*). Lucretius thus couples his critique of religious ideology—the "myths and superstitions" of religious legend—with an endorsement of the power of imagination that upends strict hierarchies of being but does not dispense with the need for careful observation of natural phenomena. As a result, nature is not subject to human fantasies about what might be possible—as would be the case were generation not governed by strict laws—at the same time as the universe as object of knowledge is opened up to speculation. The poem itself participates in this vision of a cosmos both teeming with beings and constrained in its operations, even before Lucretius famously compares the letters that make up words to the atomic elements that make up bodies. From the outset, in the invocation to Venus, the writing of the poem is made analogous to the engendering of all sorts of creatures: without Venus, "nothing comes forth to the light" (*nec sine te quicquam dias in luminis oras*) (1.22–23). The generative power of Venus comes to inhabit the poem as it does the world and all the creatures within it; it animates the production and reproduction of material bodies across species, across modes of being, and across texts.

Later on in the poem, in the fourth book, Lucretius turns to erotic desire as another key source of human anxiety. Here he is critical of the way in which images (*imagines*, which derive from *simulacra*) work to stoke a lover's yearning for a beloved, without for all that satisfying this yearning. In this section, which concludes with a description of the mechanics of human reproduction, the examples are cruder than those used early on to describe the invigorating powers of Venus: the first major image in book four of the power of erotic desire over the body is that of a young boy awakening from a sexual dream having soiled his bed. The besotted lover is at the mercy of his beloved (and of Venus herself) in that he seeks gratification of his desires where none can be attained: even the possession of the most desirable (and desired) body cannot offer to the lover any sustained satisfaction. Instead, erotic longing feeds upon itself, and threatens to become, unregulated, a form of madness. Love, like religion, produces anxiety at the very moment when it appears to promise fulfillment. The images emitted from the body of the beloved—like the stories of the priests—produce a need that they cannot seem to meet. They are too tenuous for that.

Unlike the case of religious myth, however, the problem posed by sexual desire cannot always be solved by simply turning away from the source of the images. "For these injuries from Venus," Lucretius writes, "only Venus offers / relief, and you must learn to look in other directions" (4.1073–1074). For those who wish to avoid the obsessive pursuit of love, Lucretius recommends instead a constant repetition of the sexual act, so that the "wound of love" is cured in its recurrence. Yet, unlike other kinds of appetite, erotic desire can never fully exit the domain of the simulacrum; "a picture is not enough, but it makes us want to see the body of the one we love, which is in turn never enough either" (4.1101–1104). Where the thirsty man is able to drink water, or the hungry man to eat, the lover receives within himself only images, with which his desire cannot be sated. This is not to say that the simulacra themselves are somehow immaterial. Like everything else in the universe, they are constituted by atomic particles. In this way, they are analogous to the visions that come in dreams—as in the example of nocturnal emission—or thoughts that appear in waking life, all of which take on a materiality of their own in a universe in which every thing has a body. In the case of love, however, the representations that lovers desire do nothing but further stimulate the desire that they purport to satisfy. By striving to gain possession of another's body in the act of love, humans set ourselves an impossible goal. Instead, Lucretius suggests, the lover must recognize the simulacral basis of erotic desire, and work to mitigate the drive to possess that which, by its nature, cannot be mastered.

Where both religion and love are concerned, Lucretius recommends relinquishing attachments—in the first case, to a vision of the self as immortal (and unchanging); and, in the second, to the need to subject other people to domination and possession. In the first book of the poem, the reader is asked to embrace an understanding of the human subject as both mutable and connected to the vast diversity of life forms that populate the universe (so that, while beings follow predictable patterns of growth and reproduction, they hold in common their participation in the atomic structure of all that exists). Humans are not the object of the gods' special attention. Although it is true that, in the making of each body, "one step must follow another as seeds sprout to become plants, preserving their own kind" (1.188–190), the matter of which things are made is shared among beings. "Think how letters make up words: in such a way are different bodies composed of the same elements that they all share" (1.196–198). While the discovery that all bodies are constituted of atomic particles is in one sense profoundly dehumanizing—and not only in the realization that the specifically human body becomes one creature among countless others—it is in another sense revitalizing. The act of relinquishing attachment to the wholly unique and distinct human self enables a pleasurable turn toward the proliferation of beings in general ("to travel the universe in thought and imagination," as Epicurus does).

In the Lucretian portrayal of love, lovers find themselves similarly dispossessed, since they are being asked to give up the desire to lay claim to the beloved, whose unique qualities are likewise called into question. They must enjoy—rather than struggle against—the simulacral stimulus for erotic longing, by modeling the inconstancy of their commitments after the inconstancy of the bodies that inspire them. The diaphanous substance of the simulacrum, described earlier on as "thin as spider webs or beaten gold" (4.727) and encompassing thoughts, dreams, and fantasies, is repeated in the lightness of erotic connections. The flexibility of the self is mirrored in the flexibility of the world that it inhabits, a world through which it may move nimbly, with delight rather than with fear.

The libertine rewriting of the Lucretian model, beginning in the seventeenth century and particularly developed in France, tends to rehearse this critique of religious superstition and enthrallment to a single erotic object as damaging forms of subjection. But it does so in a mode that gives increasing priority to the interpenetration of both natural and textual bodies—although Lucretius himself blurs rather than fortifies this kind of distinction—and, correspondingly, pays increasing attention to the power of the simulacrum—in the form of word, image, or idea—to assuage the kinds of harm that it is capable of bringing about. For example, in Cyrano de Bergerac's two mid-seventeenth-century narratives, *Les états et empires de la Lune* and *Les états et empires du Soleil* (often published together as *L'autre monde*, although Cyrano himself reserved this title for the journey to the moon), a proto-scientific interest in the observation of natural phenomena[29] is coupled with a form of materialism indebted in part to Epicurean atomism (even if Cyrano is nothing if not inconstant in his own philosophical attachments). On the moon, the narrator (later named "Dyrcona," an anagram of "Cyrano") meets a young man—the "fils de l'hôte"—who speaks to him at length of "l'Univers infini [qui] n'est composé d'autre chose que de ces atomes infinis, très solides, très incorruptibles."[30] The continuities among various beings—as diverse as willows, poplars, oysters, flies, frogs, sparrows, and humans—are emphasized in this model of a cosmos where Dyrcona himself is often taken to be something other than a man. (He is eventually put on trial by a society of birds who struggle to decide whether he is in fact human—and thus worthy of execution.) Cyrano's two narratives sketch the portrait of a post-Copernican universe in which all matter is in motion and where pleasure can take many forms. The various creatures that his narrator encounters range from Socrates's demon (or *daemon*), to talking animals and plants, to figures drawn from biblical and classical sources (and include the simulacrum of Descartes himself, in a twist that renders Descartes doubly Epicurean, in body and in argument). Natural philosophical and literary references proliferate and intertwine, as the narrator appears to retrace the trajectory followed by Epicurus as he is described in *DRN*, journeying beyond the confines of the known world to find evidence of the dynamic nature of matter.

Cyrano's cosmos is erotically charged, if not pornographic in the modern sense of portraying sexual acts with the aim of arousing the reader; the principle of generation is celebrated throughout, although Cyrano also describes scenes of homosexual attraction (as does Lucretius). Even as his narrator participates in some of the most significant philosophical debates of the period—debates that are often mediated by what would now be called alien life forms—the narratives are, like the Lucretian poem, designed not just to rehearse particular positions but to put them into action: not just to "tell" but to "show." Increasingly, Dyrcona's voyages reveal to him the way in which materialism enables not only a new experience of the human body—whose potentialities are encouraged rather than condemned—but an interpenetration of matter and form, of message and medium. In the journey to the sun, Cyrano's discovery of the effects of the imagination on solar bodies in motion leads him toward a recognition of thought itself as intertwined with matter, so that ideas are revealed to be directly linked to the posture or position that the body generating them assumes. In the words of the philosopher Campanella, whom Dyrcona encounters on the sun, "it is impossible that the same agitation of matter should not cause in both of us the same agitation of thought" ("il est impossible qu'un même branle de matière ne nous cause à tous deux un même branle d'esprit").[31] Here the text is more than a means of communication, since any rigid separation between "idea" and "body" has, in effect, collapsed. Cyrano's exploration of extraterrestrial life and the plurality of possible worlds upends the hierarchies of being that subtend Platonic and Aristotelian worldviews in order to posit a cosmos in which speculation can uncover new forms of delight and the agreeable "agitation" of one body be transmitted to any other in proximity to it.

Dyrcona sets off on his quest thanks to a book that has become animated of its own accord (flying from his library onto his table); his journey ends in the midst of simulacra (both theoretical and "real"). Cyrano's libertine materialism expresses what Deleuze has called "the joy of the diverse" (324) as a product of the decentering of the human in a materialist cosmos, and it does so in the exquisite embrace of the power of simulacral image, derived at least in part from text. There are echoes of Cyrano's experiment in Bernard le Bovier de Fontenelle's *Entretiens sur la pluralité des mondes* (1686), in which a philosopher discusses the nature of the post-Copernican universe with an attractive marquise, thereby making natural philosophical argument complicit in the pleasures of conversation and reading, speculation and (hypothetical) seduction.[32] Later on, in the eighteenth century, the materialist rethinking of the relationship among beings—coupled with an interest in the voluptuous intersection of body and Lucretian phantasm—reappears in the writings of authors like Julien Offray de la Mettrie (in *L'Homme machine* read alongside *L'école de la volupté* and the *Système d'Épicure*), Denis Diderot (most famously in *Le rêve de d'Alembert* and despite his turn toward Stoicism), and the marquis de Sade (where the Lucretian investment in giving up all human attachments, including to our own humanity, takes a profoundly violent turn). The eroticization of the Lucretian thematics of perception (and reception), already libidinally charged in Cyrano's tales, takes on the magnitude of an obsession in the clandestine Sadean corpus. But the idea of the erotic *imago* as the instigator of a conversion to materialism is a common trope in the obscene literature of the period. Perhaps most famously, in the 1748 novel *Thérèse philosophe*, probably authored by the marquis d'Argens, materialist argument is wedded to voluptuous compulsion, stirred by erotic tableaux (both actual and virtual). Thérèse's contemplation of erotic images leads to her losing her virginity and her self-possession, albeit at the hands of a benevolent benefactor, who subsequently demands that she write the tale of her life.

Across these works, the poetic text functions, as in Lucretius, not only as the mechanism by which nature is revealed but as the motor that enables images and pleasures to proliferate—seizing hold of the reader in an effort to guarantee their dissipation. While Diderot has an ambivalent relationship both to libertinage and Epicureanism, *Le rêve de d'Alembert* (written in 1769) takes the scene of the dreaming philosopher— immersed in a negotiation with his own phantasms—as the occasion for an exploration of the diversity (and continuity) of beings. In the account of the character mademoiselle de Lespinasse, while the sleeping d'Alembert meditates on "cet immense océan de matière" ("this immense ocean of matter"), he uses her hand to bring himself to orgasm, restaging the scene of the Lucretian wet dream (631). As the century wears on, libertine naturalism, still readable as an early form of scientific observation in Cyrano, lends increasing priority to sexual desire as the ultimate site of (pleasurable) dispossession of the human subject. Thus, the reader moves, in Sade's early poem "*La vérité, pièce trouvée parmi les papiers de La Mettrie*" (1787), in which he professes himself "*content et glorieux de mon épicurisme*" ("gloriously content in my Epicureanism") (553), from a denunciation of the "chimera" of God to a declaration of the force of the passions that renders them a "dictation" taken from nature itself: "Let us yield to their empire, and let their violence, subjugating our minds with no resistance, make with impunity laws of our pleasures" ("*Cédons à leur empire, et que leur violence, / Subjuguant nos esprits sans nulle résistance, / Nous fasse impunément des lois de nos plaisirs*") (555). Here it is to "error" (or "*écarts*," to use Sade's term, which is also one possible rendering of the Epicurean *clinamen*) that materialists deliver themselves up, and become unrecognizable to themselves and others, even as, in nature, "*tout se reproduit, . . . tout se régénère*" ("everything reproduces itself, everything regenerates") (556). While Sade's vision of error is clearly not limited to the sphere of sexuality, what he considers forms of sexual deviancy—including incest, rape, and sodomy—take pride of place in his pantheon of disorders. Whereas the dehumanizing turn of Lucretian atomism is a matter for joyous wonder in Cyrano, it becomes, with Sade, a reflection on the inevitability of human extinction in the pursuit of (inhuman) compulsions.

Inconstancy, in these texts, takes on many forms (from the figural to the moral and the ontological), but in each case materialism—with its investment in scenes of matter in motion—enables a productive intertwining of image (in the broadest sense) and body. Pleasure is animated in its representations, and the phantasm in all its materiality is explicitly put to work in the release from attachment. The French libertine reception of Lucretius thus generates a materialism that is also an endorsement of the consolatory effects of the image—and of illusion—in a cosmos defined by the contingency of life. As the texts above no doubt attest, this reception is deeply masculinist, but not exclusively so. In her *Discours sur le bonheur*, Émilie du Châtelet writes movingly of her abandonment by her lover Voltaire and her feelings about growing older.[33] "Il est à désirer d'être susceptible de passions, et . . . n'en a pas qui veut" ("So it is desirable to be susceptible to the passions, and . . . passions do not come for the asking").[34] Du Châtelet's Epicurean depiction of "sensations et . . . sentiments agréables" ("agreeable sensations and feelings," 95; 350) as the *summum bonum* of existence appears alongside an affirmation of the significance of illusion:

> Finally, I say that to be happy one must be susceptible to illusion . . .; but, you will object, you have said that error is always harmful: is illusion not an error? No: although it is true, that illusion does not make us see objects entirely as they must be in order for them to give us agreeable feelings, it only adjusts them to our nature. . . . I have cited spectacles, because illusion is easier to perceive there. It is, however, involved in all the pleasures of our life, and provides the polish, the gloss of life. . . . We cannot give ourselves illusions . . ., but we can keep the illusions that we have. . . .] (tr. Zissner and Bour (2009) 354–355)
>
> Enfin, je dis que pour être heureux il faut être susceptible d'illusion . . . mais, me direz-vous, vous avez dit que l'erreur est toujours nuisible: l'illusion n'est-elle pas une erreur? Non l'illusion ne nous fait pas voir, à la vérité, les objets entièrement tels qu'ils doivent être pour nous donner des sentiments agréables, elle les accomode à notre nature. . . . J'ai cité les spectacles, parce que l'illusion y est plus aisée à sentir. Elle se mêle à tous les plaisirs de notre vie, et elle en est le vernis. . . . On ne peut se donner des illusions . . . , mais on peut conserver les illusions qu'on a . . . . (Du Châtelet (2008) 100–101)

Here the simulacral image becomes the point upon which human desire, freed from the servitude of anxiety, converges. Rather than moving toward a suspicion of representation and its effects on us, du Châtelet's neo-Lucretian materialism sees illusion itself—best cultivated in spectacle—as the only consistent guarantor of pleasure in a universe with, in effect, no guarantees. Connected as it is to ancient debates about the nature of sensory perception and its effects, du Châtelet's emphasis on the "spectacle" of illusion—and its capacity to "adjust" the world to human nature—seems to open a portal toward modernity defined by the enmeshment of matter in image. While du Châtelet does not generalize from her own experience to that of all women, she does provide a particularly moving example of how an implicitly Lucretian position might be reworked to take account of an experience that is, in du Châtelet's terms at least, distinctively feminine. In this way she suggests the possibility of a libertine materialism that is not the sole province of either men or masculine bodies.

Notes

1. My thanks to Blanca Missé for her insightful formulation of the relationship between materialist philosophy and libertine practice as a question of desire, its expressions, and its repressions.

2. Torero-Ibad (2010) 129–138.
3. As James Steintrager puts it in *The Autonomy of Pleasure*, "Both libertine writings and the behavior they advocated—the two linked in a feedback loop of mutual information—were widely considered pernicious: threats to religion, family, health, and the state" (Steintrager (2016) 9).
4. For a foundational history of illusion as a philosophical, aesthetic, and cognitive category, see Hobson (1982).
5. For a thoughtful exploration of the relationship between the two categories in Bayle and beyond, see Bernier (2001). Serge Rivière (2003) on "the ambiguity of Voltaire's libertinage" usefully explores the conflation of the two types of libertinage in criticism of Voltaire's work and in the eighteenth century more generally.
6. Bernier (2001) 25.
7. For an outstanding account of the significance of Epicureanism to the development of seventeenth-century philosophy and natural history, see Wilson (2008). Palmer (2014) and Passannante (2011) explore the reception and dissemination of Lucretius in the Renaissance in particularly evocative ways. See also Griffin in this volume.
8. The attacks of critics of libertine thought like le père Garasse, who attempts to consolidate the bond between philosophical materialism and the licentious pursuit of pleasure, rely on imputations of debauchery to discredit all materialist positions. In his summary of the "maxims" of the libertines, Garasse (1986) 42 writes: "There is no other divinity or sovereign power in the world than NATURE, whom we must please in all things without refusing anything to our body. . . ." ("Il n'y a point d'autre divinité ny puissance souveraine au monde que la NATURE, laquelle il faut contenter en toutes choses sans rien refuser à nostre corps. . . .").
9. Bayle (1740) 1:288. Translations my own unless otherwise indicated.
10. See Jean-Pierre Cavaillé (2010) 27 on the importance of freedom—"la revendication de liberté"—for forms of thought and action understood as libertine. The debate over the philosophical signification of libertinism or libertinage is longstanding. In his article "Libertinage and rationality," Jean-Pierre Dubost (1998) 56 declares that "[l]ibertinage has no strictly philosophical core." He goes on to affirm that libertinage is fundamentally literary, rather than strictly philosophical, in nature. I will argue here that the literary emphasis of libertine materialism is part of its inheritance from the ancients and crucial to the reception and appropriation of libertine thought, on its own terms.
11. The attribution of this entry to Diderot is not definitive. The ARTFL edition of the *Encyclopédie* lists the author of both this entry and the one on "libertinage" (discussed below) as "Diderot (attribution uncertain)."
12. Bayle (1740) 4:253.
13. In the *Observations sur Hemsterhuis*, Diderot echoes Spinoza's assessment of the relationship between materialist beliefs and libertine practice. He writes, "One would say that libertinage is a necessary consequence of materialism, an assertion that strikes me as borne out by neither reason nor experience" ("On dirait que le libertinage est une conséquence nécessaire du matérialisme, ce qui ne me paraît conforme ni à la raison, ni à l'expérience") (ed. Versini (1994) 695).
14. Cavaillé (2010) 27.
15. In a brilliant examination of this divided libertine self, Elena Russo (1997) has argued that the libertine is essentially a nostalgic figure, longing for an autonomous Cartesian subject whose day is long since over and undone by the predominant Enlightenment emphasis

on the importance of sociability and relationality. This nostalgia is itself a product of modernity, as is evident in the work of Rousseau (who, in his efforts to rescue the men and women of his time from what he saw as the corrupting influence of modern society, unites a critique of progress with an investment in a return to an earlier epoch in human social life, if not a return to "nature" as such).

16. For an influential reading of Lucretius as a thinker of fluid mechanics (and his modernity in this context), see Serres (1977). For a rich and theoretically informed analysis, engaged with Serres, of the way in which Epicureanism's emphasis on the mortality of each individual life is undergirded by the "immortality" of atoms that can never be destroyed, see Goldberg (2009).
17. See Porter (2005).
18. Lucretius also advocates for a retreat from political life that resonates with the libertine withdrawal from the scene of public power and into the realm of a hidden and intimate space where relations of domination and subjection are primarily experienced in and on the body.
19. For a helpful overview of the libertine reception of Lucretius in the seventeenth century, see Spink (1960).
20. This process might also be called, at least in its inaugural moments, the poetic conversion to a materialist perception of the world.
21. Jacob (1996).
22. Girerd (2007) 93.
23. Kavanagh (2010) 4.
24. Diderot (ed. Duflo) (2002) 103, ellipses Diderot's. Moreover, this freedom brings with it a set of constraints—a grammar that inscribes itself in and on the bodies that receive it. Thus we see in the work of the marquis de Sade, for instance, how the liberation from theological superstitions—exposed as dangerous chimeras—takes the form of a new kind of submission—to nature as the latter is experienced through writing, argumentation, and the sensations of voluptuous enjoyment that emerge in the encounter with the literary work.
25. The seventeenth-century French reception (libertine and otherwise) of Lucretius passes through the reflections of Montaigne, who was interested in Lucretius's antiprovidentialism, among other aspects of *DRN*. For a wide-ranging and insightful analysis of the significance of Lucretius for early modern poetry, see Hock (2021). For analyses of Montaigne and Lucretius in the context of early modern French thought more generally, see the essays by Barbour (2007) and Ford (2007).
26. Rochester, & Love, H. (1999) 108–109.
27. For seventeenth-century libertine materialist Cyrano de Bergerac, for instance, the cosmos is a scene of fecundity where bodies, images, books, and "figures" intermingle. For a rich and detailed exploration of Cyrano's Epicureanism, see Darmon (1998).
28. La Mettrie (1996) 136.
29. Erica Harth refers to *L'autre monde* as "one of the first examples of scientific popularization" (Harth (1970) 4); Cyrano's narratives are often described as early examples of science fiction.
30. Cyrano de Bergerac (ed. Prévot) (2004) 133.
31. Cyrano de Bergerac (ed. Prévot) (2004) 274.
32. Of course, Fontenelle was not a libertine materialist; his own intellectual commitments were oriented toward Cartesianism and, to a certain extent, neo-Stoicism. On Fontenelle's Epicureanism, see Dagen (2003).

33. While the best-known authors of libertine materialist works are all men, the experience of desire as a form of dispossession is one that resonates particularly strongly with women writers.
34. Du Châtelet (2008) 95; tr. Zissner and Bour (2009) 350.

REFERENCES

Adam, A. (1986). *Les libertins au XVIIe siècle*. (Paris).
Barbour, R. (2007). "Moral and Political Philosophy: Readings of Lucretius from Virgil to Voltaire," in Gillespie and Hardie (Cambridge), 149–166.
Bartsch, S., and T. Bartscherer, eds. (2005). *Erotikon: Essays on Eros, Ancient and Modern*. (Chicago).
Bayle, P. (^{5}1740). *Dictionnaire historique et critique*. (Amsterdam).
Bernier, M. A. (2001). *Libertinage et figures du savoir: Rhétorique et roman libertin dans la Frances des Lumières (1734–1751)*. (Paris).
Cavaillé, J-P. (2010). "Libertinisme et philosophie: Catégorie historiographique et usage des termes dans les sources." *Libertinage et philosophie au XVIIIe siècle* 12: 11–32.
Dagen, J. (2003). "Fontenelle et l'épicurisme." *Revue d'Histoire littéraire de la France* 103(2): 397–414.
Du Châtelet, É. (2008). *Discours sur le bonheur*, in Mauzi (Paris), 91–135.
Du Châtelet, É. (2009). *Discourse on Happiness*, in Zinsser (Chicago), 345–365.
Cryle, P., and L. O'Connell, eds. (2003). *Libertine Enlightenment: Sex, Liberty and Licence in the Eighteenth Century*. (Basingstoke).
Darmon, J.-C. (1998). *Philosophie épicurienne et littérature au XVIIe siècle: Études sur Gassendi, Cyrano de Bergerac, La Fontaine, Saint-Évremond*. (Paris).
Deleuze, G. (1969). *Logique du sens*. (Paris).
Diderot, D., and J. le Rond d'Alembert, eds. (1751–1772). *Encyclopédie, ou dictionnaire raisonné des sciences, des arts et des métiers, etc.* ARTFL Encyclopédie Project (University of Chicago). R. Morrissey, ed. http://encyclopedie.uchicago.edu/ (accessed December 8, 2021).
Diderot, D. (1994). *Observations sur Hemsterhuis*, in Versini, 687–770.
Dubost, J.-P. (1998). "Libertinage and Rationality: From the 'Will to Knowledge' to Libertine Textuality." *Yale French Studies* 94 (Libertinage and Modernity): 52–78.
Duflo, C., ed. (2002). *Denis Diderot*, Le rêve de d'Alembert. (Paris).
Ford, P. (2007). "Lucretius in Early Modern France," in Gillespie and Hardie, 227–241.
Garasse, F. (1986). *La doctrine curieuse des beaux esprits de ce temps*, in Adam, 33–50.
Gillespie, S., and P. Hardie, eds. (2007). *The Cambridge Companion to Lucretius*. (Cambridge).
Girerd, C. (2007). *La sagesse libertine*. (Paris).
Goldberg, J. (2009). *The Seeds of Things: Theorizing Sexuality and Materiality in Renaissance Representations*. (New York).
Harth, E. (1970). *Cyrano de Bergerac and the Polemics of Modernity*. (New York).
Hobson, M. (1982). *The Object of Art: The Theory of Illusion in Eighteenth-Century France*. (Cambridge).
Hock, J. (2021). *The Erotics of Materialism: Lucretius and Early Modern Poetics*. (Philadelphia).
Hunt, L., ed. (1996). *The Invention of Pornography: Obscenity and the Origins of Modernity, 1500–1800*. (New York).
Jacob, M. (1996). "The Materialist World of Pornography," in Hunt, 157–202.

Kavanagh, T. (2010). *Enlightened Pleasures: Eighteenth-Century France and the New Epicureanism.* (New Haven, Conn.).
La Mettrie, J. O. (1996). *L'école de la volupté*, in Thomson, 113–153.
Le Brun, A., and J-J. Pauvert, eds. (1986). *Œuvres complètes du marquis de Sade*, vol. 1. (Paris).
Kennedy, D. (2002). *Rethinking Reality: Lucretius and the Textualization of Nature.* (Ann Arbor, Mich.).
Mauzi, R. (2008). *L'art de vivre d'une femme au XVIIIe siècle.* (Paris).
Palmer, A. (2014). *Reading Lucretius in the Renaissance.* (Cambridge, Mass.).
Passannante, G. (2011). *The Lucretian Renaissance: Philology and the Afterlife of Tradition.* (Chicago).
Porter, J. (2005). "Love of Life: Lucretius to Freud," in Bartsch and Bartscherer, 113–141.
Prévot, J., ed. (2004). *Cyrano de Bergerac: Les États et Empires de la Lune; Les États et Empires du Soleil.* (Paris).
Rivière, S. (2003). "Philosophical Liberty, Sexual Licence: The Ambiguity of Voltaire's Libertinage," in Cryle and O'Connell, 75–92.
Rochester, & Love, H. (1999).. *The Works of John Wilmot, Earl of Rochester.* (Oxford).
Russo, E. (1997). "Sociability, Cartesianism, and Nostalgia in Libertine Discourse." *Eighteenth-Century Studies* 30: 383–400.
Sade, D. A. F. (1986). "La vérité," in Le Brun and Pauvert, 553–559.
Serres, M. (1977). *La naissance de la physique dans le texte de Lucrèce: Fleuves et turbulences.* (Paris).
Slavitt, D., tr. (2008). *Lucretius:* De rerum natura (The Nature of Things). (Berkeley).
Spink, J. S. (1960). *French Free-Thought from Gassendi to Voltaire.* (London).
Steintrager, J. (2016). *The Autonomy of Pleasure: Libertines, License, and Sexual Revolution.* (New York).
Thomson, Ann, ed. (1996). *Julien Offray de la Mettrie:* De la volupté. (Paris).
Torero-Ibad, A. (2010). "La pratique libertine du collage comme conception de l'acte de philosopher." *Libertinage et philosophie au XVIIe siècle* 12: 129–138.
Versini, L., ed. (1994). *Denis Diderot: Œuvres.* (Paris).
Wilson, C. (2008). *Epicureanism at the Origins of Modernity.* (Oxford).
Zinsser, J. P., ed. (2009). *Émilie Du Châtelet: Selected Philosophical and Scientific Writings.* J. P. Zinsser and I. Bour, trs. (Chicago).

Index

A

Academy
  history, 266, 269
  New, 530
    contra omnia dissertatio, 259–63
    epistemology, 266–7, 269
    in utramque partem dissertatio, 259–61, 263–6
  Plato, 161–2, 169–70, 212, 216
Accius (L. Accius, poet), 284
adoption, 555–7
Adrianople, battle of, 508
adversity, as irrational force, 511
Aesara. *See* Aresas
aesthetics, 449, 451–2
Alain of Lille, 573
Albert the Great, 571
Alcuin, 570
Alexander Polyhistor, 9, 11
aliena, 94–5
allegory, 175
almsgiving, 517
Ambrose of Milan, 506–27, 528
  On Duties, 506–27
  De sacramento regenerationis sive de philosophia, 517
Anaxagoras, 466–7, 469–72, 475–6, 481
ancestors, as moral exemplars, 513
Andronicus of Rhodes, 492–3
anger, 65–8, 144, 514, 516
Anselm St, 570
Antiochus of Ascalon, 211–2, 221, 269–70, 495
antithesis, soul and body, 328–9, 335
Antonine decree, 555, 558–9
Apollonius of Tyana, 226–7
aporetic spirit, 211–2, 217
appetite, 514, 521
Apuleius, 306–9, 430, 500, 528

Apology, 354–6
On the Universe 38.1–5, 308–9
On Plato 1, 307
Archytas of Tarentum (ps.), 11–4, 18, 20
area of study (*topoi*), 181
Aresas (ps.), 6–11, 13, 20
Arians, Arianism, 507–8
Aristophanes, 153, 402
Aristotle, 4–5, 7, 12–4, 16, 18, 20, 159–60, 165–6, 491–501, 517, 571–2, 574
  'esoteric' treatises vs. 'exoteric' dialogues, 494, 500
  ethics, 219–20
  on friendship, 111–2
  poetics, 277
  on time, 413–4, 419
  zoological collections, 494, 500
Aristoxenus of Tarentum, 6, 13, 17
ascent, 513, 576
asceticism, 507, 508, 521
Asclepiades of Bithynia, 380–2
assimilation
  cultural, 558–60
  to God, 214, 220
Athanasius of Alexandria, 507
Athenaeus of Attaleia, 382–3
atomism, 305–6
atoms, 146
Atticus, 37
Augustine, 87, 376, 569–70, 572, 574–7
  Against the Academics 3.17.37, 529
  The City of God
  Confessions
    7.9.13, 531
    7.17.23, 534
    7.20.26, 537
    7.21.27, 532
    8.2.3, 532

Augustine *Confessions* (*cont.*)
    8.10, 530, 540
    9.17, 539
    13.11.12, 538
    13.17.2, 536
    22.25–28, 536
    On Genesis Against the Manicheans 2.9.12, 535
    On the Happy Life 1.4, 531
    Letters
        6.1, 530
        18, 534
        118.10, 461
    The Measure of the Soul, 540
    on time, 422–5
Aulus Gellius, 500–1
authority, Stoicism, 70
Auxentius of Milan, 507
awe, 148
Axiochus, ps.-Platonic dialogue, 431, 433

B

baptism, Christian, 517, 519
Basil of Caesarea, 507, 553–5
Bayle, Pierre, 599–601
beauty, 404–5
Being vs. Becoming, 310–1
beneficence, 510
beneficial, the, 333–4, 510–11, 514, 517
Bergerac, Cyrano de, 607–8
Bible, 507, 512–5, 517–8, 520
    John 18.36, 530
    Letter to the Colossians 2.8, 532
bio-doxography, 46–3, 470
biography, 190, 204–5, 462–4, 466, 468–70, 474, 477
body, 217–9, 510, 515–6, 519, 521
Boethius, 568, 571–3, 578–9
Bonaventure, 570, 576
Burkhardt, Jacob, 583
Byzantium, 548–62

C

Caesar (C. Iulius Caesar). *See* Lucan
Calcidius, 309–12
Callicles, 153
Calvus (C. Licinius Macer Calvus, orator), 279

capital, social, 347
cardinal virtues, 510–1, 514
Carneades
    epistemology, 270
Carthage as Rome, 552
Casaubon, Meric, 74
Cassius (Gaius Cassius Longinus), 35–6
Cato the Elder, 3–5, 17, 20–1
Cato, M. Porcius, 'the younger', 429, 434–7
    See also Lucan
causality, 213
celibacy, 521
Cereta, Laura, 584–96
    Letter to Deodata di Leno, 593–5
    Letter to Francesco Fontana, 589–92
character, 219
charity, 508, 510, 516, 519
chastity, 520
Châtelet, Émilie du, 610
choice, moral, 519
Christ, 510–3, 518, 520–1
Christian ethics, 506–27
Chrysippus, 62–6, 77, 79, 190, 199–202, 204, 361
Cicero, 3–6, 17, 20–1, 79, 91, 95, 144, 150–1, 159–70, 212, 295–301, 449, 506–27, 528, 540
    consolation, 108, 132–3, 240, 242–7, 250, 434
    on Democritus and infinitely many worlds, 416
    Dream of Scipio, 413
    knowledge of Aristotelian works, 494–6
    Letters, 34, 36, 333, 335
    Lucullus, 267, 475–6
    On Academic Scepticism, 266, 475
    On Behalf of Sestius, 35–6
    On Duties, 121, 136–7, 348, 506–27, esp. 509ff.
    On Fate, 260
    On Friendship, 108–16, 514
    On Laws, 121–8
    On Moral Ends, 34, 263–5, 325
    On the Nature of the Gods, 1.25–29, 471–4
    On the Orator, 281, 347
    Republic, 126–8, 335
    Stoic Paradoxes, 193–5
    translation of Epicurean texts, 34
    Tusculan Disputations, 120, 128–36, 257–9, 261–3, 297, 325, 350–1

Claudius Caecus, Appius, 5, 20
Cleanthes, 77, 190–1, 361
Clement of Alexandria, 515
clergy, Christian, 508–9, 514, 516, 517, 520, 521, 522
cogito, 569, 575, 577
Colonna, Vittoria, 583
Colotes, 144
Columella, 449–51
commandments, divine, 512, 520
commentary, 310
community
    Christian, 520
    human, 511
company, social, 511, 516
compassion, 517, 519
concepts (*ennoiai*), 216
conflagration, 364, 371–2
conscience, 515, 519
consolation
    Boethius, 181, 572, 578
    Cereta, 589–92
    Christian, 251
    Cicero, 108, 132–3, 240, 242–7, 250, 434
    Greek, 241, 243–5, 248–9
    grief, 241–8, 250
    Marcus Aurelius, 80
    philosophy, 240–5
    poetry, 247–51
    principate, 240, 247, 250
    rhetorical theory, 241–2, 349
    Roman Republic, 240, 247, 250–1
    Seneca, 61, 70–1, 240–9, 369, 371
    See also death
Constantinople as New Rome, 550–2
contemplation, 572, 575–6
continence, 521
contingency, 365, 372
conversion, 533
Cornutus, 190, 199–205, 275, 497–8
The Corrupting Sea, 443
corruption, the present era, 327–9
cosmology, 10–5, 17–9, 444, 449
cosmos. *See* cosmology and *kosmos*
counsel, wise, 511
courage, 510–1, 516–7
Crantor, 434

creation, 569, 571, 574, 577–8
Creator, 573–4, 576
criticism
    literary, 275, 277, 282
    stylistic, 280
cycle, history and change, 328
Cynicism, 76–78, 228–9, 230–1, 335–7
Cyrenaics, 148

D

daemon, 88–9, 91–3, 95–9
death, 46, 146, 218
    consolation, 240–51, 434
    good, 589–92
debate, 120–38
decorum (seemliness in behavior), 510–2, 514, 516
deforestation, 443–4
Deleuze, 361, 397–8
Demetrius (Cynic), 77
Democritus, 463, 466, 471, 473–6
demonology, 87–91, 93, 96, 98–9
demons, 215–6
Demosthenes, 231, 279
dependency, Roman thought on Greek, 32
Derveni Papyrus, 19–20
dialogue, 159–70, 183, 268–9
diatribe, 278, 282
didactic, 174
Diderot, Denis, 601–2, 608
Didymus of Alexandria, 507
Dio Chrysostom, 225–36
    Alexandrian Oration (32), 228–9, 231–6
    On Envy (77/78), 227, 230, 235
    Isthmian Oration (9), 231
    On Kingship (4), 230
    First Tarsian Oration (33), 232–3, 235
    Second Tarsian Oration (34), 232–5
    On Virtue (8), 230
Diogenes of Apollonia, 19, 21
Diogenes of Babylon, 276
Diogenes Laertius, 335
Diogenes of Oenoanda, 30–3, 466–7
Diogenes of Sinope, 76, 78, 230–1
Dionysius (ps.), 570–1, 577
Dionysius (Stoic), 78
Diotima, 89, 92, 98

dissertations, 173
Domitius (Ch. Domitius Ahenobarbus). *See* Lucan
doxography, 162, 461–2, 464–7, 470–3, 476
dualism, 211, 221
duty, 330, 335, 509, 512–4, 518–21
dyad
    indefinite, 213–4

E

Eccelus of Lucania (ps.), 6, 10–1, 20
ecocriticism, 442–3
education, 347, 352, 355
Edwards, Catharine, 592
effeminacy, 516
elders, company of, 516
elements, 16–9
elite, Christian vocation as, 520–1
eloquence, 352
emotion, 219–20
    good emotions, Stoic, 70–1
    See also passion
Empedocles, 17–8, 21, 463, 466–76
empiricists (medicine), 384–5
encheiridion, 175
enemies, love for, 512
Ennius, 6, 17–21, 89
Epicharmus of Syracuse, 17–21
Epictetus, 35, 65, 67, 69–70, 282, 368–9, 515
    Discourses, 75–6
        1.4.11, 181
        2.12.1–7, 183
        3.23.27–29, 184
        4.12.19, 182
    Manual, 182
Epicureanism, 167–9, 324, 335–6, 449–50, 517
    anti-Epicurean polemic, 258
    Roman masculinity, 33–7
    and sexuality, 33
    women in, 32–3
Epicurus, 143–58, 587–96
    avoiding the mob, 55
    friendship, 47–8
    Letter to Menoeceus, 305
    limits to pleasure, 51–2
    On Nature, 28
    pleasure as the highest good, 42–5

    present joys, 54
    Principal Doctrines, 31
epidromê, 174
Eriugena John Scottus, 570, 577–8
eschatology, 511, 519
eternal life, 511, 516, 518, 521
ethics, 219–20, 347, 349–50
    cosmological, 367
    etymology, 176, 199
    practical, 174
Euclid, 572
Eudorus, 211, 213
eunomia. *See* law
evil, 569
exempla, moral, 167–9, 180, 327, 329, 333, 507, 512–4
exemplarity, 95
exercise, 182
exhortation, moral, 352
exile
    consolation, 240, 242, 245–50
externals, 511, 516, 521

F

Fabianus, 77
faith, Christian, 510–1, 516, 519–20, 595
fall, the, 516, 518–9
fasting, 520
fate, 307–9, 362–3, 367, 369, 372–3
Favorinus, 217
fear, 511, 517–8
Fedele, Cassandra, 584
feminism, proto-, 585
fertility, 449–50
fitting, the, 510–2, 514, 516
    See also seemliness in behavior
flattery, 115–6, 516
forgiveness, 517
Forms, 214–6
Fortitude. *See* courage
Fortuna, 589–92
Fothergill-Payne, Louise, 586
Foucault, 361, 403–5
frank speech (*parrhêsia*), 228–36
friendship, 108–16, 144, 514, 516
    causes of, 111
    childhood friendships, 114–5

and Cyrenaics, 110
definition of, 109
dissolution of, 115
and elites, 110
and Epicureanism, 110–1
and flattery, 115–6
and frankness, 115–6
and grief, 109–10
limits on, 113
and loyalty, 112
and natural affection, 111
rareness of, 114
and revolution, 112
and self-love, 113, 115
and Stoicism, 109, 111
strains on, 112
among unequals, 114
and utility, 111
and virtue, 110–1
Fronto, 349
Fulvius Nobilior, Quintus, 17

G

Galen, 63–4, 380, 388–90, 493
    consolation, 241, 249–50
generosity, 511, 517, 519
gentlemen, 347–56, 512, 516, 520–1
Gilbert of La Porree, 573
glory, 519–20
god(s), 146, 213–6, 510–3, 516, 518–21, 569–79
    becoming like, 94–5, 99
Golden Age, 446, 450–1
Golden Verses (Pythagorean), 77–8
goodwill, 515
Goths, 508
grace, divine, 513, 516
Graver, Margaret, 588
gravitas, 508, 516
greed, 508, 516–7
Greenblatt, Stephen, 586
Gregory the Great, 570
Grief. *See* consolation
Grosseteste, Robert, 570
Guattari, Félix, 397–8
guidance, 120–38
guilt, 149
Gyges, 513, 517

H

Hadot, Pierre, 75, 361
handbooks, 173
happiness, 178, 593–5
    eudaimonia, 220, 332–4
    unattainable by changing one's abode, 54
    vita beata, 514, 516, 519
harmony, moral, 511
heaven, reward in, 511–3, 518, 521
Hecato of Rhodes, 510
hedonism, 147–50
hēgēmonikon, 362, 371, 374–5
Heraclitus, 363, 376, 466–70, 473, 476
Herennius Pontius, 5
Herillus (Stoic), 78
hierarchy of beings, 534
Hilduin, 570
history of philosophy, 212
homeland, 537
homoeomeria, 467, 469
honorable, the, 333–4, 510–2, 514
Horace, 190–2, 195–6, 198–202
    Art of Poetry, 276, 277, 279–80
    Letters, 2.1.156, 325
    Odes, 1.2, 42–8
    Odes, 2.16, 48–55.4.3, 279
hospitality, 511, 521
Hugh of St. Victor, 571, 573, 576
human beings, humanity, 511, 515, 517–9
humility, 372, 518–20

I

icons, icon-theory, and iconoclasm
    Byzantine, 553–5
Ignatius of Loyola, 75
image of God, human being as, 511
imitation, 294
immigration (to the Roman empire), 559–60
immortality
    of poets, 47
imperial images, 554–5
impulse, excessive, 62, 65
incarnation, 539
inconstancy, 601–2, 609
individual, and society, 511
ingenium, 585
inheritance, 517, 521

intellect, 218, 571–2, 538, 575, 577–8
intellectuals, Greek, 349–50
intentio, 540
intention, in moral conduct, 510, 519
interiority, 519, 534, 541
intertextuality, 285
introductory literature, 173
invulnerability, 362, 365, 369
Inwood, Brad, 61, 66
Isis, 96, 98
Italy/Italic, 3–7, 9, 11–3, 15, 17, 19–21
iucunditas, 593
iudicium. *See* judgment

J

Jerome, 515
Job, biblical exemplar, 517
jokes, 516
judgment, 65–8, 508–9, 516–21
    aesthetic, 277, 280, 283–4
    moral, 282, 284–5
Jupiter, 18–9
justice, 7, 9–13, 18, 21, 510–1, 516–7, 520
Justin Martyr, 515
Justina, empress, 507
Juvenal
    consolation, 241, 248, 250

K

Ker, James, 592
kindness, 510–1
kinship, spiritual, 555–8
knowledge, 216–7
kosmos, 214
Kraye, Jill, 583
Kristeva, Julia, 405–7

L

Lactantius, 523
lady, learned, 583–96
law, 7–8, 11–4, 16, 18
    of citizenship, 555, 558–60
    as philosophy, 549–50
leadership, Christian, 520–1
lecture (*scholae*), 179
legal fictions, 549, 554, 559–62

leisure (*otium*), 329, 335, 516
    as equivalent to *ataraxia*, 48–55
lessons, 174
libertas, 328–30
libertinage, 599–610
limits
    of human experience, 361–78 (*passim*)
linguistic theory, 276
literary form, 175
Livy, 328–9
locus amoenus, 446
Longinus, 277, 370
love, 511–2, 518–9
    filial, 111–2
    God's, 594–5
    parental, 148–9
loyalty and friendship, 112
Lucan (M. Annaeus Lucanus, poet), 275–6, 285
    on Caesar, 276, 285
    on Cato, 276
    on Domitius, 285
Lucania, 6–14, 20
Lucilius, 191–2, 195–6, 333
    literary criticism, 275
Lucretia, rape of, 168–9
Lucretius, 20–1, 28–9, 35–7, 143–58, 294, 301–6, 448, 465–70, 494, 586–96
    The Way Things Are, 143–58, 599, 603–7
        1. 301–4
        2. 594
        3. 830–846, 304–5
        4. 1153–1191, 306
        6. 1138–1285, 301
    on Epicurus, 421–2
    futility of fleeing one's country, 54
    infinitely many worlds, 416
    originality of, 28, 419–20
    political ambition, 44
    present joys, 54
    swerve, 146, 418–9
    time, 415–22
    tranquil life of gods, 47
    translation of Epicurean terminology, 420–1
    wealth, 51

M

Maecenas
  on *oratio corrupta*, 283
magic, 354
magnanimity, 510, 520
Manilius, 190
manliness, masculinity, 516, 521
Marcus Aurelius, 361, 364, 367–8, 371, 373
  Meditations, 74–5, 77–82
Marius Victorinus, 569
marriage, 400–3
Mars, 302–4
martyrs, martyrdom, 508, 510
materialism (libertine), 599–610
mathematics, 572–3
matter, 213–4
Maximus, Magnus, Western emperor, 508
Maximus of Tyre, 97
measure, in behavior, 511, 516
memory, 327–8, 339, 570
mercy, 508, 512
Messapian. *See* Oscan
methodists (medicine), 386–8
microcosm, 574, 577–9
Middle Platonism, 89
mind, 569, 572, 575–7
Mithraism, 215
Moderatus, 213
modesty, 508, 511, 514, 518, 521–2
money, use of, 520–1
monism, 221
mos maiorum (and Roman/Latin tradition), 327–8, 330–1, 333–5, 337
muliebris respublica, 584–5
Musonius Rufus, 75–8, 81, 398–407, 515
mutability, 534
myth, 212
  of Er, 218

N

narratology, 285
  Pompeius, 276
natura, 444
natural history, 445
natural selection, 146
nature, 511, 515–6, 518–9

necessity, 307–9
negotium, 326, 335, 337
Neoplatonism, 568–71, 573–4, 578–9
Neoptolemus of Parium, 276
Neopythagoreanism, 211
Nicene theology, 507–8
Nicholas of Cusa, 573
Noyes, Russell, 592
Numa Pompilius, 5
Numenius, 211, 215, 221

O

obedience, spiritual, 512
obscenity, 407
Occelus of Lucania (ps.), 6, 10–6, 20
Offray, Julien de La Mettrie, 604, 608–9
oikeiōsis, 111, 367, 372
Olivi, Peter, 570
oratory, deliberative, 349–50
order, the well-ordered person, 516, 519
Origen, 507
Oscan, 6, 17
Osiris, 90, 93, 96–7
Ovid, 97
  gods of nature/divinity, 447–8
  Metamorphoses, 447
  Narcissus, 447

P

paganism, tension with Christianity, 585–96
paideia, 225
pain, as irrational force, 511
Palmer, Ada, 586–8, 591
Panaetius, 509–10, 516–7
paradox, 190–210
  bald man, 199
  horned paradox, 202–5
  nobody paradox, 195–200
  sorites (=heap) paradox, 199–202
passion(s), 65–8, 515, 518–9, 521
patience, 517
patriotism, 517
patronage, 517
Paul, apostle, 515
Peckham, John, 570
perfection, 220, 512, 520
Peripatetics, 516–7

peroration, 351
perseverance, 511
Persius, 190–210
    on audience, 277, 279–80, 284
    and literary criticism, 275, 277–82
    Satires
        1.1–3, 196
        1.8–12, 197
        1.119–123, 198
        5.5–18, 203
        6.75–80, 200
    on technical ability, 279–81
    use of metaphors, 278, 280
persona, 91
persuasion, 352–3
pessimism, 328–9, 336
Phaethon, 370–1
Philo of Alexandria, 11–2, 507
Philo of Larissa, 269–70
Philodemus, 19, 29–30, 45, 54, 144, 154, 276, 462–5
    dialogue, 268–9
    philosophy, 512–3, 517–8
    plagiarism from scripture, 512–3
    political, 324–6, 331–2, 335
    and rhetoric, 261–2, 264–5
Philostratus, 225–7
physiognomy, 516
piety, spiritual, 510
Piso, 29, 36–7
plain living (Epicurean), 51, 53–5
Plato, 3–5, 7–9, 11–13, 18, 20–21, 87–95, 98, 530, 568, 574–5
    Gorgias, 226–8, 234
    Laws, 308, 383
    Phaedo, 217–8
    Phaedrus, 226–7, 234, 299, 446
    Republic, 219–20, 451, 517
    Symposium, 402
    Timaeus, 211–5, 309–12, 536, 539
Platonism, 211–2, 221, 507, 510, 513, 518, 568
pleasure, 27–8, 33–5, 110, 352–3, 516, 593–5
Pliny the Elder, 449–50
Pliny the Younger, 240, 242, 248, 250, 336, 451–2
Plotinus, 211, 215, 220–1, 530, 569
    Enneads
        1.6, 533

1.6.8, 537
3.2.11–12 and 18–19, 539
Plutarch, 6, 9, 18, 67, 87, 99, 249
pneuma, 18
poetic theory, Stoic, 276–7, 281
poetry, 351–2, 355
politics, 119–20, 122–8, 137, 220, 347–9
pollen, 445
Polybius, 339
Porphyry, 212, 569, 571
    Philosophy of Oracles, 536
    On the Return of the Soul, 531–2, 535
    Smith 297F, 537
    Smith 300bF, 536
    Smith 302F, 537
Posidonius, 61, 63–4, 276, 509–10
possessions, 512, 516, 519
poverty, 520
power/the powerful, attitudes to, 516–7, 521
practical wisdom (*phronêsis*), 219
pragmatism, 511, 521
prayer, 520
precarity, 364, 368, 373, 375
    See also vulnerability
pre-emotions, 65–8
premeditation of future evils, 79
princeps (prince, ruler), 324, 329, 332–4, 337
Proclus, 570, 572
progress, moral, 513
property, private, 516
propriety. See seemliness
Providence, 307–9, 514, 518, 538, 573
provocation, response to, 517–8
prudence, 510–1, 517, 520–1
psychology. See also soul
    Epicurean, 145–50, 304–5
    Peripatetic, 63–4
    Platonic, 61–4
    Stoic, 275
psychotherapy, 278, 284
public image/esteem, 508, 511, 516–7
public service, 508, 509, 517, 519, 520–1
Pythagoras, 3, 5–6, 9, 17
Pythagoreanism, 3–21, 77–8, 517

Q

Quellenforschung, 144–5
Quintilian
   Aristotle *Categories*, 497
   consolation, 240, 248

R

Rabil, Albert, 583–4
reason, 514–6, 572–8
receptacle, 311
records (*apomnêmoneumata*), 179
redemption, 511, 519
refinement, in conduct, 516
regeneration, 517, 519
regnum (tyranny), 331–2, 335–7
reincarnation, 152–3
religion, 151, 153, 215, 220
reminiscence, 540
repentance, 519
res publica vs. *imperium*, 326–7, 330
resurrection of the body, 536
retaliation, non-retaliation, 517
rhetoric, 174, 150–4, 225–36, 261–2, 264–5
   self-, 354
   Stoic, 277, 283
righteousness, in biblical terms, 520
Robin, Diana, 584
Roman comedy, 88
Romanía, 548, 552, 559–60
Rome, superiority of, 325–6
rule (*kanôn*), 178
Rutilius Namatianus, 327

S

Sade, Donatien Alphonse François marquis
   de, 608–9
sage, the/wise man, 515–6, 520
salvation, divine, 507, 513, 519
salvation-history, 513
Samnium/Samnite, 5–6
sapientia (*sophia*), 333–4, 337
Sarrazin, John, 570
scepticism, Academic, 120–37, 212, 217
Schiesaro, Alessandro, 587
science (*technie*), 164
Scipio Africanus, 513
Scripture/s, Christian *See* Bible

Second Sophistic, 88
seemliness in behavior (*decorum*), 510–2, 514, 516
self, 218, 361–78 (*passim*)
   denial of, 511, 520–1
   examination of, 77–80
   mastery of, 510, 518
   opacity of, 374–5
   rhetoric of, 354
   sacrifice of, 512
   Seneca on, 68–70
Seneca the Elder, 333
Seneca the Younger, 30, 76–78, 80, 275–8, 283, 368–75, 442, 448, 515, 586–96
   consolation, 61, 70–1, 240–9, 369, 371
   Consolation to Marcia, 61, 63, 71
   engagement with Aristotle, 498–9
   Medea, 284
   Moral Letters, 352–4
      8, 587
      66, 592
      68, 70
      92, 62–4
      99, 71
      114, 283
      115, 284
      121, 62
   natural disasters, 442
   Natural Questions, 71, 336, 349, 442
   Oedipus, 283
   On Anger, 62, 64–8, 76–7
   On Benefits, 448
   On the Happy Life, 34–5
   On Leisure, 337
   On Tranquility, 68–71
   Phaedra, 276
   Thyestes, 284, 337–8
sense impressions, 217
sex, 151, 153
Sextius, Quintus, 76–7
sexual ethics, Christian, 521
silence, 514, 518–9
silphium, 449
simulacrum, 605–7, 610
sin, original, 569–70, 578
slavery, 173, 399–400
sobriety, 511

social company, appropriate, 511, 516
social wars, 5
society, 511, 515, 522
Socrates, 81, 88–9, 93–8, 160–1, 177, 216–7,
    226–7, 232, 234, 429, 434–7
  maieutics, 262, 264, 268, 270
  and Plato, 270
sorrow
  in Seneca, 71
Sotion, 77
soul, 3, 5, 7–13, 17–20, 110, 217–9, 298–301, 514,
    519, 533, 540, 570, 572–7
  illumination of, 534
  immortality of, 540
  vehicle of, 536
soundness, inner, 511, 516
specula principis, 331–4
speech, 514, 516, 518
spiritual exercises, 75–82
Statius, 336
Stöckinger, Martin, 594
Stoicism, 3, 12, 20–1, 76, 78–80, 82, 176, 211,
    217, 219, 228, 234, 324–6, 330–7, 361–78
    (*passim*), 450, 506–27 (esp. 515–7)
  on time, 413
stories, improper, 516
Strabo, 445, 492–3
style, 348, 352–3
subconscious beliefs, 148
sublime, 364, 370
suffering, 511, 516, 518–9
suicide, 434–7
superstition (*religio*), 589–92
suspension of judgement (*epochê*), 217
Symmachus, Q. Aurelius, 507–8
symmetry argument, 433

T

Tacitus, 329, 333–4
Tarentum, 5–7, 11, 17, 20
Tatian, 515
teachers, 173, 348
temperance, 510–1, 514, 521
Tertullian, 515
Thales, 465–6, 471–2
theodicy, 514
Theodosius I, emperor, 508

theology, 571–2
theophany, 571
Theophrastus on friendship, 112
therapy, 128–36
thesis, 348
Thierry of Chartres, 573
Thom, Johan, 77
Thomas Aquinas, 571
Thrasea Paetus, 437
Thucydides
  History of the Peloponnesian War 2.47–53,
    301
time, 364, 368
Tomasini, Giacomo Filippo, 584
training, of body and soul, 75–8
tranquility, 511
translation, 87–90, 93, 98, 163–5, 293–313
  as cultural appropriation, 297–301
  Greek to Latin, 293–313
treason, 517
triad, 538
truth, 226–7
Tullia (daughter of Cicero), 108, 110
Tyrannio, 492–3

U

uncouthness, in manner, 516
union vs. disunion, 303–6
useful, the. *See* beneficial, the

V

Valentinian II, emperor, 507–8
vanity, 517
Varius Rufus, L., 432
Varro, 4, 17–8, 448, 528
Venus, 302–4
Vergil, 89–90, 92–3, 325, 415, 422–3
  Georgics, 449–50
via, 537
vice (*kakia*), 219
view from above, 80–1
virtue(s), 7–11, 75, 219–20, 510–1, 514, 516,
    592–5
  rhetoric of, 350, 352
virtus (manliness), 34–5
visibility, of virtue, 507, 512, 519
visiones, 540

Vitruvius, 445
voice, tone of, 516
voluntas, 540
voluptas, 33–5, 593–5
vulnerability, 365–6, 369, 373–4
   See also precarity

W

war, justice in, 517
wealth, 515–6, 520–1
Wildberger, Jula, 588
will, 66, 570, 572–3
William of Conches, 573
William of Lucca, 571
Wilmot, John, Earl of Rochester, 604
wisdom, 510, 512–3, 517–8
wise man, the, 515–6, 520
wish, Stoic, 70
Witt, R. G., 586
World soul, 213–5, 218

Z

Zeno of Citium, 361, 365, 517
   Republic, 78
Zeus, 18–9, 307–9
Zöller, Rainer, 66